Fodor's

JAPAN

20th Edition

Fodor's Travel Publications   New York, Toronto, London, Sydney, Auckland
www.fodors.com

A Note from the Publisher

We are especially proud of this new color edition. No other guide to Japan is as up to date or has as much practical planning information, along with hundreds of color photographs and illustrated maps. We've also included "Word of Mouth" quotes from travelers who shared their experiences with others on our forums. If you're inspired and can plan a better trip because of this guide, we've done our job.

Unfortunately, this book comes out at a challenging time for travel to Japan. On March 11, 2011, a 9.0-magnitude earthquake struck an area approximately 45 mi (72 km) east of Sendai. The earthquake and resulting tsunami caused massive destruction and death along the coast of northern Honshu but had a relatively modest impact on the rest of the country.

Clean-up from the disaster is ongoing at this writing. Most road and rail repair work is already underway, and much of that was expected to be completed by fall 2011. Repairs to some buildings are ongoing as well. But damage to the Fukushima Daichi nuclear power plant, which has been stabilized but not shut down, is still ongoing and may continue for some months.

Our writers on the ground tell us that Hakodate, Sendai, Matsu-shima, and Hirazumi (the destinations in this guide that were most directly affected by the tsunami) are slowly returning to normal. The U.S. Department of State no longer recommends that U.S. citizens avoid unnecessary travel to Japan.

Nevertheless, we urge all travelers to do careful research before traveling to the coastal areas of the Tohoku region, though we see no reason for Americans (or anyone else) to avoid travel to Japan.

Power disruptions (caused by taking several power plants offline) and ongoing repair work are possibilities for some time to come, but our writers on the ground tell us that the tourism infrastructure throughout Japan is on a solid footing. So enjoy your trip.

Itterasshai!

Tim Jarrell, Publisher

FODOR'S JAPAN

Editors: Douglas Stallings and Stephanie E. Butler

Writers: Paul Bosley, Brett Bull, Charles Canning, Nicholas Coldicott, Arudou Debito, Paige Ferrari, Rob Goss, Noriko Kitano, Misha Janette, Peter McMillan, Kevin Mcgue, Robert Morel, Aidan O'Connor, Annamarie Ruelle Sasagawa, Christal Whelan, Chris Willson

Production Editor: Evangelos Vasilakis

Maps & Illustrations: David Lindroth and Mark Stroud, *cartographers;* Bob Blake, Rebecca Baer, *map editors;* William Wu, *information graphics*

Design: Fabrizio La Rocca, *creative director;* Guido Caroti, Siobhan O'Hare, *art directors;* Tina Malaney, Nora Rosansky, Chie Ushio, Ann McBride, *designers;* Melanie Marin, *senior picture editor*

Cover Photo: (Tea ceremony) Aflo Relax/Masterfile

Production Manager: Steve Slawsky

20th Edition

ISBN 978-0-307-48049-1

ISSN 0736-9956

SPECIAL SALES

This book is available at special discounts for bulk purchases for sales promotions or premiums. Special editions, including personalized covers, excerpts of existing books, and corporate imprints, can be created in large quantities for special needs. For more information, write to Special Markets/Premium Sales, 1745 Broadway, MD 3-1, New York, NY 10019, or e-mail specialmarkets@randomhouse.com.

AN IMPORTANT TIP & AN INVITATION

Although all prices, opening times, and other details in this book are based on information supplied to us at press time, changes occur all the time in the travel world, and Fodor's cannot accept responsibility for facts that become outdated or for inadvertent errors or omissions. So **always confirm information when it matters,** especially if you're making a detour to visit a specific place. Your experiences—positive and negative—matter to us. If we have missed or misstated something, **please write to us.** Share your opinion instantly through our online feedback center at fodors.com/contact-us.

PRINTED IN CHINA

10 9 8 7 6 5 4 3 2

CONTENTS

ABOUT THIS BOOK

Our Ratings

At Fodor's, we spend considerable time choosing the best places in a destination so you don't have to. By default, anything we recommend in this book is worth visiting. But some sights, properties, and experiences are so great that we've recognized them with additional accolades. Orange **Fodor's Choice** stars indicate our top recommendations; black stars highlight places we deem **Highly Recommended**; and **Best Bets** call attention to top properties in various categories. Disagree with any of our choices? Care to nominate a new place? Visit our feedback center at www.fodors.com/feedback.

Hotels

Hotels have private bath, phone, TV, and air-conditioning, and do not offer meals unless we specify that in the review. We always list facilities but not whether you'll be charged an extra fee to use them.

Restaurants

Unless we state otherwise, restaurants are open for lunch and dinner daily. We mention dress only when there's a

> For expanded hotel reviews, visit **Fodors.com**

specific requirement and reservations only when they're essential or not accepted—it's always best to book ahead.

Credit Cards

We assume that restaurants and hotels accept credit cards. If not, we'll note it in the review.

Budget Well

Hotel and restaurant price categories from ¢ to $$$$ are defined in the opening pages of the respective chapters. For attractions, we always give standard adult admission fees; reductions are usually available for children, students, and senior citizens.

Listings
★ Fodor's Choice
★ Highly recommended
⊠ Physical address
✛ Directions or Map coordinates
🕮 Mailing address
☎ Telephone
🖷 Fax
⊕ On the Web
✍ E-mail
🎫 Admission fee
🕐 Open/closed times
Ⓜ Metro stations
▭ No credit cards

Hotels & Restaurants
🏨 Hotel
🛏 Number of rooms
♿ Facilities
🍽 Meal plans
✗ Restaurant
☎ Reservations
👔 Dress code
🚭 Smoking

Outdoors
🏌 Golf
🏕 Camping

Other
☺ Family-friendly
⇨ See also
⊠ Branch address
☞ Take note

Experience
Japan

WHAT'S WHERE

Numbers correspond to chapters.

3 Tokyo. Tokyo, home to 10% of Japan's population, would take a lifetime to fully explore. Rather than any coherent center there is a mosaic of colorful neighborhoods—Shibuya, Asakusa, Ginza, Tsukiji, Shinjuku, and dozens more—each with its own texture.

4 Side Trips from Tokyo. A quick train ride to Nikko or Kamakura will provide all your shrine and temple viewings. Hakone offers spectacular views of Mt. Fuji and numerous lakes. In Hase, the 37-foot Daibutsu—the Great Buddha—has sat for seven centuries, gazing inward.

5 Nagoya, Ise-Shima, and the Kii Peninsula. Ise Jingu (Grand Shrines of Ise)—the most important site in Japan's national religion—is found in Ise-Shima National Park. To the south, the Kii Peninsula has magnificent coastal scenery and fishing villages. Inland, the mountain monastery of Koya-san looms mythically with 120 temples.

6 The Japan Alps and the North Chubu Coast. Soaring mountains, slices of old Japan, famed lacquerware and superb hiking, skiing, and *onsen* soaking are found here. In Kanazawa is Kenroku Gar-

den, one of the three finest in the country.

7 Kyoto. Kyoto, Japan's ancient capital, represents 12 centuries worth of history and tradition in its beautiful gardens, castles, museums, and nearly 2,000 temples and shrines—Kinkaku-ji and Kiyomizu-dera top most itineraries. Here you'll also see geisha and sample *kaiseki ryori*, an elegant meal.

8 The Kansai Region. Nara may not match Kyoto's abundance of sacred sites, but its coherently arranged shrines and parks are among Japan's finest. Osaka offers a mix of bright lights, like in the Dotombori entertainment area, and tradition, such as the Osaka-jo castle. Just minutes by train from Osaka is Kobe, where European and Japanese influences have long mingled.

9 Western Honshu. Mountains divide this region into an urban south and a rural north. Hiroshima is the modern stronghold, where the sobering remnants of the charred A-Bomb Dome testify to darker times. Offshore at Miyajima, the famous torii appears to float on the water. Bizen masters craft the famous local pottery.

WHAT'S WHERE

10 Shikoku. Thanks to its isolation, this southern island has held on to its traditions and staved off the industry that blights parts of Japan. There's great hiking, dramatic scenery, some of the country's freshest seafood, and the can't-miss traditional dancing at the Awa Odori festival in Tokushima.

11 Kyushu. Rich in history and heavily reliant on the agriculture industry, lush Kyushu is the southernmost of Japan's four main islands. At Aso National Park you can look into the steaming caldera of Mt. Naka-dake, an active volcano. With its rolling hills and streetcars, Nagasaki is often called the San Francisco of Japan, a testament to the city's resurrection from the second atomic bomb.

12 Okinawa. Okinawa is known as the Hawaii of Japan. Relaxation and water sports are the main attractions of this archipelago, located some 700 km (435 mi) south of Kyushu. A paradise for snorkelers and scuba divers, the islands teem with reefs, canyons, and shelves of coral.

RUSSIA

RUSSIA

Sea of Okhotsk

45°N

HOKKAIDO

Asahikawa   Kitami

Sapporo   **14**

Muroran   Tomakomai

Kushiro

Hakodate

Hirosaki   Aomori

Hachinohe

Nihon-kai
(Sea of Japan)

13

Akita   Morioka

40°N

Sakata

Tsuruoka

Yamagata

Sado
Island

Niigata   Sendai

Nagaoka   Fukushima

Noto
Peninsula

Iwaki

Kanazawa

Fukui

Nagano   Mito

Gifu

Kyoto   Nagoya   ★TOKYO

Mt. Fuji   Yokohama

Osaka   Tsu   Shizuoka

Hamamatsu

35°N

Nachi   JAPAN

Shirahama

TAIHEIYO OCEAN
(PACIFIC OCEAN)

Japan

30°N

140°E   145°E

13 Tohoku. Zao-san draws skiers, while tourists clamor for a look at the *juhyo*, snow-covered fir trees that resemble fairy-tale monsters. Sendai is a good base for trips to Zao-san and Matsushima, a bay studded with more than 250 pine tree-covered islands. Make time for the traditional town of Kakunodate and Japan's deepest lake Tazawa-ko.

14 Hokkaido. Japan's northernmost island is also its last frontier. Glorious landscapes, hiking, and skiing adventures await. In February, the Sapporo Snow Festival dazzles with huge ice sculptures. To the south are the famous hot springs of Noboribetsu Onsen and Jigokudani (Valley of Hell), a volcanic crater that belches boiling water and sulfurous vapors.

JAPAN
TOP ATTRACTIONS

The Temples of Kyoto

(A) The former capital of Japan, Kyoto, is known for its grand, historic structures. Two of the famous Buddhist temples are the Ginkaku-ji (1474), the "Temple of the Silver Pavilion," which features the Kannon Hall and a rock-and-gravel Japanese garden, and Kinkaku-ji (1393), its golden sister that includes a gold-leaf adorned hall. Each is fronted by a spectacular lake.

Mt. Fuji

(B) Mt. Fuji, the nation's highest peak, rises 3,776 meters. One of Japan's most famous symbols, the symmetrical Fuji-san inspires artists and commoners alike. The dormant volcano sits between Yamanashi and Shizuoka prefectures. During nice weather, it can be viewed from Tokyo and Yokohama. For a closer peek, climb it in summer or see it from the Shinkansen train between Tokyo and Osaka.

Imperial Palace East Gardens

(C) Open to the public, the gardens are all that remain of the former innermost circle of defense for Edo Castle, the residence of the Tokugawa Shogun between 1603 and 1867. The gardens are accessed by three gates: Hirakawa-mon, Ote-mon, and Kitahanebashi-mon. Sculpted, rolling greenery surround stone walls, moats, and guardhouses.

Grand Shrines of Ise

(D) Located in Mie Prefecture, the Ise Jingu Shrine is arguably Japan's most revered shrine complex. Often referred to simply as Jingu, or "The Shrine," it includes more than 100 small Shinto shrines and two main shrines, Naiku and Geku. Naiku, the Inner Shrine, houses the sun goddess Amaterasu omikami. The Outer Shrine, Geku, is home to the deity for industry and agriculture, Toyouke no omikami.

Dotombori

(E) Osaka's liveliest entertainment area, Dotombori is a single street running along the Dotombori canal in the city's Namba district. It is filled with many small bars and restaurants. Be sure to sample the local specialty: *takoyaki* (battered octopus). Following large sporting events the street is at its most frenzied, with revelers sometimes diving into the canal.

Peace Memorial Park

(F) Hiroshima's Peace Memorial Park, dedicated to those killed following the atomic bomb attack, is the city's most famous tourist attraction. Inside is the Peace Memorial Museum, which provides a history of the bomb. Also in the park is the A-Bomb Dome (the former Prefectural Industrial Promotion Hall), whose curved roof stands partly intact and serves as a symbol of peace.

Maehama Beach

This spectacular 7-km stretch of sand is on the island of Niijima, a volcanic island under the jurisdiction of Tokyo. Located 163 km south of the capital (accessible by boat or ferry), the beach offers water recreation opportunities and camping. The beach also provides a view of Mt. Fuji on occasion and is the starting point for the Miyako Triathlon.

Nibutani Ainu Culture Museum

Located in the Nibutani village of Hokkaido, the museum preserves the history and traditions of the Ainu, an ethnic group indigenous to this northern island. The museum has three themes: "Ainu (Human being)," "Kamui (Gods)," and "Moshiri (the blessings of nature)." On display are examples of woven items, carvings, and canoes. Be warned that descriptions are only in Japanese.

TOP EXPERIENCES

Sumo

Sumo pits two extremely large athletes against one another in a ring (*dohyo*). A wrestler who breaches the ring's boundary or touches the ground with a body part (other than the sole of his foot) loses. Originally intended as entertainment for Shinto gods, single bouts usually last less than a minute. Tournaments, running 15 days, are held three times a year in Tokyo and once a year in Osaka, Nagoya, and Fukuoka. Novice wrestlers (*jonokuchi*) compete in the morning and top athletes (*yokozuna*) wrestle in the late afternoon. Crowds get pretty boisterous, especially for the later matches.

Ryokan

The *ryokan,* or traditional Japanese inn, offers rooms outfitted with Japanese-style interiors, such as tatami flooring and paper (*shoji*) blinds. For in-room tea service pillows and small tables make sitting very comfortable. Futons are rolled out onto the tatami at bedtime. Meals, often included in the room rate, are breakfast and dinner, both of which contain small Japanese dishes of various seafood and regional specialties. The tourist areas of Kyoto and Hakone, near Tokyo, are home to a wonderful selection of these inns.

Japanese Gardens

Gardens in the traditional Japanese style appear in parks, on castle grounds, and in front of shrines and temples. Featuring stone lanterns, rocks, ponds, a pavilion, and rolling hedges, many of the principles that influence Japanese garden design come from religion. Shintoism, Taoism, and Buddhism all stress the contemplation and re-creation of nature as part of the process of achieving understanding and enlightenment. Jisho-ji Garden and Nijo Castle Ninomaru Garden in Kyoto and Hamarikyu Gardens in Tokyo are some of Japan's more prominent gardens to visit.

Karaoke

Karaoke is a Japanese institution whose rabid popularity cannot be understated. Often used as an after-work recreation, the activity is enjoyed by millions and involves the singing of a popular song into a microphone as the instrumental track plays on the in-room sound system and its lyrics roll across a monitor. Rooms, referred to as karaoke boxes, can be rented by the hour and seat between two and 10 customers. Drinks and light snacks can be downed as song selection books are studied.

Baseball

Yakyu (baseball) is often said to epitomize the Japanese character. Players are subject to punishing preseason training regimes that test their stamina and will. In contrast to the American style of play, the sacrifice bunt is a routine tactic, often employed in the early innings. The prized quality of group harmony is evident as ballparks reverberate to repetitive theme songs created for each batter, with the fans of the Hiroshima Carp going through perhaps the most elaborate routines. Following the final out of the Japan Series, fans of the winner crowd into city streets for a night—or, if its Osaka's Hanshin Tigers, jump from a bridge into a canal—and hit the victory sales at local stores that will follow.

Seafood and Sushi

As might be expected of a nation consisting of 3,000 islands, Japan is synonymous with the fruits of the sea. Sashimi and sushi have gained popularity with restaurant goers around the world, but it's hard to imagine some other so-called delicacies catching on. The northern island

of Hokkaido boasts of the quality of its *uni* (sea urchin), while Akita Prefecture is famous for *shiokara* (raw squid intestines). Domestic tourism and television schedules are dominated by food, and city dwellers travel the length and breadth of the country on weekend excursions to taste regional specialties.

Depato

Department stores (*depato*) are towering palaces that cater to the whims of the kings and queens of global consumerism. From the ultrapolite elevator attendants to the expert package wrapper, the attention to detail is extraordinary. Established stores follow a convenient pattern in their layout. In the basement is an expansive array of elaborately presented food, ranging from handmade sweets to bento boxes. The first floor has cosmetics, and the next floors offer the latest in female fashion. Farther up you will find designer suits for men, ornate stationery, and refined home decorations. Finally, on the top floor, often with excellent urban views, is a restaurant area.

Tea Ceremony

The tea ceremony, or *chanoyu* (the Way of Tea), is a precisely choreographed program that started more than 1,000 years ago with Buddhist monks. The ritual begins as the server prepares a cup of tea for the first guest. This process involves a strictly determined series of movements and actions, including the cleansing of each utensil to be used. One by one, the participants slurp up their bowl of tea and then eat a sweet confectionary served with it. In Tokyo, the teahouse at Hamarikyu Gardens offers a wonderful chance to enjoy this tradition.

Kampai!

Whether you're out with friends, clients, or belting out a tune at the local karaoke bar, you're sure to have a drink at least once during your stay. Rice-based sake, pronounced *sa*-kay, is Japan's number one alcoholic beverage, with more than 2,000 different brands available. The sake bar Amanogawa, in the Keio Plaza Hotel Tokyo, provides a wonderful opportunity to sample different varieties. *Shochu* is made from grain and is served either on the rocks or mixed with juice or water. As to beer, Asahi and Kirin are the two heavyweights, constantly battling for the coveted title of Japan's leading brewer, but many beer fans rate Suntory's Malts brand and Sapporo's Yebisu brand as the tastiest brews in the land.

The Performing Arts

The performing arts date back hundreds of years but are still practiced in theaters across Japan. *Noh* is a minimalist dance drama where a masked actor performs very stylized moves accompanied by instrumental music. Often in conjunction with Noh are *Kyogen* performances, which are comedic plays known for their down-to-earth humor. *Kabuki* is theater performed by adult males who also portray the female roles. Fans of puppet theater may enjoy a *Bunraku* performance, in which large puppets are manipulated to the accompaniment of narrators and stringed instruments.

IF YOU LIKE

Nightlife

Cocktails with pizzazz or chicken on a stick, dreamy jazz or thumping techno beats—you'll find it all under urban Japan's neon-soaked night sky. Walking the bar-and-club crazy streets at night is a great way to discover a city's character. Tipping is not customary, but upscale establishments may have extra service charges ranging from a few hundred yen to a few thousand. Karaoke clubs and *izakaya*, traditional watering holes, are ubiquitous and a great way to mix with locals. All-night revelers might want to consider the likes of Roppongi in Tokyo or Dotombori in Osaka, while the more culturally inclined will find theaters and cinemas in every major city.

Susukino, Sapporo. Wander this northern city's entertainment district for a taste of how many Japanese wind down after work. Bars, clubs, restaurants, and karaoke joints abound.

Suntory Hall, Akasaka, Tokyo. There's no better place to catch a classical music performance than at this theater, home to perhaps the best acoustics in the country.

Sweet Basil 139, Roppongi, Tokyo. Come for dinner or just a drink at this upscale club featuring a variety of musical performances.

Metro, Kyoto. A wide range of events and guest DJs make this one of Kansai's top clubs.

Bears, Osaka. This live venue features the best of Japan's underground music.

Garden Life

Gardens are an obsession in Japan. Many urban homes have a couple of topiary trees, and Buddhist temples nationwide have immaculately maintained grounds. The best Japanese gardens are like the canvasses of master painters, in which nature is ingeniously manipulated and represented in subtly rearranged forms. Some re-create entire landscapes in miniature, and are designed for viewing from one optimal position. Others skillfully integrate immense backdrops of mountains or forest, always managing to add to the innate beauty of the natural environment. Kyoto is home to Zen gardens, minimalist affairs of raked sand, moss, and meaningfully arranged rocks.

Imperial Palace East Garden, Tokyo. An oasis of tree-lined paths, rhododendrons, and water features that provides great views of the Imperial Palace buildings.

Kenrokuen, Kanazawa. Originally landscaped in 1676, 25-acre Kenrokuen looks good all year round thanks to a wide variety of seasonal plants and trees.

Koinzan Saiho-ji, Kyoto. The so-called "Moss Temple" has an extraordinary Zen garden, though entry is extremely pricey and requires advance permission.

Suizen-ji Koen, Kumamoto. Part of this garden re-creates the 53 stations of the old Tokaido post road that was immortalized by Hiroshiga Ando in a series of woodblock prints.

Outdoor Adventure

For many people modern Japan conjures images of the concrete, neon-lighted urban jungles of Kanto and Kansai. The country's wealth of natural attractions is easily overlooked, but outdoor enthusiasts will find their every whim catered to. In winter generous snowfall makes Hokkaido and Nagano ideal destinations for skiers and snowboarders. The Japan Alps mountain range that stretches along the north side of Honshu offers excellent hiking trails, and Shikoku is well suited to cyclists. To the south, Okinawa boasts

tropical temperatures for much of the year, and its clear waters are excellent for scuba diving and snorkeling.

Niseko, Hokkaido. Australians in the know head here by the tens of thousands each winter for arguably the best skiing in Japan.

Kamikochi, Nagano. En route to this small mountain village you pass though some stunning scenery, and upon arrival a series of trails provides access to the upper reaches of the surrounding peaks.

Shikoku. The best way to enjoy this picturesque island in the Inland Sea is from the seat of a bicycle. Slow down to the local pace and spend time exploring unexpected diversions.

Manta Scramble, Okinawa. From April to June divers can observe rarely seen manta feeding on plankton in this strait between Iriomote and Kohama islands.

Holy Sites

Most modern Japanese would not express an affiliation with one religion, and both Shintoism and Buddhism play important roles in many people's lives. Shinto architecture, with the exception of Nikko's colorful shrines, tends to be plain and simple, like the style of the nation's most sacred site at Ise, emphasizing natural materials such as wood and thatch. Temples run the gamut from austere to gaudy, both in color and design. Kyoto boasts many of the finest examples of religious architecture, while in mountain areas the act of pilgrimage and supplication to the elements is almost as important as the shrines and temples themselves.

Senso-ji, Asakusa, Tokyo. Proof positive that even Japan's largest metropolis can preserve tradition. Senso-ji has a tangible Old Tokyo atmosphere from the first entrance gate, with its immense red lantern, through the narrow pedestrian streets to the huge incense burners of the temple.

Ise Jingu, Mie Prefecture. Home of Shintoism, the national religion, the Grand Shrines of Ise are majestic thatched wooden buildings concealed in expansive forested grounds.

Todai-ji, Nara. This temple's Daibutsu-den (Hall of the Great Buddha) is the largest wooden building in the world, and houses Japan's biggest Buddha figure, cast in bronze.

Kiyomizu-dera, Kyoto. The Golden Pavilion of Kinkaku-ji may feature on more postcards, but this temple's large-scale wood construction is stunning. The steep approach to Kiyomizu-dera is lined with hundreds of craft, souvenir, and food shops.

HOTEL AND RESTAURANT PLANNER

Making Reservations

The best way to book major chain hotels is through the company's Web site. The Web sites for smaller business hotels and ryokan usually lack English content online. Travel sites, such as **Rakuten** (⊕ *travel. rakuten.co.jp/en*), can assist booking these hotels. **Welcome Inns** (⊕ *www.itcj.jp*), a Japan National Tourist Organization affiliate, lists low-priced hotels in Tokyo and across the country. We highly recommend making your Tokyo hotel reservation before you arrive. Should this be impossible, head to a tourist office at the airport or major rail station for assistance.

Lodging Costs

Rates for the top foreign and domestic chains are generally in the ¥30,000–¥60,000 range (and could even go a bit higher). Business hotel rooms, with far fewer amenities, are available for under ¥20,000. A minshuku provides Japanese-style lodging and meals for roughly ¥8,000. The ryokan offers stays for between ¥10,000 and ¥30,000 that includes use of the onsen. Shoestring travelers head to hostels where a night's stay costs around ¥3,000. Capsule hotels are similarly priced.

Choosing the Right Hotel

Accommodations in Japan range from Japanese-style inns to large Western-style hotels, in all price categories. It's essential to book in advance if you're traveling during peak travel seasons and is recommended at other times.

The *ryokan,* a traditional Japanese inn, provides the most unique experience. Japanese-style interiors include tatami flooring, paper (shoji) blinds, a low table for tea service, and pillows. Futons that are rolled out in the evening serve as beds. Stays usually include traditional Japanese morning and evening meals, often with small seafood dishes and regional specialties. Lodges usually offer the use of an *onsen* (hot-spring bath), which is typically for bathing, rather than an in-room shower.

Similar to the ryokan, but less expensive, *minshuku* are Japanese-style bed-and-breakfasts. Usually family-run, these inns feature Japanese-style rooms and meals. Baths (there are usually no in-room bathing options) are part of the shared public areas, which also include toilets.

Business hotels feature Western-style digs in basic, small rooms; these are ideal for one night and are usually close to major transportation hubs. Most major cities have high-end Western-style hotels with ritzy spas, fully equipped gyms, and some of Japan's better restaurants. Many are situated in high-rise buildings and provide fantastic views of the city's skyline.

The boutique hotel arrived late to Japan, but these quirky, trendy properties have taken hold. Earth tones, funky bathrooms, and curvy, chrome fixtures dominate at these hotels, which are priced just below business hotels.

Capsule hotels—generally men-only—are the most spartan accommodations around, providing a chamber that you slide your body into laterally, much like a coffin. There are no frills here, but the price is right. Common areas with televisions and lockers for valuables and luggage come standard.

Resorts in hot-spring areas, such as Hakone or Tohoku, focus their services and amenities on the relaxation provided by onsen—either while naked or in a swimsuit.

Types of Restaurants

The Japanese love to dine out and there is something for every taste and budget. In the more popular tourist areas English menus are often available. There is nearly always someone who can speak a little English. If all else fails there are always the plastic models in the window outside to point at.

Many restaurants specialize in just one kind of food. Ramen, soba (buckwheat noodles), and udon (thick, white-wheat noodles) restaurants are hard to beat for value and reliability. Choose between table and counter seats. To order, just choose the toppings for the broth.

Okonomiyaki-ya are no-frills eateries serving thick savory pancakes. Expect tables to be fitted with a hot plate as most often diners do the cooking themselves using their choice of ingredients to fill the okonomiyaki.

In the evening *akachochin*—red lantern restaurants, so called because these hang outside their doors—establishments are a safe, inexpensive bet. Customers sit at a counter space in an informal, convivial environment. *Robata* specialize in grilled foods and to order customers simply point at what they want grilled. *Oden-ya*, which serve a variety of slowly simmered meats and vegetables, have a similar atmosphere. Again, to order just point to your desired morsels. *Izakaya*, publike dens, have counter and table service and have more extensive menus.

Sushi restaurants, usually reserved for special occasions, are a breed apart. Expect a subdued atmosphere with wooden surfaces. Sit at the counter to get to see the *itamae* (sushi chef) in action. Point at the fish in the glass case to order or ask for *omakase*—or chef's choice.

At tempura restaurants customers sit at the counter and enjoy the attention of their personal chef. Choose the course you desire (usually by how much you want to spend), which the chef will serve to you piece by piece.

Ryotei specialize in *kaiseki* (a formal multicourse meal). Expect to be greeted by kimono-clad waitresses who usher you to your private room. Leave your shoes and worries behind in the hallway, and enjoy this unforgettable experience. Those on a budget should visit at lunchtime, when many ryotei offer *kaiseki bento* at a fraction of the dinner price.

The regular bento, or Japanese box lunch of rice, fish or meat, and vegetable sides, is available everywhere from department stores to convenience stores. Sandwiches, sushi, and *onigiri* (rice balls with various fillings) are other popular to-go items.

Meals and Mealtimes

Office workers eat lunch from noon to 1, so eat later to avoid crowds. Most restaurants have lunchtime specials, which provide an opportunity for fine dining at a considerably lower price, until 2:30. Many restaurants close their doors between 3 and 5. Unless otherwise noted, the restaurants listed in this guide are open daily for lunch and dinner. For dinner at upmarket establishment ask hotel staff to make reservations—this gives the management time to locate an English menu or staff with some language skills.

Paying

These days, credit cards are widely accepted in restaurants, but this isn't a given in more informal eateries. Check that your card will be accepted before sitting down.

Menus

Many less expensive restaurants have plastic replicas of the dishes they serve, displayed in their front windows, so you can always point to what you want to eat if the language barrier is insurmountable.

TRANSPORTATION PLANNER

JR Pass

Japan Railways offers the Japan Rail Pass, an affordable way to see the country. It can be used on all JR railways, buses, and ferryboats including the Shinkansen "bullet" trains—except for Nozomi trains on the Tokaido and Sanyo lines. Hikari or Kodama trains, however, serve these same routes and are included. Passes must be purchased at an authorized JR outlet outside of Japan before your trip and are available for 7-, 14-, or 21-day periods. Activate them upon arrival at a major rail station or Narita airport. A first-class version allows access to the Shinkansen Lines' special Green Cars.

Tokyo-only Plans

JR East offers **Suica**, a rechargeable debit card in Tokyo. **PASMO**, another rechargeable prepaid card in Tokyo, can be used on subways and JR and non-JR trains. The one-day **Holiday Pass** works in the entire Tokyo–JR network on holidays, weekends, and the summer holiday period (July 20–August 31). Tokyo's other one-day passes include the **Tokunai Pass** for JR lines and the **Tokyo Free Kippu**, which also covers subways and buses.

Getting Around by Train

Japan (and Tokyo in particular) offers what is perhaps one of the world's best train and subway system: they're nearly always on time, have clean facilities, and provide a safe environment. But it's also one of the most complicated.

Shinkansen: The JR Shinkansen bullet trains travel up and down Honshu and into Kyushu. Tokyo Station is Tokyo's main hub, with lines heading north, south, and west.

Regional trains: About 70% of Japan's railways are owned by Japan Railways (JR Group), the other 30% is owned by private companies. Non-JR lines include Tokyu's Toyoko Line between Tokyo's Shibuya and Yokohama to the south. The main line of the Odakyu Company and Keio Inokashira Line use Shinjuku and Shibuya, respectively, as hubs to serve Tokyo to the west. For service to Saitama Prefecture, Tobu offers the Tojo Line, which leaves Tokyo from Ikebukuro Station. The most important JR-owned regional line in Tokyo is the In Tokyo, Yamanote Line, which loops around the city, while its Sobu and Chuo lines split that circle into east and west directions; JR trains also travel to Tokyo Disneyland.

Subways: The easiest way to explore Tokyo is via subway. There are two subway companies: Tokyo Metro and Toei. Since these are separate entities, they have separate fares, and it's cheaper to stay with one company. At the outer edges of the subway networks, private companies operate the line. If you're going far afield, be prepared to pay an additional fare.

Tokyo monorail: Beginning at Hamamatsu-cho Station, the monorail provides the simplest access to Haneda Airport.

PURCHASING TICKETS

In Tokyo (and other major cities) basic fares (train or subway) are between ¥110 and ¥310. Tickets can be purchased from machines that take coins or cash near the gates. Maps above each machine—usually in Japanese and English—give destinations. ■ TIP→ **If a station map is written only in Japanese, buy the lowest-priced ticket and adjust the fare upon arrival.** Purchase tickets for Shinkansen lines and other long-distance regional lines that require a seat reservation at a ticket windows.

1

HOW TO USE A TICKET MACHINE

Use the map above the ticket machine to determine how much money to put on your ticket. The numbers next to each stop indicate the price from your current station.

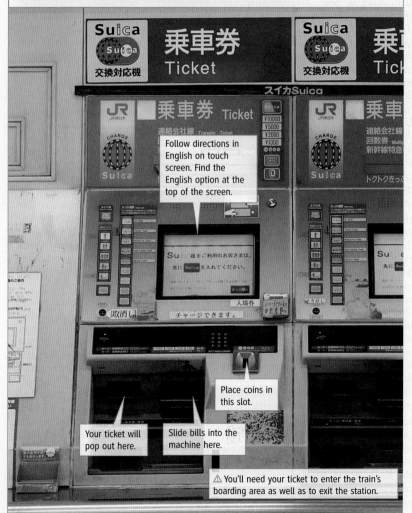

Follow directions in English on touch screen. Find the English option at the top of the screen.

Place coins in this slot.

Your ticket will pop out here.

Slide bills into the machine here.

⚠ You'll need your ticket to enter the train's boarding area as well as to exit the station.

FAQS

What time of year is the best to travel to Japan?

It depends entirely what you want to do. For simple sightseeing in Tokyo and Kyoto, the pleasant weather in spring and fall cannot be beat. Also, in April, the cherry trees start to bloom in Kansai and the baseball season kicks off. In October, Tokyo is abuzz with its international film festival and numerous design events. Summer is hot and muggy nationwide, though August is also the peak of the festival and fireworks seasons. Winter means skiing in the mountains of Hokkaido and the Japan Alps, but New Year's is one of the three big travel periods—Obon in August and Golden Week in late April/early May are the other two—where the big cities empty as everyone heads for their ancestral homes, which makes travel generally more expensive and frantic.

How expensive is Japan?

Japan has a reputation for being incredibly expensive, but things are not as they once were. Sure, that the $10 cup of coffee does indeed exist in Tokyo but so too does the $3 version at most cafés. In other words, do your homework and plan ahead. Buying a Japan Rail Pass can cut back on transportation costs if you are traveling enough. Book hotel rooms in advance online—there are bargains to be had when staying with the non-big-name foreign chains. Spending time outside big cities like Tokyo will also cut down on meal and other common expenses.

Is free Wi-Fi readily available?

Japan is considered to be one of the most technologically advanced countries on the planet, but finding free wireless access to the Internet can be challenging. Some cafés do have it, but in general Japan has not adopted the concept of free Wi-Fi. A quick search of the Web before arrival will reveal some options; probably the best bet lies in the *manga kissa* (comic-book coffee shops). At these businesses, which are scattered through all of the nation's big cities, Internet terminals are included in the fee to enter the shop, roughly ¥400 for the first hour. Or another very good option is to rent a mobile hot spot from a company like eMobile (available at international airports).

How do clothing sizes compare with Western countries?

Given the different body sizes, Japan can be very hard for clothing purchases. For simple items, such as a T-shirt, the equivalent of a typical XL size may not exist, and even if it does it might be equivalent to an L size in the West. Women may be challenged finding pant designs that fit properly around both their hips and waist. The sizes for men's shoes will generally top out at 10½. Yet the country's big cities have in recent years seen an influx of foreign retailers like Gap and H&M, which are probably a foreign traveler's most reliable options.

Will my mobile phone function?

The short answer: probably not. Though things have improved as far as foreign models functioning in Japan, renting a mobile phone at the airport is the simplest solution. Basic fees will start around $30 per week and the handsets (English-ready) have access to the Web, email, and texting. The assigned telephone number can be made known in advance if a booking is made—at a carrier like Softbank—a few days prior to pickup.

BUDGET TRAVEL TIPS

Travelers posting in the Travel Talk Forums at Fodors.com recommend the following money-saving tips.

Lodging

"A hotel's own Japanese Web site usually gives the best rates and choices—some guarantee they beat any other online quotation!" —Alec

"If there are four of you traveling together, youth hostels can be an attractive budget option. Rooms are often set up for four people, so no sharing with strangers! We've found them to be very clean and usually well located." —lcuy

"Big hotel chains (Western or Japanese) can be expensive, but Japan also has 'business hotels' that provide small basic hotel rooms at reasonable prices." —mrwunrfl

Transportation

"We used a rail pass for our travel outside of Tokyo (super), and found a Pasmo card very convenient for the subways in Tokyo." —teacherhiker

"Not only will the JR Pass get you on the Shinkansen, but it'll also get you on JR sleeper trains. Your pass entitles you to a small enclosed space (not private though), and for a surcharge you can get a private cabin. You can save one night's accommodation by traveling overnight." —Sydney2K

"Use frequent-flier miles to get around Japan. The award levels are low, just 15K or 20K miles. Once, I flew from Tokyo to Sapporo, poked around Hokkaido a bit with JR Pass, and then flew from Sapporo to Hiroshima. Then I used my JR Pass to get back to Tokyo, after a couple of stops." —mrwunrfl

Food

"Eating takeout from department store basement food halls is a excellent way to save money. You will save even more if you wait until an hour before closing when many prepared foods are marked down 25% to 50%. Makes for nice inexpensive dinners." —mjs

"I second the suggestion about grabbing food at the "depa-chika" (food section of department stores). For people who aren't fans of Japanese food or miss a hot dog or burger, try Mos Burger's Spicy Mos. One of the best fast-food burgers I've had anywhere. The convenience stores like Lawson, 7-Eleven, etc., sell hot dogs and croquettes for lunch on-the-go. The hot dogs are pretty good but the packaging of the free mustard and ketchup (similar to the ketchup packs at fast-food vendors in the U.S.) is simply amazing. Also, ramen is a great option for cheap meals! I like Jiro, but several others in the Shijuku area are good." —mdn

Shopping

"If you like beautiful fabrics or kimonos, get one from a vintage kimono shop. Japanese people do not wear vintage stuff, so these can be had for a fraction of the original price. There's one in Tokyo off Omotesando." —Cilla_Tey

"While in Tokyo, head to the Ameyoko Street Market located right in front of the JR Ueno station. There you'll find a Bangkok-style street market right in the middle of Tokyo. You can find everything from the freshest seafood to a can of Spam, real Rolex watches to fake Gucci bags, and everything else in between." —hawaiiantraveler

JAPANESE ETIQUETTE

Many Japanese expect foreigners to behave differently and are tolerant of faux pas, but they are pleasantly surprised when people acknowledge and observe their customs. The easiest way to ingratiate yourself with the Japanese is to take time to learn and respect Japanese ways.

General Tips

■ Bow upon meeting someone.

■ Japanese will often point at their nose (not chest) when referring to themselves.

■ Pointing at someone is considered rude. To make reference to someone or something, wave your hand up and down in his or her direction.

■ Direct expression of opinions isn't encouraged. It's more common for people to gently suggest something.

■ Avoid physical contact. A slap on the back or hand on the shoulder would be uncomfortable for a Japanese person.

■ Avoid too much eye contact when speaking. Direct eye contact is a show of spite and rudeness.

At Someone's Home

■ Most entertaining is done in restaurants and bars; don't be offended if you're not invited to someone's home.

■ Should an invitation be extended, a small gift—perhaps a bottle of alcohol or box of sweets—should be presented.

■ At the entryway, remove your shoes and put on the provided slippers. Remove your slippers if you enter a room with tatami flooring (straw mats). Before entering the bathroom, remove your house slippers and switch to those found near the bathroom doorway.

■ Stick to neutral subjects in conversation. The weather doesn't have to be your only topic, but you should take care not to be too nosy.

■ It's not customary for Japanese businessmen to bring wives along. If you're traveling with your spouse, don't assume that an invitation includes both of you. If you want to bring your spouse, ask in a way that eliminates the need for a direct refusal.

In Business Meetings

■ For business meetings, *meishi* (business cards) are highly recommended. Remember to place those you have received in front of you; don't shove them in your pocket. It's also good to have one side of your business card printed in Japanese.

■ Japanese position their employees based upon rank within the company. Don't be surprised if the proceedings seem perfunctory—many major decisions were made behind the scenes before the meeting started.

■ Stick to last names and use the honorific -san after the name, as in Tanaka-san (Mr. or Mrs. Tanaka). Also, respect the hierarchy, and as much as possible address yourself to the most senior person in the room.

■ Many Japanese businessmen still don't know how to interact with Western businesswomen. Be patient, and, if the need arises, gently remind them that, professionally, you expect to be treated as any man would be.

At Lodgings and Ryokan

■ When you arrive at a minshuku or ryokan, put on the slippers that are provided and make your way to your room. Remember to remove your slippers before entering your room; never step on the tatami with shoes or slippers.

■ Before entering a thermal pool, make sure you wash and rinse off entirely before getting into the water. Do not get soap in the tub. Other guests will be using the same bathwater, so it is important to observe this custom. After your bath, change into the *yukata* (robe) provided in your room. Don't worry about walking around in it—other guests will be doing the same. ⇨ *For more tips on Ryokan behavior, see "The Ryokan Experience" in Chapter 2.*

At Restaurants

■ *Oshibori* is a small hot towel provided in Japanese restaurants. This is to wipe your hands but not your face. If you must use it on your face, wipe your face first, then your hands, and never toss it on the table: fold or roll it up.

■ When eating with chopsticks, don't use the part that has entered your mouth to pick up food from communal dishes. Instead, use the end that you've been holding in your hand. Always rest chopsticks on the edge of the tray, bowl, or plate; sticking them upright in your food is reminiscent of how rice is arranged at funerals.

■ There's no taboo against slurping your noodle soup, though women are generally less boisterous about it than men.

■ Pick up the soup bowl and drink directly from it, rather than leaning over the table to sip it. Eat the fish or vegetables with your chopsticks.

■ When drinking with a friend, never serve yourself. Always pour for the other person, who will in turn pour for you. If you would rather not drink, don't refuse a refill, just sip, keeping your glass at least half full.

■ It's considered gauche to eat as you walk along a public street.

While Shopping

■ After entering a store, the staff will greet you with "*irasshaimase,*" which is a welcoming phrase. A simple smile's an appropriate acknowledgment. After that, polite requests to view an item or try on a piece of clothing should be followed as anywhere in the West. Bargaining is common at flea markets, but not so in conventional stores.

■ There's usually a plastic tray at the register for you to place your money or credit card. Your change and receipt however, will be placed in your hand. It should be noted that many small shops do not accept credit cards.

Giving Gifts

■ Gift giving is a year-round national pastime, peaking during summer's *ochugen* and the year-end *oseibo* seasons. Common gifts between friends, family, and associates include elegantly wrapped packages of fruit, noodles, or beer.

■ On Valentine's Day women give men chocolate, but on White Day in March the roles are reversed.

■ For weddings and funerals, cash gifts are the norm. Convenience stores carry special envelopes in which the money (always crisp, new bills) should be inserted.

GREAT ITINERARIES

AN INTRODUCTION TO JAPAN

Like every other nation, Japan has some sights that are more famous than others. These sights tend to be in the major cities. The following itinerary covers the barest, surface-scratching minimum in modern Tokyo and glorious Nikko; the temples and shrines of Kamakura, the power center of Japan's first shogunate; the temples of classical Kyoto; and Nara, Japan's first permanent capital. Two weeks are obviously better than one in Japan. With more time you can visit Japan's mountainous areas, Osaka, Himeji, and Hiroshima.

Day 1: Arrival

Flights from the United States tend to land in the late afternoon, so you'll want to rest up and get to bed early on your arrival day.

Days 2 and 3: Tokyo

Visit the major Tokyo sights or shops that appeal to you (⇨ *Chapter 3*). Ginza, Ueno Koen's museums, Tsukiji, the Imperial Palace grounds, and Asakusa are all among the top areas to explore. Arrange to spend your evenings in one or two of the nighttime districts, such as Roppongi or Shinjuku, or try to see a Kabuki, Noh, or Bunraku performance.

Days 4 and 5: Side-trips from Tokyo

Head to the picturesque Chusen-ji (temple) in Nikko either on your own or with a tour. Also make time to visit Kamakura, perhaps stopping in Yokohama on the way back (⇨ *Chapter 4*). These trips can all be done conveniently by train.

Days 6, 7, and 8: The Japan Alps

Take the Shinkansen train to Nagano and visit Zenko-ji (temple). Continue by train to Matsumoto and visit Karasu-jo, the Japan Folklore Museum, and the

Japan Ukiyo-e Museum. The next day travel via Kamikochi to Takayama, one of Japan's best-preserved traditional cities. Finally, on your third day head to the Asa-ichi (morning market); then see other Takayama sights—the farmhouses of Shirakawa-go village or the former samurai-controlled district of Kamisannomachi—before taking a train via Toyama to Kanazawa in the late afternoon (⇨ *Chapter 6*).

Days 9, 10, 11, and 12: Kanazawa, Kyoto, and Nara

Kanazawa has also preserved many of its traditional buildings, and it is one of the country's finest cities. Take in what sights you can, perhaps the Kenroku Garden or the Naga-machi samurai district, before catching the late-afternoon train to Kyoto (a trip of about three hours), where you'll base yourself for a few days (⇨ *Chapter 8*). In the morning, visit the sights in the eastern district (Higashiyama) in the afternoon and take in the Gion district in the evening. On your second full day in Kyoto, visit more eastern district sights as well as those in the western district sights. If you are in the city on the 25th of the month, don't miss Kitano Tenmangu market. On your third day in Kyoto, cover Central Kyoto in the morning, including To-ji market, if you're in town on the 21st of the month, and take a train to Nara (⇨ *Chapter 8*) in the afternoon to see the elegant temples, the Daibutsu (Great Buddha) of Nara Koen, and the famous deer. Return to Kyoto after dinner.

Day 13: Osaka and Kobe

This morning, take the train to Osaka (⇨ *Chapter 8*), a sprawling city of never-ending urban intrigue, where you should spend a few hours or the night. Drop your bags at your hotel (or send them onto

Kobe), and hit the consumer electronics shops in the Den Den Town; check out Senri Expo Park, or head to the Osaka Museum of History. In the afternoon, move on to Kobe, which is only 20 minutes by train. It's a port city known for beef and large foreign influence. If the Hanshin Tigers are scheduled in the evening, don't miss a chance to catch a game at the historic Koshien Stadium, midway between Kobe and Osaka. Spend the night in either Kobe or Osaka.

Day 14: Himeji and Kurashiki

Travel by train to Himeji to visit Himeji-jo, its remarkable castle (⇨ *Chapter 8, Kobe*). Continue on to Okayama and reach historic Kurashiki by early afternoon (⇨ *Chapter 9*). In the historic Bikan area of the city, there are numerous museums.

Day 15: Hiroshima

Leave Kurashiki by train in time to reach Hiroshima for lunch. Visit the Peace Memorial Park and then take the train and ferry to Miyajima, with the glorious vermilion torii in the bay. If you are up for it, take the one-hour hike up Mt. Misen. Hiroshima is known for its *okonomiyaki* (a grilled pancake of egg, meat, and eggs). Give that a try before heading to your hotel for the night (⇨ *Chapter 9*).

Day 16: Tokyo and Home

Return to Tokyo by Shinkansen train (about a four-hour trip) this morning, in time to reach Narita Airport in Tokyo for your flight home.

GREAT ITINERARIES

TOKYO IN 1 WEEK

Tokyo is a metropolis that confounds with its complexity: 34 million people occupy a greater metropolitan area that includes soaring towers of glass and steel, rolling expressways, numerous temples, parks, and square mile after square mile of concrete housing blocks. Since the end of World War II, the city has constantly reinvented itself with new building developments and cultural trends. Few things have remained static other than its pre-eminence as Japan's economic center (⇨ *Chapter 3*).

Day 1: Tsukiji and Ginza

Start *very* early (around 5 am) with a visit to the **Tokyo Central Wholesale Market** (Tokyo Chuo Oroshiuri Ichiba) in the Tsukiji district to have the finest, freshest sushi for breakfast. Take a morning stroll through **Ginza** to explore its fabled shops and *depato* (department stores). Then hit a chic restaurant or café for lunch (more-reasonably priced ones are found on the upper floors of most department stores). The **Sony Building** and its showroom of electronics are worth a stop, as are the art galleries. The skyscrapers of **Shiodome** are just down the street, in the direction of **Shimbashi**. Take a peek on the first floor of the **Shiodome Media Tower**, where aerial photos of Ginza from roughly 100 years ago exhibit how the area was once a network of canals. In the evening, head back up towards Ginza and enjoy yakitori (grilled chicken) at one of the many small restaurants in **Yuraku-cho**.

Day 2: Asakusa and Ueno

Spend the morning at **Senso-ji** and adjacent **Asakusa Jinja** in Asakusa. If you're looking for souvenir gifts—sacred or secular—allow time and tote space for the abundant selection that local vendors at

the **Nakamise Shopping Arcade** have to offer. Numerous *jinrikisha* (rickshaw) are here looking for customers to take on a tour. **Kappabashi** is a nearby street dedicated to outfitting restaurants and bars with dishes, cups, chopsticks, and even plastic food models. From there go to **Ueno** for an afternoon of museums, vistas, and historic sites. **Ueno Park** can be used for a break. Keep in mind that in the evening the crowds in Asakusa are not as intrusive as during the day, and many of the major attractions, including the five-tier pagoda of Senso-ji, are brightly lighted. A quick trip back might be worth it.

Day 3: Shibuya and Shinjuku

Start off at **Hachiko Square** and the "Scramble Crossing" and hit the nearby stores. Inside the station building is the once lost masterpiece by avant-garde artist **Taro Okamoto**, *Myth of Tomorrow*. In the afternoon see the Shinto shrine **Meiji Jingu** and walk through the nearby **Harajuku** and **Omotesando** fashion districts. Spend the rest of the afternoon on the west side of **Shinjuku**, Tokyo's 21st-century model city; and savor the view from the observation deck of architect Kenzo Tange's monumental **Tokyo Metropolitan Government Office;** cap off the day visiting **Shinjuku Gyo-en National Garden**. For those seeking a bit of excitement, the red-light district of **Kabuki-cho**, just to the east of **JR Shinjuku Station**, comes alive once the sun goes down.

Day 4: Akihabara and Imperial Palace

Spend the morning browsing in **Akihabara**, Tokyo's electronics quarter, and see the nearby Shinto shrine **Kanda Myojin**. There are also the "maid cafés," which are more a curiosity than a serious dining option. Then use the afternoon for a tour of the

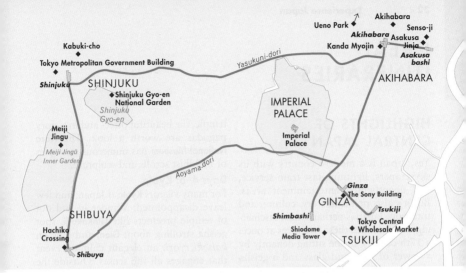

Imperial Palace and environs. The **Chidori-gafuchi National Cemetery** has a wonderful park and a boat-rental facility—both great for unwinding. If the Yomiuri Giants are in town, catch a game at **Tokyo Dome** in the evening.

Day 5: Sightseeing Loose Ends

Fill in the missing pieces: see the Buddhist temple, **Sengaku-ji** in Shinagawa; the remarkable **Edo-Tokyo Hakubutsukan** in **Ryogoku**; a tea ceremony; a Kabuki play; or a sumo tournament, if one is in town. Or visit the **Kokugikan**, National Sumo Arena, in the Ryogoku district, and some of the sumo stables in the neighborhood.

Days 6 and 7: Yokohama and Nikko

You can make Tokyo your home base for a series of side trips (⇨ *Chapter 4*). Take a train out to **Yokohama**, with its scenic port and Chinatown. There's also the preserved **Yokohama Red Brick Warehouses** that date back roughly 100 years. Short boat trips, some originating near **Yokohama Station**, that cruise through the bay are possible with a number of water ferries. A bit farther south is **Kamakura**, the 13th-century military capital of Japan. The **Great Buddha** (Daibutsu) of the **Kotoku-in** in nearby Hase is among the many National Treasures of art and architecture that draw millions of visitors a year.

Still farther off, but again an easy train trip, is **Nikko**, where the founder of the Tokugawa Shogun dynasty is enshrined. **Tosho-gu** is a monument unlike any other in Japan, and the picturesque **Lake Chuzen-ji** is in a forest above the shrine. Two full days, with an overnight stay, allows you an ideal, leisurely exploration of both. Yet another option is a trip to **Hakone**, where you can soak in a traditional onsen or climb to the summit of **Fuji-san** (Mt. Fuji).

GREAT ITINERARIES

HIGHLIGHTS OF CENTRAL JAPAN

Yes, Japan is a modern country with its skyscrapers, lightning-fast train service, and neon-lighted entertainment areas. But it's also rich in history, culture, and tradition. Japan is perhaps most fascinating when you see these two faces at once: a 17th-century shrine sitting defiantly by a tower of steel and glass and a geisha chatting on a cell phone. This part of the Kansai region might be the best place to view this contrast.

Day 1: Ise-Jingu

Ise-jingu (Grand Shrines of Ise), with their harmonious architecture and cypress-forest setting, provide one of Japan's most spiritual experiences. The Inner Shrine and Outer Shrine are roughly 6 km apart. In addition, there are 123 affiliated shrines in and around Ise City.

Day 2: Koya-san

More than 100 temples belonging to the Shingon sect of Buddhism stand on one of Japan's holiest mountains, 48 km south of Osaka. Kobo Daishi established the original **Garan-ji** temple complex in AD 816. An exploration of the atmospheric cemetery of **Okuno-in** temple takes you past headstone art and 300-year-old cedar trees. But the temple's primary function is as the mausoleum for Daishi.

Day 3: Nara

In the 8th century, Nara was the capital of Japan, and many cultural relics of that period, including some of the world's oldest wooden structures, still stand among forested hills and parkland. Be sure to visit Nara's 53-foot-high, 1,300-year-old bronze Daibutsu (Great Buddha) in **Todai-ji** temple and to make friends with the deer of **Nara Koen**. At the **Kofuku-ji**

temple, the beautiful three- and five-story pagodas are worth a look. The **Nara National Museum** has numerous examples of Buddhist scrolls and sculpture.

Days 4–6: Kyoto

For many visitors **Kyoto** *is* Japan, and few leave disappointed. Wander in and out of temple precincts like **Ginkaku-ji**, spot geisha strolling about **Gion,** and dine on *kaiseki ryori,* an elegant culinary event that engages all the senses. Outside the city center, a day trip to hillside **Arashiyama**, the gardens of the Katsura Rikyu, and the temple of Enryaku-ji atop **Hiei-zan** is a must. With nearly 2,000 temples and shrines, exquisite crafts, and serene gardens, Kyoto embodies traditional Japan. For taking some with you, the **Kyoto Handicraft Center** stocks painted screens and traditional wear. Many restaurants serve dishes based on locally sourced ingredients. Embodying this spirit is the 400-hundred-year-old **Nishiki Market,** which includes roughly 100 mom-and-pop shops offering fish and vegetables.

Day 7: Osaka

Although by no means picturesque, **Osaka** provides a taste of urban Japan outside the capital, along with a few traditional sights. The handsome castle **Osaka-jo** nestles among skyscrapers, and the neon of **Dotombori** flashes around the local Kabuki theater. Osakans are passionate about food, and you'll find some of the finest in the country here. The Hanshin Tigers have perhaps the most raucous fans in baseball, and the historic **Koshien Stadium** is the place to see them (and the Tigers) in action (though they play in the **Kyocera Osaka Dome** in August). The **Namba Grand Kagetsu Theatre** is a home to traditional *manzai* (stand-up) comedy and contemporary entertainment. Fans of electronics

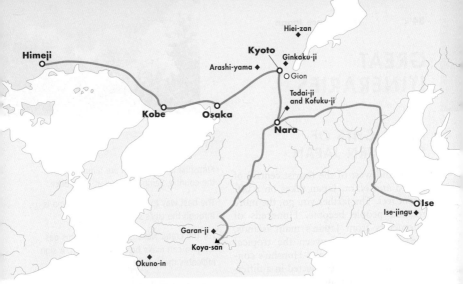

and the subculture will want to head to **Den Den Town**, which has shops selling consumer electronics and anime and manga products—much like Akihabara in Tokyo.

Day 8: Kobe

Kobe has recovered from the dark day in 1995 when it was struck by an earthquake that killed more than 5,000 people. The **Kobe Earthquake Memorial Museum** is dedicated to the event and its aftermath. Some of the first foreigners to live in Japan after the Meiji Restoration built homes in **Kitano-cho,** near the station, and the area retains an interesting mix of architectural styles. The city will forever be associated with beef, but a trip to its **Chinatown** will reveal numerous Chinese delicacies. At an elevation of 931 meters, **Mt. Rokko** is accessible by cable car and features a museum and garden. On the way up the mountain take a look at Nunobiki Falls, considered one of Japan's most picturesque falls. The city has also recently added a "life-size" statue for **Tetsujin 28** (Gigantor), the central robot in the popular manga and TV series.

Day 9: Himeji

The western Honshu city's most famous sight, **Himeji-jo,** also known as the White Egret Castle (Shirasagi-jo), dominates the skyline. The castle takes only a few hours

to see, and it's about a 15-minute walk (or a short bus ride) from the train station. Since Himeji is a short (50-minute) train ride from Kobe, it's a pleasant and unhurried day-trip destination for those based in Kobe (it's 15 minutes further if you are based in Kyoto). However, the castle is shrouded by scaffolding and under renovation through 2015 (though the interior of the main keep and other buildings in the site will be accessible during most of this period). If you get back early, use the balance of your day to buy some last-minute souvenirs.

GREAT ITINERARIES

HIGHLIGHTS OF SOUTHERN JAPAN

South and west of the tourist centers of Kyoto and Nara, Japan takes on a different feel. The farther you go, the more relaxed people become. Hundreds of kilometers from Japan's main islands, the stark divide between the tropical beaches of Okinawa and Honshu's concrete metropolises is reflected in a different culture and cuisine.

Days 1 and 2: Shikoku

The **Iya Valley** may be slightly difficult to access, but it offers untouched, deep canyons, the best river rafting in Japan, and good walking trails. For a break from Japan—and the rest of the world—visit the **Chichu Art Museum** on Naoshima Island, near Takamatsu, which integrates artworks into everyday locations, often with inspiring results (⇨ *Chapter 10*).

Day 3: Kurashiki

This rustic town, an important trading port in centuries past, retains its picturesque 17th-century buildings. The 1930s classical-style **Ohara Art Museum** houses a fine collection of European art, and Bikan Chiku is an interesting neighborhood of canals, bridges, shops, restaurants, ryokans, and museums (⇨ *Chapter 9*).

Days 4 and 5: Hiroshima

A quick glance at the busy, attractive city of Hiroshima gives no clue to the events of August 6, 1945. Only the city's **Peace Memorial Park** (Heiwa Kinen Koen)—with its memorial museum and its **A-Bomb Dome** (Gembaku Domu), a twisted, half-shattered structural ruin—serves as a reminder of the atomic bomb. From Hiroshima, make a quick trip to the island of **Miyajima** to see the famous floating torii

of **Itsukushima Jinja,** a shrine built on stilts above a tidal flat (⇨ *Chapter 9*).

Days 6 and 7: Yufuin and Mt. Aso

One of the locals' favorite pastimes is relaxing in an onsen, and in the artsy little spa town of Yufuin, on the southernmost island of Kyushu, you can soak in mineral water or bubbling mud. Nearby, five volcanic cones combine to create Japan's largest caldera at **Mt. Aso.** An immense 18 km (11 mi) by 24 km (15 mi), the stark volcanic peak contrasts vividly with the surrounding green hills. One crater, **Nakadake,** is still active, and reaching it on foot or via cable car affords views of a bubbling, steaming lake.

Days 8 and 9: Okinawa

Check out cosmopolitan **Naha,** which gives a feel for how Okinawan culture and cuisine differ from those of "mainland" Japan. Explore the main island's many reminders of its tragic fate during World War II. Take a boat to one of the smaller **Kerama** islands to relax on uncrowded, unspoiled beaches. And to truly appreciate the beauty of the ocean, get into the water—there are plenty of scuba diving and snorkeling centers.

GREAT ITINERARIES

HIGHLIGHTS OF NORTHERN JAPAN

With 80% of Japan's surface covered by mountains, the country is a dream for hikers and lovers of the great outdoors. The wilds of Hokkaido, quietly impressive Tohoku, and the vertiginous Japan Alps frequently reward exploration with spectacular scenery and experiences of traditional Japanese culture that have long-since been lost from urban areas.

Days 1 and 2: Sapporo

Sapporo is a pleasant and accessible city that serves as a good base for exploring the dramatic landscape of Hokkaido. Mountains encircle Sapporo, drawing Japanese and increasing numbers of Australian skiers in winter. Take day trips out to **Toya-ko** or **Shikotsu-ko**, picturesque caldera lakes where you can boat or fish, and the excellent **Nibutani Ainu Culture Museum** for an insight into the island's original inhabitants.

Days 3 and 4: Daisetsu-zan National Park

Japan's largest national park, **Daisetsu-san** is one of the nation's most popular spots for hiking and skiing, and reflects the essence of Hokkaido: soaring mountain peaks, hidden gorges, cascading waterfalls, forests, and hot springs. Sheer cliff walls and stone spires make for a stunning drive through the **Soun-kyo** ravine. Take a cable car up to the top of Hokkaido's tallest mountain, **Asahi-dake**; hike or ski for a couple of hours, then unwind at a hot spring below.

Days 5 and 6: Haguro-san

This mountain, the most accessible of the Dewa-san range, a trio of sacred mountains in Tohoku, is worth the trip not only for the lovely climb past cedars,

waterfalls, and shrines but also for the thatched shrine at the top. The rigorous climb itself, up 2,446 stone steps to the summit, at an elevation of 414 meters, is the main draw; however, it's possible to take a bus up or down the mountain.

Days 7–9: Japan Alps and North Chubu Coast

Nagano Prefecture, host of the 1998 Winter Olympics, is home to the backbone of the Japan Alps. Visit **Zenko-ji** temple in Nagano City before heading to the hot springs of **Yudanaka Onsen** or **Kusatsu**. Alternatively, **Kamikochi** allows you to really get away from it all—no cars are allowed into this mountain retreat. Farther west the cities of **Kanazawa** and **Takayama** offer some of the best-preserved traditional architecture in Japan, including old samurai family houses and sake breweries. Between the two is **Shirakawa-go**, where steep-roof thatched farmhouses sit snugly in a mountain valley. Stay a night to see the buildings at their best while sharing a meal around an *irori* fireplace with your fellow guests.

WHEN TO GO

Japan's most comfortable seasons are spring and fall. In spring the country is warm, with occasional showers, and flowers grace landscapes in both rural and urban areas. The first harbingers of spring are plum blossoms in early March; *sakura* (cherry blossoms) follow, beginning in Kyushu and usually arriving in Tokyo by mid-April.

Summer brings the rainy season, with particularly heavy rains and stifling humidity in June and July. Avoid July and August, unless you're visiting Hokkaido, where temperatures are more bearable. Fall relieves with clear blue skies and glorious foliage. A few surprise typhoons may occur in early fall, but the storms are usually as quick to leave.

Winter is gray and chilly, with little snow in most areas along the Pacific Ocean side of the country, where temperatures rarely fall below freezing. Hokkaido and the Japan Sea side of the country (facing Korea and Russia) are a different story, with heavy snowfalls in the winter months.

To avoid crowds, be aware of times when most Japanese are vacationing. Usually, Japanese vacation on the same holiday dates. As a result, airports, planes, trains, and hotels are booked far in advance. Many businesses, shops, and restaurants are closed during these holidays. Holiday periods include the few days before and after New Year's; Golden Week, which follows Showa Day (April 29); and mid-August at the time of the Obon festivals, when many Japanese return to their hometowns.

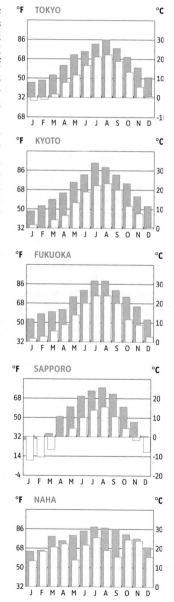

ON THE CALENDAR

	Matsuri (festivals) are very important to the Japanese, and around 30,000 are held throughout the year. Many of them originated in folk and religious rituals and date back hundreds of years. Gala matsuri take place annually at Buddhist temples and Shinto shrines, and many are associated with the changing of the seasons or for honoring the spirits of the deceased. Most are free of charge and attract thousands of visitors as well as locals. In most cases, matsuri are elaborated upon in the relevant chapters of this guide, especially when local history is involved. To find out specific matsuri dates, contact the Japan National Tourism Organization (⇨ *Visitor Information in Travel Smart*). When national holidays fall on Sunday, they are celebrated on the following Monday. Museums and sights are often closed the days after these holidays.
WINTER Jan. 1	**New Year's Day** is the "festival of festivals" for the Japanese. Some women dress in traditional kimono, and many people visit shrines and hold family reunions. Although the day is solemn, streets are often decorated with pine twigs, plum branches, and bamboo stalks.
February	During the first half of the month, more than 300 pieces of ice sculpture, some huge, populate the **Sapporo Snow Festival,** bringing some 2 million people to the city to see them.
Feb. 13-15	Akita (in Tohoku) City's **Namahage Sedo Festival** enacts in public a ritual from nearby Oga of threatening "good-for-nothings": Men in demon masks carrying buckets and huge knives issue dire warnings to loafers.
SPRING April 29	**Showa Day.** The first day of **Golden Week**—when many Japanese take vacation, and hotels, trains, and attractions are booked solid—is *not* a good time to travel within Japan.
May 15	Dating back to the 6th century, the **Aoi Festival,** also known as the Hollyhock Festival, is the first of Kyoto's three most popular celebrations. An "imperial" procession of 300 courtiers starts from the Imperial Palace and makes its way to Shimogamo Shrine to

	pray for the prosperity of the city. Today's participants are local Kyotoites.
Mid-May	Another loud Tokyo blowout, the **Kanda Festival** is all about taking the Kanda shrine's gods out for some fresh air in their *mikoshi* (portable shrines)—not to mention drinking plenty of beer and having a great time on the weekend closest to May 15.
Late May	The **Sanja Festival,** held on the third weekend of May at Tokyo's Asakusa Jinja, is the city's biggest party. Men, often naked to the waist, carry palanquins through the streets amid revelers. Many of these bare bearers bear the tattoos of the Yakuza, Japan's Mafia.
SUMMER	On Miyajima near Hiroshima, the lunar calendar determines
June	the timing of three stately barges' crossing of the bay to the island's shrine for the **Kangen-sai Festival.**
July 16-17	The **Gion Festival,** which dates back to the 9th century, is perhaps Kyoto's most popular festival. Twenty-nine huge floats sail along downtown streets and make their way to Yasaka Shrine to thank the gods for protection from a pestilence that once ravaged the city.
July 24-25	Osaka's **Tenjin Festival** is a major event, with parades of floats and nighttime fireworks and processions of 100-plus lighted vessels on the city's canals.
August	The first week's dreamlike **Neputa Festival,** held in the Tohoku city of Hirosaki, finds nightly processions of floats, populated with illuminated paintings of faces from mythology, through the streets.
Aug. 3-7	The **Nebuta Festival** in northern Tohoku's Aomori noisily celebrates an ancient battle victory with a nighttime parade of illuminated floats.
Aug. 5-7	At Yamagata's **Hanagasa Festival,** in southern Tohoku, celebrants dance through the streets in local costume among floats. Food and drink are on hand for spectators.
Aug. 6-8	Sendai's **Tanabata** celebrates two legendary astrological lovers with a theatrical rendition of their tale, and city residents decorate their streets and houses with colorful paper and bamboo streamers.

Aug. 13-16	During the **Obon Festival,** a time of Buddhist ceremonies in honor of ancestors, many Japanese take off the entire week to travel to their hometowns—try to avoid travel on these days.
Aug. 16	For the **Daimonji Gozan Okuribi,** huge bonfires in the shape of *kanji* characters illuminate five of the mountains that surround Kyoto. The most famous is the "Dai," meaning big, on the side of Mt. Daimonji in Higashiyama (Kyoto's eastern district). Dress in a cool *yukata* (cotton robe) and walk down to the banks of the Kamo-gawa to view this spectacular summer sight, or catch all five fires from the rooftop of your hotel downtown or a spot in Funaoka-yama or Yoshida-yama parks. There are *Bon* dances to honor the departed as well as the floating of lanterns in Arashiyama (the western district).
AUTUMN Oct. 22	Kyoto's **Jidai Festival,** the Festival of Eras, features a colorful costume procession of fashions from the 8th through 19th century. The procession begins at the Imperial Palace and winds up at Heian Shrine. More than 2,000 Kyotoites voluntarily participate in this festival, which dates back to 1895. For the **Kurama Fire Festival,** at Kurama Shrine, there is a roaring bonfire and a rowdy portable shrine procession that makes its way through the narrow streets of the small village in the northern suburbs of Kyoto. If you catch a spark, it is believed to bring good luck.
WINTER Dec. 23	**The Emperor's Birthday.** The Imperial Palace in Tokyo, which is usually off-limits to the public, opens its gates on this day. The only other day the public can enter the grounds is Jan. 2.
Late Dec.	City dwellers migrate to the countryside en masse for the **New Year** celebrations. Travel is *not* recommended.

DID YOU KNOW

Tokyo Tower, a knock-off of the Eiffel Tower, was built in the late 1950s to host TV transmitters as the city was trying to establish a new landmark in its skyline after the destruction of World War II.

ISOLATION AND ENGAGEMENT
A HISTORY OF JAPAN By Robert Morel

A century and a half after opening its shores to outsiders, Japan is still a mystery to many Westerners. Often misunderstood, Japan's history is much deeper than the stereotypes of samurai and geisha, overworked businessmen, and anime. Its long tradition of retaining the old while embracing the new has captivated visitors for centuries.

Much of Japanese history has consisted of the ongoing tension between its seeming isolation from the rest of the world and a desire to be a part of it. During the Edo period, Japan was closed to foreigners for some 250 years. Yet while the country has always had a strong national identity, it has also had a rapacious appetite for all things foreign. Just 50 years after opening its borders, parts of Tokyo looked like London, and Japan had become a colonial power in Asia. Much earlier, the Japanese imported Buddhism, tea, and their first writing system from China.

In the 19th century, the country incorporated Western architecture, technology, and government. More recently, the Japanese have absorbed Western fashion, music, and pop culture. Nevertheless, the country's history lives on in local traditions, festivals, temples, cities, music, and the arts.

Senso-ji Complex in Tokyo's Asakusa neighborhood

(top) Horyu-ji Inner Gate and pagoda, (bottom) Nihon Shoki, (right) Large Buddha statue at Todai-ji Temple

Ancient Japan

10,000 BC–AD 622

The first people in Japan were the hunters and fishers of the Jomon period, known for their pottery. In the following Yayoi period, hunting and fishing gave way to agriculture, as well as the introduction of rice farming and metalworking. Around AD 500 the Yamato tribe consolidated power in what is now the Kansai plain, with Yamato leaders claiming descent from the sun goddess Amaretsu and taking the title of emperor. Prince Shotoku promoted the spread of Buddhism from China and commissioned Horyu-ji Temple in Nara in 607.

- Horyu-ji Temple (Nara)
- National Museum (Tokyo)

Nara Period

710–784

As Japan's first permanent capital and urban center, Nara is often considered the birthplace of Japanese culture. Under the Emperor Shomu, who commissioned the Great Buddha at Todai-ji Temple, Buddhism rose to prominence. The first Japanese written histories, the *Kojiki* and *Nihon Shoki*, were compiled during this period, as was the *Manyoshu*, Japan's first collection of poetry. Since the country was the Eastern terminus of the Silk Road, Japan's royal family amassed an impressive collection of treasures from mainland Asia, many of which are still on display at Todai-ji Temple's Shoso-in.

- The Great Buddha at Todai-ji Temple (Nara)

Heian Period

794–1160

Partly to escape intrigues and the rising power of the Nara's Buddhist Priests, in 794 the Emperor Kammu moved the capital to Heian-kyo (now Kyoto). *Heian* translates roughly as "peace and tranquility," and during this time the Imperial court expanded its power throughout Japan. Inside the court, however, life was far from calm. This was a period of great courtly intrigue, and struggles for power between aristocrats, the powerful Fujiwara clan (the most powerful of Japan's four great noble families), and the new military class known as *bushi*. Though some emperors managed to maintain control of the court, the Heian period saw the

794–1160 The capital is moved from
Nara to Heian-kyo (now Kyoto)

1467–77 The Onin Wars initiate a
100-year period of civil war

1100   1250   1400   1550

1

IN FOCUS ISOLATION AND ENGAGEMENT: A HISTORY OF JAPAN

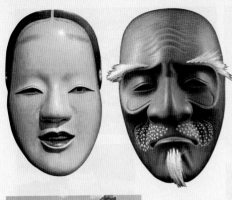

(right) Zen Garden at
the Ryoan-ji Temple,
(top) Noh masks,
(bottom) Kyoto Imperial
Palace's wooden
orange gates.

slow rise of the military class, leading to a series of wars that established them as the ruling class until well into the 19th century. Considered Japan's great classical period, this was a time when courtly arts flourished. The new Japanese *kana* script gave rise to a boom in literature. Compiled in 990, Sei Shonagon's *Pillow Book* gave a window into courtly life, and Shibuki Murasaki's *Tale of Genji* is often regarded as the world's first classic novel. Japanese *waka* poetry experienced a revival, breeding the new forms of poetry such as *tanka* that are still in use today.

■ The Imperial Palace (Kyoto)

Kamakura Period

1185–1335

As the Imperial Court lost control, the Genpei War (1180–1185) resulted in the defeat of clans loyal to the emperor in Kyoto and the rise of a new government in Kamakura. Yoritomo Minamoto named himself *Sei-i Tai Shogun* and established the *Kamakura bakufu*, a spartan military government. During this time, Japan repelled two Mongol invasions, thanks to timely typhoons that were later dubbed *kamikaze*, or divine wind. In this militaristic climate, Zen Buddhism, with its focus on self-reliance and discipline, exploded in popularity.

■ Eihiji Temple (Fukushima)
■ Hachimangu Shrine and the Great Buddha (Kamakura)

Muromachi (Ashikaga) Period

1336–1568

The heyday of the samurai, the Muromachi period was one of near constant civil war. Feudal lords known as *daimyo* consolidated their power in local fiefdoms. Peasant rebellions and piracy were common. Nevertheless, trade flourished. The movement of armies required *daimyo* to build roads, while improved communications gave birth to many merchant and artisan guilds. Trade with China grew, and in 1543 Portugal began trading with Japan, introducing firearms and Christianity. Noh theater and the tea ceremony were founded, and Kyoto's most famous temples were built in this period.

■ Kinkaku-ji Temple (Kyoto)
■ Ryoan-ji Temple (Kyoto)

(left) Matsumoto Castle, (top) three wise monkeys at Toshogu shrine, (bottom) woodcut of Kabuki actor by Utagawa Toyokuni

National Unification (Momoyama Period)

1568–1600

In 1568 Oda Nobunaga, a lord from Owari in central Japan, marched on Kyoto and took the title of Shogun. He controlled the surrounding territories until his death in 1582, when his successor, Toyotomi Hideyoshi, became the new Shogun. After unifying much of central and western Japan, he attempted unsuccessful invasions of Korea before his death in 1598. In 1600 Tokugawa Ieyasu, a top general, defeated Hideyoshi's successor in the battle of Sekihagara.

- Osaka Castle (Osaka)
- Matsumoto Castle (Matsumoto)

Edo (Tokugawa) Period

1600–1867

The Edo period ushered in 250 years of relative stability and central control. After becoming Shogun, Ieyasu Tokugawa moved the capital to Edo (present-day Tokyo). A system of *daimyo*, lords beholden to the Shogun, was established along with a rigid class system and legal code of conduct. Although Japan cut off trade with the outside world, cities flourished. By the mid-18th century, Edo's population had grown to more than 1 million, and urban centers like Osaka and Kyoto had become densely populated. Despite such rapid growth, urban life in the Edo period was highly organized, with districts managed by neighborhood associations that have persisted (in a modified way) to the present day. Popular entertainment and arts arose to satisfy the thriving merchant and artisan classes. Kabuki, flashy and sensational, overtook Noh theater in popularity, and Japan's famed "floating world" (*ukio*), with its theaters, drinking houses, and geishas emerged. Sumo, long a Shinto tradition, became a professional sport. Much of what both Japanese and foreigners consider "Japanese culture" dates to this period. But by 1853, the Shogun's hold on power was growing tenuous.

- Toshogu (Nikko)
- Katsura Imperial Villa (Kyoto) Muhammad Ali Mosque

| 1800 | 1853 U.S. Commodore Matthew Perry reopens Japan to foreign trade | 1850 | 1868 Meiji Restoration begins | 1900 | 1941 Japan attacks Pearl Harbor | 1950 |

1

IN FOCUS ISOLATION AND ENGAGEMENT: A HISTORY OF JAPAN

(top) Tokyo University, (left) wedding in Meiji Shrine, (bottom) A6M5 fighter plane at Yusyukan museum.

Meiji Period

1868–1912

The Tokugawa Shogunate's rigid class system and legal code proved to be its undoing. After U.S. Commodore Matthew Perry opened Japan to trade in March 1854, the following years were turbulent. In 1868, the last Shogun, Tokugawa Yoshinobu, ceded power to Emperor Meiji, and Japan began to modernize after 250 years of isolation. Adopting a weak parliamentary system from Germany, rulers moved quickly to develop national industry and universities. Victories over China and Russia also emboldened Japan.

- Tokyo University (Tokyo)
- Heian Shrine (Kyoto)
- Nara National Musuem (Nara)

Taisho Period

1912–1925

In the early 20th century, urban Japan was beginning to look a lot Europe and North America.

Fashion ranged from traditional *yukata* and kimono to zoot suits and bobbed hair. In 1923 the Great Kanto Earthquake and its resulting fires destroyed Yokohama and much of Tokyo. Although city planners saw this as an opportunity to modernize Tokyo's maze of streets, residents were quick to rebuild, ensuring that many neighborhood maps look much the same today as they did a century ago.

- Asakusa (Tokyo)
- The Shitamachi Museum (Tokyo)
- Meiji Shrine (Tokyo)

Wartime Japan

1926–1945

Although Japan was was increasingly liberal throughout the 1920s, the economic shocks of the 1930s helped the military gain greater control, resulting in crackdowns on left-leaning groups, the press, and dissidents. In 1931 Japan invaded Manchuria; in 1937 Japan captured Nanking, killing many civilians. Joining the Axis powers in 1936, Japan continued its expansion in Asia and in 1941 attacked Pearl Harbor. After the atomic bombings of Hiroshima and Nagasaki, the Emperor announced Japan's surrender on August 15, 1945.

- Hiroshima Peace Memorial Park (Hiroshima)
- Yasukuni Shrine Museum (Tokyo)

TIMELINE

1964 Tokyo hosts the
Summer Olympic games

2006 Shinzo Abe elected as
the country's youngest
prime minister

1989 Emperor Hirohito dies

1950   1970   1990   2010

(top) 1964 Summer Olympics, Tokyo, (bottom) manga comic books, (right) Shinjuku, Tokyo

1945–1989 Postwar Japan and the Economic Miracle

The initial postwar years were hard on Japan. More than half of Japan's total urban area was in ruins, its industry in shambles, and food shortages common. Kyoto was the only major metropolitan area in the country that escaped widespread damage. Thanks to an educated, dedicated population and smart planning, however, Japan was soon on the road to recovery. A new democratic government was formed and universal suffrage extended to all adult men and women. Japan's famous "Peace Constitution" forbade the country from engaging in warfare. With cooperation from the government, old companies like Matsushita (Panasonic), Mitsubishi, and Toyota began exporting Japanese goods en masse, while upstarts like Honda pushed their way to the top. In 1964 Japan joined the Organization for Economic Cooperation and Development's group of "rich nations" and hosted the Tokyo Olympics. At the same time, anime began gaining popularity at the box office and on TV, with Osamu Tezuka's classic *Tetsuwan Atom* (*Astro Boy*) making a splash when it aired in 1963. In the 1970s and '80s Japan became as well known for its electronics as its cars, with Nintendo, Sony, and Panasonic becoming household names abroad.

- Showa-Kan (Takayama)
- National Stadium (Yoyogi Park)

1990–PRESENT From Goods to Culture

Unfortunately, much of Japan's rapid growth in the 1980s was unsustainable. By 1991 the bubble had burst, leading to 20 years of limited economic expansion. Japan avoided an economic crisis, and most people continued to lead comfortable, if somewhat simpler, lives. After decades of exporting goods, Japan has—particularly since 2000—become an exporter of culture in the form of animation, video games, and cuisine. Japan, famous for importing ideas, has begun to send its own culture to the world.

- Shinjuku, Harajuku, and Shibuya, (Tokyo)
- Akihabara (Tokyo)
- Manga Museum (Kyoto)

A Japanese Culture Primer

WORD OF MOUTH

"If the name ends in '–ji' or '–dera' then it's a temple. Even if you are not interested in the theology, it helps to know that [Shinto shrines and Buddhist temples] employ different architectural styles. . . ."
—someotherguy

By Jared
Lubarsky

Something about Japanese culture must have led you to pick up this book and contemplate a trip to Japan. Perhaps it was a meal at your favorite sushi bar back home. It could have been the warm tones of an exquisite piece of Japanese pottery. Maybe it was a Japanese novel you read in translation—or a film. Whatever it was that sparked your interest, it's a good bet that something you find in this chapter will make your trip unforgettable.

There is a display of horsemanship called *yabusame* (now to be seen mainly at shrine festivals) in which a mounted archer, in medieval costume, challenges a narrow roped-off course lined at 80-meter intervals with small wooden targets on bamboo posts: the rider has to come down the course at full gallop, drop the reins, nock an arrow, aim and release, and take the reins again—with only seconds to set up again for the next target. Few archers manage a perfect score—but "for us," explains a yabusame official, "merely hitting the target is secondary."

Wherein the key to understanding pretty nearly every expression of traditional Japanese culture: the passionate attention to *form* and *process*. The end results are important, of course; otherwise the forms would be empty gestures. But equally important—perhaps more important—is *how you get there*. Not for nothing are so many of these disciplines, from the tea ceremony to calligraphy to the martial arts, presented to us as Ways; excellence in any one of them depends on *doing it the way it's supposed to be done*, according to traditions that may be centuries old. Philosophically, this is all about how rules can liberate: spend enough time and effort on the mastery of forms, and one day they leave the realm of conscious thought and become part of you. Not for nothing, either, are so many elements of Japanese culture rooted in the teachings of Zen Buddhism, about breaking free from the limits of the rational Self.

A TASTE OF JAPAN

By Aidan O'Connor

Get ready for an unparalleled eating adventure: from humble bowls of ramen to elaborate kaiseki feasts, a vast culinary universe awaits visitors to food-obsessed Japan.

Japan's food offerings are united by a few key philosophies. Presentation is paramount—a dedication to visual appeal means that colors and shapes are just as important as aromas, textures, and flavors. Details count—food is prepared with pride and care, and everything from a bowl's shape to a dish's finishing garnish carries meaning. Natural flavors shine through—seasonal ingredients star in minimally processed preparations, with condiments used to enhance flavors rather than mask them.

You'll find these culinary philosophies at all levels, from tiny noodle shops to lively robatayaki grills to elegant sushi restaurants. Here's what you need to know to make the most of your meals. As they say in Japan, *itadakimasho* (let's eat)!

Pressed sushi (oshizushi) and Japanese-style fried rice

THE JAPANESE MEAL

Breakfast (*asa-gohan*, literally "the morning rice") is typically eaten at home and features rice, fried fish, and miso soup. Lunch (*hiru-gohan*), mostly eaten out of the home at school or work, involves a bento lunch box of rice, grilled fish, vegetables, and pickles. The evening meal (*ban-gohan*) has the broadest range, from restaurant meals of sushi to traditional meals cooked at home.

For home-prepared meals, the basic formula consists of one soup and three dishes—a main dish of fish or meat and two vegetable side dishes. These are served together with rice, which is part of every meal. When entertain-

ing guests, more dishes will be served. Classical Japanese cooking follows the principle of "fives." An ideal meal is thought to use five cooking methods—boiling, grilling, frying, steaming, and serving raw; incorporate five colors—black or purple, white, red or orange, yellow, and green; and feature five tastes—sweet, sour, salty, bitter, and *umami* (the Japanese are credited with discovering umami, or savoriness). Ingredient quality is key, as cooking techniques are intended to coax out an ingredient's maximum natural flavor.

Staple ingredients include seafood, which plays a leading role in Japanese cuisine, with dozens of species available,

DINING ETIQUETTE

Here are a few tips to help you fit in at the Japanese table:

■ Don't point or gesture with chopsticks.

■ Avoid lingering over communal dishes with your chopsticks while you decide what to take. Do not use the end you have been eating with to remove food from the dish—use the serving chopsticks provided or the thick end of your own chopsticks.

■ When not in use, place your chopsticks on the chopstick rest.

■ Never pass food from your chopsticks to someone else's or leave chopsticks standing in your rice bowl (it resembles incense sticks at a funeral).

■ There is no taboo against slurping your noodle soup, though women are generally less boisterous about it than men.

■ Pick up the soup bowl and drink directly from it. Take the fish or vegetables from it with your chopsticks. Return the lid to the soup bowl when you are finished eating. The rice bowl, too, is to be held in your free hand while you eat from it.

■ When drinking with a friend don't pour your own. Pour for the other person first. He will in turn pour yours.

■ Japanese don't pour sauce on their rice. Sauces are intended for dipping foods into it lightly.

■ It is still considered tacky to eat as you walk along a public street.

Pouring sake into a traditional Japanese cup

from familiar choices like *maguro* (tuna) and *ebi* (shrimp) to more exotic selections like *anago* (conger eel) and *fugu* (blowfish). Meat options include chicken, pork, beef, and—in rural areas—venison and wild boar. Then there is a huge variety of vegetables and fungi (both wild and cultivated) such as *renkon* (lotus root), *daikon* (white radish), and matsutake mushrooms. Finally there is the soy bean, eaten whole as edamame, or fermented in tofu or miso.

Condiments range from tangy *shiso* (a member of the mint family) to spicy wasabi and savory soy sauce.

SUSHI

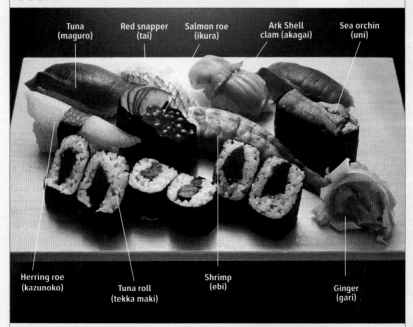

Tuna (maguro)

Red snapper (tai)

Salmon roe (ikura)

Ark Shell clam (akagai)

Sea orchin (uni)

Herring roe (kazunoko)

Tuna roll (tekka maki)

Shrimp (ebi)

Ginger (gari)

■ Sushi actually refers to anything, seafood or otherwise, served on or in vinegared rice. It is not raw fish. **Nigiri-zushi** (the sushi best known overseas) is actually a fairly recent development from Tokyo.

■ **Makizushi** is a sushi roll. These can be fat, elaborate rolls or simple sticks.

■ Other types of sushi include **chirashi-zushi** with fish and vegetables scattered artfully into the rice and, in Kyoto and Osaka, **oshizushi** in which preserved mackerel, among other fish, is pressed onto the rice. This is served in slices.

■ **Funazushi,** from around Lake Biwa near Kyoto, is perhaps the oldest type. The fish and rice are buried for six months. The rice is thrown away and the fish is eaten. This technique was historically used as a means of preserving protein. It is an acquired taste.

■ **Kaitenzushi** (conveyor belt sushi) outlets abound and are cheap. However, for the real

Hand-rolled sushi

experience, nothing matches a traditional sushi-ya.

■ Using your hands is acceptable. Dip the fish, not the rice, lightly in the soy.

■ The **beni-shoga** (pickled ginger) is a palate freshener. Nibble sparingly.

■ **Wasabi** may not be served with your sushi, as the chef often dabs a bit on the rice when making your sushi. If you want extra wasabi, ask for it.

■ Customers will often request **omakase** (tasting menu). The chef will then choose and serve the best fish, in the order he deems appropriate.

RAMEN

Scallions (negi)

Seaweed (nori)

Bamboo shoots (shinachiku)

Pork (cha-shu)

Shoyu ramen

■ Ramen is practically Japan's national dish. A ramen restaurant is never far away.

■ There are four main types: from the chilly north island of Hokkaido, there is **shio ramen** (salt ramen) and **miso ramen** (ramen in a miso broth). **Shoyu ramen** made with soy sauce is from Tokyo, while **tonkotsu ramen** (ramen in a white pork broth) is from Kyoto. Note that most ramen stocks contain meat or fish.

■ Each area has its own variation—corn and butter ramen in Sapporo; a stock made from pork and dried anchovies in northern Honshu; or Fukuoka's famed **Hakata ramen** with its milky tonkotsu broth and thin noodles with myriad toppings.

■ The reputation of a ramen restaurant depends on its stock, often a closely guarded secret.

■ Ramen is meant to be eaten with gusto. Slurping is normal.

■ Typical toppings include sliced roast pork, bean sprouts, boiled egg, **shinachiku** (fermented bamboo shoots), spring onion, **nori** (dried seaweed) and **kamaboko** (a fishcake made from white fish).

■ Beyond ramen, udon shops and soba shops also offer noodle dishes worth trying.

Miso ramen

Shio ramen

ROBATAYAKI

Grilled fish (tsukeba)

■ **Robata** means fireside, and the style of cooking is reminiscent of old-fashioned Japanese farmhouse meals cooked over a charcoal fire in an open hearth.

■ Robatayaki restaurants and izakaya taverns serving grilled foods can be found near any busy station.

■ It's easy to order at a robatayaki, because the selection of food to be grilled is lined up at the counter. Fish, meat, vegetables, tofu—take your pick.

■ Some popular choices are **yaki-zakana** (grilled fish), particularly **karei-shio-yaki** (salted and grilled flounder) and **asari saka-mushi** (clams simmered in sake).

■ Try the grilled Japanese **shiitake** (mushrooms), **ao-to** (green peppers), and the **hiyayakko** (chilled tofu sprinkled with bonito flakes, diced green onions, and soy sauce).

Matsutake mushroom

■ **O-tsukuri** (sashimi) and **katsuono tataki** (seared bonito) are very popular. The fish will vary according to the season.

■ Dipping sauces are concocted using soy, **dashi** (soup stock), and a hint of citrus such as yuzu.

■ Many robatayaki pride themselves on their wide selection of sake and shochu.

■ Most Japanese people will finish their meal with a rice dish.

TEMPURA

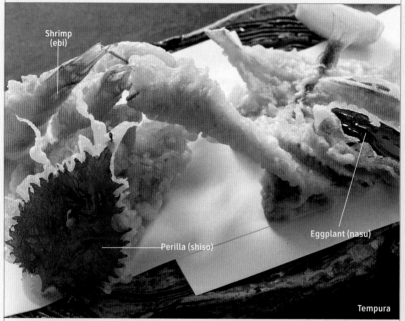

Shrimp (ebi)

Eggplant (nasu)

Perilla (shiso)

Tempura

■ Though tempura features in many busy eateries as part of a meal, it bears little resemblance to the exquisite morsels produced over the course of a full tempura meal at an intimate specialty restaurant.

■ The secret of good tempura lies in the quality of the ingredients, the freshness and temperature of the oil, and the lightness of the batter.

■ Good tempura is light and crispy, not crunchy like fried chicken.

■ Tempura is most often fried in soybean oil, but cottonseed or sesame oil also may be used.

■ Because only the freshest of ingredients will do, the menu changes with the season. Baby corn, green peppers, sweet potato, lotus root, shiitake mushrooms, and shiso leaves are the most common vegetables. In spring expect **sansai** (wild vegetables) picked that morning.

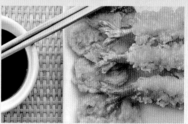

Shrimp Tempura with sweet potatoes

■ Prawns and white fish are also popular tempura items.

■ **Tsuyu** (dipping sauce) is made from dashi seasoned with soy and **mirin** (sweet rice wine). You may see a white mound of grated daikon on your plate. Add that to the tsuyu for a punch of flavor.

■ Alternatively, mixtures of salt and powdered green tea or salt and yuzu may be sprinkled on the tempura.

BENTO

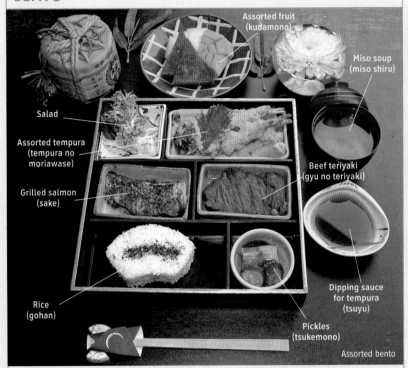

Assorted fruit
(kudamono)

Miso soup
(miso shiru)

Salad

Assorted tempura
(tempura no
moriawase)

Grilled salmon
(sake)

Beef teriyaki
(gyu no teriyaki)

Rice
(gohan)

Dipping sauce
for tempura
(tsuyu)

Pickles
(tsukemono)

Assorted bento

■ Bento boxes, the traditional Japanese box lunch, can be bought everywhere from the basement level of a luxurious department store to a convenience store.

■ A typical bento will contain rice, grilled fish, a selection of vegetable dishes, some pickles, and perhaps a wedge of orange or other fruit.

■ Every region has its **meibutsu**, or speciality dish. These are often showcased in lunch boxes available at stations or local stores.

Bento lunch box

■ Though the humble bento is usually relatively inexpensive, more ornate and intricate boxes featuring kaiseki dishes or sushi are often bought for special occasions.

■ The bento exists in an almost limitless number of variations according to the region and the season.

■ A bento is designed to be taken out and eaten on the move. They are perfect on long-distance train rides or for a picnic in the park.

BEVERAGES

Sake

■ There are more than 2,000 different brands of sake produced throughout Japan. It is often called rice wine but is actually made by a fermenting process that is more akin to beer-making. The result is a fantastically complex drink with an alcoholic content just above wine (15–17% alcohol). It is the drink of choice with sashimi and traditional Japanese food.

■ There are four main types of sake: **daiginjo, ginjo, junmai,** and **honjozo**. The first two are the most expensive and made from highly polished rice. The latter two, however, also pack flavor and character.

■ Like wine, sake can be sweet (*amakuchi*) or dry (*karakuchi*). Workaday sake may be drunk warm (*atsukan*) while the higher grades will be served chilled. Sake is the only drink that can be served at any temperature.

■ Another variety is **nama-zake**. This is unpasteurized sake and is prized for its fresh, zingy taste.

■ **Shochu** is a distilled spirit that is often 25% alcohol or more. Like vodka, it can be made from potato, sweet potato, wheat, millet, or rice. It is drunk straight, on the rocks, with water, or in cocktails.

■ Any good izakaya or robatayaki will stock a diverse selection of both sake and shochu, and staff will make recommendations.

■ Beer is, perhaps, the lubricant of choice for most social situations. Japanese beer is of a high standard and tends to be lager. It has a relatively high alcohol content at 5% or more. Recently there has been a boom in microbreweries.

JAPANESE FINE ARTS

What raises Japanese handicrafts to the level of fine arts? It is, one could argue, the standards set by the nation's *Ningen kokuho*: its Living National Treasures, who hand down these traditional skills from generation to generation.

(This page above) Japanese lacquerware; (opposite page upper right) a calligrapher at work; (opposite page bottom left) traditional Japanese papermaking

Legally speaking, these people are "Holders of Important Intangible Cultural Properties." A law, enacted in 1950, establishes two broad categories of Intangible Property. One comprises the performing arts: Kabuki, Noh, Bunraku puppet theater, and traditional music and dance. The other embraces a wide range of handicrafts, most of them in the various forms and styles of textiles, pottery, lacquerware, papermaking, wood carving, and metalworking—from all over the country. The tiny cohort of individuals and groups who exemplify these traditions at the highest levels (there are a maximum of 70 designees at any given time) receive an annual stipend; the money is intended not so much to support the title holders (Living National Treasures command very healthy sums for their work) as to help them attract and train apprentices, and thus keep the traditions alive.

CARRYING ON

Official sponsorship has proven itself a necessity in more than a few craft traditions. The weaving of *bashofu*, for example, a fabric from Okinawa, is on its way to becoming a lost art—unless the present Living National Treasure can encourage enough people to carry on with the craft. Papermaking, a cottage industry that once supported some 28,500 households nationwide, now supports only a few hundred.

LACQUERWARE

Japanese lacquerware has its origins in the Jomon period (10,000–300 BC), and by the Nara period (710–794) most of the techniques we recognize today, such as *maki-e* (literally, "sprinkled picture"), the use of gold or silver powder to underlay the lacquer, had been developed. The Edo period (1603–1868) saw the uses of lacquer extended to vessels and utensils for the newly prosperous merchant class.

The production of lacquerware starts with the refining of sap from the Japanese sumac (*urushi*). The lacquer is applied, layer upon layer, on basketry, wood, bamboo, metal, and even paper. The mirrorlike polished black and red surfaces may have inlays of mother-of-pearl or precious metals, creating motifs and designs of exquisite beauty and delicacy. Many regions in Japan are famous for their distinct lacquerware styles, among them Kyoto, Wajima, and Tsugaru. Hint: tableware with lacquer over plastic bases, rather than wood, are no less beautiful, but far less expensive and less likely to crack in dry climates.

PAPERMAKING

Washi, Japanese paper, can have a soft translucent quality that seems to belie its amazing strength and durability. It makes a splendid material for calligraphy and brush painting, and it can be fashioned into a wide variety of traditional

decorative objects. The basic ingredient is the inner bark of the paper mulberry, but leaves, fiber threads, and even gold flake can be added in later stages for a dramatic effect. The raw mulberry branches are first steamed, then bleached in cold water or snow. The fibers are boiled with ash lye, rinsed, beaten into pulp, and soaked in a tank of starchy taro solution. A screen is dipped into the tank, pulled up, and rocked to drain the solution and crosshatch the fibers. The wet sheets of paper are stacked to press out the excess liquid, then dried in the sun.

The best places to watch the papermaking process are Kurodani, near Kyoto; Mino, in central Japan; and Yame, near Kurume. Many localities are known for their unique washi products: Gifu for umbrellas and lanterns, Nagasaki for its distinctive kites, Nara for calligraphy paper.

CALLIGRAPHY

Calligraphy arrived in Japan around 500 AD with the sacred texts of Buddhism, written in *kanji* (Chinese ideograms). By 800, the *kana* syllabic alphabets of the Japanese language had also developed, and the writing of both kanji and kana with a brush, in India ink, had become an art form—a wedding of meaning and emotion that was (and still is) regarded as a revelation of the writer's individual character. The flow of the line from top to bottom, the

About 30 different styles of porcelain are made in Japan

balance of shapes and sizes, the thickness of the strokes, the amount of ink on the brush: all contribute to the composition of the work. There are five main styles of calligraphy in Japan. Two are based on the Chinese: *tensho*, typically used for seal carving; and *reisho*, for the copying of sutras. Three are solely Japanese: *kaisho*, the block style often seen in wood carving; and the flowing *sosho* (cursive) and *gyosho* styles. Sosho is especially impressive—an expression of freedom and spontaneity that takes years of discipline to achieve; retouching and erasing is impossible. Recommended reading: *The Art of Japanese Calligraphy* by Yujiro Nakata.

CERAMICS

There are some 30 different traditional styles of pottery in Japan, from unglazed stoneware to painted porcelain. Since the late 1600s, when enormous quantities of Imari and Kakiemon porcelain were exported to Europe, the achievements of Japanese potters have delighted collectors.

Although the Japanese have been making pottery for some 12,000 years, the styles we know today were developed by Chinese and Korean craftsmen who immigrated (or were forcibly brought) to Japan in the 17th century. Some of them discovered deposits of fine kaolin clay in northern Kyushu, and founded the tradition in that region of porcelains like Arita-yaki, with brilliantly colored enamel decoration over cobalt blue underglaze. Other porcelain wares include Tobe-yaki from Ehime Prefecture, Kutani-yaki from Ishikawa Prefecture, and Kiyomizu-yaki from Kyoto.

These apart, most Japanese pottery is stoneware—which has an earthier appeal, befitting the rougher texture of the clay. Stoneware from Mashiko, where celebrated potter Hamada Shoji (1894–1978) worked, is admired for its rustic brown, black, and white glazes, often applied in abstract patterns. Many regional potters use glazes on stoneware for coloristic effects, like the mottled, crusty Tokoname-yaki, with its red-iron clay. Other styles, among them the rough-surfaced Shigaraki-yaki made near Kyoto; the white or blue-white Hagi-yaki; and Bizen-yaki from Okayama Prefecture, are unglazed: their warm tones and textures are accidents of nature, achieved when the pieces take their colors from the firing process, in wood-burning through-draft kilns called *anagama* or *nobori-gama*, built on the slopes of hills. The effects depend on the choice of the wood the potter uses, where he places a particular piece in the kiln, and how he manipulates the heat, but the results are never predictable.

Main pottery towns include Hagi, Bizen, and Arita, but you can always find their products in Kyoto and Tokyo. If you do go on a pilgrimage, call ahead to local kilns and tourist organizations to verify that what you want to see will be open and to ask about sales. Recommended reading: *Inside Japanese Ceramics* by Richard L. Wilson.

TEXTILES

Run your fingers over a Japanese textile, and you touch the fabric of Japanese social history. As the caste system took shape in this country, under Buddhist and Confucian influences, it created separate populations of samurai, farmers, artisans, and merchants (in descending order). Rules and conventions emerged—enforced in the Edo period by strict sumptuary laws—about who could wear what, and on what occasions. Appearances identified people. One glance at a kimono, and you knew the wearer was a woman of middle age, the wife of a prosperous tradesman, on her way to the wedding of a family connection. Order was maintained. You were what you wore. Courtesans and actors, of course, could dress over the top; their roles gave them the license. And little by little, the merchants also found ways around the laws, to dress as befit their growing wealth and power. Evolving styles and techniques of making fabrics gave weavers and dyers and designers new opportunities to show their skills.

Western clothing follows the body line in a sculptural way; the kimono is meant as a one-size-fits-all garment in which gender matters, but size and shape are largely unimportant. Whatever the wearer's height or weight, a kimono is made from one bolt of cloth cut and stitched into panels that provide ample surface for decoration—and decorative it is indeed.

Regional styles proliferate. Kyoto's *Nishijin-ori* silk brocade is as sumptuous as a Japanese textile can be. Okinawa produces a variety of stunning fabrics; one, called *bashofu*, is made of plantain fiber threads, dyed and woven in intricate motifs, and feels like linen. Kyoto's and Tokyo's stencil dyeing techniques yield subtle, elegant geometric patterns and motifs from nature. Kanazawa's *Kaga yuzen* paste-resist dyeing on silk is famous for its flower and bird motifs, in elegant rainbow colors.

The used kimono you often see in Kyoto or Tokyo flea markets can be bargains. Also look for lighter-weight *yukata* (robes), *obi* (sashes), or handkerchiefs from Arimatsu, near Nagoya, for example. Good introductions to these craft traditions can be seen at Kyoto's Fuzoku Hakubutsukan (Costume Museum) and Nishijin Orimono (Textile Center), and the Edo period dress collection in Tokyo's National Museum.

Kaga yuzen textiles from Kanazawa exhibit a traditional flower motif

PERFORMING ARTS

Gorgeous costumes, sword fights and tearful reunions, acrobatics and magical transformations, spectacular makeup and masks, singing and dancing, ghosts and goblins, and star-crossed lovers: never let it be said that traditional Japanese culture is short on showmanship.

(This page above) A highly stylized Noh theater performance; (opposite page upper right) the Oshika Kabuki troupe; (opposite page bottom left) A Kabuki mannequin from the Edo-Tokyo Museum

The performing arts all have roots in continental Asia. Kabuki makeup as well as *gagaku* ceremonial court music and dance are Chinese-inspired; the four-string *biwa* shares a Silk Road ancestry with the Persian *oud*. Collectively, the theater traditions generate work for artisans—weavers and dyers, instrument makers, woodcarvers, and more—who make a special contribution of their own. Common features aside, the differences among them are astonishing. Kabuki is great show biz, translatable and appreciable pretty much anywhere in the world. Gagaku is virtually inaccessible, even to the vast majority of the Japanese themselves. Most of an audience that will sit riveted by the graceful, suggestive movements of *buyo* (traditional dance) will fall asleep at a dance-recitation of Noh.

MASTER PERFORMERS

The performing arts also have National Treasures, but filling the 70 allotted slots is easier than in the Fine Arts. The worlds of Japanese theater are mainly in the grip of small oligarchies—"schools"—where traditions are passed down from father to son. Some of these master performers are 9th-and even 22nd-generation holders of hereditary family stage names and specializations.

KABUKI

Tradition has it that Kabuki was created around 1600 by an Izumo shrine maiden named Okuni; it was then performed by troupes of women, who were often available as well for prostitution (the authorities soon banned women from the stage as a threat to public order). Eventually Kabuki cleaned up its act and developed a professional role for female impersonators, who train for years to project a seductive, dazzling femininity. By the latter half of the 18th century it had become Everyman's theater par excellence—especially among the townspeople of bustling, hustling Edo. Kabuki had spectacle; it had pathos and tragedy; it had romance and social satire. It had legions of fans, who spent all day at the theater, shouting out the names of their favorite actors at the stirring moments in their favorite plays.

Kabuki flowered especially in the "floating world" of Edo's red-light entertainment district. The theater was a place to see and be seen, to catch the latest trends in music and fashion, where people of all classes came together under one roof—something that happened nowhere else in the city. Strict censorship laws were put in place, and just as quickly circumvented by clever playwrights; Kabuki audiences could watch a *jidai-mono* (historical piece) set in the distant past, where the events and

characters made thinly veiled reference to troublesome contemporary events.

The Genroku era (1673–1841) was Kabuki's golden age, when the classic plays of Chikamatsu Monzaemon and Tsuruya Namboku were written, and most of the theatrical conventions and stage techniques we see today were honed to perfection. The *mie*, for example, is a dramatic pose the actor strikes at a certain moment in the play, to establish his character. The use of *kumadori* makeup, derived from Chinese opera and used to symbolize the essential elements of a character's nature, also date to this period. The exaggerated facial lines of the *kumadori*, in vivid reds and blues and greens over a white rice powder base, tell the audience at once that the wearer is a hero or villain, noble or arrogant, passionate or cold. To the Genroku also date revolving stages, trapdoors, and—most importantly—the *hanamichi*: a long, raised runway from the back of the theater, through the audience, to the main stage, where characters enter, exit, and strike their mie poses.

Kabuki traditions are passed down through generations in a small group of families; the roles and great stage names are hereditary. The repertoire does not really grow, but stars like Ichikawa Ennosuke and Bando Tamasaburo have put developed unique performance styles that still draw audiences young

and old. Alas, the venerable home of this art, the Kabuki-za Theater, was demolished in April 2010, to reopen in 2013 as part of a multistory office and entertainment complex. In the meantime, you can still see Kabuki at Tokyo's Shimbashi Enbujo Theatre, the Nissay Theatre in Yuraku-cho, and the National Theatre in Hanzomon. Recommended reading: *The Kabuki Guide* by Masakatsu Gunji.

NOH

Noh is a dramatic tradition far older than Kabuki; it reached a point of formal perfection in the 14th century and survives virtually unchanged from that period. Where Kabuki was Everyman's theater, Noh developed for the most part under the patronage of the warrior class. It is dignified, ritualized, and symbolic. Many of the plays in the repertoire are drawn from classical literature or tales of the supernatural. The texts are richly poetic, and even the Japanese find them difficult to understand. (Don't despair: the major Noh theaters usually provide synopses of the plays in English.) The action—such as it is—develops at nearly glacial speed.

The principal character in a Noh play wears a carved wooden mask. Such is the skill of the actor, and the mysterious effect of the play, that the mask itself may appear expressionless until the actor "brings it to life," at which point the mask can express a considerable range of emotions. As in Kabuki, the various roles of the Noh repertoire all have specific costumes—robes of silk brocade with intricate patterns that are works of art in themselves. Noh is not a very "accessible" kind of theater: Its language is archaic; its conventions are obscure; and its measured, stately pace can put even Japanese audiences to sleep.

More accessible is the *kyogen*, a short comic interlude traditionally performed between two Noh plays in a program. The pace is quicker, the costumes (based on actual dress of the medieval period) are simpler, and most kyogen do not use masks; the comedy depends on the satiric premise—a clever servant who gets the best of his master, for example—and the lively facial expressions of the actors.

Like Kabuki, Noh has a number of schools, the traditions of which developed as the exclusive property of hereditary families. The major schools have their own theaters in Tokyo and Kyoto, with regular schedules of performances—but if you happen to be in Kyoto on June 1–2, don't miss the Takigi Noh: an outdoor performance given at night, by torchlight, in the precincts of the Heian Shrine. There are other torchlight performances as well in Tokyo, at the Meiji Shrine (early October) and Zojoji Temple (late May), and in Nara at the Kasuga Shrine (May).

BUNRAKU

The third major form of traditional Japanese drama is Bunraku puppet theater. Itinerant puppeteers were plying their trade in Japan as early as the 10th century; sometime in the late 16th century, a form of narrative ballad called *joruri,* performed to the accompaniment of a three-string banjolike instrument called the *shamisen,* was grafted onto their art, and Bunraku was born. The golden age of Bunraku came some 200 years later, when most of the great plays were written and the puppets themselves evolved to their present form, so expressive and intricate in their movements that they require three people, acting in unison to manipulate them.

The puppets are about two-thirds human size and elaborately dressed in period costume; each one is made up of interchangeable parts—a head, shoulder piece, trunk, legs, and arms. The puppeteer called the *omozukai* controls the expression on the puppet's face and its right arm and hand. The *hidarizukai* controls the puppet's left arm and hand along with any props that it is carrying. The *ashizukai* moves the puppet's legs. The most difficult task belongs to the omozukai—a role it commonly takes some 30 years to master.

Creating the puppet heads is an art in itself, and today there are only a handful of carvers still working. As a rule, the heads are shaped and painted for specific figures—characters of different sex, age, and personality—and fitted with elaborate wigs of human hair in various styles to indicate the puppet's social standing. Able to roll their eyes and lift their eyebrows, the puppets can achieve an amazing range of facial expression.

The chanters, who provide both the narration of the play and the voices of the puppets, deliver their lines in a kind of high-pitched croak from deep in the throat. The texts they recite are considered to be among the classics of Japanese dramatic literature; the great playwright Chikamatsu Monzaemon (1653–1725) wrote for both Bunraku and Kabuki, and the two dramatic forms often adapted works from one another.

The most important Bunraku troupe is the government-supported National Bunraku Theatre in Osaka, but there are amateur and semiprofessional companies throughout the country—the most active of them on Awaji Island, near Shikoku. Periodically there are also performances in Tokyo in the small hall of the National Theater.

(Opposite page) The principal character in a Noh play wears a carved, wooden mask; (below) Bunraku puppets are about two-thirds human size.

ONSEN AND BATHING

A chain of volcanic islands on the fiery Pacific Rim, Japan has developed a splendid subculture around one of the more manageable manifestations of this powerful resource: the *onsen* thermal spa.

(This page above) A lakeside rotenburo made from natural rocks; (opposite page upper right) Gakenoyu Onsen in Nagano; (opposite page bottom left) A spa in Shirihama Onsen

The benchmark Japanese weekend excursion—be it family outing, company retreat, or romantic getaway—is the hot spring resort. Fissured from end to end with volcanic cracks and crannies, the country positively wheezes with geothermal springs. Hot water gushes and sprays almost everywhere—but most especially in the mountains; there are hot springs in every prefecture, on every offshore island—even in cities built, incautiously, above the very fault lines themselves. And to all these superheated hollows flock the Japanese in endless enthusiasm, putting many thousands of people to work, catering to their needs; onsen are as nearly recession-proof an industry as the nation has. It's not too much to say, that to understand the Japanese, to discover their innermost nature, you need to get naked with them a while in hot mineral water.

YUDEDAKO

The Japanese have a special term for that blissful state of total immersion: *yudedako*—literally "boiled octopus"—and Japanese people of all ages and both sexes will journey for miles to attain it. Getting boiled is a step on the road to sound health, good digestion, clear skin, marital harmony—to whatever it is that gives you a general sense of being at one with the universe.

2

If you're new to Japan, you might be astounded with the popularity of thermal baths. It begins to seem like the only way for a town to hope to bring in Japanese tourists is to have an onsen. Quite naturally, the Japanese have developed a subculture around one of the more manageable manifestations of this powerful resource.

THE ONSEN EXPERIENCE

An *onsen* can refer to a particular region or subregion, like Yufuin in Oita Prefecture, Kinugawa in Tochigi, or Hakone in Kanagawa: a resort destination especially well endowed with thermal springs. Or it can mean more specifically a public bathhouse with a spring-fed pool, where you pay an admission fee and soak at your leisure. (At last count, there were some 6,700 of these nationwide.) Or it could mean a lodging—one of two basic varieties—with a spring of its own. One type is the *kanko* hotel: a mega-onsen with multiple baths, in grand pharaonic styles with mosaics and waterfalls, and banquet halls and dinner shows, as well as tatami guest rooms that sleep six—and, inevitably, discos and karaoke bars and souvenir shops. The other type is the *onsen* of everyone's dreams: the picture-perfect traditional inn, a ryokan of half a dozen rooms, nestled up somewhere in the mountains all by itself, with a spectacular view

and a *rotenburo*—an outdoor pool—to enjoy it from.

THE ROTENBURO

Ah! the rotenburo! At smaller *onsen*, you can book the exquisitely crafted pool, with its stepping stones and lanterns, and bamboo screens, for a private soak: an hour or so of the purest luxury, especially by moonlight. The rotenburo is a year-round indulgence; the view from the pool might be a mountainside white with cherry blossoms in spring, or a lakefront brilliant in the red and gold of maples in autumn, or—best of all, perhaps—a winter panorama, with the snow piled high on the pines and hedges that frame the landscape, to contemplate from your snug, steamy vantage point while you slowly wrinkle yourself like a prune. Be warned: whatever the season, you'll need to make reservations well in advance, for *onsen* accommodations of any sort. Japan has more than 3,000 registered spas; collectively, they draw nearly 140 million visitors a year, and hotel space is not easy to come by.

WHAT IS AN ONSEN?

By law, an onsen is only an onsen if the water comes out of the ground at a specified minimum temperature, and contains at least one of 19 designated minerals and chemical compounds—which makes for a wide range of choices. There are iron springs with red water; there are silky-smooth alkali

springs; there are springs with radon and sulphur sodium bicarbonate: there are springs with water at a comfortable 100°F (37.8°C), and springs so hot they have bath masters to make sure you stay only for three minutes and not a fatal second longer.

One reason many Westerners are reluctant to go bathing in Japan is the fact that you have to take all your clothes off. *In front of everyone else.* There is that issue—no getting around it: Japanese communal bathing is done in the buff—but that shouldn't deter you from the experience of a truly good thing. The bath is a great equalizer: in a sense the bath *is* Japan, in its unalloyed egalitarianism. Here, rank and title are stripped away: there is no way to tell if the body boiling beside you belongs to a captain of industry or his humble employee, to an ambassador, to a pauper, to a mendicant priest—and each bather offers the other an equal degree of respect and regard; no one ever behaves in a way that might spoil the enjoyment of any other bather; no one is embarrassed or causes embarrassment.

ONSEN ETIQUETTE

Another reason you might have for your reluctance is the worrisome conviction that bathing with a bunch of strangers comes with a raft of rules—rules all those strangers know from childhood, but at least one of which you're bound to break, to your everlasting horror and shame. "What if I drop the soap in the bath?" is a typical fear.

In fact, the pitfalls are not at all so awful. There certainly are protocols to follow, but it's a short list.

1. While there are still a few spas that keep alive the old custom of *konyoku* (mixed bathing), all of them have separate entrances for men and women, announced in Japanese characters on hangings over the doors. If in doubt, ask.

2. A word of warning: body tattoos, in Japan, are indelibly associated with the *yakuza*—organized crime families and their minions—and spas commonly refuse entry to tattooed visitors, to avoid upsetting their regular clientele. The rule is strictly enforced—and could extend to that little butterfly you got on

2

your shoulder when you were young and reckless. Put a bandage over it.

3. The first room you come to inside is the dressing room. It's almost always tatami-floored: take your shoes or slippers off in the entryway. The dressing room will have lockers for your keys and valuables, and rows of wicker or plastic baskets on shelves; pick one, and put your clothes in it. If you're staying overnight at an inn with a spa of its own, you'll find a cotton kimono called a *nemaki* in your room—you sleep in it, in lieu of pajamas—and a light quilted jacket called a *hanten*. Night or day, this is standard gear to wear from your room to the spa, anywhere else around the inn, and even for a stroll out of doors. Leave them in the basket.

The spa should provide—or you should have with you—two towels: leave the bigger one in the basket, to dry off with, and take the smaller one with you next door, to the pools. (Holding this towel modestly over your nether parts is the accepted way of moving around in the spa.)

4. The pool area will have rows of washing stations along the walls: countertops with supplies of soap and shampoo, a mirror, taps and showerhead, a stool, and a bucket. Here's where you get clean—and that means *really* clean. Soap up, shower, scrub off every particle of the day's wear and tear. Take your time; use your wash towel. Leave no trace of soap. Then take your towel modestly to the pool.

You can bring the towel with you into the bath, but the onsen really would rather you didn't. Most people leave theirs at poolside, or set them folded on top of their heads. (Another protocol: spas don't insist on bathing caps, but they do want you to keep your head above water.)

And that's all there is to it. Find a pleasant spot; soak in blissful silence, if you prefer (but not too long, if you're not used to it), or feel free to strike up a conversation with a fellow soaker: *atsui desu ne*—the local equivalent of "Hot enough for you?"—is a good start, and from there, you can go anywhere. The Japanese call their friendliest, most relaxing acquaintances *hadaka no o-tsukiai*: naked encounters.

Staying at a mega-onsen? Conviviality reigns in the pools of these establishments, with all sorts of amenities to help it along. At some inns, for example, you can order a small floating table for yourself and your fellow boilers, just big enough for a ceramic flask of sake or two, and a suitable number of cups. You get to warm your insides and outsides at the same time: how bad can that be?

(Opposite page) Some onsen have single-sex bathing, some have mixed bathing; (bottom) You clean yourself thoroughly before setting foot in the onsen.

THE RYOKAN

You're likely to find Japanese hospitality polished, warm, and professional pretty much anywhere you stay—but nowhere more so than in a *ryokan*: a traditional inn.

(This page above) A traditional tatami-mat bedroom in a ryokan; (opposite page upper right) a ryokan meal served in myriad little dishes; (opposite page bottom left) bedding for a ryokan, which is laid out nightly

Ryokans are typically one- or two-story wooden buildings where the guest rooms have tatami mat floors; the bedding—stowed by day in a closet—is rolled out at night. The rooms have hardly any furniture—perhaps one low dining table and cushions on the floor, a chest of drawers with a mirror, and a scroll painting or a flower arrangement in the *tokonoma* (alcove)—but every room in a proper ryokan will have windows with sliding paper screens looking out on an exquisite interior garden. Rates are per person and include the cost of breakfast and dinner. Some inns are reluctant to accept foreign guests: the assumption is that you don't know the language or the rules of ryokan etiquette. Call well ahead for reservations: better yet, have somebody Japanese make the call for you. The venerable, top-of-the-line ryokans expect even first-time Japanese guests to have introductions from a known and respected client.

COSTS

Ryokans of august lineage and exemplary service are expensive: expect to pay ¥30,000 or even ¥50,000 per person per night with two meals. Lesser-priced inns, which can run from ¥5,000 for a single room to ¥7,000 for a double, are comfortable enough, but don't count on deluxe appointments or even a garden. The Japan National Tourism Organization has a listing of some of the latter.

2

RYOKAN ETIQUETTE

Remove your shoes as you step up from the entryway of your ryokan, and change into slippers. A maid will escort you to your room. (It might take you two or three tries thereafter to find it on your own. Ryokans pride themselves on quiet and privacy, and the rooms are typically laid out in a labyrinth of corridors, where you're seldom aware of the presence of other guests.) Slippers come off at the door; on tatami, only socks/stockings or bare feet are acceptable. Relax first with a cup of green tea, and then head for the bath. In ryokans with thermal pools (not all have them), you can take to the waters pretty much anytime between to 6 am and 11 pm; otherwise—unless you have in-room facilities—guests must stagger visits to the communal bath. The maid will make these arrangements. Be mindful of Japanese bathing rules (⇨ *Onsen and Bathing, above*); wash and rinse off thoroughly before you get in the tub for a long hot soak. After your bath, change into a nemaki, the simple cotton kimono you'll find in your room, that doubles as sleepwear—or as standard garb for an informal stroll. These days, ryokans often have private baths, but especially in more venerable establishments (even those with astronomical rates), all facilities may be shared.

Ryokans don't have legions of staff, and will appreciate it if you observe

their routines and schedules. Guests are expected to arrive in the late afternoon and eat around 6. The front doors are usually locked at 10, so plan for early evenings. Breakfast is served around 8, and checkout is at 10.

FOOD

Not every inn that calls itself a ryokan offers breakfast and dinner. Indeed, some offer only breakfast; some inns have no meals at all. Seek out those that do; it's an important part of the experience. And while some ryokans will allow you to pay a lesser rate and skip dinner, why would you do that? Dinner—a feast of local specialties in beautiful dishes of all shapes and sizes—is served in your room. When you're finished, your maid will clear the table, and lay out your futon bedding: a mattress filled with cotton wadding and (in winter) a heavy, thick comforter. In summer the comforter is replaced with a thinner quilt. In the morning the maid will gently wake you, clear away the futon, and bring in your Japanese-style breakfast: grilled fish, miso soup, pickled vegetables, and rice. If you prefer, the staff will usually be able to come up with coffee and toast, not to mention a fried egg.

BASEBALL IN JAPAN

Sumo may be the national sport, but without question, the most popular sport in Japan is baseball. It was first introduced in 1872 by Horace Wilson and has been popular ever since.

(This page above) Hanshin Tiger fans releasing balloons after the 7th-inning; (opposite page upper right) a night game at Yokohama Stadium; (opposite page bottom left) players from the Japanese Little League

Each October, two major-league teams in the United States (or one major league team from the United States and one major league team from Canada) play the best of seven games to decide the World Series. But judging from the results of the recently inaugurated World Baseball Classic (WBC) that Japan has won twice, any true world series of baseball would have to include Japan. While the Japanese professional league season is shorter than its American counterpart (130–140 games versus 162 games), the major-league season's brevity is more than made up by the company league season, the university circuit, and the spring and summer high school tournaments. In addition, there are junior high school and elementary school leagues. Many municipalities and towns even have senior leagues for people over 60 years old. The game is played everywhere: from the southern islands of Okinawa to the northern tip of Hokkaido.

CATCHING A GAME

Even if you're not a baseball fan, you should try to take in a game on any level for the spectacle. Like the players, the fans come prepared. From team colors and fan paraphernalia to songs and boxed lunches, the Japanese fans have it down. The cheering starts with the first pitch and doesn't end until the last out. Wherever you go to see a game, you will be made to feel welcome and your interest or curiosity will be rewarded.

BASEBALL-DO

Martial arts in Japan (judo, kendo, kyudo) and many other activities including the tea ceremony (*chado*) and calligraphy (*shodo*) end in the suffix *do* (pronounced "doe" as in the female deer and meaning "way"). In Japan, baseball is also a *do*, an art rather than a sport. Of course, the Japanese watch baseball as they watch any sport, but in terms of their preparation and mental approach to the game, it is a do.

All of Japan's active arts require years of practice to achieve the level of intense concentration and mindlessness that mastery requires. The idea is that if you practice something long enough and hard enough, it will become pure reflex. Then you won't have to think about what to do and when to do it. You will just do it. Major players like Toritani and Sakamoto, Nishioka and Makajima play with a fluidity and grace that is beyond athleticism, exhibiting true mastery of the sport, and the result can be breathtaking.

SPRING AND SUMMER HIGH SCHOOL TOURNAMENTS

If you're fortunate enough to be in Japan in either March or August, you can attend the high school baseball tournament held annually at Koshien Stadium in Nishinomiya (near Osaka), the mecca of Japanese baseball. In what regard is high school baseball held?

Well, the pro team that normally plays at Koshien (the Hanshin Tigers) has to hit the road for two weeks in August to make way for the summer tournament. Both high school tournaments last about two weeks. Many of the star high school players go on to be standout players in both Japan and the United States. Both Boston Red Sox pitcher Daisuke Matsuzaka and Seattle Mariners' star Ichiro Suzuki were star high school players.

TICKET PRICES

Tickets for a professional baseball game (the season runs from late March/early April to October) are a relatively good buy. At Koshien, home of the Hanshin Tigers, prices range from ¥1,900 for a seat in the outfield to ¥4,000 for a reserved seat on a lower level. When box seats are offered for sale, you can expect to pay around ¥6,000. Prices are similar at Tokyo Dome, where the Yomiuri Giants play.

Tickets for the high school baseball tournaments are even more affordable. Prices range from ¥500 for upper-reserved to ¥1,200 for lower-reserved to ¥1,600 for box seats. Seats in the bleachers are free throughout the tournaments.

Most other games (school, community, or company) are either free or, in the case of a championship game, require only a nominal fee.

JAPANESE MARTIAL ARTS

Take all that chop-socky stuff in the movies with a grain of salt: the Japanese martial arts are primarily about balance—mental, spiritual, and physical—and only incidentally about attack and self-defense.

(This page above) A practice Kendo session; (opposite page upper right) practicing Aikido throws; (opposite page bottom left) competitors at a Judo tournament

Judo and karate are now as much icons of Japanese culture as anime or consumer electronics, and just as enthusiastically embraced abroad. Judo, karate, and aikido, all essentially 20th-century developments, have gone global; it would be hard to name a country anywhere without a network of *dojos* (martial arts academies or training halls) and local organizations, affiliates of the governing bodies in Japan, certifying students and holding competitions. Judo has been an Olympic sport for men since the 1964 games in Tokyo, and for women since 1988. An estimated 50 million people worldwide practice karate, in one or another of the eight different forms recognized by the World Union of Karate-do Federations. Aikido was first introduced abroad in the 1950s; the International Aikido Federation now has affiliates in 44 member nations. Korea and Taiwan have instruction programs in kendo (fencing) that begin at the secondary school level.

LEVELS

Levels of certification are as much a part of the martial arts as they are in traditional disciplines like flower arranging or Japanese chess—the difference being that marks of rank are clearly visible. Students progress from the 10th *kyu* level to the 1st, and then from 1st *dan* to 8th (or 10th, depending on the system or school). Beginners wear white belts, intermediates wear brown, dan holders wear black or black-and-red.

KYUDO: THE WAY OF THE BOW

Archery is the oldest of Japan's traditional martial arts, dating from the 12th century, when archers played an important role in the struggles for power among samurai clans. Today it is practiced as a sport and a spiritual discipline. The object is not just to hit the target (no mean feat), but to do so in proper form, releasing the arrow at the moment the mind is empty of all extraneous thought.

KENDO: THE WAY OF THE SWORD

Fencing was a mainstay of feudal Japan, but the roots of modern kendo date to the early 18th century, with the introduction of the *shinai*—a practice sword made of bamboo slats—and the distinctive armor (*bogu*) still in use to protect the specific target areas the fencer must strike to earn points in competition. Matches are noisy affairs; attacks must be executed with foot stamping and loud spirited shouts called *kiai*.

JUDO: THE GENTLE WAY

Dr. Kano Jigoro (1860–1938) was the proverbial 90-pound weakling as a teenager; to overcome his frailty, he immersed himself at the University of Tokyo in the martial arts, and over a period of years developed a reformed version of jujutsu on "scientific principles," which he finally codified in 1884. The *ju* of judo means "softness" or "gentleness"—a reference to

its techniques of using one's opponent's strength against him—but belying the fact that this really is a rough-and-tumble contact sport.

KARATE: THE EMPTY HAND

Odd as it may sound, karate (literally: "the empty hand") doesn't quite qualify as a traditional Japanese martial art. Its origins are Chinese, but it was largely developed in the Ryukyu Kingdom (Okinawa before it was annexed), and didn't come to Japan proper until 1922. It lays stress on self-defense, spiritual and mental balance, and *kata*—formal, almost ritual sequences of movement. But it is as much about offense as defense: most of the movements end in a punch, a kick, or a strike with the knee or elbow.

AIKIDO: THE WAY OF HARMONY

The youngest of the Japanese martial arts was developed in the 1920s by Ueshiba Morihei (1883–1969), incorporating elements of both jujutsu and kendo, with much bigger doses of philosophy and spirituality. Aikido techniques consist largely of throws; the first thing a student learns is how to fall safely. Partner practice begins with a stylized strike or a punch; the intended receiver counters by getting out of the way, leading the attacker's momentum, pivoting into a throw or an arm/shoulder pin. The essential idea is to do no damage.

SUMO

This centuries-old national sport of Japan is not to be taken lightly—as anyone who has ever seen a sumo wrestler will testify.

(This page above) Two wrestlers battle in the ring; (opposite page upper right) a wrestler in traditional dress outside the arena; (opposite page bottom left) the ceremonial entrance of the tournament participants

Sheer mass, mind you, isn't necessarily the key to success—though it might seem that way. There are no weight limits or categories in sumo; contenders in the upper ranks average 350 pounds. But Chiyonofuji, one of the all-time great *yokozuna* (Grand Champions), who tipped the scales at a mere 280 pounds, regularly faced—and defeated—opponents who outweighed him by 200 pounds or more. That said, sumo wrestlers do spend a lot of their time just bulking up, consuming enormous quantities of a high-protein stew called *chanko nabe*, washed down with beer. Akebono, the first foreign-born yokozuna, weighed over 500 pounds; current Grand Champion Hakuho, from Mongolia (the profusion of non-Japanese at the top of this most traditional of Japanese institutions is no small embarrassment to the Sumo Association), started his career at 160 pounds and doubled his weight in four years.

SUMO RULES

The official catalog of sumo techniques include 82 different ways of pushing, pulling, tripping, tossing, or slapping down your opponent, but the basic rules are exquisitely simple: Except for hitting below the belt (which is all a sumo wrestler wears) and striking with a closed fist, almost anything goes. Touch the sand with anything but the soles of your feet, or get forced out of the ring, and you lose.

SUMO HISTORY

The earliest written references to sumo date back to the year 712; for many centuries it was not so much a sport as a Shinto religious rite, associated with Imperial Court ceremonies. Its present form—with the raised clay *dohyo* (platform) and circle of rice straw bales to mark the ring, the ranking system, the referee and judges, the elaborate costumes and purification rituals—was largely developed in the 16th and early 17th centuries.

THE SUMO WORLD

Sumo is very much a closed world, hierarchical and formal. To compete in it, you must belong to a *heya* (stable) run by a retired wrestler who has purchased that right from the association. The stable master, or *oyakata*, is responsible for bringing in as many new wrestlers as the heya can accommodate, for their training (every stable has its own practice ring) and schooling in the elaborate etiquette of sumo, and for every facet of their daily lives. Youngsters recruited into the sport live in the stable dormitory, doing all the community chores and waiting on their seniors while they learn. When they rise high enough in tournament rankings, they acquire servant-apprentices of their own.

All the stables in the association—now some 50 in number—are in Tokyo. Most are clustered on both sides of the

Sumida River near the green-roofed *Kokugikan* (National Sumo Arena), in the areas called Asakusabashi and Ryogoku. Come early in the day, and you can peer through the windows of the heya to watch them practice; with luck—and good connections—you might even get invited in.

There are six official sumo tournaments throughout the year: three in Tokyo (January, May and September; one each in Osaka (March), Nagoya (July), and Fukuoka (November). Wrestlers in the upper divisions fight 15 matches over 15 days. A few weeks before each tournament, a panel of judges and association *toshiyori* (elders) publish a table called a *banzuke*, which divides the 800-plus wrestlers into six ranks and two divisions, East and West, to determine who fights whom. Rankings are based on a wrestler's record in the previous tournament: win a majority of your matches and you go up in the next banzuke; lose a majority and you go down.

If you can't attend one of the Tokyo sumo tournaments, you may want to at least pay a short visit to the Sumo Museum in Tokyo (⇨ *Greater Tokyo in Chapter 3*). The museum itself is free, though it's only open weekdays. And while no explanations are in English, there are many sumo-related works of art to view.

THE GEISHA

The geisha—with her white makeup and Cupid's-bow red lip rouge, her hair ornaments, the rich brocade of her kimono—is as much an icon of Japan, instantly recognizable the world over, as Mt. Fuji itself.

(This page above) A traditional geisha performance in Kanazawa; (opposite page upper right) geishas in Kyoto; (opposite page bottom left) geishas on the streets of Kyoto

Gei stands for artistic accomplishment (*sha* simply means person), and a geisha must be a person of many talents. As a performer, she should have a lovely voice and a command of traditional dance, and play beautifully on an instrument like the *shamisen*. She must have a finely tuned aesthetic sense, and excel at the art of conversation. In short, she should be the ultimate party hostess and gracious companion. Geisha (or *geiko* in Kyoto dialect) begin their careers at a very young age, when they are accepted into an *okiya*, a sort of guildhall where they live and learn as *maiko* (apprentices). The okiya is a thoroughly matriarchal society; the owner/manager is called *o-kami-san*, who is addressed as *okaasan* ("mother"), to underscore the fact that the geishas have given up one family for another.

GEISHA LIFE

The okiya provides the apprentices with room and board, pays for their training and clothing (the latter a staggering expense), and oversees their daily lives. The maiko in turn do household chores; when they have become full-fledged geisha, they contribute a part of their income to the upkeep of the house and its all-female staff of teachers, dressers, and maids.

THE GEISHA BUSINESS

There are no free agents in the geisha world; to engage one for a party you need a referral. Geisha work almost exclusively at traditional inns (*ryokan*), restaurants (*ryotei*), and teahouses (*chaya*); the owners of one will contact an okiya with which they have a connection and make the engagement—providing, of course, that you've established yourself as a trustworthy client. That means you will understand and be prepared to pay the bill, when it shows up sometime later. Fees for a geisha's or maiko's time are measured in "sticks"—generally, one hour: the time it would take a stick of incense to burn down—and the okiya can really stick it to you. Bills are based on the number of guests at the party, and can run as high as ¥25,000 per person or more, for a two-hour engagement.

There were as many as 80,000 geisha in the 1920s; today there may be 1,000 left, most of them living and working in the Gion district of Kyoto; in Kanazawa; and in the Shimbashi, Akasaka, and Ginza districts of Tokyo. Fewer and fewer young Japanese women are willing to make the total commitment this closed world demands (even a geisha who opts to live independently will remain affiliated with her okiya for the rest of her career); fewer and fewer Japanese men of means have the taste or inclination to entertain themselves or important guests in this elegant fashion. On the other hand, the profession—while it lasts—does provide considerable job security. A geisha is valued, not solely for her beauty, but for her artistic and social skills—and her absolute discretion (what she might see and hear, for example, at a party hosted by a political bigwig for his important business connections, could topple empires). A geisha with these accomplishments will still be in demand long after the bloom of youth has fled.

A geisha will establish a variety of relations with men. She will try to develop a roster of repeat clients, and may choose one among them as a patron, for financial support and—although she is by no means, as some people imagine, a prostitute—for sexual intimacy. When a geisha marries, most often to such a client, she leaves the profession.

THE TEA CEREMONY

The Way of Tea—in Japanese, *Cha-no-yu* or *Sado*—is more than a mere ceremonial occasion to have a cuppa: it is a profound spiritual and philosophical ritual. It's also a ritual you can experience easily and relatively inexpensively.

(This page above) Guests participating in a tea ceremony; (opposite page upper right) a bowl of matcha green tea; (opposite page bottom left) an outdoor garden tea ceremony

Tea came to Japan from China in the late 8th century, first as a medicinal plant; it was the Zen monks of the 12th century who started the practice of drinking tea for a refresher between meditation sessions. Rules and customs began to evolve regarding how to drink this precious beverage, and they coalesced in the Muromachi period of the 14th and 15th centuries as the earliest form of the Cha-no-yu. The Way of Tea developed an aesthetic of its own, rooted in the Zen sense of discipline, restraint, and simplicity: an aesthetic in which the most valued tea bowls, vessels, and utensils were humble, unadorned—and even imperfect. The choreographed steps and movements of the tea ceremony were devised to focus the appreciation—in Japanese, called *wabi*—for this subdued and quiet refinement.

THE TEA PAVILION

Contemplate a Japanese tea pavilion long enough, and you begin to see how much work and thought can go into the design of something so simple. A stone path through a garden, a thatched roof, a low doorway into a single room with a *tokonoma* (alcove) and tatami floor, barely big enough for the tea master and a few guests: and yet a gateway to the infinite.

THE WAY OF TEA

The poet-priest Sen no Rikyu (1522–91) is the most revered figure in the history of Cha-no-yu. Three traditional schools of the tea ceremony, the Ura Senke, the Omote Senke, and the Mushakoji Senke—with some variations among them—maintain the forms and aesthetic principles he developed.

A full-scale formal tea ceremony, called a *chaji*, is like a drama in two acts, involving a multicourse *kaiseki* meal, two different kinds of powdered green tea, and an intermission—and can take as long as four hours to perform. Most ceremonies are less formal, confined to the serving of *usucha* ("thin tea") and a confection, for an intimate group; these are called *o-chakai*. Both forms demand a strictly determined, stately series of moves to be made by both guests and hosts.

Participants gather first in the *machiai*, a kind of waiting room or shelter in the garden, until they are invited to proceed to the teahouse. They remove their shoes, and enter the teahouse through a low doorway. It is customary to comment on the flower arrangement or scroll in the alcove. The guests sit in *seiza*, their legs tucked under them; the host enters from another small doorway, greets them, and carefully cleans the utensils: bowl, tea scoop, caddy, ladle, whisk. No matter that they are

spotless already; cleaning them is part of the ritual.

When the tea is prepared, it is served first to the principal guest, who turns the bowl in the palm of his hand, drains it in three deep careful sips, and returns it to the host. The other participants are served in turn. The guests comment on the presentation, and the ceremony is over; when they leave the pavilion, the host bows to them from the door.

You won't be expected to have the same mastery of the etiquette as a Japanese guest, but the right frame of mind will get you through, if you are invited to a tea ceremony. Make conversation that befits the serenity of the moment. (A well-known haiku poetess once said that what she learned most from Cha-no-yu was to think before she spoke.) Above all, pay close attention to the practiced movements of the host, and remember to praise the *wabi*—the understated beauty—of the utensils he or she has chosen.

Recommended reading: *The Book of Tea* by Okakura Kakuzo; *Cha-no-Yu: The Japanese Tea Ceremony* by A.L. Sadler.

JAPANESE GARDENS

Oases of calm and contemplation—and philosophical statements in their own right—Japanese gardens are quite unlike the arrangements of flowers, shrubs, and trees you find in the West.

(This page above) The garden of Hogon-in, Kyoto; (opposite page upper right) the gardens of Kinkaku-ji, Kyoto; (opposite page bottom left) Koishikawa Korakuen Garden, Tokyo

One key to understanding—and more fully enjoying—a Japanese garden is knowing that its design, like all traditional Japanese arts, emerged out of the country's unique mixture of religious and artistic ideas. From Shintoism comes the belief in the divinity or spirit that dwells in natural phenomena like mountains, trees, and stones. The influence of Taoism is reflected in the islands that serve as symbolic heavens for the souls of those who achieve perfect harmony. Buddhist gardens—especially Zen gardens, expressions of the "less is more" aesthetic of the warrior caste—evolved in medieval times as spaces for meditation and the path to enlightenment. The classic example from this period is the *karesansui* (dry landscape) style, a highly abstract composition of meticulously placed rocks and raked sand or gravel, sometimes with a single pruned tree, but with no water at all.

SHAKEI

Shakei ("borrowed landscape") is a way of extending the boundaries of the visual space by integrating a nearby attractive view—a mountain, a grove of trees, or a sweeping temple roofline, for example—framing and echoing it with plantings of similar shape or color inside the garden itself. A middle ground, usually a hedge or a wall, blocks off any unwanted view and draws the background into the composition.

GARDEN DESIGN

Historically, the first garden designers in Japan were temple priests; the design concepts themselves were originally Chinese. Later, from the 16th century on, the most remarkable Japanese gardens were created by tea masters, who established a genre of their own for settings meant to deepen and refine the tea ceremony experience. Hence the *roji*: a garden path of stepping stones from the waiting room to the teahouse itself, a transition from the ordinary world outside that prepares participants emotionally and mentally for the ceremony. Gradually, gardens moved out of the exclusive realm to which only nobles, wealthy merchants, and poets had access, and the increasingly affluent middle class began to demand professional designers. In the process, the elements of the garden became more elaborate, complex, and symbolic.

The "hide-and-reveal" principle, for example, dictates that there should be no point from which all of a garden is visible, that there must always be mystery and incompleteness in its changing perspectives: the garden *unfolds* as you walk from one view to another along the winding path. References to celebrated natural wonders and literary allusions, too, are frequently used design techniques. Mt. Fuji might be represented by a truncated cone of

stones; Ama-no-Hashidate, the famous pine-covered spit of land across Miyazu Bay, near Kyoto, might be rendered by a stone bridge; a lone tree might stand for a mighty forest. Abstract concepts and themes from myths and legends, readily understood by the Japanese, are similarly part of the garden vocabulary. The use of boulders in a streambed, for example, can represent life's surmountable difficulties; a pine tree can stand for strength and endurance; islands in a pond can evoke a faraway paradise.

Seasonal change is a highlight of the Japanese garden: the designer in effect choreographs the different plants that come into their glory at different times of year: cherry and plum blossoms and wisteria in spring; hydrangeas, peonies, and water lilies in summer; the spectacular reds and orange of the Japanese maple leaves in autumn. Even in winter, the snow clinging to the garden's bare bones makes an impressive sight. In change, there is permanence; in permanence, there is fluid movement—often represented in the garden with a water element: a pond or a flowing stream, or an abstraction of one in raked gravel or stone.

RELIGION IN JAPAN

Although both Buddhism and Shinto permeate Japanese society and life, most Japanese are blissfully unaware of the distinction between what is Shinto and what is Buddhist. A wedding is often a Shinto ceremony while a funeral is a Buddhist rite.

(This page above) A Shinto shrine near Tokyo; (opposite page upper right) a statue of Buddha at Toda-ji, Nara; (opposite page bottom left) the gates at Futura-san Jinja, Nikko

There's a saying in Japan that you're Shinto at birth (marked with a Shinto ceremony), Christian when you marry (if you choose a Western-style wedding), and Buddhist when you die (honored with a Buddhist funeral). The Japanese take a utilitarian view of religion and use each as suits the occasion. One prays for success in life at a shrine and for the repose of a deceased family member at a temple. There is no thought given to the whys for this—these things simply are. The neighborhood shrine's annual *matsuri* is a time of giving thanks for prosperity and for blessing homes and local businesses. *O-mikoshi*, portable shrines for the gods, are enthusiastically carried around the district by young local men. Shouting and much sake drinking are part of the celebration. But it's a celebration first and foremost.

RELIGION IN NUMBERS

While most Japanese— some 90 million people out of some 128 million total—identify themselves as Buddhist, most also practice and believe in Shinto, even if they don't identify themselves as Shinto followers per se. The two religions overlap and even complement each other even though most Japanese people would not consider themselves as "religious."

2

SHINTO

Shinto—literally, "the way of the *kami* (god)"—is a form of animism or nature worship based on myth and rooted to the geography and holy places of the land. It's an ancient belief system, dating back perhaps as far as 500 BC and is indigenous to Japan. The name is derived from a Chinese word, *shin tao,* coined in the 8th century AD, when divine origins were first ascribed to the royal Yamato family. Fog-enshrouded mountains, pairs of rocks, primeval forests, and geothermal activity are all manifestations of the *kami-sama* (honorable gods). For many Japanese, the Shinto aspect of their lives is simply the realm of the kami-sama and is not attached to a religious framework as it would be in the West. In that sense, the name describes more a way of thinking than a religion.

BUDDHISM

A Korean king gave a statue of Shaka—the first Buddha, Prince Gautama—to the Yamato Court in AD 538. The Soga clan adopted the foreign faith, using it as a vehicle to change the political order of the day. After battling for control of the country, they established themselves as political rulers, and Buddhism took permanent hold. Simultaneously, Japan sent its first ambassadors to China, inaugurating the importation of Chinese culture, writing, and religion into Japan.

By the 8th century, Buddhism was well established.

Japanese Buddhism developed in three waves. In the Heian period (794–1185), Esoteric Buddhism was introduced primarily by two priests, both of whom studied in China: Saicho and Kukai. Saicho established a temple on Mt. Hie near Kyoto, making it the most revered mountain in Japan after Mt. Fuji. Kukai established the Shingon sect of Esoteric Buddhism on Mt. Koya, south of Nara. In Japanese temple architecture, Esoteric Buddhism introduced the separation of the temple into an interior for the initiated and an outer laypersons' area.

Amidism (Pure Land) was the second wave, introduced by the monk Honen (1133–1212), and it flourished in the late 12th century until the introduction of Zen in 1185. Its adherents saw the world emerging from a period of darkness during which Buddhism had been in decline, and asserted that salvation was offered only to the believers in *Amida,* a Nyorai (Buddha) or enlightened being. Amidism's promise of salvation and its subsequent versions of heaven and hell earned it the appellation "Devil's Christianity" from visiting Christian missionaries in the 16th century.

In the Post-Heian period (1185 to the present) the influences of Nichiren and Zen Buddhist philosophies pushed Japanese Buddhism in new directions.

The Senso-ji Complex is the heart at soul of the Asakusa district of Tokyo.

Nichiren (1222–82) was a monk who insisted on the primacy of the Lotus Sutra, the supposed last and greatest sutra of Shaka. Zen Buddhism was attractive to the samurai class's ideals of discipline and worldly detachment and thus spread throughout Japan in the 12th century. It was later embraced as a nonintellectual path to enlightenment by those in search of a direct experience of the sublime. More recently, Zen has been adopted by a growing number of people in the West as a way to move beyond the subject/object duality that characterizes Western thought.

SHRINE AND STATE

While the modern Japanese constitution expressly calls for a separation of church and state, it hasn't always been this way. In fact, twice over the last 150 years, Shinto was the favored religion and the government used all of its influence to support it.

During the Meiji Restoration (1868), the emperor was made sovereign leader of Japan, and power that had been spread out among the shoguns was consolidated in the Imperial House. Shinto was favored over Buddhism for two reasons. First, according to Shinto, the members of the imperial family were direct descendents of the kami who had formed Japan. The second reason was more practical: many of the Buddhist temples were regional power bases that relied upon the shoguns for patronage. Relegating Buddhism to a minor religion with no official support would have a weakening effect on the shoguns, while the government could use Shinto shrines to strengthen its power base.

Indeed, Buddhism was actively suppressed. Temples were closed, priests were harassed, and priceless art was either destroyed or sold. The collections of Japanese art at the Museum of Fine Arts, Boston and the Freer Gallery in Washington, DC, were just two of the indirect beneficiaries of this policy.

During the Pacific War (the Japanese term for World War II), Shinto was again used by the military (with the complicity of the Imperial House) to justify an aggressive stance in Asia. (It should be noted that Kokuchukai Buddhism was also used to sanction the invasion of other countries.) The emperor was a god and therefore infallible. Since the

Japanese people were essentially one family with the emperor at the head, they were a superior race that was meant to rule the lesser peoples of Asia.

Once ancestor worship was allied with worship of the emperor, the state became something worth dying for. So potent was this mix that General Douglas MacArthur identified state Shinto as one of the first things that had to be dismantled upon the surrender of Japan. The emperor could stay, but shrine and state had to go.

RELIGIOUS FESTIVALS

Although there are religious festivals and holy days observed throughout the year, the two biggest events in the Japanese religious calendar are New Year's (*Oshogatsu*) and *Obon*. New Year's is celebrated from January 1 to 3. Many people visit temples the night of December 31 to ring in the New Year or in the coming weeks. Temple bells are struck 108 times to symbolize ridding oneself of the 108 human sins. This practice is called *hatsumode*. Food stalls are set up close to the popular places, and the atmosphere is festive and joyous. Many draw fortune slips called *omikuji* to see what kind of a year the oracle has in store for them.

The other major religious event in the Japanese calendar is the Obon holiday, traditionally held from August 13 to 15. Obon is the Japanese festival of the dead when the spirits come back to visit the living. Most people observe the ritual by returning to their hometown or the home of their grandparents. Graves are cleaned and respects are paid to one's ancestors. Family ties are strengthened and renewed.

VISITING A BUDDHIST TEMPLE

The first thing to do when visiting a temple is to stop at the gate (called *mon* in Japanese), put your hands together, and bow. Once inside the gate, you should stop to wash your hands at the stone receptacle usually found immediately upon entering the temple grounds. Fill one of the ladles with water using your right hand and wash your left hand first. Then refill the ladle with water using your left hand and wash your right hand. Some people also pour water in their right hand to rinse their mouth, but this is not necessary.

After washing your hands, you can ring the temple bell if you choose.

Next, light a candle in front of the main altar of the temple and place it inside the glass cabinet. Then put your hands together and bow. You can also light three sticks of incense (lighting them together is customary) and put them in the large stone or brass stand. This action is also followed with a prayer and a bow. It is important to note, however, that while some people may light both a candle and three sticks of incense, others may just do one or the other. Some may skip this part entirely.

After you finish, you can proceed to the main altar, put your hands together, bow, and pray. Many people recite one of the Buddhist sutras.

If you'd like to have a closer look at the interior of the altar building, you can climb the steps and look inside. At this time, you can also throw a coin inside the wooden box on the top step as

A worshipper bows at the Meiji Shrine in the Shibuya District of Tokyo.

The massive *torii* (entrance gates) of the Meiji Shrine are over 40 feet tall.

an offering, again putting your hands together and bowing.

Most temples have sub-altars dedicated to different Buddhist saints or deities, and you can repeat the candle, incense, and prayer steps observed at the main altar if you choose.

After praying at the main altar and/or sub-altar, you'll probably want to spend some time walking around the temple grounds. Most temples are incredibly beautiful places. Many have gardens and sculpture worthy of a visit in their own right.

Upon leaving the temple, you should stop at the gate, turn, put your hands together, and bow to give thanks.

VISITING A SHINTO SHRINE
Shrines, like temples, have gates, though they are called *torii* and are often painted bright orange. In terms of their appearance, torii look much like the mathematical symbol for pi. As with the gates of temples, one enters and exits through the torii bowing on the way in and again on the way out. However, when visiting a shrine one claps twice before bowing. This is to summon the kami. Once

you have their attention, you clap twice again to pay them homage.

Inside the shrine, you wash your hands as you would at a temple (left hand and then right hand). You then proceed to the main altar, clap twice, and bow. In a shrine, clapping twice and bowing is often repeated as there may be special trees, stones, and other holy objects situated throughout the grounds.

After you have finished visiting the shrine, you should turn around at the torii, clap twice, and bow upon leaving.

FURTHER READING
The standard work on Buddhism in Japan is Richard Bowring's *The Religious Traditions of Japan, 500–1600*. Also recommended is Kenji Matsuo's *A History of Japanese Buddhism*. Sokyo Ono's *Shinto: The Kami Way* is a good introduction to Shinto. For those wanting to learn more about Zen Buddhism, Daisetz Suzuki's *Zen and Japanese Culture* is a wonderfully clear and evocative study of the subject.

Tokyo

WORD OF MOUTH

"[Here are] free or cheap things to do: the observation deck at the top of Tokyo Metropolitan Government buildings in Shinjuku; traditional Japanese gardens like Hama Rikyu in Asakusa; the museums in Ueno Park; Meiji-jingu, Yoyogi Park, and Harajuku for people-watching; and rummaging in Akihabara."

—Alec

WELCOME TO TOKYO

TOP REASONS TO GO

★ **See Ancient Meet Modern:** In Asakusa, visit Tokyo's oldest shrine, Asakusa Jinja, before hitting Akihabara's stores for the newest gadgets.

★ **Shop 'Til You Drop:** Looking for trinkets or gifts to bring home? Scour the fashions and crafts in Shinjuku's department stores or meander down trendy Takeshita-dori for funky finds. Ginza shopping has the historic Wako department store and independent shops.

★ **Dine Like a Local:** Dine on the freshest sushi in the world, belly up to a ramen bar and slurp to your heart's content, or sample the elegant courses of a traditional *kaiseki* meal.

★ **Party All Night.** From karaoke boxes and pachinko parlors to jazz clubs and mixology bars, there's entertainment for every taste and budget. Go high-end in Ginza, drink amongst the Yakuza in Kabuki-cho, or shimmy into Shibuya's izakayas before belting out tunes in nearby karaoke bars.

1 Imperial Palace District. Kokyo, the Imperial Palace, is the center of Tokyo; nearby are several museums and Tokyo Station.

2 Akihabara and Jimbo-cho. Akihabara is famed for its electronics stores and manga shops. Jimbo-cho is filled with booksellers.

3 Ueno. Three superb national museums, a university of fine arts, and a zoo fill Ueno Park.

4 Asakusa. The sacred merges secular and ancient tradition with modernity in Asakusa.

5 Tsukiji and Shiodome. Tsukiji is home to famed sumo stables and the purported world's largest fish market. Shiodome has fashionable shops and restaurants.

6 Nihombashi, Ginza, and Marunouchi. In central Tokyo, these neighborhoods are filled with shops and offices.

7 Aoyama, Harajuku, and Shibuya. Aoyama and Harajuku are chic areas with stores and boutiques. Shibuya is a neon jungle of hip shops and eateries.

8 Roppongi. Here you'll find the massive Roppongi Hills development.

9 Shinjuku. Tokyo's government and its busiest train station share the neighborhood with the city's red-light district.

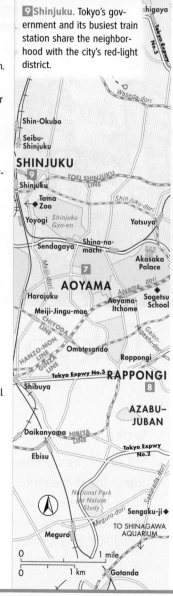

3

GETTING ORIENTED

Greater Tokyo incorporates 23 wards, 26 smaller cities, seven towns, and eight villages—altogether sprawling 88 km (55 mi) from east to west and 24 km (15 mi) from north to south with a population of 35 million people. The wards alone enclose an area of 590 square km (228 square mi), which comprise the city center and house 8 million residents. Chiyoda-ku, Chuo-ku, Shinjuku-ku, and Minato-ku are the four central business districts.

JAPANESE POP CULTURE

Step into the streets of Shibuya—or brave the crowds of preening high school fashionistas populating Harujuku's Takeshita-dori—and you'll get a crash course on Japanese pop culture that extends way behind familiar exports like Hello Kitty and Godzilla.

(Top left) Manga is a Japan-wide obsession; (top right) Distinctive manga style; (bottom right) Matriarch of Japanese kawaii, Hello Kitty.

Japanese pop culture has long been a source of fascination—and sometimes bewilderment—for foreign visitors. New fashion styles, technology, and popular media evolve quickly here, and in something of a vacuum, which leads to a constant turnover of wholly unique, sometimes wacky trends you won't find anywhere outside Japan. Luckily, you don't have to go out of your way to explore Japan's popular obsessions. You can have an immersion experience just walking through neighborhoods like Shibuya, Shinjuku, Harujuku, and Akihabara.

DID YOU KNOW?

There are more than 5 million vending machines in Japan, making it the most dense population of machines, per capita, anywhere in the world. Here, automated machines sell everything from hot drinks to live lobsters. Some use facial recognition to verify age for tobacco and beer, and even offer indecisive customers age-appropriate drink recommendations.

KAWAII

Kawaii, or "cute," isn't just a descriptor you'll hear coming out of the mouths of teenage girls, it's an aww-inducing aesthetic you'll see all over Tokyo; major airlines plaster depictions of adorable animation characters like Pikachu across the sides of their planes, and even at local police stations it's not unusual for a fluffy, stuffed-animal mascot to be on display. Duck into an arcade photo booth to take *purikura*—sticker pictures that let you choose your own kawaii background—or head to Sanrio Puroland, an entire theme park dedicated to cuteness.

KEITAI CULTURE

You can't visit Japan without marveling at the relationship people have with their cell phones or *keitai denwa*, which can operate as credit cards, TV-watching devices, and game consoles, just for starters. Japanese cell phones are so advanced, they're said to suffer from "Galapagos syndrome," a reference to the creatures of the Galapagos Islands that evolved in isolation, and subsequently have little relation to their mainland cousins. In 2003 the first novel written entirely on a cell phone was a big hit, and cell phone novels continue to be a popular literary subgenre.

J-POP IDOLS

The age of the boy band—or the girl band for that matter—is not over in

Japan. "Idol" groups are hot. Over-the-top outfits, sugar-sweet synthesized beats, and love-professing lyrics (with the occasional English word thrown in) dominate the Japanese pop charts. AKB-48, one of Tokyo's hottest groups of idols, is 48 girls strong, and performs daily at their own theater complex in Akihabara. Beloved pop groups like all-male SMAP have been pumping out hits for more than 20 years.

ANIME AND MANGA

Peek over the shoulder of a comic-book-reading businessman and you'll quickly discover that, in Japan, cartoons aren't just kids' stuff. Animation (*anime*) and comic books (*manga*) are extremely popular with readers both young and old. Comic book addicts, known as *otaku*, claim Tokyo's Akihabara as their home base. Though otaku can be translated as "nerd" or "obsessive," the term has been embraced by some. Former prime minister, Taro Aso, declared himself an otaku and confessed to reading 10 to 20 manga a week.

TOKYO'S VENDING MACHINES AND CONVENIENCE STORES

With a bright-lighted convenience store on practically every corner and a few well-stocked vending machines in between, quick shopping is truly hassle-free in Tokyo—and with the offerings ranging from novel to bizarre, an impulse buy can turn into a journey of discovery.

(Top left) Copious vending machines provide fast, cheap snacks; (Top right) limited-edition potato chip flavors; (bottom right) convenience stores offer a taste of Japanese culture.

While vending machines and convenience stores did not originate in Japan, their popularity in the country seems to have no limit. Today Japan has the world's highest density of vending machines per capita, with one machine for every 23 people. Those looking for a wider selection can head to one of the 42,000 convenience stores in the country. Canned drinks, both cold and hot, are the main staple of vending machines, but it is not uncommon to find ones offering cigarettes, batteries, snacks, ice cream cones, toiletries, fresh fruit, customized business cards, or even potted flowers. For North Americans used to convenience stores that offer little more than a candy shelf and a magazine rack, the Japanese equivalent can be a source of amazement, boasting everything from postal and courier services and digital photo printing to full hot meals.

DID YOU KNOW?

Many vending machine offerings aren't exactly healthful—sugar-laden coffee, colas, and alcohol. However, new machines are geared toward the health-conscious. Dole installed banana dispensers around Shibuya train station, targeting hurried commuters with no time for breakfast. The fruit is lightly refrigerated and gently lowered to the opening to avoid bruising. Single bananas and bunches are available.

VENDING MACHINES

If you visit Tokyo during the hot and humid summer months, it will not take long for you to understand why there is a machine selling cool drinks on every sidewalk. In winter, hot drinks warm both the stomach and hands. Long-popular drinks include Pocari Sweat, a noncarbonated sports drink with a very mild grapefruit taste; Aquarius, a comparable drink manufactured by Coca-Cola; and *Marocha Chaba no Ko*, a cold green tea available in both cans and plastic bottles. Machines sell beer and other alcoholic beverages, but you may want to avoid *shochu* alcohol sold in glass jars or paper cartons—it is overpoweringly strong. Coffee—both hot and cold—comes in small cans. Don't be surprised to see locals buy one, suck it down, and dispose of the can all during the two-minute wait for the subway. If some Japanese writing below an item is lighted in red, the machine is sold out of it. Hot drinks have a red strip below them and cold drinks are marked with blue. Automation has even spread to religion, as shrines and temples use vending machines to sell *omikuji*, fortunes written on slips of paper.

CONVENIENCE STORES

For the visitor to Tokyo, the nearest *konbini* is a treasure trove of new—and often surprising—experiences. The first convenience store opened in Japan in 1973, and like so many other concepts that have been imported into the country, the Japanese have embraced the konbini, turning it into something of their own. Beyond the usual products you might expect, Japanese convenience stores also carry full hot *bento* (boxed meal), basic clothing items, and event tickets. Services available include digital photo printing, faxing, and utility bill payments. Step into a 7-Eleven, ampm, or Family Mart and you will see familiar brands such as Pepsi and Pringles, but you are not likely to know Pepsi flavored with *shiso*, a Japanese herb, or soy sauce Pringles. Many locals indulge in the practice of *tachiyomi*, standing in front of a magazine rack and browsing the selections without actually buying anything. This practice is accepted and, for visitors, is a good way to get a sense of current trends.

TOP BUYS

3

Japanese Pringles potato chips have come in flavors such as cheese and bacon and seaweed, and new surprising combinations are rolled out every season. Another international brand that often adds a local twist is Kit Kat, which in the past has released grilled corn, Camembert cheese, and Earl Grey tea versions of its candy bars. The Japanese pronunciation, *kitto katsu*, sounds like the phrase "you are sure to pass," and so make popular gifts to students during entrance exam season. New varieties of Kit Kat debut in spring. If you are traveling with children, a fun purchase is *ramune*, a carbonated drink sold in a glass bottle sealed with a glass marble held in place by the pressure of the gas—push the marble down with your thumb to break the seal. One convenience store treat you cannot leave Japan without trying at least once is *onigiri*, a triangular rice ball containing tuna, pickled plum, or other fillings, and wrapped in sheets of dried seaweed.

TSUKIJI FISH MARKET

The fresh sashimi, grilled fish, and other sea-food seen on sale from Tokyo's street-side food stalls to its award-winning restaurants all have one thing in common: it all passes through the largest seafood market in the world, a lively center of unforgettable sights, sounds, and smells.

(Top left) Vendors bid on the freshest fish in the world; (top right) tuna sells for as much as $20,000; (bottom right) scope out the goods along with wholesalers.

It comes as no surprise that in Japan, an island nation, seafood has been a staple for centuries, and this remains just as true today even though beef and pork consumption have skyrocketed. Completed in 1935, Tsukiji Market is the main conduit through which the bounty of the oceans pass into the country. Seen from above, Tsukiji Market resembles a quarter circle. Several small city blocks at the point of the circle constitute the outer market or the *jogai shijo*. Radiating around this is the vast inner market, or *jonai shijo*. Every day more than 2,000 metric tons of seafood, worth 1.5 billion yen, changes hands here. The adventurous—and lucky—traveler can walk among the fast-dealing wholesalers at the pre-dawn market. A more leisurely visit will include a stroll through the outer market and a fresh sushi breakfast.

CONTACT INFORMATION

✉ 5–2–1 Tsukiji, Chuo-ku
☎ 03/3542–1111 ⊕ www.shijou.metro.tokyo.jp
🎟 Free ⊘ Mon.–Sat. (except 2nd and 4th Wed. of month) 5 am–3 pm
Ⓜ Toei Oedo subway line, Tsukiji-shijo Station (Exit A1); Hibiya subway line, Tsukiji Station (Exit 1).

INNER MARKET

Professional buyers and resellers deftly move through the hundreds of varieties seafood and assess them with a glance of an expert's eye at the inner market. Visitors may make purchases, but should be careful not to get in the way of the pros. Only licensed buyers can bid at the famed tuna auction, exchanging rapid-fire hand gestures with a fast-talking auctioneer. The prized catches can sell for upwards of $20,000 each.

OUTER MARKET

When Japanese consumers go to Tsukiji, they generally shop for seafood in the outer market, a collection of more than 100 separate shops, stands, and sushi restaurants. Retailers also sell dried fish, *nerimono* (fish cakes), fruits and vegetables, meat, beans, and grains. For a practical and unique souvenir, browse the shops offering Japanese kitchen utensils, both traditional wood and bamboo items and modern, cleverly designed tools. Ornately decorated dishware and chopsticks are also available. Nori (sheets of dry seaweed), essential for making sushi rolls at home, and Japanese green tea can be easily packed away to bring home.

EATING IN THE MARKET

Enjoying a sushi breakfast is an integral part of any trip to Tsukiji. There are dozens of sushi restaurants scattered throughout the outer market and it is easy to tell which are the best—they have the longest queues outside. It is well worth the wait—and the cost—as the area has the freshest sushi in the world. Daiwa Sushi (✉ *Tsukiji Oroshiurishijo 6 Bldg.*), just inside the inner market, has only one item, the chef's set (¥3,500), but it is a perennial favorite. A cheaper and quicker option is sashimi donburi, an oversize bowl of steamed rice topped with slices of raw fish, omelet, and piquant wasabi paste. Kaisendon Oedo (✉ *Tsukiji Oroshiurishijo 8 Bldg.*) is a no-frills restaurant that specializes in the dish, offering more than 30 different combinations of sashimi toppings.

3

TIPS

Get to the market by 5 am if you want to see the tuna auction, and by 7 am if you want to browse the inner market.

In busy seasons (including December), visitors are completely barred from the auctions. At other times 140 are admitted between 5 am and 6:15 am on a first-come basis.

There is pungent water on the ground, so wear hiking boots or waterproof sneakers and casual clothing.

In the inner market, be especially careful of the delivery carts that zip around, rarely slowing down when someone gets in their way.

Photography is allowed in the auction, but flashes are strictly forbidden. Taking pictures in the inner market is acceptable, but it is good practice to ask the stall keeper before snapping away.

Never touch any seafood in the auction or anywhere in the inner market.

The inner market officially closes to visitors at 9 am, and the outer market is mostly closed down by 11 am.

Updated by
Brett Bull,
Kevin Mcgue,
Nicholas
Coldicott, and
Misha Janette

The 2003 film *Lost in Translation,* by Sophia Coppola, was for many the first chance to see beyond Tokyo's historic temples and sushi to the modern, pulsating metropolis it is today. But don't think that the temples and sushi stands have gone away. This is a city of old and new, where opposites attract and new trends come and go like the tide, but history and tradition continue to be held in utmost respect.

The city is also the center of design and cutting-edge fashion. One step into the hip neighborhoods of Harajuku and Shibuya and you'll know what we mean. Dining is also a study in contrasts. People can dine at a Michelin-starred restaurant one night, and then belly up to the counter at the local ramen joint the next. And the people are as varied as their city. Residents of Aoyama may wear European designer fashion and drive fancy imports but those residing in Asakusa prefer the decidedly less flashy, including the subway system. Stop in a bar in Ginza and one might find groups of salarymen, flush with large expense accounts, entertaining clients, but down the Hibiya Line in Ebisu many of the cheap watering holes are filled with young office professionals.

Even the landscape is varied. The metropolis hosts some of the most unsightly and vast sprawls of concrete housing—extending for miles in all four directions—in the world. But it's also home to some tall buildings. In Roppongi, you'll find the city's tallest building, Tokyo Midtown (248 meters [814 feet]), and the 200-meter (656-foot) Grand Tokyo North Tower at Tokyo Station.

Whether you're gazing at the glow of Tokyo's evening lights or the green expanse of its parks or a plate of the freshest sushi imaginable or dramatically dressed people, this is a city of astonishing and intriguing beauty. If you're a foodie, artist, design lover, or cultural adventurer, then Tokyo, a city of inspiration and ideas, is for you.

PLANNING

Tokyo is a state-of-the-art financial marketplace, where billions of dollars are whisked electronically around the globe at the blink of an eye. However, most ATMs in the city shut down by 9 pm, so be sure to get enough cash when you find one. Most Citibank, Shinsei Bank (in some subway stations), and Japan Post ATMs allow international bank card transactions, but they are not always accessible. Tokyo is a safe city, so you may carry cash without fear of street crime.

WHEN TO GO

Spring and fall are the best times to visit. *Sakura* (cherry blossoms) begin blooming in Tokyo by early April. Fall has clear blue skies, though occasional typhoons occur. June brings an intense rainy season. July and August bring high temperatures and stifling humidity. Winter's gray and chilly, with Tokyo and other areas along the Pacific Coast receiving very little snow.

GETTING HERE AND AROUND

AIR TRAVEL

The major gateway to Japan is Tokyo's Narita Airport (NRT), 80 km (50 mi) northeast of the city. The new Haneda Airport International Terminal, which opened in 2010, offers flights to major international cities and is only 20 km (12 mi) south of central Tokyo. Starting in 2010, Tokyo's Haneda Airport also began Most domestic flights to and from Tokyo are out of Haneda Airport.

Flying into Haneda provides visitors with quicker access to downtown Tokyo, which is a short monorail ride away. Stop by the currency exchange and Tourist Information Desk in the second-floor arrival lobby before taking a train into the city. There are also numerous jade-uniformed concierge staff on hand to help passengers with any questions.

Airport Information Haneda Airport (HND) (☎ *03/6428-0888 [International], 03/5757-8111 [Domestic]* ⊕ *www.haneda-airport.jp/en).* **Narita Airport (NRT)** (☎ *0476/34-8000* ⊕ *www.narita-airport.jp).*

GROUND TRANSPORTATION

It takes about 90 minutes—a time very dependent on city traffic—to get from Narita to Tokyo by taxi or bus. The *Keisei Skyliner* and *Japan Railways NEX* are the easiest ways to get into the city. The Friendly Airport Limousine offers the only shuttle-bus service from Narita to Tokyo.

Japan Railways trains stop at both Narita Airport terminals. The Narita Limited Express (NEX) goes from the airport to Tokyo Station in just under an hour, then continue to Yokohama and Ofuna. All seats are reserved, and you'll need to reserve one for yourself in advance, as this train fills quickly. The Keisei Skyliner train runs every 20–30 minutes between the airport terminals and Keisei-Ueno Station. The trip takes around 40 minutes.

Contacts Airport Transport Service Co. (☎ *03/3665-7232 in Tokyo, 0476/32-8080 for Terminal 1, 0476/34-6311 for Terminal 2).* **IAE Co** (☎ *0476/32-7954 for Terminal 1, 0476/34-6886 for Terminal 2).* **Japan Railways** (☎ *03/3423-*

0111 for JR East InfoLine ⏱ *Weekdays 10–6).* **Keisei Railway** (☎ *03/3831–0131 for Ueno information counter, 0476/32–8505 at Narita Airport).*

TAXI TRAVEL

Taxis are an expensive way of getting around Tokyo, though nascent deregulation moves are easing the market a little. The first 2 km (1 mi) cost ¥710 and it's ¥80 for every additional 280 meters (400 yards). If possible, avoid using taxis during rush hours (7:30 am–9:30 am and 5 pm–7 pm). Have a Japanese person write out your destination in Japanese for the driver. Your hotel concierge will do this for you. Remember, taxi drivers do not accept tips.

TRAIN AND SUBWAY TRAVEL

Tokyo Station is the city's main hub for the JR Shinkansen bullet trains, which travel up and down Honshu and into Kyushu. Regional trains, most of which are operated by Japan Railways (JR Group), run in Tokyo and to nearby prefectures. In Tokyo, JR's Yamanote Line loops around the city, with stops in major central neighborhoods. JR's Sobu and Chuo lines split that circle into east and west directions, and it is possible to connect to Tokyo subway lines from many JR stations. Tokyu's Toyoko Line travels between the Shibuya neighborhood and Yokohama to the south. For heading to Tokyo Disneyland take the JR Keiyo Line east. The main line of the Odakyu company and Keio Inokashira Line use Shinjuku and Shibuya, respectively, as hubs to serve Tokyo to the west. For service to Saitama Prefecture, Tobu offers the Tojo Line, which leaves from Ikebukuro Station.

The easiest way to explore Tokyo is via subway. There are two subway companies: Tokyo Metro and Toei. Since these are separate entities, they have separate fares, and it's cheaper to stay with one company. The Ginza Line runs between Asakusa and Shibuya, which is also served by the north–south-running Fukutoshin Line and the east–west-bound Hanzomon Line. Similar to the JR Yamanote Line, the Oedo and Marunouchi lines loop through the city center. The Namboku Line begins in Meguro and heads through Korakuen, the station for Tokyo Dome. At the outer edges of the subway networks, private companies operate the line. If you're going far afield, be prepared to pay an additional fare.

The JR Hotline is an English-language information service, open weekdays 10–6.

Train Information JR Hotline (☎ *03/3423–0111*).

Japan Railways Group (✉ *1 Rockefeller Plaza, Suite 1410, New York, NY* ☎ *212/332–8686* ⊕ *www.japanrail.com*).

Japan Rail Pass (⊕ *www.japanrailpass.net*).

VISITOR INFORMATION

The Japan National Tourist Organization (JNTO) has an office in Tokyo. The JNTO-affiliated International Tourism Center of Japan also has more than 140 counters/offices nationwide. Look for the sign showing a red question mark and the word "information" at train stations and city centers.

Contacts **Japan National Tourist Organization (JNTO)** (✉ *2–10–1 Yurakucho, 1-chome, Chiyoda-ku, Tokyo* ☎ *03/3502–1461*).

MONEY SAVING TIPS

If you plan on visiting a lot of the city's sites, purchasing a **GRUTT Pass** (⊕ *www.museum.or.jp/grutto*) is the way to go. The pass, which is only ¥2,000, gives visitors free or discounted admission to 70 sites throughout the city including museums, zoos, aquariums, and parks. Passes can be purchased at all participating sites, as well as the Tokyo Tourist Information Center, or Family Mart and Lawson convenience stores. Keep in mind that passes expire two months after date of purchase.

EXPLORING TOKYO

IMPERIAL PALACE AND GOVERNMENT DISTRICT 皇居近辺

The Imperial Palace was built by the order of Ieyasu Tokugawa, who chose the site for his castle in 1590. The castle had 99 gates (36 in the outer wall), 21 watchtowers (of which three are still standing), and 28 armories. The outer defenses stretched from present-day Shimbashi Station to Kanda. Completed in 1640 (and later expanded), it was at the time the largest castle in the world.

This district is the core of Japan's government. It is primarily comprised of *Nagata-cho*, the Imperial Palace (*Kokyo-gaien*), the Diet (national parliament building), the Prime Minister's residence (*Kantei*), and the Supreme Court. The Imperial Palace and the Diet are both important to see, but the Supreme Court is nondescript. Unfortunately, the Prime Minister's residence is only viewable from afar, hidden behind fortified walls and trees.

The Japanese Imperial Family resides in heavily blockaded sections of the palace grounds. Tours are conducted by reservation only, and restricted to designated outdoor sections, namely, the palace grounds and the East Gardens. The grounds are open to the general public only twice a year, on January 2 and December 23 (the Emperor's Birthday), when thousands of people assemble under the balcony to offer their good wishes to the Imperial Family.

ORIENTATION

The Imperial Palace is located in the heart of central Tokyo, and the city's other neighborhoods branch out from here. The palace, in which the Imperial Family still resides, is surrounded by a moat that connects through canals to Tokyo Bay and Sumida River (Sumida-gawa) to the east. Outside the moat, large four-lane roads trace its outline, as if the city expanded from this primary location.

PLANNING

The best way to discover the Imperial Palace is to take part in one of the free tours offered by the **Imperial Household Agency** (☎ *03/3213–1111* ⊕ *www.kunaicho.go.jp*), which manages matters of the state. There are four different tours: Imperial Palace Grounds, the East Gardens (*Higashi Gyo-en*), Sannomaru Shozokan, and Gagaku Performance (in

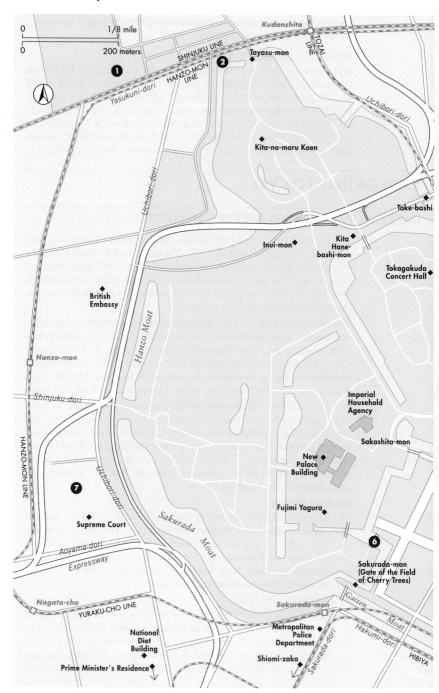

0
0

1/8 mile
200 meters

Kudanshita

SHINJUKU LINE

HANZO-MON LINE

TOZAI LINE

1

2

Tayasu-mon

Yasukuni-dori

Uchibori-dori

Kita-no-maru Koen

Uchibori-dori

Take-bashi

Inui-mon

Kita Hane-bashi-mon

Tokagakuda Concert Hall

British Embassy

Hanzo Moat

Hanzo-mon

Shinjuku-dori

HANZO-MON LINE

Uchibori-dori

Imperial Household Agency

Sakashita-mon

New Palace Building

Fujimi Yagura

7

Sakurada Moat

Supreme Court

Aoyama-dori

Expressway

6

Sakurada-mon (Gate of the Field of Cherry Trees)

Nagata-cho

YURAKU-CHO LINE

Sakurada-mon

Gaisen

Hakumi-dori

HIBIYA

National Diet Building

Metropolitan Police Department

Sakurada-dori

Shiomi-zaka

Hibumi Moat

Prime Minister's Residence

Imperial Palace and Government District

autumn only). All tours require registration a day in advance and hours change according to the season.

If you are exploring on your own, allow at least an hour for the East Garden and Outer Garden of the palace itself. Plan to visit Yasukuni Jinja after lunch and spend at least an hour there. The Yushukan (at Yasukuni Jinja) and Kogeikan museums are both small and should engage you for no more than a half hour each, but the modern art museum requires a more leisurely visit—particularly if there's a special exhibit. ■TIP→ **Avoid visiting the Imperial Palace on Monday, when the East Garden and museums are closed; the East Garden is also closed Friday.**

GETTING HERE AND AROUND

The best way to get to the Imperial Palace is by subway. Take the Chiyoda Line to Nijubashimae Station (Exit 6) or the JR lines to Tokyo Station (Marunouchi Central Exit). There are three entrance gates—Ote-mon, Hirakawa-mon, and Kita-hane-bashi-mon. You can also easily get to any of the three from the Ote-machi or Takebashi subway stations.

TOP ATTRACTIONS

Fodor's Choice ★ **Imperial Palace East Garden** 皇居東御苑 (*Kokyo Higashi Gyo-en*). The entrance to the East Garden is the Ote-mon (⇨ *below*), once the main gate of Ieyasu Tokugawa's castle. Here, you will come across the National Police Agency *dojo* (martial arts hall) and the Ote Rest House, where for ¥100 you can buy a simple map of the garden.

The **Hundred-Man Guardhouse** was once defended by four shifts of 100 soldiers each. Past it is the entrance to what was once the *ni-no-maru,* the "second circle" of the fortress. It's now a grove and garden. At the far end is the **Suwa Tea Pavilion,** an early-19th-century building relocated here from another part of the castle grounds.

The steep stone walls of the **hon-maru** (the "inner circle"), with the Moat of Swans below, dominate the west side of the garden. Halfway along is **Shio-mi-zaka,** which translates roughly as "Briny View Hill," so named because in the Edo period the ocean could be seen from here.

Head to the wooded paths around the garden's edges for shade, quiet, and benches to rest your weary feet. In the southwest corner is the Fujimi Yagura, the only surviving watchtower of the hon-maru; farther along the path, on the west side, is the **Fujimi Tamon,** one of the two remaining armories.

The odd-looking octagonal tower is the **Tokagakudo Concert Hall.** Its mosaic tile facade was built in honor of Empress Kojun in 1966. ✉ *1–1 Chiyoda, Chiyoda-ku* ☎ *03/3213–1111* 🎫 *Free* ⊗ *Mar.–Apr. 14 and Sep.–Oct. daily 9–4:30; Apr. 15–Aug. until 5; Nov.–Feb. until 4; closed Mon. and Fri.* Ⓜ *Tozai, Marunouchi, and Chiyoda subway lines, Ote-machi Station (Exit C13B).*

Tokyo Station 東京駅 (*Tokyo Eki*). The work of Kingo Tatsuno, one of Japan's first modern architects, Tokyo Station was completed in 1914. Tatsuno modeled his creation on the railway station of Amsterdam. The building lost its original top story in the air raids of 1945, but was promptly repaired. In the late 1990s, a plan to demolish the station was impeded by public outcry. Inside, it has been deepened and tunneled and

Once the site of the Imperial Palace's innermost defense circles, the East Garden now offers respite in a beautiful setting.

redesigned any number of times to accommodate new commuter lines, but the lovely old redbrick facade remains. While the historical Tokyo Station Hotel is closed for renovation (set for completion in 2012) one of the more popular attractions is the Gran Tokyo North Tower. The 200-meter-tall (656-foot-tall) glass-and-steel office building includes a branch of the high-end department store chain Daimaru. ✉ *1–9–1 Marunouchi, Chiyoda-ku* ☎ *03/3212–8011* ⊕ *www.grantokyo-nt.com* Ⓜ *Marunouchi subway line and JR lines.*

★ **Yasukuni Jinja** 靖国神社 (*Shrine of Peace for the Nation*). This shrine is not as impressive as Asakusa Shrine and Meiji Jingu, but it is still worth a visit. Founded in 1869, this shrine is dedicated to approximately 2.5 million Japanese, Taiwanese, and Koreans who have died since then in war or military service. Since 1945 Yasukuni has been a center of stubborn political debate given that the Japanese constitution expressly renounces both militarism and state sponsorship of religion. Several prime ministers have visited the shrine since 1979, causing a political chill between Japan and its close neighbors, Korea and China—who suffered under Japanese colonialism. Despite all this, hundreds of thousands of Japanese come here every year, simply to pray for the repose of friends and relatives they have lost. These pilgrimages are most frenzied on August 15, the anniversary of the conclusion of World War II, when former soldiers and ultra-right-wing groups descend upon the shrine's grounds en masse.

The shrine is not one structure but a complex of buildings that include the **Main Hall** and the **Hall of Worship**—both built in the simple, unadorned style of the ancient Shinto shrines at Ise—and the **Yushukan,** a museum of documents and war memorabilia. Also here are a

Noh theater and, in the far western corner, a sumo-wrestling ring. Sumo matches are held at Yasukuni in April, during the first of its three annual festivals. You can pick up a pamphlet and simplified map of the shrine, both in English, just inside the grounds.

Refurbished in 2002, the Yushukan presents Japan at its most ambivalent—if not unrepentant—about its more recent militaristic past. Critics charge that the newer exhibits glorify the nation's role in the Pacific War as a noble struggle for independence; certainly there's an agenda here that's hard to reconcile with Japan's firm postwar rejection of militarism as an instrument of national policy. Many Japanese visitors are moved by such displays as the last letters and photographs of young kamikaze pilots; visitors from other countries tend to find the Yushukan a cautionary, rather than uplifting, experience.

Although some of the exhibits have English labels and notes, the English is not very helpful; most objects, however, speak clearly enough for themselves. Rooms on the second floor house an especially fine collection of medieval swords and armor. Visiting on a Sunday gives one the option of foraging at the flea market that runs from morning until sundown (⇨ *Chapter 6, Shopping*). ✉ *3–1–1 Kudankita, Chiyoda-ku* ☎ *03/3261–8326* ⊕ *www.yasukuni.or.jp* ✉ *¥800* ⊙ *Grounds daily Mar.–Oct. daily 8:15–5; Nov–Feb. daily 8:15–4; Museum Apr.–Sept., daily 9–5:30; Oct.–Mar., daily 9–5* Ⓜ *Hanzo-mon and Shinjuku subway lines, Kudanshita Station (Exit 1).*

Ote-mon 大手門 (*Ote Gate*). The main entrance to the Imperial Palace East Garden, Ote-mon was in former days the principal gate of Ieyasu Tokugawa's castle. Most of the gate was destroyed in 1945 but was rebuilt in 1967 on the original plans. The outer part of the gate survived, and today it houses a fascinating photo collection of before-and-after photographs of the castle, taken about 100 years apart. ✉ *Chiyoda-ku* Ⓜ *Tozai, Marunouchi, and Chiyoda subway lines, Ote-machi Station (Exit C10).*

Two-Tiered Bridge 二重橋 (*Ni-ju-bashi*). Making a graceful arch across the moat, this bridge is surely the most photogenic spot on the grounds of the former Edo Castle. Mere mortals may pass through only on December 23 (the Emperor's birthday) and January 2 to pay their respects to the Imperial Family. The guards in front of their small, octagonal, copper-roof sentry boxes change every hour on the hour—alas, with nothing like the pomp and ceremony at Buckingham Palace. ✉ *Chiyoda-ku* Ⓜ *Chiyoda subway line, Ni-ju-bashi-mae Station (Exit 2).*

AKIHABARA 秋葉原 AND JIMBO-CHO 神保町

Akihabara is techno-geek heaven. Also known as Akihabara Electric Town, this district, which was once all about electronics, is becoming a wacky fetish district where otaku (nerds) can indulge in computer-game fantasies, hang out in kinky cafés, and buy manga (comics). Visitors don't just come here to purchase digital cameras, but to also observe one of the nation's subcultures.

If you're looking for something a little more cerebral, head to Jimbo-cho where family-run specialty bookstores of every genre abound including

Stretch Your Legs

The venue of choice for runners is the **Imperial Palace Outer Garden.** At the west end of the park, Sakurada-mon's (Gate of the Field of Cherry Trees) small courtyard is the traditional starting point for the 5-km (3-mi) run around the palace—though you can join in anywhere along the route. Jogging around the palace is a ritual that begins as early as 6 am and goes on throughout the day, no matter what the weather. Almost everybody runs the course counterclockwise, but now and then you may spot someone going the opposite way.

Looking for a challenge? Japan hosts a number of marathons throughout the year and one of the most famous is the **Tokyo Marathon** (⊕ *www.tokyo42195.org*), which is held in February. Plan ahead if you're going to sign up, because the registration deadline is at the end of August of the previous year (most of the country's running events require signing up and qualifying far more in advance than their counterparts on other shores). The marathon starts at one of Tokyo's most prominent landmarks, the Tokyo Metropolitan Government Office in Shinjuku-ku, winds its way through the Imperial Palace, past the Tokyo Tower and Asakusa Kaminari-mon Gate, and finishes at Tokyo Big Sight Exhibition Center in Koto Ward.

---

rare antiquarian and Japanese manga. The area is also home to Meiji University and Nihon University.

ORIENTATION

Akihabara is east of the Imperial Palace, right below Ueno and Asakusa. Akihabara Station is located north of Tokyo Station, on the JR Yamanote, Hibiya, and Tsukuba lines. It's right below Asakusa and Ueno districts.

Located just to the west of Akihabara, Jimbo-cho should be a very short stopover either before or after an excursion to Akihabara. The best way to get there is by taxi, which should cost about ¥800 to or from Akihabara Station.

PLANNING

Credit cards are accepted at all major electronics superstores, but bring enough cash to get around, because ATMs are difficult to find. Keep in mind that most stores in Akihabara do not open until 10 am. Weekends draw hordes of shoppers, especially on Sunday, when the four central blocks of Chuo-dori are closed to traffic and become a pedestrian mall.

GETTING HERE AND AROUND

Take the train to Akihabara Station on the JR Yamanote Line. Akihabara is a 20- to 30-minute ride from most hotels in Shinjuku or Minato-ku.

TOP ATTRACTIONS

Cospa Gee Store ジーストア. Fans of anime will enjoy this zany Japanese costume-shop experience. It's like no other in the world and a good place to pick up an original costume for Halloween. ⊠ *2F MN Bldg., 3–15–5 Soto-Kanda, Chiyoda-ku* ☎ *03/3526–6877* ☉ *Mon.–Sat. 11–8,*

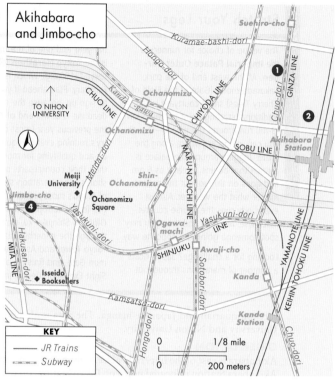

Akihabara and Jimbo-cho

Sun. and holidays 11–7 Ⓜ *JR Yamanote Line, Akihabara Station (Akihabara Electric Town Exit).*

Radio Kaikan ラジオ会館. Eight floors featuring a variety of vendors selling mini-spy cameras, cell phones disguised as stun guns, manga comics, adult toys, gadgets, and oddball hobby supplies draw otaku, other shoppers, and visitors alike. Start browsing from the top floor and work your way down. ✉ *1–15–16 Soto-Kanda, Chiyoda-ku* ☎ *03/3251–3711* ⏱ *Daily 10–7* Ⓜ *JR Yamanote Line, Akihabara Station (Akihabara Electric Town Exit).*

Thanko サンコー. As the king of wacky electronics from Japan, Thanko sells everything from recording binoculars to a smokeless ashtray to a flowerpot with a speaker mounted on its side. This showroom is a must-see for gadget geeks. ✉ *1F Machida Bldg., 3–9–10 Soto-Kanda, Chiyoda-ku* ☎ *03/3526–5472* ⊕ *www.thanko.jp* ⏱ *Mon.–Sat. 11–8, Sun. 11–7* Ⓜ *JR Yamanote Line, Akihabara Station (Akihabara Electric Town Exit).*

WORTH NOTING

Bookstores of Jimbo-cho 神保町書店街. For the ultimate browse through art books, catalogs, scholarly monographs, secondhand paperbacks, and dictionaries in almost any language, the bookstores of Jimbo-cho are the place to go. A number of the antiquarian booksellers here carry rare typeset editions, wood-block-printed books of the Edo period, and individual prints. At shops like **Isseido** and **Ohya Shobo** (both are open Monday–Saturday 10–6) it's still possible to find genuine 19th- and 20th-century prints—not always in the best condition—at affordable prices. Many of Japan's most prestigious publishing houses make their home in this area as well. The bookstores run for ½ km (¼ mi) on Yasukuni-dori beginning at the Surugadai-shita intersection. ✉ *Isseido: 1–7–4 Kanda Jimbo-cho, Chiyoda-ku* ☎ *03/3292–0071* ⊕ *www.isseido-books.co.jp* ✉ *Ohya Shobo: 1–1 Kanda Jimbo-cho, Chiyoda-ku, Jimbo-cho* ☎ *03/3291–0062* ⊕ *www.ohya-shobo.com* Ⓜ *Shinjuku and Mita subway lines, Jimbo-cho Station (Exit A7).*

UENO 上野

JR Ueno Station is Tokyo's version of the Gare du Nord: the gateway to and from Japan's northeast provinces. Since its completion in 1883, the station has served as a terminus in the great migration to the city by villagers in pursuit of a better life.

Ueno was a place of prominence long before the coming of the railroad. Since Ieyasu Tokugawa established his capital here in 1603, 36 subsidiary temples were erected surrounding the Main Hall, and the city of Edo itself expanded to the foot of the hill where the main gate of the Kan-ei-ji temple once stood.

The Meiji government turned Ueno Hill into one of the nation's first public parks. It would serve as the site of trade and industrial expositions; it would have a national museum, a library, a university of fine arts, and a zoo. The modernization of Ueno still continues, but the park is more than the sum of its museums. The Shogitai warriors failed to take everything with them: some of the most important buildings in the temple complex survived or were restored and should not be missed.

ORIENTATION

Ueno, along with Asakusa, makes up the historical enclave of Tokyo. Though the Tokyo Sky Tree transmission tower (slated for completion in 2012) can be seen from nearly all parts of these neighborhoods, traditional architecture and way of life are preserved here at the northeastern reaches of the city. Both areas can be explored in a single day, though if you have the time, it's also a good idea to devote an entire day to this place to fully appreciate its many museum exhibits and shrines.

PLANNING

Exploring Ueno can be one excursion or two: an afternoon of cultural browsing or a full day of cultural discoveries in one of the great centers of the city. ■TIP➔ Avoid Monday, when most of the museums are closed.

GETTING HERE AND AROUND

Ueno Station can be accessed by train on the Hibiya Line, Ginza Line, and JR Yamanote Line (Koen Entrance). Be sure to avoid rush hours in the morning (8–9) and evening (6–9) and bring plenty of cash for admission fees to museums and food for the day as finding an ATM may be challenging. Museums accept some major credit cards for admission; credit cards are also accepted in museum stores.

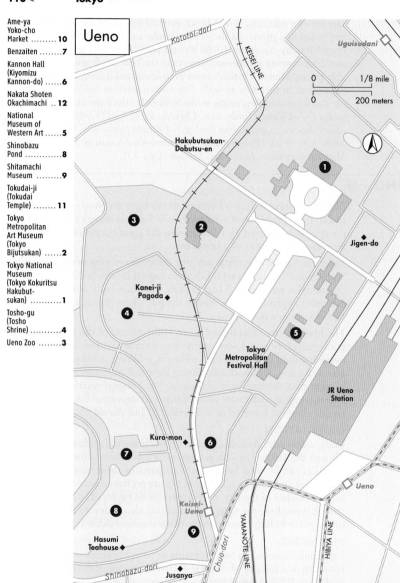

Ueno

The "ame" in Ame-ya Yoko-cho Market also means "American," referencing the many American products sold during the area's black market era.

TOP ATTRACTIONS

Ame-ya Yoko-cho Market アメヤ横丁. Not much besides Ueno Station survived the bombings of World War II, and anyone who could make it here from the countryside with rice and other small supplies of food could sell them at exorbitant black-market prices. Sugar was a commodity that couldn't be found at any price in postwar Tokyo. Before long, there were hundreds of stalls in the black market selling various kinds of *ame* (confections), most made from sweet potatoes. These stalls gave the market its name, Ame-ya Yoko-cho (often shortened to Ameyoko), which means "Confectioners' Alley." Shortly before the Korean War, the market was legalized, and soon the stalls were carrying watches, chocolate, ballpoint pens, blue jeans, and T-shirts that had somehow been "liberated" from American PXs. In years to come the merchants of Ameyoko diversified still further—to fine Swiss timepieces and fake designer luggage, cosmetics, jewelry, fresh fruit, and fish. The market became especially famous for the traditional prepared foods of the New Year, and, during the last few days of December, as many as half a million people crowd into the narrow alleys under the railroad tracks to stock up for the holiday. For a break, the area also features numerous small restaurants specializing in raw slices of tuna over rice (*maguro-don*)—cheap, quick, and very good. ⊠ *Ueno 4-chome, Taito-ku* ☉ *Most shops and stalls daily 10–7* Ⓜ *JR Ueno Station (Hiroko-ji Exit).*

Benzaiten 弁財天. Perched in the middle of Shinobazu Pond, this shrine is dedicated to the goddess Benten, one of the Seven Gods of Good Luck that evolved from a combination of Indian, Chinese, and Japanese mythology. As matron goddess of the arts, she is depicted holding a lutelike musical instrument called a *biwa*. The shrine, which was built by Abbot Tenkai, was destroyed in the bombings of 1945; the present version, with its distinctive octagonal roof, is a faithful copy. You can rent rowboats and pedal boats at a nearby boathouse. ✉ *2–1 Ueno Koen, Taito-ku* ☎ *03/3828–9502 for boathouse* ✆ *Rowboats ¥600 for 1 hr, pedal boats ¥600 for 30 mins, swan boats ¥700 for 30 mins* ◷ *Boathouse daily 9–5* Ⓜ *JR Ueno Station (Koen-guchi/Park Exit); Keisei private rail line, Keisei-Ueno Station (Ikenohata Exit).*

Kannon Hall 観音堂 (*Kiyomizu Kannon-do*). This National Treasure was a part of Abbot Tenkai's attempt to build a copy of Kyoto's magnificent Kiyomizu-dera in Ueno. His attempt was honorable, but failed to be as impressive as the original. The principal Buddhist image of worship here is the Senju Kannon (Thousand-Armed Goddess of Mercy). Another figure, however, receives greater homage. This is the Kosodate Kannon, who is believed to answer the prayers of women having difficulty conceiving children. If their prayers are answered, they return to Kiyomizu and leave a doll, as both an offering of thanks and a prayer for the child's health. In a ceremony held every September 25, the dolls that have accumulated during the year are burned in a bonfire. ✉ *1–29 Ueno Koen, Taito-ku* ☎ *03/3821–4749* ✆ *Free* ◷ *Daily 7–5* Ⓜ *JR Ueno Station (Koen-guchi/Park Exit).*

Shinobazu Pond 不忍池. Shinobazu was once an inlet of Tokyo Bay. When the area was reclaimed, it became a freshwater pond. Abbot Tenkai, founder of Kan-ei-ji on the hill above the pond, had an island made in the middle of it, which he built for **Benzaiten** (⇨ *above*), the goddess of the arts. Later improvements included a causeway to the island, embankments, and even a racecourse (1884–93). Today the pond is in three sections. The first, with its famous lotus plants, is a wildlife sanctuary. Some 5,000 wild ducks migrate here from as far away as Siberia, sticking around from September to April. The second section, to the north, belongs to Ueno Zoo; the third, to the west, is a small lake for boating. In July, the Ueno *matsuri* (festival) features food stalls and music events in the small at the pond's edge. ✉ *Shinobazu-dori, Taito-ku* ✆ *Free* ◷ *Daily sunrise–sunset* Ⓜ *JR Ueno Station (Koen-guchi/Park Exit); Keisei private rail line, Keisei-Ueno Station (Higashi-guchi/East Exit).*

NEED A BREAK?

Hasumi Teahouse 蓮見茶屋, a charming Japanese teahouse located on the bank of Shinobazu Pond, is only open in summer, when the lotus flowers cover the water. It's an open, airy café that offers perfect views of the lotus flowers in bloom and serves lunch and dinner sets: for lunch, you can get a set of tea and snacks for ¥900; for dinner you can get a set of cold beer and snacks for ¥1,000. English is not spoken, but sets are displayed in plastic models at the entrance to make ordering easier. ✉ *3 Ueno KoenTaito-ku* ☎ *03/3833–0030 (Mon.–Sat.)* ◷ *Early July–late Sept., Thurs.–Tues. noon–9* Ⓜ *Toei Oedo Line, Ueno-Okachi-machi Station (Exit 2); JR Yamanote Line, Ueno Station (Exit 6).*

Tokudai-ji 徳大寺 (*Tokudai Temple*). This is a curiosity in a neighborhood of curiosities: a temple on the second floor of a supermarket. Two deities are worshipped here. One is the bodhisattva Jizo, and the act of washing this statue is believed to safeguard your health. The other is of the Indian goddess Marici, a daughter of Brahma; she is believed to help worshippers overcome difficulties and succeed in business. ⊠ *4–6–2 Ueno, Taito-ku* ☎ *03/3831–7926* Ⓜ *JR Yamanote and Keihin-tohoku lines, Okachi-machi Station (Higashi-guchi/East Exit) or Ueno Station (Hiroko-ji Exit).*

Fodors Choice
★

Tokyo National Museum 東京国立博物館 (*Tokyo Kokuritsu Hakubutsu-kan*). This complex of four buildings grouped around a courtyard is one of the world's great repositories of East Asian art and archaeology. Altogether, the museum has some 87,000 objects in its permanent collection, with several thousand more on loan from shrines, temples, and private owners.

The Western-style building on the left (if you're standing at the main gate), with bronze cupolas, is the **Hyokeikan.** Built in 1909, it was devoted to archaeological exhibits; aside from the occasional special exhibition, the building is closed today. The larger **Heiseikan,** behind the Hyokeikan, was built to commemorate the wedding of crown prince Naruhito in 1993 and now houses Japanese archaeological exhibits. The second floor is used for special exhibitions.

In 1878, the 7th-century Horyu-ji (Horyu Temple) in Nara presented 319 works of art in its possession—sculpture, scrolls, masks, and other objects—to the Imperial Household. These were transferred to the National Museum in 2000 and now reside in the **Horyu-ji Homotsukan** (Gallery of Horyu-ji Treasures), which was designed by Yoshio Taniguchi. There's a useful guide to the collection in English, and the exhibits are well explained. Don't miss the hall of carved wooden *gigaku* (Buddhist processional) masks.

The central building in the complex, the 1937 **Honkan,** houses Japanese art exclusively: paintings, calligraphy, sculpture, textiles, ceramics, swords, and armor. Also here are 84 objects designated by the government as National Treasures. The Honkan rotates the works on display several times during the year. It also hosts two special exhibitions annually (April and May or June, and October and November), which feature important collections from both Japanese and foreign museums. These, unfortunately, can be an ordeal to take in: the lighting in the Honkan is not particularly good, the explanations in English are sketchy at best, and the hordes of visitors make it impossible to linger over a work you especially want to study. As of this writing, more attractive **Toyokan,** to the right of the Honkan, is closed for renovation and is slated to reopen in 2012. Completed in 1968 it is devoted to the art and antiquities of China, Korea, Southeast Asia, India, the Middle East, and Egypt. The more attractive **Toyokan,** to the right of the Honkan, completed in 1968, is devoted to the art and antiquities of China, Korea, Southeast Asia, India, the Middle East, and Egypt. ⊠ *13–9 Ueno Koen, Taito-ku* ☎ *03/3822–1111* ⊕ *www.tnm.go.jp* 🎟 *Regular exhibits ¥600, special exhibits approx. ¥1,500* 🕐 *Tues.–Sun. 9:30–5, times vary during special exhibitions* Ⓜ *JR Ueno Station (Koen-guchi/Park Exit).*

WORTH NOTING

Nakata Shoten Okachimachi 中田商店 御徒町店. This store probably has more shades of green than the average Tokyo park. Stuffed with cargo pants, camouflage jackets, military uniforms, and ammo boxes, Nakata Shoten is more about outfitting its customers in funky fashion than resurrecting Imperial militarism. The watches make interesting souvenirs. ✉ *6–2–14 Ueno, Taito-ku* ☎ *03/3839–6866* ✇ *Daily 10–8* Ⓜ *JR lines, Okachi-machi Station (North Exit); Toei Oedo subway line, Ueno Okachi-machi Station (Exit A7).*

National Museum of Western Art 国立西洋美術館 (*Kokuritsu Seiyo Bijutsukan*). Along with castings from the original molds of Rodin's *Gate of Hell, The Burghers of Calais,* and *The Thinker,* the wealthy businessman Matsukata Kojiro (1865–1950) acquired some 850 paintings, sketches, and prints by such masters as Renoir, Monet, Gauguin, van Gogh, Delacroix, and Cézanne. Matsukata kept the collection in Europe, but he left it to Japan in his will. The French government sent the artwork to Japan after World War II, and the collection opened to the public in 1959 in a building designed by Swiss-born architect Le Corbusier. Since then, the museum has diversified a bit; more recent acquisitions include works by Reubens, Tintoretto, El Greco, Max Ernst, and Jackson Pollock. The Seiyo is one of the best-organized, most pleasant museums to visit in Tokyo. ✉ *7–7 Ueno Koen, Taito-ku* ☎ *03/3828–5131* ⊕ *www.nmwa.go.jp* ✉ *¥420; additional fee for special exhibits* ✇ *Tues.–Thurs. and weekends 9:30–5:30, Fri. 9:30–8* Ⓜ *JR Ueno Station (Koen-guchi/Park Exit).*

☾ **Shitamachi Museum** 下町風俗資料館 (*Shitamachi Fuzoku Shiryokan*). Japanese society in the days of the Tokugawa shoguns was rigidly stratified. Some 80% of the city's land was allotted to the warrior class, temples, and shrines. The remaining 20%—between Ieyasu's fortifications on the west, and the Sumida-gawa on the east—was known as *shitamachi,* literally, "downtown" or the "lower town" (as it expanded, shitamachi came to include what today constitutes the Chuo, Taito, Sumida, and Koto wards). It was here that the common, hardworking, free-spending folk, who made up more than half the population, lived. The Shitamachi Museum preserves and exhibits what remained of that way of life as late as 1940.

The two main displays on the first floor are a merchant house and a tenement, intact with all their furnishings. This is a hands-on museum: you can take your shoes off and step up into the rooms. On the second floor are displays of toys, tools, and utensils donated, in most cases, by people who had grown up with them and used them all their lives. There are also photographs and video documentaries of craftspeople at work. Occasionally various traditional skills are demonstrated, and you're welcome to take part. This don't-miss museum makes great use of its space, and there are even volunteer guides (available starting at 10) who speak passable English. ✉ *2–1 Ueno Koen, Taito-ku* ☎ *03/3823–7451* ✉ *¥300* ✇ *Tues.–Sun. 9:30–4:30* Ⓜ *JR Ueno Station (Koen-guchi/Park Exit).*

Tokyo Metropolitan Art Museum 東京都美術館 (*Tokyo-to Bijutsukan*). ■TIP➔ **At this writing, the museum is closed for renovations until April**

2012. Check with the museum for updates. The museum displays its own collection of modern Japanese art on the lower level and rents out the remaining two floors to various art institutes and organizations. At any given time, there can be a variety of exhibits in the building: international exhibitions, work by local young painters, or new forms and materials in sculpture or modern calligraphy. ✉ *8–36 Ueno Koen, Taito-ku* ☎ *03/3823–6921* ⊕ *www.tobikan.jp* ✉ *Permanent collection free; fees vary for other exhibits (usually ¥800–¥1,400)* ⊗ *Daily 9–5; closed 3rd Mon. of month* Ⓜ *JR Ueno Station (Koen-guchi/Park Exit).*

Tosho-gu 東照宮 *(Tosho Shrine).* ■TIP→ At this writing, the shrine closed for renovations until December 2013, but the outdoor areas are still accessible. This shrine, built in 1627, is dedicated to Ieyasu, the first Tokugawa shogun. It miraculously survived all major disasters that destroyed most of Tokyo's historical structures—the fires, the 1868 revolt, the 1923 earthquake, the 1945 bombings—making it one of the few early-Edo-period buildings left in Tokyo. The shrine and most of its art are designated National Treasures.

Two hundred *ishidoro* (stone lanterns) line the path from the stone entry arch to the shrine itself. One of them, just outside the arch to the left, is more than 18 feet high, called *obaketoro* (ghost lantern). Legend has it that one night a samurai on guard duty slashed at a ghost (*obake*) that was believed to haunt the lantern. His sword was so strong, it left a nick in the stone, which can be seen today.

The first room inside the shrine is the **Hall of Worship;** the four paintings in gold on wooden panels are by Tan'yu, a member of the famous Kano family of artists, dating from the 15th century. Behind the Hall of Worship, connected by a passage called the *haiden,* is the sanctuary, where the spirit of Ieyasu is said to be enshrined.

The real glory of Tosho-gu is its so-called **Chinese Gate,** at the end of the building, and the fence on either side that has intricate carvings of birds, animals, fish, and shells of every description. The two long panels of the gate, with their dragons carved in relief, are attributed to Hidari Jingoro—a brilliant sculptor of the early Edo period whose real name is unknown (*hidari* means "left"; Jingoro was reportedly left-handed). The lifelike appearance of his dragons has inspired a legend. Every morning they were found mysteriously dripping with water and it was believed that the dragons were sneaking out at night to drink from the nearby Shinobazu Pond. Wire cages were put up to curtail this disquieting habit. ✉ *9–88 Ueno Koen, Taito-ku* ☎ *03/3822–3455* ✉ *¥200* ⊗ *Daily 9–5* Ⓜ *JR Ueno Station (Koen-guchi/Park Exit).*

🕲 **Ueno Zoo** 上野動物園 *(Ueno Dobutsuen).* First built in 1882, this is Japan's first zoo. Its two main gardens host an exotic mix of more than 900 species of animals. The deaths of its two giant pandas—Tong Tong and Ling Ling—have left the zoo without a large tourist draw, but the tigers from Sumatra, gorillas from the lowland swamp areas of western Africa, and numerous monkeys, some from Japan, make a visit to the East Garden worthwhile. The West Garden is highlighted by rhinos, zebras, and hippopotamuses, and a children's area. The process of the zoo's expansion somehow left within its confines the 120-foot, five-story Kan-ei-ji Pagoda. Built in 1631 and rebuilt after a fire in 1639, the building offers traditional Japanese tea ceremony services. ⊠ *9–83 Ueno Koen, Taito-ku* ☎ *03/3828–5171* ⊕ *www.tokyo-zoo.net/zoo/ueno* 🎫 *¥600, free on Mar. 20, May 4, and Oct. 1* ◷ *Tues.–Sun. 9:30–5* Ⓜ *JR Ueno Station (Koen-guchi/Park Exit)*.

ASAKUSA 浅草

Historically, Asakusa has been the city's entertainment hub. The area blossomed when Ieyasu Tokugawa made Edo his capital and it became the 14th-century city that never slept. For the next 300 years it was the wellspring of almost everything we associate with Japanese culture. In the mid-1600s, it became a pleasure quarter in its own right with stalls selling toys, souvenirs, and sweets; acrobats, jugglers and strolling musicians; and sake shops and teahouses—where the waitresses often provided more than tea. Then, in 1841, the Kabuki theaters moved to Asakusa.

The theaters were here for a short time, but it was enough to establish Asakusa as *the* entertainment quarter of the city—a reputation it held unchallenged until World War II, when most of the area was destroyed. Though it never fully recovered as an entertainment district, the area today is home to artisans and small entrepreneurs, children and grandmothers, hipsters, hucksters, and priests. If you have any time to spend in Tokyo, make sure you devote at least a day to exploring Asakusa.

ORIENTATION

Rich in history and traditional culture, this northeastern area of Tokyo should be top on your list of destinations. Asakusa is a border city ward that separates central Tokyo from suburban areas beyond. It's a unique spiritual and commercial, tourist, and residential area, where locals walk their dogs on the Asakusa Jinja grounds or give offerings and pray at Kannon Temple. Life in this area is slow-paced and uncomplicated. Asakusa is just east of Ueno and can be explored thoroughly in a half day, whether you go straight from Ueno or on a separate excursion.

PLANNING

Unlike most of the other areas to explore on foot in Tokyo, Senso-ji is admirably compact. You can easily see the temple and environs in a morning. The garden at Dembo-in is worth a half hour. If you decide to include Kappabashi, allow yourself an hour more for the tour. Some of the shopping arcades in this area are covered, but Asakusa is essentially an outdoor experience.

The Asakusa Tourist Information Center (Asakusa Bunka Kanko Center) is across the street from Kaminari-mon. A volunteer with some English knowledge is on duty here daily 10–5 and will happily load you down with maps and brochures.

GETTING HERE AND AROUND

Getting here by subway from Ueno Station (Ginza Line, Ueno Station to Asakusa Station, ¥160) or taxi (approximately ¥900) is most convenient. Asakusa is the last stop (eastbound) on the Ginza subway line.

Another way get to Asakusa is by river-bus ferry from Hinode Pier, which stops at the southwest corner of Sumida Koen.

CLOSE UP

A Day on the Green

Tokyo has 21 golf courses within its borders and a vast selection beyond city limits. Some are private, but that doesn't always mean nonmembers can't play. Bear in mind that you may pay twice what you would on weekdays for weekends and holidays, and just because facilities are open to tourists doesn't mean they have bilingual staff. Luckily, most have self-service systems or friendly staff. You can book tee times at *Golf in Japan* (⊕ *www.golf-in-japan.com*), an online guide to the country's course. ■TIP→ Most courses rent sets so you don't have to lug yours.

IN TOKYO
Showanomori Golf Course, Akishima. Built during the U.S. occupation, this public course offers wide fairways, a remote-control monorail cart, and some English-speaking staff, but no caddies. ⊠ *1–1–7 Tsutsujigaoka, Akishima* ⚑ *18 holes, Par 72* ☎ *042/543–1273* ⊜ *Fees ¥13,000–¥18,000; club rentals ¥2,000* Ⓜ *JR Ome Line, Akishima Station.*

Wakasu Golf Links. If convenience is what you seek, this centrally located public course is for you. Reservations are required, but carts and caddies are optional. (⊠ *3–1–2 Wakasu, Koto-ku* ⚑ *18 holes, Par 72* ⊜ *Fees ¥13,475–¥22,745; club rentals ¥3,150* ☎ *03/3522–3221* Ⓜ *Yuraku-cho Line, Shin Kiba Station.*

Yomiuri Golf Club, Inagi. Expect a strict dress code at this private club, which hosts the annual Salonpas World Ladies Championships in May. It's open to the public, you can rent golf carts, and caddies are a must, but don't count on a bilingual staff. ⊠ *3376–1 Yanokuchi, Inagi* ⚑ *18 holes, Par 72* ⊜ *Fees*

¥25,200–¥35,700; club rentals ¥5,250 ☎ *044/966–1141* Ⓜ *Odakyu Line Semi Express, Shin Yurigaoka Station.*

OUTSIDE TOKYO
Gotemba and Belle View Nagao golf clubs, Gotemba, Shizuoka. At the foot of Mt. Fuji, these courses will challenge your skills and stamina, especially on foggy days. ⊠ *1924–2 Koyama, Gotemba* ⚑ *18 holes, Par 72* ⊜ *Fees ¥5,000 for 9 holes; ¥19,000 for 18 holes; club rentals ¥3,675* ☎ *0550/87–1555* Ⓜ *Odakyu Asagiri Romance car from Shinjuku Station to Gotemba Station, 1 hr and 40 mins.*

Kasumigaura Country Club, Kasumigaura, Ibaraki. Loaded with water hazards and sand traps, this course will make you curse and sweat. The spacious clubhouse, high-end restaurant, and other luxurious facilities will make up for it, though. ⊠ *1000 Serizawa Tamatsukuri-machi, Namegata* ⚑ *18 holes, Par 72* ⊜ *Fees ¥7,800–¥18,000; club rentals ¥4,200* ☎ *0299/55–2311* Ⓜ *JR Joban from Ueno Station to Ishioka Station, 1 hr, plus taxi (30 mins, ¥6,000) to club.*

DRIVING RANGES
Lottè Kasai Golf. The granddaddy of Tokyo driving ranges sports 300 bays and a 250-yard field. ⊠ *2–4–2 Rinkai-cho, Edogawa-ku* ☎ *03/5658–5600* ⊜ *Varies but about ¥18 per ball; prepaid cards ¥3,000–¥20,000* ⊙ *Daily 24 hrs* Ⓜ *JR Keiyo Line, Kasai-Rinkai-Koen Station.*

Meguro Gorufu-jo. There is no weekday wait and an easy-to-navigate self-service system at this driving range. ⊠ *5–6–22 Kami-Meguro, Meguro-ku* ☎ *03/3713–2805* ⊜ *About ¥14 per ball* Ⓜ *Hibiya Line, Naka-Meguro Station).*

TOP EXPERIENCES: THE SENSO-JI COMPLEX

Fodor's Choice ★ **Senso-ji Complex.** Dedicated to the goddess Kannon, the Senso-ji Complex is the heart and soul of Asakusa. Come for its local and historical importance, its garden, its 17th-century Shinto shrine, and the wild Sanja Festival in May. ⌧ *2–3–1 Asakusa, Taito-ku* ☎ *03/3842–0181* 🖃 *Free* ⊙ *Temple grounds daily 6–sunset* Ⓜ *Ginza subway line, Asakusa Station (Exit 1/Kaminari-mon Exit).*

Asakusa Jinja 浅草神社 *(Asakusa Shrine).* Several structures in the

> **DID YOU KNOW?**
>
> Kamiya Bar, the first drinking establishment in Japan to call itself a "bar," was started in Asakusa in 1880 and it still stands today. Stop by for a jolt of Denki Bran, a drink that dates back to the Meiji Era. A mixture of a few different liquors and brandy, the brew—the recipe is a secret—is sold in bottles at the bar and is definitely an acquired taste. Be prepared with a chaser.

Senso-ji temple complex survived the bombings of 1945. The largest, to the right of the Main Hall, is this Shinto shrine to the Hikonuma brothers and their master, Naji-no-Nakamoto—the putative founders of Senso-ji. In Japan, Buddhism and Shintoism have enjoyed a comfortable coexistence since the former arrived from China in the 6th century. The shrine, built in 1649, is also known as Sanja Sama (Shrine of the Three Guardians). Near the entrance to Asakusa Shrine is another survivor of World War II: the east gate to the temple grounds, **Niten-mon**, built in 1618 for a shrine to Ieyasu Tokugawa and designated by the government as an Important Cultural Property. ⌧ *2–3–1 Asakusa, Taito-ku* ☎ *03/3844–1575* ⊕ *www.asakusajinja.jp.*

Belfry 時の鐘鐘楼 *(Toki-no-kane Shoro).* The tiny hillock Benten-yama, with its shrine to the goddess of good fortune, is the site of this 17th-century belfry. The bell here used to toll the hours for the people of the district, and it was said that you could hear it anywhere within a radius of some 6 km (4 mi). The bell still sounds at 6 am every day, when the temple grounds open. It also rings on New Year's Eve—108 strokes in all, beginning just before midnight, to "ring out" the 108 sins and frailties of humankind and make a clean start for the coming year. Benten-yama and the belfry are at the beginning of the narrow street that parallels Nakamise-dori. ⌧ *Taito-ku.*

NEED A BREAK?

Originally a teahouse, Waentei-Kikko 和えん亭 吉幸 is now a cozy, country-style Japanese restaurant and bar. The owner, Fukui Kodai, is a traditional Japanese *Tsugaru Shamisen* (string instrument) musician, who performs at scheduled times throughout the day. Narrow your field of vision, shut out the world outside, and you could be back in the waning days of Meiji-period Japan. This pub specializes in premium sake, with set courses of food and drink for lunch (¥2,500 to ¥3,500) and dinner (¥6,825 to ¥14,175). There's a 10% service charge for dinner. ⌧ *2-2-13 Asakusa, Taito-ku* ☎ *03/5828-8833* ⊕ *www.waentei-kikko.com* ⊙ *Thurs.–Tues. 11:30–2 and 5–10* Ⓜ *Ginza subway line, Asakusa Station (Exit 1/Kaminari-mon Exit).*

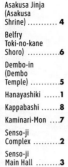

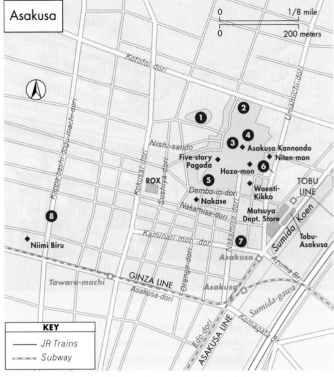

★ **Dembo-in** 伝法院 *(Dembo Temple).* Believed to have been made in the 17th century by Kobori Enshu, the genius of Zen landscape design, the garden of Dembo-in, part of the living quarters of the abbot of Senso-ji, is the best-kept secret in Asakusa. The garden of Dembo-in is usually empty and always utterly serene, an island of privacy in a sea of pilgrims. Spring, when the wisteria blooms, is the ideal time to be here.

A sign—you'll find the sign about 150 yards west of the intersection with Naka-mise-dori—in English on Dembo-in-dori leads you to the entrance, which is a side door to a large wooden gate. ■**TIP**→ **For permission to see the abbot's garden, you must first apply at the temple administration building, between Hozo-mon and the Five-Story Pagoda, in the far corner.** ⊠ *2–3–1 Asakusa, Taito-ku* ☎ *03/3842–0181 for reservations* 🎫 *Free* ⊙ *Daily 9–4; may be closed if abbot has guests* Ⓜ *Ginza subway line, Asakusa Station (Exit 1/Kaminari-mon Exit).*

Nakase 中瀬. **This is a lovely retreat from the overbearing crowds at Asakusa Kannon. The building, which is 130 years old, lends to a truly authentic Japanese experience: food is served in lacquerware bento boxes and there are an interior garden and pond, which is filled with carp and goldfish. Across Orange-dori from the redbrick Asakusa Public Hall, Nakase is expensive (lunch starts at ¥2,625; more-elaborate dinner courses top out at ¥14,700),**

Asakusa's heart and soul is the Senso-ji Complex, famous for its 17th century Shinto shrine, Asakusa Shrine, as well as its garden and the wild Sanja Festival in May.

but the experience is worth it. ✉ *1–39–13 Asakusa, Taito-ku* ☎ *03/3841–4015* ▭ *No credit cards* ⊘ *Wed.–Mon. 11:30–2 and 5–10, weekends 5–8* Ⓜ *Ginza subway line, Asakusa Station (Exit 1/Kaminari-mon Exit).*

Kaminari-mon 雷門 *(Thunder God Gate).* This is the proper Senso-ji entrance, with its huge red-paper lantern hanging in the center—a landmark of Asakusa, and picture-perfect. The original gate was destroyed by fire in 1865; the replica you see today was built after World War II. Traditionally, two fearsome guardian gods are installed in the alcoves of Buddhist temple gates to ward off evil spirits. The Thunder God (Kaminari-no-Kami) is on the left with the Wind God (Kaze-no-Kami) on the right. ■ **TIP**➔ Want to buy some of Tokyo's most famous souvenirs? Stop at **Tokiwa-do,** the shop on the west side of the gate for *kaminari okoshi* (thunder crackers), made of rice, millet, sugar, and beans.

Kaminari-mon also marks the southern extent of **Nakamise-dori,** the Street of Inside Shops. The area from Kaminari-mon to the inner gate of the temple was once composed of stalls leased to the townspeople who cleaned and swept the temple grounds. This is now kitsch-souvenir central, so be prepared to buy a few key chains, dolls, and snacks. ✉ *1 Asakusa, Taito-ku* Ⓜ *Ginza subway line, Asakusa Station (Exit 1/ Kaminari-mon Exit).*

Senso-ji Main Hall 浅草観音堂. The Main Hall and Five-Story Pagoda of Senso-ji are both faithful copies in concrete of originals that burned down in 1945. During a time when most of the people of Asakusa were still rebuilding after the fire raids, it took 13 years to raise money for the restoration of their beloved Senso-ji. To them, and those in the entertainment world, this is much more than a tourist attraction: Kabuki actors still come here before a new season of performances, and sumo wrestlers visit before a tournament to pay their respects. The large lanterns in the Main Hall were donated by the geisha associations of Asakusa and nearby Yanagi-bashi. Most Japanese stop at the huge bronze incense burner, in front of the Main Hall, to bathe their hands and faces in the smoke—it's a charm to ward off illnesses—before climbing the stairs to offer their prayers.

The Main Hall, about 115 feet long and 108 feet wide, is not an especially impressive work of architecture. Unlike in many other temples, however, part of the inside has a concrete floor, so you can come and go without removing your shoes. In this area hang Senso-ji's chief claims to artistic importance: a collection of 18th- and 19th-century votive paintings on wood. Plaques of this kind, called *ema*, are still offered to the gods at shrines and temples, but they are commonly simpler and smaller. The worshipper buys a little tablet of wood with the picture already painted on one side and inscribes a prayer on the other. The temple owns more than 50 of these works, which were removed to safety in 1945 to escape the air raids. Only eight of them, depicting scenes from Japanese history and mythology, are on display. A catalog of the collection is on sale in the hall, but the text is in Japanese only.

Lighting is poor in the Main Hall, and the actual works are difficult to see. One thing that visitors cannot see at all is the holy image of Kannon itself, which supposedly lies buried somewhere deep under the temple. Not even the priests of Senso-ji have ever seen it, and there is in fact no conclusive evidence that it actually exists.

Hozo-mon, the gate to the temple courtyard, is also a repository for sutras (Buddhist texts) and other treasures of Senso-ji. This gate, too, has its guardian gods; should either god decide to leave his post for a stroll, he can use the enormous pair of sandals hanging on the back wall—the gift of a Yamagata Prefecture village famous for its straw weaving. ⊠ *2–3–1 Asakusa, Taito-ku.*

TOP ATTRACTIONS

☺ **Hanayashiki** 花やしき. Dubbing itself as "the old park with a smile,"
★ Hanayashiki, established in 1853, is Tokyo's premier retro amusement park—think Coney Island. A haunted house, Ferris wheel, and merry-go-round await the kids who will likely be a little tired of Asakusa's historic areas. ⊠ *2–28–1 Asakusa, Taito-ku* ☎ *03/3842–8780* ⊕ *www.*

THE SANJA FESTIVAL

The Sanja Festival, held annually over the third weekend of May, is said to be the biggest, loudest, wildest party in Tokyo. Each of the areas in Asakusa has its own mikoshi (portable shrine), and, on the second day of the festival, are paraded through the streets of Asakusa to the shrine. Many of the "parishioners" take part naked to the waist, or with the sleeves of their tunics rolled up, to expose fantastic red-and-black tattoo patterns that sometimes cover their entire backs and shoulders. These are the markings of the Japanese underworld.

hanayashiki.net 🖃 ¥900–¥2,200 ⊙ *Daily 10–6, but check schedule for later closing times* Ⓜ *Ginza subway line, Asakusa Station (Exit 1/ Kaminari-mon Exit).*

★ **Kappabashi** かっぱ橋. In the 19th century, according to local legend, a river ran through the present-day Kappabashi district. The surrounding area was poorly drained and was often flooded. A local shopkeeper began a project to improve the drainage, investing all his own money, but met with little success until a troupe of *kappa*—mischievous green water sprites—emerged from the river to help him. A more prosaic explanation for the name of the district points out that the lower-ranking retainers of the local lord used to earn extra money by making straw raincoats, also called *kappa,* that they spread to dry on the bridge.

Today, Kappabashi's more than 200 wholesale dealers sell everything the city's restaurant and bar trade could possibly need to do business, from paper supplies and steam tables to the main attraction, plastic food. It is baffling to most Japanese that Kappabashi is a hot tourist attraction. ⊠ *Nishi-Asakusa 1-chome and 2-chome, Taito-ku* ⊙ *Most shops daily 9–6* Ⓜ *Ginza subway line, Tawara-machi Station (Exit 1).*

TSUKIJI 築地 **AND SHIODOME** 汐留

Although it's best known today as the site of the largest wholesale fish market in the world, Tsukiji is also a reminder of the awesome disaster of the great fire of 1657. In the space of two days, it killed more than 100,000 people and leveled almost 70% of Ieyasu Tokugawa's new capital. Ieyasu was not a man to be discouraged by mere catastrophe, however; he took it as an opportunity to plan an even bigger and better city, one that would incorporate the marshes east of his castle. Tsukiji, in fact, means "reclaimed land," and a substantial block of land it was, laboriously drained and filled, from present-day Ginza to the bay.

The common people of the tenements and alleys, who had suffered most in the great fire, did not benefit from this land project as it was first allotted to feudal lords and temples. After 1853, when Japan opened its doors to the outside world, Tsukiji became Tokyo's first foreign settlement—the site of the American delegation and an elegant two-story brick hotel, and home to missionaries, teachers, and doctors.

To the west of Tsukiji lie Shiodome and Shimbashi. In the period after the Meiji Restoration, Shimbashi was one of the most famous geisha districts of the new capital. Its reputation as a pleasure quarter is even older. In the Edo period, when there was a network of canals and waterways here, it was the height of luxury to charter a covered boat (called a *yakatabune*) from one of the Shimbashi boathouses for a cruise on the river; a local restaurant would cater the excursion, and a local geisha house would provide companionship. Almost nothing remains in Shimbashi to recall that golden age, but as its luster has faded, adjacent Shiodome has risen—literally—in its place as one of the most ambitious redevelopment projects of 21st-century Tokyo.

Shiodome (literally "where the tide stops") was an area of saltwater flats on which in 1872 the Meiji government built the Tokyo terminal—the original Shimbashi Station—on Japan's first railway line, which ran for 29 km (18 mi) to nearby Yokohama. The area eventually became Japan Rail's (JR) most notorious white elephant: a staggeringly valuable hunk of real estate, smack in the middle of the world's most expensive city that JR no longer needed and couldn't seem to sell. By 1997 a bewildering succession of receivers, public development corporations, and zoning commissions had evolved an urban renewal plan for the area, and the land was auctioned off. Among the buyers were Nippon Television and Dentsu, the largest advertising agency in Asia.

In 2002 Dentsu consolidated its scattered offices into the centerpiece of the Shiodome project: a 47-story tower and annex designed by Jean Nouvel. With the annex, known as the Caretta Shiodome, Dentsu aspired not just to a new corporate address, but an "investment in community": a complex of cultural facilities, shops, and restaurants that has turned Shiodome into one of the most fashionable places in the city to see and be seen. The 1,200-seat Dentsu Shiki Theater SEA here has become one of Tokyo's major venues for live performances; its resident repertory company regularly brings long-running Broadway hits like *Mamma Mia!* to eager Japanese audiences.

ORIENTATION

Shiodome is the southeastern transportation hub of central Tokyo. Tsukiji is a sushi-lover's dream. Perhaps getting up at 5 am to eat fish at the market isn't your idea of breakfast, but this is definitely an excellent place to taste the freshest sushi on earth, located just east of Shiodome.

PLANNING

Tsukiji has few places to spend time *in*; getting from point to point, however, can consume most of a morning. The backstreet shops will probably require no more than an hour. Allow yourself about an hour to explore the fish market; if fish in all its diversity holds a special fascination for you, take two hours. Remember that in order to see the fish auction in action, you need to get to the market before 6:30 am; by 9 am the business of the market is largely finished for the day. Sushi and sashimi will be cheaper here than in other parts of Tokyo, with sushi sets at most sushi stalls costing between ¥1,000 to ¥2,100.

GETTING HERE AND AROUND

Shidome's easily accessed by public transport: JR lines and Yurikamome Line at Shimbashi Station, Toei Oedo Line to Shiodome Station, and Asakusa Line and Ginza Line to Shimbashi Station. The connection station to the Yurikamome Monorail, a scenic ride that takes you to Odaiba in approximately 30 minutes, is also here. You can also get around quite easily on foot. There are elevated walkways that connect all the major buildings and subway and train stations.

To visit the fish market, take the subway to Tsukiji Station, which will always be the more dependable and cost-efficient option. To take the train there (depending on where you are staying), the cost will start at ¥160.

TOP ATTRACTIONS

Advertising Museum Tokyo アド・ミュージアム東京. ADMT puts the unique Japanese gift for graphic and commercial design into historical perspective, from the sponsored "placements" in 18th-century wood-block

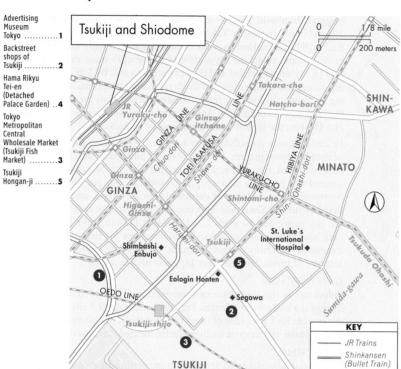

prints to the postmodern visions of fashion photographers and video directors. The museum is maintained by a foundation established in honor of Hideo Yoshida, fourth president of the mammoth Dentsu Advertising Company, and includes a digital library of some 130,000 entries on everything you ever wanted to know about hype. There are no explanatory panels in English—but this in itself is a testament to how well the visual vocabulary of consumer media can communicate across cultures. ⊠ B1F–B2F Caretta Shiodome, 1–8–2 Higashi-Shimbashi, Chuo-ku ☎ 03/6218–2500 ⊕ www.admt.jp ⊡ Free ⊘ Tues.–Fri. 11–6:30, weekends 11–4:30 Ⓜ Toei Oedo subway line, Shiodome Station (Exit 7); JR (Shiodome Exit) and Asakusa and Ginza lines (Exit 4), Shimbashi Station.

Fodor's Choice **Backstreet shops of Tsukiji** 築地6丁目. Tokyo's markets provide a vital
★   counterpoint to the museums and monuments of conventional sightseeing: they let you see how people really live in the city. If you have time for only one market, this is the one to see. The three square blocks between the Tokyo Central Wholesale Market and Harumi-dori have, naturally enough, scores of fishmongers, but also shops and restaurants. Stores sell pickles, tea, crackers and snacks, cutlery (what better place to pick up a professional sushi knife?), baskets, and kitchenware. Hole-in-the-wall sushi bars here have set menus ranging from ¥1,000

to ¥2,100; look for the plastic models of food in glass cases out front. The area includes the row of little counter restaurants, barely more than street stalls, under the arcade along the east side of Shin-Ohashi-dori, each with its specialty. If you haven't had breakfast by this point in your walk, stop at **Segawa** for *maguro donburi*—a bowl of fresh raw tuna slices served over rice and garnished with bits of dried seaweed (Segawa is in the middle of the arcade, but without any distinguishing features or English signage; your best bet is to ask someone). ■TIP→ Some 100 of the small retailers and restaurants in this area are members of the Tsukiji Meiten-kai (Association of Notable Shops) and promote themselves by selling illustrated maps of the area for ¥50; the maps are all in Japanese, but with proper frames they make great souvenirs. ⊠ *Tsukiji 4-chome, Chuo-ku* Ⓜ *Toei Oedo subway line, Tsukiji-shijo Station (Exit A1); Hibiya subway line, Tsukiji Station (Exit 1).*

★ **Hama Rikyu Tei-en** 浜離宮庭園 *(Detached Palace Garden).* Like a tiny sanctuary of Japanese tradition and nature that's surrounded by towering glass buildings, this garden is worth a visit. The land here was originally owned by the Owari branch of the Tokugawa family from Nagoya, and it extended to part of what is now the fish market. When one of the family became shogun in 1709, his residence was turned into a shogunal palace—with pavilions, ornamental gardens, pine and cherry groves, and duck ponds. The garden became a public park in 1945, although a good portion of it is fenced off as a nature preserve. None of the original buildings have survived, but on the island in the large pond is a reproduction of the pavilion where former U.S. president Ulysses S. Grant and Mrs. Grant had an audience with the emperor Meiji in 1879. The building can now be rented for parties. The stone linings of the saltwater canal work and some of the bridges underwent a restoration project that was completed in 2009. The path to the left as you enter the garden leads to the "river bus" ferry landing, from which you can leave this excursion and begin another: up the Sumida-gawa to Asakusa. ⚠ Note that you must pay the admission to the garden even if you're just using the ferry. ⊠ *1–1 Hamarikyu–Teien, Chuo-ku* ☎ *03/3541–0200* 🎫 *¥300* ⊘ *Daily 9–4:30* Ⓜ *Toei Oedo subway line, Shiodome Station (Exit 8).*

★ **Tokyo Metropolitan Central Wholesale Market** 東京中央卸売市場 *(Tsukiji Shijo).* The city's fish market used to be farther uptown, in Nihombashi. It was moved to Tsukiji after the Great Kanto Earthquake of 1923, and it occupies the site of what was once Japan's first naval training academy. Today the market sprawls over some 54 acres of reclaimed land and employs approximately 15,000 people, making it the largest fish market in the world. Its warren of buildings houses about 1,200 vendors, supplying 90% of the seafood (and some of the vegetables, meat, and fruit) consumed in Tokyo every day—some 2,000 metric tons of it. Most of the seafood sold in Tsukiji comes in by truck, arriving through the night from fishing ports all over the country. ⇨ *For more information see the feature in Where to Eat.* ⊠ *5–2–1 Tsukiji, Chuo-ku* ☎ *03/3542–1111* ⊕ *www.shijou.metro.tokyo.jp* 🎫 *Free* ⊘ *Business hrs Mon.–Sat. (except 2nd and 4th Wed. of month) 5 am–3 pm* Ⓜ *Toei*

Cherry blossoms bloom at Hama Rikyu garden.

Oedo subway line, Tsukiji-shijo Station (Exit A1); Hibiya subway line, Tsukiji Station (Exit 1).

WORTH NOTING

Tsukiji Hongan-ji 築地本願寺 *(Tsukiji Hongan Temple)*. Disaster seemed to follow this temple, which is an outpost of Kyoto's Nishi Hongwan-ji. Since it was first located here in 1657, it was destroyed at least five times, and reconstruction in wood was finally abandoned after the Great Kanto Earthquake of 1923. The present stone building dates from 1935. It was designed by Chuta Ito, a pupil of Tokyo Station architect Tatsuno Kingo. Ito's other credits include the Meiji Shrine in Harajuku; he also lobbied for Japan's first law for the preservation of historic buildings. Ito traveled extensively in Asia; the evocations of classical Hindu architecture in the temple's domes and ornaments were his homage to India as the cradle of Buddhism. But with stained-glass windows and a pipe organ as well, the building is nothing if not eclectic. Talks in English are held on the third Saturday of the month at 5:30. ⊠ *3–15–1 Tsukiji, Chuo-ku* ☎ *03/3541–1131* ⊕ *www.tsukijihongwanji.jp* 🖃 *Free* ☉ *Daily services at 7 am and 4 pm* Ⓜ *Hibiya subway line, Tsukiji Station (Exit 1).*

NIHOMBASHI 日本橋, GINZA 銀座, AND MARUNOUCHI 丸の内

Tokyo is a city of many centers. The municipal administrative center is in Shinjuku. The national government center is in Kasumigaseki. Nihombashi is the center of banking and finance, and Ginza is the center of commerce.

CLOSE UP

Cruising Like a Samurai

As during the time of the samurai, cruising in a roof-topped boat, or *yakatabune,* is the perfect means to relax amid bursting fireworks or cherry blossoms. The charm remains intact: guests are treated like royalty and are entertained while floating on the gentle waves of the Sumida or Arakawa River. Hosts within the cabin serve multiple courses of tempura and sushi and pour beer and whiskey while the boats cruise past historic bridges and along the riverbanks that make up the bay front. When the shoji (paper blinds) are opened, panoramic views of the illuminated Tokyo nightscape are a sight to behold. Observation decks offer even better viewing opportunities.

Harumiya, whose servers speak English, is a popular yakatabune company. Their boats accommodate groups of 20 to 350 and tours are run day and night, year-round. Nighttime is the best time to take a ride because of the nightscape view. Spring features the cherry blossoms in bloom; in summer, catch a break from the sweltering heat; and winter is when the year-end parties are in full swing. There are launch locations on the bay and the Arakawa River. ✉ *6–17–12 Higashisuna, Koto-ku* ☎ *03/3644–1344* ⊕ *www.harumiya. co.jp* 🍴 *Around ¥10,000 per person for 2 hrs of touring* Ⓜ *Tozai subway line, Minamisuna-cho Station (East Exit).*

When Ieyasu Tokugawa had the first bridge constructed at Nihombashi, he designated it the starting point for the five great roads leading out of his city, the point from which all distances were to be measured. His decree is still in force: the black pole on the present bridge, erected in 1911, is the Zero Kilometer marker for all the national highways and is considered the true center of Tokyo.

The early millionaires of Edo built their homes in the Nihombashi area. Some, like the legendary timber magnate Bunzaemon Kinokuniya, spent everything they made in the pleasure quarters of Yoshiwara and died penniless. Others founded the great trading houses of today—Mitsui, Mitsubishi, Sumitomo—which still have warehouses nearby.

When Japan's first corporations were created and the Meiji government developed a modern system of capital formation, the Tokyo Stock Exchange (Shoken Torihikijo) was established on the west bank of the Nihombashi-gawa (Nihombashi River). The home offices of most of the country's major securities companies are only a stone's throw from the exchange.

In the Edo period there were three types of currency in circulation: gold, silver, and copper. Ieyasu Tokugawa started minting his own silver coins in 1598 in his home province of Suruga, even before he became shogun. In 1601 he established a gold mint; the building was only a few hundred yards from Nihombashi, on the site of what is now the Bank of Japan. In 1612 he relocated the Suruga plant to a patch of reclaimed land west of his castle. The area soon came to be known informally as Ginza (Silver Mint).

Currency values fluctuated during this time and eventually businesses fell under the control of a few large merchant houses. One of the most successful of these merchants was a man named Takatoshi Mitsui, who by the end of the 17th century created a commercial empire—in retailing, banking, and trading—known today as the Mitsui Group. Not far from the site of Echigo-ya stands its direct descendant: Mitsukoshi department store.

Marunouchi lies west of Tokyo Station and extends between Hibiya Park and the Outer Garden of the Imperial Palace. After the Meiji Restoration, the area was used by the government for military purposes. Near the end of the 19th century, Iwasaki Yanosuke, the second president of Mitsubishi Corporation, bought the land, which was subsequently developed. Today, it is home numerous mixed-use office and retail complexes and the headquarters of various companies within the Mitsubishi group.

ORIENTATION

The combined areas of Marunouchi, Ginza, and Nihombashi are located beside the Imperial Palace district, to the southeast of central Tokyo. Marunouchi lies west of Tokyo Station and extends between Hibiya Park and the Outer Garden of the Imperial Palace.

PLANNING

There's something about this part of Tokyo—the traffic, the number of people, the way it urges you to keep moving—that can make you feel you've covered a lot more ground than you really have. Attack this area early in the morning but avoid rush hour (8–9) if you plan on taking the subway. None of the area's sites, with the possible exception of the Bridgestone and Idemitsu museums, should take you more than 45 minutes. The time you spend shopping, of course, is up to you. Make sure to carry bottled water. On weekend afternoons (October–March, Saturday 3–5 and Sunday noon–5; April–September, Saturday 2–6 and Sunday noon–6), Chuo-dori is closed to traffic from Shimbashi all the way to Kyo-bashi and becomes a pedestrian mall with tables and chairs set out along the street. Keep in mind that some of the museums and other sights in the area close Sunday.

GETTING HERE AND AROUND

To access Marunouchi, multiple north–south-running JR lines run between Tokyo and Yuraku-cho stations (¥130). The Yuraku-cho subway line, too, rolls through from Nagata-cho and Shin Kiba. To the east, the Ginza and Hibiya subway lines stop at Ginza Station. Slightly north is Nihombashi, which is also on the Ginza Line and only a few minutes from the bustling Ote-machi Station on the Tozai Line (¥160). By walking west from Yuraku-cho, Hibiya Park is reachable in five minutes. So is Ginza, in the opposite direction.

TOP ATTRACTIONS

Bridgestone Museum of Art ブリヂストン美術館 *(Burijisuton Bijutsukan)*. This is one of Japan's best private collections of French impressionist art and sculpture and of post-Meiji Japanese painting in Western styles by such artists as Shigeru Aoki and Tsuguji Fujita. The collection, assembled by Bridgestone Tire Company founder Shojiro Ishibashi, also includes works by Rembrandt, Picasso, Utrillo, and Modigliani. The small gallery devoted to ancient art has a breathtaking Egyptian *Sacred*

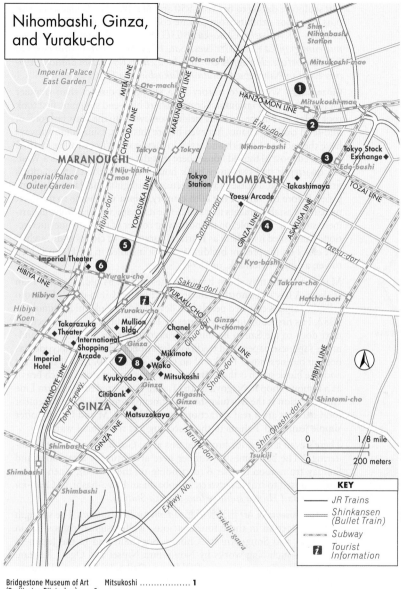

Nihombashi, Ginza, and Yuraku-cho

3

Cat sculpture dating to between 950 and 660 BC. The Bridgestone also puts on major exhibits from private collections and museums abroad. ✉ *1–10–1 Kyo-bashi, Chuo-ku* ☎ *03/3563–0241* ⊕ *www.bridgestone-museum.gr.jp* 🏷 *¥1,000* ⊘ *Tues.–Sat. 10–8, Sun. 10–6 (entrance up to 30 mins before closing)* Ⓜ *Ginza subway line, Kyo-bashi Station (Mei-jiya Exit) or Nihombashi Station (Takashimaya Exit).*

Ginza 銀座. With more history as a shopping district than trendier Omotesando and Harajuku, Ginza is where high-end shopping first took root in Japan, but the area has yielded somewhat to the "fast fashion" of mid-level clothing chains. Yet even before this shift, Ginza didn't always have the cachet of wealth and style. In fact, it wasn't until a fire in 1872 destroyed most of the old houses here that the area was rebuilt as a Western quarter. It had two-story brick houses with balconies, the nation's first sidewalks and horse-drawn streetcars, gaslights, and, later, telephone poles. Before the turn of the 20th century, Ginza was home to the great mercantile establishments that still define its character. The **Wako** department store, for example, on the northwest corner of the 4-chome intersection, established itself here as Hattori, purveyors of clocks and watches. The clock on the present building was first installed in the Hattori clock tower, a Ginza landmark, in 1894.

Many of the nearby shops have lineages almost as old, or older, than Wako's. A few steps north of the intersection, on Chuo-dori, **Mikimoto** sells the famous cultured pearls first developed by Kokichi Mikimoto in 1883. His first shop in Tokyo dates to 1899. South of the intersection, next door to the San-ai Building, **Kyukyodo** carries a variety of hand-made Japanese papers and traditional stationery goods. Kyukyodo has been in business since 1663 and on Ginza since 1880. Across the street and one block south is the **Matsuzakaya** department store, which began as a kimono shop in Nagoya in 1611. And connected to the Ginza Line Ginza Station is the **Mistukoshi** department store, where the basement food markets are a real attraction. Stores like **H&M** and **Uniqlo,** offer simple jeans and T-shirts to those seeking less traditional wares.

There's even a name for browsing this area: Gin-bura, or "Ginza wandering." The best times to wander here are Saturday afternoons and Sunday from noon to 5 or 6 (depending on the season), when Chuo-dori is closed to traffic between Shimbashi and Kyo-bashi. ✉ *Chuo-ku* Ⓜ *Ginza and Hibiya subway lines, Ginza Station.*

★ **Idemitsu Museum of Art** 出光美術館 *(Idemitsu Bijutsukan).* The strength of the collection in these four spacious, well-designed rooms lies in the Tang- and Song-dynasty Chinese porcelain and in the Japanese ceramics—including works by Nonomura Ninsei and Ogata Kenzan. On display are masterpieces of Old Seto, Oribe, Old Kutani, Karatsu, and Kakiemon ware. The museum also houses outstanding examples of Zen painting and calligraphy, wood-block prints, and genre paintings of the Edo period. Of special interest to scholars is the resource collection of shards from virtually every pottery-making culture of the ancient world. The museum is on the ninth floor of the Teikoku Gekijo building, which looks down upon the lavish Imperial Garden. ✉ *3–1–1 Marunouchi, Chiyoda-ku* ☎ *03/3213–9402* 🏷 *¥1,000* ⊘ *Tues.–Thurs.*

and weekends 10–5, Fri. 10–7 Ⓜ *Yuraku-cho subway line, Yuraku-cho Station (Exit A1).*

★ **Mitsukoshi** 三越. Takatoshi Mitsui made his fortune by revolutionizing the retail system for kimono fabrics. The emergence of Mitsukoshi as Tokyo's first *depato* (department store), also called *hyakkaten* (hundred-kinds-of-goods emporium), actually dates to 1908, with the construction of a three-story Western building modeled on Harrods of London. This was replaced in 1914 by a five-story structure with Japan's first escalator. The present flagship store is vintage 1935. Even if you don't plan to shop, this branch merits a visit. Two bronze lions, modeled on those at London's Trafalgar Square, flank the main entrance and serve as one of Tokyo's best-known meeting places. Inside, a sublime statue of Magokoro, a Japanese goddess of sincerity, rises four stories through the store's central atrium. Check out the basement floors for a taste of the food-market culture of Japanese department stores and grab a quick meal-to-go while you're there. Delicious local and international prepared food is sold here at premium prices: intricately designed *mochi* (sweet red bean) cakes, Japanese bento boxes, sushi sets, and square watermelons all sell for approximately ¥10,000. ✉ *1–4–1 Nihombashi Muro-machi, Chuo-ku* ☎ *03/3241–3311* ⊕ *www.mitsukoshi.co.jp* ⊙ *Daily 10–7, basements until 8* Ⓜ *Ginza and Hanzo-mon subway lines, Mitsukoshi-mae Station (Exits A3 and A5).*

Sukiya-bashi 数寄屋橋. The side streets of the Sukiya-bashi area are full of art galleries, which operate a bit differently here than they do in most of the world's art markets. A few, like the venerable **Nichido** (✉ *5–3–16 Ginza*), **Gekkoso** (✉ *7–2–8 Ginza*), **Yoseido** (✉ *5–5–15 Ginza*), and **Kabuto-ya** (✉ *8–8–7 Ginza*), actually function as dealers, representing particular artists, as well as acquiring and selling art. The majority, however, are rental spaces. Artists or groups pay for the gallery by the week, publicize their shows themselves, and in some cases even hang their own work. You might suspect, and with good reason, that some of these shows are vanity exhibitions by amateurs with money to spare, even in a prestigious venue like Ginza; thankfully, that's not always the case. ✉ *Chiyoda-ku* Ⓜ *Ginza, Hibiya, and Marunouchi subway lines, Ginza Station (Exit C4).*

★ **Tokyo International Forum** 東京国際フォーラム. This postmodern masterpiece, the work of Uruguay-born American architect Raphael Viñoly, is the first major convention and art center of its kind in Tokyo. Viñoly's design was selected in a 1989 competition that drew nearly 400 entries from 50 countries. The plaza of the Forum is that rarest of Tokyo rarities: civilized open space. There's a long central courtyard with comfortable benches shaded by trees. Freestanding sculpture, triumphant architecture, and people strolling are all here. The first and third Sunday of each month feature an antiques flea market in the plaza's courtyard. The Forum itself is actually two buildings. On the east side of the plaza is Glass Hall, the main exhibition space, and the west building has six halls for international conferences, exhibitions, receptions, and concert performances. Transit fans should take a stroll up the catwalks to the top, which concludes with a view of the Tokyo Station JR lines.

The Tokyo International Forum's glass atrium is the centerpiece of this arts- and culture-oriented building.

✉ *3–5–1 Marunouchi, Chiyoda-ku* ☎ *03/5221–9000* ⊕ *www.t-i-forum. co.jp* Ⓜ *Yuraku-cho subway line, Yuraku-cho Station (Exit A-4B).*

NEED A BREAK?

Amid all of Tokyo's bustle and crush, you actually can catch your breath in the Tokyo International Forum—cafés and Italian, Japanese, and French restaurants are located throughout the complex. A reasonably priced and delicious Kyoto-style vegetarian restaurant to try is **Tsuruhan.** Lunch sets start at ¥1,050 and dinner ¥3,000. Maps are available, so pick and choose. There are also ATM machines on the third floor. ✉ *3–5–1 Marunouchi, Chiyoda-ku* ☎ *03/3214–2260* ⊙ *Daily 11–3 and 5–11.*

WORTH NOTING

☾ **Kite Museum** 凧の博物館 *(Tako no Hakubutsukan).* Kite flying is an old tradition in Japan. The collection here includes examples of every shape and variety from all over the country, hand-painted in brilliant colors with figures of birds, geometric patterns, and motifs from Chinese and Japanese mythology. You can call ahead to arrange a kite-making workshop (in Japanese) for groups of children. ✉ *1–12–10 Nihombashi, Chuo-ku* ☎ *03/3271–2465* ⊕ *www.tako.gr.jp* 🎫 *¥210* ⊙ *Mon.–Sat. 11–5* Ⓜ *Tozai subway line, Nihombashi Station (Exit C5).*

Nihombashi 日本橋 *(Bridge of Japan).* Why the expressway *had* to be routed directly over this lovely old landmark back in 1962 is one of the mysteries of Tokyo and its city planning—or lack thereof. There were protests and petitions, but they had no effect. At that time, Tokyo had only two years left to prepare for the Olympics, and the traffic congestion was out of control. So the bridge, originally built in 1603, with its graceful double arch, ornate lamps, and bronze Chinese lions and uni-corns, was doomed to bear the perpetual rumble of trucks overhead—its claims overruled by concrete ramps and pillars. ⊠ *Chuo-ku* Ⓜ *Tozai and Ginza subway lines, Nihombashi Station (Exits B5 and B6); Ginza and Hanzo-mon subway lines, Mitsukoshi-mae Station (Exits B5 and B6).*

AOYAMA 青山, HARAJUKU 原宿, AND SHIBUYA 渋谷

Who would have known? As late as 1960, this was as unlikely a can-didate as any area in Tokyo to develop into the chic capital of Tokyo. Between Meiji shrine and the Aoyama Cemetery to the east, the area was so boring that the municipal government zoned a chunk of it for low-cost public housing. Another chunk, called Washington Heights, was being used by U.S. occupation forces who spent their money else-where. The few young Japanese people in Harajuku and Aoyama were either hanging around Washington Heights to practice their English or attending the Methodist-founded Aoyama University—seeking enter-tainment farther south in Shibuya.

When Tokyo won its bid to host the 1964 Olympics, Washington Heights was turned over to the city for the construction of Olympic Village. Aoyama-dori, the avenue through the center of the area, was renovated and the Ginza and Hanzo-mon subway lines were built under it. Suddenly, Aoyama became attractive for its Western-style fashion houses, boutiques, and design studios. By the 1980s the area was posi-tively *smart*. Today, most of the low-cost public housing along Omote-sando are long gone, and in its place are the glass-and-marble emporia of *the* preeminent fashion houses of Europe: Louis Vuitton, Chanel, Armani, and Prada. Their showrooms here are cash cows of their world-wide empires. Superb shops, restaurants, and amusements in this area target a population of university students, wealthy socialites, young professionals, and people who like to see and be seen.

ORIENTATION

Aoyama, Omotesando, and Harajuku, west of the Imperial Palace and just north of Roppongi, are the trendsetting areas of youth culture and fash-ion. Omotesando and Aoyama contain a laundry list of European fashion houses' flagship stores. Harajuku is a bohemian and younger fashion dis-trict that inspired Gwen Stefani to write the hit song, "Harajuku Girls," and create the "Harajuku Lovers" fashion line in 2005.

Just north of Omotesando and Aoyama, in front of the Harajuku JR Sta-tion, is Harajuku's Meiji Jingu, which is a famous hangout for dressed-up teens and crowds of onlookers.

Because it's the entertainment district for Japanese youth, Shibuya is not as clean or sophisticated as Tokyo's other neighborhoods. Rarely will you see an elderly person on the streets. Shops, cheap restaurants, karaoke lounges, bars, theaters, concert halls, and nightclubs are everywhere. With Shibuya Station connecting thousands of passengers from the suburbs into the heart of the city, it is the western frontier of central Tokyo, and the last stop of the Ginza Line.

PLANNING

Trying to explore Aoyama and Harajuku together will take a long time because there is a lot of area to cover. Ideally, you should devote an entire day here, giving yourself plenty of time to browse in shops. You can see Meiji Shrine in less than an hour; the Nezu Museum and its gardens warrant a leisurely two-hour visit. Spring is the best time of year for the Meiji Jingu Inner Garden. Just like everywhere else in this city, June's rainy season is horrendous, and the humid heat of midsummer can quickly drain your energy and add hours to the time you need to comfortably explore. The best way to enjoy this area is to explore the tiny shops, restaurants, and cafés in the backstreets.

Shibuya seems chaotic and intimidating at first, but it is fairly compact, so you can easily cover it in about two hours. Be prepared for huge crowds and some shoulder bumping. Shibuya crossing is one of the busiest intersections in the world and at one light change, hundreds rush to reach the other side. Unless you switch into shopping mode, no particular stop along the way should occupy you for more than a half hour; allow a full hour for the NHK Broadcasting Center, however, if you decide to take the guided tour. Sunday affords the best opportunity to observe Japan's younger generation in Yoyogi Koen. Three subway lines, three private railways, the JR Yamanote Line, and two bus terminals move about a million people a day through Shibuya.

GETTING HERE AND AROUND

Primary access to Shibuya is via the looping JR Yamanote Line, but the most recent point of passage is via the Fukutoshin subway line, which opened in 2008 and goes north from Shibuya up through Shinjuku and onto Ikebukuro. Old standbys are the Hanzo-mon and Ginza lines, both of which stop in Omotesando Station. The Inokashira railway goes toward Kichijoji, home to Inokashira Park, and the Toyoko railway reaches Yokohama in about 30 minutes. Hachiko Exit will be swarmed with people. Just next to it is the "scramble crossing," which leads from the station to the area's concentration of restaurants and shops. Two bus stops provide service to Roppongi to the east and Meguro and Setagaya wards to the west. On Meiji-dori, Harajuku is walkable to the north in 15 minutes, and Ebisu takes about the same going south.

TOP ATTRACTIONS

★ **Japanese Sword Museum** 刀剣博物館 *(Token Hakabutsukan)*. It's said that in the late 16th century, before Japan closed its doors to the West, the Spanish tried to establish a trade here in weapons made from famous Toledo steel. The Japanese were politely uninterested; they had been making blades of incomparably better quality for more than 600 years. At one time there were some 200 schools of sword-making in Japan; swords were prized not only for their effectiveness in battle but for the beauty of the blades and fittings and as symbols of the higher spirituality of the warrior caste. There are few inheritors of this art today. ⊠ *4–25–10 Yoyogi, Shibuya-ku* ☎ *03/3379–1386* ⊕ *www.touken.co.jp* ⊡ *¥600* ⊙ *Tues.–Sun. 10–4:30* Ⓜ *Odakyu private rail line, Sangu-bashi Station.*

★ **Meiji Shrine** 明治神宮 *(Meiji Jingu)*. The Meiji Shrine honors the spirits of Emperor Meiji, who died in 1912, and Empress Shoken. It was established by a resolution of the Imperial Diet the year after the Emperor's death to commemorate his role in ending the long isolation of Japan under the Tokugawa Shogunate and setting the country on the road to modernization. Completed in 1920 and virtually destroyed in an air raid in 1945, it was rebuilt in 1958.

A wonderful spot for photos, the mammoth entrance gates (*torii*), rising 40 feet high, are made from 1,700-year-old cypress trees from Mt. Ari in Taiwan; the crosspieces are 56 feet long. Torii are meant to symbolize the separation of the everyday secular world from the spiritual world of the Shinto shrine. The buildings in the shrine complex, with their curving, green, copper roofs, are also made of cypress wood. The surrounding gardens have some 100,000 flowering shrubs and trees.

> **TEENYBOPPER SHOPPERS HARAJUKU**
>
> On weekends the heart of Harajuku, particularly the street called Takeshita-dori, belongs to high school and junior high school shoppers, who flock there for the latest trends. Entire industries give themselves convulsions just trying to keep up with adolescent styles. Stroll through Harajuku—with its outdoor cafés, designer-ice-cream and Belgian-waffle stands, profusion of stores with names like A Bathing Ape and the Virgin Mary—and you may find it impossible to believe that Japan's most rapidly aging society in the industrial world.

An annual festival at the shrine takes place on November 3, Emperor Meiji's birthday, which is a national holiday. On the festival and New Year's Day, as many as 1 million people come to offer prayers and pay their respects. Several other festivals and ceremonial events are held here throughout the year; check by phone or on the shrine Web site to see what's scheduled during your visit. Even on a normal weekend the shrine draws thousands of visitors, but this seldom disturbs its mood of quiet serenity.

The peaceful **Inner Garden** (Jingu Nai-en), where the irises are in full bloom in the latter half of June, is on the left as you walk in from the main gates, before you reach the shrine. Beyond the shrine is the **Treasure House,** a repository for the personal effects and clothes of Emperor and Empress Meiji—perhaps of less interest to foreign visitors than to the Japanese. ✉ *1–1 Kamizono-cho, Yoyogi, Shibuya-ku* ☎ *03/3379–9222* ⊕ *www.meijijingu.or.jp* ✍ *Shrine free, Inner Garden ¥500, Treasure House ¥500* ☽ *Shrine daily sunrise–sunset; Inner Garden Mar.–Nov., daily 9–4; Treasure House daily 10–4; closed 3rd Fri. of month* Ⓜ *Chiyoda and Fukutoshin subway lines, Meiji-Jingu-mae Station; JR Yamanote Line, Harajuku Station (Exit 2).*

Meiji Shrine Outer Gardens 明治神宮外苑 *(Meiji Jingu Gai-en).* This rare expanse of open space is devoted to outdoor sports of all sorts. The Yakult Swallows play at **Jingu Baseball Stadium** (✉ *13 Kasumigaoka, Shinjuku-ku* ☎ *03/3404–8999*); the Japanese baseball season runs from April to October. The main venue of the 1964 Summer Olympics, **National Stadium** (✉ *10 Kasumigaoka, Shinjuku-ku* ☎ *03/3403–1151*) now hosts soccer matches. Some of the major World Cup matches were played here when Japan cohosted the event with Korea in autumn

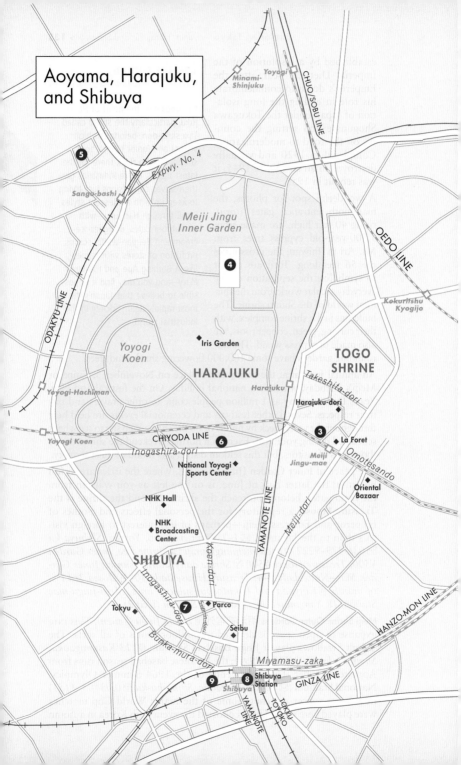

Aoyama, Harajuku, and Shibuya

5

Expwy. No. 4

Sangu-bashi

*Meiji Jingu
Inner Garden*

4

CHUO/SOBU LINE

Minami-
Shinjuku

Yoyogi

OEDO LINE

Kokuritshu
Kyogijo

ODAKYU LINE

*Yoyogi
Koen*

♦ Iris Garden

HARAJUKU

**TOGO
SHRINE**

Takeshita-dori

Harajuku

Harajuku-dori ♦

3

♦ La Foret

Yoyogi-Hachiman

CHIYODA LINE

6

Yoyogi Koen

Inogashira-dori

Meiji
Jingu-mae ♦

Omotesando

National Yoyogi ♦
Sports Center

NHK Hall ♦

Oriental
Bazaar ♦

NHK ♦
Broadcasting
Center

Meiji-dori

YAMANOTE LINE

SHIBUYA

Koen-dori

Inogashira-dori

Tokyu ♦

7 ♦ Parco

Seibu ♦

HANZO-MON LINE

Bunka-mura-dori

Miyamasu-zaka

9   **8** ☐ Shibuya
Station

GINZA LINE

Shibuya

YAMANOTE
LINE

TOKYU
TOYOKO

0   1/8 mile

0   200 meters

Sendagaya

CHUO/SOBU LINE

Expwy. No. 4

Shina-no-machi

Kaigakan

National
Stadium

Geihinkan
(Akasaka
Detached
Palace)

❶

Jingu
Baseball
Staduim

KITA-AOYAMA

HANZO-MON LINE

GINZA LINE

Gaien-nishi-dori

Gaien-mae

Aoyama-dori

Aoyama
Cemetery

Omotesando

Prada Store

Omotesando-dori

❷

Expwy. No. 3

KEY

——— JR Trains

▭▭▭ Subway

+——+ Private rail line

2002. The **Meiji Memorial Picture Gallery** (*Kaigakan*✉ *1–1 Kasumigaoka, Shinjuku-ku, Aoyama* ☎ *03/3401–5179*), across the street from the National Stadium, doesn't hold much interest unless you're a fan of Emperor Meiji and don't want to miss some 80 otherwise undistinguished paintings depicting events in his life. It's open daily 9–5 and costs ¥500. ✉ *Shinjuku-ku* ⊕ *www.meijijingugaien.jp* Ⓜ *Ginza and Hanzo-mon subway lines, Gaien-mae Station (Exit 2); JR Chuo Line, Shina-no-machi Station.*

Fodor's Choice
★ **Myth of Tomorrow** 明日の神話. This once-lost mural by avant-garde artist Taro Okamoto has been restored and mounted inside Shibuya Station. Often compared to Picasso's *Guernica,* the 14 colorful panels depict the moment of an atomic bomb detonation. The painting was discovered in 2003 in Mexico City, where in the late '60s it was originally set to be displayed in a hotel but wound up misplaced following the bankruptcy of the developer. Walk up to the Inokashira Line entrance; the mural is mounted along the hallway that overlooks Hachiko plaza. ✉ *2 Dogenzaka, Shibuya-ku* Ⓜ *JR Shibuya Station (Hachikō Exit).*

Fodor's Choice
★ **Nezu Museum** 根津美術館 (*Nezu Bijutsukan*). This recently rebuilt museum houses the private collection of traditional Japanese and Asian works of art owned by Meiji-period railroad magnate and politician Kaichiro Nezu. For the main building, architect Kengo Kuma designed an arched roof that rises two floors and extends roughly half a block through this upscale Minami Aoyama neighborhood. Inside, the 5,000-square-meter space offers a portion of the 7,000 works of calligraphy, paintings, sculptures, bronzes, and lacquerware that comprise the Nezu's collection. The museum is also home to one of Tokyo's finest gardens, featuring 5 acres of ponds, rolling paths, waterfalls, and teahouses. ✉ *6–5–1 Minami-Aoyama, Minato-ku* ☎ *03/3400–2536* ⊕ *www.nezu-muse.or.jp* 🎫 *¥1,000* ☉ *Tues.–Sun. 10–5* Ⓜ *Ginza and Hanzo-mon subway lines, Omotesando Station (Exit A5).*

★ **Ota Memorial Museum of Art** 太田記念美術館 (*Ota Kinen Bijutsukan*). The gift of former Toho Mutual Life Insurance chairman Seizo Ota, this is probably the city's finest private collection of *ukiyo-e,* traditional Edo-period wood-block prints. Ukiyo-e (pictures of the floating world) flourished in the 18th and 19th centuries. The works on display are selected and changed periodically from the 12,000 prints in the collection, which include some extremely rare work by artists such as Hiroshige, Hokusai, Sharaku, and Utamaro. ✉ *1–10–10 Jingu-mae, Shibuya-ku* ☎ *03/3403–0880* ⊕ *www.ukiyoe-ota-muse.jp* 🎫 *¥700– ¥1,000, depending on exhibit* ☉ *Tues.–Sun. 10:30–5:30; closed a few days at the end of each month; call ahead or check Web site* Ⓜ *Chiyoda and Fukutoshin subway lines, Meiji-Jingu-mae Station (Exit 5); JR Yamanote Line, Harajuku Station (Omotesando Exit).*

☺ **Yoyogi Koen** 代々木公園 (*Yoyogi Park*). This is the perfect spot to have a picnic on a sunny day. On Sunday, people come here to play music, practice martial arts, and ride bicycles on the bike path (rentals are available). Be sure to look out for a legendary group of dancing Elvis impersonators, who meet at the concrete entry plaza every Sunday and dance to classic rock and roll music. On Sunday there's a flea market along the main thoroughfare that runs through the park, opposite the National Yoyogi Sports Center. ✉ *Jinnan 2-chome, Shibuya-ku* ☎ *03/3469–6081* Ⓜ *Chiyoda and Fukutoshin subway lines, Meiji-Jingu-mae Station (Exit 2); JR Yamanote Line, Harajuku Station (Omotesando Exit).*

WORTH NOTING

Statue of Hachiko ハチ公像. Hachiko is the Japanese version of Lassie; he even starred in a few heart-wrenching films. Every morning, Hachiko's master, a professor at Tokyo University, would take the dog with him as far as Shibuya Station and Hachiko would go back to the station every evening to greet him on his return. In 1925 the professor died of a stroke. Every evening for the next seven years, Hachiko would go to Shibuya and wait there until the last train had pulled out of the station. When loyal Hachiko died, his story made headlines. A handsome bronze statute of Hachiko was installed in front of the station, funded by fans from all over the country. The present version is a replica—the original was melted down for its metal in World War II. This Shibuya landmark is one of the most popular meeting places in the city. Look for the green train car fronting the JR station; the statue is off the side, where everyone is standing. ✉ *2 Dogenzaka, Shibuya-ku* Ⓜ *JR Shibuya Station (Hachikō Exit).*

ROPPONGI 六本木

During much of the last decade of the 20th century, Roppongi was a better-heeled, better-behaved version of Shinjuku or Shibuya, without the shopping: not much happens by day, but by night the area is an irresistible draw for young clubbers with foreign sports cars and wads of disposable income. Today, this area has become an entertainment capital, attracting tourists to its bustling bar, restaurant, and nightclub scenes; English is spoken at most restaurants and shops.

Ritzy developments like Roppongi Hills and Tokyo Midtown have revitalized the area. However, since opening in 2003, the loss of some of its high-rolling tenants—the now-defunct Lehman Brothers Japan and tech company Livedoor, founded by disgraced renegade businessman Takafumi Horie—has taken a bit of the shine off Mori Tower, the main building in Roppongi Hills. Tokyo Midtown, which was completed in 2007, is home to the headquarters of Cisco Japan, FujiFilm, and game maker Konami. Further separating Roppongi from its wild ways is "Art Triangle Roppongi," a promotion campaign for three of the area's museums: the National Art Center, Tokyo; Mori Art Museum; and Suntory Museum of Art.

Azabu Juban is a prestigious residential district with many embassies in Minato-ku. Before the fire raids of 1945, Azabu Juban, like Roppongi, was a famous entertainment district with department stores, a red-light quarter, and theaters. The fires destroyed the entire neighborhood, and it was reborn as a residential area. Though the apartments may be small, this is one of the most expensive areas of the city and many celebrities, artists, and businesspeople reside here.

ORIENTATION

Roppongi is located just east of Shibuya and Aoyama, and south of the Imperial Palace. Azabu Juban is located just south of Roppongi, within seven-minute walking distance from Roppongi Hills, or a short subway ride on the Toei Oedo Line to Azabu Juban Station.

PLANNING

There are ATMs and currency exchange services at Roppongi Hills and Tokyo Midtown, as well as family- and kid-friendly activities, such as small parks and sculpture. Azabu Juban is a quick visit, and a good place to sit in a café and people-watch.

GETTING HERE AND AROUND

The best way to get to Roppongi is by subway, and there are two lines that'll take you to Roppongi Station: the Hibiya Line, which takes you right into the complex of Roppongi Hills, or the Oedo Line, with exits convenient to Tokyo Midtown.

Azabu Juban is only a short 10-minute walk from Roppongi. You can also take the Oedo Line from Roppongi to Azabu Juban Station (Exit 5), just one stop away, for ¥170.

TOP ATTRACTIONS

Mori Art Museum 森美術館. Occupying the 52nd and 53rd floors of Mori Tower, Mori Art Museum is one of the leading contemporary art showcases in Tokyo. Though lacking a permanent collection, the space is well designed (by American architect Richard Gluckman), intelligently curated, diverse in its media, and hospitable to big crowds. The nine galleries occupy 2,875 square meters for exhibits that rotate every few months and tend to focus on contemporary architecture (Le Corbusier), fashion, design, and photography. ✉ *6–10–1 Roppongi, Minato-ku* ☎ *03/5777–8600* ⊕ *mori.art.museum/jp* 💷 *Admission fee varies with exhibit* ☽ *Wed.–Mon. 10–10, Tues. 10–5* Ⓜ *Hibiya subway line, Roppongi Station (Exit 1C).*

National Art Center, Tokyo 国立新美術館. Tokyo's nightlife-happy Roppongi neighborhood has never been an art lover's destination—until now. The debut of the National Art Center adds to this town's newly burgeoning intellectual heft. Architect Kisho Kurokawa's stunning facade shimmers in undulating waves of glass. The cavernous 171,000-square-foot space houses seven exhibition areas; a library; restaurant Brasserie Paul Bocuse Le Musée, offering fine French dishes; and a museum shop. The center features traveling exhibitions that focus on modern and contemporary art. ✉ *7–22–2 Roppongi, Minato-ku* ☎ *03/5777–8600* ⊕ *www.nact.jp* ☽ *Mon., Wed., Thurs. and weekends 10–6; Fri. 10–8* 💷 *Admission fee varies with exhibit* Ⓜ *Toei Oedo and Hibiya lines, Roppongi Station (Exit 7).*

Suntory Museum of Art サントリー美術館. Based on the principle of dividing profits three ways, Suntory, Japan's beverage giant, has committed a third of its profits to what it feels is its corporate and social responsibility to provide the public with art, education, and environmental conservation. The establishment of the Suntory Art Museum in 1961 was just one of the fruits of this initiative. The museum's new home at Tokyo Midtown Gardenside is a beautiful place to view some of

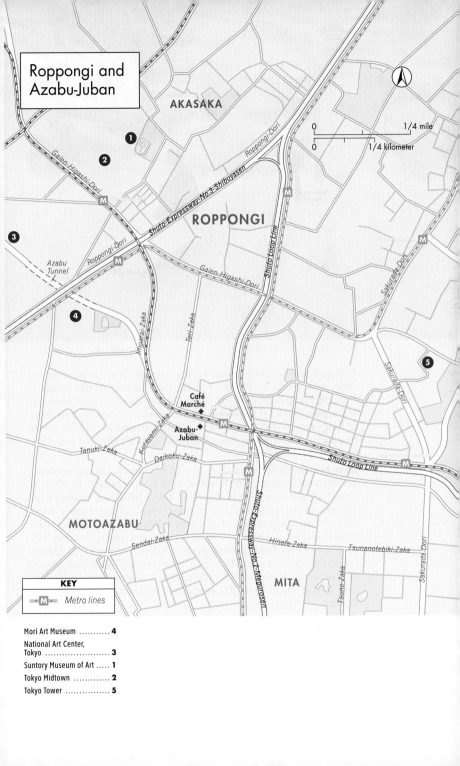

Roppongi and Azabu-Juban

AKASAKA

ROPPONGI

Gaien-Higashi-Dori

Shuto-Expressway-No.3-Shibuyasen

Roppongi-Dori

Roppongi-Dori

Azabu Tunnel

Shuto Loop Line

Gaien-Higashi-Dori

Sakurada-Dori

Imoarai-Zaka

Tori-Zaka

Sakurada-Dori

Café Marché

Azabu-Juban

Kurayami-Zaka

Tanuki-Zaka

Daikoku-Zaka

Shuto Loop Line

MOTOAZABU

Sendai-Zaka

Shuto-Expressway-No.2-Megurosen

Hinata-Zaka

Tsunanotebiki-Zaka

MITA

Tsuta-Zaka

Sakurada-Dori

0 — 1/4 mile
0 — 1/4 kilometer

KEY

Ⓜ️ Metro lines

The Mori Art Museum curates temporary, contemporary art exhibits in a sky-high space.

Tokyo's finest fine art exhibitions. Past displays have included everything from works by Picasso and Toulouse-Lautrec to fine kimonos from the Edo period. ⊠ *Tokyo Midtown Gardenside, 9–7–4 Akasaka, Minato-ku* ☎ *03/3479–8600* ⊕ *www.suntory.com/culture-sports/sma* ⊙ *Wed.–Sat. 10–8, Sun. and Mon. 10–6* 💴 *Around ¥1,300 but varies by exhibit* Ⓜ *Toei Oedo Line, Roppongi Station; Hibiya Line, Roppongi Station (Exit 8).*

Tokyo Midtown 東京ミッドタウン. The trend towards luxury, mini-city development projects, which started with Roppongi Hills in 2003, is changing the dynamic of the city. With Tokyo Midtown, Mitsui Fudosan created the tallest building in Tokyo—the 248-meter main tower rises 10 meters higher than Mori Tower at Roppongi Hills. Office, residential, and retail spaces fill out the development. Inside the complex's park is architect Tadao Ando's slope-roof design center 21_21 Design Sight, a gallery and exhibition space that covers 1,700 square meters. ⊠ *9 Akasaka, Minato-ku* ☎ *03/5413–8485* ⊕ *www.tokyo-midtown. com* Ⓜ *Toei Oedo Line, Roppongi Station; Hibiya Line, Roppongi Station.*

NEED A BREAK?

A popular local hangout in Azabu Juban at all hours of the day, Café Marche カフェロリータ is open until late. The multiple reflective wall decorations and chrome piping give a retro feel, and street-level seating allows perfect people-watching vantage points while you enjoy well-prepared pasta dishes (less than ¥1,000) and beer (Japanese or imported), cocktails, and champagne. ⊠ *1F Mademoiselle Bldg., 1–4–8 Azabu Juban,*

Minato-ku ☎ 03/6234–0122 ⏲ Mon.–Thurs. 11–2, Fri. and Sat. 11–4, Sun. 11–midnight.

WORTH NOTING

Tokyo Tower 東京タワー. In 1958 Tokyo's fledgling TV networks needed a tall antenna array to transmit signals. Trying to emerge from the devastation of World War II, the nation's capital was also hungry for a landmark—a symbol for the aspirations of a city still without a skyline. The result was the 333-meter-high (1,093 feet) Tokyo Tower, an unabashed knockoff of Paris's Eiffel Tower, and with great views of the city. The Main Observatory, set at 150 meters (492 feet) above ground, and the Special Observatory, up an additional 100 meters, quickly became major tourist attractions; they still draw many visitors a year, the vast majority of them Japanese youngsters on their first trip to the big city. A modest art gallery, the Guinness Book of World Records Museum Tokyo, and a wax museum round out the tower's appeal as an amusement complex. Enjoy live music and stunning views on the main observation-floor café during **Club 333** (⏲ *Wed. and Thurs. 7–9 pm, Fri. 7–9:30 pm*), featuring live jazz, R&B, and bossa nova performances at no extra charge. ✉ *4–2–8 Shiba-Koen, Minato-ku* ☎ *03/3433–5111* 🖅 *Main Observatory ¥820, Special Observatory ¥600 extra* ⏲ *Tower, daily 9 am–10 pm. Museums and art gallery, daily 10–9* ⊕ *www.tokyotower.co.jp* Ⓜ *Hibiya subway line, Kamiyacho Station (Exit 2).*

SHINJUKU 新宿

If you have a certain sort of love for big cities, you're bound to love Shinjuku. Come here, and for the first time Tokyo begins to seem *real:* all the celebrated virtues of Japanese society—its safety and order, its grace and beauty, its cleanliness and civility—fray at the edges.

To be fair, the area has been on the fringes of respectability for centuries. When Ieyasu, the first Tokugawa shogun, made Edo his capital, Shinjuku was at the junction of two important arteries leading into the city from the west. It became a thriving post station, where travelers would rest and refresh themselves for the last leg of their journey; the appeal of this suburban pit stop was its "teahouses," where the waitresses dispensed a good bit more than sympathy with the tea.

When the Tokugawa dynasty collapsed in 1868, 16-year-old Emperor Meiji moved his capital to Edo, renaming it Tokyo, and modern Shinjuku became the railhead connecting it to Japan's western provinces. It became a haunt for artists, writers, and students; in the 1930s Shinjuku was Tokyo's bohemian quarter. The area was virtually leveled during the firebombings of 1945—a blank slate on which developers could write, as Tokyo surged west after the war.

Now, by day the east side of Shinjuku Station is an astonishing concentration of retail stores, vertical malls, and discounters of every stripe and description. By night much of the activity shifts to the nearby red-light quarter of Kabuki-cho, which is an equally astonishing collection of bars and clubs, strip joints, hole-in-the-wall restaurants, *pachinko* parlors (an upright pinball game), and peep shows—just about anything that amuses, arouses, alters, or intoxicates is for sale. Recent crackdowns by police have limited this sort of adult activity but whatever you are after is probably still there if you know where to look.

ORIENTATION

By day, Shinjuku is a bustling center of business and government where office workers move in droves during rush hour. By night, people are inundated with flashing signs, and a darker side of Tokyo emerges, where drunken hordes leave their offices to go out for drinks, food, and sometimes, sex. Perhaps this is a rougher side of town, but Shinjuku is a fascinating place to discover at night.

PLANNING

Every day three subways, seven railway lines, and more than 3 million commuters converge on Shinjuku Station, making this the city's busiest and most heavily populated commercial center. The hub at Shinjuku—a vast, interconnected complex of tracks and terminals, department stores and shops—divides the area into two distinctly different subcities, Nishi-Shinjuku (West Shinjuku) and Higashi-Shinjuku (East Shinjuku).

Plan at least a full day for Shinjuku if you want to see both the east and west sides. Subway rides can save you time and energy as you're exploring, but don't rule out walking. The Shinjuku Gyo-en National Garden is worth at least an hour, especially if you come in early April during *sakura* (cherry blossom) season. The Tokyo Metropolitan Government Office complex can take longer than you might expect; lines for the elevators to the observation decks are often excruciatingly long. Sunday, when shopping streets are closed to traffic, is the best time to tramp around Higashi-Shinjuku. The rainy season in late June and the sweltering heat of August are best avoided.

GETTING HERE AND AROUND

From Shibuya to the south and Ikebukuro to the north, the JR Yamanote Line is one of the more common ways to reach Shinjuku Station. The Saikyo Line travels the same path but less frequently. The Keio and Oda-kyu lines serve destinations to the west, such as Shimokitazawa. Subway lines, like the Marunouchi, Shinjuku, and Toei Oedo, are best used to move to destinations in the center of the city, such as Ote-machi, Kudan-shita, and Roppongi. On foot, Kabuki-cho is accessible in minutes to the east. For the forest of office-building skyscrapers, go through the underground passage to the west and look for the towers of concrete and steel.

TOP ATTRACTIONS

Kabuki-cho 歌舞伎町. Kabuki-cho is the vice capital of Japan. When laws got stricter, prostitution just went a bit deeper underground here, where it remains—widely tolerated. ⚠ In spite of recent crackdowns by police on sex shops and hostess clubs, Kabuki-cho remains Japan's most vast adult entertainment quarter. Neon signs flash; shills proclaim the pleasures of the places you particularly want to shun. Even when a place looks respectable, ask about prices first: *bottakuri* —overcharging for food and drink—is indeed a possibility, and watered-down drinks can set you back ¥5,000 or more in a hostess or host club. You needn't be intimidated by the area though. Stop in to a street-level bar (that clearly indicates its pricing) and watch out the window as the hosts, hostesses, and local denizens

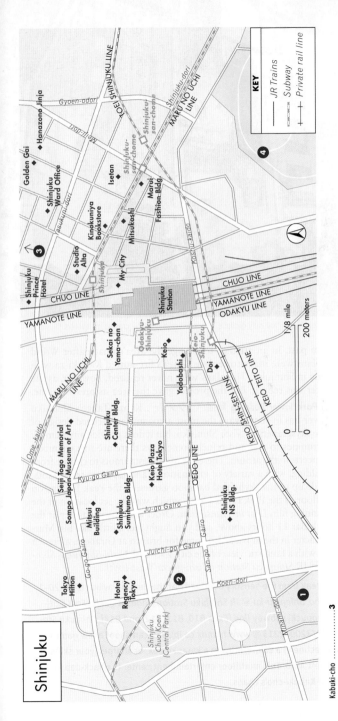

Shinjuku

Kabuki-cho **3**

Shinjuku Gyo-en
National Garden **4**

Shinjuku Park
Tower Building **1**

Tokyo Metropolitan
Government Office
(Tokyo Tocho) **2**

KEY

——— JR Trains

┄┄┄ Subway

+—+ Private rail line

Gyoen-odori

Hanazono Jinja

TOEI SHINJUKU LINE

Meiji-dori

Shinjuku-san-chome

Shinjuku-dori

MARU NO UCHI
LINE

Golden Gai

Shinjuku
Ward Office

Asukai-dori

Isetan

Marui
Fashion Bldg.

Shinjuku-
san-chome

Kinokuniya
Bookstore

Mitsukoshi

Koshu-kaido

Studio
Alta

My City

Shinjuku

Shinjuku
Prince
Hotel

CHUO LINE

CHUO LINE

Shinjuku
Station

YAMANOTE LINE

YAMANOTE LINE

ODAKYU LINE

Sekai no
Yama-chan

Odakyu-
Shinjuku

Keio

Keio-
Shinjuku

Yodobashi

Doi

KEIO SHIN-SEN LINE

KEIO TEITO LINE

1/8 mile

200 meters

MARU NO UCHI
LINE

Ome-kaido

Seiji Togo Memorial
Sompo Japan Museum of Art

Shinjuku
Center Bldg.

Chuo-dori

Kyu-go Gairo

Keio Plaza
Hotel Tokyo

OEDO LINE

Mitsui
Building

Shinjuku
Sumitomo Bldg.

Ju-go Gairo

San-go
Gairo

Shinjuku
NS Bldg.

Go-go Gairo

Juichi-go Gairo

Koen-dori

Tokyo
Hilton

Hotel
Regency
Tokyo

Shinjuku
Chuo Koen
(Central Park)

Minami-dori

0
0

Amongst the bright lights of Kabuki-cho you may glimpse Yakuza members in the crowds of revelers.

shuffle on past. In an attempt to change the area's image after World War II, plans were made to replace Ginza's fire-gutted Kabuki-za with a new one in Shinjuku. The plans were never realized, however, as the old theater was rebuilt. But the project gave the area its present name.

Shinjuku Park Tower Building 新宿パークタワー. Kenzo Tange's Shinjuku Park Tower has in some ways the most arrogant, hard-edged design of any of the skyscrapers in Nishi-Shinjuku, but it does provide any number of opportunities to rest and refuel. Some days there are free chamber-music concerts in the atrium. There are many restaurants to choose from in the building, with a variety of international and Japanese restaurants. Take a ride up to the skylighted bamboo garden of the Peak Lounge on the 41st floor of the Park Hyatt Hotel, which was the set location of the Oscar-winning film *Lost in Translation*. Order a Suntory whiskey at the New York Bar 11 floors above, and you might feel a little like Bill Murray's character in the movie. Also come for brunch at Giranole, a French brasserie with a fantastic view of the city. ⊠ *3–7–1 Nishi-Shinjuku, Shinjuku-ku* Ⓜ *JR Shinjuku Station (Nishi-guchi/West Exit).*

NEED A BREAK?

Need a break from the sensory overload? At the Humax Pavilion (⊠ *1–20–1 Kabuki-cho, Shinjuku-ku* Ⓜ *JR Shinjuku Station [Higashi-guchi/East Exit] and Marunouchi subway line [Exits B10, B11, B12, and B13], Shinjuku Station* ☎ *03/3200–2213* ⊕ *www.humax.co.jp*)**, you can shoot a few games of pool, recline in a sauna, relax in a karaoke box, or sharpen your skills at Grand Theft Auto. This multifloor entertainment center is smack-dab in the middle of Kabuki-cho's chaos.**

WORTH NOTING

Shinjuku Gyo-en National Garden 新宿御苑. This lovely 150-acre park was once the estate of the powerful Naito family of feudal lords, who were among the most trusted retainers of the Tokugawa shoguns. After World War II, the grounds were finally opened to the public. It's a perfect place for leisurely walks: paths wind past ponds and bridges, artificial hills, thoughtfully placed stone lanterns, and more than 3,000 kinds of plants, shrubs, and trees. There are different gardens in Japanese, French, and English styles, as well as a greenhouse (the nation's first, built in 1885) filled with tropical plants. ■TIP→ The best times to visit are April, when 75 different species of cherry trees—some 1,500 trees in all—are in bloom, and the first two weeks of November, during the chrysanthemum exhibition. ✉ 11 Naito-cho, Shinjuku-ku ☎ 03/3350–0151 ✉ ¥200 ⊗ Tues.–Sun. 9–4:30; also Mon. 9–4:30 in cherry-blossom season (late Mar.–early Apr.) Ⓜ Marunouchi subway line, Shinjuku Gyo-en-mae Station (Exit 1).

Tokyo Metropolitan Government Office 東京都庁 (Tokyo Tocho). Dominating the western Shinjuku skyline and built at a cost of ¥157 billion, this Kenzo Tange–designed, grandiose, city-hall complex is clearly meant to remind observers that Tokyo's annual budget is bigger than that of the average developing country. The late-20th-century complex consists of a main office building, an annex, the Metropolitan Assembly building, and a huge central courtyard, often the venue of open-air concerts and exhibitions. The building design has raised some debate: Tokyoites either love it or hate it. On a clear day, from the observation decks on the 45th floors of both towers (202 meters [663 feet] above ground), you can see all the way to Mt. Fuji and to the Boso Peninsula in Chiba Prefecture. Several other skyscrapers in the area have free observation floors—among them the Shinjuku Center Building and the Shinjuku Sumitomo Building—but city hall is the best of the lot. The Metropolitan Government Web site, incidentally, is an excellent source of information on sightseeing and current events in Tokyo. ✉ 2–8–1 Nishi-Shinjuku, Shinjuku-ku ☎ 03/5321–1111 ⊕ www.metro.tokyo.jp ✉ Free ⊗ North and south observation decks daily 9:30–5:30 Ⓜ Toei Oedo subway line, Tocho-mae Station (Exit A4).

GREATER TOKYO

The sheer size of the city and the diversity of its institutions make it impossible to fit all of Tokyo's interesting sights into neighborhoods. Plenty of worthy places—from Tokyo Disneyland to sumo stables to the old Oji district—fall outside the city's neighborhood repertoire. Yet no guide to Tokyo would be complete without them.

The 23 wards of Tokyo border four prefectures and a bay. The sheer size of the space in between those borders and the diversity of its institutions make it impossible to fit all of Tokyo's interesting sights into its neighborhoods. Plenty of worthy attractions fall outside the city's neighborhood repertoire. Yet no guide to Tokyo would be complete without them.

ORIENTATION

Since it they are so accessible, the central wards of Tokyo are often the focus for visitors. Of course, there is much more to discover in the city. The areas that lie to the west of Shibuya, south of Shinagawa, north of Ikebukuro, and east of Tokyo Station offer amusement parks, zoos, galleries, and museums.

PLANNING

For the amusement parks and zoos, visitors will want to plan to spend the entire day. The galleries and parks will only take a few hours. Be sure to plan ahead: some destinations can take over an hour to reach by train. Also keep in mind that the farther away from the city one moves the more spread out the city becomes, so plan on taking a taxi from the train station.

GETTING HERE AND AROUND

Spreading out from central Tokyo, the city spreads out like the spokes of a wheel; various railways serve areas in all cardinal directions. For Chiba Prefecture, where Tokyo Disneyland is located, take Keiyo Line, which originates at Tokyo Station. Use the same line to access Kasai Seaside Park. The Keio Line, too, starts at Shinjuku Station; Sanrio Puroland is accessible from Tama Center Station on this line.

TOP ATTRACTIONS

Fodor's Choice
★

Ryogoku 両国. Two things make this working-class Shitamachi neighborhood worth a special trip: this is the center of the world of sumo wrestling as well as the site of the extraordinary Edo-Tokyo Museum. Five minutes from Akihabara on the JR Sobu Line, Ryogoku is easy to get to, and if you've budgeted a leisurely stay in the city, it's well worth a morning's expedition.

The **Edo-Tokyo Museum** (⊠ *1–4–1 Yokoami, Sumida-ku* ☎ *03/3626–9974* ⊕ *www.edo-tokyo-museum.or.jp* ✉ *¥600; additional fees for special exhibits* ☉ *Tues.–Fri. and Sun. 9:30–5:30, Sat. 9:30–7:30*) opened in 1993, more or less coinciding with the collapse of the economic bubble that had made the project possible. Money was no object in those days; much of the large museum site is open plaza—an unthinkably lavish use of space. From the plaza the museum rises on massive pillars to the permanent exhibit areas on the fifth and sixth floors. The escalator takes you directly to the sixth floor—and back in time 300 years. You cross a replica of the Edo-period Nihombashi Bridge into a truly remarkable collection of dioramas, scale models, cutaway rooms, and even whole buildings: an intimate and convincing experience of everyday life in the capital of the Tokugawa shoguns. Equally elaborate are the fifth-floor re-creations of early modern Tokyo, the "enlightenment" of Japan's headlong embrace of the West, and the twin devastations of the Great Kanto Earthquake and World War II. If you only visit one non-art museum in Tokyo, make this it.

To get to the museum, leave Ryogoku Station by the West Exit, immediately turn right, and follow the signs. The moving sidewalk and the stairs bring you to the plaza on the third level; to request an English-speaking volunteer guide, use the entrance to the left of the stairs instead, and ask at the General Information counter in front of the first-floor Special Exhibition Gallery.

Walk straight out to the main street in front of the West Exit of Ryogoku Station, turn right, and you come almost at once to the Kokugikan (National Sumo Arena), with its distinctive copper-green roof.

If you can't attend one of the Tokyo sumo tournaments, you may want to at least pay a short visit to the **Sumo Museum** (⊠ *1–3–28 Yokoami, Sumida-ku* ☎ *03/3622–0366* ⊕ *www.sumo.or.jp* 🎫 *Free* 🕐 *Weekdays 10–4:30*), in the south wing of the arena. There are no explanations in English, but the museum's collection of sumo-related wood-block prints, paintings, and illustrated scrolls includes some outstanding examples of traditional Japanese fine art.

🕐 **Tokyo Disneyland** 東京ディズニーランド. At Tokyo Disneyland, Mickey-san and his coterie of Disney characters entertain just the way they do in the California and Florida Disney parks. When the park was built in 1983 it was much smaller than its counterparts in the United States, but the construction in 2001 of the adjacent DisneySea, with its seven "Ports of Call" with different nautical themes and rides, added more than 100 acres to this multifaceted Magic Kingdom.

There are several types of admission tickets. Most people buy the One-Day Passport (¥5,800), which gives you unlimited access to the attractions and shows at one or the other of the two parks. See the park Web site for other ticketing options. You can buy tickets in advance from any local travel agency, such as the Japan Travel Bureau (JTB).

The simplest way to get to Disneyland is by JR Keiyo Line from Tokyo Station to Maihama; the park is just a few steps from the station exit. From Nihombashi you can also take the Tozai subway line to Urayasu and walk over to the Tokyo Disneyland Bus Terminal for the 25-minute ride, which costs ¥230. ⊠ *1–1 Maihama, Urayasu* ☎ *0570/00–8632 information, 047/729–0733 guest relations* ⊕ *www.tokyodisneyresort. co.jp* 🕐 *Daily 9 am–10 pm; seasonal closings in Dec. and Jan. may vary, so check before you go.*

🕐 **Tokyo Sea Life Park** 葛西臨海水族館. The three-story cylindrical complex of this aquarium houses more than 540 species of fish and other sea creatures within three different areas: "Voyagers of the Sea" ("Maguro no Kaiyu"), with migratory species; "Seas of the World" ("Sekai no Umi"), with species from foreign waters; and the "Sea of Tokyo" ("Tokyo no Umi"), devoted to the creatures of the bay and nearby waters. To get here, take the JR Keiyo Line local train from Tokyo Station to Kasai Rinkai Koen Station; the aquarium is a 10-minute walk or so from the South Exit. ⊠ *6–2–3 Rinkai-cho, Edogawa-ku* ☎ *03/3869–5152* 🎫 *¥700* 🕐 *Thurs.–Tues. 9:30–5* Ⓜ *JR Keiyo Line, Kasai Rinkai Koen Station.*

WORTH NOTING

Sanrio Puroland サンリオピューロランド. As a theme park dedicated to the world's most famous white cat with no mouth—that would be Hello Kitty, of course—Sanrio Puroland is effectively a shrine to the concept of cuteness. An all-day passport allows for unlimited use of multiple attractions, including three theaters, a boat ride, and the Kitty Lab, where guests are allowed to experiment with what exactly is "cute." Pens, packaged snacks, and plush toys are readily available so guests don't leave empty-handed. ⊠ *1–31 Ochiai, Tama-shi* ☎ *042/339–1111* 🎫 *¥3,000– ¥4,000* ⊕ *www.puroland.co.jp* 🕐 *Weekdays 10–5, summer until 6 pm; weekends 10–8; closed Thur.* Ⓜ *Keio Line, Tama Center Station.*

WHERE TO EAT

Though Tokyoites still stubbornly resists foreign concepts in many fields, the locals have embraced outside culinary styles with gusto. While newer restaurants targeting younger diners strive for authenticity in everything from New York–style bagels to Neapolitan pizza, it is still not uncommon to see menus offering East-meets-West concoctions such as spaghetti topped with cod roe and shredded seaweed. That said, the city's best French and Italian establishments can hold their own on a global scale, with high prices to match. There is also excellent Japanese food available throughout the city, ranging from the traditional to nouveau cuisine that can be shockingly expensive.

That is not to imply that every meal in the city will drain your finances—the current rage is all about "B-class gourmet," restaurants that fill the gap between nationwide chains and fine cuisine, offering tasty Japanese and Asian food without the extra frills of tablecloths and laquerware. All department stores and most skyscrapers have at least one floor of restaurants which, while not amazing, are accessible and affordable. Street food stalls are rarer than in other parts of Asia, but are safe and cheap. ■TIP➔ **When in doubt, note that Tokyo's top-rated international hotels also have some of the city's best places to eat and drink.**

WHAT IT COSTS IN YEN				
	¢	$	$$	$$$	$$$$
AT DINNER	under ¥800	¥801–¥1,000	¥1,001–¥2,000	¥2,001–¥3,000	over ¥3,000

Prices are per person for a main course.

AKASAKA 赤坂

$$ ✕ **Ajanta** アジャンタ. In the mid-20th century, the owner of Ajanta
INDIAN came to Tokyo to study electrical engineering. He ended up changing careers and establishing what is today one of the oldest and best Indian restaurants in town. There's no decor to speak of at this restaurant which stays open until 4 am. The emphasis instead is on the variety and intricacy of South Indian cooking—and none of its dressier rivals can match Ajanta's menu for sheer depth. The curries are hot to begin with, but you can order them even hotter. Try the *masala dosa* (a savory crepe), *keema* (minced beef), or mutton curry. A small boutique in one corner sells saris and imported Indian foodstuffs. ⊠ *3–11 Niban-cho, Chiyoda-ku* ☎ *03/3264–6955* Ⓜ *Yuraku-cho subway line, Koji-machi Station (Exit 5)* ✣ *E2*.

$$$$ ✕ **Jidaiya** 時代屋. Like the Jidaiya in Roppongi, these two Akasaka
JAPANESE branches serve various prix fixe courses, including shabu-shabu, tempura, sushi, and steamed rice with seafood. The food isn't fancy, but it's delicious and filling. The rustic interior makes for a good atmosphere. ⊠ *1F Naritaya Bldg., Akasaka 3–14–3, Minato-ku* ☎ *03/3588–0489* ☉ *No lunch weekends* Ⓜ *Ginza and Marunouchi subway lines, Akasaka-mitsuke Station (Belle Vie Akasaka Exit)* ⊠ *B1 Isomura*

A Mostly Naked Free-For-All

Sumo wrestling dates back some 1,500 years. Originally a religious rite performed at shrines to entertain the harvest gods, a match may seem like a fleshy free-for-all to the casual spectator, but to the trained eye, it's a refined battle. Two wrestlers square off in a dirt ring about 15 feet in diameter and charge straight at each other in nothing but silk loincloths. There are various techniques of pushing, gripping, and throwing, but the rules are simple: except for hitting below the belt, grabbing your opponent by the hair (which would certainly upset the hairdresser who accompanies every sumo ringside), or striking with a closed fist, almost anything goes. If you're thrown down or forced out of the ring, you lose. There are no weight divisions and a runt of merely 250 pounds can find himself facing an opponent twice his size.

You must belong to one of the roughly two dozen *heya* (stables) based in Tokyo to compete. Stables are run by retired wrestlers who have purchased the right from the Japan Sumo Association. Hierarchy and formality rule in the sumo world. Youngsters recruited into the sport live in the stable dormitory, do all the community chores, and wait on their seniors. When they rise high enough in tournament rankings, they acquire their own servant-apprentices.

Most of the stables are concentrated on both sides of the Sumida-gawa near the Kokugikan. Wander this area when the wrestlers are in town (January, May, and September) and you're more than likely to see some of them on the streets, in their wood clogs and kimonos. Come 7 am–11 am, and you can peer through the doors and windows of the stables to watch

them in practice sessions. One that offers tours is the **Michinoku Stable** (✉ *1–18–7 Ryogoku*). Have a Japanese speaker complete the application form on the Web site in advance (⊕ *michinokubeya.com*) and you might be able to gain access. Another offering tours, also requiring advance reservation via the Web, is the **Kasugano Stable** (✉ *1–7–11 Ryogoku* ⊕ *www.kasuganobeya.com*).

When: Of the six Grand Sumo Tournaments (called *basho*) that take place during the year, Tokyo hosts three: in early January, mid-May, and mid-September. Matches go from early afternoon, when the novices wrestle, to the titanic clashes of the upper ranks at around 6 pm.

Where: Tournaments are held in the Kokugikan, the National Sumo Arena, in Ryogoku, a district in Sumida-ku also famed for its clothing shops and eateries that cater to sumo sizes and tastes. ✉ *1–3–28 Yokoami, Sumida-ku* ☎ *03/3623–5111* ⊕ *www.sumo.or.jp* Ⓜ *JR Sobu Line, Ryogoku Station (West Exit).*

How: The most expensive seats, closest to the ring, are tatami-carpeted loges for four people, called *sajiki*. The loges are terribly cramped and cost ¥9,200–¥11,300 per person. Cheap seats start as low as ¥3,600 for advance sales, ¥2,100 for same-day box office sales for general admission seats. For same-day box office sales you should line up an hour before the tournament. You can also get tickets through Family Mart, Circle K Sunkus, and Lawson convenience stores.

Bldg., Akasaka 5–1–4, Minato-ku ☎ *03/3224–1505* ⊕ *tokyo-jidaiya. jp/en* Ⓜ *Chiyoda subway line, Akasaka Station (Exit 1A)* ✛ *C5,* ✛ *D4.*

$$$$
JAPANESE

✕ **Kisoji** 木曽路. The specialty here is shabu-shabu: thin slices of beef cooked in boiling water at your table and dipped in sauce. Normally this is an informal, if pricey, sort of meal; after all, you do get to play with your food a bit. Kisoji, which has been serving the dish for more than 60 years, adds a dimension of posh to the experience, with all the tasteful appointments of a traditional *ryotei*—private dining rooms with tatami seating (at a 10% surcharge), elegant little rock gardens, and alcoves with flower arrangements. ✉ *3–10–4 Akasaka, Minato-ku* ☎ *03/3588–0071* Ⓜ *Ginza and Marunouchi subway lines, Akasaka-mitsuke Station (Belle Vie Akasaka Exit)* ✛ *D4.*

$$
INDIAN
★

✕ **Moti** モティ. Vegetarian dishes at Moti, especially the lentil and egg-plant curries, are very good; so is the chicken masala, cooked in butter and spices. The chefs here are recruited from India by a family member who runs a restaurant in Delhi. As its reputation for reasonably priced North Indian cuisine grew, Moti established branches in nearby Akasaka-mitsuke, Roppongi, and farther away in Yokohama. They all have the inevitable Indian friezes, copper bowls, and white elephants, but this one—popular at lunch with the office crowd from the nearby Tokyo Broadcasting System headquarters—puts the least effort into decor. ✉ *3F Kimpa Bldg., 2–14–31 Akasaka, Minato-ku* ☎ *03/3584–6649* Ⓜ *Chiyoda subway line, Akasaka Station (Exit 2)* ✛ *D4.*

$$$–$$$$
JAPANESE
☾

✕ **Ninja** 忍者. In keeping with the air of mystery you'd expect from a ninja-themed restaurant, a ninja-costumed waiter leads you through a dark underground maze to your table in an artificial cave. The menu has more than 100 choices, including some elaborate set courses that are extravagant in both proportion and price. Among the impressively presented dishes are "jack-in-the-box" seafood salad—a lacquerware box overflowing with seasonal seafood and garnished with mustard, avocado tartar, and miso paste—and the life-size bonsai-tree dessert made from cookies and green-tea ice cream. Magical tricks are performed at your table during dinner—it's slightly kitschy but entertaining nonetheless. ✉ *Akasaka Tokyu Plaza, 2–14–3 Nagata-cho, Minato-ku* ☎ *03/5157–3936* ⚐ *Reservations essential* Ⓜ *Ginza and Marunouchi subway lines, Akasaka-mitsuke Station (Tokyu Plaza Exit)* ✛ *D4.*

$$–$$$
ITALIAN
☾

✕ **Pizza Salvatore Cuomo** ピッツアサルヴァトーレクオモ. Visitors to Pizza Salvatore Cuomo instantly catch the rich aroma of the wood-burning oven that is the centerpiece of this homey, spacious restaurant. Chef Salvatore Cuomo adheres to traditional Neapolitan methods, while updating recipes with dough infused with spinach, herbs, and even squid ink. Lunch courses are filling, affordable, and quick. Though seating space is ample, expect a full house on weekdays. For dinner, classic antipasto dishes such as Caprese make for an authentic Italian meal. ✉ *Prudential Plaza Bldg., 2–13–10 Nagata-cho, Chiyoda-ku* ☎ *03/3500–5700* Ⓜ *Chiyoda and Marunouchi subway lines, Akasaka-mitsuke Station* ✛ *D4.*

$$
ITALIAN

✕ **Ristorante Carmine** カルミネ. Everybody pitched in, so the story goes, when chef Carmine Cozzolino left his job at an upscale restaurant in Aoyama and opened this unpretentious neighborhood bistro in 1987:

friends designed the logo and the interior, painted the walls (black and white), and hung the graphics, swapping their labor for meals. The five-course dinner (¥3,990–¥5,250) here could be the best deal in town. The menu changes weekly; specialties of the house include risotto primavera and Tuscan-style *filetto di pesce* (fish fillet) parmigiano. The wine list is well chosen, and the *torta al cioccolata* (chocolate cake) is a serious dessert. ⊠ *1F Nishikawa Bldg., 1–19 Saiku-cho, Shinjuku-ku* ☎ *03/3260–5066* Ⓜ *Oedo subway line, Ushigome-Kagurazaka Station (Exit 1)* ✥ *D2.*

$–$$
JAPANESE
✗ **Sawanoi** 澤乃井. The homemade udon noodles, served in a broth with seafood, vegetables, or chicken, make a perfect light meal or midnight snack. Try the *inaka* (country-style) udon, which has bonito, seaweed flakes, radish shavings, and a raw egg dropped in to cook in the hot broth. For a heartier meal, chose the *tenkama* set: hot udon and shrimp tempura with a delicate soy-based sauce. A bit run-down, Sawanoi is one of the last remaining neighborhood shops in what is now an upscale business and entertainment district. It stays open until 3 am, and a menu is available in English. ⊠ *1F Shimpo Bldg., 3–7–13 Akasaka, Minato-ku* ☎ *03/3582–2080* ▭ *No credit cards* ☉ *Closed Sun.* Ⓜ *Ginza and Marunouchi subway lines, Akasaka-mitsuke Station (Belle Vie Akasaka Exit)* ✥ *D3.*

$$$$
SUSHI
✗ **Sushi Saito** 鮨さいとう. No trip to Tokyo is complete without sampling the freshest sushi available in the world. The award-winning Sushi Saito, situated just across the street from the U.S. embassy, has only six counter seats and a discreet sign out front, but it is always fully booked. And for good reason—it has some of the best sushi in town. ⊠ *1F Jidousha kaikan Bldg., 1–9–15 Akasaka, Minato-ku* ☎ *03/3589–4412* ▵ *Reservations essential* ☉ *Closed Sun. and holidays* Ⓜ *Ginza subway line, Tameike-Sanno Station (Exit 9)* ✥ *D4.*

$$$–$$$$
CHINESE
✗ **Toh-Ka-Lin** 桃花林. Business travelers consider the Okura to be one of the best hotels in Asia. That judgment has to do with its polish, its human scale, its impeccable standards of service, and, to judge by Toh-Ka-Lin, the quality of its restaurants. The style of the cuisine here is eclectic; two stellar examples are the Peking duck and the sautéed quail wrapped in lettuce leaf. The restaurant also has a not-too-expensive mid-afternoon meal ($$) of assorted dim sum and other delicacies—and one of the most extensive wine lists in town. ⊠ *6F Hotel Okura Main Bldg., 2–10–4 Tora-no-mon, Minato-ku* ☎ *03/3505–6068* Ⓜ *Hibiya subway line, Kamiya-cho Station (Exit 4B); Ginza subway line, Tora-no-mon Station (Exit 3)* ✥ *D4.*

AOYAMA 青山

$–$$
RAMEN
✗ **Darumaya** だるまや. The classic bowl of ramen is topped with slices of pork, but Darumaya, in the fashion district of Omotesando, offers a slightly different take, topping its noodles with grilled vegetables. Vegetarians beware: the soups and sauces are not meat-free. ⊠ *1F Murayama Bldg., 5–9–5 Minami-Aoyama, Minato-ku* ☎ *03/3499–6295* ▭ *No credit cards* Ⓜ *Ginza, Chiyoda, and Hanzo-mon subway lines, Omotesando Station (Exit B1)* ✥ *B4.*

$$$
JAPANESE
✗ **Higo-no-ya** 肥後の屋. The specialty of the house is *kushi-yaki*: small servings of meat, fish, and vegetables cut into bits and grilled on

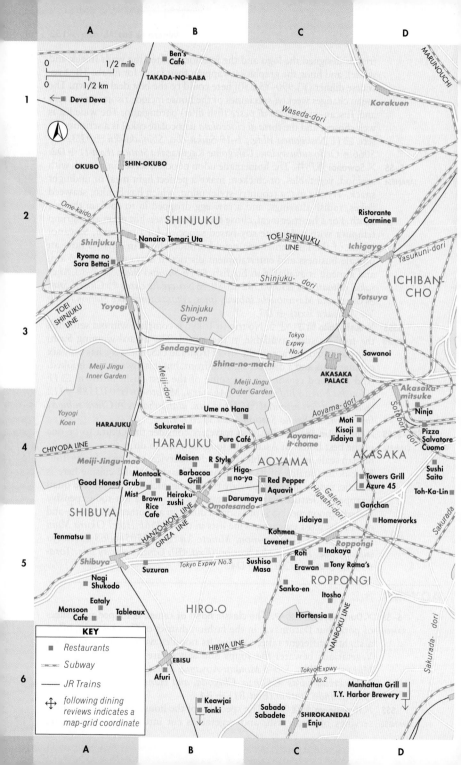

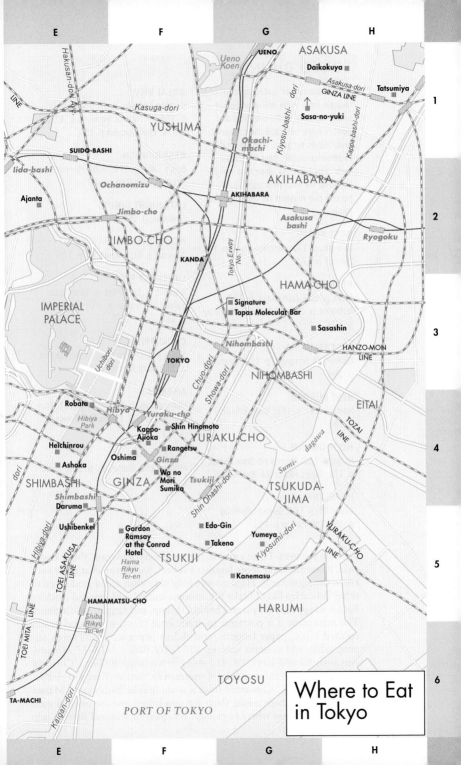

Where to Eat in Tokyo

TOKYO DINING

With hundreds of restaurants to choose from, how will you decide where to eat? Fodor's writers and editors have selected their favorite restaurants by price, cuisine, and experience in the Best Bets lists here. You can also search by neighborhood for excellent eats—just peruse our reviews on the following pages.

BEST SUSHI
Edo-gin, p. 172; Heiroku-zushi, p. 161; Takeno p. 172

BEST RAMEN
Afuri, p. 169; Darumaya, p. 153; Kohmen, p. 167; Mist, p. 161; Suzuran p. 169

BEST TEMPURA
Daikokuya Tempura, p. 157; Tenmatsu p. 169

BEST BURGER
Homeworks, p. 166; Towers Grill p. 168

MOST UNIQUE
Ninja, p. 152; Ryoma no Sora Bettei, p. 171; Tapas Molecular Bar p. 165

HOTEL DINING
Azure 45, p. 165; Gordon Ramsay, p. 159; Toh-Ka-Lin p. 153

GREAT VIEW
Gordon Ramsay, p. 159; Towers Grill, p. 168; T.Y. Harbor Brewery, p. 171; Wa no Mori Sumika p. 160

BEST BRUNCH
Ben's Café, p. 171; Good Honest Grub, p. 169; Roti p. 167

LATE NIGHT DINING
Sawanoi, p. 153; Tableaux p. 158

MOST ROMANTIC
Aquavit, p. 161; Azure 45 p. 165

LUNCH PIX FIXE
Aquavit, p. 161; Mist, p. 161; Pizza Salvatore Cuomo, p. 152; Tenmatsu p. 169

CHILD-FRIENDLY
Ninja, p. 152; Pizza Salvatore Cuomo, p. 152; Tony Roma's p. 168

AMERICAN
Homeworks, p. 166; Roti, p. 167; Tony Roma's, p. 168; T.Y. Harbor Brewery p. 171

OTHER ASIAN
Moti, p. 152; Sanko-en, p. 168; Tonki p. 163

bamboo skewers. There's nothing ceremonious or elegant about kushi-yaki; it resembles the more familiar yakitori, with somewhat more variety to the ingredients. Higo-no-ya's helpful English menu guides you to other delicacies like shiitake mushrooms stuffed with minced chicken; bacon-wrapped scallops; and bonito, shrimp, and eggplant with ginger. The restaurant is a postmodern–traditional cross, with wood beams painted black, paper lanterns, and sliding paper screens. There's tatami, table, and counter seating. ⊠ *B1 AG Bldg., 3–18–17 Minami-Aoyama, Minato-ku* ☎ *03/3423–4461* ◷ *No lunch* Ⓜ *Ginza, Chiyoda, and Hanzo-mon subway lines, Omotesando Station (Exit A4)* ⊕ *B4.*

$$–$$$
JAPANESE ✕ **Maisen** まい泉. Converted from a *sento* (public bathhouse), Maisen still has the old high ceiling (built for ventilation) and the original signs instructing bathers where to change. Bouquets of seasonal flowers help

transform the large, airy space into a pleasant dining room. Maisen's specialty is the *tonkatsu* set: tender, juicy, deep-fried pork cutlets served with a spicy sauce, shredded cabbage, miso soup, and rice. A popular alternative is the *Suruga-zen* set, a main course of fried fish served with sashimi, soup, and rice. There are no-smoking rooms upstairs. ⊠ *4–8–5 Jingu-mae, Shibuya-ku* ☎ *03/3470–0071* Ⓜ *Ginza, Chiyoda, and Hanzo-mon subway lines, Omotesando Station (Exit A2)* ✛ *B4.*

$$$ JAPANESE Fodor'sChoice ★ ✕ **Ume no Hana** 梅の花. The exclusive specialty here is tofu, prepared in more ways than you can imagine—boiled, steamed, stir-fried with minced crabmeat, served in a custard, and wrapped in thin layers around a delicate whitefish paste. Tofu is touted as the perfect high-protein, low-calorie health food; at Ume no Hana it's raised to the elegance of haute cuisine. Remove your shoes when you step up to the main room of the elegant restaurant. Latticed wood screens separate the tables, and private dining rooms with tatami seating are available. Prix fixe meals include a complimentary aperitif. ⊠ *2F Aoyama M's Tower, 2-27–18 Minami-Aoyama, Minato-ku* ☎ *03/5412–0855* Ⓜ *Ginza Line, Gaien-mae Station (Exit 1A)* ✛ *C4.*

QUICK BITES

If you're in a hurry, a visit to one branch of the MOS Burger, Freshness Burger, or First Kitchen will fit the bill. These nationwide chains offer familiar hamburgers, but they also have local variations. Yoshinoya is another popular chain, serving grilled salmon, rice, and miso soup for breakfast (until 10), and then hearty portions of rice and beef for the rest of the day.

ASAKUSA 浅草

$$ JAPANESE ✕ **Daikokuya Tempura** 大黒家天麩羅. Although tempura is available throughout the city, Asakusa prides itself on its battered, deep-fried seafood and vegetables. Daikokuya, in the center of Asakusa's historic district, is a point of pilgrimage for both locals and tourists. The menu choices are simple—*tendon* is tempura served over rice, and the tempura meal includes rice, pickled vegetables, and miso soup. Famished diners can add additional pieces of tempura for an additional fee. The light, fluffy tempura is made to order. When the line of waiting customers outside is too long, head to the shop's annex (*bekkan*) just around the corner. ⊠ *1–38–10 Asakusa, Taito-ku* ☎ *03/3844–1111* ▤ *No credit cards* ✛ *H1.*

$$ JAPANESE ✕ **Tatsumiya** たつみ屋. Here's a restaurant that's run like a formal ryotei but has the feel of a rough-cut *izakaya* (Japanese pub). Neither inaccessible nor outrageously expensive, Tatsumiya is adorned—nay, cluttered—with antique chests, braziers, clocks, lanterns, bowls, utensils, and craft work, some of it for sale. The evening meal is in the *kaiseki* style, with seven courses: tradition demands that the meal include something raw, something boiled, something vinegary, and something grilled. The kaiseki dinner is served only until 8:30, and you must reserve ahead for it. Tatsumiya also serves a light lunch, plus a variety of *nabe* (one-pot seafood and vegetable stews, prepared at your table) until 10. The pork nabe is the house specialty. ⊠ *1–33–5 Asakusa, Taito-ku*

☎ *03/3842–7373* Ⓜ *Ginza and Asakusa subway lines, Asakusa Station (Exits 1 and 3)* ✛ *H1.*

DAIKANYAMA 代官山

$$$–$$$$
ITALIAN
✕**Eataly** イータリー. The Italian luxury supermarket chain that originated in Turin has come to Tokyo. The complex, the first of its kind in Japan, is dedicated to all things Italian. In addition to shopping, there is a gelato and cake bar with outdoor seating, casual pasta and pizza restaurants open for lunch and dinner, and Guido, an elegant "slow food" dinner restaurant. ✉ *20–23 Daikanyama-cho, Shibuya-ku* ☎ *03/5784–2736* Ⓜ *Tokyu Toyoko private rail line, Daikanyama Station (Kita-guchi/North Exit)* ✛ *A5.*

$
PAN-ASIAN
✕**Monsoon Cafe** モンスーンカフェ. With several locations, Monsoon Cafe meets the demand in Tokyo for "ethnic" food—which by local definition means spicy and primarily Southeast Asian. Complementing the eclectic Pan-Asian food are rattan furniture, brass tableware from Thailand, colorful papier-mâché parrots on gilded stands, Balinese carvings, and ceiling fans. Here, at the original Monsoon, the best seats in the house are on the balcony that runs around the four sides of the atrium-style central space. Try the satay (grilled, skewered cubes of meat) platter, steamed shrimp dumplings, or *nasi goring* (Indonesian fried rice). ✉ *15–4 Hachiyama-cho, Shibuya-ku* ☎ *03/5489–3789* ⊕ *www.monsoon-cafe.jp* Ⓜ *Tokyu Toyoko private rail line, Daikanyama Station (Kita-guchi/North Exit)* ✛ *A6.*

$$$–$$$$
ECLECTIC
Fodor's Choice
★
✕**Tableaux** タブロー. The mural in the bar depicts the fall of Pompeii, the banquettes are upholstered in red leather, and the walls are papered in antique gold. Tableaux may lay on more glitz than is necessary, but the service is cordial and professional, and the food is superb. Try Zuwai-crab-and-red-shrimp spring rolls; filet mignon with creamed potatoes, seasonal vegetables, and merlot sauce; or, for dessert, the chocolate soufflé cake. The bar is open until 1:30 am. ✉ *B1 Sunroser Daikanyama Bldg., 11–6 Sarugaku-cho, Shibuya-ku* ☎ *03/5489–2201* 🎩 *Jacket and tie* ☟ *No lunch* Ⓜ *Tokyu Toyoko private rail line, Daikanyama Station (Kita-guchi/North Exit)* ✛ *A5.*

GINZA 銀座

$$$–$$$$
INDIAN
✕**Ashoka** アショカ. Since 1968, Ashoka has staked out the high ground for Indian cuisine in Tokyo—with a dining room suited to its fashionable Ginza location. The room is hushed and spacious, incense perfumes the air, the lighting is recessed, the carpets are thick, and the servers wear spiffy uniforms. The best thing to order here is the *thali,* a selection of curries, tandoori chicken, and naan served on a figured brass tray. The Goan fish curry is also excellent, as is the

> **CHECK IT OUT!**
>
> **English OK!** (⊕ *www.englishok.jp*) lists restaurants where English is spoken so people with limited or no Japanese can order food without worrying about the language barrier. Before heading out, check the Web site for maps, sample menus, and printable coupons.

The opulent décor matches Tableaux's decadent dishes.

chicken tikka: boneless chunks marinated and cooked in the tandoor. ✉ *2F Ginza Inz Bldg. 1, 3–1 Nishi Ginza, Chuo-ku* ☎ *03/3567–2377* Ⓜ *Marunouchi and Ginza subway lines, Ginza Station (Exit C9)* ✛ *E4.*

$$$$
FRENCH
✕ **Gordon Ramsay at the Conrad Hotel** ゴードン・ラムゼイ. This luxurious French restaurant in the Conrad Hotel, offers breathtaking views of the Hamarikyu Gardens and Tokyo Bay 37 floors below. There's also plenty to see inside, as the chef prepares dishes such as roasted scallops with mushroom tortellini, peas, and mint velouté with great élan in the open kitchen. Guests may even spot Ramsay himself in the kitchen during one of his frequent visits to Tokyo. ✉ *37F Conrad Tokyo, 1–9–1 Higashi-Shinbashi, Minato-ku* ☎ *03/3688–8000* ⊕ *www.gordonramsay. com* ⌂ *Reservations essential* ☾ *No lunch* Ⓜ *Toei Oedo subway line, Shiodome Station (Exit 3)* ✛ *F5.*

$$
IZAKAYA
✕ **Kanemasu** かねます. Unlike most izakaya which stay open to the wee hours of the morning, Kanemasu is open only a few hours in the evening, from 4 until around 8. There are no tables or chairs, and patrons stand around the counter while they eat and drink. So what is the attraction? The father-and-son cooking team raises izakaya fare to a new level by creating novel combinations such as *uni* (sea urchin) wrapped in strips of raw beef. The daily menu is scrawled in chalk on a blackboard, but you can always ask for *osusume* (chef's recommendation). ✉ *1–10–4 Kachidoki, Chuo-ku* ☎ *03/3531–8611* ▭ *No credit cards* ☾ *Closed Sun. and holidays* Ⓜ *Oedo subway line, Kachidoki Station (Exit A4).*

$$$$
JAPANESE
✕ **Kappo-Ajioka** 割烹 味岡. When prepared incorrectly, fugu, the highly poisonous puffer fish, is fatal, yet this doesn't stop people from trying it at this Tokyo branch of the Kansai fugu ryotei (puffer-fish restaurant).

Licensed chefs prepare the fish in every way imaginable—raw, fried, stewed—using the fresh catch flown in straight from Shimonoseki, a prime fugu-fishing region. The overall flavor is subtle and somewhat nondescript—people are drawn more to the element of danger than the taste (fatalities are rare, but a few people in Japan die each year from fugu poisoning). Try the house specialty of *suppon* (Japanese turtle) and fugu nabe, fugu sashimi, or fugu *no arayaki* (grilled head and cheeks). ■TIP➔ Reservations must be made two days in advance to order fugu. ✉ *6F New Comparu Bldg., 7–7–12 Ginza, Chuo-ku* ☎ *03/3574–8844* Ⓜ *Ginza, Hibiya, and Marunouchi subway lines, Ginza Station (Exit A5)* ✣ *F4.*

$$$$
KAISEKI

✕**Oshima** 大志満. The draw at Oshima is the *Kaga ryori* cooking of Kanazawa, a small city on the Sea of Japan known as "Little Kyoto" for its rich craft traditions. Waitresses dress in kimonos of Kanazawa's famous Yuzen dyed silk; Kutani porcelain and Wajima lacquerware grace the exquisite table settings. Seafood at Oshima is superb, but don't ignore the specialty of the house: a stew of duck and potatoes called *jibuni*. Kaiseki full-course meals are pricey, but there's a reasonable lunchtime set menu for ¥2,625. ✉ *9F Ginza Core Bldg., 5–8–20 Ginza, Chuo-ku* ☎ *03/3574–8080* Ⓜ *Ginza, Hibiya, and Marunouchi subway lines, Ginza Station (Exit A5)* ✣ *F4.*

$$$–$$$$
JAPANESE

✕**Rangetsu** らん月. Japan enjoys a special reputation for its lovingly raised, tender, marbled domestic beef. Try it, if your budget will bear the weight, at Rangetsu, in the form of this elegant Ginza restaurant's signature shabu-shabu or sukiyaki course. Call ahead to reserve a private alcove, where you can cook for yourself, or have a kaiseki meal brought to your table by kimono-clad attendants. A lunch course is available for ¥1,800 on weekends. Rangetsu is a block from the Ginza 4-chome crossing, opposite the Matsuya Department Store. ✉ *3–5–8 Ginza, Chuo-ku* ☎ *03/3567–1021* Ⓜ *Marunouchi and Ginza subway lines, Ginza Station (Exits A9 and A10)* ✣ *F4.*

$$$$
JAPANESE

✕**Wa no Mori Sumika** 和の杜すみか. A short walk from the heart of Ginza, this respite from the haute cuisine of Ginza specializes in vegetables shipped directly from farms around Japan, reflecting a recent movement in Japan toward healthier, safer eating. There are private dining rooms with tatami seating, and sunken counter seats at the window, affording a beautiful night view of lights of Ginza. The seasonal vegetables and fresh fish course (¥8,400) is like taking a tour of Japan, with the best and freshest produce from around the country appearing on your plate. ✉ *8F Duplex Bldg., 5–13–19 Ginza, Chuo-ku* ☎ *03/3547–8383* ✍ *Reservations essential* Ⓜ *Marunouchi and Ginza subway lines, Ginza Station (Exits A9 and A10)* ✣ *F4.*

$$
JAPANESE

✕**Yumeya** 夢や. Tsukishima ("moon island") is a small man-made island a stone's throw from the upscale Ginza district, which takes its name from its crescent-moon shape and is the birthplace of *monjayaki*. The watery batter is mixed with shredded cabbage and other ingredients, fried on a griddle built into the table, and eaten directly from the grill with metal spatulas. The main street in Tsukishima is filled with monjayaki establishments, and one of the best is Yumeya, which can be identified by the line of waiting patrons often outside. It can be a bit tricky to make monjayaki yourself—you need to form a ring of dry ingredients on the grill and pour the batter into the middle. The servers can also make it for you at your table. ⊠ *3–18–4 Tsukishima, Chuo-ku* ☎ *03/3536–7870* ⊟ *No credit cards* ⊗ *Closed Mon. No lunch weekdays* Ⓜ *Oedo and Yuraku-cho subway lines, Tsukishima Station (Exit 7).*

HARAJUKU 原宿

$$$$
SCANDINAVIAN

✕ **Aquavit** アクアビット. One of the handful of authentic Swedish restaurants in Tokyo, Aquavit offers a reasonably priced prix fixe dinner (and lunch). A good appetizer to try is herring sampler, which includes pickled herring and sweet varieties that change seasonally. Good main dish choices include smoked trout with celery puree, white beech mushrooms, and apple-horseradish sauce or the venison loin served with cured ham, potato dumplings, and lingonberry sauce. Got room for dessert? Don't pass up the scrumptious Swedish pancakes, which are served with ginger confit, fresh cream, and raspberries. Everything is served in a romantic dining room with ultra-modern design and furniture by Friz Hansen of Denmark. ⊠ *1F Shimizu Bldg., 2–5–8 Kita-Aoyama, Minato-ku* ☎ *03/5413–3300* ⊕ *www.aquavit-japan.com* Ⓜ *Ginza subway line, Gaien-mae Station (Exit 1B)* ✛ *B4.*

$$$$
BRAZILIAN

✕ **Barbacoa Grill** バルバッコアグリル. Carnivores flock here for the great-value all-you-can-eat Brazilian grilled chicken and barbecued beef, which the efficient waiters will keep bringing to your table on skewers until you tell them to stop. Those with lighter appetites can choose the less-expensive salad buffet and *feijoada* (pork stew with black beans); both are bargains. Barbacoa has hardwood floors, lithographs of bull motifs, warm lighting, salmon-color tablecloths, and roomy seating. This popular spot is just off Omotesando-dori on the Harajuku 2-chome shopping street (on the north side of Omotesando-dori), about 50 yards down on the left. ⊠ *4–3–24 Jingu-mae, Shibuya-ku* ☎ *03/3796–0571* Ⓜ *Ginza, Chiyoda, and Hanzo-mon subway lines, Omotesando Station (Exit A2)* ✛ *B4.*

$$
SUSHI

✕ **Heiroku-zushi** 平禄寿司. Ordinarily, a meal of sushi is a costly indulgence. The rock-bottom alternative is a *kaiten-zushi,* where sushi is literally served assembly-line style. The chefs inside the circular counter maintain a constant supply on the revolving belt on plates color-coded for price; just choose whatever takes your fancy as dishes pass by. Heiroku-zushi is a bustling, cheerful example of the genre, with fresh fish and no pretensions at all to decor. When you're done, the server counts up your plates and calculates your bill (¥126 for staples like tuna and squid to ¥367 for delicacies like eel and salmon roe). ⊠ *5–8–5 Jingu-mae, Shibuya-ku* ☎ *03/3498–3968* ⊟ *No credit cards* Ⓜ *Ginza, Chiyoda, and Hanzo-mon subway lines, Omotesando Station (Exit A1)* ✛ *B4.*

$$–$$$
RAMEN

✕ **Mist** ミスト. Exercising your plastic in Tokyo's Omotesando Hills shopping complex can be tiring. Refuel at Mist, a 21-seat "noodle studio" inside the Tadao Ando–designed complex. The look is minimalist-chic, with counter seats, a stainless-steel kitchen, and burgundy banquettes. The food, as lovely as the space, includes homemade ramen—springy, firm, and served with a savory broth. The menu boasts two styles of

3

ramen and three optional toppings. At lunch, gourmet ramen and one beverage will set you back at least ¥1,700. ⊠ *4–12–10 Jingu-mae, Shibuya-ku* ☎ *03/5410–1368* Ⓜ *Ginza, Chiyoda, and Hanzo-mon subway lines, Omotesando Station (Exit A2)* ✛ *B4.*

$–$$
CAFÉ
✕ **Montoak** モントーク. If you're into people-watching, then this two-story café on Omotesando street in the heart of one of the most fashion-conscious areas of Tokyo is the perfect place to relax on an afternoon. Order one of the scrumptious homemade tarts or cakes and a coffee, and watch the trendiest Tokyoites stroll by the full-length windows. ⊠ *6–1–9 Jingu-mae, Shibuya-ku* ☎ *03/5468–5928* Ⓜ *Ginza, Chiyoda, and Hanzo-mon subway lines, Omotesando Station (Exit A1); Chiyoda subway line, Meiji-Jingu-mae (Harajuku) Station (Exit 5)* ✛ *B4.*

$$
FRENCH
✕ **Red Pepper** レッドペッパー. This cozy bistro is a short walk down a narrow alley from Omotesando Crossing, the trendy shopping district. The atmosphere is homey, and guests squeeze into tiny antique school chairs and desks topped with candles. The cuisine is constantly changing, and most dinners ignore the printed menu in favor of the daily recommendations chalked on blackboards (mostly in Japanese) propped up here and there. You might find dishes such as button mushrooms grilled in garlic and olive oil, or porcini-and-cream-sauce fettuccine. ⊠ *1F Shimizu Bldg., 3–5–25 Kita-Aoyama, Shibuya-ku* ☎ *03/3478–1264* Ⓜ *Ginza, Chiyoda, and Hanzo-mon subway lines, Omotesando Station (Exit A3)* ✛ *B4.*

¢–$
JAPANESE
✕ **R Style** アールスタイル. Even in some of the swankiest restaurants, Japanese *wagashi* (sweets) aren't up to par. To sample authentic hand-made wagashi while sipping green tea, head to this café. The main ingredients in wagashi are adzuki beans, rice, and other grains sweetened slightly by sugarcane—making these treats a fairly healthful dessert. The intricate morsels of edible art are almost too perfectly presented to eat—almost, but not quite. Try the *konomi* (rice dumpling with adzuki conserve) or *koyomi* (bracken dumpling with soy custard) set. ⊠ *3F Omotesando Hills Main Bldg., 4–12–10 Jingu-mae, Shibuya-ku* ☎ *03/3423–1155* Ⓜ *Ginza, Chiyoda, and Hanzo-mon subway lines, Omotesando Station (Exit A2); Chiyoda subway line, Meiji-Jingu-mae (Harajuku) Station (Exit 5)* ✛ *B4.*

$$–$$$
JAPANESE
✕ **Sakuratei** さくら亭. Tucked away between two art galleries that feature works by young Japanese artists, Sakuratei defies other conventions as well: eating here doesn't always mean you don't have to cook. At this do-it-yourself *okonomiyaki* (a kind of pancake made with egg, meat, and vegetables) restaurant, you choose ingredients and cook them on the *teppan* (grill). Okonomiyaki is generally easy to make, but flipping the pancake to cook the other side can be challenging—potentially messy but still fun. Fortunately, you're not expected to do the dishes. Okonomiyaki literally means "as you like it," so experiment with your own recipe or try the house special, *sakurayaki* (with pork, squid, and onions), or *monjayaki* (a watered-down variation of okonomiyaki from the Kanto region). ⊠ *3–20–1 Jingu-mae, Shibuya-ku* ☎ *03/3479–0039* Ⓜ *Chiyoda subway line, Meiji-Jingu-mae (Harajuku) Station (Exit 5)* ✛ *B4.*

MEGURO 目黒

$$ ✕**Keawjai** ゲウチャイ. Blink and you might miss the faded sign of this
THAI little basement restaurant a minute's walk from Meguro Station. Keaw-
★ jai is one of the few places in Tokyo to specialize in the subtle complexi-
ties of Royal Thai cuisine, and despite its size—only eight tables and
four banquettes—it serves a remarkable range of dishes in different
regional styles. The spicy beef salad is excellent (and *really* spicy), as
are the baked rice and crabmeat served in a whole pineapple, and the
red-curry chicken in coconut milk with cashews. The service is friendly
and unhurried. There is also a branch in Shinjuku. ⊠ *B1 Meguro Kowa
Bldg., 2–14–9 Kami Osaki, Meguro-ku* ☏ *03/5420–7727* Ⓜ *JR Yaman-
ote and Namboku subway lines, Meguro Station (Higashi-guchi/East
Exit)* ✛ *B5.*

$–$$ ✕**Tonki** とんき. Meguro, a neighborhood distinguished for almost noth-
JAPANESE ing else culinary, has arguably the best tonkatsu restaurant in Tokyo. It's
★ a family joint, with Formica-top tables and a server who comes around
to take your order while you wait the requisite 10 minutes in line. And
people do wait in line, every night until the place closes at 10:45. Tonki
is a success that never went conglomerate or added frills to what it does
best: deep-fried pork cutlets, soup, raw-cabbage salad, rice, pickles, and
tea. That's the standard course, and almost everybody orders it, with
good reason. ⊠ *1–1–2 Shimo-Meguro, Meguro-ku* ☏ *03/3491–9928*
🕙 *Closed Tues. and 3rd Mon. of month* Ⓜ *JR Yamanote and Namboku
subway lines, Meguro Station (Nishi-guchi/West Exit)* ✛ *B5.*

NIHOMBASHI 日本橋

$$ ✕**Sasashin** 笹新. Like most izakaya, Sasashin spurns the notion of decor:
IZAKAYA there's a counter laden with platters of the evening's fare, a clutter of
rough wooden tables, and not much else. It's noisy, smoky, crowded—
and great fun. Like izakaya fare in general, the food is best described
as professional home cooking, and is meant mainly as ballast for the
earnest consumption of beer and sake. Try the sashimi, the grilled fish,
or the fried tofu; you really can't go wrong by just pointing your finger
at anything on the counter that takes your fancy. Unlike some iza-
kaya that stay open into the wee hours, this one winds down around
10:30. ⊠ *2–20–3 Nihombashi-Ningyocho, Chuo-ku* ☏ *03/3668–2456*
🍴 *Reservations not accepted* 🚫 *No credit cards* 🕙 *Closed Sun. and
3rd Sat. of month. No lunch* Ⓜ *Hanzo-mon subway line, Suitengu-mae
Station (Exit 7); Hibiya and Asakusa subway lines, Ningyocho Station
(Exits A1 and A3)* ✛ *G3.*

$$$$ ✕**Signature** シグネチャー. This elegant, award-winning French restau-
FRENCH rant on the 37th floor of the Mandarin Oriental Hotel offers wonderful
views of the Tokyo skyline as well an open kitchen where diners can
see the masterful chef Olivier Rodriguez and his staff at work. The prix
fixe lunch menu offers dishes that blend French and Japanese influences,
such as fillet of sole dusted with nori (dried seaweed). The dinner menu
includes inspired creations such as roasted veal rack with pumpkin
gnocchi and espresso-flavored gravy. A sommelier is on hand, and the
wine list includes biodynamic and organic offerings. ⊠ *37F Mandarin*

CLOSE UP

What's a Vegetarian to Do?

Tokyo has had a reputation for being a difficult place for vegetarians, but more and more Japanese are opting to go vegetarian, resulting in a rise in the number of truly vegetarian restaurants. The city's numerous Indian eateries are a safe bet, as are the handful of restaurants (such as Sasa-no-yuki) that specialize in *shojin ryori*, traditional Zen vegetarian food that emphasizes natural flavors and fresh ingredients without using heavy spices or rich sauces.

Take note that a dish may be described as meat-free even if it contains fish, shrimp, or chicken. And one should assume that salads, pastas, and soups in nonvegetarian restaurants are garnished with ham or bacon.

✕ **Brown Rice Café** ブラウンライス カフェ($$$). Tucked inside a Neal's Yard Remedies store, this café has just 10 tables and closes by 9 pm. But, if you're shopping in Harajuku, it's a great place to stop for a tempeh burger or stuffed tofu pouch. ⊠ *5–1–17 Jingu-mae, Shibuya-ku* ☎ *03/5778–5416* ⊕ *www.brown.co.jp* ⊟ *No credit cards* Ⓜ *Ginza and Hanzo-mon subway lines, Omotesando Station (Exit A1)* ⊹ *B4.*

✕ **Deva Deva Café** デヴァデヴァカフェ($). A short walk from picturesque Inokashira Park, Deva Deva Cafe is an organic oasis. Don't be surprised to see pizza, burgers, and grilled chicken on the menu of this vegan restaurant. The pizza is made with soy milk cheese; the burgers are meat-free, made with chickpeas, veggies, and herbs; and the chicken is made from soy protein. ⊠ *2–15–26 Kichijoji Hon-cho, Musashino City* ☎ *042/221 6220* ⊕ *www.devadevacafe.com* ⊟ *No credit cards* Ⓜ *JR Chuo Line, Kichijoji Station (North Exit)*

✕ **Itosho** いと正 ($$$$). At this Zen restaurant, food arrives in a procession of 13 tiny dishes, each selected according to season, texture, and color. Dinner costs between ¥8,400 and ¥10,500, and reservations must be made at least two days in advance. ⊠ *3–4–7 Azabu Juban, Minato-ku* ☎ *03/3454–6538* ⊴ *Reservations essential* ⊟ *No credit cards* Ⓜ *Namboku and Oedo subway lines, Azabu Juban Station (Exit 1)* ⊹ *C5.*

✕ **Nagi Shokudo** なぎ食堂 ($). This small restaurant hidden away on a small side street a short walk from Shibuya Station has mismatched chairs and tables and a selection of books and magazines you can browse through over a vegan meal. The ¥1,000 prix fixe lunch includes a choice of three dishes, which change daily, rice, miso soup, and a drink. In the evening, this is a great place to enjoy a light, guilt-free dinner in an arty atmosphere. ⊠ *15–10 Uguisudani-cho, Shibuya-ku* ☎ *050/1043–7751* ⊟ *No credit cards* ⊗ *Closed Sun. and holidays* Ⓜ *JR Yamanote Line, Shibuya Station (South Exit)* ⊹ *A5.*

✕ **Pure Café** ピュアカフェ ($$$). Stop along a backstreet in the upscale fashion hub of Omotesando for a daily changing menu of nutritious fare for breakfast, lunch, and dinner. ⊠ *5–5–21 Minami-Aoyama, Minato-ku* ☎ *03/5466–2611* ⊟ *No credit cards* Ⓜ *Ginza and Hanzo-mon subway lines, Omotesando Station (Exit B3)* ⊹ *B4.*

If you plan on staying in town long term, check out **Alishan** 阿里山 (⊕ *www.alishan-organic-center.com*), a vegetarian mail-order specialist.

Oriental Tokyo, 2–1–1 Nihonbashi, Chuo-ku ☎ *03/3270–8188* ⊕ *www. mandarinoriental.com/tokyo/dining/signature* ◿ *Reservations essential* Ⓜ *Ginza subway lines, Mitsukoshi-mae Station (Exit A7)* ✦ *G3.*

$$$$

JAPANESE

✕ **Tapas Molecular Bar** タパス モラキュラーバー. This award-wining restaurant occupies a mysterious place between a traditional sushi counter, a tapas bar, a science lab, and a magic show. "Chief Culinary Engineer" Jeff Ramsey, a former sushi chef, dazzles dinners with a live performance in which he creates more than 15 courses that surprise and delight. Nothing on the seasonally changing menu is what it seems, including sweet lemon slices, and the Emperor's New Mojito, an "invisible" cocktail. There are only eight seats, and seatings are at 6 and 8:30 only, so reserve as early as possible. ✉ *38F Mandarin Oriental, 2–1–1 Nihonbashi, Chuo-ku* ☎ *03/3270–8188* ⊕ *www.mandarinoriental.com/ tokyo/dining/molecular* ◿ *Reservations essential* ◷ *No lunch* Ⓜ *Ginza subway lines, Mitsukoshi-mae Station (Exit A7)* ✦ *G2.*

ROPPONGI 六本木

$$$$

FRENCH

✕ **Azure 45** アジュール フォーティーファイブ. French restaurants in Japan often focus on famous beef and poultry dishes, ignoring the fresh seafood and vegetables that are plentiful though out the country. Executive sous chef Kiyonari Araki amends this oversight at this restaurant in the Ritz-Carlton specializing in seafood. Prix fixe lunch courses offer a choice of three, four, or five dishes from a monthly changing menu. For dinner there is a "chef's tasting" menu, which is paired with wine selected by the hotel's sommelier. ✉ *Tokyo Midtown, 9–7–1 Akasaka, Minato-ku* ☎ *01/20798–688* Ⓜ *Hibiya subway line, Roppongi Station (Exit 4A); Toei Oedo Line, Roppongi Station (Exit 7)* ✦ *D4.*

$$–$$$

THAI

✕ **Erawan** エラワン. Window tables at this sprawling Thai "brasserie" on the top floor of a popular Roppongi vertical mall afford a wonderful view of the Tokyo skyline, including Tokyo Tower, at night. Black-painted wood floors, ceiling fans, Thai antiques, and rattan chairs establish the mood, and the space is nicely broken up into large and small dining areas and private rooms. The service is cheerful and professional. Specialties of the house include deep-fried prawn and crabmeat cakes, spicy roast-beef salad, sirloin tips with mango sauce, and a terrific dish of stir-fried lobster meat with cashews. For window seating, it's best to reserve ahead. ✉ *13F Roi Bldg., 5–5–1 Roppongi, Minato-ku* ☎ *03/3404–5741* Ⓜ *Hibiya subway line, Roppongi Station (Exit 3)* ✦ *C5.*

$$

JAPANESE

Fodor'sChoice

★

✕ **Ganchan** がんちゃん. The Japanese expect their yakitori joints—restaurants that specialize in bits of charcoal-broiled chicken and vegetables—to be just like Ganchan: smoky, noisy, and cluttered. The counter here seats barely 15, and you have to squeeze to get to the chairs in back. Festival masks, paper kites and lanterns, and greeting cards from celebrity patrons adorn the walls. The cooks yell at each other, fan the grill, and serve up enormous schooners of beer. Try the *tsukune* (balls of minced chicken) and the fresh asparagus wrapped in bacon. The place stays open until 1:30 am (midnight on Sunday). ✉ *6–8–23 Roppongi, Minato-ku* ☎ *03/3478–0092* ◷ *No lunch* Ⓜ *Hibiya subway line, Roppongi Station (Exit 1A)* ✦ *D4.*

Get a quintessential robatayaki experience with the delectable grilled dishes at Inayaka.

$–$$ ✕ **Homeworks** ホームワークス. Every so often, even on alien shores,
AMERICAN you've got to have a burger. When the urge strikes, the Swiss-and-bacon
special at Homeworks is an incomparably better choice than anything
you can get at one of the global chains. Hamburgers come in three
sizes on white or wheat buns, with a variety of toppings. There are also
hot teriyaki chicken sandwiches, pastrami sandwiches, and vegetarian
options like a soybean veggie burger or a tofu sandwich. Desserts, alas,
are so-so. With its hardwood banquettes and French doors open to the
street in good weather, Homeworks is a pleasant place to linger over
lunch. There's also a branch in Hiro-o. ⊠ *1F Vesta Bldg., 1–5–8 Azabu
Juban, Minato-ku* ☎ *03/3405–9884* Ⓜ *Namboku and Oedo subway
lines, Azabu Juban Station (Exit 4)* ✛ *D5.*

$$$$ ✕ **Hortensia** オルタシア. French restaurants in Tokyo tend to offer little
FRENCH in terms of variety or customer choice. This restaurant in trendy Azabu
Juban rectifies that situation by offering a prix fixe lunch which allow
dinners to choose four dishes, even if it is a quartet of mains or four
desserts. For dinner, the varieté meal offers eight courses, with each
course's main ingredient meticulously prepared in two or three ways,
such as a lobster claw served with mango confit and lobster meat paired
with caviar. The sommelier Kazuto Chiba spent years researching in
Napa Valley, and the wine list includes new entries from California,
Oregon, and Washington in addition to old French standards. ⊠ *B1F
NS Azabu Juban, 3–6–2 Azabu Juban, Minato-Ku* ☎ *03/5419–8455*
⊕ *www.lahortensia.com/en* ✛ *C5.*

$$$ ✕ **Inakaya** 田舎屋. The style here is *robatayaki*, a dining experience that
JAPANESE segues into pure theater. Inside a large U-shape counter, two cooks in
Fodor's Choice traditional garb sit on cushions behind a grill, with a cornucopia of
★

food spread out in front of them: fresh vegetables, seafood, skewers of beef and chicken. You point to what you want, and your server shouts out the order. The cook bellows back your order, plucks your selection up out of the pit, prepares it, and hands it across on an 8-foot wooden paddle. Inakaya is open from 5 pm to 5 am, and fills up fast after 7. If you can't get a seat here, there is now another branch on the other side of Roppongi Crossing. ⊠ *1F Reine Bldg., 5–3–4 Roppongi, Minato-ku* ☎ *03/3408–5040* ⌨ *Reservations not accepted* ⊘ *No lunch* Ⓜ *Hibiya subway line, Roppongi Station (Exit 3)* ✛ *C5.*

$$$$
JAPANESE

✗ **Jidaiya** 時代屋. Entering Jidaiya, which loosely translates as "period house," is like stepping into an Edo-period tavern. Most locals order from ornately drawn strips of paper that hang from high on the walls. If you are not sure what to order, leave it up to the chef (order the omakase) and you will be served a selection of shabu-shabu, tempura, sushi, rice dishes, and grilled fish. The food's not so fancy, but it's filling and delicious. ⊠ *B1 Yuni Roppongi Bldg., 7–15–17 Roppongi, Minato-ku* ☎ *03/3403–3563* Ⓜ *Hibiya subway line, Roppongi Station (Exit 2)* ✛ *C5,* ✛ *D4.*

¢–$
RAMEN

✗ **Kohmen** 光麺. This always-busy ramen shop near Roppongi Crossing sets itself appear with a polished stainless-steel-and-glass interior, but that does not mean it is any less authentic or tasty. Kohmen is known for its *tonkotsu* (pork bone) soup, and yelling "tonkotsu" over the counter will get you a basic bowl of soup with noodles topped with a slice of barbecued pork. Adding *zen bu no say* (with the works), will get you a side dish of hard-boiled egg, vegetables, dried seaweed, and other goodies you dump over your soup before eating. Kohmen is open until 6 am, making it the perfect place to stop after a night in Roppongi's entertainment district. ⊠ *7–14–3 Roppongi, Minato-ku* ☎ *03/6406–4565* ▭ *No credit cards* ✛ *B2.*

$$$$
ECLECTIC

✗ **Lovenet** ラブネット. Within the 33 private themed rooms of Lovenet, you can dine and enjoy Japan's national pastime: karaoke. Go not just for the food but the entire experience. Request the intimate Morocco suite, the colorful Candy room, or the Aqua suite, where you can eat, drink, and take a dip in the hot tub while belting out '80s hits. The Italian-trained chefs prepare Mediterranean and Japanese cuisine in the form of light snacks and full-course meals, which you order via a phone intercom system. Try the duck confit with wine sauce or a salmon-roe rice bowl. The bill is calculated based on what room you use, how long you stay, and what you order. Note that there's a two-person minimum for each room. ⊠ *3F–4F Hotel Ibis, 7–14–4 Roppongi, Minato-ku* ☎ *03/5771–5511* ⊕ *www.lovenet-jp.com* ⌨ *Reservations essential* Ⓜ *Oedo and Hibiya subway lines, Roppongi Station (Exit 4A)* ✛ *C5.*

$$–$$$
AMERICAN

✗ **Roti** ロティ. Billing itself a "modern American brasserie," Roti takes pride in the creative use of simple, fresh ingredients, and a fusing of Eastern and Western elements. For an appetizer, try the falafel and char-grilled vegetables on flat bread, or shoestring french fries with white truffle oil and parmigiano-reggiano cheese. Don't neglect dessert: the espresso-chocolate tart is to die for. Roti stocks some 60 Californian wines, microbrewed ales from the famed Rogue brewery in Oregon, and Cuban cigars. There is also a fantastic weekend brunch menu. The best seats in the house are in fact outside at one of the dozen tables around the big glass pyramid on the terrace. ⊠ *1F Piramide Bldg., 6–6–9 Roppongi, Minato-ku* ☎ *03/5785–3671* Ⓜ *Hibiya subway line, Roppongi Station (Exit 1A); Toei Oedo Line, Roppongi Station (Exit 1A)* ✛ *C5.*

$$–$$$
KOREAN

✕ **Sanko-en** 三幸園. With the embassy of South Korea a few blocks away, Sanko-en stands out in a neighborhood thick with Korean-barbecue joints. Customers—not just from the neighborhood but from nearby trendy Roppongi as well—line up at all hours (from 11:30 am to midnight) to get in. Korean barbecue is a smoky affair; you cook your own food, usually thin slices of beef and vegetables, on a gas grill at your table. The *karubi* (brisket), which is accompanied by a great salad, is the best choice on the menu. If you like kimchi (spicy pickled cabbage), Sanko-en's is considered by some to be the best in town. ⊠ *1–8–7 Azabu Juban, Minato-ku* ☎ *03/3585–6306* ⧄ *Reservations not accepted* ☉ *Closed Wed.* Ⓜ *Namboku and Oedo subway lines, Azabu Juban Station (Exit 4)* ✛ *C5.*

$$$$
SUSHI

✕ **Sushiso Masa** すし匠 まさ. If you are lucky enough to get a reservation for a few of the seven counter seats and willing to pay top dollar for it, Sushiso Masa offers a sublime sushi experience. The interior is unpretentious, and the presentation gorgeous as it is at any sushi shop. What really sets this apart is cuts of fish of the highest quality available and garnishes of rare ingredients such as *zha cai* (pickled stem of the mustard plant). ⊠ *B1F Seven Nishi-Azabu Bldg., 4–1–15 Nishi-Azabu, Minato-ku* ☎ *03/3499–9178* ⧄ *Reservations essential* ☉ *Closed Mon. No lunch* Ⓜ *Hibiya subway line, Roppongi Station (Exit 1B); Toei Oedo Line, Roppongi Station (Exit 1A)* ✛ *C5.*

$–$$
AMERICAN
☾

✕ **Tony Roma's** トニーローマ. If your kids flee in terror when a plate of sushi is placed in front of them, you may want to take them for a taste of home at this American chain world famous for its barbecued ribs. Started in Miami, Florida, in the 1970s, this casual place—one of five in Tokyo—serves kid-size portions of ribs, burgers, chicken strips, and fried shrimp. ⊠ *5–4–20 Roppongi, Minato-ku* ☎ *03/3408–2748* ⊕ *www.tonyromas.jp/en* ☉ *No lunch Sun. and holidays* Ⓜ *Hibiya subway line, Roppongi Station (Exit 3); Toei Oedo Line, Roppongi Station (Exit 3)* ✛ *C5.*

$$$$
AMERICAN

✕ **Towers Grill** タワーズグリル. While Tokyo obviously offers the best Japanese food in the world, visitors may want to take a break and visit an American-style grill. Towers Grill on the 45th floor of the Ritz-Carlton Hotel provides meals made from high-quality ingredients from around Japan including A-4-rank Tankaku beef and abalone from Sanriku. There's a great view which includes the Tokyo Sky Tree and Tokyo Tower, from which the eatery takes its name. A prix fixe lunch includes a choice of three items from a seasonally changing menu, and there are dinners with three, four, and five courses. Brunch is also available weekends and holidays. Visitors who plan to return to Tokyo may want to join the "Knife for Life" club, which provides a Laguiole steak knife engraved with the user's name. ⊠ *Tokyo Midtown, 9–7–1 Akasaka, Minato-ku* ☎ *01/2079–8688* Ⓜ *Hibiya subway line, Roppongi Station (Exit 4A); Toei Oedo Line, Roppongi Station (Exit 7)* ✛ *D4.*

SHIBUYA 原宿

$ ✕ **Afuri** 阿夫利/あふり. Ramen is the quintessential Japanese fast food
RAMEN in a bowl: thick Chinese noodles in a savory broth, with soybean paste,
diced leeks, grilled *chashu* (pork loin), and spinach. No neighborhood
in Tokyo is without at least one ramen joint—often serving only at a
counter. In Ebisu, the hands-down favorite is Afuri. Using the picture
menu, choose your ramen by inserting coins into a ticket machine, find
a seat, and hand over your ticket to the cooks who will prepare your
ramen then and there. There's limited seating, and at lunch and dinner,
the line of waiting customers extends down the street. ⊠ *1–1–7 Ebisu,*
Shibuya-ku ☎ *03/5795–0750* ▭ *No credit cards* ◷ *Closed Wed.* Ⓜ *JR*
Yamanote Line (Nishi-guchi/West Exit) and Hibiya subway line (Exit
1), Ebisu Station ✛ *B5.*

$$ ✕ **Good Honest Grub** グッドオネストグラブ. This airy, laid-back restaurant
CAFÉ has the feel of enjoying a home-cooked meal at a friend's house. Brunch
is served 10:30–4:30 on weekends and national holidays, and includes
offerings such as Greek omelets, wraps, and perhaps the best eggs Bene-
dict in town. Everything comes from the restaurant's own organic farm.
⊠ *2–20–8 Higashi, Shibuya-ku* ☎ *03/3797–9877* ✎ *Reservations not*
accepted for brunch ▭ *No credit cards* Ⓜ *JR Yamanote, Shibuya Sta-*
tion (South Exit) ✛ *B4.*

$–$$ ✕ **Suzuran** すずらん. It's said that you can judge the quality of a Tokyo
RAMEN ramen restaurant by the number of people lined up out front. If that's
true, Suzuran, a short walk from Shibuya Station, must be one of the
best in town, as people begin lining up before the restaurant opens its
doors at 11:30. Expect excellent ramen, as well as *tsukemen* (wide
noodles in a light, vinegary sauce) topped with boiled fish. Don't be
afraid of the long line outside, it moves quickly and the ramen is worth
the wait. ⊠ *3–7–5 Shibuya, Shibuya-ku* ☎ *03/3499–0434* ▭ *No credit*
cards Ⓜ *JR Yamanote, Shibuya Station (South Exit)* ✛ *B5.*

$$–$$$ ✕ **Tenmatsu** 天松. The best seats in the house at Tenmatsu, as in any
JAPANESE *tempura-ya,* are at the immaculate wooden counter, where your tidbits
★ of choice are taken straight from the oil and served immediately. You
also get to watch the chef in action. Tenmatsu's brand of good-natured
professional hospitality adds to the enjoyment of the meal. Here you can
rely on a set menu or order à la carte tempura delicacies like lotus root,
shrimp, *unagi* (eel), and kisu. Call ahead to reserve counter seating or
a full-course kaiseki dinner in a private tatami room. ⊠ *1–6–1 Dogen-*
zaka, Shibuya-ku ☎ *03/3462–2815* Ⓜ *JR Yamanote Line, Shibuya Sta-*
tion (Minami-guchi/South Exit); Ginza and Hanzo-mon subway lines,
Shibuya Station (Exit 3A) ✛ *A5.*

SHIMBASHI

$$$ ✕ **Daruma** 黒達磨. This casual eatery takes its name from the hollow
JAPANESE wooden dolls—talismans of good luck for the Japanese—that deco-
rate the interior. The specialty here is yakitori, bits of chicken meat
and cartilage grilled on skewers. Daruma serves yakitori in the style
of Hakata, an area of Fukuoka city in southern Japan, where the dish
is not limited to poultry, but includes pork and vegetables. The menu

also include horse sashimi and *mentaiko,* a marinated fish roe which is another famous delicacy from Hakata. ⊠ *2–15–8 Shimbashi, Minato-ku* ☎ *03/5512–2778* ⊘ *No lunch* ✛ *E5.*

$$$
JAPANESE

✕ **Ushibenkei**牛弁慶. Japan prides itself on producing high-quality marbleized beef. Cuts are ranked based on the ratio, distribution, and sweetness of the fat in relation to the meat, and some of the highest ranks are available for reasonable prices at this new eatery with a rustic atmosphere. For the full experience select a *gyu-nabe* ("beef pot") course, and your server will move a *shichirin,* a portable coal-burning stove, to your table and prepare a range of cow tongue, beef, tofu, and vegetables in front of your eyes. The meat is fresh enough to be safely eaten raw, so don't be surprised if you are given paper-thin cuts of beef that are only lightly seared. There are à la carte options, too. ⊠ *3–18–7 Shimbashi, Minato-ku* ☎ *03/3459–9318* ⊟ *No credit cards* Ⓜ *JR Yamanote Line, Shimbashi Station (Kasumori Exit)* ✛ *E5.*

SHINAGAWA AND 品川 AND SHIROKANEDAI 白金台

$$$$
JAPANESE

✕ **Enju** 槐樹. Happo-en, a 300-year-old-Japanese garden wrapped around a lake, is the setting for the palatial complex that houses this upscale restaurant, a shrine, and a traditional teahouse. Beautiful scenery aside, the food is what draws locals and visitors again and again. The grand exterior and pristine banquet rooms are somewhat uninviting and overly formal, but the tables overlooking the garden are a tranquil backdrop for an unforgettable meal. Among the pricey prix fixe dinners are kaiseki, shabu-shabu, sukiyaki, and tempura, and there's also a buffet dinner. Go in the afternoon for a tour of the grounds, *sado* (tea ceremony), and a seasonal Japanese set lunch for ¥2,625 or ¥3,675. For more casual dining, Café Thrush, in the same complex, has an open-air terrace with a stunning view of the garden. ⊠ *1–1–1 Shirokanedai, Minato-ku* ☎ *03/3443–3125* ⌂ *Reservations essential* Ⓜ *Mita and Namboku subway lines, Shirokanedai Station (Exit 2)* ✛ *C6.*

$$$
ECLECTIC

✕ **Manhattan Grill** マンハッタングリル. Only in hyper-eclectic Japan can you have a French-Indonesian meal at a restaurant called the Manhattan Grill in a food court dubbed the "Foodium." Chef Wayan Surbrata, who trained at the Four Seasons Resort in Bali, has a delicate, deft touch with such dishes as spicy roast-chicken salad, and steak marinated in cinnamon and soy sauce, served with shiitake mushrooms and *gado-gado* (shrimp-flavor rice crackers). One side of the minimalist restaurant is open to the food court; the floor-to-ceiling windows on the other side don't afford much of a view. The square black-and-white ceramics set off the food especially well. ⊠ *4F Atré Shinagawa, 2–18–1 Konan, Minato-ku* ☎ *03/6717–0922* Ⓜ *JR Shinagawa Station (Higashi-guchi/East Exit)* ✛ *D6.*

$$
SPANISH

✕ **Sabado Sabadete** サバドサバデテ. Catalan jewelry designer Mañuel Benito used to rent a bar in Aoyama on Saturday nights and cook for his friends, just for the fun of it. Word got around: eventually there wasn't room in the bar to lift a fork. Inspired by this success, Benito opened this Spanish restaurant. The highlight of every evening is still the moment when the chef, in his bright red cap, shouts out "Gohan desu yo!"—the Japanese equivalent of "Soup's on!"—and dishes out his bubbling-hot paella. Don't miss the empanadas or the *escalivada* (Spanish ratatouille with red peppers, onions, and eggplant). ✉ *2F Genteel Shirokanedai Bldg., 5–3–2 Shirokanedai, Minato-ku* ☎ *03/3445–9353* ▭ *No credit cards* ☾ *Closed Sun. and Mon.* Ⓜ *Mita and Namboku subway lines, Shirokanedai Station (Exit 1)* ✛ *C6.*

$$$
ECLECTIC
★

✕ **T. Y. Harbor Brewery** T.Y.ハーバーブルワリーレストラン. A converted warehouse on the waterfront houses this restaurant, a Tokyo hot spot for private parties. Chef David Chiddo refined his signature California-Thai cuisine at some of the best restaurants in Los Angeles. Don't miss his grilled mahimahi with green rice and mango salsa, or the grilled jumbo-shrimp brochettes with tabbouleh. True to its name, T. Y. Harbor brews its own beer in a tank that reaches all the way to the 46-foot-high ceiling. The best seats in the house are on the bay-side deck, open from May to October. Reservations are a good idea on weekends. ✉ *2–1–3 Higashi-Shinagawa, Shinagawa-ku* ☎ *03/5479–4555* Ⓜ *Tokyo Monorail or Rinkai Line, Ten-nozu Isle Station (Exit B)* ✛ *D6.*

SHINJUKU 新宿

$$
CAFÉ

✕ **Ben's Café** ベンズカフェ. This artsy café in the student town of Takadanobaba is one of the few locations in Tokyo that serve a full-English breakfast, available weekends 11:30–3. ✉ *1–29–21 Takadanobaba, Shinjuku-ku* ☎ *03/3202–2445* ▭ *No credit cards* Ⓜ *JR Yamanote Line, Takadanobaba Station (Waseda-guchi/Waseda Exit)* ✛ *B1.*

$$$
SUSHI

✕ **Nanairo Temari Uta** 七色てまりうた. Traditionally, *temari* were toys made from the remnants of old kimono by mothers for their children. Today they are a prime example of Japanese folk art. This restaurant is all about temari—booths are shaped like giant temari balls, and smaller versions decorate the interior. The design motif even extends to the food, which includes sushi shaped like colorful balls rather than the usual rectangles. It is fun, if a bit kitschy. ✉ *5F Humax Pavillion, 3–28–10 Shinjuku, Shinjuku-ku* ☎ *03/3226-8070* ☾ *No lunch* Ⓜ *JR Shinjuku Station (Higashi-guchi/East Exit); Marunouchi and Fukutoshin subway lines, Shinjuku Sanchome Station (Exit A5)* ✛ *B2.*

$$
JAPANESE

✕ **Ryoma no Sora Bettei** 龍馬の空別邸. Tokyoites love unique dining experiences and are also fascinated by their own history—they can revel in both in this eatery which is a tribute to Ryoma Sakamoto, a hero who helped overthrow the feudal Tokugawa Shogunate in the 1860s. When you enter from the ultramodern streets of Shinjuku, slide off your shoes, stash them in a wooden locker, and walk by a statute of the sword-wielding Sakamoto as you step into the Japan of the past. You can sit in the main dining hall which resembles a bustling historic inn, or you can phone ahead to reserve a private tatami-mat dining room. The cuisine also harkens back to the traditional rural cooking, popular before Japan opened up to the West. The house specialty is *seiromushi*, a bamboo box filled with carefully arranged seafood, poultry, or meat, steamed over a pot, served piping hot, and quickly shared with everyone at the table. ✉ *B2 141 Shinjuku Bldg., 1–4–2 Nishi-Shinjuku, Shinjuku-ku* ☎ *03/3347–2207* ⊕ *www.diamond-dining.com/shop_info/ryomanosora-bettei* ☾ *No lunch* Ⓜ *JR Shinjuku Station (Nishi-guchi/West Exit)* ✛ *A2.*

TSUKIJI 築地

$$–$$$
SUSHI
★

✕**Edo-Gin** 江戸銀. In an area that teems with sushi bars, this one maintains its reputation as one of the best. Edo-Gin serves generous slabs of fish that drape over the vinegared rice rather than perch demurely on top. The centerpiece of the main room is a huge tank where the day's ingredients swim about until they are required; it doesn't get any fresher than this. Set menus here are reasonable, especially for lunch, but a big appetite for specialties like sea urchin and *otoro* tuna can put a dent in your budget. ⊠ *4–5–1 Tsukiji, Chuo-ku* ☎ *03/3543–4401* ⊘ *Closed Sun. and Jan. 1–4* Ⓜ *Hibiya subway line, Tsukiji Station (Exit 1); Oedo subway line, Tsukiji-shijo Station (Exit A1)* ⊹ *E5.*

¢–$
JAPANESE

✕**Takeno** たけの. Just a stone's throw from the Tokyo fish market, Takeno is a rough-cut neighborhood restaurant that tends to fill up at noon with the market's wholesalers and auctioneers and personnel from the nearby Asahi newspaper offices. There's nothing here but the freshest and the best—big portions of it, at very reasonable prices. Sushi and sashimi are the staples, but there's also a wonderful *tendon* bowl, with shrimp and eel tempura on rice. Prices are not posted because they vary with the costs that morning in the market. ■TIP➜ Reservations can only be made for large parties, or if you plan to dine before 6:30 pm. ⊠ *6–21–2 Tsukiji, Chuo-ku* ☎ *03/3541–8698* ▤ *No credit cards* ⊘ *Closed Sun.* Ⓜ *Hibiya subway line, Tsukiji Station (Exit 1); Oedo subway line, Tsukiji-shijo Station (Exit A1)* ⊹ *F5.*

HIBIYA 内幸町

$$$–$$$$
CHINESE
★

✕**Heichinrou** 聘珍楼. A short walk from the Imperial Hotel, this branch of one of Yokohama's oldest and best Chinese restaurants commands a spectacular view of the Imperial Palace grounds. Call ahead to reserve a table by the window. The cuisine is Cantonese; pride of place goes to the *kaisen ryori,* a banquet of steamed sea bass, lobster, shrimp, scallops, abalone, and other seafood dishes. Much of the clientele comes from the law offices, securities firms, and foreign banks in the building. The VIP room at Heichinrou, with its soft lighting and impeccable linens, is a popular venue for power lunches. ⊠ *28F Fukoku Seimei Bldg., 2–2–2 Uchisaiwai-cho, Chiyoda-ku* ☎ *03/3508–0555* ⊘ *Closed Sun.* Ⓜ *Mita Line, Uchisaiwai-cho Station (Exit A6)* ⊹ *E4.*

YURAKU-CHO 有楽町

$$
JAPANESE
Fodor's Choice
★

✕**Robata** 炉端. Old, funky, and more than a little cramped, Robata is a bit daunting at first. But fourth-generation chef-owner Takao Inoue holds forth here with an inspired version of Japanese home cooking. He's also a connoisseur of pottery; he serves his food on pieces acquired at famous kilns all over the country. There's no menu; just tell Inoue-san (who speaks some English) how much you want to spend, and leave the rest to him. A meal at Robata—like the pottery—is simple to the eye but subtle and fulfilling. Typical dishes include steamed fish with vegetables, stews of beef or pork, and seafood salads. ⊠ *1–3–8 Yuraku-cho, Chiyoda-ku* ☎ *03/3591–1905* ▤ *No credit cards* ⊘ *Closed some Sun.*

each month. No lunch Ⓜ *JR Yuraku-cho Station (Hibiya Exit); Hibiya, Chiyoda, and Mita subway lines, Hibiya Station (Exit A4)* ✛ *E4.*

$$
IZAKAYA
✕**Shin Hinomoto** 新日の基. This izakaya is located directly under the tracks of the Yamanote Line, making the wooden interior shutter each time a train passes overhead. It's a favorite with local and foreign journalists, as the Foreign Correspondents Club is just across the street, and is actually run by a Brit, who travels down the road to Tsukiji Market every morning to buy seafood. Don't miss the fresh sashimi and buttered scallops. ✉ *2–4–4 Yuraku-cho, Chiyoda-ku* ☎ *03/3214– 8021* 🚫 *No credit cards.* ⊘ *No lunch* Ⓜ *JR Yuraku-cho Station (Hibiya Exit); Hibiya, Chiyoda, and Mita subway lines, Hibiya Station (Exit A2)* ✛ *F4.*

3

WHERE TO STAY

The bubble economy of the 1990s has resulted in Tokyo's present luxury accommodations, which rival those of any big city in the world. With hoteliers banking on research that says most visitors will pay well to be pampered, it begs the question: Are there bargains to be had? Absolutely, but you'll have to do your homework. Lower-profile business and boutique hotels are decent bets for singles or couples who do not need a lot of space, and, in addition to hostels, exchanges, and rentals (apartments and homes), the budget-conscious traveler can utilize plenty of Japanese accommodations: ryokan, minshuku, "capsule" hotels, homes, and temples.

Though not with the same dominance as other large cities in the world, Tokyo has seen the opening of a number of boutique hotels typified by small rooms in a setting that blends a utilitarian concept around quirky and stylish elements. Room interior furnishings of blacks and varying browns, the de rigueur standard, are prevalent in Tokyo, but so are such Japanese touches as paper lanterns and tatami flooring. Reception areas are simple spaces bathed in dim lights and surrounded by earthtone wall panels. Given that these accommodations often contain only a few floors, their locations are likely not easy to find. But when priced at around ¥20,000 a night, they can offer some of the best bargains in a city known for being incredibly expensive.

WHAT IT COSTS IN YEN					
	¢	$	$$	$$$	$$$$
FOR TWO PEOPLE	under ¥10,000	¥10,000– ¥20,000	¥20,000– ¥30,000	¥30,000– ¥40,000	over ¥40,000

Price categories are assigned based on the range between the least and most expensive standard double rooms in nonholiday high season. Taxes (5%, plus 3% for bills over ¥15,000) are extra.

CLOSE UP

Dining on a Budget

Tokyo offers an astounding array of top-notch Japanese and international cuisines, but quality comes at a price. However, it's possible to eat well on a budget and the recent trend for *B-kyu gurume* ("B-grade Gourmet") is making it even easier. These restaurants forgo the frills and just serve good food for affordable prices. Wallet-friendly establishments such as these can be found across the city. Here are a few of the best.

✕**Kanda Matsuya** 神田まつや (¢–$). Udon—thick noodles served chilled in summer and hot in winter—are available everywhere, even convenience stores. Matsuya offers authentic udon in a rustic atmosphere. A simple udon meal costs ¥600, or, for a bit more, get noodles topped with tempura or other goodies. ✉ *1–3 Kanda Sudacho, Chiyoda-ku* ☎ *03/3251–1556* ▭ *No credit cards* Ⓜ *Marunouchi Line, Awajicho Station (Exit A3).*

✕**Kanda Yabu Soba** かんだやぶそば (¢–$). Soba—thin noodles made from buckwheat flour and quickly dipped into a hot broth or cold dipping sauce—are the lighter cousin of udon. Because it can be eaten so quickly, soba is often sold at small stands in train stations, where it can be slurped down while waiting to change trains. Kanda Yabu Soba, set in a Japanese garden, offers a place to sit down and savor the dish. A basic soba meal costs just ¥700, but the *shun* (seasonal meal), which change 10 times a year, are excellent and affordable. ✉ *2–10 Kanda Awajicho, Chiyoda-ku* ☎ *03/3251–0287* ▭ *No credit cards* Ⓜ *JR and Marunouchi lines, Awajicho Station (Exit A3).*

✕**Santa** とんかつ三田 ($). Tonkatsu, breaded, deep-fried pork cutlets, are synonymous with cheap but filling meals. Santa offers some of the best tonkatsu in the city in large portions for affordable prices. ✉ *3–33–10 Shinjuku, Shinjuku-ku* ☎ *03/3351–5861* Ⓜ *Shinjuku Station (East Exit).*

✕**Umenoki** 梅乃木 ($$). At an izakaya, food and drink are equally important and equally good. Umenoki, in Shibuya, specializes in sashimi, which can be astronomically expensive in award-winning restaurants, but is surprisingly affordable here. You will most likely share one of the long, sunken tables with a number of other dinners, which is all part of the experience. ✉ *2–11–1 Dogenzaka, Shibuya-ku* ☎ *03/5428–6707* Ⓜ *Shibuya Station (Hachiko Exit).*

AKASAKA 赤坂

$$$–$$$$
HOTEL
🏨 **ANA InterContinental Tokyo** (ANA) インターコンチネンタルホテル東京. The ANA typifies the ziggurat-atrium style that seems to have been a requirement for hotel architecture from the mid-1980s. **Pros:** great concierge; wonderful city views; spacious lobby. **Cons:** there's a charge to use the pool and gym; room bathrooms are a bit small. ✉ *1–12–33 Akasaka, Minato-ku* ☎ *03/3505–1111* ⊕ *www.anaintercontinental-tokyo.jp* 🛏 *800 rooms, 43 suites* ♨ *In-room: a/c, safe, refrigerator, Internet. In-hotel: 7 restaurants, room service, bars, pool, gym, laundry service, parking* ◎|*No meals* Ⓜ *Ginza and Namboku subway lines, Tameike-Sanno Station (Exit 13); Namboku subway line, Roppongi-itchome Station (Exit 3)* ✛ *D4.*

$$
HOTEL
🏨 **the b akasaka** ザ・ビー赤坂. Part of the boutique chain that promotes its ability to deliver balance, breakfast, bedrooms and business, the b akasaka is a stylish option for the business traveler in the heart of the city. **Pros:** near large entertainment area; affordable. **Cons:** difficult to find; single rooms can be confining. ✉ *7–6–13 Akasaka, Minato-ku* ☎ *03/3586–0811* ⊕ *www.ishinhotels.com* 🛏 *156 rooms* ⚙ *In-room: a/c, safe, refrigerator, Wi-Fi. In-hotel: restaurant, room service, spa, laundry service* ❌ *No meals* Ⓜ *Chiyoda subway line, Akasaka Station (Exit 3B).*

$$$$
HOTEL
🏨 **The Capitol Hotel Tokyu** ザ・キャピトルホテル東急. In a break from the trend over the past decade, the newest player in the market for high-end lodging in Tokyo is a domestic chain. Tokyu reopened its Capitol hotel, whose original incarnation enjoyed a 43-year history, inside a boxy 29-floor commercial complex designed by architect Kengo Kuma in 2010. **Pros:** convenient location; beautiful and spacious pool. **Cons:** pricey; government district might not appeal to tourists. ✉ *2–10–3 Nagata-cho, Minato-ku* ☎ *03/3477–6355* ⊕ *www.capitolhoteltokyu. com* 🛏 *238 rooms, 13 suites* ⚙ *In-room: a/c, safe, refrigerator, Wi-Fi. In-hotel: 3 restaurants, room service, bar, pool, gym, spa, laundry service, Internet terminal, parking* ❌ *No meals* Ⓜ *Ginza and Namboku subway lines, Tameike-Sanno Station (Exit 5)* ✛ *D4.*

¢
HOTEL
🏨 **Capsule Inn Akasaka** かぷせるイン赤坂. The Capsule Inn is a good option if you're shaking off a few drinks once the trains stop running. **Pros:** reservations made via the Internet get a ¥500 discount; convenient location; unique experience. **Cons:** small sleeping spaces; few services; women are not allowed; communal Japanese baths only. ✉ *6–14–1 Akasaka, Minato-ku* ☎ *03/3588–1811* ⊕ *www.marroad.jp/capsule* 🛏 *201 capsules* ⚙ *In-room: no phone, a/c. In-hotel: laundry facilities* ❌ *No meals* Ⓜ *Chiyoda subway line, Akasaka Station (Exit 6)* ✛ *D4.*

$$$–$$$$
HOTEL
🏨 **Hotel New Otani Tokyo** ホテルニューオータニ東京. Opened in 1964 just prior to the Olympics and used as a setting for the 1967 James Bond film *You Only Live Twice*, the New Otani is a bustling complex in the center of Tokyo. **Pros:** beautiful garden; first-rate concierge; convenient location. **Cons:** complex layout could be off-putting; charge for Internet in some rooms. ✉ *4–1 Kioi-cho, Chiyoda-ku* ☎ *03/3265–1111* ⊕ *www.newotani.co.jp* 🛏 *1,479 rooms, 61 suites* ⚙ *In-room: a/c, safe, refrigerator, Internet. In-hotel: 34 restaurants, room service, bars, pool, gym, laundry service, parking* ❌ *No meals* Ⓜ *Ginza and Marunouchi subway lines, Akasaka-mitsuke Station (Exit 7)* ✛ *D3.*

$$$$
★
HOTEL
🏨 **Hotel Okura Tokyo** ホテルオークラ東京. Conservative dark wood in the lobby and the tiered exterior architecture at the entry have helped the Okura achieve an understated sophistication, dating back to its opening in 1962. **Pros:** friendly staff; one of Tokyo's older hotels that has kept its throwback design and feel intact; large rooms. **Cons:** navigating between buildings is confusing; a tad pricey. ✉ *2–10–4 Tora-no-mon, Minato-ku* ☎ *03/3582–0111* ⊕ *www.okura.com/tokyo* 🛏 *779 rooms, 51 suites* ⚙ *In-room: a/c, safe, refrigerator, DVD, Wi-Fi. In-hotel: 10 restaurants, room service, bars, pool, gym, spa, laundry service, parking* ❌ *No meals* Ⓜ *Hibiya subway line, Kamiya-cho Station (Exit 4B); Ginza subway line, Tora-no-mon Station (Exit 3)* ✛ *D4.*

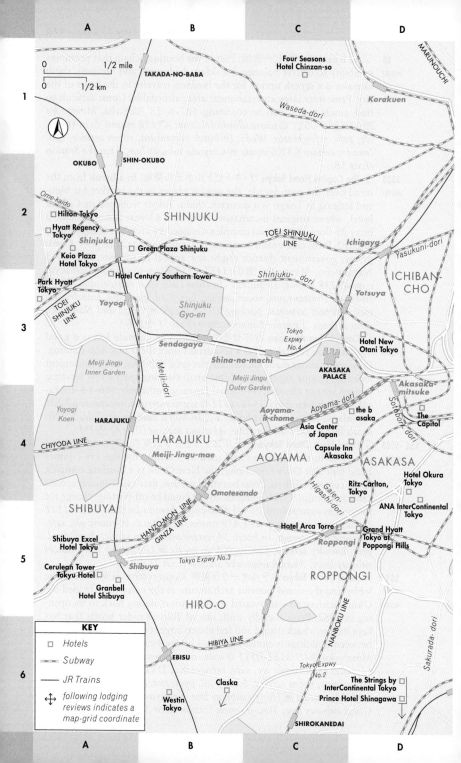

A | B | C | D

0 ⊢———⊣ **1/2 mile**
0 ⊢———⊣ **1/2 km**

Four Seasons Hotel Chinzan-so

MARUNOUCHI

Waseda-dori

Korakuen

TAKADA-NO-BABA

1

OKUBO   **SHIN-OKUBO**

Ome-kaido

SHINJUKU

TOEI SHINJUKU LINE

Ichigaya

Yasukuni-dori

2

Hilton Tokyo

Hyatt Regency Tokyo

Shinjuku

Green Plaza Shinjuku

Keio Plaza Hotel Tokyo

Hotel Century Southern Tower

Shinjuku-dori

ICHIBAN-CHO

Park Hyatt Tokyo

TOEI SHINJUKU LINE

Yoyogi

Shinjuku Gyo-en

Yotsuya

3

Sendagaya

Tokyo Expwy No.4

Hotel New Otani Tokyo

Meiji Jingu Inner Garden

Meiji-dori

Shina-no-machi

AKASAKA PALACE

Akasaka-mitsuke

Meiji Jingu Outer Garden

Aoyama-dori

Sotobori-dori

The Capitol

Yoyogi Koen

HARAJUKU

Aoyama-it-chome

the b asaka

CHIYODA LINE

4

HARAJUKU

Meiji-Jingu-mae

AOYAMA

Asia Center of Japan

Capsule Inn Akasaka

ASAKASA

Hotel Okura Tokyo

Ritz-Carlton, Tokyo

ANA InterContinental Tokyo

SHIBUYA

HANZO-MON LINE

Omotesando

GINZA LINE

Gaien-Higashi-dori

Hotel Arca Torre

Grand Hyatt Tokyo at Roppongi Hills

Shibuya Excel Hotel Tokyu

5

Tokyo Expwy No.3

Shibuya

Roppongi

ROPPONGI

Cerulean Tower Tokyu Hotel

Granbell Hotel Shibuya

HIRO-O

NANBOKU LINE

Sakurada-dori

HIBIYA LINE

EBISU

Tokyo Expwy No.2

6

Claska

The Strings by InterContinental Tokyo

Prince Hotel Shinagawa

Westin Tokyo

SHIROKANEDAI

KEY

☐ *Hotels*

▭▭ *Subway*

—— *JR Trains*

✛ *following lodging reviews indicates a map-grid coordinate*

A | B | C | D

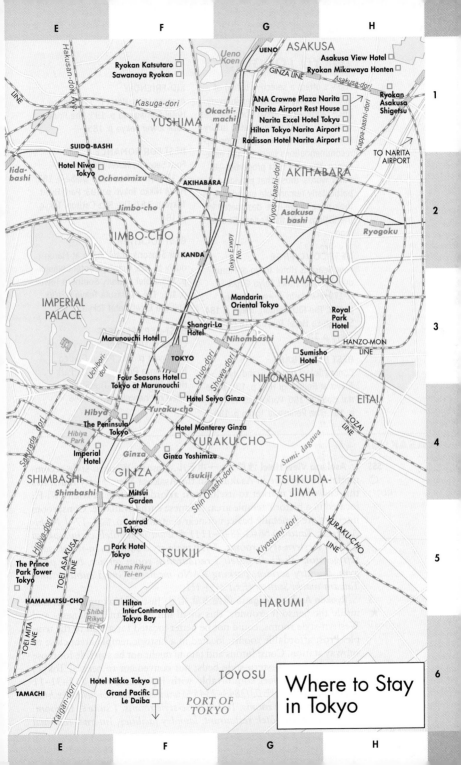

Where to Stay in Tokyo

TOKYO LODGING

Fodor's offers a selective listing of quality lodging experiences in every price range, from Tokyo's best budget beds to its most sophisticated luxury hotels. Here, we've compiled our top recommendations by price and experience. The very best properties—in other words, those that provide a particularly remarkable experience in their price range—are designated in the listings with the Fodor's Choice logo.

BEST CONCIERGE

Four Seasons Hotel Tokyo at Marunouchi p. 180; Hotel Seiyo Ginza p. 179; Mandarin Oriental, Tokyo p. 183; The Ritz-Carlton, Tokyo p. 184; Shangri-La Hotel Tokyo p. 182; Westin Tokyo p. 187

BEST HOTEL BARS

Conrad Tokyo p. 188; Grand Hyatt Tokyo at Roppongi Hills p. 184; Imperial Hotel p. 180; Park Hyatt Tokyo p. 187; The Peninsula Tokyo p. 180

KID-FRIENDLY

Asakusa View Hotel p. 178; Prince Hotel Shinagawa p. 185; The Prince Park Tower Tokyo p. 185

BEST FOR ROMANCE

Four Seasons Hotel Chinzan-so p. 182; Grand Pacific Le Daiba p. 183; Hotel Nikko Tokyo p. 183; Park Hyatt Tokyo p. 187; The Ritz-Carlton, Tokyo p. 184

BEST LOCATION

Four Seasons Hotel Tokyo at Marunouchi p. 180; Granbell Hotel Shibuya p. 185; Hotel Century Southern Tower p. 186; The Peninsula Tokyo p. 180; Shibuya Excel Hotel Tokyu p. 185

BEST-KEPT SECRETS

Claska p. 182; Hotel Century Southern Tower p. 186; Mitsui Garden Hotel Ginza Premier p. 179; Park Hotel Tokyo p. 188; The Strings by InterContinental Tokyo p. 186

ASAKUSA 浅草

$$$
HOTEL
Asakusa View Hotel 浅草ビューホテル. Upscale Western-style accommodations are rare in Asakusa, so the Asakusa View pretty much has this end of the market to itself. **Pros:** affordable; free in-room Wi-Fi; located in a historic temple area; Japanese baths available. **Cons:** room interiors are generally basic; not near central Tokyo. ⊠ *3–17–1 Nishi-Asakusa, Taito-ku* ☎ *03/3847–1111* ⊕ *www.viewhotels.co.jp/asakusa* ⊳ *330 Western-style rooms, 7 Japanese-style suites* ⚐ *In-room: safe, refrigerator, Wi-Fi. In-hotel: 5 restaurants, room service, bars, pool, gym, laundry service, parking* ⏹ *No meals* Ⓜ *Ginza subway line, Tawara-machi Station (Exit 3)* ✛ *H1.*

$
★
RYOKAN
Ryokan Asakusa Shigetsu 旅館浅草 指月. Just off Nakamise-dori and inside the Senso-ji grounds, this small inn, with both Japanese- and Western-style rooms, could not be better located for a visit to the temple. **Pros:** affordable rooms; located in a historic temple area; close to subway station. **Cons:** futons and tatami might not be suitable for those accustomed to Western-style beds; not convenient to central Tokyo; some might not feel comfortable with Japanese baths. ⊠ *1–31–11 Asakusa, Taito-ku* ☎ *03/3843–2345* ⊕ *www.shigetsu.com/e/index.html* ⊳ *6 Western-style rooms, 16 Japanese-style rooms, 1 suite* ⚐ *In-room: a/c, Internet. In-hotel: restaurant, laundry facilities, Internet terminal*

¡©¡ No meals Ⓜ *Ginza subway line, Asakusa Station (Exit 1/Kaminari-mon Exit)* ⊹ *H1.*

¢ 🏯 **Ryokan Mikawaya Honten** 旅館三河屋本店. In the heart of Asakusa, this concrete ryokan is just behind the Kaminari-mon, the gateway leading to the Senso-ji complex. **Pros:** affordable accommodations; traditional Japanese experience; interesting shopping in the area. **Cons:** futons and tatami might not be suitable for those accustomed to Western-style beds; small rooms; staff is English-challenged. ⊠ *1–30–12 Asakusa, Taito-ku* ☎ *03/3844–8807* ⇨ *19 Japanese-style rooms, 1 Western-style room* ♨ *In-room: a/c, Internet. In-hotel: laundry facilities* *¡©¡ No meals* Ⓜ *Ginza subway line, Asakusa Station (Exit 1/Kaminari-mon Exit)* ⊹ *H1.*

★
RYOKAN

3

GINZA 銀座

$$ 🏯 **Ginza Yoshimizu** 銀座吉水. With meals cooked from organic ingredients and chemical-free tatami mats in the rooms, the Yoshimizu is an environmentally friendly ryokan in the middle of Ginza. **Pros:** many shopping options nearby; central location; opportunity to have the traditional ryokan experience. **Cons:** often fully booked; Japanese baths, futon, and tatami might not suit everyone. ⊠ *3–11–3 Ginza, Chuo-ku* ☎ *03/3248–4432* ⊕ *www.yoshimizu.com* ⇨ *11 Japanese-style rooms without bath* ♨ *In-room: no phone, a/c, no TV. In-hotel: restaurant* *¡©¡ Breakfast* Ⓜ *Hibiya subway line, Higashi-Ginza Station (Exit 3 or A2)* ⊹ *F4.*

Fodor's Choice
★
RYOKAN

$$ 🏯 **Hotel Monterey Ginza** ホテルモントレー銀座. With a somewhat cheesy, faux-stone exterior that attempts to replicate 20th-century Europe, the Monterey's a bargain in the middle of Ginza. **Pros:** multiple shopping choices in area; central location; reasonable prices considering the area. **Cons:** rooms are a tad small; in-hotel dining options are limited. ⊠ *1–10–18 Ginza, Chuo-ku* ☎ *03/3562–0111* ⊕ *www.hotelmonterey. co.jp* ⇨ *224 rooms* ♨ *In-room: a/c, safe, refrigerator, Internet. In-hotel: 2 restaurants, bar, laundry service* *¡©¡ No meals* Ⓜ *Ginza subway line, Ginza Station (Exit A13)* ⊹ *F4.*

HOTEL

$$$$ 🏯 **Hotel Seiyo Ginza** ホテル西洋銀座. The grand marble staircase, the profusion of cut flowers, the reception staff in coats and tails: all combine to create an atmosphere more like an elegant private club than a hotel. **Pros:** convenient for public transport; many shopping options nearby; helpful staff. **Cons:** not suitable for children; smallish rooms. ⊠ *1–11–2 Ginza, Chuo-ku* ☎ *03/3535–1110* ⊕ *www.seiyo-ginza.com* ⇨ *51 rooms, 26 suites* ♨ *In-room: a/c, safe, refrigerator, DVD, Internet. In-hotel: 3 restaurants, room service, bars, gym, laundry service, parking* *¡©¡ No meals* Ⓜ *Ginza subway line, Kyo-bashi Station (Exit 2); Yuraku-cho Line, Ginza-Itchome Station (Exit 7)* ⊹ *F4.*

HOTEL

$$ 🏯 **Mitsui Garden Hotel Ginza Premier** 三井ガーデンホテル銀座プレミア. Chic and reasonable, this hotel, occupying the top of the 38-floor Nihonbashi Mitsui Tower, is a winner at the edge of bustling Ginza. **Pros:** affordable; convenient location. **Cons:** rooms are small; in-hotel restaurant a tad pricey; geared toward business rather than leisure travelers. ⊠ *8–13–1 Ginza, Chuo-ku* ☎ *03/3543–1131* ⊕ *www.gardenhotels.co.jp* ⇨ *361 rooms* ♨ *In-room: safe, refrigerator, Wi-Fi. In-hotel: restaurant,*

HOTEL

room service, bar, parking |O| *No meals* M *Ginza subway line, Ginza Station (A3) or JR Shimbashi Station (Ginza Exit)* ✣ *F4.*

HAKOZAKI 箱崎

$$$–$$$$
HOTEL
🏨 **Royal Park Hotel** ロイヤルパークホテル. A passageway connects this hotel to the Tokyo City Air Terminal, where you can easily catch a bus to Narita Airport, making the Royal Park a great one-night stopover point. **Pros:** convenient airport access; nice lobby; good service. **Cons:** not located near downtown; non–executive floors charged to use pool and gym. ✉ *2–1–1 Nihombashi, Kakigara-cho, Chuo-ku* ☎ *03/3667-1111* ⊕ *www.rph.co.jp* 🛏 *395 rooms, 11 suites* ♻ *In-room: a/c, safe, refrigerator, Internet. In-hotel: 6 restaurants, room service, bars, pool, gym, laundry service, parking* |O| *No meals* M *Hanzo-mon subway line, Suitengu-mae Station (Exit 4)* ✣ *H3.*

HIBIYA 日比谷

$$$$
HOTEL
🏨 **Imperial Hotel** 帝国ホテル. Though not as fashionable or spanking new as its neighbor, the Peninsula, the venerable Imperial can't be beat for traditional elegance. **Pros:** this is an old Japanese hotel with a long history; great service; large rooms. **Cons:** layout can be confusing; some rooms have dated interiors. ✉ *1–1–1 Uchisaiwai-cho, Chiyoda-ku* ☎ *03/3504-1111* ⊕ *www.imperialhotel.co.jp* 🛏 *931 rooms, 67 suites* ♻ *In-room: a/c, safe, refrigerator, Internet. In-hotel: 13 restaurants, room service, bars, pool, gym, laundry service, parking* |O| *No meals* M *Hibiya subway line, Hibiya Station (Exit 5)* ✣ *E4.*

$$$$
★
HOTEL
🏨 **The Peninsula Tokyo** ザ・ペニンシュラ東京. From the staff in caps and sharp suits, often assisting guests from a Rolls-Royce shuttling to and from Narita, to the shimmering gold glow emitting from the top floors, the 24-floor Peninsula Tokyo exudes elegance and grace. **Pros:** first-class room interiors; wonderful spa; great service. **Cons:** high prices; located near a business district. ✉ *1–8–1 Yuraku-cho, Chiyoda-ku* ☎ *03/6270-2888* ⊕ *www.peninsula.com* 🛏 *267 rooms, 47 suites* ♻ *In-room: a/c, safe, refrigerator, DVD, Wi-Fi. In-hotel: 4 restaurants, room service, bars, pool, gym, spa, laundry service, parking* |O| *No meals* M *JR Yamanote Line, Yuraku-cho Station (Hibiya-guchi/Hibiya Exit); Mita, Chiyoda, and Hibiya subway lines, Hibiya Station (Exits A6 and A7)* ✣ *F4.*

MARUNOUCHI 丸の内

$$$$
HOTEL
🏨 **Four Seasons Hotel Tokyo at Marunouchi** フォーシーズンズホテル丸の内東京. A departure from the typical large scale of most properties in the chain, this Four Seasons, set within the glistening Pacific Century Place, has the feel of a boutique hotel. **Pros:** convenient airport access; central location; helpful, English-speaking staff. **Cons:** highly priced; the only views are those of nearby Tokyo Station, but such proximity makes catching the Narita Express a snap. ✉ *1–11–1 Marunouchi, Chiyoda-ku* ☎ *03/5222-7222* ⊕ *www.fourseasons.com/marunouchi* 🛏 *48 rooms, 9 suites* ♻ *In-room: a/c, safe, refrigerator, DVD, Wi-Fi. In-hotel: restaurant, room*

Ginza Yoshimizu

Claska

Prince Park Tower Tokyo

Granbell Hotel Shibuya

Park Hyatt Tokyo

Park Hotel Tokyo

service, bar, gym, spa, laundry service, parking ⎢◎⎢ *No meals* Ⓜ *JR Tokyo Station (Yaesu South Exit)* ✢ *F3.*

$$$
HOTEL
🏨 **Marunouchi Hotel** 丸ノ内ホテル. Convenience is one reason to choose the Marunouchi Hotel, occupying the upper 11 floors of the Marunouchi Oazo Building and joining Tokyo Station via an underground walkway. **Pros:** convenient airport access; central location; helpful concierge. **Cons:** designed for business travelers; rooms are smallish; limited dining choices. ✉ *1–6–3 Marunouchi, Chiyoda-ku* ☎ *03/3217–1111* ⊕ *www.marunouchi-hotel.co.jp* 🛏 *204 rooms, 1 suite* ⎢ *In-room: a/c, safe, refrigerator, DVD, Internet. In-hotel: 3 restaurants, room service, bar, laundry service, parking* ⎢◎⎢ *No meals* Ⓜ *JR Tokyo Station (Marunouchi North Exit)* ✢ *F3.*

$$$$
Fodor's Choice
★
HOTEL
🏨 **Shangri-La Hotel Tokyo** シャングリ・ラ ホテル 東京. The Shangri-La Hotel Tokyo, which opened in 2009, offers high-end luxury, lavish interiors, and superb views of Tokyo Bay and the cityscape from the top 11 floors of Marunouchi Trust Tower Main, a 37-floor building conveniently located near Tokyo Station. **Pros:** convenient location; lavish service. **Cons:** pricey; located in a business district. ✉ *Marunouchi Trust Tower Main, 1–8–3 Marunouchi, Chiyoda-ku* ☎ *03/6739–7888* ⊕ *www.shangri-la.com* 🛏 *194 rooms, 6 suites* ⎢ *In-room: a/c, safe, refrigerator, DVD, Wi-Fi. In-hotel: 2 restaurants, room service, bar, pool, gym, spa, laundry service, parking* ⎢◎⎢ *No meals* Ⓜ *JR Tokyo Station (Yaesu North Exit)* ✢ *F3.*

MEGURO 目黒

$–$$
Fodor's Choice
★
HOTEL
🏨 **Claska** クラスカ. Hip, modern, and Japanese, Claska is Tokyo's premier boutique hotel. **Pros:** Japanese aesthetics in a modern setting; great staff; cool gift shop. **Cons:** it's five minutes by taxi from Meguro Station; dining options in immediate area are limited; often fully booked. ✉ *1–3–18 Chuo-cho, Meguro-ku* ☎ *03/3719–8121* ⊕ *www.claska.com* 🛏 *9 Western rooms, 3 Japanese rooms, 3 weekly residence rooms, 3 suites* ⎢ *In-room: a/c, DVD, Internet. In-hotel: restaurant, room service, laundry service, parking* ⎢◎⎢ *No meals* Ⓜ *Toyoko Line, Gakugei-daigaku Station (Higashi-guchi/East Exit); 5 mins by taxi from JR Meguro Station* ✢ *B6.*

MEJIRO 目白

$$$$
★
HOTEL
🏨 **Four Seasons Hotel Chinzan-so** フォーシーズンズホテル椿山荘. Boasting a European flair amid a 17-acre garden setting, the elegant and isolated Four Seasons is like a sheltered haven in the busy metropolis. **Pros:** stunning rooms; nice pool; garden views; shuttle service to subway and Tokyo Station. **Cons:** expensive room rates; isolated location. ✉ *2–10–8 Sekiguchi, Bunkyo-ku* ☎ *03/3943–2222* ⊕ *www.fourseasons. com/tokyo* 🛏 *215 rooms, 44 suites* ⎢ *In-room: a/c, safe, refrigerator, DVD, Wi-Fi. In-hotel: 3 restaurants, room service, pool, gym, spa, laundry service, parking* ⎢◎⎢ *No meals* Ⓜ *Yuraku-cho subway line, Edogawa-bashi Station (Exit 1A)* ✢ *C1.*

NIHOMBASHI 日本橋

$$$$ 🏨 **Mandarin Oriental, Tokyo** マンダリン オリエンタル 東京. Occupying
★ the top nine floors of the glistening Nihombashi Mitsui Tower is this
HOTEL hotel, a blend of harmony and outright modernity. **Pros:** wonderful spa
and concierge service; nice city views; amazing room interiors. **Cons:**
pricey; quiet area on the weekends; no pool. ✉ *2–1–1 Nihombashi
Muromachi, Chuo-ku* ☎ *03/3270–8950* ⊕ *www.mandarinoriental.com/
tokyo* 🛏 *157 rooms, 21 suites* ♿ *In-room: a/c, safe, refrigerator, DVD,
Wi-Fi. In-hotel: 4 restaurants, room service, bars, gym, spa, laundry
service, parking* ⊠ *No meals* Ⓜ *Ginza and Hanzo-mon subway lines,
Mitsukoshi-mae Station (Exit A7)* ✛ *G3.*

$ 🏨 **Sumisho Hotel** 住庄ほてる. This hotel, in a down-to-earth, friendly
★ neighborhood, is popular with budget-minded foreign visitors who pre-
HOTEL fer to stay near the small Japanese restaurants and bars of Ningyo-cho
area of Nihombashi. **Pros:** nicely priced; friendly staff; neighborhood has
small restaurants and pubs that offer great food for a good price. **Cons:**
small rooms and baths; quiet area on weekends. ✉ *9–14 Nihombashi-
Kobunacho, Chuo-ku* ☎ *03/3661–4603* ⊕ *www.sumisho-hotel.co.jp*
🛏 *72 Western-style rooms, 11 Japanese-style rooms* ♿ *In-room: a/c,
Internet. In-hotel: restaurant, laundry facilities, laundry service* ⊠ *No
meals* Ⓜ *Hibiya and Asakusa subway lines, Ningyo-cho Station (Exit
A5)* ✛ *G3.*

ODAIBA お台場

$$$$ 🏨 **Grand Pacific Le Daiba** グランパシフィックル ダイバ. A sprawling com-
HOTEL plex at the tip of a human-made peninsula in Tokyo Bay, the Grand
Pacific's a good choice for conventioneers at the nearby Tokyo Big
Site. **Pros:** great views of Tokyo Bay; large, nicely appointed rooms;
romantic setting. **Cons:** isolated location; numerous weddings booked
on weekends. ✉ *2–6–1 Daiba, Minato-ku* ☎ *03/5500–6711* ⊕ *www.
grandpacific.jp* 🛏 *860 rooms, 24 suites* ♿ *In-room: a/c, safe, refrigerator, Internet. In-hotel: 8 restaurants, room service, bars, pool, gym,
laundry service, parking* ⊠ *No meals* Ⓜ *Yurikamome rail line, Daiba
Station* ✛ *F6.*

$$$ 🏨 **Hotel InterContinental Tokyo Bay** ホテルインターコンチネンタル東京ベイ.
HOTEL Wedged between Tokyo Bay and an expressway, the InterContinental
affords pleasant views, albeit in a slightly isolated setting. **Pros:** great
views of the Rainbow Bridge and Tokyo Bay; large, nicely appointed
rooms; quiet area. **Cons:** no pool; location might be too out-of-the-
way for the sightseer. ✉ *1–16–2 Kaigan, Minato-ku* ☎ *03/5404–2222*
⊕ *www.interconti-tokyo.com* 🛏 *331 rooms, 8 suites* ♿ *In-room: a/c,
safe, refrigerator, Internet. In-hotel: 4 restaurants, room service, bar,
gym, laundry service, parking* ⊠ *No meals* Ⓜ *Yurikamome rail line,
Takeshiba Station* ✛ *F5.*

$$$–$$$$ 🏨 **Hotel Nikko Tokyo** ホテル日航東京. Like the nearby Grand Pacific
HOTEL hotel, the 16-story Nikko, whose facade follows the curve of the Tokyo
Bay shoreline, presents itself as an "urban resort" with European style.
Pros: great views of Tokyo Bay; friendly staff; romantic setting. **Cons:**
isolated location might not be ideal for the sightseer; room interiors are

a tad bland. ✉ *1–9–1 Daiba, Minato-ku* ☎ *03/5500–5500* ⊕ *www.hnt. co.jp* ⇆ *436 rooms, 17 suites* ⚲ *In-room: a/c, safe, refrigerator, Internet. In-hotel: 8 restaurants, room service, bar, pool, gym, spa, laundry service, parking* ⦿ *No meals* Ⓜ *Yurikamome rail line, Daiba Station* ✛ *F6.*

ROPPONGI 六本木

$$$$
★
HOTEL

🏨 **Grand Hyatt Tokyo at Roppongi Hills** グランドハイアット東京. Japanese refinement and a contemporary design come together perfectly at the Grand Hyatt—a truly classy hotel that provides every imaginable convenience and comfort. **Pros:** great spa; wide range of restaurants; stunning rooms. **Cons:** pricey; the complicated layout of the complex can make moving around seem like a game of Chutes and Ladders. ✉ *6–10–3 Roppongi, Minato-ku* ☎ *03/4333–1234* ⊕ *www.tokyo.grand.hyatt.com* ⇆ *361 rooms, 28 suites* ⚲ *In-room: a/c, safe, refrigerator, DVD, Wi-Fi. In-hotel: 6 restaurants, room service, bars, pool, gym, spa, laundry service, parking* ⦿ *No meals* Ⓜ *Hibiya subway line, Roppongi Station (Exit 1A); Oedo subway line, Roppongi Station (Exit 3)* ✛ *D5.*

$
HOTEL

🏨 **Hotel Arca Torre** ホテルアルカトーレ. This European-inspired hotel sits on a coveted location in the heart of one of Tokyo's premier nightlife quarters, just a few minutes' walk from the Tokyo Midtown and Roppongi Hills shopping-and-entertainment complexes. **Pros:** affordable; convenient access to nightlife. **Cons:** no room service; small rooms; neighborhood's plethora of bars and clubs makes the area noisy. ✉ *6–1–23 Roppongi, Minato-ku* ☎ *03/3404–5111* ⊕ *www.arktower. co.jp* ⇆ *76 rooms* ⚲ *In-room: a/c, refrigerator, Internet. In-hotel: 2 restaurants, laundry service* ⦿ *No meals* Ⓜ *Hibiya and Oedo subway lines, Roppongi Station (Exit 3)* ✛ *C5.*

¢–$
★
HOTEL

🏨 **Hotel Asia Center of Japan** ホテルアジア会館. Established mainly for Asian students and travelers on limited budgets, these accommodations have become popular due to their good value and easy access (a 15-minute walk) to the nightlife of Roppongi. **Pros:** affordable; this area is great for those who love the nightlife; complimentary Internet. **Cons:** just one restaurant; no room service; small rooms. ✉ *8–10–32 Akasaka, Minato-ku* ☎ *03/3402–6111* ⊕ *www.asiacenter.or.jp* ⇆ *172 rooms, 1 suite* ⚲ *In-room: a/c, refrigerator, Internet. In-hotel: restaurant, laundry service, Internet terminal* ⦿ *No meals* Ⓜ *Ginza and Hanzo-mon subway lines, Aoyama-itchome Station (Exit 4)* ✛ *C4.*

$$$$
★
HOTEL

🏨 **The Ritz-Carlton, Tokyo** ザ・リッツ・カールトン東京. Installed in the top floors of the 53-story Midtown Tower, the Ritz-Carlton provides Tokyo's most luxurious accommodations in the middle of the city. **Pros:** great views of Tokyo; romantic setting; convenient access to nightlife; stunning rooms. **Cons:** high prices; immediate area is somewhat grungy. ✉ *9–7–1 Akasaka, Minato-ku* ☎ *03/3423–8000* ⊕ *www.ritzcarlton.com* ⇆ *212 rooms, 36 suites* ⚲ *In-room: a/c, safe, refrigerator, DVD, Wi-Fi. In-hotel: 7 restaurants, room service, bar, pool, spa, laundry service, parking* ⦿ *No meals* Ⓜ *Hibiya subway line, Roppongi Station (Exit 4); Oedo subway line, Roppongi Station (Exit 7)* ✛ *D4.*

SHIBA KOEN 芝公園

$$$
☺
Fodor's Choice
HOTEL

🏨 **The Prince Park Tokyo** ザ・プリンス パークタワー東京. The surrounding parkland and the absence of any adjacent buildings make the Park Tower a peaceful setting. **Pros:** park nearby; guests have a choice of bed pillows for the large beds; there's a bowling alley and wedding chapel in the hotel; ladies only floor comes with nice amenities. **Cons:** a tad isolated; there's an extra fee to use the pool and fitness center; expensive room service. ✉ *4–8–1 Shiba-koen, Minato-ku* ☎ *03/5400–1111* ⊕ *www.princehotels.com/en/parktower* 🛏 *639 rooms, 34 suites* △ *In-room: a/c, safe, refrigerator, Internet. In-hotel: 7 restaurants, room service, bars, pool, gym, spa, laundry service, parking* ☉ *No meals* Ⓜ *Oedo subway line, Akabanebashi Station (Akabanebashi Exit)* ✛ *E5.*

SHIBUYA 渋谷

$$$$
HOTEL

🏨 **Cerulean Tower Tokyu Hotel** セルリアンタワー東急ホテル. The pricey Cerulean Tower, perched on a slope above Shibuya's chaos, has a cavernous yet bustling lobby filled with plenty of attentive, English-speaking staffers. **Pros:** friendly, attentive service; great city views; convenient location. **Cons:** pricey rates; Shibuya is one of Tokyo's more popular (read: crowded) areas; charge to use Internet, gym, and pool. ✉ *26–1 Sakuragaoka-cho, Shibuya-ku* ☎ *03/3476–3000* ⊕ *www.ceruleantower-hotel.com* 🛏 *402 rooms, 9 suites* △ *In-room: a/c, refrigerator, DVD, Internet. In-hotel: 6 restaurants, room service, bars, pool, gym, laundry service, parking* ☉ *No meals* Ⓜ *JR Shibuya Station (South Exit)* ✛ *A5.*

$$
Fodor's Choice
★
HOTEL

🏨 **Granbell Hotel Shibuya** 渋谷グランベルホテル. Location, location, location—that's the Granbell, and with a minimalist pop-art style to boot. **Pros:** reasonable rates; great location; funky design. **Cons:** small rooms; neighborhood can be noisy. ✉ *15–17 Sakuragaoka–cho, Shibuya-ku* ☎ *03/5457–2681* ⊕ *www.granbellhotel.jp* 🛏 *98 rooms, 7 suites* △ *In-room: a/c, refrigerator, Internet. In-hotel: 2 restaurants, bar, laundry service* ☉ *No meals* Ⓜ *JR Shibuya Station (West Exit)* ✛ *A5.*

$$$
HOTEL

🏨 **Shibuya Excel Hotel Tokyu** 渋谷エクセル東急. The key to this unremarkable but very convenient hotel, which is within the towering Mark City complex, is access: local shopping and cheap dining options are aplenty, Shinjuku is a five-minute train ride to the north, and the Narita Express departs from nearby Shibuya Station frequently each morning. **Pros:** affordable; convenient location; friendly staff. **Cons:** small, uninspired rooms; crowds in the area can be intimidating. ✉ *1–12–2 Dogenzaka, Shibuya-ku* ☎ *03/5457–0109* ⊕ *www.tokyuhotelsjapan.com* 🛏 *407 rooms, 1 suite* △ *In-room: a/c, refrigerator, Internet. In-hotel: 3 restaurants, room service, laundry service, parking* ☉ *No meals* Ⓜ *JR Shibuya Station (Hachiko Exit)* ✛ *A5.*

SHINAGAWA 品川

$–$$
☺
HOTEL

🏨 **Prince Hotel Shinagawa** 品川プリンスホテル. Just a three-minute walk from JR Shinagawa Station, the Prince is a sprawling complex that's part hotel (with four towers) and part entertainment village, featuring everything from a bowling alley to tennis courts to a 10-screen movie theater. **Pros:** affordable rates; multiple entertainment choices including a bowling alley and an IMAX theater; nice view of Tokyo Bay from lounge. **Cons:** complicated layout; crowded on weekends; charge for Internet. ✉ *4–10–30 Takanawa, Minato-ku* ☎ *03/3440–1111* ⊕ *www. princehotels.co.jp/shinagawa-e* 🖥 *3,679 rooms* 🛎 *In-room: a/c, refrigerator, Internet. In-hotel: 12 restaurants, room service, bar, tennis courts, pool, gym, laundry service, parking* ⽕|◎| *No meals* Ⓜ *JR Yamanote Line, Shinagawa Station (Nishi-guchi/West Exit)* ✛ *D6.*

$$$$
★
HOTEL
🏨 **The Strings by InterContinental Tokyo** ストリングスホテル東京インターコンチネンタル. Like the Conrad Tokyo up the road in Shiodome, the Strings is all about blending modernity with traditional Japanese aesthetics. **Pros:** great lobby; convenient location; nice view of the Tokyo skyline. **Cons:** expensive rates; finding elevator entrance can be challenging; no pool or spa. ✉ *2–16–1 Konan, Minato-ku* ☎ *03/4562–1111* ⊕ *www.intercontinental-strings.jp* 🖥 *200 rooms, 6 suites* 🛎 *In-room: a/c, safe, refrigerator, Internet. In-hotel: 2 restaurants, room service, bars, gym, laundry service, parking* ⽕|◎| *No meals* Ⓜ *JR Yamanote Line, Shinagawa Station (Konan Exit)* ✛ *F6.*

SHINJUKU 新宿

¢
★
HOTEL
🏨 **Green Plaza Shinjuku** グリーンプラザ新宿. Male budget travelers in Shinjuku willing to throw claustrophobia to the wind can settle in for a night at the Green Plaza, a capsule hotel in the entertainment district of Kabuki-cho. As with most capsule hotels, there are no accommodations for women. **Pros:** if you want to try a capsule hotel this is the place to do it as it's fairly priced; convenient location; public bath area offers mineral baths and saunas. **Cons:** small and limited accommodations; noisy neighborhood. ✉ *1–29–2 Kabuki-cho, Shinjuku-ku* ☎ *03/3207–5411* ⊕ *www.hgpshinjuku.jp* 🖥 *660 capsules without bath* 🛎 *In-room: no phone, a/c. In-hotel: restaurant, laundry service* |◎| *No meals* Ⓜ *Shinjuku Station (Higashi-guchi/East Exit)* ✛ *A2.*

$$–$$$
HOTEL
🏨 **Hilton Tokyo** ヒルトン東京. The Hilton, which is a short walk from the megalithic Tokyo Metropolitan Government Office, is a particular favorite of Western business travelers. **Pros:** great gym; convenient location; free shuttle to Shinjuku Station. **Cons:** in-room Internet is not free; restaurants are pricey. ✉ *6–6–2 Nishi-Shinjuku, Shinjuku-ku* ☎ *03/3344–5111* ⊕ *www.hilton.com* 🖥 *688 rooms, 127 suites* 🛎 *In-room: a/c, safe, refrigerator, Wi-Fi. In-hotel: 6 restaurants, room service, bars, pool, gym, laundry service, parking* |◎| *No meals* Ⓜ *Shinjuku Station (Nishi-guchi/West Exit); Marunouchi subway line, Nishi-Shinjuku Station (Exit C8); Oedo subway line, Tocho-mae Station (all exits)* ✛ *A2.*

$$–$$$
★
HOTEL
🏨 **Hotel Century Southern Tower** 小田急ホテルセンチュリーサザンタワー. The sparse offerings at the Century (i.e., no room service, empty refrigerators) are more than compensated for by the hotel's reasonable prices and wonderful location atop the 35-floor Odakyu Southern Tower, minutes by foot from Shinjuku Station. **Pros:** affordable; convenient location; great views. **Cons:** room amenities are basic; no room service or pool. ✉ *2–2–1 Yoyogi, Shibuya-ku* ☎ *03/5354–0111* ⊕ *www. southerntower.co.jp* 🖥 *375 rooms* 🛎 *In-room: a/c, refrigerator, Wi-Fi.*

In-hotel: 3 restaurants, bar, gym, laundry service, parking ⫶⫶◎⫶ *No meals* Ⓜ *Shinjuku Station (Minami-guchi/South Exit); Oedo and Shinjuku subway lines, Shinjuku Station (Exit A1)* ✛ *A3.*

$$–$$$
HOTEL

🏨 **Hyatt Regency Tokyo** ハイアットリージェンシー東京. The Hyatt Regency, set amid Shinjuku's skyscrapers, has the trademark Hyatt atrium-style lobby: seven stories high, with open-glass elevators soaring upward and three huge chandeliers suspended from above. **Pros:** friendly staff; affordable room rates; spacious rooms. **Cons:** rather bland exteriors and common areas; restaurant options are limited outside hotel. ✉ *2–7–2 Nishi-Shinjuku, Shinjuku-ku* ☎ *03/3348–1234* ⊕ *tokyo.regency.hyatt. com* ⇦ *726 rooms, 18 suites* ⟐ *In-room: a/c, safe, refrigerator, Internet. In-hotel: 6 restaurants, room service, bars, pool, gym, spa, laundry service, parking* ⫶⫶◎⫶ *No meals* Ⓜ *Marunouchi subway line, Nishi-Shinjuku Station (Exit C8); Oedo subway line, Tocho-mae Station (all exits)* ✛ *A2.*

$$$
HOTEL

🏨 **Keio Plaza Hotel Tokyo** 京王プラザホテル. This hotel, composed of two cereal-box-shape towers, has a reputation as a business destination that serves its guests with a classic touch. **Pros:** nice pools; affordable nightly rates; convenient location. **Cons:** rather bland exteriors and common areas; restaurant options are limited outside hotel; can be crowded if there are conventions or large groups in residence. ✉ *2–2–1 Nishi-Shinjuku, Shinjuku-ku* ☎ *03/3344–0111* ⊕ *www.keioplaza.com* ⇦ *1,431 rooms, 19 suites* ⟐ *In-room: a/c, refrigerator, Internet. In-hotel: 13 restaurants, room service, bars, pool, gym, laundry service, parking* ⫶⫶◎⫶ *No meals* Ⓜ *Shinjuku Station (Nishi-guchi/West Exit)* ✛ *A2.*

$$$$
Fodor's Choice
★
HOTEL

🏨 **Park Hyatt Tokyo** パークハイアット東京. The elevator inside the sleek, Kenzo Tange–designed Shinjuku Park Tower whisks you to the 41st floor, where this stunning hotel—immortalized in the 2003 film *Lost in Translation*—begins with an atrium lounge enclosed on three sides by floor-to-ceiling plate-glass windows. **Pros:** wonderful room interiors; great city views; top-class restaurants; discounts provided via Twitter (@ParkHyattTokyo). **Cons:** pricey; taxi is best way to get to Shinjuku Station; restaurant options are limited outside hotel. ✉ *3–7–1–2 Nishi-Shinjuku, Shinjuku-ku* ☎ *03/5322–1234* ⊕ *tokyo.park.hyatt.com* ⇦ *155 rooms, 23 suites* ⟐ *In-room: a/c, safe, refrigerator, DVD, Wi-Fi. In-hotel: 4 restaurants, room service, bars, pool, gym, spa, laundry service, parking* ⫶⫶◎⫶ *No meals* Ⓜ *JR Shinjuku Station (Nishi-guchi/West Exit)* ✛ *A3.*

$$$$
HOTEL

🏨 **Westin Tokyo** ウェスティンホテル東京. In the Yebisu Garden Place development, the Westin provides easy access to Mitsukoshi department store, the Tokyo Metropolitan Museum of Photography, the elegant Ebisu Garden concert hall, and the award-winning Taillevent-Robuchon restaurant (in a full-scale reproduction of a Louis XV château). **Pros:** beds really are heavenly; large rooms; great concierge. **Cons:** walk from station is more than 10 minutes; Internet is not free. ✉ *1–4 Mita 1-chome, Meguro-ku* ☎ *03/5423–7000* ⊕ *www.westin-tokyo.co.jp* ⇦ *418 rooms, 20 suites* ⟐ *In-room: a/c, safe, refrigerator, DVD, Wi-Fi. In-hotel: 5 restaurants, room service, bars, gym, laundry service, parking* ⫶⫶◎⫶ *No meals* Ⓜ *JR, Yamanote Line and Hibiya subway line, Ebisu Station (Higashi-guchi/East Exit)* ✛ *B6.*

SHIODOME 汐留

$$$$
HOTEL
🖥 **Conrad Tokyo** コンラッド東京. The Conrad, part of the Hilton family, welcomes you to the space age with a Japanese twist. **Pros:** modern design; fantastic bay view; fine restaurants. **Cons:** expensive; finding entrance to elevator is troublesome; charge to use pool and gym. ⊠ *1–9–1 Higashi-Shimbashi, Minato-ku* ☎ *03/6388–8000* ⊕ *conradtokyo.co.jp* 🛏 *222 rooms, 68 suites* 🛆 *In-room: a/c, safe, refrigerator, DVD, Wi-Fi. In-hotel: 4 restaurants, room service, bar, pool, gym, spa, laundry service, parking* ❑❑ *No meals* Ⓜ *JR Yamanote Line, Shimbashi Station (Shiodome Exit); Oedo subway line, Shiodome Station (Exit 9)* ✛ *F5.*

$$
Fodor's Choice
★
HOTEL
🖥 **Park Hotel Tokyo** パークホテル東京. A panorama of Tokyo or a bay view, comfortable beds, and large bathrooms greet you in the rooms of this reasonably priced boutique hotel. **Pros:** the guest rooms and public areas are stylish; affordable room rates; great concierge service. **Cons:** small rooms; few in-room frills; no pool or gym. ⊠ *1–7–1 Higashi Shimbashi, Minato-ku* ☎ *03/6252–1111* ⊕ *www.parkhoteltokyo.com* 🛏 *272 rooms, 1 suite* 🛆 *In-room: a/c, safe, refrigerator, Internet. In-hotel: 5 restaurants, room service, bar, laundry service, parking* ❑❑ *No meals* Ⓜ *JR Yamanote Line, Shimbashi Station (Shiodome Exit); Oedo subway line, Shiodome Station (Exit 10)* ✛ *E5.*

SUIDO-BASHI 水道橋

$$
HOTEL
🖥 **Hotel Niwa Tokyo** 庭のホテル 東京. Traditional and contemporary elements come together to make the Hotel Niwa Tokyo a hidden boutique gem in the middle of the city. **Pros:** affordable; quiet area; central location. **Cons:** rooms are a bit small; finding entrance is a bit challenging. ⊠ *1–1–16 Misaki-cho, Chiyoda-ku* ☎ *03/3293–0028* ⊕ *www. hotelniwa.jp* 🛏 *238 rooms* 🛆 *In-room: a/c, safe, refrigerator, Internet. In-hotel: 2 restaurants, room service, gym, laundry service* ❑❑ *No meals* Ⓜ *JR Chuo or Sobu lines, Suido-bashi Station (East Exit); Mita subway line, Suido-bashi Station (Exit A1)* ✛ *E2.*

UENO 上野

¢
RYOKAN
🖥 **Ryokan Katsutaro** 旅館勝太郎. Established four decades ago, this small, simple, economical hotel is a five-minute walk from the entrance to Ueno Koen (Ueno Park) and a 10-minute walk from the Tokyo National Museum. **Pros:** a traditional and unique Japanese experience; reasonably priced room rates; free use of computers in lobby. **Cons:** no breakfast served; baths are small; some rooms have shared Japanese baths. ⊠ *4–16–8 Ikenohata, Taito-ku* ☎ *03/3821–9808* ⊕ *www. katsutaro.com* 🛏 *7 Japanese-style rooms, 4 with bath* 🛆 *In-room: a/c, Internet. In-hotel: bicycles, laundry facilities, Internet terminal* ❑❑ *No meals* Ⓜ *Chiyoda subway line, Nezu Station (Exit 2)* ✛ *F1.*

¢–$
RYOKAN
🖥 **Sawanoya Ryokan** 澤の屋旅館. The Shitamachi area is known for its down-to-earth friendliness, which you get in full measure at Sawanoya. **Pros:** traditional Japanese experience; affordable room rates; friendly management. **Cons:** rooms are on the small side; it's a bit of a hike

to the subway station; must book well in advance; many room share Japanese baths. ✉ *2–3–11 Yanaka, Taito-ku* ☎ *03/3822–2251* ⊕ *www.sawanoya.com* ✈ *12 Japanese-style rooms, 2 with bath* ♿ *In-room: a/c, Internet. In-hotel: bicycles, laundry facilities, Internet terminal* ⦿ *No meals* Ⓜ *Chiyoda subway line, Nezu Station (Exit 1)* ✛ *F1.*

NEAR NARITA AIRPORT

Transportation between Narita Airport and Tokyo proper takes at least an hour and a half. In heavy traffic, a limousine bus or taxi ride, which could set you back ¥30,000, can stretch to two hours or more. A sensible strategy for visitors with early-morning flights home would be to spend the night before at one of the hotels near the airport, all of which have courtesy shuttles to the departure terminals; these hotels are also a boon to visitors en route elsewhere with layovers in Narita. Many of them have soundproof rooms to block out the noise of the airplanes.

$$
HOTEL
▨ **ANA Crowne Plaza Narita** ANAクラウンプラザホテル成田. With its brass-and-marble detail in the lobby, this hotel replicates the grand style of other hotels in the ANA chain. **Pros:** convenient location; pleasant staff, airport shuttle. **Cons:** small rooms; charge to use pool; in-house restaurants are the only nearby dining options. ✉ *68 Hori-no-uchi, Narita, Chiba-ken* ☎ *0476/33–1311, 0120/029–501 toll-free* ⊕ *www.anahotel-narita.com* ✈ *389 rooms, 7 suites* ♿ *In-room: a/c, safe, refrigerator, Internet. In-hotel: 3 restaurants, room service, pool, gym, parking* ⦿ *No meals.* ✛ *H1.*

$
HOTEL
▨ **Hilton Tokyo Narita Airport** ヒルトン成田. Given its proximity to the airport (a 10-minute drive), this C-shape hotel is a reasonable choice for a one-night visit. **Pros:** reasonably priced rooms; spacious lobby; airport shuttle. **Cons:** charge to use the pool and gym; standard rooms have dated furnishings. ✉ *456 Kosuge, Narita, Chiba-ken* ☎ *0476/33–1121* ⊕ *www.hilton.com* ✈ *537 rooms, 11 suites* ♿ *In-room: a/c, safe, refrigerator, Internet. In-hotel: 3 restaurants, room service, bar, golf, tennis court, pool, gym, spa, laundry service, parking* ⦿ *No meals.* ✛ *H1.*

$
HOTEL
▨ **Narita Airport Rest House.** A basic business hotel without much in the way of frills, the Rest House offers the closest accommodations to the airport itself, less than five minutes away by shuttle bus. **Pros:** day rooms available; closest rooms to the airport; hotel provides a shuttle to the airport. **Cons:** few dining choices outside the hotel; in-room furnishings are dated. ✉ *Narita International Airport, Narita, Chiba-ken* ☎ *0476/32–1212* ⊕ *www.apo-resthouse.com* ✈ *209 rooms* ♿ *In-room: a/c, refrigerator. In-hotel: restaurant, bar, laundry service, Internet terminal* ⦿ *No meals.* ✛ *H1.*

$$
HOTEL
▨ **Narita Excel Hotel Tokyuo** 成田エクセル東急. Airline crews rolling their bags through the lobby are a common sight at the Excel, a hotel with reasonable prices and friendly service. **Pros:** nice concierge; view of runway from bar; nice Japanese garden. **Cons:** small bathrooms; no outside dining options in immediate area. ✉ *31 Oyama, Narita, Chiba-ken* ☎ *0476/33–0109* ⊕ *www.tokyuhotelsjapan.com* ✈ *706 rooms, 2 suites* ♿ *In-room: a/c, safe, refrigerator, Internet. In-hotel: 4 restaurants,*

NARITA DAY ROOMS AND SHOWERS

Narita Airport is the hub between Asia and North America, so it sees many weary travelers transiting through. Since passengers on long-haul trips appreciate the chance to freshen up, the airport provides dayrooms and showers located in both terminals. Showers units can be rented for ¥500 for 30 minutes. A lounge and soaps and towels are provided. Single and twin dayrooms start at ¥1,000 per hour. Units are open from 7 am to 9 pm (9:30 in Terminal 1), and advance reservations are not accepted. ☎ *0476/33–2190 (Terminal 1), 0476/34–8537 (Terminal 2)* ⊕ *www.narita-airport.jp* 🛏 *18 shower units (8 in Terminal 1, 10 in Terminal 2), 24 dayrooms (10 singles and 3 twins in Terminal 1, 8 singles and 3 twins in Terminal 2).*

room service, bar, golf, tennis court, pool, gym, laundry service, parking |❍| *No meals.* ✚ *H1.*

$ 🖼 **Radisson Hotel Narita Airport** ラディソンホテル成田エアポート. Set on
HOTEL 28 spacious, green acres, this modern hotel feels somewhat like a resort, with massive indoor and outdoor pools. All told, it's probably the best bet for an airport stopover. **Pros:** reasonably priced rooms; high-quality bathroom toiletries by Shiseido; nice-size rooms; airport shuttle available. **Cons:** a 15-minute drive by car to the airport; no outside restaurants in the immediate area. ⊠ *650–35 Nanae, Tomisato, Chiba-ken* ☎ *0476/93–1234* ⊕ *www.radisson.com/tokyojp_narita* 🛏 *488 rooms, 2 suites* ♿ *In-room: a/c, safe, refrigerator, Internet. In-hotel: 2 restaurants, room service, bar, tennis court, pool, gym, laundry service, parking* |❍| *No meals.* ✚ *H1.*

NIGHTLIFE AND THE ARTS

As Tokyo's rich cultural history entwines itself with an influx of foreign influences, Tokyoites get the best of both worlds. An evening out can be as civilized as a night of Kabuki or as rowdy as a Roppongi nightclub. In between there are dance clubs, a swingin' jazz scene, theater, cinema, live venues, and more than enough bars to keep the social lubricant flowing past millions of tonsils nightly.

The sheer diversity of nightlife is breathtaking. Rickety street stands sit yards away from luxury hotels, and wallet-crunching hostess clubs can be found next to cheap and raucous rock bars. Whatever your style, you'll find yourself in good company if you venture out after dark.

Metropolis is a free English-language weekly magazine that has up-to-date listings of what's going on in the city; it's available at hotels, book and music stores, some restaurants and cafés, and other locations. The English-language daily newspapers *The Japan Times* and *The Daily Yomiuri* have decent entertainment features and listings in their Friday editions.

If your hotel can't help you with concert and performance bookings, call **Ticket Pia** (☎ *03/5237–9999*) for assistance in English. The **Playguide**

Agency (✉ *Playguide Bldg., 2–6–4 Ginza, Chuo-ku* ☎ *03/3561–8821* Ⓜ *Yuraku-cho subway line, Ginza Itchome Station, Exit 4*) sells tickets to cultural events via outlets in most department stores and in other locations throughout the city; you can stop in at the main office and ask for the nearest counter, but be aware that you may not find someone who speaks English. Note that agencies normally do not have tickets for same-day performances but only for advance booking.

For information on jazz events at small venues, a visit to the record shop **Disk Union** (✉ *3–31–2 Shinjuku, Shinjuku-ku* ☎ *03/5379–3551* Ⓜ *Marunouchi subway line, Shinjuku-san-chome Station [Exit A1]*) is essential. The store has flyers (sometimes in English) for smaller gigs, and the staff can make recommendations.

THE ARTS

An astonishing variety of dance and music, both classical and popular, can be found in Tokyo, alongside the must-see traditional Japanese arts of Kabuki, Noh, and Bunraku. The city is a proving ground for local talent and a magnet for orchestras and concert soloists from all over the world. Tokyo also has modern theater—in somewhat limited choices, to be sure, unless you can follow dialogue in Japanese, but Western repertory companies can always find receptive audiences here for plays in English. And it doesn't take long for a hit show from New York or London to open. Musicals such as *Mamma Mia* and *Wicked* have found enormous popularity here—although you'll find the protagonists speaking Japanese.

SHIBUYA
MUSIC
NHK Hall. The home base for the Japan Broadcasting Corporation's NHK Symphony Orchestra is probably the auditorium most familiar to Japanese lovers of classical music, as performances here are routinely rebroadcast on the national TV station. ✉ *2–2–1 Jinnan, Shibuya-ku* ☎ *03/3465–1751* Ⓜ *JR Yamanote Line, Shibuya Station (Hachiko Exit); Ginza and Hanzo-mon subway lines, Shibuya Station (Exits 6 and 7).*

TRADITIONAL THEATER
NOH **Kanze No-gakudo.** Founded in the 14th century, this is among the most important of the Noh family schools in Tokyo. The current *iemoto* (head) of the school is the 26th in his line. ✉ *1–16–4 Shoto, Shibuya-ku* ☎ *03/3469–5241* Ⓜ *Ginza and Hanzo-mon subway lines, Shibuya Station (Exit 3A).*

GINZA
TRADITIONAL THEATER
⚠ Kabuki-za, once the place to see a Kabuki show in Tokyo, has been torn down because of structural concerns. It will reopen on the same spot in spring of 2013.

KABUKI **Shimbashi Enbujo.** Dating to 1925, this theater was built for the geisha of the Shimbashi quarter to present their spring and autumn performances of traditional music and dance. Since the Kabuki-za was razed, Shimbashi Enbujo has become the top spot in Tokyo to see the nation's favorite traditional performing art. This is also the home of "Super Kabuki," a faster, jazzier modern version. Reserved seats commonly run ¥2,100–¥16,800, and there's no gallery. ⊠ *6–18–2 Ginza, Chuo-ku* ☎ *03/5565–6000* Ⓜ *Hibiya and Asakusa subway lines, Higashi-Ginza Station (Exit A6).*

YURAKU-CHO
MODERN THEATER
Takarazuka. Japan's all-female theater troupe was founded in the Osaka suburb of Takarazuka in 1913 and has been going strong ever since. Today it has not one but five companies, one of which has a permanent home in Tokyo at the 2,069-seat Tokyo Takarazuka Theater. Where else but at the Takarazuka could you see *Gone With the Wind*, sung in Japanese, with a young woman in a mustache and a frock coat playing Rhett Butler? ∎**TIP**→ Advance tickets are available only through the Play-guide agency (☎ *03/3561–8821*), with any remaining tickets sold at the theater box office on the second day. ⊠ *1–1–3 Yuraku-cho, Chiyoda-ku* ☎ *03/5251–2001* 🎫 *¥3,500–¥11,000* Ⓜ *JR Yamanote Line, Yuraku-cho Station (Hibiya Exit); Hibiya subway line, Hibiya Station (Exit A5); Chiyoda and Mita subway lines, Hibiya Station (Exit A13).*

ROPPONGI
MUSIC
Suntory Hall. This lavishly appointed concert auditorium in the Ark Hills complex has one of the best locations for theatergoers who want to extend their evening out: there's an abundance of good restaurants and bars nearby. ⊠ *1–13–1 Akasaka, Minato-ku* ☎ *03/3505–1001* Ⓜ *Ginza and Namboku subway lines, Tameike-Sanno Station (Exit 13).*

SHINJUKU
MUSIC
Nakano Sun Plaza. Everything from rock to Argentine tango is staged at this hall, located five minutes by train from Shinjuku Station. ⊠ *4–1–1 Nakano, Nakano-ku* ☎ *03/3388–1151* Ⓜ *JR and Tozai subway lines, Nakano Station (Kita-guchi/North Exit).*

New National Theater and Tokyo Opera City Concert Hall. With its 1,810-seat main auditorium, this venue nourishes Japan's fledgling efforts to make a name for itself in the world of opera. The Opera City Concert Hall has a massive pipe organ and hosts visiting orchestras and performers. Large-scale operatic productions such as *Carmen* draw crowds at the New National Theater's Opera House, while the Pit and Playhouse theaters showcase musicals and more-intimate dramatic works. Ticket prices range from ¥1,500 to ¥21,000. The complex also includes an art gallery. ⊠ *3–20–2 Nishi-Shinjuku, Shinjuku-ku* ☎ *03/5353–0788, 03/5353–9999 for tickets* ⊕ *www.operacity.jp* Ⓜ *Keio Shin-sen private rail line, Hatsudai Station (Higashi-guchi/East Exit).*

IMPERIAL PALACE AND GOVERNMENT DISTRICT
TRADITIONAL THEATER
KABUKI **National Theater** (*Kokuritsu Gekijo).* This theater hosts Kabuki companies based elsewhere; it also has a training program for young people who may not have one of the hereditary family connections but want to break into this closely guarded profession. Debut performances,

called *kao-mise,* are worth watching to catch the stars of the next generation. Reserved seats are usually ¥1,500–¥9,000. Tickets can be reserved by phone up until the day of the performance by calling the theater box office between 10 and 5. ✉ *4–1 Hayabusa-cho, Chiyoda-ku* ☎ *05/7007–9900* ⊕ *www.ntj.jac.go.jp/kokuritsu* Ⓜ *Hanzo-mon subway line, Hanzo-mon Station (Exit 1).*

CENTRAL TOKYO

NOH **National Noh Theater.** One of the few public halls to host Noh performances, this theater provides English-language summaries of the plots at performances. ✉ *4–18–1 Sendagaya, Shibuya-ku* ☎ *03/3423–1331* Ⓜ *JR Chuo Line, Sendagaya Station (Minami-guchi/South Exit); Oedo subway line, Kokuritsu-Kyogijo Station (Exit A4).*

UENO

MUSIC

Tokyo Metropolitan Festival Hall *(Tokyo Bunka Kaikan).* In the 1960s and '70s this hall was one of the city's premier showcases for orchestral music and visiting soloists. It still gets major bookings. ✉ *5–45 Ueno Koen, Taito-ku* ☎ *03/3828–2111* Ⓜ *JR Yamanote Line, Ueno Station (Koen-guchi/Park Exit).*

TRADITIONAL THEATER

RAKUGO **Suzumoto.** Built around 1857 and later rebuilt, Suzumoto is the oldest rakugo theater in Tokyo. It's on Chuo-dori, a few blocks north of the Ginza Line's Ueno Hiroko-ji stop. Tickets cost ¥2,800, and performances run continually throughout the day 12:20–4:30 and 5:20–9:10. ✉ *2–7–12 Ueno, Taito-ku* ☎ *03/3834–5906* Ⓜ *Ginza subway line, Ueno Hiroko-ji Station (Exit 3).*

GREATER TOKYO

MODERN THEATER

Cirque du Soleil. The acrobatic superstars are so popular in Japan that they have their own purpose-built theater on the edge of the Tokyo Disneyland complex. The show, *Zed,* is bigger and flashier than most temporary Cirque shows. Check any major ticket vendor for current shows and locations. The theater is located in Chiba Prefecture, 15 minutes by train from Tokyo Station. ■TIP➔ **If you're going to Disneyland, too, a combined ticket offers big savings.** ✉ *1–1 Maihama, Urayasu, Chiba* ☎ *05/7002–8666* 🎫 *¥7,800–¥18,000* ⊕ *www.cirquedusoleil.co.jp* Ⓜ *JR Keiyo, Musashino lines, Maihama Station (South Exit).*

Tokyo Dome. A 55,000-seat sports arena, the dome also hosts big-name Japanese pop acts as well as the occasional international star. ✉ *1–3–61 Koraku, Bunkyo-ku* ☎ *03/5800–9999* Ⓜ *Marunouchi and Namboku subway lines, Koraku-en Station (Exit 2); Oedo and Mita subway lines, Kasuga Station (Exit A2); JR Suido-bashi Station (Nishi-guchi/West Exit).*

NIGHTLIFE

Most bars and clubs in the main entertainment districts have printed price lists, often in English. Drinks generally cost ¥700–¥1,200, although some small exclusive bars and clubs will set you back a lot more. Be wary of establishments without visible price lists. Hostess clubs and small backstreet bars known as "snacks" or "pubs" can be particularly treacherous territory for the unprepared. That drink you've just ordered could set you back a reasonable ¥1,000; you might, on the other hand, have wandered unknowingly into a place that charges you ¥30,000 up front for a whole bottle—and slaps a ¥20,000 cover charge on top. If the bar has hostesses, it's often unclear what the companionship of one will cost you, but as an unfamiliar face, you can bet it will cost you a lot. Ignore the persuasive shills on the streets of Roppongi and Kabuki-cho, who will try to hook you into their establishment. There is, of course, plenty of safe ground: hotel lounges, jazz clubs, and the rapidly expanding Irish pub scene are pretty much the way they are anywhere else. But elsewhere it's best to follow the old adage: if you have to ask how much it costs, you probably can't afford it.

Major nightlife districts include Aoyama, Ginza, Harajuku, Roppongi, Shibuya, and Shinjuku, and each has a unique atmosphere, clientele, and price level.

AOYAMA

BARS

Radio. Koji Ozaki is the closest thing Tokyo has to a superstar bartender. This demure septuagenarian has been crafting cocktails for half a century, and he's known for both his perfectionism and creativity. Ozaki not only designed the bar he works behind and the glasses he serves his creations in (some of the best in the city), he also arranges the bar's flowers. ✉ *3–10–34 Minami-Aoyama, Minato-ku* ☎ *03/3402–2668* ⊕ *www. bar-radio.com* ☽ *Mon.–Sat. 6 pm–1 am* Ⓜ *Chiyoda, Ginza, and Hanzomon subway lines, Omotesando Station (Exit A4).*

Two Rooms. Aoyama's dressed-up drinkers hang out on the stylish terrace. Drinks are big, pricey, and modern—think martinis in multiple flavors. It adjoins a popular grill restaurant. ✉ *3–11–7 Kita-Aoyama, Minato-ku* ☎ *03/3498–0002* ⊕ *www.tworooms.jp.*

DANCE CLUBS

Le Baron de Paris. The Tokyo branch of the Paris and New York club is partly owned by superstar designer Marc Newson. As you might expect, it draws a fashionable crowd and plays host to events by trendy magazines and visiting musicians. Expect an eclectic mix of nostalgic and modern party music. Hours and prices vary greatly, so check the Web site for info. ✉ *B1, 3–8–40 Minami-Aoyama, Minato-ku* ☎ *03/3408– 3665* ⊕ *www.lebaron.jp* Ⓜ *Chiyoda, Ginza, and Hanzomon subway lines, Omotesando Station (Exit A4).*

JAZZ CLUBS

Blue Note Tokyo. The Blue Note isn't for everyone: prices are high, sets are short, and patrons are packed in tight, often sharing a table with strangers. But if you want to catch the legends—those of Herbie Hancock and Sly & the Family Stone caliber—you'll have to come here. Expect to pay upwards of ¥12,000 to see major acts, and put another ¥4,000–¥5,000 on the budget for food and drink. ✉ *6–3–16 Minami-Aoyama, Minato-ku* ☎ *03/5485–0088* ⊕ *www.bluenote.co.jp* ☽ *Shows*

The Red Lights of Kabuki-cho

CLOSE UP

Tokyo has more than its fair share of red-light districts, but the leader of the pack is unquestionably Kabuki-cho, located just north of Shinjuku Station. The land was once a swamp, although its current name refers to an aborted post–World War II effort to bring culture to the area in the form of a landmark Kabuki theater. Nowadays, most of the entertainment is of the insalubrious kind, with strip clubs, love hotels, host and hostess clubs, and thinly disguised brothels all luridly advertising their presence.

The area's also home to throngs of Japanese and Chinese gangsters, giving rise to its image domestically as a danger zone. But in truth, Kabuki-cho poses little risk to even the solo traveler. The sheer volume of people in the area each night, combined with a prominent security-camera presence, means that crime stays mostly indoors.

Despite its sordid reputation, Kabuki-cho does offer something beyond the red lights. There are eateries galore ranging from chain diners to designer restaurants. The impressive 16th-century shrine **Hanazono Jinja** (✉ 5–17–3 Shinjuku, Shinjuku-ku ☎ 03/3209–5265 💴 Free ⊙ Daily sunrise–sunset Ⓜ Marunouchi subway line, Shinjuku-san-chome Station [Exits B2 and B3]) hosts several events throughout the year, but comes alive with two must-see colorful festivals on its grounds. The weekend closest to May 28 brings the Hanazono shrine festival, in which portable shrines are paraded through the streets. The November Tori-no-Ichi festival (the exact days in November vary each year) is held here and at several shrines throughout Tokyo, but Hanazono is the most famous place to buy the festival's *kumade*: big rakes decorated with money, mock fruit, and other items people would like to "rake in." People buy them for luck, and replace them every year.

Also here is Golden Gai, probably Tokyo's most atmospheric drinking area.

—Nicholas Coldicott

---

usually Mon.–Sat. at 7 and 9:30, Sun. at 6:30 and 9 Ⓜ *Chiyoda, Ginza, and Hanzo-mon subway lines, Omotesando Station (Exit A3).*

HARAJUKU

BARS

Harajuku Taproom. Expat Bryan Baird runs an acclaimed microbrewery in the shadow of Mt. Fuji. In 2010 he opened this great taproom that serves his range of brews, as well as decent Japanese-style pub grub. ✉ *1–20–13 Jingu-mae, Shibuya-ku* ☎ *03/6438–0450* ⊕ *www.bairdbeer. com* ⊙ *Weekdays 5–midnight, weekends noon–midnight.*

Montoak. Positioned halfway down the prestigious shopping street Omotesando-dori, within spitting distance of such fashion giants as Gucci, Louis Vuitton, and Tod's, this hip restaurant-bar is a great place to rest after testing the limits of your credit card. With smoky floor-to-ceiling windows, cushy armchairs, and a layout so spacious you won't believe you're sitting on one of Tokyo's most exclusive streets, the place attracts a hipper-than-thou clientele but never feels unwelcoming.

Go techno in Shibuya at Womb.

The bar food consists of canapés, salads, cheese plates, and the like. Drinks start at ¥700. ✉ *6–1–9 Jingu-mae, Shibuya-ku* ☎ *03/5468–5928* ⊕ *www.montoak.com* ✆ *Daily 11 am–3 am* Ⓜ *Chiyoda subway line, Meiji-Jingu-mae Station (Exit 4).*

SHIBUYA

BEER HALLS AND PUBS

What the Dickens. This spacious pub, in the Ebisu section of Shibuya, feels more authentically British than many of its rivals, thanks partly to a menu of traditional pub grub. It hosts regular live music (funk, folk, jazz, rock, reggae—anything goes here) and other events. ✉ *4F, 1–13–3 Ebisu-Nishi, Shibuya-ku* ☎ *03/3780–2099* ⊕ *www.whatthedickens.jp* ✆ *Tues. and Wed. 5 pm–1 am, Thurs.–Sat. 5 pm–2 am, Sun. 5 pm–midnight* Ⓜ *Hibiya subway line, Ebisu Station (Nishi-guchi/West Exit).*

DANCE CLUBS

★ **Womb.** Well-known techno and break-beat DJs make a point of stopping by this Shibuya überclub on their way through town. The turntable talent, local and international, and four floors of dance and lounge space make Womb Tokyo's most consistently rewarding club experience. ✉ *2–16 Maruyama-cho, Shibuya-ku* ☎ *03/5459–0039* ⊕ *www. womb.co.jp* 💳 *Around ¥3,500* ✆ *Daily 10 pm–early morning* Ⓜ *JR Yamanote Line, Ginza and Hanzo-mon subway lines, Shibuya Station (Hachiko Exit for JR and Ginza, Exit 3A for Hanzo-mon).*

GAY BARS

Chestnut & Squirrel. Chestnut & Squirrel (the name translates in Japanese as a certain female body part) is the place to be for lesbians on Wednesday nights in Tokyo. The bar's cheap drinks (cocktails and most beers ¥500), friendly, unpretentious vibe, and mix of foreign and Japanese customers give it the feel of a friendly neighborhood bar. ✉ *3F O-ishi Bldg., 3–7–8 Shibuya, Shibuya-ku* ☎ *No phone* ⊕ *www. chestnutandsquirrel.com* ⊗ *Wed. 7:30 pm–late.*

IZAKAYA

Tachimichiya. With its traditional Japanese dishes, wide range of sakes and shochus, and rustic interior, Tachimichiya is a classic izakaya in all ways but one: its love of punk rock. The wall is adorned with posters of the Sex Pistols, the Ramones, and the Clash, who also provide the sound track. The theme is fun rather than overbearing, and the food alone is good enough to warrant a visit. It's located in Daikanyama, two minutes by train from Shibuya Station. ✉ *B1, 30–8 Sarugaku-cho, Shibuya-ku* ☎ *03/5459–3431* ⊗ *Weekdays 6 pm–4 am, weekends 6 pm–midnight* Ⓜ *Tokyu Toyoko Line, Daikanyama Station.*

Watami. One of Tokyo's big izakaya chains—with a half dozen branches in the youth entertainment district of Shibuya alone—Watami is popular for its seriously inexpensive menu. Seating at this location ranges from a communal island bar to Western-style tables to more-private areas. ✉ *4F Satose Bldg., 13–8 Udagawacho, Shibuya-ku* ☎ *03/6415–6516* ⊗ *Sun.–Thurs. 5 pm–3 am, Fri. and Sat. 5 pm–5 am* Ⓜ *JR Yamanote Line, Ginza and Hanzo-mon subway lines, Shibuya Station (Hachiko Exit for JR and Ginza, Exit 6 for Hanzo-mon).*

KARAOKE

Shidax. The Shidax chain's corporate headquarters—in an excellent Shibuya location, across from Tower Records—has 130 private karaoke rooms, a café, and a restaurant. ✉ *1–12–13 Jinnan, Shibuya-ku* ☎ *03/5784–8881* ⊗ *¥760 per hr* ⊗ *Daily 11 am–8 am* Ⓜ *JR, Ginza, and Hanzo-mon subway lines, Shibuya Station (Exit 6).*

ASAKUSA

BARS

Fodor's Choice
★

Kamiya Bar. Tokyo's oldest Western-style bar hasn't had a face-lift for decades, and that's part of what draws so many drinkers to this bright, noisy venue. The other major attraction is the Denki Bran, a delicious but hangover-inducing liquor (comprising gin, red wine, brandy, and curaçao) that was invented here and is now stocked by bars throughout Japan. ✉ *1–1–1 Asakusa, Taito-ku* ☎ *03/3841–5400* ⊗ *Daily 11:30 am–10 pm* Ⓜ *Asakusa and Ginza subway lines, Asakusa Station (Exit A5).*

GINZA

BARS

Star Bar. It's often said that Ginza has all the best bars, and Star Bar may be the best of the lot. Owner-bartender Hisashi Kishi is the Director of Technical Research for the Japan Bartenders Association, and his attention to detail is staggering. The drinks aren't cheap, but you get what you pay for. Try one of Kishi's Sidecars. ✉ *B1, 1–5–13 Ginza, Chuo-ku* ☎ *03/3535–8005* ⊕ *www.starbarginza.com* ⊗ *Weekdays 6 pm–2 am; Sat. 6 pm–midnight* Ⓜ *JR Yamanote Line, Yuraku-cho Station (Kyobashi Exit).*

CLOSE UP

Tokyo-Style Nightlife

Tokyo has a variety of nightlife options, so don't limit yourself to your hotel bar in the evenings. Spend some time relaxing the way the locals do at izakaya, karaoke, and live houses—three unique forms of contemporary Japanese entertainment.

IZAKAYA

Izakaya (literally "drinking places") are Japanese pubs that can be found throughout Tokyo. If you're in the mood for elegant decor and sedate surroundings, look elsewhere; these drinking dens are often noisy, bright, and smoky. But for a taste of authentic Japanese-style socializing, a visit to an izakaya is a must—this is where young people start their nights out, office workers gather on their way home, and students take a break to grab a cheap meal and a drink.

Typically, izakaya have a full lineup of cocktails, a good selection of sake, draft beer, and lots of cheap, greasy Japanese and Western food; rarely does anything cost more than ¥1,000. Picture menus make ordering easy, and because most cocktails retain their Western names, communicating drink preferences shouldn't be difficult.

KARAOKE

In buttoned-down, socially conservative Japan, karaoke is one of the safety valves. Employees, employers, husbands, wives, teenage romancers, and good friends all drop their guard when there's a microphone in hand. The phenomenon started in the 1970s when cabaret singer Daisuke Inoue made a coin-operated machine that played his songs on tape so that his fans could sing along. Unfortunately for Inoue, he neglected to patent his creation, thereby failing to cash in

as karaoke became one of Japan's favorite pastimes. Nowadays it's the finale of many an office outing, a cheap daytime activity for teens, and a surprisingly popular destination for dates.

Unlike most karaoke bars in the United States, in Japan the singing usually takes place in the seclusion of private rooms that can accommodate groups. Basic hourly charges vary but are usually less than ¥1,000. Most establishments have a large selection of English songs, stay open late, and serve inexpensive food and drink, which you order via a telephone on the wall. Finding a venue around one of the major entertainment hubs is easy—there will be plenty of young touts eager to escort you to their employer. And unlike most other touts in the city, you won't end up broke by following them.

LIVE HOUSES

Tokyo has numerous small music clubs known as "live houses." These range from the very basic to miniclub venues, and they showcase the best emerging talent on the local scene. Many of the best live houses can be found in the Kichijoji, Koenji, and Nakano areas, although they are tucked away in basements citywide. The music could be gypsy jazz one night and thrash metal the next, so it's worth doing a little research before you turn up. Cover charges vary depending on who's performing but are typically ¥3,000–¥5,000 ($25–$41).

BEER HALLS AND PUBS

Ginza Lion. This bar, in business since 1899 and occupying the same stately Chuo-dori location since 1934, is remarkably inexpensive for one of Tokyo's toniest addresses. Ginza shoppers and office workers alike drop by for beer and ballast—anything from yakitori to spaghetti. Beers start at ¥590. ⊠ 7–9–20 Ginza, Chuo-ku ☎ 03/3571–2590 ⊙ Daily 11:30 am–11 pm Ⓜ Ginza, Hibiya, and Marunouchi subway lines, Ginza Station (Exit A3).

YURAKU-CHO

BARS

Fodor's Choice ★ **Peter.** Like most of Tokyo's high-end hotels, the Peninsula has a high-rise bar. But unlike many hotel bars, especially the high-rise, five-star varieties that are dimly lighted with a jazz piano and ultracomposed staff, Peter has an entrance in a rainbow of colors, eye-catching cocktails, and occasional DJs. This 24th-floor spot's decor of chrome trees and rainbow lights is defiantly anti-zeitgeist, but lots of fun. ⊠ 24F Peninsula Tokyo, 1–8–1 Yuraku-cho, Chiyoda-ku ☎ 03/6270–2763 ⊕ www.tokyo.peninsula.com ⊙ Daily 11:30 am–10 pm Ⓜ Hibiya and Mita subway lines, Hibiya Station (Exit A6).

IZAKAYA

Takara. This high-class izakaya in the sumptuous Tokyo International Forum is a favorite with foreigners because of its English-language menu and extensive sake list. ⊠ B1, 3–5–1 Marunouchi, Chiyoda-ku ☎ 03/5223–9888 ⊙ Weekdays 11:30 am–2:30 pm and 5:30 pm–11 pm, weekends 11:30 am–3:30 pm and 5:30 pm–10 pm Ⓜ Yuraku-cho subway line, Yuraku-cho Station (Exit A-4B).

ROPPONGI

BARS

A971. With a plum spot on the edge of Roppongi's Midtown complex, A971 has been popular right from its opening. It has an airy, modern feel, faces a spacious patio, and often hosts house music DJs. It's standing room only on the weekends, which means plenty of socializing, usually of the flirtatious kind. ⊠ Tokyo Midtown East, 9–7–2 Akasaka, Minato-ku ☎ 03/5413–3210 ⊕ www.a971.com ⊙ Mon.–Thurs. 10 am–5 am, Sun. 10 am–midnight Ⓜ Hibiya and Oedo subway lines, Roppongi Station (Exit 8).

Agave. In most Roppongi hot spots, tequila is pounded one shot at a time. Not so at Agave: this authentic Mexican cantina treats the spirit with a little more respect, and your palate will be tempted by a choice of more than 400 tequilas and mescals. A single shot can cost between ¥800 and ¥10,000, but most of the varieties here aren't available anywhere else in Japan, so the steep prices are worth paying. ⊠ 7–15–10 Roppongi, Minato-ku ☎ 03/3497–0229 ⊙ Mon.–Thurs. 6:30 pm–2 am, Fri. and Sat. 6:30 pm–4 am Ⓜ Hibiya and Oedo subway lines, Roppongi Station (Exit 3).

DANCE CLUBS

★ **Eleven.** One of Tokyo's top clubs, Eleven occupies two basement floors and hosts the best of Tokyo's homegrown DJs as well as big names like Francois K, Frankie Knuckles, and Joaquin Joe Claussell. ⊠ 1–10–11

Nishi-Azabu, *Minato-ku* ☎ *03/5775–6206* ⊕ *www.go-to-eleven.com* ✉ *¥3,000–¥3,500* ⊘ *10 pm–5 am.*

Super-Deluxe. This isn't quite a dance club. You could call it an experimental party space, with each night hosting a different kind of event. It's home to Pecha Kucha, a popular evening of presentations by creative types; but you might also find a techno night, underground-film screenings, a performance-art event, or anything else the imagination can conjure up. ✉ *B1, 3–1–25 Nishi-Azabu, Minato-ku* ☎ *03/5412–0516* ⊕ *www.super-deluxe.com* ⊘ *Daily 6 pm–late* Ⓜ *Hibiya and Oedo subway lines, Roppongi Station (Exit 1C).*

Warehouse 702. Nightlife in Roppongi tends to be raucous and lowbrow, so serious clubbers should head to nearby Azabu Juban for this spacious subterranean venue with a great sound system and consistently high-quality DJs. ✉ *B1, 1–4–5 Azabu Juban, Minato-ku* ☎ *03/6230–0343* ⊕ *www.warehouse702.com* ✉ *Around ¥3,500* ⊘ *Wed.–Mon. 11 pm–5 am* Ⓜ *Nanboku and Oedo subway lines, Azabu Juban Station (Exit 7).*

JAZZ CLUBS

Fodor's Choice
★

Sweet Basil 139. An upscale jazz club near Roppongi Crossing, Sweet Basil 139 (no relation to the famous New York Sweet Basil) is renowned for local and international acts that run the musical gamut from smooth jazz and fusion to classical. A large, formal dining area serves Italian dishes that are as good as the jazz, making this spot an excellent choice for a complete night out. With a spacious interior and standing room for 500 on the main floor, this is one of the largest and most accessible jazz bars in town. Prices range from ¥2,857 to ¥12,000 depending on who's headlining. ✉ *6–7–11 Roppongi, Minato-ku* ☎ *03/5474–0139* ⊕ *stb139.co.jp* ⊘ *Mon.–Sat. 6–11 pm; shows at 8* Ⓜ *Hibiya and Oedo subway lines, Roppongi Station (Exit 3).*

KARAOKE

Big Echo. One of Tokyo's largest karaoke chains, Big Echo has dozens of locations throughout the city. Cheap hourly rates and late closing times make it popular with youngsters. The Roppongi branch is spread over three floors. ✉ *7–14–12 Roppongi, Minato-ku* ☎ *03/5770–7700* ✉ *¥500–¥600 per hr* ⊘ *Daily 6 pm–5 am* Ⓜ *Hibiya and Oedo subway lines, Roppongi Station (Exit 4).*

★ **Lovenet.** Despite the misleading erotic name, Lovenet is actually the fanciest karaoke box in town. Luxury theme rooms of all descriptions create a fun and classy setting for your dulcet warbling. Mediterranean and Japanese food is served. ✉ *7–14–4 Roppongi, Minato-ku* ☎ *03/5771–5511* ⊕ *www.lovenet-jp.com* ✉ *From ¥2,000 per hr* ⊘ *Daily 6 pm–5 am* Ⓜ *Hibiya and Oedo subway lines, Roppongi Station (Exit 4A).*

Pasela. This 10-story entertainment complex on the main Roppongi drag of Gaien-Higashi-dori has seven floors of karaoke rooms with more than 10,000 foreign-song titles. A Mexican-themed bar and a restaurant are also on-site. ✉ *5–16–3 Roppongi, Minato-ku* ☎ *0120/911–086* ⊕ *www.pasela.co.jp* ✉ *¥400–¥1,260 per hr* ⊘ *Mon.–Thurs. 5 pm–10 am, Fri.–Sun. 2 pm–8 am* Ⓜ *Hibiya and Oedo subway lines, Roppongi Station (Exit 3).*

SHINJUKU

BARS

Donzoko. This venerable bar claims to be Shinjuku's oldest—established in 1951—and has hosted Yukio Mishima and Akira Kurosawa among many other luminaries. It's also one of several bars that claim to have invented the popular *chu-hai* cocktail (shochu with juice and soda). But for all its history, Donzoko has a young and vibrant atmosphere, with its five floors usually packed. ⊠ *3–10–2 Shinjuku, Shinjuku-ku* ☎ *03/3354–7749* ⊗ *Weekdays 6 pm–1 am; weekends 5 pm–midnight* Ⓜ *Marunouchi and Shinjuku subway lines, Shinjuku-san-chome Station (Exit C3).*

★ **New York Bar.** Even before *Lost in Translation* introduced the Park Hyatt's signature lounge to filmgoers worldwide, New York Bar was a local Tokyo favorite. All the style you would expect of one of the city's top hotels combined with superior views of Shinjuku's skyscrapers and neon-lighted streets make this one of the city's premier nighttime venues. The quality of the jazz on offer equals that of the view. Drinks start at ¥800, and there's a cover charge of ¥2,000 after 8 *pm* (7 *pm* on Sunday). ⊠ *52F Park Hyatt Hotel, 3–7–1–2 Nishi-Shinjuku, Shinjuku-ku* ☎ *03/5322–1234* ⊗ *Sun.–Wed. 5 pm–midnight, Thurs.–Sat. 5 pm–1 am* Ⓜ *JR Shinjuku Station (Nishi-guchi/West Exit).*

GAY BARS

Advocates Cafe. Almost every great gay night out begins at this welcoming street-corner pub, where the patrons spill out onto the street. This is the perfect place to put back a few cocktails (¥700–¥900), meet new people, and get a feeling for where to go next. The crowd is mixed and very foreigner-friendly. ⊠ *2–18–1 Shinjuku, Shinjuku-ku* ☎ *03/3358–3988* ⊕ *www.advocates-cafe.com* ⊗ *Mon.–Sat. 6 pm–4 am, Sun. 6 pm–1 am.*

Arty Farty. Cheap and cheesy, Arty Farty is a fun club, complete with a ministage and stripper pole. Those with aversions to Kylie or Madonna need not bother. Draft beer starts at ¥500, and the alcohol selection is comprehensive. The crowd is mixed and foreigner-friendly. ⊠ *2F Dai 33 Kyutei Bldg., 2–11–7 Shinjuku, Shinjuku-ku* ☎ *03/5362–9720* ⊗ *Sun.–Thurs. 7 pm–3 am, Fri. and Sat. 7 pm–5 am.*

Dragon Men. Despite the name, Tokyo's swanky gay lounge Dragon Men also welcomes women. Remodeled in 2007, Dragon is a neon-deco space that would look right at home in New York or Paris. The location could be better: it's behind a drugstore, and the outdoor tables face a ramshackle wall, but when the place is crammed on weekends with cuties of all persuasions, who's looking? ⊠ *1F Stork Nagasaki, 2–11–4 Shinjuku, Shinjuku-ku* ☎ *03/3341–0606* ⊗ *Sun.–Thurs. 6 pm–3 am, Fri. and Sat. 6 pm–4 am.*

GB. The men-only GB has been running for two decades, and carries a whiff of the old days when things were less mainstream. Video monitors blast contemporary and classic dance hits. On weekends the place is packed with gentlemen in their twenties through fifties cruising via strategically placed mirrors. ⊠ *B1 Shinjuku Plaza Bldg., 2–12–3 Shinjuku,*

TOKYO'S GAY BARS

Gay culture in Japan is a little different than that in the West. Most of it takes place well under the radar, which can be both a blessing and a curse; there are fewer options, but there's also less of the prejudice you might experience elsewhere. People are more likely to be baffled than offended by gay couples and some hotels may "not compute" that a same-sex couple would like a double bed. Still it's a very safe city to visit and with a little digging you'll find a scene more vibrant than you—or many Tokyoites—might expect. The city's primary queer hub is Ni-chome in the Shinjuku district. Take the Shinjuku or Marunouchi subway line to Shinjuku-Sanchome Station (Exit C7). Ni-chome is sometimes likened to its more notorious neighbor Kabuki-cho, its name also spoken in hushed tones and accompanied by raised eyebrows. Ni-chome, however, is more subtle in its approach. Although queer and queer-friendly establishments can be found sprinkled in other areas (Shibuya, Daikanyama Shinbashi, and Ebisu), none quite match Ni-chome for variety or accessibility.

Shinjuku-ku ☎ *03/3352–8972* ⊕ *gb-tokyo.tripod.com* ⊗ *Sun.–Thurs. 8 pm–2 am, Fri. and Sat. 8 pm–3 am.*

Motel #203. One of Ni-chome's newest bars, Motel is a posh but relaxed bar for "women who love women." It's a cozy den of vintage lamps, leather sofas, and plush cushions, with no cover charge. The bar's owner is an icon in the Tokyo lesbian scene and also runs a popular monthly dance party, called "Girlfriend," usually the last Saturday of every month at nearby Bar Hijo-guchi, or Bar Exit. Motel is women-only except Thursday, which is mixed. ⊠ *203 Sunnocorpo Shinjuku Bldg., 2–7–2 Shinjuku, Shinjuku-ku* ☎ *03/6383–4649* ⊕ *www.bar-motel.com* ⊗ *Wed.–Mon. 8 pm–4 am.*

JAZZ CLUBS

Intro. This small basement bar features one of the best jazz experiences in Tokyo: a Saturday "jam session" that stretches until 5 am (¥1,000 entry fee). Other nights of the week occasionally bring unannounced live sets by musicians just dropping by, but usually it's the owner's extensive vinyl and CD collection that the regulars are listening to. Simple Japanese and Western food is available. ⊠ *B1 NT Bldg., 2–14–8 Takadanobaba, Shinjuku-ku* ☎ *03/3200–4396* ⊕ *www. intro.co.jp* ⊗ *Sun.–Thurs. 6:30 pm–midnight, Fri. 6:30 pm–1 am, Sat. 5 pm–5 am* Ⓜ *JR Takadanobaba Station (Waseda Exit).*

Shinjuku Pit Inn. Most major jazz musicians have played at least once in this classic Tokyo club. The veteran Shinjuku Pit stages mostly mainstream fare with the odd foray into the avant-garde. Afternoon admission is ¥1,300 weekdays, ¥2,500 weekends; evening entry is typically ¥3,000. Better-known local acts often cost a little more. ⊠ *B1 Accord Shinjuku Bldg., 2–12–4 Shinjuku, Shinjuku-ku* ☎ *03/3354–2024* ⊗ *Daily, hrs vary* ⊕ *www.pit-inn.com* Ⓜ *Marunouchi subway line, Shinjuku-san-chome Station.*

CENTRAL TOKYO
KARAOKE

Smash Hits. If karaoke just isn't karaoke to you without drunken strangers to sing to, Smash Hits has the answer. An expat favorite, it offers thousands of English songs and a central performance stage. The cover charge gets you two drinks and no time limit. ⊠ *5–2–26 Hiro-o, Shibuya-ku* ☎ *03/3444–0432* ⊕ *www.smashhits.jp* ⊠ *¥3,500* ☯ *Tues.–Sat. 7 pm–3 am* Ⓜ *Hibiya Line, Hiroo Station (Exit 2).*

ELSEWHERE IN TOKYO
BEER HALLS AND PUBS

Popeye. Of the staggering 70 beers on tap here, most are top-quality Japanese microbrews, from pilsners to IPAs to barley wines. The owner is one of Japan's leading authorities on beer, and his passion is reflected in the quality of the brews. Popeye is always packed, so get there early or be prepared to wait. ⊠ *2–18–7 Ryogoku, Sumida-ku* ☎ *03/3633–2120* ⊕ *www.40beersontap.com* ☯ *Mon.–Sat. 5 pm–11:30 pm.*

DANCE CLUBS

Ageha. This massive bay-side venue has the city's best sound system and most diverse musical lineup. The cavernous Arena hosts well-known house and techno DJs, the bar plays hip-hop, a summer-only swimming-pool area has everything from reggae to break beats, and inside a chill-out tent there's usually ambient or trance music. Because of its far-flung location and enormous capacity, Ageha can be either a throbbing party or an embarrassingly empty hall, depending on the caliber of the DJ. Free buses to Ageha depart every half hour between 11 pm and 4:30 am from the stop opposite the Shibuya police station on Roppongi-dori, a three-minute walk from Shibuya Station (there are also return buses every half hour from 11:30 pm to 5 am). ⊠ *2–2–10 Shin-Kiba, Koto-ku* ☎ *03/5534–1515* ⊕ *www.ageha.com* ⊠ *Around ¥3,500* Ⓜ *Yuraku-cho subway line, Shin-Kiba Station.*

JAZZ CLUBS

Hot House. This could very well be the world's smallest jazz club. An evening here is like listening to live jazz in your living room with five or six other jazz lovers on your sofa. It's so small, in fact, that you can't get through the front door once the pianist is seated, so don't show up late. Live acts are trios at most, with no space for drums or amplifiers. Simple, home-style Japanese cooking helps make this a truly intimate experience. ⊠ *B1 Liberal Takadanobaba, 2–14–8 Takadanobaba, Shinjuku-ku* ☎ *03/3367–1233* ☯ *Show times vary from 8:30 pm to early morning* Ⓜ *JR Takadanobaba Station (Waseda Exit).*

LIVE HOUSES

Showboat. A small, basic venue in western Tokyo that's been going strong for more than a decade, Showboat attracts both amateur and semiprofessional performers. Ticket prices vary by act but are typically around ¥2,000 and often include one drink. ⊠ *B1 Oak Hill Koenji, 3–17–2 Koenji Kita, Suginami-ku* ☎ *03/3337–5745* ⊕ *www.showboat.co.jp* ☯ *Daily 6 pm–early morning* Ⓜ *JR Sobu and JR Chuo lines, Koenji Station (Kita-guchi/North Exit).*

Kabukicho, in Shinjuku, is a brightly lit hub for bars, pachinko parlors, and restaurants, as well as tattooed Yakuza.

SHOPPING

You didn't fly all the way to Tokyo to buy European designer clothing, so shop for items that are Japanese-made for Japanese people and sold in stores that don't cater to tourists. This city is Japan's showcase. The crazy clothing styles, obscure electronics, and new games found here are capable of setting trends for the rest of the country—and perhaps the rest of Asia.

Also, don't pass up the chance to purchase Japanese crafts. Color, balance of form, and superb workmanship make these items exquisite and well worth the price you'll pay. Some can be quite expensive; for example, Japanese lacquerware carries a hefty price tag. But if you like the shiny boxes, bowls, cups, and trays and consider that quality lacquerware is made to last a lifetime, the cost is justified.

Horror stories abound about prices in Japan—and some of them are true. Yes, a cup of coffee can cost $10, if you pick the wrong coffee shop. A gift-wrapped melon from a department-store gourmet counter can cost $150. And a taxi ride from the airport to central Tokyo does cost about $200. But most people take the convenient airport train for $9, and if you shop around, you can find plenty of gifts and souvenirs at fair prices.

Japan has been slow to embrace the use of credit cards, and even though plastic is now accepted at big retailers, some smaller shops only take cash. So when you go souvenir hunting, be prepared with a decent amount of cash; Tokyo's low crime rates make this a low-risk proposi-

All That Tokyo Jazz

CLOSE UP

The Tokyo jazz scene is one of the world's best, far surpassing that of Paris and New York with its number of venues playing traditional, swing, bossa nova, rhythm and blues, and free jazz. Though popular in Japan before World War II, jazz really took hold of the city after U.S. forces introduced Charlie Parker and Thelonius Monk in the late 1940s. The genre had been banned in wartime Japan as an American vice, but even at the height of the war, fans were able to listen to their favorite artists on Voice of America radio. In the 1960s Japan experienced a boom in all areas of the arts, and jazz was no exception. Since then, the Japanese scene has steadily bloomed, with several local stars—such as Sadao Watanabe in the 1960s and contemporary favorites Keiko Lee and Hiromi Uehara—gaining global attention.

Today there are more than 120 bars and clubs that host live music, plus hundreds that play recorded jazz. Shinjuku, Takadanobaba, and Kichijoji are the city's jazz enclaves. Famous international acts regularly appear at big-name clubs such as the Blue Note, but the smaller, lesser-known joints usually have more atmosphere. With such a large jazz scene, there's an incredible diversity to enjoy, from Louis Armstrong tribute acts to fully improvised free jazz—sometimes on successive nights at the same venue.

If you time your visit right, you can listen to great jazz at one of the city's more than 20 annual festivals dedicated to this adopted musical form. The festivals vary in size and coverage, but two to check out are the Tokyo Jazz Festival and the Asagaya Jazz Street Festival.

Tokyo Jazz Festival. On the last weekend in September, the festival takes over the Tokyo International Forum in Marunouchi. Though the 5,000-seat hall lacks the intimacy you might seek in a jazz show, the lineup is usually an impressive mix of local talent and international stars. ☎ 03/5777–8600 ⊕ www.tokyo-jazz.com

Asagaya Jazz Street Festival. Held the last weekend of October, the predominantly mainstream affair takes places in some less-than-mainstream places, with venues ranging from a Shinto shrine to a Lutheran church (most within walking distance of Asagaya Station). Look for festival staff at the station to help guide you, but they may not speak English. Previous headliners have included the Mike Price Jazz Quintet and vocalist Masamichi Yano. The festival gets crowded, so come early to ensure entry. ☎ 03/5305–5075

—James Catchpole

tion. The dishonor associated with theft is so strong, in fact, that it's considered bad form to conspicuously count change in front of cashiers.

Japan has an across-the-board 5% value-added tax (V.A.T.) imposed on luxury goods as well as on restaurant and hotel bills. This tax can be avoided at some duty-free shops in the city (don't forget to bring your passport). It's also waived in the duty-free shops at the international airports, but because these places tend to have higher profit margins, your tax savings there are likely to be offset by the higher markups.

Stores in Tokyo generally open at 10 or 11 am and close at 8 or 9 pm.

AKIHABARA AND JIMBO-CHO

SPECIALTY STORES

ANTIQUES

Yasukuni Jinja. Every Sunday, from sunrise to sunset, antiques-hunters can search and explore this flea market, which boasts 100 booths run by professional collectors. It's located near the Yasukuni Jinja, so when you're finished shopping, stroll over to the shrine to learn about the controversy that surrounds it. ✉ *3–1–1 Kudan-Kita, Chiyoda-ku* ☎ *03/3261–8326* Ⓜ *Hanzo-mon and Shinjuku subway lines, Kudan-shita Station (Exit 1).*

BOOKS

Bookstores of Jimbo-cho. The site of one of the largest concentrations of used-book stores in the world, the Jimbo-cho area is a bibliophile's dream. In the ½-km (¼-mi) strip along Yasukuni-dori and its side streets you can find centuries-old Japanese prints, vintage manga, and even complete sets of the *Oxford English Dictionary*. Most shops have predominately Japanese-language selections, but almost all stock some foreign titles, with a few devoting major floor space to English books. Kitazawa Shoten, recognizable by its stately entranceway, carries lots of humanities titles. Tokyo Random Walk is the retail outlet of Tuttle Publishing, which puts out books on Japanese language and culture. The large Japanese publisher Sanseido has its flagship store here; the fifth floor sells magazines and postcards in addition to books. The stores in the area are usually open 9 or 9:30 to 5:30 or 6, and many of the smaller shops close Sunday or Monday. Ⓜ *Mita, Shinjuku, and Hanzo-mon subway lines, Jimbo-cho Station (Exit A5).*

DOLLS

Beishu. Colorful and often made from precious metals, the delicate dolls handcrafted at this shop have found their way into some of Japan's larger department stores, museums, and even the Imperial Palace. ✉ *1–23–3 Yanagibashi, Taito-ku* ☎ *03/3834–3501* ◷ *Daily 9:30–5:30* Ⓜ *JR Sobu Line, Asakusa subway line, Asakusa-bashi Station (Exit A3).*

Kyugetsu. In business for more than a century, Kyugetsu sells every kind of doll imaginable. ✉ *1–20–4 Yanagibashi, Taito-ku* ☎ *03/5687–5176* ◷ *Weekdays 9:15–6, weekends 9:15–5:15* Ⓜ *Asakusa subway line, JR Sobu Line, Asakusa-bashi Station (Exit A3).*

ELECTRONICS

LAOX. One of the big Akihabara chains, LAOX has several locations in the area. The seven-story main branch is duty free, with three floors dedicated to export models. English-speaking staff members are always on call. ✉ *1–2–9 Soto-Kanda, Chiyoda-ku* ☎ *03/3253–7111* ◷ *Sun.–Thurs. 10–8, Fri. and Sat. 10–9* Ⓜ *JR Yamanote Line, Akihabara Station (Electric Town Exit).*

Sofmap. One Akihabara retailer that actually benefited from the bursting of Japan's economic bubble in the early '90s is Sofmap, once known as a used-PC and software chain with a heavy presence in Tokyo. Now its multiple branches also sell electronics, music, and mobile phones. Most are open daily until 7:30 or 8. ✉ *3–13–8 Soto-Kanda, Chiyoda-ku*

☎ 03/3253–3399 ⊗ Daily 11–8 Ⓜ JR Yamanote Line, Akihabara Station (Electric Town Exit).

AOYAMA AND OMOTESANDO

MALLS AND SHOPPING CENTERS

Glassarea. Virtually defining Aoyama elegance is this small cobblestone shopping center, which draws well-heeled young professionals to its boutiques, restaurants, and housewares shops. *⊠ 5–4–41 Minami-Aoyama, Minato-ku ☎ 03/5778–4450 ⊗ Most shops daily 11–8 Ⓜ Ginza, Chiyoda, and Hanzo-mon subway lines, Omotesando Station (Exit B1).*

Gyre. Near the Harajuku end of Omotesando, this mall houses luxury-brand shops such as Chanel and Bulgari as well as the only MoMA design store outside New York City. *⊠ 5–10–1 Jingu-mae, Shibuya-ku ☎ 03/5468–5801 ⊗ Daily 11–10 Ⓜ Chiyoda and Fukutoshin subway lines, Meiji-Jingu-mae Station (Exit 4).*

Omotesando Hills. Architect Tadao Ando's latest adventure in concrete is Tokyo's newest monument to shopping. The six wedge-shape floors include some brand-name heavy hitters (Yves Saint Laurent and Harry Winston) and a wide range of smaller stores whose shelves showcase mid- to high-end shoes and bags. *⊠ 4–12–10 Jingu-mae, Shibuya-ku ☎ 03/3497–0293 ⊗ Daily 11–9 Ⓜ Hanzo-mon, Ginza, and Chiyoda subway lines, Omotesando Station (Exit A2).*

SPECIALTY STORES

ANTIQUES

★ **Fuji-Torii.** An English-speaking staff, a central Omotesando location, and antiques ranging from ceramics to swords are the big draws at this shop, in business since 1948. In particular, Fuji-Torii has an excellent selection of folding screens, lacquerware, painted glassware, and *ukiyo-e* (wood-block prints). *⊠ 6–1–10 Jingu-mae, Shibuya-ku ☎ 03/3400–2777 ⊗ Wed.–Mon. 11–6; closed 3rd Mon. of month Ⓜ Chiyoda and Fukutoshin subway lines, Meiji-Jingu-mae Station (Exit 4).*

Morita. This Aoyama shop carries antiques and new *mingei* (Japanese folk crafts) in addition to a large stock of textiles from throughout Asia. *⊠ 5–12–2 Minami-Aoyama, Minato-ku ☎ 03/3407–4466 ⊗ Daily 10–7 Ⓜ Ginza, Chiyoda, and Hanzo-mon subway lines, Omotesando Station (Exit B1).*

CERAMICS

Tsutaya. *Ikebana* (flower arrangement) and *sado* (tea ceremony) goods are the only items sold at this Kotto-dori shop, but they come in such stunning variety that a visit is definitely worthwhile. Colorful vases in surprising shapes and traditional ceramic tea sets make for unique souvenirs. *⊠ 5–10–5 Minami-Aoyama, Minato-ku ☎ 03/3400–3815 ⊗ Daily 10–6:30 Ⓜ Ginza, Chiyoda, and Hanzo-mon subway lines, Omotesando Station (Exit B3).*

CLOTHING BOUTIQUES

10 Corso Como Comme des Garçons. Milanese lifestyle guru Carla Sozzani helped create this spacious boutique for designer Rei Kawakubo's Comme des Garçons lines, which include Junya Watanabe men's and women's wear. Also on offer are local cult brands like Toga. The staff isn't too busy being hip to help you out. ⊠ *5–3 Minami-Aoyama, Minato-ku* ☎ *03/5774–7800* ⊙ *Daily 11–8* Ⓜ *Ginza, Chiyoda, and Hanzo-mon subway lines, Omotesando Station (Exit A5).*

Bape Exclusive Aoyama. Since the late 1990s, no brand has been more coveted by Harajuku scenesters than the A Bathing Ape label (shortened to Bape) from DJ–fashion designer Nigo. At the height of the craze, hopefuls would line up outside Nigo's well-hidden boutiques for the chance to plop down ¥7,000 for a T-shirt festooned with a simian visage or a *Planet of the Apes* quote. Bape has since gone aboveground, with Nigo expanding his business empire to Singapore, Hong Kong, New York, Paris, Los Angeles, and London. Here in Tokyo, you can see what all the fuss is about at a spacious boutique that houses the Bape Gallery on the second floor. ⊠ *5–5–8 Minami-Aoyama, Minato-ku* ☎ *03/3407–2145* ⊙ *Daily 11–7* Ⓜ *Ginza and Hanzo-mon subway lines, Omotesando Station (Exit A5).*

★ **Comme des Garçons.** Sinuous low walls snake through Rei Kawakubo's flagship store, a minimalist labyrinth that houses the designer's signature clothes, shoes, and accessories. Staff members will do their best to ignore you, but that's no reason to stay away from one of Tokyo's funkiest retail spaces. ⊠ *5–2–1 Minami-Aoyama, Minato-ku* ☎ *03/3406–3951* ⊙ *Daily 11–8* Ⓜ *Ginza, Chiyoda, and Hanzo-mon subway lines, Omotesando Station (Exit A5).*

Issey Miyake. The otherworldly creations of internationally renowned designer Miyake are on display at his flagship store in Aoyama, which carries the full Paris line. Keep walking on the same street away from Omotesando Station and you'll find his menswear, Pleats Please, Haat and Me stores just a stone's throw away. ⊠ *3–18–11 Minami-Aoyama, Minato-ku* ☎ *03/3423–1408* ⊙ *Daily 11–8* Ⓜ *Ginza, Chiyoda, and Hanzo-mon subway lines, Omotesando Station (Exit A4).*

Fodor's Choice ★ **Prada.** This fashion "epicenter," built in 2003 and designed by Herzog and de Meuron, is one of the most buzzed-about architectural wonders in the city. Its facade is comprised of a mosaic of green glass "bubble" windows: alternating convex and concave windows create distorted reflections of the surrounding area. Many world-renowned, nearby boutiques have tried to replicate the significant impact the Prada building has had on the Omotesando, but none have been unable to match this tower. Most visitors opt for a photo in front of the cavelike entrance that leads into the basement floor. ⊠ *5–2–6 Minami-Aoyama, Minato-ku* ☎ *03/6418–0400* ⊙ *Daily 11–8* Ⓜ *Ginza, Chiyoda, and Hanzo-mon subway lines, Omotesando Station (Exit A5).*

Undercover. This stark shop houses Paris darling Jun Takahashi's cult clothing. Racks of men's and women's punkish duds sit under a ceiling made of a sea of thousands of hanging lightbulbs. ⊠ *5–3–18 Minami-*

Mix with Tokyo's most glamorous residents at Prada's architecturally dazzling Omotesando store.

Aoyama, Minato-ku ☎ *03/3407–1232* ⊘ *Daily 11–8* Ⓜ *Ginza, Chiyoda, and Hanzo-mon subway lines, Omotesando Station (Exit A5).*

FOLK CRAFTS

★ **Oriental Bazaar.** The four floors of this popular tourist destination are packed with just about anything you could want as a traditional Japanese (or Chinese or Korean) handicraft souvenir: painted screens, pottery, chopsticks, dolls, and more, all at very reasonable prices. ⊠ *5–9–13 Jingu-mae, Shibuya-ku* ☎ *03/3400–3933* ⊘ *Fri.–Wed. 10–7* Ⓜ *Chiyoda and Fukutoshin subway lines, Meiji-Jingu-mae Station (Exit 4).*

FOODSTUFFS AND WARES

Ⓒ **Ginza Natsuno.** This two-story boutique sells an incredible range of chopsticks, from traditional to pop-motifs, and wooden to crystal-encrusted sticks that can be personalized. Children's chopsticks and dishes are available here, too. ⊠ *4–2–17 Jingu-mae, Shibuya-ku* ☎ *03/3403–6033* ⊘ *Mon.–Sat. 10–8, Sun. 10–7* Ⓜ *Ginza, Chiyoda, and Hanzo-mon subway lines, Omotesando Station (Exit A2).*

Tea-Tsu. Some people ascribe Japanese longevity to the beneficial effects of green tea. Tea-Tsu sells a variety of leaves in attractive canisters that make unique gifts. Customers can sample tea and tea-flavored desserts while browsing the leaves and tea sets. ⊠ *5–10–17 Minami-Aoyama, Minato-ku* ☎ *03/3498–5300* ⊘ *Tues.–Sun. 11–7* Ⓜ *Ginza, Chiyoda, and Hanzo-mon subway lines, Omotesando Station (Exit B1).*

HOUSEWARES

Franc Franc Village. This concept shop by the popular interior chain sells fun, colorful goods like placemats, rice bowls, and stationery for reasonable prices. It also houses the mini Monocle shop, curated by the culture magazine of the same name, which has a selection of small goods for the person who already has everything like smart phone accessories and obscure coffee-table books. ⊠ *3–11–13 Minami-Aoyama, Minato-ku* ☎*03/5413–2511* ⊘ *Daily 11–10* Ⓜ *Ginza, Chiyoda, and Hanzo-mon subway lines, Omotesando Station (Exit A3).*

Sempre. Playful, colorful, and bright describe both the products and the space of this Kotto-dori housewares dealer. Among the great finds here are interesting tableware, glassware, lamps, office goods, and jewelry. ⊠ *5–13–3 Minami-Aoyama, Minato-ku* ☎*03/5464–5655* ⊘ *Mon.–Sat. 11–8, Sun. 11–7* Ⓜ *Ginza, Chiyoda, and Hanzo-mon subway lines, Omotesando Station (Exit B3).*

KIMONO

Gallery Kawano. Kawano, in the high-fashion district of Omotesando, sells kimonos and kimono fabric in a variety of patterns. ⊠ *4–4–9 Jingu-mae, Shibuya-ku* ☎*03/3470–3305* ⊘ *Daily 11–6* Ⓜ *Ginza, Chiyoda, and Hanzo-mon subway lines, Omotesando Station (Exit A2).*

TOYS

Kiddy Land. Commonly regarded as Tokyo's best toy store, Kiddy Land also carries kitsch items that draw in Harajuku's teen brigade. As of this writing, the store is in a temporary location while the original building gets a face-lift. It is expected to return to 6–1–9 Jingu-mae by fall o2012. Check with the store for updates (the phone number, station, and business times will all remain the same despite the move). ⊠ *6–14–2 Jingu-mae, Shibuya-ku* ☎*03/3409–3431* ⊘ *Weekdays 11–9, weekends 10:30–9* Ⓜ*JR Yamanote Line, Harajuku Station (Omotesando Exit); Chiyoda and Fukutoshin subway lines, Meiji-Jingu-mae Station (Exit 4).*

ASAKUSA AND UENO

SHOPPING STREETS AND ARCADES

Ame-ya Yoko-cho Market. Everything from fresh fish to cheap import clothing is for sale at this bustling warren of side streets between Okachi-machi and Ueno stations. In the days leading up to New Year's, the area turns into mosh-pit mayhem as shoppers fight for fish and snacks to serve over the holidays. The name of the market is often shortened to Ameyoko. Most shops and stalls are open daily 10–7. ⊠ *Ueno 4-chome, Taito-ku* Ⓜ*JR Ueno Station (Hiroko-ji Exit), JR Okachi-machi Station (Exit A7).*

Nakamise-dori. This narrow street is heaven for those seeking out traditional knickknacks and souvenirs. It is just as lively as it was when it was established in the Edo period, although now shops sells cheap sushi key chains and T-shirts alongside traditional hairpieces and silk screens. The entrance is marked by the giant red lantern at the Kaminari-mon, and ends at the grounds of the Senso-ji Complex. Most shops are open daily 10–6. ⊠ *Asakusa 2-chome, Taito-ku* ☎*03/3844–3350* Ⓜ *Ginza subway line, Asakusa Station (Exit 1).*

Nishi-Sando. Kimono and *yukata* (cotton kimono) fabrics, traditional accessories, swords, and festival costumes at very reasonable prices are all for sale at this Asakusa arcade. It runs east of the area's movie theaters, between Rok-ku and the Senso-ji Complex. ⊠ *Asakusa 2-chome, Taito-ku* Ⓜ *Ginza subway line, Asakusa Station (Exit 1).*

SPECIALTY STORES

FOODSTUFFS AND WARES

Tokiwa-do. Come here to buy some of Tokyo's most famous souvenirs: *kaminari okoshi* (thunder crackers), made of rice, millet, sugar, and beans. The shop is on the west side of Asakusa's Thunder God Gate, the Kaminari-mon entrance to Senso-ji. ⊠ *1–3–2 Asakusa, Taito-ku* ☎ *03/3841–5656* 🕙 *Daily 9–8:30* Ⓜ *Ginza subway line, Asakusa Station (Exit 1).*

PAPER

Origami Kaikan. In addition to shopping for paper goods at Yushima no Kobayahi's store, you can also tour a papermaking workshop and learn the art of origami. ⊠ *1–7–14 Yushima, Bunkyo-ku* ☎ *03/3811–4025* 🕙 *Mon.–Sat. 9–6* Ⓜ *JR Chuo and Sobu lines, Ochanomizu Station (West Exit); Chiyoda subway line, Yushima Station (Exit 5).*

SWORDS AND KNIVES

Ichiryo-ya Hirakawa. A small, cluttered souvenir shop in the Nishi-Sando arcade, Ichiryo-ya carries antique swords and reproductions and has some English-speaking salesclerks. ⊠ *2–7–13 Asakusa, Taito-ku* ☎ *03/3843–0051* 🕙 *Wed. and Fri.–Mon. 11–6* Ⓜ *Ginza subway line, Asakusa Station (Exit 1) or Tawara-machi Station (Exit 3).*

TRADITIONAL WARES

★ **Fuji-ya.** Master textile creator Keiji Kawakami's cotton *tenugui* (teh-*noo*-goo-ee) hand towels are collector's items, often framed instead of used as towels. Kawakami is an expert on the hundreds of traditional towel motifs that have come down from the Edo period: geometric patterns, plants and animals, and scenes from Kabuki plays and festivals. When Kawakami feels he has made enough of one pattern of his own design, he destroys the stencil. The shop is near the corner of Dembo-in Dori, on the street that runs parallel behind Naka-mise dori. ⊠ *2–2–15 Asakusa, Taito-ku* ☎ *03/3841–2283* 🕙 *Fri.–Wed. 10–6* Ⓜ *Ginza subway line, Asakusa Station (Exit 6).*

Hyaku-suke. This is the last place in Tokyo to carry government-approved skin cleanser made from powdered nightingale droppings. Ladies of the Edo period—especially the geisha—swore by the cleanser. These days this 100-year-old-plus cosmetics shop sells little of the nightingale powder, but its theatrical makeup for Kabuki actors, geisha, and traditional weddings—as well as unique items like seaweed shampoo, camellia oil, and handcrafted combs and cosmetic brushes—makes it a worthy addition to your Asakusa shopping itinerary. ⊠ *2–2–14 Asakusa, Taito-ku* ☎ *03/3841–7058* 🕙 *Wed.–Mon. 11–5* Ⓜ *Ginza subway line, Asakusa Station (Exit 6).*

Jusan-ya. A shop selling handmade boxwood combs, this business was started in 1736 by a samurai who couldn't support himself as a feudal retainer. It has been in the same family ever since. Jusan-ya is on Shinobazu-dori, a few doors west of its intersection with Chuo-dori in Ueno. ⊠ *2–12–21 Ueno, Taito-ku* ☎ *03/3831–3238* 🕙 *Mon.–Sat.*

10–6:30 Ⓜ *Ginza subway line, Ueno Hiroko-ji Station (Exit 3); JR Yamanote Line, Ueno Station (Shinobazu Exit).*

Naka-ya. If you want to equip yourself for Senso-ji's annual Sanja Festival in May, this is the place to come. Best buys here are *sashiko hanten,* which are thick, woven, firemen's jackets, and *happi* coats, cotton tunics printed in bright colors with Japanese characters. Some items are available in children's sizes. ✉ *2–2–12 Asakusa, Taito-ku* ☎ *03/3841–7877* ◷ *Daily 10–6:30* Ⓜ *Ginza subway line, Asakusa Station (Exit 6).*

Yono-ya. Traditional Japanese coiffures and wigs are very complicated, and they require a variety of tools to shape them properly. Tatsumi Minekawa, the current master at Yono-ya—the family line goes back 300 years—deftly crafts and decorates very fine boxwood combs. Some combs are carved with auspicious motifs, such as peonies, hollyhocks, or cranes, and all are engraved with the family benchmark. ✉ *1–37–10 Asakusa, Taito-ku* ☎ *03/3844–1755* ◷ *Thurs.–Tues. 10:30–6* Ⓜ *Ginza subway line, Asakusa Station (Exit 1).*

DAIKANYAMA AND NAKAMEGURO

SHOPPING STREETS AND ARCADES

Boutiques along Meguro River. Just one block behind Nakameguro Station is the Meguro River, a canal beside which a number of hip cafés and clothing boutiques are concentrated. The crowd here is decidedly artsy and ecologically minded. There's barely a chain store to be found, and many of the cozy shops tout locally sourced vegan and organic food and clothing. Many are also open until 10 for the nighttime strolling clientele. ✉ *Between Kami-meguro 1-chome and Aobadai 1-chome, Meguro-ku* Ⓜ *Tokyu Toyoko and Hibiya subway lines, Nakameguro Station (Main Exit).*

SPECIALTY STORES

CLOTHING BOUTIQUES

Harcoza. This is one of those "only in Tokyo" shops, with a quirky selection of clothing and accessories such as a bonsai tree watch and rings made of solidified croissants and desserts. Downstairs is a gallery that features work from underground artists. ✉ *2–15–9 Ebisu-nishi, Shibuya-ku* ☎ *03/6416–0725* ◷ *Wed.–Mon. 11–7:30* Ⓜ *Tokyu Toyoko Line, Daikanyama Station (West Exit).*

CLOTHING CHAINS

Mangart Beams T. This small but intriguing boutique sells manga alongside designer-made T-shirts inspired by the comic books. Even better, new designs rotate overhead on a conveyor belt. ✉ *2F, 19–6 Sarugakucho, Shibuya-ku* ☎ *03/5428–5952* ◷ *Daily 11–8* Ⓜ *Tokyu Toyoko Line, Daikanyama Station (Komazawa-dori Exit).*

HOUSEWARES

Zero First Design. Kyu-Yamate-dori at Daikanyama is a well-known hub of interior goods stores, and this one is full of unique and modern pieces from both local and international designers. And even though it is a fair walk from Daikanyama Station it is still the go-to place for local discerning style aficionados. ✉ *2–3–1 Aobadai, Meguro-ku*

Shopping in Kappabashi

A wholesale-restaurant-supply district might not sound like a promising shopping destination, but Kappabashi, about a 10-minute walk west of the temples and pagodas of Asakusa, is worth a look. Ceramics, cutlery, cookware, folding lanterns, and even kimono can all be found here, along with the kitschy plastic food models that appear in restaurant windows throughout Japan. The best strategy is to stroll up and down the 1-km (½-mi) length of Kappabashi-dogu-machi-dori and visit any shop that looks interesting. Most stores here emphasize function over charm, but some manage to stand out for their stylish spaces as well. Most Kappabashi shops are open until 5:30; some close Sunday. To get here, take the Ginza subway line to Tawara-machi Station.

Kappabashi Soshoku. Come here for *aka-chochin* (folding red-paper lanterns) like the ones that hang in front of inexpensive bars and restaurants. ⊠ *3–1–1 Matsugaya, Taito-ku* ☎ *03/3844–1973* ⏱ *Mon.–Sat. 9:30–5:30.*

Kawahara Shoten. The brightly colored bulk packages of rice crackers, shrimp-flavored chips, and other Japanese snacks sold here make offbeat gifts. ⊠ *3–9–2 Nishi-Asakusa, Taito-ku* ☎ *03/3842–0841* ⏱ *Mon.–Sat. 9–5:30.*

⏱ **Maizuru.** This perennial tourist favorite manufactures the plastic food that's displayed outside almost every Tokyo restaurant. Ersatz sushi, noodles, and even beer cost just a few thousand yen. You can buy tiny plastic key holders and earrings, or splurge on a whole Pacific lobster, perfect in coloration and detail down to the tiniest spines on its legs. ⊠ *1–5–14 Nishi-*

Asakusa, Taito-ku ☎ *03/3843–1686* ⏱ *Daily 9–6.*

Noren-no-Nishimura. This Kappabashi shop specializes in *noren*—the curtains that shops and restaurants hang to announce they're open. The curtains are typically cotton, linen, or silk, most often dyed-to-order for individual shops. Nishimura also sells premade noren of an entertaining variety—from white-on-blue landscapes to geisha and sumo wrestlers in polychromatic splendor—for home decorating. They make wonderful wall hangings and dividers. ⊠ *1–10–10 Matsugaya, Taito-ku* ☎ *03/3841–6220* ⏱ *Mon.–Sat. 10–5.*

Soi Furniture. The selection of lacquerware, ceramics, and antiques sold at this Kappabashi shop is modest, but Soi displays the items in a primitivist setting of stone walls and wooden floor planks, with up-tempo jazz in the background. ⊠ *3–17–3 Matsugaya, Taito-ku* ☎ *03/3843–9555* ⏱ *Daily 10–6.*

★ **Tsubaya Hochoten.** Tsubaya sells high-quality cutlery for professionals. Its remarkable selection is designed for every imaginable use, as the art of food presentation in Japan requires a great variety of cutting implements. The best of these carry the Traditional Craft Association seal: hand-forged tools of tempered blue steel, set in handles banded with deer horn to keep the wood from splitting. Be prepared to pay the premium for these items: a cleaver just for slicing soba can cost as much as ¥50,000. ⊠ *3–7–2 Nishi-Asakusa, Taito-ku* ☎ *03/3845–2005* ⏱ *Mon.–Sat. 9–5:45, Sun. 9–5.*

☎ 03/5489–6101 ⊙ *Daily 11–8* Ⓜ *Tokyu Toyoko Line, Daikanyama Station (Komazawa-dori Exit).*

LACQUERWARE

Fodor'sChoice **Yamada Heiando.** With a spacious, airy layout and lovely lacquerware
★ goods, this fashionable Daikanyama shop is a must for souvenir hunters—and anyone else who appreciates fine design. Rice bowls, sushi
trays, bento lunch boxes, *hashioki* (chopstick rests), and jewelry cases
come in traditional blacks and reds, as well as patterns both subtle and
bold. Prices are fair—many items cost less than ¥10,000—but these
are the kinds of goods for which devotees of Japanese craftsmanship
would be willing to pay a lot. ⊠ *Hillside Terrace G Block 202, 18–12
Sarugakucho, Shibuya-ku* ☎ 03/3464–5541 ⊙ *Mon.–Sat. 10:30–7, Sun.
10:30–6:30* Ⓜ *Tokyu Toyoko Line, Daikanyama Station (Komazawa-dori Exit).*

GINZA

SHOPPING STREETS AND ARCADES

International Shopping Arcade. A somewhat ragtag collection of shops in
Hibiya, this arcade holds a range of goods, including cameras, electronics, pearls, and kimonos. The shops are duty-free, and most of the sales
staff speaks decent English. If you listen carefully you'll hear the rumble
of cars passing above on the freeway that is the roof of the building.
⊠ *1–7–23 Uchisaiwai-cho, Chiyoda-ku* Ⓜ *Chiyoda and Hibiya subway
lines, Hibiya Station (Exit A13).*

DEPARTMENT STORES

Fodor's Choice
★
Matsuya. On the fourth floor, the gleaming Matsuya houses an excellent selection of Japanese fashion, including Issey Miyake, Yohji Yamamoto, and Comme Ça Du Mode. The Louis Vuitton shops on the first and second floors are particularly popular with Tokyo's brand-obsessed shoppers. ✉ *3–6–1 Ginza, Chuo-ku* ☎ *03/3567–1211* ☉ *Daily 10–8* Ⓜ *Ginza, Marunouchi, and Hibiya subway lines, Ginza Station (Exits A12 and A13).*

Matsuzakaya. The Matsuzakaya conglomerate was founded in Nagoya and still commands the loyalties of shoppers with origins in western Japan. It houses affordable fashion chains like Forever21 and Muji with less emphasis on luxury. ✉ *6–10–1 Ginza, Chuo-ku* ☎ *03/3572–1111* ☉ *Daily 10:30–7:30* Ⓜ *Ginza, Marunouchi, and Hibiya subway lines, Ginza Station (Exits A3 and A4).*

★
Mitsukoshi. Mitsukoshi was Japan's first department store chain, and this Ginza branch has been open since 1930. It is the largest department store in the area, with a sprawling grass-covered terrace on the ninth floor that provides a respite from the shopping bustle and the modern architecture of a glittery annex. ✉ *4–6–16 Ginza, Chuo-ku* ☎ *03/3562–1111* ☉ *Daily 10–8* Ⓜ *Ginza, Marunouchi, and Hibiya subway lines, Ginza Station (Exits A6, A7, and A8).*

Fodor's Choice
★
Muji. This chain features generically branded housewares and clothing at reasonable prices. You'll find a large selection of Bauhaus-influenced furniture, appliances, and bedding at the massive flagship branch in Yuraku-cho. If you're a bit overwhelmed by all the options, relax at the dining area that boasts—what else?—Muji meals. ✉ *3–8–3 Marunouchi, Chiyoda-ku* ☎ *03/5208–8241* ☉ *Daily 10–9* Ⓜ *JR Yamanote Line, Yuraku-cho subway line, Yuraku-cho Station (JR Kyobashi Exit, subway Exit D9).*

Wako. Wako is well known for its high-end watches, glassware, jewelry, and accessories, as well as having some of the handsomest, most sophisticated window displays in town. The clock atop this curved 1930s-era building is illuminated at night, making it one of Tokyo's more recognized landmarks. ✉ *4–5–11 Ginza, Chuo-ku* ☎ *03/3562–2111* ☉ *Mon.–Sat. 10:30–6* Ⓜ *Ginza, Marunouchi, and Hibiya subway lines, Ginza Station (Exits A9 and A10).*

SPECIALTY STORES

CLOTHING CHAINS

Uniqlo. Uniqlo offers customers a chance to wrap themselves in simple, low-priced items from the company's own brand. This supersize location sells men's, women's, and children's clothing right on the main Ginza drag. ✉ *5–7–7 Ginza, Chuo-ku* ☎ *03/3569–6781* ☉ *Daily 11–9* Ⓜ *Ginza, Hibiya, and Marunouchi subway lines, Ginza Station (Exit A2).*

ELECTRONICS

★
Apple Store. This very stylish showroom displays the newest models from Apple's line of computer products. The Genius Bar on the second floor offers consulting services should you need advice on how to resuscitate a comatose iPad or MacBook. ✉ *3–5–12 Ginza, Chuo-ku* ☎ *03/5159–8200* ☉ *Daily 10–9* Ⓜ *Ginza, Hibiya, and Marunouchi subway lines, Ginza Station (Exit A13).*

The Power of Tea

Green tea is ubiquitous in Japan. But did you know that besides being something of a national drink, it's also good for you? Green tea contains antioxidants twice as powerful as those in red wine; these help reduce high blood pressure, lower blood sugar, and fight cancer. A heightened immune system and lower cholesterol are other benefits attributed to this beverage.

Whether drinking green tea for its healing properties, good taste, or as a manner of habit, you'll have plenty of choices in Japan. Pay attention to tea varietals, which are graded by the quality and parts of the plant used, because price and quality runs the spectrum within these categories. For the very best Japanese green tea, take a trip to the Uji region of Kyoto.

Bancha (common tea). This second-harvest variety ripens between summer and fall, producing leaves larger than those of sencha and a weaker-tasting tea.

Genmai (brown rice tea). This is a mixture, usually in equal parts, of green tea and roasted brown rice.

Genmaicha (popcorn tea). This is a blend of bancha and genmai teas.

Gyokuro (jewel dew). Derived from a grade of green tea called *tencha* (divine tea), the name comes from the light-green color the tea develops when brewed. Gyokuro is grown in the shade, an essential condition to develop just this type and grade.

Hojicha (panfried tea). A panfried or oven-roasted green tea.

Kabusecha (covered tea). Similar to gyokuru, kabusecha leaves are grown in the shade, though for a shorter period, giving it a refined flavor.

Kukicha (stalk tea). A tea made from stalks by harvesting one bud and three leaves.

Matcha (rubbed tea). Most often used in the tea ceremony, matcha is a high-quality, hard-to-find powdered green tea. It has a thick, paintlike consistency when mixed with hot water. It is also a popular flavor of ice cream and other sweets in Japan.

Sencha (roasted tea). This is the green tea you are most likely to try at the local noodle or bento shop. Its leaves are grown under direct sunlight, giving it a different flavor from cousins like gyokuro.

Sony Building. Test drive the latest Sony gadgets at this retail and entertainment space in the heart of Ginza. The first- to fourth-floor showrooms allow parents to fiddle with digital cameras and computers from Japan's electronics leader while kids will enjoy playing with interactive displays of electric trains and weight-sensitive musical stairs. The Opus theater on the eighth floor shows movie trailers on a super-high-definition 3-D screen that also features games and events to coincide with movie releases. Take a break by browsing the Internet for free or at one of the cafés or pubs on the floors above the showroom. ⊠ *5–3–1 Ginza, Chuo-ku* ☎ *03/3573–2371* ☽ *Daily 11–7* Ⓜ *JR Yamanote Line, Yuraku-cho Station (Ginza Exit); Ginza, Hibiya, and Marunouchi subway lines, Ginza Station (Exit B9).*

Sukiya Camera. The cramped Nikon House branch of this two-store operation features enough Nikons—old and new, digital and film—that it could double as a museum to the brand. Plenty of lenses and flashes are available as well. ✉ *4–2–13 Ginza, Chuo-ku* ☎ *03/3561–6000* ⊗ *Mon.–Sat. 10–7:30, Sun. 10–7* Ⓜ *JR Yamanote Line, Yuraku-cho Station (Ginza Exit); Ginza, Hibiya, and Marunouchi subway lines, Ginza Station (Exit B10).*

JEWELRY

Ginza Tanaka. From necklaces to precious metals shaped into statues, this chain of jewelry stores has crafted a reputation as one of Japan's premier jewelers since its founding in 1892. ✉ *1–7–7 Ginza, Chuo-ku* ☎ *03/5561–0491* ⊗ *Daily 10:30–7* Ⓜ *Yuraku-cho subway line, Ginza 1-Chome Station (Exit 7).*

Fodor'sChoice
★
Mikimoto. Kokichi Mikimoto created his technique for cultured pearls in 1893. Since then his name has been associated with the best quality in the industry. Mikimoto's tower in Ginza is a boutique devoted to nature's ready-made gems; the building, like the pearls it holds, dazzles visitors with its facade that resembles Swiss cheese. ✉ *2–4–12 Ginza, Chuo-ku* ☎ *03/3562–3130* ⊗ *Mon.–Sat. 11–7:30, Sun. 11–7* Ⓜ *Ginza, Hibiya, and Marunouchi subway lines, Ginza Station (Exit C8).*

KIMONO

Hayashi. This store in the Yuraku-cho International Arcade, under the train tracks, specializes in ready-made kimono, sashes, and dyed yukata. ✉ *2–1–1 Yuraku-cho, Chiyoda-ku* ☎ *03/3501–4012* ⊗ *Mon.–Sat. 10–7, Sun. 10–6* Ⓜ *JR Yamanote Line, Yuraku-cho Station (Ginza Exit); Hibiya subway line, Hibiya Station (Exit A5).*

Tansu-ya. This small but pleasant Ginza shop, part of a chain with locations throughout Japan and abroad, has attractive used kimono, yukata, and other traditional clothing in many fabrics, colors, and patterns. The helpful staff can acquaint you with the somewhat complicated method of putting on the garments. ✉ *3–4–5 Ginza, Chuo-ku* ☎ *03/3561–8529* ⊗ *Mon.–Sat. 11–7, Sun. 11–6* Ⓜ *Ginza, Hibiya, and Marunouchi subway lines, Ginza Station (Exit A13).*

PAPER

Itoya. The 10 stories of this paper emporium are filled with locally crafted and import stationery, much of which is designed to translate traditional motifs onto contemporary office tools. ✉ *2–7–15 Ginza, Chuo-ku* ☎ *03/3561–8311* ⊗ *Mon.–Sat. 10:30–8, Sun. 10:30–7* Ⓜ *Ginza, Hibiya, and Marunouchi subway lines, Ginza Station (Exit A2).*

★
Kyukyodo. Kyukyodo has been in business since 1663—and in Ginza since 1880—selling its wonderful handmade Japanese papers, paper products, incense, brushes, and other materials for calligraphy. ✉ *5–7–4 Ginza, Chuo-ku* ☎ *03/3571–4429* ⊗ *Mon.–Sat. 10–7:30, Sun. 11–7* Ⓜ *Ginza, Hibiya, and Marunouchi subway lines, Ginza Station (Exit A2).*

SWORDS AND KNIVES

Fodor'sChoice
★
Nippon Token *(Japan Sword).* Wannabe samurai can learn how to tell their *toshin* (blades) from their *tsuka* (sword handles) with help from the English-speaking staff at this small shop, which has been open since the Meiji era (1868–1912). Items that range from a circa-1390

Continued on page 227

SHOP TOKYO

By Misha Janette

Tokyo, the most retail-dense city in the world, lures even the most reluctant shoppers with promises of every product imaginable. Travel back in time at department and specialty stores selling traditional ceramics and lacquerware, or leap into the future in Akihabara and other gadget-oriented neighborhoods. Fashionistas watch trends in Harajuku morph before their eyes, while those with more highbrow sensibilities browse the jewelry at stalwarts like Mikimoto.

Each Tokyo neighborhood has its own specialty, style, mood, and type of customer. Local production still thrives in the city's backstreets despite an influx of global chains and mega-corporations. Keep in mind, however, that nearly all of the locally produced goods will cost a pretty penny; the Japanese are meticulous in design and quality, and tend to prefer small-scale production to large output. Here in Tokyo you will find that one-offs and limited-edition items are often the norm rather than the exception.

For clothing, sizing is still the biggest roadblock to really getting the most from Tokyo boutiques. But with the abundance of quirky trends sometimes it's enough just to window-shop.

Above: A Harajuku boutique shows off wild new trends.

WHAT TO BUY

MANGA

Manga, or Japanese comic books, have had an incredible influence on pop culture around the world. The inherently Japanese-style illustrations are fun to look at, and the simple language is great for studying. Book-Off, a well-known used manga chain, sells comics at rock-bottom prices, sometimes ¥100 each.

INNERWEAR

The Japanese are known for their electronics, but did you know their textile and fiber industry is also one of the most advanced in the world? The sweat-repelling, heat-conducting, UBAV/UVB-blocking and aloe-vera dispensing underthings available at Tokyo department stores are probably already in every Japanese person's top drawer at home.

FLAVORED SNACKS

Japan is the land of limited-edition products, and every season brings new, adventurous flavors in finite quantities. All it takes is a trip to the local convenience store to find melon- or Sakura-flavored Kit-Kat bars, or sweet Mont Blanc-flavored Pepsi. We dare you to try them.

PHONE ACCESSORIES

Cell phones and their accoutrement have become a fashion statement all their own. Phone straps, small plastic models that hang from one's phone, are the most popular. They come in all forms, from Asahi beer bottles to Hello Kitty dolls. There are also matching plastic "no peek" sheets that prevent others from spying on your phone's screen.

HOUSEWARES

Tokyoites appreciate fine design, and this passion is reflected in the exuberance of the city's *zakka* shops—retailers that sell small housewares. The Daikanyama and Aoyama areas positively brim with these stores, but trendy zakka can be found throughout the city. Handmade combs, chopsticks, and towels are other uniquely Japanese treasures to consider picking up while in Tokyo.

RECORDS

Tokyo's small specialty music stores are a real treat: local music and imports from around the world are usually available on both vinyl and CD. Out-of-print or obscure vinyl editions can run well over ¥10,000, but collectors will find the condition of the jackets to be unmatched.

SOCKS

As it's customary in Japanese houses to remove one's shoes, socks are more than mere padding between foot and shoe. It's no surprise, then, that the selection of socks goes well beyond black and white. Stripes, polka-dots, Japanese scenery, and monograms are just some of the depictions you'll find at the high-end sock boutiques. The complicated weaving techniques mean they will also cost more than the average cotton pair.

SAKE SETS

Sake is a big deal here, and the type of sake presented to another can make or break business deals and friendships. Better than just a bottle are the gift sets that include the short sake glasses and oversized bottles in beautiful packaging fit for royalty.

JEWELRY

Japan has always been known for its craftsmen who possess the ability to create finely detailed work. Jewelry is no exception, especially when cultured pearls are used. Pearls, which have become something of a national symbol, are not inexpensive, but they are much cheaper in Japan than elsewhere.

WASHLETTE TOILET SEATS

It may seem ludicrous, but the Japanese "washlette" toilet seat is perhaps the best innovation of this millennium. The seats are heated, come with deodorizers, and may even play music to mask any "rude" sounds. Even better, some can be retrofitted to old toilets—just be sure to check your seat measurements before leaving home.

CHARCOAL

Japanese women have been using charcoal, or *takesumi*, in their beauty routines for centuries, believing it cleans out the pores and moisturizes the skin. Charcoal-infused formulas are used in soaps, cleansers, cremes, and masques, and often are naturally colored pitch-black like squid ink.

FOLK CRAFTS

Japanese folk crafts, called *mingei*—among them bamboo vases and baskets, fabrics, paper boxes, dolls, and toys—achieve a unique beauty in their simple and sturdy designs. Be aware, however, that simple does not mean cheap. Long hours of labor go into these objects, and every year there are fewer craftspeople left, producing their work in smaller and smaller quantities. Include these items in your budget ahead of time: The best—worth every cent—can be fairly expensive.

EXPERIENCING JAPANESE DEPATO

The impressive architecture at the Prada flagship matches the designer wares inside.

A visit to a Japanese *depato* (department store) is the perfect Cliff's Notes introduction to Japanese culture. Impeccable service combines with the best luxury brands, gourmet food, and traditional goods—all displayed as enticing eye candy.

These large complexes are found around major train stations and are often owned by the conglomerate rail companies who make their profit when visitors take the train to shop there. The stores themselves commonly have travel agencies, theaters, and art galleries on the premises, as well as reasonably priced and strategically placed restaurants and cafés.

ARRIVE EARLY
The best way to get the full experience is to arrive just as the store is opening. Err on the early side: Tokyo's department stores are exacting in their opening times. White-gloved ladies and gents bow to waiting customers when the doors open on the hour. Early birds snatch up limited-edition food and goods before they sell out. There's never a dearth of reasons to come: local celebrity appearances, designer Q&A sessions, and fairs.

ANATOMY OF A DEPATO
The first floors typically house cosmetics, handbags, and shoes, with the next few floors up going to luxury import brands. On many a top floor you'll find gift packages containing Japan's best-loved brands of sake, rice crackers, and other foods. Department stores also typically devote one floor to traditional Japanese crafts, including ceramics, paintings, and lacquerware.

Don't miss the *depachika* (food departments) on the basement levels, where an overwhelming selection of expensive Japanese and Western delicacies are wrapped with the utmost care. More affordable versions come packed deli-style to be taken home for lunch or dinner.

Shibuya's depato attract trendsetters.

BEST DEPATO FOR...

Most department stores are similar and house the same brands. But some have distinctive characteristics.

The Trendy Dresser: Seibu in Shibuya and Ikebukuro is known for its collection of fashion-forward tenants.

Emerging Designers: Isetan in Shinjuku oozes style and has ample space on the fourth floor dedicated to up-and-coming designers.

Gifts: Shinjuku's Takashimaya is the place to buy souvenirs for discerning friends back home.

Traditional Crafts: Mitsukoshi in Nihombashi will leave those looking for a bit of Old Japan wide-eyed.

TIPS FOR DEPATO SHOPPING

■ Major department stores accept credit cards and provide shipping services.

■ It's important to remember that, unlike most of the Western world, goods must be purchased in the department where they were found. This goes for nearly every multilevel shop in Japan.

■ Nowadays, most salesclerks speak some English. If you're having communication difficulties, someone will always come to the rescue.

■ On the first floor you'll invariably find a general information booth with maps of the store in English.

■ Some department stores close one or two days a month. To be on the safe side, call ahead.

Depato interiors are often dramatic.

FASHIONABLE TOKYO

The Japanese fashion scene has gone through many changes since Yohji Yamamoto's solemn, deconstructed garments and Rei Kawakubo's Comme des Garçons clothing lines challenged norms in the 1980s. While these designers and their ilk are still revered, it's Tokyo's street fashion that keeps the city on the world's radar.

Clockwise from top left: An orange-haired Harajuku Girl; manga-influenced street fashion; girls from Shibuya ogle a mobile phone.

Thanks to Gwen Stefani's "Harajuku Girls" and Quentin Tarantino's *Kill Bill*, images of the Gothic Lolita—a fashion subculture typified by a Victorian porcelain-doll look punctuated by dark makeup and macabre accessories—have seeped into Western popular culture. New subcultures, or "tribes," like the Harajuku Girls emerge, take hold in Tokyo, and evolve (or get thrown aside) with blazing speed. The "forest girl" tribe's aesthetic draws from sources such as the American prairie and traditional German attire in loose layers, often in organic and vintage materials. The "skirt boys" are among the mens' tribes. These cool boys stomp around in boots and skirts that Japanese menswear designers have been favoring on the runway in recent years.

Japanese fashion continues to awe and inspire; international designers come to Tokyo for ideas. This means you might already be wearing something from Tokyo without even knowing it!

SIZING UP JAPANESE SIZES

Japanese garments, even if they are not a troublesome and common "one-size-fits-all," run considerably smaller than American items. The female aesthetic tends to favor loose and roomy shapes so is far more forgiving than the menswear, which is often cut impossibly small and tight.

Shibuya brands often carry items in nothing more than an arbitrary "one-size-only" on the racks that may not fit many Westerners at all. Many designers, in deference to the growing foreign market, are starting to offer larger sizes. The internationally recognized brands, department stores, and bigger boutiques, including Opening Ceremony in Shibuya, are the best bets for finding a range of sizes.

Shoes tend to run small, often stopping at 27 cm (U.S. size 9) for men and 24 cm (U.S. size 8) for women. What's more, Japanese shoes are often made a little wider than their Western counterparts.

Above: Harajuku Girls wear dramatic costume-like outfits.

A TALE OF TWO NEIGHBORHOOD STYLES

You don't need to be an industry insider attending Japan's Fashion Week shows to get a sense of Tokyo's multiple styles; you just need to stroll the neighborhoods where every sidewalk is a catwalk.

Japanese street fashion begins and ends along the maze-like backstreets of **Harajuku**, referred to as "Ura-Hara." You'll find many of Tokyo's most popular and promising up-and-coming brands' boutiques, although it might take sharp eyes to spot the often-obstructed store signs. Tokyo's youngest shoppers come for the newest fashions and to show off their costume-like vestments. Visit on a Sunday to see them in full regalia. If the throngs of tweens prove too much, there are other incredible street-fashion shopping areas. Shimokitazawa and Koenji are known for their used-clothing shops and a young fashion scene that's just as lively as that of Harajuku.

For a different take, go to **Shibuya**, where women and men have cultivated a distinctive fashion and lifestyle. The so-called Shibuya style is vivid, brash, and hyper, and comes with its own idols, models, and magazines. Malls such as 109, which is the center of this movement's universe, dedicate their retail space wholly to this world.

More than 50,000 people, including many visitors to Tokyo, attend the biannual **Tokyo Girls Collection**, daylong events of Shibuya-style fashion shows and musical performances by pop big acts. JTB offers full package tours around the event starting at ¥8,000 per person.

FIVE EMERGING DESIGNERS

Limi Feu: Limi, Yohji Yamamoto's daughter, takes a hint from him in her loose, monotone, punk attire, but injects it with a cool, feminine touch. ⊕ www.limifeu.com

Matohu: This unisex brand creates looks based on traditional and colorful Japanese clothing, namely robes, by incorporating ancient dye and weaving techniques into 21st-century designs. ⊕ www.matohu. com/en

N. Hoolywood: Daisuke Obana's menswear line has been on the top of Japanese editors' lists since 2002. He adds contemporary design elements to used clothing, and his attire tends to be loose and casual. ⊕ www. n-hoolywood.com

Tao Comme des Garçons: The youngest in line to the avant-garde Comme des Garçons throne is a wunderkind with knitwear. Expect ingenious mixed-and-matched textures, vivid colors, and patterns.

Somarta: This brand is known for its intricate, seamless knitwear and other experimental textiles developed using Japanese technology. The new menswear line called Molfic follows the same innovative ethos in its seasonless designs. ⊕ www. somarta.jp

Top to bottom: Limi Feu, N. Hoolywood, Somarta

samurai sword to inexpensive reproductions will allow you to take a trip back in time, but make sure your wallet is ready for today's prices. ⊠ *3–8–1 Toranomon, Minato-ku* ☎ *03/3434–4321* ⊙ *Weekdays 9:30–6, Sat. 9:30–5* Ⓜ *Hibiya and Ginza subway lines, Tora-no-mon Station (Exit 2).*

Token Shibata. A tiny, threadbare shop incongruously situated near Ginza's glittering department stores, Token Shibata sells well-worn antique swords. ⊠ *5–6–8 Ginza, Chuo-ku* ☎ *03/3573–2801* ⊙ *Mon.– Sat. 9:30–6:30* Ⓜ *Ginza, Hibiya, and Marunouchi subway lines, Ginza Station (Exit A1).*

HARAJUKU

MALLS AND SHOPPING CENTERS

★ **Laforet.** This mall is so earnest about staying on the tip of Harajuku fashion trends that it changes out stores every six months. While shop genres vary, from Gothic Lolita to bohemian chic, they all target fashion-conscious teenagers. Rumor has it that many of the West's top fashion designers still come here to look for inspiration for their next collections. ⊠ *1–11–6 Jingu-mae, Shibuya-ku* ☎ *03/3475–0411* ⊙ *Daily 11–9* Ⓜ *Chiyoda and Fukutoshin subway lines, Meiji-Jingu-mae Station (Exit 5).*

SHOPPING STREETS AND ARCADES

Cat Street. With its avant-garde crafts stores, funky T-shirt shops, and hipster boutiques, this pedestrian strip serves as a showcase for Japan's au courant designers and artisans. Cat Street is the place to experience bohemian Tokyo in all its exuberance. ⊠ *Between Jingu-mae 3-chome and Jingu-mae 6-chome, Shibuya-ku* Ⓜ *Chiyoda and Fukutoshin subway lines, Meiji-Jingu-mae Station (Exits 4 and 5).*

Takeshita-dori. Teenybopper fashion is all the rage along this Harajuku mainstay, where crowds of schoolkids look for the newest, low-priced addition to their ever-changing, outrageous wardrobes. ⊠ *Jingu-mae 1-chome, Shibuya-ku* Ⓜ *JR Harajuku Station (Takeshita-Dori Exit).*

SPECIALTY STORES
CLOTHING CHAINS

Beams. Harajuku features a cluster of no fewer than 11 Beams stores that provide Japan's younger men and women with extremely hip threads. With branches ranging from street wear to high-end import brands as well as a record store, uniform gallery, and funky "from Tokyo" souvenir shop that sells anime figurines, shopping here will ensure that you or your kids will be properly stocked with the coolest wares from the city. ⊠ *3–24–7 Jingu-mae, Shibuya-ku* ☎ *03/3470–3947* ⊙ *Daily 11–8* Ⓜ *JR Harajuku Station (Takeshita-Dori Exit); Chiyoda and Fukutoshin subway lines, Meiji-Jingu-mae Station (Exit 4).*

Uniqlo UT Store. This Harajuku post takes a fashion-forward approach by housing its large variety of T-shirts in a space that resembles a futuristic convenience store or vending machine. The shirts are stuffed into plastic canisters and lined up on shelves that reach the ceiling. ⊠ *6–10–8*

Gothic styles influence the striking outfits worn by Harajuku Girls.

Jingu-mae, Shibuya-ku ☎ *03/5468–7313* ⊘ *Daily 11–9* Ⓜ *Chiyoda and Fukutoshin subway lines, Meiji-Jingu-mae Station (Exit 4).*

SHIBUYA

MALLS AND SHOPPING CENTERS

Parco. Parco, owned by the Seibu conglomerate, is actually a gathering of vertical malls filled with small retail shops and boutiques, all in walking distance of one another in the commercial heart of Shibuya. Parco Part 1 caters to a young crowd and stocks many casual brands from the local runways for men and women. Part 3 sells a mixture of fashion and hip interior goods. The nearby Zero Gate complex houses the basement restaurant-nightclub La Fabrique, and Quattro, behind it, is a popular concert venue. ✉ *15–1 Udagawa-cho, Shibuya-ku* ☎ *03/3464–5111* ⊘ *Daily 10–9* Ⓜ *Ginza, Fukutoshin, and Hanzo-mon subway lines, Shibuya Station (Exits 6 and 7).*

Shibuya 109. This nine-floor outlet is a teenage girl's dream. It's filled with small stores whose merchandise screams kitsch and trend. Many weekend afternoons will see dance groups and fashion shows on the stage at the front entrance. ✉ *2–29–1 Dogenzaka, Shibuya-ku* ☎ *03/3477–5111* ⊘ *Daily 10–9* Ⓜ *JR Yamanote Line, Ginza, Fukutoshin, and Hanzo-mon subway lines, Shibuya Station (Hachiko Exit for JR, Exit 3 for subway lines).*

SPECIALTY STORES
BOOKS
Tower Records. This branch of the U.S.-based chain carries an eclectic collection of English-language books at more reasonable prices than most bookstores in town. It also has one of the best selections of foreign magazines in Tokyo. ✉ *1–22–14 Jinnan, Shibuya-ku* ☎ *03/3496–3661* ⊙ *Daily 10–11* Ⓜ *JR Yamanote Line, Hanzo-mon, Fukutoshin, and Ginza subway lines, Shibuya Station (Hachiko Exit for JR, Exit 6 for subway).*

CLOTHING CHAINS
★ **Journal Standard.** This is not a chain dedicated to outfitting copy editors and reporters in shirts and ties. In fact, this branch is frequented by young couples looking for the season's *it* fashions. To the south of it is the Journal Standard Café with a bakery and an outside terrace that is perfect for people-watching. ✉ *1–5–6 Jinnan, Shibuya-ku* ☎ *03/5457– 0700* ⊙ *Daily 11:30–8* Ⓜ *JR Yamanote Line, Ginza, Fukutoshin, and Hanzo-mon subway lines, Shibuya Station (Hachiko Exit for JR, Exits 6 and 7 for subways).*

HOUSEWARES
Fodor's Choice **Tokyu Hands.** This housewares chain is dedicated to providing the do-it-
★ yourselfer with all the tools, fabrics, and supplies he or she may need to
☺ tackle any job. There's a selection of plastic models and rubber Godzilla action figures on the seventh floor of the Shibuya branch. It's not unusual to see Japanese hobbyists spending an entire afternoon browsing in here. ✉ *12–18 Udagawa-cho, Shibuya-ku* ☎ *03/5489–5111* ⊙ *Daily 10–8:30* Ⓜ *JR Yamanote Line, Ginza, Fukutoshin, and Hanzo-mon subway lines, Shibuya Station (Hachiko Exit for JR, Exits 6 and 7 for subway).*

RECORD STORES
Manhattan Records. The hottest hip-hop, reggae, and R&B vinyl can be found here, and a DJ booth pumps out the jams from the center of the room. Don't expect a lot advice from the staff—no one can hear you over the throbbing tunes. ✉ *10–1 Udagawa-cho, Shibuya-ku* ☎ *03/3477–7166* ⊙ *Daily noon–9* Ⓜ *JR Yamanote Line, Ginza, Fukutoshin, and Hanzo-mon subway lines, Shibuya Station (Hachiko Exit for JR, Exits 6 and 7 for subway).*

IKEBUKURO

DEPARTMENT STORES
Seibu. Even Japanese customers have been known to get lost in this mammoth department store; the main branch is in Ikebukuro. The Shibuya branch, which still carries an impressive array of merchandise, is smaller and more manageable. Seibu has an excellent selection of household goods, from furniture to lacquerware and quirky interior design pieces, in its stand-alone Loft shops (often next door to Seibu branches, or occasionally within the department store itself). ✉ *1–28–1 Minami Ikebukuro, Toshima-ku* ☎ *03/3981–0111* ⊙ *Mon.–Sat. 10–9, Sun. 10–8* Ⓜ *JR Yamanote Line, Marunouchi, Fukutoshin, and Yurakucho subway lines, Ikebukuro Station (Minami-guchi/South Exit); Seibu Ikebukuro Line, Seibu Ikebukuro Station (Seibu Department Store Exit); Tobu Tojo Line, Tobu Ikebukuro Station (Minami-guchi/*

South Exit) ✉ *21–1 Udagawa-cho, Shibuya-ku* ☎ *03/3462–0111*
⊘ *Sun.–Wed. 10–8, Thurs.–Sat. 10–9* Ⓜ *JR Yamanote Line, Ginza and Hanzo-mon subway lines, Shibuya Station (Hachiko Exit for JR, Exits 6 and 7 for subway lines).*

SPECIALTY STORES

PAPER

Kami-no-Takamura. Specialists in *washi* and other papers printed in traditional Japanese designs, this shop also carries brushes, inkstones, and other tools for calligraphy. At the entrance is a gallery showcasing seasonal traditional stationery and the work of local artists. ✉ *1–1–2 Higashi-Ikebukuro, Toshima-ku* ☎ *03/3971–7111* ⊘ *Daily 11–6:45* Ⓜ *JR Yamanote Line, Marunouchi and Fukutoshin subway lines, Ikebukuro Station (East Exit for JR, Exit 35 for subway).*

SHINJUKU

DEPARTMENT STORES

Isetan. One of Tokyo's oldest and largest department stores, Isetan is known for its high-end fashions, including a selection of larger sizes not found in most Tokyo stores. The basement's food court, which includes both traditional and modern prepared cuisine, is one of the city's largest in a department store. ✉ *3–14–1 Shinjuku, Shinjuku-ku* ☎ *03/3352–1111* ⊘ *Daily 10–8* Ⓜ *JR Yamanote Line, Marunouchi subway line, Shinjuku Station (Higashi-guchi/East Exit for JR, Exits B2, B3, B4, and B5 for subway line).*

Marui. Marui, easily recognized by its red-and-white logo, burst onto the department store scene in the 1980s by introducing an in-store credit card—one of the first stores in Japan to do so. Now the five Marui buildings together comprise the largest department store in the area by a large margin. This includes Marui Curren, Marui Annex, and Marui Men where youngsters flock to the stores in search of petite clothing, accessories, and sportswear. Marui Honkan is the chain's main location. ✉ *3–30–13 Shinjuku, Shinjuku-ku* ☎ *03/3354–0101* ⊘ *Mon.–Sat. 11–9, Sun. 11–8:30* Ⓜ *JR Yamanote Line, Shinjuku Station (Higashi-guchi/East Exit); Marunouchi, Shinjuku, and Fukutoshin subway lines, Shinjuku San-chome Station (Exit A1).*

★ **Takashimaya.** In Japanese, *taka* means "high"—a fitting word for this store, which is beloved for its superior quality and prestige. Gift-givers all over Japan seek out this department store; a present that comes in a Takashimaya bag makes a statement regardless of what's inside. The third floor, with shops by Prada, Celine, Fendi, Cartier, and many others, is one of the toniest retail spaces in the district. The lower-level food court carries every gastronomic delight imaginable, from Japanese crackers and Miyazaki beef to one of the largest gourmet dessert courts in the city. The annexes boast a large-scale Tokyu Hands and Kinokuniya bookstore as well. *Takashimaya Times Sq., 5–24–2 Sendagaya, Shibuya-ku* ☎ *03/5361–1111* ⊘ *Sun.–Fri. 10–8, Sat. 10–8:30* Ⓜ *JR Yamanote Line, Shinjuku Station (Minami-guchi/South Exit); Fukutoshin subway line, Shinjuku San-chome Station (Exit E8).*

SPECIALTY STORES

BOOKS

Kinokuniya. The mammoth Kinokuniya bookstore, an annex of Takashi-maya (⇨ *above*) devotes most of its sixth floor to English titles, with an excellent selection of travel guides, magazines, and books on Japan. ✉ *Takashimaya Times Sq., 5–24–2 Sendagaya, Shibuya-ku* ☎ *03/5361–3300* ⊗ *Sun.–Fri. 10–8, Sat. 10–8:30* Ⓜ *JR Yamanote Line, Shinjuku Station (Minami-guchi/South Exit); Fukutoshin subway line, Shinjuku San-chome Station (Exit E8).*

CLOTHING CHAINS

Don Quixote. This 24-hour discount store has chains all around the country. The generally tight quarters aren't recommended for those with claustrophobia, but junk collectors will love the costumes, odd cosmetics, family-size bags of Japanese snacks, and used luxury handbags and watches. It's all haphazardly stacked from the floor to the ceiling. ✉ *1–16–5 Kabuki-cho, Shinjuku-ku* ☎ *03/5291–9211* ⊗ *Daily 24 hrs* Ⓜ *Marunouchi, Oedo, and Shinjuku subway lines, JR Yamanote Line, Keio and Odakyu lines, Shinjuku Station (Higashi-guchi/East Exit).*

ELECTRONICS

Bic Camera. This large discount-electronics chain in the Odakyu Halc building sells far more than just cameras. Bic is well known for its vast selection of energy and economically efficient electronics at extremely competitive prices. ✉ *1–5–1 Nishi-Shinjuku, Shinjuku-ku* ☎ *03/5326–1111* ⊗ *Daily 10–9* Ⓜ *Marunouchi, Oedo, and Shinjuku subway lines, JR Yamanote Line, Keio and Odakyu lines, Shinjuku Station (Nishi-guchi/West Exit).*

Yodobashi Camera. This discount-electronics superstore near Shinjuku Station carries a selection comparable to that of Akihabara's big boys. It is comprised of a number of annexes, including a watch, hobby, and professional camera building, that together span an entire block. ✉ *1–11–1 Nishi-Shinjuku, Shinjuku-ku* ☎ *03/3346–1010* ⊗ *Daily 9:30 am–10 pm* Ⓜ *Marunouchi, Shinjuku, and Oedo subway lines, JR Yamanote Line, Keio and Odakyu lines, Shinjuku Station (Nishi-guchi/West Exit).*

FOLK CRAFTS

Bingo-ya. Although it is a good taxi ride away from Shinjuku, this tasteful four-floor shop allows you to complete your souvenir shopping in one place. The store carries traditional handicrafts—including ceramics, toys, lacquerware, Noh masks, fabrics, and lots more—from all over Japan. ✉ *10–6 Wakamatsu-cho, Shinjuku-ku* ☎ *03/3202–8778* ⊗ *Tues.–Sun. 10–7* Ⓜ *Oedo subway line, Wakamatsu Kawada Station (Kawada Exit).*

RECORD STORES

Fodor's Choice
★

Disk Union. Vinyl junkies rejoice. The Shinjuku flagship of this chain offers Latin, rock, and indie at 33 rpm. Other stores clustered within the nearby blocks have punk, metal, and jazz. Be sure to grab a store flyer that lists all of its branches since each usually specializes in one music genre or other. Oh, and for you digital folk: CDs are available, too. ✉ *3–31–4 Shinjuku, Shinjuku-ku* ☎ *03/3352–2691* ⊗ *Mon.–Sat. 11–9, Sun. 11–8* Ⓜ *Marunouchi, Oedo, and Shinjuku subway* *lines, JR Yamanote Line, Keio and Odakyu lines, Shinjuku Station (Higashi-guchi/East Exit).*

ROPPONGI

MALLS AND SHOPPING CENTERS

🜋 **Axis.** Classy and cutting-edge housewares, fabrics, and ceramics are sold at this multistory design center on the main Roppongi drag of Gaien-Higashi-dori. Savoir Vivre has an excellent selection of ceramics. Kids can play at the basement toy store or on the miniature replica cars on the first floor. The JIDA Gallery on the fourth floor shows the best of what's current in Japanese industrial design. ⊠ *5–17–1 Roppongi, Minato-ku* 🕿 *03/3587–2781* 🕙 *Most shops Mon.–Sat. 11–7* Ⓜ *Hibiya and Oedo subway lines, Roppongi Station (Exit 3); Namboku subway line, Roppongi Itchome Station (Exit 1).*

★ **Midtown Tokyo.** Opened in 2007, it is one of the newer shopping and business multiplexes in the city. An airy, open structure houses exclusive boutiques such as Restir and hotels like the Ritz Carlton, and it is also known for its concentration of cafés by the world's top pâtissiers. ⊠ *9–7–3 Akasaka, Minato-ku* 🕿 *03/3475–3100* 🕙 *Most shops daily 11–9* Ⓜ *Hibiya and Oedo subway lines, Roppongi Station (Exit 8); Chiyoda subway line, Nogizaka Station (Exit 3).*

Roppongi Hills. You could easily spend a whole day exploring the retail areas of this minicity. The shops here emphasize eye-catching design and chichi brands. Finding a particular shop, however, can be a hassle given the building's Escher-like layout. ⊠ *6–10–1 Roppongi, Minato-ku* 🕿 *03/6406–6000* 🕙 *Most shops daily 11–9* Ⓜ *Hibiya and Oedo subway lines, Roppongi Station (Roppongi Hills Exit).*

SPECIALTY STORES
ANTIQUES

Nogi Jinja. This antiques fair at the Nogi shrine is the longest running in the city with a history of more than 35 years. On the second Sunday of every month (except November) about 40 veteran dealers offer their traditional wares at negotiable prices. ⊠ *8–11–27 Akasaka, Minato-ku* 🕿 *04/2691–4687* 🕙 *5–3:30* Ⓜ *Chiyoda subway line, Nogizaka Station (Exit 1).*

CERAMICS

Noritake. The Akasaka showroom of this internationally renowned brand carries fine china and glassware in a spacious setting. ⊠ *7–8–5 Akasaka, Minato-ku* 🕿 *03/3586–0059* 🕙 *Weekdays 10–6* Ⓜ *Chiyoda subway line, Akasaka Station (Exit 7).*

Savoir Vivre. In Roppongi's swanky Axis Building, this store sells contemporary and antique tea sets, cups, bowls, and glassware. ⊠ *3F Axis Bldg., 5–17–1 Roppongi, Minato-ku* 🕿 *03/3585–7365* 🕙 *Daily 11–7* Ⓜ *Hibiya and Oedo subway lines, Roppongi Station (Exit 3).*

CLOTHING BOUTIQUES

Restir. In the Midtown Tokyo complex, this is possibly the most exclusive and fashion-forward boutique in the city. The first floor is decorated in graphite and black mirrors and comes replete with a DJ booth for private parties. ⊠ *9–7–4 Akasaka, Minato-ku* 🕿 *03/5413–3708* 🕙 *Daily*

11–9 Ⓜ *Hibiya and Oedo subway lines, Roppongi Station (Exit 8); Chiyoda subway line, Nogizaka Station (Exit 3).*

JEWELRY

Tasaki Pearl Gallery. Tasaki sells pearls at slightly lower prices than Mikimoto. The store has several showrooms and hosts an English-language tour that demonstrates the technique of culturing pearls and explains how to maintain and care for them. ⊠ *1–3–3 Akasaka, Minato-ku* ☎ *03/5561–8880* ⊗ *Weekdays 9–7, weekends 9–6* Ⓜ *Ginza subway line, Tameike-Sanno Station (Exit 9).*

NIHOMBASHI AND TOKYO

MALLS AND SHOPPING CENTERS

Coredo. Unlike other big stores in the Nihombashi area, this sparkling mall has a contemporary feel thanks to an open layout and extensive use of glass and wood. Housewares shops cover the third floor and fashion can be found on the first two floors. ⊠ *1–4–1 Nihombashi, Chuo-ku* ☎ *03/3272–4939* ⊗ *Mon.–Sat. 11–9, Sun. 11–8* Ⓜ *Ginza, Tozai, and Asakusa subway lines, Nihombashi Station (Exit B12).*

Marunouchi and Shin-Marunouchi Buildings. These neighboring shopping, office, and dining mega-complexes have brought some much-needed retail dazzle to the area. Between the two of them are about 300 stores, covering clothing, jewelry, housewares, and more. ⊠ *2–4–1 Marunouchi, Chiyoda-ku* ☎ *03/5218–5100* ⊗ *Mon.–Sat. 11–9, Sun. 11–8* Ⓜ *Marunouchi subway line, Tokyo Station (Marunouchi Bldg. Exit); JR Yamanote Line, Tokyo Station (Marunouchi Minami-guchi/South Exit).*

DEPARTMENT STORES

Fodor'sChoice
★
Mitsukoshi. Founded in 1673 as a dry-goods store, Mitsukoshi later played one of the leading roles in introducing Western merchandise to Japan. It has retained its image of quality and excellence, with a particularly strong representation of Western fashion designers. The store also stocks fine traditional Japanese goods—don't miss the art gallery and the crafts area on the sixth floor. With its own subway stop, bronze lions at the entrance, and an atrium sculpture of the Japanese goddess Magokoro, this flagship store merits a visit even if you're not planning on buying anything. ⊠ *1–4–1 Nihombashi Muro-machi, Chuo-ku* ☎ *03/3241–3311* ⊗ *Daily 10–7* Ⓜ *Ginza and Hanzo-mon subway lines, Mitsukoshi-mae Station (Exits A3 and A5).*

SPECIALTY STORES

BOOKS

Maruzen. There are English titles on the fourth floor as well as art books; this flagship branch of the Maruzen chain also hosts the occasional art exhibit. ⊠ *1–6–4 Marunouchi, Chiyoda-ku* ☎ *03/5288–8881* ⊗ *Daily 9–9* Ⓜ *JR Yamanote Line, Tokyo Station (North Exit); Tozai subway line, Otemachi Station (Exit B2C).*

Yaesu Book Center. English-language paperbacks, art books, and calendars are available on the seventh floor of this celebrated bookstore. ⊠ *2–5–1 Yaesu, Chuo-ku* ☎ *03/3281–1811* ⊗ *Mon.–Sat. 10–9, Sun. 10–8* Ⓜ *JR Yamanote Line, Tokyo Station (Yaesu South Exit 5).*

FOODSTUFFS AND WARES

Yamamoto Noriten. The Japanese are resourceful in their uses of products from the sea. Nori, the paper-thin dried seaweed used to wrap maki sushi and *onigiri* (rice balls), is the specialty here. If you plan to bring some home with you, buy unroasted nori and toast it yourself at home; the flavor will be far better than that of the preroasted sheets. ⊠ *1–6–3 Nihombashi Muro-machi, Chuo-ku* ☎ *03/3241–0261* ◎ *Daily 9–6:30* Ⓜ *Hanzo-mon and Ginza subway lines, Mitsukoshi-mae Station (Exit A1).*

HOUSEWARES

Pass the Baton. This eccentric store is brimming with zakka (tschotskes) that are donated from the coffers of local fashion designers, artists, magazine editors, and celebrities. The goods are fixed up and resold, with a portion of the profit going to charity. It is tucked inside the Brick Square complex, next to an English rose garden. ⊠ *2–6–1 Marunouchi, Chiyoda-ku* ☎ *03/6269–9555* ◎ *Mon.–Sat. 11–9, Sun. 11–8* Ⓜ *Marunouchi subway line, Tokyo Station (Marunouchi Bldg. Exit); JR Yamanote Line, Tokyo Station (Marunouchi Minami-guchi/South Exit).*

PAPER

Ozu Washi. This shop, which was opened in the 17th century, has one of the largest washi showrooms in the city and its own gallery of antique papers. ⊠ *3–6–2 Nihombashi-Honcho, Chuo-ku* ☎ *03/3662–1184* ◎ *Mon.–Sat. 10–7* Ⓜ *Ginza and Hanzo-mon subway lines, Mitsukoshi-mae Station (Exit A4).*

SWORDS AND KNIVES

Kiya. Workers shape and hone blades in one corner of this shop, which carries cutlery, pocketknives, saws, and more. Scissors with handles in the shape of Japanese cranes are among the many unique gift items sold here, and custom-made knives are available, too. Kiya is located in the Coredo Muro-machi complex. ⊠ *2–2–1 Nihombashi-Muromachi, Chuo-ku* ☎ *03/3241–1333* ◎ *Daily 10–8* Ⓜ *Ginza subway line, Mitsukoshi-mae Station (Exit A4).*

Side Trips from Tokyo

WORD OF MOUTH

"I had a wonderful time visiting Mt Fuji. Magnificent! And it was only one of the 60 days a year where you got a clear view, so I was very fortunate. Beautiful cruise on a volcanic lake and amazing cable car ride too. . . . It would be criminal not to take a day trip to Mt Fuji!"

—Hagan

SIDE TRIPS FROM TOYKO

TOP REASONS TO GO

★ **Peerless Fuji:** Climb Japan's tallest mountain or catch a glimpse of it from Fuji-Hakone-Izu National Park.

★ **Rustic Japan:** Escape the endless modernity of Tokyo in Nikko, where the Tosho-gu area shrines and temples transport you centuries back into the country's past and the Kegon Falls just transport you.

★ **Zen and the Art of Travel:** Kita-Kamakura is home to two preeminent Zen temples, Engaku and Kencho. In Hase gaze on the Great Buddha or explore inside the giant statue.

★ **Go to China Without Boarding a Plane:** In Yokohama, a port city, sample authentic Chinese goods, spices, and crafts in Chinatown. For a bit of whimsy and a great view, ride Yokohama's Ferris wheel.

1 Fuji-Hakone-Izu National Park and Mt. Fuji. Fuji-Hakone-Izu National Park lies southwest of Tokyo. Its chief attraction, of course, is Mt. Fuji. South of it, the Izu Peninsula projects out into the Pacific, with Suruga Bay to the west and Sagami Bay to the east. The beaches and rugged shoreline of Izu, its forests and highland meadows, and its numerous hot-springs inns and resorts make the region a favorite destination for the Japanese.

2 Nikko. Nikko is not simply the site of the Tokugawa Shrine but also of a national park, Nikko Kokuritsu Koen, on the heights above it. The centerpiece of the park is Chuzenji-ko, a deep lake some 21 km (13 mi) around, and the 318-foot-high Kegon Falls, Japan's most famous waterfall.

3 Kamakura. Kamakura is an ancient city—the birthplace, one could argue, of the samurai way of life. Minamoto no Yoritomo, the country's first shogun, chose this site, with its rugged hills and narrow passes, as the seat of his military government. The warrior elite took much of their ideology—and their aesthetics—from Zen Buddhism, endowing splendid temples that still exist today. A walking tour of Kamakura's Zen temples and Shinto shrines is a must for anyone with a day to spend out of Tokyo.

4 Yokohama. Yokohama is Japan's largest port and has an international character that rivals—if not surpasses—that of Tokyo. Its waterfront park and its ambitious Minato Mirai bay-side development project draw visitors from all over the world.

GETTING ORIENTED

Kamakura and Yokohama are close enough to Tokyo to provide ideal day trips, and as it's unlikely that you'll stay overnight in either city, no accommodations are listed for them. Mt. Takao, less than an hour from Shinjuku, can be visited in one day. Nikko is something of a toss-up: you can easily see Tosho-gu and be back in Tokyo by evening. But when the weather turns glorious in spring or autumn, why not spend some time in the national park, staying overnight at Chuzenji, and returning to the city the next day? Mt. Fuji and Hakone, on the other hand—and more especially the Izu Peninsula—are pure resort destinations. Staying overnight is an intrinsic part of the experience, and it makes little sense to go without hotel reservations confirmed in advance.

4

Updated by
Kevin Mcgue

While there's plenty to keep you occupied in Tokyo for days, the urge to get out and explore beyond the city limits should not be ignored. The city's a great base for numerous day trips including visits to the iconic Fuji-san (Mt. Fuji) in Fuji-Hakone-Izu National Park, one of Japan's most popular resort areas; Nikko, a popular vacation destination for Tokyo residents and the home of Tosho-gu, the astonishing shrine to the first Tokugawa shogun Ieyasu; the ancient city of Kamakura which has great historical and cultural sights; and Yokohama, a port city with an international character all its own—it's home to the country's largest Chinatown.

One caveat: the term "national park" does not quite mean what it does elsewhere in the world. In Japan, pristine grandeur is hard to come by; there are few places in this country where intrepid hikers can go to contemplate the beauty of nature for very long in solitude. If a thing's worth seeing, it's worth developing. This world view tends to fill Japan's national parks with bus caravans, ropeways, and gondolas, scenic overlooks with coin-fed telescopes, signs that tell you where you may or may not walk, fried-noodle joints and vending machines, and shacks full of kitschy souvenirs. That's true of Nikko, and it's true as well of Fuji-Hakone-Izu National Park.

PLANNING

RESTAURANTS
The local specialty in Nikko is a soybean-based concoction known as *yuba* (tofu skin); dozens of restaurants in Nikko serve it in a variety of dishes you might not have believed possible for so prosaic an ingredient. Other local favorites are *soba* (buckwheat) and *udon* (wheat-flour) noodles—both inexpensive, filling, and tasty options for lunch.

Three things about Kamakura make it a good place to dine. It's on the ocean (properly speaking, on Sagami Bay), which means that fresh seafood is everywhere; it's a major tourist stop; and it has long been a prestigious place to live among Japan's worldly and well-to-do (many successful writers, artists, and intellectuals call Kamakura home). On a day trip from Tokyo, you can feel confident picking a place for lunch almost at random.

Yokohama, as befits a city of more than 3 million people, lacks little in the way of food: from quick-fix lunch counters to elegant dining rooms, you'll find almost every imaginable cuisine. Your best bet is Chinatown—Japan's largest Chinese community—with more than 100 restaurants representing every regional style. If you fancy Italian, Indian, or even Scandinavian, this international port is still guaranteed to provide an eminently satisfying meal.

HOTELS

In both Nikko and the Fuji-Hakone-Izu area, there are modern, Western-style hotels that operate in a fairly standard international style. More common, however, are the traditional *ryokan* (inns). The main difference between these lodging options is that Western-style hotels are situated in prime tourist locations whereas ryokans stick strictly to Japanese-style rooms and are found in less touristy locations. The undisputed pleasure of a ryokan is to return to it at the end of a hard day of sightseeing, luxuriate for an hour in a hot bath with your own garden view, put on the *yukata* (cotton kimono) provided for you (remember to close your right side first and then the left), and sit down to a catered private dinner party. There's little point to staying at a Western-style hotel, unless you want to say you've had the experience and survived. These places do most of their business with big, boisterous tour groups; the turnover is ruthless and the cost is way out of proportion to the service they provide.

The price categories listed here are for double occupancy, but you'll find that most kanko and ryokan normally quote per-person rates, which include breakfast and dinner. Remember to stipulate whether you want a Japanese or Western breakfast. If you don't want dinner at your hotel, it's usually possible to renegotiate the price, but the management will not be happy about it; the two meals are a fixture of their business. The typical ryokan takes great pride in its cuisine, usually with good reason: the evening meal is an elaborate affair of 10 or more different dishes, based on the fresh produce and specialties of the region, served to you—nay, *orchestrated*—in your room on a wonderful variety of trays and tableware designed to celebrate the season.

WHAT IT COSTS IN YEN				
	¢	$	$$	$$$	$$$$
Restaurants	under ¥800	¥800–¥1,000	¥1,000–¥2,000	¥2,000–¥3,000	over ¥3,000
Hotels	under ¥8,000	¥8,000–¥12,000	¥12,000–¥18,000	¥18,000–¥22,000	over ¥22,000

Restaurant prices are per person for a main course at dinner. Hotel price categories reflect the range of least- to most-expensive standard double rooms in nonholiday high season, with no meals, unless otherwise noted. Taxes (5%) are included.

FUJI-HAKONE-IZU NATIONAL PARK 富士箱根伊豆国立公園

Fuji-Hakone-Izu National Park, southwest of Tokyo between Suruga and Sagami bays, is one of Japan's most popular resort areas. The region's main attraction, of course, is Mt. Fuji, a dormant volcano—it last erupted in 1707—rising to a height of 12,388 feet. The mountain is truly beautiful; utterly captivating in the ways it can change in different light and from different perspectives. Its symmetry and majesty have been immortalized by poets and artists for centuries. ■TIP→ In spring and summer, Mt. Fuji often hides behind a blanket of clouds. Keep this in mind if seeing the mountain is an important part of your trip.

Apart from Mt. Fuji itself, each of the three areas of the park—the Izu Peninsula, Hakone and environs, and the Five Lakes—has its own unique appeal. Izu is defined by its dramatic rugged coastline, beaches, and *onsen* (hot springs). Hakone has mountains, volcanic landscapes, and lake cruises, plus onsen of its own. The Five Lakes form a recreational area with some of the best views of Mt. Fuji. And in each of these areas there are monuments to Japan's past.

Although it's possible to make a grand tour of all three areas at one time, most people make each of them a separate excursion from Tokyo.

Trains will serve you well in traveling to major points anywhere in the northern areas of the national-park region and down the eastern coast of the Izu Peninsula. For the west coast and central mountains of Izu, there are no train connections; unless you are intrepid enough to rent a car, the only way to get around is by bus.

Especially in summer and fall, the Fuji-Hakone-Izu National Park area is one of the most popular vacation destinations in the country, so most towns and resorts have local visitor information centers. Few of them have staff members who speak fluent English, but you can still pick up local maps and pamphlets, as well as information on low-cost inns, pensions, and guesthouses.

FUJI-SAN (MT. FUJI) 富士山

Fodor's Choice ★   **Fuji-san.** There are six routes to the summit of the 12,388-foot-high mountain but only two, both accessible by bus, are recommended: from Go-gome (Fifth Station), on the north side, and from Shin-Go-gome (New Fifth Station), on the south. The climb to the summit from Go-gome takes five hours and is the shortest way up; the descent takes three hours. From Shin-Go-gome the ascent is slightly longer and stonier, but the way down, via the *sunabashiri,* a volcanic sand slide, is faster. The quickest route is to ascend from Go-gome and descend to Shin-Go-gome via the sunabashiri. ⇨ *For more information on Mt. Fuji, see Peerless Fuji in this chapter.*

GETTING HERE AND AROUND

Take one of the daily buses directly to Go-gome from Tokyo; they run July through August and leave from Shinjuku Station. The journey takes about two hours and 40 minutes from Shinjuku and costs ¥2,600.

Continued on page 250

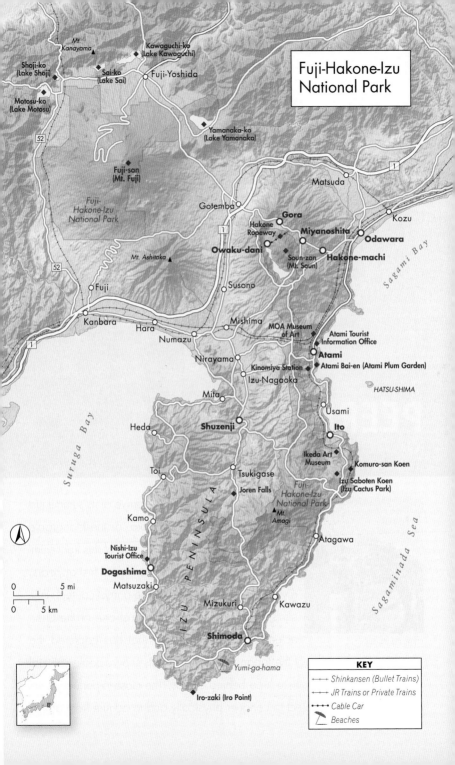

Fuji-Hakone-Izu National Park

Mt. Kanayama

Kawaguchi-ko (Lake Kawaguchi)

Shoji-ko (Lake Shoji)

Sai-ko (Lake Sai)

Fuji-Yoshida

Motosu-ko (Lake Motosu)

52

Yamanaka-ko (Lake Yamanaka)

Fuji-san (Mt. Fuji)

Fuji-Hakone-Izu National Park

Matsuda

Gotemba

Gora

Hakone Ropeway

Miyanoshita

Kozu

Mt. Ashitaka

Owaku-dani

Soun-zan (Mt. Soun)

Hakone-machi

Odawara

1

52

Fuji

Susono

Sagami Bay

Kanbara

Hara

Mishima

MOA Museum of Art

Atami Tourist Information Office

1

Numazu

Nirayama

Kinomiya Station

Atami

Atami Bai-en (Atami Plum Garden)

Izu-Nagaoka

HATSU-SHIMA

Mita

Usami

Heda

Shuzenji

Ito

Suruga Bay

Ikeda Art Museum

Komuro-san Koen

Toi

Tsukigase

Joren Falls

Izu Saboten Koen (Izu Cactus Park)

Kamo

Fuji-Hakone-Izu National Park

Sagaminada Sea

Nishi-Izu Tourist Office

Mt. Amagi

Dogashima

Atagawa

Matsuzaki

IZU PENINSULA

0   5 mi

0   5 km

Mizukuri

Kawazu

Sagaminada Sea

Shimoda

Yumi-ga-hama

Iro-zaki (Iro Point)

KEY

Shinkansen (Bullet Trains)

JR Trains or Private Trains

Cable Car

Beaches

PEERLESS FUJI

by Peter MacMillan

Climbing Mt. Fuji

Mount Fuji greets hikers who arrive at its summit just before dawn with the *go-raiko,* or the Honorable Coming of the Light. The reflection of this light shimmers across the sky just before the sun first appears, giving the extraordinary sunrise a mystical feel. Fujisan's early morning magic is just one of the characteristics of the mountain that has captured the collective imagination of the Japanese, along with its snowy peak, spiritual meaning, and propensity to hide behind clouds. The close-to-perfectly symmetrical cone is an object to conquer physically and to admire from afar.

Japan is more than 70% mountainous, and Fuji is its tallest mountain. It appears in literature, art, and culture from the highest level to the most ordinary in countless ways. In a word, Fuji is ubiquitous.

Since ancient times Mt. Fuji has been an object of worship for both Shinto and Buddhist practitioners. Shrines devoted to Konohana-Sakuya Hime, Mt. Fuji's goddess, dot the trails. So sacred is Fuji that the mountaintop torii gate at the Okumiya of Sengen Taisha Shrine (though at Fuji's foot, the shrine also encompasses the mountain above the 8th station) states that this is the greatest mountain in the world. Typically the gate would provide the shrine's name. Here, the torii defines not the shrine but the sacred space of the mountain.

Rising to 12,385 feet (3,776 meters) Mt. Fuji is an active volcano, but the last eruption was in 1707. Located on the boundaries of Shizuoka and Yamanashi prefectures, the mountain is an easy day trip west of Tokyo, and on clear days you can see the peak from the city. In season, hikers clamber to the peak, but it is gazing upon Fuji that truly inspires awe and wonder. No visit to Japan would be complete without at least a glimpse of this beautiful icon.

(top left) Mt. Fuji's famous morning light draws visitors, (top right) the summit is often surrounded by clouds, (bottom right) the trails are rocky and rugged at tiimes.

THE SYMBOLISM OF FUJI-SAN

ARTISTIC FUJI

Mt. Fuji is one of the world's most painted and photographed mountains. But rising above all the visual depictions are Katsushika Hokusai's *Thirty-six Views of Mt. Fuji* and his *One Hundred Views of Mt. Fuji*. The latter is a stunning work and considered his masterpiece. However, the *Thirty-Six Views* is more famous because the images were printed in full color, while the *One Hundred Views* was printed in monochrome black and gray. His *Great Wave off Kanagawa* is one of the most famous prints in the history of art.

Hokusai believed that his depictions would get better and better as he got older, and they did; his *One Hundred Views* was completed when he was 75. He was also obsessed with achieving immortality. In creating the *One Hundred Views of Mt. Fuji*, a mountain always associated with immortality, he hoped to achieve his own. History proved him right.

LITERARY FUJI

There are thousands of literary works related to Fuji, including traditional and modern poems, haiku, Noh dramas, novels, and plays. In the Man'yoshu, 8th-century poet Yamabe no Akahito famously extolled Fuji: "When I sail out/on the Bay of Tago/every where's white-/Look! Snow's piling up/ on the peak of Fuji." Matsuo Basho, in another well known poem, wrote about not being able to see the mountain: "How lovely and intriguing!/ Covered in drifting fog,/ the day I could not see Fuji." There are many times of the year when Fuji hides behind the clouds, so don't be disappointed if you miss it. Like the great haiku poet, see the mountain in the eye of your heart.

(top) Katsushika Hokusai's *Red Fuji*, (bottom) *Great Wave off Kanagawa* by Katsushika Hokusai

SEE FUJI-SAN FROM AFAR

Like the poets and artists who have found inspiration in gazing at Fuji-san, you, too, can catch a glimpse of the snow-capped cone on the horizon. On a clear day, most likely in winter when the air is dry and the clouds lift, the following experiences provide some of the best Fuji views.

SEE FUJI

Atop Tokyo. Visit the Tokyo City View observation promenade on the 52nd floor of the Mori Tower in Roppongi. You can walk all around this circular building and take in the spectacular views of Tokyo and, when the weather is fine, Fuji. While you're here, don't miss the sky-high Mori Art Museum, a contemporary art space on the 52nd and 53rd floors. The evening view of the city is also splendid, but Fuji will be slumbering under the blanket of nightfall.

From Hakone. Part of Fuji-Hakone-Izu National Park, the same park Fuji calls home, and an easy day trip from Tokyo, Hakone is a playground of hiking trails, small art museums, an onsen, and more. Head to the beautiful gar-

den at Hakone Detached Palace for scenic views of Fuji-san. Early morning and late evening will provide the best chance for clear skies.

Speeding out of town. The classic view of Fuji is from the Shinkansen traveling from Tokyo to Kyoto. Some of the world's fastest transportation technology hums beneath you when, suddenly, the world's most beautiful and sacred mountain appears on the left. This striking combination of the ancient and cutting-edge is at the heart of understanding Japan. Make sure not to fall asleep!

(top) Shinkansen speeding past Fuji, (bottom) Fuji from inside Hakone National Park i

CLIMBING FUJI-SAN
FROM KAWAGUCHIKO TRAIL

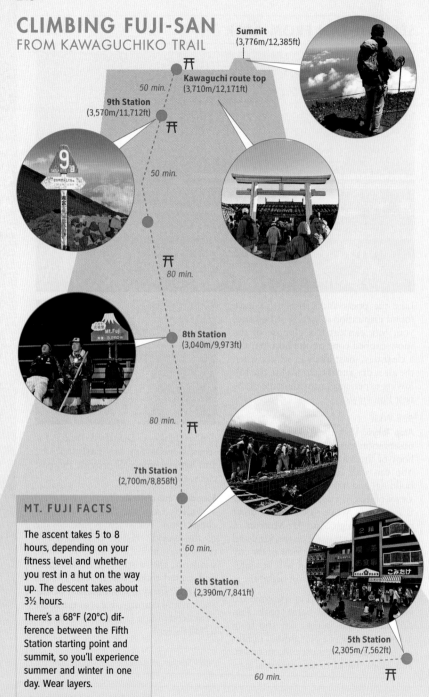

Summit
(3,776m/12,385ft)

Kawaguchi route top
(3,710m/12,171ft)

50 min.

9th Station
(3,570m/11,712ft)

50 min.

80 min.

8th Station
(3,040m/9,973ft)

80 min.

7th Station
(2,700m/8,858ft)

60 min.

6th Station
(2,390m/7,841ft)

5th Station
(2,305m/7,562ft)

60 min.

MT. FUJI FACTS

The ascent takes 5 to 8 hours, depending on your fitness level and whether you rest in a hut on the way up. The descent takes about 3½ hours.

There's a 68°F (20°C) difference between the Fifth Station starting point and summit, so you'll experience summer and winter in one day. Wear layers.

A photographer capturing view from Mt. Fuji

Although many Japanese like to climb Mt. Fuji once in their lives, there's a saying in Japanese that only a fool would climb it twice. You, too, can make a once-in-a-lifetime climb during the mountain's official open season from July through August. Unless you're an experienced hiker, do not attempt to make the climb at another time of year.

TRAIL CONDITIONS

Except for the occasional cobblestone path, the routes are unpaved and at times steep, especially toward the top. Near the end of the climb there are some rope banisters to steady yourself, but for the most part you'll have to rely on your own balance.

Fuji draws huge crowds in season, so expect a lot of company on your hike. The throngs grow thicker in August during the school break and reach their peak during the holiday Obon week in mid-August; it gets so crowded that hikers have to queue up at certain passes. Trails are less crowded overnight. Go during the week and in July for the lightest crowds (though the weather is less reliable). Or accept the crowds and enjoy the friendships that spring up among strangers on the trails.

TRAILS OVERVIEW

If you're in good health you should be able to climb from the base to the summit. That said, the air is thin, and it can be humbling to struggle for oxygen while some 83-year-old Japanese grandmother blithely leaves you in her dust (it happens).

Most visitors take buses as far as the Fifth Station and hike to the top from there (⇨ *See Mt. Fuji listing in this chapter for more information on buses*). The paved roads end at this halfway point.

Four routes lead to Mt. Fuji's summit—the **Kawaguchiko, Subashiri, Gotemba,** and **Fujinomiya**—and each has a corresponding Fifth Station that serves as the transfer point between bus and foot. Depending on which trail you choose, the ascent takes between 5 and 10 hours. Fujinomiya is closest to the summit; Gotemba is the farthest.

We recommend Kawaguchiko (Fuji-Yoshida) Trail in Yamanashi, as its many first-aid centers and lodging facilities (huts) ensure that you can enjoy the climb. ■TIP→ **Those interested in experiencing Fuji's religious and spiritual aspects should walk this trail from the mountain's foot. Along the way are small shrines that lead to the torii gate at the top, which signifies Fuji's sacred status.** While the food and cleanliness standards at mountain huts are subpar, they provide valuable rest spots and even more valuable camaraderie and good will among travelers. For further details on mountain huts and the climb see the Fuji-Yoshida City Official Web site: ⊕ *www.city. fujiyoshida.yamanashi.jp/div/ english/html/index.html*

AT THE TOP

Once you reach the top of Mt. Fuji, you can walk along the ridge of the volcano. A torii gate declares that Fuji is the greatest mountain in the world. It also marks the entrance to the **Fuji-san Honmiya Sengen Taisha Shrine** (at the foot of the mountain near the Kawaguchiko Trail is the shrine's other facility). Inside the shrine, head to the post office where you can mail letters and postcards with a special Mt. Fuji stamp. There's also a chalet at the top for those captivated enough to stay the night.

NIGHT HIKES

The most spectacular way to hike Mt. Fuji is to time the climb so that you arrive at sunrise. Not only is the light famously enchanting, but the sky is also more likely to be clear, allowing for views back to Tokyo. Those who choose this have a few options. Start from the Kawaguchiko Fifth Station on the Kawaguchi Trail around 10 PM (or later, depending on the sunrise time) and hike through the night, arriving at the summit between 4:30 and 5 AM, just as the sun begins to rise. A better alternative is to begin in the afternoon or evening and hike to the Seventh or Eighth Station, spend a few hours resting there, and then depart very early in the morning to see the sun rise. ■ TIP➡ The trail isn't lit at night, so bring a headlamp to illuminate the way. Avoid carrying flashlights, though, as it is important to keep your hands free in case of a fall.

COMMEMORATE YOUR VISIT

Purchase a walking stick at the base of Mt. Fuji and, as you climb, have it branded at each station. By the time you reach the top you'll have the perfect souvenir to mark your achievement.

(top) First glimpse of the go-raiko, (bottom) Mt. Fuji at dawn

Walking sticks for sale

DID YOU KNOW?

Although earlier meanings of the word *Fuji* include "peer-less," and "immortal one," the current way of writing Fuji implies "wealthy persons of military status." The mountain called *fuji-san* (not *fuji-yama*) in Japanese.

Mt. Fuji is one of the world's most symmetrical mountains.

Reservations are required; book seats through the Fuji Kyuko Highway Bus Reservation Center, the Keio Highway Bus Reservation Center, the Japan Travel Bureau (which should have English-speaking staff), or any major travel agency.

To return from Mt. Fuji to Tokyo, take an hour-long bus ride from Shin-Go-gome to Gotemba (¥1,500). From Gotemba take the JR Tokaido and Gotemba lines to Tokyo Station (¥1,890), or take the JR Line from Gotemba to Matsuda (¥480) and change to the private Odakyu Line from Shin-Matsuda to Shinjuku (¥750).

ESSENTIALS

Buses from Tokyo Fuji Kyuko Highway Bus Reservation Center (☎ 03/5376–2222). Japan Travel Bureau (☎ 03/5796–5454). Keio Highway Bus Reservation Center (☎ 03/5376–2222). Tokai Bus Company (☎ 0557/36–1112 for main office, 0558/22–2511 Shimoda Information Center).

IZU PENINSULA 伊豆半島

GETTING HERE AND AROUND

Having your own car makes sense only for touring the Izu Peninsula, and only then if you're prepared to cope with less-than-ideal road conditions, lots of traffic (especially on holiday weekends), and the paucity of road markers in English. It takes some effort—but exploring the peninsula *is* a lot easier by car than by public transportation. From Tokyo take the Tomei Expressway as far as Oi-matsuda (about 84 km [52 mi]); then pick up Routes 255 and 135 to Atami (approximately

28 km [17 mi]). From Atami drive another 55 km (34 mi) or so down the east coast of the Izu Peninsula to Shimoda.

■ TIP→ One way to save yourself some trouble is to book a car through the Nippon or Toyota rental agency in Tokyo and arrange to pick it up at the Shimoda branch. You can then simply take a train to Shimoda and use it as a base. From Shimoda you can drive back up the coast to Kawazu (35 minutes) and then to Shuzenji (30 minutes). It is possible to drop off the car in Tokyo but only at specific branches, so visit your rental-car company's Web site or call them in advance.

Once you are on the Izu Peninsula itself, sightseeing excursions by boat are available from several picturesque small ports. From Dogashima, you can take the Dogashima Marine short (20 minutes, ¥920) or long (45 minutes, ¥1,240) tours of Izu's rugged west coast. The Fujikyu Kogyo company operates a daily ferry to Hatsu-shima from Atami (25 minutes, ¥2,340 round-trip) and another to the island from Ito (23 minutes, ¥1,150). Izukyu Marine offers a 40-minute tour (¥1,530) by boat from Shimoda to the coastal rock formations at Iro-zaki.

Sunrise Tours operates a tour to Hakone, including a cruise across Lake Ashi and a trip on the gondola over Owaku-dani (¥15,000 includes lunch and return to Tokyo by Shinkansen; ¥12,000 includes lunch and return to Tokyo by bus). ■ TIP→ These tours are an economical way to see the main sights all in one day and are ideal for travelers with limited time. Sunrise tours depart daily from Tokyo's Hamamatsu-cho Bus Terminal and some major hotels.

Trains are by far the easiest and fastest ways to get to the Fuji-Hakone-Izu National Park area. The gateway station of Atami is well served by comfortable express trains from Tokyo, on both JR and private railway lines. These in turn connect to local trains and buses that can get you anywhere in the region you want to go. Call the JR Higashi-Nihon Info Line (10–6 daily, except December 31–January 3) for assistance in English.

The *Kodama* Shinkansen from JR Tokyo Station to Atami costs ¥3,880 and takes 51 minutes; JR Passes are valid. The JR local from Atami to Ito takes 25 minutes and costs ¥320. Ito and Atami are also served by the JR Odoriko Super Express (not a Shinkansen train) also departing from Tokyo Station; for correct platform, check the schedule display board. The Tokyo–Ito run takes 1¾ hours and costs ¥4,190; you can also use a JR Pass. The privately owned Izukyu Railways, on which JR Passes are not valid, makes the Ito–Shimoda run in one hour for ¥1,570.

The Izu–Hakone Railway Line runs from Tokyo to Mishima (one hour, 36 minutes; ¥4,090), with a change at Mishima for Shuzenji (31 minutes, ¥500); this is the cheapest option if you don't have a JR Pass. With a JR Pass, a Shinkansen–Izu Line combination will save about 35 minutes and will be the cheapest option. The Tokyo–Mishima Shinkansen leg (62 minutes) costs ¥4,400; the Mishima–Shuzenji Izu Line leg (31 minutes) costs ¥500.

ESSENTIALS

Buses from Tokyo Fuji Kyuko Highway Bus Reservation Center (☎ 03/5376–2222). **Keio Highway Bus Reservation Center** (☎ 03/5376–2222). **Tokai Bus Company** (☎ 0557/36–1112 for main office, 0557/22–2511 Shimoda Information Center).

Rental-Car Contacts Nippon Rent-a-Car (☎ 03/3485–7196 English operator available on weekdays 10 am–5 pm ⊕ www.nipponrentacar.co.jp). **Toyota Rent-a-Car** (☎ 0070/800–0100 toll-free, 03/5954–8008 English operator available 8–8 ⊕ www.toyota-rl-tyo.co.jp/rentacar/syasyu/info-e.html).

Tour Contacts Dogashima Marine (☎ 0558/52–0013). **Fujikyu Kogyo** (☎ 0557/81–0541). **Izukyu Marine** (☎ 0558/22–1151). **Sunrise Tours** (☎ 03/5796–5454 ⊕ www.jtbgmt.com/sunrisetour).

Tourist Information Atami Tourist Association (⊠ 12–1 Ginza-cho, Atami ☎ 0557/85–2222). **Nishi-Izu Tourist Office** (⊠ Dogashima, Nishi-Izu-cho, Kamo-gu ☎ 0558/52–1268). **Shimoda Tourist Association** (⊠ 1–1 Soto-ga-oka, Shimoda ☎ 0558/22–1531).

Train Information Izukyu Corporation (☎ 0557/53–1111 for main office, 0558/22–3202 Izukyu Shimoda Station). **JR Higashi-Nihon Info Line** (☎ 03/3423–0111). **Odakyu Reservation Center** (☎ 03/3481–0130).

ATAMI 熱海

100 km (60 mi) southwest of Tokyo Station.

The gateway to the Izu Peninsula is Atami. Most Japanese travelers make it no farther into the peninsula than this town on Sagami Bay, so Atami itself has a fair number of hotels and traditional inns.

When you arrive, collect a map from the **Atami Tourist Information Office** at the train station.

GETTING HERE AND AROUND

From JR Tokyo Station, take the Tokaido Acty Express to Atami, which is the last stop (one hour, 34 minutes, ¥1,890) or the Kodama Shinkansen (49 minutes, ¥3,570).

ESSENTIALS

Visitor Information Atami Tourist Information Office (☎ 0557/85–2222).

WHAT TO SEE

Atami Plum Garden 熱海梅園 *(Atami Bai-en).* The best time to visit the garden is in late January or early February, when its 850 trees bloom. If you do visit, also stop by the small shrine that's in the shadow of an enormous old camphor tree. The shrine is more than 1,000 years old and is popular spot for people who are asking the gods for help with alcoholism. The tree is more than 2,000 years old and has been designated a National Monument. It's believed that if you walk around the tree once, another year will be added to your life. Atami Bai-en is always open to the public and is 15 minutes by bus from Atami or an eight-minute walk from Kinomiya Station, the next stop south of Atami served by local trains. ⊠ 1169–1 Baien-cho, Atami ☎ 0557/85–2222 ☑ Free.

Hatsu-shima 初島. If you have the time and the inclination for a beach picnic, it's worth taking the 25-minute high-speed ferry (round-trip ¥2,340) from the pier. There are nine departures daily between 7:30 and

CLOSE UP

A Healing Headache

While earthquakes are an annoying, everyday fact of life in Japan, they also provide one of the country's greatest delights: thermal baths. Wherever there are volcanic mountains—and there are a lot—you're sure to find springs of hot water, called *onsen,* that are rich in all sorts of restorative minerals. Any place where lots of spas have tapped these sources is an *onsen chiiki* (hot-springs resort area). The Izu Peninsula is particularly rich in onsen. It has, in fact, one-fifth of the 2,300-odd officially recognized hot springs in Japan.

Spas take many forms, but the ne plus ultra is that small secluded Japanese mountain inn with a *rotemburo* (an open-air mineral-spring pool). For guests only, these pools are usually in

a screened-off nook with a panoramic view. A room in one of these inns on a weekend or in high season should be booked months in advance. (High season is late December to early January, late April to early May, the second and third weeks of August, and the second and third weeks of October.) More typical is the large resort hotel, geared mainly to groups, with one or more large indoor mineral baths of its own. Where whole towns and villages have developed to exploit a local supply of hot water, there will be several of these large hotels, an assortment of smaller inns, and probably a few modest public bathhouses, with no accommodations, where you just pay an entrance fee for a soak of whatever length you wish.

5:20. You can easily walk around the island, which is only 4 km (2½ mi) in circumference, in less than two hours. Use of the **Picnic Garden** (open daily 10–3) is free. ☎ *0557/81–0541 for ferry.*

★ **MOA Museum of Art** 美術館 *(MOA Bijutsukan).* This museum houses the private collection of the messianic religious leader Mokichi Okada. Okada (1882–1955), who founded a movement called the Sekai Kyusei Kyo (Religion for the Salvation of the World), also acquired more than 3,000 works of art; some are from the Asuka period (6th and 7th centuries). Among these works are several particularly fine *ukiyo-e* (Edo-era wood-block prints) and ceramics. On a hill above the station and set in a garden full of old plum trees and azaleas, the museum also affords a sweeping view over Atami and the bay. ⊠ *26–2 Momoyama, Atami* ☎ *0557/84–2511* 🔁 *¥1,600* ⏰ *Fri.–Wed. 9:30–5.*

Oyu Geyser 大湯間欠泉 *(Oyu Kanketsusen).* Located just a 15-minute walk south east from Atami Station, the geyser used to gush on schedule once every 24 hours but stopped after the Great Kanto Earthquake of 1923. Not happy with this, the local chamber of commerce rigged a pump to raise the geyser every five minutes. ⊠ *3 Kamijuku-cho, Atami.*

WHERE TO STAY

Hotel reviews have been abbreviated in this book. For expanded reviews, please go to Fodors.com.

$$$$

★

RYOKAN

🏠 **Atami Taikanso** 熱海大観荘. The views of the sea must have been the inspiration for Yokoyama Taikan, the Japanese artist who once owned this villa. **Pros:** spotlessly clean rooms. **Cons:** eating dinner may take most of your evening. ⊠ *7–1 Hayashi-ga-oka-cho, Atami* ☎ *0557/81–8137* ⊕ *www.atami-taikanso.com* ⤶ *44 Japanese-style rooms with bath* ⌂ *In-hotel: restaurant, pool* ⦿ *Some meals.*

$$$–$$$$
HOTEL

▥ **New Fujiya Hotel** ニュー富士屋ホテル. Only the top rooms have a view of the sea at this modern, inland resort hotel that's a great base for sightseeing. **Pros:** a number of shared hot-spring baths. **Cons:** nothing of the comfortable, at-home service of a ryokan. ⊠ *1–16 Ginza-cho, Atami* ☎ *0557/81–0111* ⤶ *158 Western-style rooms with bath, 158 Japanese-style rooms with bath* ⌂ *In-hotel: 3 restaurants, bar, pool* ⦿ *Some meals.*

ITO 伊東

16 km (10 mi) south of Atami.

There are some 800 thermal springs in the resort area surrounding Ito, 16 km (10 mi) south of Atami. These springs—and the beautiful, rocky, indented coastline nearby—remain the resort's major attractions, although there are plenty of interesting sights here. Some 150 hotels and inns serve the area.

Ito traces its history of associations with the West to 1604, when William Adams (1564–1620), the Englishman whose adventures served as the basis for James Clavell's novel *Shogun,* came ashore.

Four years earlier Adams had beached his disabled Dutch vessel, *De Liefde,* on the shores of Kyushu and became the first Englishman to set foot on Japan. The authorities, believing that he and his men were Portuguese pirates, put Adams in prison, but he was eventually befriended by the shogun Ieyasu Tokugawa, who brought him to Edo (present-day Tokyo) and granted him an estate. Ieyasu appointed Adams his adviser on foreign affairs. The English castaway taught mathematics, geography, gunnery, and navigation to shogunal officials and in 1604 was ordered to build an 80-ton Western-style ship. Pleased with this venture, Ieyasu ordered the construction of a larger oceangoing vessel. These two ships were built at Ito, where Adams lived from 1605 to 1610.

This history was largely forgotten until British Commonwealth occupation forces began coming to Ito for rest and recuperation after World War II. Adams's memory was revived, and since then the Anjin Festival (the Japanese gave Adams the name *anjin,* which means "pilot") has been held in his honor every August. A monument to the Englishman stands at the mouth of the river.

GETTING HERE AND AROUND

From JR Tokyo Station or Shinagawa Station, take the Tokaido Line (2 hours, 15 minutes, ¥2,210) or the Super Odoriko Express (1 hour, 40 minutes, ¥4,190) to Ito Station.

ESSENTIALS

Visitor Information Ito Tourist Association (⊠ *1–8–3 Yukawa, Ito* ☎ *0557/37–6105* ⊕ *www.itospa.com.*

WHAT TO SEE

Ikeda 20th-Century Art Museum 池田20世紀美術館 *(Ikeda 20-Seiki Bijutsukan).* The museum, which overlooks Lake Ippeki, houses works by Picasso, Dalí, Chagall, and Matisse, plus a number of wood-block prints. The museum is a 15-minute walk north west from Izu Cactus Park. ✉ *614 Totari* ☎ *0557/45–2211* 🖅 *¥900* 🕙 *Thurs.–Tues. 10–4:30.*

Izu Cactus Park 伊豆シャボテン公園 *(Izu Shaboten Koen).* The park consists of a series of pyramidal greenhouses that contain 5,000 kinds of cacti from around the world. At the base of Komuro-san (Mt. Komuro), the park is 20 minutes south of Ito Station by bus. ✉ *1317–13 Futo* ☎ *0557/51–5553* 🖅 *¥1,800* 🕙 *Mar.–Oct., daily 9–5; Nov.–Feb., daily 9–4.*

Komuro-san Koen 小室山公園 *(Mt. Komuro Park).* On the east side of the park there are 3,000 cherry trees of 35 varieties that bloom at various times throughout the year. You can take a cable car to the top of the mountain. The park is about 20 minutes south of Ito Station by bus. ✉ *1428 Komuro-cho, Ito* ☎ *0557/45–1444* 🖅 *Free; round-trip cable car to mountain top ¥400* 🕙 *Daily 9–4.*

WHERE TO STAY

Hotel reviews have been abbreviated in this book. For expanded reviews, please go to Fodors.com.

$$$–$$$$
RYOKAN
🛏 **Hanafubuki** 花吹雪. This traditional Japanese inn, which is located in the Jogasaki forest, has modern, comfortable rooms, but still retains classic elements like tatami mats, screen sliding doors, and *chabudai* (low dining tables) with *zabuton* (cushion seating). **Pros:** an authentic Japanese experience. **Cons:** meals are available to nonguests, so the dining room can be a bit crowded. ✉ *1041 Yawatano Isomichi, Ito* ☎ *0557/54–1550* ⊕ *www.hanafubuki.co.jp* 🔄 *12 Japanese-style rooms with bath, 2 Western-style rooms with bath, 3 family rooms with bath* ⚒ *In-hotel: restaurant, bar* ⌾ *Some meals.*

$$$$
HOTEL
🛏 **Hatoya Sun Hotel** ホテルサンハトヤ. Located along a scenic coastline, Hatoya Hotel is in the Ito onsen resort area. **Pros:** live entertainment at dinner. **Cons:** a lot of guests with children make this a bit noisy. ✉ *572–12 Yukawa Tateiwa, Ito* ☎ *057/38–4126* 🔄 *187 Japanese-style rooms with bath, 3 Western-style rooms with bath, 1 mixed Western-Japanese style room with bath* ⚒ *In-room: refrigerator (some). In-hotel: restaurant, bar, pool, parking (free)* ⌾ *Some meals.*

EN ROUTE
South of Ito the coastal scenery is lovely—each sweep around a headland reveals another picturesque sight of a rocky, indented shoreline. There are several spa towns en route to Shimoda. Higashi-Izu (East Izu) has numerous hot-springs resorts, of which **Atagawa** is the most fashionable. South of Atagawa is **Kawazu**, a place of relative quiet and solitude, with pools in the forested mountainside and waterfalls plunging through lush greenery.

SHIMODA 下田

35 km (22 mi) south of Ito city.

Of all the resort towns south of Ito along Izu's eastern coast, none can match the distinction of Shimoda. Shimoda's encounter with the West began when Commodore Matthew Perry anchored his fleet of black ships off the coast here in 1853. To commemorate the event, the three-day Black Ship Festival (Kurofune Matsuri) is held here every year in mid-May. Shimoda was also the site, in 1856, of the first American consulate.

The **Shimoda Tourist Office**, in front of the station, has the easiest of the local English itineraries to follow. The 2½-km (1½-mi) tour covers most major sights. On request, the tourist office will also help you find local accommodations.

GETTING HERE AND AROUND

From JR Shinagawa Station, take the Tokaido Line to Atami, change to the Ito Line, and take it to the final stop, Izukyu Shimoda Station (three hours, ¥3,780).

ESSENTIALS

Visitor Information Shimoda Tourist Office (☎ *0558/22–1531*).

WHAT TO SEE

Hofuku-ji 宝福寺. The first American consul to Japan was New York businessman Townsend Harris. Soon after his arrival in Shimoda, Harris asked the Japanese authorities to provide him with a female servant; they sent him a young girl named Okichi Saito, who was engaged to be married. The arrangement brought her a new name, Tojin (the Foreigner's) Okichi, much disgrace, and a tragic end. When Harris sent her away, she tried, but failed to rejoin her former lover. The shame brought upon her for working and living with a Westerner and the pain of losing the love of her life drove Okichi to drown herself in 1892. Her tale is recounted in Rei Kimura's biographical novel *Butterfly in the Wind* and inspired Puccini's *Madame Butterfly*, although some skeptics say the story is more gossip than fact. Hofuku-ji was Okichi's family temple. The museum annex displays a life-size image of her, and just behind the temple is her grave—where incense is still kept burning in her memory. The grave of her lover, Tsurumatsu, is at Toden-ji, a temple about midway between Hofuku-ji and Shimoda Station. ⊠ *18–26–1 Shimoda, Shimoda* ☎ *0558/22–0960* ⊡ *¥300* ⊗ *Daily 8–5.*

Ryosen-ji 了仙寺. This is the temple in which the negotiations took place that led to the United States–Japan Treaty of Amity and Commerce of 1858. The **Treasure Hall** (Homotsu-den) contains more than 300 original artifacts relating to Commodore Perry and the "black ships" that opened Japan to the West. ⊠ *3–12–12 Shimoda, Shimoda* ☎ *0558/22–2805* ⊡ *Treasure Hall ¥500* ⊗ *Daily 8:30–5.*

WHERE TO STAY

Hotel reviews have been abbreviated in this book. For expanded reviews, please go to Fodors.com.

¢   🏠 **Pension Sakuraya** ペンション桜家. There are a few Western-style
HOTEL   bedrooms at this family-run inn just a few minutes' walk from Shimoda's main beach, but the best lodgings are the Japanese-style corner rooms, which have nice views of the hills surrounding Shimoda. **Pros:** very homey atmosphere; Japanese bath available. **Cons:** rooms are a bit cramped. ⊠ *2584–20 Shira-hama, Shimoda* ☎ *0558/23–4470* 🛏 *4 Western-style rooms with bath, 5 Japanese-style rooms without bath* ⊕ *izu-sakuraya.jp/english* ⚹ *In-hotel: restaurant, laundry facilities, Internet terminal* ⬦⬤ *Some meals.*

$$$–$$$$ 🏠 **Shimoda Prince Hotel** 下田プリンスホテル. This modern V-shape resort
HOTEL   hotel faces the Pacific and is steps away from a white-sand beach. **Pros:** an excellent view of the sea. **Cons:** the restaurants are on the pricey

side. ✉ *1547–1 Shira-hama, Shimoda* ☎ *0558/22–2111* 🌐 *www.princehotels.co.jp* 🛏 *70 Western-style rooms with bath, 6 Japanese-style rooms with bath* ♿ *In-hotel: 2 restaurants, bar, tennis courts, pool* 🍴 *Some meals.*

$$$–$$$$
HOTEL

🏨 **Shimoda Tokyu Hotel** 下田東急ホテル. Perched just above the bay, the Shimoda Tokyu has impressive views of the Pacific from one side (where rooms cost about 10% more) and mountains from the other. **Pros:** nice views of the ocean. **Cons:** restaurants quite expensive compared to Tokyo standards. ✉ *5–12–1 Shimoda, Shimoda* ☎ *0558/22–2411* 🌐 *www.tokyuhotels.co.jp* 🛏 *107 Western-style rooms with bath, 8 Japanese-style rooms with bath* ♿ *In-hotel: 3 restaurants, bar, pool* 🍴 *Breakfast.*

4

IRO-ZAKI (IRO POINT) 石廊崎
11 km (8 mi) south of Shimoda.

If you visit Iro-zaki, the southernmost part of the Izu Peninsula, in January, you're in for a special treat: a blanket of daffodils covers the cape.

GETTING HERE AND AROUND
From Izukyu Shimoda Station on the Izu Kyuko Line, take Tokai Bus Minami Izu Line to Iro-zaki Minami-guchi Stop (15 minutes).

WHAT TO SEE
Iro-zaki Jungle Park 石廊崎ジャングルパーク. From the bus stop at the end of the line from Shimoda Station, it's a short walk to the park's 3,000 varieties of colorful tropical plants. Beyond the park you can walk to a lighthouse at the edge of the cliff that overlooks the sea; from here you can see the seven islands of Izu. ✉ *546–1 Iro-zaki, Minami-Izu* ☎ *0558/65–0050* 🎟 *¥900* 🕐 *Daily 8–5.*

DOGASHIMA 堂ヶ島
16 km (10 mi) northeast of Mishima.

The sea has eroded the coastal rock formations into fantastic shapes near the little port town of Dogashima, including a tombolo, or a narrow band of sand, that connects the mainland to a small peninsula with a scenic park.

The **Nishi-Izu Tourist Office** is near the pier, in the small building behind the bus station.

GETTING HERE AND AROUND
Dogashima is not directly accessible by train. From Shinjuku Station, take Odakyu Asagiri express train to Numazu Station (two hours, 1 minute, ¥3,280), and change to the Express Bus Super Romance (two hours, 15 minutes) to Dogashima. From Tokyo Station, take the JR Shinkansen to Mishima (44 minutes, ¥3,890), change to the Izu Hakone Line to Shuzenji (35 minutes, ¥5,000) and take the Tokai bus to the Dogashima stop. There is also an express Tokai Bus, Minami Izu Line, which will take you from Shimoda Station to Dogashima (55 minutes).

ESSENTIALS

Visitor Information Nishi-Izu Tourist Office (☎ *0558/52–1268*).

TOURS

Dogashima Marine Sightseeing Boat. Sightseeing boats from Dogashima Pier makes 20-minute runs to see the rocks (¥920). In an excess of kindness, a recorded loudspeaker—which you can safely ignore—recites the name of every rock you pass on the trip. ☎ *0558/52–0013*

WHERE TO STAY

Hotel reviews have been abbreviated in this book. For expanded reviews, please go to Fodors.com.

$$$$
HOTEL ⬚ **Dogashima New Ginsui** 堂ヶ島ニュー銀水. Surrounded by its very own secluded beach, every guest room overlooks the sea at the New Ginsui, which sits atop cliffs above the water. *2977–1 Nishina, Nishi-Izu-cho* ☎ *0558/52–2211* ⊕ *www.dougashima-newginsui.jp* 🖙 *121 Japanese-style rooms with bath* ⚹ *In-hotel: restaurant, pools, spa, laundry service* 🍽 *Some meals.*

SHUZENJI 修善寺
25 km (15 mi) south of Mishima by Izu-Hakone Railway.

Shuzenji—a hot-springs resort in the center of the peninsula, along the valley of the Katsura-gawa (Katsura River)—enjoys a certain historical notoriety as the place where the second Kamakura shogun, Minamoto no Yoriie, was assassinated early in the 13th century. Don't judge the town by the area around the station; most of the hotels and hot springs are 2 km (1 mi) to the west.

If you've planned a longer visit to Izu, consider spending a night at **Inoshishi-mura** いのしし村, en route by bus between Shimoda and Shuzenji. The scenery in this part of the peninsula is dramatic, and the dining specialty at the local inns is roast mountain boar. In the morning, a pleasant 15-minute walk from Inoshishi-mura brings you to **Joren Falls** (Joren-no-taki). Located on the upper part of the Kano River, these falls drop 82 feet into a dense forest below. This area has some nationally protected flora and fauna species, and because of the cool temperatures, hiking here is popular in summer.

GETTING HERE AND AROUND

The train is by far the easiest way to get to Shuzenji. The Izu–Hakone Railway Line runs from Tokyo to Mishima (one hour, 36 minutes, ¥4,090), with a change at Mishima for Shuzenji (31 minutes, ¥500); this is the cheapest option if you don't have a JR Pass. With a JR Pass, a Shinkansen–Izu Line combination will save about 35 minutes and will be the least expensive. The Tokyo–Mishima Shinkansen leg (62 minutes) costs ¥4,400; the Mishima–Shuzenji Izu Line leg (31 minutes) costs ¥500.

WHERE TO STAY

Hotel reviews have been abbreviated in this book. For expanded reviews, please go to Fodors.com.

¢
RYOKAN ⬚ **Goyokan** 五葉館. This family-run ryokan on Shuzenji's main street has rooms that look out on the Katsura-gawa, plus gorgeous stone-lined (for men) and wood-lined (for women) indoor hot springs. **Pros:** among

CLOSE UP

Ryokan Etiquette

Guests are expected to arrive at ryokan in the late afternoon. When you do, put on the slippers that are provided and a maid will escort you to your room. Remember to remove your slippers before entering your room; never step on the tatami (straw mats) with shoes or slippers. Each room will be simply decorated—one small low table, cushions on the tatami, and a scroll on the wall—which will probably be shoji (sliding paper-paneled walls).

In ryokan with thermal pools, you can take to the waters anytime, although the pool doors are usually locked from 11 pm to 6 am. In ryokan without thermal baths or private baths in guest rooms, visits must be staggered. Typically the maid will ask what time you would like to bathe and fit you into a schedule. Make sure you wash and rinse off entirely before getting into the bath. Do not get soap in the tub. Other guests will be using the same bathwater, so it is important to observe this custom. After your bath, change into the yukata provided in your room. Don't worry about walking around in it—other guests will be doing the same.

Dinner is served around 6. At the larger, newer ryokan, meals will be in the dining room; at smaller, more personal ryokan, it is served in your room. When you are finished, a maid will clear away the dishes and lay out your futon. In Japan *futon* means bedding, and this consists of a thin cotton mattress and a heavy, thick comforter, which is replaced with a thinner quilt in summer. The small, hard pillow is filled with grain. The less expensive ryokan (under ¥7,000 for one) have become slightly lackadaisical in changing the quilt cover with each new guest; in an inoffensive a way as

possible, feel free to complain—just don't shame the proprietor. Around 8 am, a maid will gently wake you, clear away the futon, and bring in your Japanese-style breakfast, which will probably consist of fish, pickled vegetables, and rice. If this isn't appealing, politely ask if it's possible to have coffee and toast. Checkout is at 10 am.

Make sure you call or e-mail as far in advance as possible for a room—inns are not always willing to accept foreign guests because of language and cultural barriers. It is nearly impossible to get a room in July or August. Many top-level ryokan require new guests to have introductions and references from a respected client of the inn to get a room; this goes for new Japanese guests, too. On the other hand, inns that do accept foreigners without introduction sometimes treat them as cash cows, which means they might give you cursory service and a lesser room. If you don't speak Japanese, try to have a Japanese speaker reserve a room for you; this will convey the idea that you understand the customs of staying in a traditional inn.

4

the best-priced rooms in the area. **Cons:** doesn't have the cozy feel of a true ryokan. ⊠ *765–2 Shuzenji-cho, Tagata-gun* ☎ *05/5872–2066* ⊕ *www.goyokan.co.jp* ⇨ *11 Japanese-style rooms without bath* ⌂ *In-room: refrigerator* ⦿ *Breakfast.*

$$
RYOKAN

🏠 **Kyorai-An Matsushiro-kan** 去来庵 松城館. Although this small family-owned inn is nothing fancy, the owners make you feel like a guest in their home. They also speak some English. **Pros:** nice shared hot-spring bath. **Cons:** the decor throughout is rather dated. ⊠ *55 Kona, Izunokuni* ☎ *05/5948–0072* ⇨ *16 Japanese-style rooms, 14 with bath* ⌂ *In-hotel: restaurant* 🖃 *No credit cards* ⦿ *Some meals.*

$$$$
RYOKAN

🏠 **Ochiairou Murakami** 落合楼村上. This traditional ryokan was built in the Showa period and though it has been renovated and modernized, the main wooden structure remains true to its original design. **Pros:** there's free pickup from Yugashima bus terminal; there's a lovely garden on the grounds. **Cons:** you may have to wait for the shared baths. ⊠ *1887–1 Yugashima, Izu* ☎ *05/5885–0014* ⇨ *15 Japanese-style rooms with bath* ⌂ *In-hotel: restaurant* ⦿ *Some meals.*

$$$$
RYOKAN
★

🏠 **Ryokan Sanyoso** 旅館三養荘. The former villa of the Iwasaki family, founders of the Mitsubishi conglomerate, is as luxurious and beautiful a place to stay as you'll find on the Izu Peninsula. **Pros:** a truly authentic ryokan and furnishings; Japanese bath available. **Cons:** the most expensive ryokan in the area. ⊠ *270 Mama-no-ue, Izunokuni* ☎ *05/5947–1111* ⇨ *3 Western-style, 30 Japanese-style, and 7 mixed Western-Japanese-style rooms with bath* ⌂ *In hotel: bar* ⦿ *Some meals.*

HAKONE 箱根

The national park and resort area of Hakone is a popular day trip from Tokyo and a good place for a close-up view of Mt. Fuji (assuming the mountain is not swathed in clouds, as often happens in summer). ■ **TIP→** On summer weekends it often seems as though all of Tokyo has come out to Hakone with you. Expect long lines at cable cars and traffic jams everywhere.

TIMING

You can cover the best of Hakone in a one-day trip out of Tokyo, but if you want to try the curative powers of the thermal waters or do some hiking, then stay overnight. Two of the best areas are around the old hot-springs resort of Miyanoshita and the western side of Koma-ga-take-san (Mt. Koma-ga-take).

GETTING HERE AND AROUND

The typical Hakone route, outlined here, may sound complex, but this is in fact one excursion from Tokyo so well defined that you really can't get lost—no more so, at least, than any of the thousands of Japanese tourists ahead of and behind you. The first leg of the journey is from Odawara or Hakone-Yumoto by train and cable car through the mountains to Togendai, on the north shore of Ashi-no-ko (Lake Ashi). The long way around, from Odawara to Togendai by bus, takes about an hour—in heavy traffic, an hour and a half. The trip over the mountains, on the other hand, will take about two hours. Credit the difference to the Hakone Tozan Tetsudo Line—possibly the slowest train you'll ever ride. Using three switchbacks to inch its way up the side of the mountain, the train takes 54 minutes to travel the 16 km (10 mi) from Odawara to Gora (38 minutes from Hakone-Yumoto). The steeper it gets, the grander the view.

Trains do not stop at any station en route for any length of time, but they do run frequently enough to allow you to disembark, visit a sight, and catch another train.

Within the Hakone area, buses run every 15 to 30 minutes from Hakone-machi buses to Hakone-Yumoto Station on the private Odakyu Line (40 minutes, ¥930), and Odawara Station (one hour, ¥1,150), where you can take either the Odakyu Romance Car back to Shinjuku Station or a JR Shinkansen to Tokyo Station. The buses are covered by the Hakone Free Pass.

Sunrise Tours operates a tour to Hakone, including a cruise across Lake Ashi and a trip on the gondola over Owaku-dani (¥15,000 includes lunch and return to Tokyo by Shinkansen; ¥12,000 includes lunch and return to Tokyo by bus). ■TIP→ These tours are an economical way to see the main sights all in one day and are ideal for travelers with limited time. Sunrise Tours depart daily from Tokyo's Hamamatsu-cho Bus Terminal and some major hotels.

ESSENTIALS

Buses from Tokyo Fuji Kyuko Highway Bus Reservation Center (☎ 03/5376–2222). **Keio Highway Bus Reservation Center** (☎ 03/5376–2222). **Tokai Bus Company** (☎ 0557/36–1112 for main office, 0558/22–2511 Shimoda Information Center).

Tour Contacts Sunrise Tours (☎ 03/5796–5454 ⊕ www.jtbgmt.com/sunrisetour).

Tourist Information Hakone-machi Tourist Association (✉ 698 Yumoto, Hakone-machi ☎ 0460/5–8911).

TOP ATTRACTIONS

Fodor's Choice
★ **Hakone Kowakien Yunessun** 箱根小涌園 ユネッサン. This complex on the hills overlooking Hakone offers more than the average onsen. There is a shopping mall modeled on a European outdoor market, a swim-suit rental shop, a massage salon, and game center in addition to all the water-based attractions. The park is divided into two main zones, called Yunessun and Mori no Yu ("Forest Bath"). In the Yunessun side, you need to wear a swimsuit, and can visit somewhat tacky re-creations of Turkish and ancient Roman baths. You can also take a dip in coffee, green tea, sake, or red wine. It is all a bit corny, but fun. Younger visitors will enjoy the waterslides on "Rodeo Mountain." In the more secluded Mori no Yu side, you can go au naturel in a variety of indoor and outdoor, single-sex baths. When signing in at reception, get a waterproof digital wristband that allows you to pay for lockers and drink machines within the complex. ✉ 1297 Ninotaira Hakone-machi, Ashigarashimo-gun ☎ 0460/82–4126 ⊕ www.yunessun.com/english/ ☜ ¥3,500 for the Yunessun zone, ¥1,800 for the Mori no Yu zone, ¥4,000 for both ☉ Mar.–Oct.: Yunessun daily 9–7, Mori no Yu daily 11–8. Nov.– Feb.: Yunessun daily 9–6, Mori no Yu daily 11–8.

Hakone Kowakien Yunessun offers a varied and unusual onsen experience.

★ **Hakone Open-Air Museum** 箱根彫刻の森美術館 *(Hakone Chokoku-no-mori Bijutsukan)*. Only a few minutes' walk from the Miyanoshita Station (directions are posted in English), the museum houses an astonishing collection of 19th- and 20th-century Western and Japanese sculpture, most of it on display in a spacious, handsome garden. There are works here by Rodin, Moore, Arp, Calder, Giacometti, Takeshi Shimizu, and Kotaro Takamura. One section of the garden is devoted to Emilio Greco. Inside are works by Picasso, Léger, and Manzo, among others. ☒ *1121 Ni-no-taira* ☎ *0460/82–1161* ⊕ *www.hakone-oam.or.jp* ▤ *¥1,600* ⊘ *Mar.–Nov., daily 9–5; Dec.–Feb., daily 9–4.*

★ **Hakone Ropeway.** At the cable-car terminus of Soun-zan, a gondola called the Hakone Ropeway swings up over a ridge and crosses the valley called **Owaku-dani,** also known as "Great Boiling Valley," on its way to Togendai. The landscape here is desolate, with sulfurous billows of steam escaping through holes from some inferno deep in the earth—yet another reminder that Japan is a chain of volcanic islands. At the top of the ridge is one of the two stations where you can leave the gondola. From here, a ¾-km (½-mi) walking course wanders among the sulfur pits in the valley. Just below the station is a restaurant; the food here is truly terrible, but on a clear day the view of Mt. Fuji is perfect. Remember that if you get off the gondola at any stage, you—and others in the same situation—will have to wait for someone to make space on a later gondola before you can continue down to Togendai and Ashi-no-ko (but again, the gondolas come by every minute). ☒ *1–15–1 Shiroyama, Odawara* ☎ *0465/32–2205* ⊕ *www.hakoneropeway.co.jp*

CLOSE UP

The Road to the Shogun

In days gone by, the town of Hakone was on the Tokaido, the main highway between the imperial court in Kyoto and the shogunate in Edo (present-day Tokyo). The road was the only feasible passage through this mountainous country, which made it an ideal place for a checkpoint to control traffic. The Tokugawa Shogunate built the Hakone-machi here in 1618; its most important function was to monitor the *daimyo* (feudal lords) passing through—to keep track, above all, of weapons coming into Edo, and womenfolk coming out.

When Ieyasu Tokugawa came to power, Japan had been through nearly 100 years of bloody struggle among rival coalitions of daimyo. Ieyasu emerged supreme because some of his opponents had switched sides at the last minute, in the Battle of Sekigahara in 1600. The shogun was justifiably paranoid about his "loyal" barons—especially those in the outlying domains—so he required the daimyo to live in Edo for periods of time every two years. When they did return to their own lands, they had to leave their wives behind in Edo, hostages to their good behavior. A noble lady coming through the Hakone Sekisho without an official pass, in short, was a case of treason.

The checkpoint served the Tokugawa dynasty well for 250 years. It was demolished only when the shogunate fell, in the Meiji Restoration of 1868. An exact replica, with an exhibition hall of period costumes and weapons, was built as a tourist attraction in 1965.

✉️ ¥970 *(without Hakone Free Pass)* 🕐 *Mar.–Nov., daily 8:45–5:15; Dec.–Feb., daily 9:15–4:15.*

Miyanoshita 宮ノ下. The first stop on the train route from Hakone-Yumoto, this is a small but very pleasant and popular resort. As well as hot springs, this village has antiques shops along its main road and several hiking routes up the ¾-km- (½-mi-) tall Mt. Sengen. If you get to the top, you'll be rewarded with a great view of the gorge.

WORTH NOTING

Ashi-no-ko 芦ノ湖 *(Lake Ashi).* From Owaku-dani, the descent by gondola to Togendai on the shore of Lake Ashi takes 25 minutes. There's no reason to linger at Togendai; it's only a terminus for buses to Hakone-Yumoto and Odawara and to the resort villages in the northern part of Hakone. Head straight for the pier, a few minutes' walk down the hill, where boats set out on the lake for Hakone-machi. Look for the **Hakone Sightseeing Cruise** (✉️ *1–15–1 Shiroyama, Odawara* ☎️ *0465/32–6830* 🌐 *www.hakone-kankosen.co.jp* ✉️ *¥300* 🕐 *Summer, 40-min intervals; winter, 50-min intervals. Mar.–Nov., daily 9:30–5; Dec.–Feb., daily 9:30–4).* The ride is free with your Hakone Free Pass; otherwise, buy a ticket (¥970) at the office in the terminal. A few ships of conventional design ply the lake; the rest are astonishingly corny Disney knockoffs. One, for example, is rigged like a 17th-century warship. With still water and good weather, you'll get a breathtaking reflection of the mountains in the waters of the lake as you go. If a cruise is not what

Passengers floating over the Owaku-dani valley on the Hakone Ropeway can see Fuji looming—on a clear day, of course.

you're after, go exploring and fishing with hired boats from **Togen-dai Boat House** (☎ *090/1448–1834*) or **Ashinoko Fishing Center Oba** (☎ *0460/84–8984*).

Gora 強羅. This small town is at the end of the train line from Odawara and at the lower end of the Hakone Tozan Cable Car. It's a good jumping-off point for hiking and exploring. Ignore the little restaurants and souvenir stands here: get off the train as quickly as you can and make a dash for the cable car at the other end of the station. If you let the rest of the passengers get there before you, and perhaps a tour bus or two, you may stand 45 minutes in line.

Hakone-machi 箱根町. The main attraction here is the **Hakone Barrier** (Hakone Sekisho). The barrier was built in 1618 and served as a checkpoint to control traffic until it was demolished during the Meiji Restoration of 1868. An exact replica was built as a tourist attraction in 1965 and is only a few minutes' walk from the pier, along the lakeshore in the direction of Moto-Hakone. Last entry is 30 minutes before closing time. ⊠ *1 Hakone-machi* ☎ *0460/83–6635* 🎟 *¥300* ☉ *Mar.–Nov., daily 9–5; Dec.–Feb., daily 9–4:30.*

Hakone Museum of Art 箱根美術館 *(Hakone Bijutsukan)*. A sister institution to the MOA Museum of Art in Atami, Hakone Museum of Art is at the second stop of the Hakone Tozan Cable Car. The museum, which consists of two buildings set in a garden, houses a modest collection of porcelain and ceramics from China, Korea, and Japan. ⊠ *1300 Gora* ☎ *0460/82–2623* 🌐 *www.moaart.or.jp* 🎟 *¥900* ☉ *Apr.–Nov., Fri.–Wed. 9:30–4:30; Dec.–Mar., Fri.–Wed. 9:30–4.*

Soun-zan 早雲山 *(Mt. Soun).* The Hakone Tozan Cable Car travels from Gora to Soun-zan, departing every 20 minutes; it takes 10 minutes (¥410; free with the Hakone Free Pass) to get to the top. It's ideal for those wanting to spend a day hiking. There are four stops en route, and you can get off and reboard the cable car at any one of them if you've paid the full fare.

WHERE TO STAY

Hotel reviews have been abbreviated in this book. For expanded reviews, please go to Fodors.com.

WHAT THE . . . ?

No, your eyes are not playing tricks on you. Those are in fact local entrepreneurs boiling eggs in the sulfur pits in Owaku-dani. Locals make a passable living selling the eggs, which turn black, to tourists at exorbitant prices. A popular myth suggests that eating one of these eggs can extend your life by seven years. What do you have to lose?

GORA

$$$$ **Gora Tensui** 強羅天翠. The Gora Tensui, which opened in 2007, is
RYOKAN unique in that it's something of a cross between a boutique hotel and a Japanese-style inn. **Pros:** four rooms have a private onsen on a terrace. **Cons:** no Japanese food in the restaurant. ⊠ *1320–276 Gora, Ashigarashimo-gun, Hakone-machi* ☎ *0460/86–1411* ⊕ *www.gora-tensui.com/index_english.html* 📑 *17 rooms with private bath* ⚒ *In-hotel: restaurant* ♒ *Some meals.*

LAKE ASHI

$$–$$$ **Hakone Prince Hotel** 箱根プリンスホテル. The location of this resort
HOTEL complex is perfect, with the lake in front and the mountains of Koma-
★ ga-take in back. **Pros:** lovely quaint cottages surrounded by nature; Japanese bath available. **Cons:** a bit remote from nearby sightseeing spots. ⊠ *144 Moto-Hakone, Hakone-machi* ☎ *0460/3–1111* ⊕ *www. princehotels.co.jp* 📑 *142 Western-style rooms with bath, 116 Western-style cottages with bath* ⚒ *In-hotel: 2 restaurants, room service, bar, tennis courts, pools* ♒ *Breakfast.*

MIYANOSHITA

$$$ **Fujiya Hotel** 富士屋ホテル. Built in 1878, this Western-style hotel with
HOTEL modern additions is showing signs of age, but that somehow adds to
★ its charm. **Pros:** wonderful, friendly service. **Cons:** rooms and bath decor are rather dated. ⊠ *359 Miyanoshita, Hakone-machi* ☎ *0460/2–2211* ⊕ *www.fujiyahotel.co.jp* 📑 *149 Western-style rooms with bath* ⚒ *In-hotel: 3 restaurants, room service, bar, golf course, pools* ♒ *Some meals.*

SENGOKU

¢ **Fuji-Hakone Guest House** 富士箱根ゲストハウス. A small, family-run
HOTEL Japanese inn, this guesthouse has simple tatami rooms with the bare essentials. **Pros:** friendly staff; inexpensive rates. **Cons:** difficult to access from nearest transportation, especially at night. ⊠ *912 Sengoku-hara (103 Moto-Hakone for Moto-Hakone Guest House), Hakone-machi* ☎ *0460/84–6577 for Fuji-Hakone, 0460/83–7880 for Moto-Hakone* 📑 *14 Japanese-style rooms without bath in Fuji-Hakone, 5 Japanese-style rooms without bath in Moto-Hakone* ♒ *Some meals.*

CLOSE UP

Hakone Freebies

Many places in Hakone accept the Hakone Free Pass. It's valid for three days and is issued by the privately owned Odakyu Railways. The pass covers the train fare to Hakone and allows you to use any mode of transportation including the Hakone Tozan Cable Car, the Hakone Ropeway, and the Hakone Cruise Boat. In addition to transportation, Free Pass holders get discounts at museums such as the Hakone Museum of Art, restaurants, and shops. The list of participants is pretty extensive and it always changes, so it's a good idea to check out the Web site for a complete list

of participating companies and terms and conditions.

The Hakone Free Pass (¥5,500) and the Fuji-Hakone Free Pass (¥7,200) can be purchased at the **Odakyu Sightseeing Service Center** (☎ 03/5321–7887 ⊕ www.odakyu-group.co.jp) inside JR Shinjuku Station, near the West Exit, or by credit card over the phone. Allow a couple of days for delivery to your hotel. If you have a JR Pass, it's cheaper to take a Kodama Shinkansen from Tokyo Station to Odawara and buy the Hakone Free Pass there (¥4,130) for travel within the Hakone region only.

¢

RYOKAN

🖼 **Lodge Fujimien** ロッジ富士見苑. This traditional ryokan, complete with an on-site onsen, has all the trimmings of an expensive ryokan, for a fraction of the price. **Pros:** affordable rates; convenient location. **Cons:** its accessible location leads to occasional overcrowding. ⊠ *1245 Sengoku-hara, Hakone* ☎ *0460/84–8675* ⊕ *www.fujimien.com* 🛏 *21 Japanese-style rooms with bath, 5 Western-style rooms with bath* ☺ *In-hotel: restaurant, parking (free)* ⊟ *No credit cards* �🍴*Some meals.*

FUJI GO-KO (FUJI FIVE LAKES) 富士五湖

To the north of Mt. Fuji, the Fuji Go-ko area affords an unbeatable view of the mountain on clear days and makes the best base for a climb to the summit. With its various outdoor activities, such as skating and fishing in winter and boating and hiking in summer, this is a popular resort area for families and business conferences.

The five lakes are, from the east, Yamanaka-ko, Kawaguchi-ko, Sai-ko, Shoji-ko, and Motosu-ko. Yamanaka and Kawaguchi are the largest and most developed as resort areas, with Kawaguchi more or less the centerpiece of the group.

TIMING
You can visit this area on a day trip from Tokyo, but unless you want to spend most of it on buses and trains, plan on staying overnight.

GETTING HERE AND AROUND
Direct bus service runs daily from Shinjuku Station in Tokyo to Lake Kawaguchi every hour between 7:10 am and 8:10 pm. Buses go from Kawaguchi-ko Station to Go-gome (the fifth station on the climb up Mt. Fuji) in about an hour; there are eight departures a day until the

climbing season (July and August) starts, when there are 15 departures or more, depending on demand. The cost is ¥1,700.

The transportation hub, as well as one of the major resort areas in the Fuji Five Lakes area, is Kawaguchi-ko. Getting there from Tokyo requires a change of trains at Otsuki. The JR Chuo Line Kaiji and Azusa express trains leave Shinjuku Station for Otsuki on the half hour from 7 am to 8 pm (more frequently in the morning) and take approximately one hour. At Otsuki, change to the private Fuji-Kyuko Line for Kawaguchi-ko, which takes another 50 minutes. The total traveling time is about two hours, and you can use your JR Pass as far as Otsuki; otherwise, the fare is ¥1,280. The Otsuki–Kawaguchi-ko leg costs ¥1,110. Also available are two direct-service rapid trains for Kawaguchi-ko that leave Tokyo in the morning at 6:08 and 7:10 on weekdays, 6:09 and 7:12 on weekends and national holidays.

The Holiday Kaisoku Picnic-go, available on weekends and national holidays, offers direct express service from Shinjuku, leaving at 8:10 and arriving at Kawaguchi-ko Station at 10:37. From March through August, JR puts on additional weekend express trains for Kawaguchi-ko, but be aware that on some of them only the first three cars go all the way to the lake. Coming back, you have a choice of late-afternoon departures from Kawaguchi-ko that arrive at Shinjuku in the early evening. Check the express timetables before you go; you can also call either the JR Higashi-Nihon Info Line or Fuji-kyuuko Kawaguchi-ko Station for train information.

ESSENTIALS

Buses from Kawaguchi Fuji Kyuko Gotemba Reservation Center (☏ *0550/82–2555*). Fuji Kyuko Lake Kawaguchi Reservation Center (☏ *0555/72–2922*).

Buses from Tokyo Fuji Kyuko Highway Bus Reservation Center (☏ *03/5376–2222*). Keio Highway Bus Reservation Center (☏ *03/5376–2222*). Tokai Bus Company (☏ *0557/36–1112 for main office, 0558/22–2511 Shimoda Information Center*).

Train Information Fuji-kyuuko Kawaguchi-ko Station (☏ *0555/72–0017*). JR Higashi-Nihon Info Line (☏ *03/3423–0111*). Odakyu Reservation Center (☏ *03/3481–0130*).

Visitor Information Fuji-Kawaguchiko Tourist Association (✉ *890 Funatsu, Kawakuchiko-machi, Minami-Tsuru-gun* ☏ *0555/72–2460*).

WHAT TO SEE

Fuji-kyu Highland 富士急ハイランド. The largest of the recreational facilities at Lake Kawaguchi, Fuji-kyu Highland has an impressive assortment of rides, roller coasters, and other amusements, but it's probably not worth a visit unless you have children in tow. In winter there's superb skating here, with Mt. Fuji for a backdrop. Fuji-kyu Highland is about 15 minutes' walk east from Kawaguchi-ko Station. ✉ *5–6–1 Shin Nishi Hara, Fujiyoshida* ☏ *0555/23–2111* 🎫 *Full-day Free Pass ¥4,800, entrance only ¥1,200* ⊙ *Weekdays 9–5, weekends 9–8.*

Fuji Museum 富士博物館 *(Fuji Hakubutsukan)*. One of the little oddities at Lake Kawaguchi is this museum, located on the lake's north shore, next to the Fuji Lake Hotel. The first floor holds conventional exhibits of local geology and history, but upstairs is an astonishing collection of—for want of a euphemism—phalluses (you must be 18 or older to view the exhibit). Mainly made from wood and stone and carved in every shape and size, these figures played a role in certain local fertility festivals. ⊠ *3964 Funatsu, Fujikawaguchiko-machi, Minami Tsurugen* ☏ *0555/73–2266* 🔲 *1st fl. ¥200, 1st and 2nd fl. ¥500* ⊗ *Mar.–Oct., daily 9–4; Nov.–Feb., Sat.–Thurs. 9–4; closed 3rd Tues. of month.*

Kawaguchi-ko 河口湖 *(Lake Kawaguchi)*. A 5- to 10-minute walk from Kawaguchi-ko Station, this is the most developed of the five lakes. It's ringed with weekend retreats and vacation lodges—many of them maintained by companies and universities for their employees. Excursion boats depart from a pier here on 30-minute tours of the lake. The promise, not always fulfilled, is to have two views of Mt. Fuji: one of the mountain itself and the other inverted in its reflection on the water.

Motosu-ko 本栖湖 *(Lake Motosu)*. Lake Motosu is the farthest west of the five lakes. It's also the deepest and clearest of the Fuji Go-ko. It takes about 50 minutes to get here by bus.

Sai-ko 西湖 *(Lake Sai)*. Between Lakes Shoji and Kawaguchi, Lake Sai is the third-largest lake of the Fuji Go-ko, with only moderate development. From the western shore there is an especially good view of Mt. Fuji. Near Sai-ko there are two natural caves, an ice cave and a wind cave. You can either take a bus or walk to them.

Shoji-ko 精進湖 *(Lake Shoji)*. Many consider Lake Shoji, the smallest of the lakes, to be the prettiest. There are still remnants of lava flow jutting out from the water, which locals perch upon while fishing.

Shoji Trail 精進口ルート. This trail leads from Lake Shoji to Mt. Fuji through Aoki-ga-hara (Sea of Trees). Beware. This forest has an underlying magnetic lava field that makes compasses go haywire.

Tenjo-san 天上山 *(Mt. Tenjo)*. A gondola along the shore of Lake Kawaguchi (near the pier) quickly brings you to the top of the 3,622-foot-tall mountain. From the observatory here the whole of Lake Kawaguchi lies before you, and beyond the lake is a classic view of Mt. Fuji.

Yamanaka-ko 山中湖 *(Lake Yamanaka)*. The largest of the Fuji Go-ko, Lake Yamanaka) is 35 minutes by bus to the southeast of Kawaguchi. It's also the closest lake to the popular trail up Mt. Fuji that starts at Go-gome, and many climbers use this resort area as a base.

WHERE TO STAY

Hotel reviews have been abbreviated in this book. For expanded reviews, please go to Fodors.com.

KAWAGUCHI-KO

$$$–$$$$
HOTEL

🔲 **Fuji View Hotel** 富士ビューホテル. This hotel on Lake Kawaguchi is a little threadbare but comfortable. The terrace lounge affords fine views of the lake and of Mt. Fuji beyond. **Pros:** comparatively inexpensive lodgings. **Cons:** rooms are rather small. ⊠ *511 Katsuyama-mura, Fuji-Kawaguchiko-machi* ☏ *0555/83–2211* ⊕ *www.fujiyahotel.*

4

co.jp ⮐40 *Western-style rooms with bath, 30 Japanese-style rooms with bath* ⬧ *In-hotel: 2 restaurants, golf course, tennis courts* ⦿| *Some meals.*

YAMANAKA-KO

$$
HOTEL

🏨 **Hotel Mount Fuji** 富士山ホテル. This is the best resort hotel on Lake Yamanaka and has all the facilities for a recreational holiday including on-site game and karaoke rooms and a nature walk on the grounds.

Pros: comfortable rooms; convenient facilities. **Cons:** one of the more expensive options in the area. ✉ *1360–83 Yamanaka, Yamanaka-komura* ☎ *0555/62–2111* ⊕ *www.mtfuji-hotel.com* ⮐*150 Western-style rooms with bath, 1 Japanese-style room with bath* ⬧ *In-hotel: 3 restaurants, pool, parking (free)* ⦿| *Some meals.*

¢–$
HOTEL

🏨 **Inn Fujitomita** 旅館ふじとみた. One of the closest lodging options to the Mt. Fuji hiking trails, this inexpensive inn is a launching point for treks around the Fuji Go-ko area. **Pros:** spacious rooms; pleasant surrounding grounds. **Cons:** very crowded during climbing season. ✉ *13235 Shibokusa, Oshinomura, Minami-Tsuru-gun* ☎ *0555/84–3359* ⊕ *www. tim.hi-ho.ne.jp/innfuji* ⮐*10 Japanese-style rooms, 3 with bath* ⬧ *In-room: no TV (some). In-hotel: restaurant, tennis courts, pool, laundry facilities* ⦿| *Some meals.*

NIKKO 日光

130 km (81 mi) north of Tokyo.

"Think nothing is splendid," asserts an old Japanese proverb, "until you have seen Nikko." Nikko, which means "sunlight," is a popular vacation spot for the Japanese, for good reason: its gorgeous sights include a breathtaking waterfall and one of the country's best-known shrines. In addition, Nikko combines the rustic charm of a countryside village (complete with wild monkeys that have the run of the place) with a convenient location not far from Tokyo.

GETTING HERE AND AROUND

Buses and taxis can take you from Nikko to the village of Chuzenji and nearby Lake Chuzenji; one-way cab fare from Tobu Nikko Station to Chuzenji is about ¥6,000. ⚠ There is no bus service between Tokyo and Nikko. Local buses leave Tobu Nikko Station for Lake Chuzenji, stopping just above the entrance to Tosho-gu, approximately every 30 minutes from 6:15 am until 7:01 pm. The fare to Chuzenji is ¥1,100, and the ride takes about 40 minutes. The last return bus from the lake leaves at 7:39 pm, arriving back at Tobu Nikko Station at 9:17 pm.

It's possible, but unwise, to travel by car from Tokyo to Nikko. The trip will take at least three hours, and merely getting from central Tokyo to the toll-road system can be a nightmare. Coming back, especially on a Saturday or Sunday evening, is even worse.

The limited express train of the Tobu Railway has two direct connections from Tokyo to Nikko every morning, starting at 7:30 am from Tobu Asakusa Station, a minute's walk from the last stop on Tokyo's Ginza subway line; there are additional trains on weekends,

WORD OF MOUTH

"Mt Fuji, Hakone, Nikko and Kamukura would be on top of the [day trips] list."—Cilla_Tey

holidays, and in high season. The one-way fare is ¥2,620. All seats are reserved. Bookings are not accepted over the phone; they can only be bought at Asakusa Station. During summer, fall, and weekends, buy tickets a few days in advance. The trip from Asakusa to the Tobu Nikko Station takes about two hours, which is quicker than the JR trains. If you're visiting Nikko on a day trip, note that the last return train is at 7:43 pm, requiring a quick and easy change at Shimo-Imaichi, and arrives at Asakusa at 9:35 pm. If you have a JR Pass, use JR (Japan Railways) service, which connects Tokyo and Nikko, from Ueno Station. Take the Tohoku–Honsen Line limited express to Utsunomiya (about 1½ hours) and transfer to the train for JR Nikko Station (45 minutes). The earliest departure from Ueno is at 5:10 am; the last connection back leaves Nikko at 8:03 pm and brings you into Ueno at 10:48 pm. (If you're not using the JR Pass, the one-way fare will cost ¥2,520.)

More expensive but faster is the Yamabiko train on the north extension of the Shinkansen; the one-way fare, including the surcharge for the express, is ¥4,920. The first one leaves Tokyo Station at 6:04 am (or Ueno at 6:10 am) and takes about 50 minutes to Utsunomiya; change there to the train to Nikko Station. To return, take the 9:46 pm train from Nikko to Utsunomiya and catch the last Yamabiko back at 10:37 pm.

VISITOR INFORMATION

You can do a lot of preplanning for your visit to Nikko with a stop at the Japan National Tourist Organization office in Tokyo, where the helpful English-speaking staff will ply you with pamphlets and field your questions about things to see and do. Closer to the source is the Tourist Information and Hospitality Center in Nikko itself, about halfway up the main street of town between the railway stations and Tosho-gu, on the left; don't expect too much in the way of help in English, but the center does have a good array of guides to local restaurants and shops, registers of inns and hotels, and mapped-out walking tours.

ESSENTIALS

Tourist Information Nikko Tourist Information and Hospitality Center (☎ *0288/54–2496*).

Tours JTB Sunrise Tours (☎ *03/5796–5454* ⊕ *www.jtbusa.com*).

Train Contact Japan Railways (☎ *03/3423–0111* ⊕ *www.japanrail.com*).

EXPLORING

The town of Nikko is essentially one long avenue—Sugi Namiki (Cryptomeria Avenue)—extending for about 2 km (1 mi) from the railway stations to Tosho-gu. You can easily walk to most places within town. Tourist inns and shops line the street, and if you have time, you might want to make this a leisurely stroll. The antiques shops along the way may turn up interesting—but expensive—pieces like armor fittings, hibachi, pottery, and dolls. The souvenir shops here sell ample selections of local wood carvings.

TOSHO-GU 東照宮

The Tosho-gu area encompasses three UNESCO World Heritage sights—Tosho-gu Shrine, Futarasan Shrine, and Rinnoji Temple. These are known as *nisha-ichiji* (two shrines and one temple) and are Nikko's main draw. Signs and maps clearly mark a recommended route that will allow you to see all the major sights, which are within walking distance of each other. You should plan for half a day to explore the area.

A multiple-entry ticket is the best way to see the Tosho-gu precincts. The ¥1,000 pass gets you entrance to Rinno-ji (Rinno Temple), the Taiyu-in Mausoleum, and Futara-san Jinja (Futara-san Shrine); for an extra ¥300 you can also see the Sleeping Cat and Ieyasu's tomb at Taiyu-in (separate fees are charged for admission to other sights). There are two places to purchase the multiple-entry ticket: one is at the entrance to Rinno Temple, in the corner of the parking lot, at the top of the path called the Higashi-sando (East Approach) that begins across the highway from the Sacred Bridge; the other is at the entrance to Tosho-gu, at the top of the broad Omote-sando (Central Approach), which begins about 100 yards farther west.

TOP ATTRACTIONS

★ **Futara-san Jinja** 二荒山神社 *(Futara-san Shrine).* Nikko's holy ground is far older than the Tokugawa dynasty, in whose honor it was improved upon. Futara-san is sacred to the Shinto deities Okuni-nushi-no-Mikoto (god of the rice fields, bestower of prosperity), his consort Tagorihime-no-Mikoto, and their son Ajisukitaka-hikone-no-Mikoto. Futara-san actually has three locations: the Main Shrine at Tosho-gu; the Chugushi (Middle Shrine), at Chuzenji-ko; and the Okumiya (Inner Shrine), on top of Mt. Nantai.

The bronze torii at the entrance to the shrine leads to the **Chinese Gate** (Kara-mon), gilded and elaborately carved; beyond it is the **Hai-den,** the shrine's oratory. The Hai-den, too, is richly carved and decorated, with a dragon-covered ceiling. The Chinese lions on the panels at the rear are by two distinguished painters of the Kano school. From the oratory of the Taiyu-in a connecting passage leads to the **Sanctum** (Hon-den)—the present version of which dates from 1619. Designated a National Treasure, it houses a gilded and lacquered Buddhist altar some 9 feet high, decorated with paintings of

THE UBIQUITOUS TORII

Wondering what those gatelike structures are with two posts and two crosspieces? They are torii and are used as gateways to Japanese Shinto temples.

CLOSE UP

Ieyasu's Legacy

In 1600, Ieyasu Tokugawa (1543–1616) won a battle at a place in the mountains of south-central Japan called Seki-ga-hara that left him the undisputed ruler of the archipelago. He died 16 years later, but the Tokugawa Shogunate would last another 252 years.

The founder of such a dynasty required a fitting resting place. Ieyasu (ee-eh-ya-su) had provided for one in his will: a mausoleum at Nikko, in a forest of tall cedars, where a religious center had been founded more than eight centuries earlier. The year after his death, in accordance with Buddhist custom, he was given a *kaimyo*—an honorific name to bear in the afterlife. Thenceforth, he was Tosho-Daigongen: the Great Incarnation Who Illuminates the East. The imperial court at Kyoto declared him a god, and his remains were taken in a procession of great pomp and ceremony to be enshrined at Nikko.

The dynasty he left behind was enormously rich. Ieyasu's personal fief, on the Kanto Plain, was worth 2.5 million *koku* of rice. One koku, in monetary terms, was equivalent to the cost of keeping one retainer in the necessities of life for a year. The shogunate itself, however, was still an uncertainty. It had only recently taken control after more than a century of civil war. The founder's tomb had a political purpose: to inspire awe and to make manifest the power of the Tokugawas. It was Ieyasu's legacy, a statement of his family's right to rule.

Tosho-gu was built by his grandson, the third shogun, Iemitsu (it was Iemitsu who established the policy of national isolation, which closed the doors of Japan to the outside world for more than 200 years). The mausoleum and shrine required the labor of 15,000 people for two years (1634–36). Craftsmen and artists of the first rank were assembled from all over the country. Every surface was carved and painted and lacquered in the most intricate detail imaginable. Tosho-gu shimmers with the reflections of 2,489,000 sheets of gold leaf. Roof beams and rafter ends with dragon heads, lions, and elephants in bas-relief; friezes of phoenixes, wild ducks, and monkeys; inlaid pillars and red-lacquer corridors: Tosho-gu is everything a 17th-century warlord would consider gorgeous, and the inspiration is very Chinese.

animals, birds, and flowers, in which resides the object of all this veneration: a seated wooden figure of Iemitsu himself. ✉ *Take the avenue to the left as you're standing before the stone torii at Tosho-gu and follow it to the end* 🎟 *¥200, ¥1,000 multiple-entry ticket includes admission to Rinno Temple and Taiyu-in Mausoleum* ☉ *Apr.–Oct., daily 8–5; Nov.–Mar., daily 9–4.*

★ **Rinno-ji** 輪王寺 *(Rinno Temple)*. This temple belongs to the Tendai sect of Buddhism, the head temple of which is Enryaku-ji, on Mt. Hiei near Kyoto. The main hall of Rinno Temple, called the **Sanbutsu-do**, is the largest single building at Tosho-gu; it enshrines an image of Amida Nyorai, the Buddha of the Western Paradise, flanked on the right by Senju (Thousand-Armed) Kannon, the goddess of mercy, and on the left by Bato-Kannon, regarded as the protector of animals. These three

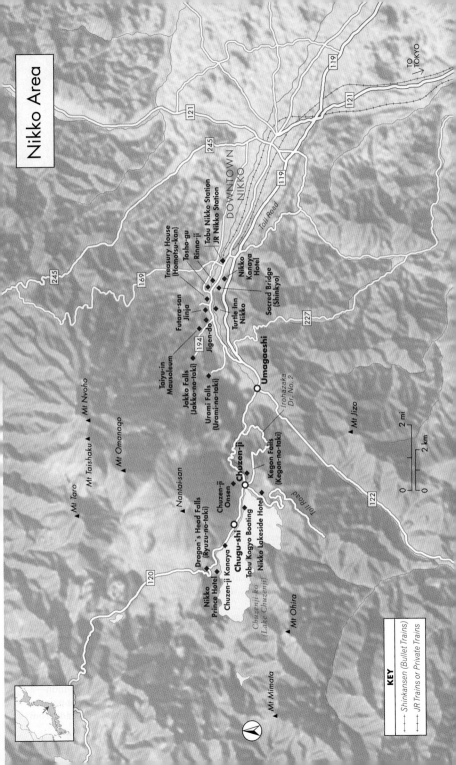

Nikko Area

KEY

⊢—⊣ *Shinkansen (Bullet Trains)*
⊢—⊣ *JR Trains or Private Trains*

TO TOKYO

119

121

121

245

119

DOWNTOWN NIKKO

Toll Road

Treasury House (Homotsu-kan)
Tosho-gu
Rinno-ji
Tobu Nikko Station
JR Nikko Station

Nikko Kanaya Hotel

169

Futara-san Jinja

Jigen-do

194

Sacred Bridge (Shinkyo)

Turtle Inn Nikko

Taiyu-in Mausoleum

Jakko Falls (Jakko-no-taki)

Urami Falls (Urami-no-taki)

245

227

Umagaeshi

Irohazaka Dr. No. 2

Mt Jizo

Mt Taro

Mt Nyoho

Mt Taishaku

Mt Omanago

Nantai-san

Chuzen-ji Onsen

Chuzen-ji

Kegon Falls (Kegon-no-taki)

Dragon's Head Falls (Ryuzu-no-taki)

120

Nikko Prince Hotel

Chuzen-ji Kanaya

Chugu-shi

Tobu Kogyo Boating

Nikko Lakeside Hotel

Chuzenji-ko (Lake Chuzenji)

Mt Ohira

Toll Road

122

Mt Mimata

0   2 mi
0   2 km

The gold-leaf detailing at Rinno Ji complements the gold on the three famed Buddhas in Sanbutsudoh Hall.

images are lacquered in gold and date from the early part of the 17th century. The original Sanbutsu-do is said to have been built in 848 by the priest Ennin (794–864), also known as Jikaku-Daishi. The present building dates from 1648.

In the southwest corner of the Rinno Temple compound, behind the abbot's residence, is an especially fine Japanese garden called **Shoyo-en**, created in 1815 and thoughtfully designed to present a different perspective of its rocks, ponds, and flowering plants from every turn on its path. To the right of the entrance to the garden is the **Treasure Hall** (Homotsu-den) of Rinno Temple, a museum with a collection of some 6,000 works of lacquerware, painting, and Buddhist sculpture. The museum is rather small, and only a few of the pieces in the collection— many of them designated National Treasures and Important Cultural Properties—are on display at any given time. ⊠ *2300 Yamauchi, Nikko* ⌨ *Rinno Temple ¥1,000, multiple-entry ticket includes admission to the Taiyu-in Mausoleum and Futara-san Shrine; Shoyo-en and Treasure Hall ¥400* ⊙ *Apr.–Oct., daily 8–5, last entry at 4; Nov.–Mar., daily 8–4, last entry at 3.*

★ **Taiyu-in Mausoleum** 大猷院廟. This grandiose building is the resting place of the third Tokugawa shogun, Iemitsu (1604–51), who imposed a policy of national isolation on Japan that was to last more than 200 years. Iemitsu, one suspects, had it in mind to upstage his illustrious grandfather; he marked the approach to his own tomb with no fewer than six different decorative gates. The first is another Nio-mon—a Gate of the Deva Kings—like the one at Tosho-gu. The dragon painted on the ceiling is by Yasunobu Kano. A flight of stone steps leads from here to the second gate, the Niten-mon, a two-story structure protected front and back by carved and painted images of guardian gods. Beyond it, two more flights of steps lead to the middle courtyard. As you climb the last steps to Iemitsu's shrine, you'll pass a bell tower on the right and a drum tower on the left; directly ahead is the third gate, the remarkable **Yasha-mon**, so named for the figures of *yasha* (she-demons) in the four niches. This structure is also known as the Peony Gate (Botan-mon) for the carvings that decorate it.

SEEKING YOUR FORTUNE?

Make sure you visit **Gohoten-do**, in the northeast corner of Rinno Temple, behind the Sanbutsu-do. Three of the Seven Gods of Good Fortune are enshrined here, which are derived from Chinese folk mythology. These three Buddhist deities are Daikoku-ten and Bishamon-ten, who bring wealth and good harvests, and Benzai-ten, patroness of music and the arts. You might leave Tokyo rich and musical.

As you exit the shrine, on the west side, you come to the fifth gate: the **Koka-mon**, built in the style of the late Ming dynasty of China. The gate is normally closed, but from here another flight of stone steps leads to the sixth and last gate—the cast copper **Inuki-mon**, inscribed with characters in Sanskrit—and Iemitsu's tomb. ⊠ *2300 Sannai, Nikko* ⊠ *¥1,000 multiple-entry ticket includes admission to Rinno Temple and Futara-san Shrine* ⊙ *Apr.–Oct., daily 8–5; Nov.–Mar., daily 8–4.*

Fodor's Choice ★ **Tosho-gu** 東照宮. With its riot of colors and carvings, inlaid pillars, red-lacquer corridors, and extensive use of gold leaf, this 17th-century shrine to Ieyasu Tokugawa is magnificent, astonishing, and never dull.

The west gate of Rinno Temple brings you to Omote-sando, which leads uphill to the stone torii of the shrine. The **Five-Story Pagoda** of Tosho-gu—a reconstruction dating from 1818—is on the left as you approach the shrine. The 12 signs of the zodiac decorate the first story. The black-lacquer doors above each sign bear the three hollyhock leaves of the Tokugawa family crest.

From the torii a flight of stone steps brings you to the front gate of the shrine—the Omote-mon, also called the Nio-mon (Gate of the Deva Kings), with its fearsome pair of red-painted guardian gods. From here the path turns to the left. In the first group of buildings you reach on the left is the **Sacred Stable** (Shinkyu). Housed here is the white horse—symbol of purity—that figures in many of the shrine's ceremonial events. Carvings of pine trees and monkeys adorn the panels over the stable. And where the path turns to the right, you'll find a granite font where visitors can purify themselves before entering the inner precincts of Tosho-gu. The **Sutra Library** (Rinzo), just beyond the font, is a repository for some 7,000 Buddhist scriptures, kept in a huge revolving bookcase nearly 20 feet high; it's not open to the public.

As you pass under the second (bronze) torii and up the steps, you'll see a belfry and a tall bronze candelabrum on the right and a drum tower and a bronze revolving lantern on the left. The two works in bronze were presented to the shrine by the Dutch government in the mid-17th

Tosho-gu honors Ieyasu Tokugawa, the first Shogun and founder of Tokyo.

century. Behind the drum tower is the **Yakushi-do,** which enshrines a manifestation of the Buddha as Yakushi Nyorai, the healer of illnesses. The original 17th-century building was famous for a huge India-ink painting on the ceiling of the nave, *The Roaring Dragon,* so named for the rumbling echoes it seemed to emit when visitors clapped their hands beneath it. The painting was by Yasunobu Enshin Kano (1613–85), from a family of artists that dominated the profession for 400 years. The Kano school was founded in the late 15th century and patronized by successive military governments until the fall of the Tokugawa Shogunate in 1868. The Yakushi-do was destroyed by fire in 1961, then rebuilt; the dragon on the ceiling now is by Nampu Katayama (1887–1980).

The centerpiece of Tosho-gu is the **Gate of Sunlight** (Yomei-mon), at the top of the second flight of stone steps. A designated National Treasure, it's also called the Twilight Gate (Higurashi-mon)—implying that you could gape at its richness of detail all day, until sunset. And rich it is indeed: 36 feet high and dazzling white, the gate has 12 columns, beams, and roof brackets carved with dragons, lions, clouds, peonies, Chinese sages, and demigods, painted vivid hues of red, blue, green, and gold. On one of the central columns, there are two carved tigers; the natural grain of the wood is used to bring out the "fur." As you enter the Yomei-mon, there are galleries running east and west for some 700 feet; their paneled fences are also carved and painted with nature motifs.

The portable shrines that appear in the Tosho-gu Festival, held yearly on May 17–18, are kept in the **Shinyo-sha,** a storeroom to the left as you come through the Twilight Gate into the heart of the shrine. The paintings on the ceiling, of *tennin* (Buddhist angels) playing harps, are by Tan-yu Kano (1602–74).

Mere mortals may not pass through the **Chinese Gate** (Kara-mon), which is the "official" entrance to the Tosho-gu inner shrine. Like its counterpart, the Yomei-mon, on the opposite side of the courtyard, the Kara-mon is a National Treasure— and, like the Yomei-mon, is carved and painted in elaborate detail with dragons and other auspicious figures. The Main Hall of Tosho-gu is enclosed by a wall of painted and carved panel screens; opposite the right-hand corner of the wall, facing the shrine, is the **Kito-den,** a hall where annual prayers were

once offered for the peace of the nation. For a very modest fee, Japanese couples can be married here in a traditional Shinto ceremony, with an ensemble of drums and reed flutes and shrine maidens to attend them.

The **Main Hall** (Hon-den) of Tosho-gu is the ultimate purpose of the shrine. You approach it from the rows of lockers at the far end of the enclosure; here you remove and store your shoes, step up into the shrine, and follow a winding corridor to the Oratory (Hai-den)—the anteroom, resplendent in its lacquered pillars, carved friezes, and coffered ceilings bedecked with dragons. Over the lintels are paintings by Mitsuoki Tosa (1617–91) of the 36 great poets of the Heian period, with their poems in the calligraphy of Emperor Go-Mizuno-o. Deeper yet, at the back of the Oratory, is the Inner Chamber (Nai-jin)—repository of the Sacred Mirror that represents the spirit of the deity enshrined here. To the right is a room that was reserved for members of the three principal branches of the Tokugawa family; the room on the left was for the chief abbot of Rinno Temple, who was always chosen from the imperial line.

Behind the Inner Chamber is the Innermost Chamber (Nai-Nai-jin). No visitors come this far. Here, in the very heart of Tosho-gu, is the gold-lacquer shrine where the spirit of Ieyasu resides—along with two other deities, whom the Tokugawas later decided were fit companions. One was Hideyoshi Toyotomi, Ieyasu's mentor and liege lord in the long wars of unification at the end of the 16th century. The other was Minamoto no Yoritomo, brilliant military tactician and founder of the earlier (12th-century) Kamakura Shogunate (Ieyasu claimed Yoritomo for an ancestor).

■TIP➔ Don't forget to recover your shoes when you return to the courtyard.

Between the Goma-do and the **Kagura-den** (a hall where ceremonial dances are performed to honor the gods) is a passage to the **Gate at the Foot of the Hill** (Sakashita-mon). Above the gateway is another famous symbol of Tosho-gu, the Sleeping Cat—a small panel said to have been carved by Hidari Jingoro (Jingoro the Left-handed), a late-16th-century master carpenter and sculptor credited with important contributions to numerous Tokugawa-period temples, shrines, and palaces. A separate admission charge (¥520) is levied to go beyond the Sleeping Cat, up the flight of 200 stone steps through a forest of cryptomeria to **Ieyasu's tomb.** The climb is worth it for the view of the Yomei-mon and Kara-mon from above; the tomb itself is unimpressive. ⊠ *Sannai, Nikko* ⌑ *Free, Ieyasu's tomb ¥520* ☺ *Apr.–Oct., daily 9–5; Nov.–Mar., daily 9–4.*

THREE LITTLE MONKEYS

While in the Sacred Stable, make sure to look at the second panel from the left. The three monkeys, commonly known as "Hear no evil, Speak no evil, See no evil," have become something of a Nikko trademark; the image has been reproduced on plaques, bags, and souvenirs. While the phrase's true origins are uncertain, scholars and legend suggest it originated from this shrine as a visual interpretation of the religious phrase, "If we do not hear, see, or speak evil, we ourselves shall be spared all evil." As for the monkeys, it's been said that a Chinese Buddhist monk introduced the image to Japan in the 8th century.

OFF THE BEATEN PATH

Located on the northern shore of peaceful Yunoko (Lake Yuno), these isolated hot springs were once a popular destination for 14th-century aristocrats. Today, the area is still known for its hot springs—being able to soak in an *onsen* (hot springs) all year long, even when temperatures drop below zero, will always be a major plus—but they are now controlled by separate resorts. Besides the healing and relaxing effects of the baths, visitors come for the hiking trails, fishing, camping, skiing, bird-watching, and mountain-climbing opportunities. ■ **TIP→** Try to avoid the fall season, as it's peak visitor time and there are always delays. You can get to the Yumoto onsen by taking the Tobu Operated Buses, which leave Tobu Nikko and JR Nikko stations. There are one or two services an hour depending on the time of the day. A one-way trip from central Nikko takes about 80 minutes and costs ¥1,650.

WORTH NOTING

☺ **Edo Wonderland** 日光江戸村 *(Nikko Edo Mura),* a living-history theme park a short taxi ride from downtown, re-creates an 18th-century Japanese village. The complex includes sculpted gardens with waterfalls and ponds and 22 vintage buildings, where actors in traditional dress stage martial arts exhibitions, historical theatrical performances, and comedy acts. You can even observe Japanese tea ceremony rituals in gorgeous tatami-floor houses, as well as people dressed as geisha and samurai. Strolling stuffed animal characters and acrobatic ninjas keep kids happy. Nikko Edo Mura has one large restaurant and 15 small food stalls serving period cuisine like *yakisoba* (fried soba) and *dango* (dumplings). ⊠ *470–20 Karakura, Nikko* ☎ *0288/77–1777* ⌑ *¥4,500 unlimited day pass includes rides and shows* ☺ *Mid-Mar.–Nov., daily 9–5; Dec.–mid-Mar., daily 9:30–4.*

Jigen-do 慈眼堂. Tenkai (1536–1643), the first abbot of Rinno Temple, has his own place of honor at Tosho-gu: the Jigen-do. The hall, which was founded in 848, now holds many of Rinno Temple's artistic

The three monkeys, who "see no evil, speak no evil, hear no evil," perch on the paneling of Tosho-gu's Sacred Stable.

treasures. To reach it, take the path opposite the south entrance to Futara-san Shrine that passes between the two subtemples called Jogyo-do and Hokke-do. Connected by a corridor, these two buildings are otherwise known as the Futatsu-do (Twin Halls) of Rinno Temple and are designated a National Cultural Property. The path between the Twin Halls leads roughly south and west to the Jigen-do compound; the hall itself is at the north end of the compound, to the right. At the west end sits the Go-oden, a shrine to Prince Yoshihisa Kitashirakawa (1847–95), the last of the imperial princes to serve as abbot. Behind it are his tomb and the tombs of his 13 predecessors. ⊠ *2300 Sannai, Nikko* ☏ *Free* ☉ *Apr.–Nov., daily 8–5; Dec.–Mar., daily 9–4.*

Monument to Masasuna Matsudaira 松平正綱の杉並木寄進碑. Opposite the Sacred Bridge, at the east entrance to the grounds of Tosho-gu, this monument pays tribute to one of the two feudal lords charged with the construction of Tosho-gu. Matsudaira's great contribution was the planting of the wonderful cryptomeria trees (Japanese cedars) surrounding the shrine and along all the approaches to it. The project took 20 years, from 1628 to 1648, and the result was some 36 km (22 mi) of cedar-lined avenues—planted with more than 15,000 trees in all. Fire and time have taken their toll, but thousands of these trees still stand in the shrine precincts, creating a setting of solemn majesty the buildings alone could never have achieved. Thousands more line Route 119 east of Nikko on the way to Shimo-Imaichi. ⊠ *Moritomo, Nikko.*

Sacred Bridge 神橋 *(Shinkyo).* Built in 1636 for shoguns and imperial messengers visiting the shrine, the original bridge was destroyed in a flood; the present red-lacquer wooden structure dates to 1907. Buses leaving from either railway station at Nikko go straight up the main street to the bridge, opposite the first of the main entrances to Tosho-gu. Open again after a year of renovation, the bridge is free to cross, but closes at 4 or 5 pm, depending on the season. The Sacred Bridge is just to the left of a modern bridge, where the road curves and crosses the Daiya-gawa (Daiya River). ⊠ *2307 Sannai, Nikko* ⌨ *¥500* ⊙ *Apr.–Oct., daily 9–5; Nov.–Mar., daily 9–4.*

Treasury House 宝物館 *(Homotsu-kan).* An unhurried visit to the precincts of Tosho-gu should definitely include the Treasury house as it contains a collection of antiquities from its various shrines and temples. From the west gate of Rinno Temple, turn left off Omote-sando, just below the pagoda, onto the cedar-lined avenue to Futara-san Jinja. A minute's walk will bring you to the museum, on the left. ⊠ *2280 Sannai, Nikko* ☎ *0288/54–2558* ⌨ *¥500* ⊙ *Apr.–Oct., daily 9–5; Nov.–Mar., daily 9–4.*

CHUZENJI-KO 中禅寺湖

More than 3,900 feet above sea level, at the base of the volcano known as Nantai-san, is Chuzenji-ko (Lake Chuzenji), renowned for its clean waters and fresh air. People come to boat and fish on the lake and to enjoy the surrounding scenic woodlands, waterfalls, and hills.

TOP ATTRACTIONS

Fodor's Choice
★

Kegon Falls 華厳滝 *(Kegon-no-taki).* More than anything else, the country's most famous falls are what draw the crowds of Japanese visitors to Chuzenji. Fed by the eastward flow of the lake, the falls drop 318 feet into a rugged gorge; an elevator (¥530) takes you to an observation platform at the bottom. The volume of water over the falls is carefully regulated, but it's especially impressive after a summer rain or a typhoon. In winter the falls do not freeze completely but form a beautiful cascade of icicles. The elevator is just a few minutes' walk east from the bus stop at Chuzenji village, downhill and off to the right at the far end of the parking lot. ⊠ *2479–2 Chugushi, Nikko* ☎ *0288/55–0030* ⊙ *Daily 8–5.*

NEED A BREAK?

Take a breather at the **Ryuzu-no-taki Chaya** (⊠ *2485 Chugushi, Nikko* ☎ *0288/55–0157* ⊙ *Daily 11–5*), a charming, but rustic, tea shop near the waterfalls. Enjoy a cup of green tea, a light meal, or Japanese sweets like rice cakes boiled with vegetables and dango (sweet dumplings) while you gaze at the falling waters.

Urami Falls 裏見滝 *(Urami-no-taki).* "The water," wrote the great 17th-century poet Basho, "seemed to take a flying leap and drop a hundred feet from the top of a cave into a green pool surrounded by a thousand rocks. One was supposed to inch one's way into the cave and enjoy the falls from behind." ■TIP→ The falls and the gorge are striking—but you should make the climb only if you have good hiking shoes and are willing to get wet in the process. ⊠ *The steep climb to the cave begins at the Arasawa bus stop, with a turn to the right off the Chuzenji road.*

Tobu Kogyo Boating. Explore Lake Chuzenji on chartered 60-minute boat rides. ⊠ *2478 Chugushi, Nikko, Tochigi-ken* ☎ *0288/55–0360* ⌨ *¥150– ¥1,500 depending on route chosen* ⊙ *Dec.–Mar., daily 9:30–3:30.*

DID YOU KNOW?

The 97-meter-high Kegon Falls draws visitors from all over Japan and the world. The spectacular sight near Lake Chuzenji Lake is also home to 12 other waterfalls. Behind and next to Kegon, these falls drip out of cracks in the volcano, Nantai-san. Try to spot a few of them once you've taken in Kegon's grandeur.

WORTH NOTING

Chugu-shi 中宮祠. A subshrine of the Futara-san Shrine at Tosho-gu, this is the major religious center on the north side of Lake Chuzenji, about 1½ km (1 mi) west of the village. The **Treasure House** (Homotsu-den) contains an interesting historical collection, including swords, lacquerware, and medieval shrine palanquins. ✉ *Shrine free, Treasure House ¥300* ⊙ *Apr.–Oct., daily 8–5; Nov.–Mar., daily 9–4.*

Chuzen-ji 中禅寺 *(Chuzen Temple)*. A subtemple of Rinno Temple, at Tosho-gu, the principal object of worship here is the **Tachi-ki Kannon**, a 17-foot-tall standing statue of the Buddhist goddess of mercy, said to have been carved more than 1,000 years ago by the priest Shodo from the living trunk of a single Judas tree. The bus trip from Nikko to the national park area ends at Chuzenji village, which shares its name with the temple established here in 784. ✉ *Turn left (south) as you leave the village of Chuzenji and walk about 1½ km (1 mi) along the eastern shore of the lake* ✉ *¥500* ⊙ *Apr.–Oct., daily 8–5; Mar. and Nov., daily 8–4; Dec.–Feb., daily 8–3:30.*

Dragon's Head Falls 竜頭滝 *(Ryuzu-no-taki)*. If you've budgeted an extra day for Nikko, you might want to consider a walk around the lake. A paved road along the north shore extends for about 8 km (5 mi), one-third of the whole distance, as far as the "beach" at Shobu-ga-hama. Here, where the road branches off to the north for Senjogahara, are the lovely cascades of Dragon's Head Falls. To the left is a steep footpath that continues around the lake to Senju-ga-hama and then to a campsite at Asegata. The path is well marked but can get rough in places. From Asegata it's less than an hour's walk back to Chuzenji village.

Jakko Falls 寂光滝 *(Jakko-no-taki)*. Falling water is one of the special charms of the Nikko National Park area; people going by bus or car from Tosho-gu to Lake Chuzenji often stop off en route to see these falls, which descend in a series of seven terraced stages, forming a sheet of water about 100 feet high. About 1 km (½ mi) from the shrine precincts, at the Tamozawa bus stop, a narrow road to the right leads to an uphill walk of some 3 km (2 mi) to the falls.

Umagaeshi 馬返し. In the old days, the road became too rough for horse riding, so riders had to alight and proceed on foot; the lake is 4,165 feet above sea level. From Umagaeshi the bus climbs a one-way toll road up the pass; the old road has been widened and is used for the traffic coming down. The two roads are full of steep hairpin turns, and on a clear day the view up and down the valley is magnificent—especially from the halfway point at **Akechi-daira** (Akechi Plain), from which you can see the summit of **Nantai-san** (Mt. Nantai), reaching 8,149 feet. Hiking season lasts from May through mid-October; if you push it, you can make the ascent in about four hours. ⚠ Wild monkeys make their homes in these mountains, and they've learned the convenience of mooching from visitors along the route. Be careful—they have a way of not taking no for an answer. Do not give in to the temptation to give them food—they will never leave you alone if you do. ✉ *About 10 km (6 mi) from Tobu Station in Nikko, or 8 km (5 mi) from Tosho-gu.*

WHERE TO EAT

LAKE CHUZENJI

$$$ ✕ **Nantai** なんたい. The low tables,
JAPANESE antiques, and pillows scattered
on tatami flooring make visitors
feel like they're dining in a tradi-
tional Japanese living room. Try the
Nikko specialty, *yuba* (tofu skin),
which comes with the *nabe* (hot
pot) for dinner. It's the quintessen-
tial winter family meal. The sea-
food here is fresh and both the trout
and salmon are recommended.
Each meal comes with rice, pick-
les, and selected side dishes like soy-
stewed vegetables, tempura, udon,
and a dessert. ✉ *2478–8 Chugushi,
Nikko* ☎ *0288/55–0201.*

**FEELING
ADVENTUROUS?**

If you want to avoid the hairpin
turns, try the **ropeway** that runs
from Akechi-daira Station directly
to the Akechi-daira lookout. It
takes three minutes and the
panoramic views of Nikko and
Kegon Falls are priceless. ✉ *709–5
Misawa, Hosoo-machi, Nikko*
☎ *0288/55–0331* 🎫 *¥390* 🕐 *Apr.–
Oct., daily 8:30–4; Nov.–Mar., daily
9–3.*

4

DOWNTOWN NIKKO

$$$$ ✕ **Fujimoto** ふじもと. At what may be Nikko's most formal Western-style
FRENCH restaurant, finer touches include plush carpets, art deco fixtures, stained
and frosted glass, a thoughtful wine list, and a maître d' in black tie.
The menu combines elements of French and Japanese cooking styles
and ingredients; the fillet of beef in mustard sauce is particularly excel-
lent. Fujimoto closes at 7:30, so plan on eating early. ✉ *2339–1 Sannai,
Nikko* ☎ *0288/53–3754* 🕐 *Closed Thurs.*

$$$$ ✕ **Gyoshintei** 堯心亭. This is the only restaurant in Nikko devoted to
JAPANESE *shojin ryori*, the Buddhist-temple vegetarian fare that evolved centuries
ago into haute cuisine. Gyoshintei is decorated in the style of a *ryotei*
(traditional inn), with all-tatami seating. It differs from a ryotei in that it
has one large, open space where many guests are served at once, rather
than a number of rooms for private dining. Dinner is served until 7.
✉ *2339–1 Sannai, Nikko* ☎ *0288/53–3751* 🕐 *Closed Thurs.*

$$$$ ✕ **Masudaya** ゆば亭ますだや. Masudaya started out as a sake maker
KAISEKI more than a century ago, but for four generations now, it has been the
town's best-known restaurant. The specialty is yuba, which the chefs
transform, with the help of local vegetables and fresh fish, into sump-
tuous high cuisine. The building is traditional, with a lovely interior
garden; the assembly-line-style service, however, detracts from the ambi-
ence. Masudaya serves a nine-course *kaiseki*-style meal at table seating
for ¥3,990, and an 11-course meal at tatami seating for ¥5,450. Meals
here are prix fixe. ✉ *439–2 Ishiya-machi, Nikko* ☎ *0288/54–2151*
🍽 *Reservations essential* ▭ *No credit cards* 🕐 *Closed Thurs. No dinner.*

$$$$ ✕ **Meiji-no-Yakata** 明治の館. Not far from the east entrance to Rinno
CONTINENTAL Temple, Meiji-no-Yakata is an elegant 19th-century Western-style stone
house, originally built as a summer retreat for an American diplomat.
The food, too, is Western style; specialties of the house include fresh
rainbow trout from Lake Chuzenji, roast lamb with pepper sauce, and
melt-in-your-mouth filet mignon made from local Tochigi beef. High

ceilings, hardwood floors, and an air of informality make this a very pleasant place to dine. The restaurant opens at 11 am in summer and 11:30 am in winter; it always closes at 7:30. ✉ *2339–1 Sannai, Nikko* ☎ *0288/53–3751* ⏱ *Closed Wed.*

$$$
JAPANESE ✕ **Sawamoto** 澤本. Charcoal-broiled *unagi* (eel) is an acquired taste, and there's no better place in Nikko to acquire it than at this restaurant. The place is small and unpretentious, with only five plain-wood tables, and service can be lukewarm, but Sawamoto is reliable for a light lunch or dinner of unagi on a bed of rice, served in an elegant lacquered box. Eel is considered a stamina builder: just right for the weary visitor on a hot summer day. ✉ *1019 Bandu, Kami Hatsuishi-machi, Nikko* ☎ *0288/54–0163* ▭ *No credit cards* ⏱ *No dinner.*

WHERE TO STAY

Hotel reviews have been abbreviated in this book. For expanded reviews, please go to Fodors.com.

LAKE CHUZENJI

$$$$
HOTEL 🛏 **Chuzenji Kanaya** 中禅寺金谷ホテル. A boathouse and restaurant on the lake give this branch of the Nikko Kanaya on the road from the village to Shobu-ga-hama the air of a private yacht club. **Pros:** clean; Western-style rooms. **Cons:** the most expensive hotel in the area. ✉ *2482 Chu-gushi, Chuzen-ji, Nikko* ☎ *0288/51–0001* ⊕ *www.kanayahotel. co.jp/english/chuzenji/index.html* 🛏 *60 rooms, 54 with bath* ⚐ *In-hotel: restaurant* ⏱◎ *Some meals.*

$$–$$$
HOTEL 🛏 **Nikko Lakeside Hotel** 日光レイクサイドホテル. In the village of Chuzenji at the foot of the lake, the Nikko Lakeside has no particular character, but the views are good and the transportation connections (to buses and excursion boats) are ideal. **Pros:** close to the lake and hot spring baths. **Cons:** room decor is a bit dated. ✉ *2482 Chu-gushi, Chuzen-ji, Nikko* ☎ *0288/55–0321* 🛏 *100 rooms with bath* ⚐ *In-hotel: 2 restaurants, bar, tennis court, bicycles* ⏱◎ *Some meals.*

DOWNTOWN NIKKO

$$$–$$$$
HOTEL 🛏 **Nikko Kanaya Hotel** 日光金谷ホテル. This family-run operation is a
★ little worn around the edges after a century of operation, but it still has the best location in town: across the street from Tosho-gu. **Pros:** spacious; well-appointed. **Cons:** rooms are rather pricey. ✉ *1300 Kami Hatsuishi-machi, Nikko* ☎ *0288/54–0001* ⊕ *www.kanayahotel.co.jp/ english/nikko/index.html* 🛏 *77 rooms, 62 with bath* ⚐ *In-hotel: 2 restaurants, bar, pool* ⏱◎ *Some meals.*

¢
HOTEL 🛏 **Turtle Inn Nikko** タートルイン日光. This Japanese Inn Group member provides friendly, modest, cost-conscious Western- and Japanese-style accommodations with or without a private bath. **Pros:** cozy atmosphere; English-speaking staff, Japanese bath available. **Cons:** rooms are a bit on the small side. ✉ *2–16 Takumi-cho, Nikko* ☎ *0288/53–3168* 🛏 *7 Western-style rooms, 3 with bath; 5 Japanese-style rooms without*

KUSATSU ONSEN

For an authentic Japanese experience and a bit of relaxation, head to the onsen of Kusatsu. Half a dozen hot springs dot the area. If you are traveling to Kusatsu from Nikko, you will need to backtrack to JR Omiya Station, where you can take the Kusatsu #3 Express to Naganohara-Kusatsuguchi Station (2 hours, ¥3,820). If you are coming from Tokyo, take the JR Kusatsu Limited Express from Ueno Station to Naganohara-Kusatsuguchi Station (2 hours, ¥4,620). From Naganohara-Kusatsuguchi Station take the JR bus to Kusatsu Onsen Bus Terminal (30 min, ¥1,000).

Kusatsu Onsen Center
草津温泉館. This onsen, surrounded by a wooded area, offers six different types of indoor and outdoor baths, including one in a cave, as well as steam baths. ⊠ 464–35 Kusatasu, Kusatsu-cho, Azuma-gun ☎ 02/7988-2500 ☜ ¥800 ⊗ Daily 10:30–7.

★ **Otaki no Yu**大滝乃湯. Otaki no Yu is one of the biggest and most popular of the Kusatsu onsen. A wase-yu, one of the indoor bathing options, is comprised of three separate tubs of gradually increasing temperature, allowing your body to acclimate to the hottest temperature. Outside there is an enormous wooden bath that accommodates 1,000 (swim-suited) bathers. ⊠ 596–13 Kusatasu, Kusatsu-machi, Azumagu ☎ 02/7988-2600 ⊕ www.kusatsu-onsen.ne.jp ☜ ¥800 ⊗ Daily 9–9.

Sai No Kawara Outdoor Bath
西の河原露天風呂. Sai No Kawara has giant outdoor baths, separated for men and women. The water creates a current—walk against the waves for a natural massage. The water temperature also varies from place to place, so if the water is too hot or cool for you, simply rove to another area. ⊠ 521–3 Kusatasu, Kusatsu-cho, Azuma-gun ☎ 02/7988-6167 ☜ ¥500 ⊗ Apr.–Nov., daily 7 am–8 pm; Dec.–Mar., daily 9–8.

bath ⊕ www.turtle-nikko.com ⚿ In-room: Internet. In-hotel: restaurant ⦿ Some meals.

KAMAKURA 鎌倉

Kamakura, about 40 km (25 mi) southwest of Tokyo, is an object lesson in what happens when you set the fox to guard the henhouse.

For the aristocrats of the Heian-era Japan (794–1185), life was defined by the imperial court in Kyoto. Who in their right mind would venture elsewhere? In Kyoto there was grace and beauty and poignant affairs of the heart; everything beyond was howling wilderness. Unfortunately, it was the howling wilderness that had all the estates: the large grants of land, called *shoen*, without which there would be no income to pay for all that grace and beauty.

By the 12th century two clans—the Taira (*ta-ee-ra*) and the Minamoto, themselves both offshoots of the imperial line—had come to dominate the affairs of the Heian court and were at each other's throats in a struggle for supremacy. In 1160 the Taira won a major battle that should have secured their absolute control over Japan, but in the process they made one serious mistake: having killed the Minamoto leader Yoshitomo (1123–60), they spared his 13-year-old son, Yoritomo (1147–99), and sent him into exile. In 1180 he launched a rebellion and chose Kamakura—a superb natural fortress, surrounded on three sides by hills and guarded on the fourth by the sea—as his base of operations.

The rivalry between the two clans became an all-out war. By 1185 Yoritomo and his half brother, Yoshitsune (1159–89), had destroyed the Taira utterly, and the Minamoto were masters of all Japan. In 1192 Yoritomo forced the imperial court to name him shogun; he was now de facto and de jure the military head of state. The emperor was left as a figurehead in Kyoto, and the little fishing village of Kamakura became—and for 141 years remained—the seat of Japan's first shogunal government.

The Minamoto line came to an end when Yoritomo's two sons were assassinated. Power passed to the Hojo family, who remained in control, often as regents for figurehead shoguns, for the next 100 years. In 1274 and again in 1281 Japan was invaded by the Mongol armies of China's Yuan dynasty. On both occasions typhoons—the original kamikaze (literally, "divine wind")—destroyed the Mongol fleets, but the Hojo family was still obliged to reward the various clans that had rallied to the defense of the realm. A number of these clans were unhappy with their portions—and with Hojo rule in general. The end came suddenly, in 1333, when two vassals assigned to put down a revolt switched sides. The Hojo regent committed suicide, and the center of power returned to Kyoto.

Kamakura reverted to being a sleepy backwater town on the edge of the sea, but after World War II, it began to develop as a residential area for the well-to-do. Nothing secular survives from the days of the Minamoto and Hojo; there wasn't much there to begin with. The warriors of Kamakura had little use for courtiers, or their palaces and gardened villas; the shogunate's name for itself, in fact, was the Bakufu—literally, the "tent government." As a religious center, however, the town presents an extraordinary legacy. Most of those temples and shrines are in settings of remarkable beauty; many are designated National Treasures. If you can afford the time for only one day trip from Tokyo, you should probably spend it here.

GETTING HERE AND AROUND

A bus from Kamakura Station (Sign 5) travels to most of the temples and shrines in the downtown Kamakura area, with stops at most access roads to the temples and shrines. However, you may want to walk out as far as Hokoku-ji and take the bus back; it's easier to recognize the end of the line than any of the stops in between. You can also go by taxi to Hokoku-ji—any cab driver knows the way—and walk the last leg in reverse.

Bus companies in Kamakura don't conduct guided English tours. However, if your time is limited or you don't want to do a lot of walking, the Japanese tours hit the major attractions. These tours depart from

Kamakura Station eight times daily, starting at 9 am; the last tour leaves at 1 pm. Purchase tickets at the bus office to the right of the station.

On weekends the Kanagawa Student Guide Federation offers a free guide service. Students show you the city in exchange for the chance to practice their English. Arrangements must be made in advance through the Japan National Tourist Organization in Tokyo. You'll need to be at Kamakura Station between 10 am and noon.

Sunrise Tours runs daily English-language trips from Tokyo to Kamakura; these tours are often combined with trips to Hakone. You can book through, and arrange to be picked up at, any of the major hotels. Check to make sure that the tour covers everything you want to see, as many include little more than a passing view of the Great Buddha in Hase. Given how easy it is to get around—most sights are within walking distance of each other, and others are short bus or train rides apart—you're better off seeing Kamakura on your own.

Traveling by train is by far the best way to get to Kamakura. Trains run from Tokyo Station (and Shimbashi Station) every 10 to 15 minutes during the day. The trip takes 56 minutes to Kita-Kamakura and one hour to Kamakura. Take the JR Yokosuka Line from Track 1 downstairs in Tokyo Station (Track 1 upstairs is on a different line and does not go to Kamakura). The cost is ¥780 to Kita-Kamakura, ¥890 to Kamakura (or use your JR [Japan Railways] Pass). It's now also possible to take a train from Shinjuku, Shibuya, or Ebisu to Kamakura on the Shonan-Shinjuku Line, but these trains depart less frequently than those departing from Tokyo Station. Local train service connects Kita-Kamakura, Kamakura, Hase, and Enoshima.

To return to Tokyo from Enoshima, take a train to Shinjuku on the Odakyu Line. There are 11 express trains daily from here on weekdays, between 8:38 am and 8:45 pm; 9 trains daily on weekends and national holidays, between 8:39 am and 8:46 pm; and even more in summer. The express takes about 70 minutes and costs ¥1,220. Or you can retrace your steps to Kamakura and take the JR Yokosuka Line to Tokyo Station.

VISITOR INFORMATION

Both Kamakura and Enoshima have their own tourist associations, although it can be problematic getting help in English over the phone. Your best bet is the Kamakura Station Tourist Information Center, which has a useful collection of brochures and maps. And since Kamakura is in Kanagawa Prefecture, visitors heading here from Yokohama can preplan their excursion at the Kanagawa Prefectural Tourist Association office in the Silk Center, on the Yamashita Park promenade.

ESSENTIALS

Tour Contacts Japan National Tourist Organization (✉ *Tokyo* ☎ *03/3201–3331* ⊕ *www.jnto.go.jp*). **Kanagawa Student Guide Federation** (☎ *03/3201–3331*). **Sunrise Tours** (☎ *03/5796–5454* ⊕ *www.jtbgmt.com/sunrisetour/index.aspx*).

Tourist Information Enoshima Tourist Association (☎ *0466/37–4141*). **Kamakura Station Tourist Information Center** (☎ *0467/22–3350*). **Kamakura**

Tourist Association (☎ 0467/23–3050). **Kanagawa Prefectural Tourist Association** (☎ 045/681–0007 ⊕ www.kanagawa-kankou.or.jp).

Train Contact Japan Railways (☎ 03/3423–0111 ⊕ www.japanrail.com).

EXPLORING

There are three principal areas in Kamakura, and you can easily get from one to another by train. From Tokyo head first to Kita-Kamakura for most of the important Zen temples, including Engaku-ji (Engaku Temple) and Kencho-ji (Kencho Temple). The second area is downtown Kamakura, with its shops and museums and the venerated shrine Tsuru-ga-oka Hachiman-gu. The third is Hase, a 10-minute train ride southwest from Kamakura on the Enoden Line. Hase's main attractions are the great bronze figure of the Amida Buddha, at Kotoku-in, and the Kannon Hall of Hase-dera. There's a lot to see in Kamakura, and even to hit just the highlights will take you most of a busy day.

KITA-KAMAKURA 北鎌倉

Hierarchies were important to the Kamakura Shogunate. In the 14th century it established a ranking system called Go-zan (literally, "Five Mountains") for the Zen Buddhist monasteries under its official sponsorship.

TOP ATTRACTIONS

★ **Engaku-ji** 円覚寺 *(Engaku Temple)*. The largest of the Zen monasteries in Kamakura, Engaku-ji was founded in 1282 and ranks second in the Five Mountains hierarchy. Here, prayers were to be offered regularly for the prosperity and well-being of the government; Engaku Temple's special role was to pray for the souls of those who died resisting the Mongol invasions in 1274 and 1281. The temple complex currently holds 18, but once contained as many as 50, buildings. Often damaged in fires and earthquakes, it has been completely restored.

Among the National Treasures at Engaku Temple is the **Hall of the Holy Relic of Buddha** (Shari-den), with its remarkable Chinese-inspired thatched roof. Built in 1282, it was destroyed by fire in 1558 but rebuilt in its original form soon after, in 1563. The hall is said to enshrine a tooth of the Gautama Buddha himself, but it's not on display. In fact, except for the first three days of the New Year, you won't be able to go any farther into the hall than the main gate. Such is the case, alas, with much of the Engaku Temple complex: this is still a functioning monastic center, and many of its most impressive buildings are not open to the public. The accessible National Treasure at Engaku Temple is the **Great Bell** (Kosho), on the hilltop on the southeast side of the complex. The bell—Kamakura's most famous—was cast in 1301 and stands 8 feet tall. It's rung only on special occasions, such as New

> **TIMING TIP**
>
> If your time is limited, you may want to visit only Engaku Temple and Tokei Temple in Kita-Kamakura before riding the train one stop to Kamakura. If not, follow the main road all the way to Tsuru-ga-oka Hachiman-gu and visit four additional temples en route.

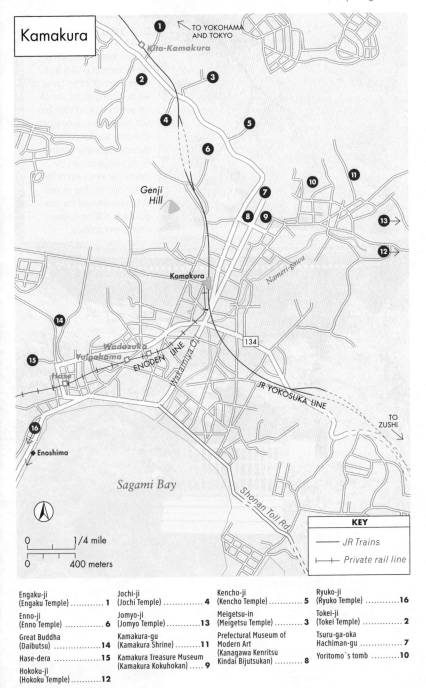

Kamakura

TO YOKOHAMA
AND TOKYO

Kita-Kamakura

Genji
Hill

Kamakura

Nameri-gawa

134

ENODEN LINE

Wadosuka

Yuigahama

Hase

Wakamiya Oji

JR YOKOSUKA LINE

TO
ZUSHI

Enoshima

Sagami Bay

Shonan Toll Rd.

0   1/4 mile

0   400 meters

KEY

— *JR Trains*

|—|—|—|— *Private rail line*

Engaku-ji (Engaku Temple) **1**	Jochi-ji (Jochi Temple) **4**	Kencho-ji (Kencho Temple) **5**	Ryuko-ji (Ryuko Temple) **16**
Enno-ji (Enno Temple) **6**	Jomyo-ji (Jomyo Temple) **13**	Meigetsu-in (Meigetsu Temple) **3**	Tokei-ji (Tokei Temple) **2**
Great Buddha (Daibutsu) **14**	Kamakura-gu (Kamakura Shrine) **11**	Prefectural Museum of Modern Art (Kanagawa Kenritsu Kindai Bijutsukan) **8**	Tsuru-ga-oka Hachiman-gu **7**
Hase-dera **15**	Kamakura Treasure Museum (Kamakura Kokuhokan) **9**		Yoritomo`s tomb **10**
Hokoku-ji (Hokoku Temple) **12**			

Year's Eve. Reaching the bell requires a trek up a long staircase, but once you've made it to the top you can enjoy tea and traditional Japanese sweets at a small outdoor café. The views of the entire temple grounds and surrounding cedar forest from here are tremendous.

The two buildings open to the public at Engaku Temple are the **Butsunichi-an,** which has a long ceremonial hall where you can enjoy *sado* (Japanese tea ceremony), and the **Obai-in.** The latter is the mausoleum of the last three regents of the Kamakura Shogunate: Tokimune Hojo, who led the defense of Japan against the Mongol invasions; his son Sadatoki; and his grandson Takatoki. Off to the side of the mausoleum is a quiet garden with apricot trees, which bloom in February. As you exit Kita-Kamakura Station, you'll see the stairway to Engaku Temple just in front of you. ⊠ *409 Yama-no-uchi, Kita-Kamakura* 🕾 *0467/22–0478* 🖅 *Engaku Temple ¥300* ⏰ *Nov.–Mar., daily 8–4; Apr.–Oct., daily 8–5.*

★ **Enno-ji** 円応寺 *(Enno Temple).* In the feudal period, Japan acquired from China a belief in Enma, the lord of hell, who, with his court attendants, judged the souls of the departed and determined their destination in the afterlife. Kamakura's otherwise undistinguished Enno-ji (Enno Temple) houses some remarkable statues of these judges—as grim and merciless a court as you're ever likely to confront. To see them is enough to put you on your best behavior, at least for the rest of your excursion. Enno Temple is a minute's walk or so from Kencho Temple, on the opposite (south) side of the main road to Kamakura. ⊠ *A few minutes' walk along the main road to the south will bring you to Tsuru-ga-oka Hachiman-gu in downtown Kamakura. 1543 Yama-no-uchi, Kita-Kamakura* 🕾 *0467/25–1095* 🖅 *¥200* ⏰ *Mar.–Nov., daily 9–4; Dec.–Feb., daily 9–3.*

★ **Kencho-ji** 建長寺 *(Kencho Temple).* Founded in 1250, this temple was the foremost of Kamakura's five great Zen temples, and it lays claim to being the oldest Zen temple in all of Japan. It was modeled on one of the great Chinese monasteries of the time and built for a distinguished Zen master who had just arrived from China. Over the centuries, fires and other disasters have taken their toll on Kencho Temple, and although many buildings have been authentically reconstructed, the temple complex today is half its original size. Near the Main Gate (San-mon) is a bronze bell cast in 1255; it's the temple's most important treasure. The Main Gate and the Lecture Hall (Hatto) are the only two structures to have survived the devastating Great Kanto Earthquake of 1923. Like Engaku Temple, Kencho Temple is a functioning temple of the Rinzai sect, where novices train and laypeople can come to take part in Zen meditation. ⊠ *The entrance to Kencho Temple is about halfway along the main road from Kita-Kamakura Station to Tsuru-ga-oka Hachiman-gu, on the left. 8 Yama-no-uchi, Kita-Kamakura* 🕾 *0467/22–0981* 🖅 *¥300* ⏰ *Daily 8:30–4:30.*

★ **Tokei-ji** 東慶寺 *(Tokei Temple).* A Zen temple of the Rinzai sect, Tokei-ji holds special significance for the study of feminism in medieval Japan. More popularly known as the Enkiri-dera, or Divorce Temple, it was founded in 1285 by the widow of the Hojo regent Tokimune as a refuge for the victims of unhappy marriages. Under the shogunate, a husband of the warrior class could obtain a divorce simply by sending his wife back to her family. Not so for the wife: no matter what cruel and unusual treatment her husband meted out, she was stuck with him. If she ran away, however, and managed to reach Tokei Temple without being caught, she could receive sanctuary at the temple and remain there as a nun. After three years (later reduced to two), she was officially declared divorced. The temple survived as a convent through the Meiji Restoration of 1868. The last abbess died in 1902; her headstone is in the cemetery behind the temple, beneath the plum trees that blossom in February. Tokei Temple was later reestablished as a monastery.

The **Matsugaoka Treasure House** (Matsugaoka Hozo) of Tokei Temple displays several Kamakura-period wooden Buddhas, ink paintings, scrolls, and works of calligraphy, some of which have been designated by the government as Important Cultural Objects. The library, called the Matsugaoka Bunko, was established in memory of the great Zen scholar D. T. Suzuki (1870–1966).

Tokei Temple is on the southwest side of the JR tracks (the side opposite Engaku Temple), less than a five-minute walk south from the station on the main road to Kamakura (Route 21—the Kamakura Kaido), on the right. ⊠ *1367 Yama-no-uchi, Kita-Kamakura* ☎ *0467/22–1663* ⊑ *Tokei Temple ¥100, Matsugaoka Treasure House additional ¥300* ⊘ *Tokei Temple Apr.–Oct., daily 8:30–5; Nov.–Mar., daily 8:30–4. Matsugaoka Treasure House Mon.–Thurs. 9:30–3:30.*

WORTH NOTING

Jochi-ji 浄智寺 *(Jochi Temple).* In the Five Mountains hierarchy, Jochi-ji was ranked fourth. The buildings now in the temple complex are reconstructions; the Great Kanto Earthquake of 1923 destroyed the originals. The garden here is exquisite. Jochi Temple is on the south side of the railway tracks, a few minutes' walk farther southwest of Tokei Temple in the direction of Kamakura. ⊠ *Turn right off the main road (Rte. 21) and cross over a small bridge; a flight of moss-covered steps leads up to the temple. 1402 Yama-no-uchi, Kita-Kamakura* ☎ *0467/22–3943* ⊑ *¥200* ⊘ *Daily 9–4:30.*

Meigetsu-in 明月院 *(Meigetsu Temple).* This temple is also known as Ajisai-dera (the hydrangeas temple), because when the flowers bloom in June, it becomes one of the most popular places in Kamakura. The gardens transform into a sea of color—pink, white, and blue—and visitors can number in the thousands. A typical Kamakura light rain shouldn't deter you; it only showcases this incredible floral display to its best advantage. Meigetsu-in features Kamakura's largest *yagura* (a tomb cavity enclosing a mural) on which 16 images of Buddha are carved. From Tokei Temple walk along Route 21 toward Kamakura for about 20 minutes until you cross the railway tracks; take the immediate left turn onto the narrow side street that doubles back along the tracks. This street bends to the right and follows the course of a little stream called the Meigetsu-gawa to the temple gate. ⊠ *189 Yama-no-uchi, Kita-Kamakura* ☎ *0467/24–3437* ⊑ *¥300* ⊘ *Nov.–May and July–Oct., daily 9–4; June, daily 8:30–5.*

DOWNTOWN KAMAKURA 鎌倉市

Downtown Kamakura is a good place to stop for lunch and shopping. Restaurants and shops selling local crafts, especially the carved and lacquered woodwork called Kamakura-*bori*, abound on Wakamiya Oji and the street parallel to it, Komachi-dori.

When the first Kamakura shogun, Minamoto no Yoritomo, learned he was about to have an heir, he had the tutelary shrine of his family moved to Kamakura from nearby Yui-ga-hama and ordered a stately avenue to be built through the center of his capital from the shrine to the sea. Along this avenue would travel the procession that brought his son— if there were a son—to be presented to the gods. Yoritomo's consort did indeed bear him a son, Yoriie (yo-*ree*-ee-eh), in 1182; Yoriie was brought in great pomp to the shrine and then consecrated to his place in the shogunal succession. Alas, the blessing of the gods did Yoriie little good. He was barely 18 when Yoritomo died, and the regency established by his mother's family, the Hojo, kept him virtually powerless until 1203, when he was banished and eventually assassinated. The Minamoto were never to hold power again, but Yoriie's memory lives on in the street that his father built for him: Wakamiya Oji, "the Avenue of the Young Prince."

TOP ATTRACTIONS

Hokoku-ji 報国寺 *(Hokoku Temple)*. Visitors to Kamakura tend to overlook this lovely little Zen temple of the Rinzai sect that was built in 1334, but it's worth a look. Over the years it had fallen into disrepair and neglect, until an enterprising priest took over, cleaned up the gardens, and began promoting the temple for meditation sessions, calligraphy exhibitions, and tea ceremony. Behind the main hall are a thick grove of bamboo and a small tea pavilion—a restful oasis and a fine place to go for *matcha* (green tea). The temple is about 2 km (1 mi) east on Route 204 from the main entrance to Tsuru-ga-oka Hachiman-gu; turn right at the traffic light by the Hokoku Temple Iriguchi bus stop and walk about three minutes south to the gate. ⊠ 2–7–4 Jomyo-ji ☎ 0467/22–0762 ⊠ ¥200, tea ceremony ¥500 ☽ Daily 9–4.

★ **Tsuru-ga-oka Hachiman-gu** 鶴岡八幡宮 *(Minamoto Shrine)*. This shrine is dedicated to the legendary emperor Ojin, his wife, and his mother, from whom Minamoto no Yoritomo claimed descent. At the entrance, the small, steeply arched, vermilion **Drum Bridge** (Taiko-bashi) crosses a stream between two lotus ponds. The ponds were made to Yoritomo's specifications. His wife, Masako, suggested placing islands in each. In the larger **Genji Pond**, to the right, filled with white lotus flowers, she placed three islands. Genji was another name for clan, and three is an auspicious number. In the smaller **Heike Pond,** to the left, she put four islands. Heike (*heh*-ee-keh) was another name for the rival Taira clan, which the Minamoto had destroyed, and four—homophonous in Japanese with the word for "death"—is very unlucky indeed.

On the far side of the Drum Bridge is the **Mai-den.** This hall is the setting for a story of the Minamoto celebrated in Noh and Kabuki theater. Beyond the Mai-den, a flight of steps leads to the shrine's Main Hall (Hon-do). To the left of these steps is a ginkgo tree that—according to

An Ancient Soap Opera

Once a year, during the Spring Festival (early or mid-April, when the cherry trees are in bloom), the Mai-den hall at Tsuru-ga-oka Hachiman-gu is used to stage a heartrending drama about Minamoto no Yoritomo's brother, Yoshitsune. Although Yoritomo was the tactical genius behind the downfall of the Taira clan and the establishment of the Kamakura Shogunate in the late 12th century, it was his dashing half brother who actually defeated the Taira in battle. In so doing, Yoshitsune won the admiration of many, and Yoritomo came to believe that his sibling had ambitions of his own. Despite Yoshitsune's declaration of allegiance, Yoritomo had him exiled and sent assassins to have him killed. Yoshitsune spent his life fleeing from one place to another until, at the age of 30, he was betrayed in his last refuge and took his own life.

Earlier in his exile, Yoshitsune's lover, the dancer Shizuka Gozen, had been captured and brought to Yoritomo and his wife, Masako. They commanded her to dance for them as a kind of penance. Instead she danced for Yoshitsune. Yoritomo was furious, and only Masako's influence kept him from ordering her death. When he discovered, however, that Shizuka was carrying Yoshitsune's child, he ordered that if the child were a boy, he was to be killed. A boy was born. Some versions of the legend have it that the child was slain; others say he was placed in a cradle, like Moses, and cast adrift in the reeds.

legend—was witness to a murder that ended the Minamoto line in 1219. From behind this tree, a priest named Kugyo leapt out and beheaded his uncle, the 26-year-old Sanetomo, Yoritomo's second son and the last Minamoto shogun. The priest was quickly apprehended, but Sanetomo's head was never found. Like all other Shinto shrines, the Main Hall is unadorned; the building itself, an 1828 reconstruction, is not particularly noteworthy. ✉ *To reach Tsuru-ga-oka Hachiman-gu from the east side of Kamakura Station, cross the plaza, turn left, and walk north along Wakamiya Oji. Straight ahead is the first of three arches leading to the shrine, and the shrine itself is at the far end of the street.* 2–1–31 Yuki-no-shita ☎0467/22–0315 ✉Free ⊙ Daily 9–4.

Yoritomo's tomb 頼朝の墓. The man who put Kamakura on the map, so to speak, chose not to leave it when he died: it's only a short walk from Tsuru-ga-oka Hachiman-gu to the tomb of the man responsible for its construction, Minamoto no Yoritomo. If you've already been to Nikko and have seen how a later dynasty of shoguns sought to glorify its own memories, you may be surprised at the simplicity of Yoritomo's tomb. To get here, cross the Drum Bridge at Tsuru-ga-oka Hachiman-gu and turn left. Leave the grounds of the shrine and walk east along the main street (Route 204) that forms the T-intersection at the end of Wakamiya Oji. A 10-minute walk will bring you to a narrow street on the left—there's a bakery called Bergfeld (⇨ *see review below*) on the corner that leads to the tomb, about 100 yards off the street to the north and up a flight of stone steps. Yoritomo's tomb is located behind Tsuru-ga-oka Hachiman-gu Yoritomo's tomb. ✉Free ⊙ Daily 9–4.

WORTH NOTING

Jomyo-ji 浄明寺 *(Jomyo Temple)*. Founded in 1188, this one of the Five Mountains Zen monasteries. Though it lacks the grandeur and scale of the Engaku and Kencho, it still merits the status of an Important Cultural Property. This modest single-story monastery belonging to the Rinzai sect is nestled inside an immaculate garden that is particularly beautiful in spring, when the cherry trees bloom. Its only distinctive features are its green roof and the statues of Shaka Nyorai and Amida Nyorai, who represent truth and enlightenment, in the main hall. To reach it from Hokoku-ji, cross the main street (Route 204) that brought you the mile or so from Tsuru-ga-oka Hachiman-gu, and take the first narrow street north. A tea ceremony with Japanese green tea takes place in this lovely setting. The monastery is about 100 yards from the corner. ⊠ *3–8–31 Jomyo-ji* ☎ *0467/22–2818* 🖳 *Jomyo Temple ¥100, tea ceremony ¥500* ⊙ *Daily 9–4.*

Kamakura-gu 鎌倉宮 *(Kamakura Shrine)*. This Shinto shrine was built after the Meiji Restoration of 1868 and was dedicated to Prince Morinaga (1308–36), the first son of Emperor Go-Daigo. When Go-Daigo overthrew the Kamakura Shogunate and restored Japan to direct imperial rule, Morinaga—who had been in the priesthood—was appointed supreme commander of his father's forces. The prince lived in turbulent times and died young: when the Ashikaga clan in turn overthrew Go-Daigo's government, Morinaga was taken into exile, held prisoner in a cave behind the present site of Kamakura Shrine, and eventually beheaded. The **Treasure House** (Homotsu-den), on the northwest corner of the grounds, next to the shrine's administrative office, is of interest mainly for its collection of paintings depicting the life of Prince Morinaga. To reach Kamakura Shrine, walk from Yoritomo's tomb to Route 204, and turn left; at the next traffic light, a narrow street on the left leads off at an angle to the shrine, about five minutes' walk west. ⊠ *154 Nikaido* ☎ *0467/22–0318* 🖳 *Kamakura Shrine free, Treasure House ¥300* ⊙ *Daily 9–4.*

Kamakura Treasure Museum 鎌倉国宝館 *(Kamakura Kokuhokan)*. This museum was built in 1928 as a repository for many of the most important objects belonging to the shrines and temples in the area; many of these are designated Important Cultural Properties. The museum, located along the east side of the Tsuru-ga-oka Hachiman-gu shrine precincts, has an especially fine collection of devotional and portrait sculpture in wood from the Kamakura and Muromachi periods; the portrait pieces may be among the most expressive and interesting in all of classical Japanese art. ⊠ *2–1–1 Yuki-no-shita* ☎ *0467/22–0753* 🖳 *¥300* ⊙ *Tues.–Sun. 9–4.*

Prefectural Museum of Modern Art 神奈川県立美術館 *(Kanagawa Kenritsu Kindai Bijutsukan)*. On the north side of the Heike Pond at Tsuru-ga-oka Hachiman-gu, this museum houses a collection of Japanese oil paintings and watercolors, wood-block prints, and sculpture. ⊠ *2–1–53 Yuki-no-shita* ☎ *0467/22–5000* 🖳 *¥800–¥1,200, depending on exhibition* ⊙ *Tues.–Sun. 9:30–4:30.*

HASE 長谷

TOP ATTRACTIONS

Fodor's Choice ★   **Great Buddha** 大仏 *(Daibutsu)*. The single biggest attraction in Hase ("*ha*-seh") is the Great Buddha—sharing the honors with Mt. Fuji, perhaps, as the quintessential picture-postcard image of Japan. The statue of the compassionate Amida Buddha sits cross-legged in the temple courtyard, the drapery of his robes flowing in lines reminiscent of ancient Greece, his expression profoundly serene. The 37-foot bronze figure was cast in 1292, three centuries before Europeans reached Japan; the concept of the classical Greek lines in the Buddha's robe must have come over the Silk Route through China during the time of Alexander the Great. The casting was probably first conceived in 1180, by Minamoto no Yoritomo, who wanted a statue to rival the enormous Daibutsu in Nara. Until 1495 the Amida Buddha was housed in a wooden temple, which washed away in a great tidal wave. Since then the loving Buddha has stood exposed, facing the cold winters and hot summers, for more than five centuries.

■**TIP→** It may seem sacrilegious to walk inside the Great Buddha, but for ¥20 you can enter the figure from a doorway in the right side and explore his stomach, with a stairway that leads up to two windows in his back, offering a stunning view of the temple grounds (open until 4:15 pm). To reach Kotoku-in and the Great Buddha, take the Enoden Line from the west side of JR Kamakura Station three stops to Hase. From the East Exit, turn right and walk north about 10 minutes on the main street (Route 32). ✉ *4–2–28 Hase, Hase* ☎ *0467/22–0703* 💴¥200 🕙 *Apr.–Sept., daily 7–6; Oct.–Mar., daily 7–5:30.*

Fodor's Choice ★   **Hase-dera** 長谷寺. The only temple in Kamakura facing the sea, this is one of the most beautiful, and saddest, places of pilgrimage in the city. On a landing partway up the stone steps that lead to the temple grounds are hundreds of small stone images of Jizo, one of the bodhisattvas in the Buddhist pantheon. Jizo is the savior of children, particularly the souls of the stillborn, aborted, and miscarried; the mothers of these children dress the statues of Jizo in bright red bibs and leave them small offerings of food, heartbreakingly touching acts of prayer.

The **Kannon Hall** (Kannon-do) at Hase-dera enshrines the largest carved-wood statue in Japan: the votive figure of Juichimen Kannon, the 11-headed goddess of mercy. Standing 30 feet tall, the goddess bears a crown of 10 smaller heads, symbolizing her ability to search out in all directions for those in need of her compassion. No one knows for certain when the figure was carved. According to the temple records, a monk named Tokudo Shonin carved two images of the Juichimen Kannon from a huge laurel tree in 721. One was consecrated to the Hase-dera in present-day Nara Prefecture; the other was thrown into the sea in order to go wherever the sea decided that there were souls in need, and that image washed up on shore near Kamakura. Much later, in 1342, Takauji Ashikaga—the first of the 15 Ashikaga shoguns who followed the Kamakura era—had the statue covered with gold leaf.

The **Amida Hall** of Hase-dera enshrines the image of a seated Amida Buddha, who presides over the Western Paradise of the Pure Land.

DID YOU KNOW?

The Daibutsu of Kamakura, cast in the 13th century, was originally housed indoors, but weather disasters in the 14th and 15th centuries destroyed multiple reconstructions its temple. Starting in 1495 the Buddha has meditated al fresco. Built in the Chinese Sung style, this bronze Buddha weighs in at 121 tons.

Hase-dera, in Kamakura, is dedicated to unborn children. The beautiful temple faces the sea.

Minamoto no Yoritomo ordered the creation of this statue when he reached the age of 42; popular Japanese belief, adopted from China, holds that your 42nd year is particularly unlucky. Yoritomo's act of piety earned him another 11 years—he was 53 when he was thrown by a horse and died of his injuries. The Buddha is popularly known as the *yakuyoke* (good-luck) Amida, and many visitors—especially students facing entrance exams—make a point of coming here to pray. To the left of the main halls is a small restaurant where you can buy good-luck candy and admire the view of Kamakura Beach and Sagami Bay. ✉ *To reach Hase-dera from Hase Station, walk north about 5 mins on the main street (Rte. 32) towards Kotoku-in and the Great Buddha, and look for a signpost to the temple on a side street to the left. 3–11–2 Hase, Hase* ☎ *0467/22–6300* 🎫 *¥300* ⊘ *Mar.–Sept., daily 8–5:30; Oct.–Feb., daily 8–4:30.*

NEED A BREAK?

Kaiko-an 海光庵 is a spacious tearoom inside the temple grounds that offers dango (sweet rice dumplings on a stick), green tea, and sweets. Rest your feet, grab a table by the windows, and take in the breathtaking views of the ocean. ✉ *3–11–2 Hase, Hase* ☎ *0467/22–6300* ▭ *No credit cards* ⊘ *Mar.–Sept., daily 8–5:30; Oct.–Feb., daily 8–4:30.*

RYUKO-JI AND ENOSHIMA 龍口寺・江ノ島

Ryuko-ji 龍口寺 *(Ryuko Temple).* The Kamakura story would not be complete without the tale of Nichiren (1222–82), the monk who founded the only native Japanese sect of Buddhism and who is honored here. Nichiren's rejection of both Zen and Jodo (Pure Land) teachings brought him into conflict with the Kamakura Shogunate, and the Hojo regents sent him into exile on the Izu Peninsula in 1261. Later allowed to return, he continued to preach his own interpretation of the Lotus Sutra—and to assert the "blasphemy" of other Buddhist sects, a stance that finally persuaded the Hojo regency, in 1271, to condemn him to death. The execution was to take place on a hill to the south of Hase. As the executioner swung his sword, legend has it that a lightning bolt struck the blade and snapped it in two. Taken aback, the executioner sat down to collect his wits, and a messenger was sent back to Kamakura to report the event. On his way he met another messenger, who was carrying a writ from the Hojo regents commuting Nichiren's sentence to exile on the island of Sado-ga-shima.

> **WORD OF MOUTH**
>
> "From the Kamakura train station we boarded a local bus to Daibutsu—the Great Buddha. And great it was, an impressive 13 meter-high structure meditating in a lovely space surrounded by pine trees. Although we couldn't climb into the Buddha's ear, for a mere ¥20 each we were able to climb inside up to the Buddha's tummy (the statue is made of cypress wood with a copper patina), definitely a first for all of us!" —fourfortravel

Followers of Nichiren built Ryuko Temple in 1337, on the hill where he was to be executed, marking his miraculous deliverance from the headsman. There are other Nichiren temples closer to Kamakura—Myohon-ji and Ankokuron-ji, for example. But Ryuko not only has the typical Nichiren-style main hall, with gold tassels hanging from its roof, but also a beautiful pagoda, built in 1904. To reach it, take the Enoden Line west from Hase to Enoshima—a short, scenic ride that cuts through the hills surrounding Kamakura to the shore. ✛ *From Enoshima Station walk about 100 yards east, keeping the train tracks on your right, and you'll come to the temple.* ✉ *3–13–37 Katase, Fujisawa* ☎ *0466/25–7357* 🎟 *Free* ☉ *Daily 6–4.*

OFF THE BEATEN PATH

The Sagami Bay shore in this area has some of the closest beaches to Tokyo, and in the hot, humid summer months it seems as though all of the city's teeming millions pour onto these beaches in search of a vacant patch of rather dirty gray sand. Pass up this mob scene and press on instead to **Enoshima** 江ノ島. The island is only 4 km (2½ mi) around, with a hill in the middle. Partway up the hill is a shrine where the local fisherfolk used to pray for a bountiful catch—before it became a tourist attraction. Once upon a time it was quite a hike up to the shrine; now there's a series of escalators, flanked by the inevitable stalls selling souvenirs and snacks. The island has several cafés and restaurants, and on clear days some of them have spectacular views of Mt. Fuji and the Izu Peninsula. To reach the causeway from Enoshima Station to the island, walk south from the station for about 3 km (2 mi), keeping the Katase-gawa (Katase River) on your right. To return to Tokyo from Enoshima, take a train to Shinjuku on the Odakyu Line. From the island walk back across the causeway and take the second bridge over the Katase-gawa. Within five minutes you'll come to Katase-Enoshima Station. Or you can retrace your steps to Kamakura and take the JR Yokosuka Line to Tokyo Station.

WHERE TO EAT

KITA-KAMAKURA

$$$$
JAPANESE
★

✕ **Hachinoki**   **Kita-Kamakura-ten** 鉢の木北鎌倉店. Traditional shojin ryori (the vegetarian cuisine of Zen monasteries) is served in this old Japanese house on the Kamakura Kaido (Route 21) near the entrance to Jochi Temple. The seating is mainly in tatami rooms with beautiful antique wood furnishings. If you prefer table seating, visit the annex building. Allow plenty of time; this is not a meal to be hurried through. Meals, which are prix fixe only, are served Tuesday to Friday 11 to 2:30, weekends 11 to 3. ⊠ *350 Yama-no-uchi, Kita-Kamakura* ☎ *0467/23–3722* ⊘ *Closed Wed.*

$$–$$$
JAPANESE

✕ **Kyorai-an** 去来庵. A traditional Japanese structure houses this restaurant known for its excellent Western-style beef stew. Also on the menu are pasta dishes, rice bouillon, homemade cheesecake, and wine produced in the Kita-Kamakura wine region. Half the seats are on tatami mats and half are at tables, but all look out on a peaceful patch of greenery. Kyorai-an is on the main road from Kita-Kamakura to Kamakura on the left side; it's about halfway between Meigetsu Temple and Kencho Temple, up a winding flight of stone steps. Meals are served Monday to Thursday 11:30 to 2:30, weekends and holidays 11 to 3 and 5 to 7. ⊠ *157 Yamanouchi, Kamakura* ☎ *0467/24–9835* ✍ *Reservations essential* ▭ *No credit cards* ⊘ *No dinner Mon.–Thurs.*

DOWNTOWN KAMAKURA

¢
CAFÉ

✕ **Bergfeld** ベルグフェルド. If you need to take a break during your walking tour of Kamakura, you may want to stop by this quaint café and bakery. It serves German cakes and cookies that are surprisingly authentic—the baker trained in Germany. There are a few small tables outside, and cozy tables inside where you can enjoy coffee and cakes before resuming your tour. Many Japanese who visit from other parts of the country bring back the bakery's butter cookies as souvenirs. ⊠ *3–9–24 Yukinoshita, Kamakura* ☎ *0467/24–2706* ▭ *No credit cards* ⊘ *Closed Tues. and the 3rd Thurs. of the month.*

¢
JAPANESE

✕ **Kaisen Misaki-ko** 海鮮三崎港. This *kaiten-zushi* (sushi served on a conveyor belt that lets you pick the dishes you want) restaurant on Komachi-dori serves eye-poppingly large fish portions that hang over the edge of their plates. All the standard sushi creations, including tuna, shrimp, and egg, are prepared here. Prices range from ¥170 to ¥500. The restaurant is on the right side of the road just as you enter Komachi-dori from the East Exit of Kamakura Station. As in any kaiten-zushi joint, simply stack up your empty dishes to the side. When you are ready to leave, the dishes will be counted and you will be charged accordingly. ⊠ *1–7–1 Komachi, Kamakura* ☎ *0467/22–6228* ▭ *No credit cards.*

$$–$$$
INDIAN

✕ **T-Side** ティーサイド. Authentic, inexpensive Indian fare and a second-floor location that looks down upon Kamakura's main shopping street make this restaurant a popular choice for lunch and dinner.

done well, the various *thali* (sets) are a good value, and the kitchen also serves some Nepalese dishes. T-Side is at the very top of Komachi-dori on the left as you enter from Kamakura Station. ⊠ *2–11–11 Komachi, Kamakura* ☎ *0467/24-9572* ⊕ *www.kamakura-t-side.com* ⊟ *No credit cards.*

HASE

$$$–$$$$

CHINESE

✕ **Kaiserro** 華正樓. This establishment, in an old Japanese house, serves the best Chinese food in the city. The dining-room windows look out on a small, restful garden. Make sure you plan for a stop here on your way to or from the Great Buddha at Kotoku-in. ⊠ *3–1–14 Hase, Hase* ☎ *0467/22–0280* ⌓ *Reservations essential.*

THE POWER OF THE JAPANESE BLADE

In the corner of the enclosure where the Chinese Gate and Sanctum are found, an antique bronze lantern stands some 7 feet high. Legend has it that the lantern would assume the shape of a goblin at night; the deep nicks in the bronze were inflicted by swordsmen of the Edo period—on guard duty, perhaps, startled into action by a flickering shape in the dark. This proves, if not the existence of goblins, the incredible cutting power of the Japanese blade, a peerlessly forged weapon.

4

YOKOHAMA 横浜

In 1853, a fleet of four American warships under Commodore Matthew Perry sailed into the bay of Tokyo (then Edo) and presented the reluctant Japanese with the demands of the U.S. government for the opening of diplomatic and commercial relations. The following year Perry returned and first set foot on Japanese soil at Yokohama—then a small fishing village on the mudflats of the bay, some 20 km (12½ mi) southwest of Tokyo.

Two years later New York businessman Townsend Harris became America's first diplomatic representative to Japan. In 1858 he was finally able to negotiate a commercial treaty between the two countries; part of the deal designated four locations—one of them Yokohama—as treaty ports. With the agreement signed, Harris lost no time in setting up his residence in Hangaku-ji, in nearby Kanagawa, another of the designated ports. Kanagawa, however, was also one of the 53 relay stations on the Tokaido, the highway from Edo to the imperial court in Kyoto, and the presence of foreigners—perceived as unclean barbarians—offended the Japanese elite. Die-hard elements of the warrior class, moreover, wanted Japan to remain in isolation and were willing to give their lives to rid the country of intruders. Unable to protect foreigners in Kanagawa, in 1859 the shogunate created a special settlement in Yokohama for the growing community of merchants, traders, missionaries, and other assorted adventurers drawn to this exotic new land of opportunity.

The foreigners (predominantly Chinese and British, plus a few French, Americans, and Dutch) were confined here to a guarded compound about 5 square km (2 square mi)—placed, in effect, in isolation—but not for long. Within a few short years the shogunal government collapsed, and Japan began to modernize. Western ideas were welcomed, as were Western goods, and the little treaty port became Japan's principal gateway to the outside world. In 1872 Japan's first railway was built, linking Yokohama and Tokyo. In 1889 Yokohama became a city; by then the population had grown to some 120,000. As the city prospered, so did the international community and by the early 1900s Yokohama was the busiest and most modern center of international trade in all of East Asia.

Then Yokohama came tumbling down. On September 1, 1923, the Great Kanto Earthquake devastated the city. The ensuing fires destroyed some 60,000 homes and took more than 40,000 lives. During the six years it took to rebuild the city, many foreign businesses took up quarters elsewhere, primarily in Kobe and Osaka, and did not return.

Over the next 20 years Yokohama continued to grow as an industrial center—until May 29, 1945, when in a span of four hours, some 500 American B-29 bombers leveled nearly half the city and left more than half a million people homeless. When the war ended, what remained became—in effect—the center of the Allied occupation. General Douglas MacArthur set up headquarters here, briefly, before moving to Tokyo; the entire port facility and about a quarter of the city remained in the hands of the U.S. military throughout the 1950s.

By the 1970s Yokohama was once more rising from the debris; in 1978 it surpassed Osaka as the nation's second-largest city, and the population is now inching up to the 3.5 million mark. Boosted by Japan's postwar economic miracle, Yokohama has extended its urban sprawl north to Tokyo and south to Kamakura—in the process creating a whole new subcenter around the Shinkansen Station at Shin-Yokohama.

The development of air travel and the competition from other ports have changed the city's role in Japan's economy. The great liners that once docked at Yokohama's piers are now but a memory, kept alive by a museum ship and the occasional visit of a luxury vessel on a Pacific cruise. Modern Yokohama thrives instead in its industrial, commercial, and service sectors—and a large percentage of its people commute to work in Tokyo. Is Yokohama worth a visit? Not, one could argue, at the expense of Nikko or Kamakura. But the waterfront is fun and the museums are excellent.

GETTING HERE AND AROUND

From Narita Airport, a direct limousine-bus service departs once or twice an hour between 6:45 am and 10:20 pm for Yokohama City Air Terminal (YCAT). YCAT is a five-minute taxi ride from Yokohama Station. JR Narita Express trains going on from Tokyo to Yokohama leave the airport every hour from 8:13 am to 1:13 pm and 2:43 pm to 9:43 pm. The fare is ¥4,180 (¥6,730 for the first-class Green Car coaches). Or you can take the limousine-bus service from Narita to Tokyo Station and continue on to Yokohama by train. Either way, the journey will take more than two hours—closer to three, if traffic is heavy.

The Airport Limousine Information Desk phone number provides information in English daily 9 to 6; you can also get timetables on its Web site. For information in English on Narita Express trains, call the JR Higashi-Nihon Info Line, available daily 10 to 6.

Most of the things you'll want to see in Yokohama are within easy walking distance of a JR or subway station, but this city is so much more negotiable than Tokyo that exploring by bus is a viable alternative. Buses, in fact, are the best way to get to Sankei-en. The city map available in the visitor centers in Yokohama has most major bus routes marked on it, and the important stops on the tourist routes are announced in English. The fixed fare is ¥210. One-day passes are also available for ¥600. Contact the Sightseeing Information Office at Yokohama Station (JR, East Exit) for more information and ticket purchases.

One subway line connects Azamino, Shin-Yokohama, Yokohama, Totsuka, and Shonandai. The basic fare is ¥200. One-day passes are also available for ¥740. The Minato Mirai Line, a spur of the Tokyu Toyoko Line, runs from Yokohama Station to all the major points of interest, including Minato Mirai, Chinatown, Yamashita Park, Moto-machi, and Basha-michi. The fare is ¥180–¥200, and one-day unlimited-ride passes are available for ¥450.

There are taxi stands at all the train stations, and you can always flag a cab on the street. ■TIP➡ Vacant taxis show a red light in the windshield. The basic fare is ¥710 for the first 2 km (1 mi), then ¥80 for every additional 350 meters (0.2 mi). Traffic is heavy in downtown Yokohama, however, and you will often find it faster to walk.

Teiki Yuran Bus offers a full-day (9–3:45) sightseeing bus tour that covers the major sights and includes lunch at a Chinese restaurant in Chinatown. The tour is in Japanese only, but pamphlets written in English are available at most sightseeing stops. Buy tickets (¥5,300) at the bus offices at Yokohama Station (east side) and at Kannai Station; the tour departs daily at 9:45 am from Bus Stop 14, on the east side of Yokohama Station. A half-day tour is also available, with lunch (9:30–1:20, ¥3,000) or without (2–5:45, ¥2,300).

The sightseeing boat *Marine Shuttle* makes 40-, 60-, and 90-minute tours of the harbor and bay for ¥1,000, ¥1,600, and ¥2,200, respectively. Boarding is at the pier at Yamashita Park. Boats depart roughly every hour between 10:20 am and 6:30 pm. Another boat, the *Marine Rouge,* runs 90-minute tours departing from the pier at 11, 1:30, and 4, and a special two-hour evening tour at 7 (¥2,800).

JR trains from Tokyo Station leave approximately every 10 minutes, depending on the time of day. Take the Yokosuka, the Tokaido, or the Keihin Tohoku Line to Yokohama Station (the Yokosuka and Tokaido lines take 30 minutes; the Keihin Tohoku Line takes 40 minutes and cost ¥450). From there the Keihin Tohoku Line (Platform 3) goes on to Kannai and Ishikawa-cho, Yokohama's business and downtown areas. If you're going directly to downtown Yokohama from Tokyo, the blue commuter trains of the Keihin Tohoku Line are best.

The private Tokyu Toyoko Line, which runs from Shibuya Station in Tokyo directly to Yokohama Station, is a good alternative if you leave from the western part of Tokyo. ■TIP➡ The term "private" is important because it means that the train does not belong to JR and is not a subway line. If you have a JR Pass, you'll have to buy a separate ticket. Depending on which Tokyu Toyoko Line you catch—the Limited Express, Semi

Express, or Local—the trip takes between 25 and 44 minutes and costs ¥260.

Yokohama Station is the hub that links all the train lines and connects them with the city's subway and bus services. Kannai and Ishikawa-cho are the two downtown stations, both on the Keihin Tohoku Line; trains leave Yokohama Station every two to five minutes from Platform 3. From Sakuragi-cho, Kannai, or Ishikawa-cho, most of Yokohama's points of interest are within easy walking distance; the one notable exception is Sankei-en, which you reach via the JR Keihin Tohoku Line to Negishi Station and then a local bus.

VISITOR INFORMATION

The Yokohama International Tourist Association arranges visits to the homes of English-speaking Japanese families. These usually last a few hours and are designed to give *gaijin* (foreigners) a glimpse into the Japanese way of life.

The Yokohama Tourist Office, in the central passageway of Yokohama Station, is open daily 9 to 7 (closed December 28–January 3). The head office of the Yokohama Convention & Visitors Bureau, open weekdays 9 to 5 (except national holidays and December 29–January 3), is in the Sangyo Boeki Center Building, across from Yamashita Koen.

ESSENTIALS

Airport Transportation Airport Limousine Information Desk (☎ 03/3665–7220 ⊕ www.limousinebus.co.jp). **JR Higashi-Nihon Info Line** (☎ 03/3423–0111).

Bus Information Sightseeing Information Office (☎ 045/465–2077).

Emergencies Ambulance or Fire (☎ 119). **Police** (☎ 110). **Washinzaka Hospital** (✉ 169 Yamate-cho, Naka-ku ☎ 045/623–7688). **Yokohama Police Station** (✉ 2–4 Kaigan-dori, Naka-ku ☎ 045/623–0110).

Tourist Information Yokohama Convention & Visitors Bureau (✉ 2 Yamashita-cho, Naka-ku ☎ 045/221–2111). **Yokohama International Tourist Association** (☎ 045/641–4759). **Yokohama Tourist Office** (✉ Yokohama Station, Nishi-ku ☎ 045/441–7300).

Tours Marine Shuttle (☎ 045/671–7719 Port Service reservation center). **Teiki Yuran Bus** (☎ 045/465–2077).

EXPLORING

Large as Yokohama is, the central area is very negotiable. As with any other port city, much of what it has to offer centers on the waterfront—in this case, on the west side of Tokyo Bay. The downtown area is called Kannai (literally, "within the checkpoint"); this is where the international community was originally confined by the shogunate. Though the center of interest has expanded to include the waterfront and Ishikawa-cho, to the south, Kannai remains the heart of town.

Think of that heart as two adjacent areas. One is the old district of Kannai, bounded by Basha-michi on the northwest and Nippon-odori on the southeast, the Keihin Tohoku Line tracks on the southwest, and

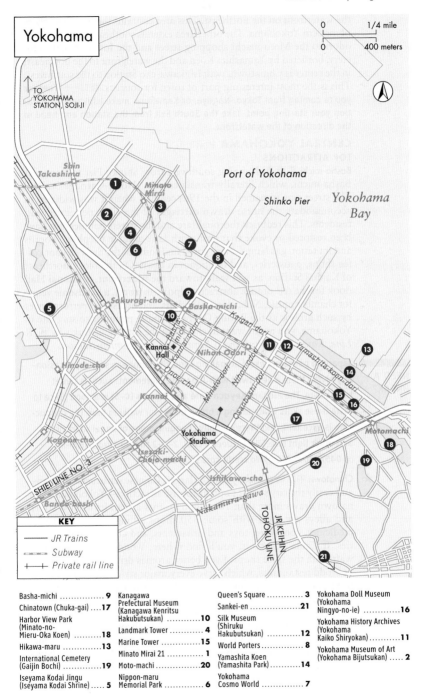

Yokohama

0 ___ 1/4 mile
0 ___ 400 meters

TO
YOKOHAMA
STATION, SOJI-JI

Port of Yokohama

Shinko Pier

Yokohama Bay

Shin Takashima

Minato Mirai

Sakuragi-cho

Basha-michi

Kaigan-dori

Hinode-cho

Kannai Hall

Nihon Odori

Yamashita-koen-dori

Kannai

Minato-dori

Ninon-odori

Osanbashi-dori

Motomachi

Kogane-cho

Yokohama Stadium

Isezaki-Chojo-machi

Ishikawa-cho

SHIEI LINE NO. 3

Banba-bashi

Nakamura-gawa

TOHOKU LINE

JR KEIHIN

KEY

— JR Trains
⋯⋯ Subway
+—+ Private rail line

the waterfront on the northeast. This area contains the business offices of modern Yokohama. The other area extends southeast from Nippon-odori to the Moto-machi shopping street and the International Cemetery, bordered by Yamashita Koen and the waterfront to the northeast; in the center is Chinatown, with Ishikawa-cho Station to the southwest. This is the most interesting part of town for tourists. ■TIP→ Whether you're coming from Tokyo, Nagoya, or Kamakura, make Ishikawa-cho Station your starting point. Take the South Exit from the station and head in the direction of the waterfront.

CENTRAL YOKOHAMA 横浜市街
TOP ATTRACTIONS

Basha-michi 馬車道. Running southwest from Shinko Pier to Kannai is Basha-michi, which literally translates into "Horse-Carriage Street." The street was so named in the 19th century, when it was widened to accommodate the horse-drawn carriages of the city's new European residents. This redbrick thoroughfare and the streets parallel to it have been restored to evoke that past, with faux-antique telephone booths and imitation gas lamps. Here you'll find some of the most elegant coffee shops, patisseries, and boutiques in town. On the block northeast of Kannai Station, as you walk toward the waterfront, is **Kannai Hall** (look for the red-orange abstract sculpture in front), a handsome venue for chamber music, Noh, classical recitals, and occasional performances by such groups as the Peking Opera. If you're planning to stay late in Yokohama, you might want to check out the listings. ⊠ *Naka-ku* Ⓜ *JR Line, Kannai Station; Minato Mirai Line, Basha-michi Station.*

NEED A BREAK?

Japanese pâtissiers excel at making exquisite European sweets, occasionally giving them a new twist with Japanese ingredients such as sweet bean paste. The elegant **Keyuca Café and Sweets** (¢–$) is a good place to taste these skills while taking a break from your walking tour. The cappuccino is excellent, and there's a daily changing menu of bagel sandwiches and other light fare. ⊠ *B1 Queen's East, 2–3–2 Minato-Mirai, Nishi-ku* ☎ *045/640–1361* 🚫 *No credit cards* 🕐 *Daily 11–8.*

★ **Chinatown** 中華街 *(Chuka-gai).* The largest Chinese settlement in Japan—and easily the city's most popular tourist attraction—Yokohama's Chinatown draws more than 18 million visitors a year. Its narrow streets and alleys are lined with some 350 shops selling foodstuffs, herbal medicines, cookware, toys and ornaments, and clothing and accessories. If China exports it, you'll find it here. Wonderful exotic aromas waft from the spice shops. Even better aromas drift from the quarter's 160-odd restaurants, which serve every major style of Chinese cuisine: this is the best place for lunch in Yokohama. Chinatown is a 10-minute walk southeast of Kannai Station. When you get to Yokohama Stadium, turn left and cut through the municipal park to the top of Nihon-odori. Then take a right, and you'll enter Chinatown through the Gembu-mon (North Gate), which leads to the dazzling red-and-gold, 50-foot-high Zenrin-mon (Good Neighbor Gate). ⊠ *Naka-ku* Ⓜ *JR Line, Ishikawa-cho Station; Minato Mirai Line, Motomachi-Chukagai Station.*

Get a taste of China in Japan with a visit to the restaurants and shops of Yokohama's Chinatown.

Harbor View Park 港の見える丘公園 *(Minato-no-Mieru-Oka Koen)*. The park—a major landmark in this part of the city, known, appropriately enough, as the Bluff *(yamate)*—was once the barracks of the British forces in Yokohama. Come here for spectacular nighttime views of the waterfront, the floodlit gardens of Yamashita Park, and the Bay Bridge. Foreigners were first allowed to build here in 1867, and it has been prime real estate ever since—an enclave of consulates, churches, international schools, private clubs, and palatial Western-style homes. ⊠ *Naka-ku* Ⓜ *JR Line, Ishikawa-cho Station; Minato Mirai Line, Motomachi-Chukagai Station.*

Hikawa-maru 氷川丸. Moored on the waterfront, more or less in the middle of Yamashita Park, is the *Hikawa-maru*. It was built in 1929 by Yokohama Dock Co. and was launched on September 30, 1929. For 31 years, she shuttled passengers between Yokohama and Seattle, Washington, making a total of 238 trips. A tour of the ship evokes the time when Yokohama was a great port of call for the transpacific liners. The *Hikawa-maru* has a French restaurant, and in summer there's a beer garden on the upper deck. ⊠ *Naka-ku* ☎ *045/641–4361* 🎫 *¥500* ⏱ *Apr.–June, Sept., and Oct., daily 9:30–7; July and Aug., daily 9:30–7:30; Nov.–Mar., daily 9:30–6:30* Ⓜ *JR Line, Ishikawa-cho Station; Minato Mirai Line, Motomachi-Chukagai Station.*

Silk Museum シルク博物館 *(Shiruku Hakubutsukan)*. The museum, which pays tribute to the period at the turn of the 20th century when Japan's exports of silk were all shipped out of Yokohama, houses an extensive collection of silk fabrics and an informative exhibit on the silk-making process. People on staff are very happy to answer questions. In the same building, on the first floor, are the main offices of the Yokohama International Tourist Association and the Kanagawa Prefectural Tourist Association. The museum is at the northwestern end of the Yamashita Park promenade, on the second floor of the Silk Center Building. ⊠ *1 Yamashita-cho, Naka-ku* ☎ *045/641–0841* 🖾 *¥500* 🕙 *Tues.–Sun. 9–4* Ⓜ *Minato Mirai Line, Nihon Odori Station (Exit 3).*

WORTH NOTING

International Cemetery 横浜山手外国人墓地 *(Gaikokujin Bochi).* This Yokohama landmark is a reminder of the port city's heritage. It was established in 1854 with a grant of land from the shogunate; the first foreigners to be buried here were Russian sailors assassinated by xenophobes in the early days of the settlement. Most of the 4,500 graves on this hillside are English and American, and about 120 are of the Japanese wives of foreigners; the inscriptions on the crosses and headstones attest to some 40 different nationalities whose citizens lived and died in Yokohama. From Moto-machi Plaza, it's a short walk to the north end of the cemetery. ⊠ *Naka-ku* 🕙 *No entry after 4 pm* Ⓜ *JR Line, Ishikawa-cho Station; Minato Mirai Line, Motomachi-Chukagai Station.*

Kanagawa Prefectural Museum of Cultural History 神奈川県立歴史博物館 *(Kanagawa Kenritsu Rekishi Hakubutsukan).* One of the few buildings in Yokohama to have survived both the Great Kanto Earthquake of 1923 and World War II, the museum is a few blocks north of Kannai Station (use Exit 8) on Basha-michi. Most exhibits here have no explanations in English, but the galleries on the third floor showcase some remarkable medieval wooden sculptures (including one of the first Kamakura shogun, Minamoto no Yoritomo), hanging scrolls, portraits, and armor. The exhibits of prehistory and of Yokohama in the early modern period are of much less interest. ⊠ *5–60 Minami Naka-dori, Naka-ku* ☎ *045/201–0926* 🖾 *¥300, special exhibits ¥800* 🕙 *Tues.–Sun. 9–4:30; closed last Tues. of month and the day after a national holiday* Ⓜ *JR Line, Sakuragi-cho and Kannai stations.*

Marine Tower マリンタワー. For an older generation of Yokohama residents, the 348-foot-high decagonal tower, which opened in 1961, was the city's landmark structure; civic pride prevented them from admitting that it falls lamentably short of an architectural masterpiece. The tower has a navigational beacon at the 338-foot level and purports to be the tallest lighthouse in the world. At the 328-foot level, an observation gallery provides 360-degree views of the harbor and the city, and on clear days in autumn or winter, you can often see Mt. Fuji in the distance. Marine Tower is in the middle of the second block northwest from the end of Yamashita Park, on the left side of the promenade. ⊠ *15 Yamashita-cho, Naka-ku* ☎ *045/641–7838* 🖾 *¥700* 🕙 *Jan. and Feb., daily 9–7; Mar.–May, Nov., and Dec., daily 9:30–9; June, July, Sept., and Oct., daily 9:30–9:30; Aug., daily 9:30 am–10 pm* Ⓜ *JR Line, Ishikawa-cho Station; Minato Mirai Line, Motomachi-Chukagai Station.*

Moto-machi 元町. Within a block of Ishikawa-cho Station is the beginning of this street, which follows the course of the Nakamura-gawa (Nakamura River) to the harbor where the Japanese set up shop 100 years ago to serve the foreigners living in Kannai. The street is now lined with smart boutiques and jewelry stores that cater to fashionable young Japanese consumers. ⊠ *Naka-ku* Ⓜ *JR Line, Ishikawa-cho Station; Minato Mirai Line, Motomachi-Chukagai Station.*

Yamashita Koen 山下公園 *(Yamashita Park).* This park is perhaps the only positive legacy of the Great Kanto Earthquake of 1923. The debris of the warehouses and other buildings that once stood here were swept away, and the area was made into a 17-acre oasis of green along the waterfront. The fountain, representing the Guardian of the Water, was presented to Yokohama by San Diego, California, one of its sister cities. From Harbor View Park, walk northwest through neighboring French Hill Park and cross the walkway over Moto-machi. Turn right on the other side and walk one block down toward the bay to Yamashita-Koen-dori, the promenade along the park. ⊠ *Naka-ku* Ⓜ *JR Line, Ishikawa-cho Station; Minato Mirai Line, Motomachi-Chukagai Station.*

Yokohama Doll Museum 横浜人形の家 *(Yokohama Ningyo-no-ie).* This museum houses a collection of some 4,000 dolls from all over the world. In Japanese tradition, dolls are less to play with than to display—either in religious folk customs or as the embodiment of some spiritual quality. Japanese visitors to this museum never seem to outgrow their affection for the Western dolls on display here, to which they tend to assign the role of timeless "ambassadors of good will" from other cultures. The museum is worth a quick visit, with or without a child in tow. It's just across from the southeast end of Yamashita Park, on the left side of the promenade. ⊠ *18 Yamashita-cho, Naka-ku* ☎ *045/671–9361* 🎫 *¥500* ⏱ *Daily 10–6; closed 3rd Mon. of month* Ⓜ *JR Line, Ishikawa-cho Station; Minato Mirai Line, Motomachi-Chukagai Station.*

Yokohama History Archives 横浜開港資料館 *(Yokohama Kaiko Shiryokan).* Within the archives, housed in what was once the British Consulate, are some 140,000 items recording the history of Yokohama since the opening of the port to international trade in the mid-19th century. Across the street is a monument to the U.S.–Japanese Friendship Treaty. To get here from the Silk Center Building, at the end of the Yamashita Park promenade, walk west to the corner of Nihon-odori; the archives are on the left. ⊠ *3 Nihon-odori, Naka-ku* ☎ *045/201–2100* 🎫 *¥200* ⏱ *Tues.–Sun. 9:30–5* Ⓜ *Minato Mirai Line, Nihon-odori Station.*

AROUND YOKOHAMA

TOP ATTRACTIONS

Iseyama Kodai Jingu 伊勢山皇大神宮 *(Iseyama Kodai Shrine).* A branch of the nation's revered Grand Shrines of Ise, this the most important Shinto shrine in Yokohama—but it's only worth a visit if you've seen most everything else in town. The shrine is a 10-minute walk west of Sakuragi-cho Station. ⊠ *64 Miyazaki-cho, Nishi-ku* ☎ *045/241–1122* 🎫 *Free* ⏱ *Daily 9–7* Ⓜ *JR Line, Sakuragi-cho Station; Minato Mirai Line, Minato Mirai Station.*

Landmark Tower ランドマークタワー. The 70-story tower in Yokohama's Minato Mirai is Japan's tallest building, although the Tokyo Sky Tree broadcast tower is poised to take that title when construction is completed in 2011. The observation deck on the 69th floor has a spectacular view of the city, especially at night; you reach it via a high-speed elevator

Landmark Tower and the Ferris wheel create a lovely skyline along Yokohama Bay.

that carries you up at an ear-popping 45 kph (28 mph). The Yokohama Royal Park Hotel occupies the top 20 stories of the building. On the first level of the Landmark Tower is the **Mitsubishi Minato Mirai Industrial Museum,** with rocket engines, power plants, a submarine, various gadgets, and displays that simulate piloting helicopters—great fun for kids.

The Landmark Tower complex's **Dockyard Garden,** built in 1896, is a restored dry dock with stepped sides of massive stone blocks. The long, narrow floor of the dock, with its water cascade at one end, makes a wonderful year-round open-air venue for concerts and other events; in summer (July–mid-August), the beer garden installed here is a perfect refuge from the heat. ⊠ *3–3–1 Minato Mirai, Nishi-ku* ☎ *045/224–9031* ▦ *Elevator to observation deck ¥1,000, museum ¥300* ☉ *Museum Tues.–Sun. 10–5* Ⓜ *JR Line, Sakuragi-cho Station; Minato Mirai Line, Minato Mirai Station.*

Minato Mirai 21 みなとみらい21. If you want to see Yokohama urban development at its most self-assertive, then this is a must. The aim of this project, launched in the mid-1980s, was to turn some three-quarters of a square mile of waterfront property, lying east of the JR Negishi Line railroad tracks between the Yokohama and Sakuragi-cho stations, into a model "city of the future." As a hotel, business, international exhibition, and conference center, it's a smashing success. ⊠ *Nishi-ku* Ⓜ *JR Line, Sakuragi-cho Station; Minato Mirai Line, Minato Mirai Station.*

★ **Sankei-en** 三渓園. Opened to the public in 1906, this was once the estate and gardens of Tomitaro Hara (1868–1939), one of Yokohama's wealthiest men, who made his money as a silk merchant before becoming a patron of the arts. On the extensive grounds of the estate he created is a kind of open-air museum of traditional Japanese architecture, some of which was brought here from Kamakura and the western part of the country. Especially noteworthy is **Rinshun-kaku,** a villa built for the Tokugawa clan in 1649. There's also a tea pavilion, Choshu-kaku, built by the third Tokugawa shogun, Iemitsu. Other buildings include a small temple transported from Kyoto's famed Daitoku-ji and a farmhouse from the Gifu district in the Japan Alps (around Takayama). ✉ *58–1 Honmoku San-no-tani, Naka-ku* ☎ *045/621–0635* 💰 *Inner garden ¥300, outer garden ¥300, farmhouse ¥100* 🕐 *Inner garden daily 9–4, outer garden and farmhouse daily 9–4:30* Ⓜ *JR Keihin Tohoku Line to Negishi Station and a local bus (number 54, 58, or 99) bound for Honmoku; Yokohama Station (East Exit) and take the bus (number 8 or 125) to Honmoku Sankei-en Mae. It will take about 35 mins.*

WORTH NOTING

Nippon-maru Memorial Park 日本丸メモリアルパーク. The centerpiece of the park, which is on the east side of Minato Mirai 21, where the O-oka-gawa (O-oka River) flows into the bay, is the *Nippon-maru,* a full-rigged three-masted ship popularly called the "Swan of the Pacific." Built in 1930, it served as a training vessel. The *Nippon-maru* is now retired, but it's an occasional participant in tall-ships festivals and is open for guided tours. Adjacent to the ship is the **Yokohama Maritime Museum,** a two-story collection of ship models, displays, and archival materials that celebrate the achievements of the Port of Yokohama from its earliest days to the present. ✉ *2–1–1 Minato Mirai, Nishi-ku* ☎ *045/221–0280* 💰 *Ship and museum ¥600, ship only ¥200* 🕐 *Museum closed Mon.* Ⓜ *JR Line, Sakuragi-cho Station; Minato Mirai Line, Minato Mirai Station.*

Queen's Square クイーンズスクエア. The courtyard on the northeast side of the Landmark Tower connects to this huge atrium-style vertical mall with dozens of shops (mainly for clothing and accessories) and restaurants. The complex also houses the Pan Pacific Hotel Yokohama and Yokohama Minato Mirai Hall, the city's major venue for classical music. ✉ *2–3–1 Minato-Mirai, Nishi-ku* ☎ *045/222–5015* ⊕ *www.qsy. co.jp* 🕐 *Shopping 11–8, restaurants 11 am–11 pm* Ⓜ *JR Line, Sakuragi-cho Station; Minato Mirai Line, Minato Mirai Station.*

World Porters ワールドポーターズ. This shopping center, on the opposite side of Yokohama Cosmo World, is notable chiefly for its restaurants that overlook the Minato Mirai area. Try arriving at sunset; the spectacular view of twinkling lights and the Landmark Tower, the Ferris wheel, and hotels will occasionally include Mt. Fuji in the background. Walking away from the waterfront area from World Porters will lead to **Aka Renga** (Redbrick Warehouses), two more shopping-and-entertainment facilities. ✉ *2–2–1 Shinko, Naka-ku* ☎ *045/222–2000* 💰 *Free* 🕐 *Daily 10–9, restaurants 10–11* Ⓜ *JR Line, Sakuragi-cho Station; Minato Mirai Line, Minato Mirai Station.*

Yokohama Cosmo World よこはまコスモワールド. This amusement-park complex claims—among its 30 or so rides and attractions—the world's largest water-chute ride at 13 feet long and four stories high. The Ferris wheel towers over Yokohama. It's west of Minato Mirai and

Queen's Square, on both sides of the river. ⊠ *2–8–1 Shinko, Naka-ku* ☎ *045/641–6591* ✉ *Park free, rides ¥300–¥700 each* ◷ *Mid-Mar.– Nov., weekdays 11–9, weekends 11–10; Dec.–mid-Mar., weekdays 11–8, weekends 11–9* Ⓜ *JR Line, Sakuragi-cho Station; Minato Mirai Line, Minato Mirai Station.*

Yokohama Museum of Art 横浜美術館 *(Yokohama Bijutsukan)*. Designed by Kenzo Tange and housed at Minato Mirai 21, the museum has 5,000 works in its permanent collection. Visitors will see paintings by both Western and Japanese artists, including Cézanne, Picasso, Braque, Klee, Kandinsky, Ryusei Kishida, and Taikan Yokoyama. ⊠ *3–4–1 Minato Mirai, Nishi-ku* ☎ *045/221– 0300* ✉ *¥500* ◷ *Mon.–Wed. and weekends 10–5:30, Fri. 10–7:30 (last entry)* Ⓜ *JR Line, Sakuragi-cho Station; Minato Mirai Line, Minato Mirai Station.*

OFF THE BEATEN PATH

Soji-ji 総持寺. One of the two major centers of the Soto sect of Zen Buddhism, Soji-ji, in Yokohama's Tsurumi ward, was founded in 1321. The center was moved here from Ishikawa, on the Noto Peninsula (on the Sea of Japan, north of Kanazawa), after a fire in the 19th century. There's also a Soji-ji monastic complex at Eihei-ji in Fukui Prefecture. The Yokohama Soji-ji is one of the largest and busiest Buddhist institutions in Japan, with more than 200 monks and novices in residence. The 14th-century patron of Soji-ji was the emperor Go-Daigo, who overthrew the Kamakura Shogunate; the emperor is buried here, but his mausoleum is off-limits to visitors. However, you can see the **Buddha Hall**, the **Main Hall**, and the **Treasure House**. To get to Soji-ji, take the JR Keihin Tohoku Line two stops from Sakuragi-cho to Tsurumi. From the station walk five minutes south (back toward Yokohama), passing Tsurumi University on your right. Look out for the stone lanterns that mark the entrance to the temple complex. ⊠ *2–1–1 Tsurumi, Tsurumi-ku* ☎ *045/581–6021* ✉ *¥300* ◷ *Daily dawn–dusk; Treasure House Tues.–Sun. 10–4.*

WHERE TO EAT

$$$–$$$$
SEAFOOD
★

✕ **Aichiya** 愛知屋. The "house of Aichi Prefecture" specializes in dishes of crab shipped in from Aichi. The merchandise is displayed in its pre-prepared state in cases and tanks at the front of the restaurant. There is crab soup, grilled crab, stewed crab, crab salad, and so on. A fall and winter course boasts *fugu* (blowfish), a delicacy that must be prepared by licensed experts, so as to avoid allowing the fish's poisonous organs from seeping into the meat. ⊠ *7–156 Isezaki-cho, Naka-ku* ☎ *045/251– 4163* ⊟ *No credit cards* ◷ *Closed Mon. No lunch.*

$$$
JAPANESE

✕ **Chano-ma** 茶の間. This stylish eatery serves modern Japanese cuisine. There are bedlike seats that you can lounge on while eating and a house

DJ spins tunes during dinner. While you're there, make sure you try the miso sirloin steak or grilled scallops with tasty citron sauce drizzled on top, served with a salad. It does get crowded here on the weekends, so come early to avoid a long wait. Try coming at lunchtime and you can take advantage of the ¥1,000 set-lunch special. ⊠ *3F Red Brick Warehouse Bldg. 2, 1–1–2 Shinkou, Naka-ku* ☎ *045/650–8228* Ⓜ *Minato Mirai Line, Basha-michi Station; JR Negishi Line, Sakuragi-cho and Kannai stations.*

$$$$
CHINESE
★

✕ **Kaseiro** 華正樓. Surprisingly, Chinese food can be hit-or-miss in Japan, but not at Kaseiro. This elegant restaurant, with red carpets and gold-tone walls, is the best of its kind in the city, serving authentic Beijing cuisine, including, of course, Peking Duck and shark-fin soup. The consistently delicious dishes, combined with the fact that both the owner and chef are from Beijing, make this restaurant a well-known favorite among locals and travelers alike. ⊠ *186 Yamashita-cho, Chinatown, Naka-ku* ☎ *045/681–2918* ⌂ *Jacket and tie.*

$$$$
JAPANESE

✕ **Motomachi Bairin** 元町梅林. The area of Motomachi is known as the wealthy, posh part of Yokohama; restaurants here tend to be exclusive and expensive, though the service and quality justify the price. This restaurant is an old-style Japanese house complete with a Japanese garden and five private tatami rooms. The ¥12,000, 27-course banquet includes some traditional Japanese delicacies such as sashimi, shiitake mushrooms, and chicken in white sauce; deep-fried burdock; and broiled sea bream. ⊠ *1–55 Motomachi, Naka-ku* ☎ *045/662–2215* ⌂ *Reservations essential* ▭ *No credit cards* ☉ *Closed Mon.*

$$$$
JAPANESE

✕ **Rinka-en** 隣華苑. If you visit the gardens of Sankei-en, you might want to have lunch at this traditional country restaurant, which serves kaiseki-style cuisine. Meals here are prix fixe. The owner is the granddaughter of Hara Tomitaro, who donated the gardens to the city. ⊠ *52–1 Honmoku San-no-tani, Naka-ku* ☎ *045/621–0318* ⌂ *Reservations essential* ⌂ *Jacket and tie* ▭ *No credit cards* ☉ *Closed Wed. and Aug.*

$$–$$$
ITALIAN

✕ **Roma Statione** ローマステーション. Opened more than 40 years ago, Roma Statione, between Chinatown and Yamashita Park, remains a popular venue for Italian food. The owner, whose father studied cooking in Italy before returning home to open this spot, is also the head chef and has continued using the original recipes. The house specialty is seafood: the spaghetti *vongole* (with clam sauce) is particularly good, as is the spaghetti *pescatora* and the seafood pizza. An added bonus is the impressive selection of Italian wines. ⊠ *26 Yamashita-cho, Naka-ku* ☎ *045/681–1818* ▭ *No credit cards* Ⓜ *Minato Mirai Line, Motomachi-Chukagai Station (Exit 1).*

$$$$
SCANDINAVIAN

✕ **Scandia** スカンディア. This Scandinavian restaurant near the Silk Center and the business district is known for its smorgasbord. It's popular for business lunches as well as for dinner. Scandia stays open until midnight, later than many other restaurants in the area. Expect dishes like steak tartare, marinated herring, and fried eel, and plenty of rye bread. ⊠ *1–1 Kaigan-dori, Naka-ku* ☎ *045/201–2262* ▭ *No credit cards.*

$$$$
STEAK

✕ **Serina Romanchaya** 瀬里奈 浪漫茶屋. The hallmarks of this restaurant are *ishiyaki* steak, which is grilled on a hot stone, and shabu-shabu—thin

4

slices of beef cooked in boiling water at your table and dipped in one of several sauces; choose from sesame, vinegar, or soy. Fresh vegetables, noodles, and tofu are also dipped into the seasoned broth for a filling, yet healthful meal. ⊠ *B1 Shin-Kannai Bldg., 4–45–1 Sumiyoshi-cho, Naka-ku* ☎ *045/681–2727.*

$$$
ITALIAN
☺
✕ **Yokohama Cheese Cafe** 横浜チーズカフェ. This is a cozy and inviting casual Italian restaurant, whose interior looks like an Italian country home. There are candles on the tables and an open kitchen where diners can watch the cooks making pizza. On the menu: 18 kinds of Napoli-style wood-fire–baked pizzas, 20 kinds of pastas, fondue, and other dishes that include—you guessed it—cheese. The set-course menus are reasonable, filling, and recommended. ⊠ *2–1–10 Kitasaiwai, Nishi-ku* ☎ *045/290–5656* Ⓜ *JR Yokohama Station.*

Nagoya, Ise-Shima, and the Kii Peninsula

WORD OF MOUTH

"We stayed recently at the Westin Nagoya Castle and liked it. . . . Nagoya-jo is one of my favorites in Japan as they have elevators. . . . The Noh theatre is right next door to the castle, so you can catch a Noh performance if you time it right."

—hawaiiantraveler

WELCOME TO NAGOYA, ISE-SHIMA, AND THE KII PENINSULA

TOP REASONS TO GO

★ **The Shrines:** The Grand Shrines of Ise, rebuilt every two decades for the last 1,500 years, are the most sacred in Japan.

★ **Shopping:** Nagoya's Noritake is one of the world's largest porcelain makers. Seto, Tajimi, and Tokoname produce ceramics, Arimatsu tie-dyed fabrics, Gifu paper lanterns and umbrellas, and Seki samurai swords.

★ **Japan at Work and Play:** Tour the factories of Toyota and Noritake. See the annual sumo tournament in July or Chunichi Dragons baseball games.

★ **Relive Japan's Modernization:** Meiji-mura holds more than 60 original Meiji-era buildings (1868–1912)—including the foyer of Frank Lloyd Wright's Imperial Hotel—that were reconstructed here.

★ **Eat Fish from the Bird's Mouth:** In *ukai* cormorants capture *ayu* (sweetfish), but rings around the birds' necks prevent them from swallowing their catch, which is taken by fishermen.

1 Nagoya. An ancient transport, business, and cultural hub, Nagoya combines the best of old and contemporary Japan. To the north, along the edge of the Gifu and Nagano mountains, are cormorant fishing and craft centers.

2 Ise-Shima National Park. Many people get no farther than the shrines at Ise, but just to the south is a world of bays ringed by fishing villages and oyster farms.

GETTING ORIENTED

Nagoya is between Tokyo and Kyoto, and we recommend spending a couple of days exploring the sights. The city serves as a jumping-off point for traveling south and west to Ise-Shima and the Kii Peninsula. Nagoya is on a wide plain in the main urban and industrial corridor that runs along the south side of Honshu from Tokyo as far west as Kobe. The mountains of the southern Japan Alps rise just north and east of the city, and to the west is the lush Kii Peninsula.

5

3 Kii Peninsula. Traveling west and inland on the Kii Peninsula, time slows down, with few roads and only one coastal railway line. The peninsula rewards patient explorers with beautiful wilderness and the shrines of the Kumano Kodo pilgrimage road.

4 Koya-san. Koya-san is the headquarters of the 1,200-year-old Shingon Buddhist sect and has overnight temple accommodation. This small, isolated mountain town, dotted by 117 temples, is a calm and spiritual retreat.

TOYOTA: NAGOYA'S MAINSTAY

It may sound like the kind of activity reserved for only the most dedicated of motorheads, but you don't need to be into cars to be awed by the Toyota museum and plant tour.

(This page above) Workers assembling a car in a Toyota plant; (opposite page upper right) the Prius assembly line at Toyota's Tsutsumi Plant; (opposite page bottom left) finished cars roll off the assembly line

Few things in Japan are as ubiquitous as Toyota. Working men drive Toyota trucks, families get about in its station wagons, and executives are rarely seen in anything other than a Toyota luxury sedan or limo. Even the Emperor gets driven about in one of the Aiichi automaker's creations—a custom-made, $500,000 Toyota Century Royal. Though the company has had its troubles in recent years—with heavy financial losses during the global financial crisis and then the recall of more than 8 million cars and trucks worldwide in 2009 and 2010—in Japan, Toyota is still synonymous with quality and innovation. And it's not hard to see why if you head to Toyota City (yes, a city named after the company) for a tour of one of Toyota's high-tech car plants.

WHAT'S IN A NAME?

Although the motor company was founded by Kiichiro Toyoda and early models were branded with his surname, Toyoda soon decided to drop the "da" for a "ta", and the Toyota brand was born. The reason? Firstly, "ta" sounds clearer, but more importantly, when written in katakana Toyota (トヨタ) uses 8 brush strokes, a number considered to be fortuitous. Toyoda (トヨダ) uses 10.

TOURING TOYOTA

For many the quintessential Japanese company, Toyota was a prominent figure in Japan's remarkable postwar recovery. Its success has in large part been attributed to its pioneering and integrated approach to production and management—the Toyota Production System—based around "just-in-time" production and *jidoka* (automation with a human touch). With the former, Toyota makes only what is needed, when it is needed. The latter is Toyota's way of building quality control into each stage of the production process—as you'll hear on the tour, each worker on the Toyota production line has the power to bring the entire line to a halt if they discover a defect.

The tour itself, in the company of an English-speaking guide and up to 40 other visitors, starts at 11 am with a quick bus trip to one of three nearby plants—the Motomachi Plant, where Toyota makes its Crown, Mark X, and Estima models; the Takaoka Plant, where the Corolla and iQ models are produced; or the Tsutsumi Plant, which rolls out Camry, Premio, and Prius autos. Whichever plant you end up at, the first stop, the welding shop, is designed to wow. It's a blur of machinery and sparks as state-of-the-art robots apply more than 90% of the 3,000+

welding spots it takes to secure almost 400 different parts to each car.

After that, it's briefly back on the bus and off to the main part of the tour—an hour walking above the sprawling assembly shop, watching the workers below rapidly attaching parts as the cars flow ceaselessly along the production line. All the while, against a backdrop of beeps, flashing lights, and noisy air jet blasts, the guide reels off an astonishing list of facts and figures: about 38,000 boxes of parts pass through each factory daily; a single car needs almost 30,000 parts; and around 300 cars roll off the line a day at each plant.

TOURING DETAILS

You need to be at the Kaikan (Exhibition Hall) by 10:30 am to sign in for the 11 o'clock tour, which gives ample time to explore the museum's slick exhibits on environmentally friendly technology, motor sports, safety, and Toyota's global CSR initiatives. You'll also be able to get hands-on with the latest Toyota and Lexus models, catch a quick musical performance given by Toyota's partner robot, and see a demonstration of the futuristic i-unit, a single-passenger concept vehicle that was created for the Aiichi Expo in 2005. For more details of how to reserve a tour (reservations are essential) and how to get to the Kaikan, see the separate listing.

Updated by
Rob Goss

Nagoya punches well above its weight. The present-day industries of Japan's fourth-largest city are a corollary to its *monozukuri* (art of making things) culture. This is manifested in the efficiency of Toyota's production lines, but traditional crafts including ceramics, tie-dyeing, and knife making are still very much alive. Nagoya's GDP is greater than Switzerland's, but this economic prowess is matched by a capacity to pleasantly surprise any visitor.

Nagoya purrs along contentedly, burdened neither by a second-city complex nor by hordes of tourists, and it has an agreeable small-town atmosphere. A substantial immigrant population, by Japanese standards, includes many South Americans working in local factories and provides international flavor to the city's food and entertainment choices. Among the legacies of the city's hosting of the 2005 World Expo are a well-developed tourism and transportation infrastructure.

On arrival, you will first notice the twin white skyscrapers sprouting from the ultramodern station, almost a city in itself. An extensive network of underground shopping malls stretches out in all directions below the wide, clean streets around Nagoya Station and in downtown Sakae. Above ground are huge department stores and international fashion boutiques. The even taller building opposite the station is the headquarters of the sales division of auto-making giant Toyota, the driving force of the local economy.

Within two hours' drive of the city are the revered Grand Shrines of Ise, Japan's most important Shinto site, and to the south are the quiet fishing villages of Ise-Shima National Park. On the untamed Kii Peninsula, steep-walled gorges and forested headlands give way to pristine bays, and fine sandy beaches await in Shirahama. Inland is the remarkable mountain temple town of Koya-san. Add to this some memorable *matsuri* (festivals), and this corner of Japan becomes far more than just another stop on the Shinkansen train.

See the glossary at the end of this book for definitions of the common Japanese words and suffixes used in this chapter.

PLANNING

WHEN TO GO

Spring is the most popular season, especially early April when cherry trees bloom. Nagoya gets extremely humid in July and August, but in autumn the trees turn color under blue skies. Sea breezes make coastal areas bearable in summer. Cold winds blow into Nagoya from the ski grounds to the north in winter, but Wakayama Prefecture remains mild. The weather can be changeable along the coastline of Ise-Shima, and if you're heading inland on the Kii Peninsula be prepared for hilly terrain.

GETTING HERE AND AROUND

In Nagoya subways are the easiest way to get around. Outside the city the extensive rail network will take you to most places of interest, although buses may be necessary on the remote Kii Peninsula.

AIR TRAVEL

Nagoya's compact, user-friendly Chubu International Airport (referred to locally as "Centrair") serves overseas flights and is a hub for domestic travel. Many major airlines have offices in downtown Nagoya, 45 km (28 mi) northeast of the airport, including Japan Airlines (JAL) and All Nippon Airways (ANA), both of which fly from Nagoya to most major Japanese cities. The Meitetsu Airport Limited Express train makes the 28-minute run between Centrair and Nagoya Station for ¥1,200. This price includes a seat-reservation fee.

Airline Contacts All Nippon Airways (☎ 0120/029–709 ⊕ www.ana.co.jp). **Japan Airlines** (☎ 052/265–3369 ⊕ www.jal.co.jp).

Airport Contacts Chubu Kokusai Kuko (Centrair) (☎ 0569/38–1195 daily 6:40 am–10 pm ⊕ www.centrair.jp). **Meitetsu Airport Limited Express** (✉ Meitetsu Customer Center ☎ 052/582–5151 operators available weekdays 8–7, weekends 8–6 ⊕ www.meitetsu.co.jp).

BUS TRAVEL

Highway buses operated by JR and Meitetsu connect Nagoya with major cities, including Tokyo and Kyoto. The fare is half that of the Shinkansen trains, but the journey takes three times longer.

City buses crisscross Nagoya, running either north–south or east–west. The basic fare is ¥200 and ¥100 for children—pay when you get on the bus. A one-day bus pass costs ¥600, and a combination bus/subway pass costs ¥850 (¥600 on weekends and national holidays). Detailed information on bus travel can be collected at the Tourist Information Office in the center of Nagoya Station, and day- and combination-passes are available at bus terminals and subway stations.

Bus Contacts JR Tokai Bus (☎ 052/563–0489 daily 9–7). **Meitetsu Highway Bus** (☎ 052/582–0489 daily 8–7). **Nagoya City Transportation Bureau** (☎ 052/522–0111 daily 8–7 ⊕ www.kotsu.city.nagoya.jp).

CAR TRAVEL

The journey on the two-lane expressway from Tokyo to Nagoya takes about 5 hours; from Kyoto allow 2½ hours. Major highways also connect Nagoya to Nagano, Takayama, Kanazawa, and Nara. Japanese highways are jam-prone, with holiday season traffic jams out of Tokyo

CLOSE UP

Festivals

Nagoya and the surrounding cities host a wide variety of matsuri (festivals) throughout the year. Running the gamut from chaotic to tranquil and beautiful to bizarre, these annual events bring the culture and traditions of the area to life in ways that castles, museums, and temples cannot. We have picked out a few of the best, but whenever you visit check with the Tourist Information Center or Nagoya International Center for upcoming festivals. All these events are free.

FEBRUARY

Hadaka (Naked) Festival. For 1,200 years, thousands of men aged 23 and 42 (unlucky ages in Japan) have braved the winter cold wearing nothing but *fundoshi* (loincloths). Their goal, in an event that regularly results in serious injury to participants, is to touch the *shin otoko* (the one truly "naked man") and transmit their bad spirits to him before he reaches Konomiya shrine and submits to cleansing rituals. Eagerness to achieve this task often leads to dangerous stampedes, but the crowds of more than 100,000 are well protected from harm. The festival is held in the first half of February—contact Nagoya City Tourist Information Center in JR Nagoya Station for details. Konomiya Station is 15 minutes north of Nagoya on the Meitetsu Gifu Line, and the shrine is a 10-minute walk from the station.

MARCH

Honen Festival. The 1,500-year-old Tagata-jinja in Komaki is home to one of Japan's infamous male fertility festivals. On March 15 large crowds gather to watch and take pictures of a 6-foot, 885-pound *owasegata* (phallus) being carried between two shrines and

offered to the *kami* (god) for peace and a good harvest. The festival starts at 10 am and climaxes with face-size "lucky" rice cakes being tossed into the crowd just before 4 pm. The closest station is Tagata-jinja-mae on the Meitetsu Komaki Line. Change at Inuyama if you are traveling from Nagoya. The train takes one hour.

JULY

Owari Tsushima Tenno Festival. The main feature of this charming, low-key event is five boats decorated with 365 paper lanterns (for the days of the year) arranged into a circular shape and 12 more (representing the months) hanging from a mast. The festival occurs the fourth Saturday and Sunday in July. Haunting traditional music accompanies the boats as they drift lazily around the river and the lanterns and fireworks reflect in the water. Tsushima is 25 minutes west of Nagoya on the Meitetsu Bisai Line. Follow the crowds west from the station for about 15 minutes to the shrine and festival area.

AUGUST

Domannaka. More than 20,000 dancers in troupes of up to 150 dancers each arrive from all over Japan to take over Nagoya's streets and public spaces. Started in 1999, this energetic festival has rapidly gained popularity. It mixes hip-hop beats with spiced-up traditional dance moves and colorful costumes. Domannaka takes place over a weekend in late August. The exact dates and locations change from year to year, so get the latest details from Nagoya City Tourist Information Center in JR Nagoya Station.

sometimes reaching 100 km (60 mi) in length. Signage is confusing, so be sure to get a car with satellite navigation or a good road map.

Wide main streets make Nagoya relatively easy to navigate. Road signs in the city often point to places out of town, however, so a detailed map is advised.

TRAIN TRAVEL

Frequent bullet trains run between Tokyo and Nagoya. The ride takes 1 hour, 48 minutes on the *Hikari* Shinkansen and 2½ hours on the slower *Kodama* Shinkansen, and costs ¥10,380. The trip west to Kyoto takes 50 minutes, and Shin-Osaka just over 1 hour. JR Passes are not accepted on the faster *Nozomi* Shinkansen, which does the journey from Tokyo in 1 hour, 43 minutes and costs ¥10,580. Less-expensive Limited Express trains proceed from Nagoya into and across the Japan Alps—to Takayama, Toyama, Matsumoto, and Nagano.

ABOUT THE RESTAURANTS

Restaurants in Nagoya and on the peninsulas are slightly less expensive than in Tokyo. Your cheapest options are the noodle shops, *donburi* (rice bowl) chains, and *kaiten* (revolving) sushi and curry houses. Franchised restaurants often have English alongside Japanese on their menus, but don't expect the staff to know more than a few words.

ABOUT THE HOTELS

Nagoya's lodging ranges from *ryokan* (traditional Japanese inns) and efficient business hotels to large luxury palaces. At Koya-san, temple accommodation is a fascinating experience. Furnishings in temples are spartan but sufficient, and the food is strictly vegetarian. You may be invited to attend early-morning prayer service. In addition to holidays, hotels can be busy in October and November owing to conferences held in Nagoya and autumn foliage outside the city. The large hotels in downtown Nagoya have English-speaking staff, but it's advisable to ask the Tourist Information Center to make reservations for you outside the city.

For a short course on accommodations in Japan, see Accommodations in Travel Smart.

WHAT IT COSTS IN YEN					
	¢	$	$$	$$$	$$$$
Restaurants	under ¥800	¥800–¥1,000	¥1,000–¥2,000	¥2,000–¥3,000	over ¥3,000
Hotels	under ¥8,000	¥8,000–¥12,000	¥12,000–¥18,000	¥18,000–¥22,000	over ¥22,000

Restaurant prices are per person for a main course, set meal, or equivalent combination of smaller dishes at dinner. Hotel prices are for a double room with private bath, excluding service and tax.

VISITOR INFORMATION

The **Nagoya International Center** 名古屋国際センター, or Kokusai Senta, as it's locally known, is a wise stop on any Nagoya itinerary. Multilingual staff have a wealth of information on Nagoya and the surrounding area, and the center publishes a monthly newsletter, "Nagoya

Calendar," which gives up-to-date advice, information, and event listings in English. It is one stop from JR Nagoya Station on the Sakura-dori subway line or a seven-minute walk through the underground walkway that follows the line.

Contacts Nagoya International Center ✉ *1–47–1 Nakono, Nakamura-ku* ☎ *052/581–0100* ⊕ *www.nic-nagoya.or.jp/en* ⊙ *Tues.–Sun. 9–7).*

NAGOYA 名古屋

366 km (227 mi) southwest of Tokyo, 190 km (118 mi) east of Osaka, 148 km (92 mi) east of Kyoto.

In 1612, shogun Ieyasu Tokugawa established Nagoya by permitting his ninth son to build a castle here. Industry and merchant houses sprang up in the shadow of this magnificent fortress, as did pleasure quarters for samurai. Supported by taxing the rich harvests of the surrounding Nobi plain, the Tokugawa family used the castle as its power center for the next 250 years.

After the Meiji Restoration in 1868, when Japan began trade with the West in earnest, Nagoya developed rapidly. When the harbor opened to international shipping in 1907, Nagoya's industrial growth accelerated, and by the 1930s it was supporting Japanese expansionism in China with munitions and aircraft. This choice of industry was Nagoya's downfall; very little of the city was left standing after World War II.

Less than two months after the war, ambitious and extensive reconstruction plans were laid, and Nagoya began its remarkable comeback as an industrial metropolis. Planners laid down a grid system, with wide avenues intersecting at right angles. Hisaya-odori, a broad avenue with a park in its 328-foot-wide median, bisects the city. At Nagoya's center is an imposing 590-foot-high television tower (useful for getting your bearings). Nagoya-jo is north of the tower, Atsuta Jingu to the south, Higashiyama-koen east, and the JR Station west. The Sakae subway station serves as the center of the downtown commercial area. Today Nagoya is home to 2.3 million people living in a 510-square-km (197-square-mi) area.

GETTING HERE AND AROUND

BY AIR

International flights from major airlines arrive at Nagoya's Chubu International Airport, and frequent bullet trains make it easy to access Nagoya from Tokyo and Kyoto.

BY BUS

The golden **Nagoya Sightseeing Route Bus,** known to locals as the *Meguru,* provides cheap tours of the city. The service runs on a loop from Nagoya Station, via Noritake Garden, Nagoya-jo, the Tokugawa Art Museum, and Sakae. A hop-on, hop-off ticket for the day, which can be bought on the bus, costs ¥500, and offers discounts for certain attractions.

Bus Contacts **Nagoya Sightseeing Route Bus** (☎ *052/521–8990* ⊕ *www.ncvb. or.jp/routebus/en).*

BY TAXI

Taxis are parked at all major stations and hotels. Elsewhere it is still far easier to wave one down on the street than to call one of the Japanese-speaking reservation numbers. The initial fare is ¥500. A ride from Nagoya Station to Nagoya-jo costs about ¥1,200.

BY TRAIN AND SUBWAY

All Nagoya's stations have bilingual maps, and many trains have English announcements. The Higashiyama Line snakes from the west into JR Nagoya Station and then goes due east, cutting through the city center at Sakae. The Meijo Line runs in a loop, passing through the city center at downtown Sakae. A spur line, the Meito, connects Kanayama to Nagoya Port. The Tsurumai Line runs north–south through the city, then turns from the JR Station to Sakae to cross the city center. A fourth line, the Sakura-dori, cuts through the city center from the JR Station, paralleling the east–west section of the Higashiyama Line. The basic fare is ¥200. A one-day pass for Nagoya's subways costs ¥740, while a combination bus/subway pass is ¥850 on weekdays and ¥600 (Weekend Eco Pass) on weekends or national holidays.

The JR trains are the easiest for jumping on and off, but they do not serve all destinations. Meitetsu and Kintetsu stations are lacking in English signage, though Meitetsu prints a handy English-language guide to their network with instructions on how to purchase tickets. You can pick up a copy at Meitetsu Nagoya Station or Chubu International Airport.

Nagoya's subway system is user-friendly, with signs and announcements in English, and it can get you to almost all places of interest in the city. If you are staying a few days, consider purchasing a *Yurika* discount ticket for multiple trips. Yurika tickets can also be used on city buses and some Meitetsu trains.

JR Nagoya Station 名古屋駅 is like a small city, with a variety of shops in, under, and around the station complex. The main **Nagoya City Tourist Information Center** is in the station's central corridor. English-speaking staff can supply sightseeing information, subway maps, and details of upcoming events. Smaller information centers are in three other parts of the city—**Sakae, Kanayama,** and **Nagoya Port.**

Train Contacts **JR Central Japan** (☎ 050/3772–3910 daily 6–midnight ⊕ www. jr-central.co.jp). **Kintetsu** (☎ 052/561–1604 daily 9–7). **Meitetsu** (✉ Meitetsu Customer Center ☎ 052/582–5151 ⊘ Weekdays 8–7, weekends 8–6 ⊕ www. meitetsu.co.jp).

VISITOR INFORMATION

Kanayama (✉ North Exit of Kanayama Station ☎ 052/323–0161 ⊘ Daily 9–7). **Nagoya City Tourist Information Center** (☎ 052/541–4301 ⊘ Daily 9–7). **Nagoya Port** (✉ Next to Nagoya-ko subway station ☎ 052/654–7000 ⊘ Tues.–Sun. 9–5).

Sakae (✉ Oasis 21 Bus Station and Shopping Center ☎ 052/963–5252 ⊘ Daily 10–8).

5

The Tokugawa Art Museum in Nagoya owns the original 12th-century scrolls for *The Tale of Genji*.

EXPLORING

TOP ATTRACTIONS

★ **Tokugawa Art Museum** 徳川美術館 *(Tokugawa Bijutsukan)*. The seldom-displayed 12th-century hand scrolls of *The Tale of Genji*, widely recognized as the world's first novel, are housed here. Even when the scrolls are not available, beautiful relics of the lifestyle of the aristocratic, premodern samurai class—including swords and armor, tea-ceremony artifacts, Noh masks, clothing, and furnishings—fascinate visitors. If you're visiting specifically to see the scrolls, call the museum to make sure they are on display; if not, look for a later copy in Room 6. Or visit the Hosa Library rooms, which house an incredible collection of other ancient scrolls and texts, some dating to the 8th century. If you've got time, it's worth paying an additional ¥150 for entry to the adjacent **Tokugawaen** 徳川園, an attractive Japanese garden modeled in the Edo style. Tokugawa Art Museum is a 10-minute walk south of Ozone Station, which is on the Meijo subway line and the JR Chuo Line. ⌂ *1017 Tokugawa-cho, Higashi-ku* ☏ *052/935–6262* ⊕ *www.tokugawa-art-museum.jp* ✉ *¥1,200* ⏱ *Museum Jan. 4–mid-Dec., Tues.–Sun. 10–5; garden Jan. 4–mid-Dec., Tues.–Sun. 9:30–5:30.*

Fodor's Choice ★ **Toyota Plant Tour** トヨタ工場見学. Dropping in at an automobile factory might not be everyone's idea of holiday fun, but a Toyota Plant Tour makes all those dry books about *kaizen* (improvement) and the Japanese postwar economic miracle come to life. The tour starts at the **Toyota Kaikan** トヨタ会館 (Toyota Exhibition Hall), with impressive exhibits on environmentally friendly technology, safety, and motor sports. Then a company bus whisks you to one of several giant factories in the vicinity, where a guide takes you around the main welding and assembly shops—hives of modern manufacturing activity where man and machine operate as one. English guides are available at the Kaikan and factory for the two- to three-hour tour. The Kaikan is about 90 minutes from Nagoya Station. Take the JR Tokaido Line Special Rapid service to Okazaki Station, then the Aichi Kanjo local service (platform #0) to Mikawa Toyota Station, from where it's a 15-minute walk or five-minute taxi to the Kaikan. At Okazaki, be sure to get on one of the front two carriages of the Aichi Kanjo Line; only these carriages go as far as Toyota Mikawa. ■ TIP→ Reservations are required for the plant tour, and should ideally be made at least two weeks in advance; this can be done in English, either online or by phone. ⊠ *Toyota Kaikan Exhibition Hall 1, Toyota-cho* ☎ *0565/23–3922* ⊕ *www.toyota.co.jp/en/about_toyota/ facility/toyota_kaikan* ⊠ *Free* ⊘ *Mon.–Sat. 9:30–5 except national and summer holidays, and Toyota company holidays.* Tours once a day weekdays *from 10:30.*

WORTH NOTING

OFF THE
BEATEN
PATH

Arimatsu-Narumi Shibori Kaikan 有松鳴海絞会館 *(Arimatsu Tie-Dyeing Museum).* Arimatsu has been producing *shibori* (tie-dyed cotton) for 400 years. The active tie-dyeing houses and traditional clay-wall buildings line a preserved stretch of the old road that connected Edo-era Tokyo with Kyoto. At Arimatsu-Narumi Tie-Dyeing Museum (Arimatsu-Narumi Shibori Kaikan), for ¥300 you can learn about the history and techniques of the dyeing process and see demonstrations of current production. The museum sells samples of the cloth, which features striking bright white designs on the deepest indigo, as well as tie-dyed clothing and home furnishings like tablecloths. You can also try making your own tie-dyed souvenirs at one of the regular workshops, which require a reservation and start at ¥1,050. Arimatsu Station is 20 minutes south of Nagoya on the Meitetsu Nagoya Line. ⊠ *60–1 Hashi-higashi-minami, Arimatsu-cho, Midori-ku* ☎ *052/621–0111* ⊕ *www. shibori-kaikan.com* ⊠ *Free* ⊘ *Thurs.–Tues. 9:30–5.*

Atsuta Jingu 熱田神宮. A shrine has stood at the site of Atsuta Jingu for 1,700 years. After Ise, this is the country's most important Shinto shrine. The **Homotsukan** (Treasure House) is reputed to house one of the Emperor's three imperial regalia—the Kusanagi-no-Tsurugi (Grass-Mowing Sword)—and although it is never on public display, there are many other worthy artifacts to see. Nestled among 1,000-year-old trees, making it easy to spot from the train, the shrine is an oasis of tradition in the midst of modern industrialism. Sixty festivals and 10 religious events are held here each year—check with the tourist office to see what's going on. From Meitetsu Nagoya Station take the Meitetsu Nagoya Line south to Jingumae Station. The shrine is across the road from the West Exit. ⊠ *Atsuta-ku* ☎ *052/671–4151* ⊕ *www.atsutajingu. or.jp/en/intro* ⊠ *Shrine free, Treasure House ¥300* ⊘ *Daily 9–4:30; closed last Wed. and Thurs. of month.*

Nagoya-jo 名古屋城. This castle is notable for its size and for the pair of gold-plated dolphins—one male, one female—mounted atop the *donjon* (principal keep). Built on land artificially raised from the flat Nagoya plain, the castle is protected by vast stone walls and two picturesque

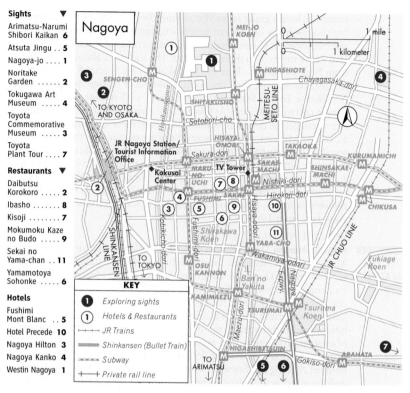

Nagoya

MEI-JO KOEN

HIGASHIOTE

Chayagasaka-dori

SENGEN-CHO

SHIYAKUSHO

Horikawagawa

TO KYOTO
AND OSAKA

Sotobori-cho

HISAYA-ONORI-dori

TAKAOKA

KURUMAMICHI

JR Nagoya Station/
Tourist Information
Office

Sakura-dori

SHINSAKAE-MACHI

Kokusai
Center

MARU-NO-UCHI

TV Tower

SAKAE-MACHI

Nishiki-dori

Hirokoji-dori

CHIKUSA

FUSHIMI

Hisaya-odori

Kobikicho-dori

Shirakawa
Koen

YABA-CHO

Wakamiya-odori

Fukiage
Koen

Fushimi-dori

OSU
KANNON

Ban'no
Yakuta

Maezu-dori

JR CHUO LINE

KAMIMAEZU

TSURUMAI

Tsuruma
Koen

SHINKANSEN LINE

TO
TOKYO

HIGASHIBETSUIN

TO
ARIMATSU

Gokiso-dori

ARAHATA

KEY

❶ *Exploring sights*

① *Hotels & Restaurants*

┝┷┥ *JR Trains*

═══ *Shinkansen (Bullet Train)*

╌╌╌ *Subway*

┼─┼ *Private rail line*

moats. The current castle is a 1959 reconstruction of the 1612 original, and an elevator whisks you between floors. Between the entrance and the top floor, which has 360-degree views of modern-day Nagoya, are five floors of exhibits. On the third floor is an evocative re-creation of Edo-era streets, complete with sound effects. The fifth floor has several hands-on exhibits, including a full-scale replica of the 2,673-pound female dolphin that you can clamber all over. Inside the east gate a traditional teahouse built of *hinoki* (Japanese cypress) stands in the otherwise unspectacular **Ninomaru Tei-en** (Ninomaru Gardens), where a traditional tea ceremony costs ¥500. Nagoya-jo's east gate is one block north of the Shiyakusho (City Hall) subway station. ⊠ *Honmaru, Nishi-ku* ☎ *052/231–1700* 🎟 *¥500* ☉ *Castle daily 9–4:30, garden daily 9–5.*

Noritake Garden ノリタケの森. Delicate colors and intricate hand-painted designs characterize the china of Noritake, one of the world's largest manufacturers of porcelain. Its garden complex includes a craft center—effectively a mini-factory where workers demonstrate the 15-step manufacturing process from modeling to glazing to hand painting. You can even paint a design and transfer it to a piece of china. Workshops run 10 am to 4 pm and cost from ¥1,800 plus the price of shipping your piece once it has been fired (only plates can be shipped overseas). The upper floors house a small museum displaying "Old Noritake" works with art nouveau and art deco influences. Browsing is free in the "Celabo" area in the Welcome Center, which shows the diverse industrial applications of ceramics, from circuit boards to racing helmets. There's the odd bargain to be found in the outlet section of the company shop. Noritake Garden is a 15-minute walk north of JR Nagoya Station or five minutes from the Kamejima subway station. ✉ *3–1–36 Noritake-Shinmachi, Nishi-ku* ☎ *052/561–7114 craft center, 052/561–7290 shop* ☉ *Craft center Tues.–Sun. 10–5, shop Tues.–Sun. 10–6* 💰 *Craft center and museum ¥500; joint entrance with Toyota Commemorative Museum ¥800.*

♻ **Toyota Commemorative Museum of Industry and Technology** 産業技術記念館. Housed in the distinctive redbrick buildings of the company's original factory, this museum is dedicated to the rise of Nagoya's most famous company. Toyota's textile-industry origins are explored in the first of two immense halls, with an amazing selection of looms illustrating the evolution of spinning and weaving technologies over the last 200 years. The second, even larger hall focuses on the company's move into auto manufacturing. The museum's main aim is to interest today's Japanese schoolchildren in Nagoya's traditional monozukuri (art of making things) industrial culture, and the intimidatingly large halls are broken up into interactive display areas. In the Technoland room you can try out a wind tunnel, navigate a virtual reality maze, and use a massive lever to easily lift a 265-pound engine. The museum is a 20-minute walk north of JR Nagoya Station or 10 minutes from the Kamejima subway station. ✉ *4–1–35 Noritake-Shinmachi, Nishi-ku* ☎ *052/551–6115* ⊕ *www.tcmit.org* ☉ *Tues.–Sun. 9:30–5* 💰 *Museum ¥500; joint entrance with Noritake Garden ¥800.*

WHERE TO EAT

Nagoya Station and Sakae have the highest concentrations of restaurants.

$$–$$$
IZAKAYA

✕ **Daibutsu Korokoro** 大仏ころころ. This *izakaya* (traditional) restaurant has several twists, the main one being the decor. Modern Japanese restaurants should all look like this—dark wood, discreet lighting, and a maze of private dining rooms. A 9½-foot-tall bronze Buddha is in the middle of the restaurant. If anything, the fancy trappings slightly overshadow the food, which includes decent sashimi sets and some inventive tofu dishes. The restaurant is across from the main post office, 1½ blocks north of JR Nagoya Station's Sakura-dori Exit. ✉ *B1 Kuwayama Bldg., 2–45–19 Meieki, Nakamura-ku* ☎ *052/581–9130.*

$$–$$$
JAPANESE
★

✕ **Ibasho** いば昇. This fabulous old wooden restaurant serves a Nagoya specialty, *hitsumabushi* (chopped eel smothered in miso sauce and served on rice), which fills the restaurant with a mouthwatering, grilled-charcoal aroma. Some of the seating is at low tables on raised tatami-mat flooring, though there are also rustic tables and chairs overlooking a small Japanese garden. Ibasho is on Motoshigecho-dori, two blocks west from Exit 1 of Sakae subway station. The restaurant closes at 8 pm. ✉ *3–13–22 Nishiki, Naka-ku* ☎ *052/951–1166* 💳 *No credit cards* ☉ *Closed Sun. and the 2nd and 3rd Mon. of each month.*

On the Menu

Nagoya cuisine is considered hearty, and is famous for its *aka miso* (red miso). Dishes featuring this sticky, sweet paste include *misonikomi udon*, thick noodles cooked in an earthenware pot of miso soup with chicken, egg, wood mushrooms, and green onions (you may want the chili pepper served on the side); *hitsumabushi*, chopped eel cooked in miso; and *miso katsu*, pork cutlet with miso-flavored sauce.

Other local specialties include *kishimen*, velvety smooth flat white noodles; *tebasaki*, deep-fried spicy chicken wings; and *uiro*, a sweet cake made of rice powder and sugar, eaten during the tea ceremony. The highly prized *ko-chin* is a specially fattened and extremely tender kind of chicken.

$$$$
JAPANESE

✕ **Kisoji** 木曽路. Come here for reasonably priced *shabu-shabu*—thinly sliced beef and vegetables that you boil in broth in the center of your table and then dip into various sauces before eating. Set courses run from ¥3,800 to ¥10,000. There are Western-style tables and chairs, but waitresses wear kimonos. Kisoji is two blocks northwest of the Sakae intersection, on the corner of Nishiki-dori and Shichiken-cho. ✉ *3–20–15 Nishiki, Naka-ku* ☎ *052/951–3755.*

$$–$$$
JAPANESE
★

✕ **Mokumoku Kaze no Budo** モクモク風の葡萄. In a perfect world, all school and office canteens would be a bit more like this. For ¥2,300 (¥1,800 at lunchtime) you get all you can eat from a generously stocked buffet of healthy vegetable, fish, and meat dishes, plus drinks and dessert, all made from locally sourced produce. It is on the seventh floor of the La Chic mall in Sakae. ✉ *7F La Chic, 3–6–1 Sakae, Naka-ku* ☎ *052/241–0909.*

$$
IZAKAYA

✕ **Sekai no Yama-chan** 世界の山ちゃん. Pepper-coated *tebasaki* (deep-fried spicy chicken wings) are the specialty at the main branch of Nagoya's most well-known izakaya chain, though you can also get other decent izakaya fare, such as sashimi. With most dishes costing around ¥400 to ¥500, the prices are good, too. Yama-chan is a no-frills place with a mix of traditional and Western-style seating, and the atmosphere is lively. It's a five-minute walk from Exit 13 of Sakae Station, directly behind the Hotel Precede. ✉ *4–9–6 Sakae, Naka-ku* ☎ *052/242–1342* ⊕ *www.yamachan.co.jp.*

$–$$
JAPANESE

✕ **Yamamotoya Sohonke** 山本屋総本家. *Misonikomi udon* (udon noodles in a hearty, miso-based broth with green onions and mushrooms) dominates the menu at this simple restaurant. A big, steaming bowl of this hearty, cold-chasing specialty starts at just ¥976. It is halfway between the Fushimi and Yaba-cho subway stations, across the road from the eye-catching Nadya Park Building. ✉ *3–12–19 Sakae, Naka-ku* ☎ *052/241–5617* ▭ *No credit cards.*

WHERE TO STAY

Nagoya's hotels are concentrated in three major areas: the district around JR Nagoya Station, downtown Fushimi and Sakae, and the Nagoya-jo area.

Hotel reviews have been condensed for this book. Please go to Fodors. com for full reviews of each property.

$ **Fushimi Mont Blanc Hotel** 伏見モンブランホテル. Centrally located and HOTEL   comparatively inexpensive, this business hotel is a good alternative to the more expensive luxury hotels. **Pros:** affordable; good front desk service; less than 10 minutes' walk into central Sakae. **Cons:** rooms feel a little claustrophobic; can be noisy at times. ⊠ *2–2–26 Sakae, Naka-ku* ☎ *052/232–1121* ⊕ *www.montblanc-hotel.co.jp* ⌂ *In-room: a/c, refrigerator, Internet. In-hotel: 2 restaurants, laundry facilities, laundry service* ⑩ *No meals.*

$$–$$$ **Hotel Precede Nagoya** ホテルプリシード名古屋. Bridging the divide HOTEL   between perfunctory business hotels and more-deluxe accommodations, this hotel has garnered good reviews from Japanese travelers. **Pros:** good value; convenient location for shoppers and party animals; spacious single rooms. **Cons:** budget travelers will find cheaper rooms elsewhere. ⊠ *4–6–1 Sakae, Naka-ku* ☎ *052/263–3411* ⊕ *www.hotel-precede.com* ⌂ *In-room: a/c, refrigerator, Internet. In-hotel: 2 restaurants, laundry service, Internet terminal, parking (paid)* ⑩ *No meals.*

$$$$ **Nagoya Hilton** ヒルトン名古屋. This large business hotel is a reli-HOTEL   able, albeit expensive, option in Nagoya. **Pros:** attentive and flexible ★   staff; convenient location; excellent restaurants. **Cons:** Internet costs extra; tiny swimming pool. ⊠ *1–3–3 Sakae, Naka-ku* ☎ *052/212–1111* ⊕ *www.hilton.com* ↵ *434 rooms, 16 suites* ⌂ *In-room: a/c, safe, Internet. In-hotel: 4 restaurants, bar, room service, tennis court, pool, gym, laundry service, parking (paid), some pets allowed* ⑩ *No meals.*

$$$–$$$$ **Nagoya Kanko Hotel** 名古屋観光ホテル. The Imperial Family and pro-HOTEL   fessional ballplayers are among those served by Nagoya's oldest hotel. Fodor's Choice   **Pros:** exceptional service; free parking; good breakfast buffet. **Cons:** ★   might be a little old-fashioned for some. ⊠ *1–19–30 Nishiki, Naka-ku, Aichi-ken* ☎ *052/231–7711* ⊕ *www.nagoyakankohotel.co.jp* ↵ *375 rooms, 7 suites* ⌂ *In-room: a/c, safe (some), refrigerator, Internet. In-hotel: 5 restaurants, room service, bar, gym, laundry service, parking (free)* ⑩ *No meals.*

$$$$ **The Westin Nagoya Castle** ウェスティンナゴヤキャッスルホテル. Perched HOTEL   on the bank of the Nagoya Castle moat, this hotel is a perennial favorite among elderly travelers and has a more relaxed atmosphere than some of the other places in the city. **Pros:** close to the castle; 1 pm check-in is perfect for sightseers; good facilities. **Cons:** inconvenient for every-where except the castle; in a particularly quiet part of town. ⊠ *3–19 Hinokuchi-cho, Nishi-ku* ☎ *052/521–2121* ⊕ *www.castle.co.jp/wnc* ↵ *195 rooms, 5 suites* ⌂ *In-room: a/c, safe (some), Internet. In-hotel: 8 restaurants, room service, bars, pool, gym, spa, children's programs, laundry service, parking (free)* ⑩ *No meals.*

5

NIGHTLIFE

Sakae has a high concentration of restaurants and bars. By day couples and families pack its streets, flitting between boutiques and department stores; at night the area fills with pleasure seekers of all stripes. Most of the good bars are to be found in the narrow streets to the southwest of the Sakae subway station and in the immediate vicinity of the TV tower. Anywhere designated as a "snack" establishment (a kind of hostess club) is best avoided unless you've got money to burn on overpriced drinks and female company.

Elephant's Nest. Close to Exit 5 of the Fushimi subway station, toward the Hilton hotel, is this popular English-style pub that has Guinness (¥1,000 per pint) on tap, dartboards, and live soccer on the TV. The food, including fish-and-chips, is okay, too. Happy hour is from 5:30 to 7. ⊠ *3–1–4 Sakae, Naka-ku* ☎ *052/232–4360* ⊘ *Sun.–Thurs. 5:30–1, Fri. and Sat. 5:30–2.*

iD Café. The young crowd gathers at the wild, five-floor club. On weekday evenings entrance costs ¥1,500, including three drinks. The price rises to ¥2,000 on weekends, as does the number of drinks. ⊠ *Mitsukoshi Bldg., 3–1–15 Sakae, Naka-ku* ☎ *052/251–0382.*

Marumikanko Building. Nagoya is regularly included on international DJs' tour schedules, although you might have to head out on a weekday night to catch the biggest names. Expect to pay between ¥1,500 and ¥2,500 for admission (usually including a couple of drinks) at most clubs, depending on the event. Three of the city's best clubs can be found in this building, two blocks south of Hirokoji-dori. **Café Domina** (☎ *052/264–3134* ⊕ *www.cafe-domina.com*), in the basement, leans toward more abstract and bass-heavy fare. **Club JB's** (☎ *052/241–2234* ⊕ *www.club-jbs.jp*), also in the basement, is a stronghold for house and techno. **Underground** (☎ *052/242–1388* ⊕ *www.underground.co.jp*), on the third and fourth floors, serves up a steady diet of hip-hop and R&B without the ghetto pretensions of some of the other joints in town. ⊠ *4–3–15 Sakae, Naka-ku.*

SPECTATOR SPORTS

In Nagoya you will find Japanese sports fans just as entertaining as the action on the field. Ask Tourist Information about upcoming events and where to buy tickets.

BASEBALL

The Chunichi Dragons play home games at the 40,500-capacity Nagoya Dome. Two leagues of six teams make up Japanese professional baseball, and the Dragons have won the Central League pennant seven times and the Japan Series twice. In recent years the team is in a groove, reaching the Japan Series in 2004 and 2006 before finally winning it—for the first time since 1954—in 2007. They came close again in 2010, this time losing a nail-biting Japan Series to Chiba Lotte Marines in extra innings in game seven. Fans here are a bit different—they sing well-drilled songs for each of the batters on their own team, but sit in stony silence when the opposing team is at bat. The season runs from

April to October, and tickets for the upper-tier "Panorama" seats start at ¥1,500, rising to ¥5,800 for those behind home plate. Other than when a big team such as the Yomiuri Giants or Hanshin Tigers is in town, tickets are usually available at the stadium.

SOCCER

The remarkably loyal fans that turn up in the thousands to cheer on Nagoya Grampus finally had something to cheer about in 2010, as the team romped to a first J-League Division One title. Until then, Grampus had a reputation as perennial underachievers, always seeming to hang around mid-table in J-League 1—despite having had star players such as Gary Lineker and Dragan Stojkovic (now the head coach)—and managing a couple of Emperor's Cup wins. From March to December they play half their home games in Nagoya at the 20,000-seat Mizuho Stadium, where the running track dissipates the atmosphere, and half at the futuristic 45,000-seat Toyota Stadium. Tickets on game day range in price from ¥2,000 to ¥7,000

SUMO

In mid-July Nagoya's Aichi Prefectural Gymnasium, situated next to the castle, hosts one of the three sumo tournaments held outside Tokyo each year. The arena holds 8,000 people, and you are almost guaranteed a good view of the *dohyo* (ring). Tickets, with costs starting at ¥2,800, are often available on the day of the tournament, but it's better to make advance reservations, particularly in the second half of the two-week event. The venue is a two-minute walk from Exit 7 of the Shiyakusho subway station. ✉ *Aichi Prefectural Gymnasium, 1–1 Ninomaru, Naka-ku* ☎ *052/962–9300 ticket sales during the tournament* ⊕ *www.sumo.or.jp* ▭ *AE, DC, MC, V.*

SOUTH GIFU-KEN

Old Japan resonates in the foothills of the Hida Sanmyaku (Hida Mountains), just north of Nagoya. Ancient customs and crafts, such as cormorant fishing and umbrella-, lantern-, pottery-, and sword making, are still practiced, and the nation's oldest castle, Inuyama-jo, has seen it all for almost 500 years. Gifu is the main center of *ukai* (cormorant fishing). Inuyama also offers the fishing experience, and it boasts a superior castle and, in Meiji-mura, an outstanding museum.

GIFU 岐阜

30 km (18 mi) northwest of Nagoya.

Gifu's main attraction is its 1,300-year tradition of cormorant fishing. The city center spreads several blocks north from the JR and Meitetsu stations. Extensive rebuilding after World War II didn't create the prettiest place, but there is plenty going on. *Wagasa* (oiled paper umbrellas) are handmade in small family-owned shops, and *chochin* (paper lanterns) and laquered *uchiwa* fans are also produced locally. If you are interested in seeing these items being made, ask Tourist Information for workshops that allow visitors.

GETTING HERE AND AROUND

Gifu is a 20-minute ride on the JR Tokaido Line or Meitetsu Nagoya Line from Nagoya. Gifu Park is 15 minutes by bus or 30 minutes on foot north from JR Gifu Station.

A city Tourist Information Office is on the second floor of the train station, just outside the ticket gates.

ESSENTIALS

Visitor Information Tourist Information Office (✉ *JR Gifu Station* ☎ *058/262–4415* ◷ *Dec.–Feb., daily 10–6; Mar.–Nov., daily 10–7*).

WHAT TO SEE

Gifu City Museum of History 岐阜市歴史博物館. In Gifu Park, five minutes' walk south of the cable-car station, is this well-presented hands-on-museum. On the second floor you can dress up in traditional clothing and play old Japanese games such as *bansugoroku* (similar to backgammon). ✉ *2–18–1 Omiya-cho* ☎ *058/265–0010* ✐ *¥300* ◷ *Tues.–Sun. 9–5.*

Gifu-jo 岐阜城. The castle, perched dramatically on top of Mt. Kinka, overlooks the city center and Nagara River. The current building dates from 1951; the 16th-century structure was destroyed by an 1891 earthquake. A cable-car ride up from Gifu Park (¥600 one-way, ¥1,050 round-trip) gets you to the castle in 10 minutes, or you can walk the 2.3-km (1.5-mi) path to the 329-meter summit in about an hour. Take any bus (except the N80 service) from bus stops 12 and 13 to Gifu Park (¥200). ✉ *Gifu-jo, Omiya-cho* ☎ *058/263–4853* ✐ *¥200* ◷ *Mid-Mar.–mid-Oct. daily 9–5:30; mid-Oct.–mid-Mar., daily 9:30–4:30.*

Nawa Insect Museum 名和昆虫博物館. Located in Gifu Park, this museum houses disturbingly large beetles, colorful butterflies, and other bugs. ✉ *2–18 Omiya-cho* ☎ *058/263–0038* ✐ *¥500* ◷ *Late July–Aug., Fri.–Wed. 10–5; Sept.–late July, Fri.–Wed. 9–6.*

OFF THE
BEATEN
PATH

Sangyo Shinko Center 産業振興センター *(Seki Swordsmith Museum)*. Seki has a 700-year-old sword-manufacturing heritage, and you'll appreciate the artistry and skill of Japanese sword smiths at this museum dedicated to their craft. Three types of metal are used to form blades, which are forged multiple times and then beaten into shape with a hammer. Demonstrations are held three times a day (at 10, 1:30, and 2:30) on January 2 and the first Sunday of March, April, June, and November. Special displays occur during the Seki Cutlery Festival the second weekend of October. Seki is 30 minutes northeast of Gifu via the Meitetsu Minomachi Line. ✉ *9–1 Minamikasuga-cho, Seki* ☎ *0575/23–3825* ✐ *¥200* ◷ *Wed.–Mon. 9–4:30.*

Shoho-ji 正法寺. The temple building is rather run-down, but it houses Japan's third-largest Buddha. This imposing incarnation of Shaka Nyorai (Great Buddha) is 45 feet tall and constructed of pasted-together paper *sutra* (prayers) coated with clay and stucco and then lacquered and gilded; it took 38 years to complete. From Gifu Park, walk two blocks south. ✉ *8 Daibutsu-cho* ☎ *058/264–2760* ✐ *¥150* ◷ *Apr.–Nov., daily 9–5; Dec.–Mar., daily 9–4.*

Nighttime cormorant fishing (called ukai) is a top attraction in Gifu.

Ukai 鵜飼い. Cormorant fishing (in which a fisherman uses a live, captive cormorant as a means of catching fish in the river) can be seen for free from the banks of the Nagara-gawa, just east of Nagara Bridge at around 7:30 pm each evening from May 11 to October 15. Or you can buy a ticket for one of approximately 130 boats, each carrying from 10 to 30 spectators. Allow two hours for an ukai outing—an hour and a half to eat and drink (bring your own food if you haven't arranged for dinner on board) and a half hour to watch the fishing. Boat trips (¥3,300) begin at around 6 pm nightly; reservations, made through Gifu City Cormorant Fishing Sightseeing Office or the Tourist Information Center, are essential. There's no fishing on the autumn full moon. ☎ *058/262–0104 Gifu City Cormorant Fishing Sightseeing Office, 058/262–4415 Tourist Information Office.*

WHERE TO EAT

$–$$
JAPANESE
✕ **U no Iori U** 鵜の庵鵜. Cormorants strut around the Japanese garden outside this café, where the specialty is *ayu* (sweetfish). The owner boasts of upholding the 1,300-year-old local ukai tradition, and the ayu are prepared every way imaginable. Most popular are *ayu-zosui*, a rice porridge, and *ayu-no-narezushi*, a kind of reverse sushi with the ayu stuffed full of rice. It is 1½ blocks west of Ryokan Sugiyama. ✉ *94–10 Naka-Ukai, Nagara* ☎ *058/232–2839* ▭ *No credit cards* ☽ *No dinner (closes at 4).*

WHERE TO STAY

Hotel reviews have been condensed for this book. Please go to Fodors. com for full reviews of each property.

$ 🏨 **Hotel Resol Gifu** ホテルリソル岐阜. This tall, relatively modern hotel
HOTEL   has larger-than-average, Western-style rooms. **Pros:** more spacious
than the average business hotel; close to station; 1 pm check-out available. **Cons:** often booked up well in advance. ✉ *5–8 Nagazumi-cho*
☎ *058/262–9269* 📠 *058/264–1330* ⊕ *www.resol-gifu.com* 🛏 *119
rooms* ⌂ *In-room: a/c, refrigerator, Internet. In-hotel: restaurant, laundry service, spa, parking (paid)* ⍾ *No meals.*

$$$$ 🏨 **Ryokan Sugiyama** 旅館すぎ山. Across the Nagara River from the cas-
RYOKAN   tle, Sugiyama is a tasteful blend of traditional and modern. **Pros:** good
food; ideally positioned for ukai watchers. **Cons:** not cheap; decor a little threadbare in places. ✉ *73–1 Nagara* ☎ *058/231–0161* 📠 *058/233–
5250* ⊕ *www.usyounoie-sugiyama.co.jp* 🛏 *45 rooms* ⌂ *In-room: a/c,
safe, refrigerator. In-hotel: restaurant, parking (free)* ⍾ *Some meals.*

INUYAMA 犬山

22 km (14 mi) east of Gifu, 32 km (20 mi) north of Nagoya.

Inuyama sits along the Kiso River, on the border between Aichi and
Gifu prefectures. A historically strategic site, the city changed hands
several times during the Edo period. You can see cormorant fishing here
from June 1 to October 15; tickets are available from major hotels for
¥2,200 to ¥5,000.

GETTING HERE AND AROUND

Access Inuyama on the Meitetsu Kakamigahara Line via Gifu or on the
Meitetsu Inuyama Line via Nagoya. A good way to see the Kiso-gawa
is on a tame raft. To travel the hour-long, 13-km (8-mi) river trip, take
the train on the Meitetsu Hiromi Line from Inuyama to Nihon-Rhine-
Imawatari. Several companies, including Kisogawa Kanko, offer trips
for a fixed rate. Call the Tourist Information Office in the station for
information on traveling the river and fishing.

Contacts Kisogawa Kanko (☎ *0574/28–2727* 🛏 *¥3,400*). **Tourist Information
Office** (☎ *0568/61–6000*).

WHAT TO SEE

★   **Inuyama-jo** 犬山城. Inuyama's most famous sight is Inuyama-jo, also
known as Hakutei-jo (White Emperor Castle). Built in 1537, it is the
oldest of the 12 original castles in Japan. The castle is exceedingly pretty,
and stands amid carefully tended grounds on a bluff overlooking the
Kiso River. Climb up the creaky staircases to the top floor for a great
view of the river, city, and surrounding hills. The gift shops at the foot
of the castle hill are good for browsing. From Inuyama-Yuen Eki, walk
southwest along the river for 15 minutes. ✉ *65-2 Inuyama-kita-koken*
☎ *0568/61–1711* 🛏 *¥500* ⊘ *Daily 9–4:30.*

Jo-an Teahouse 茶室如庵. In Uraku-en, a traditional garden attached to
the grounds of the Meitetsu Inuyama Hotel, sits the Jo-an Teahouse.
The teahouse was constructed in Kyoto in 1618 and moved to its present site in 1971. Admission to the garden is pricey, so it's worth paying
an extra ¥500 to be served green tea in the traditional style. Uraku-en is
less than ½ km (¼ mi) from Inuyama-jo, behind the Meitetsu Inuyama

Hotel. ✉ *1 Gomon-saki* ☎ *0568/61–4608* 🍵 *Teahouse and gardens* *¥1,000* 🕐 *Mar.–Nov., daily 9–5; Dec.–Feb., daily 9–4.*

Kiso-gawa 木曽川. The pretty stretch of the river that flows beneath cliff-top Inuyama-jo has been dubbed the Japanese Rhine.

Fodor'sChoice **Meiji-mura** 明治村. Situated in attractive countryside, this expansive
★ site—considered one of Japan's best museums—has more than 60 buildings originally constructed during the Meiji era (1868–1912), when Japan ended its policy of isolationism and swiftly industrialized. The best way to experience the exhibits is to wander about, stopping to look at things that catch your eye. There's an English pamphlet you receive upon entry to help guide you. If you get tired of walking, transport options within Meiji-mura include a tram originally from Kyoto, a steam train from Yokohama, and an old village bus; you can buy an ¥800-day pass that covers all three. Among the exhibits are a surprisingly beautiful octagonal wood prison from Kanazawa, a Kabuki theater from Osaka that hosts occasional performances, and the former homes of renowned writers Soseki Natsume and Lafcadio Hearn. The entrance lobby of legendary American architect Frank Lloyd Wright's Imperial Hotel, where Charlie Chaplin and Marilyn Monroe were once guests, is arguably the highlight. It opened on the day of the Great Kanto Earthquake in 1923, 11 years after the death of Emperor Meiji, and though it is not strictly a Meiji-era building, its Mayan-influenced detailing and sense of grandeur and history are truly unique. Buses run from Inuyama Station to Meiji-mura at 6 and 36 minutes past the hour from 9 to 3. The ride takes 20 minutes and costs ¥410. ✉ *1 Uchiyama* ☎ *0568/67–0314* ⊕ *www.meijimura.com* 🎫 *¥1,600* 🕐 *Mar.–Oct., daily 9:30–5; Nov.–Feb., Tues.–Sun., 9:30–4.*

WHERE TO STAY

Hotel reviews have been condensed for this book. Please go to Fodors.com for full reviews of each property.

$$ 🏨 **Meitetsu Inuyama Hotel** 名鉄犬山ホテル. On the south bank of the
HOTEL Kiso-gawa, this hotel has winning views of the river, castle, and hills. **Pros:** convenient for accessing local sights; excellent on-site hot-spring baths. **Cons:** younger travelers are likely to feel a little out of place. ✉ *107–1 Kita-Koken* ☎ *0568/61–2211* 🖷 *0568/62–5750* ↳ *92 Western-style rooms, 34 Japanese-style rooms* ♨ *In-room: a/c, safe, refrigerator, Internet (some). In-hotel: 4 restaurants, room service, bars, parking (free)* ⊟ *AE, DC, MC, V* ⊘ *No meals.*

HIKING

Tsugao-san 継鹿尾山. A hike to Tsugao-san reveals more pleasant scenery near Inuyama-jo. Start on the paved riverside trail at the base of Inuyama-jo. Follow the trail east past the Japan Monkey Park, then north to Jakko-in (built in AD 654), where the maples blaze in fall. Along the route are good views of the foothills stretching north from the banks of the Kiso-gawa. You can climb Tsugao-san or continue northeast to Obora Pond and southeast to Zenjino Station, where you can catch the Meitetsu Hiromi Line two stops back to Inuyama Station. The train passes through Zenjino at least three times an hour. From Inuyama-jo to Zenjino Station is an 8-km (5-mi) hike. Allow 2½ hours from the castle to the top of Tsugao-san; add another hour if you continue to Zenjino via Obora Pond.

IGA UENO 伊賀上野

95 km (59 mi) southwest of Nagoya, 67 km (42 mi) east of Kyoto, 39 km (24 mi) east of Nara, 88 km (55 mi) east of Osaka.

This small city halfway between Nagoya and Nara has some interesting claims to fame. Noted haiku poet Matsuo Basho was born here in the 1640s, and it was home to one of Japan's leading ninja schools. Iga Ueno is accessible from Nagoya, Kyoto, Nara, and Osaka on the JR Line.

WHAT TO SEE

★ **Iga-Ryu Ninja Museum** 伊賀流忍者博物館. The city makes the most of its major attraction. The Iga-Ryu school of *ninjutsu* (ninja arts) was one of the top two training centers for Japan's ancient spies and assassins in the 14th century. At the *ninja yashiki* (ninja residence), a guide dressed in ninja costume explains how they were always prepared for attack. The hidden doors and secret passages are ingenious, but it can't have been a relaxed existence. Energetic demonstrations of ninja weapons like throwing stars, swords, daggers, and sickles are fun, and for an extra fee you can try out the throwing star or even dress up as a ninja. Two exhibitions round out the tour. The first gives background on ninja history and techniques, and the second displays the disguises and encryption used by the Iga ninja, as well as the inventive tools that enabled them to walk on water and scale sheer walls. The museum is in Ueno Park, a 10-minute walk up the hill from Iga Ueno Station. ✉ *117–13–1 Ueno Marunouchi* ☎ *0595/23–0311* ⊕ *www.iganinja.jp/en* 🎫 *¥700, ¥200 to practice throwing stars, ¥500 to dress up as a ninja* ⏰ *Daily 9–5; demonstrations of weapons mid-Mar.–Nov., Wed.–Mon. 11–3; Dec.–mid-Mar., weekends and holidays 11–3.*

Iga Ueno-jo 伊賀上野城. This castle stands today because of one man's determination and wealth. The first castle built here was destroyed by a rainstorm in 1612, before it was completed. More than 300 years later, local resident Katsu Kawasaki financed a replica that sits atop vertiginous 98-foot stone walls—be careful when it's windy. Kawasaki also paid for the Haiku Poetry Master's Pavilion, built in memory of Japan's famous wandering poet, Matsuo Basho, which stands near the castle in Ueno Park. ☎ *0595/21–3148* 🎫 *¥500* ⏰ *Daily 9–5.*

ISE-SHIMA NATIONAL PARK 伊勢志摩国立公園

Hanging like a fin underneath central Honshu, Ise-Shima is a scenic and sacred counterweight to Japan's overbuilt industrial corridor. Ise-Shima National Park, which holds the supremely venerated shrines of Ise Jingu, extends east from Ise to Toba (the center of the pearl industry), and south to the indented coastline and pine-clad islands near Kashikojima. The bottom hook of the peninsula, around to Goza via Daio, has some of the prettiest coves on the Ago Bay, each one home to oyster nets and small groups of fishing boats.

ISE 伊勢

107 km (66 mi) south of Nagoya, 158 km (98 mi) east of Kyoto, 127 km (79 mi) east of Nara, 143 km (89 mi) east of Osaka.

When you step off the train, you may feel that Ise is a drab city, but hidden in two forests of towering cedar trees are the most important and impressive Shinto shrines in Japan. Indeed, the city's income comes mainly from the pilgrims who visit Geku and Naiku, the Outer and Inner shrines, respectively. Near the Inner Shrine you'll find an array of shops hawking souvenirs to the busloads of tourists and a few spots to eat such local specialties as *Ise udon* (udon noodles with a thick broth) and *akafuku* (sweet rice cakes). The busiest times at Ise Jingu are during the Grand Festival, held October 15–17 every year, when crowds gather to see the pageantry, and on New Year's Eve and Day, when hundreds of thousands come to pray for good fortune.

GETTING HERE AND AROUND

Ise can be reached from Kyoto, Nara, and Osaka by the JR and Kintetsu lines, with the latter's Limited Express service from Nagoya being the fastest option. The city has two stations five minutes apart, Ise (JR and Kintetsu) and Uji-Yamada (Kintetsu only). From either station it's only a 10-minute walk through town to the Outer Shrine. A frequent shuttle bus makes the 6-km (4-mi) trip between Geku and Naiku; a bus also goes directly from the Inner Shrine to Uji-Yamada Station.

You can arrange a full-day tour to Ise and the Mikimoto Pearl Island at Toba from Nagoya (¥20,000) through **JTB Sunrise Tours.**

Ise Tourist Information Center is across the street from the Outer Shrine, and has information about both Ise and the surrounding area.

Contacts **Ise Tourist Information Center** (☎ 0596/28–3705 ⊕ www.ise-kanko. jp/english/index.html ☉ 8:30–5).

JTB Sunrise Tours Central Japan (Nagoya) (☎ 052/211–3065 ⊕ www.jtb-sunrisetours.jp).

WHAT TO SEE

Fodor'sChoice **Ise Jingu** 伊勢神宮 *(Grand Shrines of Ise).* The shrines are rebuilt every ★ 20 years in accordance with Shinto tradition. To begin a new generational cycle, exact replicas of the previous halls are erected with new wood, using the same centuries-old methods, on adjacent sites. The old buildings are then dismantled. The main halls you see now—the 61st set—were completed in 1993 at an estimated cost of more than ¥4.5 billion. For the Japanese, importance is found in the form of the buildings; the vintage of the materials is of little concern. You cannot enter any of the buildings, but the tantalizing glimpses of the main halls that you catch while walking the grounds add to the mystique of the site. Both Grand Shrines exhibit a natural harmony that the more-contrived buildings in later Japanese architecture do not. If you are pressed for time, head for the more impressive Naiku first.

Deep in a park of ancient Japanese cedars, **Geku** (⊠ *279 Toyokawa-machi*), dating from AD 477, is dedicated to Toyouke O-kami, goddess of agriculture. Its buildings are simple, predating the influx of

The Grand Shrine of Ise is rebuilt every 20 years, in accordance with the Shinto tradition.

6th-century Chinese and Korean influence. It's made from unpainted hinoki (cypress), with a closely cropped thatched roof. You can see very little of the exterior of Geku—only its roof and glimpses of its walls—and none of the interior. Four fences surround the shrine, and only the Imperial Family and their envoys may enter.

The same is true for the even more venerated **Naiku** (✉ *1 Uji-kan-machi, 6 km [4 mi] southwest of Geku*). Naiku is where the Yata-no-Kagami (Sacred Mirror) is kept, one of the three sacred treasures of the imperial regalia. The shrine, said to date from 4 BC, also houses the spirit of the sun goddess Amaterasu, who Japanese mythology says was born of the left eye of Izanagi, one of the first two gods to inhabit the earth. According to legend, Amaterasu was the great-great-grandmother of the first mortal emperor of Japan, Jimmu. Thus, she is revered as the country's ancestral goddess-mother and guardian deity. The Inner Shrine's architecture is simple. If you did not know its origin, you might call it classically modern. The use of unpainted cypress causes Naiku to blend into the ancient forest encircling it. To get to Naiku, take Bus 51 or 55 from Uji-Yamada Station or in front of Geku to the Naiku-mae bus stop, which is right in front of the shrine. The ride takes about 20 minutes. Geku is a five-minute walk southwest of Ise Station or a 10-minute walk west of Uji-Yamada Station. ⊕ *www.isejingu.or.jp/english/index.htm* ◷ *Sunrise–sunset* ✉ *Free.*

WHERE TO EAT

$$–$$$ ✕ **Izakaya Toramaru** 虎丸. This izakaya (traditional-style) restaurant
IZAKAYA   won't open on days when they aren't able to get a fresh delivery of fish, which tells you how seriously they take their food. Though there

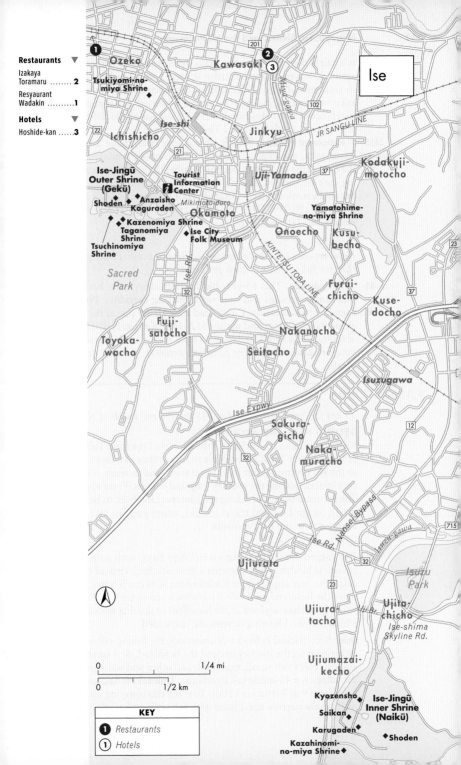

Restaurants ▼

Izakaya
Toramaru **2**

Resyaurant
Wadakin **1**

Hotels ▼

Hoshide-kan **3**

Ise

① Ozeko

②
Kawasaki
③

┃201┃

┃102┃

Tsukiyomi-no-
miya Shrine ◆

Miya-gawa

Ise-shi

JR SANGU LINE

┃22┃ Ichishicho

Jinkyu

Uji-Yamada

Kodakuji-
motocho

┃21┃

┃37┃

**Ise-Jingū
Outer Shrine
(Gekū)**
◆
Shoden ◆ ◆Anzaisho
Kaguraden

Tourist
Information
Center
Mikimoto-doro
Okamoto

Yamatohime-
no-miya Shrine

┃23┃

◆◆Kazenomiya Shrine
Taganomiya
Shrine
Tsuchinomiya
Shrine
◆ ◆Ise City
Folk Museum

Onoecho

Kusu-
becho

KINTETSU TOBA LINE

*Sacred
Park*

Ise Rd.

Furuí-
chicho

Kuse-
docho

┃32┃

┃37┃

**Fuji-
satocho**

Nakanocho

Toyoka-
wacho

Seitacho

Isuzugawa

Ise Expwy

Sakura-
gicho

Naka-
muracho

┃12┃

┃32┃

Nansei Bypass

┃715┃

Ise Rd.

Isuzu-gawa

┃32┃

*Isuzu
Park*

0 ———————— 1/4 mi

0 ———————— 1/2 km

Ujiurata

┃23┃

Ujiura-
tacho

Ujita-
chicho
*Ise-shima
Skyline Rd.*
Uji Br.

Ujiumazai-
kecho

Kyozensho ◆

Saikan ◆

**Ise-Jingū
Inner Shrine
(Naikū)**

Karugaden ◆

◆ Shoden

Kazahinomi-
no-miya Shrine ◆

KEY

① *Restaurants*

① *Hotels*

is a fairly diverse menu, the main draw here is the expertly prepared sashimi, served in haphazardly shaped pottery dishes. Ask the staff to recommend a good drink from the extensive selection of Japanese sake and shochu. Izakaya Toramaru is housed in a replica warehouse two blocks east of Hoshide-kan. ⊠ *2–13–6 Kawasaki* ☎ *0596/22–9298* ⊟ *No credit cards* ⊗ *Closed Thurs. No lunch.*

$$$$
JAPANESE
★ ✕ **Restaurant Wadakin** 和田金. If you love beef, make a pilgrimage to Matsusaka, one express train stop north of Ise. Wadakin claims to be the originator of Matsusaka beef's fame; the cattle are raised with loving care on the restaurant's farm out in the countryside. Sukiyaki or the chef's steak dinner will satisfy your cravings. ⊠ *1878 Naka-machi, Matsusaka* ☎ *0598/21–1188* ⊟ *No credit cards* ⊗ *Closed 4th Tues. of month and 1st Tues. in Dec.*

WHERE TO STAY

Hotel reviews have been condensed for this book. Please go to Fodors. com for full reviews of each property.

$–$$
RYOKAN
★ 🏠 **Hoshide–kan.** This 85-year-old traditional-style inn has wood-decorated tatami rooms and narrow, squeaking corridors. **Pros:** foreigner friendly; good location. **Cons:** dead zone after 9 pm; at the mercy of the elements in summer and winter. ⊠ *2–15–2 Kawasaki* ☎ *0596/28–2377* 🖷 *0596/27–2830* ➴ *10 Japanese-style rooms with shared bath* ⚄ *In-hotel: restaurant, laundry facilities, Internet, parking (free)* ⦿ *Some meals.*

KASHIKOJIMA 賢島

25 km (16 mi) south of Toba, 145 km (90 mi) south of Nagoya.

GETTING HERE AND AROUND

Kashikojima can be reached on the Kintetsu Line from Toba or Nagoya or by bus from Toba. It's possible to follow the coast from Kashikojima to the Kii Peninsula, but there is no train, and in many places the road cuts inland, making the journey long and tedious. From Kashikojima or Toba you are better off taking the Kintetsu Line back to Ise to change to the JR Sangu Line and travel to Taki, where you can take the JR Kisei Line south to the Kii Peninsula.

WHAT TO SEE

★ The jagged coastline at Ago-wan (Ago Bay), with calm waters and countless hidden coves, presents a dramatic final view of the Ise Peninsula. The best approach to Kashikojima is to catch a bus to Goza, the tip of the headland, and ride a ferry back across the bay. From the boat you'll get a close-up look at the hundreds of floating wooden rafts from which the pearl-bearing oysters are suspended.

Daio 大王. Tucked behind a promontory, the fishing village is an interesting stop on the journey around the headland. At a small fish market you can buy fresh squid, mackerel, and other seafood. Standing above the village is a 46-meter-tall lighthouse, **Daiozaki todai,** open to visitors daily from 9 to 4 (entry is ¥200). To reach this towering white structure, walk up the narrow street lined with fish stalls and pearl souvenir shops

CLOSE UP

The Pearl Divers

At Toba, before Kokichi Mikimoto (1858–1954) perfected a method for cultivating pearls here in 1893, *Ama,* or female divers (women were believed to have bigger lungs), would dive all day, bringing up a thousand oysters, but they wouldn't necessarily find a valuable pearl. Pearl oysters are now farmed, and the famous female divers are a dying breed. On the outlying islands, however, women do still dive for abalone, octopus, and edible seaweed. The quickest and cheapest way to get from Ise to Toba is an 18-minute ride on the JR Line for ¥230.

Mikimoto Pearl Museum
ミキモト真珠博物館 *(Mikimoto Shinju no Hakubutsukan).* The museum on Pearl Island, 500 yards southeast from Toba Station, explores the history of pearl diving in Japan. ☎ *0599/25–2028* ⊕ *www.mikimoto-pearl-museum. co.jp* ✉ *¥1,500* ⊙ *Apr.–Nov., daily 8:30–5:30; Dec., daily 9–4:30; Jan.– Mar., daily 8:30–5.*

Toba Tourist Information Center. Outside Exit 1 of Kintetsu Toba Station, you'll find an English map of the main attractions. ☎ *0599/25–2844* ⊙ *9–5:30.*

at the back of the harbor. From this lighthouse you can see **Anorizaki todai,** a stone lighthouse built in 1973, 11 km (7 mi) east.

WHERE TO STAY

Hotel reviews have been condensed for this book. Please go to Fodors. com for full reviews of each property.

$-$$
RYOKAN

🍴 **Daioso** 大王荘. Staying at this small, family-run ryokan next to the harbor in Daio allows you to enjoy the peaceful evening after the tourists have left and witness the early-morning activity of the fishermen. **Pros:** reasonably priced; on the harbor; good if you like fish. **Cons:** some spoken Japanese essential; Western-style rooms are drab. ✉ *244 Namigiri, Shima-gun* ☎ *0599/72–1234* 🖨 *0599/72–0489* 🛏 *3 Western-style rooms; 4 Japanese-style rooms, 2 with bath* ⚅ *In-room: a/c, safe, refrigerator (some), Internet. In-hotel: restaurant, parking (free)* 🍽 *Some meals.*

$
MINSHUKU
★

🍴 **Ishiyama-so** 石山荘. On tiny Yokoyama-jima in Ago-wan, this small inn has painted its name in large letters on the red roof. **Pros:** idyllic setting; doesn't get much more remote than this. **Cons:** no frills; limited dining options if you don't eat in; no private baths. ✉ *Yokoyama-jima, Kashikojima, Ago-cho, Shima-gun* ☎ *0599/52–1527* 🖨 *0599/52–1240* 🛏 *2 Western-style rooms, 4 Japanese-style rooms, all with shared bath* ⚅ *In-room: a/c, safe. In-hotel: Wi-Fi hotspot* ▭ *No credit cards* 🍽 *No meals.*

KII PENINSULA 紀伊半島

Beyond Ise-Shima, the Kii Peninsula has magnificent marine scenery, coastal fishing villages, beach resorts, and the temple mountain of Koyasan. Wakayama Prefecture, which constitutes much of the Kii Peninsula, has a population of only 1 million, and life here moves at a relaxed pace.

From Shingu you can reach all three great shrines of the Kumano Kodo pilgrimage route. Nearby Yoshino-Kumano National Park has pristine gorges, holy mountains, and another ancient Buddhist site at Yoshino-san, where gorgeous hillside sakura flower in early April.

SHINGU 新宮

138 km (86 mi) southwest of Taki, 231 km (144 mi) southwest of Nagoya.

GETTING HERE AND AROUND

You can reach Shingu by JR Limited Express from Taki or Nagoya. The Shingu Tourist Association Information Center is to the left as you exit the station.

ESSENTIALS

Visitor Information Shingu Tourist Association Information Center (☎ 0735/22–2840 ⊗ *Daily 9–5:30*).

WHAT TO SEE

Shingu is home to one of the three great shrines of the Kumano Kodo, **Hayatama-taisha** 速玉大社 (daily 9–4:30). One of the few north–south roads penetrating the Kii Peninsula begins in town and continues inland to Nara by way of Doro-kyo (Doro Gorge). A drive on this winding, steep, narrow road, especially on a bus, warrants motion-sickness pills. The mossy canyon walls outside your window and the rushing water far below inspire wonder, but frequent sharp curves provide plenty of anxiety. Continue north on the road past Doro-kyo to reach **Hongu** 本宮 shrine (⊗ *Daily 9–4:30*), which has attractive wooden architecture and a thatched roof.

WHERE TO STAY

Hotel reviews have been condensed for this book. Please go to Fodors. com for full reviews of each property.

$–$$ 🏨 **Shingu UI Hotel.** Better than the average business hotel, fair-size rooms
HOTEL   and an easily accessible location make this a good option if you're staying overnight in Shingu. **Pros:** convenient base for day-trippers; decent service. **Cons:** perfunctory decor; showing its age. ⊠ *3–12 I-no-sawa* ☎ *0735/22–6611* 🖷 *0735/22–4777* 🛏 *82 rooms* ⚒ *In-room: a/c, refrigerator, Internet (some). In-hotel: restaurant, bar, laundry service, parking (free)* ⍾ *No meals.*

DORO-KYO 瀞峡

20 km (12 mi) north of Shingu.

The wide ocean views of the coastal journey to Shingu give way to gorges and mountainsides of a deep mossy green when you pass through the tunnel five minutes north of the city. Up the Kumano River, the walls of the steep-sided Doro-kyo rise above you. Farther up, sheer 150-foot cliffs tower over the Kumano-gawa. Tours of the gorge (¥4,800) depart from Shingu Station and can be booked through the Shingu Tourist Association Information Center. A bus goes as far as Shiko, and then a flat-bottomed, fan-driven boat travels upriver to Doro-hatcho and back again. Outside seats on the boats are the best. You can book a trip at the information center at Shingu Station.

NACHI

13 km (8 mi) southwest of Shingu.

GETTING HERE AND AROUND
Nachi can be reached by hourly JR services via Shingu. The trip takes 19 minutes and costs ¥230. From Nachi Station, a 20-minute bus ride (¥470) gets you to the shrine and waterfall.

WHAT TO SEE
Nachi Taisha 那智大社. Reputed to be 1,400 years old, this is perhaps the most impressive of the Kumano Kodo shrines, and it overlooks **Nachi-no-taki** 那智の滝, the highest waterfall in Japan, which drops 430 feet into a rocky river. At the bus stop near the falls a large torii gate marks the start of a short path that leads to a paved clearing near the foot of the falls. A 15-minute climb up the mossy stone path opposite the souvenir shops is the temple. You can ride an elevator to the top of the bright red pagoda for an on-high view of the waterfall. Next to the shrine is the 1587 Buddhist temple **Seiganto-ji**, starting point for a 33-temple Kannon pilgrimage through western Honshu. Many visitors walk here from a point several kilometers away on the road to Nachi Station. The temple grounds offer mountain views to the southwest. ⊠ *1 Nachi-san, Nachi-Katsuura-cho* ☎ *Shrine free, elevator ¥200* ☉ *Daily 9–4:30.*

Shio-no-misaki 潮岬. Eight km (5 mi) from Kushimoto, this is Honshu's southernmost point. Stationed high above the rocky cliffs is a white lighthouse that unfortunately closes before sunset (☎ *¥200* ☉ *9–4*). Adjacent to the lighthouse is a good spot for picnics and walking on the cliff paths. The beach looks inviting, but sharp rocks and strong currents make swimming a bad idea.

SHIRAHAMA 白浜

82 km (51 mi) west of Nachi, 178 km (111 mi) south of Osaka.

Rounding the peninsula, 54 km (34 mi) northwest of Shio-no-misaki, Shirahama is a small headland famous for its pure white-sand beach. If you're wondering why it looks and feels so different from the other beaches, it's because this sand is imported from Australia. Hot springs are dotted along the beach and around the cape. The climate, which allows beach days even in winter, makes Shirahama an inviting base for exploring the area. While it can be intolerably busy in July and August, it is otherwise pretty laid-back. JR trains from Nachi and Osaka run to Shirahama. A 17-minute bus ride from the train station gets you to the beachside town.

WHAT TO SEE
Fodor'sChoice **Sakino-yu Onsen** 崎の湯温泉. Soak in this open-air hollow among the
★ wave-beaten rocks facing the Pacific, where it's said that emperors Saimei (594–661) and Mommu (683–707) once bathed. It's at the south

end of the main beach, below Hotel Seamore. 🎫 ¥300 🕐 *Thurs.–Tues. dawn–dusk.*

Shirara-yu Onsen しらら湯温泉. At the north end of the beach, locals come and go all day to bathe and chat. The baths overlook the beach and ocean from the second floor of this old wooden building, and on the first floor is an open lounge area. You can rent or buy towels, but bring your own toiletries. 🎫 ¥300 🕐 *Wed.–Mon. 7–11, Tues. noon–11.*

KOYA-SAN 高野山

63 km (39 mi) east of Wakayama, 64 km (40 mi) southeast of Osaka.

This World Heritage Site is the headquarters of the Shingon sect of Buddhism, founded by Kukai, also known as Kobo Daishi, in AD 816.

GETTING HERE AND AROUND

If you approach Koya-san by cutting across the Yoshino-Kumano National Park by bus from Shingu or Hongu on Route 168, get off the bus at Gojo and backtrack one station on the JR Line to Hashimoto; then take the Nankai Line. If you are coming from Osaka, take the Nankai Line from Namba Station, which sometimes requires a change of train at Hashimoto Station.

By rail, the last leg of the trip is a five-minute cable-car ride (¥380) from Gokuraku-bashi Station. JR Passes are not valid for the cable car. The lift deposits you at the top of 3,000-foot Koya-san, where you can pick up a map and hop on a bus to the main attractions, which are about 2½ km (1½ mi) from the station and 4 km (2½ mi) from each other on opposite sides of town. Two buses leave the station when the cable car arrives, which is every 20 or 30 minutes. One goes to Okuno-in Cemetery, on the east end of the main road, and the other goes to the Dai-mon, to the west. Koya-san Tourist Association office at the intersection in the center of town can be reached by either bus for ¥280.

ESSENTIALS

Visitor Information Koya-san Tourist Association office (✉ 600 Koya-san, Koya-cho, Ito-gun ☎ 0736/56–2616).

WHAT TO SEE

Dai-mon 大門 *(Big Gate)*. Every year a million visitors pass through Koya-san's **gate** to enter the great complex of 117 temples and monasteries. Traveling to Koya-san takes you through mountain wilderness, but the town itself is sheltered and self-contained. The main buildings are imposing, while the minor temples are in a wide range of styles and colors, each offering small-scale beauty in its decor or garden. Monks, pilgrims, and tourists mingle in the main street, the sneaker-wearing, motorcycle-riding monks often appearing the least pious of all.

Danjo Garan 壇上伽藍 *(Sacred Precinct)*. The Danjo Garan boasts several outsize halls. The most striking is the **Kompon-daito** *(Great Stupa)*. This red pagoda with an interior of brightly colored beams contains five large seated gold Buddhas. Last rebuilt in 1937, the two-story structure has an unusual style and rich vermilion color. From Kongobu-ji walk down the temple's main stairs and take the road to the right of the parking lot

Koya-san is a World Heritage Site and the headquarters of the Shingon sect of Buddhism.

in front of you; in less than five minutes you will reach Danjo Garan. 📷 *Kompon-daito ¥200* 🕐 *Daily 8:30–5.*

Kongobu-ji 金剛峯寺. On the southwestern side of Koya-san, Kongobu-ji is the chief temple of Shingon Buddhism. It was first built in 1592 as the family temple of Hideyoshi Toyotomi, and rebuilt in 1861 to become the main temple of the Koya-san community. The screen-door artwork and rock garden, the largest in Japan, are noteworthy. 📷 *¥500* 🕐 *Daily 8:30–4:30.*

★ **Okuno-in** 奥の院. If time is limited, head for this memorial park first. Many Japanese make pilgrimages to the mausoleum of Kobo Daishi or pay their respects to their ancestors buried here. Arrive early in the morning, before the groups take over, or even better, at dusk, when it gets wonderfully spooky.

Exploring this cemetery is like peeking into a lost and mysterious realm. Incense hangs in the air, and you can almost feel the millions of prayers said here clinging to the gnarled branches of 300-year-old cedar trees reaching into the sky. The old-growth forest is a rarity in Japan, and among the trees are buried some of the country's most prominent families, their graves marked by mossy pagodas and red-robed bodhisattvas.

You can reach Okuno-in by way of the 2½-km (1½-mi) main walkway, which is lined with more than 100,000 tombs, monuments, and statues. The lane enters the cemetery at Ichi-no-hashi-guchi; follow the main street straight east from the town center for 15 minutes to find this small bridge at the edge of the forest.

The path from Okuno-in-mae ends at the refined **Toro-do** 灯籠堂 (*Lantern Hall*), named after its 11,000 lanterns. Two fires burn in this hall; one has reportedly been alight since 1016, the other since 1088. Behind the hall is the mausoleum of Kobo Daishi. The hall and the mausoleum altar are extremely beautiful, with subtle lighting and soft gold coloring. ✆ *Free* 🕐 *Lantern Hall Apr.–Oct., daily 8–5; Nov.–Mar., daily 8:30–4:30.*

Reihokan 霊宝館 (*Treasure Hall*). Here you'll find a collection of more than 5,000 well-preserved Buddhist relics, some dating back 1,000 years. The New Wing houses themed exhibitions of sculpture, painting, and artifacts. The Old Wing (confusingly marked "Exit") has a permanent exhibition of Buddha and bodhisattva figures and calligraphic scrolls. The museum is across the road from the Danjo Garan. ✆ *¥600* 🕐 *May–Oct., daily 8:30–5:30; Nov.–Apr., daily 8:30–4:30.*

WHERE TO STAY

Koya-san has no modern hotels; however, 52 of the temples offer Japanese-style accommodations—tatami floors, futon mattresses, and traditional Japanese shared baths. You eat the same food as the priests. Dinner and breakfast is *shojin ryori,* vegetarian cuisine that uses locally made tofu. Prices start from ¥9,500 per person, including meals. All the temples are open to foreign guests, but only half will cater to non-Japanese speakers. An advance reservation is advisable, especially in October and November, when crowds come for the autumn leaves, and the August holidays. Arrangements can be made through Koya-san Tourist Association, the Nankai Railway Company office in Namba Station (Osaka), and the Japan Travel Bureau in most Japanese cities.

Hotel reviews have been condensed for this book. Please go to Fodors. com for full reviews of each property.

$–$$ 🏯 **Eko-in** 恵光院. Eko-in is a friendly temple, close to Okuno-in, where
TEMPLE   you can take part in morning prayers and the morning fire ceremony. **Pros:** good vegetarian food; several of the younger monks speak good English; very welcoming to foreigners. **Cons:** some single rooms have no locks and are only separated by sliding doors ✉ *497 Koya-san* ☎ *0736/56–2541* 📠 *0736/56–2891* ⊕ *www.ekoin.jp* ⇆ *37 rooms* ᚼ *In-room: a/c, safe* ❘◯❘ *Some meals.*

$–$$ 🏯 **Rengejo-in** 蓮華定院. Rengejo-in is an especially lovely temple where
TEMPLE   both the head priest and his mother speak English. **Pros:** excellent vegetarian food; very accommodating to foreigners. **Cons:** opposite end of town from Okuno-in; may prove a little too austere for some. ✉ *700 Koya-san* ☎ *0736/56–2233* 📠 *0736/56–4743* ⇆ *46 Japanese-style rooms* ᚼ *In-room: no phone, a/c, safe* ▭ *No credit cards* ❘◯❘ *Some meals.*

The Japan Alps and the North Chubu Coast

WORD OF MOUTH

"We really enjoyed Kanazawa. The Kanazawa castle park and the Kenrokuen Gardens are a must. It was especially beautiful since it was during cherry blossom season."

—panda2ac

"Matsumoto Castle is gorgeous."

—gertie3751

WELCOME TO THE JAPAN ALPS AND THE NORTH CHUBU COAST

TOP REASONS TO GO

★ **Onsen:** The salty, calcium-rich waters of coastal thermal spas and iron- and sulfur-heavy springs in the mountains make your skin smooth, your bones strong, and set your mind at ease.

★ **Hiking:** The Japan Alps offer staggering views and a serious workout. Trails wind through peaks and ridges, and summer brings wildflowers to the highland slopes and valleys.

★ **Skiing:** The resorts around Nagano attract outdoor enthusiasts, particularly on weekends. Shiga Kogen, near Yudanaka, and Happo-o-ne, near Hakuba, are among the best areas.

★ **Glimpses of Feudal Japan:** Visit the former samurai quarters in Kanazawa's Naga-machi section. Matsumoto Castle evokes the history of a strictly hierarchical society.

★ **Folk Art:** Kanazawa is renowned for dyed silk, gilded crafts, and pottery; Matsumoto has excellent wood craftsmanship. Lacquer is a specialty of the Noto Peninsula.

1 The Japan Alps. The Alps are divided into three ranges: the northern Hida Mountains, the central Kiso range, and the southern Alps. The northern region is the most popular for hiking and skiing and is easily accessed from Matsumoto or Nagano. The jagged snow-capped peaks interspersed with high basins reach elevations of 9,850 feet. Mostly forested, they are covered with alpine flora in the warmer months. Hot springs are scattered throughout this volcanic region.

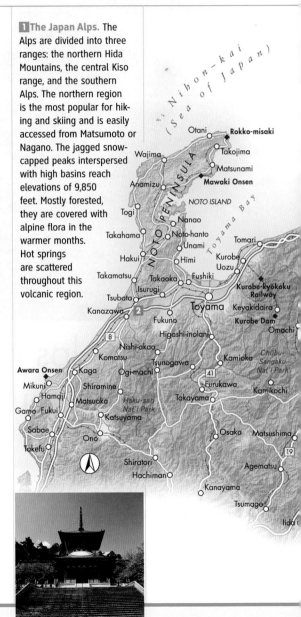

GETTING ORIENTED

The label "Japan Alps" does not refer to a defined political region; it's a name for the mountains in Chubu, the middle district. Chubu encompasses nine prefectures in the heart of Honshu, three of which—Gifu, Nagano, and Yamanashi—make up the central highlands. Between the Alps and the Sea of Japan is a narrow coastal belt known as Hokuriku, comprised of Kanazawa, Fukui, and the rugged coastline of the Noto Peninsula. Heavy snowfall in winter and hot summers make this region ideal for growing rice. Niigata and Sado Island form the northeastern coast.

2 Kanazawa and the North Chubu Coast. Ishikawa Prefecture stretches long and narrow from north to south; thus the topographies of the Noto Peninsula and the Ishikawa's southern Kaga region are significantly different. Kanazawa, the administrative, economic, and cultural center of Kaga, is also renowned for traditional crafts. The Noto Peninsula has both rugged cliffs on its northern Sea of Japan side and calmer bays in the south.

GASSHO-ZUKURI FARMHOUSES

It's tempting to think of traditional domestic architecture in Japan, with its paper windows and tatami mats and sliding screens as, well, insubstantial. The moment you see a gassho-zukuri farmhouse, that temptation will disappear.

(This page above) A Doboruku Matsuri procession; (opposite page upper right) a snowy winter in Shirokawa-go; (opposite page bottom left) gassho-zukuri farmhouses in Shirakawa-go

The term *gassho-zukuri* in Japanese means "praying hands." As hands come together, fingertips touching, in Buddhist observance, so lie the sloping, gable roofs of these remarkable farmhouses, watertight layers of reed thatching 3 feet thick or more, over massive wooden beams, set at a steep 60-degree angle to keep the snow from piling up. The mountain forests of Gifu and Toyama prefectures in the Japan Alps, where most of these houses survive, get some of the heaviest snow falls in Japan—12 feet of it, from November through March, is not uncommon—and no less a roof would do. The houses, four and sometimes five stories high, are usually built on a north–south axis, so the angle offers the least resistance to the winter wind. They are a masterfully practical architectural adaptation to challenging weather conditions, but they also have a certain beauty.

STRONGLY BUILT

Gassho-zukuri houses represent one of the crowning achievements of traditional Japanese carpentry. Astonishingly, these houses were built without nails, pegs, or brackets. Complex joinery, ropes, and strips of hazel wood hold the beams together, the joints tightened with small wedges, typically with no diagonal bracing. They are flexible enough to withstand winter storms and even earthquakes.

A PRACTICAL HOUSE

Like most traditional farmhouses, the gassho-zukuri was a living and working space for one, two, or even four generations of an immediate and extended family and their hired help—often 30 people or more—under the one pitched roof. Sleeping quarters were on the first and second floors; in the medieval period, the ground floor was also used for the making of niter (for gunpowder) in summer—tribute paid to the feudal lord in lieu of taxes—and *washi* (Japanese paper) in winter. The triangular top stories were reserved for silkworm cultivation. Stables were connected to the living space, so no one had to go outdoors during the long, cold winter months—except, alas, to the outhouse.

In the center of the huge open room on the main floor was—and still is—the *irori,* a charcoal fire pit with a huge wooden pot hook suspended over it for cooking. In winter, it was the only source of heat in the house; the higher your standing in the family, the closer you got to sit by the fire. The hearth sent billows of smoke upward to cure meats and dry food set on a metal grill suspended from the ceiling; the rising heat also kept the precious silkworms warm. Centuries of smoke would darken the walls and beams of the house, giving them as well a protective coating against insects, but the smoke takes its toll on the thatching, which has to be replaced

every 30 or 40 years. When there's a roof to be done, the whole community pitches in, like an Amish barn-raising, laying some 20 truckloads' worth of new reeds in two or three days.

SEEING THE GASSHO-ZUKURI TODAY

At one time, it was estimated that there were more than 1,800 of these extraordinary farmhouses in the mountain villages of central Japan, between the castle towns of Nagoya and Kanazawa, many dating back to the 17th century. Today, only some 150 remain—the largest number of them in the villages of Shirakawa-go and Takayama on the border of Toyama and Gifu prefectures, which together were declared a UNESCO World Heritage Site in 1959. Access to them is by no means easy, but since the 1990s these villages have become increasingly popular tourist destinations, especially for domestic travelers; many of the houses in Ogi-machi village (*see* ⇨ *Shirakawa-go, below*) have been converted to *minshuku* (guesthouses) to accommodate visitors to this area. Another group of gassho-zukuri farmhouses can be found in Hida no Sato (Hida Folk Village), an open-air historical museum in the Gifu city of Takayama (*see the listing, below*).

Updated by
Annamarie
Sasagawa

No trip to Japan is complete without spending a few days in this central alpine region. Until the 20th century brought highways and railways to central Japan, villages here were largely isolated from the rest of the country. Unique traditions still linger in this region of snow-topped mountains, coastal cliffs, open-air hot springs, and superb hiking and skiing.

Come here for traditional architecture in towns like Tsumago and Magome, or to wander around thatch-roofed farmhouses in Takayama and Shirakawa-go village. Visit Buddhist temples such as Fukui's Eihei-ji, a major Zen center, Nagano's Zenko-ji, and Kanazawa's Nichiren Myoryu-ji (locally called Ninja-dera or the temple of the Ninja).

Central Japan is justly famous for its festivals. Takayama's biannual town festival draws crowds from all over the country. Sado Island parties for days on end during its annual Earth Celebration, hosted by taiko drum group Kodo, and the tiny town of Nanao on the Noto Peninsula lets it all hang out during its riotous Seihakusai festival. When they're not dancing in the streets, local craftspeople produce some of Japan's best ceramics, pottery, dyed silk, wood carvings, and lacquerware.

Escape summer city heat by trekking in the Japan Alps or strolling through the car-free alpine village of Kamikochi. When the winter snows start to fall, ski fields in Nagano and Niigata offer endless fresh powder, and the many hot springs and sake breweries in the region are a weary snowbunny's dream.

⇨ *See the glossary at the end of this book for definitions of the common Japanese words and suffixes used in this chapter.*

PLANNING

WHEN TO GO

Temperatures vary widely from the coastal areas to the mountains. Hikers should bring warm clothes even in summer. Cherry-blossom season in April is beautiful; May, June, and September are when transportation is safe and reliable, and not too crowded. At the height of summer, from mid-July to the end of August, the Alps and coastal regions are the prime getaway for those fleeing the stagnant heat of urban Japan—expect throngs of tourists and lofty prices. The skiing season peaks over Christmas and New Year's. Winter's heavy snows make driving around the Alps difficult or impossible, and only a few buses and trains run per day. It's fine if you're sticking to the major cities, but unless you've got skiing to do, and a direct train to get there, winter is not ideal for exploring the countryside.

HOW MUCH TIME?

A quick loop of the major towns and destinations—the Alps, the Noto-anto (Noto Peninsula), the Chubu Coast, and Sado Island—takes more than a week. To enjoy the unique scenery and culture of the region, it is best to choose two or three cities as sightseeing hubs. In the Alps region, frequent trains run north and south through the mountain valleys, while cutting across the mountains east to west and visiting smaller towns requires more planning. Local tourist offices can supply you with detailed bus and train information for the surrounding area.

GETTING HERE AND AROUND

Travel in the Alps is largely restricted to the valleys and river gorges that run north and south. The only east–west route is through the mountains, between Matsumoto and Takayama. It's easier to go along the coast and through the foothills of Fukui, Ishikawa, Toyama, and Niigata, except in winter when Fukui gets hit with furious blizzards. In Noto-hanto, buses and trains can be relied on for trips to key places.

AIR TRAVEL

The major airport in the area is Komatsu Kuko in Kanazawa, although there are daily flights from Fukuoka, Osaka, and Sapporo to Matsumoto and Toyama for those wanting to reach the Alps quickly. Since the opening of Noto Airport in Wajima, you can reach the Noto Peninsula in one hour from Tokyo. The recently opened Chubu International Airport (Centrair) near Nagoya has frequent domestic and international flights.

BUS AND TRAIN TRAVEL

Whether to take the bus or the train isn't usually a choice, because there is often only one form of public transportation to the place you're going. Not all train lines in Nagano Prefecture are JR, so budget in additional charges if you are traveling on a rail pass.

Tokyo–Nagano Shinkansen service has effectively shortened the distance to the Alps from the east: the trip on the Nagano Shinkansen takes only about 90 minutes. From Kyoto and Nagoya the Alps are three hours away on the Hokuriku and Takayama lines. Unless you are coming from Niigata, you will need to approach Takayama from the south (connections through Maibara are the speediest) on JR. To get to Kanazawa from Tokyo, you can either connect through Maibara or Echigo Yuzawa.

CAR TRAVEL

To really explore the area, rent a car in Kanazawa or Toyama to make the loop of the Noto Peninsula at your own pace. Another good route is between Kanazawa and Takayama via Shirakawa-go.

An economy-size car costs about ¥8,000 per day or ¥50,000 per week. Reserve the car in a city like Kanazawa, Nagano, or Matsumoto, or before you leave Tokyo, Nagoya, or Kyoto—not many people speak English in rural Japan. Tollways are convenient but expensive and less scenic than the many beautiful highways in the region.

In winter certain roads through the central Japan Alps are closed, and the road into Kamikochi is inaccessible from November through April.

ABOUT THE RESTAURANTS

Traditional Japanese *ryotei* specialize in seasonal delicacies while casual eateries serve delicious home-style cooking and regional dishes. Western fare is easy to come by, especially in larger cities like Kanazawa, which is famed for the local Kaga cuisine.

ABOUT THE HOTELS

Accommodations run the gamut from Japanese-style inns to large, modern hotels. *Ryokan* and *minshuku* (guesthouses) serve traditional Japanese food, and usually highlight regional specialties. Hotels in the bigger cities have a variety of Western and Japanese restaurants. Japanese inns mostly include two meals in the room rate. In summer, it's advisable to book as far in advance as possible.

Most hotels have a high-speed Internet connection in the room or an Internet terminal for guest use, but ryokan rarely do. Hotel lobbies and areas around the stations often have free Wi-Fi access, sometimes available in the rooms.

WHAT IT COSTS IN YEN					
	¢	$	$$	$$$	$$$$
Restaurants	under ¥800	¥800–¥1,000	¥1,000–¥2,000	¥2,000–¥3,000	over ¥3,000
Hotels	under ¥8,000	¥8,000–¥12,000	¥12,000–¥18,000	¥18,000–¥22,000	over ¥22,000

Restaurant prices are per person for a main course, set meal, or equivalent combination of smaller dishes at dinner. Hotel prices are for a double room, excluding service and tax.

VISITOR INFORMATION

Offices of the JR Travel Information Center and Japan Travel Bureau are at major train stations. They can help you book local tours, hotel reservations, and travel tickets. You shouldn't assume English will be spoken, but usually someone speaks sufficiently well for your basic needs. Where public transportation is infrequent, such as the Noto-

On the Menu

Every microregion in Japan's alpine region has its specialties and unique style of preparing seafood from the Sea of Japan. Vitamin-rich seaweed such as *wakame* or *kombu* is a common ingredient, sometimes served in miso soup with tiny *shijimi* clams.

In Toyama spring brings tiny purple-hue baby firefly squid (*hotaru-ika*) to the menu, which are boiled in soy sauce or sake and eaten whole with a tart mustard-miso sauce. Try the seasonal *ama-ebi* (sweet shrimp) and *masu-zushi* (thinly sliced trout sushi that's been pressed flat). In winter, crabs abound, including the red, long-legged *beni-zuwaigani.*

Speaking of crabs, Fukui has huge (some 28 inches leg to leg) *echizen-gani* crabs. When boiled with a little salt and dipped in rice vinegar, they're pure heaven. In both Fukui and Ishi-kawa, restaurants serve *echizen-soba* (homemade buckwheat noodles with mountain vegetables) with sesame oil and bean paste for dipping.

The seafood-based *Kaga-ryori* (Kaga cuisine) is common to Kanazawa and Noto-hanto. *Tai* (sea bream) is topped with mountain fern brackens, greens, and mushrooms. At Wajima's early-morning fish market near the tip of Noto-hanto and at Kanazawa's *omi-cho* market you have your choice of everything from abalone to seaweed, and nearby restaurants will cook it for you.

In Niigata Prefecture try *noppei-jiru*, a hot (or cold) soup with *sato-imo* (a type of sweet potato) as its base, and mushrooms, salmon, and a few other local ingredients. It goes well with hot rice and grilled fish. *Wappa-meshi* is steamed rice garnished with local ingredients, especially wild vegetables,

chicken, fish, and shellfish. In autumn try *kiku-no-ohitashi*, a side dish of chrysanthemum petals marinated in vinegar. Like other prefectures on the Nihon-kai coast, Niigata has outstanding fish in winter—*buri* (yellowtail), flatfish, sole, oysters, abalone, and shrimp. A local specialty is *namban ebi*, raw shrimp dipped in soy sauce and wasabi. It's butter-tender and especially sweet on Sado-ga-shima. Also on Sado-ga-shima, take advantage of the excellent wakame dishes and *sazae-no-tsuboyaki* (wreath shell-fish) broiled in their shells with a soy or miso sauce.

The area around Matsumoto is known for its wasabi and chilled *zarusoba* (buckwheat noodles), a refreshing meal on a hot day, especially with a cold glass of locally brewed sake. Eel steamed inside rice wrapped in bamboo leaves is also popular.

Sansai soba (buckwheat noodles with mountain vegetables) and *sansai-ryori* (wild vegetables and mushrooms in soups or tempura) are specialties in the mountainous areas of Takayama and Nagano. Local river fish like *ayu* (smelt) or *iwana* (char) are grilled on a spit with *shoyu* (soy sauce) or salt. *Hoba miso* is a dark, slightly sweet type of miso roasted on a large magnolia leaf.

Nagano is also famous for *ba-sashi* (raw horse meat), *sakura nabe* (horse-meat stew cooked in an earthenware pot), and boiled baby bees. The former two are still very popular; as for the latter, even locals admit they're something of an acquired taste.

6

CLOSE UP

Get Your Festival On

Takayama's spring and fall festivals (April 14 and 15 and October 9 and 10) transform the usually quiet town into a rowdy, colorful party, culminating in a musical parade of intricately carved and decorated *yatai* (floats) and puppets. Flags and draperies adorn local houses, and at night the yatai are hung with lanterns. Book rooms well ahead and expect inflated prices. April's Sanno Matsuri is slightly bigger than October's Hachi-man Matsuri.

During Kanazawa's Hyaku-man-goku Matsuri (early June) parades of people dressed in ancient Kaga costumes march through the city to the sound of folk music. Torchlit Noh theater performances, ladder-top acrobatics by Kaga firemen, and singing and dancing in parks create a contagious atmosphere of merrymaking.

Of the *many* festivals on the Noto-hanto, the most impressive are Nanao's Seihakusai festival, a 400-year-old tradition where three huge 30-ton wooden *Hikiyama* (Towering Mountain) floats with unpivoted wheels are hauled around the city streets by locals, held May 3–5, and Issaki Hoto Matsuri, held the first Saturday of August.

hanto and Sado-ga-shima, local tours are available; however, the guides speak only Japanese.

THE JAPAN ALPS

The Japan Alps cover a region known as Shinshu, between the north and south coasts of the Chubu area. There are 10 peaks above 9,800 feet that attract both skiers and hikers, but the region also has many parks and forests for less-strenuous nature exploring.

Roads and railways through the Japan Alps follow the valleys. This greatly lengthens trips such as the three-hour Matsumoto–Takayama ride. Route maps for Shinkansen and JR lines are at any train station or bookstore. Some routes only have a few trains a day. The last train or bus may leave as early as 7 pm.

Buses are not as convenient as trains, but some scenic routes are recommended. Any bus station, always right by the train station, has maps and schedules. The local tourist information office—also in or near the train station—will help you decipher timetables and fares.

KARUIZAWA 軽井沢

145 km (90 mi) northwest of Tokyo, 72 km (45 mi) southeast of Nagano

When Archdeacon A.C. Shaw, an English prelate, built his summer villa here in 1886 at the foot of Mt. Asama in southeastern Nagano Prefecture, he sparked the interest of fashionable, affluent Tokyoites, who soon made it their preferred summer destination. Some became patrons of the arts, which led to the opening of galleries and art museums. Pamphlets on current exhibitions are at the tourist office.

Emperor Akihito met the Empress Michiko on a tennis court here in the 1950s. Two decades later John Lennon and Yoko Ono lolled at her family's *besso* (summerhouse) and the Monpei Hotel. In Kyu-Karuizawa, near the Karuizawa train station, more than 500 branches of trendy boutiques sell the same goods as their flagship stores in Tokyo.

GETTING HERE AND AROUND

Coming from Tokyo, Karuizawa is a nice stop en route to the hot-spring towns of Kusatsu and Yudanaka or Matsumoto and Kamikochi. The town itself is easy to explore by foot, taxi, or bicycle. Naka-Karuizawa Station, one stop (five minutes) away on the Shinano Tetsudo Line, is a gateway to Shiraito and Ryugaeshi waterfalls, the Yacho wild bird sanctuary, and hiking trails. ■ TIP→ Karuizawa is very crowded from mid-July to the end of August. If you are visiting during this time, book your accommodation well in advance.

VISITOR INFORMATION

Karuizawa Tourist Information Service is inside the JR Station.

Contact **Karuizawa Tourist Information Service** (☎ *0267/42–5538* ⊕ *www. town.karuizawa.nagano.jp/html/english/index.html*).

WHAT TO SEE

6

Asama-san 浅間山. This active volcano of more than 8,000 feet threatens to put an end to the whole "Highlands Ginza" below. For a view of the glorious Asama-san in its entirety, head to the observation platform at **Usui-toge** 碓氷峠 (Usui Pass). You can also see neighboring Myogi-san, as well as the whole Yatsugatake, a range of eight volcanic peaks. Walk northeast along shop-filled Karuizawa Ginza street to the end, past Nite-bashi, and follow the trail through an evergreen forest to the pass. A lovely view justifies the 1½-hour walk. Two to three buses leave per hour if you want a ride back..

Shiraito-no-taki and Ryugaeshi-no-taki 白糸の滝と竜返しの滝 *(Shiraito and Ryugaeshi falls)*. Hiking paths get crowded during the tourist season, but the falls make a good afternoon excursion in the off-season. To get to the trailhead at Mine-no-Chaya, take the bus from Naka-Karuizawa. The ride takes about 25 minutes. From the trailhead it's about a 1½-km (1-mi) hike to Shiraito. The trail then swings southeast, and 3 km (2 mi) farther are the Ryugaeshi Falls. For a longer hike, walk back to town via Mikasa village. It takes about an hour and 15 minutes. Or catch the bus bound for Karuizawa (10 minutes) from the parking lot.

Yacho-no-mori 野鳥の森 *(Wild Bird Forest)*. This sanctuary is home to some 120 bird species. You can watch the birds' habitat from two observation huts along a 2½-km (1½-mi) forest course. To get here, take a five-minute bus ride from Naka-Karuizawa Station to Nishiku-iriguchi, and then walk up the small road for 400 meters. The narrow entrance is past the café, restaurant, and onsen on the left. Alternatively, you can bike to the sanctuary's entrance in about 15 minutes. Bikes can be rented at Naka-Karuizawa Station for ¥800 per hour or ¥2,000 a day. ✉ *Nagakura Hoshino, Karuizawa-cho* ☎ *0267/45–7777.*

WHERE TO EAT

$$ × **Kastanie** カスターニエ. The tiled bar counter and wooden tables cov-

MEDITERRANEAN ered with red-and-white-checked cloths are as inviting as the staff of this terraced restaurant a few blocks north of the Karuizawa Station. Most dishes are seasonal, but try the grilled vegetable Veronese spaghetti and the salmon and Camembert pizza. Meat plates include herbed, grilled chicken or sizzling rib-roast steak. Look for the sign hanging from the second floor. ⊠ *Kitasakagun* ☎ *0267/42–3081* ⊟ *No credit cards* ⊘ *Closed Mon.*

NAGANO AND ENVIRONS 長野とその周辺

135 mi northwest of Tokyo, 45 mi northwest of Karuizawa, 155 mi northeast of Nagoya.

Nagano Prefecture is called the "Roof of Japan," home to the northern, central, and southern Japan Alps and six national parks that offer year-round recreational activities. Active volcanoes include Mt. Asama on the border between Nagano and Gunma prefectures and Mt. Ontake in Nagano Prefecture, which is a destination for religious pilgrims.

GETTING HERE AND AROUND

Nagano is 97 minutes from Tokyo's Ueno Station by Shinkansen, 40 minutes from Karuizawa by Shinkansen, and three hours from Nagoya by JR Limited Express. It's a convenient base for visiting some of the surrounding onsen and mountains, though you can easily see the main sights around Zenko-ji in half a day.

VISITORINFORMATION

You'll find tourist information offices in Kusatsu, Nagano, and Yamaouchi.

Contacts Kusatsu Information Center (⊠ *3–9 Kusatsu-machi, Kusatsu* ☎ *0279/88–0800* ⊕ *www.kusatsu-onsen.ne.jp*). **Nagano Tourist Office** (⊠ *692–2 Habashita, Minami Nagano* ☎ *026/234–7165* ⊕ *www.go-nagano. net/english*). **Yamanouchi Information Center** (⊠ *Yamanouchi-machi* ☎ *0269/33–1107*).

NAGANO 長野

Rimmed by mountains, Nagano has been a temple town since the founding of Zenko-ji temple in the 7th century. Before the 1998 Winter Olympics a new Shinkansen line was built connecting Tokyo and Nagano, and new highways were added to handle the car and bus traffic. Suddenly the fairly inaccessible Alps region was opened to visitors. Yet as the excitement faded, a rather forlorn air descended. This lifts with vigor in ski season, when visitors swarm the surrounding mountains.

WHAT TO SEE

★ **Zenko-ji** 善光寺. Nagano's unusual temple is the final destination each year for millions of religious pilgrims. Since the 7th century this nonsectarian Buddhist temple has accepted believers of all faiths and admitted women when other temples forbade it. Each morning the head priest (Tendai sect) and head priestess (Jodo sect) hold a joint service to pray for the prosperity of the assembled pilgrims (usually on tour packages).

Zenko-ji in Nagano is a non-sectarian Buddhist temple that accepts believers of all faiths.

Line up outside to be blessed by the priest, who taps his rosary on each head. You then pass the incense burner, waving the smoke over yourself for good fortune and health. Inside, rub the worn wooden statue of the ancient doctor Binzuru (Pindola Bharadvaja in Sanskrit) for relief of aches and pains. A faithful disciple of Buddha, Binzuru is famous for stories of his miraculous powers and ability to fly. After the service, descend into the pitch-black tunnel in the basement to find the iron latch on the wall—seizing it is said to bring enlightenment.

The temple is a 3-km (2-mi) walk from the station, or you can arrange a taxi through your hotel the night before. The starting time for the morning service ranges from 5:30 to 7 am, depending on the season, a minute later or earlier each day. From 9:30 you can hop on the Gururin-go bus for the 10-minute trip (¥100) to the temple gate. ⊠ *4–9–1 Motoyoshi* ☎ *026/234–3591* 🖻 *¥500* ⊘ *Inner sanctuary daily 1 hr before morning prayer–4 (winter), 4:30 (summer).*

YUDANAKA ONSEN 湯田中温泉

Photographs of snow-covered white macaques cavorting in open-air thermal pools have made Yudanaka Onsen famous. Northeast of Nagano, nine open-air hot springs are between Yudanaka Onsen and Shibu Spa Resort. The onsen where the monkeys soak is known as Jigoku-dani (Hell Valley), and is just east of Yudanaka and Shibu. Yudanaka is the last stop on the Nagano Dentetsu Line; the trip from Nagano takes 40 minutes and costs ¥1,230. Several spas string out from here. The area is not unlike Yellowstone National Park, with its bubbling, steaming, sulfurous volcanic vents and pools. Considerable development, however, including more than 100 inns and hotels, several streets, and shops, ends the comparison. The spas are the gateway to Shiga Kogen (Shiga Heights), site of Olympic alpine skiing and the snowboarding slalom. There are several inexpensive ryokan in Yudanaka, which makes an overnight trip worthwhile if you have time.

WHAT TO SEE

Jigoku-dani Yaen Koen 地獄谷野猿公苑. You may have seen videos or photos of the Japanese white macaques steaming in this snow-covered onsen in winter, though they live here year-round. But when snow is on the ground, they are a big draw; just don't feed or touch them—or look them in the eye. The train goes as far as Yudanaka; from there, take a taxi or public bus to Kanbayashi Onsen, from which it is a 40-minute walk. From early December to late March, you can catch a "Snow Monkey Holiday Minibus" from Yudanaka or Shibu Onsen to a parking lot about 10 minutes on foot from the monkey onsen. The bus doesn't run every day, so check the schedule in advance. A return bus ride plus park entry is ¥1,500 from Shibu Onsen (¥700 for just return bus) or ¥1,700 from Yudanaka (¥800 for bus only). You need to buy your tickets in cash at least the day before, and then call the bus company on the day you plan to ride to reserve a seat (your hotel can help). ✉ 6845 Yamanouchi-machi, Shimotakai-gun ☎ 0269/33–8636 Snow Monkey Holiday Minibus tickets and reservations, 0269/33–2921 Shibu Onsen Ryokan Association (for information) ⊕ www.jigokudani-yaenkoen. co.jp ✍ ¥500 ⊘ Apr.–Oct., daily 8:30–5; Nov.–Mar., daily 9–4.

KUSATSU 草津

★ The highly touted hot springs at Kusatsu contain sulfur, iron, aluminum, and even trace amounts of arsenic. Just inside the border of Gunma Prefecture, the springs are reached in summer (April–November) by a bus route across Shiga Kogen from Yudanaka, or year-round from Karuizawa. The yu-batake (hot-spring field) gushes over 1,000 gallons of boiling, sulfur-laden water per minute before it's cooled in seven long wooden boxes and sent to more than 130 ryokan in the village. The open field is beautifully lighted up at night.

WHAT TO SEE

Netsu-no-yu 熱の湯 (Fever Bath). This is the main and often unbearably hot public bath next door to the yu-batake. You can't actually bathe here, but you can watch one of several daily yumomi shows from April to November (10, 10:30, 3:30, 4, 4:30, and 5, extra early morning shows in October and no 5 pm show April), in which locals churn the waters with long wooden planks until the baths reach a comfortable temperature. ✉ 414 Kusatsu-cho ☎ 0279/88–3613 ✍ ¥500 ⊘ Daily 10–5.

Sai-no-kawara Dai-rotemburo 西の河原大露天風呂. For a dip in the open air, try the 5,500-square-foot milky bath at the western end of Kusatsu village, with pleasing scenery by day and stars by night. The spa is a 15-minute walk west from the Kusatsu bus terminal. ✉ 521–3 Kusatsu-machi ☎ 0279/88–6167 ✍ ¥500 ⊘ Apr.–Nov., daily 7 am–8 pm; Dec.–Mar., daily 9 am–8 pm.

WHERE TO EAT AND STAY

Hotel reviews have been condensed for this book. Please go to Fodors. com for full reviews of each property.

$$$$
JAPANESE
✕**Restaurant Sakura** さくら. A few blocks southwest of Zenko-ji, the famous sake distiller Yoshinoya has a restaurant attached to the sake factory and warehouses. From 9 to 5 you can tour for free, ending with a sampling of fresh sake. Sakura has an open-air terrace and a glass-walled interior. The Sakura *bento* (box lunches) for ¥1,890 holds seasonal delights like the pungent Matsutake mushroom. ✉ *941 Nishinomon-cho* ☎ *026/237–5000* ⏱ *Closed the 4th Wed. of each month. Sake factory occasionally closed for special events—call first.*

$$
HOTEL
🏨**Nagano Sunroute Hotel** ホテルサンルート長野. A coffee table and two easy chairs are squeezed into each compact Western-style room, which is all you need if you're en route to other Alps destinations. **Pros:** convenient location next to the station. **Cons:** small rooms for the price. ✉ *1–28–3 Minami-Chitose* ☎ *026/228–2222* 🖷 *026/228–2244* 🛏 *143 rooms* ⚅ *In-room: a/c, refrigerator, Internet. In-hotel: restaurant, laundry service* 🍴 *No meals.*

$–$$
RYOKAN
★
🏨**Uotoshi Ryokan** 魚敏旅館. This small ryokan in the steamy bath village of Yudanaka has a 24-hour, hot springs-fed *hinoki* (cypress) bathtub. **Pros:** the chance to try your hand at Japanese archery is a rare treat. **Cons:** somewhat out of the way. ✉ *2563 Sano, Yamanouchi-machi, Shimo-Takai-gun* ☎ *0269/33–1215* 🖷 *0269/33–0074* 🌐 *www.avis. ne.jp/~miyasaka* 🛏 *8 Japanese-style rooms without bath* ⚅ *In-room: a/c, Internet. In-hotel: restaurant* 🍴 *Breakfast.*

MATSUMOTO 松本

64 km (40 mi) southwest of Nagano, 282 km (175 mi) northwest of Tokyo, 185 km (115 mi) northeast of Nagoya.

Snowcapped peaks surround the old castle town of Matsumoto, where the air is cool and dry on the alpine plateau. More interesting and picturesque than Nagano, this gateway to the northern Alps is one of the best bases for exploring the area. Full of good cafés and restaurants, Matsumoto is also a center for traditional crafts including *tensan*, fabric woven from silk taken from wild silkworms; Matsumoto *shiki* or lacquerware; Azumino glass; and wood crafts. Old merchant houses stand along Nakamachi Street, south of the castle. Several influential educators, lawyers, and writers from this city have impacted Japan's sociopolitical system in the past.

Though it only takes a day to visit the main sights in town, Matsumoto's restaurants, cafés, and relaxed atmosphere make it a hard place to leave. It is worth staying a night or two to visit the outlying museums and onsen. Matsumoto is also a good base to visit Kamikochi to the west, or the post towns of Magome and Tsumago to the south.

GETTING HERE AND AROUND

Fuji Dream Airlines (FDA), code-sharing with Japan Airlines, has daily flights between Matsumoto and Fukuoka, Kagoshima, and Sapporo. Trains are also available: Matsumoto is 1 hour from Nagano on JR Shinonoi Line, 1 hour from Tokyo Shinjuku Station on JR Chuo Line

Matsumoto-jo is also called "Crow Castle" because of its black walls.

"Azusa" express, and 2¼ hours from Nagoya on JR Chuo Line's "Wide View Hinano" express. By highway bus it's 3¼ hours east of Takayama.

Contact Fuji Dream Airlines (☎ *050/3786–0489* ⊕ *www.fujidreamairlines.com [Japanese only]*).

VISITOR INFORMATION

Matsumoto is very compact, so grab a map at the Tourist Information Center at the JR Station and head for the old part of town near the Chitose-bashi Bridge at the end of Hon-machi-dori. Alternatively, Matsumoto's Town Sneaker shuttle bus (¥150–¥190) stops at the main sights, and the tourist office can direct you to one of the many locations lending free bicycles.

Contact Tourist Information Center (✉ *3–7 Marunoichi* ☎ *0263/32–2814* ⊕ *welcome.city.matsumoto.nagano.jp*).

WHAT TO SEE

OLD TOWN

★ **Kyu Kaichi Gakko** 開智学校 *(Kaichi Primary School)*. Built in 1873, the former Kaichi Primary School houses more than 80,000 educational artifacts from the Meiji Restoration, when education was to become the unifying tool for the rapid modernization of post-feudal Japan. The displays in the former classrooms include wall charts (used prior to the introduction of textbooks) and 19th-century desks and writing slates. The building was used as a school until 1960. Its bizarre style reflects the architecture of the period: a mishmash of diverse Occidental elements fashioned from Japanese materials. A big, fancy cupola sits atop the shingled roof; the white walls made of mortar are dotted with red, slatted windows; and the front door, hidden in the shadow of the blue, grandiose balcony, is protected by a skillfully carved dragon. ⊠ *2–4–12 Kaichi* ☎ *0263/32–5725* 🖃 *¥300* 🕓 *Tues.–Sun. 8:30–5.*

★ **Matsumoto-jo** 松本城 *(Matsumoto Castle).* Nicknamed Karasu-jo (Crow Castle) for its black walls, this castle began as a small fortress with moats in 1504. It was remodeled into its current three-turreted form between 1592 and 1614, just as Japan became a consolidated nation under a central government. The civil wars ended and the peaceful Edo era (1603–1868) began, rendering medieval castles obsolete. Its late construction explains why the 95-foot-tall *tenshukaku* (stronghold or inner tower) is the oldest surviving tower in Japan—no battles were ever fought here. Exhibits on each floor break up the challenging climb up very steep stairs to the top. If you hunker down to look through rectangular openings (broad enough to scan for potential enemies) on the sixth floor, you'll have a gorgeous view of the surrounding mountains. At the end of July there is a *taiko* (Japanese drums) festival and on November 3 and 4 the Matsumoto Castle Festival features a samurai parade.

In the southwest corner of the castle grounds, which bloom in spring with cherry trees, azaleas, and wisteria, the **Nihon Minzoku Shiryokan** (Japan Folklore Museum) exhibits samurai wear, Edo-period agricultural implements, and explanations of Matsumoto's development. In January an ice-sculpture exhibition is held in the museum's park. The castle is a 20-minute walk from the station. ⊠ *4–1 Marunouchi* ☎ *0263/32–2902 for castle, 0263/32–0133 for museum* 🖃 *Castle and museum ¥600* 🕓 *Daily 8:30–5.*

NEED A BREAK?

Old Rock. Two blocks before the Chitose-bashi Bridge, which takes you from Hon-machi dori across the river to the castle, this Japanese version of a traditional British pub serves fish-and-chips, pizza, and (sometimes) roast beef. Guinness, Kilkenny, Boddingtons, Stella Artois, and local Karuizawa beer are on draft. It's close to Parco department store, between the station and castle. ⊠ *2-3-20 Chuo* ☎ *0263/38-0069* 🕓 *Daily 11:30-2:30 and 6-midnight.*

WEST OF THE STATION

Two of the city's best museums are west of the JR Station. It's too far to walk, and there's no bus. You can take the Kamikochi train (on the private Matsumoto Dentetsu Line) four stops to Oniwa Station and walk 10 minutes. The museums can be hard to find though, so the ¥2,000 taxi ride, albeit expensive, is recommended.

Matsumoto Rekishi no Sato *(Matsumoto History Village).* Next to the Ukiyo-e Hakubutsukan is Japan's oldest palatial wooden court building and the former site of the Matsumoto District Court. Displays pertain to the history of law enforcement from the feudal period to the modern era. ⊠ *2196–01 Shimadachi, Koshiba* ☎ *0263/47–4515* 🖃 *¥400* 🕓 *Tues.–Sun. 9–4:30.*

★ **Nihon Ukiyo-e Hakubutsukan** 日本浮世絵博物館 *(Japan Wood-Block Print Museum).* The museum is devoted to the lively, colorful, and widely popular *ukiyo-e* wood-block prints of Edo-period artists. Highlights include Hiroshige's scenes of the Tokaido (the main trading route through Honshu in feudal Japan), Hokusai's views of Mt. Fuji, and Sharaku's Kabuki actors. Based on the enormous holdings of the wealthy Sakai family, the museum's 100,000 pieces (displays rotate every three months) include some of Japan's finest prints and represent the largest collection of its kind in the world. ✉ *2206–1 Shimadachi, Koshiba* ☎ *0263/47–4440* ⊕ *www.ukiyo-e.co.jp/jum-e* ✍ *¥1,200* ⊘ *Tues.–Sun. 10–5.*

AROUND MATSUMOTO

The local train to the Daio horseradish farm and the Rokuzan Art Museum journeys through vibrant green fields, apple orchards, and miles of rice paddies.

Daio Wasabi Nojo 大王わさび農場 *(Daio Wasabi Farm).* At the largest wasabi farm in the country, the green horseradish roots are cultivated in flat gravel beds irrigated by melted snow from the Alps. The chilly mineral water is ideal for the durable wasabi.

You should try some of the farm's products, which range from wasabi cheese to wasabi chocolate and wasabi ice cream. You can pickle your own horseradish in one of the 20-minute workshops (¥1,000). The farm is 10 stops (one on the express) north along the JR Oito Line from Platform 6 in Matsumoto Station. To reach the farm from Hotaka Station, you can rent a bike, take a 40-minute walk along a path from the train station (the station attendant will direct you), or hop in a taxi for about ¥1,300. ✉ *1692 Hotaka* ☎ *0263/82–8112* ✍ *Free* ⊘ *May–Oct., daily 8:30–5:20; Nov.–Apr., daily 9–4:30.*

Rokuzan Bijutsukan 碌山美術館 *(Rokuzan Art Museum).* The museum displays the work of Rokuzan Ogiwara, a sculptor who was influenced by Auguste Rodin and pioneered modern sculptural styles in Japan. He is especially known for his female figures and male figures in heroic poses. This ivy-covered brick building with a stunning bell tower is in Hotaka, 10 stops north of Matsumoto Station on the JR Oito Line. From Hotaka Station it's a 10-minute walk to the museum. ✉ *5095–1 Oaza-hotaka* ☎ *0263/82–2094* ✍ *¥700* ⊘ *May–Oct., daily 9–5; Nov.–Apr., Tues.–Sun. 9–4.*

WHERE TO EAT

$$$
JAPANESE
Fodor's Choice
★

✕ **Kura** 蔵. For a surprisingly small number of yen you can feast in this 90-year-old Meiji-era warehouse in the center of town. Kura serves a large assortment of sushi and traditional fare: the *aji tataki* (horse-mackerel sashimi) and tempura are particularly tasty. The stoic owner expertly prepares your meal, but should his wife spot you relishing the food, you're in for some disarming hospitality—she has an arsenal of potent *ji-zake* (locally brewed sake) and a heart of gold. From the station, take a left onto Koen-dori. Take a left after the Parco department store, and you'll see the restaurant's whitewashed facade and curved black eaves on the left. ✉ *1–10–22 Chuo* ☎ *0263/33–6444* ⊘ *Closed Mon.*

$$
JAPANESE

✕ **Yakitori Yume-ya** 焼き鳥夢屋. Adorned in retro, prewar decor, Yume-ya specializes in old-style yakitori (skewered, grilled meat and vegetables). Cozy up to the narrow counter for food and drinks, or sit outside during the warmer months. Little English is spoken, but the cooks are happy to explain the menu with exaggerated gestures. ⊠ *Showa Yokocho Bldg., 1–13–11 Chuo* ☎ *0263/33–8430* ▭ *No credit cards* ⊗ *Closed Sun. No lunch.*

WHERE TO STAY

Hotel reviews have been condensed for this book. Please go to Fodors. com for full reviews of each property.

$$$–$$$$
HOTEL
🏨 **Hotel Buena Vista** ホテルブエナビスタ. One of Matsumoto's more expensive hotels, the Buena Vista has a glowing marble lobby, a coffeehouse, a café-bar, four restaurants (two Japanese, one Chinese, one French), and a sky lounge called **Sorpresa** that serves French food. **Pros:** large rooms; good location. **Cons:** buffet dinner is pricey. ⊠ *1–2–1 Hon-jo* ☎ *0263/37–0111* 🖷 *0263/37–0666* ⊕ *www.buena-vista.co.jp* ⋑ *200 rooms* ⌂ *In-room: a/c, refrigerator, Internet. In-hotel: 4 restaurants, bar* ❮◉❯ *No meals.*

$$
HOTEL
🏨 **Hotel New Station** ホテルニューステーション. Although good-value business hotels are often sterile, this one has a cheerful staff and a lively restaurant that serves freshwater *iwana* (char)—an area specialty. **Pros:** inexpensive; excellent staff; near the station. **Cons:** small rooms. ⊠ *1–1–11 Chuo* ☎ *0263/35–3850* 🖷 *0263/35–3851* ⊕ *www.hotel-ns.co.jp* ⋑ *95 rooms* ⌂ *In-room: a/c, Internet. In-hotel: restaurant* ❮◉❯ *No meals.*

$$$$
RYOKAN
★
🏨 **Kikunoyu** 菊の湯. This stately hot-spring ryokan was built in the *honmune-zukuri* or traditional private-house style. **Pros:** relaxing getaway; staff speak some English. **Cons:** not a good base for other sightseeing. ⊠ *1–29–7 Asama-onsen, Nagano-ken* ☎ *0263/46–2300* 🖷 *0263/46–0015* ⊕ *www.kikunoyu.com* ⋑ *17 Japanese-style rooms* ⌂ *In-room: a/c, refrigerator. In-hotel: restaurant, Internet terminal* ❮◉❯ *Some meals.*

NIGHTLIFE

Eonta エオンタ. This jazz bar has been popular with locals since the 1970s. The owner plays songs from his 1,000-plus CDs. A corner with sofas is for those who listen only. Toasted sandwiches, light meals, and good coffee are served. It's in a quasi-dilapidated two-story building a few blocks southeast of the castle. ⊠ *9–7 Ota 4-chome* ☎ *0263/33–0505* ⊕ *www.getnagano.com/en/places/nightlife* ⊗ *Thurs.–Tues. 4 pm–midnight.*

HAKUBA 白馬

★ *64 km (40 mi) north of Matsumoto, 48 km (30 mi) northwest of Nagano.*

In the northwestern part of Nagano Prefecture, Hakuba Village 白馬村 lies beneath the magnificent Hakuba Range, the best of the northern Japan Alps. Hakuba means "white horse," because the main peak, Mt. Shirouma-dake (9,617 feet), resembles a horse. This is an all-year resort area for trekking, skiing, and climbing around the 9,500-foot mountains among rare alpine flora, insects, and wildlife. Gondola and chairlifts carry you up to ridges with panoramic views. More than 850 lodging facilities serve the 3.7 million annual visitors. Olympic alpine runs and ski jumps await winter sports fans, and summer visitors can still find snow, especially in the Grand Snowy Gorge.

Hakuba Village, at the foot of the Hakuba Range of mountains, is green in spring and summer and a major skiing center in winter.

Since the main attractions of Hakuba are hiking and skiing in the mountains, plan to stay at least two days to take advantage of the surroundings. The ski season in Hakuba runs from December to the first week of May. The hiking season is late June until the end of September, though the trails can be crowded in August. In July the mountains are covered in fields of wildflowers, making for a spectacular sight.

GETTING HERE AND AROUND
Both the JR Limited Express and the JR Oito Line run from Matsumoto to Hakuba. From Nagano the bus will take about an hour.

VISITOR INFORMATION
The **Hakuba Village Office of Tourism,** to the right as you exit the train station, provides basic maps (mostly in Japanese). Near the Alpico bus terminal and Happo bus stop is the **Happo-o-ne Tourism Association.** The staff can help you reserve a hotel room, but for the peak summer and winter seasons, you should book in advance. Run by a Canadian and Japanese couple, **Evergreen Outdoor Center** offers a variety of outdoor tours year-round. It is also a good place to get information on outdoor activities in the Hakuba area.

Contacts Evergreen Outdoor Center (✉ *Wadanomori Visitor Center, 4683–2 Happo Hakuba, Wadano* ☎ *0261/72–5150*). **Hakuba Village Office of Tourism** (☎ *0261/72–5000* ⊕ *vill.hakuba.nagano.jp/english*). **Happo-o-ne Tourism Association** (☎ *0261/72—3066*).

WHAT TO SEE

Happo-o-ne Ski Resort 八方尾根スキー場. Japan's first parallel jumping hills were constructed with critical points of 393 feet and 295 feet, and each has a scaffold structure for the in-run and landing slope. These ski jumps can also be used in spring and summer. The Champion and Panorama courses have starting points of an altitude of 5,510 feet, with separate courses for men (vertical drop 2,755 feet) and women (vertical drop 2,555 feet). The downhill course for super-giant slalom starts lower. This ridge stretches to the east from Mt. Karamatsu (8,843 feet), with breathtaking views if the mist doesn't roll in. Even in summer a sweater or light jacket may be needed. You can reach the first cairn via three connecting gondolas (five minutes to Happo Gondola Station, then eight minutes by gondola for Usagidaira, and an additional 10 minutes by alpine lift). From here the jewel-like Happo Pond is a 6-km (4-mi) hike. For more-ambitious hikers, three more hours gets you to the top of Mt. Karamatsu-dake. It's a five-minute, 3-km (2-mi) bus ride from Hakuba to Happo and then a 15-minute walk through the resort of Swiss-like chalets and hotels to the gondola station. The round-trip fare is ¥2,600, and the lower gondola operates from 8 am to 5 pm (from 7 am in July); the higher chairlift stops at 4:30 pm. ✉ *5734–1 Hokujo Happo, Kitaajimi-gun* ☎ *0261/72–3066* ⊕ *www.hakuba-happo.or.jp/en.*

Mt. Shirouma-dake 白馬岳. Hiking at the bottom of Hakuba Grand Snowy Gorge (Daisekkei), one of Japan's largest gorges (3½ km [2 mi]), which is snowy all year round, requires warm clothes even in midsummer, when temperatures can dip below freezing. More than 100 types of alpine flowers grace the nearby fields in summer. From the trailhead at Sarukura Village heading west, it's 1 hour, 45 minutes to the gorge through the forest. If you are lucky, you may see snow grouse, a protected species in Japan. For climbers who want to scale Mt. Shirouma, which takes six hours to the top (two huts are on the way for overnight stays), proper equipment is necessary. The trail southwest of Sarukura to Yarigatake—a shorter hike of three hours—leads to the highest outdoor hot spring, **Yari Onsen**, at an elevation of 6,888 feet. The onsen is part of an overnight lodge with rates from ¥8,900, which include two meals; you pay ¥300 just to use the onsen. The lodge is open from mid-July to the end of September. Adequate hiking gear is necessary for the longer trails. Sarukura is a 40-minute bus ride from Hakuba Station. Equipment like snowshoes and crampons can be rented in Hakuba Village. ☎ *0261/72–2002 Yari Onsen lodge reservations* ✑ *¥300.*

Tsugaike Shizen-en 栂池自然園 *(Tsugaike Natural Park). This* alpine marshland dazzles with a wide variety of rare alpine flora from early June to late October and is graced with gold and crimson leaves from September to October. It is a three-hour walk to take in the entire park. Getting there requires a one-hour bus ride (early June to late October) from Hakuba Oike Station, two stops north of Hakuba Station. ✉ *131 Naka Otani-bei, Otari-mura, Kita-Azumi-gun district* ☎ *0261/82–2233 (Otari Village tourism office)* ✑ *¥300* ☉ *Mid-May–early Nov., daily.*

WHERE TO STAY

Hotel reviews have been condensed for this book. Please go to Fodors. com for full reviews of each property.

$$
INN
🈁 **Pension Noichigo Pension** 野いちご. A five-minute walk (or ski) from the Happo-o-ne lift, family-run Noichigo feels more like a European pension than a Japanese inn. **Pros:** excellent location for hiking and skiing; friendly and knowledgeable owners. **Cons:** fewer luxury amenities than larger hotels. ⊠ *4869 Wadano-no-mori, Wadano* ☎ *0261/72–4707* ⊕ *www.janis.or.jp/users/noichigo/top_page_english.html* 🛏 *6 rooms* ⌂ *In-room: a/c (some), Internet. In-hotel: restaurant* ▭ *No credit cards* ⍩ *Some meals.*

KISO VALLEY 木曾谷(木曾路)

★ *89 km (55 mi) south of Matsumoto.*

This deep and narrow valley is cut by the Kiso River and walled in by the central Alps to the east and the northern Alps to the west. From 1603 to 1867 the area was called Nakasendo (center highway), because it connected western Japan and Kyoto to Edo (present-day Tokyo).

After the Tokaido highway was built along the Pacific coast and the Chuo train line was constructed to connect Nagoya and Niigata, the 11 once-bustling post villages, where travelers and traders once stopped to refresh themselves and share news, became ghost towns. Two villages, Tsumago and Magome, have benefited from efforts to retain the memory of these old settlements. Traditional houses have been restored along the sloping stone streets and power lines have been buried underground. Walking through these historical areas, you can almost imagine life centuries ago, when the rustic shops were stocked with supplies for travelers instead of the traditional crafts now offered for sale.

EN ROUTE
You can hike the **old trade route** between Magome and Tsumago. The full 500-km (310-mi) post road connecting Tokyo and Kyoto was constructed during the 8th century. Hiking the section between Magome and Tsumago is a hilly three-hour trip. At points the road becomes a dirt pathway winding through forests of cedar past small shrines and a pair of waterfalls. There's a daily baggage delivery service between the two towns (¥500 per bag) from late July to the end of August. It is available on weekends and public holidays the rest of the year. Make arrangements at tourist information offices.

GETTING HERE AND AROUND

The central valley town of Nagiso is one hour south of Matsumoto on the JR Chuo Line. Tsumago is a 10-minute bus ride (¥300) from JR Nagiso Station. Magome is closer to JR Nakatsugawa Station, which is 12 minutes south on the same line. Both towns are served by buses from the Nagiso and Nakatsugawa stations, so you can take a bus to one village and return from the other. Local buses between Magome and Tsumago are infrequent. A taxi costs about ¥3,000. To get to Takayama from here, take the JR Chuo Line from Nakatsugawa or Nagiso to Tajimi, change to a local JR Takayama Line train to Mina-Ota, then an express train to Takayama (total four hours). There are

Traditional houses have been restored along Magome's sloping streets.

also infrequent buses from Nakatsugawa to Gero, which is 45 minutes from Takayama by express train. There are also direct highway buses from Magome to Tokyo's Shinjuku Station (4½ hours).

VISITOR INFORMATION

The staff at Magome Tourist Information Office—in the village center along the old post road—can help you reserve a hotel room. The Tsumago Tourist Information Office, in the center of town, has the same services as the Magome tourist office.

Contacts Magome Tourist Information Office (☎ 0573/69–2336 ⊙ *Daily 9–5*). **Tsumago Tourist Information Office** (☎ 0264/57–3123 ⊙ *Daily 9–5*).

WHERE TO STAY

Hotel reviews have been condensed for this book. Please go to Fodors. com for full reviews of each property.

$$$
RYOKAN
★

📷 **Hatago Matsushiro-ya** 旅籠松代屋. This small ryokan in Tsumago has been a guesthouse since 1804. **Pros:** traditional setting; beautiful building. **Cons:** no private bath or toilets; paper walls mean little privacy. ⊠ *807 Azuma-Terashita, Minami-Nagiso-machi, Kiso-gun* ☎ *0264/57– 3022* 🛏 *7 Japanese-style rooms without bath* ♿ *In-room: a/c, no phone* 🖃 *No credit cards* ⊙ *Closed Wed.* ⅊ *Some meals.*

$
MINSHUKU

📷 **Magome Chaya** 馬籠茶屋. The friendly English-speaking owners of this reasonably priced Magome guesthouse in the center of town welcome foreign visitors. **Pros:** central location; friendly staff; hotel has a kitchen for guest use. **Cons:** small rooms; no private baths. ⊠ *4206 Magome, Nakatsugawa* ☎ *0573/69–2038* 🛏 *13 Japanese-style rooms without bath* ♿ *In-room: a/c* 🖃 *No credit cards* ⅊ *Some meals.*

$$$
MINSHUKU

🏠 **Onyado Daikichi** 御宿大吉. The windows in all six tatami rooms of this minshuku face the wooded valley. The chef prepares local specialties such as horse-meat sashimi, mountain vegetables, and fried grasshoppers, but more-familiar Japanese food is also on the menu. Owner Nobuko-san welcomes foreign guests and even speaks a little English. There are shared Japanese baths. **Pros:** lovely views; traditional setting. **Cons:** no private baths. ✉ *Tsumago, Nagiso-machi, Kiso-gun* ☎ *0264/57–2595* 📠 *0274/57–2203* 📠 *6 Japanese-style rooms without bath* ⚲ *In-room: a/c. In-hotel: restaurant* ⊟ *No credit cards* 🍽 *Some meals.*

KAMIKOCHI 上高地

48 km (30 mi) west of Matsumoto, 64 km (40 mi) east of Takayama.

The incomparably scenic route from Matsumoto to Takayama winds over the mountains and through Chubu-Sangaku National Park (Chubu-Sangaku Kokuritsu Koen) via Kamikochi. Travel is only possible after the last week of April or the first week of May, when plows have removed the almost 30 feet of winter snow. If you spend the night in Kamikochi, which is surrounded by virgin forests of birch, larch, and hemlock, consider renting a rowboat at Taisho-ike (Taisho Pond) for the spectacular view of the snow-covered peaks.

Unless you plan to do some serious hiking, Kamikochi is best done as a day trip from Takayama or Matsumoto. Plan to arrive in the morning, though, as it is worth spending the entire day here.

GETTING HERE AND AROUND

No cars are allowed in Kamikochi. Take the Matsumoto Electric Railway from Matsumoto Station to Shin-Shimashima, the last stop. The ride takes 30 minutes and departs once or twice an hour. At Shin-Shimashima Station, cross the road for the bus to Naka-no-yu and Kamikochi (¥1900, or ¥2400 for a bus-and-train combo ticket). There are also buses from Matsumoto to Kamikochi, departing twice daily when the road is open (late April–November; ¥2400). To get here from Takayama, take a bus to Hirayu Onsen (one hour; ¥1,530) and change to another bus for Kamikochi (25 minutes; ¥1,130). There are some direct buses in summer from Takayama.

VISITOR INFORMATION

Up-to-date bus and road information is available at the Matsumoto and Takayama tourist offices. Kamikochi is where the trails for some of the most famed alpine ascents begin; favorite peaks are Mt. Yariga-take and Mt. Hotaka-dake. Most maps are in Japanese, but some English information is available from tourist info offices. Planning in advance is essential; climbs range from a few days to a week, and the trails can be crowded in summer.

WHERE TO STAY

Hotels and ryokan here close from mid-November to late April.

Hotel reviews have been condensed for this book. Please go to Fodors. com for full reviews of each property.

Kamikochi's Imperial Hotel is a branch of the famous hotel in Tokyo.

$$$$ Imperial Hotel 上高地帝国ホテル. This rustic alpine lodge is owned by
HOTEL   Tokyo's legendary Imperial Hotel, and staff members are borrowed from
Fodor's Choice   that establishment for summer. **Pros:** luxurious accommodations. **Cons:**
★   more expensive than other lodgings in the area. ⊠ *Azumi-kamikochi,
Matsumoto, Nagano-ken* ☎ *0263/95–2006, 03/3592–8001 Nov.–Mar.,
212/692–9001 in U.S.* ⊟ *0263/95–2412* ⊕ *www.imperialhotel.co.jp*
⇆ *75 rooms* ☐ *In-room: a/c, safe, refrigerator. In-hotel: 3 restaurants,
bar* ⫶⊙⫶ *Some meals.*

$$$–$$$$ Taisho-ike Hotel 大正池ホテル. This small mountain resort is perched
HOTEL   on the rim of the brilliant-blue Taisho Pond. **Pros:** lovely views; com-
fortable Western-style rooms. **Cons:** Japanese-style rooms aren't recom-
mended. ⊠ *Azumi-kamikochi, Matsumoto* ☎ *0263/95–2301* ⊟ *0263/
95–2522* ⊕ *www.taisyoike.co.jp/english* ⇆ *21 Western-style rooms, 6
Japanese-style rooms* ☐ *In-room: a/c, no phone. In-hotel: restaurant*
⫶⊙⫶ *Some meals.*

SPORTS AND THE OUTDOORS

HIKING

As you approach Kamikochi, the valley opens onto a row of tower-
ing mountains: Oku-Hotaka-san is the highest, at 10,466 feet. Mae-
Hotaka-san, at 10,138 feet, is on the left. To the right is 9,544-foot
Nishi-Hotaka-san. The icy waters of the Azusa-gawa flow from the
small Taisho Pond at the southeast entrance to the basin.

There are many hiking trails in the river valley around Kamikochi.
One easy three-hour walk east starts at **Kappabashi**, a small suspen-
sion bridge over the crystal clear Azusa-gawa, a few minutes northeast
of the bus terminal. Along the way is a stone sculpture of the British

explorer Reverend Walter Weston, the first foreigner to ascend these mountains. Continuing on the south side of the river, the trail cuts through a pasture to rejoin the river at Myoshin Bridge. Cross here to reach Myoshin-ike (Myoshin Pond). At the edge of the pond sits the small Hotaka Jinja Kappabashi (Water Sprite Bridge). To see the beautiful **Taisho-ike** 大正池 (Taisho Pond), head southeast from Kappabashi for a 20-minute walk. You can rent a boat (¥800 per half hour), or continue 90 minutes farther east to **Tokusawa,** an area with camping grounds and great mountain views.

TAKAYAMA 高山

267 km (166 mi) north of Nagoya, 80 km (50 mi) north of Matsumoto.

Takayama, originally called Hida, is a tranquil town whose rustic charms are the result of hundreds of years of peaceful isolation in the Hida Mountains. Downtown, shops and restaurants mingle with museums and inns along rows of traditional wood-lattice buildings. A peculiar-looking ball of cedar leaves suspended outside a storefront indicates a drinking establishment or brewery. Nicknamed "Little Kyoto," Takayama has fewer crowds and wider streets, not to mention fresh mountain air and gorgeous scenery.

Takayama's hugely popular festivals, spring's Sanno Matsuri (April 14–15) and the smaller autumn Hachi-man Matsuri (October 9–10), draw hundreds of thousands of spectators for parades of floats. Hotels are booked solid during Matsuri time, so if you plan to join the festivities, make reservations several months in advance.

Outside of festival time, it is easy to see all the main attractions here in a day, two at the most. Though it's decidedly touristy, many people like using Takayama as a hub to visit Kamikochi and the surrounding area.

GETTING HERE AND AROUND

Takayama has connections north to Toyama by JR train (four departures daily). The ride takes about two hours (with up to an hour waiting for connections) and costs ¥1,620. From Toyama trains go east to Niigata or west to Kanazawa and the Noto-hanto. It's easy to get to Takayama by bus from Matsumoto for ¥3,400. A highly recommended detour to Kamikochi—available May through early November—increases the fare to ¥6,260.

Laid out in a compact grid, Takayama can be explored on foot or bicycle. Several shops rent bikes; ask at the tourist information office for details.

VISITOR INFORMATION

The Hida Tourist Information Office, in front of the JR Station, is open from April to October, daily 8:30–6:30; and from November to March, daily 8:30–5. The English-speaking staff provides maps and helps with accommodations, both in town and in the surrounding mountains.

Contact Hida Tourist Information Office (☎ *0577/32-5328* ⊕ *www.hida.jp/english*).

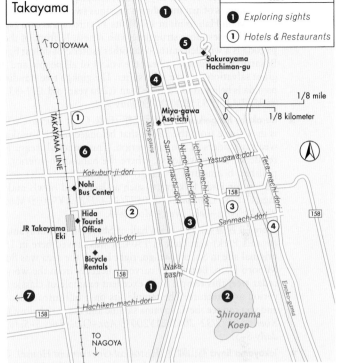

Takayama

KEY

❶ *Exploring sights*

① *Hotels & Restaurants*

TO TOYAMA

Sakurayama
Hachiman-gu

Miya-gawa
Asa-ichi

1/8 mile

1/8 kilometer

TAKAYAMA LINE

Miya-gawa

Yasugawa-dori

San-no-machi-dori

Ni-no-machi-dori

Ichi-no-machi-dori

Tera-machi-dori

Kokubun-ji-dori

Nohi
Bus Center

Hida
Tourist
Office

JR Takayama
Eki

Hirokoji-dori

Sanmachi-dori

158

158

158

Bicycle
Rentals

158

Naka-
bashi

Hachiken-machi-dori

158

TO
NAGOYA
↓

Shiroyama
Koen

Enoko-gawa

6

WHAT TO SEE

Hida Minzoku Kokokan 飛騨民俗考古館 *(Archaeology Museum)*. This mansion once belonged to a physician who served the local daimyo (feudal lord). It has mysterious eccentricities—hanging ceilings, secret windows, and hidden passages—all of which suggest ninja associations. Displays include wall hangings, weaving machines, and other Hida regional items. ⊠ *82 Kamisanno-machi* ☎ *0577/32–1980* ☞ *¥500* ⊙ *Mar.–Oct., daily 9–5; Nov.–Feb., daily 9:30–4:30.*

Fodor'sChoice
★

Hida no Sato 飛騨の里 *(Hida Folk Village)*. These traditional farmhouses, dating from the Edo era, were transplanted from all over the region. Many of the houses are A-frames with thatch roofs called gassho-zukuri (praying hands). You're free to go inside the buildings. Twelve of the buildings are "private houses" displaying folk artifacts like tableware and weaving tools. Another five houses are folk-craft workshops, with demonstrations of *ichii ittobori* (wood carving), *Hida-nuri* (Hida lacquering), and other traditional regional arts. It's possible to walk here from Takayama Station but the roads are busy; it's better to buy a combination bus/folk village ticket at the bus station next to Takayama Station. ⊠ *1–590 Kami-Okamoto-cho, Gifu* ☎ *0577/34–4711* ☞ *¥700; ¥900 for combination bus/village ticket* ⊙ *Daily 8:30–5.*

Kokubun-ji 国分寺. The city's oldest temple, dating from 1588, houses many objects of art, including a precious sword used by the Heike clan. In the Main Hall (built in 1615) sits a figure of Yakushi Nyorai, a Buddha who eases those struggling with illness. In front of the three-story pagoda is a wooden statue of another esoteric Buddhist figure, Kannon Bosatsu, who vowed to hear the voices of all people and immediately grant salvation to those who suffer. The ginkgo tree standing beside the pagoda is believed to be more than 1,200 years old. ⊠ *1–83 Sowa-machi* ☎ *0577/32–1395* 🖃 *¥300* 🕓 *Daily 9–4.*

★ **Kusakabe Mingeikan** 日下部民芸館 *(Folk-Craft Museum)*. This museum is in a house from the 1880s that belonged to the Kusakabe family— wealthy traders of the Edo period. This national treasure served as a residence and warehouse, where the handsome interior, with heavy, polished beams and an earthy barren floor, provides an appropriate setting for Hida folk crafts such as lacquered bowls and wood carvings. ⊠ *1–52 Ojin-machi* ☎ *0577/32–0072* 🖃 *¥500* 🕓 *Mar.–Oct., daily 9–4:30; Nov.–Feb., Wed.–Mon. 9–4.*

Shoren-ji 照蓮寺. The main hall of Shoren-ji in Shiroyama Koen (Shiroyama Park) was built in 1504. It was moved here in 1961 from its original site in Shirakawa-go, right before the area was flooded by the Miboro Dam. Beautifully carved, allegedly from the wood of a single cedar tree, this temple is an excellent example of classic Muromachi-period architecture. The temple sits on a hill surrounded by gardens, and you can see the Takayama skyline and the park below. ⊠ *Shiroyama Koen* ☎ *0577/32–2052* 🖃 *¥200* 🕓 *Apr.–Oct., daily 8–5:30; Nov.–Mar., daily 8–5.*

★ **Takayama Jinya** 高山陣屋 *(Historical Government House)*. This rare collection of stately buildings housed the 25 officials of the Tokugawa Shogunate who administered the Hida region for 176 years. Highlights include an original storehouse (1606), which held city taxes in sacks of rice, a torture chamber (curiously translated as the "law court"), and samurai barracks. Free guided tours in English are available upon request and take 30–50 minutes. In front of the house, fruit, vegetables, and local crafts are sold at the **Jinya-mae Asa-ichi**, morning market, open from April to October, daily 6–noon, and from November to February, daily 7–noon. From the JR Station, head east on Hirokoji-dori for a few blocks to the old section of town. Before the bridge, which crosses the small Miya-gawa, turn right, pass another bridge, and the Takayama Jinya is on your right. ⊠ *1–5 Hachiken-machi* ☎ *0577/32–0643* 🖃 *¥420* 🕓 *Apr.–Oct., daily 8:45–5; Nov.–Mar., daily 8:45–4:30.*

★ **Takayama Matsuri Yatai Kaikan** 高山屋台会館 *(Takayama Float Exhibition Hall)*. This community center displays four of the 11th-, 17th-, and 18th-century *yatai* (festival floats) used in Takayama's famous Sanno and Hachi-man festivals. More than two centuries ago Japan was ravaged by the bubonic plague, and yatai were built and paraded through the streets to appease the gods. Because this seemed to work, locals built bigger, more elaborate yatai to prevent further outbreaks. The delicately etched wooden panels, carved wooden lion-head masks for dances, and elaborate tapestries are remarkable. Technical wizardry is also involved, as each yatai contains puppets, controlled by rods and wires, that perform amazing, gymnast-like feats. ✉ *178 Sakura-machi* ☎ *0577/32–5100* ⚄ *¥820* ⊙ *Mar.–Nov., daily 8:30–5; Dec.–Feb., daily 9–4:30.*

WHERE TO EAT AND STAY

Hotel reviews have been condensed for this book. Please go to Fodors. com for full reviews of each property.

$$$$

JAPANESE

★

✗ **Kakusho** 角正. This restaurant is known for its *shojin* ("temple food"), which includes *sansai ryori,* light dishes of mountain vegetables soaked in a rich miso paste and served with freshwater fish grilled with salt or soy sauce. Occasionally this treat is served atop a roasted magnolia leaf and called *hoba-miso.* The owner, Sumitake-san, can translate the menu for you. From Miya-gawa, head east on the Sanmachi-dori, crossing four side streets (including the one running along the river), walk up the hill, and take a left at the top. There is no English sign out front, but a white *noren* (hanging cloth) hangs in the entrance way of this Edo-era house. You might want to steer toward the semiformal. It's directly across from a small pay parking lot. ✉ *2 Babacho-dori* ☎ *0577/32–0174* ⚅ *Reservations essential* ▭ *No credit cards.*

$$

JAPANESE

★

✗ **Suzuya** 寿々や. Suzuya's recipes have been passed down over several generations. The house specialty is the superb and inexpensive sansairyori, a time-honored mountain cuisine. Suzuya is in a traditional Hidastyle house, and the dining room is intimate and wood beamed. There's an English menu, and the staff is used to serving foreign guests. From the station, turn onto Kokubunji-dori and take a right after five blocks. ■TIP➜ Lunch is served until 3 pm, and dinner begins at 5. Try to go during off-hours to avoid tour groups. ✉ *24 Hanakawa* ☎ *0577/32–2484.*

$$$–$$$$

HOTEL

🛏 **Hida Plaza Hotel** ひだホテルプラザ. This is the best internationalstyle hotel in town. **Pros:** luxurious; central location. **Cons:** lacks the personal touch of many area ryokan and inns. ✉ *2–60 Hanaoka-cho* ☎ *0577/33–4600* ⊕ *www.hida-hotelplaza.co.jp* ⟿ *136 Western-style rooms, 89 Japanese-style rooms, 2 suites* ⚅ *In-room: a/c, safe, refrigerator, Internet. In-hotel: 4 restaurants, room service, bar, pool, gym, laundry service* ⎟◯⎟ *No meals.*

$$

MINSHUKU

★

🛏 **Yamakyu** 山久. Cozy, antiques-filled nooks with chairs and coffee tables become small lounges in this old Tera-machi minshuku. **Pros:** warm, cozy atmosphere; excellent food. **Cons:** early-to-bed curfew means less freedom; some private toilets but no private baths. ✉ *58 Tensho-ji-machi* ☎ *0577/32–3756* ⟿ *20 Japanese-style rooms without bath* ⚅ *In-room: a/c. In-hotel: restaurant* ▭ *No credit cards* ⎟◯⎟ *Some meals.*

NIGHTLIFE

Nightlife in sleepy Takayama revolves around locally produced beer and sake. Try one of the many small Japanese-style bars, or *izakaya,* that line the streets to the north of Kokubunji Street.

Red Hill. Two blocks east and one block south of City Hall is this bar, popular with the foreign locals. ✉ *1–4 Sowa-cho* ☎ *0577/33–8139* ⊙ *Tues.–Sun. 7 pm–midnight.*

6

SHIRAKAWA-GO 白川郷

80 km (50 mi) northwest of Takayama.

It's speculated that the Shirawaka-go area—and particularly Ogi-machi, an Edo-era hamlet deep within, was originally populated by survivors of the powerful Taira family, who were nearly killed off in the 12th century by the rival Genji family. The majority of the residents living here still inhabit gassho-zukuri houses. Their shape and materials enable the house to withstand the heavy regional snow, and in summer the straw keeps the houses cool. Household activities center on the *irori* (open hearth), which sends smoke up through the timbers and thatch roof. Meats and fish are preserved (usually on a metal shelf suspended above the hearth) by the ascending smoke, which also prevents insects and vermin from taking up residence in the straw.

Shirakawa-go makes for a good day trip from Kanazawa or Takayama, or as a stop on the way to either. Several of the old houses are now minshuku, making Ogi-machi village a relaxing place to stay overnight.

GETTING HERE AND AROUND

It's more convenient to drive to Shirakawa-go and Ogi, but it's possible to get there by public transportation. A bus departs from Nagoya at 9 am daily, taking three hours and costing ¥3,500. You'll also find daily bus service between Shirakawa-go and Kanazawa, departing Kanazawa at 8:45 am, 12:35 pm, and 4 pm, and from Shirakawa-go at 10:20 am, 1:50 pm, and 4:50 pm (1 hour; ¥1,800). Bus services stop from about the end of October until March or April, and it is best to reserve a seat through tourist offices in advance. From Takayama, buses go year-round four to six times daily for ¥2,400 one-way, ¥4,300 round-trip.

VISITOR INFORMATION

Many old houses in Ogi-machi village function as minshuku. To stay in one, make reservations through the Ogi-machi Tourist Office, open daily 9–5. It's next to the Gassho-shuraku bus stop in the center of town.

Contacts Ogi-machi Tourist Office (✉ *57 Ogi-machi, Shirakawa-mura* ☎ *0576/96–1013*).

WHAT TO SEE

★ **Shirakawa-go Gassho-zukuri Village** 白川郷合掌造り村. Opposite Ogi-machi, on the banks of the Sho-gawa, this open-air museum has 25 traditional gassho-zukuri farmhouses. The houses were transplanted from four villages that fell prey to the Miboro Dam, built upriver in 1972. Over the years a colony of artisans has established itself in the village. You can watch them creating folk crafts like weaving, pottery, woodwork, and hand-dyeing in a few of the preserved houses. Many of the products are for sale. Each house charges a small admission fee. ✉ *Ogi-machi, Shirakawa mura, Ono-gun* ☎ *0576/96–1231* 🎫 *¥150 per house* 🕐 *Daily 8:30–5.*

KANAZAWA AND THE NORTH CHUBU COAST

The center of culture and commerce in the Hokuriku region, Kanazawa ranks among Japan's best-loved cities. To the east are snowcapped mountains, including the revered (and hikeable) Haku-san. To the north stretches the clawlike peninsula of the Noto-hanto, where lush rolling hills and rice fields meet scenic coastlines. Farther north along the Nihon-kai are the hardworking industrial capitals of Toyama and Niigata, and offshore the secluded Sado Island.

KANAZAWA 金沢

225 km (140 mi) northeast of Kyoto, 257 km (160 mi) north of Nagoya, 153 km (95 mi) northwest of Takayama, 343 km (213 mi) southwest of Niigata.

Twenty-first-century Kanazawa presents an extraordinary union of unblemished Old Japan and a modern, trendsetting city. More than 300 years of history have been preserved in the earthen walls and flowing canals of Naga-machi, the former samurai quarter west of downtown; the cluster of Buddhist temples in Tera-machi on the southern bank of the Sai-gawa River; and the wooden facades of the former geisha district, located north of the Asano-gawa river. Modern art, fashion, music, and international dining thrive in the downtown core of Korinbo, and in the shopping districts of Tate-machi and Kata-machi. The Japan Sea provides great seafood and a somewhat dreary climate. Fortunately, cold, gray, and wet weather is offset by friendly people and only adds to the sad, romantic air of the city.

In the feudal times of the Edo period, the prime rice-growing areas around Kanazawa (known then as the province of Kaga) made the ruling Maeda clan the second wealthiest in the country. Harvests came in at more than *hyaku-man-goku* (1 million *koku,* the Edo-period unit of measurement based on how much rice would feed one person for a year). This wealth funded various cultural pursuits such as silk dyeing, ceramics, and the production of gold-leaf and lacquerware products.

This prosperity did not pass unnoticed. The fear of attack by the Edo daimyo inspired the Maeda lords to construct one of the country's most massive castles amid a mazelike network of narrow, winding lanes that make the approach difficult and an invasion nearly impossible. These defensive tactics paid off, and Kanazawa enjoyed 300 years of peace and prosperity. Nevertheless, seven fires over the centuries reduced the once-mighty Kanazawa-jo to just the remaining castle walls and a single, impressive gate.

Between sightseeing, shopping, and sampling Kanazawa's many restaurants and cafés, it is worth staying here a couple of nights. Though the atmosphere of the city changes with each season, it is an excellent place to visit any time of the year.

GETTING HERE AND AROUND

The flight from Tokyo's Haneda Kuko to Komatsu Kuko in Kanazawa takes one hour on Japan Airlines (JAL) or All Nippon Airlines (ANA); allow 40 minutes for the bus transfer to downtown Kanazawa, which

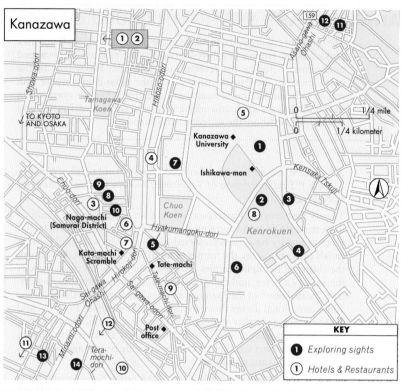

Kanazawa

KEY

1 Exploring sights

① Hotels & Restaurants

Sights ▼		Restaurants ▼		Hotels ▼	
Gyokusenen	3	Fumuroya	12	APA Hotel Eki-mae	1
Higashi-no-Kuruwa	11	Itaru	7	Hotel Nikko Kanazawa	2
Ishikawa Kenritsu Bijutsukan	6	Kincharyo	6	Kanazawa New Grand Hotel	4
Ishikawa Prefectural Products Center	4	Legian	3	Nakayasu Ryokan	5
Kanazawao Castle Park	1	Miyoshian	8	Yogetsu	11
Kenrokuen	2	Noda-ya	9		
Kutani Kosen Gama	13	Sugi no I	10		
Kyu-Saihitsuan	8				
Myoryu-ji	14				
Naga-machi	10				
Nomura-ke	9				
Oyama Jinja	7				
Shima-ke	12				
21 Seiki Bijutsukan	5				

costs ¥1,100. By train, Kanazawa is 2 hours from Kyoto; 3 hours from Nagoya; 2½ hours from Takayama (requiring a change of trains at Toyama); and 3 hours, 40 minutes from Niigata—all by JR Limited Express. The three-hour direct bus between Kanazawa and Takayama is also an option; there are two daily, and the cost is ¥4,200 one-way.

Ideal for tourists, the city's *shu-yu basu* (loop bus) departs every 15 minutes from 8:30 am to 9 pm from Gate 0 of Kanazawa Station's East Exit, and delivers you to the major tourist sites. Stops are announced in English and displayed on a digital board at the front of the bus. A single ride costs ¥200; the day pass is ¥500. You can purchase the pass from the Hokutetsu bus ticket office in front of Kanazawa Station.

Kanazawa is a good place to rent a car to explore the Noto-hanto and other parts of the Japan Sea Coast. Eki Rent-a-Car at the East Exit from the train station is one reliable option.

Rental Car Contact Eki Rent-a-Car (⊠ *Kanazawa Station* ☎ *076/265–6639*).

VISITOR INFORMATION
The Kanazawa Information Office has two desks at the train station and staff that will help you find accommodations. An English speaker is on duty from 10 am to 6 pm from the Kanazawa Goodwill Guide Network, which offers free guide and interpreting services.

Contact Kanazawa Information Office (☎ *076/232–6200* 🖶 *076/238–6210* ◷ *Daily 9–7*).

WHAT TO SEE

Fodor's Choice ★ **Gyokusenen** 玉泉園 *(Gyokusen Garden).* This tiny, intimate garden was built by Kim Yeocheol, who later became Naokata Wakita when he married into the ruling Kanazawa family. Yeocheol was the son of a Korean captive brought to Japan in the late 16th century. He became a wealthy merchant, using his fortune to build this quiet getaway. The garden's intimate tranquillity stems from the imaginative and subtle arrangement of moss, maple trees, and small stepping stones by the pond. Two waterfalls that gracefully form the Chinese character for *mizu* (water) feed the pond. The garden is markedly different from the bold strokes of Kenroku Garden. You can have tea here for ¥600. ⊠ *8–3 Kosho-machi* ☎ *076/221–0181* 💴 *¥500* ◷ *Thurs.–Tues. 9–4.*

Higashi-no-Kuruwa 東の郭 *(the Eastern Pleasure Quarter).* The high-class entertainment district of Edo-period Kanazawa was near the Asano-gawa. Now the pleasures are limited to viewing quaint old geisha houses recognizable by their wood-slat facades and latticed windows. Many have become tearooms, restaurants, or minshuku. If you are lucky, you might see a geisha scuttling to an appointment. Take the JR bus from Kanazawa Station (¥200) to Hachira-cho, just before the Asano-gawa Ohashi. Cross the bridge and walk northeast into the quarter.

Ishikawa Kenritsu Bijutsukan 石川県立美術館 *(Ishikawa Prefectural Art Museum).* Come here to see the country's best permanent collection of *Kutani-yaki* (colorful overglaze-painted porcelain), dyed fabrics, and old Japanese paintings. ⊠ *2–1 Dewa-machi, southwest of Kenrokuen* ☎ *076/231–7580* 💴 *¥350* ◷ *Daily 9–4:30.*

The intimate Gyokusen Garden is one of the most impressive sights in Kanazawa.

Ishikawa Prefectural Products Center 石川県観光物産館 (*Ishikawa-ken Kanko Bussankan*). Located near Gyokusen Garden, the center serves as a place where you can both buy traditional crafts from the region and see demonstrations of Yuzen dyeing, pottery, and lacquerware production. ✉ *2–2– Kenroku-cho* ☎ *076/222-7788* 💴 *¥700, includes admission to Gyokusen Garden* 🕐 *Apr.–Nov., daily 9–4:30; Dec.–Mar., Fri.–Wed. 9–4:30.*

Kanazawao Castle Park 金沢城公園. The area surrounding the castle is a suitable place to start exploring Kanazawa. Recently restored, the castle's sprawling grounds and gardens make a good stop on the way to Kenroku Garden. Though most of the castle is a reproduction, the original **Ishikawa-mon** (Ishikawa Gate) remains intact—its thick mossy stone base is topped with curving black eaves and white lead roof tiles. The tiles could be melted down and molded into ammunition in case of a prolonged siege. To reach the castle, take any bus (¥200) from Gate 11 at the bus terminal outside the JR Station or walk 30 minutes. ✉ *1–1 Marunouchi* ☎ *076/234-3800* 💴 *Free* 🕐 *Mar.–mid-Oct., daily 7–6; mid-Oct.–Feb., daily 8–5.*

★ **Kenrokuen** 兼六園 (*Kenroku Garden*). Across the street from the Kanazawa Castle is the largest of the three most famous landscaped gardens in the country (the other two are Mito's Kairaku Garden and Okayama's Koraku Garden). The Maeda lord Tsunanori began construction of Kenrokuen in 1676, and by the early 1880s it had become 25 sprawling acres of skillfully wrought bridges and fountains, ponds, and waterfalls. The garden changes with the seasons: spring brings cherry blossoms; brilliant azaleas foretell the arrival of summer; autumn paints the maples deep yellow and red; and in winter the pine trees are strung with long ropes, tied from trunk to bough, for protection against heavy snowfalls. Kenrokuen means "Garden of Six Qualities" (*ken-roku* means "integrated six"). The garden was so named because it exhibited the six superior characteristics judged necessary by the Chinese Sung Dynasty for the perfect garden: spaciousness, artistic merit, majesty, abundant water, extensive views, and seclusion. Despite the promise of its last attribute, the gardens attract a mad stampede of visitors—herded by megaphone—during cherry-blossom season (mid-April) and Golden Week (late April and early May). Early morning is the most sensible time for a visit, when the grounds are a little more peaceful and relaxing. ⊠ *1 Kenroku-cho* ☎ *076/234–3800* 🖂 *¥300* ⊙ *Mar.–mid-Oct., daily 7–6; mid-Oct.–Feb., daily 8–5.*

Kutani Kosen Gama 九谷光仙窯 *(Kutani Pottery Kiln)*. You can watch artisans making the local Kutani pottery, which is noted for its vibrant color schemes, at this spot, which was established in 1870. ⊠ *5–3–3 No-machi* ☎ *076/241–0902* 🖂 *Free* ⊙ *Mon.–Sat. 8:30–noon and 1–5, Sun. 8:30–noon.*

Kyu-Saihitsuan 長町友禅館 *(Saihitsuan Yuzen Silk Center)*. A few houses have been carefully restored in the Samurai district, including the Saihitsuan Yuzen Silk Center, where you can watch demonstrations of Yuzen silk painting —a centuries-old technique in which intricate floral designs with delicate white outlines are meticulously painted onto silk used for kimonos—and of course buy the products. It's behind the Tokyu Hotel, five blocks southwest of Oyama Jinja. ⊠ *2–6–16 Naga-machi* ☎ *076/264–2811* 🖂 *¥350* ⊙ *Daily 9–4:30.*

Fodor'sChoice
★

Myoryu-ji 妙立寺. On the south side of the Sai-gawa is the intriguing and mysterious Myoryu-ji. Its popular name, Ninja-dera (Temple of the Ninja), suggests it was a clandestine training center for martial-arts masters who crept around in the dead of night armed with *shuriken* (star-shape blades). In fact, the temple was built to provide an escape route for the daimyo in case of invasion. Ninja-dera was built by Toshitsune in 1643, when the Tokugawa Shogunate was stealthily knocking off local warlords and eliminating competition. At first glance, it appears a modest yet handsome two-story structure. Inside, however, you find 29 staircases, seven levels, myriad secret passageways and trapdoors, a tunnel to the castle hidden beneath the well in the kitchen, and even a *seppuku* room, where the lord could perform an emergency ritual suicide. Unfortunately (or fortunately, considering all the booby traps), visitors are not permitted to explore the hidden lair alone. You must join a Japanese-language tour and follow along with your English pamphlet. ⊠ *1–2–12 No-machi* ☎ *076/241–0888* 🖂 *¥800* ⊙ *Mar.–Nov., daily 9–4:30; Dec.–Feb., daily 9–4.*

Naga-machi 長町 *(Samurai district)*. Behind the modern Korinbo 109 shopping center, Seseragi-dori leads to the samurai district where the Maeda clan lived. Narrow, snaking streets are lined with beautiful, golden adobe walls 8 feet high, footed with large stones and topped with black tiles.

Nomura-ke. This elegant house in Naga-machi was rebuilt more than 100 years ago by an industrialist named Nomura. Visit the Jodan-no-ma drawing room made of cypress, with elaborate designs in rosewood and ebony. Then pass through the sliding doors, adorned with the paintings of Sasaki Senkai of the illustrious Kano School, to a wooden veranda. Rest your feet here, and take in the stunning little garden with weathered lanterns among pine and maple trees, and various shrubs and bonsai. Stepping stones lead to a pond dotted with moss-covered rocks and brilliant orange-flecked carp. In the upstairs tearoom you can enjoy a cup of *macha* (green tea) for ¥300 and a bird's-eye view of the gardens. ✉ *1–3–32 Naga-machi* ☎ *076/221–3553* 💴 *¥500* ⊙ *Apr.–Sept., daily 8:30–5:30; Oct.–Mar., daily 8:30–4:30.*

Oyama Jinja 尾山神社. Built in 1599, Oyama Jinja was dedicated to Lord Toshiie Maeda, the founder of the Maeda clan. The shrine's unusual three-story gate, **Shin-mon,** was completed in 1875. Previously located atop Mt. Utatsu, the square arch and its stained-glass windows were to believed to once function as a lighthouse, guiding ships in from the Japan Sea to the Kanaiwa Port, 6 km (4 mi) northwest. You're free to walk around the shrine. ✉ *11–1 Oyama-cho* ☎ *076/231–7210* 💴 *Free.*

Shima-ke 志摩家. This elegant former geisha house constructed in the early 19th century is now a museum open to the public. ✉ *1–13–21 Higashi-yama* ☎ *076/252–5675* 💴 *¥400* ⊙ *Tues.–Sun. 9–6.*

21 Seiki Bijutsukan 金沢21世紀美術館 *(21st-Century Museum of Contemporary Art).* This circular building was created to entwine a museum's architecture with the art exhibits, and for exhibition designers to take cues from the architecture. Transparent walls and scattered galleries encourage visitors to choose their own route. Previous exhibitions have included a Gerhard Richter retrospective, a video installation by Mathew Barney, and the work of Japanese photographer Araki Nobuyoshi. It's south of Kanazawa Park, next to City Hall. ✉ *1–2–1 Hirosaka* ☎ *076/220–2800* 🌐 *www.kanazawa21.jp/en* 💴 *Varies by exhibition* ⊙ *Tues.–Fri. 10–6, weekends 10–8.*

WHERE TO EAT

$$$
JAPANESE
✕ **Fumuroya** 不室屋. Not far from the Omi-Cho market, this store specializes in wheat gluten, called *ofu,* and its adjacent lunch restaurant offers a set lunch for ¥3,150 of *jibu ni,* a stew made with chicken (instead of the usual duck), ofu, and shiitake mushrooms. It closes at 6. ✉ *2–3–1 Owari-cho* ☎ *0762/224–2886* ⌂ *Reservations essential* ⊙ *No dinner.*

$$$$
JAPANESE
✕ **Itaru** いたる. Slip into Itaru for a taste of good Kaga-ryori at a reasonable price. Although the staff speaks little English, there are English menus available to help you out. For a sampling of local cuisine, try the set course that varies seasonally. Watching the cooks behind the counter adds to the overall dining experience. Also on the menu is a good selection of local sake. ✉ *2–7–5 Kata-machi* ☎ *0762/24–4156* ▭ *No credit cards* ⊙ *No lunch.*

$$$–$$$$
JAPANESE
★
✕ **Kincharyo** 金茶寮. The menu changes seasonally in the showpiece restaurant of the Kanazawa Tokyu Hotel. The lacquered, curved countertop of the sushi bar is beautiful. Superb dinner courses range from

tempura sets (¥4,042–¥8,085) to mixed *kaiseki* (full meal); nine items cost ¥5,775). In spring your meal may include *hotaru-ika* (firefly squid) and *iidako* (baby octopus) no larger than your thumbnail. The lunch kaiseki bento costs from ¥1,300 to ¥3,600. ⊠ *3F Kanazawa Tokyu Hotel., 2–1–1 Korinbo* ☎ *076/263–5511.*

$
INDONESIAN
★
✕ **Legian** レギャン. You might be surprised to find a funky Balinese eatery alongside the Sai-gawa. But if you try the *gado-gado* (vegetables in a spicy sauce), *nasi goreng* (Indonesian-style fried rice), or chicken *satay* (grilled on a skewer, with peanut sauce), you'll be happily surprised. Indonesian beer and mango ice cream are also available. It's open late (Monday–Thursday until 12:30 am, Friday and Saturday until 4:30 am), and after dinner the atmosphere gets quite lively, with more of a nightclub atmosphere. From Kata-machi Scramble (the area's central intersection), turn right just before Sai-gawa Bridge, and follow the narrow lane along the river. ⊠ *2–31–30 Kata-machi* ☎ *076/262–6510* ▭ *No credit cards* ☾ *Closed Wed. No lunch.*

$$$$
JAPANESE
★
✕ **Miyoshian** 三芳庵. Excellent bento and fish and vegetable dinners have been made here for nearly 100 years in the renowned Kenroku Garden. Prices are still reasonable—the Kaga kaiseki course is less than ¥3,000. In the annex macha tea is served with Japanese pastries from Morihachi, a confectioner with a 360-year history. ⊠ *1 Kenroku-cho* ☎ *076/221–0127* ☾ *Closed Tues.*

¢
CAFÉ
✕ **Noda-ya** 野田屋. Slip into this little tea shop for a scoop of delicious *macha sofuto kurumu* (green tea ice cream) or a cup of tea. You can sit in the little garden in back or on benches out front. At the far end of the Tate-machi shopping street the heavenly scent of roasting green tea leaves wafts out the door. The café is open daily from 9 to 7:30. ⊠ *3 Tate-machi* ☎ *076/221–0982* ▭ *No credit cards.*

$$$$
JAPANESE
✕ **Sugi no I** 杉の井. This elegant restaurant in Tera-machi, on the south bank of the Sai-gawa River close to the Sakura-bashi Bridge, serves Kaga specialties like duck stew with wheat gluten called jibu ni and *gori no tsukuda ni,* tiny soy-simmered river fish on Kutani china, Oribe pottery, and lacquerware. There is a special ladies' course (that anyone can order) for ¥3,675. For a surcharge of ¥500 per person you can usually have a private room overlooking the garden. In traditional Japanese style, the meal finishes with rice, pickles, and soup; in autumn the broth is clear with herbs and a shrimp dumpling. Full-course dinners start at ¥15,000. ⊠ *3–11 Kyokawa-machi* ☎ *0762/43–2288* ⚑ *Reservations essential.*

WHERE TO STAY

Hotel reviews have been condensed for this book. Please go to Fodors. com for full reviews of each property.

$$
HOTEL
★
🏨 **APA Hotel Eki-mae** アパホテル金沢駅前. This hotel is so close to the JR Station it's practically inside it. **Pros:** directly next to JR Station; classy. **Cons:** a 30-minute walk from the sights and nightlife of Kata-machi. ⊠ *1–9–28 Hiroka* ☎ *076/231–8111* 🖷 *076/231–8112* ⊕ *www. apahotel.com* ⮐ *456 rooms* ⚑ *In-room: a/c, refrigerator, Internet. In-hotel: 2 restaurants, bar, laundry service, laundry facilities, Internet terminal* ⦿ *No meals.*

$$$$
HOTEL
★

🏨 **Hotel Nikko Kanazawa** ホテル日光金沢. The exotic lobby of this 30-story hotel is more reminiscent of Singapore than Japan, with tropical plants, cherry-oak slatted doors, and colonial-style furniture. **Pros:** near JR Station; spacious rooms. **Cons:** it's a long walk to Kata-machi's sights and nightlife. ⊠ *2–15–1 Hon-machi* ☎ *076/234–1111* 📠 *076/234–8802* ⊕ *www.jalhotels.com* 🛏 *256 rooms, 4 suites* ⚙ *In-room: a/c, Internet. In-hotel: 4 restaurants, bars, pool, gym, laundry service, parking (paid)* 🍴 *No meals.*

$$$–$$$$
HOTEL

🏨 **Kanazawa New Grand Hotel** 金沢ニューグランドホテル. Stepping into this hotel's sleek black-and-cream marble lobby is a refreshing break from the dreary concrete of the main drag outside. **Pros:** good location halfway between JR Station and Kata-machi; restaurant serves some of the city's best contemporary French cuisine. **Cons:** few interesting places in the immediate vicinity. ⊠ *4–1 Minami-cho* ☎ *076/233–1311* 📠 *076/233–1591* ⊕ *www.new-grand.co.jp* 🛏 *100 Western-style rooms, 2 Japanese-style rooms, 2 suites* ⚙ *In-room: a/c, Internet. In-hotel: 5 restaurants* 🍴 *No meals.*

$$$
RYOKAN

🏨 **Nakayasu Ryokan** 中安旅館. Just north of Kenroku Garden, this family-run ryokan dates from 1920. **Pros:** helpful staff; reasonable rates; close to Kenroku Garden; free bicycles. **Cons:** some rooms have shared baths. ⊠ *23 Jukken-machi* ☎ *076/232–2228* 📠 *076/252–4444* ⊕ *nakayasu-ryokan.co.jp* 🛏 *21 Japanese-style rooms* ⚙ *In-room: a/c. In-hotel: Internet, restaurant, room service, bicycles, parking (free)* ▤ *No credit cards* 🍴 *Some meals.*

¢
MINSHUKU

🏨 **Yogetsu** 陽月. In a century-old geisha house in the Eastern Pleasure Quarter, Yogetsu is a small, stylish minshuku. **Pros:** quiet location; charming atmosphere. **Cons:** fewer amenities than major hotels. ⊠ *1–13–22 Higashiyama* ☎ *076/252–0497* 🛏 *5 Japanese-style rooms without bath* ⚙ *In-room: a/c (some). In-hotel: restaurant* ▤ *No credit cards* 🍴 *Breakfast.*

NIGHTLIFE

All-night fun can be found in the center of town. ■TIP→ Be warned: these places don't take credit cards.

Apre. Free billiard tables make this bar a scene on weekends. When it opens at 8 pm, the tables fill up, and the action is competitive. It's tricky to find, so don't hesitate to call for directions. It's closed Monday. ⊠ *Laporto Bldg., 1–3–9 Kata-machi* ☎ *076/221–0090.*

Pole-Pole. Pronounced "po-ray-po-ray, this reggae bar is run by the same jolly owner as Legian, and is just behind the restaurant. If you want to sit, arrive before midnight. The two dark, cramped rooms get so full that the crowd spills out into the hallway. Pole-Pole is closed Sunday but open until 5 am the rest of the week. ⊠ *2–31–31 Kata-machi* ☎ *076/260–1138.*

Eihei-ji, southeast of Fukui, is one of two headquarters of the Soto Zen school of Buddhism.

FUKUI 福井

80 km (50 mi) southwest of Kanazawa, 177 km (110 mi) north of Nagoya.

★ **Eihei-ji** 永平寺. One of the two headquarters of Soto Zen, Eihei-ji is 19 km (12 mi) southeast of Fukui. Founded in 1244, the extensive complex of 70 temple buildings is spread out on a hillside surrounded by hinoki and *sugi* (cedar) trees more than 100 feet tall, some as old as the original wooden structures. This temple offers a rare glimpse into the daily practice of the 200 or so monks (and a few nuns) in training. They are called *unsui,* or cloud water, the traditional name for mendicant monks wandering in search of a teacher. The rigorous training remains unchanged since Dogen started this monastery. Each monk only has one tatami mat (1 meter by 2 meters), to eat, sleep, and meditate on. The mats are lined in rows on raised platforms in a communal room. All activities, from using the bathroom to cleaning out the incense tray, are considered to be meditations, and so visitors are expected to dress modestly and explore in silence. Students of Zen or those interested in meditation can do short retreats of one to three days and lodge at the temple (for ¥8,000 a night, including two meals), with at least two weeks' advance notice in writing. The easiest way to get to Eihei-ji from Fukui is by train to Eihei-ji Guchi Station and by bus from there to the temple. ✉ *5–15 Shihi Eiheiji-cho, Yoshida-gun* ☎ *0776/63–3102* 🎫 *¥500* ⏲ *Daily 5–5.*

WHERE TO STAY

Hotel reviews have been condensed for this book. Please go to Fodors. com for full reviews of each property.

$–$$ ☒ **Hotel Akebono Bekkan** ホテルアケボノ別館. Think of this small, two-
HOTEL story wooden hotel as a weekend retreat—the owners can arrange training sessions in Zen meditation and classes in pottery and paper-making. **Pros:** convenient location; benefits of a hotel with the comfort of a ryokan. **Cons:** not all rooms have baths. ☒ *3–10–12 Chuo* ☎ *0776/ 22–1000* 🖷 *0776/22–8023* ⊕ *www.riverge.com* 🛏 *10 Japanese-style rooms, 5 with bath* ☐ *In-room: a/c. In-hotel: restaurant, Wi-Fi hotspot* ↻◎ *No meals.*

NOTO-HANTO (NOTO PENINSULA) 能登半島

Thought to be named after an *Ainu* (indigenous Japanese) word for "nose," the Noto-hanto, a national park, juts out into the Nihon-kai and shelters the bays of both Nanao and Toyama. Steep, densely forested hills line the eroded west coast, which is wind- and wave-blasted in winter and ruggedly beautiful in other seasons. The eastern shoreline is lapped by calmer waters and has stunning views of Tate-yama (Mt. Tate), the Hida Mountains, and even of some of Nagano's alpine peaks more than 105 km (70 mi) away.

A quick sightseeing circuit of the Noto-hanto, from Hakui to Nanao, can be done in six to eight hours, but to absorb the peninsula's remarkable scenery, stay two or three days, stopping in Wajima and at one of the minshuku along the coast; arrangements can be made through tourist information offices in Kanazawa, Nanao, or Wajima.

GETTING HERE AND AROUND

Nanao, on east coast of peninsula, and Wajima, on the north coast of Noto-hanto, are accessible by JR Limited Express via Kanazawa. You can also fly in to Noto Airport from Tokyo (two flights with ANA per day) and take the "Furusato taxi" shuttle bus to nearby towns. The peninsula is a good place to explore by car. If you aren't driving from Kanazawa, book a car at Nissan Rent-a-Car at Wakura Station. You can also combine train and bus trips or guided tours, which can be arranged in Kanazawa. From Anamizu the private Noto Line goes northeast to Takojima, the region's most scenic route. The line to Wajima turns inland after Hakui and misses some of the peninsula's best sights, so it makes sense to get off the train at Hakui and continue up the coast to Wajima by bus.

Rental Car Contact Nissan Rent-a-Car (☒ *14–27 Yube, oIshisaki-machi, Nanao* ☎ *0767/62–0323*).

Visitor Information Kanazawa Information Office (☎ *076/232–6200* 🖷 *076/238–6210*). **Wajima Tourist Office** (☎ *0768/22–1503* ⊘ *Daily 10–6*).

WHAT TO SEE

Hakui 羽咋. The train from Kanazawa runs along the coast until Hakui, 40 minutes from Kanazawa. Some buses from here continue along the scenic coastal to Myojo-ji temple and Wajima (others go by the inland route). If you have your own bike you can cycle along the coastal path as far as beautiful Gan-mon (Sea Gate), some 26 km (16 mi) away, where you can stop for lunch. Just north of Chirihama, a formerly popular and now unkempt beach, the scenery improves.

Myojo-ji 妙成寺. This less-visited but well-tended temple complex is a few miles north of Hakui on the bus route from Kanazawa. The temple, founded in 1294 and belonging to the Nichiren sect of Buddhism, has a five-story pagoda from the 1600s. A very large, colorful Buddha statue sits inside a squat wooden building. The influence of mainland Asia is visible in the gargantuan, wooden guardian deities. A recording on the bus announces where to get off for Myojo-ji. It's a 10-minute walk to the temple from the bus stop. ⊠ *1 Yo Taki-dani-machi, Hakui* ☎ *0767/27–1226* 💴 *¥500* 🕙 *Daily 8–5.*

EN
ROUTE

Although you can take the inland bus directly north from Kanazawa or Hakui to Monzen, the longer (70-minute) bus ride along the coast is recommended for its scenic value. The 16-km (10-mi) stretch between Fuku-ura and Sekinohana, known as the Noto Seacoast (Noto-Kongo), has fantastic wind- and wave-eroded rocks, from craggy towers to partly submerged checkerboard-pattern platforms. Among the best is Gan-mon, a rock cut through the center by water. Gan-mon is about 45 minutes north of Hakui and is a stop on tour-bus routes.

6

Soji-ji 總持寺. The Zen temple complex at Monzen once served as the Soto sect's headquarters. Though a fire destroyed most of the buildings in 1818 and the sect moved its headquarters to Yokohama in 1911, this is still an important training temple. As at major Zen temple Eihei-ji in Fukui, near the Kansai region, lay practitioners may stay for a few days (although the temple hesitates to accept lone female travelers since room doors don't lock). Strolling paths traverse the lush grounds, where you can see some spectacular red maples and an elaborately carved gate. The Soji-ji-mae bus stop is in front of the temple; use a bus or walk 10 minutes from Monzen Station to reach it. It also can be accessed from the Anamizu bus station on the Noto Chuo bus bound for Monzen (32 minutes). ⊠ *1–18 Monzen, Wajima, Monzen-cho* 💴 *¥400, ¥6,500 for overnight stays* 🕙 *Daily 8–5.*

Wajima 輪島. Only 16 km (10 mi) and one bus stop up the road from Monzen, this fishing town at the tip of the peninsula is also known for its gorgeous lacquerware.

Asa-ichi 朝市. The morning market in Wajima is held daily here, except on the second and fourth Wednesday of each month (in the market is open every day in August). You can buy seafood, fruit, vegetables, local crafts, and lacquerware from elderly women wearing indigo *monpei* (field pants). The smaller *yu-ichi* (evening market) starts around 3 pm and runs until sunset. Almost anyone can point you in the right direction. ⊠ *Asa-ichi dori, Kawai-cho* ☎ *0768/22–7653* 🕙 *Daily 8–11:30 and 3–sunset.*

Wajima Shikki Kaikan 輪島漆器会館 *(Lacquerware Hall)*. To observe the traditional lacquerware manufacturing process, visit the Lacquerware Hall. The production of a single piece involves more than 20 steps from wood preparation and linen reinforcement to the application of layers of lacquer, carefully dried and polished between coats. Wajima

Shikki Kaikan is in the center of town on the north side of Route 249, just before Shin-bashi (New Bridge). From the station, turn left when you exit and walk straight (northwest) about four blocks until you hit Route 249. Turn left again—there's a Hokuriku Bank on the corner—and continue southwest along Route 249 for about four blocks. ⊠ 24–55 Kawai-machi, Wajima ☎ 0768/22–2155 ⛭ ¥200 ⊙ Daily 8:30–5.

NEED A BREAK?

Shin-puku. Various sashimi and sushi *teishoku* (sets) are reasonably priced at this small but beautiful sushi bar a 10-minute walk from the train station in Wajima. From the station, turn left as you exit and walk northwest (left) about four blocks until you hit the main road, Route 249. Then turn right and walk northeast about three blocks along Route 249. One block past the Cosmo gas station (on the left), Shin-puku is on the right, and is open daily until 10 pm. ⊠ 41 Kawai-cho, Wajima ☎ 0768/22–8133 ⊙ Daily 11:30–2 and 4:30–midnight.

Sosogi 曾々木. From Wajima an hourly bus runs to this small village 20 minutes to the northeast, passing the terraced fields of **Senmaida,** where rice paddies descend from the hills to the sea.

Rokko-zaki 禄剛崎 *(Cape Rokko).* From Sosogi, you can continue around the peninsula's northern tip by bus, past a small lighthouse, and down to the northern terminus of the Noto Railway Line at Takojima. Unless you have a car, however, the views and scenery don't quite justify the infrequency of the public transportation.

Suzu 珠洲. The same hourly bus that runs between Wajima and Sosogi continues on to this town on the *uchi* (inside) coast. Just south of Suzu, near Ukai Station, is a dramatic offshore rock formation called *Mitsuke-jima,* a huge wedge of rock topped with lush vegetation, connected to the shore with a pebbly path popular with lovers. It is said that Kobo Daishi gave it the nickname of *Gunkan Island*, or Battleship Island, because it resembles a warship sailing to attack.

Mawaki Onsen 真脇温泉. Southeast of Suzu is this open-air **onsen.** Artifacts, including pottery from the *Jomon* (straw-rope pattern) archaeological period (13,000 BC–300 BC) have been found here. Mawaki is also well known for its wonderful hilltop view, which overlooks the rice fields and fishing villages along the edge of Toyama Bay. One bath-and-sauna complex is made of stone, the other of wood; on alternate weeks they open to men and women. A hotel is connected to the bath complex. To get here, hike up the hill or take a short taxi ride from Jomon Station on the Noto Line. Mawaki can also be reached in 2¼ hours by car from Kanazawa along a scenic toll road, or in 2½ hours by train (with a change in Wakura). On your way south to Mawaki Onsen are numerous opportunities for hiking, swimming, and camping. ⊠ 19–39 Mawaki, Noto-cho, Housu-gun ☎ 0768/62–4567 🖷 0768/62–4568 ⛭ ¥450 ⊙ Mon. 1–9 pm, Tues.–Sun. 10 am–10 pm.

Nanao 七尾. This town is best known for its festivals. Seihakusai festival, a 400-year-old tradition held May 3–5, is essentially three days of nonstop partying. Huge (26-foot) 10-ton floats resembling ships called *deka-yama* (big mountains) are paraded through the streets. At midnight the floats become miniature Kabuki stages for dance performances by costumed children. Since Seihakusai festival is celebrated during Golden Week, when almost everyone in Japan is on vacation, it's a wild scene. The men pulling the floats are given generous and frequent libations of beer and sake, and the crowd also suffers no shortage of refreshments.

Takaoka 高岡, the southern gateway to the Noto Peninsula, has Japan's third-largest **Daibutsu** (Great Buddha), standing 53 feet high and made of bronze. Also in Takaoka, a 400-meter walk from the station, is **Zuiryu-ji**, a delightful Zen temple that doubles as a youth hostel. A sprawling park, **Kojo-koen**, not far from the station, is particularly stunning in autumn, with its red-and-silver maples. Takaoka is mostly known for its traditions of copper-, bronze-, and iron-smithing, and remains a major bell-casting center.

WHERE TO STAY

Hotel reviews have been condensed for this book. Please go to Fodors. com for full reviews of each property.

$$
MINSHUKU

Fukasan 深三. Conveniently near the morning market and only one street up from the harbor, this two-story wooden minshuku is infused with the warmth of the hosts, who have furnished the interior with locally made crafts. **Pros:** excellent location for visiting the morning market; traditional atmosphere. **Cons:** fewer amenities than a larger hotel. ⊠ *4–4 Kawai-machi, Wajima* ☎ *0768/22–9933* 🖷 *0768/22–9934* 🛏 *4 Japanese rooms* ☾ *In-room: a/c. In-hotel: restaurant* ▭ *No credit cards* ☐ *Some meals.*

$$–$$$
HOTEL

Mawaki Po-re Po-re 真脇ポーレポーレ. This little hotel, built into a hillock, connects with the bath complex at Mawaki and has great views of the sea and surrounding hills. **Pros:** choice of Western or Japanese-style rooms. **Cons:** somewhat out of the way. ⊠ *19–110 Aza-Mawaki, Noto-cho, Housu-gun* ☎ *0768/62–4700* 🖷 *0768/62–4702* 🛏 *5 Western-style rooms, 5 Japanese-style rooms, 1 suite* ☾ *In-room: a/c, safe. In-hotel: restaurant* ☐ *Breakfast.*

$
MINSHUKU
Fodor's Choice
★
☻

Shunran Village 春欄の里. More than 30 traditional houses in this farming village at the end of the peninsula have been turned into minshuku, offering visitors the chance to experience rural Noto life, albeit with no hotel-style amenities at all in most cases. **Pros:** friendly staff; some English spoken; rare chance to experience rural life. **Cons:** access difficult without a car; no bath or toilet in rooms. ⊠ *16–9 Miya-chi, Noto-cho, Hosu-gun* ☎ *0768/67–8001* ✉ *shunran@shunran.info* 🛏 *In-room: no phone (some), a/c (some), no TV (some)* ▭ *No credit cards* ☐ *Some meals.*

TOYAMA 富山

18 km (11 mi) southeast of Takaoka, 61 km (38 mi) east of Kanazawa, 282 km (175 mi) north of Kyoto

Busy, industrial Toyama is beautified by Toyama-joshi Koen (Toyama Castle Park), a spread of greenery with a reconstructed version of the original 1532 castle. Toyama Bay is the habitat of the glowing hotaru ika, or firefly squid. Their spawning grounds stretch for 15 km (9 mi)

The Kurobe-Kyokoku Railway operates from April through November through the deepest valley in Japan.

along the coast from Uozu to the right bank of Toyama City's Jouganji River and about 1½ km (¾ mi) from shore. From March until June, their spawning season, the females gather close to the seabed and come to the surface from dusk until midnight. From the early morning until dawn the sea magically glows from the squids' photophores, blue-white light-producing organs that attract their prey. This phenomenon has been designated a Special Natural Monument. Sightseeing boats provide close-up views.

GETTING HERE AND AROUND

All Nippon Airways has five flights daily between Tokyo and Toyama. Toyama is 30 minutes from Takaoka by JR local, one hour from Kanazawa by JR Limited Express, and three and four hours north of Kyoto and Nagoya, respectively, by JR. Toyama has a network of streetcars that can take you to most destinations within town. Other than as a base to see some of the surrounding area, there is not much reason to linger in Toyama. It makes for a convenient overnight stop, however.

Visitor Information Toyama Tourist Information Office (☎ 0764/44–3200 www.info-toyama.com/english).

WHAT TO SEE

Kurobe-kyokoku Railway 黒部峡谷鉄道. A slow, open-air train operates from April through November along the river of the deepest valley in Japan, Kurobe-kyokoku (Kurobe Gorge) to Keyakidaira. On the 20-km (12½-mi), 90-minute ride the old-fashioned tram chugs past gushing springs and waterfalls, and you might even see wild monkeys or *serow*, a type of native mountain goat. One of the best views is from the 125-foot-long, 128-foot-high bridge, Atobiki-kyo. Bring a windbreaker, even in summer, as it's a cold and damp ride. Kuronagi-onsen, Kanetsuri-onsen, and Meiken-onsen, which supply water to Unazuki-onsen and other hot springs, are along the trolley route. You can get off at any one of those springs and enjoy the spa. To get to Unazuki from Toyama Station, take the JR Line to Uozu Station and switch to the Chitetsu Line (30 minutes). A 1-km (½-mi) walk from Keyaki-daira Station leads to the precipitous cliff over the Sarutobi-kyo valley and a view of the Kurobe River. ⊠ *11 Kurobe Keikoku-guchi, Kurobe City* ☏ *0765/62–1011 for ticket reservations only* 🖶 *0765/62–1724 for ticket reservations only* ⊕ *www.kurotetu.co.jp/en* 🎫 *¥1,440 one-way* ⊗ *Mid-Apr.–mid-Nov., daily (exact departures vary by date).*

NIIGATA 新潟

155 mi northeast of Toyama, 205 mi northwest of Tokyo.

The coast between Kurobe and Niigata is flat and not so interesting. Two towns along the way, Naoetsu and Teradomari, serve as ferry ports to Ogi and Akadomari, respectively, on Sado-ga-shima. From Niigata ferries go to Sado-ga-shima and even Hokkaido. In the skiing season people fly into Niigata before traveling by train to the northern Alps for quick access to ski resorts.

GETTING HERE AND AROUND

Niigata is 3 hours from Toyama on the JR Hokuriku Line, 1½ hours or 2 hours, 15 minutes from Tokyo by Shinkansen and Toki local line respectively. Niigata serves as a waypoint en route to Sado-ga-shima.

VISITOR INFORMATION

Niigata Kotsu Information center is found to the left of the Ryotsu bus terminal and offers tours of Sado-ga-shima covering Skyline Drive, where public buses don't run. Tours, from May to November, depart daily from Ryotsu and cost ¥6,440. You'll also find city maps, ferry schedules, and help finding a hotel there.

Contact Niigata Kotsu Tourist Information (☏ *025/283–1188 wwww. enjoyniigata.com/english* ⊗ *Daily 8:30–5:15*).

WHAT TO SEE

Hoppo Bunka Keikan 北方文化博物館 *(Northern Culture Museum).* On the banks of the Agano River on the Kamabara Plain the museum is a 40-minute bus ride from Niigata Station. This former estate was established in the Edo period by the Ito family, which, by the 1930s, was the largest landowner in the Kaetsu area, with 8,352 acres of paddy fields, more than 2,500 acres of forest, and 78 overseers who controlled no fewer than 2,800 tenants. The family also owned about 60 warehouses, which stored 1,800 tons of rice every autumn. Ito Mansion, built in 1887, was their home for generations until the Land Reform Act of 1946, which compelled landowners to sell off their paddy land holdings above 7.5 acres. Their mansion with its valuable art collection became this museum, which has two restaurants and coffee shops. The house has 65 rooms, a special art gallery, gardens, a tearoom, and an annex for study called "Sanrakutei" where everything—pillars, furniture, and even tatami mats—is triangular or diamond shape. The garden is laid out in the traditional style of the Kamakura and Muromachi periods (14th–15th century). Its five teahouses are in different parts of the garden (two of them built later), and numerous natural rocks—mostly from Kyoto—are artistically arranged around the pond. At Niigata ask the Tourist Information office to point you in the direction of the right bus, which takes 40 minutes. Alternatively, by taxi it takes 25 minutes. ✉ *2–15–25 Somi* ☎ *025/385–2001* 🖃 *¥800* ☉ *Apr.–Nov. 9–5; Dec.–Mar. 9–4:30.*

WHERE TO EAT AND STAY

Hotel reviews have been condensed for this book. Please go to Fodors. com for full reviews of each property.

$$–$$$
JAPANESE
★

✕ **Inaka-ya** 田舎家. Their specialty, *wappa-meshi* (rice steamed in a wooden box with toppings of salmon, chicken, or crab), makes an inexpensive and excellent lunch. The *yanagi karei hitohoshi-yaki* (grilled flounder), *nodo-kuro shioyaki* (grilled local whitefish), and *buri teriyaki* (yellowtail) will make your mouth water. Inaka-ya, which closes between lunch and dinner from 2 to 5, is found in the heart of Furu-machi, the local eating and drinking district. ✉ *1457 Kyuban-cho, Furu-machi-dori* ☎ *025/223–1266* 🖃 *No credit cards.*

$$
SEAFOOD

✕ **Marui** 丸伊. This is the place for fresh fish. For starters, order the *nami nigiri* (standard sushi set) for ¥1,400, plus a bottle of chilled sake, the local Kitayuki brand, for ¥1,260. Then glance at what your neighbors have ordered and ask for what looks good. You can't go wrong with the freshest fish, abalone, sea urchin, and squid in town. Marui closes during mid-afternoon. It's one block off the Furu-machi arcade, around the corner from Inaka-ya. ✉ *8–1411 Higashibori-dori* ☎ *025/228–0101.*

$$
HOTEL

🏨 **Niigata Toei Hotel** 新潟東映ホテル. For an inexpensive business hotel a block and a half from the station, this ranks the best. **Pros:** near Niigata Station; rooftop beer garden from June to September. **Cons:** the usual small business hotel rooms. ✉ *1–6–2 Benten* ☎ *025/244–7101* 🖷 *025/241–8485* 🛏 *133 rooms* 👍 *In-room: a/c, Internet. In-hotel: 2 restaurants, bar* 🍴 *No meals.*

$$$$
HOTEL

🏨 **Okura Hotel Niigata** ホテルオークラ新潟. This is a sophisticated, first-class hotel on the Shinano-gawa, ½ km (¼ mi) from the station. **Pros:** the highest-class hotel in Niigata; good location. **Cons:** more expensive than other lodgings. ✉ *6–53 Kawabata-cho Chuo-ku* ☎ *025/224–6111, 0120/10–0120 toll-free in Japan* 🖷 *025/224–7060* 🌐 *www.okura-niigata.com* 🛏 *263 Western-style rooms, 2 Japanese-style rooms* 👍 *In-room: a/c, refrigerator, Internet. In-hotel: 6 restaurants, room service, bar, laundry service, Internet terminal* 🍴 *No meals.*

SADO ISLAND (SADO-GA-SHIMA) 佐渡島

84 km (52 mi) west of Niigata.

Sado is known as much for its unblemished natural beauty as for its melancholy history. Revolutionary intellectuals, such as the Buddhist monk Nichiren, were banished to Sado to endure harsh exile as punishment for treason. When gold was discovered on Sado during the Edo period (1603–1868), the homeless and poverty-stricken were sent to Sado to work as forced laborers in the mines. This long history of hardship has left a tradition of soulful ballads and folk dances. Even the bamboo grown on the island is said to be the best for making *shakuhachi,* the flutes that accompany the mournful music.

May through September is the best time to visit Sado. In January and February the weather is bitterly cold, and at other times storms can prevent sea and air crossings. Although the island is Japan's fifth largest, it's still relatively small, at 530 square km (331 square mi). Two parallel mountain chains running along the north and south coasts are split by a wide plain, and it is here that the island's cities are found. Despite the more than 1 million tourists who visit the island each year (more than 10 times the number of inhabitants), the pace is slow.

Sado's usual port of entry is **Ryotsu** 両津, the island's largest township. The town's center runs between Kamo-ko (Kamo Lake) and the coast, with most of the hotels and ryokan on the shore of the lake. Kamo-ko is connected to the sea by a small inlet running through the middle of town. Ryotsu's Ebisu quarter has the island's largest concentration of restaurants and bars. Give yourself at least two days to take advantage of the beauty of Sado Island. For music lovers, the Kodo Earth Celebration in mid-August is not to be missed.

GETTING HERE AND AROUND

Sado Kisen has two main ferry routes, both with regular ferry and hydrofoil service. From Niigata to Ryotsu the journey takes 2½ hours, with six or seven crossings a day; the one-way fare is ¥2,320 for ordinary second class, ¥3,360 for first class, and ¥6,470 for special class. The jetfoil (¥6,220 one-way, ¥11,250 round-trip within five days) takes one hour, with 10 or 11 crossings daily in summer, three in winter, and between three and eight at other times of the year (depending on the weather). The bus from Bay No. 6 in front of the JR Niigata Station takes 15 minutes (¥200) to reach the dock for ferries sailing to Ryotsu.

Between Ogi and Naoetsu the hydrofoil cost is the same as the Niigata–Ryotsu crossing, but the Naoetsu ferry terminal is a ¥150 bus ride or ¥900 taxi ride from Naoetsu Station.

Depending on the season, one to three ferries sail between Teradomari (a port between Niigata and Naoetsu) and Akadomari, taking two hours. The fare is ¥2,760. The port is five minutes on foot from the Teradomari bus station, and 10 minutes by bus from the JR train station (take the Teradomari-ko bus).

Frequent bus service is available between major towns on Sado-ga-shima. The 90-minute bus ride from Ryotsu to Aikawa departs every 30 minutes and costs ¥740. Two-day weekend passes for unlimited bus travel are ¥2,000, and are available at the Ryotsu and Ogi ports and in the towns of Sawata and Aikawa. In hop-on, hop-off zones it is possible to flag the bus driver or get off anywhere on most routes, which is very convenient for sightseeing.

From May through November, four- and eight-hour tours of the island depart from Ryotsu and Ogi. These buses have a magnetic attraction to souvenir shops. The best compromise is to use the tour bus for the mountain skyline drive (¥4,500), then rent a bike to explore on your

The main attraction in Ogi, on Sado Island, is a trip on a traditional taraibune fishing boat.

own. You can make bus-tour reservations directly with the Niigata Kotsu Regular Sightseeing Bus Center.

Ferry Contacts Sado Kisen (✉ *353 Ryotsu Ebisu* ☎ *0259/27–5111* ⊗ *Daily 8–5).*

Tour Information Niigata Kotsu Regular Sightseeing Bus Center ☎ *0259/52–3200.*

Visitor Information Sado Tourism Association. ☎ *0259/57–5000* ⊕ *www. visitsado.com/en.* **Senkaku Bay Tourism** (☎ *0259/75–2221).*

WHAT TO SEE

The simplest way explore Sado is to take the bus from Ryotsu west to Aikawa. Before gold was discovered here in 1601 it was a town of 10,000 people. The population swelled to 100,000 before the gold was exhausted. Now it's back to a tenth that size.

Ogi 小木. The trip from Sawata to Ogi takes 50 minutes, the highlight being the beautiful *benten-iwa* (rock formations) just past Tazawaki. Take a window seat on the right-hand side of the bus. You can use Ogi as a port for returning to Honshu by ferry (2½ hours to Naoetsu) or on the hydrofoil (1 hour). Ogi's chief attractions are the **taraibune** たらい舟, round, tublike boats used for fishing. You can rent one (¥500 for a 30-minute paddle), and with a single oar paddle your way around the harbor. Taraibune can also be found in Shukunegi on the Sawasaki coast, where the water is dotted with rocky islets and the shore is covered with rock lilies in summer.

CLOSE UP

Heartbeat of Sado Island

A hawk flies overhead as the sky deepens to the indigo of the kimonos the two women are wearing. With an elegant flick, the *batchi* resounds against the stretched hide of the taiko drum and a rhythm begins. Soon all the members of **Kodo** 鼓童 bound onto the outdoor stage with their vibrant and distinctive blend of ensemble taiko, percussion, flute, song, and dance. The annual three-day **Earth Celebration**, held in August, kicks off.

On the second and third evenings Kodo are joined by artists they meet on tour, ranging from African and Asian drummers to a Romanian brass band, Fanfare Cio Carlia, and Carlos Nuñez, the Galician bagpipe revivalist. On-stage collaborations offer surprises; cleated *geta* (Japanese clogs)

were custom-made for New York tap star Tamango to dance with.

Kodo (which can mean heartbeat, child, or drum) was started in the 1960s to revive Japanese folk music. About 20 core members live communally on Sado Island with their families, growing rice and vegetables organically. To play the largest *odaiko*, an 800-pound, double-headed drum, takes immense stamina; and all members train intensively.

Not only is this an opportunity to catch Kodo on their home turf, but there are fringe events, workshops, a flea market, local festivals, and a pierside send-off when the ferry leaves. Tickets and accommodation should be booked well in advance through their Web site, ⊕ *www.kodo.or.jp.*

6

Osado Skyline Drive 大佐渡スカイライン. The most scenic drive on Sado is the Osado Skyline Drive. No public buses follow this route. You must take either a tour bus from Ryotsu or a taxi from Aikawa across the skyline drive to Chikuse (¥4,500), where you connect with a public bus either to Ryotsu or back to Aikawa. You can do the route in reverse as well.

Sado Kinzan 佐渡金山 *(Sado Mine).* Aikawa's mine has been a tourist attraction since operations halted in the 1980s. There are about 325 km (250 mi) of underground tunnels, some running as deep as 1,969 feet. Parts of this extensive digging are open to the public. Robots illustrate how Edo-period slaves worked in the mine. The robots are quite lifelike, and they demonstrate the appalling conditions endured by the miners. The mine is a tough 40-minute uphill walk or a five-minute taxi ride (about ¥900) from the bus terminal. The return is easier. ☎ *0259/74–2389* ✉*¥1,200* ⊙ *Apr.–Oct., daily 8–5:30; Nov.–Mar., daily 8–sunset (last entry for tours at 3:30).*

★ **Senkaku-wan** 尖閣湾 *(Senkaku Bay).* North of Aikawa along this bay is the most dramatic stretch of coastline on Sado-ga-shima. Boat tours of the bay leave regularly.

To reach the southwestern tip of Sado, first take a bus to Sawata from Aikawa or Ryotsu, and then transfer to the bus for Ogi; en route you may want to stop at the town of **Mano** 真野, where the exiled emperor Juntoku (1197–1242) is buried at the **Mano Goryo** (Mano Mausoleum).

★ **Shukunegi** 宿根木. This town has become a sleepy backwater town since it stopped building small wooden ships to traverse the waters between Sado and Honshu. It has, however, retained its simple lifestyle and traditional buildings that date back more than a century. You can reach Shukunegi from Ogi on a sightseeing boat or by bus. Both take about 20 minutes; consider using the boat at least one way for the view of the cliffs that an earthquake created 250 years ago.

WHERE TO EAT AND STAY

You can make hotel reservations at the information counters of Sado Kisen ship company at Niigata Port or Ryotsu Port.

Hotel reviews have been condensed for this book. Please go to Fodors. com for full reviews of each property.

$$
JAPANESE
★

✕ **Uoharu** 魚春. At the ferry terminal in Ogi, ask to be directed toward the area clustered with restaurants. In a corner of the three-story building is a fish shop at ground level with a restaurant upstairs. You can either choose your fish fresh off ice or try one of the excellent lunches like the sashimi, abalone steak (*awabi*), or sea urchin (*sazae*) sets from a menu with pictures. The restaurant usually closes at 5 pm but sometimes accepts reservations for the evening. ⊠ *415–1 Ogi-machi Ogi* ☎ *0259/86–2085* ▭ *No credit cards* ☉ *Closed Sat. No dinner without prior reservation.*

$$$$
HOTEL

▥ **Sado Royal Hotel Mancho** 佐渡ロイヤルホテル万長. This is the best hotel on Sado's west coast. It caters mostly to Japanese tourists; no English is spoken, but the staff nevertheless make the few visiting Westerners feel welcome. **Pros:** excellent views; friendly staff. **Cons:** no English spoken. ⊠ *58 Orito, Aikawa-orito* ☎ *0259/74–3221* 🖷 *0259/74–3738* ⟿ *74 rooms* ⌂ *In-room: a/c. In-hotel: restaurant* ⍾ *Some meals.*

$
INN
★

▥ **Sado Seaside Hotel** 佐渡シーサイドホテル. One kilometer (½ mile) from Ryotsu Port, this is more a friendly inn than a hotel. **Pros:** friendly staff; good value. **Cons:** no Western-style rooms. ⊠ *80 Sumiyoshi* ☎ *0259/27–7211* 🖷 *0259/27–7213* ⊕ *www2u.biglobe.ne.jp/~sado/ englishpage.htm* ⟿ *13 Japanese-style rooms, 5 with bath* ⌂ *In-room: a/c. In-hotel: restaurant, laundry service* ⍾ *No meals.*

SPORTS AND THE OUTDOORS

BOAT TOURS

From the waters of Senakaku Bay, you can look back at the fantastic, sea-eroded rock formations and 60-foot cliffs. You get off the boat at Senkaku-wan Yuen (Senkaku Bay Park), where you can picnic, stroll, and gaze at the varied rock formations offshore. From the park, return by bus from the pier to Aikawa. To reach the bay, take a 15-minute bus ride from Aikawa to Tassha for the 40-minute sightseeing cruise. The one-way cruise boat runs April–November (¥800, glass-bottom boat ¥1,000). For more information on boat tours, contact Senkaku Bay Tourism (⇨ *Visitor Information, above*).

Kyoto

WORD OF MOUTH

"Fushimi-Inari Taisha is a Shinto shrine with thousands of red torii gates that you walk through up a hill and into a forest. It is an amazing sight and experience. It got dark on us and the lanterns went on in the gates."

—Orcas

WELCOME TO KYOTO

TOP REASONS TO GO

★ **Architecture:** Despite modernization, about 27,000 traditional houses remain. The preservation districts include Sannen-zaka, Gion Shin-bashi, and the canal street leading to Kamigamo Jinja.

★ **Gardens:** Chinese-influenced gardens symbolize paradise on Earth. The *karesansui* (rock gardens) of Zen temples signify the eternal quest for wholeness; the most famous of these is at Ryoan-ji.

★ **Crafts:** Traditional craftspeople still work here. There's no shortage of art and antiques shops; secondhand kimonos are a bargain; and ceramics, lacquerware, and woven bamboo make great souvenirs.

★ **Live Culture:** Professional dancers and performers, geisha are revered as an embodiment of culture, with their opulent kimonos, hair ornaments, and artistic skills.

★ **Festivals:** Experience one of Kyoto's many festivals, many occurring between May and October.

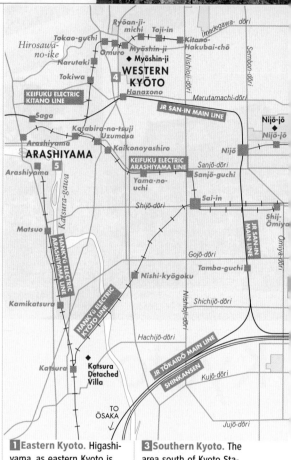

1 Eastern Kyoto. Higashi-yama, as eastern Kyoto is known, is chockablock with temples and shrines. The Gion shopping and entertainment neighborhood is also here.

2 Central Kyoto. Here are the hotels, the business district, and the Kiya-machi entertainment area.

3 Southern Kyoto. The area south of Kyoto Station has its share of gems, including. To-ji and the unforgettable Fushimi-Inari Taisha.

4 Western Kyoto. Although it's not as dense with sights as eastern Kyoto, this neighborhood includes many temples and gardens.

GETTING ORIENTED

Central Kyoto is fairly compact and easily navigable. Its grid layout, originally modeled on Xi'an in China, makes this Japan's most rational urban space. The city map is not difficult to understand. Broad avenues running east–west are numbered, giving you a handy opportunity to practice your Japanese. Counting to eight—ichi, ni, san, shi, go, roku, shichi, hachi—gives you most of these main arteries: Ichijo-dori, Nijo-dori, Sanjo-dori, and so on. Several important avenues don't follow this numbering system, notably Oike-dori, running in front of city hall, and Maruta-machi-dori and Imadegawa-dori, on the northern and southern sides of the Imperial Palace. Streets running north–south aren't numbered, but sights are clustered around a few main thoroughfares. Karasuma-dori bisects Kyoto Station in the middle of the city. East of the Kamogawa River, the Higashiyama neighborhood holds many of the city's most popular sights, all connected by the congested Higashi-oji-dori.

7

5 Arashiyama. Just outside the city, the exquisite villa Katsura Rikyu, the lovely Tenryu-ji, and beautiful riverside parks are in Arashiyama.

6 Northern Kyoto. Far from the center of the city, the main attractions of northern Kyoto are the mountaintop Buddhist enclave of Enryaku-ji on Hiei-zan and the charming countryside of Ohara.

Updated by Christal Whelan and Paul Bosley

The astonishing number of temples, shrines, and palaces that adorn the city make Kyoto's architecture its most famous feature abroad. Japan's capital for more than 1,000 years, Kyoto was the center not only for politics, but religion, philosophy, art, culture, and cuisine. Every one of Japan's refined cultural arts blossomed from seeds that were planted here, including the tea ceremony, Kabuki theater, Zen, and Tantric Buddhism.

Breathtaking sights are abundant, though some places truly stand out. Many tourists come away most impressed by Kyoto's great temples, such as Kiyomizu-dera in the city's eastern mountains, and the forest-cloaked Fushimi-Inari Taisha, a shrine pathway through a miles-long chain of towering vermilion gates. Visitors also flock to cultural hubs like the Museum of Traditional Crafts, showcasing the city's artisanal legacy, and Sanjusangen-do, with its 1,000 golden statues of Kannon.

Kyoto residents have a fierce sense of propriety about nearly everything, ranging from good table manners to family pedigree. This strict code has some notorious consequences for locals—who are not considered true Kyotoites unless they can trace their lineage back four generations—but certain benefits for visitors. The Kyoto mind-set insists that nothing made here should be of less than exquisite craftsmanship and stellar design. This philosophy means that whether browsing for gifts in a handkerchief shop, sightseeing at a local temple, or sitting down to a 12-course dinner, whatever you encounter is likely to be top-notch. As a visitor here you're a guest of the city, and Kyoto will make sure you leave with wonderful memories.

PLANNING

With hundreds of temples and shrines and several former imperial and shogunal residences, Kyoto has a lot to see. Keep this in mind and don't run yourself ragged. Balance a morning at temples or museums with an afternoon in traditional shops, and a morning at the market with the rest of the day in Arashiyama or at one of the imperial villas. We highly recommend a visit to at least one of the mountaintop temple complexes, such as Enryaku-ji on Hiei-zan or Daigo-ji. Remember that you must apply in advance (anywhere from one to several days) to visit attractions that require permits, such as the Imperial Palace, the imperial villas Katsura Rikyu and Shugaku-in, and Koinzan Saiho-ji.

WHEN TO GO

Cherry-blossom time in spring (usually the first week of April) and the glorious autumn foliage in early November are remarkable, though the city can be extremely crowded and very expensive. Except for the depths of winter and the peak of summer heat in August, Kyoto's climate is mild enough—though often rainy, especially mid-June to mid-July—to make sightseeing pleasant for most of the year. In the high season (May–October) the large numbers of visitors can make accommodations scarce.

GETTING HERE AND AROUND

Kyoto has an excellent public transportation system, so getting around the city is a snap. Buses are frequent and reliable, though the thick crowds can make them run slightly behind schedule. JR trains and five private light-rails and subways service the city, and are especially useful for reaching outlying sights and making day trips to nearby cities.

AIR TRAVEL

International and some domestic flights land at Kansai International Airport, near Osaka. Osaka's Itami Aiport handles all regional flights. To get to downtown Kyoto from Kansai, take the JR Haruka Limited Express, a train that departs every 30 minutes (75 minutes; ¥3,490). From Itami, buses depart approximately every 20 minutes from 8:10 am to 9:20 pm (55–90 minutes; ¥1,280–¥1,370). MK Taxi offers a shuttle bus from both Kansai (¥3,500) and Itami (¥2,300); reserve in advance.

BUS TRAVEL

Buses in Kyoto are quick, reliable, and punctual, making them an excellent form of transportation. City bus 100 is designed around the tourist route, connecting all the major sightseeing spots. Pick up route maps at the Kyoto Tourist Information Center.

Within the city the standard fare is ¥220, which you pay when leaving the bus; outside the city limits the fare varies according to distance. Several special transportation passes are available, including the following: a one-day city bus pass for ¥500, valid for use inside the inner-city area; Kyoto sightseeing one-day (¥1,200) or two-day (¥2,000) passes that cover travel on city buses, the subway, and private Kyoto Line buses; and the *torafika kyo* pass, which provides ¥3,300 worth of transport via city bus or subway for ¥3,000. Passes are sold at travel agencies, main bus terminals, and information centers in Kyoto Station.

SUBWAY TRAVEL

Kyoto has a 28-station subway system. The Karasuma Line runs north to south from Kokusai Kaikan to Takeda. The Tozai Line runs between Nijo in the west and Roku-jizo in the east. Purchase tickets at the vending machines in stations before boarding. Fares increase with distance traveled and begin at ¥210. Service runs 5:30 am–11:30 pm.

TAXI TRAVEL

Taxis are readily available in Kyoto. Fares for smaller-size cabs start at ¥640 for the first 2 km (1 mi), with a cost of ¥100 for each additional 500 meters. Many taxi companies provide guided tours of the city, priced per hour or per route. Keihan Taxi has four-hour tours from ¥18,000 per car; MK Taxi runs similar tours starting at ¥18,000 for three hours. There are fixed fares for some sightseeing services that start and end at Kyoto Station. A 7½-hour tour of the city's major sights will cost in the region of ¥26,000 with any of the 17 taxi companies, including Keihan Taxi and MK Taxi.

Contacts Keihan Taxi (☎ 075/622–4000). **MK Taxi** (☎ 075/778–4141 ⊕ www. mk-group.co.jp).

TRAIN TRAVEL

Frequent Shinkansen trains run between Tokyo and Kyoto, taking 2 hours and 40 minutes. The one-way reserved fare is ¥13,220. JR train service between Osaka and Kyoto costs ¥540 and takes 30 minutes; trains connecting with Shin-Osaka take 15 minutes and cost ¥1,380. Keihan and Hankyu lines express trains take 40 minutes and cost between ¥390 and ¥460. They depart every 15 minutes from Osaka's Yodoyabashi and Umeda stations.

For travel to Kyoto's northern reaches, change from the Keihan subway line to the Eizan Railway by transferring at Imadegawa-dori/Demachi-Yanagi Station. The Eizan has two lines, the Kurama Line, running north to Kurama, and the Eizan Line, running northeast to Yase. The Hankyu Line, which runs west as far as Katsura Rikyu, connects with the subway at Karasuma Station. From Shijo-Omiya Station the Keifuku Arashiyama Line runs to western Kyoto. JR also runs to western Kyoto on the San-in Main Line.

TOURS

Several private companies offer guided tours of Kyoto. One of the best is Kyoto-Tokyo Private Tours, run by Ian Roepke, a consultant to the *Kyoto Visitor's Guide*; the company offers half-day and full-day tours of the city. A seasoned guide who can shed insight into the mysterious world of the geisha, Peter MacIntosh of Kyoto Sights and Nights leads late-afternoon walks through the old teahouse districts. The Japanese guide known as Johnnie Hillwalker has been giving his popular all-walking tours of Kyoto since 1996 and has been a tour guide for almost 50 years; he loves storytelling and slow walking but takes sabbatical from December through February. Sunrise Tours organizes half-day morning and afternoon deluxe coach tours highlighting different city attractions. Volunteer guides can be requested by calling the Utano Youth Hostel. The Kyoto International Community House can arrange home visits.

Contacts Johnnie Hillwalker (☎🖷 075/622–6803 ⊕ web.kyoto-inet.or.jp/ people/h-s-love). **Kyoto International Community House** (✉ 2–1 Torii-cho, Awata-guchi, Sakyo-ku ☎ 075/752–3010). **Kyoto Sights and Nights** (☎ 090/5169–1654 ⊕ www.kyotosightsandnights.com). **Kyoto-Tokyo Private**

DID YOU KNOW?

Kyoto's Gion District is the city's geisha district (and has been since the 16th century). You can still see geishas in traditional dress traveling to their appointments in the early evening.

Tours (⊕ *www.kyoto-tokyo-private-tours.com*). **Sunrise Tours** (☎ *075/341–1413* ⊕ *www.jtbgmt.com/sunrisetour/kyoto*). **Utano Youth Hostel** (✉ *29 Nakayama-cho, Uzumasa, Ukyo-ku* ☎ *075/462–2288*).

VISITOR INFORMATION

One of Kyoto's best resources, the Tourist Information Center, is on the second floor of Kyoto Station. Heading away from of the tracks, take the escalator up one flight; the information desk is next to the entrance of Isetan Department Store. The office publishes pamphlets with descriptions of five self-guided walking tours, including maps. The tours range in length from about 40 to 80 minutes. The office is open daily 8:30 to 7, but closes the second and fourth Tuesday of each month. To get the lay of the land, newcomers should obtain an up-to-date bus map, a tourist map, and a copy of the free monthly *Kyoto Visitor's Guide* here.

Visitors require special permission from the Imperial Household Agency to visit three sights in Kyoto: Kyoto Imperial Palace, Katsura Rikyu, and Shugaku-in Imperial Villa. It's best to obtain permission at least a few days in advance, but the permission to visit the Imperial Palace can often be obtained for a same-day visit by stopping in at the agency's office, which is in the northwest corner of the Imperial Palace's park; you can also apply for permission on the agency's Web site.

Contacts Imperial Household Agency (✉ *3 Kyoto Gyoen-nai, Kamigyo-ku* ☎ *075/211–1215* ⊕ *sankan.kunaicho.go.jp*).

Kyoto Tourist Information Center (✉ *2F JR Kyoto Station, Karasuma-dori, Shimogyo-ku* ☎ *075/343–0548*).

Kyoto Visitor's Guide (⊕ *www.kyotoguide.com*).

EXPLORING KYOTO

EASTERN KYOTO

East of the Kamogawa River, in the neighborhoods known as Higashi-yama (literally, Eastern Mountain) and Okazaki, are some of Kyoto's most dazzling shrines and temples, stretching from solemn Sanjusangen-do in the south to the elegant Ginkaku-ji in the north. The cobbled streets of the Gion district are mysterious during the day, and even more so at night. Just west of the river, taverns along the alleyways of Ponto-cho and bars and restaurants on Kiya-machi are the city's most happening neighborhoods after dark.

GETTING AROUND

Subway lines crisscross eastern Kyoto, making them a great way to get around. Maps detailing the extensive bus network are available at tourist information centers. Buses run on major roads like Shichijo-dori, Shijo-dori, and Higashi-oji-dori. But the best way to explore these neighborhoods is on foot. Starting from anywhere, you can't walk 10 minutes in any direction without encountering a landmark.

CLOSE UP

A Brief History of Kyoto

Although Kyoto was Japan's capital for more than 10 centuries, the real center of political power was often elsewhere, be it Kamakura (1192–1333) or Edo (1603–1868). Until 710 Japan's capital moved with the accession of each new emperor. When it was decided that this expense was too great, Nara was chosen as the permanent capital. This experiment lasted 74 years, during which Buddhists rallied for, and achieved, tremendous political power. In an effort to thwart them, Emperor Kammu moved the capital to Nagaoka for a decade and then, in 794, to Kyoto.

Until the end of the 12th century, the city flourished under imperial rule. The city's nobility, known as "cloud dwellers," cultivated an extraordinary culture of refinement called *miyabi*. But when imperial power waned, the city saw the rise of the samurai class employed to protect the noble families' interests. Ensuing clashes between various clans led to the Gempei War (1180–85), from which the samurai emerged victorious. The *bushido* (or warrior spirit) found a counterpart in the minimalism of Zen Buddhism's austerity. The past luxury of miyabi was replaced with Zen's respect for frugality and discipline.

This period also brought devastating civil wars. Because the various feuding clans needed the Emperor's support to claim legitimacy, Kyoto, as imperial capital, became the stage for bitter struggles. The Onin Civil War (1467–77) was particularly devastating for Kyoto. Two feudal lords, Yamana and Hosokawa, disputed who should succeed the reigning shogun. Yamana camped in the western part of the city with 90,000 troops, and Hosokawa settled in the eastern part with 100,000 troops. Central Kyoto was the battlefield, and many of the city's buildings were destroyed.

Ieyasu Tokugawa, founder of the Tokugawa shogunate, eventually moved the country's political center to Edo. Kyoto remained the imperial capital, and the first three Tokugawa shoguns paid homage to the city by restoring old temples and building new villas in the early 1700s. Much of what you see in Kyoto dates from this period. When Emperor Meiji was restored to power in the late 1860s his capital and Imperial Court were moved to Tokyo. Commerce flourished, though, and Kyoto continued as the center of traditional culture.

7

TOP ATTRACTIONS

Eikan-do 永観堂. Next to the Nanzen-ji temple complex, Eikan-do was built after the original temple, dating from 855, was destroyed in the 15th century. Visitors come throughout the year to see the lifelike Amida Buddha statue with a turned head, which is said to have once come alive to dance with a reveling priest. The temple draws the most visitors in autumn, when people come to see the colorful foliage, and in November, when there's an excellent display of painted doors. ✉ *48 Eikando-cho, Higashiyama-ku* 📧 *Dec.–Oct. ¥600, Nov. ¥1,000* 🕙 *Dec.–Oct., daily 9–4; Nov., daily 9–9.*

Fodor'sChoice ★ **Ginkaku-ji** 銀閣寺. The Temple of the Silver Pavilion was intended to dazzle the courtly world with its opulence, but the current structure is an exercise in elegance and restraint. Yoshimasa Ashikaga spent years constructing his retirement villa in a conspicuous homage to his grandfather's Golden Pavilion on the opposite end of town. Carefully sculpted gardens surround a two-story mansion that the shogun originally intended to be wrapped in silver leaf. During construction in the 1470s, a tumultuous war and government unrest meant funds for the audacious project dried up. What remains is a quintessentially peaceful place. High earthen walls frame a modest compound of buildings giving way to extensive gardens. The lovely Silver Pavilion, which stares down at its reflection in the water, sits among the rolling moss-covered hillsides, dark pools, and an enormous dry garden, called the Sea of Sand. To reach Ginkaku-ji from Kyoto Station, take Bus 5, 11, or 17 to the Ginkaku-ji-michi bus stop. ⊠ *1 Ginkaku-ji-cho, Sakyo-ku* 🖃 *¥500* 🕙 *Mid-Mar.–Nov., daily 8:30–5; Dec.–mid-Mar., daily 9–4:30.*

NEED A BREAK?

Ginkaku-ji-yu Sento 銀閣寺湯. **A remnant of a former era when private homes did not have bathing facilities, this neighborhood *sento* (public bath) is very popular for its hot, cold, and herbal baths. Men and women bathe in separate rooms, but the etiquette is the same: Enter the bathing area naked, and wash and rinse yourself thoroughly (use the stool and basin) before dipping into the communal tubs. Small towels are used as washcloths, then wrung tightly and used for drying afterwards. Soap and a towel can be purchased on-site, or you can bring your own toiletries. Lockers have bracelet keys or baskets in which to place your clothes. ⊠ *Ishibashi-cho 32-1, Sakyo-ku, Jodoji* 🕿 *075/771–8311* 🖃 *¥410* 🕙 *Sun. and Mon. 3:30 pm–12:30 am.***

Kotoimo Honpo 古都芋本舗. **Just down the road from Ginkaku-ji, this shop is a good place to stop for something cool as it specializes in ice cream and *mochi* (rice dough). Flavors change with the seasons: in spring, ice cream is made from fragrant cherry leaves; in summer, mango; in autumn and winter, sweet potato; and year-round you can get *hoji-cha* (roasted green tea), *macha* (green tea), and vanilla for ¥250. You can also get white or black sesame mochi filled with sweet potato paste (¥150). A popular retro-drink is *ramune* (lemonade) in a Codd-neck bottle which contains a marble held under pressure. Duck inside and sit on the benches, or find a stone seat along the canal. ⊠ *Ishibashi-cho 58, Sakyo-ku, Jodoji* 🕿 *075/752–1221* 🕙 *Daily 9–6.***

Gion Corner ギオンコーナー. Because Westerners rarely have the opportunity to experience Japanese traditional arts, this theater's 50-minute show brings a sampling of five together—gagaku (court music), *kyomai* (Kyoto-style dance), Bunraku (puppet theater), *kyogen* (comic drama), and koto (Japanese harp). Before the show there is a tea ceremony. ⊠ *Yasaka Hall, 570-2 Minamigawa Gion-machi, Higashiyama-ku* 🕿 *075/561–1119* 🕙 *Mar.–Nov., daily at 7 pm and 8 pm; Dec.–Feb., daily at 7 pm (without Bunraku)* 🖃 *¥3,150.*

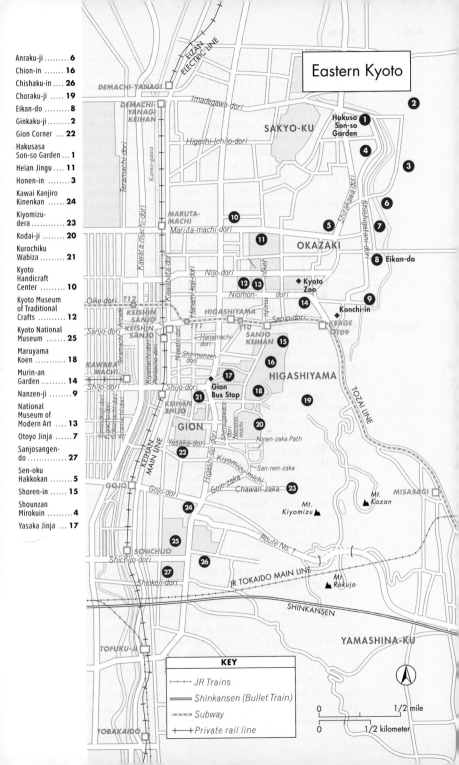

Eastern Kyoto

Heian Jingu 平安神宮. The massive vermilion and white walls of Heian Jingu are one of Kyoto's best-known landmarks. Built in the 1890s to commemorate the 1,100th anniversary of Kyoto's founding, Heian Jingu pays homage to the two emperors who bookend the city's era of national prominence: Kammu, who brought the imperial throne here in 794, and Komei, whose reign ending in 1866 saw the sun set on Kyoto's days as the capital. An assertion of Kyoto's unfaded splendor, Heian Jingu was built as a slightly smaller replica of the Imperial Palace, destroyed in 1227. The architecture reveals China's strong influence on the early Japanese court. The astonishing red torii gate, the biggest in Japan, and the three elaborate gardens behind the main shrine are particularly impressive. The complex makes a wonderful backdrop for several annual events, most famously the brazier-lighted dramas of Takigi No every June 1 and 2, and the thousands of performers in period dress for the Jidai Costume Festival on October 22. You can get here via Bus 5, 32, 46, or 100 to Kyoto Kaikan Bijutsukan-mae, Tozai subway to Higashiyama, or Keihan subway to Sanjo-dori. ⊠ *Okazaki-nishi Tenno-cho, Sakyo-ku* ☎ *075/761–0221* ⊠ *Gardens ¥600* ⏱ *Mid-Mar.–Aug., daily 8:30–5:30; Sept., Oct., and early Mar., daily 8:30–5; Nov.–Feb., daily 8:30–5:40.*

Fodor'sChoice   **Kiyomizu-dera** 清水寺. Pilgrims have climbed Higashiyama's cobble-
★   stone streets lined with tea shops and craft vendors to this gorgeous mountainside temple for centuries. In a forest on Kyoto's eastern flank, Kiyomizu-dera's tremendous gates and pagodas are marvels to behold. The main hall's huge veranda, jutting out over the valley, has become one of the city's quintessential images. Hundreds of clean-hewn timbers support the large deck and gracefully angular cypress-shingle roof. Finding the courage to set out on a daring new adventure is often likened to "taking a leap from the veranda of Kiyomizu."

The temple was founded in 780, but the buildings you see today date from 1633. Inside the towering gateway is a small shrine that is well worth exploring. Take off your shoes before descending the stairway for a metaphoric journey into the soul; in the dark passageway below the temple, quietly follow a chain of thick wooden beads to an ancient tablet carved with the Sanskrit rune for heart. (It's fine to touch the tablet.) Past the main hall, the quirky Jishu-jinja shrine is dedicated to Okuni Nushi-no-mikoto, a deity considered to be a powerful match-maker. Many young people visit the shrine to seek help in finding their life partners. They try to walk between two stones placed 18 meters (59 feet) apart, with their eyes closed. It's said that love will materialize for anyone who can walk in a straight line between the two.

Farther down the path, the "Sound of Feathers" waterfall tumbles down in three perfect streams before a raised platform. You can catch some of its water by using one of the long-handled silver cups; drinking from the falls supposedly helps with health, longevity, and academic success. If you need more to fortify you, enjoy some noodle soup, hot tea, or cold beer from one of the old stalls below the trellised balcony. To get here, take Bus 100 or 206 to Gojo-zaka or Kiyomizu-michi, where a 10-minute uphill walk takes you to the temple. ⊠ *Kiyomizu 1-chome, Higashiyama-ku* ⊠ *¥300* ⏱ *Daily 6–6.*

Ginkaku-ji (Temple of the Silver Pavilion) was built in the late 15th century as a retirement villa for Shogun Yoshimasa Ashikaga.

<table>
</table>

NEED A BREAK?

Bunnosuke Jaya. On the road to Kiyomizu-dera, a wooden archway covered in *senja-fuda* (name cards pilgrims affix on the entryways to shrines and temples) leads to this charming courtyard teahouse. The specialty here is *amazake*, a nonalcoholic drink often served hot with a touch of ginger. The interior is adorned with an eclectic collection of kites and folk dolls. ⊠ *Kiyomizu 3-cho, Higashiyama-ku* ☎ *075/561–1972* ⊘ *Thurs.–Tues. 10:30–5:30.*

Kurochiku Wabiza くろちく倭美坐. Fine traditional crafts, including reasonably priced dolls, ceramics, lacquerware, prints, incense, textiles, and bonsai, can be found here. From Kyoto Station, take Bus 206 to the Gion stop. The center is on the Shijo-dori in the Gion Kurochiku Building. ⊠ *275 Gion-machi Kitagawa Higashiyama-ku* ☎ *075/541–9660* ⊘ *Daily 10–7.*

★ **Murin-an Garden** 無隣庵庭園. In a departure from traditional Japanese gardens, this garden has rolling expanses of English-style lawns that reflect the melding of Japanese and Western elements. This blending of styles is also visible in the architecture of a house that once belonged to soldier and statesman Arimoto Yamagata. Backed by a sweep of hills, Murin-an has paths that meander past converging streams and a three-tier waterfall. The south side of the garden is almost always in shadow, creating wonderful contrasts. ⊠ *31 Nanzenji-Kusakawa-cho, Sakyo-ku* ⊡ *¥400* ⊘ *Daily 9–4:30.*

★ **Nanzen-ji** 南禅寺. Several magnificent temples share this corner of the forested foothills between Heian Jingu and Ginkaku-ji. The most

Getting to Know Gion

Japan's traditional and modern worlds intersect where Shijo-dori crosses Hanami-koji-dori in the district of Gion. To the south, cobblestone streets lead past wood-fronted teahouses displaying red paper lanterns, while a block northward are high-rises chock-full of bars. Eastward is Yasaka Jinja's commanding orange-and-white arched gate; westward are the city's best department stores.

Gion remains Kyoto's center for high culture, including venues offering Kabuki, Noh, and Bunraku puppetry theater. Perhaps more famous to foreign visitors is the floating world of geisha entertainment, brought into the spotlight recently by the film adaptation of Arthur Golden's *Memoirs of a Geisha*. Wandering around Hanami-koji-dori at night you're sure to see *maiko-san* and *gekko-san*, the modern equivalents of apprentice and senior geisha, on their way to appointments at exclusive teahouses behind curtained doorways.

prominent is Nanzen-ji, with its awesome gateway. A short distance away you'll enjoy Nanzen-in's serene beauty, Kochi-in's precise garden, and Murin-an's expansive lawns.

Like Ginkaku-ji, the villa of Nanzen-ji was turned into a temple on the death of its owner, Emperor Kameyama (1249–1305). By the 14th century this had become the most powerful Zen temple in Japan, which spurred the Tendai monks to destroy it. The 15th-century Onin Civil War demolished the buildings again, but some were reconstructed during the 16th century. Nanzen-ji has again become one of Kyoto's most important temples, in part because it's the headquarters of the Rinzai sect of Zen Buddhism.

Monks in training are still taught at the temple. You enter through the enormous 1628 **San-mon** (Triple Gate), the classic "gateless" gate of Zen Buddhism that symbolizes entrance into the most sacred part of the temple precincts. From the top floor of the gate you can view Kyoto spread out below. Whether or not you ascend the steep steps, give a moment to the statue of Goemon Ishikawa. In 1594 this Robin Hood–style outlaw tried but failed to kill the daimyo (feudal lord) Hideyoshi Toyotomi. He hid in this gate until his capture, after which he was boiled in a cauldron of oil. His story is still enacted in many Kabuki plays.

On your way to see the major temples and gardens within the complex, don't overlook Nanzen-ji's other attractions. The **Hojo** (Abbots' Quarters) is a National Treasure. Inside, screens with impressive 16th-century paintings divide the chambers. These wall panels of the *Twenty-Four Paragons of Filial Piety and Hermits* were created by Eitoku Kano (1543–90) of the Kano School—in effect the Kano family, because the school consists of eight generations of one bloodline (Eitoku was from the fifth generation). Enshu Kobori created what's commonly known as the Leaping Tiger Garden, an excellent example of the karesansui style, attached to the Hojo. The large rocks are grouped with clipped

The original Kiyomizu-dera was built six years before the founding of Kyoto; the current structure dates to 1633.

azaleas, maples, pines, and moss, all positioned against a plain white well behind the raked gravel expanse. The greenery effectively connects the garden with the lush forested hillside beyond.

Past Nanzen-ji's three-tiered gateway, quiet **Nanzen-in** (✉ *Nanzenji-Fukuchi-cho, Sakyo-ku* ☎ *075/771–0365* 💴 *¥300* 🕙 *Daily 8:40–4*) has a peaceful garden that is well worth exploring. A curiously modern brick aqueduct cuts through the maples leading up to Emperor Kameyama's mausoleum.

Recognized by garden aficionados around the world as one of Japan's finest, **Konchi-in** 金地院 (✉ *86 Fukuchi-cho, Nanzen-ji, Sakyo-ku* 💴 *¥400* 🕙 *Mar.–Nov., daily 8:30–5; Dec.–Feb., daily 8:30–4:30*) was first established in the 15th century. It was moved inside Nanzen-ji's temple complex in 1605 and landscaped by designer Enshu Kobori several decades later. Shadow-dappled stone pathways wind past moss-covered hills to a pond hugged close by maple and cherry trees. There's a lovely temple building and a dry garden whose solemn rocks figure a crane and turtle symbolizing wisdom and longevity. Kochi-in is on the path leading up to Nanzen-ji, just before the main gate. A climb to the top of this temple's pagoda affords superb views of the eastern mountains. ✉ *Nanzenji-Fukuchi-cho, Sakyo-ku* 💴 *Abbotts' Quarters ¥500, Triple Gate ¥500* 🕙 *Mar.–Nov., daily 8:40–5; Dec.–Feb., daily 8:40–4:30.*

NEED A BREAK?

Taian-en 大安苑. **In a garden within the Nanzen-ji temple complex that was designed by renowned Showa designer, Ogawa Jihei the 11th (whose predecessor Ogawa Jihei 7th designed the garden at Heian Jingu), this**

Continued on page 420

THE PHILOSOPHER'S PATH

哲学の道

A STROLL THROUGH KYOTO'S EASTERN HILLS AND TEMPLES

by
Christal Whelan

"If my heart can become pure and simple, like that of a child, I think there probably can be no greater happiness." —Kitaro Nishida

Tucked away in the lush foothills of the Eastern Mountains of Kyoto, the Philosopher's Path winds along a canal lined with cherry trees and through a quiet residential neighborhood. With notable Buddhist temples, imperial tombs, Shinto shrines, and quaint shops, the route has become one of the city's most popular walking courses.

Although it traverses an area rich in antiquity, the Philosopher's Path is a modern promenade, receiving its name in the early Showa era (1926–1989) after its counterpart in Heidelberg. Later, the path became associated with the legacy of the philosopher Kitaro Nishida (1870–1945), renowned for his synthesis of Eastern and Western thought, who walked the path daily. Today many follow in Nishida's foot-steps along the canal and likewise bear witness to the drama of the changing seasons. Flanked by two bridges—the Nyakaou-ji and Ginkaku-ji—and a Zen temple at both extremes, this mile offers a perfect balance of Japanese his-tory, culture, cuisine, art, and devotion to nature all within a single walk.

(opposite) The Philosopher's Path, (top) Tea house on the Philosopher's Path

Ginkaku-ji

THE ROUTE (NORTH TO SOUTH)

If you decide to follow this route from south to north, simply reverse the walk.

Begin your morning at **Ginkaku-ji**, the Silver Pavilion. Although it was once the aesthetic and cultural center of a nation, fires over the years have ravaged the complex and left only two original buildings, both now National Treasures—the Kannon-den and the Toku-do. These graceful structures are thatched with layers of thin cypress shingles. On the apex of the Kannon-den a bronze phoenix stands perched prophetically, and the paper windows shimmer with reflections from the rippling pond below. Exquisite dry sand and classical stroll gardens are by Soami, a master landscape designer of the medieval period. The

road away from Ginkaju-ji, down an incline, leads to the Philosopher's Path on the left. On the corner, refreshment can be found at the **Kotoimo Hompo**. The only public toilet along this route is located down the staircase from here in the parking lot.

Heading south, the outdoor chapel at **Shounzan Mirokuin** is dedicated to the bodhisattva Jizo, who protects children and those in dire straits. This temple belongs to Shugendo, a fusion of mountain veneration, Shinto, and Japanese Tantric Buddhism (here, Tendai). Normally closed, the temple opens to the public on August 28, from 1 to 3 pm, when the ascetic practitioners called *yamabushi* hold a religious procession that culminates in a *saito-goma*, or outdoor fire ceremony.

Follow the path markers and cross the bridge to **Honen-in Temple.** The thatched entrance gate and the temple grounds are the highlights here since the temple interior is closed to the public most

of the year. To the right of the entry is a building used for contemporary year-round art exhibitions. Across the street, at the foot of the temple, is Honen-in's **Mori no sentaa** (Friends of the Forest Center), devoted to the study and preservation of nature; with reservations two weeks in advance, the Center offers guided nature hikes ($) up Mt. Daimonji.

The nearby temple of **Anraku-ji** runs Café Momiji on its premises, an art gallery nearby (**Hanairo**), and hosts the popular *kabocha kuyo*, a service conducted since 1790 in honor of pumpkin-squash (July 25, 9–3).

The nearby **Otoyo Jinja** is an ancient Shinto shrine that

Sen-oku Museum

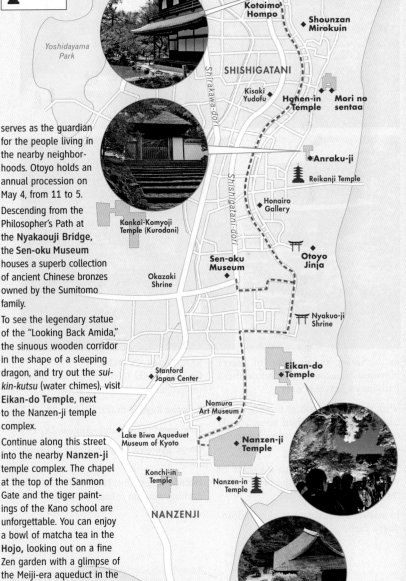

KEY

- - - *The route*
⛩ *Shrine*
🏯 *Temple*

Imadegawa-dori

Ginkaku-ji-gu Sento
Ginkaku-ji

Hakusasonsou
Son-so

Kotoimo Hompo

Shounzan Mirokuin

Yoshidayama Park

SHISHIGATANI

Shirakawa-dori

Kisaki Yudofu

Honen-in Temple

Mori no sentaa

Anraku-ji

Reikanji Temple

Shishigatani-dori

Honairo Gallery

Konkai-Komyoji Temple (Kurodani)

Sen-oku Museum

Okazaki Shrine

Otoyo Jinja

⛩ Nyakuo-ji Shrine

Stanford Japan Center

Eikan-do Temple

Nomura Art Museum

Lake Biwa Aqueduet Museum of Kyoto

Nanzen-ji Temple

Konchi-in Temple

Nanzen-in Temple

NANZENJI

---

serves as the guardian for the people living in the nearby neighborhoods. Otoyo holds an annual procession on May 4, from 11 to 5.

Descending from the Philosopher's Path at the **Nyakaouji Bridge,** the **Sen-oku Museum** houses a superb collection of ancient Chinese bronzes owned by the Sumitomo family.

To see the legendary statue of the "Looking Back Amida," the sinuous wooden corridor in the shape of a sleeping dragon, and try out the *sui-kin-kutsu* (water chimes), visit **Eikan-do Temple,** next to the Nanzen-ji temple complex.

Continue along this street into the nearby **Nanzen-ji** temple complex. The chapel at the top of the Sanmon Gate and the tiger paintings of the Kano school are unforgettable. You can enjoy a bowl of matcha tea in the **Hojo,** looking out on a fine Zen garden with a glimpse of the Meiji-era aqueduct in the background, or visit **Taian-en** for a quieter respite.

7

IN FOCUS THE PHILOSOPHER'S PATH

THE PATH IN ALL SEASONS

In the **spring**, the eruption of cherry blossoms transforms the Philosopher's Path into a heavenly pink.

With the **summer** comes fireflies, flourishes of hydrangea, bird song, cicada cries, and murmur of water tumbling over rocks.

The **autumn** gives way to a palette of yellows, oranges, and the deep red of the Japanese maple.

In **winter** snows blanket the Philosopher's Path.

SEASONAL EVENTS

Go-san Okuribi (Sending off ceremony on five mountains): August 16

Kabocha Kuyo (Anraku-ji): July 25, 9–3

Saito goma (Mirokuin): August 28, 1–3

Otoyo gyoretsu (Otoyo Jinja): May 4, 11–5

Eikando (Light Up): Nov. 6–30, 5:30–9, evening autumn foliage viewing

(top left) Spring cherry blossoms; (top right) summer strolling; (bottom left) Ginkaku-ji in winter; (bottom right) the fall Eikando festival

PRACTICAL INFO

GETTING THERE

You can begin your walk at either end of the pathway—Ginkaku-ji or Nanzen-ji. If you choose Nanzen-ji, take the subway (Tozai line) from Sanjo-Keikan and get off at Keage, or catch Bus 5 from Kyoto Station to Nazen-ji Eikando-mae. From either, it is a 10-minute walk. To start from Ginkaku-ji, catch Bus 17, 5, or 100 and get off at Ginkaku-ji-mae. An easy walk up Imadegawa to Ginkaku-ji-michi leads into the temple.

TIMING

With no stops along the way, the entire course takes just under an hour. But if you stop at the suggested points of interest, allow three hours or more. You can begin at any time, but should bear in mind that Gingaku-ji closes at 4:30 or 5 depending on the season. A visit to Ginkaku-ji is probably best done as early as possible (it opens at 8:30 am) to beat the crowds at one of Kyoto's most frequented temples.

FUEL UP

If you begin the walk at Gingaku-ji, then you will wind up at Taian-en for either lunch or dinner, depending on what hour you set out. The trip from north to south allows you to end up sipping from a frothy bowl of green tea in Nanzen-ji's **Hojo** or sitting down to a traditional bento lunch or dinner. A trip in the reverse (from Nanzen-ji to Ginkaku-ji) leads to something more luxurious; you can finish with a nice cleansing at **Ginkaku-ji-yu Sento**, a traditional neighborhood bathhouse. At this end, dinner at either **Kisaki Yudofu**, or for more sumptuous *kaiseki* feast, try the teahouse at the **Hakusasa Son-so** (down the hill from Ginkaju-ji) in its garden (reservations required).

SHUIN-CHO

From whichever end you do start, be sure to pick up a *shuin-cho* at your starting temple (¥1,300). These small, cloth-covered books have thick, blank sheets for collecting ink stamps and calligraphic signatures from each temple you visit. There is a nominal fee for these signatures, but they're worth every yen for such an authentic souvenir of Japan's ancient capital.

Creation of a dry landscape garden, or *karesansui*, at Honen-in temple restaurant opened in 2010. The two waterfalls are fed from the Biwa Canal and mountain streams, and a gorgeous gnarled red pine is the centerpiece. Bento lunches (¥1,800) are served in a tatami room level with a garden that emphasizes maples. On the second floor is Ankoan, a Japanese-style café that serves coffee, tea, and alcoholic beverages, where a dessert prix-fixe is ¥800. ⊠ *Nanzenji-Kusakawa-machi 81, Sakyo-ku* ☎ *075/752–4333.*

Fodor's Choice
★

Sanjusangen-do 三十三間堂. One of Kyoto's most awe-inspiring spectacles, this 400-foot-long hall holds 1,000 golden statues of the many-limbed Kannon. Enthroned in the center of the hall is a 6-foot-tall version of the deity that was carved by Tankei, a sculptor of the Kamakura period (1192–1333). In the corridor behind are the 28 guardian deities who protect the Buddhist universe. Notice the frivolous-faced Garuda, a bird that feeds on dragons. In the back of the hall are explanations of the significance of Kannon's various poses. From Kyoto Station take Bus 206, 208, or 100 to the Sanjusangen-do-mae stop. The temple is to the south, beyond the Hyatt Regency. ⊠ *657 Sanjusangen-do Mawari-cho, Higashiyama-ku* ☞ ¥600 ☉ *Apr.–mid-Nov., daily 8–5; mid-Nov.–Mar., daily 9–4.*

**OFF THE
BEATEN
PATH**

Sannen-zaka and Ninen-zaka 三年坂と二年坂. With their cobbled paths and delightful wooden buildings, these two lovely winding streets are the finest extant examples of Old Kyoto. This area is one of four historic preservation districts in the city, and the shops along the way sell snacks, souvenirs, and local crafts like pottery, dolls, and bamboo baskets. From Kiyomizu-dera turn right halfway down Kiyomizu-zaka. ⊠ *Higashiyama-ku.*

Yasaka Jinja 八坂神社. The magnificent vermilion-and-white gate of Kyoto's central shrine retains an essential role in the city's fiscal good fortune: in addition to the good-luck charms people flock here to buy, you will see the names of the city's biggest stores and companies adorning each glowing lantern hanging from the main hall's eaves, each of them sponsors seeking to gain financial favor. The shrine was built in the 7th century above an underground lake to ensure that the god who resides in the east—the blue water dragon—receives the fresh water needed to ensure healthy Earth energy. The original enshrined Shinto deity, Susano-no-Mikoto, later came to be associated with the Buddhist spirit Gozu Ten-no, a protector against pestilence and god of prosperity. Also known as Gion Shrine, Yasaka hosts the Gion Festival, which started in 869 as a religious ritual to rid the city of a terrible plague that originated in Kyoto and swiftly spread all over Japan. From Kyoto Station take Bus 206 or 100 to the Gion bus stop; the shrine is just off Higashi-oji-dori. ⊠ *625 Gion-machi, Kitagawa, Higashiyama-ku* ☞ *Free* ☉ *Daily 24 hrs.*

WORTH NOTING

Anraku-ji Temple 安楽寺. This small temple in the foothills of Higashi-yama dates back to the 12th century, when the priest Honen began to preach a novel means of salvation accessible to anyone, the recitation of the name of Amida Buddha (*nenbutsu*). Two of Honen's disciples, Anraku and Juren, preached this new and then-heretical faith in the

Sanjusangen-do contains 1,000 small statues of Kannon, a bodhisattva (enlightened being) in addition to a 6-foot-tall version with 1,000 hands.

countryside outside the usual surveillance. Two ladies in the Imperial Court, Matsumushi and Suzumushi, who were also said to be concubines of Emperor Go-Toba (1180–1239), inspired by the teachings, became nuns. Convinced that the monks had seduced the two ladies, the Emperor had the monks seized and beheaded. The court ladies then took their own lives. Then Honen was himself exiled as a heretic. When he was finally permitted to return to Kyoto in 1212, the elderly priest had Anraku-ji built to honor his faithful disciples and their two converts. The tombs of all four are on the temple grounds. Today Anraku-ji is a living, family-run temple, devoted to the arts and international exchanges. The temple recently opened Café Momiji on the premises, and it is open from 11 to 5 most days, also serving as an event space. Nearby the Gallery Hana-iro sponsors exhibitions of contemporary art. ⊠ *Shishigadani, Gosho-no-dancho 21, Sakyo-ku* ☎ *075/771–5360* ⊕ *anrakuji-kyoto.com* ⊡ *Free* ⊘ *Daily 11–5.*

Chion-in 知恩院. The headquarters of the Jodo sect of Buddhism, Chion-in is impressive enough to have been cast in the film *The Last Samurai* as a stand-in for Edo Castle. Everything here is on a massive scale. The imposing tiered gateway is the largest in the country, and the bell inside the temple grounds, cast in 1633, is the heaviest in all Japan, requiring 17 monks to ring it. (They don't do it every day, but at least you can understand why.) If you're lucky enough to be in Kyoto over New Year's you can hear the progression of 108 booming gongs meant to release temple goers from the worldly desires of the old year and welcome in the clarity of a new one (it's also nationally televised). The temple buildings are fun to explore, especially since you can take a good look at the exposed *uguisu-bari* (nightingale floor), constructed to "sing" unexpectedly in order to expose intruders. Walk underneath the corridor to examine the way the boards and nails are placed to create this inventive burglar alarm. Like most Kyoto temples, Chion-in's history includes a litany of fires and earthquakes, and most of the buildings you see date from the early 1600s. Not all the buildings here are open to the public. From Kyoto Station, take Bus 206 to the Gion stop. The temple is north of Maruyama Koen. ⊠ *400 Rinka-cho, Higashiyama-ku* ▧ *¥500* ⊙ *Daily 9–4.*

Chishaku-in 智積院. Paintings by Tohaku Hasegawa and his son Kyuzo—some of the best examples of the Momoyama period—are the best reason to visit this temple. Hasegawa painted exclusively for Zen temples in his later years, with masterpieces ranging from lyrical monochrome ink creations to bolder, more colorful works like the screen paintings exhibited here. Rich in detail, the screens evoke the seasons with the images of cherry, maple, pine, and plum as well as autumn grasses. The paintings, from the 16th century, were originally created for an earlier temple on the same site. From Kyoto Station, take Bus 206 or 208 to the Higashiyama-Shichijo stop. Chishaku-in is at the end of Shichijo-dori where it terminates at Higashi-oji-dori. ⊠ *Hisgashiyama-Shichijo, Higashiyama-ku* ▧ *¥500* ⊙ *Daily 9–4.*

Choraku-ji 長楽寺. A procession of stone lanterns lines the steep path to this tiny temple, founded by Emperor Kammu with the priest Saicho in 805. In 1185, after the Minamoto clan's defeat of the Taira clan in the momentous Genpei War, the last survivor found refuge here. Note the 11-faced statue of Kannon, evocative of the deity's Indian origins. The temple is number seven on Kyoto's new Thirty-Three Kannon Pilgrimage. Choraku-ji is east of Maruyama Koen. ⊠ *626 Maruyama-cho, Higashiyama-ku* ▧ *¥500* ⊙ *Daily 9–5.*

Hakusasa Son-so Garden 白沙村荘庭園. Down the hill from Ginkaku-ji, about 100 yards before the street crosses a canal, sits a century-old villa with an impeccable garden. This was once the home of painter Kansetsu Hashimoto, who created a unique style of painting that combined various Japanese periods and drew inspiration from Chinese imagery. The house contains many of Hashimoto's sketches and paintings, as well as works by both Chinese and Japanese contemporaries and an enthralling collection of Greek and Persian pottery. An exquisite stone garden and a teahouse are also open to the public. If you book at least two days in advance, it's possible to experience a complete tea ceremony. For a very special kaiseki dinner in a private room overlooking the luxurious garden with a carp pond, reservations are required (¥12,000 per person); lunch here is also available (¥4,500). To get here from Kyoto Station, take Bus 5 or 100 to the Ginkaku-ji-michi stop and walk east along the canal. Hakusa Son-so will be on the right. ⊠ *37 Ishibashi-cho, Jodoji, Higashiyama-ku* ▧ *¥800* ☎ *075/751–0446* ✉ *hakusasonso@gmail.com* ⊙ *Daily 10–5; last entry at 4:30.*

Honen-in 法然院. Near Ginkaku-ji on the Philosopher's Path this bamboo forest is a great place to escape from Kyoto's hustle and bustle. Flanking a flagstone pathway inside the temple's thatched gateway, two long regular mounds of sand are raked daily into shapes symbolizing the changing seasons. As you explore the surrounding green forest (if you arrive early in the morning, you can see the priests raking it clean) and stroll through the verdant garden, you may see the tombs of several notables, including novelist Junichiro Tanizaki, economist Hajime Kawakami, and artist Heihachiro Fukuda. The temple, built in 1680, is on a site chosen in the 13th century by Honen, founder of the populist Jodo sect of Buddhism. Year-round, monks place 25 flowers before the Amida Buddha statue in the main hall, representing the 25 bodhisattvas who accompany the Buddha to receive the souls of the newly deceased.

Across the street from Honen-in, at the foot of the temple, is Honen-in's **Mori no sentaa** (*Friends of the Forest Center* ⊠ *Shishigatani-Goshonodan-cho, Sakyo-ku* ☎ *075/752–4583* ☑ *¥1,000*), devoted to the study and preservation of nature. With reservations two weeks in advance, the center offers guided nature hikes up Mt. Daimonji (1,529 feet). ⊠ *Shishigatani-Goshonodan-cho, Sakyo-ku* ☎ *075/771–2420* ☑ *Free* ⊙ *Daily 6–4.*

Kawai Kanjiro Memorial House 河井寛次郎記念館 (*Kawai Kanjiro Kinen-kan*). The house and workshop of prolific potter Kanjiro Kawai has been transformed into a museum showcasing his distinctive works. One of the leaders of the *Mingei* (folk art) movement in the 1920s, Kawai's skill is evident in the asymmetrical vases, bowls, and pots on display in the house. Besides the fascinating workshop and enormous kiln preserved in an inner courtyard, the house itself is magnificent. It's a terrific opportunity for those who have never been inside a Japanese home. The house is a little hard to find, located in an alley just southwest of the Higashi-oji-dori and Gojo-dori intersection. To get here, take Bus 100 or 206 to Gojo-zaka. Walking west (downhill) on Gojo-dori, take the first left. ⊠ *569 Kanei-cho, Gojo-zaka, Higashiyama-ku* ☎ *075/561–3585* ☑ *¥900* ⊙ *Tues.–Sun. 10–5.*

Kodai-ji 高台寺. In the heart of ancient Higashiyama's cobbled streets, the elegant Momoyama-era temples and teahouses of Kodai-ji are set in an expansive garden of serene pools swimming with orange carp, hills of carefully tended moss, a forest of tall bamboo, and an expanse of raked gray sand. Many of the splendid paintings and friezes inside the main temples were relocated from Fushimi Castle, parts of which were used to construct Kodai-ji in the early 1600s. The temple was a memorial to Hideyoshi Toyotomi, commissioned by his wife Nene. (The road running in front of the temple is alternately called Higashiyama-dori or Nene-no-michi.) On the hills overlooking the main temple are teahouses designed by tea master Sen-no-Rikyu; they are identifiable by their umbrella-shape bamboo ceilings and thatched roofs. Evening illumination shows in April, November, and December are a great way to see the park after dark. (Avoid holiday weekends, when the place is packed.) The temple is a five-minute walk east of the Higashiyama Yasui bus stop (take number 206 or 207). ⊠ *Shimogawara-cho, Higashiyama-ku* ☎ *075/561–9966* ☑ *¥600* ⊙ *Daily 9–5.*

Kyoto Handicraft Center 京都ハンディクラフトセンター. Here you'll find seven floors filled with dolls, kimonos, pottery, swords, woodblock prints, and one of the best collections of English-language books on Japan. The eye-popping selection and reasonable prices mean this duty-free commercial center is a great place for browsing. Regular demonstrations of traditional craft techniques and hands-on workshops make this place tourist-oriented, though not a tourist trap. Everything is of high quality. To get here, take Bus 202 or 206 to Kumano Jinja-mae or Bus 5, 32, 46, or 100 to Kyoto Kaikan Bijutsukan-mae. The building is across Maruta-machi-dori from Heian Jingu. ✉ *21 Entomi-cho Shogo-in, Sakyo-ku* ☎ *075/761–5080* ⊙ *Daily 10–7.*

Kyoto Museum of Traditional Crafts 京都伝統産業ふれあい館 *(Kyoto Fureaikan).* Fascinating displays reveal the painstaking care taken with Kyoto's traditional crafts. Dioramas, pictures, videos, and live artisans at work show how a wide range of crafts, from everyday items like pottery and textiles to precious objects like jewelry and kimonos. The souvenir shop sells goods of the highest quality. The museum faces Heian Jingu. ✉ *B-1F Miyako Messe, 9–1 Seishoji-cho, Okazaki, Sakyo-ku* ☎ *075/762–2670* ⊡ *Free* ⊙ *Tues.–Sun. 9–5 (last entry at 4:30).*

Kyoto National Museum 京都国立博物館 *(Kokuritsu Hakubutsukan).* At this writing, the museum is undergoing an extensive renovation; the New Collections Hall is scheduled to open in fall 2013. The building itself is an enthralling piece of the Kyoto landscape, but its lackluster permanent collection doesn't rate as must-see. The Meiji-era brick structure holds an extensive collection of sculptures, textiles, ceramics, and metalwork. It is worth checking on the temporary exhibitions, which can bring some real treasures. The museum is on the corner of Shichijo-dori and Higashi-oji-dori, across from Sanjusangen-do and Chishaku-in. From Kyoto Station take Bus 206 or 208 to the Sanjusangen-do-mae stop. ✉ *527 Chaya-machi, Higashiyama-ku* ☎ *075/541–1151* ⊕ *www.kyohaku.go.jp* ⊡ *¥500* ⊙ *Jan. 8–Nov. 23, Tues.–Sun. 9:30–5:30.*

Maruyama Koen 円山公園 *(Maruyama Park).* Many people cut through this park, which lies near Yasaka Jinja and between Chion-in and Gion, when sightseeing. It is a popular venue for drinking sake outdoors, and with its ancient weeping cherry tree, it is a favorite spot during the cherry-blossom season with vendors making their rounds to supply refreshment. From Kyoto Station, take Bus 206 to the Higashiyama stop; the park is north of Kodai-ji. ✉ *Higashiyama-ku.*

National Museum of Modern Art 京都国立近代美術館 *(Kindai Bijutsukan).* This small but excellent museum is known for its collection of 20th-century Japanese paintings, emphasizing the artistic movements in the Kansai region. You'll also see ceramic treasures by Kanjiro Kawai, Rosanjin Kitaoji, Shoji Hamada, and others. There are frequent exhibitions of contemporary artists. The museum is on the road to Heian Jingu. Take Bus 5 or 100 to Kyoto Kaikan Bijustsukan-mae. ✉ *Enshoji-cho, Okazaki, Sakyo-ku* ☎ *075/761–4111* ⊡ *¥420* ⊙ *Tues.–Sun. 9:30–5.*

Otoyo Jinja 大豊神社. Built in 887, this small shrine was built as a prayer for the recovery of the Emperor Uda from a serious illness. Its long pathway is lined with stone lanterns, and the main buildings enshrine Sukunahikona no mikoto, Emperor Ojin, and Sugawara Michizane. It is considered the guardian shrine for people who live in the adjacent neighborhoods of Shishigadani, Honenin, and Nanzenji. The shrine's annual procession in May involves some 50 people, two horses, and a *mikoshi* (portable shrine). ☒ *Shishigadani, Miyanomae-machi Kanyuchi, Sakyo-ku* ☏ *075/771–1351* 🎫 *Free* ⊙ *Daily 9–5.*

Sen-oku Hakkokan 泉屋博古館. This refined museum presents the extraordinary collection of ancient Chinese bronzes collected by Kichizaemon Sumitomo for over 30 years, until his death in 1926. As 15th head of the Sumitomo family, widely known for its expertise in electric wire manufacturing, Kichizaemon's interest in metal was as artistic as scientific. In the years following the collapse of Qing Dynasty in 1912, when many of China's treasures appeared in foreign markets, Kichizaemon amassed the most outstanding collection outside China. The Sumitomo Collection represents objects crafted more than 3,000 years ago during the Shang and Zhou periods (1600–221 BC) as well as some more recent: ritual implements, musical instruments, mirrors, bells, and calligraphy. ☒ *Miyanomae-cho 24, Shishigadani, Sakyo-ku* ☏ *075/771–6411* ⊕ *www.sen-oku.or.jp* 🎫 *¥730* ⊙ *Mid-Mar.–June and Sept.–mid-Dec., Tues.–Sun. 10:30–5.*

★ **Shoren-in** 青蓮院. Paintings by the Kano School are on view at this Tendai sect temple, a five-minute walk north of Chion-in. Although the temple's present building dates from 1895, the sliding doors and screens inside are centuries older. They are the work of the 16th-century painter Motonobu Kano, who is known for combining simple Chinese ink painting with Japanese ornamental styles. An immense camphor tree near the entrance makes the grounds a pleasant place to wander, and koto (harp) concerts are sometimes held in the evenings; in fall and spring the temple is lighted up from 6 pm to 10 pm. From Kyoto Station take Bus 206 to the Higashiyama-Sanjo stop. ☒ *69–1 Sanjobo-cho, Awataguchi, Higashiyama-ku* ☏ *075/561–2345* 🎫 *¥500* ⊙ *Daily 9–5.*

Shounzan Mirokuin 祥雲山弥勒院. A popular neighborhood chapel called "Shawase no Jizo" or "Happy Jizo" by locals, it houses a lovely image of Jizo in an orange-red robe holding a child on his left arm and a pilgrim's staff in his right hand. As the bodhisattva who descends into the darkest hells to save those in need, Jizo is also the protector of children and the guardian of travelers, and his image is frequently found along roads and paths where devotees clothe him in colored bibs and caps. While the chapel is open year-round, the main temple that enshrines Dainichi Nyorai, or the Cosmic Buddha, is open only from April to early May. This temple represents the ascetic mountain tradition—a fusion of Shinto, Tantric Buddhism, and mountain veneration—known as Shugendo. In August, Shugendo practitioners affiliated with the temple gather to conduct a *saito goma,* an outdoor fire ceremony for purification. It is a colorful and dynamic expression of their commitment and also open to the public. ☒ *Jodoji Minamida-cho 29, Sakyo-ku* ☏ *075/771–2277* 🎫 *Free* ⊙ *Daily.*

CENTRAL KYOTO

The two major sights in central Kyoto are the opulent Nijo Castle and the more modest Imperial Palace. The latter requires permission, and you must join a guided tour. Central Kyoto is a big shopping destination: west of the Kamogawa to Karasuma-dori and on the north–south axis between Shijo-dori and Oike-dori, there are department stores, specialty shops, and restaurants.

GETTING AROUND

Buses and several subway lines service all of central Kyoto's sights, but taxis may be more cost effective way for groups to get around. Out-of-the-way sights are best accessed by train.

TOP ATTRACTIONS

★ **Higashi-Hongan-ji** 東本願寺. Very close to Kyoto Station, this temple is the first of the city's ancient sights to confront visitors arriving by bus. Its strong walls, mighty gates, and high-roofed main hall are impressive enough to make some newcomers believe they are looking at the Imperial Palace. In the current complex, largely a reconstruction in 1895, everything is dwarfed by the cavernous main hall, the second-largest wooden structure in Japan. During construction of the temple, female devotees had their hair cut and woven into the strong, thick rope needed to drag the heavy timber. A ragged section of one of these *kezuna* is on display inside the **Daishi-do**, a double-roofed structure that is admirable for its gracefully curving lines. From Kyoto Station walk 500 yards northwest. ⊠ *Karasuma Shichijo-agaru, Shimogyo-ku* ⬛ *Free* ☾ *Daily 9–4.*

Fodor's Choice
★ **Nijo-jo** 二条城. In the early Edo period, the first Tokugawa shogun, Ieyasu, stripped all power from Kyoto's Imperial Court by consolidating a new military and political center at his far-off fortress in Tokyo. Nijo Castle, begun in 1603, is a grandiose and unequivocal statement of the shogunate's power. Nijo-jo's wide exterior moat and towering walls are the castle's exterior face, but once inside a second moat and defensive wall become visible. This had less to do with defense than it did with reinforcing the castle's social statement: access to the inner sanctum depended on a visitor's status within the shogunate's hierarchy, and the powers-that-be could remind anyone of their place in the system. Anyone who was permitted inside was as much a hostage as a guest, a feeling surely driven home by the castle's ingenious nightingale floors, which "sing" as you walk across them, revealing your movements at all times. (You can see how they work by looking underneath the balcony as you walk through the garden.)

The Tokugawa shoguns were rarely in Kyoto. Ieyasu stayed in the castle three times; the second shogun stayed twice, including the time in 1626 when Emperor Gomizuno-o was granted an audience. After that, for the next 224 years, no Tokugawa shogun visited Kyoto, and the castle started to fall into disrepair. Only when the Tokugawa shogunate was under pressure from a failing economy did the 14th shogun, Tokugawa Iemochi (1846–66), come to Kyoto to confer with the Emperor. The 15th and last Tokugawa shogun, Yoshinobu, famously returned power to the Emperor in 1867, the central event of the Meiji Restoration. Since

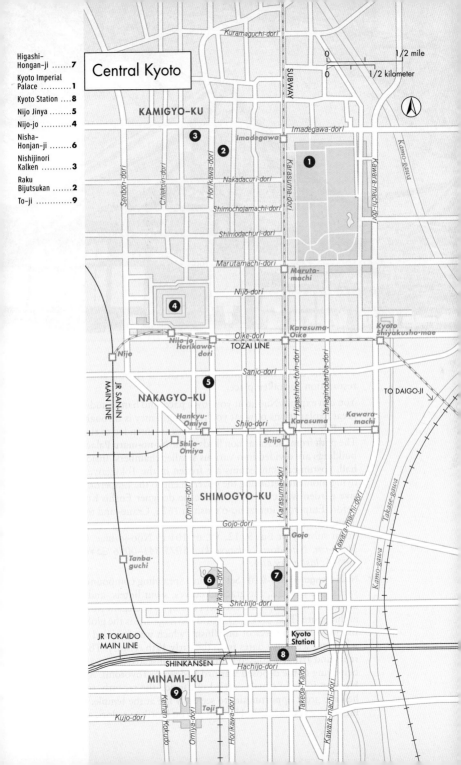

Central Kyoto

0   1/2 mile
0   1/2 kilometer

Kuramaguchi-dori

SUBWAY

KAMIGYO-KU

Imadegawa-dori

❸

Imadegawa

❷

❶

Nakadacuri-dori

Horikawa-dori

Chieton-dori

Senbon-dori

Karasuma-dori

Kawara-machi-dori

Kamo-gawa

Shimochojamachi-dori

Shimodachuri-dori

Marutamachi-dori

Maruta-machi

Nijō-dori

❹

Oike-dori

Karasuma-Oike

Kyoto Shiyakusho-mae

Nijo-jo Horikawa-dori

TOZAI LINE

☐ **Nijo**

Sanjo-dori

❺

NAKAGYO-KU

Higashimo-toin-dori

Yanaginobanba-dori

TO DAIGO-JI

Hankyu-Omiya

Shijo-dori

Karasuma

Kawara-machi

☐ *Shijo-Omiya*

☐ *Shijo*

SHIMOGYO-KU

Omiya-dori

Gojo-dori

Karasuma-dori

Kawara-machi-dori

Takase-gawa

☐ *Gojo*

☐ *Tanba-guchi*

❻

❼

Horikawa-dori

Shichijo-dori

Kamo-gawa

**JR TOKAIDO
MAIN LINE**

**Kyoto
Station**

❽

SHINKANSEN

Hachijo-dori

Takeda-Kaido

Kawara-machi-dori

MINAMI-KU

❾

Toji

Keihan Kokudo

Omiya-dori

Horikawa-dori

Kujo-dori

JR SAN-IN MAIN LINE

Nijo-jo was constructed in 1603 as the residence of Ieyasu Tokugawa, the founder of the shogunate.

1939, the castle has belonged to the city of Kyoto, and considerable restoration has taken place.

You can explore Nijo-jo at your own pace, and handy audio guides give great explanations of what you're seeing. Entry is through the impressive **Kara-mon gate**, whose sharp angles are intended to slow an attack. The path from the Kara-mon leads to the **Ni-no-maru Palace**, whose five buildings are divided into various smaller chambers. Inside the central **hall**, costumed mannequins are frozen in the Tokugawa shogunate's dying moment, returning the government to the Emperor. The impressive garden was created by landscape designer Enshu Kobori shortly before Emperor Gomizuno-o's visit in 1626. Crane- and tortoise-shape islands symbolize strength and longevity. You can get to the castle via Tozai subway or Bus 9, 12, 50, or 101 to Nijo-jo-mae. ⊠ *Horikawa Nishi-iru, Nijo-dori, Nakagyo-ku* ☎ *075/841–0096* 🖼 *¥600* ⊙ *Daily 8:45–5; last entry at 4.*

★ **Nishi-Hongan-ji** 西本願寺. Set within a sprawling compound with courtyards and gardens, the graceful curves, stout lintels, and ornate gold accents of this temple are excellent examples of elegant Momoyama-era architecture. This UNESCO World Heritage Site is the global center for the Jodo Shinshu sect of Buddhism, which was founded in 1272, but what you see today dates from the early 17th century. The fascinating relics and artifacts housed within were confiscated from various palaces belonging to the deposed warlord Hideyoshi Toyotomi. As at Higashi-Hongan-ji, daily rituals carried out inside the recently restored main hall are great opportunities to see daily life at the temple. Daily morning service is at 6. Nishi-Hongan-ji is on Horikawa-dori, a block north

MR. MONKEY WAS NO MONKEYMAN

Hideyoshi Toyotomi was quite a man. Though most of the initial work of unifying Japan in the late 16th century was accomplished by the warrior Nobunaga Oda (he was ambushed a year after defeating the monks on Hiei-zan), it was Hideyoshi who completed the job. Not only did he end civil strife, he also restored the arts. For a brief time (1582–98), Japan entered one of the most colorful periods of its history. How Hideyoshi achieved his feats is not exactly known. He was brought up as a farmer's son, and his nickname was Saru-san (Mr. Monkey) because he was small and uncomely. According to one legend—probably started by Hideyoshi himself—he was the son of the Emperor's concubine. She had been much admired by a man to whom the Emperor owed a favor, so the Emperor gave the concubine to him. Unknown to either of the men, she was soon pregnant with Hideyoshi. Whatever his origins (he changed his name frequently), he brought peace to Japan after decades of civil war.

of Shichijo-dori. Visits are permitted year-round (except when special events are observed). Japanese-language tours of the "Shoin" are given by appointment only; there are no guided tours in English. ⊠ *Gakurin-cho, Higashi-nakasuji, Rokujo-sagaru, Shimogyo-ku* ☎ *075/371–5181* 🎫 *Free* ☉ *Nov.–Feb., daily 5:30–5; Mar.–May, Sept., and Oct., daily 5:30 am–5:30 pm; Apr.–Aug., daily 6–6; admission is by reservation only.*

To-ji 東寺. Established by imperial edict in 796 and called Kyo-o-gokoku-ji, To-ji was built to guard the city. It was one of the only two temples that Emperor Kammu permitted to be built in the city—he had had enough of the powerful Buddhists while in Nara. The temple was later given to the priest Kukai (Kobo Daishi), who founded the Shingon sect of Buddhism at the turn of the 9th century.

Fires and battles during the 16th century destroyed the temple buildings, but many were rebuilt, including in 1603 the Kon-do (Main Hall), which blends Chinese and Japanese elements. The Ko-do (Lecture Hall), on the other hand, has managed to survive the ravages of war since it was built in 1491. Inside this hall are 15 original statues of Buddhist gods, making up a mandala, considered masterpieces of the Heian era (750–1150). There is a daily morning service at 6 in the Daishi-do with devotional chanting.

On the 21st of each month a market, known locally as Kobo-san, is held. Antique kimonos, fans, and other artifacts can be found at bargain prices if you know your way around the savvy dealers. A smaller antiques market is held on the first Sunday of the month. The temple is a 10-minute walk southwest of Kyoto Station. You can walk from there, or take the Kintetsu subway line one stop. Bus 207 also runs past To-ji. ⊠ *1 Kujo-cho, Minami-ku* 🎫 *Free, main buildings ¥500* ☉ *Mar. 20–Sept. 19, daily 8:30–5:30; Sept. 20–Mar. 19, daily 8:30–4:30.*

7

WORTH NOTING

Kyoto Imperial Palace 京都御所 *(Kyoto Gosho)*. Although it tops the list of must-see sights for many tourists, the Imperial Palace leaves many underwhelmed. In fact, you are prohibited from entering any of the buildings on the rather sedate hour-long tour. The original building burned down in 1788, as did several of the replacements. The present structure dates from 1855. It's hardly palatial, though fine in its way; the ingenious cypress-bark roof is particularly attractive. And the park-like setting is very pretty.

To see the palace, you must receive permission to enter from the Imperial Household Agency *(see ⇨ Visitor Information in Planning at the beginning of this chapter)*. You can usually arrange a same-day visit by showing your passport at the office in the park's northwest corner, or you can make a request on the Web site. Guided tours in English begin at the Seishomon entrance, inside the park. Tours run weekdays at 10 and 2. ⊠ *Kunaicho, Kyoto Gyoen-nai, Kamigyo-ku* ☎ *075/211–1215* ⊕ *sankan.kunaicho.go.jp* ☒ *Free* ☯ *Office weekdays 8:45–noon and 1–5.*

Kyoto Station 京都駅. Kyoto's train station, derided as an eyesore by some and hailed as a masterpiece by others, is more than just the city's central point of arrival and departure: the station houses a hotel, a theater, a department store, and dozens of shops and restaurants with great views of the city from the 16th floor. ⊠ *137 Karasuma-dori Shiokoji-sagaru, Shimogyo-ku.*

Nijo Jinya 二条陣屋. A short walk south of Nijo-jo is the less-visited Nijo Jinya, a former merchant house built in the 17th century. The house later became an inn for traveling daimyo, or feudal lords. The house is crammed with built-in safeguards against attack, including hidden staircases, secret passageways, and hallways too narrow to allow the wielding of a sword. Fascinating hour-long tours through the warren of rooms are in Japanese; reservations are required. ⊠ *137 Sanbo Omiya-cho, Nakagyo-ku* ☎ *075/841–0972* ☒ *¥1,000* ☯ *Tours in Japanese only, Thurs.–Tues. 10–4.*

Nishijin-ori Kaikan 西陣会館 *(Nishijin-ori Textile Center)*. The Nishijin district, which still has some old wooden warehouses hugging the canals, hangs onto the artistic thread of traditional Japanese silk weaving. The Nishijin-ori Textile Center is a fascinating place to learn about the weaving industry. Hands-on lessons let you weave your own garment: for ¥1,800 you'll get a great souvenir and the experience is easy and fun. Reserve ahead and you can try on various different kimonos, and even rent one for a night on the town. Try to catch at least one of the seven daily fashion shows that feature traditional clothing. To get here, take Bus 9, 12, 51, or 59 to the Horikawa-Imadegawa stop. ⊠ *Horikawai-Imadegawa-Minami-Iru, Kamigyo-ku* ☎ *075/451–9231* ⊕ *www.nishijin.or.jp* ☒ *Free* ☯ *Daily 9–5.*

Raku Bijutsukan 樂美術館 *(Raku Museum)*. Any serious collector of tea-ceremony artifacts is likely to have a Raku bowl in his or her collection. The Raku Museum displays more than 1,000 bowls and vessels of astonishing beauty. As a potter's term in the West, *raku* refers to a low-temperature firing technique, but the word originated with this family, who made exquisite tea bowls for use in the shogun's tea ceremonies. The museum is to the east of Horikawa-dori, three blocks south of Imadegawa-dori; take the Karasuma subway line to Imadegawa Station or Bus 9 or 12 to Ichi-jo-modori-bashi. ✉ *Aburakoji-ichijo sagaru, Kamigyo-ku* ☎ *075/414–0304* 💴 *Around ¥900, depending on exhibition* ◷ *Tues.–Sun. 10–4.*

SOUTHERN KYOTO

The most interesting southern Kyoto sights are three religious structures: Tofuku-ji, Fushimi-Inari Taisha, and Byodo-in; the latter is actually in the tea-producing city of Uji. Both Fushimi-Inari Taisha and the temple Daigo-ji in southern Kyoto are on mountains with trails to explore.

GETTING AROUND

The temples and shrines in southern Kyoto are far from one another, so traveling time can eat into your day. If you visit Tofuku-ji, consider combining it with a visit to Fushimi-Inari Taisha, farther south.

TOP ATTRACTIONS

★ **Byodo-in** 平等院 *(Temple of Equality).* South of Kyoto in Uji, this temple was originally the villa of a 10th-century member of the influential Fujiwara family. The **Amida-do** is also known as the Phoenix Hall, thanks to its two protruding wings that make the building resemble the legendary bird; the hall is depicted on the ¥10 coin; it is surrounded by a garden. Built in the 11th century by the Fujiwaras, the Amida-do is considered one of Japan's most beautiful religious buildings—something of an architectural folly—where heaven is brought close to Earth. Jocho, one of Japan's most famous 11th-century sculptors, crafted a magnificent statue of Amida Buddha here; his hand mudra indicates that the Buddha rests in the highest of the nine paradises. The Aji Pond in front symbolizes the lotus lake of Amida's paradise. In the museum alongside you can see 52 small wooden *kuyo* or reverent *bosatsu* (enlightened beings) floating on clouds, playing celestial music.

Uji is a famous tea-producing district, and the slope up to the temple is lined with shops where you can sample the finest green tea and pick up a small package to take home. It's possible to set up a visit to a tea farm through the Kyoto Tourist Information Center. The shrines and temples surrounding the Uji River are also pleasant to explore. To get to Uji, take the JR Nara Line to Uji Station. Byodo-in is a 12-minute walk east toward the river from the station. ✉ *116 Ujirenge, Uji* ☎ *0774/21–2861* 💴 *¥600; additional ¥300 for Phoenix Hall* ◷ *Phoenix Hall daily 9:30–4:10, garden daily 8:30–5:30; Museum daily 9–5.*

NEED A BREAK? Taiho-an 対鳳庵. **Opposite Byodo-in, this is an authentic tea-ceremony building set in a delightful garden near the swift Uji River. Here you can enjoy a cup of green tea with a seasonal Japanese sweet, or if you book in advance, the full tea ceremony for ¥500. The teahouse is open daily**

7

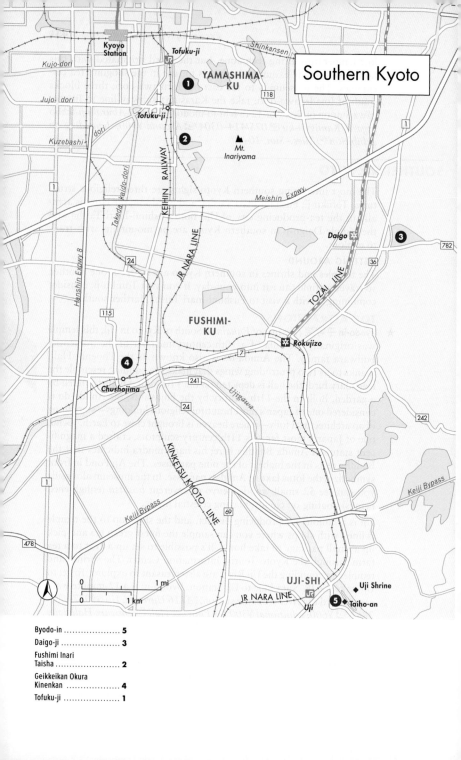

Southern Kyoto

Kyoyo Station

Tofuku-ji

YAMASHIMA-KU

Tofuku-ji

Mt. Inariyama

Daigo

FUSHIMI-KU

Rokujizo

Chushojima

Meishin Expwy

KEIHIN RAILWAY

JR NARA LINE

Takeda Kaido-dori

Hanshin Expwy 8

TOZAI LINE

KINKETSU KYOTO LINE

Uji River

Keiji Bypass

Keiji Bypass

UJI-SHI

Uji Shrine

Uji

Taiho-an

Kujo-dori

Jujo-dori

Kuzebashi-dori

Shinkansen

0   1 mi
0   1 km

from 10 to 4 (except December 21 through January 9). ⊠ *2 Ujitogawa, Uji*
☎ *0774/23–3334* ⊘ *Closed Dec. 21–Jan. 9.*

Fodor'sChoice
★
Fushimi-Inari Taisha 伏見稲荷大社. Many visitors find Fushimi-Inari Tai-sha's thousands of red lacquered gates to be the quintessential image of Japan. This is the central headquarters for 40,000 shrines nation-ally that do service to Inari, the god of rice, sake, and prosperity. The shrine's 10,000 torii gates, donated by the thankful, are unforgettable. They trace a path up the mountainside, broken up at irregular intervals with shrines, altars, mausoleums, and thousand upon thousand of foxes in stone and bronze. As Japan's underpinnings have shifted from agri-culture to other forms of business, Inari has been adopted as a patron deity for any kind of entrepreneurial venture, and the gates in the path are donated by businesses from around the country seeking a blessing. Walking the whole circuit takes about three hours, or a bit longer if you stop at the shops selling snacks along the way. In 2011, the shrine celebrates its 1,300th anniversary with festivities from October 7 to 10. To get here, take the JR Nara Line to Inari Station or Keihan Railway to Fushimi-Inari Station. ⊠ *68 Fukakusa Yabu-no-uchi-cho, Fushimi-ku* 🖃 *Free* ⊘ *Daily sunrise–sunset.*

★ **Gekkeikan Okura Kinenkan** 月桂冠大倉記念館 *(Gekkeikan Okura Museum).* Not far from Fushimi-Inari Taisha is a district of old white-walled sake breweries and warehouses, some dating to the early Edo era. Gekkeikan, founded in 1637, is one of the oldest breweries. The museum details the brewing process, and there are free tastings. The brewery is a five-minute walk from Chushojima Station, on the Keihan Line, or a 10-minute walk from Momoyama Goryo-mae Station, on the Kintetsu Kyoto Line. Reservations must be made in advance. ⊠ *247 Minamihama-cho, Fushimi-ku* ☎ *075/623–2056* ⊕ *www.gekkeikan. co.jp* 🖃 *¥300* ⊘ *Daily 9:30–4:30 by reservation only.*

WORTH NOTING

Daigo-ji 醍醐寺. The main temple of this mountain enclave founded in 874 is set in the foothills, and many smaller temples stand on the ridges above. Its five-story pagoda, which dates from 951, is reputed to be the oldest existing structure in Kyoto. By the late 16th century the temple had begun to decline in importance and showed signs of neglect. Then Hideyoshi Toyotomi paid a visit one April, when the temple's famous cherry trees were in bloom. Hideyoshi ordered the temple restored. The **Sanbo-in**, with its Momoyama-period thatched roof, has bold colorful paintings of Chinese village scenes; the paintings, which incorporate gold leaf, were done by the Kano School. The intriguing garden com-bines elements of the *chisen-kaiyu* (stroll garden with a pond) and the *karesansui*, or dry garden. From the temple you can continue up the mountain (about an hour's hike) to several sub-temples. The temple holds the Daigo-ichi, a monthly bazaar on the 29th with food and clothing stalls that line the temple walkways. To reach Daigo-ji, in the southeast suburb of Yamashina, take the Tozai subway line to Daigo Station; follow the signs for a 10-minute walk to the nearby hills. ⊠ *22 Higashi Oji-cho, Fushimi-ku* 🖃 *¥600* ⊘ *Mar.–Nov., daily 9–4:30; Dec.– Feb., daily 9–3:30.*

7

Tofuku-ji 東福寺. A fabulous gateway arch—the oldest Zen gateway in Japan and a National Treasure, constructed in accordance to strict Buddhist guidelines—attracts many visitors to this expansive medieval complex of 24 temples. At 22 meters tall, the gate is a sight to see, both inside and out. Its friezes, attributed to the prominent Heian-era sculptor Teicho, depict scenes of the Buddha and his disciples. The temple, of the Rinzai sect of Zen Buddhism, was established in 1236 and ranks as one of the most important in Kyoto, along with the Myoshin-ji and Daitoku-ji. Arranged around the main hall are four contrasting gardens, both dry gravel and landscaped, including a stroll garden. Autumn, with the burnished color of the maple trees, is an especially fine time for visiting. There are at least three ways to get to Tofuku-ji, which is southeast of Kyoto Station: Bus 208 from Kyoto Station, a JR train on the Nara Line to Tofuku-ji Station, or a Keihan Line train to Tofuku-ji Station. From the station it's a 15-minute walk to the temple. ⊠ *15–777 Hon-machi, Higashiyama-ku* ☎ *075/561–0087* ⊕ *www.tofukuji.jp/english. html* ⊠ *¥400* ⊗ *Daily 9–4 (Dec.–Mar. until 3:30).*

> **HIDDEN CHRISTIANS**
>
> Japan's so-called Hidden Christians are descended from early converts to Christianity as introduced to Japan in 1549 by the Spanish Jesuit missionary, Francis Xavier. Christianity initially flourished under the warlord Oda Nobunaga, but after his death edicts outlawed the religion in 1614 and 1640. Churches were burned, Christians executed (or exiled), and a system to ferret out remaining Christians instituted. An estimated 150,000 Christians went underground at this time, only beginning to reemerge in the Meiji period.

WESTERN KYOTO

Western Kyoto's most iconic sights are the opulent golden temple at Kinkaku-ji and the dazzling rock garden at Ryoan-ji, but the city's western precincts are filled with remarkable religious architecture. The sprawling temple complexes Daitoku-ji and Myoshin-ji are well worth a visit, as is the blossom-covered Kitano Tenman-gu, which hosts a fabulous market each month.

GETTING AROUND

The sights in the northern and western parts of this area can be reached easily using city buses. For Katsura Rikyu rail is best; and to reach Koinzan Saiho-ji, you can take Bus 29 from Karasuma Shijo.

TOP ATTRACTIONS

Fodor's Choice
★

Kinkaku-ji 金閣寺 *(Temple of the Golden Pavilion).* Possibly the world's most ostentatious retirement cottage, the magnificent gold-sheathed Kinkaku-ji was built by Shogun Yoshimitsu Ashikaga (1358–1409). He ordered it built in 1393 in anticipation of the time when he would quit politics—the following year, in fact—to manage the affairs of state through the new shogun, his 10-year-old son. On Yoshimitsu's death, his son followed his father's wishes and converted the villa into a temple.

Kinkaku-ji was burned down in 1950 and was rebuilt in 1955; its three stories were then covered in gold leaf.

The current temple was reconstructed in the 1950s after a monk set fire to the standing structure. (His internal conflict is the focus of Yukio Mishima's 1956 famous novel *Temple of the Golden Pavilion*, published the year after construction had finished.) The top two stories are coated with gold leaf, as per Yoshimitsu's original vision, a spectacular sight when reflected in the pond's still waters. To get here, take Bus 12, 59, 101, 102, 204, or 205 to Kinkaku-ji-mae. ⊠ *1 Kinkaku-ji-cho, Kita-ku* 🖃 *¥400* ⏱ *Daily 9–5.*

★ **Kitano Tenman-gu** 北野天満宮. In February and March, the gorgeous plum blossoms that blanket the gardens surrounding this shrine make it a great place to warm your spirit during the sometimes desolate winter. The rest of the year, the shrine's biggest draw is its fabulous market. Held on the 25th of every month, the market draws vendors selling everything from gooey fried octopus balls and black soy bean tea to kimonos and woodblock prints. To get here, take Bus 50, 101, or 201 to Kitano Tenman-gu-mae. ⊠ *Imakoji-agaru, Onmae-dori, Kamigyo-ku* 🖃 *Shrine free, plum garden ¥600* ⏱ *Shrine Apr.–Sept., daily 5–5; Oct.– Mar, daily 5:30–5:30. Plum garden Feb. and Mar., daily 10–4.*

★ **Myoshin-ji** 妙心寺. Surrounded by thick stone walls, this complex holds some great treasures within its 47 temples. The biggest tourist draw is in the lecture hall of the main temple, with its stunning painting of a dragon stretching across the expansive ceiling. In rendering the lifelike creature, the painter made clever use of a perspective to make it seem like the dragon's eyes glare at you wherever you walk. Japan's oldest bell is also at daily use in Myoshin-ji, tolling out the hour for meditation since 698. Shunko-in, one of the 47, keeps a Hidden Christian bell;

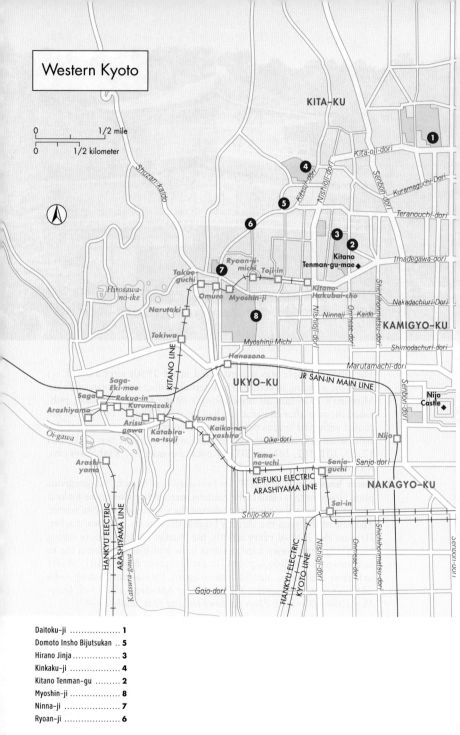

Western Kyoto

KITA-KU

0 ——— 1/2 mile
0 ——— 1/2 kilometer

Shuzan Kaido

Kita-oji-dori

1

Kuramaguchi-Dori

4

Kitsuji-dori

Nishioji-dori

Senbon-dori

Teranouchi-dori

5

6

3

2

Kitano
Tenman-gu-mae ◆

Imadegawa-dori

Ryoan-ji-
michi

Toji-in

7

Takao-
guchi

Omuro

Myoshin-ji

Kitano-
Hakubai-cho

Shichihonmatsu-dori

Nakadachiuri-Dori

Hirosawa-
no-ike

8

Ninnaji Omaee Kaido

Nishioji-dori

KAMIGYO-KU

Narutaki

Shimodachuri-dori

Tokiwa

Myoshinji Michi

Hanazono

Marutamachi-dori

KITANO LINE

JR SAN-IN MAIN LINE

UKYO-KU

Senbon-dori

Saga-
Eki-mae

Nijo
Castle

Saga

Rakuo-in

Arashiyama

Kurumazaki

Arisu-
gawa

Uzumasa

Katabira-
no-tsuji

Kaiko-no-
yashiro

Nijo

Oike-dori

Sanjo-
guchi

Sanjo-dori

Arashi-
yama

Yama-
no-uchi

KEIFUKU ELECTRIC
ARASHIYAMA LINE

NAKAGYO-KU

Oi-gawa

Sai-in

HANKYU ELECTRIC
ARASHIYAMA LINE

Katsura-gawa

Shijo-dori

HANKYU ELECTRIC
KYOTO LINE

Nishioji-dori

Omaee-dori

Shichihonmatsu-dori

Senbon-dori

Gojo-dori

made in Portugal, the bell was placed in Nanban-ji Church, the first Christian church in Kyoto in 1576 and the center of Catholic missionary activity until the religious persecution brought about its destruction. Buses 61, 62, and 63 stop at Myoshin-ji-mae; otherwise take a JR Sagano Line train to Hanazono-cho. ⊠ *1 Hanazono Myoshinji-cho, Ukyo-ku* ☏ *¥500 for lecture hall (20-min guided tour required), ¥400 for most smaller temples* ⊗ *Nov.–Mar., daily 9:10–3:40; Apr.–Oct., daily 9:10–4:40.*

Ninna-ji 仁和寺. With a five-tier pagoda at its center, this temple sits in a parklike setting. It's surrounded by late-blooming cherry trees that attract crowds every May. Emperor Omuro's palace stood here in the late 9th century, but the buildings you see today were constructed in the 17th century. The Hon-do (Main Hall), moved here from the Imperial Palace, is well worth a look. Ninna-ji is a 10-minute walk west of Ryoan-ji and a five-minute walk northwest of Myoshin-ji's north gate. Take either Bus 26 or 59 to the Omuro-ninna-ji, or a JR Sagano Line train to Hanazono-cho. ⊠ *33 Ouchi Omuro, Ukyo-ku* ☏ *¥800* ⊗ *Daily 9–5.*

★ **Ryoan-ji** 龍安寺. The solemn stones set into the sand at Ryoan-ji's rock garden has become one of Japan's quintessential images. The simple arrangement can be viewed as an oasis for contemplation or a riddle to train the mind. From any single vantage point, only 14 of the 15 stones can be seen. In the Buddhist tradition, 15 is a number that signifies completion, and it is supposed that the garden's message is that, in this world, completion is not possible. As mystical as the experience may be for some, you will be hard up to get time alone with your thoughts. The destination draws crowds by the busloads. If you need a moment to yourself, head to the small restaurant on the temple grounds. Buses 50, 55, and 59 stop at Ryoan-ji-mae. ⊠ *13 Goryoshita-cho, Ryoan-ji, Ukyo-ku* ☏ *¥300* ⊗ *Mar.–Nov., daily 8–5; Dec.–Feb., daily 8:30–4:30.*

WORTH NOTING

Daitoku-ji 大徳寺 Two dozen temples can be found in this walled compound, a holy place for the Rinzai sect of Zen Buddhism. The original temple was founded in 1319, but fires during the Onin Civil War destroyed it in 1468. Most buildings you see today were built under the patronage of Hideyoshi Toyotomi in the late 16th century. Several of the smaller temples are well worth exploring.

Daisen-in 大仙院 is best known for its excellent landscape paintings by the renowned Soami (1465–1523), as well as the famed Muromachi-era garden, attributed to Soko Kogaku (1465–1548). Circling the building, the moody rock-and-gravel garden depicts the flow of life in the movement of a river, swirling around rocks, over a waterfall, and finally into an ocean of nothingness.

Ryogen-in 龍源院 has five small gardens of gravel, stone, and moss. The A-Un garden includes a stone with ripples emanating from it, thought to symbolize the cycle of life, from the "a" sound said at birth to the "un" said at death, encompassing all in between.

Koto-in 高桐院 is famous for its long, maple-tree-lined approach and the single stone lantern central to the main garden.

Zuiho-in 瑞法院 has Hidden Christian roots, and its rock garden suggests an abstract cross; a statue of Mary is evidently buried under the stone lantern in an adjacent garden.

There are several ways to get to the temple complex from downtown Kyoto. Take the Karasuma subway to Kita-oji Station, where any bus going west along Kita-oji-dori will take you to the Daitokuji-mae stop. Buses 12, 204, and 206 make the same stop. ⊠ *53 Murasakino Daitokuji-cho, Kita-ku* ☎ *075/491–0019* ✉ *Compound free, Daisen-in ¥400, Ryogen-in ¥350, Koto-in ¥400, Zuiho-in ¥400* ☉ *Daily; temple hrs vary, with most open from 9 to 4:30 or 5.*

NEED A BREAK?

Ichiwa いち和 **has been serving tea and** *aburi mochi*—**skewered rice-flour cakes charcoal-grilled and dipped in sweet miso sauce—since the Heian era (750–1150). You can enjoy the treats under the eaves of a 17th-century house as you watch visitors on their way to and from Imamiya Shrine. Ichiwa is just outside the shrine, northwest of Daitoku-ji.** ⊠ *69 Imamiya-cho, Murasakino, Kita-ku* ☎ *075/492–6852* ☉ *Thurs.–Tues. 10–5.*

Domoto Insho Bijutsukan 堂本印象美術館 *(Insho Domoto Art Museum).* An artist of tremendous versatility, Insho-san (as he was affectionately known) worked in wood, stained-glass, oils, and watercolors. The narrative paintings of the 20th-century artist hold wide appeal because they depict scenes from everyday life. Yet his use of classical Japanese painting's muted color palate with a more abstract, sometimes cubist, approach to figures makes his work very appealing. To get here, take Bus 12, 15, 50, 51, 55, or 59 to Ritsumeikan Daigaku-mae. ⊠ *26-3 Kamiyanagi-cho, Hirano, Kita-ku* ☎ *075/463–0007* ✉ *¥500* ☉ *Tues.–Sun. 9:30–5.*

Hirano Jinja 平野神社. Near Kinkaku-ji, the gorgeous cherry blossoms at this modest shrine have been the focus of an annual spring festival since 985. The pale pink petals contrast with vermilion lanterns lining the lanes of this Heian-style complex. The shrine was brought here from Nagaoka, the country's capital after Nara and before Kyoto. The four buildings you can visit date from the 17th century. Recently installed next to a 400-year-old camphor tree is a huge magnetic boulder from Iwate, chosen for the power it is said to contain. Access is via Bus 50, 52, or 100 to Kitano Tenmongu-mae. From there, the shrine is a 10-minute walk north. ⊠ *Miyamoto-cho 1, Hirano, Kita-ku* ✉ *Free* ☉ *Daily 6–5.*

ARASHIYAMA

Beyond the city is the semirural hillside area of Arashiyama, which lies along and above the banks of the Oi-gawa (the local name for the Katsura-gawa as it courses through this area). The pleasure of Arashiyama, the westernmost part of Kyoto, is the same as it has been for centuries. The gentle foothills of the mountains, covered with cherry and maple trees, are splendid. The sights are spaced apart, connected by a pathway that meanders along the hillside, through fields and a peaceful bamboo grove, and past several craft shops and restaurants.

The Katsura Rikyu includes Japan's oldest surviving stroll garden, which dates to the 17th century.

It's no wonder that the aristocracy of feudal Japan came here to escape famine, riots, and political intrigue.

GETTING AROUND

The easiest ways to get to Arashiyama are by the JR San-in Main Line from Kyoto Station to Saga Station, or via the Keifuku Electric Railway to Arashiyama Station (which is just south of Saga Station).

TOP ATTRACTIONS

Fodor's Choice ★ **Adashino Nembutsu-ji** 化野念仏寺. The most unusual feature of this temple is the cemetery, where about 8,000 stone Buddhas are packed together, a solemn sea of quiet mourners. The statues honor the vast number of nameless dead who fell victim to the tumult of pre-Edo Japan and were burned here in mass pyres. The temple's main hall, built in 1712, contains an arresting statue of Amida Buddha carved by Kamakura-era sculptor Tankei. On August 23 and 24, a ceremony called Sento-kuyo is held here, with more than 1,000 candles lighted for the peaceful repose of ancestor spirits. Whatever time of year you visit, make sure to come in late afternoon, when the shadows beneath the statues take on animated character. From Kyoto Station, take Bus 72 to Arashiyama Toriimoto. ✉ *17 Adashino-cho, Saga-toriimoto, Ukyo-ku* ☎ *075/861–2221* 🎫 *¥500* 🕐 *Mar.–Nov., daily 9–4:30; Dec.–Feb., daily 9–4.*

Fodor's Choice ★ **Katsura Rikyu** 桂離宮 (*Katsura Imperial Villa*). The setting for this villa is a perfect example of Japanese integration of nature and architecture. Here you find Japan's oldest surviving stroll garden, dating to the 17th century, with pathways that take you through an encyclopedia of famous Japanese natural sites and literary references, such as the

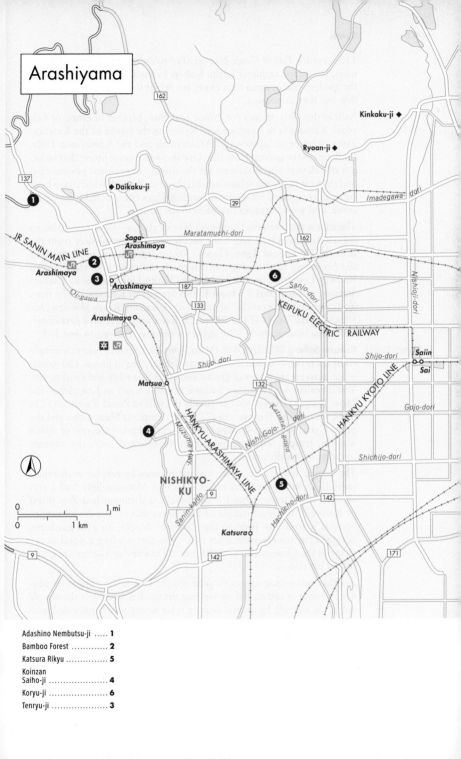

Arashiyama

Kinkaku-ji ◆

Ryoan-ji ◆

137

● 1

Daikaku-ji ◆

Imadegawa-dori

JR SANIN MAIN LINE

Saga-Arashimaya

Maratamuchi-dori

162

29

Arashimaya

● 2

JR

● 3

Arashimaya

187

● 6

Sanjo-dori

Oi-gawa

133

KEIFUKU ELECTRIC RAILWAY

Nishioji-dori

Arashimaya ○

Shijo-dori

Shijo-dori

Saiin

Sai

Matsuo ○

132

HANKYU KYOTO LINE

Gojo-dori

HANKYU ARASHIMAYA LINE

Muzume Hwy.

Katsura-gawa dori

Nishi-Gojo-gawa

● 4

NISHIKYO-KU

0   1 mi
0   1 km

● 5

Hachicho-dori

Shichijo-dori

Sanin-kaido

9

142

171

Katsura ○

9

142

11th-century *Tale of Genji*. Not satisfied to create simply beautiful pictures, landscape architect Enshu Kobori focused on the rhythm within the garden: spaces open then close, are bright then dark; views are visible and then concealed.

Built in the 17th century for Prince Toshihito, brother of Emperor Go-yozei, Katsura is in southwestern Kyoto on the banks of the Katsura-gawa, with peaceful views of Arashiyama and the Kameyama Hills. Look out at the garden from the three *shoin* (a type of house that incorporates alcoves and platforms for the display of personal possessions) and the four rustic tea arbors around the central pond, which have been strategically placed for optimal vistas. Bridges constructed from earth, stone, and wood connect five islets in the pond.

The villa is fairly remote from other historical sites—allow several hours for a visit, for which you must secure advance permission from the Imperial Household Agency *(see ⇨ Visitor Information in Planning at the beginning of this chapter)*. To reach the villa, take the Hankyu Railway Line from one of the Hankyu Kyoto Line stations to Katsura Station, or catch Bus 33 from Kyoto Station to Katsura Rikyu mae. You can also take a taxi for about ¥800. ✉ *Katsura Rikyu Shimizu-cho, Ukyo-ku* ☎ *075/211–1215* 💴 *Free* ⏲ *Tours weekdays on a first-come-first-serve basis daily 9–3:30; agency weekdays 8:45–noon and 1–5.*

Fodor's Choice ★ **Koinzan Saiho-ji** 供隠山西芳寺 *(Moss Temple)*. Entrance into this temple complex transports you into an extraordinary sea of green: 120 varieties of moss create waves of greens and blues that eddy and swirl gently. You'll realize why Koinzan Saiho-ji is also known as Kokedera—the Moss Temple. The site was originally the villa of Prince Shotoku (572–621). During the Tempyo era (729–749) Emperor Shomu charged the priest Gyoki to create 49 temples in the central province, one of which was this temple. The original garden represented Jodo, the western paradise of Buddhism.

The temple and garden, destroyed many times by fire, lay in disrepair until 1338, when the chief priest of nearby Matsuno-jinja had a revelation here. He convinced Muso Soseki, a distinguished Zen priest of Rinzen-ji, the head temple of the Rinzai sect of Zen Buddhism, to convert it from the Jodo to the Zen sect. Soseki, an avid gardener, designed the temple garden on two levels surrounding a pond in the shape of the Chinese character for heart. Present-day visitors are grateful for his efforts.

Another interesting aspect to your temple visit is the obligatory *shakyo,* writing of sutras. Before viewing the garden, you enter the temple and sit at a small, lacquered writing table where you're provided with a brush, ink, and a thin sheet of paper with Chinese characters in light gray. After rubbing your ink stick on the ink stone, dip the tip of your brush in the ink and trace over the characters. A priest explains in Japanese the temple history and the sutra you are writing. If time is limited, you don't have to write the entire sutra; when the priest has ended his explanation, simply place what you have written on a table before the altar and proceed to the garden. You do need advance permission to visit the temple, and there are several ways to do this. You can send the temple a request along with a stamped, self-addressed postcard, or you could simply ask your hotel's concierge if he or she can call for you. It's also possible to arrange a visit through the Kyoto Tourist Information Center. To reach the temple, take the Hankyu Line train from Arashiyama to Matsuno Station; buses from JR Station stop at here. ✉ *56 Jingatani-cho, Matsuo, Nishikyo-ku* ☎ *075/391–3631* 🎫 *¥3,000* 🕐 *Daily 9–5 with advance permission only.*

★ **Koryu-ji** 広隆寺. One of Kyoto's oldest temples, Koryu-ji was founded in 622 by Kawakatsu Hata in memory of Prince Shotoku (572–621). Shotoku, known for issuing the Seventeen-Article Constitution, a set of Confucian-inspired moral dictates, was the first powerful advocate of Buddhism after it was introduced to Japan in 552. In the **Hatto** (Lecture Hall) of the main temple stand three statues, each a National Treasure. The center of worship is the seated figure of Buddha, flanked by the figures of the Thousand-Handed Kannon and Fukukenjaku-Kannon. In the **Taishi-do** (Prince Hall) is a wooden statue of Prince Shotoku, thought to have been carved by him personally. Another statue of Shotoku in this hall was probably made when he was 16 years old.

The most famous of the Buddhist images in the Reiho-den (Treasure House) is the statue of **Miroku Bosatsu,** who according to Buddhist belief is destined to appear on Earth in the far-off future to save those unable to achieve enlightenment. Japan's first registered National Treasure, this rustic wooden statue is thought to date from the 6th or 7th century and might have been carved by Shotoku himself. Of all the Buddhas in Kyoto, this may be the most captivating. The epitome of serenity, the statue gently rests the fingers of its right hand against its cheek (one finger, sadly, was broken off when an ardent student clutched the statue in the late 1960s). Once a year, on November 22, the central Buddha which is hidden here—the Buddha of medicine (Yakushi)—is shown to the public. From Kyoto Station take the JR San-in Main Line to Hanazono Station and then board Bus 61. From Shijo-Omiya Station, in central Kyoto, take the Keifuku Electric Arashiyama Line to Uzumasa Station. From central or western Kyoto, take Bus 61, 62, or 63 to the Uzumasa-koryuji-mae stop. ✉ *Hachioka-cho, Uzumasa, Ukyo-ku* 🎫 *¥700* 🕐 *Mar.–Nov., daily 9–5; Dec.–Feb., daily 9–4:30.*

★ **Tenryu-ji** 天龍寺. For good reason this is known as the Temple of the Heavenly Dragon: in the 14th century, Emperor Go-Daigo, who had brought an end to the Kamakura shogunate, was forced from his throne by Takauji Ashikaga. After Go-Daigo died, Takauji had twinges of conscience. That's when Priest Muso Soseki had a dream in which a golden dragon rose from the nearby Oi-gawa. He told the shogun about his dream and interpreted it to mean the spirit of Go-Daigo was not at peace. Worried about this ill omen, Takauji completed Tenryu-ji in 1339 on the same spot where Go-Daigo had his favorite villa. Apparently the late emperor's spirit was appeased. Construction took several years and was partly financed by a trading mission to China, which brought back treasures of the Ming Dynasty. In the Hatto (Lecture Hall), where today's monks meditate, a huge "cloud dragon" is painted on the ceiling. The temple was often ravaged by fire, and the current buildings are as recent as 1900; the painting of the dragon was rendered by 20th-century artist Shonen Suzuki.

The **Sogenchi garden** of Tenryu-ji dates from the 14th century and is one of the most notable in Kyoto. Muso Soseki, an influential Zen monk and skillful garden designer, created the garden to resemble Mt. Horai in China. It is famed for the arrangement of vertical stones in its large pond and as one of the first gardens to use "borrowed scenery," incorporating the mountains in the distance into the design of the garden.

If you visit Tenryu-ji at lunchtime, consider purchasing a ticket for Zen cuisine served at **Shigetsu**, within the temple precinct. The price for lunch in the large dining area overlooking a garden begins at ¥3,500 (more-elaborate courses cost ¥5,500 and ¥7,500), and includes admission to the garden itself. Here you can experience the Zen monks' philosophy of "eating to live" rather than "living to eat." Although you won't partake in the monk's daily helping of gruel, a salted plum, and pickled radishes, you will try Zen cuisine prepared for festival days. The meal includes sesame tofu served over top-quality soy sauce, a variety of fresh boiled vegetables, miso soup, and rice. The *tenzo*, a monk specially trained to prepare Zen cuisine, creates a multicourse meal that achieves the harmony of the six basic flavors—bitter, sour, sweet, salty, light, and hot—required for monks to practice Zen with the least hindrance to body and mind. Advance reservations are required.

Take the JR San-in Main Line from Kyoto Station to Saga Station or the Keifuku Electric Railway to Arashiyama Station. From Saga Station walk west; from Arashiyama Station walk north. ✉ *68 Susuki-no-bamba-cho, Saga-Tenryu-ji, Ukyo-ku* ☎ *075/882–9725, 075/882–9725 for Shigetsu reservations* 📧 *Garden ¥500, temple ¥100, Shigetsu lunch ¥3,500–¥7,500 (includes garden)* ⊙ *Apr.–Oct., daily 8:30–5:30; Nov.–Mar., daily 8:30–5; lunch at Shigetsu by reservation only.*

WORTH NOTING

Bamboo forest 竹林. Dense bamboo forests—with their rows upon rows of long, ringed, smooth stems—provide a feeling of composure and tranquillity. The sound of wind blowing through bamboo, of stems knocking against one another and leaves rustling, is revered in Japan. Nowadays, bamboo forests are few and far between. This one, on the way to Okoeni Sanso from Tenryu-ji, is a delight. The forest is a short walk from the Saga-Arashiyama train station. ✉ *Ukyo-ku.*

NORTHERN KYOTO

The mountain Hiei-zan and the Ohara region are the focal points in the northern suburbs of Kyoto. For several centuries Ohara was a sleepy Kyoto backwater surrounded by mountains. Although it's now catching up with the times, it retains a feeling of Old Japan. Hiei-zan is a fount of Kyoto history. On its flanks the priest Saicho founded Enryaku-ji in the 8th century and with it the vital Tendai sect of Buddhism. It's an essential Kyoto sight, and walking on forested slopes among its 70-odd temples is a good reason to make the trek to Hiei-zan.

GETTING AROUND

The sights in northern Kyoto are spread out and must be reached by a combination of train, bus, and cable car. It's best to make this a day trip to allow some time to explore Ohara and Hiei-zan. If you're booked on a tour to the Shugaku-in Imperial Villa on the same day, then you'll probably only have time to explore one or the other.

TOP ATTRACTIONS

Fodor's Choice
★
Enryaku-ji. With a view over the mountain ranges and the sound of chanting filling the air, this extensive complex of ancient temples and worship halls leaves many visitors reflecting on just how far their journey has taken them.

Enryaku-ji was established to protect the northern frontier when Emperor Kammu founded the city in the late 8th century. Because police were prohibited from entering the temple grounds, the whole mountainside became a refuge for thieves, brigands, and fugitives. To protect itself, Enryaku-ji developed its own zealous and well-trained militia, rivaling those of many feudal lords. No imperial army could manage a war without the support of Enryaku-ji, and at times Enryaku-ji's forces would slaughter monks of rival Buddhist sects. Not until the 16th century was there a force strong enough to attack the temple. Nobunaga Oda, the general who helped unify Japan and ended more than a century of civil strife, sacked the monastery in 1571. In the battle many monks were killed, and most buildings were destroyed. The structures standing today were built in the 17th century.

The **Kompon Chu-do** hall dates from 1642 and has a stunning copper roof in the *irimoya-zukuri* layered style. Its dark, cavernous interior conveys the mysticism for which the sect is known. Giant pillars and a coffered ceiling shelter the central altar surrounded by religious images. You can kneel with worshippers on a dais above the shadowy recess containing the smaller altars, an arrangement that supposedly allows you to come face-to-face with the enshrined deities. Even if you don't see a vision of the supernatural, you can enjoy a closer look at the ornate oil lanterns hanging before the altar, each representing a stage of enlightenment. Near the main hall, a mausoleum contains the remains of Saicho, who oversaw Enryaku-ji's construction. The echoing of the monks' wooden sandals follows you as you explore Enryaku-ji's other buildings; pay particular attention to the Shaka-do, the oldest structure in the complex.

To access the cable cars that take visitors to the base of the temple, take JR Kosei Line trains to Eizan Station, Keihan Line trains to Hiei-zan Sakamoto Station, or the Eiden/Eizan Line from Demachi-Yanagi Station to Yase-Yuen Station. Kyoto Line buses 16, 17 and 18 also run to Yase-Yuen. *Enryaku-ji* ⊠ *4220 Sakamoto-hon-machi, Otsu* ☎ *077/578–0001* ⊕ *www.hieizan.or.jp* 🖃 *¥800, cable car ¥550* ⊙ *Mar.–Nov., daily 8:30–4:30; Dec.–Feb., daily 9–4.*

★
Jikko-in 実光院. At this seldom-visited temple you can sit, relax, and have a taste of the tea ceremony. To enter, ring the gong on the outside of the gate. Once inside you can wander through the carefully cultivated garden with its natural waterfall, serene pond, and tiny teahouse framed

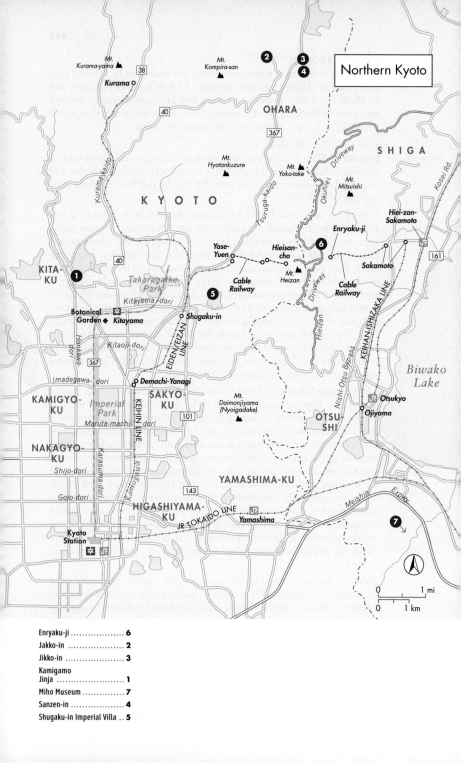

Northern Kyoto

KYOTO

OHARA

SHIGA

Mt. Kurama-yama ▲
Kurama
38

Mt. Kompira-san ▲

❷
❸
❹

40

367

Mt. Hyotankuzure ▲

Mt. Yoko-take ▲

Okuhiei Driveway

Mt. Mitsuishi ▲

Tsuruga-kaido

Kosei Rd.

Kurama-kaido

Hiei-zan-Sakamoto

Yase-Yuen
Hieisan-cho
❻ Enryaku-ji

Cable Railway
Mt. Heizan ▲

Hiei Driveway

Sakamoto

Cable Railway

KEIHAN-ISHIZAKA LINE

161

KITA-KU ❶

Takaragaike Park

Kitayama-dori

Botanical Garden ◆ Kitayama

❺ Shugaku-in

EIDEN-EIZAN LINE

Kitaoji-dori

Honkawa-dori

Imadegawa-dori

Demachi-Yanagi

KAMIGYO-KU

Imperial Park

SAKYO-KU

101

Mt. Daimonjiyama (Nyoigadake) ▲

KEIHIN LINE

Maruta-machi-dori

Karasuma-dori

NAKAGYO-KU

Shijo-dori

Kamogawa-dori

Gojo-dori

367

Nishi-Otsu Bypass

OTSU-SHI

❼ Otsukyo

Ojiyama

Biwako Lake

YAMASHINA-KU

143

HIGASHIYAMA-KU

JR TOKAIDO LINE

Yamashina

Meishin Expwy

❼

Kyoto Station ❀

0 ——— 1 mi
0 ——— 1 km

against the hills. Various strains of cherry trees are planted around the lake so you can see the blossoms throughout the year. Inside the temple, the main lintel holds 36 portraits of Chinese poets by members of the Kano School. To get here, take Kyoto Line Bus 17 or 18; the 90-minute journey from Kyoto Station costs ¥580. From the Ohara bus stop, walk northeast for about seven minutes along the signposted road. Jikko-in is 200 yards from Sanzen-in. ✉ *187 Ohara Shorin'in-cho, Sakyo-ku* ☎ *075/744-2537* 🎫 *¥700* 🕙 *Daily 9–4:30.*

Kamigamo Jinja 上賀茂神社. One of Kyoto's oldest shrines, Kamigamo Jinja is a terrific example of rich Heian architecture. With charming bridges, sand sculptures, and vermilion gateways, Kamigamo Jinja was built in the 8th century by the Kamo family and has always been associated with Kamo Wakeikazuchi, a god of thunder, rain, and fertility. Now the shrine is famous for its annual horse race—held on May 5— and its hollyhock festival, which started in the 6th century when people thought that the Kamigamo deities were angry at being neglected. Held on May 15, it includes 500 people in Heian period costumes processing on horseback or in ox-drawn carriages. On June 30, a purification ritual takes place in which throngs of people cast paper effigies into the river beneath the flickering glare of charcoal braziers. The canal street that leads up to the shrine has many *machiya* (elongated town houses), some of which are more than 400 years old. To get to the shrine, take Bus 9 north Kamigamojinja-mae or Kamigamo Misono-bashi. Or take the subway north to Kitayama Station, from which the shrine is 20 minutes on foot northwest. ✉ *339 Motoyama, Kamigamo, Kita-ku* 🎫 *Free* 🕙 *Daily 9–4.*

★ **Sanzen-in** 三千院. This small temple of the Tendai sect was founded by the renowned priest Dengyo-Daishi (767–822). The temple is a *monzeki,* meaning the abbot has traditionally been of royal blood. The Hon-do (Main Hall) was built by Priest Eshin (942–1017), who probably carved the temple's Amida Buddha. The Buddha is flanked by two seated attendants: the goddess of wisdom, Daiseishi, to the right; and the goddess of compassion, Kannon, to the left. Unusual for a Buddhist temple, Sanzen-in faces east, not south. Note its ceiling, on which a painting depicts the descent of Amida, accompanied by 25 bodhisattvas, to welcome the believer. Full of maple trees and moss, the gardens are serene in any season. In autumn the colors are magnificent, and the approach to the temple up a gentle slope—with the river on one side and small shops on the other—enhances the anticipation for the burnt-gold trees guarding the old, weathered temple. Snow cover in winter is also magical. Take Kyoto Line Bus 17 or 18 north for 90 minutes from Kyoto Station to Ohara. From the Ohara bus station walk northeast for about seven minutes along the signposted road. ✉ *540 Ohara Raigoin-cho, Sakyo-ku* 🎫 *¥700* 🕙 *Mar.–Nov., daily 8:30–5; Dec.–Feb., daily 8:30–4:30.*

WORTH NOTING

Jakko-in 寂光院. After a devastating fire, this small monastery surrounded by a quiet garden was completely rebuilt in 2005. The temple's history goes back much further. In April 1185, after a two-year struggle, the Taira clan met its end in a naval battle against the rival Minamoto

7

Sanzen-in, a temple of the Tendai Buddhist sect, faces east, not south, as is the case with most Buddhist temples.

clan. Seeing that all was lost, the Taira women drowned themselves, taking with them the eight-year-old emperor Antoku. His mother, the 29-year-old Kenreimon-in, leaped into the sea, but Minamoto soldiers hauled her back on board their ship.

She alone survived and lived here as a nun in solitude in a 10-foot-square cell made of brushwood and thatch for 27 years, until her death ended the Taira line. You may need to ask for directions to her mausoleum, which is higher up the hill, away from the throng of visitors and along the path by the side of the temple. When Kenreimon-in came to Jakko-in it was far removed from Kyoto. Now Kyoto's sprawl reaches this far and beyond, but the temple, hidden in trees, is still a place of solitude. From Kyoto Station take Kyoto Line Bus 17 or 18 for a 90-minute ride and get out at the Ohara bus stop; the fare is ¥480. Walk 20 minutes or so along the road leading to the northwest. ⊠ 676 *Oharakusao-cho, Sakyo-ku, Sakyo-ku* 🖀 *¥600* ☺ *Mar.–Nov., daily 9–5; Dec.–Feb., daily 9–4:30.*

Miho Museum ミホミュージアム *(Miho Bijutsukan).* The distance from Kyoto may make getting here seem daunting, but the Miho Museum is well worth the trip, thanks both to its phenomenal architecture and impressive worldly collection. Conceived by architect I. M. Pei, the building uses many of the same design elements and construction techniques employed at his extension for the Louvre in Paris. The exquisite collection consists of more than 2,000 pieces, including Syrian floor mosaics, Iranian metal ornaments, Egyptian statuary, Afghani Buddha icons, and Roman frescos. Roughly 250 pieces are on display at any one time in temporary exhibitions that change seasonally. An on-site restaurant sells bento meals with organic ingredients for about ¥1,000, and a tearoom serves Japanese and Western beverages and desserts. From Kyoto Station, take the JR Tokaido Line to Ishiyama Station; from there the Teisan Line bus to the museum takes 50 minutes. Buses to Miho, which cost ¥800 one-way, run on the hour from 9 to 6. ⊠ *300 Momodani, Shiga-ken, Shigariki* ☏ *0748/82–3411* ⊕ *www.miho. jp* ☞ *¥1,000* ☺ *Mid-Mar.–mid-June and Sept.–mid-Dec., Tues.–Sun. 10–5; last entry at 4.*

Shugaku-in Imperial Villa 修学院離宮 *(Shugaku-in Rikyu).* The focus of this compound is not the opulent villas but the sumptuous gardens. The grounds are held to be one of the great masterpieces of gardening. The manicured trees, lawns, and flowers are especially lovely thanks to the neighboring rice fields and orchards.

The Upper and Lower villas were built in the 17th century by the Tokugawa family to entertain the Emperor; the Upper Villa provides nice views of northern Kyoto. The Middle Villa was added later as a palace home for Princess Bunke, daughter of Emperor Go-mizunoo. Permission is required to visit the villa, best obtained a few days in advance from the Imperial Household Agency *(see ⇨ Visitor Information in Planning at the beginning of this chapter).* Although all guided tours are in Japanese, there are free English-language audio guides. From Kyoto Station, Bus 5 takes about an hour. Or you can ride 20 minutes north on a Keifuku Eizan Line train from the Demachi-Yanagi terminus, which is northeast of the intersection of Imadegawa-dori and the Kamogawa. ⊠ *Yabusoe Shugaku-in, Sakyo-ku* ⊕ *sankan.kunaicho. go.jp* ☞ *Free* ☺ *Weekdays 9–3 (first come, first served).*

WHERE TO EAT

Attuned to subtle seasonal changes, Kyoto cuisine emphasizes freshness and contrast. From the finest *ryotei* (high-class Japanese restaurants) to the smallest *izakaya* (pub), the distinctive elements of gracious hospitality, subtle flavors, and attention to decor create an experience that engages all the senses. Both elaborate establishments and casual shops usually offer set menus at lunchtime, at a considerably lower price than dinner. Although the finest traditional *kaiseki ryori* (the elaborate, multicourse, often expensive meal) is costly, this experience is highly recommended at least once during your visit to Japan.

If you find yourself with an unintelligible menu, ask for the *o-makase,* or chef's recommendation and you can specify your budget in some instances. The custom of dining early, from 6 pm until 8 pm, still endures in very traditional restaurants, but many restaurants are open until 10 or 11 pm. If possible, let the hotel staff make reservations for you where necessary. For more-formal restaurants try to book at least two days in advance; bookings are often not accepted for the following day if called in after 4 pm. Keep in mind that not all restaurants accept credit cards.

WHAT IT COSTS IN YEN				
	¢	$	$$	$$$	$$$$
At Dinner	under ¥800	¥800–¥1,000	¥1,000–¥2,000	¥2,000–¥3,000	over ¥3,000

Restaurant prices are per person for a main course, set meal, or equivalent combinations of smaller dishes.

EASTERN KYOTO 洛東

$
IZAKAYA

×**Gion Kappa Nawate** 祇園かっぱ縄手. In contrast to the expensive kaiseki ryori restaurants favored by tourists, residents seek out just-plain-folks places like this one. It's a late-night izakaya specializing in *robata-yaki*, which is to say a casual bar-restaurant with a charcoal grill and great selection of meat, poultry, and vegetable dishes. Here it's common to order a variety of dishes to share. If there are no tables, find a seat at the long counter. The restaurant is two blocks north of Shijo-dori in the heart of Gion. Everything dish is ¥390, even the drinks. The friendly middle-aged men who work there enjoy using their broken English with tourists. ⊠ *Sueyoshi-cho, Nawate-dori Shijo-agaru, Higashiyama-ku* ☎ *075/531–1112* ▭ *No credit cards* ☾ *No lunch.*

$$$$
JAPANESE
Fodor'sChoice
★

×**Kikunoi** 菊乃井. The care lavished on every aspect of dining is unparalleled here thanks to the conscientious attention of Kikunoi's owner, world-renowned chef and authority on Kyoto cuisine, Yoshihiro Murata. A lifetime study of French and Japanese cooking, a commitment to using the finest local ingredients, and a playful creative sense make every exciting meal hum with flavor. Once seated in a private dining room, you are brought a small *sakizuke,* or appetizer, the first of up to 14 courses, each exquisitely presented and unfailingly delicious. Dishes like cedar-smoked barracuda fillets, citrus-infused matsutake mushroom soup, or sashimi served on chrysanthemum petals keenly accord to the nuances of each new season. This restaurant is on the northern edge of Kodai-ji temple. Evening courses start at ¥15,500, lunches at ¥4,200. ⊠ *Gion Maruyama Makuzugahara, Kawahara-cho 459, Higashiyama-ku* ☎ *075/561–0015* ⊕ *kikunoi.jp* ✍ *Reservations essential.*

$$$$
JAPANESE

×**Kikusui** 菊水. Near Nanzen-ji temple, Kikusui serves elegant kaiseki ryori meals with an aristocratic flair. Dine on tatami mats at low tables or at table-and-chair seating, all overlooking an elegant Japanese garden. The subtle flavors of the set menus are intended to be offset by the scenic view, where a canopy of pink and white cherry blossoms accents the light spring menus and fiery red and orange maples highlight the warm flavors of stews in autumn. *Kyo-no-aji,* smaller versions of kaiseki ryori served for lunch, let you savor Kikusui's elegant setting and fine cuisine for ¥5,000. ⊠ *31 Fukui-cho, Nazen-ji, Sakyo-ku* ☎ *075/771–4101* ⊕ *kyoto-kikusui.com* ✍ *Reservations essential.*

$$$$
JAPANESE

×**Kisaki Yudofu** 喜さ起京湯どうふ. Kisaki is a place for a hearty and healthy meal. Though some dishes include meat or chicken, the cuisine here relies mostly on fresh vegetables, including plenty of pickles and seaweed. An expert in tofu, the hospitable, English-speaking owner,

Kikunoi is one of the most famous restaurants in Kyoto serving Kyokaiseki ryori, a finely crafted, multicourse feast.

Emiko, will cater to special requests. Tempura, warmed tofu, and hot pots cooked at the table are the staples in this attractive two-story restaurant along the Philosopher's Path overlooking maple and cherry trees. Try the *Kisaki nabe* that includes pork, chicken, beef, chrysanthemum, shiitake, and spinach. This is the place to be in August during the Okuribi Festival, when it is possible to watch the distant hillside fires lighted in the shape of a ship on its symbolic journey to the Buddhist Pure Land. Just be aware that even though the restaurant closes at 9, the last order is taken at 7:30. ⊠ *Minamida-cho 173-19, Jodoji, Sakyo-ku* ☎ *075/751–7406* ▭ *No credit cards* ☉ *Closed Wed.*

$$$$
JAPANESE
✕ **Kyo-machiya Suishin** 京町家すいしん. Not far from Gion Kaburenjo Theater, a black-and-white latticed storefront conceals a vegetable lover's paradise. The dining area is raised so that those seated on floor cushions are at eye level with the busy chefs in the open kitchen. Hollowed-out flooring beneath the tables and at the long bar make tatami-mat dining possible without stiff knees. For a nice primer on Kyoto's essential dishes, opt for the *Fushimi* menu or the more-extensive *Gosho* menu. Suishin brings out the flavors of local organic vegetables, fish, and meats with a conspicuously restrained hand, creating flavors so light they seem to float in your mouth. Look for a lantern above the door. ⊠ *181 Zaimoku-cho, Ponto-cho, Nakagyo-ku* ☎ *075/221–8596* ⊕ *suishin.co.jp.*

$$$$
JAPANESE
★
✕ **Kyoto Gion Oishimbo** 京都祇園おいしんぼ. The menu at this restaurant in the heart of Gion hits just the right balance. Choose between two courses or order à la carte. Excellent preparation and presentation take the simple, unpretentious *o-banzai* (home-style) dishes to another level. Seishu Oishinbo, the house sake, makes everything taste even better.

As is common for old houses in the neighborhood, the tatami-matted rooms on the first floor overlook a small courtyard garden. The restaurant is just off Gion's main drag. ⊠ *Gion-cho Minamigawa 570-123, Higashiyama-ku, Hanami komichi* ☎ *075/541–6100* ⊕ *kyoto-oishinbo. com* ⚲ *Reservations essential.*

$$$$
JAPANESE

✕**Minoko** 美濃幸. Disappear behind a blue curtain off the cobbled streets of Gion into a Japanese fairy tale. Rooms connected by charming wooden passages look out onto an expansive garden, and tables are set with simple but sumptuous decorations, like grand lacquered tables and regal kimonos. The decor sets the scene perfectly for a delicious, if not overly daring, kaiseki ryori meal. The kindly proprietors seem old enough to remember the Meiji Restoration, but their attention to the quality of your meal is unfailing. Inquire about the cozy *ko-cha-shitsu,* or "small tearoom" that's perfect for a romantic dinner for two. Minoko is less than a block from Yasaka Jinja's southern gate. Only minimal English is spoken, so have your concierge make the reservation for you. ⊠ *480 Kiyoi-cho, Shimogowara-dori, Gion, Higashiyama-ku* ☎ *075/561–0328* ⚲ *Reservations essential* ⊗ *Closed 2nd and 4th Wed. of each month.*

$$$$
SUSHI

✕**Nontaro** 呑太呂. In the heart of Kyoto's busy nightlife district, Nontaro has been the place for sushi for decades. Beefy chefs on impossibly tall wooden geta sandals serve the freshest cuts of richly flavorful sushi, mixing staples like ginger-tinged mackerel with innovative surprises like aloe heart dabbed with horseradish. Nontaro serves its sushi in a traditional style, which has fallen by the wayside almost everywhere else. Each delicate roll is dropped directly onto the red-lacquer countertop for you to grab and gobble up, and running water in a narrow channel lets you wash your hands after each go. In etiquette-over-everything Kyoto, finger food feels totally scandalous. A take-out bento box, perfect for sightseeing or temple-hopping, is ¥3,680. A lunch course is between ¥2,000 and ¥5,000. ⊠ *Hanami-koji Shijo-agaru, Higashi-yama-ku* ☎ *075/561–3189* ⊕ *gion-nontaroh.jp* ⚲ *Reservations essential* ⊗ *Closed New Year's Day and during Obon Festival.*

$$
JAPANESE
★

✕**Omen** おめん. This branch of a Kyoto chain is perfect for an inexpensive home-style lunch. On the Philosopher's Path between Ginkaku-ji and Nanzen-ji, it's an ideal place to recharge between sights. Omen refers to the house specialty: *men* means noodles, and Omen's fabulous udon noodle soup is fantastic. Served broken down to its components— a basket of noodles and a platter of seasonal vegetables beside a bowl of steaming broth—it's meant to be consumed at a leisurely pace. Add what you like to the broth, plus some roasted sesame to taste. The salted mackerel is also excellent. The restaurant is country-style and comfortable, with a choice of counter stools, tables and chairs, or tatami mats. Reservations are accepted only on weekdays. ⊠ *74 Ishi-bashi-cho, Jodoji, Sakyo-ku* ☎ *075/771–8994* ⊕ *omen.co.jp* ⊗ *Closed Thurs.*

$$$$
JAPANESE

✕**Ponto-cho Robin** 先斗町魯ビン. An adventurous menu sets Ponto-cho Robin ahead of the competition. Charcoal-color walls, rich wooden staircases, and a great view of the river from this 150-year-old town house are a great setting for dishes like sea urchin in wasabi broth, grilled river fish, and the ever-popular *kami-nabe,* a hot pot made of paper and cooked on an open flame at your table: gimmicky but mesmerizing, it's actually pretty tasty. Seating on the riverfront deck is lovely in summer. ⊠ *137–4 Wakamatsu-cho, Ponto-cho, Nakagyo-ku* ☎ *075/222–8200* ⌂ *Reservations essential* ⊘ *No lunch.*

¢ ✕ **Rakusho** 洛匠. This is an excellent spot to recharge with tea and sweets
JAPANESE while wandering through the cobbled lanes of Gion. The house specialty
★ is *warabi-mochi,* a treat made from steamed and pounded rice that has a gelatin-like consistency. The green color and subtle spice comes from the mountain herb *yomogi.* The dish is served on a heap of golden *kinako,* made from toasted soybeans, to add a delightful sweetness. Don't feel shy about licking your bamboo spoon to enjoy the last bit. The restaurant also serves ice cream and a variety of other Japanese treats along with excellent green tea. You'll find it on the northern end of Higashiyama's cobbled Nene-no-michi. ⊠ *Kodai-ji Kitamon-mae-dori, Washio-cho 516, Higashiyama-ku* ☎ *075/561–6892* ⊕ *rakusyou. co.jp* ⌂ *Reservations not accepted* ▭ *No credit cards.*

$ ✕ **Ramen Santoka** らーめん山頭火. Inspired by the classic food movie,
JAPANESE *Tampopo,* this great soup shop has all the standards: salt, soy, or miso ramen noodles with veggies, pork, or seaweed. Part of a chain born in Hokkaido, this location sits here in a good location with a view of a rock garden. Ramen Santoka stays open until 2 am, or until the soup runs out. ⊠ *137 Yamato-oji-dori, Sanjo-sagaru Higashigawa, Dai-kokucho, Higashiyama-ku* ☎ *075/532–1335* ⊕ *santouka.co.jp.*

$$$$ ✕ **Tozentei** 陶然亭. Among the antiques stores and kimono shops on
JAPANESE Shinmonzen-dori, Tozentei emphasizes to-the-letter traditional Japanese cooking. Meals here, made with only local produce, are old-school enough to please a shogun. Grumpy gray windows frame this intimate hideaway that fits only 14. ⊠ *Nishmonzen Yamato-oji-dori Higashi-iru, Higashiyama-ku* ☎ *075/561–8024* ⌂ *Reservations essential* ⊘ *Closed Sun.*

$$$$ ✕ **Yagenbori** やげんぼり. Waitresses in exquisite kimonos serve posh iza-
JAPANESE kaya fare inside this 130-year-old teahouse on a cobbled corner by the romantic Shirakawa River, just north of Shijo-dori in Gion. The decor, featuring original paintings by renowned woodblock revivalist Clifton Karhu, is a feast for the eyes. The feast on the table is less exciting, especially for those familiar with Japanese cuisine, but sashimi served in icy tureens, delicious warm yuba tofu skin, and *kamaboko* fish soup are all good. Don't miss the *hoba* miso—bean paste with mushrooms and green onions that is wrapped in a giant oak leaf and grilled at your table—on the à la carte menu. The excellent box lunch is a bargain at ¥2,800. ⊠ *Sueyoshi-cho, Kiridoshi-kado, Gion, Higashiyama-ku* ☎ *075/551–3331* ⊕ *yagenbori.co.jp.*

¢–$ ✕ **Yojiya Café** よーじや. This immensely popular café is a treasure no lon-
CAFÉ ger hidden along the Philosopher's Path. Located in a traditional house that overlooks a low-lying garden with a pond and miniature bridge, the café consists of a tatami room with a glass wall; there are no tables, just soft cushions for seats maximize the view. It's an especially cozy and comfortable place to take a rest in winter. Yojiya's specialty is desserts that blend traditional and Western flavors. Try the macha cappuccino or a dessert set to get a good sense of what's on offer. Customers are

7

CLOSE UP

On the Menu

Compared with the style of cooking elsewhere in Japan, *Kyoto-ryori* (Kyoto cuisine) is lighter and more delicate, stressing the natural flavor of ingredients over enhancement with heavy sauces and broths. *O-banzai* (Kyoto home cooking) is served at many restaurants at reasonable prices. The freshness and quality of the ingredients is paramount, and chefs carefully handpick only the best. *Sosaku ryori* (creative cuisine) is becoming popular as chefs find inspiration in other cultures while retaining light and subtle flavors.

Kyoto is also the home of *shojin ryori*, the Zen vegetarian-style cooking best sampled on the grounds of one of the city's Zen temples, such as Tenryu-ji in Arashiyama. Local delicacies like *fu* (glutinous wheat cakes) and *yuba* (soy-milk skimmings) have found their way into the mainstream of Kyoto ryori, but were originally devised to provide protein in the traditional Buddhist diet.

For a reasonably priced alternative to the kaiseki ryori (the elaborate, multicourse, often expensive meal), the *kaiseki bento* (box lunch) served by many ryotei is a good place to start. Box lunches are so popular in Kyoto that restaurants compete to make their bento unique, exquisite, and delicious.

served from small lacquered trays. Don't leave without visiting the small, elegant shop at the rear of the garden that sells natural cosmetics. ✉ *Honenin-cho 15, Shishigadani, Sakyo-ku* ☎ *075/754–0017* ⊕ *www. yojiya.co.jp* ☐ *No credit cards* ☹ *Closed Tues. No dinner.*

CENTRAL KYOTO

$$ ✕ **Ask a Giraffe** アスクアジラフ. The eclectic decor and accessible menu
CAFÉ   make this longtime place an expat favorite. Sandwiches, salads, and
☺   pasta dishes are always fantastic. The yearly menu is full of great choices like mouthwatering tuna steak and the uniquely Japanese staple *omuraisu* (a fried-rice omelet). Coffees and cakes round out the selection. It's in the Shinpu-kan shopping center inside George's. ✉ *Karasuma-dori Anekoji-sagaru 586-2, Nakagyo-ku* ☎ *075/257–8028* ⊕ *giraffe.georges.co.jp.*

$$$$ ✕ **Ca' Del Viale** カデルヴィアーレ. The signature dish in this well-
ITALIAN   regarded trattoria is handmade pasta topped with a tomato sauce fla-
★   vorful enough to satisfy the most road weary traveler. The antipasti include carefully selected organic vegetables and fine Italian ham. Such entrées as tender pork steaks or grilled fish in orange-infused balsamic vinegar are excellent, and the decadent desserts are a great way to finish a meal: the lychee mousse alone is worth the visit. Savoring your multicourse meal on the terrace will cap off your day nicely. Lunch courses start from ¥1,500. ✉ *Nishino Kyosenbon, Sanjo Nishi-iru, Nakagyo-ku* ☎ *075/812–2366* ⊕ *watanabechef.com* ⟋ *Reservations essential* ☹ *Closed Mon. No lunch Tues.*

$$ ✕ **Café Bibliotic HELLO!** カフェビブリオテックハロー. The banana trees that
CAFÉ mask this airy two-story town-house café are visible from several blocks
away. The three lunch options change regularly and range from steak
sandwiches to rice and curry dishes. Drinks like Moroccan chai or
the playful seasonal smoothies (strawberry, mint, and ginger anyone?)
complement desserts like mango and coconut cream or French toast
with candied almonds. Browse the wall of books while you're waiting.
✉ *Nijo-dori Yanaginobana, Higashi-iru, Nakagyo-ku* ☎ *075/231–8625*
▭ *No credit cards.*

$ ✕ **Café Indépendants** カフェ アンデパンダン. This laid-back spot, espe-
CAFÉ cially popular at lunch, serves good daily specials, including curries,
salads, and soups. A devoted clientele of students and artists comes for
the cheap, bountiful lunch plates, the friendly service, and the convivial
atmosphere. The setting is a Meiji-era building's brick-and-plaster base-
ment, with funky mosaic tiles and lots of exposed masonry. It's located
on the south side of Sanjo-dori one block in from the Tera-machi shop-
ping arcade. ✉ *1928 Bldg., Sanjo-dori, Nakagyo-ku* ☎ *075/255–4312*
⊕ *cafe-independants.com* ▭ *No credit cards.*

$$$$ ✕ **Giro Giro Hitoshina** 枝魯枝魯ひとしな. Quickly becoming one of Kyo-
JAPANESE to's most popular restaurants, Giro Giro has a lively atmosphere, excel-
Fodor's Choice lent food, and great location on the sleepy Takase-gawa River. Sit at the
★ counter surrounding the busy chefs or grab a table upstairs—both offer
views of people walking along the river wishing they could trade places
with you. The set menu changes monthly to showcase seasonal dishes
and fresh ingredients. The chef's style has been described as "punk kai-
seki ryori" cuisine; what this means is that you can have a multicourse,
kaiseki-style menu without all of the strict convention. Expect an elabo-
rate *hassun* (appetizer) tray followed by seven more varying courses.
You will be hard-pressed to find a better high-end value than this. Giro
Giro is easiest to find by walking the narrow lane along the Takase-
gawa; look for the glow of the massive window a few blocks north
of Gojo-dori. ✉ *420–7 Nanba-cho, Nishi Kiya-machi-dori, Higash-
igawa, Matsubarashita, Shimogyo-ku* ☎ *075/343–7070* ⊕ *guiloguilo.
com* ⌂ *Reservations essential* ♡ *Closed last Mon. of month. No lunch.*

$$$ ✕ **Kerala** ケララ. Imported spices and the fresh, local vegetables are the
INDIAN secrets to this Indian restaurant's success. Dishes may not be as spicy as
you would expect, but the spinach, lamb, and chickpea curries—not to
mention the tandoori chicken—are sumptuous and flavorful. The house
special chicken Kerala curry is the most popular dish and runs ¥1,500.
This second-story restaurant opposite the Royal Hotel has a blend of
modern and traditional Indian furnishings and extremely reasonable
evening set courses. ✉ *Kawara-machi-dori Sanjo-agaru Nishigawa,
Nakagyo-ku* ☎ *075/251–0141.*

$$$$ ✕ **Mankamero** 萬亀楼. Since 1722, Mankamero's specialty has been
JAPANESE *yusoku ryori,* cuisine intended for members of the Imperial Court.
Fodor's Choice Every step of the meal is incredibly elaborate, down to the ceremoni-
★ ally dressed chef who prepares your dishes using specially made utensils.
A dramatic, if repellently named, course is the "dismembered fish," in
which each part of a single fish is prepared and served on a series of
pedestal trays. Prices reflect the aristocratic experience—up to ¥30,000

7

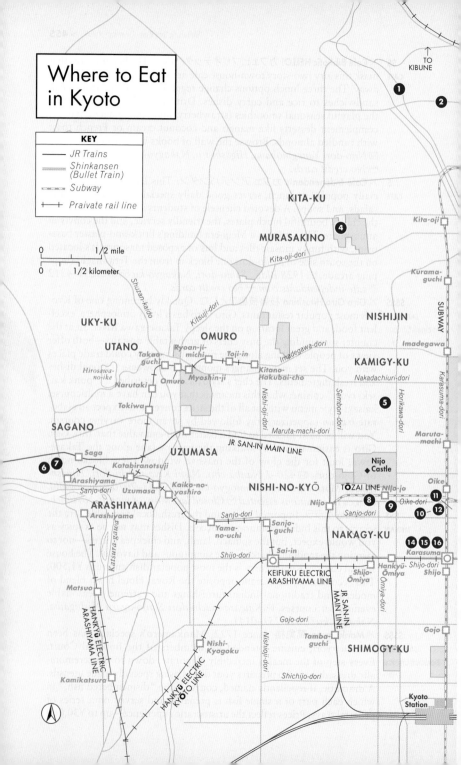

Where to Eat in Kyoto

KEY

- —— JR Trains
- ══ Shinkansen (Bullet Train)
- ╌╌ Subway
- ┼┼ Praivate rail line

0 ──── 1/2 mile
0 ──── 1/2 kilometer

TO KIBUNE

1 **2**

KITA-KU

MURASAKINO

Kita-oji

Kita-oji-dori

4

Kurama-guchi

SUBWAY

NISHIJIN

Kitsuji-dori

UKY-KU

UTANO

OMURO

Ryoan-ji-michi

Toji-in

Imadegawa-dori

Imadegawa

KAMIGY-KU

Takao-guchi

Omuro

Myoshin-ji

Kitano-Hakubai-cho

Nakadachiuri-dori

Karasuma-dori

Hirosawa-no-ike

Narutaki

Nishi-oji-dori

Sembon-dori

Horikawa-dori

Tokiwa

5

Maruta-machi-dori

Maruta-machi

SAGANO

Saga

JR SAN-IN MAIN LINE

UZUMASA

Nijo Castle

Oike

6 **7**

Katabiranotsuji

Arashiyama

Kaiko-no-yashiro

NISHI-NO-KYŌ

TŌZAI LINE

Nijo-jo

11

Sanjo-dori

Uzumasa

Nijo

8 **9**

Oike-dori

10 **12**

ARASHIYAMA

Arashiyama

Sanjo-dori

Yama-no-uchi

Sanjo-guchi

Sanjo-dori

NAKAGY-KU

14 **15** **16**

Katsura-gawa

Shijo-dori

Sai-in

KEIFUKU ELECTRIC ARASHIYAMA LINE

Shijo-Ōmiya

Hankyū-Ōmiya

Karasuma

Shijo-dori

Shijo

Matsuo

HANKYŪ ELECTRIC ARASHIYAMA LINE

Omiya-dori

JR SAN-IN MAIN LINE

Gojo-dori

Gojo

Nishi-Kyogoku

Tamba-guchi

Kamikatsura

HANKYŪ ELECTRIC KYŌTO LINE

Nishioji-dori

SHIMOGY-KU

Shichijo-dori

Kyoto Station

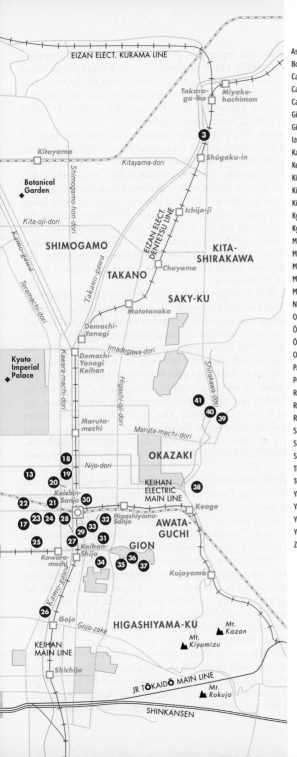

per person for the full repertoire. A wonderful *take-kago* (bamboo box) lunch set is within reach of commoners at ¥6,325, revealing a series of steamed surprises. Mankamero is on the west side of Inokuma-dori north of Demizu-dori. Look for the blue-tile roof. ☒ *Inokuma-dori, Demizu-agaru, Ebisu-cho 387, Kamigyo-ku* ☎ *075/441–5020* ⊕ *mankamerou.com* ⌂ *Reservations essential.*

$$$$
JAPANESE
Fodor's Choice
★

✗ **Manzaratei Nishiki** まんざら亭. The unpretentious vibe, the sense of adventure, and the superb cuisine—Japanese-based with other Asian and European influences—have made Manzaratei a local favorite. Depending on the season, the ample menu offers handmade soba, oven-roasted chicken, or spring rolls with citrusy *ponzu* dressing. Outdoor dining in the warmer months and counter seating on both floors of the two-story town house let you mingle with other patrons; for more-intimate evenings, ask for a table upstairs under the eaves. The restaurant is a block north of the intersection of Shijo-dori and Karasuma-dori. An English menu is available. ☒ *Karasuma Nishiki-koji, 317 Nishi-iru, Uradeyama-cho* ☎ *075/257–5748* ⊕ *manzara.co.jp* ⌂ *Reservations essential* ☽ *No lunch.*

$$$$
JAPANESE

✗ **Mishima-tei** 三島亭. Five generations of chefs have preserved the delicious sukiyaki recipe served here since 1873. At the street-level butcher's counter, housewives line up to pay top dollar for the high-quality beef, but your feast awaits upstairs in the large tatami-matted dining room, one of the many cheerful garden rooms, or the endearing teahouse (our favorite). A kimono-clad attendant will help get you started cooking everything at your table. Sukiyaki varies between restaurants: Mishima-tei favors thin slices of beef and a platter of vegetables which you eat by dipping anything hot off the pan into cooling, flavorful raw egg before popping it into your mouth. The ¥6,000 Mini Course belies its name in terms of quantity. At the west entrance of the Tera-machi arcade, it's easy to find. ☒ *Tera-machi, Sanjo-sagaru, Higashi-iru, Nakagyo-ku* ☎ *075/221–0003* ⊕ *mishima-tei.co.jp* ⌂ *Reservations essential* ☽ *Closed Wed.*

$$$$
JAPANESE

✗ **Mukadeya** 百足屋. Homestyle o-banzai cooking is the specialty of this sophisticated restaurant found in a beautiful machiya (town house). Bonito sashimi, simmered pumpkin, and gingery ground chicken are artfully presented on lacquer trays, feasts for the eyes that taste even better than they look. Though only three set choices are available, you will find a rich variety of local seasonal fare often numbering between eight and 12 courses. You'll be greeted warmly by kimono-clad hostesses then seated near a cheerful courtyard garden; the experience feels expansive and inviting. Even though the restaurant is not far from the Karasuma-Shijo intersection, it is rather tricky to find. Let a taxi driver help you find your way to Mukadeya's front door. ☒ *381 Mukadeya-cho, Shin-machi-dori, Nishiki-agaru, Nakagyo-ku* ☎ *075/256–7039* ⌂ *Reservations essential* ☽ *Closed Wed.*

$$$$
FRENCH

✗ **Ogawa** おがわ. The best in Kyoto-style nouvelle cuisine is served in this intimate spot across from the Takase-gawa canal. Dishes depend on the chef's whims as much as on what's in season, but the menu might include buttery risotto-like rice pilaf topped with delicate sea urchin; duck meat and foie gras in bite-size portions; and hors d'oeuvres such as oyster gratin, crab-and-scallop stew, and wild mushroom tempura. The fruit and vegetable salads are exceptional, and the take-all-you-want dessert tray with tarts, tortes, and pastries is the icing on the cake. With advance notice the chef will even grant special-order requests. ✉ *Kiya-machi Oike-agaru Higashi-iru, Nakagyo-ku* ☎ *075/256–2203* ⊕ *r-ogawa.com* ⚬ *Reservations essential* ⊗ *Closed Tues.*

$$$
JAPANESE
☾

✕ **Oiwa** 大岩. *Kura* storehouses were built of thick plaster and separated from other buildings to protect them from fire and theft: the kimono merchants who used to own this one have long since retired, and the treasure stored inside these days is fine *kushikatsu* cooking featuring bite-size bits of meat and vegetables skewered, battered, deep-fried, and served with a variety of sauces. Usually considered a laborer's snack, kushikatsu seems an incongruous choice for Oiwa's French-trained chefs, but their interpretation offers a richness and elegance found nowhere else. Order by the skewer or ask for the set meal. There's even a menu for small children. The restaurant is along the Takase-gawa River. ✉ *Kiya-machi-dori, Nijo-sagaru, Nakagyo-ku* ☎ *075/231–7667* ⊕ *www.kushi-oiwa.co.jp* ▭ No credit cards ⊗ *No lunch Wed. and weekends.*

$$
SOBA
★

✕ **Omen** おめん. This branch of the famed soba noodle shop is convenient to the downtown shopping area. It's a perfect place to pop in for a delicious lunch of udon noodle soup and off the main road just enough to provide a break from the Shijo crowds. Add some crushed roasted sesame for an extra kick. ✉ *Goko-machi Shijo-agaru, Nakagyo-ku* ☎ *075/255–2125* ⊕ *omen.co.jp* ⊗ *Closed Thurs.*

$$$$
STEAK

✕ **Omi** 近江. This excellent steak restaurant specializes in Omi beef (of the same high-end wagyu grade as well-known Kobe beef and celebrated by Japanese gourmets). You'll be ushered through corridors to the dining room and seated around a *hori-gotatsu* (recessed grill) or at a counter in a pristine tatami room. Excellent seafood platters are also popular, as is the lunch menu which is ¥5,000. The restaurant is in a Meiji-era town house connected to an annex of the Hotel Fujita Kyoto. A drink beside the duck pond in hotel's bar is a great way to end the evening. Private rooms are available upon request. ✉ *Hotel Fujita Kyoto, Nijo-dori, Kiya-machi Kado, Nakagyo-ku* ☎ *075/212–1347* ⚬ *Reservations essential.*

$
CAFÉ

✕ **PAUSA.** An expat favorite, this jazzy café offers an exciting selection of dishes so varied and delicious you'll want to keep coming back. Try the Okinawan-style stir-fries, the Vietnamese-style pancakes, or the rice dishes with vegetables and bean curd. Whatever you choose, top it off with a soul-warming café au lait. Well-deserved popularity has led to this becoming a local chain, but this branch is our favorite. ✉ *38–1 Benkeiseki-cho, Fuyacho-dori, Sanjo-agaru, Nakagyo-ku* ☎ *075/212–2310* ▭ No credit cards ⊗ *Closed last Wed of month.*

$$$$
JAPANESE

✕ **Shinsen-en Heihachi** 神泉苑平八. Facing Nijo Castle's southern wall, this touristy restaurant is situated within the only remaining garden from the original Imperial Palace. The 1,200-year-old Sacred Spring Garden dates from 794, when the Emperor Kammu established Kyoto as the nation's capital. Shinsen-en Heihachi's charming shrine, pond, and vermilion bridge are essentially all that remain. You can dine

7

Somushi Kocha-ya is a Korean-style teahouse and restaurant on Shijo-dori.

looking out at the pond, or, if seating is available, on a boat floating leisurely in the middle of it. Lunch courses beginning at ¥3,800 are a better buy than the ¥8,400-and-up dinners. There are not as many à la carte options, but single items start at a more affordable ¥800. ⊠ *Oike-dori, Shinsenen Higashi-iru Mon-mae 167, Nakagyo-ku* ☎ *075/841–0811* ⊕ *heihachi-web.com.*

$

KOREAN

Fodor's Choice

★

✕ **Somushi Tea House** 素夢子 古茶家. Dark-wood furnishings create a provocative and intimate environment for sampling the bountiful brews at Kyoto's top Korean teahouse. Unlike Japanese and Chinese teas, which pull flavor from leaves or powder, the house favorites here are brewed full of berries, spices, and herbs. The intense aromas are complemented by a menu of vegetable stews, stuffed fritters, and innovative versions of Korean staples like organic *bibimbap* (a rice bowl topped with various ingredients). Reserve ahead to sample the Gozen menu, with nine bronze pots filled with royal cuisine good enough to leave you wishing you were an ancient Seoul nobleman. Seating is in a cozy private room at the back, on cushions at floor-level tables, or at a robust wooden counter with a better chance to chat with the convivial proprietors. *Karasuma Sanjo Nishi-iru, Mikura-cho 73Nakagyo-ku* ☎ *075/253–1456* ⊕ *somushi.com* ⊘ *Closed Wed.*

$$$$

VIETNAMESE

✕ **Tiem An Huong Viet** ティエム・アン・フォーン・ヴィェット. Tucked away in a small street, the jade-color walls and dark Vietnamese furnishings of this delightful eatery are reminiscent of a classy Hanoi café. Classics like *pho* noodle soup are excellent, and the menu is full of dishes that are great for sharing: a house favorite is *ban xeo*, a huge do-it-yourself pancake you assemble with choices of vegetables, shrimp, fragrant herbs, and spicy dipping sauce. It is one block north and one block east of the

Karasuma-Oike intersection. ✉ *Oshikoji-dori, Higashi-ura-in, Nishi-iru 118, Nakagyo-ku* ☎ *075/253–1828* 🖃 *No credit cards* 🕲 *Closed Tues. (usually).*

$$$$ ✕ **Yoshikawa** 吉川. Adjacent to a well-reputed inn of the same name,
JAPANESE Yoshikawa serves full-course kaiseki ryori dinners. The lavish spread includes soup, vegetables, grilled or baked fish, and the light, crisp tempura that is the house specialty. Roasted duck is available for those who don't eat raw fish. Tempura dinners include 13 pieces of fried fish, meat, and vegetables. A special shabu-shabu set is offered to hotel guests, and a geisha visit can even be arranged by the hotel staff. The establishment boasts a breathtaking Enshu-style landscaped garden that greatly complements the experience. ✉ *Tomino-koji, Oike-sagaru, Nakagyo-ku* ☎ *075/221–5544* ⊕ *kyoto-yoshikawa.co.jp* ⟁ *Reservations essential* 🕲 *Closed Sun.*

$$$$ ✕ **Zezekan Pocchiri** 膳處漢 ぽっちり. Feast on Beijing-style cuisine in this
CHINESE impressive Taisho-era warehouse with antique glass windows and an inner courtyard garden. The fascinating mural of ornate *pocchiri* clasps used by geisha-like maiko-san to secure their belts gives the place its name. Evening meals include a parade of small appetizers and more-substantial dishes like spicy tofu stir-fries, chicken stews, and delicately flavored sea bream. For ¥11,000 you can order a meal inspired by Imperial Court cuisine, featuring savory Peking duck and seasonal delicacies like spiny lobster and crab stew. The detached bar stocks a good selection of Chinese aperitifs and European wines, and stays open until 11. ✉ *Nishiki-koji, Muromachi-Nishi-iru, Tenjinyama-cho 283-2* ☎ *075/257–5766* ⟁ *Reservations essential.*

ARASHIYAMA

$$$ ✕ **Bodegon** ボデゴン. This tile-floor Spanish restaurant in Arashiyama
SPANISH brings paella to a neighborhood most famous for its tofu. Nestled among the tatami-matted restaurants on the neighborhood's main drag, Bodegon combines Spanish flavors in food and wine with Kyoto hospitality. This is a great place to dine after a day of sightseeing, and you'll be happy to linger in this scenic district after the crowds thin out. ✉ *1 Susuki-no-bamba-cho, Saga, Tenryu-ji, Ukyo-ku* ☎ *075/872–9652* 🕲 *Closed Thurs.*

$$$$ ✕ **Sagano** 嵯峨野. Amid Arashiyama's lush bamboo forests, this quiet
JAPANESE retreat offers a fine example of *yudofu* cooking derived from the monastic tradition. The set meal includes delicacies like *abura-age* (fried tofu with black sesame seeds). Standing in front of a backdrop of antique woodblock prints, women in kimonos prepare your meal before your eyes. If you prefer a bit more privacy, you can walk through the garden to private rooms in the back. If weather permits, choose one of the low tables in the courtyard garden. Reservations are a good idea year-round, particularly during the peak foliage season in November. ✉ *45 Susuki-no-bamba-cho, Saga, Tenryu-ji, Ukyo-ku* ☎ *075/861–0277* 🖃 *No credit cards.*

7

NORTHERN KYOTO

$$$$
JAPANESE
★

✕ **Izusen** 泉仙. Where better to try vegetarian cuisine than in the heart of one of northern Kyoto's biggest temple complexes? In the garden of Daiji-in, a subtemple of massive Daitoku-ji, soups and sauces bring out the flavors of fu and yuba, wheat gluten and soy milk skin, alongside seasonal vegetable dishes. The monastic shojin ryori cuisine is presented in a series of red-lacquer bowls of diminishing sizes, one fitting inside another as the meal goes on. Low tables in the temple garden are perfect for soaking up the richness of the outdoors, and cheerful tatami rooms are great for inclement weather. ✉ *4 Daitoku-ji-cho, Murasakino, Kita-ku* ☎ *075/491–6665* ⊕ *kyoto-izusen.com* ⊘ *Closed Thurs.*

$$$$
JAPANESE

✕ **Kamigamo Akiyama** 上賀茂秋山. The refined menu at this rustic counter-seating restaurant showcases Kyoto's excellent home-style cooking. The lunch and dinner menus often include duck meat, river eel, or fish sashimi. Inventive desserts round out the meals, like soft mochi rice paste swirled in chocolate and roasted soybean powder. Akiyama is a few blocks east of Kamigamo Jinja along the canal. ✉ *58 Okamoto-cho, Kamigamo, Kita-ku* ☎ *075/711–5136* 🍴 *Reservations essential* ⊘ *Closed Wed. and last Thurs. of month.*

$$$$
JAPANESE
★

✕ **Yamabana Heihachi-Jaya** 山花 平八茶屋. Off the beaten path in the northeastern corner of Kyoto, this roadside inn is well known not only for its excellent full-course kaiseki ryori dinners, duck hot pots, boar stew, and delicious boxed lunches with mountain potatoes and barley rice, but also for the sauna in which patrons relax before dining. The *kamaburo* is fashioned from thick clay and heated from beneath the floor by a pine fire. After a soothing sauna, change into a cotton kimono and retire to the large dining room or an intimate private room for an exquisitely relaxing meal. This is an unforgettable way to round off a day exploring Hiei-zan and Ohara. ✉ *8–1 Kawagishi-cho, Yamabana, Sakyo-ku* ☎ *075/781–5008* ⊕ *heihachi.co.jp* 🍴 *Reservations essential.*

WHERE TO STAY

No other Japanese city can compete with Kyoto for style and grace. For the ultimate experience of Kyoto hospitality, stay in a *ryokan,* a traditional Japanese inn. Though often costly, a night in a ryokan guarantees you beautiful traditional Japanese surroundings, excellent service, and two elegant meals (breakfast and dinner) in most cases. But you don't have to limit yourself to the traditional. Kyoto is a tourist city, so accommodations range from luxurious hotels to small guesthouses. Service in this city is impeccable; the information desks are well stocked, and concierges or guest-relations managers are often available in the lobby to respond to your needs.

Hotel reviews have been condensed for this book. Please go to Fodors. com for full reviews of each property.

WHAT IT COSTS IN YEN					
	¢	$	$$	$$$	$$$$
For 2 People	under ¥8,000	¥8,000–¥12,000	¥12,000–¥18,000	¥18,000–¥22,000	over ¥22,000

Hotel prices are for a room with private bath, including service and 5% tax.

EASTERN KYOTO

$
B&B
B&B Juno. This delightful bed-and-breakfast is in a quiet residential neighborhood just north of downtown's hustle and bustle. **Pros:** great breakfast; close to good restaurants; central location. **Cons:** books up quickly; only Japanese-style rooms with shared baths are available. ☒ *Jodoji Nishidacho 115-8, Sakyo-ku* ☎ *No phone* ⊕ *www.gotokandk. com/casa.html* ↵ *3 Japanese-style rooms with shared bath* ⚒ *In-room: a/c, refrigerator. In-hotel: Wi-Fi hotspot* ▭ *No credit cards* ⦿ *Breakfast.*

$$$$
RYOKAN
★
☾
Gion Hatanaka 祇園 畑中. A stone's throw from Yasaka Jinja, this comfortable, modern ryokan is located in the heart of Gion, a location that gives you easy access to many of the temples in eastern Kyoto. **Pros:** great location; modern facilities; relaxed vibe. **Cons:** rooms short on character; basic decor. ☒ *Yasaka Jinja, Minami-mon-mae, Gion, Higashiyama-ku* ☎ *075/541–5315* ⊕ *www.thehatanaka.co.jp* ↵ *21 Japanese-style rooms* ⚒ *In-room: a/c, safe. In-hotel: restaurant* ⦿ *Some meals.*

$$$–$$$$
HOTEL
Fodor's Choice
★
Hyatt Regency ハイアットリージェンシー京都」. The central location and friendly staff make the Hyatt Regency the city's best luxury hotel. **Pros:** terrific staff; great location; extravagant Continental breakfast. **Cons:** somber exterior; chain-hotel feel. ☒ *644–2 Sanjusangen-do-mawari, Higashiyama-ku* ☎ *075/541–1234* ⊕ *kyoto.regency.hyatt.jp* ↵ *184 rooms* ⚒ *In-room: a/c, safe, refrigerator, DVD, Internet. In-hotel: 4 restaurants, bar, gym, spa, laundry service* ⦿ *No meals.*

$
RYOKAN
Ryokan Yuhara 旅館ゆはら. Drawing many repeat visitors, the Ryokan Yuhara lets you save a few yen while exploring Kyoto. **Pros:** friendly innkeepers; family-friendly atmosphere. **Cons:** strict curfew; all shared bathrooms. ☒ *188 Kagiya-cho, Shomen-agaru, Kiya-machi-dori, Higashiyama-ku* ☎ *075/371–9583* ↵ *10 Japanese-style rooms with shared bath* ⚒ *In-room: a/c, safe* ⦿ *No meals.*

$$$–$$$$
HOTEL
Westin Miyako Hotel ウエティン都ホテル. Located at the foot of the mountains, the Westin Miyako feels far from the city while retaining great access to downtown (the Keage subway stop is nearby). **Pros:** free transfer from Kyoto Station; good restaurants; helpful concierge. **Cons:** far from downtown. ☒ *Sanjo-Keage, Higashiyama-ku* ☎ *075/771–7111* ⊕ *www.westinmiyako-kyoto.com* ↵ *320 rooms* ⚒ *In-room: a/c, Internet. In-hotel: 9 restaurants, bars, pools, gym* ⦿ *No meals.*

$$$–$$$$
RYOKAN
Yachiyo 八千代. An excellent traditional ryokan, Yachio is known for its impressive garden, eager staff, and excellent meals. **Pros:** lavish bathrooms; lots of space; Western breakfast option. **Cons:** not all rooms have views. ☒ *34 Nanzenji-Fukuchi-cho, Sakyo-ku* ☎ *075/771–4148* ⊕ *www.ryokan-yachiyo.com* ↵ *25 rooms, 20 with bath* ⚒ *In-room: a/c, safe. In-hotel: restaurant* ⦿ *Some meals.*

7

Fodor'sChoice ★

Hyatt Regency Kyoto

Kyoto Brighton

Hotel Granvia Kyoto

CENTRAL KYOTO

$$$-$$$$
HOTEL

🖬 **ANA Hotel Kyoto** 京都全日空ホテル. This is not the best of the city's chain hotels, though the hallways were recently refurbished. But the location, directly across from Nijo Castle, is dynamite. **Pros:** ideal location; near shopping. **Cons:** stale decor; shabby carpeting. ⊠ *Nijo-jo-mae, Horikawa-dori, Nakagyo-ku* ☎ *075/231–1155* ⊕ *www.ana-hkyoto.com* ⟿ *303 rooms* ⌂ *In-room: a/c, safe, refrigerator. In-hotel: 7 restaurants, bar, pool, gym* ⦿❙ *No meals.*

$$$$
RYOKAN

🖬 **Hiiragiya** 柊家旅館. Join the ranks of celebrities, aristocrats, and royalty who have lodged under the holly-leaf crest of this elegant inn. **Pros:** excellent location; multilingual staff; holly-infused soaps and bath oils. **Cons:** meal plans not very flexible. ⊠ *Nakahakusan-cho, Fuyacho-Anekoji-agaru, Nakagyo-ku* ☎ *075/221–1139* ⊕ *www.hiiragiya.co.jp* ⟿ *28 Japanese-style rooms* ⌂ *In-room: a/c, safe, refrigerator, Internet. In-hotel: room service, laundry facilities* ⦿❙ *Some meals.*

$$$-$$$$
HOTEL

🖬 **Hotel Fujita Kyoto** ホテルフジタ京都. Reasonable rates and river views make this hotel a good bargain. **Pros:** near nightlife; close to the sights; quiet rooms. **Cons:** could use refurbishing; not the most multilingual staff. ⊠ *Kamogawa Nijo-ohashi Tamoto, Nakagyo-ku* ☎ *075/222–1511* ⊕ *www.fujita-kyoto.com* ⟿ *189 rooms* ⌂ *In-room: a/c, safe, refrigerator. In-hotel: 6 restaurants, bar* ⦿❙ *No meals.*

$$$-$$$$
HOTEL
Fodor'sChoice
★
☾

🖬 **Hotel Granvia Kyoto** ホテルグランヴィア京都. A fusion of ultramodern design with traditional Japanese style is what you'll find at this popular hotel above Kyoto Station. **Pros:** good location; interesting architecture; plenty of amenities. **Cons:** charge for pool and gym; crowded area. ⊠ *Kyoto Station, Karasuma Chuo-guchi Shiokoji-sagaru Karasuma-dori, Shimogyo-ku* ☎ *075/344–8888* ⊕ *www.granvia-kyoto.co.jp/e/index.html* ⟿ *539 rooms* ⌂ *In-room: a/c, Internet. In-hotel: restaurant, pool, gym* ⦿❙ *No meals.*

$$$$
RYOKAN
★

🖬 **Kinmata** 斤又. Only a few hundred feet from the bustling thoroughfare of Shijo-dori, this high-class ryokan offers a trip back in time. **Pros:** antique furnishings; authentic construction; great location. **Cons:** tough futons; unofficial midnight curfew; no private baths; books up fast. ⊠ *Goko-machi Shijo Agaru, Nakagyo-ku* ☎ *075/221–1039* ⊕ *www.kinmata.com* ⟿ *7 Japanese-style rooms with shared bath* ⌂ *In-room: a/c. In-hotel: restaurant* ⦿❙ *Some meals.*

¢–$
HOTEL

🖬 **K's House Kyoto** ケイズハウス京都. True, K's House bills itself first and foremost as a backpacker hostel, but the modern architecture, smart facilities, helpful multilingual staff, and central location make it a great find. **Pros:** clean facilities; cheap all-you-can-eat buffet; chance to meet fellow travelers. **Cons:** rooms are small; spartan decor; towels must be rented except in en-suite rooms; only a minority of rooms have private baths. ⊠ *418 Nayacho, Shichijo-agaru, Dotemachi-dori, Shimogyo-ku* ☎ *075/342–2444* ⊕ *kshouse.jp* ⟿ *140 rooms* ⌂ *In-room: a/c, no phone, safe. In-hotel: bicycles, laundry facilities, Internet terminal, Wi-Fi hotspot* ⦿❙ *No meals.*

$$$$
HOTEL
Fodor'sChoice
★
☾

🖬 **Kyoto Brighton Hotel** 京都ブライトンホテル. One of the city's best hotels, the Kyoto Brighton has an elegant design sense and thorough dedication to good hospitality. **Pros:** conscientious staff; great decor; great restaurants. **Cons:** expensive rates. ⊠ *Nakadachiuri,*

7

Shin-machi-dori, Kamigyo-ku ☎ *075/441–4411, 800/223–6800 in U.S.* ⊕ *www.brightonhotels.co.jp* ⇗ *183 rooms, 2 suites* ⮣ *In-room: a/c, safe, refrigerator, Internet. In-hotel: 5 restaurants, bars, pool, spa* ⍰ *No meals.*

$$$–$$$$
HOTEL
☺   🏨 **Kyoto Kokusai Hotel** 京都国際ホテル. A location just across the street from Nijo Castle provides excellent views from the rooftop lounge and many of the rooms. **Pros:** convenient access to public transportation; good facilities. **Cons:** some rooms overdue for renovation. ✉ *Nijojo-mae, Horikawa-dori, Nakagyo-ku* ☎ *075/222–1111* ⊕ *kyoto-kokusai. com* ⇗ *277 rooms* ⮣ *In-room: a/c, safe, refrigerator. In-hotel: 5 restaurants, bar* ⍰ *No meals.*

$–$$
RYOKAN   🏨 **Matsubaya Ryokan** 松葉家旅館. This simple ryokan welcomed its first guest, a monk from the nearby temple, in 1884. You won't find kimono-clad attendants here, but you also won't find wallet-emptying rates. **Pros:** friendly staff; cheap and tasty breakfast. **Cons:** bland rooms; staff speaks little English; dinner not available. ✉ *Kamijuzuya-machi-dori, Higashi Nito-in, Nishi-iru, Shimogyo-ku* ☎ *075/351–3727* ⊕ *www. matsubayainn.com* ⇗ *8 Japanese-style rooms, 7 with bath* ⮣ *In-room: a/c, safe, refrigerator, Wi-Fi. In-hotel: laundry facilities, Internet terminal, parking (paid)* ⍰ *No meals.*

$$$$
HOTEL
☺   🏨 **New Miyako Hotel** 新都ホテル. This gleaming white edifice with two protruding wings looks like it would be at home in any American city. **Pros:** friendly staff; pleasant facilities. **Cons:** slightly stuffy room decor. ✉ *17 Nishi-Kujoin-cho, Minami-ku* ☎ *075/661–7111* ⊕ *www. miyakohotels.ne.jp/newmiyako* ⇗ *714 rooms* ⮣ *In-room: a/c, safe, refrigerator, Internet. In-hotel: 4 restaurants, bars* ⍰ *No meals*

$$$–$$$$
RYOKAN   🏨 **Nishiyama Ryokan** 西山旅館. A central location, friendly staff, and surprisingly top-notch kaiseki and hot-pot dinners make this hotel a good find. **Pros:** helpful concierge; flexible meal plans. **Cons:** thin futons; cramped, shared bathrooms. ✉ *Goko-machi-dori, Nijo-sagaru, Nakagyo-ku* ☎ *075/222–1166* ⊕ *www.ryokan-kyoto.com* ⇗ *34 Japanese-style rooms, 1 Western-style room, all with shared bath* ⮣ *In-room: a/c, safe, refrigerator. In-hotel: restaurant, laundry facilities, Internet terminal* ⍰ *No meals*

¢–$
HOTEL
★
☺   🏨 **Palace Side Hotel** パレスサイドホテル. A great option for travelers on a budget, this hotel has a good location, convenient access to public transportation, and a very helpful, multilingual concierge. **Pros:** very reasonable rates; central location; massage therapists on call. **Cons:** lots of wear and tear; cramped bathrooms; lousy Continental breakfast. ✉ *Karasuma-dori, Shimo-dachiuri-agaru, Kamigyo-ku* ☎ *075/415–8887* ⊕ *www.palacesidehotel.co.jp* ⇗ *120 rooms* ⮣ *In-room: a/c, kitchen (some). In-hotel: restaurant, Internet terminal* ⍰ *No meals*

$$$$
HOTEL
☺   🏨 **Rihga Royal Hotel Kyoto** リーガロイヤルホテル京都. Even the smallest rooms at this well-established chain hotel are warm and inviting, with delicate shoji windows and elegant bath furnishings. **Pros:** close to the station; deluxe rooms; excellent decor. **Cons:** ¥2,500 extra for pool and sauna. ✉ *1-Taimatsucho, Shiokoji-sagaru, Higashi Horikawa-dori, Shimogyo-ku* ☎ *075/341–1121, 800/877–7107 in U.S.* ⊕ *www.rihga. com* ⇗ *494 rooms* ⮣ *In-room: a/c, Internet. In-hotel: 6 restaurants, bar, pool* ⍰ *No meals.*

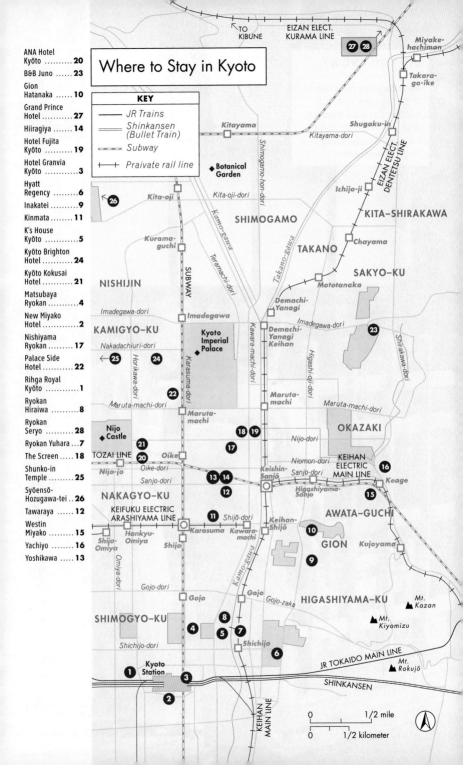

Where to Stay in Kyoto

KEY

— JR Trains

═ Shinkansen
(Bullet Train)

╍ Subway

╋ Praivate rail line

TO KIBUNE

EIZAN ELECT. KURAMA LINE

Miyake-hachiman

Takara-ga-ike

Shugaku-in

EIZAN ELECT. DENTETSU LINE

Kitayama

Kitayama-dori

◆ Botanical Garden

Shimogamo-hon-dori

Ichijo-ji

KITA–SHIRAKAWA

Kita-oji

Kita-oji-dori

SHIMOGAMO

Kamo-gawa

Chayama

TAKANO

SAKYO-KU

Kurama-guchi

SUBWAY

Teramachi-dori

Takano-gawa

Mototanaka

Shirakawa-dori

NISHIJIN

Imadegawa-dori

Imadegawa

Demachi-Yanagi

Imadegawa-dori

KAMIGYO-KU

Nakadachiuri-dori

Kyoto Imperial Palace

Kawara-machi-dori

Demachi-Yanagi Keihan

Higashi-oji-dori

Horikawa-dori

Karasuma-dori

Maruta-machi

Maruta-machi-dori

OKAZAKI

Maruta-machi-dori

Maruta-machi

Nijo-dori

KEIHAN ELECTRIC MAIN LINE

Nijo Castle ◆

Oike

Niomon-dori

Sanjo-dori

Keage

TOZAI LINE

Nijo-jo

Oike-dori

Sanjo-dori

Keishin-Sanjo

Higashiyama-Sanjo

NAKAGYO-KU

AWATA-GUCHI

KEIFUKU ELECTRIC ARASHIYAMA LINE

Shijō-dori

Keihan-Shijo

GION

Kujoyama

Hankyu-Omiya

Shijo-Omiya

Karasuma

Kawara-machi

Shijo

Omiya-dori

Kamo-gawa

Gojo-dori

Gojo

Gojo

Gojo-zaka

HIGASHIYAMA-KU

Mt. Kazan

SHIMOGYO-KU

Shichijo-dori

Shichijo

Mt. Kiyomizu

Kyoto Station

JR TOKAIDO MAIN LINE

Mt. Rokujō

SHINKANSEN

KEIHAN MAIN LINE

MAIN LINE

0 ——— 1/2 mile
0 ——— 1/2 kilometer

DID YOU KNOW?

Tawaraya is the most famous of Kyoto's many ryokan. It was founded more than 300 years ago and is still run by the same Okazaki family, now 11 generations later.

$ **Ryokan Hiraiwa** 旅館平岩. One of several budget lodgings near the
RYOKAN Takase-gawa, Ryokan Hiraiwa appeals to travelers seeking the traditional feeling of tatami-mat rooms. **Pros:** easy access to many sights;
friendly staff. **Cons:** bland rooms; only a few private baths. ✉ *314
Hayao-cho Kaminokuchi-agaru, Ninomiyacho-dori, Shiogyo-ku*
☎ *075/351–6748* ⇄ *18 Japanese-style rooms* ⚮ *In-room: a/c, safe,
refrigerator. In-hotel: restaurant, laundry facilites, Internet terminal*
🍽 *No meals.*

$$$–$$$$ **The Screen** ザスクリーン. This personalized boutique hotel has gained
HOTEL a foothold in this competitive market thanks to its chic interiors. **Pros:**
good location; close to boutiques; pampering feel. **Cons:** restaurant
service can be slow. ✉ *640–1 Shimogoryomae-cho, Nakagyo-ku*
☎ *075/252–1113* ⊕ *www.screen-hotel.jp* ⇄ *13 rooms* ⚮ *In-room: a/c,
safe, refrigerator, DVD. In-hotel: restaurant, room service, bar, spa,
Internet terminal* 🍽 *No Meals.*

$$$$ **Tawaraya** 俵屋. The most famous of Kyoto's traditional inns, Tawa-
RYOKAN raya has been host to dignitaries, presidents, and royalty. **Pros:** excellent
Fodor'sChoice reputation; doting, incomparable service. **Cons:** extremely expensive;
★ must reserve dinner a day in advance. ✉ *Fuyacho-Aneyakoji-agaru,
Nakahakusan-cho, Nakagyo-ku* ☎ *075/211–5566* ⇄ *18 Japanese-
style rooms* ⚮ *In-room: a/c, Internet. In-hotel: laundry service* 🍽 *Some
meals.*

$$$$ **Yoshikawa** 吉川. This traditional inn is within walking distance of
RYOKAN the downtown shopping area. **Pros:** excellent indoor garden; terrific
meals. **Cons:** expensive rates; fixed meal times. ✉ *Tomino-koji, Oike-
sagaru, Nakagyo-ku* ☎ *075/221–5544* ⊕ *kyoto-yoshikawa.co.jp* ⇄ *9
Japanese-style rooms* ⚮ *In-room: a/c, Internet. In-hotel: restaurant*
🍽 *Some meals.*

WESTERN KYOTO

$ **Shunko-in Temple.** Visiting Kyoto's temples gives you a taste of the
TEMPLE city's history, but staying in one is a more intimate way of experiencing
the past. **Pros:** insider tour; plenty of atmosphere. **Cons:** modern rooms;
books up fast; no meal service of any kind on premises. ✉ *42 Myoshinji-
cho, Hanazono, Ukyo-ku* ☎ *075/462–5488* ⊕ *www.shunkoin.com* ⇄ *6
Japanese-style rooms, 2 with bath* ⚮ *In-room: a/c, no TV* ⊟ *No credit
cards* 🍽 *No meals.*

$$$$ **Syoenso-Hozugawa-tei** 松園荘保津川亭. In the mountains northwest
RYOKAN of Kyoto, this ryokan allows you to soak in your own *rotemburo* (out-
door hot tub) overlooking a private garden. **Pros:** healthful hot springs;
mountain views. **Cons:** far from city center; expensive rates; no private
baths. ✉ *Yunohana-onsen, Kameoka City* ☎ *0771/22–0903* ⊕ *www.
syoenso.com* ⇄ *56 Japanese-style rooms, all with shared bath* ⚮ *In-
room: a/c, safe. In-hotel: restaurant* 🍽 *Some meals.*

NORTHERN KYOTO

$$$–$$$$ **Grand Prince Hotel** グランドプリンスホテル京都. Although some dis-
HOTEL tance north of the city center, the deluxe Prince Hotel is regal enough to
make you feel like visiting royalty. **Pros:** excellent breakfast; responsive

7

staff. **Cons:** far from the city's sights; dated decor. ✉ *Takaraga-ike, Sakyo-ku* ☎ *075/712–1111, 800/542–8686 in U.S.* ⊕ *www.princejapan. com* ⇨ *309 rooms* ♿ *In-room: a/c, safe, refrigerator, Wi-Fi. In-hotel: 4 restaurants, bar* ⏐◯⏐ *No meals.*

$$$–$$$$
RYOKAN
⚏ **Ryokan Seryo** 芹生. After a long day of sightseeing, there is nothing more relaxing than an outdoor natural hot spring in the mountains. **Pros:** peaceful atmosphere; great food. **Cons:** far from the city; communal hot spring is open to the public during business hours. ✉ *22 Shorinin-cho, Ohara, Sakyo-ku* ☎ *075/744–2301* ⊕ *www.seryo.co.jp* ⇨ *7 Japanese-style rooms,(3 with bath; 1 Western-style room* ♿ *In-room: a/c, safe. In-hotel: restaurant* ⏐◯⏐ *Some meals.*

NIGHTLIFE AND THE ARTS

THE ARTS

Kyoto is known for its traditional performances—particularly dance and Noh theater. All dialogue is in Japanese, but sometimes there are synopses available. From time to time world-class musicians play the intimate venues, including David Lindley, Ron Sexsmith, and Michelle Shocked. The most convenient source for information is your hotel concierge or guest-relations manager, who may even have a few tickets on hand. For further information on Kyoto's arts scene check the music and theater sections of the monthly magazine *Kansai Scene,* at bookshops for ¥300; you can also find information on the Web site ⊕ *www.kanseiscene.com.* Another source is the *Kyoto Visitor's Guide* (*see* ⇨ *Visitor Information, above*), which devotes a few pages to "This Month's Theater." Look at the festival listings for temple and shrine performances. It's available free from the Kyoto Tourist Information Center on the ninth floor of the Kyoto Station Building; the staff can also provide you with information.

PERFORMING ARTS COMPLEXES
EASTERN KYOTO

Gion Corner Theater ギオンコーナ. Some call it a tourist trap, but for others it's a comprehensive introduction to Japanese performing arts. The one-hour show here combines court music and dance, ancient comic plays, Kyoto-style dance performed by maiko (apprentice geisha), and puppet drama. Segments are also offered on the tea ceremony, flower arranging, and koto music. Before attending a show, walk around Gion and Ponto-cho. You're likely to see beautifully dressed geisha and maiko on their way to work. It's permissible to take their picture—"*Shashin o tottemo ii desu ka?*"—but as they have strict appointments, don't delay them.

For tickets, contact your hotel concierge or call the theater directly. The show costs ¥3,150—a bargain considering that it would usually cost 10 times as much to watch maiko and geisha perform. Two performances are held nightly at 7 and 8, from March through November. No performances are offered August 16. ✉ *Gion Hanami-koji, Higashiyama-ku* ☎ *075/561–1119.*

The Saio-dai, an unmarried woman, represents the Emperor in the Aoi (Hollyhock) Matsuri, which takes place in mid-May.

SEASONAL DANCES

In the **Miyako Odori** in April and the **Kamo-gawa Odori** in May and October, geisha and maiko dances and songs pay tribute to the seasonal splendor of spring and fall. The stage settings are spectacular.

EASTERN KYOTO

Gion Kaburenjo Theater 祇園歌舞練場. Tickets to performances at this theater cost from ¥2,000 to ¥4,500. ☒ *Gion Hanami-koji, Higashiyama-ku* ☏ *075/561–1115.*

CENTRAL KYOTO

Ponto-cho Kaburenjo Theater 先斗町歌舞伎練場. Tickets to performances cost between ¥2,000 and ¥4,000. ☒ *Ponto-cho, Sanjo-sagaru, Nakagyo-ku* ☏ *075/221–2025.*

KABUKI

Kabuki developed in the Edo era as a theatrical art with lavish costumes and sets and dynamic all-male performances. Though Kabuki is faster-paced than Noh, a single performance can easily take half a day. Devotees pack bentos to eat while watching shows. Kyoto hosts traveling Kabuki performances periodically, since most of the troupes are based in Tokyo. Especially anticipated in Kyoto is the annual month-long **Kaomise** *(Face Showing)* Kabuki Festival in December, featuring top Kabuki stars and introducing upcoming artists. Tickets range from ¥5,500 to ¥27,000 and need to be booked weeks in advance.

EASTERN KYOTO

Minami-za 南座. The beautifully renovated theater, the oldest in Japan, hosts Kabuki performances year-round. ☒ *Shijo Kamo-gawa, Higashiyama-ku* ☏ *075/561–1155.*

NOH

Kyoto is the home of Japan's most ancient form of traditional theater, Noh, which is more ritualistic and sophisticated than Kabuki. Some understanding of the plot of each play is necessary to enjoy a performance, which is generally slow-moving and solemnly chanted. The carved masks used by the main actors express a whole range of emotions, though the mask itself may appear expressionless until the actor "brings it to life." Noh performances are held year-round and range from ¥3,000 to ¥13,000. Particularly memorable are outdoor Noh performances, especially **Takigi Noh**, held outdoors by firelight on the nights of June 1 and 2 in the precincts of the Heian Jingu. For more information about performances, contact the Kyoto Tourist Information Center.

EASTERN KYOTO

Kanze Kaikan Noh Theater 観世会館. This is the oldest of Kyoto's Noh theaters, and it sometimes hosts Noh orientation talks. The theater does not offer programs in English. ⊠ *44 Enshoji-cho, Okazaki, Sakyo-ku* ☎ *075/771–6114.*

CENTRAL KYOTO

Oe Nogakudo 大江能楽堂. Only a five minute walk from the Karasuma subway station, this is an intimate theater with a beautiful wooden interior (though seating is scarce). ⊠ *Oshikoji-dori, Nakagyo-ku* ☎ *075/ 561–0622.*

Shin Kongo Noh Theater 金剛能楽堂. This is the only Kongo-style Noh theater in Japan. ⊠ *Karasuma-dori, Ichijo-sagaru, Kamigyo-ku* ☎ *075/ 441–7222.*

NIGHTLIFE

Though Kyoto's nightlife is more sedate than Osaka's, the areas around the old geisha quarters downtown thrive with nightclubs and bars. The Kiya-machi area along the small canal near Ponto-cho in central Kyoto is packed full of bars, restaurants, and a few dance clubs and is as close to a consolidated nightlife area as you'll get in Kyoto. It's full of small watering holes with red lanterns (indicating inexpensive places) or small neon signs in front. It's also fun to walk around the Gion in eastern Kyoto and Ponto-cho in central Kyoto to try to catch a glimpse of a geisha or maiko stealing down an alleyway on her way to or from an appointment.

BARS AND CLUBS

EASTERN KYOTO

A-Bar. This tucked-away gem is located one block west of Kiyamachi-dori and three blocks north of nearby Shijo-dori on the second floor of the Reiho building. With its wood-paneling, the one-room izakaya doesn't look like much, but it regularly fills up with a healthy mix of expats and locals. It's a great place to share your stories with fellow travelers as the long communal tables guarantee you a chance to make new friends. Watch out for flying bottle caps, though; the popular manager, Tsue, has a knack for popping open beer bottles with chopsticks (he has been featured on TV for this talent). Cash only, and it opens at

Metro is one of the best music clubs in the Kansai region.

5. ✉ *Reiho Bulding 2F, Nishi Kiyamachi-dori, Nakagyo-ku, Shijo-agaru* ☎ *075/213–2129* ⊕ *a-bar.net.*

★ **The Gail Irish Pub** ゲールアイリッシュパブ. North of the Minami-za theater in Gion, this convivial pub entertains patrons with Irish music and sporting events on TV. Have a chat with the locals to find out what's happening around town. If you want more than a drink, the menu offers classic fish-and-chips, plus Irish stew and a beef-and-Guinness pie. ✉ *2F 236 Otobiru, Nijuichiken-cho, Yamat-oji, Kawabata Shijo-agaru* ☎ *075/525–0680* ⊕ *www.tadgspub.com.*

★ **Metro** クラブメトロ. One of the best clubs in Kansai, Metro has an extremely wide range of regular events, from salsa to reggae, as well as frequent guest appearances by famous DJs from Tokyo and abroad. ✉ *2F Ebisu Bldg., 82 Shimotsutsumi-cho, Maruta-machi-sagaru, Kawabata-dori, Sakyo-ku* ☎ *075/752–4765* ⊕ *www.metro.ne.jp.*

CENTRAL KYOTO

Café Independants カフェエンデパンダン. As its name suggests, this bar hosts a spectrum of indie rock, jazz, and blues artists, making it a good place to tap into the underground music scene. Trestle tables line the graffiti-covered walls of this basement venue with some tasty dishes on offer. The café also usually has fluent English-speaking staff on hand. ✉ *1928 Bldg., Sanjo-dori, Goko-machi, Nakagyo-ku* ☎ *075/255–4312* ⊕ *cafe-independants.com.*

Le Club Jazz ルクラブジャズ. You can hear live jazz, blues, and soul gigs on Tuesday, and jam sessions every night from Thursday to Monday. There's a ¥2,000 cover charge on weekends, which includes two drinks. The club is diagonally opposite Café Independents, near the bustling west entrance of the Tera-machi shopping arcade. ✉ *2F Sanjo Arimoto Bldg., Sanjo-Goko-machi Nishi-iru, Kamigyo-ku* ☎ *075/211–5800.*

★ **Taku Taku** ライブハウス磔磔. This bar is an enduring live-music venue, tending toward rock and blues, that occasionally features some stellar performers. You can find it in an old kura, or storehouse, in the backstreets southwest of the Takashimaya department store. ✉ *Tominokoji-dori, Bukkoji-sagaru, Shimogyo-ku* ☎ *075/351–1321.*

Yoramu ヨラム. Israeli sake aficionado Yoram has an extensive range of the delicate rice wine, from unfiltered to aged, fruity to dry, all available by the glass. A tasting set of three kinds of sake starts at ¥1,200. The dishes on the menu have all been chosen to complement the drink. The cozy bar is south of Nijo-dori, east of Higashino-toin-dori. During the day it's a soba shop run by Yoram's partner. ✉ *Nijo-dori, Nakagyo-ku* ☎ *075/ 213–1512.* ⊕ *sakebar-yoramu.com* ⊘ *Closed Sun.–Tues.*

SHOPPING

Most shops slide their doors open at 10, and many shopkeepers partake of the morning ritual of sweeping and watering the entrance to welcome the first customers. Shops lock up at 6 or 7 in the evening. Stores often close sporadically once or twice a month (closings are irregular), so it helps to call in advance if you're making a special trip. On weekends downtown can be very crowded.

A shopkeeper's traditional greeting to a customer is *o-ideyasu* (Kyoto-ben, the Kyoto dialect, for "honored to have you here"), voiced in the lilting Kyoto intonations with the required bowing of the head. When a customer makes a purchase, the shopkeeper will respond with *o-okini* ("thank you" in Kyoto-ben), a smile, and a bow. Take notice of the careful effort and adroitness with which purchases are wrapped; it's an art in itself. American Express, MasterCard, Visa, and to a lesser degree traveler's checks, are widely accepted.

Kyoto's *depato* (department stores) are small in comparison to their mammoth counterparts in Tokyo and Osaka. They still carry a wide range of goods and are great places for one-stop souvenir shopping. Wandering around the food halls is a good way to build up an appetite. Prices drop dramatically during end-of-season sales. You can call at the beginning of the month to find out about scheduled closures.

Kyoto has several popular seasonal fairs, from local area pottery sales to the national antiques fairs, usually held in May, June, and October. Several temple markets take place in Kyoto each month. These are great places to pick up bargain kimonos or unusual souvenirs. They're also some of the best spots for people-watching.

SHOPPING DISTRICTS

Kyoto is compact and relatively easy to navigate. Major shops line both sides of **Shijo-dori,** which runs east–west, and **Kawara-machi-dori,** which runs north–south. Concentrate on Shijo-dori between Yasaka Jinja and Karasuma Station as well as Kawara-machi-dori between

Sanjo-dori and Shijo-dori. Some of modern Kyoto's shopping districts are near Kyoto Station in central Kyoto. **Porta** ポルタ, under Kyoto Station, hosts more than 200 shops and restaurants in a sprawling subterranean arcade. **Aeon Mall** イオンモール is very new and has the feel of a large Western mall. Along with a lot more you can catch a movie, go to The Gap, or even eat ribs at Tony Roma's. It's on the south side of Kyoto Station.

Roads leading to **Kiyomizu-dera** run uphill, yet you may hardly notice the steepness for all of the alluring shops that line the way. Be sure to peek in for unique gifts. Food shops offer sample morsels, and tea shops serve complimentary cups of tea.

SHUINCHO

The *shuincho* is a booklet usually no larger than 4 by 6 inches, usually covered with brocade, composed of blank sheets of heavyweight paper that continuously fold out. You can find them at gift stores or at temples for as little as ¥1,000. Use them to collect ink stamps from places you visit while in Japan. Stamps and stamp pads are ubiquitous in Japan—at sights, train stations, and some restaurants. Most stamps are given for free; at temples monks will write calligraphy over the stamp for a small fee.

Shin-Kyogoku, a covered arcade running between Tera-machi-dori and Kawara-machi-dori, is another general-purpose shopping area with many souvenir shops.

EASTERN KYOTO
ART AND ANTIQUES

There are several places in eastern Kyoto that are good destinations if you are looking for antiques. **Nawate-dori,** in eastern Kyoto's Higashiyama-ku between Shijo-dori and Sanjo-dori, is noted for fine antique textiles, ceramics, and paintings.

Shinmonzen-dori, also in Higashiyama-ku, holds the key to shopping for art and antiques in Kyoto. It's an unpretentious little street of two-story wooden buildings between Higashi-oji-dori and Hanami-koji-dori, just north of Gion. What gives the street away as a treasure trove are the large credit-card signs jutting out from the shops. There are no fewer than 17 shops specializing in scrolls, *netsuke* (small carved figures to attach to Japanese clothing), lacquerware, bronze, woodblock prints, paintings, and antiques. Shop with confidence, because shopkeepers are trustworthy and goods are authentic. Pick up a copy of the pamphlet *Shinmonzen Street Shopping Guide* from your hotel or from the Kyoto Tourist Information Center.

BAMBOO

The Japanese wish their sons and daughters to be as strong and flexible as bamboo. Around many Japanese houses are small bamboo groves, for the deep-rooted plant withstands earthquakes. On the other hand, bamboo is so flexible it can bend into innumerable shapes. Bamboo groves used to flourish on the hillsides surrounding Kyoto, but the groves are in decline. The wood is carefully cut and dried for several months before being stripped and woven into baskets and vases.

Kagoshin かごしん. This store has been in operation since 1862. Basket weavers here use more than 50 varieties of bamboo in intricate designs. ⊠ *Ohashi-higashi, Sanjo-dori, Higashiyama-ku* ☎ *075/771–0209* ⊗ *Mon.–Sat. 9–6.*

CERAMICS

Asahi-do 朝日堂. In the heart of the pottery district near Kiyomizu-dera, Asahi-do specializes in Kyoto-style hand-painted porcelain, and offers the widest selection of any pottery store in the area. ⊠ *1–280 Kiyomizu, Higashiyama-ku* ☎ *075/531–2181* ⊗ *Daily 9–6.*

DOLLS

Ningyo were first used in Japan in the purification rites associated with the Doll Festival, an annual family-oriented event on March 3. Kyoto ningyo are made with fine detail and embellishment.

Nakanishi Toku Shoten 中西京子商店. This store sells old museum-quality dolls. The owner, Mr. Nakanishi, turned his extensive doll collection into the shop two decades ago and has since been educating customers with his vast knowledge of the doll trade. ⊠ *359 Moto-cho, Yamato-oji Higashi-iru, Furumonzen-dori, Higashiyama-ku* ☎ *075/561–7309* ⊗ *Daily 10–5.*

KIMONOS AND ACCESSORIES

Kasagen 傘元. Umbrellas protect kimonos from the scorching sun or pelting rain. Head for Kasagen to purchase authentic oiled-paper umbrellas. The shop has been around since 1861, and its umbrellas are guaranteed to last for years. ⊠ *284 Gion-machi, Kitagawa, Higashiyama-ku* ☎ *075/561–2832* ⊗ *Daily 10–9.*

LACQUERWARE

Monju 文殊. Monju sells authentic lacquered trays, bowls, incense holders, and tea containers. Unlike the inexpensive, plastic, faux lacquerware sold at some souvenir shops, real lacquerware has a wooden base, which is then coated with natural lacquer made from the Asian sumac tree. Gold and silver powder is used in the more lavish *maki-e* lacquerware. You can even buy chopsticks with their own carrying case to use instead of the disposable ones supplied in restaurants. This shop is on Shijo-dori in Gion. ⊠ *Hanami-koji Higashi-iru, Shijo-dori, Higashiyama-ku* ☎ *075/525–1617* ⊗ *Fri.–Wed. 10:30–7:30.*

TEMPLE MARKETS

Chion-in 知恩院. A market specializing in homemade goods is held here on the 15th of each month. To get to the Chion-in market, take Bus 206 from Kyoto Station to Hyakumanben. ⊠ *400 Hayashi-shita-cho 3-chome, Yamato-oji, Higashi-hairu, Shimbashi-dori, Higashiyama-ku.*

CENTRAL KYOTO

ART AND ANTIQUES

Tera-machi-dori, between Oike-dori and Maruta-machi in Nakagyo-ku, is known for antiques of all kinds and tea-ceremony utensils.

CERAMICS

Tachikichi たち吉. This store on Shijo-dori west of Kawara-machi has five floors full of contemporary and antique ceramics. One floor is an art gallery that hosts exhibits of very fine ceramics by Japanese and

CLOSE UP

Kyoto Crafts

Temples, shrines, and gardens can't be taken home with you. You can, however, pack up a few *omiyage* (mementos) for which this city is famous. The ancient craftspeople of Kyoto served the Imperial Court for more than 1,000 years, and the prefix *kyo-* before a craft is synonymous with fine craftsmanship.

Kyo-ningyo, exquisite display dolls, have been made in Kyoto since the 9th century. Constructed of wood coated with white shell paste and clothed in elaborate, miniature patterned-silk brocades, Kyoto dolls are considered the finest in Japan. Kyoto is also known for fine ceramic dolls and *Kyo-gangu*, its local varieties of folk toys.

Kyo-sensu are embellished folding fans used as accoutrements in Noh theater, tea ceremonies, and Japanese dance. They also have a practical use—to keep you cool. Unlike other Japanese crafts, which have their origin in Tang Dynasty China, the folding fan originated in Kyoto.

Kyo-shikki refers to Kyoto lacquerware, which also has its roots in the 9th century. The making of lacquerware, adopted from the Chinese, is a delicate process requiring patience and skill. Finished lacquerware products range from furniture to spoons and bowls, which are carved from cypress, cedar, or horse-chestnut wood. These pieces have a brilliant luster; some designs are decorated with gold leaf and inlaid mother-of-pearl.

Kyo-yaki is the general term applied to ceramics made in local kilns; the most popular ware is from Kyoto's Kiyomizu district. Often colorfully hand-painted in blue, red, and green on white, these elegantly shaped teacups, bowls, and vases are thrown on potters' wheels located in the Kiyomizu district and in Kiyomizu-danchi in Yamashina. Streets leading up to Kiyomizu-dera—Chawan-zaka, Sannen-zaka, and Ninen-zaka—are sprinkled with kyo-yaki shops.

Kyo-yuzen is a paste-resist silk-dyeing technique developed by 17th-century dyer Yuzen Miyazaki. Fantastic designs are created on plain white silk pieces through the process of either *tegaki yuzen* (hand-painting) or *kata yuzen* (stenciling).

Nishijin-ori is the weaving of silk. *Nishijin* refers to a Kyoto district producing the best silk textiles in all Japan, which are used to make kimonos. Walk along the narrow backstreets of Nishijin and listen to the persistently rhythmic looms.

7

---

international artists. In business since 1872, Tachikichi has an excellent reputation. ⊠ *Shijo-dori, Tominokoji, Nakagyo-ku* ☎ *075/255–3507* ⊕ *tachikichi.co.jp* ☉ *Thurs.–Tues. 10–7.*

DEPARTMENT STORES

Daimaru 大丸. This store mainly appeals to more expensive and conservative tastes, and is on the main Shijo-dori shopping avenue. Its basement food hall is the best in town. ⊠ *Shijo-Karasuma, Shimogyo-ku* ☎ *075/211–8111* ☉ *Daily 10–7:30.*

Fujii Daimaru 藤井大丸. This store, directly opposite the Tera-machi mall on Shijo-dori, is a funkier branch of the old matron Daimaru. ⊠ *Shijo-Tera-machi, Shimogyo-ku* ☎ *075/211–8181* ☉ *Daily 10–8.*

Isetan 伊勢丹. This department store in the Kyoto Station Building has 13 floors, including a restaurant floor, a cosmetics floor, an amusement arcade, and an art gallery. It closes periodically on Tuesday. ⊠ *Karasuma-dori, Shimogyo-ku* ☎ *075/352–1111* ⊘ *Daily 10–7:30.*

Takashimaya 高島屋. This store on Kawara-machi-dori is Japan's most established and sophisticated depato, with designer and luxury goods at matching prices. You'll find accommodating, English-speaking salespeople and a convenient money-exchange counter. The restaurant floor is rather grand, with a concierge service for diners. ⊠ *Shijo-Kawara-machi, Shimogyo-ku* ☎ *075/221–8811* ⊘ *Daily 10–7:30.*

FOLK CRAFTS

Kuraya Hashimoto 蔵屋橋元. This shop has one of the best collections of antique and newly forged swords and will ship them for you. ⊠ *Nishihorikawa-dori, Oike-agaru, southeast corner of Nijo-jo, Nakagyo-ku* ☎ *075/821–2791* ⊘ *Thurs.–Tues. 10–6.*

Ryushido 龍枝堂. Here, you can stock up on calligraphy and *sumi* supplies, including writing brushes, ink sticks, ink stones, paper, paperweights, and water stoppers. ⊠ *Nijo-agaru, Tera-machi-dori, north of Nijo, Kamigyo-ku* ☎ *075/252–4120* ⊘ *Daily 10–6.*

Yamato Mingei-ten やまと民芸店. On Kawara-mach-dori near the BAL Building downtown, this shop has an ever-changing selection of folk crafts, including ceramics, metalwork, paper, lacquerware, and textiles from all over Japan. ⊠ *Kawara-machi, Takoyakushi-agaru, Nakagyo-ku* ☎ *075/221–2641* ⊘ *Wed.–Mon. 10–8:30.*

INCENSE

Kungyoku-do 薫玉堂. On Horikawa-dori opposite Nishi-Hongan-ji, Kungyoku-do has been dealing in fine woods, herbs, and spices for 400 years. ⊠ *Horikawa-dori, Nishi-Hongan-ji-mae, Shimogyo-ku* ☎ *075/371–0162* ⊘ *Daily 9–5:30; closed 1st and 3rd Sun. of month.*

KIMONOS AND ACCESSORIES

Shimmering new silk kimonos can cost more than ¥1,000,000—they are art objects, as well as couture—while equally stunning old silk kimonos can cost less than ¥3,000. You can find used kimonos at some local end-of-the-month temple markets.

Aizen Kobo 愛染工房. Two blocks west of the textile center on Imadegawa-dori and a block south, Aizen Kobo specializes in the finest handwoven and hand-dyed indigo textiles. Pure Japanese indigo dye, with its famed rich color, may soften but will never fade. The shop is in a traditional weaving family home, and the friendly owners will show you their many dyed and woven goods, including garments designed by Hisako Utsuki, the owner's wife. ⊠ *Omiya Nishi-iru, Nakasuji-dori, Kamigyo-ku* ☎ *075/441–0355* ⊘ *Mon.–Sat. 9–5:30.*

Jusan-ya 十三や. Probably the most famous—and surely one of the oldest—of the numerous accessories stores that can be found in the relatively quiet Gojo neighborhood, this shop specializes in *tsugekushi* (boxwood combs). *Kanzashi*, the hair ornaments worn with kimonos, are also available. ⊠ *Shinkyogoku Higashi-iru, Shijo-dori, Shimogyo-ku* ☎ *075/221–2008* ⊘ *Daily 10–6.*

花呈瑞色
薰風和琴

瑞霖

Miyawaki Baisen-an 宮脇賣扇庵. The most famous fan shop in all of Kyoto has been in business since 1823. It delights customers not only with its fine collection of lacquered, scented, painted, and paper fans, but also with the Old World atmosphere that emanates from the building that houses the shop. ⊠ *Tominokoji Nishi-iru, Rokkaku-dori, Nakagyo-ku* ☎ *075/221–0181* ⊗ *Daily 9–6.*

YAYA yufu やゝ游風. Just steps from Shijo subway station's Exit 5, this quaint kimono shop offer original attire and antique accessories. Its English-speaking staff member, Megumi, is kind, inviting, and extremely knowledgeable about the traditional art of kimono, as well as its blend with modern styles. Your time spent trying on different combinations with her is sure to be a fun fashion experience to send you home with a real piece of lovely Kyoto. Many of the goods sold here are painstakingly tracked down at Kyoto estate sales and flea markets. Who knows how many generations back that *tsugekushi* goes? ⊠ *319-3 Kamiyanagi-cho, Karasuma-higashi-iru, Bukkoji-dori, Shimogyo-ku* ☎ *075/341–8777* ⊕ *yaya2002.com* ⊗ *Thurs.–Mon. 12–7.*

MARKETS

Nishiki-koji 錦小路. Kyoto has a wonderful food market, which is north of Shijo-dori and branches off the Tera-machi-dori covered arcade in central Kyoto. Look for delicious grilled fish dipped in soy sauce for a tasty snack or fresh Kyoto sweets. Try to avoid the market in late afternoon, when housewives come to do their daily shopping. The market is long and narrow; in a sizable crowd there's always the possibility of being pushed into the display of fresh fish. ⊠ *Nishiki-koji-dori, Nakagyo-ku.*

NOVELTIES

☺ **Loft** ロフト. This store has five floors jam-packed with kitsch, from beauty products to anime merchandise. Kids and teenagers love browsing here, and you're sure to find some unusual souvenirs and gifts. ⊠ *Kawaramachi-nishi, Takoyakushi-dori, Nakagyo-ku* ☎ *075/255–6210* ⊗ *Daily 11–9.*

TEMPLE MARKETS

To-ji 東寺. The largest and most famous temple market takes place on the 21st of each month. Hundreds of stalls display fans, kimonos, antiques, and trinkets, which attract many collectors. The temple also hosts a smaller antiques market on the first Sunday of the month. ⊠ *1 Kujo-cho, Minami-ku.*

Kitano Tenman-gu 北野天満宮. This vibrant flea market overflows into the side streets surrounding the grounds on the 25th of each month, with kimono and Japanese crafts at reasonable prices. ⊠ *Imakoji-agaru, Onmae-dori, Kamigyo-ku.*

The Kansai Region

WORD OF MOUTH

"Give Osaka at least two nights. It is a fantastic place to make your adjustment to Japan. The shopping is about the best in all of Japan at the Namba walk and Dotombori areas of Namba and you can get used to the subway/train transport systems without the confusion that is Tokyo."

—hawaiiantraveler

WELCOME TO
THE KANSAI REGION

TOP REASONS TO GO

★ **Architecture:** Skyscrapers share Osaka's 1,500-year-old skyline with 4th-century burial mounds, while Nara's wealth of classical temples, pagodas, and shrines are outstanding.

★ **Food:** Osaka has been *nihon no daidokoro* (Japan's kitchen) since the 17th century. The region's tender, highly marbleized Kobe beef is world famous.

★ **Nada no Sake:** The sake breweries of Nada, in western Kobe, use *miyamizu* (mineral-rich water) and Yamada Nishiki rice, grown near Mt. Rokko.

★ **Shopping:** Locals in old wooden shops sell Nara's famous crafts: *sumi* (ink sticks) for calligraphy and ink painting, Nara *sarashi* (fine handwoven, sun-bleached linen), and akahadayaki pottery.

★ **Todai-ji Temple Complex:** The complex in Kobe includes the Daibutsu-den, home to the monumental Great Buddha. The 8th-century San-gatsu-do houses Tenpyo-era statues.

1 Osaka. The people's eccentric friendliness in Japan's third-largest city plays against its rough-and-tumble urban background.

2 Nara. Visitors come for Nara's expansive parks and temples only to be enchanted by its rustic side streets and quiet sense of history.

3 Kobe. The city's relaxed cosmopolitan vibe blends into the waterfalls and *onsen* (thermal spas) of Arima.

GETTING ORIENTED

Osaka sits between Kobe to the west and Nara to the east and has the Kansai region's main international airport, which serves all three cities. Travel to either Kobe or Nara from Osaka takes about 30 minutes, and it's about an hour from Kobe to Nara, and vice-versa. Kyoto is the other major tourist destination in the Kansai region, and it is covered in a separate chapter.

8

NARA'S SACRED DEER

Of all the attractions in Nara, there is one that no visitor can miss. At some point, as you wander between temples, the city's sacred deer will come to inspect you. Cute they may be, just remember they are also wild animals, and coexistence with humans is not always trouble-free, neither for the deer nor their two-legged admirers.

Nara's deer have been part of the landscape of the city for as long as any of the temples, and they rival Todai-ji (with its Daibutsu, the famed statue of Buddha) as the favorite attraction for many tourists, Japanese especially. Red and flecked with white in summer, their coats turn gray in winter; today there are some 1,200 deer freely roaming around Nara Park and the surrounding hills. After such a long time cohabiting with humans they are, of course, only too familiar with us. And they are used to deference: traffic stops when they decide to cross the road, and they are likely to make their interest in being hand-fed known as soon as they approach you.

(This page above) A deer nibbling the grass in Nara Koen; (opposite page upper right) feeding the deer; (opposite page bottom left) Nara's deer can be assertive.

FEEDING THE DEER

Many tourists buy special biscuits, *shika senbei* (deer crackers), that are available at kiosks dotted around the park. The deer have learned how to appeal and cajole. Some will even bow their head meekly to request food. More often, however, they are not so demure and will jostle for that treat. As they can smell the crackers it is best not to hide them in a bag or pocket.

Normally, Nara's deer and humans get on harmlessly enough, but visitors should be wary of mothers in May and June, when they will be fiercely protective of their fawns. Likewise, young males can be unpredictable in the rutting season in fall.

THE LEGEND OF THE DEER

Legend has it that in 768 a white deer carried the deity Takemikazuchi-no-Mikoto, one of the first four deities of Kasuga Taisha, from a distant province called Hitachi (now known as Ibaraki, north of Tokyo) all the way to Nara. As a reward, the deer was hailed as divine—and would be forever untouchable. Ever since, the deer inhabiting the Kasuga hills, now part of Nara Park, were considered messengers of the gods and have been both protected and revered. In fact, it was only after World War II that the animals were stripped of their divine status, though they are no less cherished. In fact, they are designated as "'national natural treasures" by the government, and punishment for harming them can be draconian. One hapless, would-be poacher found this out as recently as 2010, when he tried to bag some illicit venison but ended up with a stretch in jail.

SHIKA NO TSUNOKIRI

Partly to protect visitors, but chiefly to stop the deer from hurting each other, there is an antler-cutting ceremony each

October. The *shika no tsunokiri* has changed little in 300 years. The bucks are chased into a special enclosure near Kasuga Taisha by *seko* (beaters) in traditional garb. The seko use *juji* (nets made of bamboo with rope), which they hurl at the animals, hook the antlers, and then pull the bucks in. A Shinto priest next gives each animal some purified water before sawing off its antlers. All males over four years face the same indignation. The fully grown antlers do not have nerves or veins, so they will not bleed and no lasting harm is done, but the buck does not undergo the ordeal without a struggle.

SENTO-KUN

So popular are the deer with tourists that when Nara recently celebrated 1,300 years since its founding and was looking for a character that would embody everything about the city, the winning entry was *Sento-kun*. Looking suspiciously like an impish Buddha with antlers, he did not go down well with some of the city's more conservative figures who thought him disrespectful to the Buddha. Sento-kun has, however, proved enormously popular with visitors ever since and, if nothing else, is confirmation that Nara's deer are as big a draw as any of the magnificent temples or shrines.

8

SAKE, THE JAPANESE DRINK

Sake, or *nihonshu,* is the essential Japanese drink. Ranging in taste from fruity and bright to rich and mellow, there is a nihonshu for virtually every palette. Many sake breweries offer free tours and tastings to tourists.

(This page above) Assorted sake bottles, some decorated; (opposite page upper right) sake in its different varieties; (opposite page bottom left) sake from Hokkaido

Sake is brewed throughout Japan, and brewery tours are common. If you are in Kansai, you may want to visit one of the breweries in Nada, which accounts for over a quarter of Japan's sake production. Thanks to a near-perfect combination of rice, water, brewing techniques, and its location next to the port of Kobe, Nada has been Japan's premier sake-brewing region since the 18th century. Many breweries offer tours in both Japanese and English, followed by free tastings and a chance to buy the hard-to-find sake produced there. Unfortunately, few breweries allow guests to enter the actual brewing area. To visit a brewery, call ahead for reservations since tours may only be available on certain days. If you don't have time for a brewery visit, most souvenir shops sell local sake. Just ask for *ji-zake* (local sake).

KOBE SHU-SHIN-KAN BREWERY

Kobe Shu-shin-kan Brewery (☎ 078/841–1121 ⊕ *www.shushinkan.co.jp/guide/english.html*), in business since 1751, is one of the few that opens its brew house to tours. Sake is only brewed from October to March, but the rest of the year visitors can still see the facilities and learn about the process. To book a tour call the day before. There's also a shop (☉ *Daily 10–6*) and restaurant.

IMPORTANT SAKE TERMS

Like wine, nihonshu is nuanced and complex. It is officially separated into different grades depending on how much of the rice grain remains after polishing. Since the glutinous, low-protein inner cores of rice kernels produce the best sake, more polishing results in better sake. Anyone at a liquor store, souvenir shop, or restaurant should be able to give you further recommendations.

DAI-GINJOSHU

The highest grade of sake, *dai-ginjoshu* rice is polished so that only 50% of the grain remains. These sake are usually complex, light, and crisp. If you only try one nihonshu in Japan, make sure it is a dai-ginjoshu.

GINJOSHU

The second-highest level sake, *ginjoshu* uses rice with 60% of the grain remaining. Ginjoshu usually has a clear, crisp flavor and slightly fruity bouquet.

HONJOZOSHU

Honjozoshu rice is polished so that under 70% of the grain remains. These sake are less complex than Ginjoshu and Dai-Ginjoshu, but still light and fragrant. Quite affordable, they are an excellent companion to most Japanese food.

FUTSUSHU

Literally "normal sake," *futsushu* is the table wine of nihonshu. Some varieties are quite tasty, while others are best avoided. Most hot sake, or *atsukan,* is this variety.

JUNMAISHU

Junmai ("pure rice") indicates a sake that has been brewed using only white rice, pure water, and the fermenting agent *koji*. Not one of the four official grades of nihonshu, there are Junmai Honjozoshu (often called simply Junmaishu), Junmai Ginjoshu, and Junmai Dai-Ginjoshu. Junmai sake often has a mellow, smooth flavor.

NAMAZAKE

Bottled without aging, these unpasteurized sakes are known for their refreshing crispness. *Namazake* is only available for a short time after being brewed and must be refrigerated. While breweries release namazake at different times, spring is the most popular season.

NIGORIZAKE

Nigorizake is only slightly filtered, giving it a cloudy white appearance. Nigori sake has heavier, sweeter taste than other sake.

NIHONSHUDO

This indicates whether a sake is sweet or dry. Dry sake has a positive number while sweet sake has a negative. For those new to nihonshudo, sake in the +/-5 range is some of the most popular.

8

Updated by
Robert Morel

Stretching from Mie Prefecture in the east to Hyogo Prefecture in the west, the Kansai region is both a snapshot of archetypal Japan and a showcase for the country's diversity. As home to Japan's capitals for nearly a millennium, Kansai is the undisputed seat of Japanese culture and tradition. It is the birthplace of Japan's traditional theater styles—Noh, Kabuki, and Bunraku—as well as the tea ceremony, Japanese Buddhism, and *ikebana* (flower arrangement). Thanks to Kobe and Osaka, it was also the heart of Japanese trade and industry until Tokyo surpassed it in the 1970s.

After the Kanto (Tokyo) region, Kansai is Japan's most populous and economically important area. Most major companies have offices in Kansai and a few, like Panasonic and Nintendo, still have their headquarters in the region. Though much of the shipping and manufacturing industry has moved overseas, the cities of Kansai have responded by investing heavily in science, research, and technology businesses.

Because of its size and location, the geography of Kansai is as varied as the culture. The Kii Mountain range in southern Mie and Nara prefectures quickly gives way to the stunning rural coastline of Wakayama. Most of the region's population is concentrated around the four cities of Osaka, Kyoto, Kobe, and Nara, all in southern Kansai. Northern Kansai, including Lake Biwa and the Japan Sea coast, is quite rural. Thanks to the tempering effect of the inland sea, the climate of Kansai is generally mild, though summers are renowned for their humidity.

Kansai deserves its reputation as the culinary center of Japan. Whether it be delicate temple food in Kyoto and Nara, hearty Osaka fare, or Kobe's cosmopolitan fusion of Japanese and Western cuisines, no other region has such a range of local specialties. Kyoto may be the Kansai's main draw, but to sample the diversity of Japan's cities, make time to see Osaka, Kobe, and Nara. Within an hour's train ride, each city has its own unique culture, cuisine, and attractions. No other region of Japan produces such urban variety in such a small area.

Osaka's urban energy complements its offbeat fashions and reputation as Japan's culinary capitol. For urban explorers, the side streets of America-mura, Minami-horie, or Shin-Sekai offer countless surprises. Anime fans can visit Den Den Town for the latest games, anime goods, and "maid" cafés (where waitresses dress in French parlor maid uniforms).

In Kobe's East-meets-West cosmopolitan mix, travelers can wander Chinatown and have tea in a 19th-century European mansion before taking a cable car up Mt. Rokko for the romantic night view or a stay at Arima Onsen. For foodies, the city is home to Kobe beef and Japan's largest concentration of sake distilleries.

Nara is home to Japan's most famous World Heritage Site, where visitors can feed (or fend off) Nara Park's gregarious deer and see the stunning Todai-ji and Horyu-ji temples. The charming old houses of Nara-machi have become restaurants, galleries, and cafés—the perfect places to find souvenirs and sample local specialties like nara-zuke (vegetables pickled in sake).

Each city may not be for everyone, but to skip all three is to miss out on a chance to see some of Japan's most unique urban landscapes.

PLANNING

For many tourists, Osaka is a day trip, but it is also an excellent base from which to explore the surrounding Kansai region—Kyoto, Nara, and Kobe are each 30 minutes away by train. Osaka is also the most convenient jumping-off point for a trip to the mountainside monasteries of Koya-san, two hours away on the Nankai private rail line.

8

WHEN TO GO

Spring (March to May) and fall (September to November) are the best times to visit the Kansai region. The cherry blossoms flower mid-March to early April, and the autumn leaves are brightest late October to early November. Though summer (June to August) is very hot and sticky, winter is relatively balmy. There's an erratic rainy season, mostly in June.

GETTING HERE AND AROUND
AIR TRAVEL
Many international carriers fly into Kansai International Airport (KIX) south of Osaka, which handles all of the Kansai region's international flights as well as connecting domestic flights to major Japanese cities. The airport, constructed on reclaimed land in Osaka Bay, is easy to navigate and is an interesting sight in its own right. Exiting customs on the first floor, you will find English-language tourist information and direct access to the limousine buses that run to many downtown hotels and destinations (roughly 60 minutes depending on the destination). Japan Airlines (JAL) and All Nippon Airways (ANA) have ongoing domestic flights to major cities from KIX. Osaka is about 30 to 70 minutes from KIX, Kobe about 40 minutes, and Nara about 90 minutes.

About 60% of domestic flights use Itami Airport, roughly 30 minutes northwest of Osaka. Travel to Kobe from Itami Airport takes about 40 minutes, 55 minutes to Nara.

Airline Contacts **Air Canada** (☎ 0120/048–048). **All Nippon Airways** (☎ 0120/02–9222). **Japan Airlines** (☎ 0120/255–931 international, 0120/25–5971 domestic). **Northwest Airlines** (☎ 0120/120–747). **Skymark** (☎ 050/3116–7370).

Airport Contacts **Kansai International Airport** (✉ 1–Banchi, Senshu-kuko Kita, Izumisano ☎ 07/2455–2500 ⊕ www.kansai-airport.or.jp/en/index.asp).

BUS TRAVEL

There are also a number of highway buses to Osaka from most cities in Japan, and from Osaka it's an easy trip to either Kobe or Nara. There are many bus companies, but JR Bus is one of the most popular.

Bus Contacts **JR West Bus** (✉ 1–3–23 Hokko, Konohana-ku ☎ 06/6466–9990).

TRAIN TRAVEL

Hikari Shinkansen trains from Tokyo Station to Shin-Osaka Station take about 3 hours and cost ¥13,950; the trip to Kobe from Tokyo takes 3½ hours and costs ¥14,670. The Nozomi Shinkansen trains cost a bit more and are about 30 minutes faster, but you can't use a JR Pass on these trains.

Nara can be reached from either Osaka or Kobe, but there are no direct trains from Tokyo. From Osaka's Kintetsu Namba Station, Nara is a 31-minute ride on the hourly Limited Express (¥1,040) or 35 minutes by Ordinary Express train (¥540), which leaves every 20 minutes. The JR Line from Tenno-ji Station takes 50 minutes and costs ¥450; from JR Namba it costs ¥540 and takes 40 minutes; from Osaka Station it takes one hour and costs ¥780.

From Kobe, take the JR Tokaido Line rapid train from San-no-miya Station to Osaka (around 25 minutes) and transfer to one of the trains listed here.

ABOUT THE RESTAURANTS

Thanks to its history and unique culture, the Kansai region offers an unparalleled variety of Japanese cuisine. In addition to the local specialties of Osaka, Kobe, and Nara, Kansai has the same inexpensive chain restaurants as Tokyo and a good variety of international food. Outside tourist areas, restaurant staff may not speak English but often exhibit Kansai's signature friendliness, going out of their way to help.

ABOUT THE HOTELS

Hotels in Kansai are slightly cheaper than those in Tokyo. Business hotels and international hotels comprise most of the lodging offerings in the larger cities, while traditional *ryokan* (traditional inns) are common in more-rural destinations like Arima Onsen. Because of Kyoto's popularity during Golden Week (beginning of May), cherry-blossom season (mid-March to early April), and its autumn foliage (October and November), hotels in the surrounding cities are often booked solid. If you are traveling during one of these times, reserve a room early. Unless otherwise noted, expect private baths, air-conditioning, and basic TV in all rooms. Large international-chain hotels have English-speaking staff, but it's advisable to ask a tourist information center to make reservations for you outside the city.

For a short course on accommodations in Japan, see Accommodations in Travel Smart.

WHAT IT COSTS IN YEN					
	¢	$	$$	$$$	$$$$
Restaurants	under ¥800	¥800–¥1,000	¥1,000–¥2,000	¥2,000–¥3,000	over ¥3,000
Hotels	under ¥8,000	¥8,000–¥12,000	¥12,000–¥18,000	¥18,000–¥22,000	over ¥22,000

Restaurant prices are per person for a main course, set meal, or equivalent combinations of smaller dishes. Hotel prices are for a double room with private bath, excluding service and 5% tax.

VISITOR INFORMATION

There's a regional visitor information center in Kansai International Airport. Each city has its own visitor information centers as well.

Contacts ☎ *06/4804–3824*. **Kansai Tourist Information Center** (✉ *1F Passenger Terminal Bldg., Kansai International Airport*).

OSAKA

8

From Minami's neon-lighted Dotombori and historic Tenno-ji to the high-rise class and underground shopping labyrinths of Kita, Osaka is a city that pulses with its own unique rhythm. Though Osaka has no shortage of tourist sites, it is the city itself that is the greatest attraction. Home to some of Japan's best food, most unique fashions, and warmest locals, Osaka does not beg to be explored—it demands it. More than anywhere else in Japan, it rewards the whimsical turn down an interesting side street or the chat with a random stranger. People do not come here to see the city, they come to experience it.

Excluded from the formal circles of power and aristocratic culture in 16th-century Edo (Tokyo), Osaka took advantage of its position and as Japan's trading center, developing its own art forms such as Bunraku puppet theater and Rakugo comic storytelling. It was in Osaka that feudal Japan's famed Floating World—the dining, theater, and pleasure district—was at its strongest and most inventive. Wealthy merchants and common laborers alike squandered fortunes on culinary delights, turning Osaka into "Japan's Kitchen," a moniker the city still has today. Though the city suffered a blow when the Meiji government canceled all of the samurai class's outstanding debts to the merchants, it was quick to recover. At the turn of the 20th century, it had become Japan's largest and most prosperous city, a center of commerce and manufacturing.

Today Osaka remains Japan's iconoclastic metropolis, refusing to fit Tokyo's norms and expectations. Unlike the hordes of Tokyo, Osakans are fiercely independent. As a contrast to the neon and concrete surroundings, the people of Osaka are known as Japan's friendliest and most outgoing. Ask someone on the street for directions in Tokyo and you are lucky to get so much as a glance. Ask someone in Osaka and you get a conversation.

⇨ *See the glossary at the end of this book for definitions of the common Japanese words and suffixes used in this chapter.*

ORIENTATION AND PLANNING

ORIENTATION

The main areas of the city, Kita (north) and Minami (south), are divided by two rivers: the Dojima-gawa and the Tosabori-gawa. Between Kita and Minami is Naka-no-shima, an island and the municipal center of Osaka. The bay area, to the west of the city center, is home to the Osaka Aquarium, the Suntory Museum, and Universal Studios Japan (USJ). The Shinkansen stops at Shin-Osaka, three stops (about five minutes) north of Osaka Station on the Mido-suji subway line. To the north of Shin-Osaka is Senri Expo Park.

Kita. Kita (north of Chuo Dori) is Osaka's economic hub and contains Osaka's largest stations: JR Osaka and Hankyu Umeda. The area is crammed with shops, department stores, and restaurants. Nearby are a nightlife district, Kita-shinchi; Naka-no-shima and the Museum of Oriental Ceramics; Osaka-jo (Osaka Castle); and Osaka Koen (Osaka Park).

Minami. Restaurants, bars, department stores, and boutiques attract Osaka's youth to Minami (south Chuo Dori); theatergoers head to the National Bunraku Theatre and electronics-lovers to Den Den Town. For a glimpse of old Osaka, visit Tenno-ji Temple and Shin Sekai. The main stations are Namba, Shin-sai-bashi, Namba Nankai, and Tenno-ji. There's easy access to the Municipal Museum of Fine Art and Sumiyoshi Taisha (Sumiyoshi Grand Shrine).

PLANNING

HOW MUCH TIME?

You can see the major sights and get a glimpse of the city in a couple of days. If you want to do some shopping, try the local cuisine, and get a taste of the energy that makes Osaka unique, plan on spending two to three nights here.

GETTING HERE AND AROUND

AIRPORT TRANSFERS Frequent trains run from KIX to Tenno-ji and Shin Osaka (JR Kansai Airport Express Haruka, 30 and 45 minutes), JR Kyo-bashi Station (Kansai Airport Rapid, 70 minutes), and the Nankai Namba Station (Nankai Rapid Limited Express, 30 minutes).

Buses from Itami Airport operate at intervals of 15 minutes to one hour (depending on your destination), daily 6 am–9 pm, and take passengers to seven locations in Osaka: Shin-Osaka Station, Umeda, Namba (near the Nikko and Holiday Inn hotels), Ue-hon-machi, Abeno, Sakai-higashi, and Osaka Business Park (near the Hotel New Otani). Buses take 25–50 minutes, depending on the destination, and cost ¥490–¥620.

SUBWAY TRAVEL Osaka's subway system is extensive and efficient, running from early morning until nearly midnight at intervals of three to five minutes.

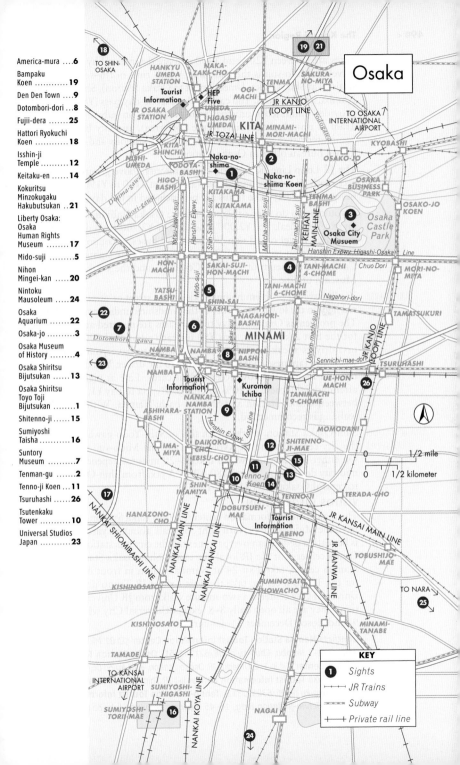

Osaka

KEY

- 1 Sights
- JR Trains
- Subway
- Private rail line

Fares are between ¥200 and ¥400 and are determined by the distance traveled. Mido-suji is the main line, which runs north–south and has stations at Shin-Osaka, Umeda (next to Osaka Station), Shin-sai-bashi, Namba, and Tenno-ji. You can purchase a one-day pass (¥850)—which provides unlimited municipal transportation on subways, the New Tram (a tram line that runs to the port area), and city buses—at the commuter ticket machines in major subway stations and at the Japan Travel Bureau office in Osaka Station.

The JR Loop Line (Kanjo-sen) circles the city above ground and intersects with all subway lines. Fares range from ¥120 to ¥190, or you can use your JR Pass; these trains are not included in the day-pass price.

If you plan to do a lot of sightseeing the Osaka Unlimited pass is also an excellent deal. For ¥2,000 (one day) or ¥2,700 (two days) you get unlimited travel on all non-JR trains and buses, a coupon book, and free admission to many of Osaka's most popular sights like Osaka Castle, the Museum of Oriental Ceramics, and the Osaka Municipal Museum of Fine Art.

TAXI TRAVEL You'll have no problem hailing taxis on the street or at taxi stands. (A red light in the lower left corner of the windshield indicates availability.) The problem is Osaka's heavy traffic. Fares are metered at ¥550–¥640 for the first 2 km (1 mi), plus ¥90 for each additional 500 yards. Few taxi drivers speak English, so it's advisable to have your destination written in Japanese characters to show to the driver. You don't need to tip, and many taxis now accept credit cards. Late at night, generally after midnight, there's a 20% surcharge. Expect to pay ¥1,500 for trips between Osaka Station and Shin-sai-bashi/Namba. Within localities, walking is recommended.

TRAIN STATION TRANSFERS Shin-Osaka Station, on the north side of Shin-Yodo-gawa, is linked to the city center by the JR Kyoto Line and the Mido-suji subway line. On either line the ride, which takes 6–20 minutes depending on your mid-city destination, costs ¥180–¥230. A taxi from Shin-Osaka Station to central Osaka costs ¥1,500–¥2,700.

VISITOR INFORMATION

The main visitor information center is at JR Osaka Station. To get there from the Mido-suji Exit, turn right and walk about 50 yards. The office is beneath a pedestrian overpass, next to the city bus station. The Shin-Osaka center is at the JR local line exit at Shin-Osaka Station. For the Namba center, take Exit 24 at Namba Station in front of Starbucks; for the Tenno-ji center, take the East Exit of JR Tenno-ji Station. The Universal City center is a two-minute walk from JR Universal City Station. They are all open daily 8–8 (except Universal City which opens at 9) and closed December 31–January 3.

Contacts Namba Station Tourist Information Center (✉ *B1 Mido-suji Grand Bldg., 2-2-3 Namba, Chuo-ku* ☎ *06/6211–3551*). **Osaka Station Tourist Information Center** (✉ *3-1-2 Umeda, JR Osaka Station, Kita-ku* ☎ *06/6345–2819*). **Shin-Osaka Tourist Information Center** (✉ *JR Shin-Osaka Station, Higashi-Yodo-gawa-ku* ☎ *06/6305–3311*). **Tenno-ji Station Tourist Information Center** (✉ *1F JR Tenno-ji Station Bldg., 10–45 Hidenin-cho, Tenno-ji-ku* ☎ *06/6774–*

Osaka's aquarium is one of the best in Japan and also one of the world's largest.

3077). **Universal City Tourist Information Center** (✉ *6–2–61 Shimaya, Universal City Walk, Konohana-ku* ☎ *06/4804–3824*).

EXPLORING OSAKA

Most of Osaka's museums are closed Monday. One exception is Senri Expo Park, which closes (along with its museums) Wednesday. Museums stay open on Monday national holidays, closing the following day instead. Likewise, Senri Expo Park stays open on Wednesday holidays, closing Thursday instead.

KITA

Culture by day and glamour by night: Kita (north of Chuo Dori) is the place to come for the museums of Naka-no-shima, the city's deluxe department stores, and the chance to lose yourself (intentionally or not) in one of Japan's largest underground shopping labyrinths. At night take in the view from the Umeda Sky Building or the Ferris wheel at the HEP Five department store before you explore Osaka's upscale entertainment district, Kita-shinichi.

TOP ATTRACTIONS

Fodor's Choice ★

Osaka Aquarium 海遊館 *(Kaiyukan)*. This eye-catching red, gray, and blue building is Japan's best aquarium outside of Okinawa and one of the world's largest. More than 11,000 tons of water hold a multitude of sea creatures, including whale sharks, king penguins, giant spider crabs, jellyfish, and sea otters. You can stroll through 15 different re-created environments, including the rivers and streams of Japanese and Ecuadorian forests, the icy waters around Antarctica, the dark depths of

Venice of the East

When Tokyo was but a fishing village and Kyoto a mountain hamlet, big things were happening in Osaka. The Osaka-Nara region was the center of the emerging Japanese (Yamato) nation into the 9th century, and in 645 Emperor Kotoku (596–654) made Osaka his capital. He called it Naniwa, but the city's imperial ascendancy was brief. Until the 8th century capital cities were relocated upon an emperor's death. As a result, Osaka was the royal seat for a fleeting nine years. Despite changes in its political fortunes, Osaka developed as a trade center, a role its waterways had destined it to play. Exchange wasn't limited to commerce. Buddhism and Chinese characters filtered into the fledgling Japanese society through Osaka to Nara, and from Nara to the rest of the country.

By 1590 Hideyoshi Toyotomi (1536–98), the first *daimyo* (warlord) to unite Japan, had completed construction of Osaka Castle to protect his realm against the unruly clans of Kyoto. He designated Osaka a merchant city to consolidate his position. After Toyotomi died, Tokugawa Ieyasu's (1543–1616) forces defeated the Toyotomi legacy at the Battle of Sekigahara in 1600. Osaka's strategic importance was again short-lived, as Tokugawa moved the capital to Edo (now Tokyo) in 1603. Osaka grew rich supplying the new capital with rice, soy sauce, and sake as Edo transformed its agricultural land into city suburbs. All copper produced in Japan was exported through Osaka, and the National Rice Exchange was headquartered in Dojima, near Kita-shinchi: "70% of the nation's wealth comes from Osaka" was the catchphrase of the era. Some of Japan's business dynasties were founded during the economic boom of the 17th century, and they prevail today—Sumitomo, Konoike, and Mitsui among them.

By the end of the Genroku Era (1688–1704) Osaka's barons were patronizing Bunraku puppetry and *Kamigata Kabuki* (comic Kabuki). Chikamatsu Monzaemon (1653–1724), writer of *The Forty-Seven Ronin,* penned the tragedies, which quickly became classics. Ihara Saikaku (1642–93) immortalized the city's merchants in the risqué *Life of an Amorous Man* and *The Great Mirror of Male Love.* When Tokyo became the official capital of Japan in 1868 there were fears that the "Venice of the East" would suffer. But expansion of the spinning and textile industries assured prosperity, and earned Osaka a new epithet— "Manchester of the East."

As a consequence of the Great Kanto Earthquake in 1923, Osaka became Japan's main port and by 1926 the country's largest city. Chemical and heavy industries grew during World War I, and were prime targets for American bombers during World War II. Much of Osaka was flattened, and more than a third of the prefecture's 4.8 million people were left homeless. During the postwar years many Osaka companies moved their headquarters to Tokyo. Even so, Osaka was rebuilt and went on to host Asia's first World Expo in 1970. It has since fashioned itself as a city of cutting-edge technology, trend-setting, and a unique way of life. The Osaka City Government plans to revive the "Water City" appellation for Osaka, but for now the heritage of the city's waterways lives on in its place-names: *bashi* (bridge), *horie* (canal), and *semba* (dockyard).

Osaka-jo, originally built in the 1580s and reconstructed in 1931, is on a hill above the Osaka-jo Koen-mae Station.

the Japan Sea, and the volcanically active Pacific Ring of Fire. The surrounding Tempozan Harbor Village also contains the Suntory Museum, cruises that ply Osaka Bay on a reproduction of the *Santa María,* and various shops and restaurants. There are often street performances outside on weekends. To get here, take the Chuo subway line to Osaka-ko Station; the aquarium is a five-minute walk northwest from the station. ⊠ *1–1–10 Kaigan-dori, Minato-ku* ☎ *06/6576–5501* ⊕ *www.kaiyukan. com/language/eng* ⌨ *¥2,000* ⊙ *Tues.–Sun. 10–8; last entry at 7.*

Fodor's Choice **Osaka-jo** 大阪城 *(Osaka Castle).* Osaka's most visible tourist attraction
★ and symbol, Osaka Castle exemplifies the city's ability to change with the times. Originally built in the 1580s, the castle is now an impressive five-story ferroconcrete reconstruction (completed in 1931). Instead of leaving a collection of steep wooden staircases and empty rooms, Osaka turned its castle into an elevator-equipped museum celebrating the history of its creator, Hideyoshi Toyotomi, the first *daimyo* (territorial lord) to unite Japan.

For those more interested in aesthetics than artifacts, the castle itself is impressive and the eighth-floor donjon offers a stunning view of Osaka's urban landscape. Watching the sun set behind Osaka's skyscrapers is reason enough for a visit. The surrounding garden makes for a relaxing break from the energy of the city as well. From Osaka-jo Koen-mae Station it's about a 10-minute walk up the hill to the castle. You can also take the Tani-machi subway line from Higashi-Umeda Station (just southeast of Osaka Station) to Tani-machi 4-chome Station. From here it's a 15-minute walk. ⊠ *1–1 Osaka-jo, Chuo-ku* ☎ *06/6941–*

3044 ⊕ *www.osakacastle.net* ✉ *Castle* ¥600, *garden additional* ¥210 ⊗ *Daily 9–5; last entry at 4:30.*

Osaka Shiritsu Toyo Toji Bijutsukan 大阪市立東洋陶磁美術館 *(Museum of Oriental Ceramics).* Located in Naka-no-shima Koen, Osaka's oldest park, the Museum of Oriental Ceramics houses more than 900 pieces of Chinese, Korean, and Japanese ceramics. Though only a fraction is on display at a given time, the collection is one of the finest in the world and includes 15 works designated as National Treasures or Important Cultural Properties. Those interested in art and ceramics should put this at the top of their must-see list. To get here take the Sakai-suji subway line to Kita-hama or the Mido-suji subway line to Yodoya-bashi and walk north across the Tosabori-gawa to the museum. ✉ *1–1 Naka-no-shima, Kita-ku* ☎ *06/6223–0055* ✉ ¥500 ⊗ *Tues.–Sun. 9:30–5; last entry at 4:30.*

WORTH NOTING

Bampaku Koen 万博公園 *(Senri Expo Park).* Originally the site of Expo 1970, one of Osaka's defining postwar events, Senri Expo Park still draws visitors thanks to regular weekend events. This 647-acre park contains sports facilities, various gardens, and an amusement park; the National Museum of Ethnology and the Japan Folk Art Museum; and an enormous statue by Taro Okamoto called the Tower of the Sun. Located outside the city center, the park offers an interesting look at how Osaka has tried to make the most of the site of a former World Expo. Unless you are particularly interested in one of the museums, or have extra time and need a break from the city, the park is easily skipped. To get to the park, take the Mido-suji subway line to Senri-Chuo Station (20 minutes from Umeda); then take the monorail to Bampaku Koen-mae (10 minutes). ✉ *Senri, Suita* ☎ *06/6877–3339 for Senri Expo Park* ✉ *Gardens* ¥150–¥310 *each, Expo Land* ¥1,100; *see separate entries for other facilities* ⊗ *Thurs.–Tues. 9:30–5.*

Hattori Ryokuchi Koen 服部緑地公園. Come for the park's open-air **Museum of Old Japanese Farmhouses** (Nihon Minka Shuraku Hakubut-sukan), and wander about full-size traditional rural buildings such as the giant *gassho-zukuri* (thatch-roof) farmhouse from Gifu Prefecture. The park also has horseback-riding facilities, tennis courts, a youth hostel, and an open-air stage that hosts concerts and other events in summer. There's even an outdoor Kabuki theater. An English-language pamphlet is available. Take the Mido-suji subway line from Umeda to Ryokuchi Koen Station. The park is a 10-minute walk away. ✉ *1–1 Hat-tori Ryokuchi, Toyonaka* ☎ *06/6862–4946 park office, 06/6862–3137 museum* ✉ *Park free, museum* ¥500 ⊗ *Daily 9:30–5; last entry at 4:30.*

Kokuritsu Minzokugaku Hakubutsukan 国立民族学博物館 *(National Museum of Ethnology).* The National Museum of Ethnology exhibits textiles, masks, and contraptions from around the world with sensi-tivity and respect. Displays on the Ainu (the original inhabitants of Hokkaido) and other aspects of Japanese culture are particularly infor-mative. Information sheets explaining the sections of the museum are available on request and supplement the English-language brochure included with admission. The museum is on the east side of the main road that runs north–south through Senri Expo Park. ⊠ *Senri Expo Park, Senri, Suita* ☎ *06/6876–2151* ⊕ *www.minpaku.ac.jp/english* ⊠ *¥420* ⊗ *Thurs.–Tues. 10–5; last entry at 4:30.*

Nihon Mingei-kan 日本民芸館 *(Japan Folk Crafts Museum, Osaka)*. The exhibits of "beauty from day-to-day life" at this museum in Senri Expo Park explore the diversity and intricacy of Japanese handicrafts from Hokkaido to Okinawa. The textiles, wood crafts, and bamboo ware in simple displays evoke Japan's traditional past; they make quite a contrast to Osaka's modernity. ⊠ *10–5 Bampaku Koen, Senri Expo Park, Senri, Suita* ☎ *06/6877–1971* ⊠ *¥700* ⊗ *Thurs.–Tues. 10–5; last entry at 4:30.*

🕙 **Osaka Museum of History** 大阪歴史博物館. Informative as it is enjoyable, the Osaka Museum of History seeks to immerse visitors in the city's history from pre-feudal times to the early 20th century. Full of life-size displays and hands-on activities, the museum does an excellent job of offering attractions for children and adults. There are two paths through the exhibits, a "Highlight Course" (to get a hint of Osaka's past in under an hour) and the "Complete Course" (for a more immersive experience). It makes an excellent stop on the way to Osaka Castle. To get here take the Chuo or Tani-machi subway line to Tani-machi 4-Chome Station and take Exit 9 or 2. ⊠ *1–32 Otemae, 4-chome, Chuo-ku* ☎ *06/6946–5728* ⊕ *www.mus-his.city.osaka.jp* ⊠ *¥600* ⊗ *Mon., Wed., Thurs., and weekends 9:30–5; Fri. 9:30–8.*

Suntory Museum. Osaka native Tadao Ando is Japan's most famous architect, and a global figurehead of the minimalist movement. The Suntory Museum, his Osaka masterpiece, has rotating art and culture exhibitions from around the world as well as an IMAX Theater. You can also see his work at the JR Universal City Station on the Yumesaki Line and at the cinematheque in Tenno-ji Park. ⊠ *1–5–10 Kaigan-dori, Minato-ku* ☎ *06/6577–0001* ⊕ *www.suntory.co.jp/culture/smt* ⊠ *¥1,000 gallery, ¥1,600 gallery and IMAX Theater* ⊗ *Thurs.–Tues. 10–8; last entry at 7:30.*

Tenman-gu 天満宮. This 10th-century shrine is the main site of the annual **Tenjin Matsuri,** held July 24 and 25, one of the three largest and most enthusiastically celebrated festivals in Japan. Dozens of floats are paraded through the streets, and more than 100 vessels, lighted by lanterns, sail along the canals amid fireworks. The festival started as an annual procession to bestow peace and prosperity on the shrine's faithful. It is dedicated to Sugawara no Michizane, the Japanese patron of scholars. Sugawara was out of favor at court when he died in 903. Two years later plague and drought swept Japan—Sugawara was exacting revenge from the grave. To appease Sugawara's spirit he was deified as Tenjin-sama. He is enshrined at Tenman-gu. On the 5th, 15th, and 25th of each month students throughout Japan visit Tenman-gu shrines to pray for academic success. Tenman-gu is a short walk from either JR Tenman-gu Station or Minami-Mori-machi Station on the Tani-machi-suji subway line. ⊠ *2–1–8 Tenjin-bashi, Kita-ku* ☎ *06/6353–0025* ⊠ *Free* ⊗ *Apr.–Sept., daily 5:30 am–sunset; Oct.–Mar., daily 6 am–sunset.*

🕐 **Universal Studios Japan** ユニバーサルスタジオジャパン. The 140-acre Universal Studios Japan (USJ) combines the most popular rides and shows from Universal's Hollywood and Florida movie-studio theme parks with special attractions designed specifically for Japan. Popular rides include those based on *Jurassic Park, Spider-Man,* and *E.T.* The Japan-only Snoopy attraction appeals to the local infatuation with all things cute, as do the daily Hello Kitty parades. Restaurants and food outlets abound throughout the park, and the road from JR Universal City Station is lined with the likes of Hard Rock Cafe and Bubba Gump Shrimp, local fast-food chain MOS Burger, and Ganko Sushi. Tickets are available at locations throughout the city, including branches of Lawson convenience stores and larger JR stations, as well as at USJ itself. Due to high demand on weekends and during holiday periods, tickets must be bought in advance and are not available at the gate. The park is easily reached by direct train from JR Osaka Station (about 20 minutes) or by changing to a shuttle train at JR Nishi-kujo Station on the Loop Line. ⊠ *2–1–33 Sakurajima, Konohana-ku* ☎ *06/6465–3000* ⊕ *www.usj.co.jp* 💲 *¥6,100* 🕐 *Daily 10–10.*

MINAMI

Tradition by day and neon by night, Minami is the place to come for Osaka history: Japan's oldest temple, a breathtaking collection of Japanese art in the Municipal Museum of Fine Art, and a mausoleum bigger than the pyramids. And then youth culture takes over when it comes to nightlife neonside: this is where future fashionistas forge the haute couture of tomorrow. Amid all this modernity are glimpses of an older Osaka in sites like Shin Sekai and Tenno-ji Temple.

TOP ATTRACTIONS

America-mura アメリカ村 *(America Village)*. Though it takes its name from the original shops that sold cheap American fashions and accessories, America-mura, or Ame-mura (*ah*-meh *moo*-ra) as it's called, is now a bustling district full of trendy clothing stores, record stores, bars, cafés, and clubs that cater to teenagers and young adults. To see the variety of styles and fashions prevalent among urban youth, Ame-mura is *the* place to go in Osaka. Pick up an English Ame-mura guide map at any of the stores in the neighborhood. ⊠ *West side of Mido-suji, 6 blocks south of Shin-sai-bashi Station, Chuo-ku.*

Den Den Town でんでんタウン. All the latest anime, video games, computers, cameras, phones, MP3 players, and other electronic gadgets are on display here. Even if you are not in the market for electronics, a stroll through Den Den Town provides an interesting look at Japan's anime, video game, and computer subcultures. "Den Den" is derived from the word *denki,* which means electricity. ⊠ *2 blocks east of Namba Station, Naniwa-ku.*

★ **Dotombori-dori** 道頓堀通り. If you only have one night in Osaka, Dotombori-dori is the place to go. Once Osaka's old theater district, Dotombori-dori is now a neon-lighted pedestrian street filled with restaurants, shops, and the shouts of countless touts each proclaiming (usually falsely) that their restaurant is the only one worth visiting. Though the area has become increasingly touristy, spending some time

The Shinsaibashi district is one of Osaka's busiest shopping areas.

in Dotombori-dori and the surrounding area on a weekend evening is the essential Osaka experience. Stop at the recently renovated Ebisu-bashi to watch street musicians attract crowds as spiky-haired twentysomethings practice the art of *nampa* (the elaborate, amusing, and uniquely Japanese method of chatting people up). Stroll along the riverfront walkways to avoid the crowds. Or slip into Hozenji Yokocho Alley just two blocks south of Dotombori-dori to splash water on the moss-covered statues at Hozenji Shrine or dine in any of the excellent restaurants hidden away on this quiet street. ✉ *From Umeda, take Mido-suji subway line to Namba and walk north 2 blocks up Mido-suji, Chuo-ku.*

Osaka Shiritsu Bijutsukan 大阪市立美術館 *(Municipal Museum of Fine Art)*. The building isn't too impressive, but the exceptional collection of 12th- to 14th-century classical Japanese art on the second floor is. Other collections include the works of Edo-period artist Korin Ogata, more than 3,000 examples of modern lacquerware, and a collection of Chinese paintings and artifacts. Take the Loop Line or the Mido-suji subway line to Tenno-ji Station, or the Tani-machi subway to Shitenno-ji-mae. The museum is in Tenno-ji Koen, southwest of Shitenno-ji. ✉ *1–82 Chausuyama-cho, Tenno-ji-ku* ☎ *06/6771–4874* ⊕ *www.osaka-art-museum.jp/english/index.html* 🎟 *¥300 includes entry to Tenno-ji Koen* ⊗ *Tues.–Sun. 9:30–5; last entry at 4:30.*

★ **Shin Sekai** 新世界. Stepping into Shin Sekai (translation: New World) is a chance to see the Osaka of a generation ago. Built in 1912, the neighborhood was meant to emulate New York and Paris (complete with its own Eiffel Tower). After the war, the area fell into neglect and became one of the few dangerous areas in Osaka. Over the past decade, Shin Sekai has cleaned up its act while retaining its unique retro feel. On weekends you'll find families, college students, and tourists lining up to try *kushi katsu,* the neighborhood's specialty of batter-fried meat and vegetables on skewers. Near Tenno-ji Park and Shitenno-ji Temple, Shin Sekai is an excellent evening stop. After dinner, visit Tsutenkaku Tower for lovely night views of Osaka and to meet Biliken, the neighborhood deity. The easiest way to get to Shin Sekai is from Exit 2 of the Dobutuenn-mae subway on the Mido-suji Line. Cross the street in the direction of the towering pachinko parlor, and walk through Jan Jan Yokocho, the covered shopping street that leads to Shin Sekai. ⊠ *Ebisu-Higashi, Naniwa-ku* ⊕ *www.shinsekai.ne.jp/en/* ✉ *Free.*

Shitenno-ji 四天王寺. Tenno-ji, as this temple is popularly known, is one of the most important historic sights in Osaka and the oldest temple in Japan. Founded in 593, architecturally it's gone through hell, having been destroyed by fire many times. The last reconstruction of the Main Hall (Kon-do), Taishi-den, and the five-story pagoda in 1965 has maintained the original design and adhered to the traditional mathematical alignment. What has managed to survive from earlier times is the 1294 stone torii that stands at the main entrance. (Torii are rarely used at Buddhist temples.)

The founder, Umayado no Mikoto (573–621), posthumously known as Prince Shotoku (Shotoku Taishi), is considered one of early Japan's most enlightened rulers for his furthering of Buddhism and his political acumen. He was made regent over his aunt, Suiko, and set about instituting reforms and establishing Buddhism as the state religion. Buddhism had been introduced to Japan from China and Korea in the early 500s, but it was seen as a threat to the aristocracy, who claimed prestige and power based upon their godlike ancestry. On the 21st of every month the temple has a flea market that sells antiques and baubles; go in the morning for a feeling of Old Japan.

Three train lines will take you near Shitenno-ji. The Tani-machi-suji subway line's Shitenno-ji-mae Station is closest to the temple and the temple park. The Loop Line's Tenno-ji Station is several blocks south of the temple. The Mido-suji subway line also has a Tenno-ji stop, which is next to the JR Station. ⊠ *1–11–18 Shitenno-ji, Tenno-ji-ku* ☎ *06/6771–0066* ✉ *¥300* ⊗ *Apr.–Sept., daily 8:30–4:30; Oct.–Mar., daily 8:30–4.*

Sumiyoshi Taisha 住吉大社 *(Sumiyoshi Grand Shrine).* In a city of former mariners it's no surprise that locals revere Sumiyoshi Taisha, since it's dedicated to the guardian deity of sailors. According to legend, the shrine was founded by Empress Jingu in 211 to express her gratitude for her safe return from a voyage to Korea. Sumiyoshi Taisha is one of three shrines built prior to the arrival of Buddhism in Japan (the other two are Ise Jingu in Mie Prefecture and Izumo Taisha in Tottori Prefecture). According to Shinto custom, shrines were torn down and rebuilt at set intervals to the exact specifications of the original. Sumiyoshi was last replaced in 1810. Sumiyoshi is also famous for its *taiko-bashi* (arched bridge), given by Yodo-gimi, the consort of Hideyoshi Toyotomi, who bore him a son.

Every June 14 starting at 1 pm, a colorful rice-planting festival takes place here with traditional folk performances and processions. Sumiyoshi Matsuri, a large and lively festival, is held from July 30 to August 1. A crowd of rowdy young men carries a 2-ton portable shrine from Sumiyoshi Taisha to Yamato-gawa and back; this is followed by an all-night street bazaar. To reach the shrine, take the 20-minute ride south on the Nankai Main Line from Nankai Namba Station to Sumiyoshi Koen Station. ⊠ 2–9–89 Sumiyoshi, Sumiyoshi-ku ☎ 06/6672–0753 🖙 Free ☉ Apr.–Oct., daily 6–5; Nov.–Mar., daily 6:30–5.

Tenno-ji Koen 天王寺公園 (Tenno-ji Park). The best place to get away from the noise and concrete of the city, this park contains not only the **Municipal Museum of Fine Art** and the garden of **Keitaku-en,** but also the **Tenno-ji Botanical Gardens** (Tenno-ji Shokubutsuen). Also within the park is a prehistoric burial mound, **Chausuyama Kofun,** that was the site of Tokugawa Ieyasu's camp during the siege of Osaka-jo in 1614–15. Visit in the morning or evening when the park is at its quietest. Take the Loop Line from Osaka Station to Tenno-ji Station. The park is on the left side of the road going north to Shitenno-ji. ⊠ 6–74 Chausuyama-cho, Tenno-ji-ku ☎ 06/6771–8401 🖙 ¥150 park only, ¥300 with Municipal Museum of Fine Art ☉ Tues.–Sun. 9:30–4:30; last entry at 4.

Tsuruhashi. Koreans are the largest ethnic minority in Japan, and more of them live in Osaka than anywhere else. Known as zainichi, they have only recently begun to proclaim their traditional heritage and use their Korean names after decades—in some cases centuries—of "assimilation." Since 2000, a wave of Korean tarento (talent) has swept into Japan. The most popular was the actor Bae Yong-jun, affectionately known as Yon-sama. You may not be able to see Yon-sama in person, but you'll get an eyeful of him from the posters outside restaurants and Korean groceries and music stores in Tsuruhashi, Osaka's Korea Town. For a fun evening feasting on excellent, affordable yaki-niku (Korean-style barbecue) take the West Exit of JR Tsuruhashi Station and step into any one of the restaurants lining the narrow street. Many also specialize in Kobe beef, an added treat.

Tsutenkaku Tower 通天閣. Nearly every major city in Japan has its tower, and while they all offer lovely views, most are not much to look at themselves. Shin Sekai's Tsutenkaku breaks this trend by looking decidedly strange. Built in 1912 with the rest of Shin Sekai, the original tower merged Paris's Arc de Triomphe and Eiffel Tower into a single design. Though the original was dismantled to supply iron for Japan's war effort, it was designed and rebuilt by the local citizens in 1956. On the face of the tower is Japan's largest clock (changing color by the minute); the top displays different-color LED lights to indicate the weather. Charmingly gaudy, Tsutenkaku is considered one of the most authentic symbols of Osaka. The observation deck provides one of the city's best night views and a chance to meet Billiken, Shin Sekai's deity of "things as they ought to be." ⊠ 1–18–6 Ebisu Higashi, Naniwa-ku

☎ 06/6641–9559 ⊕ www.tsutenkaku.co.jp ⊠ ¥600 ⊙ Daily 9–9; last entry at 8:30.

WORTH NOTING

Fujii-dera 藤井寺. An 8th-century, 1,000-handed statue of Kannon, the goddess of mercy, is this temple's main object of worship. The seated figure is the oldest Buddhist sculpture of its kind, and it's only on view on the 18th of each month. To get here, take the Mido-suji subway line to Tenno-ji Station, then transfer to the Kintetsu Minami–Osaka Line and take it to Fujii-dera Station. The temple is a few minutes' walk away. ⊠ 1–16–21 Fujii-dera, Fujii-dera ☎ 0721/938–0005 ⊠ Free ⊙ Statue on view 18th of month.

Isshin-ji Temple 一心寺. The ultramodern gate and fierce guardian statues of Isshin-ji Temple are a stark contrast to the nearby Shitenno-ji Temple. Dating back to 1185, the temple is now known for its Okotsubutsu—a Buddha statue made of the cremated remains of more than 200,000 people laid to rest at Isshin-ji. Far from morbid, the statue is meant to reaffirm one's respect for the deceased and to turn them into an object of everyday worship. An Okotsubutsu is made every 10 years, the first in 1887. Though 12 Okutsubutsu have been made, due to a direct hit to the temple during World War II, only the five crafted after the war remain. To get here take the Sakisuji Subway to Ebisu Cho Station and walk east along Isshin-ji-mae. The temple is on the right soon after passing under the expressway. ⊠ 2–8–69 Tenno-ji-ku, Tenno-ji-ku ☎ 06/6771–0444 ⊕ www.isshinji.or.jp ⊠ Free ⊙ Daily 9–5.

Keitaku-en 慶沢園. Jihei Ogawa, master gardener of the late Meiji period, spent 10 years working the late Baron Sumitomo's circular garden into a masterpiece. The woods surrounding the pond are a riot of color in spring, when the cherry blossoms and azaleas bloom. Keitaku-en is adjacent to Shiritsu Bijutsukan in Tenno-ji Koen. ⊠ Tenno-ji-ku ⊠ Included in Tenno-ji Koen admission ⊙ Tues.–Sun. 9:30–4:30; last entry at 4.

Liberty Osaka: Osaka Human Rights Museum リバティおおさか. In a country that often falls back on the myth of everyone living in egalitarian harmony, Liberty Osaka is one of the city's more unique sights. The museum delves into issues of discrimination in Japan against ethnic groups, women, the homeless, sexual minorities, and many other groups. In addition to the English audio guide, each section has a documentary video with English subtitles, and visitors are given a 30-page booklet detailing the museum's contents. The highly informed volunteer staff is happy to answer questions about the permanent and special rotation exhibits. Although it's less centrally located than some of Osaka's other sights, Liberty Osaka is highly recommended for anyone interested in issues regarding discrimination. To get here take the JR Loop Line to Ashihara Station and walk south along the main road 656 yards. The museum will be on your right. ⊠ 3–6–36 Naniwa-Nishi, Naniwa-ku ☎ 06/6561–5891 ⊕ www.liberty.or.jp ⊠ ¥500 ⊙ Tues.–Sun. 10–5; closed 4th Fri. of each month.

Mido-suji 御堂筋. Osaka's Champs Élysées, the ginko-tree-lined Mido-suji boulevard is Osaka's most elegant thoroughfare and home to its greatest concentration of department stores. To the east of Mido-suji is the Shin-sai-bashi-suji arcade, one of Osaka's best shopping and entertainment streets. If you're in town on the second Sunday in October, try to catch the annual Mido-suji Parade, with its colorful procession of floats and musicians. The Shin-sai-bashi stop (Exit 7) on the Mido-suji subway line is in the heart of the city's shopping districts. ⊠ *Chuo-ku.*

Nintoku Mausoleum 仁徳天皇陵古墳. The 4th-century mausoleum of Emperor Nintoku is in the city of Sakai, southeast of Osaka. The mausoleum was built on an even larger scale than that of the pyramids of Egypt—archaeologists calculate that the central mound of this site covers 1.3 million square feet. Construction took more than 20 years and required a total workforce of about 800,000 laborers. Japan has been pushing hard to have the masusoleum declared a UNESCO World Heritage Site. Surrounding the Emperor's burial place are three moats and pine, cedar, and cypress trees. You can walk around the outer moat to get an idea of the size of the mausoleum and the grounds. However, entry into the mausoleum is not allowed. From Tenno-ji Station, take the JR Hanwa Line to Mozu Station (a half-hour ride). From there the mausoleum is within a five-minute walk. ⊠ *7 Daisen-cho, Sakai* ☎ *0722/41–0002.*

WHERE TO EAT

You can find a particularly broad range of Japanese food in Osaka, from the local snack foods, *okonomiyaki* (a thick pancake filled with cabbage and other ingredients) and *takoyaki* (tasty, grilled octopus in batter) to full kaiseki restaurants. The seafood from the Seto Inland Sea is always fresh, as is the tender beef used at the many Korean barbecue restaurants in Osaka's Korea Town, Tsuruhashi. French and Mexican cuisines are also popular in Osaka.

The department stores around Osaka Station are "gourmet palaces," each with several floors of restaurants. The Hankyu Grand Building and the Daimaru at JR Osaka Station have the best selection. Under Osaka Station is the Shin-Umeda Shokudokai—a maze of narrow alleys lined with *izakaya* (lively after-work drinking haunts). The beer and hot snacks comfort many an overworked salaryman on the commute home.

For some energetic dining neonside, head to Dotombori-dori and Soemon-cho (pronounced *so*-eh-mon cho), two areas along Dotombori-gawa packed with restaurants and bars. Kimono-clad *mama-sans* serve the city's expense-accounters at Kita-shinchi, in south Kita-ku, the city's most exclusive dining quarter.

KITA

$$$ ✕ **Bat-ten Yokato** バッテンよかとぉ. Located in the basement of Kita-
JAPANESE Shinichi's Aspa Building, the hip, low-ceilinged Batsuten Yofuto serves up a wide selection of very good yakitori (skewered meat and vegetables) in a fun, cozy atmosphere. Sitting at the long bar, customers can watch the cooks work and call out requests. In addition to the quality of the food, the fact that the staff is obviously having a good time makes this an excellent place to try one of the most popular foods in Japan.

On the Menu

CLOSE UP

Osakans are passionate about food. In fact, they coined the word *kuidaore*—to eat until you drop. They expect restaurants to use the freshest ingredients. For centuries the nearby Seto Inland Sea has allowed easy access to fresh seafood. Osakans continue to have discriminating palates and demand their money's worth.

Osakan cuisine is flavored with a soy sauce lighter in color and milder in flavor than the soy used in Tokyo. One local delicacy is *okonomiyaki*, something between a pancake and an omelet, filled with cabbage, mountain yams, pork, shrimp, and other ingredients. *Osaka-zushi* (Osaka-style sushi), made in wooden molds, has a distinctive square shape. *Unagi* (eel) remains a popular local dish; grilled unagi is eaten in summer for quick energy.

Fugu (blowfish), served boiled or raw, is a winter delicacy.

The thick, white noodles known as *udon* are a Japanese staple, but Osakans are particularly fond of *kitsune* udon, a local dish (now popular throughout Japan) in which the noodles are served with fried tofu known as *abura-age*. Another Osaka invention is *takoyaki*, griddle dumplings with octopus, green onions, and ginger smothered in a delicious sauce. Sold by street vendors in Dotombori, these tasty snacks also appear at every festival and street market in Kansai. And for heavier fare, Osaka is famous for kushi katsu, skewered, deep-fried meat and vegetables. If you don't want to fall over, try to leave the table *hara-hachi bunme*, 80% full.

✉ *1–11–24 Kita-shinichi, Chuo-ku* ☎ *06/4799–7447* ✍ *Reservations not accepted* ▭ *No credit cards* ⊗ *Closed Sun.*

$$$$
JAPANESE
★
✕ **Isshin** 一新. Only 16 seats grace this *kappo* (counter) restaurant to the east of Kita-shinichi, where the food is prepared and then immediately served by the chef. Ordering the *omakase* (chef's suggestion) dispenses with menu anxiety. The quality and quantity reflect Osaka's reputation for good food at reasonable prices. Sashimi, tempura, crab, and whatever is in season will be on the menu with a range of premium sakes to accompany them. Isshin is east of Mido-suji and Shin-mido-suji near the American consulate. Go down the street with the convenience store on your right and Isshin is about 100 yards on the left. ✉ *B1 Oshima Bldg., 4–12–2 Nishi-Tenma, Kita-ku* ☎ *06/4709–3020.*

$$$
FRENCH
Fodor's Choice
★
✕ **La Baie** ラ・ベ. The city's premier hotel restaurant serves extremely good French food. The elegant—yet relaxed—atmosphere, seasonal menus, and extensive wine list make La Baie an excellent choice for modern French cuisine. With its high ceiling, 18th-century paintings, and dark-wood accents, the interior is elegant yet relaxed, and the service is impeccable. The weekday lunch courses are a good way to sample some of the best French cuisine in Osaka. ✉ *Ritz-Carlton Osaka, 2–5–25 Umeda, Kita-ku* ☎ *06/6343–7020.*

$$
MEXICAN
✕ **Los Inkas** ロスインカス. Hugely popular with the local Latin community, Los Inkas is always busy, and the up-tempo music makes it a good place for a party. Many dishes are Peruvian, though other Latin cuisines, including Mexican, are represented. Menu highlights include *ceviche*

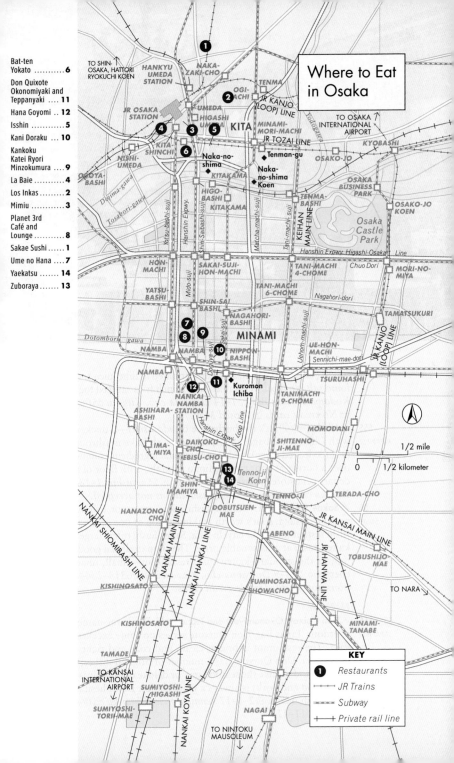

La Baie, in the Ritz-Carlton, Osaka, is the city's best hotel restaurant.

mixto (shrimp, octopus, and fish marinated in lime juice and spices) and *lomo saltado* (beef, vegetables, and french fries sautéed together). ✉ *2F Kodama Leisure Bldg., 1–14 Doyama-cho, Kita-ku* ☎ *06/6365–5190* ▬ *No credit cards* ⊘ *Closed Mon.*

$$$
JAPANESE
✗ **Mimiu** 美々卯. It's the birthplace of *udon-suki*—a thick, noodle stew with Chinese cabbage, clams, eel, yams, shiitake mushrooms, *mitsuba* (a three-leaved green), and other seasonal ingredients simmered in a pot over a burner at your table. Mimiu is on the 10th floor of the Hanshin department store opposite Osaka Station. ✉ *Hanshin, 1–13–13 Umeda, Kita-ku* ☎ *06/6345–6648* ✍ *Reservations not accepted.*

$$
SUSHI
✗ **Sakae Sushi** 栄すし. *Kaiten* sushi (aka "conveyor belt sushi") originated in Osaka, so it's worth making a stop at one of the many kaiten sushi restaurants in the city. In Kita, Sakae Sushi offers large cuts of tasty kaiten sushi at a reasonable price. The shop itself is a good representation of the standard kaiten sushi restaurant—small, unadorned, and energetic. ✉ *5–9 Douyama-cho, Kita-ku* ☎ *06/6313–2344* ✍ *Reservations not accepted* ▬ *No credit cards.*

MINAMI

$$ – $$$
JAPANESE
✗ **Don Quixote Okonomiyaki and Teppanyaki.** While the name suggests an overdone Tapas Bar, Don Quixote serves up some excellent okonomiyaki. The restaurant is bright, clean, and cozy and right in the heart of Namba. Don Quixote has a number of original dishes, but starting with a standard like the seafood mix or deluxe okonomiyaki (a mixture of seafood and pork) is always a good choice. Don't hesitate to ask for an English menu. ✉ *2–8–17 Sennichi-mae, Chuo-ku* ☎ *06/6644–8313* ⊘ *Daily 11–11.*

$$$$ ✕**Hana Goyomi.** Dining at the Swissôtel's flagship restaurant is an ele-
JAPANESE gant escape from the crowds of Osaka. The seasonal kaiseki dinners
★ are presented with exquisite attention to detail, bringing out the flavor
of each ingredient. The restaurant offers separate seating a the sushi
bar, tempura counter, tables, and even four private rooms. Choose from
one of the seasonal set menus, or leave your dinner in the hands of the
skilled chefs. Not only can guests order from any of the menus at Hana
Goyomi, but the staff is also happy to serve Kobe beef from Minami, the
hotel's teppanyaki restaurant. ⊠ *Swissôtel, 5–1–60 Namba, Chuo-ku*
☎ *06/6646–5127* ⊕ *www.swissotel.com/osaka.*

$$$$ ✕**Kani Doraku** かに道楽. The most famous restaurant on Dotombori-
SEAFOOD dori—the enormous mechanical crab is a local landmark—Kani Doraku
has fine crab dishes at reasonable prices. The lunch a crab set, with
large portions of crab, costs around ¥4,000; crab for dinner costs more
than ¥6,000. If you prefer a quick snack, a stand outside sells crab legs
(¥500 for two). An English-language menu is available. Reserve ahead
on weekends. ⊠ *1–6–18 Dotombori, Chuo-ku* ☎ *06/6211–8975.*

$$$ ✕**Kankoku Katei Ryori Minzokumura** 韓国家庭料理民俗村. Popular with
KOREAN Korean celebrities, this restaurant eschews glitz for tradition. *Katei*
means "home-style" in Japanese, and the Korean hot pot, teppanyaki,
sumibiyaki (charcoal-grilled), and seafood hot pot set menus won't
break the bank. It opens early (3 pm) and closes late (4 am). ⊠ *1–22
Soemon-cho, Unagidani, Chuo-ku* ☎ *06/6212–2640.*

$$ ✕**Planet 3rd Café and Lounge** プラネットサード. Planet 3rd, part of the
CAFÉ Wired Café group, is a hip hangout on the fringe of America-mura. The
food is tasty—consisting mostly of sandwiches, curries, and sweets—
and the atmosphere is cool and laid back. In the morning the café
serves breakfast from 7 am. The computers at the front are free use for
customers. ⊠ *1–5–24 Nishi-Shin-sai-bashi, Chuo-ku* ☎ *06/6282–5277*
⊕ *www.cafecompany.co.jp* ⊟ *No credit cards.*

$$$$ ✕**Ume no Hana** 梅の花. Healthy prix-fixe, multicourse menus of tofu-
VEGETARIAN based cuisine—particularly refreshing on hot summer days—are the
specialty here. This is a good spot to take a break from shopping in
Shin-sai-bashi, and during the day you can order one of the cheaper
lunch sets. The private dining rooms are in a traditional Japanese style
with pottery and ikebana. Reserve ahead for weekends and evenings.
⊠ *11F Shin-sai-bashi OPA Bldg., 1–4–3 Nishi-Shin-sai-bashi, Chuo-ku*
☎ *06/6258–3766.*

$$$ ✕**Yaekatsu** 八重勝. For a real taste of Osaka, line up for kushi katsu
JAPANESE outside Shin Sekai's Yaekatsu. This no-frills, counter-only restaurant
has the reputation of being one of Osaka's oldest and best places to
get kushi katsu. Around dinnertime the line stretches the length of the
shop, so go early, or be prepared to wait. Yaekatsu is in Shin Sekai's
Jan Jan Yokocho shopping street. Coming from Dobutsuen-mae Sta-
tion, the shop is halfway down the shopping street on your left. The
sign is only in Japanese, so don't hesitate to ask someone where it is.
⊠ *3–4–13 Ebisu-higashi, Naniwa-ku* ☎ *06/6643–6332* ⌕ *Reservations
not accepted* ⊟ *No credit cards* ☉ *Closed Thurs.*

$$$$ ✕**Zuboraya** づぼらや. Zuboroya is one of Osaka's best known fugu
JAPANESE (blowfish) restaurants. Though there are now shops in other parts of

8

town, the Shin Sekai location is the original. In addition to fugu sashimi, the store has fugu nabe (hot pot), and many other varieties. For less-adventurous diners, Zuboraya serves a range of Japanese foods, like sushi, tempura, and shabu-shabu. ⊠ *2–5–5 Ebisu-higashi, Naniwa-ku* ☎ *06/6633–5529* ⊕ *www.zuboraya.co.jp.*

WHERE TO STAY

Osaka is known more as a business center than as a tourist destination, so hotel facilities are usually excellent, but their features are rarely distinctive, except at the high end of the scale. The city has modern accommodations for almost every taste. Choose accommodations based on location rather than amenities. Note that most hotels offer special rates much lower than the listed rack rates. Call hotels or check their Web sites for information on specials.

Hotel reviews have been condensed for this book. Please go to Fodors. com for full reviews of each property.

KITA

$$$$ 🛏 **ANA Crowne Plaza Osaka** 大阪全日空ホテル. One of Osaka's oldest
HOTEL   deluxe hotels, the ANA overlooks Naka-no-shima Koen. The 24-story building is a handsome white-tile structure with some unusual architectural features like great fluted columns in the lobby. **Pros:** centrally located. **Cons:** there are few shops and attractions directly adjacent to the hotel. ⊠ *1–3–1 Dojima-hama, Kita-ku* ☎ *06/6347–1112* 🖨 *06/6347–9208* ⊕ *www.anacrowneplaza-osaka.jp/english* 🛏 *493 rooms* ⏢ *In-room: a/c, safe, refrigerator, Internet. In-hotel: 5 restaurants, bar, pool, gym, parking (paid)* ⑩ *No meals.*

$$$$ 🛏 **Hilton Osaka** ヒルトン大阪. Glitz and glitter lure tourists and expense-
HOTEL   accounters to the Hilton Osaka, across from JR Osaka Station in the
★   heart of the business district. **Pros:** the Deluxe and Executive floors have some of the most stylish rooms in the city. **Cons:** other than the stylish interior, there is little that sets this hotel apart from less-expensive ones. ⊠ *8–8 Umeda, 1-chome, Kita-ku* ☎ *06/6347–7111* 🖨 *06/6347–7001* ⊕ *www.hilton.co.jp/osaka* 🛏 *525 rooms* ⏢ *In-room: a/c, safe (some), refrigerator, Internet. In-hotel: 7 restaurants, pool, gym, parking (paid)* ⑩ *No meals.*

$$$$ 🛏 **Hotel New Otani Osaka** ホテルニューオータニ大阪. Indoor and out-
HOTEL   door pools, a rooftop garden, tennis courts, and a sparkling marble atrium make this amenities-rich hotel a popular choice for Japanese and Western travelers. **Pros:** rooms facing the castle afford beautiful views; many amenities. **Cons:** not as centrally located as the Umeda or Shin-sai-bashi/Namba hotels. ⊠ *4–1 Shiromi, 1-chome, Chuo-ku* ☎ *06/6941–1111* 🖨 *06/6941–9769* ⊕ *www.osaka.newotani.co.jp* 🛏 *525 rooms, 53 suites* ⏢ *In-room: a/c, safe (some), refrigerator, Internet. In-hotel: 9 restaurants, bars, tennis courts, pool, gym, bicycles, Internet terminal, parking (paid)* ⑩ *No meals.*

$$$$ 🛏 **Rihga Royal Hotel** リーガロイヤルホテル大阪. Built in the 1930s, the
HOTEL   Royal contains more than 20 restaurants, bars, and karaoke rooms,
★   and no fewer than 60 shops—in addition to more than 1,000 rooms and suites. **Pros:** nature themes and imperial visits set it apart from

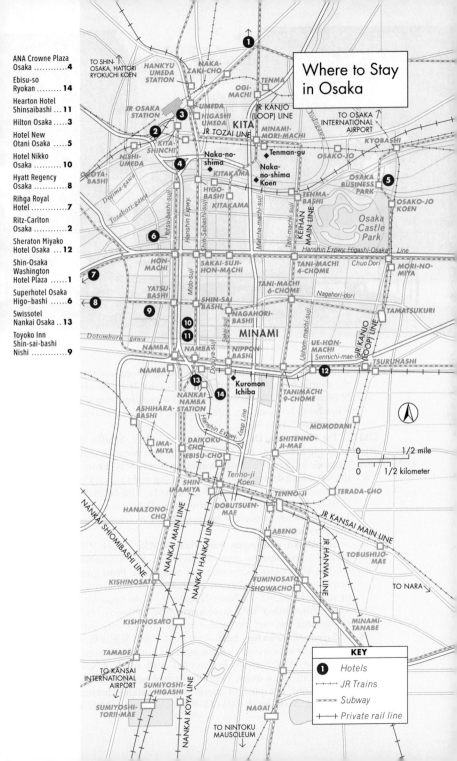

Where to Stay in Osaka

KEY

- **1** Hotels
- JR Trains
- Subway
- Private rail line

The Ritz-Carlton, Osaka, is the city's most luxurious hotel.

similar hotels. **Cons:** less than convenient location requires taking the shuttle bus to transportation. ⊠ *5–3–68 Naka-no-shima, Kita-ku* ☎ *06/6448–1121* 🖷 *06/6448–4414* ⊕ *www.rihga.com* ⇗ *980 rooms, 53 suites* ⌂ *In-room: a/c, safe, Internet. In-hotel: 20 restaurants, bars, pools, gym* ❍ *No meals.*

$$$$
HOTEL
Fodor's Choice
★

🖻 **The Ritz-Carlton, Osaka** リッツカールトン大阪. Smaller than Osaka's other top hotels, the Ritz-Carlton combines a homey feel and European elegance in the city's most luxurious place to stay. **Pros:** luxurious to the last detail; deluxe rooms have stunning night views. **Cons:** the most expensive hotel in town. ⊠ *2–5–25 Umeda, Kita-ku* ☎ *06/6343–7000* 🖷 *06/6343–7001* ⊕ *www.ritzcarlton.com* ⇗ *292 rooms* ⌂ *In-room: a/c, DVD, Internet. In-hotel: 4 restaurants, room service, bar, pool, gym, spa, parking (paid).*

$$
HOTEL

🖻 **Shin-Osaka Washington Hotel Plaza** 新大阪ワシントンホテルプラザ. Part of a no-nonsense chain of business hotels throughout the country, the Washington is the smartest of its kind. **Pros:** great location if you have an early Shinkansen to catch. **Cons:** not very close to sights or nightlife. ⊠ *5–5–15 Nishi-Nakajima, Yodo-gawa-ku* ☎ *06/6303–8111* 🖷 *06/6308–8709* ⊕ *washington.jp/* ⇗ *490 rooms* ⌂ *In-room: a/c, refrigerator, Internet. In-hotel: 4 restaurants, parking (paid).*

$
HOTEL

🖻 **Superhotel Osaka Higo-bashi** スーパーホテル大阪肥後橋. A member of the popular nationwide chain of business hotels, this Superhotel is in a quiet, leafy neighborhood five minutes' walk south of Naka-no-shima. **Pros:** located in a quiet, centrally located neighborhood; reasonably priced. **Cons:** not much of interest within walking distance. ⊠ *1–20–1 Edo-bori, Nishi-ku* ☎ *06/6448–9000* 🖷 *06/6448–2400* ⇗ *80 rooms*

⚓ *In-room: no phone, a/c, Internet. In-hotel: laundry facilities, Internet terminal* ⍟ *Breakfast.*

MINAMI

$
RYOKAN
⌂ **Ebisu-so Ryokan** えびす荘旅館. Osaka's only member of the inexpensive Japanese Inn Group is a partly wooden structure with 15 Japanese-style rooms. **Pros:** friendly innkeepers; excellent location. **Cons:** simple accommodations; no private baths. ✉ *1–7–33 Nippon-bashi-nishi, Naniwa-ku* ☎ *06/6643–4861* ⇗ *15 Japanese-style rooms without bath* ⚓ *In-room: a/c* ⍟ *Breakfast.*

$–$$
HOTEL
⌂ **Hearton Hotel Shin-sai-bashi** ハートンホテル心斎橋. For travelers on a budget, the Hearton Hotel Shin-sai-bashi offers a good location at a very reasonable price. **Pros:** well situated for shopping and nightlife; inexpensive. **Cons:** small, simple rooms. ✉ *1–5–24 Nishi-Shin-sai-bashi, Chuo-ku* ☎ *06/6251–3711* ⊕ *www.heartonhotel.com/hearton_hotel_shinsaibashi.htm* ⇗ *302 rooms* ⚓ *In-room: a/c, refrigerator, Internet.* ⍟ *No meals.*

$$$$
HOTEL
⌂ **Hotel Nikko Osaka** ホテル日航大阪. A striking white tower in the colorful Shin-sai-bashi Station area, the Nikko is within easy reach of Osaka's nightlife. Price depends on amenities, as the twin and double rooms are all the same size. **Pros:** excellent location between the shopping and nightlife areas of Shin-sai-bashi, Namba, and America-mura. **Cons:** priced slightly higher than less centrally located hotels of the same caliber. ✉ *1–3–3 Nishi-Shin-sai-bashi, Chuo-ku* ☎ *06/6244–1111* 📠 *06/6245–2432* ⊕ *www.hno.co.jp* ⇗ *640 rooms, 5 suites* ⚓ *In-room: a/c, refrigerator, Internet. In-hotel: 3 restaurants, bars, Internet terminal, parking (paid)* ⍟ *No meals.*

$$$$
HOTEL
⌂ **Hyatt Regency Osaka** ハイアットリージェンシー大阪. If Universal Studios Japan is on your itinerary, the Hyatt, in the Nanko development area, is quite convenient to the park, and Kansai International Airport is a 45-minute bus ride away. **Pros:** larger than average rooms; located near Universal Studios. **Cons:** not a convenient location for experiencing the city. ✉ *1–13 Nanko-Kita, Suminoe-ku* ☎ *06/6612–1234* 📠 *06/6614–7800* ⊕ *www.hyattregencyosaka.com* ⇗ *500 rooms, 7 suites* ⚓ *In-room: a/c, refrigerator, Internet. In-hotel: 11 restaurants, bars, pool, gym, spa, Internet terminal, parking (free)* ⍟ *No meals.*

$$$–$$$$
HOTEL
⌂ **Sheraton Miyako Hotel Osaka** 都ホテル大阪. Renovated in 2007, the Miyako is an excellent base for exploring Osaka as well as taking day trips to Kyoto and Nara. **Pros:** excellent location; great value if you book online; airport shuttle available. **Cons:** less luxurious than some of its pricier rivals. ✉ *6–1–55 Ue-hon-machi, Tenno-ji-ku* ☎ *06/6773–1111* 📠 *06/6773–3322* ⊕ *www.miyakohotels.ne.jp/osaka* ⇗ *575 rooms, 2 suites* ⚓ *In-room: a/c, Internet. In-hotel: 10 restaurants, bars, pool, gym* ⍟ *No meals.*

$$$$
HOTEL
★
⌂ **Swissôtel Nankai Osaka** スイスホテル南海大阪. With mellow contemporary art and European-style furnishings the standard rooms at this high-end hotel are some of the best in the city. **Pros:** best location in Osaka; connected to Nankai Namba Station for easy airport access. **Cons:** one of the most expensive hotels in the area. ✉ *5–1–60 Namba Chuo-ku* ☎ *06/6646–1111* 📠 *06/6648–0331* ⊕ *www.swissotel.com/osaka* ⇗ *548 rooms, 5 Western-style suites, 1 Japanese-style suite*

8

♧ *In-room: a/c, Internet. In-hotel: restaurants, bar, pool, gym* ❶*No meals.*

¢ ▣ **Toyoko Inn Shin-sai-bashi Nishi** 東横イン心斎橋西. A 10-minute walk
HOTEL west of the Shin-sai-bashi subway station and close to the laid-back
cafés of Minami-horie, the Toyoko Inn is a good-value, comfortable
business hotel. **Pros:** inexpensive; located near the Minami hot spots.
Cons: small rooms; few amenities. ✉ *1–9–22 Kita-horie, Nishi-ku*
✆ *06/6536–1045* ✆ *06/6536–1046* ⓕ *www.toyoko-inn.com/eng* ⇄ *144
rooms* ♧ *In-room: a/c, refrigerator, Internet. In-hotel: Internet terminal*
❶ *CP.*

NIGHTLIFE AND THE ARTS

THE ARTS

BUNRAKU

National Bunraku Theatre. Fans of theater will not want to miss the chance
to see a performance at Osaka's National Bunraku Theatre. Registered
by UNESCO as a World Intangible Cultural Heritage in 2003, Bunraku
is not your average puppet show. The 3-foot-tall puppets require three
handlers, and the stories, mostly originating in Osaka, contain all the
drama and tension (if not the sword fights) of a good samurai drama.
The National Bunraku Theatre is Japan's premier place to watch this
300-year-old art form. An "Earphone-Guide" (¥650 rental) explains
the action and context in English as the play unfolds. Performances
are usually twice daily (late morning and late afternoon) on weekends. To get here take the Sennichimae or Sakai-suji subway lines to
Nippon-bashi Station and take Exit 7. The theater is just before passing
under the Hanshin Expressway. ✉ *1–12–10 Nippon-bashi, Chuo-ku*
✆ *0570/07–9900* ⓕ *www.ntj.jac.go.jp* ✉ *¥2,300–¥5,800.*

*For more information on Bunraku, see "Japanese Performing Arts" in
Chapter 2, A Japanese Culture Primer.*

NIGHTLIFE

Osaka has a diverse nightlife scene. The Kita (North) area surrounds
JR Umeda Station; and the Minami (South) area is between the Shin-
sai-bashi and Namba districts and includes part of Chuo-ku (Central
Ward). Many Japanese refer to Minami as being "for kids," but there
are plenty of good restaurants and drinking spots for more-seasoned
bon vivants. Osaka's hip young things hang out in America-mura, in
the southern part of Chuo-ku, with its innumerable bars and clubs. Kita
draws a slightly more adult crowd, including businesspeople.

BARS

Café Absinthe カフェ・アブシンス. After browsing the fashions in Minami-
horie's boutiques, pop into Café Absinthe in neighboring Kita-horie for
Mediterranean food and good music. Live performances usually start
at around 9. The music and the crowd are very international and very
laid-back. ✉ *1–16–18 Kita-horie, Nishi-ku* ✆ *06/6534–6635.*

DANCE CLUBS

Club Karma. If you're looking for serious techno or all-night dancing, Club Karma hosts all-night drum 'n' bass/techno events on weekends and on nights before national holidays (cover from ¥2,500). On non-event nights it's a scenester bar serving good food to hip music. ⊠ *B1F Zero Bldg., 1–5–18 Sonezaki-shinchi, Kita-ku* ☎ *06/6344–6181.*

JAZZ

Blue Note. Jazz fans should head to Umeda and this high-end club where the best of the international and national jazz scenes plays two sets nightly. Tickets aren't cheap: expect to pay anywhere from ¥5,000 to ¥12,000. ⊠ *B2 Herbis Plaza Ent, 2–2–22 Umeda, Kita-ku* ☎ *06/6342–7722.*

Mr. Kelly's. This club on the ground floor of the Sun Garden Hotel regularly features a jazz trio plus a guest vocalist as well as regular touring musicians. The cover charge starts at ¥3,000 for a double bill. ⊠ *2–4–1 Sonezaki Shinchi, Kita-ku* ☎ *06/6342–5821.*

ROCK AND ALTERNATIVE

Bears. This tiny basement, which reaches capacity with 70 people, is the city's single most interesting venue for live music. It's ground zero for the region's avant-garde musical underground. Bears is out of the way and very smoky, and this adds to the underground feel. Events start and finish early, so get here by 6:30. There's something on every evening. ⊠ *B1 Shin-Nihon Namba Bldg., 3–14–5 Namba-naka, Naniwa-ku* ☎ *06/6649–5564.*

Club Quattro. Up-and-coming Japanese rock bands and popular Western bands play here. The sound system is excellent. ⊠ *8F Shin-sai-bashi Parco Bldg., 1–9–1 Shin-sai-bashi-suji, Chuo-ku* ☎ *06/6281–8181.*

SPECTATOR SPORTS

BASEBALL

Kyocera Domu Osaka *(Osaka Dome).* The Orix Buffaloes are the local team, but it is the Hanshin Tigers from Nishi-no-miya, between Kobe and Osaka, that prompt young men to jump into the Dotombori River in excitement. The Tigers are based in historic Koshien Stadium near Kobe, but they play here for their season opener and during the month of August. The Hanshin department store has 10% discounts when the Tigers win, and you can see their black-and-yellow colors all over the city. Osaka Dome looks like a spaceship and has pleasing-to-the-eye curved edges in a city dominated by the gray cube. Tickets cost as little as ¥1,600. Buy them at the gate, at branches of Lawson convenience store in the city, or by telephone from Ticket Pia. The dome is next to Osaka Domu-mae Chiyozaki subway station on the Nagahori Tsurumi-ryokuchi Line. ⊠ *3–2–1 Chiozaki, Nishi-ku* ☎ *06/6363–9999 Ticket Pia.*

SOCCER

There has been a soccer boom in Japan since the World Cup was cohosted by South Korea and Japan in 2002. Two J-League soccer teams, Gamba Osaka and Cerezo Osaka, play in Osaka. Tickets start at ¥1,500 for adults, and the season runs from March to November.

Bampaku EXPO Memorial Stadium. The Gamba Osaka play at this stadium in the north part of the city. Access is via the Osaka Monorail to Koen Higashi-guchi Station. ⊠ *3–3 Senri Bampaku Koen, Suita-shi* ☎ *06/6875–8111.*

Nagai Stadium. The Cerezo Osaka play at this stadium in south Osaka, close to Nagai Station on the JR Hanwa Line or Mido-suji subway line. ⊠ *2–2–19 Nagai-Higashi, Sumiyoshi-ku* ☎ *06/6692–9011.*

SUMO

Osaka Furitsu Taiikukaikan *(Osaka Prefectural Gymnasium).* The sumo scene has become a hotbed of international rivalry as Bulgarians, Estonians, and some Russians with attitude have been edging the local talent out of the *basho* (ring). From the second Sunday through the fourth Sunday in March, one of Japan's six sumo tournaments takes place in Osaka. Most seats, known as *masu-seki,* are prebooked before the tournament begins, but standing-room tickets (¥1,000) and a limited number of seats (¥3,000) are available on the day of the event. The ticket office opens at 9 am, and you should get in line early. The stadium is a 10-minute walk from Namba Station. ⊠ *3–4–36 Namba-naka, Naniwa-ku* ☎ *06/6631–0120.*

SHOPPING

As with everything else in Osaka, the city rewards shoppers with a sense of adventure. Though Osaka is full of shopping complexes, towering department stores, and brand-name shops, you must step away from the main streets and explore neighborhood shops and boutiques to find the best deals, newest electronics, and cutting-edge fashions. Osaka's miles of labyrinthine underground shopping complexes offer an escape from summer heat and are an experience in and of themselves. The network of tunnels and shops in underground Umeda is the most impressive (and confusing). Fortunately, signs and maps are plentiful and the information desk staff speaks English.

There are specialized wholesale areas throughout the city, and many have a few retail shops as well. One such area is **Doguya-suji,** just east of Nankai Namba Station and the Takashimaya department store. This street is lined with shops selling nothing but kitchen goods—all sorts of pots, pans, utensils, and glassware are piled to the rafters. Though most customers are in the restaurant trade, laypeople shop here, too. Feel free to wander around: there's no obligation to buy. A trip here could be combined with a visit to nearby **Den Den Town,** known for its electronic goods. Also in this neighborhood, east of the main entrance to Doguya-suji, is **Kuromon Ichiba,** the famous market district where chefs select the treats—fruits, vegetables, meat, and much more—cooked up at the city's restaurants that evening.

SHOPPING COMPLEXES AND MALLS

Hilton Plaza West and East have international brands like Max Mara, Dunhill, Chanel, and Ferragamo. Herbis Ent Plaza is a local high-end shopping complex connected to the Hilton Plaza West complex. These three shopping complexes are opposite Osaka Station. To the east of the Hankyu Grand Building is NU Chayamachi—a collection of small boutiques, both local and foreign, and some good cafés.

> ### CRAFTS SHOPPING
>
> At one time famous for its traditional crafts—particularly *karaki-sashimono* (ornately carved furniture), fine Naniwa Suzu-ki pewterware, and *uchihamono* (Sakai cutlery)—Osaka lost much of its traditional industry during World War II. The simplest way to find Osakan crafts is to visit one of the major department stores.

Herbis Ent Plaza (✉ *2–2–22 Umeda, Kita-ku* ☎ *06/6343–7500*).
Hilton Plaza East (✉ *1–8–6 Umeda, Kita-ku* ☎ *06/6348–9168*).
Hilton Plaza West (✉ *2–2–2 Umeda, Kita-ku* ☎ *06/6342–0002*).
Namba Parks (✉ *2–10–70, Naniwa-ku* ☎ *06/6644–7100*).
NU Chayamachi (✉ *10–12 Chayamachi, Kita-ku* ☎ *06/6373–7371*).

DEPARTMENT STORES

All major Japanese *depato* (department stores) are represented in Osaka. Hankyu is headquartered here. They're open 10–7, but usually close one day a month, on a Wednesday or Thursday. The food hall in the basement of Hanshin department store is the city's best. If you want to take a break from shopping, head to the roof of HEP Five, where you can ride an enormous Ferris wheel.

Daimaru (✉ *1–7–1 Shin-sai-bashi-suji, Chuo-ku* ☎ *06/6343–1231*).
Hankyu (✉ *8–7 Kakuta-cho, Kita-ku* ☎ *06/6361–1381*).
Hanshin (✉ *1–13–13 Umeda, Kita-ku* ☎ *06/6345–1201*).
HEP Five (✉ *5–15 Kakuda-cho, Kita-ku* ☎ *06/6342–0002* 🎟 *Ferris wheel ¥500* ⏰ *Building and Ferris wheel daily 11–11, shops daily 11–9*).
Takashimaya (✉ *5–1–5 Namba, Chuo-ku* ☎ *06/6631–1101*).

DESIGNER STORES

Though it is being slowly invaded by chain stores, Osaka's famed **America-mura** is still a good place to find hip young fashions. For original boutiques and cutting-edge styles, head to the streets of **Minami-semba** and **Minami-horie** to the west.

Evisu Tailor. This company is jean designer to the stars—Madonna included. Anyone wearing a pair of handmade raw-denim Evisus is recognized by the conspicuous seagull logo on the back pockets. The main shop is in Minami-semba, a 10-minute walk north of Minami-horie. ✉ *4–10–19 Minami-semba, Chuo-ku* ☎ *06/6241–1995*.

SOZ. This store is the brainchild of Hideki Tominaga, an Osaka native. He created the Mini Carpenter Block—an art toy of colorful, interlocking, plastic pieces that he believes helps develop creativity. The Mini Carpenter Block has taken on a life of its own, with SOZ stores throughout the world and a recent exhibit at Paris's Louvre Museum.

8

The cutest of his creations is Mr. Pen, whom you may want to buy after seeing the king penguins at the Osaka Aquarium. Take the Namba Parks Exit from the Mido-suji subway station. ⊠ *3F Namba Parks, 2–10–70, Naniwa-ku* ☎ *06/6641–4683.*

ELECTRONICS

Although some Japanese electronic goods may be cheaper in the United States than in Japan, many electronics products are released on the Japanese market six to 12 months before they reach the West. The reason to buy in Japan is to find something you won't find elsewhere, not to find a bargain.

Den Den Town was once the home of more than 300 small retail shops specializing in electronics, cameras, and watches. Today, shoppers are more likely visit Den Den Town for computer games, scale models, and an assortment of anime-related goods. Shops are open 10–7 daily. Take your passport, and make your purchases in stores with signs that say "Tax-Free" in order to qualify for a 5% discount. The area is near Ebisu-cho Station on the Sakai-suji subway line (Exit 1 or 2), and Nippon-bashi Station on the Sakai-suji and Sennichi-mae subway lines (Exit 5 or 10).

Yodobashi Camera. If you haven't the time to spend exploring Den Den Town, head to this enormous electronics department store in Umeda. Don't be put off by the name: they sell far more than just cameras. On the north side of JR Osaka Station, opposite the Hotel New Hankyu, the store is impossible to miss. ⊠ *1–1 Ofuka-cho, Kita-ku* ☎ *06/4802–1010* ☉ *Daily 9:30–9.*

NARA

Nara is a place of synthesis, where Chinese art, religion, and architecture fused with Japanese language and Shinto traditions. The city was established in 710 and was then known as Heijo-Kyo (citadel of peace). Fujiwara-no-Fuhito, father-in-law of Emperor Mommu, was responsible for the city's creation. His grandson, the future Emperor Shomu, later graced the new capital with its wealth of temples, pagodas, and shrines.

Buddhism had come to Japan in the 6th century. Along with *kanji* (Chinese characters) and tea, it spread throughout the archipelago. Emperor Shomu hoped that making the new capital the center of Buddhism would unite the country and secure his position as head of an emergent nation state. The grandest of the Buddhist temples built in Nara during this era was Todai-ji, which Emperor Shomu intended as a nexus for all the temples of his realm. But after 84 years the citadel of peace fell victim to the very intrigue that the Emperor had tried to suppress. In 794, the capital moved to Kyoto and Nara lost prominence, as did the Kegon sect that still manages Todai-ji today.

Now Nara is a provincial city whose most obvious role is a historical one, and Todai-ji is a monument rather than a political stronghold. Nara is a site of renewal and reinvention that has overcome typhoons, fires, and wars to remain a city of superlatives. Its position in the national consciousness as the birthplace of modern Japanese culture is well secured as it celebrated its 1,300th anniversary in 2010.

ORIENTATION AND PLANNING

ORIENTATION

Almost at the center of the Japanese archipelago, Nara is on the Yamato plain, with Osaka to the west and Kyoto to the north. Much of what you'll come to Nara to see is in picturesque Nara Koen (Nara Park), which is a short distance east of the two main stations. The commercial shopping district is south of Kintetsu Nara Station, while Sanjo-dori, west of Nara Koen and Nara-machi, has the two main tourist shopping areas. Horyu-ji, Yakushi-ji, and Toshodai-ji, the major temples of western Nara, are all on one bus route or can be reached by JR train.

Nara Koen. The broad and undulating Nara Koen was created out of wasteland in 1880 and sits east of the Kasuga Mountain and the cleared slopes of Wakakusa-yama, in a dense forest. The park is home to some 1,200 tame deer, the focus of much local lore and legend.

Nara-machi. This was the "new" area of Nara at the beginning of the Edo period (1603–1868). Today its lanes and alleys are still lined by old wooden houses with latticed windows and whitewashed walls. Many of these old houses have been converted into galleries, museums, and shops.

Western Nara. Horyu-ji Temple has the oldest wooden structures in the world and is considered the apotheosis of classical Japanese architecture. Toshodai-ji Temple is where Ganjin, the first Buddhist monk to come to Japan from China, taught Japanese monks and legitimized the spread of Buddhism throughout the country.

PLANNING

HOW MUCH TIME?

Most visitors miss the best that Nara has to offer on a hurried day trip from Kyoto, Osaka, or Kobe. If time is an issue, the city is compact and well connected enough to explore all the temples and shrines in Nara Koen and spend a full morning or afternoon shopping and walking the streets of Nara-machi in one day. To make the most of this pleasant and relaxing city, an overnight stay is recommended. The city and park just beg to be discovered at a leisurely pace rather than packed into half-day time slot, not to mention the grand Horyu-ji Temple on the outskirts of the city, less than 15 minutes away by train. The tranquil evening atmosphere makes for a nice breather from Kyoto and Osaka's hustle and bustle.

GETTING HERE AND AROUND

AIRPORT TRANSFERS   The hourly airport limousine bus from KIX takes 90 minutes and costs ¥1,800. From Itami, buses leave hourly, take 55 minutes, and cost ¥1,440.

BUS TRAVEL   Two local bus routes circle the main sites (Todai-ji, Kasuga Taisha, and Shin-Yakushi-ji) in the central and eastern parts of the city: Bus 1 runs counterclockwise, and Bus 2 runs clockwise. Both stop at JR Nara Station and Kintetsu Nara Station and have a flat fare of ¥180.

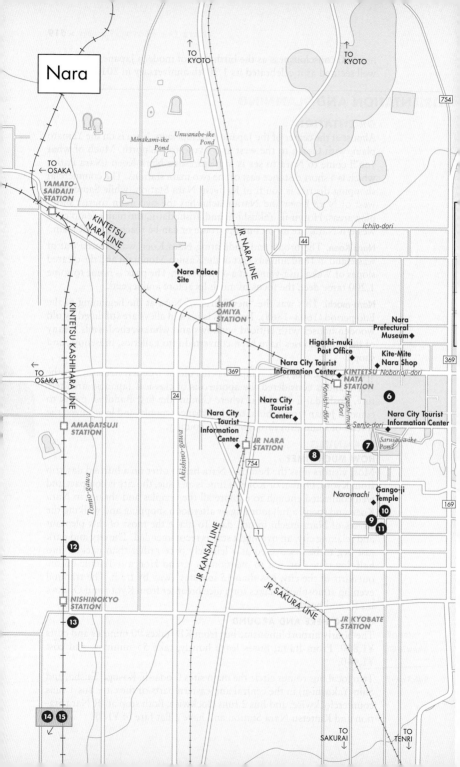

Nara

TO KYOTO

TO KYOTO

754

TO OSAKA

YAMATO-SAIDAIJI STATION

KINTETSU NARA LINE

Minakami-ike Pond

Unwanabe-ike Pond

Ichijo-dori

JR NARA LINE

Nara Palace Site

44

SHIN OMIYA STATION

Nara Prefectural Museum

KINTETSU KASHIHARA LINE

369

Higashi-muki Post Office

Kite-Mite Nara Shop

TO OSAKA

Nara City Tourist Information Center

KINTETSU NARA STATION

Noborioji-dori

369

369

24

Nara City Tourist Center

Konishi-dori

Higashi-muki

6

AMAGATSUJI STATION

Nara City Tourist Information Center

JR NARA STATION

Sanjo-dori

Nara City Tourist Information Center

Akishino-gawa

754

Sarusawa-ike Pond

7

8

Tomio-gawa

Nara-machi

Gango-ji Temple

9

10

1

11

12

JR KANSAI LINE

JR SAKURA LINE

169

NISHINOKYO STATION

JR KYOBATE STATION

13

14 **15**

TO SAKURAI

TO TENRI

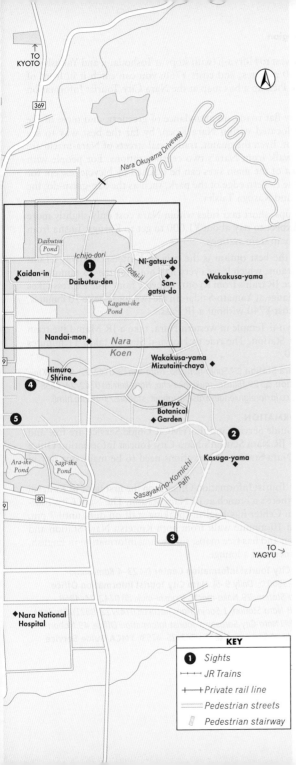

KEY

1 *Sights*

├──┤ *JR Trains*

┼──┼ *Private rail line*

══ *Pedestrian streets*

▯ *Pedestrian stairway*

Bus 97 heads west to Horyu-ji (with stops at Toshodai-ji and Yakushi-ji), takes about 50 minutes, and costs ¥760; you can catch it in front of either station. Pick up a bus map at the Nara City Tourist Information Center.

FOOT TRAVEL With relatively flat roads, an abundance of greenery, and most of the major sights located within Nara Koen, by far the best way to see Nara is on foot. Even the quaint, traditional streets of Nara-machi are a 10-minute walk from Nara's two central stations. For people with less time, most of the main sites can be reached by bicycle, except for those along the eastern edge of the park, such as the San-gatsu-do, the Ni-gatsu-do, and Kasuga Taisha.

TAXI TRAVEL For small groups, short taxi rides within Nara cost only slightly more than buses. Expect to pay about ¥1,000 to get to Kasuga Taisha from either of the main train stations.

TRAIN TRAVEL From Kyoto, the best option is the private Kintetsu Railway's Limited Express trains, which leave every half hour for the 33-minute trip (¥1,110). Three JR trains from Kyoto run every hour. The express takes 45 minutes (change at Yamato-Saidai-ji); the two locals take 70 minutes. All JR trains cost ¥740 without a JR Pass.

To get to Horyu-ji Temple in western Nara, take a JR Main Line train from JR Nara Station. The ride to Horyu-ji Station takes 11 minutes and costs ¥210.

Contacts JR Nara Station (✉ *Sanjo-hon-cho, Nara-ken* ☎ *0742/22–9821*). **Kintetsu Nara Station** (✉ *29 Higashi-mukinaka-cho, Nara-ken* ☎ *0742/24–4858* ⊕ *www.kintetsu.co.jp/foreign/english/useful/about_stations/3-4-nara.html*).

VISITOR INFORMATION

The Student Guide Service and the YMCA Guide Service are free and leave from the JR Nara Station's Nara City Tourist Information Office and Kintetsu Nara Station. Reservations need to be made one day in advance.

The Nara City Tourist Information Office is on the first floor of Kintetsu Nara Station; there's a branch at JR Nara Station. The Nara City Tourist Information Center has English-speaking staff on duty until 7 pm. The center is a 10-minute walk from both Kintetsu Nara Station and JR Nara Station and has free maps, sightseeing information in English, a souvenir corner, and a lounge.

Contacts Nara City Tourist Information Center (✉ *23–4 Kami-sanjo-cho* ☎ *0742/22–3900* ☉ *Daily 9–5*). **Nara City Tourist Information Office** (✉ *Kintetsu Nara Station, 29 Naka-machi, Higashi-muki* ☎ *0742/24–4858* ☉ *Daily 9–5*✉ *JR Nara Station, 1 Sanjo, Hon-machi* ☎ *0742/22–9821*). **Student Guide Service** (✉ *Nara City Sarusawa Tourist Information Office, 49 Nobori-oji-cho, north side of Sarusawa-ike* ☎ *0742/26–4753*). **YMCA Guide Service** (☎ *0742/45–5920*).

EXPLORING NARA

NARA KOEN 奈良公園

Nara Koen has the city's popular tourist sites. Even so, it is wide enough to accommodate thousands of giggling schoolchildren and other Japanese tourists, yet still feel spacious and quiet. Be warned that it is home to many divine messengers of god—the tame deer seen just about everywhere.

TOP ATTRACTIONS

★ **Kasuga Taisha** 春日大社. Famous for the more than 2,000 stone *mantoro* (lanterns) that line the major pathways, Kasuga Taisha is at once a monument to those who have paid tribute to the shrine's Shinto gods by dedicating a lantern, and to the Shinto tradition of worshipping nature. The lighting of the lanterns on three days of the year attracts large crowds that whisper with reverential excitement. February 3 is the Mantoro Festival, celebrating the beginning of spring, and August 14–15 is the Chugen Mantoro Festival, when the living show respect to their ancestors by lighting the way back to Earth for them on their annual visit. As people take photographs with their mobile phones, the new messengers (men with loudspeakers) direct the well-behaved crowds. Kasuga Taisha was founded in 768 and for centuries, according to Shinto custom, the shrine was reconstructed every 20 years on its original design—not merely to renew the materials but also to purify the site. It's said that Kasuga Taisha has been rebuilt more than 50 times; its current incarnation dates from 1893. After you pass through the *torii* (orange gate), the first wooden structure you'll see is the **Hai-den** (Offering Hall); to its left is the **Naorai-den** (Entertainment Hall). To the left of Naorai-den are the four **Hon-den** (Main Shrines). They are designated as National Treasures, all built in the same Kasuga style and painted vermilion and green—a striking contrast to the dark wooden exterior of most other Nara temples.

To get to Kasuga Taisha from Nara Koen, walk east past the Five-Story Pagoda until you reach a torii. This path will lead you to the shrine. ✉ *160 Kasuga-no-cho* ☎ *0742/22–7788* 🎬 *Kasuga Shrine Museum* ¥400; shrine's outer courtyard free; inner precincts with 4 Hon-den structures and gardens ¥500 ⊙ Museum daily 9–4; inner precincts Nov.–Mar., daily 7–4:30; Apr.–Oct., daily 6:30–5:30.

Fodor's Choice **Todai-ji Temple Complex** 東大寺. The temple complex was conceived by
★ Emperor Shomu in the 8th century as the seat of authority for Buddhist Japan. Construction was completed in 752, and even though the Imperial Household later left Nara, Todai-ji and its Great Buddha remained. An earthquake damaged it in 855, and in 1180 the temple was burned to the ground. Its reconstruction met a similar fate during the 16th-century civil wars. A century later only the central buildings were rebuilt; these are what remain today. Among the structures, the Daibutsu-den is the grandest, with huge beams that seemingly converge upward toward infinity.

To get to Todai-ji, board Bus 2 from the front of either the JR Station or Kintetsu Nara Station and exit at Daibutsu-den. Cross the street to the path that leads to the Todai-ji complex. You can walk from Kintetsu

8

Todai-ji's Daibatsu-den houses a 53-foot statue of the Buddha.

Nara Station in about 15 minutes by heading east on Noborioji-dori, the avenue running parallel to the station. In Nara Koen turn left onto the pedestrians-only street, lined with souvenir stalls and restaurants, that leads to Todai-ji. A taxi from JR or Kintetsu Nara station costs about ¥1,000.

The important temples and structures are close together; allow about three hours to see everything, allowing for time to feed the deer.

The **Daibutsu-den** 大仏殿 *(Hall of the Great Buddha)* is a rare example of monumentality in the land of the diminutive bonsai. Unfortunately the *kutsu-gata* (shoe-shape) gilt ornaments that decorate the roof ridge of the Daibutsu-den did a lamentable job in their supposed ability to ward off fire. The current Daibutsu-den was restored in 1709 at two-thirds its original scale. At 157-feet tall and 187-feet wide, it's still considered the largest wooden structure in the world. If you want to ward off illness, follow the lead of those lighting incense at the huge bronze urn and waving it all over their bodies.

Inside the Daibutsu-den is the **Daibutsu,** a 53-foot bronze statue of the Buddha. His hand alone is the size of six tatami mats. The Daibutsu was originally commissioned by Emperor Shomu in 743. After numerous unsuccessful castings, this figure was finally made in 749. A statue of this scale had never been cast before in Japan, and it was meant to serve as a symbol to unite the country. The Daibutsu was dedicated in 752 in a grand ceremony attended by the then-retired Emperor Shomu, the Imperial Court, and 10,000 priests and nuns. The current Daibutsu is an amalgamation of work done in three eras: the 8th, 12th, and 17th centuries.

Patience may be a virtue, but here there is a fast track to enlightenment. Apparently, if you can squeeze through the hole in the pillar behind the Daibutsu you've achieved it. In a cruel irony, wisdom is thus bestowed upon children with ease while their elders struggle on.

A peaceful pebble garden in the courtyard of **Kaidan-in** 戒檀院 belies the ferocious expressions of the Four Heavenly Guardian clay statues inside. Depicted in full armor and wielding weapons, they are an arresting sight. *Kaidan* is a Buddhist word for the terrace on which monks are ordained; the Chinese Buddhist Ganjin (688–763) administered many induction ceremonies of Japanese Buddhists here. The current structure dates from 1731. Kaidan-in is in northwestern Nara Koen, west of the Daibutsu-den.

The soaring **Nandai-mon** 南大門 *(Great Southern Gate)*, the entrance to the temple complex, is supported by 18 large wooden pillars, each 62 feet high and nearly 3⅓ feet in diameter. The original gate was destroyed in a typhoon in 962 and rebuilt in 1199. Two outer niches on either side of the gate contain fearsome wooden figures of Deva kings, who guard the great Buddha within. They are the work of master sculptor Unkei, of the Kamakura period (1185–1335). In the inner niches are a pair of stone *koma-inu* (Korean dogs), mythical guardians that ward off evil.

Named for a ritual that begins in February and culminates in the spectacular sparks and flames of the Omizu-tori festival in March, the **Ni-gatsu-do** 二月堂 *(Second Month Temple)* was founded in 752. It houses important images of the Buddha that are, alas, not on display to the public. Still, its hilltop location and veranda afford a commanding view of Nara Koen.

Behind the Ni-gatsu-do is a lovely **rest area**, where free water and cold tea are available daily from 9 to 4. Although no food is sold, it's a quiet spot to picnic, unhindered by the antlered messengers.

The **San-gatsu-do** 三月堂 *(Third Month Temple)*, founded in 733, is the oldest original building in the Todai-ji complex. It takes its name from the *sutra* (Buddhist scripture) reading ceremonies held here in the third month of the ancient lunar calendar (present-day February to April). You can sit on benches covered with tatami mats and appreciate the 8th-century National Treasures that crowd the small room. The principal display is the lacquer statue of Fukukensaku Kannon, the goddess of mercy, whose diadem is encrusted with thousands of pearls and gemstones. The two clay *bosatsu* (bodhisattva) statues on either side of her, the Gakko (Moonlight) and the Nikko (Sunlight), are fine examples of the *Tenpyo* period (Nara period), the height of classical Japanese sculpture. The English pamphlet included with admission details all the statues in the San-gatsu-do. ✉ *Todai-ji Temple Complex, 406–1 Zoushi-chou, Nara Koen, Central Nara* 🕾 *¥500* ◷ *Apr.–Sept., daily 7:30–5:30; Oct., daily 7:30–5; Nov.–Feb., daily 8–4:30; Mar., daily 8–5.*

NEED A BREAK?

Wakakusa-yama Mizutani-chaya 若草山水谷茶屋**. At the foot of Wakakusa-yama and down some stone steps is a delightful old thatched-roof farmhouse. You can order simple noodle dishes (¥650–¥750) and *mat-cha* whisked green tea (¥650). Alternatively, enjoy a cold beer (400) under

FIRE FESTIVALS AND LIGHT-UPS IN NARA

To light up doesn't mean to have a cigarette in Japan. In fact, most light-ups are at temples and shrines where, unlike most public spaces in Japan, smoking is banned. Here are the more dramatic illuminations on the Nara festival calendar.

JANUARY

Wakakusa-yama Yaki (Grass Burning Festival). On the night before the second Monday in January, 15 priests set Wakakusa-yama's dry grass afire while fireworks illuminate Kofuku-ji's Five-Story Pagoda in one of Japan's most photographed rituals. This rite is believed to commemorate the resolution of a boundary dispute between the monks and priests of Todai-ji and Kofuku-ji. The fireworks start at 5:50 and the grass fire is lighted at 6.

FEBRUARY

Mantoro (Lantern Festival). On February 3 the 2,000 stone and 1,000 bronze lanterns at Kasuga Taisha are lighted to mark the traditional end of winter called *setsubun*. It takes place between 6 pm and 8:30 pm.

MARCH

Shuni-e Omizutori (Water Drawing Festival). From March 1 to 14 priests circle the upper gallery of the Ni-gatsu-do (Second Month Hall) wielding 21-foot-long *taimatsu* (bamboo torches) weighing more than 160 pounds, while sparks fall on those below. Catching the embers burns out sins and wards off evil. This festival is more than 1,200 years old, a rite of repentance to the Eleven-Headed Kannon, an incarnation of the Goddess of Mercy. These evening events happen March 1–11 and 13, 7–7:20; March 12, 7:30–8:15; March 14, for five minutes from 6:30 to 6:35.

JULY–OCTOBER

Light-up Promenade. Sights including Yakushi-ji, Kofuku-ji, and Todai-ji are illuminated at night in July, August, September 7–10, and October 6–10.

AUGUST

Toka-e. From August 1 to 15 Nara Koen is aglow with more than 7,000 candles from 7 to 9:45 pm.

Chugen Mantoro (Mid-year Lantern Festival). For more than 800 years the thousands of lanterns at Kasuga Taisha have been lighted to guide ancestors back to Earth on their annual pilgrimage, in Obon on August 14–15 from 7 to 9:30 pm.

the canopy of maple trees. ⊠ *30 Kasugano-cho* ☎ *0742/22–0627* ⊗ *Thurs.–Tues. 10–4 (food served 11–2).*

WORTH NOTING

Kofuku-ji 興福寺. The **Kofuku-ji Temple's Five-Story Pagoda** dominates the skyline. Built in 1426, it's an exact replica of the original pagoda built here in 730 by Empress Komyo, which burned to the ground. At 164 feet, it is the second tallest in Japan, a few centimeters shorter than the pagoda at To-ji Temple in Kyoto. To the southwest of the Five-Story Pagoda, down a flight of steps, is the **Three-Story Pagoda.** Built in 1114, it is renowned for its graceful lines and fine proportions.

While the Five-Story Pagoda is Kofuku-ji's most eye-catching building, the main attraction is the first-rate collection of Buddhist statues in the **Tokondo** (Great Eastern Hall). A reconstruction dating from the 15th-century, the hall was built to speed the recovery of the ailing Empress Gensho. It is dominated by a statue of Yakushi Nyorai (Physician of the Soul) and is flanked by Four Heavenly Kings and Twelve Heavenly Generals. In contrast to the highly stylized and enlightened Yakushi Nyorai, the seated figure on the left is a statue of a mortal, Yuima Koji. A lay devotee of Buddhism, Yuima was respected for his eloquence but perhaps more revered for his belief that enlightenment could be accomplished through meditation even while mortal passions were indulged. Although Kofuku-ji Temple is no longer a religious mecca, you may see older Japanese writing on *ema* (votive plaques) left by pilgrims to ensure the happiness and safety of their families. The exquisite incense and the patina of the gold leaf on the drapery of the Yakushi Nyorai create a reflective experience.

Ironically, the architecturally contrasting concrete-and-steel **Kokuhokan** (National Treasure House), north of Kofuku-ji, houses the largest and most varied collection of National Treasure sculpture and other works of art. The most famous is a statue of Ashura, one of the Buddha's eight protectors, with three heads and six arms.

Kofuku-ji is a five-minute walk west of Nara Kokuritsu Hakubutsukan (Nara National Museum) in the central part of Nara Koen, and it's an easy 15-minute walk from the JR or Kintetsu Station. ✉ *48 Noborioji-cho* ☎ *0742/22–7755* 🎫 *Great Eastern Hall ¥300, National Treasure House ¥600, pass for both ¥ 800* 🕙 *Daily 9–5.*

Nara Kokuritsu Hakubutsukan 奈良国立博物館 *(Nara National Museum)*. One of the earliest examples of Western-style Meiji architecture, the Nara National Museum was completed in 1889 to much controversy over its decidedly non-Japanese design. True to Nara's reputation as the seat of Japanese culture, the museum houses sculpture from China, Korea, and Japan, though its collection focuses mainly on the Nara and Heian periods. The West Wing has paintings, calligraphy, ceramics, and archaeological artifacts from Japan, some dating back to the 10th-century BC. The East Wing is used for temporary exhibitions. During the driest days of November the Shoso-in Repository, behind the Todai-ji, displays some of its magnificent collection. ✉ *50 Noborioji-cho* ☎ *0742/22–7771* 🎫 *¥500* 🕙 *Tues.–Sun. 9:30–5; enter by 4:30.*

Shin-Yakushi-ji 新薬師寺. This temple was founded in 747 by Empress Komyo (701–760) in gratitude for the recovery of her sick husband, Emperor Shomu. Only the Main Hall, which houses many fine objects from the Nara period, remains. In the center of the hall is a wooden statue of Yakushi Nyorai, the Physician of the Soul. Surrounding this statue are 12 clay images of the Twelve Divine Generals who protected Yakushi. Eleven of these figures are originals. The generals stand in threatening poses, bearing spears, swords, and other weapons, and wear terrifying expressions. ✉ *1289 Takabatake-cho* ☎ *0742/22–3736* 🎫 *¥600* 🕙 *Daily 9–5.*

8

Nara-machi is a maze of lanes and alleys lined with old warehouses and *machiya* (traditional wooden houses) that have been converted into galleries, shops, and cafés. A lot of locals still live here, so the smell of grilled mackerel at lunchtime or roasted tea in the afternoon wafts through the air. Many of the old shops deal in Nara's renowned arts and crafts, such as akahadayaki pottery, ink, and linen. In recent years, Nara-machi has also become home to younger artisans with a contemporary take on the city's traditional crafts. A free map, available from any Nara City Tourism Information Office, guides you to the main shops, museums, and galleries, as do English signposts. Nara-machi is a good change of pace from temple viewing.

Remember that stores can close irregularly. From the southwest corner of Sarusawa-ike, with the pond notice board on your left, walk straight until you come to a main road, on the other side of which is the center of Nara-machi.

WHAT TO SEE

Akahadayaki 赤膚焼. A potter's wheel is in the window of Akahadayaki, where beautiful ceramic candleholders (*tokaki*) illuminate the rooms with leaf and geometric patterns. The tokaki and ceramics at Akahadayaki are all handmade, original designs. ✉ *18 Shibashinya-cho, Nara-machi* ☎ *0742/23–3110* ☺ *Thurs.–Tues. 10:30–5.*

Kai 界. Rooted in tradition, Kai houses a collection of shops with new takes on traditional Japanese arts and crafts. In addition to being a café and gallery, Kai is also the work space and storefront for various local artisans. With artists producing everything from paintings to wood carvings to glass jewelry, this is an excellent stop for unique souvenirs. ✉ *12–1 Wakido-cho, Nara-machi* ☎ *0742/24–3056* ⊕ *www.kai.st* ☺ *Tues.–Sun. 11–6.*

Kobaien 古梅園. Nara accounts for about 90% of Japan's sumi-ink production, and for 400 years Kobaien has made fine ink sticks for calligraphy and ink painting. More recently, some types of sumi-ink have been used for tattooing. ✉ *7 Tsubai-cho, Nara-machi* ☎ *0742/23–2965* ☺ *Weekdays 9–5.*

Koshi-no-ie ならまち格子の家. This well-to-do merchant's house has been thoroughly restored. It's like a quick trip through the Edo period. English pamphlets are available. ✉ *44 Gango-ji-cho, Nara-machi* ☎ *0742/23–4820* ☞ *Free* ☺ *Tues.–Sun. 9–5.*

Nara-machi Shiryokan 奈良町資料館 *(Nara-machi Historical Library and Information Center)*. So just what are those red cloth animals on pieces of rope outside houses in Nara? Called *migawarizaru* (substitute monkeys), they are hung on the eaves of houses to ward off illness and accidents. There is a monkey for every member of a household ready to suffer illness and accidents in place of its owner. The migawarizaru are just one tradition that has lived on in Nara-machi. The Nara-machi Shiryokan displays many other artifacts relating to the history of this neighborhood. ✉ *12 Nishi Shinya-cho, Nara-machi* ☎ *0742/22–5509* ☺ *Weekends and national holidays only, 10–4.*

Horyu-ji's wooden buildings are among the world's oldest.

"Yu" Nakagawa 遊中川. "Yu" Nakagawa specializes in handwoven, sun-bleached linen textiles, a Nara specialty known as Nara *sarashi*. This shop sells *noren* (two-panel curtains put on business entranceways to show that they are open), handbags, slippers, and other linen crafts incorporating traditional Nara motifs. ✉ *31–1 Ganrin-in-cho, Nara-machi* ☎ *0742/22–1322* ☉ *Daily 11–6:30.*

WESTERN NARA 奈良西部

Horyu-ji is home to some of the oldest wooden buildings in the world. Just east of Horyu-ji is Chugu-ji, with one of the finest sculptures in Japan, the 7th-century Miroku Bodhisattva. A short bus ride back toward Nara brings you to Yakushi-ji and Toshodai-ji temples, both religious and political centers during the Nara period. To visit all four temples in one day go to Horyu-ji by the JR Main Line first (Chugu-ji is a 10-minute walk from Horyu-ji) and proceed to Toshodai-ji and Yakushi-ji by bus.

TOP ATTRACTIONS

Horyu-ji 法隆寺. Horyu-ji is the jewel in the crown of classical Japanese architecture. In the morning, elderly locals on their way to work pray in front of the temple with an intensity the younger generation usually displays toward manga and *puri-kura* (photo stickers). Founded in 607 by Prince Shotoku (573–621), Horyu-ji's original wooden buildings are among the world's oldest. The first gate you pass through is the **Nandai-mon**, which was rebuilt in 1438 and is thus a relatively young 500 years old. The second gate, **Chu-mon** (Middle Gate), is the 607 original. Unlike most Japanese gates, which are supported by two pillars at the ends, central pillars support this gate. Note their entasis, or swelling at the center, an architectural feature from ancient Greece that traveled as far as Japan. Such columns are found in Japan only in the 7th-century structures of Nara.

After passing through the gates, you enter the temple's western precincts. The first building on the right is the **Kon-do** (Main Hall), a two-story reproduction of the original 7th-century hall, which displays Buddhist images and objects from as far back as the Asuka period (552–645). The Five-Story Pagoda to its left was disassembled in World War II to protect it from air raids, after which it was reconstructed with the same materials used in 607. Behind the pagoda is the **Daiko-do** (Lecture Hall), destroyed by fire and rebuilt in 990. Inside is a statue of Yakushi Nyorai (Physician of the Soul) carved from a camphor tree.

From the Daiko-do, walk past the Kon-do and Chu-mon; then turn left and walk past the pond on your right. You come to two concrete buildings known as the **Daihozo-den** (Great Treasure Hall), which display statues, sculptures, ancient Buddhist religious articles, and brocades. Of particular interest is a miniature shrine that belonged to Lady Tachibana, mother of Empress Komyo. The shrine is about 2½ feet high; the Buddha inside is about 20 inches tall.

Todai-mon (Great East Gate) opens onto Horyu-ji's eastern grounds. The octagonal **Yumedono** (Hall of Dreams) was so named because Prince Shotoku used to meditate in it.

To get here, take a JR Kansai Main Line train to Horyu-ji Station (¥210). The temple is a short shuttle ride or a 15-minute walk. Alternatively, Bus 52, 60, or 97 to Horyu-ji is a 50-minute ride from the JR Nara Station or Kintetsu Nara Station (¥760). The Horyu-ji-mae bus stop is in front of the temple. ⊠ *1–1 Ikaruga-cho, Horyu-ji, Ikoma-gun, Nara-ken, Western Nara* ☎ *0745/75–2555* 🎫 *¥1,000* ⊗ *Feb. 22–Nov. 3, daily 8–5; Nov. 4–Feb. 21, daily 8–4:30; last entry 30 mins before closing.*

WORTH NOTING

Chugu-ji 中宮寺. Chugu-ji was originally the home of Prince Shotoku's mother in the 6th century and is now a Buddhist nunnery. This temple houses an amazing wooden statue of the Miroku Bodhisattva, the Buddha of the Future. His gentle countenance has been a famous image of hope since it was carved, sometime in the Asuka period (552–645). Chugu-ji is a few minutes' walk north of the Yumedono. ⊠ *1–1–2 Ikaruga-cho, Horyu-j Kita, Ikoma-gun, Nara-ken, Western Nara* ☎ *0745/75–2106* 🎫 *¥500* ⊗ *Daily 9–4.*

Toshodai-ji 唐招提寺. The main entrance to Toshodai-ji, which was built in 751, is called the Path of History, since in Nara's imperial days dignitaries and priests trod this route; today it is lined with clay-walled houses, gardens, and the occasional shop selling crafts or nara-zuke.

At the temple's entrance entasis pillars support the **Nandai-mon** (Great South Gate). Beyond the Nandai-mon is the **Kon-do** (Main Hall), a superb example of classical Nara architecture. It was restored in 2009. Inside the hall is a lacquer statue of Vairocana Buddha, the same incarnation of Buddha that is enshrined at Todai-ji. The halo surrounding him was originally covered with 1,000 Buddhas; now there are 864.

Try, Try, Try Again

Toshodai-ji Temple was built in 751 for Ganjin, a Chinese priest who traveled to Japan at the invitation of Emperor Shomu. At that time, Japanese monks had never received formal instruction from a Buddhist monk. The invitation was extended by two Japanese monks who had traveled to China in search of a Buddhist willing to undertake the arduous and perilous journey to Japan.

It seemed that Ganjin would never make it to Japan. On his first journey some of his disciples betrayed him. His second journey resulted in a shipwreck. During the third trip his ship was blown off course, and on his fourth trip government officials refused him permission to leave China. Before his next attempt, he contracted an eye disease that left him blind. He persevered, nonetheless, and finally reached Japan in 750. Ganjin shared his knowledge of Buddhism with his adopted country and served as a teacher to many Japanese abbots as well as Emperor Shomu. He is also remembered for bringing the first sampling of sugar to Japan. Every June 6, to commemorate his birthday, the Miei-do (Founder's Hall) in the back of the temple grounds displays a lacquer statue of Ganjin that dates from 763.

In back of the Kon-do sits the **Daiko-do** (Lecture Hall), formerly an assembly hall of the Nara Imperial Court, the only remaining example of Nara palace architecture.

Toshodai-ji is a 10-minute walk from the rear gate of Yakushi-ji along the Path of History. From central Nara or Horyu-ji, take Bus 52 or 97 to the stop in front of Toshodai-ji. ⊠ *13–46 Gojo-cho, Western Nara* ☎ *0742/33–7900* 🖃 *¥600* ⊙ *Daily 8:30–5.*

Yakushi-ji 薬師寺. The two pagodas that tower over Yakushi-ji Temple are an analogy of past and present Japan. Yakushi-ji's **East Pagoda** dates from 1285, and has such an interesting asymmetrical shape that it inspired Boston Museum of Fine Arts curator Ernest Fenollosa (1853– 1908), an early Western specialist in Japanese art, to remark that it was as beautiful as "frozen music." Its simple, dark brown beams with white ends contrast starkly with its flashier, vermilion-painted 20th-century neighbor, the **West Tower,** built in 1981. For many, the new goes against the "imperfect, impermanent, and incomplete" principles of the old *wabi-sabi* aesthetic; but we think the contrast thrusts Yakushi-ji right into the 21st-century. Officially named one of the Seven Great Temples of Nara, Yakushi-ji was founded in 680 and moved to its current location in 718. From central Nara take either the Kintetsu Line train, changing at Yamato-Saidai-ji to Nishinokyo, or Bus 52 or 97 to Yakushi-ji; from Horyu-ji or Chugu-ji, take Bus 97 to Yakushi-ji-mae. ⊠ *457 Nishinokyo-cho, Western Nara* ☎ *0742/33–6001* 🖃 *¥500–¥800, depending on event/season* ⊙ *Daily 8:30–5.*

8

WHERE TO EAT

It's a sin to visit Nara and not have a *kaiseki* dinner (an aesthetically arranged 7- to 12-course set meal using the freshest ingredients) if you can afford the splurge. It's usually an evening meal, but most kaiseki restaurants serve mini-kaiseki at lunchtime for day-trippers that are considerably more affordable. Most traditional restaurants are small and have set courses. Nara retires early, and restaurants close around 10 pm, taking last orders around 9 pm. Small restaurants and iza-kaya (after-work drinking haunts that serve an array of small dishes and drinks) are dispersed throughout the two main shopping streets, Higashi-muki Dori (a pedestrian arcade) and Konishi-dori, close to Kintetsu Nara Station.

When ordering food, start by asking for an *osusume* (a suggestion) and go from there. Don't be embarrassed or afraid to communicate, even without Japanese, as people in Nara look after their visitors. But keep in mind that each time you eat some delicious sashimi or order tempura you add ¥600–¥900 to your bill. Learning a language can be expensive! Expect to pay about ¥750 for a large bottle of beer. Because English-speaking staff and English menus aren't givens, ask a staff member from your hotel to help make arrangements. Alternatively, stay in a ryokan, where a kaiseki dinner is included in the room rate.

NARA KOEN AREA

$$$$
JAPANESE
★

✕ **Onjaku** 温石. Hidden down a quiet street just south of Ara-ike in Nara Koen is this intimate restaurant serving exquisitely presented traditional kaiseki meals. Within the faded wooden walls, a common architectural motif in Nara, you can sit at a rustic counter or in one of two serene tatami rooms. Choose from one of the two set meals. Both lunch and dinner here are short and served early (noon–1 for lunch, 6–7:30 for dinner). ✉ *1043 Kita-temma-cho, Nara Koen Area* ☎ *0742/26–4762* ⚐ *Reservations essential* 🍽 *No credit cards* ⊗ *Closed Tues.*

$$$$
JAPANESE

✕ **To-no-chaya** 塔の茶屋. One of Nara's most distinctive meals is *cha-gayu* (green-tea-flavored rice porridge). During the day To-no-chaya serves a light meal of this special dish, with sashimi and vegetables, plus a few sweetened rice cakes for dessert. The restaurant was named To-no-chaya, which means "tearoom of the pagoda," for its views of the Five-Story Pagoda of Kofuku-ji. Bento-box meals are served 11:30–4 (¥3,000). You must reserve ahead for cha-gayu in the evening. ✉ *47 Noborioji-cho, Nara Koen Area* ☎ *0742/22–4348* 🍽 *No credit cards* ⊗ *Closed Tues.*

$$$$
JAPANESE
★

✕ **Tsukihitei** 月日亭. Deep in the forest behind Kasuga Taisha, Tsukihitei has the perfect setting for kaiseki. From the walk up a wooded path to the tranquillity of your own tatami room, everything is conducive to experiencing the beautiful presentation and delicate flavors—as Hellen Keller did when she dined at Tsukihitei in 1948. When reserving a table, enlist the help of a good Japanese speaker to select a set meal for you, and allow yourself to be regaled. The lunch sets cost between ¥10,000 and ¥15,000, not exactly cheap but cheaper than dinner. ✉ *158 Kasugano-cho, Nara Koen Area* ☎ *0742/26–2021* ⚐ *Reservations essential.*

$$$$
JAPANESE
★
✕ **Uma no Me** 馬の目. In a little 1920s farmhouse just north of Ara-ike pond in Nara Koen this delightful restaurant with dark beams and pottery-lined walls serves delicious home-style cooking. Everything is prepared from scratch. Recommended is the ¥3,500 lunch course with seasonal vegetables, tofu, and fried fish. As there is only one set meal, ordering is no problem. ✉ *1158 Takabatake-cho, Nara Koen Area* ☏ *0742/23–7784* ⚲ *Reservations essential* ▭ *No credit cards* ☾ *Closed Thurs.*

$$–$$$
JAPANESE
✕ **Yamazakiya** 山崎屋. Pungent nara-zuke will lure you into this well-known shop and adjoining restaurant. Inside, white-capped prep cooks busily prepare packages of pickles that you can try with cha-gayu or a meal of tempura. The set menus are on display, making ordering simple. This is a good place to escape the crowds on Higashi-muki Dori, the main shopping street. Nara Kintetsu Station and Nara Koen are within a five-minute walk. ✉ *5 Minami-machi-cho Higashi-muki Dori, Nara Koen Area* ☏ *0742/27–3715* ☾ *Closed Mon.*

$$$$
JAPANESE
★
✕ **Yanagi-ja-ya** 柳茶屋. At this main branch of this Nara institution in Nara Koen, just past the Five-Story Pagoda, you may find yourself just popping in to try some *warabi mochi* for morning or afternoon tea. Delicious morsels made from warabi (bracken fern root) are tossed in soybean flour and sweetened with brown sugar syrup. At a second branch, the unassuming exterior belies an elegant interior. You're transported to a bygone age in a secluded tatami room overlooking a garden where you'll be served simple bento meals of sashimi, stewed vegetables, and tofu in black-lacquer boxes. Lunch costs ¥4,000–¥6,000. ✉ *4–48 Noborioji-cho, Nara Koen Area* ☏ *0742/22–7560* ⚲ *Reservations essential* ▭ *No credit cards* ☾ *Closed Mon. No dinner.* ✉ *49 Noborioji-cho, Nara Koen Area* ☏ *0742/22–7460* ⚲ *Reservations essential* ▭ *No credit cards* ☾ *Closed Wed.*

NARA-MACHI

$$$$
JAPANESE
✕ **Harishin** はり新. Harishin's Kamitsumichi bento, with a selection of sashimi, tofu, fried shrimp, vegetables, and homemade plum liqueur, is a bargain for ¥2,900. Harishin is traditional and quite rustic. You sit in either a large tatami room overlooking a garden or around a large *irori* (hearth). ✉ *15 Nakashinya-cho, Nara-machi* ☏ *0742/22–2669* ☾ *Closed Mon.*

$$$$
SUSHI
✕ **Hiraso** 平宗. At Hiraso you can try *kakinoha-zushi,* sushi wrapped in a persimmon leaf. What's more, you can take it away in a light wooden box wrapped with precision. Most set menus at Hiraso include cha-gayu, which is usually made with mushrooms or seasonal vegetables. Another featured Nara delicacy is *kakisuga,* dried persimmon, dusted with *kudzu* (flour made from the East Asian kudzu vine) or arrowroot powder and cooked tempura style. Hiraso has tables and chairs, but the tatami alcoves are more intimate. It's open all day, and take-out sushi is available from 10 to 8:30. On a clear day, the take-out kakinoha-zushi makes for a satisfying lunch in Nara Park. ✉ *30–1 Imamikado-cho, Nara-machi* ☏ *0742/22–0866* ☾ *Mon. take-out only.*

$$
JAPANESE
✕ **Naracafe Youan** 由庵. Naracafe Youan doubles as an organic café and an informal information center. Its excellent lunch sets are made with locally sourced food and are artistically presented—a kind of a rustic

8

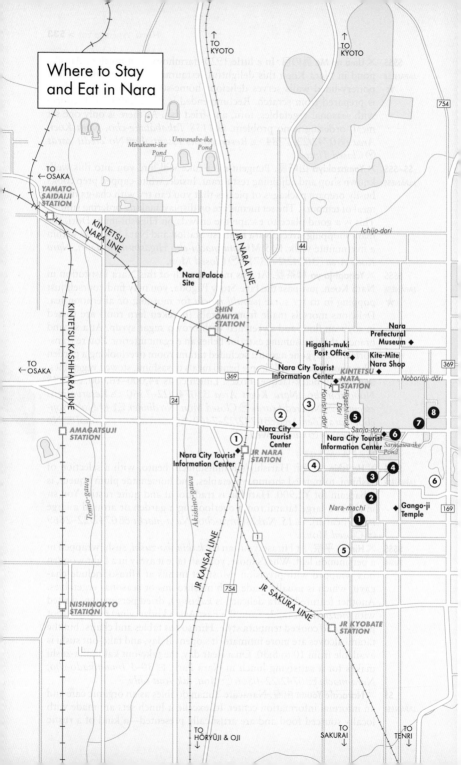

Where to Stay and Eat in Nara

TO
KYOTO

TO
KYOTO

754

Minakami-ike
Pond

Unwanabe-ike
Pond

TO
← OSAKA

YAMATO-
SAIDAIJI
STATION

KINTETSU
NARA LINE

Ichijo-dori

JR NARA LINE

44

Nara Palace
Site

SHIN
OMIYA
STATION

Nara
Prefectural
Museum

KINTETSU
KASHIHARA LINE

Higashi-muki
Post Office

Kite-Mite
Nara Shop

Nara City Tourist
Information Center

KINTETSU
NARA
STATION

Noboriōji-dōri

369

TO
← OSAKA

369

Konishi-dōri

Higashi-muki Dōri

③

⑤

⑧

24

②

Nara City
Tourist
Center

Sanjo-dori

⑥

⑦

①

Nara City Tourist
Information Center

JR NARA
STATION

Nara City Tourist
Information Center

Sarusawa-ike
Pond

④

③

④

⑥

AMAGATSUJI
STATION

Tomio-gawa

Akishino-gawa

②

Nara-machi

①

Gango-ji
Temple

169

JR KANSAI LINE

⑤

1

NISHINOKYO
STATION

JR SAKURA LINE

754

JR KYOBATE
STATION

TO
HŌRYŪJI & OJI

TO
SAKURAI

TO
TENRI

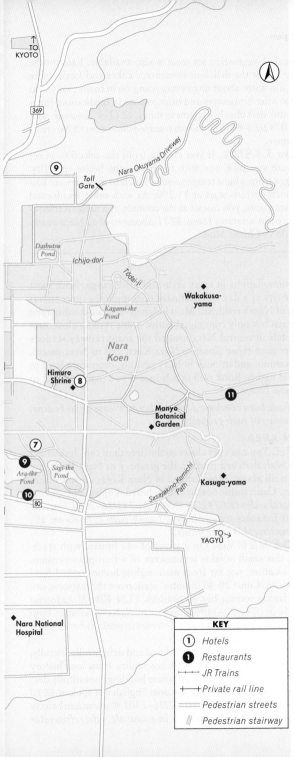

KEY

1 *Hotels*

1 *Restaurants*

⊢—⊣ *JR Trains*

+—+ *Private rail line*

▨▨ *Pedestrian streets*

▨ *Pedestrian stairway*

café-kaiseki meal. A vegetarian set meal is also available. Later in the afternoon, stop by for the delicious homemade cakes and fresh coffee or tea and find out more about any events going on in town that week. The owners also offer homestays and offer lessons in meditation, Japanese cooking, and shakuhachi (Japanese flute). ⊠ *13–1 Takamikaido, Nara-machi* ☎ *0742/26–4455* ⊕ *www.naracafe-youan.com* ⊟ *No credit cards* ⊗ *No dinner.*

$$$$ ✕**Tempura Asuka** 天ぷら飛鳥. If you choose from the selection of set
JAPANESE   meals, make sure you pick one with tempura—the house specialty. Other fare ranges from a light tempura-soba lunch to an elaborate kaiseki dinner. Lunch options start at ¥1,200. As with other less-formal Nara-machi restaurants, you can sit at the counter, at a table overlooking the garden, or in a tatami room. ⊠ *11 Shonami-cho, Nara-machi* ☎ *0742/26–4308* ⊗ *Closed Mon.*

WHERE TO STAY

Nara has accommodations in every style and price range. Since most people treat the city as a day-trip destination, at night the quiet streets are the domain of Nara's residents. Most lodgings have air-conditioning and TVs in rooms but only communal baths. Some ryokan close Sunday nights. Hotels in central Nara around the main railway stations are often noisier than those closer to Nara Koen and in Nara-machi. In spring and autumn and at peak holiday periods, rooms are hard to find on weekend nights. Book well in advance if you plan to travel to Nara during these times.

Hotel reviews have been condensed for this book. Please go to Fodors. com for full reviews of each property.

NARA KOEN AREA

$$$$ 🏠 **Edo-San** 江戸三. You can't get closer to the deer than this. Individual
RYOKAN   cottages, some with thatched roofs in the greenery of Nara Koen, are what Edo-San is all about. **Pros:** located in Nara Koen; closest neighbors are the deer. **Cons:** traffic nearby can be heard; English not spoken. ⊠ *1167 Takabatake-cho* ☎ *0742/26–2662* 🖷 *0742/26–2663* ⊕ *www. edosan.jp* ➦ *10 Japanese-style cottages, 1 with bath* ⌂ *In-room: a/c. In-hotel: parking (free)* ❣◎❣ *Some meals.*

$$ 🏠 **Hotel Nara Club** 奈良倶楽部. On a street of old houses with tradi-
HOTEL   tional gardens, this small hotel is reminiscent of a European pension. **Pros:** peaceful location; not far from main sights; home-cooked food using local produce. **Cons:** 20-40 minutes' walk from the stations; single, twin, and family rooms, but no doubles. ⊠ *21 Kita Mikado-cho* ☎ *0742/22–3450* 🖷 *0742/22–3490* ⊕ *www.naraclub.com/e/index.html* ➦ *8 rooms* ⌂ *In-room: a/c, refrigerator, Internet (some). In-hotel: Internet terminal, parking (free)* ❣◎❣ *No meals.*

$$$$ 🏠 **Kankaso** 観鹿荘. At once exquisitely refined and delightfully friendly,
RYOKAN   Kankaso exemplifies the best of Japanese hospitality. **Pros:** long history
★   of serving foreign guests; traditional Japanese building; beautifully decorated; very convenient to Nara Koen. **Cons:** English not spoken. ⊠ *10 Kasugano-cho* ☎ *0742/26–1128* 🖷 *0742/26–1301* ⊕ *www.kankaso.jp* ➦ *9 Japanese-style rooms, 5 with bath* ⌂ *In-room: a/c, safe, refrigerator*

The Nara Hotel was built in 1909.

(some), Internet. In-hotel: restaurant, bar, parking (paid) ⑩ *Some meals.*

$$$$
HOTEL
Fodor's Choice
★

▦ **Nara Hotel** 奈良ホテル. No wonder the Emperor stays here. Built in 1909, the hotel is a beautiful synthesis of Japanese and Western architecture. **Pros:** very spacious rooms; top-class service; imperial atmosphere **Cons:** nothing here comes cheap. ✉ *1093 Takabatake-cho, Nara-ken* ☎ *0742/26–3300* 🖷 *0742/23–5252* ⊕ *www.narahotel.co.jp* ⇨ *129 rooms, 3 suites* ⚓ *In-room: a/c, refrigerator, Internet. In-hotel: 2 restaurants, bar, laundry service, parking (free)* ⑩ *No meals.*

NARA-MACHI

$
RYOKAN

▦ **Ryokan Seikanso** 旅館静観荘. Of the many inexpensive, small ryokan in Nara-machi, this family-run establishment is the best pick for its spotlessness and attentive service. **Pros:** cheap and cheerful; great breakfasts; friendly service. **Cons:** rooms are clean but getting on in years; shared bathing and toilet facilities only. ✉ *29 Higashikitsu-ji-cho* 🖷 *0742/22–2670* ⇨ *9 Japanese-style rooms, all with shared bath* ⚓ *In-room: no phone, a/c, Internet. In-hotel: parking (free)* ⑩ *No meals.*

WESTERN NARA

$$–$$$
HOTEL

▦ **Hotel Fujita Nara** ホテルフジタ奈良. Centrally situated between JR Nara Station and Nara Koen, this modern hotel is often the best deal in town. **Pros:** central location; bicycle rental available. **Cons:** reasonable prices are rising steadily. ✉ *47–1 Shimo Sanjo-cho* ☎ *0742/23–8111* 🖷 *0742/22–0255* ⊕ *www.fujita-nara.com* ⇨ *114 rooms, 3 suites* ⚓ *In-room: a/c, refrigerator, Internet (some). In-hotel: 2 restaurants, bar, bicycles, Wi-Fi hotspot, parking (paid)* ⑩ *No meals.*

$$$
HOTEL

⊞ **Hotel Nikko Nara** ホテル日航奈良. Nara's largest hotel provides comfort in plush surroundings. **Pros:** directly connected to JR Nara Station; courteous staff. **Cons:** rooms and bathrooms are relatively small. ⊠ *8–1 Sanjo-hon-machi* ☎ *0742/35–8831* 🖷 *0742/35–6868* ⊕ *www. nikkonara.jp* ⇱ *330 rooms, 1 suite* ⚒ *In-room: a/c, refrigerator, Internet. In-hotel: 4 restaurants, laundry service, Internet terminal, parking (paid)* ¶⊙¶ *No meals.*

$$
RYOKAN

⊞ **Ryokan Nanto** 旅館南都. The quietest ryokan on the city side of Nara Koen, Nanto has airy tatami rooms of a simplicity fit for a Zen-practicing samurai. **Pros:** family-friendly; located right between the two stations. **Cons:** credit cards not accepted. ⊠ *29 Kamisanjo-cho* ☎ *0742/22–3497* 🖷 *0742/23–0882* ⊕ *www.basho.net/nanto* ⇱ *13 Japanese-style rooms, 3 with bath* ⚒ *In-room: a/c. In-hotel: restaurant, parking (paid)* ⊟ *No credit cards* ¶⊙¶ *Breakfast.*

$$$$
RYOKAN

⊞ **Tsubakiso** 旅館椿荘. Friendly service and an internal garden make for a relaxed stay in this quiet mix of old and new. **Pros:** lovely garden; central yet quiet location; vegetarian meals available upon request. **Cons:** communal bathing is not for the shy. ⊠ *35 Tsubai-cho* ☎ *0742/22–5330* 🖷 *0742/27–3811* ⇱ *7 Japanese-style rooms, 3 with bath* ⚒ *In-room: a/c, refrigerator, Internet. In-hotel: Internet terminal, Wi-Fi hotspot, parking (paid)* ¶⊙¶ *Some meals.*

SHOPPING

Nara is especially known for traditional arts and crafts, including aka-hadayaki pottery, ink, and linen. Nara-machi has the highest concentration of traditional shops (*see the Nara-machi section in Exploring Nara, above*) as well as those selling contemporary takes on the traditional. The area around Todai-ji has many touristy souvenir shops, though few that stand out. The Nara City Tourism Information Office can supply you with an English-language guide and map.

Kite-Mite Nara Shop. For an overview of the arts and crafts of Nara Prefecture, visit the Kite-Mite Nara Shop on your way to Nara Koen. A brochure in English is available. ⊠ *38–1 Noborioji-cho* ☎ *0742/26– 8828* ⊙ *Tues.–Sun. 10–6).*

KOBE

Kobe resonates with a cool, hip vibe, a condition of its internationalism and its position between mountains and sea. With more than 44,000 *gaijin* (foreigners) living in the city, representing more than 120 countries, Kobe may be Japan's most diverse city. It has great international cuisine, from Indonesian to French. It also has some of the best Japanese cuisine, especially the famous Kobe beef.

Kobe's diversity is largely attributable to its harbor. The port was a major center for trade with China dating back to the Nara period (710– 794). Kobe's prominence increased briefly for six months in the 12th century when the capital was moved from Kyoto to Fukuhara, now western Kobe. Japan acquiesced to opening five ports, and on January 1, 1868, international ships sailed into Kobe's harbor. American

Continued on page 545

THE ART OF MONOZUKURI
By Jared Lubarsky

8

TRADITIONAL JAPANESE CRAFTS

The Japanese take pride in their *monozukuri*: their gift for making things. And well they should, with traditions of craftsmanship centuries old to draw on, an itch for perfection, a loving respect for materials, and a profound aesthetic sense of what can be done with them.

There are really two craft traditions in Japan. In the first are the one-of-a-kind works of art—inlaid furniture and furnishings with designs in gold and mother-of-pearl, brocaded textiles, Tea Ceremony utensils, and so on—made by master artisans for wealthy patrons. These days, the descendants of these masters swell the ranks of Japan's *ningen koku-ho*, the official roster of Living National Treasures, who keep their crafts alive and set the standards of excellence. In the other are the humble charms of the *mingei* (folk craft) tradition: work in clay and bamboo, lacquer and native wood, iron and hand-forged steel—things made by nameless craftsmen for everyday use. Over the centuries the two traditions have enriched each other, and together they put Japanese craft work up among the best presents you can bring home from anywhere.

Top, clockwise: Kiyomizu pottery, ningyo doll, Darumas. Bottom: kokeshi doll

JAPANESE CERAMICS

Shopping for imari porcelain

Mashiko ware

If one Japanese folk tradition can be said to have contributed more than any other to Japan's collective cultural heritage, it must be pottery—admired by collectors and craftspeople all over the world. The tradition dates back more than 2,000 years, though pottery-making began to flourish as a real art form in the 16th century. Most Japanese pottery, apart from some porcelain and earthenware, is stoneware—formed into a wonderful variety of vases, cups, bowls, and platters and fired in climbing kilns on the slopes of hills.

Just visiting the regions where distinctive styles have developed would make a great *wanderjahr* in Japan. The village of Arita in Kyushu is famous for **imari** porcelain, with patterns of flowers and birds in bright enamel colors over blue and red underglazes. The folk pottery of **Mashiko**, in Tochigi Prefecture (northeast of Tokyo and southeast of Nikko), is admired for its rough textures and simple, warm colors. **Hagi** ware, from Western Honshu, is known for the rugged and rustic shapes of its Tea Ceremony bowls and cups. The red-brown **Bizen** ware from Okayama prefecture (also in Western Honshu)—one of the six remaining pottery centers of medieval Japan—is unglazed; every piece takes its unique colors and tones from the wood ash in the kiln. But you may also be interested in **Kyo-yaki** ceramics and porcelain from Kyoto, **Akahadayaki** pottery from Nara, or the **Jo-yachi** (glazed) pottery of Okinawa.

Hagi ware

Imari-Arita ware

Mashiko ware

Tobe ware

Kokutani ware

Bizen ware

Suzu ware

Matsushiro ware

Kutani ware

WHERE TO FIND: Most department stores in cities all over Japan have several different kinds of ceramics, though you'll find more regional specialties in the areas where they are produced. At first glance, Japanese ceramics may seem priced for a prince's table, but keep an eye out for seasonal sales; you can often find affordable pieces you will want to keep forever.

TOKYO SOURCE

Almost everyone passes through Tokyo on a trip to Japan. If you want to get an overview of traditional crafts or buy some souvenirs, the **Japan Traditional Craft Center** (✉ *Metropolitan Plaza 1-3F, 1-11-1 Nishi-Ikebukuro* ☎ *03/5954-6066* ⊕ *www.kougei.or.jp*) is open daily 11–7 and sells crafts from all over the country, in most of the important categories from paper to tools to pottery, under its own seal of approval.

TYPES OF JAPANESE CRAFTS

Although you'll find regional craft specialties all over Japan, in every mega-metropolis and small village, the best overall selection of stores will be found in Tokyo, Kyoto, and Nara. But you can save money by looking for regional crafts closer to the source.

Hina ningyo dolls

Furoshiki

DOLLS

Traditional dolls, meant primarily for display and not as playthings, come in many different styles. **Kokeshi** dolls, which date from the Edo period, are long cylinders of wood with painted features. **Daruma** are papier-mâché dolls painted red, round as Humpty-Dumpties, representing a Buddhist priest who legend says meditated in the lotus position for so long that his arms and legs atrophied. **Hakata** dolls, from Kyushu, are ceramic figurines in traditional costume, such as geisha, samurai, or festival dancers. **Kyo-ningyo**, from Kyoto, are made of wood coated with white shell paste and then clothed in elaborate costumes.

WHERE TO FIND: Buy Kyo-ningyo in Kyoto, Hakata in Kyushu (especially in Fukuoka). Kokeshi come from the Tohoku region. Daruma can be purchased at temples all over Japan, but they come from Takasaki, north of Tokyo.

PRINTED FABRICS

Stencil-dyed fabrics were an important element of the Edo (old Tokyo) craft tradition, and survive in a range of motifs and intricate geometric designs—especially for light summer kimonos, room dividers, and cushion covers. **Furoshiki**—large cotton squares for wrapping, storing, and carrying things—make great wall hangings, as do the smaller cotton hand towels called **tenugui**, which are used as towels or as a head-covering in Kendo (Japanese sword-fighting).

WHERE TO FIND: Furoshiki and tenugui can be found all over Japan, but some stores specialize in them.

Kokeshi

Tenugui

8

KIMONOS

Most Japanese women, unless they work in traditional restaurants, nowadays only wear kimonos rented for special occasions like weddings and coming-of-age ceremonies. A new one, in brocaded silk, can cost ¥1 million ($11,000) or more. Reluctant to pay that much for a bathrobe or a conversation piece? You might settle for a secondhand version—about ¥10,000 ($82) in a flea market, for one in decent condition—or look instead for cotton summer kimonos, called **yukata**, in a wide variety of colorful designs; you can buy one new for ¥7,000–¥10,000.

WHERE TO FIND: Kimonos are sold all over Japan, but you might want to look in Kyoto's Temple Markets for a reasonably priced, used kimono. Kyushu is also known for reasonably priced kimonos.

Wajima nuri, lacquerware

LACQUERWARE

For its history, diversity, and fine workmanship, lacquerware rivals ceramics as the traditional Japanese craft nonpareil. One warning: lacquerware thrives on humidity. Cheaper pieces usually have plastic rather than wood underneath, and because these won't shrink and crack in dry climates, they make safer—but no less attractive—buys.

WHERE TO FIND: Lacquerware can be found all over Japan, but it is a specialty of the Noto Peninsula (particularly Wajima). It's also very widely made in Kyushu.

Kimonos

Lacquerware being handcrafted in Wajima

Washi (Sugihara paper)

PAPER

What packs light and flat in your suitcase, won't break, doesn't cost much, and makes a great gift? The answer is **washi** (handmade paper, usually of mulberry fibers), which the Japanese craft in a myriad of colors, textures, and designs and fashion into an astonishing number of useful and decorative objects. Look for stationery, greeting cards, single sheets in color and classical motifs for gift wrapping and origami, and washi-covered jewelry boxes.

WHERE TO FIND: There are washi manufacturers all over Japan, but some of the most famous types are **Mino Washi** calligraphy paper from Gifu (see Nagoya, Ise-Shima, and the Kii Peninsula); **Tosa Washi** from Kochi (see Shikoku); and **Yama Washi** from Fukuoka (Kyushu).

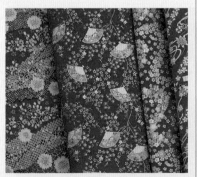

Patterned Washi

SWORDS AND KNIVES

Supple and incredibly strong, hand-forged steel was for centuries the stuff of samurai swords and armor. Genuine antique swords seldom come on the market now (imitations sold as flashy souvenirs are not really worth considering), and when they do they fetch daunting prices. But the same craftsmanship is still applied to a range of kitchen knives and cleavers, comparable in both quality and price to the best Western brands.

A set of japanese knife in a shop in Tokyo

WHERE TO FIND: You can find Japanese knives in any big-city department store, or look for them on the side streets of Kappabashi, the restaurant wholesale supply district in Tokyo. But the center for Japanese knife- and sword-making is the city of Seki, a few miles northeast of Gifu (see Nagoya, Ise-Shima, and the Kii Peninsula).

Tanto Japanese sword

and European sailors and traders soon settled in Kobe, and their culture and technology spread throughout the city. Cinema and jazz made their debut in Kobe, and that legacy is ongoing. Many original residences have survived, and the European structures contrast strikingly with the old Japanese buildings and modern high-rises.

Prior to 1995, Kobe was Japan's busiest port. But on January 17, 1995, an earthquake with a magnitude of 7.2 hit the Kobe area, killing more than 6,400 people, injuring almost 40,000, and destroying more than 100,000 homes. Communication lines were destroyed, damaged roads prevented escape and relief, and fires raged throughout the city. Kobe made a remarkable and quick recovery.

The city now pulses with the activity of a modern, industrialized city. The colorful skyline reflects off the night water, adding to Kobe's reputation as a city for lovers. Don't come to Kobe looking for traditional Japan; appreciate its urban energy, savor its international cuisine, and take advantage of its shopping.

ORIENTATION AND PLANNING

ORIENTATION

Kobe lies along the Seto Inland Sea in the center of Honshu, a little west of Osaka and several hours east of Hiroshima. Smaller than Tokyo and Osaka, Kobe is more accessible and less formidable. It is large enough, however, to keep you occupied with new attractions and events no matter how frequently you visit.

Divided into approximately 10 distinctive neighborhoods, the city extends from the business-oriented region near the harbor to the lower slopes of Mt. Rokko. Penned in by natural boundaries, Kobe expanded its territory with three man-made islands in the harbor.

Two man-made islands rest in the middle of the harbor. **Rokko Island** is home to numerous foreign companies, a number of shopping plazas, and the Sheraton hotel, and is where foreigners now tend to settle. **Port Island** features conference centers, an amusement park, and the Portopia Hotel. Port Island is linked with downtown by a fully computerized monorail—with no human conductor—that extends south to the Kobe airport.

Downtown. San-no-miya Station, in the city center, marks the heart of Kobe's entertainment and nightlife area. Every night passersby linger to hear musicians in a small park just north of the station. Moto-machi's stores are to the west, and most of the business district lies south of San-no-miya.

Kintano-cho. Kobe's original European and American settlers built elegant residences, now known as *ijinkan,* on the city's northern slopes. Many of the preserved ijinkan have been turned into museums. Small boutiques, international cafés, and a few antiques shops seduce visitors to meander along Kitano-zaka and Pearl Street.

North of Kobe. The impressive Nunobiki Falls are surprisingly accessible from downtown, just behind the Shin-Kobe Station. Rokko-san (*san* means "mountain") is a little farther out, providing great views and

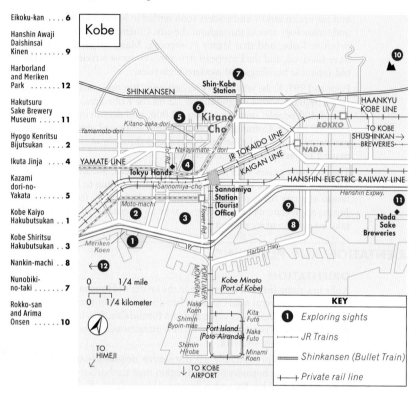

cool mountain air. Arima Onsen, on the other side of Rokko-san, is one
of Japan's oldest hot-springs destinations.

PLANNING

The big attractions of Kobe can be covered in a day or two. Hit the
Great Hanshin-Awaji Earthquake Museum and the Kobe City Museum
in the morning. Follow this with a stroll around Kitano-cho and a café
stop, and wind down the day at Harborland for dinner. On a second
day head up Rokko-san and to the resort town of Arima, where you
can soak in mineral hot springs and wander the quaint streets.

WHEN TO GO

Except for the cold days of winter and the humid days of midsummer,
Spring, especially at cherry-blossom time, and autumn are the best seasons to visit.

HOW MUCH TIME?

Although Kobe's main sights could be covered in a day, a two-day stop
in the city would not only give you enough time to see most of the sights,
it would also give you enough meal times to enjoy the numerous food
choices and relax into the city's laid-back rhythm. Put aside a third day
for getting out of the city and into the mountains of Rokko-san and the
hot springs at the famous resort of Arima.

GETTING HERE AND AROUND

AIRPORT TRANSFERS
From Kansai International Airport, take the JR Kansai Airport Express Haruka to Shin-Osaka and change to the JR Tokaido Line for Kobe's JR San-no-miya Station, a 75-minute (¥3,320) trip, not including transfer times. For a quicker trip, ignore the train and take the comfortable limousine bus (70 minutes; ¥1,800), which drops you off in front of San-no-miya Station.

From Osaka Itami Airport, buses to San-no-miya Station leave from a stand between the airport's two terminals approximately every 20 minutes 7:45 am–9:10 pm. The trip takes about 40 minutes (¥1,020).

Kobe Airport handles mainly domestic flights, is 18 minutes from JR San-no-miya Station via the Portliner (¥320 one-way).

Airport Contacts Kobe Airport Terminal (✉ *1 Kobe Kuko, Chuo-ku* ☎ *078/304–7777* ⊕ *www.kairport.co.jp/eng/index.html*).

SUBWAY TRAVEL
Kobe's main subway line runs from Tanigami in the far north of the city, and passes through Shin-Kobe and San-no-miya stations before continuing west to the outskirts of town. Another line runs along the coast from San-no-miya and links up with the main line at Shin-Nagata Station. Fares start at ¥180 and are determined by destination. The San-no-miya–Shin-Kobe trip costs ¥200.

The Portliner was the first digitally driven monorail in the world, and departs from San-no-miya Station every six minutes from 6:05 am until 11:40 pm on its loop to and around Port Island. The ride affords a close-up view of Kobe Harbor.

TRAIN TRAVEL
The Shinkansen (bullet train) stops at the Shin-Kobe Station, just north of San-no-miya. The two are connected by the Seishin-Yamate Line that extends north from San-no-miya Station to the Shin-Kobe Station. Shin-Kobe also connects to Arima.

The trip between Osaka Station and Kobe's San-no-miya Station takes 20 minutes on the JR Tokaido Line rapid train, which leaves at 15-minute intervals throughout the day; without a JR Pass the fare is ¥390. The Hankyu and Hanshin private lines run between Osaka and Kobe for ¥310.

The City Loop bus starts at San-no-miya and circles through Meriken Park, Harborland, and Kitano before returning to San-no-miya. Taxis are easy to find at San-no-miya Station, but can also be found at any *noriba,* or taxi stand.

Purchase tickets from a vending machine; you surrender them upon passing through the turnstile at your destination station. Fares depend on your destination.

Three rail lines, JR, Hankyu, and Hanshin, cut straight through the city from one side to the other, and converge at San-no-miya Station. Most of the city is a 10-minute walk from a train station, making trains the most convenient way to get around.

VISITOR INFORMATION

Kobe Tourist Information Center offers detailed maps, in English, of all the neighborhoods, with attractions and streets clearly marked. Also pick up a "Kobe Guide" and a "Visitor's Welcome Book," which has coupons on museums, activities, and hotels. The English-speaking staff can help book rooms, find tours, and give recommendations. The Kobe Information Center is near the West Exit of JR San-no-miya; another branch is located at the JR Shin-Kobe Station. The Japan Travel Bureau can arrange for hotel reservations, train tickets, package tours, and more throughout the country.

Visitor Information Japan Travel Bureau (⊠ *JR San-no-miya Station* ☎ *078/231–4118*). **Kobe Information Center** (⊠ *JR San-no-miya Station* ☎ *078/322–0220* ⊙ *Daily 9–7⊠ Shin-Kobe Station* ☎ *078/241–9550* ⊙ *Daily 10–6*). **Kobe Tourist Information Center** (⊠ *At West Exit of JR San-no-miya Station* ☎ *078/271–2401*).

EXPLORING KOBE

DOWNTOWN KOBE

In 1868, after nearly 200 years of isolation, Kobe's port opened to the West, and Kobe became an important gateway for cultural exchange. Confined to a small area by its natural boundaries, the city has kept its industrial harbor within the city limits. The harbor's shipping cranes project incongruously against the city's sleek skyscrapers, but the overall landscape manages to blend together beautifully. The harbor is approximately a 20-minute walk southwest of the San-no-miya area.

TOP ATTRACTIONS

Fodor's Choice ★
Hanshin Awaji Daishinsai Kinen *(Great Hanshin-Awaji Earthquake Memorial).* In 1995, the Great Hanshin-Awaji Earthquake killed 6,433 people and destroyed much of Kobe's harbor and vast areas of the city. Using documentary footage and audio, an introductory film shows the frightening destruction wrought upon this modern city. A re-created post-quake display, film screenings, and high-tech exhibits convey the sorrows and memories of the event. This excellent museum has English pamphlets and electronic guides and English-speaking volunteers are on hand. It's a 10-minute walk from the South Exit of JR Nada Station, one stop east of JR San-no-miya Station. ⊠ *1–5–2 Wakinohama Kaigan-dori, Chuo-ku* ☎ *078/262–5050* ⊕ *www.dri.ne.jp/english/index.html* 🎟 *¥800 to both Disaster Reduction and Human Renovation exhibits; ¥500 each for either one* ⊙ *Tues.–Sun. 9:30–4:30.*

Harborland and Meriken Park ハーバーランドとメリケンパーク. A trip to Kobe is incomplete without a waterside visit. Within Meriken Park broken slabs of thick concrete and crooked lightposts are preserved as part of the Port of Kobe Earthquake Memorial Park. Across the grassy park the Kobe Maritime Museum's roofline of white metal poles, designed like the billowing sails of a tallship, contrast beautifully with the crimson Port Tower. The top of the tower provides a 360-degree view of Kobe. A walkway connects to **Mosaic,** Harborland's outdoor shopping mall. You can eat dinner at any of the restaurants on the waterfront. The nighttime view is stunning, with Port Tower and the Maritime Museum lighted up. Nearby, a small Ferris wheel rotates lazily, the colors of its flashing lights bouncing off the sides of nearby ships. Meriken Park and Harborland are a 10-minute walk south of Moto-machi Station.

You can learn about earthquakes at the Hanshin Awaji Daishinsai Kinen.

Fodor'sChoice **Hyogo Kenritsu Bijutsukan** 兵庫県立美術館 *(Hyogo Prefectural Museum of*
★ *Art)*. This striking concrete edifice was designed by acclaimed architect
Tadao Ando. Ando works primarily with concrete, and is known for
his use of light and water, blending indoors and outdoors and utilizing
flowing geometric paths in his designs. He has innumerable works in
Japan, and designed the Museum of Modern Art in Fort Worth and the
Pulitzer Foundation for the Arts building in St. Louis. The permanent
exhibition features art from prominent 20th-century Japanese painters
Ryohei Koiso and Heizo Kanayama, Kobe natives who specialized in
Western techniques. The museum rotates its vast collection, displaying
fantastic modern works from Japanese artists as well as sculptures by
Henry Moore and Auguste Rodin. It also hosts international exhibi-
tions. It's a 10-minute walk from the South Exit of JR Nada Station,
one stop east of JR San-no-miya Station. ⊠ *1–1–1 Wakinohama Kaigan-
dori, Chuo-ku* ☎ *078/262–0901* ⊕ *www.artm.pref.hyogo.jp* ✉ *¥500*
☉ *Tues.–Sun. 10–6.*

★ **Kobe Shiritsu Hakubutsukan** 神戸市立博物館 *(Kobe City Museum)*. This
museum specializes in work from the 16th and 17th centuries, focusing on reciprocal cultural influences between East and West. The first
floor has a variety of displays on the West's impact on Japan in the
second half of the 17th century. Other exhibits document the influence
of Western hairstyles for women and the arrival of electric and gas
lamps. The museum also has an impressive collection of woodcuts, old
maps, archaeological artifacts, and Namban-style art, namely prints,
silkscreens, and paintings from the late 16th to 17th century, usually

8

depicting foreigners in Japanese settings. The historical exhibits are fascinating, but it is the artwork from this period that is the real draw.

From San-no-miya Station, walk south on Flower Road to Higashi-Yuenchi Koen. Walk through the park to the Kobe Minato post office, across the street on the west side. Then head east along the street in front of the post office toward the Oriental Hotel. Turn left at the corner in front of the hotel, and the City Museum is in the old Bank of Tokyo building at the end of the block. ⊠ *24 Kyo-machi, Chuo-ku* ☎ *078/391–0035* ✑ *¥200; more for special exhibitions* ⊙ *Tues.–Sun. 9:30–5.*

WORTH NOTING

Hakutsuru Sake Brewery Museum 白鶴酒造資料館. Nada, one of Kobe's westernmost neighborhoods, is home to a number of museums and breweries—many offering free sake tasting. The most popular is the Hakutsuru Sake Brewery Museum. At the door is a sake barrel of immense proportions. Traditional tools and devices, videos in English, and life-size figures of traditionally clad brewers demonstrate the sake-brewing process. The tour ends with free tasting. It's a five-minute walk south from Hanshin Sumiyoshi Station. ⊠ *4–5–5 Sumiyoshi-minami-machi, Higashinada-ku* ☎ *078/822–8907* ✑ *Free* ⊙ *Tues.–Sun. 9:30–4:30.*

Ikuta Jinja 生田神社. Legend has it that this shrine was founded by Empress Jingu in the 3rd century, making it one of Japan's oldest. An impressive orange torii, rebuilt after the 1995 earthquake, stands amid the bustle of modern Kobe, welcoming tourists and religious observers alike. Every year two Noh plays, *Ebira* and *Ikuta Atsumori*, at Ikuta's Autumn Festival (Akimatsuri) retell parts of the 12th-century *Genpei* war. It's around the corner from Tokyu Hands department store, about 450 yards west of San-no-miya Station. ⊠ *1–2–1 Shimoyamate-dori, Chuo-ku* ✑ *Free* ⊙ *Daily 7–7.*

Kobe Kaiyo Hakubutsukan 神戸海洋博物館 *(Kobe Maritime Museum and Kawasaki Good Times World)*. The Maritime Museum is the stunning building with a billowing roofline of metal-pipe sails. It showcases detailed ship models, opening with a 27-foot model of the HMS *Rodney,* the British flagship that led a 12-ship flotilla into Kobe Harbor on January 1, 1868. A model of the *Oshoro Maru,* one of Japan's earliest sailing ships, is adorned with pearls, rubies, gold, and silver. There are also displays of modern tankers. **Kawasaki Good Times World** is also inside the museum. High-tech displays and interactive models showcase the Kawasaki company's products, from Jet Skis to the Shinkansen bullet train, and its history. Visitors can ride a helicopter flight simulator and see a robot work at a Rubik's Cube. Admission is included in the fee for the museum. Nearby is Kobe's Port Tower, which looks not unlike the Sydney Tower (*see* ⇨ *Harborland and Meriken Park, above*). ⊠ *2 Meriken Koen, Hatoba-cho, Chuo-ku* ☎ *078/327–8983* ✑ *¥500 for museum, ¥600 for Port Tower, ¥800 for both* ⊙ *Tues.–Sun. 10–5.*

Nankin-machi 南京町. If you're heading to Meriken Park or Harborland, consider a short stop in Kobe's Chinatown. The area was originally a center for Chinese immigrants to Kobe, though it is now mostly popular with Japanese tourists for souvenirs and food. It's a lot more Japan-like than one would expect China to be. To find Nankin-machi from Moto-machi Station, walk on the port side and enter the neighborhood through the large fake-marble gate.

NEED A BREAK?

✕ **Free Café Harimaya Station.** True to its name, the Harimaya Station offers coffee, tea, juices, and a selection of traditional Japanese snacks for no charge. Harimaya Honten Confectionery established the café to "share the delightful taste of Japanese rice crackers" and educate people about environmental problems and possible solutions. Located just south of Kobe's *Chuka-gai* (Chinatown) it is a refreshing rest stop. There is also a counter in the back where patrons can order Harimaya rice crackers. ⊠ *1–2–7 Sakae-machi-dori, Chuo-ku* ☎ *078/392–1030* ⊕ *www.harimayahonten.co.jp/pc_english* ⏱ *Daily.*

KITANO-CHO

Wealthy foreigners, including Americans, English, and Germans, settled in the Kitano area in the late 19th century, bringing Western-style domestic architecture. Their homes are referred to in Kobe as *ijinkan* (pronounced "choo-eh-keh"), and the district is extremely popular with Japanese tourists, who enjoy the rare opportunity to see old-fashioned Western houses. Some residences are still inhabited by Westerners, but more than a dozen 19th-century ijinkan in Kitano-cho are open to the public. A few of them are worth exploring, but seeing them all can be repetitive. The curious mélange of Japanese and Western Victorian and Gothic architecture makes for a good neighborhood walk. The streets are littered with small boutiques, cafés, and a few antiques shops, including Nanae. Try Bistrot Café de Paris for a bite of French cuisine if you get hungry.

To get to Kitano-cho, walk 15 minutes north along Kitano-zaka-dori from San-no-miya Station or 10 minutes west along Kitano-dori from Shin-Kobe Station. Yamamoto-dori (nicknamed Ijinkan-dori) is Kitano's main east–west street, and the ijinkan are on the small side streets ascending the hill. Tourist information centers offer detailed area maps with all attractions marked in English.

8

TOP ATTRACTIONS

Eikoku-kan 英国館 (English House). This typically old-fashioned Western house (pronounced "eh-ee-ko koo-kan") was constructed in 1907 by an Englishman named Baker and served as a makeshift hospital during World War II. Now it's a house museum by day and an English pub by night. Antique baroque and Victorian furnishings dominate the interior, there are several downstairs bars, and, as if belonging to a decadent member of the royal family, a bottle of champagne rests in the bathtub. A classic black Jaguar in the driveway and an enormous moose head on the wall complete the English atmosphere. ⊠ *2–3–16 Kitano-dori, Chuo-ku* ☎ *078/241–2338* 💴 *¥700* ⏱ *Museum daily 9–5; pub daily 5 pm–1 am.*

Kazami dori-no-Yakata 風見鶏の館 (*Weathercock House*). More elaborate than any other Kobe ijinkan, this one, built by a German trader in

1910, stands out strikingly in red brick at the north end of Kitano-cho. It is listed as an Important Cultural Property. The interior reflects various traditional German architectural styles, including that of a medieval castle. Its architecture makes this the most famous ijinkan, but the interiors are spartan, with few additional attractions. ⊠ *3–13–3 Kitano-cho, Chuo-ku* ☎ *078/242–3223* 💴 *¥300* 🕙 *Apr.–Nov, daily 9–6; Dec.–Mar, daily 9–5; closed 1st Tues. of Mar., June, Sept., and Dec.*

NORTH OF KOBE

Thanks to Kobe's mountain backdrop, hiking is a popular local pastime. From Shin-Kobe Station it's a short climb to the Nunobiki Falls. For a good mountain day hike, try going up Rokko-san; from Hankyu Kobe Line Rokko Station you can take a bus or taxi to Rokko Cable-Shita cable-car station ("Shita" means down or bottom). From there you can either hike all the way up the mountain or take the cable car partway. You may see wild boar—harmless unless provoked—in the forested mountains.

> **DISAPPEARING DOLLS**
>
> If you make it to Arima, the *Arima ningyo fude* (Arima doll brush) makes a nice souvenir. Made for calligraphy, the brushes have handles wrapped in colorful silk thread, and a little doll pops out of the handle when writing. The doll disappears when the brush is laid down. Legend has it that long ago Emperor Kotoku greatly desired a son. After he visited Arima Springs his wish was granted and a son was born. Made for more than 1,300 years, the dolls symbolize the birth of Prince Arima. The brushes are handmade locally, and their beautiful designs make them popular gift items.

TOP ATTRACTIONS

Nunobiki-no-taki 布引の滝 *(Nunobiki Falls).* In the bustle of this modern city, you wouldn't think that one of Japan's most impressive waterfalls would be just behind the train station. Nunobiki Falls has four gushing cascades in the forests of Mt. Rokko. References to their beauty have appeared in Japanese literature since the 10th century. They are a 20-minute walk from behind the Shin-Kobe Station. After the falls you can pick up the Shin-Kobe Ropeway, which stops just above the falls before continuing on to the Nunobiki Herb Park. The stopping point provides a beautiful view of the city, especially at night. The signs leading you to the falls are in Japanese, but the concierge at the Crown Plaza ANA Hotel can provide English-language hiking maps. ⊠ *Chuo-ku.*

★ **Rokko-san and Arima Onsen** 六甲山と有馬温泉. Three cable cars scale Mt. Rokko, providing spectacular views of the city. For convenience, take the Shin-Kobe Ropeway up to the Nunobiki Herb Park. It departs just east of the Shin-Kobe Station. You can do this trip in a half day, but you may want a full day to explore Arima Onsen. Ideally, time the trip so you'll descend soon after dusk, when the city lights shine against the black sea.

The Rokko cable also has staggering views of lush forests. On the mountain are various recreational areas, including the oldest golf course

Himeji-jo, about 50 km (31 mi) west of Kobe, can be reached in about 40 minutes by train.

in Japan, designed in 1903 by the English merchant Arthur H. Gloom, and the summerhouses of Kobe's wealthier residents.

To get to Rokko-san, take the Hankyu Kobe Line from Hankyu San-no-miya Station to Hankyu Rokko Station (¥180). From there take a taxi or a bus to Rokko Cable-Shita Station. A funicular railway travels up the mountain to Rokko-sanjo Station (¥570). You can return to Kobe by cable car or by rail. Take the Kobe Dentetsu to Tanigami Station and change for the subway back to San-no-miya (¥900).

The Japanese were already enjoying the thermal waters at **Arima Onsen** before the 7th century. Arima is on the north slope of Rokko-san and consists of a maze of tiny streets and traditional houses. Some 30 ryokan use the thermal waters' reputed curative powers to attract guests. Although the water gushes up freely from springs, some ryokan charge as much as ¥10,000 for use of their baths. Go instead to the public bath, **Arima Onsen Kaikan,** in the center of the village near the bus terminal. Here ¥520 gets you a soak in the steaming waters. Arima Onsen Kaikan is open daily 8 am–10 pm (closed the first and third Tuesday of the month). Take the subway north from JR Shin-Kobe Station, transferring at Tanigami and ending at Arima (¥900).

HIMEJI

Himeji City is about 50 km west of Kobe and is most easily accessed via the JR Express (Sanyo Line), which will deposit you in JR Himejo Station after 40 minutes of travel time from Kobe (the trip from Kyoto on the same line takes an additional 15 minutes).

Fodor's Choice ★ **Himejo-jo.** Also known as Shirasagi-jo (White Egret Castle), Himeji Castle is visible as soon as you exit the station. Universally loved, it dazzles the city from atop a nearby hill. A visit to Himeji-jo could well be one of the high points of your trip to Japan, especially if you can manage to see the brilliantly lighted white castle soaring above cherry blossoms or pine branches at night. Thanks to frequent rail service, it should be easy to hop off, visit the castle, and jump on another train two hours later.

Himeji-jo could be regarded as medieval Japan's crowning achievement of castle design and construction. It arrived at its present state of perfection after many transformations, however. It was first a fortress in the year 1333 and was transformed into a castle in 1346. Radically enlarged by Terumasa Ikeda in the period 1601–1610, it has remained essentially the same ever since, surviving numerous wars and—perhaps even more miraculously—never once falling victim to the scourge of fire.

The five-story, six-floor main *donjon* (stronghold) stands more than 100 feet high and is built into a 50-foot-high stone foundation. Surrounding this main donjon are three smaller ones; all four are connected by covered passageways. Attackers would have had to cross three moats, penetrate the outer walls, and then withstand withering attack from the four towers and the more than 30 other buildings within. It was an impregnable fortress then, and its grace and grand proportions still inspire awe. Filmmaker Akira Kurosawa used Himeji-jo's exterior and the castle's grounds in his 1985 movie *Ran*.

Although not completely necessary for getting around or understanding the features of this amazing castle, informative, detailed free guided tours in English are usually available from volunteer guides, though they cannot be booked in advance; ask about the availability of a guide when you buy your entry ticket. Tours usually take 90 minutes.

Major renovation work on the main castle's rooftop will affect the visitor experience through early 2015. Scaffolding completely obscures the main castle exterior, and at this writing, the castle keep was expected to be off-limits through March 2011, after which the interior will partially reopen to visitors; an observation platform will also be available during the renovation (accessible by elevator); reservations for the Observation Platform are recommended, though same-day tickets may be available on occasion (the reservations line may be in Japanese only, so it may be wise to have your hotel concierge make these arrangements). The castle interior is expected to be off-limits again from mid-2014 through the end of the renovation period in 2015. Other buildings remain open during the renovation.

From the central north exit of JR Himeji Station, the castle is a 15- to 20-minute walk or a five-minute bus ride; also, bicycles are available free at the Tourist Office next door. The bus departs from the station plaza, on your left as you exit. ⊠ *Honmati 68, Hyogo, Himeji* ☎ *0792/85–1146* ⊕ *www.himeji-castle.gr.jp/index/english/index.html* ▱ *¥600, ¥400 during renovation (Apr. 2010–Mar. 2015), ¥200 for Observation Platform* ۝ *Sept.–May, daily 9–4; Jun.–Aug., daily 9–5.*

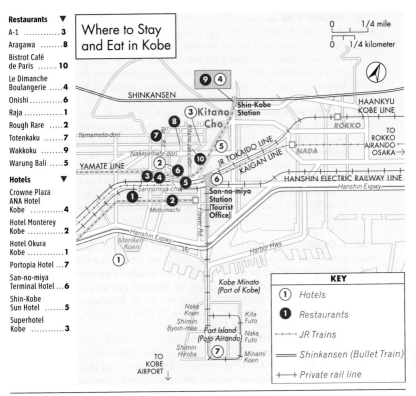

WHERE TO EAT

Kobe is the place to find international cuisine, especially dishes from Europe and Southeast Asia. Excellent restaurants are found practically anywhere but are especially prevalent north of San-no-miya Station and in the Kitano area. For a quick snack, stop by one of the city's delicious bakeries.

$$$$ ✕ **A-1.** A-1 has a relaxed atmosphere and serves thick slices of Kobe beef.
STEAK The teppanyaki steak (broiled on a hot plate) is cooked in a spice, wine, and soy marinade and served with charcoal-grilled vegetables and crisp garlic potatoes. The "small" is enough to fill you up, and costs ¥5,400. Four shops are about town, but the main one is conveniently north of Hankyu San-no-miya Station, across from the B-Kobe hotel. ⊠ *B1F Lighthouse Bldg., 2–2–9 Shimoyamate-dori, Chuo-ku* ☎ *078/331–8676.*

$$$$ ✕ **Aragawa** あら皮. Japan's first steak house is famed for its superb,
STEAK hand-fed Kobe beef from one farm in the nearby city of Sanda. The
Fodor's Choice melt-in-your-mouth *sumiyaki* (charcoal-broiled) steak is worth its
★ weight in yen and only served with mustard and pepper. (Don't even think about asking for other condiments.) The dining room's dark-wood paneling and lovely chandelier give it a European air. Be prepared to spend a minimum of ¥28,000 for your main course. ⊠ *2–15–18 Nakayamate-dori, Chuo-ku* ☎ *078/221–8547* ⊙ *Closed Sun.*

$$ ✕**Bistrot Café de Paris** ビストロカフェドパリ. This lively café offers
FRENCH delectable French cuisine and has a popular outdoor terrace—a true
rarity in Japan at a prime location. The menu ranges from couscous
to bouillabaisse. Midway up the hill on Kitano-zaka, it's great for
people-watching and is a good stop while cruising the Kitano district.
Lunch sets start at around ¥1,000, dinners around ¥3,000. ⌧ *1–7–21
Yamamoto-dori, Chuo-ku* ☎ *078/241–9448.*

$ ✕**Le Dimanche Boulangerie.** Even among Kobe's many excellent bakery-
CAFÉ cafés, Le Dimanche stands out. The owners make some of the best arti-
sanal bread in the city, seamlessly integrating Japanese and European
elements. Unique specialties include their *renkon* (lotus root) tartine,
crème brûlée croissant, and signature *viennois aux airelles* (Viennese
cranberry roll). The second-floor café is bright and airy, with rustic
hardwood floors and tables. It's the perfect spot for a light snack while
browsing the many botiques along Tor Road. ⌧ *3–12–16 Kitanagasa-
dori, Chuo-ku* ☎ *078/331–8760* ⊕ *le-dimanche.jp* ▭ *No credit cards*
☽ *No dinner.*

$$$$ ✕**Onishi** 大西. Onishi has a well-deserved reputation, both with Japa-
STEAK nese locals and longtime foreign residents, for serving fine Kobe beef.
★ Steaks are cooked by master chefs in the middle of an enormous coun-
ter—hot plate around which diners sit. Baseball players and sumo wres-
tlers are among the celebrity patrons. ⌧ *3F Kitanofenikusu Bldg.,
1–17–6 Nakayamate-dori, Chuo-ku* ☎ *078/332–4029* ▭ *No credit
cards* ☽ *Closed Sun. and Mon. No lunch.*

$$ ✕**Raja** ラジャ. Raja's mellow ambience is matched by delicious Indian
INDIAN food. The restaurant is now in its second generation; the friendly
★ owner/chef is the son of the reputed first Indian chef in Kobe. Among
their home-style Indian food of spicy curries and samosas, vegetarians
can find something *mecha oishii* (very delicious). Raja attributes the
excellence of their tandoori chicken
to using the highest grade charcoal
available in Japan. It's located
on the west end of Chinatown,
near Moto-machi. Dinner sets
start from ¥3,200. ⌧ *B1F Sano-
tatsu Bldg., 2–7–4 Sakae-machi,
Chuo-ku* ☎ *078/332–5253.*

$$ ✕**Rough Rare** ラフレア. This funky,
ECLECTIC laid-back, two-story café attracts a
young, stylish clientele. A DJ booth
is upstairs for the restaurant's occa-
sional music events. Pasta, burgers,
salads, and *omuraisu* (a Japanese
omelet filled with ketchup-flavored
rice) are served. The food isn't
gourmet, but the restaurant is just
plain cool. ⌧ *18–2 Akashi-cho,
near Daimaru department store,
Chuo-ku* ☎ *078/333–0808* ▭ *No
credit cards.*

REARED ON BEER

Around the world, Kobe beef is
legendary for its succulence and
taste. Cows receive daily mas-
sages, and in summer they ingest
a diet of sake and beer mash.
They are descended from an
ancient line of *wagyu* (Japanese
cows) known to be genetically
predisposed to higher marbling.
True Kobe beef comes from only
262 farms in the Tajima region of
Hyogo Prefecture (of which Kobe
is the capital), each of which raise
an average of five animals. The
best beef restaurants are mostly
in the central Chuo-ku district, and
Kobe beef is on the menu at the
top hotels.

$$$$
CHINESE

✕**Totenkaku** 東天閣. This Chinese restaurant has been famous among Kobe residents since 1945 for its Peking duck, flown in fresh from China. Built at the turn of the 20th century, Totenkaku is in one of Kobe's ijinkan, the F. Bishop House. With tall ceilings, red carpets, luxurious curtains, and artwork from China, the building itself is worth the proverbial cost of admission. You can keep the price down by ordering one of the Chinese noodle specialties to fill you up, or by going at lunchtime, when you can have a set meal for just ¥2,100, but some of the special dishes can cost up to ¥31,000. ⊠ *3–14–18 Yamamoto-dori, Chuo-ku* ☎ *078/231–1351.*

$$$$
STEAK

✕**Wakkoku** 和黒. Wakkoku is a swank restaurant in the shopping plaza underneath the Oriental hotel. The beef is sliced thin and cooked before you on a teppanyaki grill along with fresh vegetables and served with pepper, mustard, and soy sauce for dipping. The food is delicious. Wakkoku uses three-year-old cows that have never been bred, which assures their highest-quality beef of unbelievable tenderness. Lunch sets start at ¥2,940 and go up to ¥5,040. The pricier option uses the highest-quality meat, a small but noticeable difference. ⊠ *Kitano-cho, 1-chome, Chuo-ku* ☎ *078/262–2838.*

$$–$$$
INDONESIAN

✕**Warung Bali** ワルン・バリ. The dulcet sounds of the gamelan drift about Warung Bali, a tidy Indonesian restaurant serving Balinese food. The *tempeh goring* (tempeh with shrimp paste, tomato, and chili peppers) and tofu with peanut sauce are simply amazing. Owner and chef Made Widjaja is on hand to do more than inspire Japanese to eat *nasi campur* (rice topped with meats, vegetables, and peanuts, and eggs) with their hands; he speaks fluent English and can custom-make dishes, a relief for vegetarians dining in Japan. ⊠ *1F Onaga Bldg., 2–4–5 Kita-nagasa Dori, Chuo-ku* ☎ *078/321–6080* ⊟ *No credit cards.*

8

WHERE TO STAY

Kobe is an industrialized city that caters to business travelers. There are many comfortable, well-situated business hotels, almost all of which have rooms with air-conditioning, private bath, and TV.

Hotel reviews have been condensed for this book. Please go to Fodors. com for full reviews of each property.

$$$$
HOTEL
Fodor'sChoice
★

🏨 **Crowne Plaza ANA Hotel Kobe** クラウンプラザアナ神戸. The tallest building in Kobe, this stunning luxury hotel stands out prominently at night, a brightly lighted needle-thin tower jutting into the sky. **Pros:** nice views of the city; only a few steps away from the bullet train station; unusual in a luxury hotel, in-room Internet service is free. **Cons:** slightly outside central Kobe. ⊠ *Kitano-cho, 1-chome, Chuo-ku, Hyogo-ken* ☎ *078/291–1121* 🖷 *078/291–1151* ⊕ *www.ichotelsgroup.com* ⇄ *580 rooms, 12 suites* ⌕ *In-room: a/c, Internet. In-hotel: 7 restaurants, room service, bar, pool, gym* ⊙ *No meals.*

$$$$
HOTEL

🏨 **Hotel Monterey Kobe** ホテルモントレー神戸. With its Mediterranean-style courtyard fountains and European furnishings, the Hotel Monterey takes you off Kobe's busy streets and into modern Italy. **Pros:** Italian styling; large rooms; great location; in-room Internet is free. **Cons:** not a very Japanese experience. ⊠ *2–11–13 Shimoyamate-dori, Chuo-ku* ☎ *078/392–7111* 🖷 *078/322–2899* ⇄ *164 rooms* ⌕ *In-room: a/c, Internet. In-hotel: restaurant, Wi-Fi hotspot, parking (paid)* ⊙ *No meals.*

$$$$ ⊡ **Hotel Okura Kobe** ホテルオークラ神戸. A 35-story hotel on the wharf
HOTEL in Meriken Koen, this is one of the city's best. **Pros:** high-level customer
★   service; choice of Western or Japanese rooms; great views. **Cons:** the
extras and restaurant meals are pricey. ⊠ *Meriken Koen, 2–1 Hatoba-
cho, Chuo-ku* ☎ *078/333–0111* 🖷 *078/333–6673* ⊕ *www.kobe.
hotelokura.co.jp* ↩ *457 Western-style rooms, 5 Japanese-style rooms,
12 suites* ⌂ *In-room: a/c, refrigerator, Internet. In-hotel: 5 restaurants,
room service, bar, pools, gym* ⍥ *No meals.*

$$$$ ⊡ **Portopia Hotel** ポートピアホテル. A huge hotel with every facility imag-
HOTEL inable, rooms here overlook the port, and the restaurants and lounges
on the top floors have panoramic views of Rokko-san and Osaka Bay.
Pros: lots of facilities. **Cons:** a little dated; not very convenient for downtown sightseeing. ⊠ *6–10–1 Minatojima Naka-machi, Chuo-ku* ☎ *078/
302–1111* 🖷 *078/302–6877* ⊕ *www.portopia.co.jp* ↩ *745 rooms* ⌂ *In-
room: a/c, refrigerator, Internet. In-hotel: 10 restaurants, room service,
bar, tennis court, pools, gym* ⍥ *No meals.*

$$$ ⊡ **San-no-miya Terminal Hotel** 三宮ターミナルホテル. In the terminal build-
HOTEL ing above JR San-no-miya Station, this hotel is extremely convenient,
particularly if you need to catch an early train. **Pros:** great location for
access to public transportation. **Cons:** basic facilities (but Kobe is just
outside your door). ⊠ *8–1–2 Kumoi-dori, Chuo-ku* ☎ *078/291–0001*
🖷 *078/291–0020* ⊕ *www.sth-hotel.co.jp* ↩ *190 rooms* ⌂ *In-room: a/c,
refrigerator, Wi-Fi* ⍥ *No meals.*

$ ⊡ **Shin-Kobe Sun Hotel** 新神戸サンホテル. This old-fashioned busi-
HOTEL ness hotel was built in the early boom years after World War II. **Pros:**
good public bathing facilities. **Cons:** the rooms have seen better days.
⊠ *2–1–9 Nunobiki-cho, Chuo-ku* ☎ *078/272–1080* 🖷 *078/272–1080*
↩ *159 rooms* ⌂ *In-room: a/c, refrigerator, Wi-Fi* ⍥ *Breakfast.*

¢   ⊡ **Superhotel Kobe.** This business hotel features rooms built according
HOTEL to a formula, with just two set prices, one for singles and one for
doubles. **Pros:** bargain price for a central location. **Cons:** small rooms;
semi-double rather than double beds. ⊠ *2–1–11 Kano-cho, Chuo-ku*
☎ *078/261–9000* 🖷 *078/261–9090* ↩ *87 rooms* ⌂ *In-room: no phone,
a/c, Internet* ⍥ *No meals.*

NIGHTLIFE

Kobe's compactness is an advantage—virtually all the best bars are
within walking distance of each other. Kobe is regarded as the center
of Japan's thriving jazz scene.

Booze Up Bar. Entering Booze Up feels like stepping onto the retro set of
a Quentin Tarantino movie. Soul and funk LPs are artfully blended one
to the other on dual turntables. Tasty pizzas and pastas are served up
alongside good cocktails. Can ya dig it? Just northwest of Tokyu Hands
department store. ⊠ *2–15–3 Shimoyamate-dori* ☎ *078/322–2873.*

Polo Dog. Polo Dog is regularly packed with foreigners, both longtime
residents and travelers passing through, and it usually has live music
on weekends, when the place can get loud. The bar serves burgers, sal-
ads, and excellent garlic french fries. It's arrayed with 1950s and '60s
Americana and is known for having the cheapest drinks in town. ⊠ *2F*

The Crowne Plaza Kobe is the tallest building in town.

K Bldg., 1–3–21 San-no-miya-cho, 1 street south of Center Gai, near Flower Rd., Chuo-ku ☎ *078/331–3945.*

Sone. The city's most famous jazz club, in existence since 1961, is run by the Sone family. Four sets of live music are played every night, starting at 6:50, and the action often centers on a piano trio with rotating guest vocalists. The musicians are a mix of Japanese and visiting foreigners. Spacious and relaxed, Sone serves pizza, pasta, and salads. There's a cover charge of ¥900. ✉ *1–24–10 Nakayamate-dori* ☎ *078/221–2055.*

SHOPPING

SHOPPING AREAS

Kobe's historic shopping area is known as **Moto-machi.** It extends west for 2 km (1 mi) from JR Moto-machi Station. Much of the district is under a covered arcade, which starts opposite the Daimaru department store and runs just north of Nankin-machi. Moto-machi is more of a functional shopping area, selling housewares (including antiques), imported foods, and electronics, with restaurants scattered between.

Nearly connected to the Moto-machi arcade, the **San-no-miya Center Gai** arcade extends from the department store Sogo to the Moto-machi area for 1 km (½ mi). Because it's next to San-no-miya Station, this is a good stop for a bite to eat. Center Gai has a hipper vibe than the Moto-machi district. Next to Sogo is a branch of the Loft department store, home to crafts and lifestyle accessories spread over four floors. The building also houses a branch of the Kinokuniya bookstore, which has a small English-language selection.

Piazza Kobe and Motoko Town make up the narrow shopping district running under the JR train tracks from San-no-miya to Moto-machi. The shops range from Italian leather shoes and handmade accessories to Chinese apothecaries and small electronics. Not for the claustrophobic, it is an excellent chance to see Japan living up to its reputation to make use of every last inch of space.

BOUTIQUE ROW

Kobe's trendy crowd shops in the exclusive stores on Tor Road, which stretches north–south on a tree-lined slope into Kitano-cho. Fashionable boutiques selling Japanese designer brands and imported goods alternate with chic cafés and restaurants. The side streets are fun to poke about.

SPECIALTY STORES

Kinoshita Pearl. Established in 1938, Kinoshita pearl remains a small boutique with unique designs and quality service. While the store offers many classic designs, it has a range of high-end "casual" pearl jewelry as well. Just note that casual in Kobe still comes with a high price tag. ✉ *1–1–7 Yamamoto-dori, Chuo-ku* ☎ *078/221–3170* ⊕ *www.kinoshitapearl.co.jp* ⊗ *Thurs.–Tues. 10–6.*

Nanae. This darling and inexpensive antiques shop in Kitano-cho has a large collection of high-quality used *yukata* (lightweight summer kimonos) that shoppers can try on and a collection of ceramics, laquerware, and antiques. Nanae, the owner, enjoys explaining the history behind the pieces. ✉ *1F Kurata Bldg., 2–14–26 Yamamoto-dori, Chuo-ku* ☎ *078/222–8565* ⊗ *Daily 10:30–7.*

Naniwa-ya. This store sells excellent Japanese lacquerware at reasonable prices; it has been in operation since before World War I. ✉ *3–8 Moto-machi-dor i, 4-chome, Moto-machi* ☎ *078/341–6367* ⊗ *Thurs.–Tues. 11–6.*

Sakae-ya. This store sells traditional Japanese dolls, from *Oshie* (three-dimensional pictures made of silk) to *kimekomi* dolls (animals representing the zodiac calendar) to the traditional samurai and kimono-clad ladies. The tiny shop is packed with cloth for dollmaking, cupboards for hiding doll-making supplies, and, of course, dolls. ✉ *8–5 Moto-machi-dori, 5-chome, Moto-machi* ☎ *078/341–1307* ⊗ *Tues.–Sun. 10–5:30.*

Santica Town is an underground shopping mall with 120 shops and 30 restaurants. It extends for several blocks beneath Flower Road south from San-no-miya Station. It's closed the third Wednesday of the month. ✉ *1–10–1 San-no-miya, Chuo-ku, Hyogo-ken* ⊗ *Daily 10–8.*

Tasaki Shinju, the main shop of this pearl company, not only sells pearls but also exhibits astounding works of "pearl" art, including a model of the "Akashi Pearl Bridge" and a rooster with an impossibly long pearl tail. ✉ *Tasaki Bldg., 6–3–2 Minatojima, Naka-machi, Port Island* ☎ *078/303–7667* ⊗ *Daily 9–6.*

Tor Deco. This Tor Road boutique specializes in beautiful handcrafted glass accessories, gifts, and housewares. It features the work of artisans from around the country, each with their own unique style. ✉ *2–4–12 Nakayamate-dori, Chuo-ku* ☎ *078/322–0468* ⊕ *www.tor-deco.com* ⊗ *Thurs.–Tues. 10–8.*

Western Honshu

WORD OF MOUTH

"You can take a local train from Hiroshima JR station to the Miya-jima rail station. It's about 15 minutes or so from memory, then the ferry to Miyajima Island. [It's a] very pretty place, and you can spend a few hours wandering around there. If you have JR Pass, you take the JR Ferry for free as well."

—gearsau

WELCOME TO
WESTERN HONSHU

TOP REASONS TO GO

★ **Photogenic Icons:** Beside Miyajima, the O-torii rises from the Inland Sea. An hour from Matsue is the austere Izumo Taisha, a Shinto shrine reputed to ensure marital happiness.

★ **Fabulous Seafood:** Great seafood abounds: oysters (*kaki*) in Hiroshima; *anago* (conger eel) in Miyajima; *uni-don* (sea urchin over rice) in Hagi; *mamakari* (a sardinelike fish) in Kurashiki; and little black *shijimi* clams in Matsue.

★ **Lessons of the Past:** Although A-Bomb Dome in Hiroshima is held in great reverence, the city has embraced the future with its energetic multinational vibe.

★ **Gardens:** Okayama is home to one of Japan's top three gardens, the spacious and lush Korakuen, which surrounds the stunning black U-jo, or "Crow Castle."

★ **The People:** Though English is not widely spoken and foreigners may garner stares, locals will go above and beyond to help puzzled tourists.

MI SHIMA

1 San-yo. San-yo comprises the sunny southern coastline of western Honshu; the region's major cities are Okayama and Hiroshima. Though the entire stretch is heavily populated and industrialized, bright spots worth a look are Kurashiki, Okayama, and Miyajima, near Hiroshima.

2 San-in. Remote as it is, a trip through the surreal landscape of San-in may come closest to providing the best of what Japan has to offer. Romantic destinations worth some extra travel time include the hidden hamlets of Hagi and Tsuwano, and the enchanting lakeside city of Matsue.

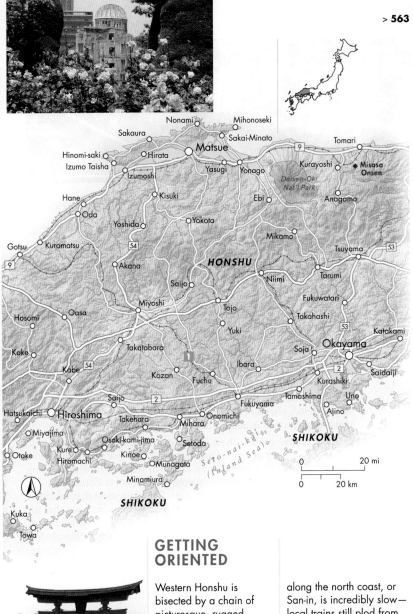

GETTING ORIENTED

Western Honshu is bisected by a chain of picturesque, rugged mountains called the Chugoku San-chi. These mountains run east–west, making north–south travel a difficult proposition. Keep in mind that travel along the north coast, or San-in, is incredibly slow—local trains still plod from village to village—so if you are pressed for time to get to Hagi or Tsuwano, use Yamaguchi as your base; for Matsue, Kurashiki and Okayama work best.

Updated by
Paige Ferrari

Like disparate siblings, the two coasts of western Honshu have distinctly different personalities. Taken together, they embody the ancient and modern—those two seemingly bipolar time frames that exist in a more profound juxtaposition in Japan than perhaps in any other country in the world.

While the southern coast, or San-yo, has basically gone along with Japan's full-steam-ahead efforts to set the pace for the developed world, you can still encounter pockets of dramatic Old World charm among the modern and shockingly new. The San-in coast, on the other hand has largely escaped the scourge of overdevelopment, yet you may be surprised to learn that everything you'd want in a city can be found up there, concentrated in and around lovely Matsue.

Happily, neither coast is short on history, religious significance, scenic beauty, or culinary delights. Hiroshima survived one of history's most horrible events to become a lively, famously friendly, forward-looking city. Kurashiki has a remarkably preserved old-style district that can whisk you back to Edo times with a stroll down willow-draped canals and stylishly tiled warehouses. Hagi is a scenic bayside town that for 500 years has been the center of Hagi-yaki ceramics, coveted light-color and smooth-texture earthenware glazed with mysteriously translucent milky colors.

⇨ *See the glossary at the end of this book for definitions of the common Japanese words and suffixes used in this chapter.*

PLANNING

Travel along San-yo is easy, and the weather is usually mild. Coming from Tokyo or Osaka, Okayama and Kurashiki are natural first stops and gateways to the larger region. If you seek adventure along San-in, budget time for slow trains, layovers, incomplete or changeable information, and the like. It is possible to get from Yamaguchi up to

Matsue in a harried day, but you'll have more fun if you take a couple of days or more.

WHEN TO GO

San-yo is the sunniest region in Japan, and almost any time is a good time to visit. The northern shore, or San-in, does get a strong dose of winter, but the reward is a wonderfully long, delightful spring. Like most of Japan, western Honshu gets oppressively muggy by midsummer, but the wind off the Nihon-kai cools the San-in coast. Summer festivals and autumn colors are spectacular throughout the region, and these always attract many tourists; reserve well ahead if you are traveling then.

GETTING HERE AND AROUND

AIR TRAVEL

Hiroshima Kuko is the region's major airport, with many daily flights to Haneda Kuko in Tokyo and direct daily flights to Kagoshima, Okinawa, Sendai, and Sapporo. Other airports in western Honshu—at Izumo, Tottori, and Yonago—have daily flights to Tokyo. JAS and ANA fly out of Iwami Airport, which serves Hagi, Tsuwano, and Masuda, to Tokyo and Osaka.

BOAT AND FERRY TRAVEL

Hiroshima is a ferry hub. Seto Nai-kai Kisen Company runs eight boats daily to Miyajima (¥1,800 one-way)

Contacts Seto Nai-kai Kisen Company (✉ *12–23 Ujinakaigan, 1-chome, Minami-ku, Hiroshima* ☎ *082/253–1212* 🖷 *082/505–0134* ⊕ *www. setonaikaikisen.co.jp*).

BUS TRAVEL

You won't likely need highway buses, except for making the one-hour run between Yamaguchi and Hagi (knocking three hours off the train-travel time). Two companies operate bus routes: JR and Bocho bus lines. Japan Rail Passes are only valid for use on the JR buses.

Bus Contacts Bocho Bus Center (☎ *0856/72–0272*).

CAR TRAVEL

All the major cities and most of the towns listed here will have at least a basic choice of car-rental outlets. If you know a little Japanese and can handle both middle-of-nowhere navigation and hectic urban traffic situations, you might consider renting a car and exploring western Honshu at your own pace—but you'll also need a good Japanese map atlas or GPS in your car.

TRAIN TRAVEL

By far the easiest way to travel to western Honshu and along its southern shore is by Shinkansen from Tokyo, Kyoto, and Osaka. Major Shinkansen stops are Okayama, Hiroshima, and Shin-Yamaguchi. It takes approximately four hours on the Shinkansen to travel to Hiroshima from Tokyo, and less than half that from Osaka.

JR express trains run along the San-yo and San-in coasts, making a loop beginning and ending in Kyoto. Crossing from one coast to the other in western Honshu requires traveling fairly slowly through the mountains.

9

Local trains and buses run between major towns on the San-in coast, but still nowhere near as often or as quickly as in San-yo. It is always advisable to reserve seats on the popular routes between big cities and to holiday destinations during peak season. Most stations now have tourist offices with English speakers that can help with this.

ABOUT THE RESTAURANTS

Western Honshu is one of the best regions to sample local Japanese seafood, with regional specialties from the Nihon-kai (Japan Sea) and Seto Nai-kai (Inland Sea). The oysters in Hiroshima, sea eel on Miyajima, and sashimi and sushi on the San-in coast are all superb. Matsue's location means that a variety of both freshwater and saltwater fish are available. Most reasonably priced restaurants have a visual display of the menu in the window, if not photos on the menu pages. If you cannot order in Japanese and no English is spoken, you can always lead the waiter to the window display and point. If you're adventurous, it is always fun to ask, "*Osusume?*" which means "(What do you) recommend?"

ABOUT THE HOTELS

Accommodations cover a broad spectrum, from pensions and *minshuku* (private residences that rent rooms) to large, modern resort hotels that have little character but all the facilities you'd expect of an international chain. Large city and resort hotels have Western and Japanese restaurants. In summer or on holiday weekends hotel reservations are necessary. Unless otherwise noted, rooms have private baths, air-conditioning, and basic TV service.

⇨ *For a short course on accommodations in Japan, see Lodging in Travel Smart*

WHAT IT COSTS IN YEN				
	¢	$	$$	$$$	$$$$
Restaurants	under ¥800	¥800–¥1,000	¥1,000–¥2,000	¥2,000–¥3,000	Over ¥3,000
Hotels	Under ¥8,000	¥8,000–¥12,000	¥12,000–¥18,000	¥18,000–¥22,000	Over ¥22,000

Restaurant prices are per person for a main course, set meal, or equivalent combinations of smaller dishes. Hotel prices are for a double room with private bath, excluding service and tax. In Japan, it is common for hotels and *ryokan* (traditional Japanese inns) to list prices per person, not just per room.

VISITOR INFORMATION

Most major towns and nowadays even the small ones have tourist information centers that offer free maps and brochures. They can also help you secure accommodations. Except for the internationally known places, though, you should not assume that extensive English is spoken.

THE SAN-YO REGION 山陽地方

San-yo means "sunny side of the mountain range," and the southern region along the Inland Sea is celebrated for its mild, clear climate. Although it's highly developed, to say the least, and you can't see or appreciate much of its beauty from the train or the highway, it's wonderfully easy to stop and get a closer look at it.

OKAYAMA 岡山

672 km (418 mi) west of Tokyo, 188 km (117 mi) southeast of Matsue.

The city of Okayama claims to have the most sunny days in Japan, and the disposition of the locals tends to reflect this. A beautiful black castle is set amid a spacious and luxuriant garden, justly rated among Japan's top three castles.

GETTING HERE AND AROUND

The JR Shinkansen will whisk you away from Tokyo to Okayama in 3 hours, 17 minutes (¥16,860), or from Matsue you can reach the city in 2 hours, 27 minutes by JR Yakumo Express (¥5,870).

Hop on one of the frequent streetcars plying Momotaro-dori, the main boulevard heading east from the Shinkansen Station (¥100) to get around town. To get to the castle, park, and museums ride three stops east and walk southeast. For ¥520 you can buy a combined park-castle admission ticket.

The Shinkansen Station makes Okayama an attractive base for visiting the historic charms of Kurashiki—only an 11-minute local JR train hop to the west.

Should you need a map of Okayama or city information, head to the Tourist Information Office in the underground shopping center to the right of the JR Station's East Exit.

ESSENTIALS

Currency Exchange Chugoku Bank (✉ *1–15–20 Marunouchi* ☎ *086/223–3111*).

Visitor Information Okayama Tourist Information Office (☎ *086/222–2912* 🕐 *Daily 9–6*).

WHAT TO SEE

★ **Koraku Garden** 後楽園 *(Korakuen)*. This is one of the country's finest gardens (and officially listed as one of the top three), with charming tea arbors, green lawns, ponds, and hills that were created at the turn of the 18th century on the banks of the Asahi-gawa. Gardens in Japan, whether dry, wet, or a combination of both, are constructed with many elements in mind, but the goal is always to engender feelings of peace and tranquillity. They are a form of visual meditation, so to speak. Korakuen scores high in all relevant areas. The maple, apricot, and cherry trees give the 32-acre park plenty of flowers and shade. The riverside setting, with Okayama-jo in the background, is delightful. The garden's popularity increases in peak season (April through August), but this is perhaps the largest park in Japan, so you won't feel hemmed

9

The Koraku Garden in Okayama was built in the early 18th century

in by crowds. Bus 20 (¥160) from Platform 2 in front of the JR Station goes directly to Korakuen. ⊠ *1–5 Korakuen* ☎ *086/272–1148* 💳 *¥350* 🕐 *Apr.–Sept., daily 7:30–6; Oct.–May, daily 8–5.*

Museum of Oriental Art 岡山市立オリエント美術館 *(Orient Bijutsukan).* On display at any time are at least 2,000 items from an impressive collection. Special exhibitions vary, but they generally show how Middle Eastern art reached ancient Japan via the Silk Road, and items range from Persian glass goblets and ornate mirrors to early stringed instruments. To reach the museum from the JR Station, take the streetcar (¥140) bound for Higashiyama directly north for 10 minutes. The museum is across Asahi-gawa from Korakuen (about a 10-minute walk). ⊠ *9–16 Tenjin-cho* ☎ *086/232–3636* 💳 *¥300* 🕐 *Tues.–Sun. 9–5.*

Okayama-jo 岡山城. Painted an unexpectedly attractive shadowy black, and set off dramatically by lead tiles and contrasting white vertical-slat shutters, Okayama's castle is known locally as U-jo ("Crow Castle"). Though it was built in the 16th century, only the "moon-viewing" outlying tower survived World War II. A ferroconcrete replica was painstakingly constructed to scale in 1966. The middle floors now house objects that represent the region's history, including a collection of armor and swords and a palanquin you can climb into to have your photo taken. Unlike many other castles with great views, this one has an elevator to take you up the six floors. A five-minute walk across the bridge brings you from the South Exit of Korakuen to the castle. Boats are available for rent on the river below. ⊠ *2–3–1 Marunouchi* ☎ *086/225–2096* 💳 *¥300* 🕐 *Daily 9–5.*

WHERE TO EAT AND STAY

Hotel reviews have been condensed for this book. Please go to Fodors. com for full reviews of each property.

$$$–$$$$
JAPANESE
✕ **Musashi** 武蔵. You'll find healthful, vegetable-laden Okayama-style cuisine at this delightful eatery. For lunch we recommend the unbeatable *bara-zushi teishoku*, or bits and pieces of sushi with a vegetables prix-fixe, a feast for only ¥1,050. Musashi is about a seven-minute walk straight out along the boulevard from the East Exit of JR Okayama Station, on the left just past 7-Eleven. ✉ *1–7–18 Nodaya-cho* ☎ *086/222–3893* ◷ *Closed Sun.*

$$$$
HOTEL
🏨 **Hotel Granvia Okayama** ホテルグランヴィア岡山. This large, luxurious hotel makes a comfortable base for exploring the area. **Pros:** best location in town; large, posh rooms; nice breakfast included. **Cons:** pool and other amenities cost extra; be careful with the touchy in-room bar—don't move a thing unless you mean to buy it. ✉ *1–5 Ekimoto-cho* ☎ *086/234–7000* 🖷 *086/234–7099* 🛏 *323 Western-style rooms, 3 Western-style suites, 2 Japanese-style suites* ⚒ *In-room: a/c. In-hotel: 8 restaurants, bar* ⏣ *Breakfast.*

KURASHIKI 倉敷

★ *749 km (465 mi) west of Tokyo, 196 km (122 mi) west of Shin-Osaka.*

From the 17th through the 19th century, this vital shipping port supplied Osaka with cotton, textiles, sugar, reeds, and rice. Today Kurashiki thrives on income from tourism. If your views were limited to what you see just outside the station, you'd be forgiven for thinking Kurashiki is just another overindustrialized modern Japanese city. We strongly recommend, however, walking 10 minutes southeast of the station to Bikan Chiku, a neighborhood of canals, bridges, shops, restaurants, ryokans, and museums.

You can see most of Kurashiki's sights in a day, but it's worth staying longer, perhaps in a splendid old ryokan, to fully appreciate the time-machine aspect of the place. The Bikan district is artfully lighted up at night, and a stroll down the willow-draped canals after a sumptuous meal can be an unforgettably romantic journey. Note that virtually the entire town shuts down on Monday.

GETTING HERE AND AROUND

Kurashiki is three hours, 28 minutes west of Tokyo or one hour west of Shin-Osaka by the Shinkansen and San-yo Line. In town, you can stroll leisurely through the streets taking in the scenery.

ESSENTIALS

Kurashiki Tourist Information Office (☎ *086/426–8681 main branch, 086/422–0542 Bikan branch* ◷ *Apr.–Oct., daily 9–6; Nov.–Mar., daily 9–5:15*), on the right outside the second-floor South Exit from the JR Station, has knowledgeable locals who provide useful maps and information. Another office is in the Bikan district, at the first bend of the canal, on the right a block past the Ohara Art Museum, just across the bridge from the Ryori-Ryokan Tsurugata. They sell tickets for the 20-minute canal-boat tours (summer only) for ¥300, and provide information on the museums located around the Bikan area.

WHAT TO SEE

★ **Ohara Art Museum** 大原美術館 *(Ohara Bijutsukan)*. In the old town, this museum is not to be missed. In 1930, noted art collector and founder Magosaburo Ohara built this Parthenon-style building to house a collection of Western art with works by El Greco, Corot, Manet, Monet, Rodin, Gauguin, Picasso, Toulouse-Lautrec, and many others. They were shrewdly acquired for him by his friend Kojima Torajiro, a talented Western-style artist whom he dispatched to Europe for purchases. The museum is wonderfully compact and can be appreciated in a single morning or an afternoon. Two wings exhibit Japanese paintings, tapestries, wood-block prints, and pottery—including works by Shoji Hamada and Bernard Leach—as well as modern and ancient Asian art, much of it also brought home from trips made by Torajiro at Ohara's behest. ⊠ *1–15–Chuo* ☎ *086/422–0005* ⊠ *¥1,000* ☉ *Tues.–Sun. 9–5.*

WHERE TO EAT

$$–$$$ ✕ **Hamayoshi** 浜吉. Three tables and a counter make up this intimate
JAPANESE restaurant specializing in fish from the Seto Nai-kai. Sushi is one option; another is *mamakari,* a kind of vinegared sashimi sliced from a small fish caught in the Inland Sea. Other delicacies are *shako-ebi,* or mantis-shrimp, and lightly grilled *anago,* or sea eel. No English is spoken, but an English menu is available, and the owner will be happy to help you order and instruct you on how to enjoy the chef's delicacies. Hamayoshi is on the main street leading from the station, just before the Kurashiki Kokusai Hotel. Unlike many restaurants here, it's open on holidays. ⊠ *2–19–30 Achi* ☎ *086/421–3430* ⊕ *www.kurashiki.co.jp/hamayoshi* ☉ *Closed Mon.*

$$$–$$$$ ✕ **Kiyu-tei** 亀遊亭. For the best reasonably priced grilled steak in town,
STEAK come to this attractive Kurashiki-style restaurant. The entrance to the restaurant is through a nearly hidden courtyard behind a gate across the street from the entrance to the Ohara Art Museum. ⊠ *1–2–20 Chuo* ☎ *086/422–5140* ☉ *Closed Mon.*

$ ✕ **KuShuKuShu (9494)** くしゅくしゅ. Feeling a bit restless? Want to get out
IZAKAYA of the ryokan or hotel? Want something different to eat but are afraid that there is no nightlife in old Bikan-Chiku town? You'll be happy to be wrong, and happy to find this lively little *izakaya* (traditional restaurant) that has been a Kurashiki favorite for 22 years. Cool music and loud laughter can be heard from here when all else on the streets is locked up tight. Unwind to an eclectic mix of traditional white stucco, black wooden beams, bright lights, and jazz. Though the staff doesn't speak English, an English menu is available. Scores of tasty à la carte snacks, such as grilled meats or cheese and salami plates—and low-priced beer and sake—add to the fun. It's tucked along the east side of the covered Ebisu-dori shopping arcade halfway between the station and Kanryu-ji. ⊠ *2–16–41 Achi* ☎ *086/421–0949* ▭ *No credit cards* ☉ *No lunch.*

WHERE TO STAY

Hotel reviews have been condensed for this book. Please go to Fodors. com for full reviews of each property.

$$-$$$
HOTEL

☒ **Kurashiki Kokusai Hotel** 倉敷国際ホテル. The town's oldest Western-style hotel welcomes guests with a black-tile lobby and dramatic Japanese wood-block prints. **Pros:** location is near the good stuff; welcoming, capable staff. **Cons:** not right on the old canals; rooms, though large, are dated. ☒ *1–1–44 Chuo* ☎ *086/422–5141* 🖷 *086/422–5192* 📞 *106 Western-style rooms, 4 Japanese-style rooms* 🛏 *In-room: a/c. In-hotel: restaurant, bar, parking (free)* ⭘ *No meals.*

$$$$
RYOKAN

☒ **Ryokan Kurashiki** 旅館倉敷. Refurbished in a newly polished old-style splendor, this is perhaps the most luxurious place to submit to the ritual of pleasures sought by wealthy Japanese at a traditional ryokan more than 300 years ago. **Pros:** great food in great quantities; lots of antiques and period pieces; private in-room baths. **Cons:** remodeled rooms have less personality, style, and space; the restaurant menu is only available in Japanese. ☒ *4–1 Hon-machi* ☎ *086/422–0730* 🖷 *086/422–0990* ⊕ *www.ryokan-kurashiki.jp/en/top.php* 📞 *5 rooms* 🛏 *In-room: a/c. In-hotel: restaurant* ⭘ *Some meals.*

$$$-$$$$
RYOKAN

☒ **Ryori-Ryokan Tsurugata** 旅館鶴形. Treat yourself to a stay—or perhaps just a fantastic dinner—at this charming ryokan built in 1774. **Pros:** best local value for this type of accommodation; steeped in tradition; some rooms have private baths. **Cons:** ancient tradition means a slower pace than Westerners are used to. ☒ *1–3–15 Chuo* ☎ *086/424–1635* 🖷 *086/424–1650* 📞 *11 Japanese-style rooms, 3 with bath* 🛏 *In-room: a/c. In-hotel: restaurant* ⭘ *Some meals.*

¢
HOTEL

☒ **Toyoko Inn Kurashiki Station South Exit** 東横イン倉敷駅南口. This reasonably priced hotel is one of Kurashiki's most popular, as it offers basic, reliably comfortable rooms at a great value, and only minutes away from the station's South Exit. **Pros:** location; free breakfast; free Internet. **Cons:** perhaps a bit too modern given the location; it's a shame to stay anywhere but Bikan Chiku in Kurashiki. ☒ *2–10–20 Achi* ☎ *086/430–1045* 🖷 *086/430–1046* 📞 *154 rooms* 🛏 *In-room: a/c, Internet. In-hotel: Wi-Fi hotspot* ⭘ *Breakfast.*

HIROSHIMA 広島

342 km (213 mi) west of Shin-Osaka, 864 km (537 mi) from Tokyo.

On August 6, 1945, at 8:15 am, a massive chunk of metal known as *Little Boy* fell from an American plane, and the sky ignited and glowed for an instant. In that brief moment, however, it became as hot as the surface of the sun in Hiroshima, until then a rather ordinary workaday city in wartime Japan. Half the city was leveled by the resulting blast, and the rest was set ablaze. Rain impregnated with radioactive fallout then fell, killing many that the fire and 1,000-mph shock wave had not. By the end of this mind-boggling disaster, more than 140,000 people died.

Modern Hiroshima's Peace Memorial Park 平和祈念公園 (*Heiwa Kinen Koen*) is at the northern point of the triangle formed by two of Hiroshima's rivers, the Ota-gawa (also called Hon-kawa) and Motoyasu-gawa. Monuments to that day abound in the park, but only one original site bears witness to that enormous release of atomic energy 60 years ago: the A-Bomb Dome. Its gloomy shadows are now surrounded by a vibrant, rebuilt city. As if to show just how earnestly Hiroshima has redefined itself, only a short walk to the east is Nagarekawa-cho, the city's most raucous nightlife district.

GETTING HERE AND AROUND

The streetcar (tram) is an easy form of transport in Hiroshima. Enter the middle door and take a ticket from the automatic dispenser. Pay the driver at the front door when you leave. All fares within city limits are ¥150. A one-day pass is ¥600, available for purchase at the platform outside JR Hiroshima Station. There are seven streetcar lines; four either depart from the JR Station or make it their terminus. Stops are announced by a recording, and each stop has a sign in *romaji* (romanized Japanese) posted on the platform. To reach Peace Memorial Park, take Streetcar 2 or 6 to the Gembaku-Domu-mae stop and cross over Motoyasu-gawa on the Aioi-bashi; you can also take Streetcar 1 to Chuden-mae for a five-minute walk to Peace Memorial Museum.

Buses also joust with the traffic on Hiroshima's hectic streets; the basic fare is ¥200. Information in English can be gathered at any of the Hiroshima Tourist Information Offices. The Hiroshima Bus Company's red-and-white Bus 24 to Heiwa Koen leaves you only a two-minute walk to the Peace Memorial Museum

Taxis can be hailed throughout the city. Look for cabs that have the " 空車" light on the dashboard illuminated, indicating they are ready to pick up passengers. The fare for the first 1½ km (1 mi) is ¥570 for small taxis, ¥620 for larger ones, then ¥70 for every 300 meters.

Two excellent, English-speaking Tourist Information Offices are in JR Hiroshima Station: the South Exit office, on the first floor, is the main one; the other is on the first floor at the Shinkansen (North) Exit. The main tourist office, the Rest House in Peace Memorial Park is next to the Motoyasu fork of the river, between the Children's Peace Monument and the Flame of Peace.

ESSENTIALS

Currency Exchange Hiroshima Bank (✉ 1–3–8 Kamiya-cho, Naka-ku ☎ 082/247–5151).

Internet Futaba @ Café GIGA (✉ Hiroshima Eki-Mae, 2–22 Matsubara-cho, Minami-ku ☎ 082/568–4792).

Visitor Information International Conference Center Hiroshima (☎ 082/242–7777 ☾ May–Nov., daily 9–7; Dec.–Apr., daily 10–6). **Rest House in Peace Memorial Park** (☎ 082/247–6738 ☾ Apr.–Sept., daily 9:30–6; Oct.–Mar., daily 8:30–5). **Tourist Information Offices** (☎ 082/261–1877 SouthExit, 082/263–6822 North Exit ☾ Daily 9–5:30).

WHAT TO SEE

Fodor's Choice ★ **A-Bomb Dome** 原爆ドーム *(Gembaku Domu)*. This ruin is a poignant symbol of man's self-destructiveness. It was the city's old Industrial Promotion Hall, and it stands in stark contrast to the new Hiroshima, which hums along close by. Despite being directly below the bomb blast, the building did not collapse into rubble like the rest of the city. Eerie, twisted, and charred, the sturdy domed structure of iron and concrete has stood darkly brooding next to the river, basically untouched since that horrible morning. A visit to A-Bomb Dome is a sobering reminder of nuclear destruction, and at dusk the sad old building's foreboding, derelict appearance can be emotionally overwhelming. The site is just outside the official northeast boundary of Peace Memorial Park. Take Streetcar 2 or 6 from Hiroshima Station to the Gembaku-Domu-mae stop. ⊠ *Heiwa Kinen Koen.*

Children's Peace Monument 原爆の子像 *(Genbaku-no-ko-zo).* You may wish to pause a moment here before leaving the park. Many consider this the most profound memorial in Peace Memorial Park. The figure is of Sadako, a young girl who at age 10 developed leukemia as a result of exposure to the atomic radiation that lingered long after the blast. She believed that if she could fold 1,000 paper *senbazuru* (cranes)—a Japanese symbol of good fortune and longevity—her illness would be cured. She died before finishing the thousand, and it is said that her schoolmates finished the job for her. Her story has become a folktale of sorts, and it inspired a nationwide paper crane–folding effort among schoolchildren that continues to this day. The colorful chains of paper cranes—delivered daily from schools all over the world—are visually and emotionally striking. ⊠ *Heiwa Kinen Koen.*

Flame of Peace 平和の灯 *(Heiwa no Tomoshibi).* The flame burns behind the Memorial Cenotaph. It will be extinguished only when all atomic weapons are banished. In the meantime, every August 6, the citizens of Hiroshima float paper lanterns down the city's rivers for the repose of the souls of the atomic-bomb victims. ⊠ *Heiwa Kinen Koen.*

Hiroshima Children's Museum 広島子供文化科学館 *(Kodomo Bunka Kagakukan).* The city's hands-on children's museum is a good diversion for the kids. The joyful noise of excited children alleviates the somber mood of Peace Memorial Park. Kids get a kick out of conducting their own science "experiments." To get here, leave the Peace Memorial Park via Aioi-bashi at the North Entrance and walk north and east, keeping the river on your left and the baseball stadium on your right. A planetarium is next door. ⊠ *5–83 Moto-machi, Naka-ku* ☎ *082/222–5346* ⊠ *Center free; planetarium ¥500* ⊙ *Tues.–Sun. 9–5.*

Hiroshima-jo 広島城. Hiroshima's castle was originally built by Terumoto Mori on the Ota-gawa delta in 1589. He named the surrounding flatlands *Hiro-Shima,* meaning "wide island," and it stuck. The Imperial Japanese Army used the castle as headquarters in World War II, and with its significant depot of munitions it was one of the targets of the bomb. It was destroyed in the blast. In 1958 the five-story donjon (main tower) was rebuilt to its original specifications. Unlike many castles in Japan, it has lots of brown wood paneling that gives it a warm appearance, and it stands in intriguing contrast to the modern city that has evolved around it. Inside are exhibits from Japan's feudal Edo period (17th–19th century). It's a 15-minute walk north from the A-Bomb Dome. ⊠ *21–1 Moto-machi, Naka-ku* ☎ *082/221–7512* ⊕ *www.rijo-castle.jp* ⊠ *Castle and museum ¥360* ⊙ *Apr.–Sept., daily 9–5:30; Oct.–Mar., daily 9–4:30.*

9

Continued on page 581

Hiroshima is a city on which an atomic bomb was dropped.
Hiroshima is a city with many memorials for the lives lost.
Hiroshima is a city which continually seeks peace.

Part of a translated poem at the entrance to Hiroshima's Peace Museum

A WALK THROUGH HIROSHIMA'S
PEACE MEMORIAL
PARK

By Paige Ferrari

Peace Park is both the physical and emotional center of Hiroshima. Some of the monuments here, such as the Memorial Cenotaph, have become internationally recognizable icons for peace. Others are lesser-known, but nonetheless powerful, monuments dedicated to specific groups and individuals who lost their lives on August 6, 1945. After a visit to the museum, walking through the park provides time for reflection. Like Hiroshima itself, the park honors an unhappy history while presenting an optimistic view for the future. Atomic bomb survivors—known as *Hibakusha*—and rowdy, yellow-capped groups of school kids alike visit the park throughout the year to remember the past. Though the details of the atomic bomb's impact are grim, the overwhelming message is one of hope and peace. Visitors of all backgrounds and nationalities should feel welcome here.

Paper lanterns float on the Motoyasu River during Hiroshima's annual Peace Ceremony.

STARTING FROM THE PEACE MUSEUM

As you exit the ❶ **Peace Museum** and stand under the elevated section, walk straight along the path towards the iconic A-Bomb Dome.

Framing the dome is the ❷ **Memorial Cenotaph.** The dome is shaped like a traditional Japanese house and records the names of 260,000 who ultimately perished from the initial bombing or, later, from its effects. The epitaph is translated: "Let all souls here rest in peace, for we shall not repeat the evil." Each year on August 6, thousands gather here to remember the events of past.

Continuing along the main path, which runs to the left of the Cenotaph, you'll pass by the ❸ **Pond for Peace.** Its water is intended as a symbolic offering for the victims who were unable to quench their thirst after the bomb's detonation and subsequent black rain.

At the end of the pond burns the ❹ **Flame of Peace,** first lit during the 1964 Tokyo Olympics. The structure itself resembles a pair of cupped hands. Hiroshima residents will tell you that this flame is not an eternal one. It will be extinguished the day the world is free of all nuclear weapons.

Ahead and on your left is what many visitors find to be Peace Park's most moving offering, the ❺ **Children's Peace Monument.** The statue and the cases of paper cranes behind it are dedicated to all the children who died in the blast and from radiation-related sicknesses after, including Sadako Sasaki, whose determination to fold 1,000 paper cranes before she succumbed to leukemia at age 12, is one of Hiroshima's most heartbreaking and enduring stories. Brightly colored paper cranes, on display in a series of glass cases behind the monument, are brought from

around the world but especially by groups of Japanese elementary school students.

Break off the path and walk to your left. Here, in a wooded region at the edge of the park, you'll find a cluster of specific monuments. These include the ❻ **Monument for the Korean A-Bomb Victims,** the ❼ **A-bombed Gravestone,** and the ❽ **Atomic Memorial Mound.** The mound is a particularly solemn place. Constructed on the 10-year anniversary of the bombing, it was an area once used as a crematorium and now holds the ashes of roughly 70,000 victims.

Walking towards the tip of the park, you'll come upon the ❾ **Peace Bell,** built in 1964.

A map of the world without borders is carved on the bell, and all visitors are welcome to strike the bell. The bell's sound is intended to remind all who hear it of the reverberations of nuclear power. Nearby, at the narrow tip of the park near the Aioi-bashi bridge, stands the ❿ **Peace Clock Tower.** Built in 1967, the clock chimes each morning at 8:15, the moment the bomb was dropped.

Walk across the ⓫ **Aioi-bashi Bridge.** This bridge, with its characteristic T-shape, was selected as the target for the bombing. On the opposite side of the bridge you can walk around the ⓬ **A-Bomb Dome,** once the city's Industrial Promotions Hall.

To visit the bomb's nearby hypocenter, walk past the A-Bomb Dome as if you're returning to the museum. To your left, across a small street outside the park perimeter, you'll see a black temple and a white temple standing side by side, bisected by a small street. In front of the white building is a statue with a shadow permanently burned into the pedestal, a product of thermal radiation. Walk down the street between these buildings for a block, then walk half a block to your right to find yourself standing in front of what used to be ⓭ **Shima Hospital,** the bomb's hypocenter. A small plaque shows what the area looked like directly after the blast, but otherwise there is little to distinguish it from the surrounding commercial area.

Find your way back to the trail in front of the A-Bomb Dome. Walking back towards the museum you'll come upon the ⑭ **Memorial Tower for Mobilized Students** on your left. On the day of the bombing, children as young as 12 were working outside, demolishing buildings in order to create fire-breaks that would minimize the damage from potential air attacks. Of the 8,400 students working that day, nearly 6,400 died.

As you cross the Motoyasu Bridge back onto the main park grounds, ahead on your right you'll see the ⑮ **Rest House** and tourist information center. Walking back towards the museum's main building, the modern-looking building ahead of you is the ⑯ **Hiroshima National Peace Memorial Hall for the Atomic Bomb Victims**, opened in 2002. Inside you can hear survivor stories and visit the research library, which houses over 100,000 memoirs written by survivors. The basement of the center provides a breathtaking artist's rendition of a 360-degree view from the hypocenter.

Walking more towards the museum itself, you'll find the

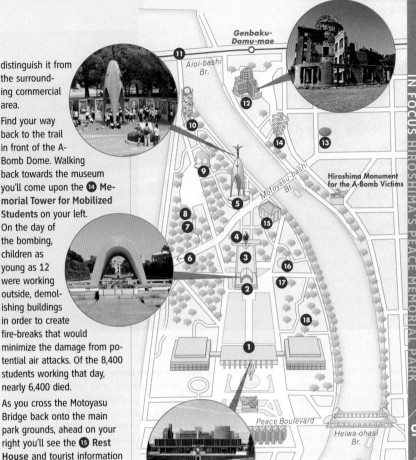

⑰ **Monument dedicated to Sankichi Toge**, who was 28 at the time of the bombings. After the war, Toge protested nuclear weapons through his poetry, including the one that is on the monument. A lock of Sankichi's hair and his pen are buried on the monument, the Japanese side of which faces towards his home.

Directly in front of the museum's snack and gift store,

you'll find a small, cordoned-off ⑱ **Chinese Parasol Tree**. This tree is also an A-bomb survivor. Despite being scorched in the blast, new leaves started to bud and develop the next year. Today, it is a symbol for the tenacity of life and rebirth.

This is a good space to end your walk, although you should feel free to cross Heiwa Dori (Peace Boulevard) to take in some of the smaller, scattered monuments, or simply take some time to rest and reflect.

9

TOTAL DESTRUCTION

A-Bomb Dome today

Looking at bustling Hiroshima today, there is little evidence of the almost total destruction that visited the city on August 6, 1945. The first atomic bomb was dropped on Japan at 8:15 AM and exploded approximately 1,900 feet above the city, centered on the Shima Hospital (the actual target, the Aioi-bashi Bridge, was missed). The intial blast radius was approximately 1 square mile, and the fireball resulting from the explosion engulfed approximately 4.4 square miles; fires eventually destroyed about 69% of the buildings of Hiroshima. In the initial blast, 70,000 to 80,000 people were killed immediately, with as many as 180,000 more killed eventually by injuries sustained in the bombing or by radiation and its after-effects. The destruction in the city was almost complete in the blast- and fire-ravaged areas, and very few structures survived. The city's Industrial Promotions Hall (now better known

as the **A-Bomb Dome**) was less than 500 feet from ground zero and was one of the few structures in the immediate blast radius to survive. Compared to the destruction in Nagasaki three days later, the number of dead and the amount of destruction in Hiroshima was considerably more because the city is built on a flat river plain.

Atomic bomb mushroom clouds over Hiroshima.

The A-Bomb Dome in the bomb's immediate aftermath in 1945

Ground Zero before the bombing shows a busy city; each circle is approximately 1/5 mi.

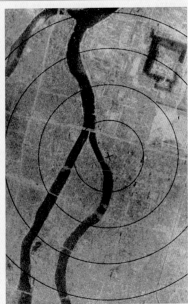

Ground Zero after the bombing (same scale). Note the almost complete lack of standing structures.

PLANNING YOUR TRIP TO PEACE MEMORIAL PARK

HISTORY

Before the atomic bomb, the area now home to Peace Park was known as the Nakajima District. Nakajima was a lively, urban center populated by around 6,500 residents. In 1949, it was decided that this area—decimated on account of being so near the bomb's hypocenter—would be reborn as a monument for peace. The park was designed by Kenzo Tange, after his design won in an international architecture competition.

THE ROUTE

The park and surrounding monuments are not structured on a grid. Visitors are welcome to make their own trail and wander off the main paths to explore. This is merely a suggested walking tour, hitting major points of interest.

TIMING

The park can be experienced in as little as an hour, with a trip to the **Cenotaph, Peace Flame**, and adjoining **A-Bomb Dome** area, but visitors with more time should take the opportunity to walk a meandering circle around the museum. Visiting the area's nearly 60 monuments can easily fill an afternoon. The park is particularly vivid in the summer, when the oleander flowers—a gift from sister-city Honolulu—are in full bloom.

GETTING HERE AND BACK

Riding the streetcar from JR Hiroshima Station is an easy way to reach **Peace Park**. Take the number 1 tram bound for Hiroshima Port via Kamiyacho, disembarking at Chuden-Mae. From Chuden-Mae, it's a 5-minute walk to the front of the Peace Museum.

Riding the number 2 or 6 tram will also take you to the Genbakudomu-mae stop (in front of the A-Bomb dome.) Within the city, streetcar fares are a flat ¥150, payable when you get off.

Memorial Cenotaph in Hiroshima

VISITOR CENTER

The **Hiroshima Peace Museum** has maps and information for English speakers.

The International Hall, located opposite the museum in the same building, also offers assistance, in addition to English-language newspapers and magazines.

WHAT'S NEARBY

The park is surrounded by a bustling commercial area, with no shortage of restaurants. Indeed, many visitors are surprised to find a regular commercial center so close to Peace Memorial Park. There are also a few tourist-friendly eateries along the riverside, including Kakifune Kawana, a floating restaurant that boasts some of the best oysters in town. (See "Where to Eat" in this chapter for more information on this and other restaurants.)

Hiroshima National Peace Memorial Hall for the Atomic Bomb Victims 原爆死没者追悼平和祈念館 *(Kokuritsu Hiroshima Hibakusha Tsuito Heiwa Kinen-kan)*. The memorial recounts the stories of known victims of the atomic devastation. In addition to the extensive archives of names, a collection of victims' photos lends immediacy to one of the most shocking moments in history. Heartbreaking firsthand accounts and memoirs of survivors are available for viewing. ✉ *1–6 Nakajima-cho, Heiwa Kinen Koen* ☎ *082/543–6271* 🖷 *082/543–6273* 🎫 *Free* ⊙ *Apr.–July, daily 9–6; Aug. 1–15, daily 8:30–7; Aug. 16–Nov., daily 8:30–6; Dec.–Mar., daily 9–5.*

Hiroshima Kenritsu Bijutsukan 広島県立美術館 *(Hiroshima Prefectural Art Museum)*. Next to the Shukkei Garden, this museum is a visual treat. Standouts include two particularly surrealistic pieces: a typically fantastical piece by Salvador Dalí called *Dream of Venus;* and Ikuo Hirayama's much closer-to-home *Holocaust at Hiroshima.* Hirayama, who became one of Japan's most acclaimed artists, was a junior-high-school student at the time the A-bomb was dropped. ✉ *2–22 Kaminobori-cho, Naka-ku* ☎ *082/221–6246* ⊕ *www1.hpam-unet.ocn.ne.jp/english* 🎫 *¥500 for museum only; museum and Shukkei Garden ¥600* ⊙ *Tues.–Sun. 9–5, Sat. until 7; entry closes 30 mins before museum.*

Hon-dori 本通り. Around Hiroshima's central district are hundreds of shops. Take the tram that runs from the main station to stop T-31 (Hon-dori), or simply walk east across the north bridge out of Peace Park. The big department stores are at the east end of the arcade, near the Hatchobori streetcar stop: Sogo (closed Tuesday) is open from 10 to 8; Fukuya (closed Wednesday) and Tenmaya (closed Thursday) are open from 10 to 7:30; and Mitsukoshi (closed Monday) is open from 10 to 7. Many restaurants, including a big, gorgeous Andersen's, a popular bakery chain (one block down on the right from T-31), and several modern hotels, are also found here. ✉ *Hon-dori.*

Memorial Cenotaph 原爆死没者慰霊碑 *(Gembaku Shibotsusha Irei-hi)*. Designed by Japanese architect Kenzo Tange, the cenotaph resembles the primitive A-frame houses of Japan's earliest inhabitants. Buried inside is a chest containing the names of those who died in the destruction and aftermath of the atomic bomb. On the exterior is the inscription (translated): "Rest in peace, for the error shall not be repeated." The cenotaph stands before the north side of the Heiwa Kinen Shiryokan. ✉ *Heiwa Kinen Koen.*

Peace Memorial Museum 平和祈念資料館 *(Heiwa Kinen Shiryokan)*. A visit to the museum may be too intense an experience for some. Displays of models, charred fragments of clothing, melted ceramic tiles, lunch boxes, watches, and shocking photographs tell Hiroshima's story of death and destruction. The heat-ray-photographed human shadow permanently imprinted on granite steps can take you well beyond sadness, and the Dalí-esque watch forever stopped at 8:15 is chilling. Most exhibits have brief explanations in English, and more-detailed information is on the audio tour, which you can rent for ¥150. ✉ *Heiwa Kinen Koen* ☎ *082/241–4004* 🎫 *¥50* ⊙ *Mar.–July and Sept.–Nov., daily*

9

8:30–6; Aug., daily 8:30–7; Dec.–Feb., daily 8:30–5. Last admission 30 mins before museum closes.

Shukkei-en 縮景園. This garden laid out in 1630 by Lord Naga-akira Asano (the name means "shrunken scenery garden") resembles one once found around a famed lake in Hangzhou, China, which the *daimyo* (lord) wanted to re-create for leisurely strolls. The water is dotted with tiny rocky islets sprouting gnarled pine trees. Small bridges cross above lots of colorful carp, a fish venerated for its long and vigorous life. Shukkei-en is east of Hiroshima-jo castle on the banks of the Kyo-bashi-gawa. Return to the JR Station on Streetcar 9; at the end of the line transfer to Streetcar 1, 2, or 6. If you purchase a combined ticket (¥600) for the garden and the Prefectural Art Museum, you must visit the museum first and enter the garden from the museum. ⊠ *2–11 Kamiya-cho, Naka-ku* ☎ *082/221–3620* ⊕ *shukkeien.jp* ✆ *¥250* ⊙ *Apr.–Sept., daily 9–6; Oct.–Mar., daily 9–5.*

WHERE TO EAT

$$$
JAPANESE
✕ **Hiroshima Station** 広島駅. If you don't have enough time to go out on the town for lunch or dinner, try the beer garden–restaurant area in the station's basement or the restaurants on the second and sixth floors of the Asse Department Store. You'll find restaurants of all types, from in-and-out cheapies to elegant eateries—many are branches of famous establishments elsewhere in the city. Enter the Asse complex from the South Exit of the JR Hiroshima Station. ⊠ *JR Hiroshima Station Bldg., 9–1 Matsubara-cho, Higashi-ku* ☎ *082/248–2391.*

$$$$
SEAFOOD
★
✕ **Kakifune Kanawa** かき船かなわ *(Kanawa Oyster Boat).* Hiroshima is known for its oysters, and Kanawa, on a barge moored on the Motoyasu-gawa, near Peace Memorial Park, gets its oysters from a particularly salty area of the Inland Sea. It's believed that these waters impart the firm flesh and sweet, robust taste that loyal customers love to splurge on. It's not cheap, but the oysters are worth every yen. An English menu makes it all very easy, and dining is on tatami mats, with relaxing river views. ⊠ *3–1 Ohashi, Ohte-machi, moored on river at Heiwa-Ohashi, Naka-ku* ☎ *082/241–7416* ⊕ *www.kanawa.co.jp.*

$$$
JAPANESE
✕ **Kamameshi Suishin Honten** 酔心. Famous for its *kamameshi,* or rice casseroles, this restaurant (part of a large chain) serves the freshest fish from the Seto Nai-kai—*fugu,* or puffer fish, oysters, and eel, to name but a few. If you prefer your fish cooked, try the rockfish grilled with soy sauce. English menus (and Japanese-style rooms with *horikotatsu* pits to hang your legs in) are available. ⊠ *6–7 Tate-machi, Naka-ku* ☎ *082/247–4411* ⊙ *Closed Wed.*

$$
JAPANESE
✕ **Okonomi Mura** お好み村 *(Village of Okonomiyaki).* In this enclave 20 shops serve *okonomi-yaki,* literally, "as you like it grilled." Okonomi-yaki is best described as an everything omelet, topped with bits of shrimp, pork, squid, or chicken, cabbage, and bean sprouts. Different areas of Japan make different okonomi-yaki; in Hiroshima the ingredients are layered rather than mixed, and they throw in lots of fried noodles. Seating in these lively shops, which are generally open late, is either at a wide counter in front of a grill or at a table with its own grill. This complex is near the Hon-dori shopping area, just west of Chuo-dori.

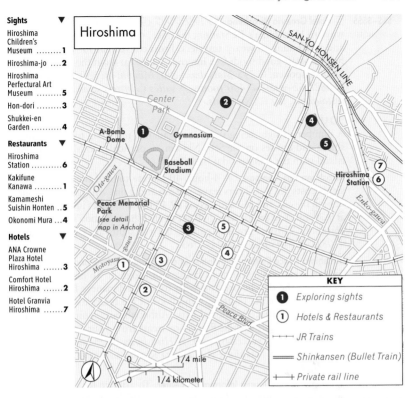

Hiroshima

KEY

❶ Exploring sights

① Hotels & Restaurants

┼──┼ JR Trains

═══ Shinkansen (Bullet Train)

┼─┼ Private rail line

✉ *Shintenchi Plaza, 2–4F, 5–13 Shintenchi, Naka-ku* ☎ *082/241–2210* ⊕ *okonomimura.jp* ▭ *No credit cards.*

WHERE TO STAY

Hotel reviews have been condensed for this book. Please go to Fodors. com for full reviews of each property.

$$$$
HOTEL
★
🏨 **ANA Crowne Plaza Hotel Hiroshima** クラウンプラザホテル広島. This reliable and popular hotel was renovated in 2007 and remains one of the very best in town. **Pros:** spacious double rooms; free Internet access in rooms and lobby. **Cons:** bring your own laptop as on-site rentals are expensive. ✉ *7–20 Naka-machi, Naka-ku* ☎ *082/241–1111* 🖨 *082/241–9123* 🛏 *430 rooms, 1 suite* 🚻 *In-room: a/c, Internet. In-hotel: 6 restaurants, pool, gym, Wi-Fi hotspot* ⏐❶⏐ *Breakfast.*

$–$$
HOTEL
🏨 **Comfort Hotel Hiroshima** コンフォートホテル広島. This affordable hotel stands near Peace Memorial Park, and it's also just a short walk from the happening nightspots. **Pros:** free Western and Japanese buffet breakfast and complimentary coffee available 24-hours a day; 10-minute walk to Peace Park and Hon-dori shopping street. **Cons:** tiny bathrooms; spartan furnishings; thin walls transmit some noise. ✉ *3–17 Koma-chi, Naka-ku* ☎ *082/541–5555* 🖨 *082/541–0096* 🛏 *282 Western-style rooms* 🚻 *In-room: a/c, Wi-Fi. In-hotel: Internet terminal* ⏐❶⏐ *Breakfast.*

9

$$$–$$$$
HOTEL

[☒] **Hotel Granvia Hiroshima** ホテルグランヴィア広島. Connected by walk-ways to Hiroshima's JR Station, this nice, relaxing hotel is convenient and welcoming to weary travelers. **Pros:** convenient for train access; helpful staff; good food; free Internet. **Cons:** far from the action; little English spoken. ⊠ *1–5 Matsubara-cho, Minami-ku* ☎ *082/262–1111* 🖷 *082/262–4050* ⌨ *400 rooms, 4 suites* ⌂ *In-room: a/c. In-hotel: 5 restaurants, bar* ⦿ *No meals.*

TOURS

A number of sightseeing tours are available, including tours of Hiroshima and cruises on the Seto Nai-kai, in particular to Miyajima, the island with the famous tidal-basin torii.

Hiroshima Bus Company. A 4-hour, 40-minute tour of the city's major sights costs ¥3,500. Tours leave at 9 am and 2 pm. An eight-hour tour of both the city and Miyajima costs ¥9,470, and includes lunch. It leaves at 9:30 am. You depart from in front of Hiroshima Station's Shinkansen entrance. All tours are in Japanese, but the sights are gaijin-friendly. ☎ *082/545–7950* 🖷 *082/545–7963.*

Hiroshima Peace Culture Foundation International Relations and Cooperation Division. The foundation has a home-visit program. To make arrangements, go the day before you wish to visit a Japanese home to the International Center on the ground floor of the International Conference Center in Peace Memorial Park. Although not required, bringing an inexpensive gift such as flowers or treats from your home country helps to ensure a successful visit. ⊠ *Hiroshima International Conference Center, 1–5 Nakajima-cho, Heiwa Kinen Koen* ☎ *082/242–8879* 🖷 *082/242–7452.*

Hiroshima Station Tourist Information Center. To arrange for a sightseeing taxi ahead of time, telephone the local visitor information center. A three-hour tour runs approximately ¥12,960. Because these taxi drivers are not guides, you should rent an audio guide that describes key sights in English. These special taxis can be picked up from a special depot in front of Hiroshima Station at the Shinkansen entrance. ☎ *082/261–1877.*

MIYAJIMA 宮島

Miyajima's majestic orange O-torii, or big gate, is made of several stout, rot-resistant camphor-tree trunks, and is famed for the illusion it gives of "floating" over the water. The torii is one of Japan's most enduring scenic attractions, but most of the time it actually presides over brownish tidal sand flats, so you will want to time your visit for when the tide is in. Ferry offices and hotels can give you a tidal forecast—don't forget to ask.

Behind the sea gate is the elegant shrine Itsukushima Jinja. For a few hundred yen you can walk the labyrinthine wooden boardwalks out over the tidal basin and pick your spots to snap those perfect photos.

To get to the shrine and to see the torii, go right from the pier on the path that leads through the village, which is crowded with restaurants, hotels, and souvenir shops. As you pass through the park, expect to

Miyajima's O-torii sits at the entrance to a cove and is in the water at high tide.

be greeted by herds of fearless deer. Don't show or let them smell any food, or else you'll become too popular; they do have little horns, and they are known to head-butt those who disappoint them!

GETTING HERE AND AROUND

The easiest, least expensive way to get to Miyajima is to take the train on the JR San-yo Line from Hiroshima Station to Miyajima-guchi Station. From Miyajima-guchi Station, a three-minute walk takes you to the pier where ferries depart for Miyajima. The train takes about 25 minutes (¥400) and departs from Hiroshima every 15–20 minutes. The first train leaves Hiroshima at 5:55 am; the last ferry returns from Miyajima at 10:14 pm. There are two boats, but the JR Rail Pass is only valid on the JR-operated boat (¥340 round-trip without Rail Pass). Allow a minimum of three hours for the major sights of Miyajima, or just one hour to get photos of O-torii and the shrine. Bicycle rentals are available at the Miyajima ferry terminal, offering a quick way to scoot around the island.

Inside the ferry terminal (common to both lines), tucked in the entrance to a novelty and snack shop, is the English-speaking Miyajima Tourist Association.

ESSENTIALS

Visitor Information Miyajima Tourist Association (☎ *0829/44–2011* ⊙ *Daily 9–7*).

WHAT TO SEE

Go-ju-no-to 五重の塔 *(Five-Storied Pagoda)*. Atop a small hill overlooking Itsukushima Jinja, this pagoda is lacquered in bright orange, like the shrine and gate, and dates from 1407. At night, it's extra gorgeous—you'll want a roll of high-speed film or a steady hand for digital photos.

Itsukushima Jinja 厳島神社. This shrine was founded in AD 593 and dedicated to the three daughters of Susano-o-no-Mikoto, the Shinto god of the moon—also of the oceans, moon-tugged as they are. It has been continually repaired and rebuilt, and the present structure is a 16th-century copy of 12th-century buildings. The orange woodwork next to the glaring white walls is surprisingly attractive, especially when complemented by a blue sky and sea. The deck has the best frontal views of the torii. ⊠ *1—1 Miyajima-cho* 💲 *¥300* 🕐 *Mar.–Oct., daily 6:30–6; Nov.–Feb., daily 6:30–5:30.*

Momijidani Koen 紅葉谷公園 *(Red Maple Valley Park)*. Many people spend only half a day on Miyajima, but if you have more time, take a stroll through the park that is inland from Itsukushima Jinja. A steeply priced cable car goes a mile up, stopping nearly at the summit of **Misen-dake** (Mt. Misen). It's a short hike from the upper terminus to the top of the mountain, where you can look out over Seto Nai-kai and all the way to Hiroshima. 💲 *Cable car ¥1,000 one-way, ¥1,800 round-trip; park free.*

★ **O-torii** 大鳥居. Miyajima's sea gate stands nearly 50 feet tall at the entrance to the cove where the ancient Shinto shrine is. This, the 18th version, was built in 1875, and has become one of the nation's most recognizable symbols. Hotels and ferry operators have tide charts so you can maximize your photo opportunities; otherwise you may gasp in surprise to find the mythic gate suspended over drab sand flats.

If you stay overnight on the island, and if the weather cooperates, you're guaranteed to get some photos to die for, because the gate is lighted up in spectacular fashion and looks hallucinatory set against the black night air and calm reflecting water. The nearby five-story pagoda and the shrine are also illuminated.

WHERE TO STAY

Hotel reviews have been condensed for this book. Please go to Fodors. com for full reviews of each property.

$$$$
RYOKAN

🛏 **Iwaso Ryokan** 岩惣. For traditional elegance, it's easy to like this venerable Japanese inn. **Pros:** the oldest and most famous lodging on the island; everyone important has stayed here; delicious 12-course meals; new wing is wheelchair-accessible. **Cons:** Making reservations online requires some knowledge of Japanese; sure, you'll feel just like the royalty that signed their guest book—until you get the bill; the *onsen* (thermal spa) may be a bit too hot and stuffy for some. ⊠ *345 Miyajima-cho* 📞 *0829/44–2233* 📠 *0829/44–2230* 🌐 *www.iwaso.com* 🛏 *38 Japanese-style rooms, 33 with bath* ⚒ *In-room: a/c. In-hotel: restaurant* 🍴 *Some meals.*

$$$$
RYOKAN
★

🛏 **Ryokan Jukei-so** 聚景荘. This charming and relatively modernized hillside ryokan has been around for more than a century. **Pros:** great views, inside and out; quiet hillside retreat; unobtrusive, respectful service.

Yamaguchi – Gateway to San-in

Yamaguchi (山口) is a small town, but one where you're likely to experience a disarming level of hospitality. It's also a logical base for striking out for territory hinterlands like Hagi and Tsuwano, especially if accommodations are fully booked in those romantic hideaways. The Shinkansen at nearby Shin-Yamaguchi will get you there, and—if you have the time to look around—the English-speaking Tourist Information Office will happily provide you with a map. For overnight stays, the Sunroute Hotel Yamaguchi is a basic, affordable option, about a 10-minute walk from the station.

You're likely make new friends if you duck in for a bite at favorite local restaurants like Tojima-zushi (sushi) or Domani, (an Italian restaurant that turns into an okonomi-yaki joint past 8 pm); both are located in the covered shopping mall about a five-minute walk up the street from JR Yamaguchi Station.

If you're more interested in resting your travel-weary body than grabbing a meal, pop your bags in a coin locker and head one train stop over to the Yuda Onsen, where the healing sulfur baths will leave you feeling rejuvenated and ready for the next leg of your journey.

Cons: a bit boring if peace and quiet isn't your thing. ⊠ *50 Miyajima-cho* ☎ *0829/44–0300* 🖨 *0829/44–0388* ⇄ *13 Japanese-style rooms* 🛏 *In-room: a/c. In-hotel: restaurant* ⦿ *Some meals.*

THE SAN-IN REGION 山陰地方

If you are looking for adventure in a "real Japan" setting, you have come to the right place. Though the endless narrow ridges of steep mountains can make access from the south difficult, slow, and expensive, this hard fact of geography has kept the entire north stretch of western Honshu delightfully isolated. Any effort to explore it pays off in dividends of great scenery, precious local crafts, tasty seafood, rich history, and genuinely welcoming people.

HAGI 萩

117 km (73 mi) north of Yamaguchi.

Hagi is virtually surrounded by two branches of the Abu-gawa—the river's south channel, Hashimoto-gawa, and the river's northeast fork, Matsumoto-gawa. Rising in great semicircles behind the sleepy town are symmetrical waves of shadowy mountains, while before it stretches a sparkling blue sea.

Hagi is rich with history, and, owing to its remoteness, retains the atmosphere of a traditional castle town—though, unfortunately, its castle was a casualty of the Meiji Restoration. Turning away from feudalism to support the new order, the city was of critical importance in the 1865 to 1867 movement to restore power to the emperor. Japan's first prime minister, Hirobumi Ito (1841–1909), was a Hagi native.

Hagi is also famous for Hagi-yaki, a type of earthenware with soft colors and milky, translucent glazes ranging from beige to pink. The esteemed local ceramics industry began in the 16th century when a Mori general brought home captive Korean potters (perhaps his consolation for a failed invasion) to create pottery for their new masters. The visually soothing Hagi-yaki is second only to Raku-yaki as the most coveted pottery in Japan, and it does not come cheaply, except during the annual price-friendly Hagi-yaki Festival every May 1–5.

GETTING HERE AND AROUND

The fastest way to Hagi is by JR bus (Rail Pass accepted), crossing the mountains in just one hour for ¥1,680 from Yamaguchi City. The bus departs from the front of the train station. A JR bus also leaves from the Shinkansen Exit of Shin-Yamaguchi for an 80-minute ride for ¥1,970. Buses run one per hour between 6 am and 7 pm. Some buses stop at Hagi Station, the Hagi Bus Center, or Higashi-Hagi Station; all stop at the last two. Return buses follow the same plan. The ideal way to explore Hagi is by bicycle, and you can rent a bike for between ¥800 and ¥1,000 per day near the stations or shopping arcades. A local bus system (red bus) loops around town for ¥100 a ride or ¥500 for a full day.

City information is available from English-speaking staff at the Hagi City Tourist Bureau next to Hagi Station. For local information at Higashi-Hagi Station, try Hagi Tourist Office in the building to the left of the station, on the left side of the shopping arcade. The City Tourist Office is downtown in Hagi City Hall.

ESSENTIALS

Currency Exchange Yamaguchi Bank (⌧ *16–1 Higashi Tamachi* ☎ *0838/22–0380*).

Visitor Information City Tourist Office (⌧ *495–4 Emukai* ☎ *0838/25–3131* ☉ *Mon.–Sat. 9–5*). **Hagi City Tourist Bureau** (☎ *0838/25–1750* ☉ *Daily 9–5:45*). **Hagi Tourist Office** (☎ *0838/22–7599* 🖷 *0838/24–2202*).

WHAT TO SEE

If you've just arrived by bus, you won't be impressed by the run-down buildings around the Hagi Bus Center. That's okay—there's no need to linger here. Head three short blocks north, then left onto Tamachi Mall, and then west through the quaint older sections of town for 15 minutes to see the park and castle ruins. If you need to make a Tourist Info stop first, head south two blocks and then west two more, to Hagi City Hall.

Horiuchi 堀内. This is the old samurai section of town. From Shizuki Koen, cross the canal (on the middle bridge) to the east side, and head toward downtown. The tomb of **Tenju-in** is a memorial to Terumoto Mori, who in the early 16th century founded the tenacious clan that ruled the Choshu area for 13 generations. Next you come to the **Outer Gate of Mori**; the **Toida Masuda House Walls** are on your right as you head south. Dating from the 18th century, these are the longest mud walls in the area. At the next chance, turn right and head west to the ancient, wooden **Fukuhara Gate**.

Jo-zan Gama 城山窯 *(Jo-zan Kiln)*. Stop in at this pottery studio near Shizuki Koen, perhaps the best place to browse through and purchase magnificent pottery. Usually you are welcome to enter the studios and see the kilns across the street. Classes for a chance to make your own may be available. Bicycles can be rented here as well. ⊠ *Hagi-jo-ato, Horiuchi* ☎ *0838/25–1666* ⊗ *Daily 8–5.*

★ **Shizuki Koen** 指月公園. Hagi's westernmost end is bounded on three sides by the sea. This large, lovely park contains the Hagi-jo ruins and Hana-no-e Teahouse. **Hagi-jo** was one of many castles destroyed by the Meiji government around 1874 for being an embarrassing symbol of backward ways. The dramatic seaside location, with its stupendous mountain backdrop, must have made the castle a truly superb sight in its day, but alas, we can only imagine, since the walls and moats are all that remain.

The **Hana-no-e Teahouse** is a bare-bones oasis of Zen, set amid meditative gardens and judiciously pruned greenery. The attendants make the classic, slightly bitter *matcha* tea (¥500) for you while you reflect upon the transient nature of life—or consider where you'd like to go next.

Mori House, south of the park, is a long narrow building once home to samurai foot soldiers in the late 18th century. The rooms are sparse and placed one next to the other. This arrangement allowed the soldiers to leap into rank-and-file assembly just outside at a moment's notice. ⊠ *O-aza Horiuchi* ☎ *0838/25–1826* ⊠ *¥210, includes admission to Hagi-jo grounds, Hana-no-e Teahouse, and Mori House* ⊗ *Apr.–Oct., daily 8–6:30; Nov.–Feb., daily 8:30–4:30; Mar., daily 8:30–6.*

Tamachi Mall 田町モール. This is the busiest street in Hagi, with some 130 shops selling local products from Yamaguchi Prefecture. The shopping mood is addictive, the wares gorgeous, and the shopkeepers friendly, so your money can go quickly. Tamachi Mall is six blocks southwest from the dated, Jetson's-style Hagi Grand Hotel, across the Matsumoto-gawa from Higashi-Hagi Station. ⊠ *Central Hagi.*

WHERE TO EAT

$$$–$$$$
JAPANESE
Fodor's Choice
★

✕**Chiyo** 千代. A *tsubaki* course, at ¥3,150, includes squid and scallops cooked before you with butter on a sizzling-hot river stone, and such goodies as fugu—as sashimi or cooked tempura-style—stuffed with foie gras. Zingy homemade pickles reset your palate for each successive treat. Women beautifully dressed in formal wear serve you in a classically elegant manner, and off to the right of the intimate 10-seat counter are views of a mossy green and flowery window garden. All seating is Japanese style and no English menu is available. ⊠ *20–4 Imafuruhagi-machi, Yamaguchi-ken* ☎ *0838/22–1128* ⊗ *Closed Mon. No dinner Sun.*

$–$$
JAPANESE

✕**Sobaho Fujita-ya** 蕎麦舗ふじたや. Colorful local characters come to this casual restaurant for beer and sake and *seiro-soba* (thin buckwheat noodles served in steaming hot baskets), and hot tempura served on fragrant handmade cypress trays. The restaurant is usually open by 11:30 (or when the noodles are ready), but it closes at 6 (or when all the noodles are gone), so only a very early dinner is possible here. ⊠ *59 Kumagaya-cho* ☎ *0838/22–1086* ▭ *No credit cards* ⊗ *Closed Wed.*

9

$$$–$$$$
JAPANESE

✕ **Wafu Resutoran Nakamura** 中村. Set-menu courses at this reliable and popular traditional restaurant typically offer a variety of fish, mountain vegetables, miso soup, and steamed rice. Nakamura has tatami and Western seating but no English-language menu. You can select your food from the tempting window display. Reservations are accepted here and recommended for larger parties. ✉ *394 Hijiwara* ☎ *0838/22–6619* ☾ *No lunch in summer.*

WHERE TO STAY

Hotel reviews have been condensed for this book. Please go to Fodors. com for full reviews of each property.

$$$–$$$$
HOTEL

🏨 **Hagi Tanaka Hotel** 萩たなかホテル. Enticingly close to the hypnotic Mt. Kasa, its baths tap an onsen, and delectable morsels from the bay are served for dinner in your room. **Pros:** wonderful hot spring baths; great local cuisine; clean, new rooms still embody fine old traditions. **Cons:** not much English spoken here; remote location. ✉ *707–10 Koshigahama* ☎ *0838/25–0001* 🖷 *0838/24–1111* ⊕ *www.hagitanakahotel. jp* ⇗ *92 Japanese-style rooms* ♿ *In-room: a/c. In-hotel: bar* ❖❘ *Some meals.*

$$$$
RYOKAN

🏨 **Hokumon Yashiki** 北門屋敷. An elegant ryokan built upon the ruins of an old Mori clan estate, with fine touches of understated luxury, the Hokumon Yashiki pampers you in a style the ruling elite were surely accustomed to in the good old days. **Pros:** unique interior design melds traditional Japanese style with European elements; top-notch hospitality; one of the most conspicuously traditional inns in the world. **Cons:** nothing lively for miles around; Web site in Japanese only. ✉ *210–12 Horiuchi* ☎ *0838/22–7251* 🖷 *0838/25–8144* ⇗ *42 Japanese-style rooms without bath, 5 Western-style rooms* ♿ *In-room: a/c* ❖❘ *Some meals.*

$
HOTEL

🏨 **Urban City Hotel Hasegawa** ビジネスホテル長谷川. If you want a cheap, decent place to crash near the Hagi Bus Center, this business hotel is adequate—and right across the street. **Pros:** convenient to the old part of town; cheap. **Cons:** feels like you're staying in a ghost town; rooms are as minimalist as can be. ✉ *17 Karahi-machi* ☎ *0838/22–0450* 🖷 *0838/22–4884* ⇗ *13 Western-style rooms, 5 Japanese-style rooms* ♿ *In-room: a/c. In-hotel: restaurant, bar* ❖❘ *No meals.*

TSUWANO 津和野

93 km (58 mi) northeast of Hagi; 50 km (31 mi) northeast of Yamaguchi; 63 km (39 mi) northeast of Shin-Yamaguchi.

Fodor's Choice
★

This hauntingly beautiful town, tucked into a narrow north–south valley at the foot of conical Aono-yama and its attendant dormant volcanic mountain friends, may be the most picturesque hamlet in all Japan. If you catch it on a clear day, the view from the old castle ruins simply takes your breath away. Even when it's cloudy, the mist hangs romantically among the trees and ridges. The stucco-and-tile walls hearken back to ancient times, like those in Hagi and Kurashiki, and the clear, carp-filled streams running beside the streets can induce even tired, jaded travelers to take a leisurely stroll or bike ride backward through time.

Dancers dress as white egrets in Tsuwano's Sagi-mai Shinji festival.

It's easy to see why Tsuwano has come to be known as "Little Kyoto," and it's easier still to imagine how a gifted spirit and intellect could soar here. The towering Japanese literary figure Ogai Mori, novelist and poet, was born (in 1862) and lived here, until, at the age of 12, he went off and enrolled at Tokyo University's preparatory program in medicine.

GETTING HERE AND AROUND

Tsuwano can be reached by train: it's 2 hours, 23 minutes northeast of Hagi by JR (¥1,620); 1 hour, 13 minutes northeast of Yamaguchi by JR Yamaguchi Line (¥950); or 1 hour northeast of Shin-Yamaguchi by JR Super Oki Express (¥2,770). Though JR trains from Yamaguchi are quick and easy, JR train routes from Hagi to Tsuwano involve a change and long layovers in Masuda. You can also take a bus from Hagi's Bocho Bus Center directly to Tsuwano, which takes around two hours (¥2,080).

In Tsuwano all sights are within easy walking distance. You can also rent a bicycle from one of the four shops near the station plaza (two hours ¥500; all day ¥800).

Bus Contacts Bocho Bus Center (☎ 0856/72–0272).

ESSENTIALS

The Tourist Information Office is inside the Photograph Gallery to the right of the railway station. It has free brochures, and staff members will help you reserve accommodations. As with most places in town, little English is spoken here.

Visitor Information Tourist Information Office (☎ 0856/72–1771 ⊙ Daily 9–5).

WHAT TO SEE

Nagomi-no-Sato. Tsuwano puts its geothermal gifts to good use at the spa at this volcanic spring. Inside and out, the tubs have great views of the surrounding gumdrop-shape volcanic peaks. It's west of everything else in town, across the river from the Washibara Hachiman-gu (a shrine where traditional horseback archery contests are held the second Sunday of April every year), but still not too far to get to by rented bike. ⌂ *256-O-aza Washibara* ☎ *0856/72–4122, 0120/26–4753 toll-free* ⌨ *¥500* ⊘ *Hot springs daily 10–8 except 2nd and 4th Thurs. of month; restaurant daily 10–10, except 1st and 3rd Thurs. of month*

Old House of Ogai Mori 森鴎外旧宅 / 森鴎外記念館. While spartan, the house is, perhaps, worth a visit if only to commemorate the achievements of this gifted genius who called Tsuwano his home. Ogai Mori (1862–1922), son of the head physician to the daimyo of Shimane, became a doctor at the young age of 19 and, in spite of courting trouble for his outspoken criticism of Japan's backward ways compared to the West, went on to become the author of such acclaimed novels as *The Wild Geese* and *Vita Sexualis*. He was also a prominent figure in the fledgling government behind the Meiji Restoration. From Tsuwano Station it's a 12-block walk south along the main road, or take the bus and get off at Ogai Kyukyo-mae. ⌂ *1–230 Machida, Kanoashi-gun* ☎ *0856/72–3210* ⌨ *¥600* ⊘ *Tues.–Sun. 9–5.*

Taikodani Inari Jinja 太鼓谷稲荷神社 *(Taiko Valley Inari Shrine). This* is one of the five most revered Inari shrines in Japan. Inari shrines are connected with the fox, a Shinto symbol of luck and cleverness. People come to pray for good fortune in business and health. A series of 1,174 red wooden gates are suspended above steps that climb up the western side of the valley to the shrine, and the journey is a nice hike with a jaw-dropping view of the valley waiting for you at the top. From the station, follow the streamside Tono-machi-dori past the Katorikku Kyokai (Catholic church), but before crossing the river turn right onto the small lane. The lane leads to the tunnel-like approach through the gates to the structure high on a cliffside. You can also take a bus that approaches by a back road; the Tourist Information Office can help with this. **Yasaka Jinja** is another shrine on the site, where every July 20 and 27 sees the famous Heron Dance Festival.

Tsuwano-jo (Tsuwano Castle). The local castle was another casualty of the Meiji Restoration in the late 19th century, but from the derelict ruins there is an awesome panoramic view of the dormant volcanic cone of Aono-yama to the east, surrounding similar peaks, and the entire valley stretching out below. To get up here you can hike a marked trail that leads from Taikodani Inari Jinja or take a chairlift from below the Inari shrine for ¥450 round-trip. The chairlift takes only five minutes, and from the top it's about a 15-minute moderate hike to the castle foundations. ⊘ *Daily 10–5.*

OFF THE BEATEN PATH **Otometoge Maria Seido** 乙女峠マリア聖堂. Between 1868 and 1870, in an effort to disperse Christian strongholds and cause them extreme hardship—in the hope that the believers would recant their faith—the Tokugawa Shogunate sent 153 Christians from Nagasaki to Tsuwano, where they were imprisoned and tortured. Many gave in, but 36 died for their faith. Otometoge Maria Seido (St. Mary's Chapel at the Pass of the Virgin) was built in 1948 to commemorate the plight of the 36 martyrs, which is portrayed in the stained-glass windows. The chapel is a 1-km (½-mi) walk from Tsuwano Station. Go right out of the station, make another right at the first street (which leads to Yomei-ji), and just after crossing the tracks turn right again and walk up the hill. Every May 3 a procession begins at the church in town and ends in the chapel courtyard, where a large outdoor mass is celebrated.

WHERE TO EAT

$–$$

SUSHI

✕ **Sushi Kappo Aoki** 寿司割烹あおき. An old-fashioned, rustic-decor sushi restaurant with a few tables on tatami mats and a long bar counter with stools, Aoki has a cheerful staff and reasonable prices. It's also within easy walking distance of Tsuwano Station. Try the *jyo-nigiri* (deluxe sushi set); it will likely include a slice or two of tasty, chewy koi, or local carp. That and a frosty mug of beer set you back only ¥1,900. The restaurant stays open until 10 pm. ⊠ *78–10 Ushioro-da, Kanoashi-gun* ☎ *0856/72–0444* ▭ *No credit cards* ☉ *Closed Tues.*

$$$–$$$$

JAPANESE

Fodor's Choice

★

✕ **Yuki** 遊亀. Carp dishes—yes, carp—and delectable mountain vegetables maintain Yuki's highly venerated reputation. They have *ayu*, or river smelt, and other things, but for only ¥2,800 you can get the Tsuwano *teishoku*, a gourmet carp course that offers a smattering of everything a fat and happy carp can become: there's chewy carp sashimi (with a wonderful lemony-mustard-thyme dipping sauce); tender deep-fried carp; carp steeped so long in soy sauce, sake, and brown sugar that it is dense and even slightly dry but very delicious; and carp boiled in a tangy miso soup until it's almost flaky. This is bona-fide stamina food, and tastes way better than you might think—these are not like the carp you and your uncles pulled out of those old muddy ponds! The dining room is chock-full of old farm and country-life implements, and there's even a stream burbling at your feet. Come early, as they close at around 7 pm, and after 3 early dinner is served by reservation only. ⊠ *271–4 Ushioro-da, Kanoashi-gun, Shimane-ken* ☎ *0856/72–0162* ▭ *No credit cards.*

WHERE TO STAY

Hotel reviews have been condensed for this book. Please go to Fodors. com for full reviews of each property.

$–$$

MINSHUKU

Fodor's Choice

★

🏠 **Tsuwano Lodge** 津和野ロッジ. Relax and revel in style at this lodge tucked among the rice paddies and bamboo groves along the way to the Washibara Hachiman-gu shrine. **Pros:** rooftop bath; fantastic, multicourse meal is a great value; frog-song lullabies in season; bicycles for rent. **Cons:** rustic and isolated, in an already quite remote place; there are no private baths here. ⊠ *Ushihara Guchi 345, Kanoashi-gun, Shimane-ken* ☎ *0856/72–1683* 📠 *0856/72–2880* ⤶ *8 Japanese-style rooms without bath* ⚲ *In-room: a/c. In-hotel: restaurant* ▭ *No credit cards* ⍓ *Breakfast.*

$$

MINSHUKU

🏠 **Wakasagi-no-Yado** 民宿若さぎの宿. Despite their limited English, the family that runs this small but satisfactory inn is eager to help overseas tourists and will meet you at Tsuwano Station, only an eight-minute walk away. **Pros:** nice location; heartwarming hospitality; bicycles for rent on-site. **Cons:** small, spartan rooms; no private bathrooms; reservations requests can be made in Japanese only ✉ *Mori-mura, Kanoashi-gun* ☎🖷 *0856/72–1146* ➲ *7 Japanese-style rooms without bath* 🛁 *In-room: a/c* ▤ *No credit cards* ⊙ *Closed Nov. 11–Dec. 30* ⊚ *Breakfast.*

MATSUE 松江

Fodor's Choice
★ *194 km (121 mi) northeast of Tsuwano, 172 km (107 mi) northwest of Kurashiki.*

Matsue is a city blessed with so much overwhelming beauty and good food that you will wonder what to look at, what to eat, and what to do first. It's where the lake named Shinji-ko empties into the lagoon called Naka-umi, which connects directly with the Sea of Japan. This makes Matsue a seafood lover's paradise; specialties include both kinds of eel, all kinds of shrimp, shellfish, carp, sea bass, smelt, whitebait, and the famous black shijimi clams from Shinji-ko. The water also provides the city with a lovely network of canals.

Matsue also attracts and holds onto some of the country's most welcoming and interesting people, both foreign and native. This remote realm is a traveler's favorite, and once you've come here you'll surely be back—it's that kind of place. In the 1890s, the famed journalist-novelist Lafcadio Hearn came here and promptly fell in love, first with the place, and then with a local woman—a samurai's daughter, no less. In true journalistic fashion he proceeded to let the entire world know about it.

GETTING HERE AND AROUND

Japan Rail can get you to Matsue from Tsuwano (2 hours, 34 minutes northeast by JR Super Oki Express, ¥5,870) or Kurashiki, Okayama (2 hours, 17 minutes northwest by JR Yakumo Limited Express, ¥5,550). Most sights in Matsue are within walking distance of each other. Where they are not, the buses fill in. The bus station faces the train station.

ESSENTIALS

The Matsue Tourist Information Office is outside JR Matsue Station and open daily 9–6. You can collect free maps and brochures and use the Internet (also for free). The Shimane Tourist Association offers a substantial discount of 30% to 50% for foreigners at nine of its tourist attractions; the current list includes the castle and four museums. You need only present your passport or foreigner's registration card at the entrance to these places.

Currency Exchange San-in Godo Bank (✉ *10 Sakana-cho* ☎ *0120/31–5180*). **Shimane Bank** (✉ *2–35 Tohon-cho* ☎ *085/224–4000*).

Visitor Information Matsue Tourist Information Office (✉ *665 Asahi-machi* ☎ *0852/21–4034* 🖷 *0852/27–2598*).

WHAT TO SEE

Lafcadio Hearn Memorial Hall 小泉八雲記念館 *(Koizumi Yakumo Kinenkan).* The Hearn museum has a good collection of the author's manuscripts and other artifacts related to his life in Japan. It's adjacent to

Matsue-jo is one of the most striking buildings in the region; it has been standing since its construction in 1611.

Koizumi Yakumo Kyukyo, Hearn's former residence in Matsue. Two minutes from the Memorial Hall is the Hearn Kyukyo bus stop, where a bus goes back to the center of town and the station. ✉ 322 Okudani-cho 📞 0852/21–2147 💴 ¥300 🕐 Apr.–Sept., daily 8:30–6:30; Oct.–Mar., daily 8:30–5.

Lafcadio Hearn Residence 小泉八雲旧宅 (Koizumi Yakumo Kyukyo). The celebrated writer's house has remained unchanged since he left Matsue in 1891. Born of an Irish father and a Greek mother, Lafcadio Hearn (1850–1904) spent his early years in Europe and moved to the United States to become a journalist. In 1890 he traveled to Yokohama, Japan, and made his way to Matsue, where he began teaching. There he met and married a samurai's daughter named Setsu Koizumi. He later took posts in Kumamoto, Kobe, and Tokyo. Disdainful of the materialism of the West, he was destined to be a lifelong Japanophile and resident. He became a Japanese citizen, taking the name Yakumo Koizumi. His most famous works were Glimpses of Unfamiliar Japan (1894) and Japan: An Attempt at Interpretation (1904). ✉ 315 Kitahori-cho 📞 0852/23–0714 💴 ¥350 🕐 Mar.–Nov., daily 9–5; Dec.–Feb., daily 10–4:40.

Matsue English Garden 松江イングリツシユ　ガーデン. This garden is of the same scale, arrangement, and style of any traditional English garden. There's an outdoor rest area, fountain plaza, sunken garden, indoor garden, "white" garden, pergola, cloister courtyard, landscape garden, rose terrace, and laburnum arch. If you've covered everything else, try this place—it's quite stunning, and it was put together in only five years by a jovial English gardener named Keith Gott. The garden is out on the lakeshore northwest of town, at Nishi-Hamasada. It's

9

one stop (five minutes; get off at English Garden-mae Station) west of Matsue Shinji-ko Onsen Station by the Ichibata Railway, so it can be seen on the way to or from Izumo Taisha. ✉ *369 Nishi-Hamadasa-cho* ☎ *0852/36–3030* 🖃 *Free* ⌚ *Apr.–Sept., daily 9–5; Oct.–Mar., daily 9–4.*

★ **Matsue-jo** 松江城. Start a tour of Matsue at the enchanting and shadowy castle and walk in the castle park, **Shiroyama Koen,** under aromatic pines. Constructed of exactly such wood, the castle was completed in 1611. Not only did it survive the Meiji upheavals intact, but it was, amazingly, never ransacked during the civil war–type turbulence of the Tokugawa Shogunate. Perhaps it's the properties of the wood, or the angles, or the mysterious tricks of light and shadows, but this castle truly feels *alive* and is a certified must-see sight of the region.

Built by the daimyo of Izumo, Yoshiharu Horio, for protection, Matsue-jo's donjon (main tower), at 98 feet, is the second tallest among originals still standing in Japan. Crouching as it does below and behind the surrounding lofty pines, Matsue-jo is slightly spooky, even in daytime. Despite its foreboding aspect, the castle seems to beckon you inside for a peek. By all means, obey the call! This is a fabulously preserved walk-in time capsule, with six interior levels belied by a tricky facade that suggests only five. The lower floors display an appropriately macabre collection of samurai swords and armor. The long climb to the castle's uppermost floor is definitely worth it for the view encompasses the city, Lake Shinji, the Shimane Peninsula, and—if weather conditions permit—the distant mystical snowy peak of Daisen.

The castle and park are a 1-km (½-mi) stroll northwest from Matsue Station, or take the Lakeline Bus from Terminal 7 in front of the station and get off at Otemae; the fare is ¥150. ✉ *1–5 Tono-machi* ☎ *0852/21–4030* 🖃 *¥550* ⌚ *Apr.–Sept., daily 8:30–6; Oct.–Mar., daily 8:30–4:30.*

Meimei-an Teahouse 明々庵. Built in 1779, this is one of Japan's best-preserved teahouses. For ¥400 you can contemplate the mysteries of Matsue-jo, and for ¥400 more, you get tea and a sweet. To get here, leave Shiroyama Koen, the castle park, at its East Exit and follow the moat going north; at the top of the park a road leads to the right, northwest of the castle. The teahouse is a short climb up this road. ✉ *278 Kitahori-cho* ☎ *0852/21–9863* 🖃 *¥400, ¥800 with tea* ⌚ *Daily 9–5.*

Samurai Residence 武家屋敷 *(Buke Yashiki).* Built in 1730, this house belonged to the well-to-do Shiomi family, chief retainers to the daimyo. Note the separate servant quarters, a shed for the palanquin, and slats in the walls to allow cooling breezes to flow through the rooms. Buke Yashiki is on the main road at the base of the side street on which Meimei-an Teahouse is located (keep the castle moat on your left). ✉ *305 Kitahori-cho* ☎ *0852/22–2243* 🖃 *¥300* ⌚ *Apr.–Sept., daily 8:30–6; Oct.–Mar., daily 8:30–4:30.*

Shinji-ko 宍道湖. When dusk rolls around, you'll want to position yourself well. You won't get a better sunset than the one seen every night over the town's lake. As locals do, you can watch it from Shinji-ko Ohashi, the town's westernmost bridge, but the best spot is south of the bridge, along the road, down near water level in **Shirakata Koen,** the narrow lakeside park just west of the NHK Building and the hospital.

This is a great place to kick back and enjoy some tasty local microbrews and portable sushi. A very popular *yuhi*, or sunset, spot is the patio of the Prefectural Art Museum, visible and adjacent to the park above.

WHERE TO EAT

$$–$$$
JAPANESE
Fodor's Choice
★

✕ **Kawakyo** 川京. This is the best place to try the seven famous delicacies from Shinji-ko: *suzuki* (or *hosho-yaki*), sea bass wrapped in *washi* (paper) and steam-baked over hot coals; *unagi* (freshwater eel) split, broiled, and basted in sweet soy sauce; *shirao*, a small whitefish often served as sashimi or cooked in vinegar-miso; *amasagi* (smelt), teriyaki-grilled or cooked in tempura; *shijimi*, small black-shelled clams served in miso or other soup; *koi*, string-bound, washi-wrapped, steam-baked carp; and *moroge-ebi*, steamed shrimp. Especially good is the hosho-yaki. The staff is very outgoing, as is the regular crowd. Don't forget to request one of the delicious *ji-zake* (locally made sake) samplers. Reservations are a good idea. Kawakyo is in the block just east of the middle (Matsue Ohashi) bridge, a block north of the river. ⊠ *65 Suetsugu Hon-machi, Shimane-ken* ☎ *0852/22–1312* 🚫 *No credit cards* 🕐 *Closed Sun. No lunch.*

$–$$
SOBA

✕ **Ohashi** 大橋. If you're pressed for time but want to grab a decent lunch, try some *warigo* soba, a local buckwheat noodle specialty. Ohashi is right inside the Shamine department store next to the station and has a filling, healthful Yakumo Gozen set course for ¥1,000. An early dinner is also possible since the restaurant is open until 8:15. ⊠ *472–2 Asahi-machi* ☎ *0852/26–6551* 🚫 *No credit cards* 🕐 *Closed every 3rd Tues.*

$–$$
SOBA

✕ **Yakumo-an** 八雲庵. A colorful garden surrounds the dining area at this traditional house that serves good soba. Recommended dishes include the *sanshurui soba* (three kinds of soba) for ¥750. Take the top dish and, leaving the garnishes in, pour the broth into it, then dunk the noodles as you go. Drink the leftover broth, too; it's full of B vitamins and good for your metabolism. ⊠ *308 Kitabori-cho, north of castle* ☎ *0852/22–2400* 🚫 *No credit cards* 🕐 *Daily 9–4:30.*

WHERE TO STAY

$$$$
RYOKAN
★

🏠 **Naniwa Issui** なにわ一水. A swanky ryokan near the Matsue Shinji-ko Onsen Station (for easy Izumo Taisha access), Naniwa Issui is envied for its amazing views out over the big lake—and for its onsen. **Pros:** unbeatable access to everything this city and region has to offer; private balcony onsen put you in the lap of luxury. **Cons:** you'll need take taxis or walk 7–10 minutes to the JR Matsue Shinji-ko bus stop. ⊠ *63 Chidori-cho* ☎ *0852/21–4132* 🖨 *0852/21–4162* 🛏 *29 Japanese-style rooms* ⚒ *In-room: a/c. In-hotel: restaurant* ⏐○⏐ *Some meals.*

$–$$
RYOKAN

🏠 **Ryokan Terazuya** 旅館寺津屋. The same family has maintained a tradition of heartwarming hospitality at this charming riverside ryokan since 1893. **Pros:** high level of hospitality will inspire a deeper appreciation of Japan; station pickup service. **Cons:** don't expect to practice your Nihongo as the master will insist on using his excellent English; no private baths; noise from the street and nearby Shirakata Shrine tends to carry over. ⊠ *60–3 Tenjin-machi* ☎ *0852/21–3480* 🖨 *0852/21–3422* 🛏 *9 Japanese-style rooms without bath* ⚒ *In-room: a/c* 🚫 *No credit cards* ⏐○⏐ *Some meals.*

9

IZUMO TAISHA

37 km (23 mi) west of Matsue.

Oldest of all Japan's Shinto shrines, **Izumo Taisha** has been of tremendous cultural significance—second only to the great shrine at Ise—since the 6th century. The main building was last rebuilt in 1744. In ancient days it was the largest wooden building in the country, but since the 13th century, each time it was rebuilt, it was scaled to half its former size, and it is now *only* 24 meters tall. The original must have been a humbling thing to stand in front of! Nature has arrayed a shrine of its own to compliment the ornate but somehow subdued structures: a lofty ridge of forested peaks rises behind, a boulevard of fragrant ancient pines lines the approach, and lush green lawns flank both sides. Pilgrims come here primarily to pray for success in courtship and marriage.

Although this is Japan's oldest Shinto shrine, the *hon-den* (main building) dates from 1744 and most of the other were buildings from 1688 onward. The newest were built in 1874. The architectural style, with its saddled crests and ornamental roof fixtures resembling crossed swords, is said to be unique to the Izumo region, but some similarities with the main Shinto shrine of Ise Jingu on the Kii Peninsula can be noted. The taisha is dedicated to a male god, Okuninushi, the creator of the land and god of marriage and fortune. Instead of clapping twice, as at other shrines, you should clap four times—twice for yourself, and twice for your current or future partner. According to folklore, if you successfully throw a ¥5 coin so that it sticks up into the sacred hanging strands of the enormously thick 5-ton, 25 foot-long twisted straw rope, or *shimenawa*, suspended above the entrance to the main building, you will be doubly assured of good luck in marriage. As you will undoubtedly see, it is almost impossible to do without some kind of cheating—which may say something about the difficulties of marriage.

Two rectangular buildings on either side of the compound are believed to house the visiting millions of Shinto gods during the 10th lunar month of each year. In the rest of Japan the lunar October is referred to as Kannazuki, "month without gods," while in Izumo, October is called Kamiarizuki, "month with gods." The shrine is a five-minute walk north, to the right along the main street, from Izumo Taisha-mae Station. ⊠ *Izumo Taisha, Izumo* ☎ *0853/53–2298* 🎫 *Free* ⊙ *Daily 8:30–5:30.*

GETTING HERE AND AROUND

The shrine is most easily seen on a day trip from Matsue, and the easiest way is to go from Matsue Shinji-ko Onsen Station. Buses run often between it and Matsue Station for ¥200. It takes one hour on the Ichibata Dentetsu (electric railway, ¥790), from Matsue Shinji-ko Onsen Station. After about 50 minutes you'll need to change trains at Kawato Station for the final 10-minute leg to Izumo Taisha-mae Station. You can also get there by taking the JR train from Matsue Station to JR Izumo Station, then transferring to the Ichibata Bus for a 30-minute ride, ¥490, to the Izumo Taisha Seimon stop.

Shikoku

WORD OF MOUTH

"A hidden gem that is a MUST if you are an art fan is Naoshima . . . all I can say is wow. Best place I've been in my life."

—kitty_chan81

WELCOME TO SHIKOKU

TOP REASONS TO GO

★ **Get Off the Concrete:** Discover Shikoku's natural charms by rafting, hiking, walking, and swimming. Best of all, bicycle across the Seto Inland Sea on a series of island-hopping bridges.

★ **Get Your Hands Dirty:** Try a martial art, make soba noodles, dye fabrics, and learn a two-step in time for the summer dances.

★ **Get Down, Get Funky:** Festivals mark every weekend between April and October leading up to the biggest dance festivals in the nation—Yosakoi and Awa Odori.

★ **Get Personal:** Encounter Shikoku's legendary hospitality first-hand.

★ **Get Real:** Shikoku may very well be the closest a tourist can get to "the real Japan," with its time-forgotten towns like Uchiko and Nishi-Iya, unique landmarks like Dogo Onsen and Kompira-san, and acres of rice.

1 Takamatsu and Eastern Shikoku. In Kagawa and Tokushima prefectures natural spectacles like the giant whirlpools in Tokushima and artistic attractions like Takamatsu's Ritsurin Garden springboard you to small towns and craft workshops nearby.

GETTING ORIENTED

Shikoku has four prefectures—Kagawa in the northeast, Tokushima below it, Ehime in the west, and Kochi along the entire Pacific coast. This chapter is arranged as an itinerary beginning in Kagawa's Takamatsu and moving through Tokushima to the central Iya Valley, south to Kochi, and finally north towards Ehime's Matsuyama. The reverse loop is just as practicable. The advantage of finishing around Matsuyama is the easy access by bus or bicycle to Hiroshima, or by ferry to Hiroshima, Kyushu, Kobe, or Osaka—perfect for a direct link to Kansai Airport if it's time to go home.

10

2 Kochi and Central Shikoku. The mile-high mountains of central Shikoku are largely undeveloped—it's just too steep to build anything! Visit two great escapes: the isolated Iya Valley, with its steep gorges and mountain villages that are best explored on a rafting trip down the vibrant Yoshino River, and the rowdy, fun-loving city of Kochi, which you'll find on the sun-kissed Pacific coast.

3 Matsuyama and Western Shikoku. Matsuyama mixes small-town character with an exciting urban landscape. Come for Japan's best eating, fashion, and in-city sights outside of Honshu. See the superb cliff-top castle and dreamlike Dogo Onsen, the oldest hot spring in Japan, and venture into the surrounding mountain villages.

Updated by Annamarie Sasagawa

Shikoku, the smallest of Japan's four main islands, isn't somewhere many tourists manage to visit. The island is mountainous and mostly rural, but what Shikoku lacks in urban adventure it makes up for in an abundance of natural beauty, unique traditions, and very enthusiastic hospitality.

"Shikoku" means "four kingdoms," and refers to the ancient regions of Awa, Sanuki, Iyo, and Tosa, which are now Tokushima, Kagawa, Ehime, and Kochi prefectures. It's been a travel destination for Japanese people since the 8th century, when Shingon Buddhist priest Kobo Daishi established an 88-temple pilgrimage circuit. In the Edo era, non-samurai Japanese didn't have the right to travel freely, so going on a shogunate-approved pilgrimage to Shikoku was one of the few ways to explore the country.

Visiting Shikoku now doesn't involve convincing the shogun of your piety, though it does require a bit of planning. There are fewer English speakers here than on Honshu, and transport connections are less frequent. Coming here is well worth the effort, though. Locals are proud of their island and extend endless hospitality to the few foreigners who make the trip. You won't find a match for Shikoku hospitality elsewhere in Japan, nor for its ancient hot springs, mountain temples, farm villages, or summer dance festivals.

PLANNING

Your trip will almost certainly start at one of the island's northern cities: coming from Kansai your most likely access is via Takamatsu or Tokushima in eastern Shikoku; from Hiroshima or western Honshu it's Matsuyama in the west. Because Shikoku's rewards lie off the beaten path, exploring involves the challenges of a road less traveled. Public transportation is infrequent and English competence minimal. On the other hand, locals here will be more excited to socialize with you here than anywhere else in the country. Use the cities for access to small towns and natural getaways, and tailor your route to suit your aims and schedule. If you only have a few days, a good itinerary is Matsuyama, the Iya Valley, and Naoshima or the Shimanami Kaido bridges. If you have a week, add in a trip to Kochi.

WHEN TO GO

Shikoku's unspoiled scenery offers some perfect locations in which to bask in the fleeting glories of springtime cherry blossoms and autumn foliage without the usual Honshu crowds. Summer is festival time throughout the country, but Shikoku has the best of the bunch: the epic dance festivals **Yosakoi** in Kochi, held August 9–12, and Tokushima's **Awa Odori**, held August 12–15. Winter is mild on the island, but the roads in to Iya can ice up, and the early autumn typhoons that batter Kochi and southern Ehime can disrupt transport.

GETTING HERE AND AROUND

Trains and buses are the easiest ways to travel, though in rural areas they can be infrequent and irregular. Missing a train doesn't always mean just waiting for the next one: the next one might not come until October. Check schedules and find out when renting a car will save you time and money. Ask tourist information centers (not JR ticket windows) to help you plan. Driving is a fantastic way to explore the countryside, but be ready for challenging mountain roads.

AIR TRAVEL

All Nippon Airways (ANA) and Japan Airlines (JAL) provide domestic flights to and from Shikoku's four major cities: Takamatsu, Kochi, Matsuyama, and Tokushima. International connections through Seoul and Taipei are rarely cost-effective; use bus, train, or ferry connections to airports in Tokyo or Osaka.

Contacts All Nippon Airways (ANA) (☎ *800/235–9262 in U.S. and Canada, 0570/029–222 in Japan* ⊕ *www.anaskyweb.com*). **Japan Airlines (JAL)** (☎ *800/525–3663 in U.S. and Canada, 0570/025–071 in Japan* ⊕ *www.jal.co.jp*).

BOAT TRAVEL

Cities and small ports offer ferry connections to Tokyo, Osaka, Kobe, western Honshu, and Kyushu. Use the respective ferry companies' sites to check timetables or ask tourist information offices to help; reservations are rarely necessary if you don't have a vehicle, though you do need to make a reservation for an overnight ferry. Popular routes are Tokushima–Tokyo (19 hours), Matsuyama–Kobe/Osaka (6–8 hours), Matsuyama–Hiroshima (3 hours), Matsuyama–Beppu (5 hours), and Yawatahama–Beppu (1½ hours).

BUS TRAVEL

Short-haul and overnight buses connect Shikoku's four major cities to a number of cities on Honshu and with each other—useful when no direct train route exists, like between Matsuyama and Kochi or Tokushima. Buses also provide access to far-flung coastal and mountain regions.

CAR TRAVEL

Shikoku's narrow roads present challenges, but having your own transportation provides a priceless escape into the island's mountainous interior and secluded small towns. The easiest rental-car service is **ToCoo** トクー, with branch connections in all of Shikoku's airports and cities. Make reservations through the English Web site. (You must have an

On the Menu

Every corner of Shikoku has a special dish, cuisine, or crop. Ehime is famous for *mikan*—clementines—and between November and March you can't walk a country mile without a farmer handing you a bag. Ehime is also the nation's main cultivator of *tai*, or red snapper; *tai-meshi* is rice that's cooked with chunks of the fish, usually in a flaming tin pot. Kagawa-ken's *sanuki-udon* is widely thought to be the nation's best, and Tokushima-ken's delicious *Iya-soba*, made from the valley's hearty strand of buckwheat flour, is even

tastier if you've pounded the dough yourself at a *soba dojo*. Sand-grown at Naruto are the best *satsumaimo*, purple Japanese sweet potatoes, and *imo-taki* are popular across the island in autumn, during potato-baking parties for watching the full moon. The most renowned cuisine styles are in Kochi: *tosa-ryori* and *sawachi-ryori*, different ways of serving enormous amounts of delicious fish, particularly slices of lightly seared *katsuo* (skipjack tuna).

international driving permit). Tourist information centers have good maps illustrating Shikoku's major roads and highways, and getting around is pretty straightforward.

■TIP➔ **Get off the highways!** Don't miss out on seeing some of the "Real Japan" you came here for. Fishing towns and rice-farming villages are all over the island, and although expressway travel will save you a little time, you'll never see what life is like outside Shikoku's cities when you stick to them. Try the rewarding, easily navigable numbered prefectural routes (you'll also save on the exorbitant tolls). Get directions at the information centers and enjoy the countryside.

Contact **ToCoo** (⊕ *www2.tocoo.jp*).

TRAIN TRAVEL

Shikoku is belted around by a single rail track with branches going off to the interior. Since it is just the single track in most places, expect irregular schedules and long waits for local trains as express ones hurtle by. The JR Pass is good on all normal and express trains. Some train lines on Shikoku (mostly in rural Kochi) are not owned by JR, so you will have to pay a small extra fee to use your JR Pass on these lines. A ¥15,700 Shikoku Free Kippu is good for three days of unlimited train use. Shikoku is the rare place in Japan where a rail pass may not save you money; plan your trip carefully to determine if it's worth it.

Contact **JR Pass** (⊕ *www.japanrailpass.net*).

ABOUT THE RESTAURANTS

Three of Shikoku's four main cities—Takamatsu, Kochi, and Matsuyama—specialize in a variety of cuisines at very reasonable prices. In smaller towns expect places to close at 8 pm.

ABOUT THE HOTELS

Accommodations on Shikoku range from *ryokan* and *minshuku* (guest houses) in old homes to international hotels and lavish *onsen (thermal spa)* resorts. Unless otherwise noted, all hotel rooms have private baths, phones, and air-conditioning. Large city and resort hotels serve Western and Japanese food. Reservations are essential during major festivals and Japanese holiday periods.

⇨ *For a short course on accommodations in Japan, see Lodging in Travel Smart.*

WHAT IT COSTS IN YEN					
	¢	$	$$	$$$	$$$$
RESTAURANTS	under ¥800	¥800–¥1,000	¥1,000–¥2,000	¥2,000–¥3,000	over ¥3,000
HOTELS	under ¥8,000	¥8,000–¥12,000	¥12,000–¥18,000	¥18,000–¥22,000	over ¥22,000

Restaurant prices are per person for a main course, set meal, or equivalent combinations of smaller dishes. Hotel prices are for a double room with private bath, excluding service and tax.

VISITOR INFORMATION

Tourist information centers in Shikoku's main cities might have the only skilled English speakers you meet on the island. Use them for advice, transportation info, reservations, recommendations, maps, and local news. Foreign tourists are still relatively rare on Shikoku, so be specific about what you're interested in, and ask a lot of questions. Information centers are listed throughout the chapter.

Japan Travel Phone is a nationwide **English-language hotline** providing travel information and assistance. Call from yellow, blue, or green public phones (not red phones); insert a ¥10 coin, which will be returned.

Contact Japan Travel Phone English-language hotline (☎ *0120/444–800 or 0088/224–800* ⊘ *Daily 9–5*).

10

TAKAMATSU AND EASTERN SHIKOKU

TAKAMATSU 高松

71 km (44 mi) south of Okayama.

If you're coming to Shikoku by train or ferry from Honshu, your first stop will likely be Takamatsu, the capital of Kagawa Prefecture. Takamatsu combines urban verve with a relaxed down-home atmosphere. There is something Parisian in the air here: the locals' unwavering devotion to taking things slow, the city's wide sunlit boulevards, funky shops and cafés, and the prefectural government's dedication to funding the arts make Takamatsu the perfect place to slow down, look around, and adjust to Shikoku time.

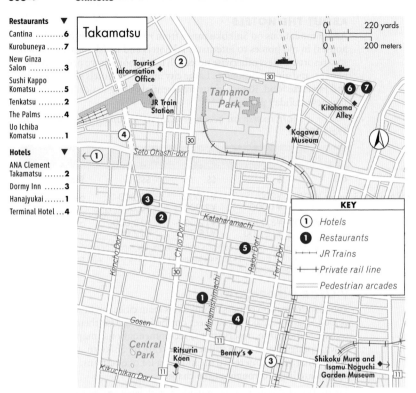

Takamatsu

KEY
① Hotels
❶ Restaurants
⊢⊢⊢ JR Trains
+——+ Private rail line
═══ Pedestrian arcades

GETTING HERE AND AROUND

It takes one hour to get here from Okayama by JR. Buses from Tokyo are 10 hours; Nagoya 7 hours; Osaka 4 hours; Kyoto or Shin-Kobe 3 hours, 30 minutes; Sannomiya 2 hours, 25 minutes; Matsuyama 2 hours, 30 minutes; Kochi 2 hours; and Tokushima 1 hour, 30 minutes. Ferries from Osaka and Kobe arrive in 2 hours, 20 minutes.

You're most likely to set off exploring from Takamatsu's northern tip, where the JR Station, bus platforms, and ferry port bracket a wide piazza around the Clement Hotel. At the northwest corner of the grassy, highly missable **Tamamo Castle park**, continue straight along the park's edge towards the **Kagawa Museum** and **Kitahama Alley**, or turn left down broad Chuo-dori to hit the city. Ten minutes on foot will bring you to the covered Hyogo-machi shopping arcade and within easy striking distance of the city's other sights. The city's biggest draw, the 120-acre **Ritsurin Garden**, is a 20 minute walk farther south.

The east-lying districts Yashima and Mure are home to two more captivating attractions: the historical preserve **Shikoku Mura** and the **Isamu Noguchi Garden Museum**, a superb sculpture park in a studio of the late master. Just outside of the main city, both sites are easy to access by car or local train.

VISITOR INFORMATION

A squat **Information Office** in front of the JR Station is the place for maps, timetables, and travel advice. Some staff speak English quite well, so use them to help plan your next move. If you need more multilingual help or local events info, try **IPAL**, a cultural exchange office in the central Chuo-koen. Ask for their city map, better than the standard one, the latest *Kagawa Journal* events newsletter, and a **Kagawa Welcome Card**, great for discounts on sights. You can print the card off their Web site, too.

Contacts Information Office (☎ 087/851–2009). **IPAL** (☎ 087/837–5908 ⊕ www.i-pal.or.jp ⊗ Tues.–Sun. 9–6). **Kagawa Welcome Card** (⊕ www.21kagawa.com/visitor/kanko/index.htm).

CHEAP BICYCLES

Why let walking from sight to sight eat up your whole day? Take advantage of the cheap bicycle rental available from an underground garage near the JR Station. For ¥100 per day, the whole city will open up to you. Explore some out-of-the way spots, like the two skinny piers and cute lighthouses off the sun port north of the station, perfect for watching the sunset. To make things even more convenient, bikes can be returned to several locations around Takamatsu.

WHAT TO SEE

Fodor's Choice ★ **Isamu Noguchi Garden Museum** イサムノグチ庭園博物館. A wonderland of sculpture both playful and profound, the installations and extensive outdoor facility embrace you with the nuances of Noguchi's creativity. The sensitivity and expressiveness of the Japanese-American sculptor are so potent here in his former studio and home that you'll feel as if he's giving the tour himself. The site holds hundreds of his works in stone and other media, although the emphasis tends away from the paper sculpture with which Noguchi is most often associated abroad. Officially visitation requires at least two weeks' advance reservation by mail or fax, but the rules are not as strict as they sound. Phoning ahead will usually get you admitted, but if you do make arrangements in advance, you may be able to meet with an English-speaking curator. The museum is a 10-minute taxi ride from JR Yashima Station, or go two stops farther on the Kotoden Shido Line to Kotoden Yakuri Station before hopping a cab or walking for 20 minutes. Note that the museum closes August 13 to 16 and December 29 to January 5 annually. ⊠ 3519 Mure, Mure-cho ☎ 087/870–1500 ☎ 087/845–0505 ⊕ www.isamunoguchi.or.jp ☎ ¥2,100 ⊗ Tues., Thurs., and Sat. at 10, 1, and 3 by appointment.

Kagawa Museum 香川県立ミュージアム. Just south of the decaying castle park, this museum emphasizes interactive learning with hands-on exhibits—everything from sword making to wood-block-printing to producing (and playing with) Japanese toys—and an engaging permanent collection. You won't need a lick of Japanese to enjoy walking in a Neolithic hut, crawling with a magnifying glass on the giant photo map of Kagawa, or dressing up in full samurai armor and lush ceremonial kimonos. The museum staff will help you don the costumes and even take a Polaroid for you, and it's all included in the entry fee. ⊠ 5–5 Tamamo-cho ☎ 087/822–0002 ⊕ www.pref.kagawa.jp/kmuseum ☎ ¥400 ⊗ Tues.–Thurs. and weekends 9–4:30, Fri. 9–7.

Ritsurin-koen 栗林公園. If you have time for only one thing in Takamatsu, make it a visit here. Built by a feudal lord in the 17th century, this garden became public property after the 19th-century Meiji Restoration and is now a registered National Treasure. Ritsurin contains close to a thousand sculpted pine trees, six carp-filled lakes, and two wooden teahouses where samurai used to gather to perform the tea ceremony and compose haiku. Give yourself about two hours to stroll through the garden, and don't miss Kikugetsu-tei teahouse, which serves green tea and snacks daily 9 to 4:30. The garden is especially peaceful in the early morning or late afternoon. English maps are available at the entrance. It's a 10-minute taxi ride from Takamatsu Station, a 3-minute walk from JR Ritsurin Kita-guchi Station, or a 10-minute walk from Koto-den Ritsurin Koen Station. ⊠ *1–20–16 Ritsurin-cho* ☎ *087/833–7411* ⊕ *www.pref.kagawa.jp/ritsurin* ✉ *¥400* ☉ *Daily sunrise–sunset.*

★ **Shikoku Mura** 四国村. Located in the Yashima district just east of central Takamatsu, this open-air museum consists of traditional buildings that have been relocated from around Shikoku. The park does a fabulous job of illustrating how life on Shikoku has changed throughout the centuries. Enter the park by crossing a very rickety vine bridge or play it safe and use the sidewalk detour. The route through the park is clearly marked, and English information boards are thoughtful and thorough. Highlights of the park include a village Kabuki theater relocated from Shodo-shima island, thatched-roof farmhouses brought from mountain villages, fishermen' huts, sugarcane-pressing sheds, and lighthouse keeper's residences.

On a hill above the sugarcane-pressing shed is **Shikoku Mura Gallery** 四国村ギャラリー, a Tadao Ando–designed concrete-and-glass art gallery that looks like it was relocated to the park from central Tokyo. Inside the gallery are works by Renoir, Picasso, and Leonard Foujita, but the highlight of the gallery is the outdoor water garden.

Access is by Kotoden or JR trains: take the Kotoden Shido Line 20 minutes to Kotoden-Yashima Station and walk 5 minutes to the park, or take the JR Kotoku Line 15 minutes to Yashima 屋島 Station and walk 10 minutes to the park. Going by car, take Route 11 toward Tokushima and turn left at the first McDonalds on the right. ⊠ *91 Yashima-Naka-machi* ☎ *087/843–3111* ⊕ *www.shikokumura.or.jp* ✉ *¥800* ☉ *Apr.– Oct., daily 8:30–6; Nov.–Mar., daily 8:30–5:30.*

NEED A BREAK?

Waraya わら家. Locals take fierce pride in Kagawa's local culinary specialty *sanuki-udon*, and people travel distances beguiling good sense to partake at this restored riverside house at the base of Shikoku Mura. Stop here for lunch (¢–$) and enjoy the rustic waterwheel. Remember: people say the noodles taste better if you slurp them loudly and although quiet eating isn't rude *per se*, why would you forgo the extra flavor? If you're with a party of three or more, don't pass up the family-size noodle barrel for the most fun for your buck. ⊠ *91 Yashima-Naka-machi* ☉ *Weekdays 10–6:30, weekends 10–9.*

Continued on page 614

THE HENRO: SHIKOKU'S 88-TEMPLE PILGRIMAGE

By Annamarie
Ruelle Sasagawa

On the mountainous island of Shikoku, 88 sacred temples have welcomed Buddhist pilgrims for over 1,000 years. Leave your everyday world behind, and walk in the footsteps of tradition on Shikoku's ancient pilgrimage trail.

10

Shikoku's 88-Temple Pilgrimage is an 870-mile Buddhist pilgrimage route encircling the island of Shikoku. The pilgrimage dates from the 9th century and is the longest of Japan's ancient pilgrimage trails.

Unlike Europe's Camino de Santiago de Campostela pilgrimage, in which pilgrims travel toward a sacred destination, all 88 temples on the Shikoku circuit are considered equally sacred; thus, there is no start- or end-point. A pilgrim completes the journey by traveling full-circle.

Although eight of the 88 temples belong to other sects of Buddhism, the Shikoku pilgrimage is a Shingon Buddhist tradition. It's unique among Japan's Buddhist pilgrimage routes in its devotion to Kobo Daishi, the founder of Shingon Buddhism. Each temple on the route, no matter which Buddhist deity it enshrines, also houses a small building dedicated to the spirit of this ancient monk.

(top left) Chikurin-ji, (top right) Byodo-ji, (bottom right) Kumatani-ji

KOCHI ONE DAY LOOP: TEMPLES 31-33

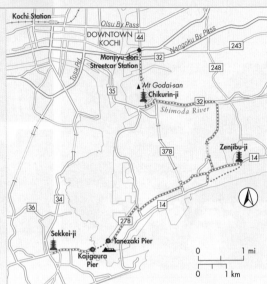

Most tourists—even those with plenty of time to spare—won't be able to travel the entire circuit. But if you have been drawn to Shikoku, you will certainly want to get a taste of the pilgrimage experience even if you don't have two full months to hike the whole route. You won't be alone; many westerners want to partake and can be seen hiking along with the other foot pilgrims (who are in short supply these days since most go on group bus tours). You don't need to don full pilgrim garb to get a taste of this experience, but you may want to buy a *Shuin-cho* (calligraphy book) to gather stamps from the various temples if you haven't already purchased one (these are available at all the larger temples). Kochi is a particularly good place to visit a few temples since there are three within reasonable walking distance. Try this one-day, 15-mile walk that takes you to the three pilgrimage temples within Kochi's city limits: **Chikurin-ji, Zenjibi-ji,** and **Sekkei-ji.** Allow a full day (approximately 9 hours) to complete this loop. You'll find some small shops and vending machines along the way where you can get snacks and drinks, but be sure to pack a lunch.

From Kochi Station, take the streetcar to Monjiyu-dori station, changing at Hari-maya Bashi. (20 minutes, ¥190). Walk south from the station and cross the canal. The big hill in front of you is Mt. Godai-san.

Chikurin-ji

Chikurin-ji

Zenjibu-ji

Sekkei-ji

Turn left after the bridge, and keep an eye out for small white signs with red arrows and a stenciled silhouette of a pilgrim. Follow these signs past a shrine and up Mt. Gogai-san to **Chikurin-ji** (#31).

After visiting Chikurin-ji, follow the trail south down Mt. Godai-san. It's a steep descent. When you get to the bottom, cross the Shimoda River and turn left. Again,

look for signs that mark the pilgrim trail. After about an hour on this trail, go through the tunnel on your left. After the tunnel, you'll see a pond and **Zenjibu-ji** (#32), atop a small hill. Zenjibu-ji was also founded in 724 AD (on some road signs it's also called Mine-ji).

Walk southwest from Zenjibu-ji along the coast for about 90 minutes. When you reach the end of the pen-

insula, take the free small ferry across. **Sekkei-ji** (#33), is about 1 mi west of the ferry stop on the other side. It's a Rinzai Zen temple that was founded in AD 815.

Nagahama Shucho-jo bus stop is a 3-minute walk from Sekkei-ji. Buses run from here back to Kochi station (25 minutes, ¥440).

WHO WAS KOBO DAISHI?

10

Kukai, or Kobo Daishi—as he is more widely known by the honorific title bestowed after his death—was a Buddhist priest, founder of Shingon Buddhism, an esoteric form of Buddhism that focuses on rituals instead of abstract meditation. He was a scholar, calligrapher, pilgrim, and all-round adventurer.

Born to an aristocratic family in Kagawa prefecture on Shikoku in AD 774, he went to Nara in 791 to study Confucian classics, where he became interested in Buddhism. In 804, he used his family connections to join an expedition to China, where he studied esoteric Buddhism in Xi'an for two years with the Chinese master Hui-kuo.

After returning to Japan, he became the head priest of Nara's Todai-ji temple in 810. In 819, he founded the monastery town of Koya-san high in the mountains of Wakayama prefecture. For the next 16 years, Kobo Daishi traveled between Koya-san, the courts and universities of Kyoto, and pilgrimage sites around Japan. In 835, he died—or according to Shingon Buddhist tradition did not die but rather left this world to enter eternal meditation in a cave in Koya-san, where he's still believed to be.

Kobo Daishi felt a lifelong tension between academic learning and the lessons of travel that resonates with many Japanese today.

Statue of Kobo Daishi

HISTORY OF THE PILGRIMAGE

THE PILGRIMAGE BEGINS

The cost and difficulty of travel kept the numbers of pilgrims low until the Tokugawa era (1603–1868). Shogun **Ieyasu Tokugawa**'s rise to power in 1603 brought political stability to Japan after a century of civil war. Increased prosperity among peasants and better roads made travel possible for many who could never travel before.

Keen to prevent rural rebellion, however, the shogun quickly forbade commoners from traveling freely. The only way for a peasant to travel legally was by obtaining permission to make a pilgrimage. Shikoku was a popular destination for these "passport pilgrims." The pilgrims surged in numbers, quickly turning Shikoku's sleepy temple towns into rather lively places, and so they have remained.

A LULL IN FOOT TRAFFIC

The fun stopped when Japan entered the Meiji era (1868–1912). In the face of growing European influence in Asia, Japan's new imperial government scrambled to transform the nation into a modern power. As part of this modernization effort, Japan's ruling elite promoted a return to "pure" Japanese values, favoring Shinto, Japan's indigenous religion, over Buddhism, an import from mainland Asia.

During this period of anti-Buddhist sentiment, pilgrim numbers dropped, and six of the pilgrimage's 88 temples were destroyed, damaged, or relocated. World War II left Japan's citizens with little extra money to donate to the temples or pilgrims.

THE MODERN PILGRIMAGE

As Japan's economic recovery took hold, pilgrims once again began to arrive on Shikoku. Rising incomes and the time pressures of urban life soon created a market among would-be pilgrims for faster ways to complete the circuit. The first pilgrimage bus tours began in the 1950s, and the majority of pilgrims have traveled by car or bus ever since.

(top left) Yakuo-ji, (top middle) Ieyasu Tokugawa, (top right) Gokuraku-ji, (top bottom) Nagao-ji

WALKING THE PILGRIMAGE

It takes about two months to walk the entire 870-mile pilgrimage circuit. All 88 temples now have road access, so it's possible to do the pilgrimage by car or motorcycle in just under two weeks. By bicycle, the circuit takes about a month.

WHEN TO GO: Spring (mid-March to mid-April), brings cherry blossoms and mild weather to Shikoku and is the most popular pilgrimage season. Autumn (early October to mid-November) is also a good time to go. The rainy season (June) is best avoided; winter can be quite cold, summer hot and humid.

WHERE TO START: Although the temples are numbered, you don't have to start at #1. Start wherever is convenient and complete the circle, ideally in a clockwise fashion. However, a superstition among pilgrims says that if you travel counterclockwise (*gyaku-uchi*) you're more likely to encounter Kobo Daishi en route.

WHERE TO STAY: About a third of the 88 temples provide accommodation and meals to pilgrims for about ¥6,000 per person, but space at temple lodgings (*shukubo*) fills up fast with bus tour groups. Some temples also provide free basic accommodation in wooden sheds called *tsuyado*, which are not much more than a roof over your head. You must bring your own blankets and food. In villages near smaller temples, you'll find many *minshuku* at about the same cost as temple lodging. English isn't widely spoken on Shikoku, so some Japanese skills will make things smoother.

GEAR: To walk the pilgrimage, you'll need sturdy shoes, raingear, a warm jacket, a bilingual map, mobile phone, and enough cash to survive between major cities.

If you want to look like a Japanese pilgrim, you'll need some extra gear. A white pilgrim's overcoat (*oizuru*) indicates to the world that you're on a spiritual journey and are prepared to die en route. Black Chinese characters on a pilgrim's *oizuru* read "two people walking together" and remind lonely pilgrims that Kobo Daishi is walking with them.

You'll also need a conical straw hat, a sutra book, an embroidered stole, a set of Buddhist rosary beads, a bell, a wooden staff, and a Shuin-cho in which to collect seals from each temple (the book is not unlike the Spanish *credencial* used by pilgrims on the Camino de Santiago de Campostela) and is also available in places like Kyoto and Nara. Larger temples on Shikoku sell all these accessories, and they make good souvenirs, though they aren't at all necessary to do the walk.

TOURS: Bus tours are given in Japanese only, but the Japan-based travel company Sasa Trails (⊕ *www.sasatrails.com*) organizes guided one- or two-day tours to some of Shikoku's pilgrimage temples.

Pilgrims walking along a Shikoku beach

WHERE TO EAT

Dozens of great restaurants and stores are scattered along the central Marugame-machi arcade and the side streets lacing it to Raion-dori. The city's late bedtime makes it easy to move from a meal to nightlife spot before finding a second dinner later on.

$$
MEDITERRANEAN
✕ **Cantina.** Housed in an old warehouse facing the waterfront, Cantina serves up Mediterranean food, although some dishes come with a Japanese twist, such as the tuna and cod roe spaghetti. Grab a seat on the outdoor patio and watch the sun go down. Anything you order will be good, but try the seafood paella or prosciutto and mozzarella salad. ⊠ *3–2 Kitahama-cho, Kitahama Alley* ☎ *087/811–7718* ▭ *No credit cards.*

$$
MEXICAN
✕ **Kurobuneya** 黒船屋. In this second-floor Kitahama Alley establishment you'll find good Mexican fare next to Japanese *izakaya* (traditional bar) staples, and a wide range of cocktails, beer, and seasonal sake. The friendly owner will happily take a break from mixing drinks and playing jazz records to give you all the (somewhat quirky) Shikoku travel advice you'll ever need. ⊠ *3–2 Kitahama-cho, Kitahama Alley C* ☎ *087/826–3636* ▭ *No credit cards* ☉ *Closed Mon. No lunch.*

$$
JAPANESE
★
✕ **New Ginza Salon** ギンザサロン. This lovely little bistro compliments a swanky-chic decor with cuisine so unpretentiously good that you'll imagine whatever today's special is has always been your favorite dish. The New Ginza excels at using very standard Japanese kitchen ingredients in dishes that soar above the tired tastes of standard kitchen fare. The antique tables and plush chairs create a perfect setting for their delicious lunch plates, colorful dinner menu, and excellent handmade pastries. Don't worry about the Japanese-only menu—decide on fish, chicken, or meat and order one of the day's three prix-fix sets. ⊠ *2–4–11 Hyogo-machi* ☎ *087/823–7065* ▭ *No credit cards* ☉ *No dinner Sun.*

$$
HAWAIIAN
✕ **The Palms.** On cushy divans under the cheesy beach dioramas, Hawaiian food and imported beer might not transport you to Oahu, but they make for a great start to a Takamatsu night. Strike up conversation with the affable proprietor Kengo and his superfriendly regulars, or strum the in-house ukulele at the bar. ⊠ *2F, 2–9–7 Kawara-machi* ☎ *087/862–3444* ▭ *No credit cards* ☉ *Closed Wed.*

$$$$
★
JAPANESE
✕ **Sushi Kappo Komatsu** 寿司割烹小松. This intimate restaurant in the Raion-dori arcade specializes in sushi from the Seto Inland Sea and traditional kaiseki-style (full meal) cuisine. Ingredients are top quality and service is attentive. There's no English menu, and the staff speak very little English, so bring your phrasebook or just order the ¥3,700 omakase (chef's choice) sushi set. Sit at the long counter if you're in the mood to meet locals, or ask for a private booth. It's hard to spot as there's no English sign, so ask for directions. ⊠ *1F Lady Bldg., 10–16 Gobo-machi* ☎ *087/816–3812* ☉ *Closed Sun. No lunch.*

$$$
JAPANESE
✕ **Tenkatsu** 天勝. Find your favorite fish in the pool at Tenkatsu and it will be on your plate a few minutes later. Forgo the tatami tables to sit close to the action at the big black countertop. This interior design doesn't overwhelm, but the food makes up for it. Plastic displays and a picture menu help you choose the dish (choosing the fish is rather more

KITAHAMA ALLEY

The former warehouse town of Kitahama Alley escaped the wrecking ball and now houses an enclave of funky shops, craft workspaces, restaurants, cafés, and a large gallery space. This grass-roots venture is the work of a young cohort of entrepreneurs. English-speakers are easy to find. What's more challenging is finding the place itself: the salt-blasted wooden and metal buildings look so derelict you might pass by without realizing it. Kitahama Alley is a 10-minute walk from Takamatsu Station. Follow the coastline east past Tamamo Koen until a canal cuts back toward the city and you'll see the warehouses on your right. Poke into stores like **Depot** (which sells funky home and kitchen items) and **Peekabooya** (with baby clothes on offer more fashionable than anything in your own wardrobe). For eating, try second-floor **Juke Joint Kurobuneya** with good Mexican fare next to Japanese izakaya staples, and a Japanese take on Mediterranean food at Cantina next door.

intuitive). *Nabe* hot pots in autumn and winter are house favorites. ✉ *7–5 Hyogo-machi* ☎ *087/821–5380.*

$$$$
JAPANESE
✗ **Uo Ichiba Komatsu** 魚市場小松. The simmering energy of a cantina thrives in this upscale three-floor restaurant. Flags and banners hang above tanks full of eels and fish waiting to be selected for your plate, and the chefs do a dazzling job preparing the freshest, most sumptuous seafood. Other Japanese fare is also top-notch. Dinner is lively, but the set menus at lunch are considerably cheaper. It's located just across from Kawaroku Hotel, off Marugame-machi arcade. ✉ *9–5 Hyakken-machi* ☎ *087/826–2056* ☾ *Closed Sun. No lunch.*

WHERE TO STAY

Hotel reviews have been condensed for this book. Please go to Fodors. com for full reviews of each property.

$$$$
HOTEL
🏨 **ANA Hotel Clement Takamatsu** 全日空ホテルクレメント高松. This branch of the upscale ANA hotel chain is Takamatsu's premier Western-style hotel. **Pros:** convenient location; spacious rooms. **Cons:** only fourth-floor rooms are nonsmoking; overpriced breakfast. ✉ *1–1 Hamamo-cho* ☎ *087/811–1111* 🖨 *087/800–2222* ⊕ *www.anahotels.com/eng/index. html* ⤙ *300 rooms* ♿ *In-room: a/c, refrigerator, Internet. In-hotel: restaurant, laundry service, parking (paid)* ♒ *No meals.*

$$
HOTEL
★
🏨 **Dormy Inn** ドーミーイン. This branch of the national chain feels almost too good to be true. **Pros:** great value; great location; opened in 2008. **Cons:** no in-room cots for a third body; garish in-room robes. ✉ *1–10–10 Kawara-machi* ☎ *087/832–5489* ⊕ *www.hotespa.net/business/en* ⤙ *48 rooms* ♿ *In-room: a/c, refrigerator, DVD, Internet. In-hotel: restaurant, laundry facilities* ♒ *No meals.*

$$$$
RYOKAN
★
🏨 **Hanajyukai** 花樹海. This is our top choice in Takamatsu for a luxury ryokan experience, and best of all it overlooks both the city and sea from a flower-covered mountainside. **Pros:** friendly staff; new tatami in all rooms in 2008; opting out of breakfast and dinner can cut down the cost. **Cons:** away from downtown; harsh Western rooms face the cliff side; little-to-no English help. ✉ *3–5–10 Nishitakara-cho* ☎ *087/861–5580*

10

🖨 *087/834–9912* ⊕ *www.hanajyukai.jp* ⇌ *40 Japanese-style rooms, 5 Western-style rooms* ⚮ *In-room: a/c, refrigerator. In-hotel: restaurant, bar, laundry facilities* ❗❗*Some meals.*

$ ⌤ **Terminal Hotel.** A stylish full renovation in the summer of 2008 has
HOTEL   bumped the Terminal Hotel up the ranks of Takamatsu's most fashionable places to stay. **Pros:** close to the station; air purifiers in rooms. **Cons:** cramped lobby; English Web site is difficult to navigate. ✉ *10–17 Nishinomarucho* 🖨 *087/822–3731* ⊕ *www.webterminal.co.jp* ⇌ *48 rooms* ⚮ *In-room: a/c, Internet. In-hotel: Internet terminal* ❗❗*No meals.*

NIGHTLIFE

Benny's ベニーズ. For a change of pace and music, head to Benny's. Sofas encourage mingling with the friendly clientele, and if there's no local band play, you can always pick up an instrument and jam down. Benny will accompany you on blues harmonica if you ask him. All drinks are ¥500. It's located in the Kawara-machi Building. ✉ *6F Kawara-machi Bldg., 1–9–9 Kawara-machi-dori* 🖨 *090/2891–6481* ⏰ *Closed Sun.*

NAOSHIMA 直島

20 km (12 mi) northeast of Takamatsu.

In past centuries, pirate attacks were the biggest surprise travelers encountered on the Seto Inland Sea. Now, it's the art museums of Naoshima. This tiny island in the inland sea between Takamatsu and Okayama boasts three world-class contemporary art museums as well as an installation art project. If you're a fan of or are just curious about contemporary art, don't miss this unexpected highlight.

GETTING HERE AND AROUND

Access Naoshima by ferry from Takamatsu or Okayama. Ferries from Takamatsu to Naoshima's Miyanoura Port take 25 minutes on the fast boat (foot passengers only) or one hour on the regular car ferry. From Okayama, ferries depart from Uno Port (access is by bus or train from Okayama Station) and take 15 to 20 minutes to reach Miyanoura.

Getting around Naoshima is best done by bicycle, on the town bus, or in the island's one taxi. The town bus costs ¥100 per ride and goes to all major sights. Bicycles are available for ¥500 a day. In Miyanoura, you can rent them from Café Ougiya or Café Little Plum (call ahead to reserve a bike at Little Plum; it's first-come, first-served at Ougiya); in Honmura, bikes can be rented at Cafe Restaurant Garden (*see* ⇨ *Where to Eat, below*). There aren't many bikes available on the island, so consider renting one in Takamatsu and bringing it across on the car ferry (there's a charge of ¥300 each way to bring a bike on the ferry). Be warned: the route from Miyanoura to Chichu Art Museum and Benesse House is a steep climb!

Outside of the two villages, Miyanoura and Honmura, which can be covered on foot in about five minutes, the only other major sites on Naoshima are its art museums. Although there are postal addresses, most business do not have physical addresses; if you need directions here, it's faster to ask using the name of the establishment.

The majority of the Chichu Art Museum is underground.

Contacts Café Little Plum (☎ *087/892–3751*). **Café Ougiya** (☎ *087/892–3642*). **Naoshima Taxi** (☎ *087/892–3036*).

VISITOR INFORMATION

Naoshima's **Information Center** is at Miyanoura Port

Contact Naoshima Visitor Information Center (☎ *087/892–2299* ⊕ *www.naoshima.net* ⊗ *Daily 8:30–6*).

WHAT TO SEE

007 Museum 007 記念館. If all the contemporary art on Naoshima has you feeling bit too contemplative, head to this small museum a two-minute walk from Miyanoura Port. There's no deep meaning to the exhibits here: it's James Bond paraphernalia collected by island residents who really *really* want the movie version of *The Man with the Red Tattoo* to be filmed on Naoshima. It's a must-see mishmash of kitsch and hope—provided you're a James Bond fan. ✉ *2310 Miyanoura* ☎ *087/892–2299 Naoshima tourist info* ✉ *Free* ⊗ *Daily 9–5*.

★ **Art House Project** 家プロジェクト. Art House Project artists take empty houses and other structures left behind by islanders who have gone to seek work in the city and turn them into installation art projects. Art, memory, and everyday life blend together as you wander through the seven "houses" (including a temple and shrine) in Honmura while around you villagers go about their daily business. If you have time for only one house, don't miss James Turrell's Minamidera. ✉ *Honmura* ☎ *087/892–3223 for Benesse House* ⊕ *www.benesse-artsite.jp* ✉ *¥1,000 for all 7 sites* ⊗ *Daily 10:30–4*.

10

Benesse House Museum ベネッセハウス ミュージアム. Installation art exhibits are scattered around the road leading to this top-class contemporary art museum. Inside, full-length windows illuminate a rotating collection of installation pieces in natural sunlight. The museum is open later than others on the island, so if you only have one day here, save this museum for the evening. ✉ *3418 Naoshima-cho, Gotanji* ☎ *087/892–3223* ⊕ *www.benesse-artsite.jp* 🎫 *¥1,000* ⏰ *Daily 8 am–9 pm.*

★ **Chichu Art Museum** 地中美術館. Never mind what's inside, the building itself is art. *Chichu* literally means "inside the earth," and this Tadao Ando–designed museum, built into a hillside overlooking Naoshima's south coast, lives up to its name. View works by Monet, Walter de Maria, and James Turrell in natural light. The Monet gallery is breathtaking. Buy tickets at the ticket office 50 meters down the road; during busy times, you'll probably have to wait to enter. ✉ *3449–1 Naoshima* ☎ *087/892–3755* ⊕ *www.benesse-artsite.jp* 🎫 *¥2,000* ⏰ *Mar.–Sept., Tues.–Sun. 10–6; Oct.–Feb., Tues.–Sun. 10–5.*

Lee Ufan Museum 李禹煥美術館. Between Benesse House and the Chichu Art Musuem is this museum devoted to Korean artist Lee Ufan. Yet another Tadao Ando creation, it opened in June 2010 and aims to encourage a "slightly out-of-the-ordinary encounter with art, architecture, and nature." Decide for yourself how ordinary the experience is, but it's not one to pass up. Wear comfortable shoes; you'll be standing a lot. ✉ *1390 Azakura-ura* ☎ *087/840–8285* ⊕ *www.benesse-artsite.jp* 🎫 *¥1,000* ⏰ *Mar.–Sept., Tues.–Sun. 10–6; Oct.–Feb., Tues.–Sun. 10–5.*

★ **Naoshima Bath I ♥ Yu** 直島銭湯 I ♥湯. Two minutes on foot from Miyanoura Port is Japan's funkiest functioning public bath (*yu* means hot water). Created in 2009 by artist Shinro Otake, the bathhouse contains, among other things, an aircraft cockpit, the bottom of a ship, and an elephant statue sourced from a museum of erotica. What's not to love? Take the plunge; you won't have another chance to bathe with art. Towels, shampoo, and soap are for sale inside. ✉ *2252–2 Miyanoura* ☎ *087/892–2626* ⊕ *www.benesse-artsite.jp/en/naoshimasento* 🎫 *¥500* ⏰ *Weekdays 2–9, weekends 10–9.*

WHERE TO EAT AND STAY

While it's possible to see the major sights on Naoshima in one (very long) day, staying overnight on the island lets you take things at a more leisurely pace. After the day-trippers leave on the late afternoon ferry, the island feels like a different place altogether. So if you have the time, staying overnight is well worth it. Accommodation on Naoshima ranges from basic guesthouses to luxury rooms at Benesse House. Rooms book out quickly on weekends and during summer holidays, so if you plan to come here then, book as far in advance as possible. Naoshima cafés keep relaxed island hours; they're usually open from 10 or 11 am to sundown.

Hotel reviews have been condensed for this book. Please go to Fodors. com for full reviews of each property.

$ ✕ **Cafe Restaurant Garden** ガーデン. Stop at this Honmura café in an old
CAFÉ farmhouse for unexpectedly delicious pizza, fresh orange juice, and

Naoshima apple cake. If your knees aren't up for sitting on the tatami, ask for the room with plush couches and lounge chairs. The café also rents bicycles so you can explore the island. ⊠ *Honmura, next to the ocean* ☎ *087/892–3301* ▤ *No credit cards* ⊗ *Closed Mon.*

$

CAFÉ

✕**Shioya**ダイナー. This 1950s-style café next to the bathhouse in Miyanoura serves up hot dogs, BLT sandwiches, and whatever else the friendly owners feel like making that day. It's also the perfect spot for a post-bath beer. ⊠ *Next to Naoshima bath, Miyanoura* ☎ *087/892–3290* ▤ *No credit cards* ⊗ *Closed Mon.*

$$$$

HOTEL

⊞ **Hotel Benesse House** ベネッセハウス. Naoshima Bath House is your chance to bathe with art; here, you can sleep with it. **Pros:** 24-hour access to the art museum; views of the inland sea. **Cons:** staff hard to find; food bland. ⊠ *3418 Naoshima-cho, Gotanji* ☎ *087/892–3223* ⊕ *www.benesse-artsite.jp* ▱ *65 rooms* ⚓ *In-room: a/c, no TV. In-hotel: restaurants, Internet terminal* ⍾ *No meals.*

$$$

RYOKAN

⊞ **Oomiyake Ryokan** おおみやけ旅館. Miyake-san, the owner of this small ryokan in Honmura, spent decades in France and Morocco before returning to Naoshima to turn his 17th-century family home into a ryokan. **Pros:** traditional building; friendly owners; café next door. **Cons:** sliding screen walls mean little privacy; no private baths except in the annex guesthouse; no meals served in the ryokan. ⊠ *Honmura* ☎ *087/892–2328* ⊕ *www.oomiyake.jp* ▱ *4 Japanese-style rooms* ⚓ *In-room: no a/c, no TV* ▤ *No credit cards* ⍾ *No meals.*

KOTOHIRA 琴平

45 km (28 mi) south of Takamatsu.

Konpira-san shrine is the draw here: this mountaintop Shinto shrine draws pilgrims from all over Japan. Other than the shrine, there's not much else in town. The place is eerily quiet after sundown, and you'll want to stay elsewhere.

GETTING HERE AND AROUND

Kotohira is one hour from Takamatsu by JR or Kotoden train. JR lines run south 40 minutes to Awa Ikeda for easy access to Iya or Kochi; otherwise, a change at Tadotsu gives access to Matsuyama. There are two stations in town, JR and Kotoden. Ditch your bags in coin lockers at either train station (if they won't fit, gift shops at the shrine will watch them for you), and pick up a map at the local information center located smack between the two stations before heading to the mountain.

10

VISITOR INFORMATION

Kotohira Information Center (☎ *087/775–3500* ⊗ *Daily 10–7*).

WHAT TO SEE

Konpira Shrine 金刀比羅宮. According to legend, this shrine, which is also known as Kotohira-gu (琴平宮), was founded in the 1st century. It's stood on top of Mt. Zozu ever since, protecting sailors and seafarers. Visiting requires a bit of effort; you'll have to climb 785 steps to the impressive main shrine and 583 more to the final lookout. It's also possible to go by taxi to the upper gate, or even hire two sturdy locals to carry you up in a straw basket (availability varies; look for them at the base of the mountain). The first half of the climb is crowded with souvenir shops and tourists, but once you climb past the shops it gets a lot more peaceful. You're able to glimpse the ocean as you climb, and the noise of the town fades away to rustling trees and birdsong. The **Treasure House**, on your right after you pass through the stone gate, houses masks used in Noh and Kabuki theater. The **Shoin** is an Edo-period hall with artifacts and screens painted by Okyo Maruyama. ✉ *892–1 Kotohira* ☎ *0877/75–2121* 🖥 *Shrine free, ¥500 for Treasure House, ¥400 for Shoin* ☉ *Treasure House and Shoin usually daily 8:30– 5; hrs change with exhibitions. Shrine open all hrs.*

NEED A BREAK?

Kinryo Sake Museum and Brewery 金陵の郷. After the long climb up and down from Konpira Shrine, you may want some refreshment, or at least a diversion. When you reach the bottom, congratulate yourself with a stop at this sake museum and brewery marked by an enormous sake bottle fountaining into the street in front of the temple stairs. You can't really miss it. Entry is ¥310. Sample the wares for ¥100 a shot. ✉ *623 Kotohira* ☎ *0877/73–4133* 🖥 *¥310* ☉ *Mon., Tues., Thurs., and Fri. 9–4.*

TOKUSHIMA 徳島

70 km (43 mi) southeast of Takamatsu and from Awa Ikeda.

Tokushima literally means "virtuous island"—ironic, considering the local residents' fondness for drinking, dancing, and hard partying. The city's annual **Awa Odori** dance festival is Japan's biggest, but there's fun to be had year-round in the city and surrounding area. Most visitors stay near the city center or in Naruto, a nearby peninsula famous for giant whirlpools that churn and thunder in the rocky straights below the cliffs. Nearby, the ambitious Otsuka Museum attracts huge crowds for its bizarre and breathtaking archive of the world's art. In surrounding hamlets you can try your hand at local crafts like indigo-dyeing or papermaking as they've done it for centuries. Back in the city proper you'll learn to dance the Awa Odori, either in a special performance hall or with the million others dancing the streets every summer during the Awa Odori Festival. Tokushima's major sights can be covered in a well-planned day or two, giving you plenty of time in the mountains and gorges of Iya after moving on.

GETTING HERE AND AROUND

Tokushima is accessible by JR train: 1 hour, 15 minutes from Takamatsu; 1 hour, 30 minutes from Awa Ikeda; 2 hours, 25 minutes from Kochi; 3 hours, 40 minutes from Matsuyama; 3 hours, 20 minutes from Shin-Osaka; 1 hour, 30 minutes from Okayama. Highway and JR buses are also an option. Highway buses depart from Takamatsu (1 hour, 30 minutes); Kochi (2 hours, 40 minutes); Matsuyama (3 hours, 10 minutes); Kobe (2 hours); Kyoto, Osaka, or Kansai Airport (3 hours); or overnight from Tokyo. By JR bus it's 2 hours, 25 minutes from Osaka, Kobe, or Shin-Kobe. There are ferries from Tokyo (19 hours) and Wakayama (2 hours).

Buses leave Tokushima for Naruto on the hour between 9 and 3, taking 63 minutes and costing ¥690; the return has more varied times, so check the schedule. The boat quay at Naruto Kanko-ko is a few stops before the end of the line, about an eight-minute walk from Uzu-no-michi. There are also trains to Naruto Station; catch a bus or taxi from there to the coast. Going by car from Tokushima takes roughly a half hour. ■ **TIP→** Tokushima's best sights are far from the city center and not well serviced by public transportation. Arranging to hire your own car in to access the craft centers and whirlpools makes for a better, easier time.

VISITOR INFORMATION

Before hitting the town, head up by glass elevator to the sixth floor of the Clement Tower Station Building to TOPIA, the best tourist information center in western Japan. The city employs a native English speaker there nearly full time who can provide bus schedules, train times, tide calendars (necessary for seeing the whirlpools at their best), and a good battle plan for tackling it all.

Contact TOPIA (⊠ *Clement Plaza, 6F, 1-61 Terashima Honcho Nishi* ☎ *088/656–3033* ⊕ *www.topia.ne.jp/e_index.htm* ⊗ *Daily 10–6*).

WHAT TO SEE

Awa Odori Kaikan 阿波踊り会館. The Awa Odori Festival happens every summer over Obon, festival of the dead, and if you miss it you can still get a dose at this museum and theater. *Odori* means "dance," and at the Kaikan silk-robed professionals perform the famous local step nightly. But shine your shoes: when the troupe leader starts talking to the audience, he's looking for volunteers. Everyone will be thrilled to see you try, so stand up! They'll give you some fragmented English directions and, thankfully, it's a very easy dance. The first volunteering round is for men, the second for women; each has different steps to learn. You might get a prize for participating, and one special award goes to the biggest fool on the floor—this honor is a staple of the festival, and it's not always the foreigners who win. The best show is at 8 pm. Arrive early and browse the gift shop or treat yourself to a ropeway ride up the mountain for a lovely view of the city. The third floor of the building is a museum dedicated to the Awa Odori Festival. ⊠ *20 Shin-machi-bashi, 2-chome* ☎ *088/611–1611* ⊡ *Museum ¥300, afternoon dance ¥500, evening dance ¥700. Ropeway ¥1,000 round-trip* ⊗ *Gift shop daily 9–9. Museum daily 9–5. Performances at 2, 3, 4, and 8 pm; also at 11 am on weekends. Closed 2nd Wed. in Oct.–Feb., closed 2nd Wed. in Jun.*

Awa Washi Dento 阿波和紙伝統産業会館 (*Hall of Awa Handmade Paper*). Trek out to this paper museum to make your own postcards and browse the phenomenal gift shop; it goes from sheets of softer-than-silk wrapping paper to peerless fans and parasols. It's also something of a pain to get to by train; the trip takes one hour to Awa-Yamakawa Station, then you walk 15 minutes to the hall. ⊠ *136 Kawahigashi* ☎ *0883/42–6120* ⊕ *www.awagami.or.jp* ⊡ *¥300* ⊗ *Tues.–Sun. 9–5.*

○ **The House of Indigo** 藍の館. At Ai-no-Yakata, you can try the ancient craft of dyeing cloth in cauldrons of blue-black, pungent indigo. Someone at the desk will show you a price chart for items—cotton handkerchiefs are only ¥500, silk scarves close to ¥2,000. Towels come out splendidly, but you have to ask for the separate price chart (the word is *ta-o-ru*). It's fun, and you'll be delighted with what you make. Snoop around the 400-year-old craft center when you're finished. One of the proprietors performs daily on the *shaku-hachi*, a thick-bodied wooden flute, and he'll play anytime you ask. From Tokushima Station hop a 20-minute bus to Higashi Nakatomi. Walk down the hill behind you and follow the indigo signs. ⊠ *Aizumi-cho, Tokumei Aza Maesunishi* ☎ *088/692–6317* 🖾 *¥300* ⊗ *Daily 9–5.*

Naruto Whirlpools 鳴門の渦潮. The thunderous roar of giant whirlpools fills the cliffs around the Naruto Kaikyo (the Naruto Straits), splitting the peaceful sky and green mountainsides asunder with a chaos of furious, frothing sea. See the whirlpools from a glass-bottomed gantry 45 meters above the water or, better still, from the deck of a tour boat down in the belly of the beast. The walkway, called **uzu-no-michi,** which is under the Onaruto Bridge, gives a great view of the pools and the seacoast, but you'll wish you had chosen the boats. There are a few companies with different-size vessels and marginally different prices (¥1,500–¥2,500). All the rides are exhilarating. Two of the best boat tours are Wonder Naruto and Aqua Eddy, both run by the Naruto Kanko Kisen company (*see* ⇨ *Tours, below*).Which tour you select will depend on what time you arrive and what time the pools reach their active peak on that day. The whirlpools are formed when the pull of changing tides forces a huge volume of seawater through the narrow, rocky bottleneck. The tide calendar will let you know what time to see the pools at their best on any given day; the straits will froth furiously for a good hour on each end of the peak. ⊠ *Naruto Koen* ☎ *088/683–6262* 🖾 *Park free, uzu-no-michi ¥500* ⊗ *Park always open. Uzu-no-michi Mar.–Sept., daily 9–6; Oct.–Feb., daily 9–5. Closed 2nd Mon. in Mar., June, Sept., and Dec.*

★ **Otsuka Museum of Art** 大塚美術館. From uzu-no-michi a boardwalk rings the high coastline; walk south for 10 minutes and you'll come to this surreal and ambitious exhibition space that has a collection of Western art from all over the world . . . sort of. More than a thousand great works of art have been precisely reproduced on ceramic tiles and arranged throughout the enormous facility by era and location. More than a Greatest Hits of Art, you'll find well-known and obscure works on display. Surround yourself with a room full of Rubens altars, stand alone in the Sistine Chapel or before Picasso's *Guernica,* wander through replicated French churches, Greek tombs, a banquet hall from Pompeii, and countless other sights you'd thought were one-of-a-kind. Indeed, these pieces are unique, and seeing them can be confounding, as you feel moved by the power of a thousand stunning pictures of pictures. It is a unique and enlightening experience. ⊠ *65–1 Aza Tosadomari-ura Fukuike, Naruto-cho* ☎ *088/687–3737* ⊕ *www.o-museum.or.jp* 🖾 *¥3,150* ⊗ *Tues.–Sun. 9:30–5; last entry at 4.*

WHERE TO EAT

Tokushima is well served by slick bars and restaurants, so you'll eat well here. Although Tokushima has a thriving nightlife scene, it's not welcoming: there's a bit of a divide between expats and locals, and the foreigner-friendly places feel grubby and cheap. Get the partying out of your system in Takamatsu.

$$$–$$$$
JAPANESE
★
✕**Wine** 和いん. Excellent Japanese cuisine balances the traditional with the experimental, and the funky decor is as good a reason to come as the food. Across three floors and dozens of differently crafted environs you'll find cushioned corner nooks, normal sit-down tables, latticed-in private chambers, and other one-of-a-kind settings to relish in your meal. The friendly staff will help you decipher the Japanese menu. But you can't go wrong with the ¥3,500 set course: seven wide-ranging dishes include staples like seasonal sashimi and vegetables, and a three-hour all-you-can-drink (two hours on Friday). ✉ *1F, 12–1 Konya-machi* ☎ *088/657–7477* ⊘ *No lunch.*

$
JAPANESE
★
✕**YRG.** The secret favorite of Tokushima's burgeoning young-and-cool demographic and those expats who stay aloof from the binge-drinking scene downtown, YRG's laid-back atmosphere and hip but unpretentious decor make it the best lunch or dinner spot in Tokushima. Takao, the English-speaking proprietor, decides the set menus daily, aiming for nutritionally balanced yet provocative comfort food: it's home-cooking *plus*. Drink menus are inside kid's books from a dozen countries on shelves and tables. Wi-Fi is available. Coming out of the JR Station you'll see two smaller streets and one major one branch off to the left; take the middle street and walk two minutes to just before it terminates. ✉ *1–33–4 Terashima Honcho Higashi* ☎ *088/656–7889* ▭ *No credit cards* ⊘ *Closed Thurs.*

WHERE TO STAY

Although they often show up on hotel searches, the expensive resorts like Grand Hotel Kairakuen and the Best Western Kochi feel old and worn-out, and they don't deal well with non-Japanese-speaking guests. Better choices exist among the newer business hotels by the station.

Hotel reviews have been condensed for this book. Please go to Fodors. com for full reviews of each property.

$$
HOTEL
🏨**Agnes Hotel** アグネスホテル. The friendly atmosphere among staff and patrons could have to do with the delicious French pastries served downstairs, all baked on premises with high-quality imported ingredients and seasonal fruits, but surely the root is the Agnes's proprietor Takashi, gregarious in English and Japanese and dying to make your stay enjoyable. **Pros:** a minute away from the station; bilingual manager; terrific pastries. **Cons:** no doubles, just singles and twins; spartan decor. ✉ *1–28 Terashima Honcho Nishi* ☎ *088/626–2222* ⊕ *www.*

SAIL TOKUSHIMA

Although Tokushima best serves you as a hub for accessing its surroundings, it's a charming city in its own right. Take advantage of the half-hour river tours running from Ryokoku-bashi near the Toyoko Inn. Weekdays from September through June, tours run every 40 minutes from 1 to 3:40. In July and August, tours start at 5 pm, and on weekends (and likely any other time—they are not strict about the schedule) the adorable old men running it will take you any time you show up. Write your name in the book and drop ¥100 in the box on the pier before boarding.

10

agneshotel.jp ⇘ *76 rooms* ⟲ *In-room: a/c, Internet. In-hotel: restaurant* ⦿ *No meals.*

$$ ⚏ **Hotel Sunroute** ホテルサンルート. Luxurious but affordable, this hotel
HOTEL comes with good English assistance, great city access—it's located across from the JR Station—and excellent amenities. **Pros:** nice bathrooms; international clientele. **Cons:** loud music! ✉ *1–5–1 Moto-machi* ☎ *088/653–8111* ⊕ *www.sunroute-tokushima.com* ⇘ *177 rooms* ⟲ *In-room: a/c, refrigerator, DVD, Internet. In-hotel: laundry service* ⦿ *No meals.*

$$$$ ⚏ **Renaissance Resort Naruto** ルネッサンスリゾート鳴門. Stretching along
HOTEL the sandy beaches at Naruto, this resort hotel is peerless for comfort, service, luxury, and access to the sights and surroundings of Naruto. **Pros:** sumptuous rooms and facilities; great access to Naruto. **Cons:** far from city center; no swimming on the beach. ✉ *16–45 Oge Tosa-domariura* ☎ *088/687–2580* ⊟ *088/687–2211* ⊕ *www.renaissance-naruto.com* ⇘ *167 Western-style rooms, 41 Japanese-style rooms* ⟲ *In-room: a/c, refrigerator, DVD. In-hotel: restaurant, pool, laundry facilities* ⦿ *No meals.*

$ ⚏ **Toyoko Inn** 東急イン. Clean, fresh facilities and easy city access make
HOTEL for a relaxing stay at Shikoku's newest branch of this comfortable chain hotel, which opened in October 2008. **Pros:** two-minute walk from the station; close to YRG. **Cons:** rooms could be bigger, no Wi-Fi. ✉ *1–5 Ryogokuhon-cho* ☎ *088/657–1045* ⊕ *www.toyoko-inn.com* ⇘ *139 rooms* ⟲ *In-room: a/c, safe, refrigerator, Internet. In-hotel: laundry facilities, Internet terminal* ⦿ *No meals.*

TOURS

Naruto Kanko Kisen. This tour company offers boat tours of the Naruto whirlpools on two ships: *Wonder Naruto* and *Aqua Eddy*. Tours on *Wonder Naruto* take 30 minutes, cost ¥1,530, and depart every 40 minutes, from 9 to 4:20 daily. *Aqua Eddy* tours take 25 minutes, cost ¥2,200, and depart every half hour from 9:15 to 4:15 daily. Reservations are mandatory for *Aqua Eddy* but not required for Wonder Naruto. You can book online through their Japanese Web site or by phone. Both ships depart from the small pier in Kameura Port, at the southwest end of Naruto Koen Park.

✉ *Naruto Koen Kameura Kanko-ko* ☎ *088/687–0101* 💳 *¥1,530 or ¥2,200* ⊘ *Daily 9–4:15.*

NIGHTLIFE

Bourbon Street. An expat-run bar in the maze of drinking holes downtown, Bourbon Street gets its name for the frequent jazz shows (often highlighting the soaring voice of Vivian, the proprietress). It's just a few years old, but the great drink selection and comradely atmosphere are sure to stick around. ✉ *1F Toku Bldg., 1–73–1 Sakae-machi* ☎ *088/626–5758* ⊘ *Daily 8 pm–3 am.*

The Iya Valley's most famous attractions are its Kazura-Bashi (vine bridges).

CENTRAL SHIKOKU

IYA VALLEY AND OBOKE-KOBOKE GORGES 祖谷と大歩危小歩危

Fodor's Choice
★

25 km (16 mi) southwest of Awa Ikeda, 105 km (65 mi) west of Tokushima, 135 km (84 mi) east of Matsuyama.

In the Iya Valley, mountain villages cling to the side of improbably steep hills while turquoise rivers rush through the ravines below. This remote region was once so isolated that it became the retreat of choice for Heike clan warriors after they lost an epic battle to their Minamoto rivals in the 12th century. To get to Iya now, you don't have to string your own vine bridges across ravines like the Heiki did—although some of the bridges remain—you can access the valley by bus or car. But if you want to feel you've escaped modern Japan for a hidden world, you can't do better than here.

Next to Iya, the Yoshino River roars through Okobe and Koboke gorges, which is where you'll find Japan's best white-water rafting. Try your hand at making delicious Iya soba or local crafts, or trek deeper into the valley to hike to the swordlike summit of Mt. Tsurugi.

GETTING HERE AND AROUND

After some local government mergers in 2006, the villages in the Iya Valley were combined to become "Miyoshi City." Don't be fooled by "city" moniker, though—Miyoshi City is actually a collection of rural villages administered from the small riverside town of Awa Ikeda, 32 km (20 mi) north of the Iya Valley. Access Iya by taking the express Nampu train which runs between Okayama and Kochi to Oboke Station, a small station in the foothills of the Iya Valley. From Oboke, Yonkoh buses run to Nishi-Iya Village eight times a day in summer (April–November) and four times a day in winter (¥640). Infrequent buses also run from Awa Ikeda city (1 hour, 15 minutes). If you're comfortable driving on narrow mountain roads, a car offers the best way to see the valley. The closest rental-car offices are in Awa Ikeda, but renting in Tokushima and driving into the valley via Route 438/439 over Mt. Tsurugi makes sense because of the beautiful scenery, as does renting in Kochi and driving in via Route 32, which follows the Yoshino River. ■TIP→ **If you drive to Iya, rent the smallest car possible. Mountain roads are narrow and corners are tight!**

VISITOR INFORMATION

Miyoshi City Office of Tourism has an excellent English Web site with information and downloadable maps for the Iya Valley.

Contact Miyoshi City Office of Tourism (⊕ *www.miyoshinavi.jp/english*).

WHAT TO SEE

Chiiori House プロジェクト. Chiiori began when popular artist and Japanese-culture appreciator Alex Kerr stumbled upon the abandoned house during his college years and bought it on the spot. Restoring the house has involved help from two communities: Chiiori's neighbors in Iya; and an international network of preservationists, tourists, and volunteers. Countless hands have contributed to restoring Chiiori, especially to the taxing job of maintaining its thatch roof. Now that most villagers have tin roofs, thatch fields are hard to come by, and caretakers are still stockpiling thatch to redo the roof in the near future. They always welcome volunteer laborers or visitors: call the house to arrange a visit (they ask a small donation from daytime visitors). It's possible to stay overnight at the house for a donation. Facilities are self-serve and basic, and outside of summer it can get quite chilly, but you won't find this kind of serenity anywhere else. No credit cards are accepted. ⊠ *209 Higashi-Iya Aza-Tsurui, Miyoshi City, Tokushima-ken* ☎ *0883/88–5290* ⊕ *www.chiiori.org* ✉ *Donation requested* ☾ *Thurs.–Tues. 11–5.*

Kazura-Bashi かずら橋. Iya's most famous features are its three vine bridges that span its gorges. These bridges are called *kazura-bashi* (literally, "vine bridges"). The most-visited kazura-bashi, referred to by most signs, maps, and local residents simply as "Kazura-bashi," is 20 minutes from Oboke Station. A less-visited pair are closer to Mt. Tsurugi. The bridges date back 800 years, to the aftermath of the momentous Gempei War, when the defeated Heike clan fled to these valleys after losing to the rival Minamoto clan. If the refugees were attacked, they could cut the bridges' vines at a moment's notice. These days, thin steel wires reinforce the precarious planks, and fresh vines are restrung every three years, but it still feels death-defying to cross the boards over the rivers. To visit the more popular bridge, follow signs to Kazura-bashi from Route 32 or Route 45. If you're driving, park in the cheaper pay parking lots up the hill. The tall waterfall down the path is free, but you'll pay to cross the bridge. ⊠ *Nishi-Iya Sanzon Village, Miyoshi City,*

CLOSE UP

Make Like Indiana Jones

If a day or two spent rafting, canyoning, and bridge walking (with a night in a hot spring) leaves you wanting more, grab your bullwhip and fedora and head farther into the valley. Mt. Tsurugi, the "Fufu-bashi" (so-called "husband and wife" vine bridges), and a handful of onsen-hotels and craft workshops await you. Driving there is not complicated per se—follow signs toward Higashi-Iya and Tsurugi-san— but the narrow mountain roads are challenging, and you'll want someone to mark the way on a map. You can also take a Yonkoh bus from West Iya to Kubo transfer to a smaller bus bound for Mt. Tsurugi, and get off at the Kazura-bashi bus stop. Buses are infrequent, so check the schedule

carefully to avoid getting stranded in the hills. The *taiken*, literally *experiences*, offered by local artisans are unique activities. Making delicious buckwheat soba noodles is rewarding, especially since this region is famous for its hearty strand of buckwheat, but making tofu or hiring a local Sherpa to climb Tsurugi-san with you are great fun, too. For a full listing of these taiken, check ⊕ *iya.jp/takumi/e. htm.* For logistical help, turn to the good folks at Miyoshi City Office of Tourism or your ryokan. But remember, the trouble with hidden paradises is that they're *hidden.* A car, some basic Japanese, and some gusto will help you get the most out of being here.

Tokushima-ken ☎ *0883/72–7620 for Miyoshi City Office of Tourism* ✉ *¥500 to cross bridge* ☻ *Daily dawn–dusk.*

WHERE TO STAY
Hotel reviews have been condensed for this book. Please go to Fodors. com for full reviews of each property.

$$
RYOKAN
Fodor's Choice
★

🏨 **Iya Onsen** 祖谷温泉. Perched on the edge of a steep ravine above the Iya River, this upscale hot spring inn is one of Japan's three "secret" baths. (If you ask locals where the other two are, ironically, nobody seems to know.) **Pros:** amazing views; traditional Iya cuisine; outdoor riverside bath. **Cons:** limited English; far from Iya Village. ✉ *367–2 Matsuo Matsumoto, Ikeda-cho, Tokushima-ken* ☎ *0883/75–2311* ⊕ *www.iyaonsen.co.jp/english* 🛏 *20 rooms* 🛁 *In-room: a/c, refrigerator, Internet, safe. In-hotel: restaurant, parking (free)* ⦿ *Some meals.*

10

$$
RYOKAN
★
🕑

🏨 **Kazuraya Ryokan** 旅館かずらや. Iya's most cheerful family, the Hiraguris, run this traditional inn just up the road from Kazura-bashi. **Pros:** traditional Iya cooking; family hospitality. **Cons:** limited English. ✉ *78 Kantei, Nishi-Iya Sanzon Village, Miyoshi City* ☎ *0883/87–2831* 🛏 *18 rooms* 🛁 *In-room: a/c, safe. In-hotel: Internet terminal, parking (free)* 🗖 *No credit cards* ⦿ *Some meals.*

SPORTS AND THE OUTDOORS
WHITEWATER RAFTING
If you have time for nothing else in the region, rafting down through rocky gorges on the wild Yoshino River should be your top priority. Several companies guide trips down the river.

White-water rafting is a popular activity in the Iya Valley.

Fodor's Choice
★

Happy Raft ハッピーラフト. This is your best bet for well-trained bilingual guides and friendly service. Half-day trips are ¥7,000 in high season, but you'll wish you had done the full day for ¥15,500. After spending a morning or day letting Happpy Raft make you happy, move on through Iya, or try a longer combination rafting-and-canyoning trip. Staff are great resources for travel tips in the area. Happy Raft is south of Oboke Station on Route 32. It's technically just inside the Kochi border but much closer to Iya than Kochi city. ✉ *10–4 Iwahara Otoyo-cho Nagaoka-gun, Kochi* ☎ *088/775–0500* ⊕ *www.happyraft.com/en.*

KOCHI 高知

170 km (105 mi) southwest of Takamatsu; 175 km (108 mi) southwest of Tokushima; 155 km (96 mi) southeast of Matsuyama; 110 km (68 mi) northeast of Nakamura, near the southern Ehime border.

Kochi has earned a reputation for being different. The locals are rough-talking, boisterous, and social, and their spirited city has an attitude far from the Japanese mainstream. The famous **Yosakoi Dance Festival,** one of Japan's most popular summer events, is an explosion of parades and performances that fills the city for days. For weeks before and after, the streets shake with excitement, making summer the best time to visit. Kochi smacks of a brash, square-shouldered gumption simply not found anywhere else in Japan, and it richly rewards a short swagger through.

GETTING HERE AND AROUND

Kochi is 2 hours, 10 minutes from Takamatsu; 2 hours from Tokushima; 4 hours from Matsuyama; 3 hours, 30 minutes from Osaka; or 2 hours from Nakamura near the Ehime border by train. By bus it is 2 hours, 30 minutes from Matsuyama.

Half the city's best attractions are in striking distance of **Harimaya-bashi** Bridge, a 10-minute walk south of the train station. Taxis from the station run about ¥550. Streetcars go from the station to just about anywhere you want to go for ¥180, and the tram lines are easily navigable. Yosakoi Gururin buses travel the city center; access farther-flung sights like Katsurahama Beach, Chikurin-ji Temple, and the Makino Botanical Garden by the My Yu bus in front of Kochi Station (for ¥900). Renting a bicycle is another option; OK Parking rents bikes for ¥500 a day. To get there, walk from the station toward **Harimaya-bashi,** turn right at the Louis Vuitton shop, and look for the parking garage on your left after the fourth traffic light.

VISITOR INFORMATION

The **Tourist Information Booth** at Kochi Station has few regular English-speakers, but they'll put a great effort into helping you anyway. Make sure to grab their excellent English city and prefecture map, as well as the helpful *Welcome to Kochi* magazine.

Contact Tourist Information Booth (☎ *088/826–3337* ⊕ *www.attaka.or.jp/ foreign/english/index.html* ⊗ *Daily 9–5*).

WHAT TO SEE
DOWNTOWN

Harimaya-bashi Bridge (播磨屋橋) is at the center of Kochi's best-known story, retold in a Yosakoi song, about a Buddhist priest caught here buying a hairpin for a lover, thus breaking his vow of celibacy for an affair that ended in tragedy. The arched red bridge still spans a canal downtown; see what's for sale there these days, or else try shopping in the twisting, tunneled arcades and the shops and side streets that sprout off from them. Locals come out to dine, chat, and dance (yes, dance) in parks and at outdoor cafés until the wee hours. Even in this, Kochi is a world apart from the general Japanese stigma against eating, lounging, and horsing around in public. When the stores and bars finally close, there's always a ramen cart or two doing business on the sidewalk, so pull up a stool and dig in! Kochi people won't pay you a lot of mind until you start talking to them, but many are multilingual, affable, and easy to engage.

★ **Hirome-ichiba** ひろめ市場. The best place to mingle with the locals is at their two popular markets. Kochi goes for culinary treasure over material stuff, and while the busy, hivelike market has interesting pottery, jewelry, and photographs, everyone's really here for the food. This exciting maze of mini-restaurants and food counters has enough strange, delicious food that you couldn't try everything in a year. Displays, pictures, and abundant people traffic will help you ask for what you want, and you can always point to someone else's plate across the broad wooden tables. It's at the western end of the main arcade, close to the castle, about 15 minutes by foot from JR Kochi Station. Look for the mass of bicycles parked around a squat coffee stand beside the entrance, a big orange-and-green sign above the hangar-bay door, and a large crowd of well-fed locals. ⊠ *2–3–1 Obiya-machi* ☎ *088/822–5287* ⊙ *Daily 8–11 (some stalls open at 7 on Sun., market occasionally closed Wed.).*

★ **Kochi Castle** 高知城. Go west through the markets and arcades downtown to find the barrel-chested body of Kochi-jo, which has a slightly different feel from other Japanese castles, more rough-hewn and well lived-in. The view from the topmost watchtower is splendid, and walking up the enormous steps or through the daimyo's receiving chambers is like being transported to the Edo period. From the station, hop a green Yosakoi Gururin bus for a short ¥100 ride. Walking from Harimaya-bashi should take 15 minutes. ⊠ *1–2–1 Marunouchi* ☎ *088/824–5701* ⊠ *¥400* ⊙ *Daily 9–5; last entry at 4:30.*

Nichiyo-ichi Sunday Market 日曜市. This popular market offers a mile of bizarre fruits and vegetables (some looking like they're from other planets) and tasty walking-food, but also local crafts, kitsch, and an army of fellow browsers. It's not the place for good souvenir shopping, but why not try some *yuzu-an* in a pastry pocket? This Kochi specialty replaces red-bean in normal desserts with a paste made from sour yellow yuzu fruit grown in the prefecture. Nichiyo-ichi runs along broad, palm-lined Otetsuji-dori street, parallel to the arcade and just north of it. The market goes along the street east from Harimaya-bashi right up to the gates of the castle. ⊠ *Nichiyo-ichi* ⊙ *Sun. sunrise–sunset.*

⊙ **Yokoyama Memorial Manga Museum** 横山隆一記念まんが館. The playful, modern museum celebrates the life and work of Japan's first great cartoonist, hometown boy Ryuichi Yokoyama. His most popular character, Fuku-chan, is still widely loved, as the crowds of schoolkids reading comics in the museum's free *manga* (comics) library will attest. The museum offers an introduction to this talented creator's life and work, and it's a lot of fun: the cartoons inspire and delight, and no language skill is required to enjoy most of the visual humor. Look through World War II propaganda cartoons (from the other side), interactive print stations, dioramas, model railroads, and tons of comic strips. ⊠ *3F and 5F Cul-Port, Kochi Culture Plaza, 2–1 Kutanda* ☎ *088/883–5029* ⊠ *¥400* ⊙ *Tues.–Sun. 9–6.*

OUTSIDE THE CITY CENTER

Chikurin-ji 竹林寺. Buddhist pilgrims had been communing with nature in the gardens of this temple long before the giant ferns moved in next door at the Makino Botanical Garden. This Japanese garden of this austere mountaintop temple is a registered National Treasure and dates from the 13th century. Its simple arrangement of ponds, rocks, and pine trees is a soothing contrast to the vibrant foliage of Makino, and it is particularly peaceful in the late afternoon. Linger at the temple a while, and you're likely to encounter white-clad Shingon Buddhist pilgrims visiting the temple on their way around the island. ⊠ *3577 Godaisan* ☎ *088/088–3085* ⊠ *¥500 garden, temple free)* ⊙ *Daily 9–5.*

Katsurahama 桂浜. The prefecture may be known for its great surfing and swimming beaches, but the city's beach is not one of them. Rocks and breakers prohibit any fun in the water, and the pebbly sand isn't comfortable for picnicking, but the view from a cliff-top shrine is great (moon-watching from this spot is depicted in many ukiyo-e prints). Katsurahama is best known for the giant statue of **Sakamoto Ryoma,** Kochi's local-born historic hero, staring grimly out to sea from his big black pedestal.

☺ **Makino Botanical Garden** 牧野植物園. The city's best attraction lies away
Fodor'sChoice from downtown Kochi. Planted in honor of Kochi botanist Tomitaro
★ Makino, this Eden-like valley of flowers and trees lies hidden atop Mt. Godaisan. Different trails for each season show off the best nature has to offer. Hours can disappear as you walk through the azaleas, camellias, chrysanthemums, and thousands of other plants in this huge and lovingly tended landscape (don't miss the giant ferns, so big you can actually sit in them). You're encouraged to leave the paths and explore on your own—for as Makino wrote, "to commune with nature we need to make ourselves free and jump into her." You'll find more of his quotes, recollections, philosophy, and drawings in a fascinating museum inside the park. ✉ *4200–6 Godaisan* ☎ *088/882–2601* 🎫 *¥700* ⊙ *Daily 9–5.*

Sakamoto Ryoma Kinenkan 坂本龍馬記念館 (*Sakamoto Ryoma Memorial Museum*). Ryoma was a radical and a revolutionary during the turbulent times before the Meiji Restoration, and the political changes he instigated were big enough to get him killed; at this museum jutting fabulously over the sand and surf, you can see the blood-splashed screen from the room where he was assassinated, and learn about his life and politics. You'll finally know who the cowboyish samurai is plastered on every street corner in Kochi. One stop before Katsurahama on an orange Kenkotsu bus, the trip takes 40 minutes. ✉ *830 Urado-Shiroyama* ☎ *088/841–0001* ⊕ *www.kochi-bunkazaidan.or.jp/~ryoma/english1.htm* 🎫 *¥400* ⊙ *Daily 9–5.*

Sekkei-ji 雪蹊寺. This Rinzai Zen temple dates from the 9th century and is Temple 33 on the Shikoku 88-Temple pilgrimage route. Its patron deity is Yakushi Nyorai, the Buddha of medicine and healing. ✉ *857–3 Nagahama* ☎ *088/837–2233* 🎫 *Free* ⊙ *Daily dawn–dusk.*

Zenjibu-ji 禅師峰寺. This Shingon Buddhist temple was founded in the 8th century and is Temple 32 on the Shikoku 88-Temple pilgrimage route. Also called Mine-ji, the temple is devoted to Kannon, the Buddha of mercy and compassion. ✉ *3084 Tochi, Nankoku* ☎ *088/865–9430* 🎫 *Free* ⊙ *Daily dawn–dusk.*

OFF THE
BEATEN
PATH
Muroto Cape 室戸岬. A surreal coastline of rocks, steep precipices, and surf awaits you at far-off Muroto. The road east from Kochi follows a rugged shoreline cut by inlets and indentations along a rockscape out of Dr. Seuss, where the Pacific Black Current has shaped enormous terraces going down to the sea. It's about a 2½-hour drive along the coast road out to the cape, or a long bus ride to the black-sand beaches at Murotomisaki-mae. A concrete promenade lets you walk the farthest tip of sea-sculpted land. Children may be most interested in the **Muroto Dolpin Center** (✉ *6810–162 Ugeihama, Muroto Misaki-cho, Muroto City* ☎ *0887/22–1245* ⊕ *www.muroto-dc.jp* ⊙ *Daily 9–4*), a

10

conservationist NGO that lets you swim with dolphins. The full experience costs ¥8,400 for adults, ¥5,250 for kids, but prices are discounted from November through February and there are considerably cheaper options; kids must be over 43 inches tall. It's off Route 55 on the western side of the peninsula, a five-minute walk from Muruto Eigyosho bus stop, 50 minutes past Nahari Station.

To get to Muroto by public transport, take a 1½-hour train ride to Nahari Station on the private Tosa Kuroshio train (¥1,300, JR Pass not valid), and a one-hour bus ride from there (¥1,050). It's a trek; check return schedules carefully.

WHERE TO EAT

¢–$
JAPANESE

✕**Faust** ファウスト. This delightful café-restaurant is just off the main drag. Sit outdoors and people-watch on the cobbled lane, or head indoors to the fancy, intimate third floor. The first floor is dinerlike, the second acceptable, but sitting in the literati-chic upper level and getting to order from the same cheap, delicious menu is having your cake and eating it, too. The cake, incidentally, is excellent. ✉ *1–2–22 Hon-machi* ☎ *088/873–4111* ▭ *No credit cards.*

¢–$
JAPANESE
★

✕**Myojin-Maru** 明神丸. Inside Hirome-ichiba, just follow your nose, but don't leave without trying the *katsuo tataki,* Kochi's regional fish specialty and the only item on the menu. Look for the orange flames erupting from this stall's window. Fresh cuts of katsuo are seared to perfection by a cook perilously close to being engulfed by the flames that he's feeding with big handfuls of straw. Most katsuo for Kochi come from the port town Kure to the southwest, and this shop belongs to the captain of Kure's largest fishing vessel. The fish is served on beds of rice or drizzled with citrusy ponzu sauce, and you'll never get enough of it. ✉ *Inside Hirome-ichiba, 2–3–1 Obiya-machi Arcade* ☎ *088/820–5101* c*No credit cards.*

$$$$
JAPANESE

✕**Tosahan** 土佐藩. If you want to see Kochi's refined side, try a Tosa ryori course at Tosahan. Dark-wood beams, tatami floors, and red-paper lanterns create a rich atmosphere. A picture menu and displays make ordering easy. Katsuo is the specialty, along with *nabe* hot pots, and anything you get will be more or less perfect. Look for the giant backlighted poster of Ryoma, Kochi's claim-to-fame samurai, glowering at you a few blocks into Obiya-machi arcade. ✉ *1–2–2 Obiya-machi Arcade* ☎ *088/821–0002.*

$$$–$$$$
JAPANESE

✕**Tosa Ryori Tsukasa** 土佐料理 司高知本店. Set courses range from bento-box to jaw-dropping sashimi feasts: *sawachi ryori,* lavish fish platters that are a Kochi specialty. The staff recommend the katsuo—in Japanese it's *sasuga Kochi,* "just as you'd expect in Kochi"—but consider the shabu-shabu meat and veggie sets, which your servers will teach you to cook on a special table in your private tatami room. Be careful with seating; the main area on the first floor is a bland cafeteria, so indicate that you want an upstairs tatami room instead. ✉ *1–2–15 Harimaya-cho* ☎ *088/873–4351.*

WHERE TO STAY

Hotel reviews have been condensed for this book. Please go to Fodors. com for full reviews of each property.

$ 🏨 **7Days Hotel** セブンデイズホテル. The 7Days and its slightly plusher
HOTEL   annex are primarily business hotels, but they stand out from the pack for their pampering, comfortable feel. **Pros:** spacious rooms; nice digs. **Cons:** mostly twins available; away from entertainment. ✉ *2–13–6 and 2–13–17 Harimaya-cho, Kochi-ken* ☎ *088/884–7100 or 088/884–7111* ⊕ *www.7dayshotel.com* 🛏 *134 rooms* ♿ *In-room: a/c, refrigerator, Internet. In-hotel: restaurant, laundry facilities, laundry service, Internet terminal* ⏐◎⏐ *No meals.*

$$ 🏨 **Best Western Kochi** ベストウェスタン高知. Formerly the Washington,
HOTEL   this hotel's location on Otetsuji-dori puts you right by the castle, on top of the Sunday market, and in the best spot to get home after a night out feasting and rollicking your way through town. **Pros:** in the heart of the city; easy for non-Japanese speakers. **Cons:** unexciting rooms. ✉ *1–8–25 Otetsuji* ☎ *088/826–6611* 🛏 *172 rooms* ♿ *In-room: a/c, Wi-Fi. In-hotel: restaurant* ⏐◎⏐ *No meals.*

$$$ 🏨 **Hotel Shin-Hankyu** 新阪急ホテル. This Western-style luxury chain
HOTEL   hotel feels almost out of place in gruff Kochi city, which can either mean a missed opportunity to experience Kochi hospitality or a relaxing escape from the verve of the streets and nightlife. **Pros:** friendly staff helpful with city orientation; close to city center. **Cons:** slightly twee next to the down-to-earth city; only four double rooms (the others are twins). ✉ *4–2–50 Hon-machi* ☎ *088/873–1111* ⊕ *www.hankyu-hotel. com* 🛏 *238 Western-style rooms, 4 Japanese-style rooms* ♿ *In-room: a/c, refrigerator, Internet. In-hotel: 4 restaurants, bar, pool, gym, laundry service* ⏐◎⏐ *No meals.*

$$$$ 🏨 **Jyoseikan** 城西館. "Fit for a king" is an expression we take for
HOTEL   granted, but watch yourself—Jyoseikan is where the Emperor stays when the Royal Family comes to Kochi. **Pros:** spacious tatami rooms; close to the castle and Sunday market. **Cons:** easy to get lost walking back at night; few English-speaking staff. ✉ *2–5–34 Kami-machi, Kochi-ken* ☎ *088/875–0111* ⊕ *www.jyoseikan.co.jp* 🛏 *72 Japanese-style rooms* ♿ *In-room: a/c, Internet, refrigerator. In-hotel: restaurant* ⏐◎⏐ *No meals.*

MATSUYAMA AND WESTERN SHIKOKU

MATSUYAMA 松山

160 km (100 mi) southwest of Takamatsu; 120 km (75 mi) west of Awa Ikeda; 195 km (120 mi) west of Tokushima; 155 km (95 mi) northwest of Kochi; 75 km (46 mi) from Hiroshima (hydrofoil); 160 km (100 mi) to Oita (ferry).

Shikoku's largest city, Matsuyama prides itself on a great history, friendly disposition, fantastic cultural attractions, and a love for fine food, intense fashion, and haiku. You'll be quickly captivated by the sights and feel of the city, and you can join in the fun; bathe at Dogo Onsen, Japan's oldest hot spring, hit the fashion avenue downtown, or go restaurant crawling through the best spots on the island. Denizens

10

say it's *sumi-yasui* (easy living) here, and you'll find Matsuyama one of the most rewarding stops along your route.

GETTING HERE AND AROUND
BOAT TRAVEL

You can also get to Matsuyama by sea. By hydrofoil it takes 90 minutes from Hiroshima or, by regular ferry, two hours, 30 minutes. The ferry will take you four hours from Beppu in Kyushi, and overnight (about eight hours) from Osaka or Kobe. Except for the Orange Ferry from Osaka, all ferries to Matsuyama arrive at Matsuyama Kanko Ko Terminal. Get from the terminal to central Matsuyama by taking a direct Iyotetsu bus to Matsuyama Shi-eki (¥500; about 30 minutes), by taxi (about ¥3,000; 20 minutes), or by taking a shuttle bus to Iyotetsu Takahama train station and taking the train from there to Matsuyama Shi-eki (¥400; 45 minutes). There are also direct buses from Kanko Ko Terminal to Dogo Onsen (¥600; 40 minutes).

From Hiroshima: The Setonaikai Kisen and Ishizaki Kisen companies run hydrofoils from Hiroshima Port 14 times a day each, for a one-way fare of ¥6,900 (both companies). The Ishizaki Kisen slow ferry from Hiroshima makes 10 trips a day and costs ¥3,500 one-way.

From Kansai: From Osaka, both the Orange Ferry and Diamond Ferry companies run overnight boats, with the Orange Ferry sometimes stopping for passenger pickup in Kobe. On the Orange Ferry, berths in an eight-person room go for ¥6,500; a private cabin for two is ¥10,500 per person, and a spot on the tatami mat floor is ¥5,500. The Orange Ferry offers a 30% discount on return tickets if your trip is less than two weeks and also offers discounts on the bus from Toyo Port to Matsuyama. If Matsuyama is your last stop in Japan and you're flying home from Kansai Airport, you can also book a direct bus with Orange Ferry from the Osaka Port to Kansai Airport. The Orange Ferry arrives at Toyo Port, 50 km (31 mi) east of Matsuyama. Buses (operated by either JR or Iyotetsu Bus Company) connect Matsuyama with Toyo Port. On the Diamond Ferry, which leaves from Matsuyama Kanko Ko, berths in a four-, eight-, or 12-person room are ¥8,100. Beds in a two-person cabin are ¥9,100 per person. Book online for a 20% discount

From Kyushu: The Diamond Ferry departs once a day in the evening from Beppu Port in Kyushu. A tourist-class ticket is ¥3,300 one-way per adult. Book online for a 20% discount

■TIP➔ The Orange Ferry or Diamond Ferry that run between Osaka and Matsuyama Port (Diamond) or Toyo Port (Orange) feel like floating luxury hotels, with chandeliers, simulated hot-spring baths, cotton *yukata* (robe), and nice cafeterias.

Contacts **Diamond Ferry** (☎ 0120/56–3268 ⊕ www.ferry-sunflower.co.jp [in Japanese only]). **Orange Ferry** (☎ 0898/64–4121 ⊕ www.orange-ferry.co.jp [Japanese only]). **Ishizaki Kisen** (☎ 089/951–0128 ⊕ www.ishizakikisen.co.jp). **Setonaikai Kisen** (☎ 082/253–1212 ⊕ www.setonaikaikisen.co.jp).

Dogo Onsen, Japan's oldest hot spring, is the biggest draw in Matsuyama.

PUBLIC TRANSPORTATION

The best way to get around Matsuyama is by tram. Rides in the city cost ¥150 each, paid when you get off the tram. A day-pass is ¥600 and can be bought from the tram driver. No. 5 trams run from the JR Station to Dogo Onsen, and most of the city's best spots are on the way. The stop in the center of Matsuyama is Okaido-mae on Ichiban-cho street, in front of the city's busy arcades and the restaurant mile surrounding them. Uphill across from the arcades, a five-minute walk past the Starbucks and through one of Matsuyama's cutest shopping streets (the work of several recent years of public works and private investment) will bring you to Matsuyama Castle's ropeway. It's especially nice at night thanks to waist-high streetlights and tall fishbowl lampposts. ■TIP➔ If you're traveling with kids, don't miss a ride on the special Botchan steam trams that putter around the city. Trains run between Shi-eki and Dogo Onsen eight to 10 times a day. A one-way trip is ¥300.

TRAIN TRAVEL

By train Matsuyama is 2 hours, 10 minutes from Takamatsu; 1 hour, 30 minutes from Awa Ikeda; 3 hours from Tokushima; 3 hours from Kochi; and 7 hours from Tokyo. By bus it is about 3 hours to Kochi or Tokushima. There are two main train stations in the city, JR Matsuyama and Matsuyama Shi-eki. JR trains and buses arrive at the JR Station, which is a bit far from the city center. Local buses, trams, and Iyotetsu trains go to the more-central Shi-eki Station.

VISITOR INFORMATION

There are tourist information offices at JR and Shi-eki stations. English maps are available even if an English speaker is not. For real assistance with anything, head to the Ehime Prefectural International Center. EPIC is a peerless resource for advice on the city and region. The desk staff will bend over backwards to help you with event info, transport tips, hotel reservations, and even rental bikes (for a refundable ¥1,000 deposit). It's next to the Kenmin Bunka Kaikain, or People's Cultural Hall, off Tram 5's Minami-machi stop.

Contacts City Tourist Information Office (⊠ *Matsuyama Station* ☏ *089/931– 3914*). **Ehime Prefectural International Center (EPIC)** (⊠ *1–1 Dogo Ichiman* ☏ *089/917–5678* ⊕ *www.epic.or.jp/english/index.html*).

WHAT TO SEE

Matsuyama is easy to navigate and is served by a good tram network. There is one central, enormous central landmark, Matsuyama Castle and the moat surrounding it. Orientation is not difficult, though it's a large and not particularly well-organized city; the hastiness with which sections have been developed—and the antiquity of other areas—has left many grimy sectors and dead zones, but for visitors the action is concentrated around a few locations.

★ **Dogo Onsen** 道後温泉. Mention Matsuyama to anyone, and Dogo Onsen will be the first place they recommend. It has been the city's number-one attraction since time began for this nation. Dogo is the oldest hot spring in Japan, with a history stretching back almost 3,000 years. Japan's first written text mentions it as a favorite of gods, emperors, and peasants alike, and it's still in daily use by locals and tourists. The main wooden building at present-day Dogo dates from 1894 and looks like a fairy-tale castle; the only thing that's changed significantly is the view.

The best value is the ¥800 course for a bath with some frills. Head upstairs and you'll get a basket with towels and a lightweight *yukata* robe. Staff will point you to the Kami-no-Yu, or the Water of the Gods. The gods apparently liked it simple; the great granite tub is plainer than the modern multibath complexes, but the water feels terrific. Come wash away your cares and concerns. Baths are gender-segregated.

■**TIP**➔ Remember your onsen procedure: go into the bathroom with your teeny towel, and wash and rinse yourself (and rinse your towel!) before getting into the bath. Don't worry much about bathing faux pas like dropping your towel in the water. On laid-back Shikoku, and especially at Dogo, no one is too fussy. Even tattoos are usually no problem.

After you bathe, don the soft yukata and relax upstairs. Your ticket includes green tea and *sembei* crackers, served in a serene public tatami room. Relaxing in this second-story terrace is one of the great joys of coming to Dogo. Technically, your ticket allows you to stay for up to an hour, but if it's not busy, staff aren't strict about the time limit. Stay and sip free tea refills, or explore the upstairs quarters where writer Soseki Natsume stayed and worked during his time in Matsuyama. (Dogo was about the only thing he liked about the city, although Matsuyama inexplicably claims him as a favorite son.) ⊠ *5–6 Yuno-machi, Dogo*

☎ *089/921–5141* 🖛 *¥400–¥1,500* ⊙ *Kami-no-Yu Tub: daily 6–11; last entry at 10; pricier Rei-no-yu Tub: daily 6–10; last entry 9.*

Ehime Museum of Art 愛媛県立美術館. The modern building at the city's center could have a bigger permanent collection, but the selection of recent Japanese art is terrific and the traveling exhibition spaces are extensive. ✉ *Horinouchi* ☎ *089/932–0010* 🖛 *Depends on exhibit* ⊙ *Tues.–Sun. 9:40–6.*

★ **Ishite-ji Temple** 石手寺. Ishite-ji is like an ancient, Buddhist-themed amusement park. It's Temple 51 on the Shikoku 88-Temple pilgrimage route, offering more fun things to see and do than at any other holy site. Without a doubt it's the best temple on Shikoku. As sprawling and unkempt as the city around it, its surprises are, like the temple cats, too numerous to count. Ghastly statues and lovely bridges wait in the forest, a scrambling rock pathway leads up the back of the mountain, and two spooky caves are yours to explore (even most locals don't know about them). The obvious draws are wonderful, too—a pagoda and huge temple buildings, painted panels, golden statues, a giant mandala on the stairway to the main shrine, a wood-carved *kami* (spirit) with a sword you can heft, a huge bronze bell to ring for a hundred yen, and a cauldron of ash to light incense in. Pass a stone dragon at the entrance and a strip of *omiyage* paper-fortune merchants, and you'll see a table for making origami cranes; they'll be added to the heavy, colorful bunches hanging around pillars everywhere, and in return you can take home a white placard on which the monks have written a sutra. Don't miss the cave behind the main temple building. The darkness is not total, but it feels impossibly long, and when you finally emerge on the other side—past startling wooden statues and 88 stone Buddhas (one for each temple on the pilgrimage)—you'll be confronted by a 100-foot statue of the Kobo Daishi striding across the mountains. Remember those huge sandals you saw at the gate? They're his. Don't miss Ishite-ji's regular festival, held on the 20th day of every month. ✉ *2–9–21 Ishite* ☎ *089/977–0870* 🖛 *Free* ⊙ *Temple always open. Shops and caves daily (closed 4–5).*

Itami Juzo Memorial Museum. Alongside Akira Kurosawa and Hayao Miyazaki, the late Juzo Itami is regarded as one of Japan's most innovative and captivating directors. His films are known for their affectionate and absurdist look at mundane scenes of Japanese life. Each film starred his wife Nobuko Miyamoto as an everywoman lead countered by an off-the-wall supporting role, sometimes played by Itami himself. Best-known films include almost-a-Western *Tampopo,* centering on a bedraggled ramen-shop owner trying to make the perfect soup; and *Ososhiki,* the story of an idiosyncratic family coming together for a funeral. If you haven't seen them, they're musts for any Japan tourist; if you have, then you'll love the museum, curated by Miyamoto herself, showcasing video clips and objects from Itami's life. Tobe-bound buses from Shieki take 20 minutes to Amayama-bashi; backtrack two minutes to the museum. ✉ *1–6–10 Higashi Ishii* ☎ *089/969–1313* ⊕ *itami-kinenkan.jp* 🖛 *¥800* ⊙ *Wed.–Mon. 10–6.*

10

Matsuyama Castle 松山城. Large, well kept, and mighty, Matsuyama-jo is one of the cooler castles in Japan. Inside you can watch footage of the post–World War II reconstruction; the hand labor is astonishing, from the shaping and joining of wood to the stamping out of straw wattle for the walls. There is no concrete, no rebar, and only enough nails to hold down the floorboards. Dark-wood passageways carry the smell of old smoke, from the numerous fires the castle has suffered. For daytime visits, ride the ropeway up and walk about 20 minutes to the castle. Don't miss the lovely Ninomaru garden just west of the castle, and exit from there to Ichiban-cho, a few blocks west of the Okaido arcade, or take the ropeway down again. ⊠ *5 Maru-no-uchi* ☎ *089/921–4873* 🖅 *Castle ¥500, ropeway ¥500 round-trip, or a ¥1,000 comprehensive ticket* ☽ *Feb.–Nov., daily 9–5; Dec. and Jan., daily 9–4:30.*

OFF THE BEATEN PATH

Twin Stadiums. Watch Ehime's minor-league baseball team, the Mandarin Pirates, at **Botchan Stadium** 坊ちゃんスタジアム for an affordable taste of Japan's baseball mania. Even more fun are the high-school games: Japan is nuts for high-school baseball, and Ehime's teams have been national competitors the last few years, so home games are boisterous and well attended. Get schedules and information at EPIC. Next door, Japan's finest martial-arts stadium stands out like a black-roof fortress: watch or try a class in any number of arts, any time of day at the **Ehime Ken-Budokan** 愛媛県武道館.

WHERE TO EAT

$$$–$$$$
ECLECTIC
★

✕ **Amitie** アミティエ. The alleys and side streets east off Okaido offer an endless number of great dinner spots, but for lunch this is our favorite. Cuisine and presentation are excellent without being snooty, the interior is funky without being crass or grimy. Sit upstairs and strike up conversation with your neighbors; the convivial hosts and softly worn wooden interior engender affability. Amitie is outside Bijutsukan-mae tram stop, across the moat from the art museum. ⊠ *6–23 Minami Horibata-cho* ☎ *089/998–2811.*

$$
INDIAN

✕ **Ladkey's** ラルキー. Come here for top-quality Pakistani/Indian food prepared by chef Ladkey, who hails from northern India. The ¥3,200, two-hour all-you-can-eat-and-drink course is a closely kept secret of Matsuyama's expat population. A picture menu helps you order. Lunch sets come with salads and choice of naan or saffron rice. It's located between Shieki and the art museum. ⊠ *5–9 Hanazono-cho* ☎ *089/948–0885* 🖃 *No credit cards.*

$
THAI

✕ **Mirai Kanai** ミライ・カナイ. A laid-back international clientele, extensive list of cocktails, nightly Thai-food themed specials, and a low-key attitude about almost everything will make you think you've found a portal to Chiang Mai. It's one block down a side street just across from the castle ropeway entrance. ⊠ *2–5–1 Kiyo-cho* ☎ *089/934–0108* 🖃 *No credit cards.*

¢
CAFÉ

✕ **NY Kitchen Sakura** ニューヨークキッチン サクラ. This laid-back café is a great place to stop for cake, tea, drinks, or light meals. It's in the Niban-cho shopping district just south of Mitsukoshi department store. ⊠ *3–7–14 Niban-cho* ☎ *089/948–0020* 🖃 *No credit cards* ☽ *Closed Sun.*

$$$–$$$$
SUSHI
✕ **Taihei Sushi** 大平寿司. At this totally unremarkable counter with totally sumptuous sushi, dinner times are crowded and fun. A ¥2,500 or ¥3,500 fixed course gets you eight to 10 different kinds of sushi, with soup. There's zero English ability in-house but folks are friendly; if you're unsated, start pointing to what looks good. Look for the purple-and-white polka-dot curtain on Yasaka-dori, north of Sanban-cho. ✉ *2–6–19 Sanban-cho* ☎ *089/934–0007* ▭ *No credit cards* ⊗ *Closed Sun. No lunch.*

$$
ECLECTIC
✕ **Tipitina's.** Funky and unpretentious decor, the friendly bilingual staff, and a menu of delicious share-me-size dishes will endear you to this second-floor izakaya-cum-bistro with a faux-cowhide door. The menu is eclectic, ranging from cheese fondue to Vietnamese spring rolls. Try the "magical drink." It's located on Yasaka-dori corner one block north of Sanban-cho. ✉ *2–6–18 Sanban-cho* ☎ *089/921–7011* ▭ *No credit cards* ⊗ *No lunch.*

¢–$
CAFÉ
✕ **Un Petit Peu** アン・プチ・プー. Delicious handmade custards and crepes across two cute floors, along with corner views of Matsuyama's busy night scene, make this comfy coffee-and-pastry shop a perfect part of any evening out. It's been so popular with such a wide demographic that construction began on a second location only five months after this one opened in May 2008. In the ineffable Japanese accent, "An Poochi Poo" is on the corner of Niban-cho and Yasaka-dori. It's open from 3 pm until late. ✉ *1–10–9 Niban-cho* ☎ *089/931–8550* ▭ *No credit cards* ⊗ *Closed Sun. No lunch.*

$$$$
JAPANESE
★
✕ **Yushoku Shunsai Mejina** 遊食旬菜 meji菜. It's Japanese style at its best in this tiny oasis in Chifune-machi. One block north of Shi-eki Station, Mejina offers elegant lunch or dinner kaiseki courses served on delicate ceramic tableware and with impeccable service. There's no English menu, but you can't go wrong with the set meals. Try the lunch bento for ¥980 or the dinnertime omakase kaiseki set, which you need to reserve one day in advance, for ¥3,150. ✉ *5–6–3 Chifune-machi* ☎ *089/998–2118* ▭ *No credit cards.*

WHERE TO STAY

Hotel reviews have been condensed for this book. Please go to Fodors. com for full reviews of each property.

$$$$
HOTEL
🏨 **ANA Hotel Matsuyama** 松山全日空ホテル. The biggest international hotel downtown, the ANA is just next to Mitsukoshi department store on Ichiban-cho. **Pros:** next to city center; easy access to sights. **Cons:** somewhat generic rooms. ✉ *3–2–1 Ichiban-cho* ☎ *089/933–5511* ⊕ *www.anahotelmatsuyama.com* �’ *327 rooms* ♿ *In-room: a/c, refrigerator, Internet. In-hotel: 4 restaurants, bar* ❨◯❩*No meals.*

$–$$
HOTEL
🏨 **Hotel Checkin Matsuyama** チェックイン松山. This hotel is at the epicenter of restaurants and nightlife in downtown Matsuyama. **Pros:** prime city location; parking; hotel bath draws water from Dogo Onsen. **Cons:** lower floors can be a bit noisy from the street; breakfast area can be crowded. ✉ *2–7–3 Sanban-cho* ☎ *089/998–7000* ⊕ *www.checkin.co.jp/ matsuyama* �’ *270 rooms* ♿ *In-room: a/c, refrigerator, Internet. In-hotel: restaurant, laundry facilities, Internet terminal, parking (paid)* ❨◯❩*No meals.*

10

$

HOTEL

🖼 **Hotel Dogo Yaya** ホテル道後やや. The owners of Yume Kura opened a more affordable alternative to visitors seeking luxury accommodation in Dogo in July 2010. **Pros:** close to Dogo; fashionable facilities, choice of geta sandals to wear to the bath. **Cons:** minimal English-language support; some rooms have small windows. ⌂ *6–1 Dogo Tako-cho, Dogo* ☎ *089/907–1181* ⊕ *www.yayahotel.jp* ⇗ *68 rooms* ⌂ *In-room: a/c, refrigerator, Internet, safe. In-hotel: restaurant, bar, parking (paid)* ❙⊙❙ *Breakfast.*

$–$$

HOTEL

🖼 **Hotel Patio Dogo** ホテルパティオドウゴ. Even after staying here it's hard to believe a hotel this nice and in this excellent location can be so affordable. **Pros:** nice bathrooms; May 2008 renovation; excellent location. **Cons:** C rooms cramped; far from nightlife. ⌂ *Dogo Onsen Honkanmae, Dogo* ☎ *089/941–4128* ⊕ *www.patio-dogo.co.jp* ⇗ *101 rooms* ⌂ *In-room: a/c, refrigerator, Wi-Fi. In-hotel: restaurant, laundry service* ❙⊙❙ *No meals.*

$$$

HOTEL

🖼 **JAL City Matsuyama** JALシティ松山. Overlooking the moat and castle just east of the JR Station, this Western-style hotel has comfortable rooms and great city access. **Pros:** friendly staff; good city and tram access. **Cons:** unexciting rooms; far from both Dogo and downtown. ⌂ *1–10–10 Ohte-machi* ☎ *089/913–2580* ⊕ *matsuyama.jalcity.co.jp* ⇗ *120 rooms* ⌂ *In-room: a/c, refrigerator, DVD, Internet. In-hotel: 2 restaurants* ❙⊙❙ *No meals.*

$$$–$$$$

RYOKAN

🖼 **Yume Kura** 夢蔵. A high-class ryokan built in 2006 just behind Dogo Onsen, Yume Kura delivers the royal treatment in a great location. **Pros:** location; volcanic spring bathtubs; memory-foam beds; bath-gear baskets to carry to Dogo Onsen. **Cons:** no double beds; no in-room dinner service; meals not optional (but breakfast-only option is available). ⌂ *4–5 Dogo Yutsuki-cho, Dogo* ☎ *089/931–1180* ⊕ *www.yume-kura. jp* ⇗ *7 Japanese-style rooms* ⌂ *In-room: a/c, refrigerator, DVD. In-hotel: restaurant, parking (free)* ❙⊙❙ *Some meals.*

NIGHTLIFE

Indie's Kashimashi. Don't be fooled by the underwhelming first-floor café: head downstairs to the chic bar floor underneath this popular early-to-late nightspot to see what the buzz is all about. There's no English menu, which may render the delicious Italian kitchen upstairs inaccessible, but wine and excellent cocktails make up for it. Cakes and pastries arrive daily from an off-site bakery. It's on Yasaka-dori between Niban-cho and Sanban-cho. ⌂ *B1F, 2–1–1 Niban-cho Mitsuwa Bldg.* ☎ *089/913–0769* ⊙ *Mon.–Thurs. 6 pm–3 am, Fri. and Sat. 6–4, Sun. 6–1.*

Salon Kitty. These compact quarters host some of Japan's biggest-name bands in intimate shows at great prices. Tastes lean towards rock and J-punk; recent guests include Bump of Chicken and the Cro-Magnons, bands that can easily sell out the Japan Budokan. Call to find out who's coming up. ⌂ *5F, 138 Kawahara-cho* ☎ *089/945–0020.*

SHOPPING

Matsuyama is the fashion capital of Shikoku, and a stroll down its main shopping arcades, **Okaido** and **Gintengai,** will leave you reeling from the getups, ranging from gorgeous to grotesque. Nowhere else outside Tokyo does fad-fashion get this high a priority. Okaido begins at the

Starbucks on Ichiban-cho and goes south for a kilometer until turning right into the Gintengai; Gintengai empties out by a large Takashimaya department store and the city bus and tram terminal, Shi-eki. Follow the tram lines a few blocks past a Mr. Donut to find Ladkey's, a terrific Indian restaurant with good lunch specials but a temperamental owner. A block farther to Matsuyama's best lunch place, Amitie, across from the castle moat and Ehime Museum of Art. The tram stop here is Bijutsukan-mae.

Okaido, Gintengai, and Shi-eki complete a square adjacent to the castle's moat. Inside is **Chifune-machi**, bursting with clothing stores, cafés, and other shops. You won't stumble on any hidden temples or ancient ruins, but there's plenty of good shopping and city life. Walk the square of the same area on the *other* side of Okaido after dark, and you'll hit a staggering number of great restaurants. The two best streets to follow both run parallel to the main arcade. For the first, head into Okaido from the Starbucks, and go left at the first stoplight (this is Niban-cho), then make a right to find foody heaven. No spot on the strip is terribly expensive, and each place has a lot of character and great food. A few blocks farther east, the main artery, Yasaka-dori, demarcates the restaurant miles from the red-light district; lots of great places to eat and drink line both sides. Places for late-night coffees and deserts have multiplied recently; newcomer Un Petit Peu is on Niban-cho between Okaido and Yasaka-dori, in the opposite direction from the old town. Local favorite NY Kitchen Sakura is on the other side of Okaido and one block past the red London bus hair salon. The pink cherry-blossom beer is better in someone else's glass, but the coffees and cakes are wonderful.

UCHIKO 内子

50 km (30 mi) south of Matsuyama.

This small farming town in the mountains south of Matsuyama was a major producer of Japanese paper and wax until the early 20th century. Now, it's a peaceful mountain town of old merchant houses, candle and umbrella workshops, and an impressive turn-of-the-20th-century Kabuki theater. Mid-century, it also became famous as the hometown of novelist Oe Kenzaburo, the second Japanese writer to win the Noble Prize in literature.

Uchiko is small enough to cover on foot, and strolling through this old town is the best way to experience it. From Uchiko Station, follow a wooden sign pointing left to the old shopping street **Yokaichi**, where the only change for centuries has been the height of plants against the beige-orange walls. You won't need more than a morning to poke through the fun shops, full of good, cheap omiyage *souvenirs*: straw pinwheels, tea leaves, sour *tsukemono pickles,* and local sake.

WHAT TO SEE

One of Uchiko's more-unexpected sights is the mountainous **sleeping Buddha** *statue inside Kosho-ji Temple, just up the road from the town's junior high school. The temple was founded in the 15th century, but*

10

the Buddha statue dates from 1998. Its relative youth doesn't detract from its impressive serenity.

Omori's Wax Workshop 大森和蠟燭屋. The highlight of Yokaichi street is this shop, where an old man and his sons make distinctive candles by hand (the smaller ones are as surprisingly inexpensive as the larger are surprisingly costly). It's the large candle shop in the shopping arcade. ✉ *2214 Uchiko* ☎ *0893/43–0385* ⊗ *Tues.–Thurs. and weekends 9–5.*

Uchiko Townhouse Museum 内子町立町家資料館. Just 50 meters northeast from Omori's Wax Workshop, this museum is an 18th-century town house that once belonged to a wealthy family and is now open to the public. ✉ *3023 Uchiko* ☎ *0893/44–2118* 💳 *Free* ⊗ *daily 9–4:30.*

Uchiko Za 内子座. This theater was built in 1916 and has been hosting Kabuki and Bunraku performances ever since. It also hosts a drum performance by the famous Kodo Taiko group every October. It's a must-see if you're in town in October. When there are no performances scheduled, you can view the interior for a small admission fee. ✉ *2102 Uchiko* ☎ *0893/44–2840* 💳 *¥300* ⊗ *Daily 9–4:30.*

> ## THE DEMON BULL
>
> So-called "demon bulls" (*ushi-oni*) are common in Shikoku and Kansai folklore. This fearsome creature has the body of a bull and the head of a demon, and will set a curse on the family of anyone who injures or angers it. Uwajima residents were traditionally particularly wary of demon bulls and still hold an annual *ushi-oni* festival from July 22 to 24 at Warai-jinja shrine to pacify the demons, just in case.

UWAJIMA 宇和島

90 km (56 mi) south of Matsuyama, 130 km (80 mi) west of Kochi.

Uwajima's claims to fame are its sumo-style bullfights and a notorious sex museum located next to the local Shinto fertility shrine, which has displays that would make Jenna Jameson blush. One way to get around Uwajima is by bicycle; you can rent bikes from EkiRentacar next to the train station for ¥100 per hour.

WHAT TO SEE

Uwajima Tourist Information. There's a tourist information booth inside the station, but the main tourist information office is in the ferry terminal about a 10-minute walk away. The main office sells stickers with Uwajima's demon bull for ¥50—these make great souvenirs! ✉ *1–318–16 Benten-cho* ☎ *089/522–3934* ⊗ *Daily 9–6.*

Taga Jinja 多賀神社. The town's infamous sex museum is located at this Shinto fertility shrine not far from the station. It's easy to zip past the entrance, but once there you can tell you've arrived. No, that's no giant squid. And just beyond the squid is the museum, called **Deko Boko Jindou** (literally a shrine honoring "things that poke out, things that go in"). The three-floor collection is astonishing. What is that samurai doing? It's best to leave the kids at the castle for this one (the castle is

The Tatara Ohashi Bridge is part of the Shimanami Sea Road that connects Shikoku with western Honshu.

up the arcade and to the right). ⊠ *1340 Fujie* ☎ *089/522–3444* ✆ *¥800* ⊗ *Daily 8–5.*

Togyu 闘牛. After the sex museum, Uwajima's other attraction is this sport in which two bulls lock horns and push, à la sumo, for control of a ring. The bullfights date back to the 18th century, and if you can make it during one of the six annual tournaments, you'll have a great time. The stadium is at the foot of Maru-yama, a 30-minute walk from Uwajima Station. ⊠ *1 Akebono-cho* ☎ *0895/22–3934 Uwajima tourist info* ✆ *¥2,500 for bullfights* ⊗ *Tournaments Jan. 2, 1st Sun. in Apr., July 24, Aug. 14, and 4th Sun. in Oct.*

SHIMANAMI KAIDO しまなみ街道

Beginning in Imabari, 45 km (28 mi) north of Matsuyama.

ⓒ
Fodor'sChoice
★

By far the most scenic way to travel between Shikoku and western Honshu is the **Shimanami Kaido** (*Shimanami Sea Road*). This series of 10 long bridges connects Imabari (just north of Matsuyama) with Onomichi (just east of Hiroshima) by way of a series of islands in the Seto Inland Sea. Most of the islands on the Shimanami route were accessible only by ferry until the bridges were completed in 1999, and despite the new infrastructure they still run on island time. A trip over the Shimanami bridges lets you take in fishing villages, tangerine orchards, pearl farms, seaweed pastures, and stretches of sparking sea. It's the only bridge between Shikoku and Honshu on which you can cycle, and it has quickly become one of the most popular cycling routes in western Japan.

Biking the Shimanami Kaido is a safe, exciting experience that anyone with a reasonable level of fitness can accomplish. The bridges were built with cyclists in mind: a separate cycling track runs along each bridge, so you won't deal with car traffic for almost the entire ride. Cycling paths are clearly marked on the islands, and maps are readily available. The cycling isn't strenuous, so don't get discouraged by the first big corkscrew pathway up from Imabari to the Kurushima Ohashi, or the unattractive hills on the first island, Oshima. After that it's clear sailing.

Biking straight to Onomichi takes about six hours, but you don't have to cycle the whole way: leave the bikes on any of the islands' rental stations and take a ferry or bus the rest of the way across. Staff at the rental stations have all the schedules and are very helpful. Your hotel can even send your luggage ahead.

VISITOR INFORMATION

ICIEA 今治市国際交流協会. The shop workers in Imbari won't speak much English, so if you have communication problems go through Imabari's helpful International Organization. ⊠ *1–1–16 Kitahorai-cho, Imabari, Ehime-ken* ☎ *089/834–5763* ⊕ *iciea.imabari-cc.ac.jp* ☉ *Weekdays 8:30–5:15.*

BICYCLE RENTALS

Sunrise Itoyama. Rental bikes here are ¥500 a day plus a ¥1,000 refundable deposit (kept if you return the bike to a different rental station). ⊠ *2–8–1 Sunaba-cho, Imabari* ☎ *089/841–3196* ☉ *May–Sept., daily 8–8; Oct.–Mar., daily 8–5.*

WHAT TO SEE

★ **Oyamazumi Jinja** 大山祇神社. Omishima, three islands over from Imabari, is home to this shrine. In the 8th century victorious warriors started leaving their weaponry here after battle as thanks for divine favor. The museum on the grounds of the shrine holds more than two-thirds of the nation's designated National Treasures in swords, spears, breastplates, and helmets. ⊠ *3327 Miya-ura, Oshima-cho* ☎ *089/782–0032* ☜ *¥1,000* ☉ *Daily 8:30–4:30.*

WHERE TO STAY

Hotel reviews have been condensed for this book. Please go to Fodors. com for full reviews of each property.

$$
MINSHUKU
▥ **Minshuku Kohan** 民宿湖畔. If you're taking two days to cycle the Shimanami, Omishima Island is a good place to break the journey. **Pros:** friendly owners; filling meals. **Cons:** minimal English-language support. ⊠ *5828–2 Miyaura, Oshima-cho* ☎ *0897/82–0871* ▱ *6 rooms* ☖ *Inroom: no phone, a/c (some). In-hotel: beachfront, some pets allowed* ▤ *No credit cards* ▥ *Some meals.*

Kyushu

WORD OF MOUTH

"Nagasaki is a very interesting city . . . Dejima is no longer an island, but it's a well-preserved open-air museum. Some other western buildings are worth visiting, too, such as the Glover Mansion and Garden."

—someotherguy

WELCOME TO KYUSHU

TOP REASONS TO GO

★ **Diverse Cities:** Fukuoka has free-wheeling nightlife, Nagasaki radiates Old World charm, Kumamoto's castle contrasts with traffic-heavy streets, and Kagoshima's palm trees calm travelers.

★ **Gastronomy Domain:** Find the sought-after Hakata ramen in Fukuoka. Nagasaki has *chanpon* (seafood and vegetable noodle soup), and Kagoshima has *kurobuta tonkatsu* (breaded pork cutlet).

★ **Inside the Volcano:** Mt. Aso is notoriously active, as is Sakura-jima, across the bay from Kagoshima. Hot springs are found throughout Kyushu.

★ **Into the Wild:** With its lava flows, outlying islands, rugged mountains, and national parks, Kyushu is an adventurer's dream. Most trails require only good shoes, water, and some time.

★ **Remote Access:** A high-speed train links Kumamoto with Kagoshima in an hour, and in another hour, you can be on the hot sand of Ibusuki's beaches.

1 Fukuoka. After landing at one of the most convenient airports in the world, you can be downtown in six minutes by subway. Fabulous dining, ultramodern shopping, and nicely humming nightlife are among the joys that this vibrant city has to offer.

2 Nagasaki. Consistently rated by the Japanese a favorite destination, Nagasaki has maintained its rich and colorful international past even in the face of the devastation brought on by the plutonium bomb that ended World War II. Today you'll still see the spirit of entrepreneurship that helped the city rebuild itself.

3 Kumamoto. The Herculean effort to restore Kumamoto's massive 17th-century castle was completed just in time for its 400-year anniversary in 2007. Impressive and menacing, its black facade and angular aspects give it the appearance of a sinister hideout. Suizen-ji Joju-en, a luxurious garden, is another highlight.

4 Aso-san (Mt Aso). Aso National Park contains lakes, fields, and this chain of five volcanic peaks situated inside the largest caldera in the world.

5 Kagoshima. The mild climate and easygoing vibe draw comparisons to Naples, Italy, but locals fear that one day the smoking, rumbling cone of Sakura-jima out in the bay will make Pompeii a more apt analogy. Famous hot-sand baths and remote beaches are found along the southern reaches of the prefecture.

Nihon-kai (Sea of Japan)

Oka
Hirado   Karatsu
Yamanaka   Imabuku   Ochi
Maetsuyoshi   Kusuku
Nakiri   Imari   Arita   34   Saga
Sasebo   Kashima
Tokuman   Kawatana
Kakinoura
Kashinoura   Omura   Isahaya
Mieda   34   57   Shimabara
Nagasaki   Obama
Fukahori   Arie
Nomo   *Tachibana-Wan*   *Shimabara-wan*

0   20 mi
0   20 km

Hondo
Kami-jima
Shimo-jima
Ushibuka
Minamata
Tajiri
Akune   Izumi
Miyanojo
Naka-koshiki   Sendai
Kushikino
Koshiki-kaikyo   Ijuin   3
Izaku
Oura   Kawanabe
Miyagahama
Makurazuki

Ariake-kai
Amakusa-nada
Yatsushiro-kai

GETTING ORIENTED

Situated perfectly as the gateway to the continent of Asia, Kyushu is quite close to the Korean Peninsula. It's considerably west and a little south of Tokyo. A good route starts with a flight or Shinkansen run into Hakata/Fukuoka in the north, moves down to Nagasaki on the west coast by express train, winds eastward by bus or train to the central city of Kumamoto, with a possible side trip to Aso-san (Mt. Aso), and a jaunt south to the city of Kagoshima via the fancy high-speed train, then farther south by local train to the thermal spa resort area of Ibusuki, famous for its hot-sand baths, where you can be heat-treated on the pictur-esque, breezy beach.

6 Kirishima-yaku Kokuritsu Koen. This mountainous national park northeast of Kagoshima rivals Takachiho as one of the most sacred places in the country.

7 Yufuin. Yufuin is a delightful and popular upscale hot-springs resort beneath the dramatic twin-peaked mountain known as Yufu-dake.

TAKACHIHO, THE CRADLE OF MYTH

Deep in the sacred mountains, a spiritual place full of atmosphere, is the birthplace of Japanese mythology. A visit to the Takachiho region takes you to the places where the gods first alighted on Earth, hid in caves, and created the first water spring.

(This page above) The ritual Kaguro dance performed in Takachiho; (opposite page upper right) Ama-no-Iwato Shrine; (opposite page bottom left) Takachiho Gorge

These days, one of the biggest booms in the domestic Japanese travel market is the draw of spiritual places and power spots. More than one million Japanese visit Takachiho every year, yet few foreigners are aware of this fascinating and important region of the country. Be one of the first to get in on the trend. A visit to Takachiho takes you to a magical and mysterious region that is still intact, not unlike how it was generations ago. There you can find the spots where, according to the myths, the gods, who are still worshipped as a part of everyday Japanese life, first came to Earth. There you can see the wonderful *Kagura* dances to the gods that have been performed since ancient times. Talk a walk in the mountains, imbibe the sacred waters of mountain springs, and find your own path.

DANCING TO THE GODS

Kagura is an ancient ritual dance to give thanks to the gods that has been performed since ancient times. It is performed throughout the night in homes between December and January. Visitors are welcome for a small fee. A shortened, but excellent, tourist version can be seen every night from 8 pm at Kagura Hozonkan, in the grounds of Takachiho Shrine. Make sure not to miss it.

VISITING TAKACHIHO

Both Takachiho and Takachiho-no-Mine (*see* ⇨ *Kirishima-yaku Kokuritsu Koen*) claim to be the places where Amaterasu's grandson descended to Earth to establish the Japanese Imperial Family. Many years ago officials from both towns went to court, but the judge deferred, ruling that each town had the right to believe it was the actual place where the gods descended to Earth. Both places are very spiritual and worthy of a visit.

The best way to spend time in Takachiho is to visit some of the more-remote places you can't visit on a half-day trip. This will take you out into the mountains and steep valleys and enable you to marvel at how the people of ancient times in these parts could create such marvelous myths perfectly matching their environment. You'll marvel even more at the sense that these myths are still a part of everyday life in this region. There are dozens of places to visit. Here are just a few of the main attractions. *For information on reaching Takachiho, see* ⇨ *Kumamoto.*

WHAT TO SEE

Make sure to get a guidebook and even a guide from the excellent local **Takachiho Tourist Office** (☎ *0982/73–1213* ⊕ *takachiho-kanko.info*), which can connect you with an English-speaking

guide. But go to some places by yourself to enjoy the atmosphere.

Ama-no-Iwato Shrine 天岩戸神社. This shrine contains the cave where the sun goddess Amaterasu hid until Ame-no-Uzume managed to lure her out. If you apply at the entrance, a Shinto priest will take you into the sacred precinct and across the valley so you can see the actual cave. ⊠ *1073–1 Iwato, Takachiho-cho, Nishiusuki-gun* ⊠ *Free* ۞ *Dawn–dusk*

Ama-no-Yasugawara 天安河原. A dark but deeply spiritual place, this huge, dark cave faces onto a small river. According to the myth, the gods gathered here to figure out how to get Amaterasu out of her cave. Visitors pile stones on top of each other to leave their wishes, and the place is filled with little stone piles creating an otherworldly atmosphere. ⊠ *Iwato, Takachiho-cho, Nishiusuki-gun* ⊠ *Free* ۞ *Dawn–dusk*

Takachiho Gorge 高千穂峡. This is an impressive ravine of the Gokase River with many waterfalls cascading into it. You can walk along a hiking path at the edge or see it by renting a boat from the booth on the river below the parking lot (¥1,500/30 minutes for up to three people), though boats are not always available. ⊠ *Mitai, Takachiho-cho, Nishiusuki-gun* ⊠ *Gorge free, boat rental 1,500* ۞ *Sept.–July 19, daily 8:30–5, July 20–Aug., daily 7:30–6.*

Updated
by Peter
McMillan

Kyushu's landscape couldn't be more varied, with active yet accessible volcanoes, numerous thermal spas, endless fields of rice and famous potatoes, forested mountains capped by winter snows, busy harbors along lively seacoasts, and pleasant seaside retreats.

Kyushu has been inhabited and favored for human settlement for more than 10,000 years, and ruins and artifacts thousands of years old suggest that the region was the most important gateway for human contact between Japan and the rest of Asia. The most rapid anthropological changes occurred from about 300 BC to AD 300, when rice became widely cultivated and complex pottery and tools began to appear, thus conveniently framing the Yayoi period. Continuous trade with China brought prosperity and culture, and advanced ceramics were introduced—and then produced—by Korean masters who were employed and enslaved by the local fiefdoms of the 16th and 17th centuries.

It was also through Kyushu that Western knowledge, weapons, religion, and cooking methods first made their way into Japan. In the mid-1500s Nagasaki saw the arrival of fleets of enterprising and courageous European merchants and missionaries, and the resulting frenzy of trade in ideas and goods continued unabated until the Tokugawa Shogunate slammed the door shut on the whole show in the early 1600s. What brought things to a halt was a plague of panic induced by an alarming new phenomenon: Christianity.

The Portuguese and other Catholics not afraid to preach to the natives were expelled and permanently barred. The Dutch, however, were considered more money-minded, and therefore less threatening, and were permitted to stay—under scrutiny and isolation. They were housed within the enclave of Dejima, a man-made island in Nagasaki Harbor, where they were encouraged to keep bringing in coveted goods but were constantly guarded and watched. For the next 200 years, this profitable little arrangement would be the only form of contact the West would have with Japan until the arrival of Perry's forceful "Black Ship."

Today Kyushu is a fascinating mix of old and new, nature and culture. Much of the remote and rugged interior—such as that surrounding Mt.

11

Aso's fuming cone—is still an isolated wilderness, yet the amenities of modern life are well supplied in cities and coastal resorts.

⇨ *See the glossary at the end of this book for definitions of the common Japanese words and suffixes used in this chapter.*

PLANNING

WHEN TO GO

In early spring it's pleasantly warm, and the greenery is at its best. May and June usher in heavy rains, and July and August are intensely muggy. September is summery, but watch for typhoons, which can blow in at any time until late October. Autumn colors, appearing in late October or early November, are nice, particularly in the north. In January and February the mountains of central Kyushu receive a little snowfall, and that's when the Siberian cranes show up for the gentle winter the region enjoys.

GETTING HERE AND AROUND

Travel in Kyushu is for the most part straightforward, with trains providing the bulk of the transport. Highway buses are useful for certain routes. Frequent and inexpensive ferries ply the bays and ports, linking Kyushu with offshore islands. During holiday seasons you'll want to reserve seats on express trains, but with most buses and ferries turning up 20 minutes prior to departure you should get on board with no trouble.

AIR TRAVEL

Air routes link Kyushu's major cities with Tokyo and Osaka. Fukuoka, Nagasaki, and Kagoshima have the most frequent and useful daily connections and offer some international flights. When using domestic carriers like ANA you need not enter and return from the same city: it's easy to fly into Fukuoka and out of Kagoshima, for example.

Airline Contacts All Nippon Airways *(ANA)* (☎ *0120/029–222*). **Japan Airlines** (☎ *0120/25–5971*). **Skymark** (☎ *050/3116–7370*).

BUS TRAVEL

Buses make useful connections around Kyushu, and if you don't have a JR Rail Pass, they are often much cheaper than the trains. For example, the bus between Nagasaki and Kumamoto is half the price and takes about the same time; plus you don't have to make any changes or wait for connections, as you do with trains. A highway bus makes a trip between Kumamoto to Yufuin, either direct or with a stopover at the Aso-san crater.

CAR TRAVEL

Car rental is a good idea in Kyushu if you have lots of time and if you explore the more-out-of-the-way places such as Aso-san. All the major rental outfits have offices in the big cities near the JR stations.

TRAIN TRAVEL

High-speed train service now links Kumamoto with Kagoshima, via a quick and easy change in Yatsushiro. The new Tsubame (Swallow) train is chic, posh, spacious, and uncrowded. Express trains making the popular run between Fukuoka and Nagasaki are jammed on weekends and holidays, so book at least a day ahead.

ABOUT THE RESTAURANTS

Fresh fish is served everywhere on Kyushu. Appetites are on the hearty side here, so there's lots of meat, too. Local specialties abound and are often reasonably priced. In the bigger cities like Fukuoka, Nagasaki, Kumamoto, and Kagoshima—and along the stylish new streets of Yufuin—you'll find plenty of Western-style restaurants.

ABOUT THE HOTELS

You can find the usual American hotel chains, with all the familiar extras, in places like Fukuoka and Nagasaki. The rural areas surrounding Aso and Kagoshima have snug little inns with views of the surrounding peaks. In Yufuin nearly all hotels and *ryokan* (guesthouses) offer soothing thermal mineral water baths. Unless otherwise noted, all hotel rooms have private baths. Reservations are essential during the long national holidays, particularly Golden Week (late April–early May), Obon (mid-August), and New Year's (first week of January) when Japanese tourists flock to the island.

WHAT IT COSTS IN YEN					
	¢	$	$$	$$$	$$$$
RESTAURANTS	under ¥800	¥800–¥1,000	¥1,000–¥2,000	¥2,000–¥3,000	over ¥3,000
HOTELS	under ¥8,000	¥8,000–¥12,000	¥12,000–¥18,000	¥18,000–¥22,000	over ¥22,000

Restaurant prices are per person for a main course, set meal, or equivalent combinations of smaller dishes. Hotel prices are for a double room, excluding 5% tax and tip.

VISITOR INFORMATION

Every major city has tourist information offices near shopping, sightseeing, and eating areas, and one or more near the high-speed train exit of each JR train station. Generally, one English speaker is on duty during peak travel hours. The bigger hotels usually have front-desk employees who speak and understand some English; they are good sources for information on local sights and restaurant recommendations.

FUKUOKA 福岡

1,175 km (730 mi) west of Tokyo, 622 km (386 mi) west of Shin-Osaka.

Fukuoka is a good base to begin exploring Kyushu. To get a sense of the city, walk along the meandering Naka-gawa river. The stunning Canal City shopping complex, a 15-minute walk west of Hakata Station, is full of great people-watching, shops, and dining. You'll find a bit of everything, from global coffee and fast-food outlets to famous local ramen.

For night owls, there's plenty happening in the west-central downtown alleys in an area known as Tenjin at truly astounding hours. Friday nights only begin at midnight, usually with a huge and hearty bowl of *tonkotsu* (pork-bone soup) ramen—often referred to as "Hakata ramen"—a rich, tasty staple that locals seem to depend on for their legendary all-night stamina.

On the Menu

The most celebrated dish in Fukuoka is *tonkotsu ramen*, a strongly flavored pork-bone-based soup with extra-thin noodles, scallions, and strips of roasted pork. Usually it gets heaps of garlic, chili pepper, and other toppings. Wherever you are on Kyushu, *ramen* can never be too far, and it's always good.

Popular in Nagasaki, *shippoku* consists of elaborately prepared dishes that blend the flavors of Asia and Europe. Served Chinese style on a revolving round tabletop and perfect for large groups, shippoku is not a solitary affair. Another Nagasaki favorite, *chanpon*, consists of Chinese-style noodles, vegetables, and shellfish in a thick soup. *Sara udon* has the chan-pon ingredients fried crispy instead of boiled.

Ba-sashi (raw horse meat) is a Kumamoto specialty. Perhaps an easier-to-swallow delicacy is *karashi renkon*, slices of lotus root stuffed with mustard and/or cayenne and deep-fried. Compared to the subdued flavors of most Japanese cuisine, these dishes attest to the region's bolder palate.

In Kagoshima, don't pass up a chance to try the famed *kurobuta tonkatsu*, or breaded fried pork cutlet from locally bred black pigs. There's also *satsuma-age*, a fried-fish cake stuffed with ingredients like garlic, cheese, meat, potato, or burdock root. *Imo-jochu*, a much-loved regional spirit distilled from sweet potatoes, helps wash down these goodies.

The Naka-gawa divides the city. Everything west of the river is known as Fukuoka, while everything east—including the station and airport—is referred to as Hakata, so trains or planes might say to or from Hakata rather than Fukuoka. But don't be confused: Hakata is just a *ku*, or district, of the whole place, which is still Fukuoka.

GETTING HERE AND AROUND

Fukuoka Airport is Kyushu's main airport. It's just two stops away—only six minutes—from Fukuoka's Hakata train station on the Kuko subway line. All Nippon Airways (ANA), Japan Airlines (JAL), and Skymark Airlines (SKY) fly the 1½-hour route to Fukuoka Airport from Tokyo's Haneda Airport. JAL also flies once daily (1¾ hours) between Tokyo's Narita International Airport and Fukuoka Airport. ANA and JAL have 12 direct flights (1¼ hours) between Osaka and Fukuoka.

The Kyushu Kyuko Bus Company makes the two-hour trip between Fukuoka's Tenjin Bus Center and Nagasaki. Frequent buses make the four-hour trip between Fukuoka (departing from Hakata Kotsu Bus Center and Tenjin Bus Center) and Kagoshima.

JR Shinkansen trains travel between Tokyo and Hakata Station in Fukuoka (5½ hours) via Osaka and Hiroshima. The regular fare is ¥22,000 and there are 15 daily runs. Regular JR Express trains also travel this route, but take at least twice as long.

After World War II Fukuoka was rebuilt with wide, tree-lined avenues arranged on an easy-to-navigate Western-style grid. The subway system connects the downtown attractions with a convenient extension to the international airport. The two major transportation hubs are Hakata Station and Tenjin Station. Tenjin, in the heart of downtown Fukuoka, is the terminal for both subway lines. The Kuko Line runs to Hakata Station and on to Fukuoka (Hakata) Airport, and the Hakozaki Line runs out toward the bay. Fares start at ¥200.

A low-cost bus (¥100) operates in the city center. Most city buses leave from **Hakata Kotsu Bus Center** across the street from Hakata Station, and from Tenjin Bus Center.

Airport Information Fukuoka Airport (☎ *092/483–7003*).

Bus Contacts Kyushu Kyuko Bus Company (☎ *092/734–2500 or 092/771–2961*).

Bus Depots Hakata Kotsu Bus Center (☎ *092/431–1171* 🚌 *¥100*). **Tenjin Bus Center** (☎ *092/734–2500 or 092/771–2961*).

VISITOR INFORMATION

The **Fukuoka International Association** has an English-speaking staff, and English-language newspapers and periodicals are available for visitors to read. **Fukuoka Station Information** offers information on travel, sightseeing, and accommodations.

Contact JTB Kyushu, Tenjin branch (✉ *1F Tenjin Bldg., 2–12–1 Tenjin* ☎ *092/731–5221* ☺ *Weekdays 10–7:30, weekends 10–6*).

EXPLORING FUKUOKA

Canal City キャナルシティ. To while away the hours people-watching, go for a stroll around this astounding area. Restaurants range from upscale dining to takeout, and there are countless cafés, shops, hotels, and a huge cinema in the area. At one end is a zigzagging water-lined patio-scape where folks go to see and be seen. At the other end is a futuristic half-dome structure ingeniously tiered with balconies lined with shops and cafés, and it's all done up in an eye-catching palette of salmon pinks and pastel blues. The tantalizing sight lines, liberal use of glass, open space, and clever angles make it seem as though you can see into, over, and under everything else in the structure. ✉ *1–2 Sumiyoshi, Hakata-ku* ☎ *092/282–2525* ⊕ *www.canalcity.co.jp.*

Ohori Koen 大濠公園. The lake in this park was once part of an impressive moat surrounding Fukuoka's castle. A leisurely 2-km (1-mi) path follows its perimeter. In early April the pink and white flowers of the park's 2,600 cherry trees present a dazzling display. Within the park is the **Fukuoka City Art Museum** 福岡市美術館, which houses a few notable works by Dalí, Miró, Chagall, and Warhol. Across from it is a traditional Japanese garden. From Hakata Station, take the subway to Ohori Koen Station; it's a 20-minute ride. ✉ *1–6 Ohorikoen, Chuo-ku* ☎ *092/714–6051* ⊕ *www.fukuoka-art-museum.jp* 🚌 *Park free, museum ¥200, garden ¥240* ☺ *Museum and garden, Tues.–Sun. 9:30–5:30 (July and Aug. 9:30–7:30).*

Shofuku-ji 聖福寺. The monk Eisai (1141–1215) returned from a long stint in China to introduce Zen Buddhism to Japan and planted the first tea-bush seeds. Nowadays most tea is grown in other regions such as

Shizuoka, but you can still buy the green tea from this region, with its legendary hue and flavor, in stores as far away as Tokyo. Eisai also established Shofuku-ji, Japan's first Zen temple, which the inscription on the main gate by Emperor Gotoba commemorates. In Zen tradition, the grounds and structure reflect the calm, austere nature of this deeply meditative philosophy. The bronze bell in the belfry was designated an Important Cultural Property. The temple is a 15-minute walk northwest from Hakata Station, or a five-minute Nishitetsu bus ride from the station to the nearby Oku-no-do stop (you can pick up the bus on the main road in front of Hakata Station's West Exit). ⊠ *6–1 Gokusho-machi, Hakata-ku* ☎ *092/291–0775* ⊕ *www.shofukuji.or.jp/index.html* ⊡ *Free* ⊙ *Daily 9–5.*

WHERE TO EAT

$$$
JAPANESE

✕ **Bassin** バサン. Inside the fancy Plaza Hotel Tenjin, Bassin (locals pronounce it "Bah-san") has wooden counters and furniture set off against cream-color walls and art deco lamps. Try the garden salad with seaweed dressing or the marinated tofu. Unique dishes include grilled chicken in a burdock-root sauce, and stewed snapping-turtle meat with summer vegetables. More-elaborate Japanese courses run ¥3,500–¥7,000. ⊠ *Plaza Hotel Tenjin, 1–9–63 Daimyo, Chuo-ku* ☎ *092/739–3210* ⊕ *www.plaza-hotel.net/bassin/index.html.*

¢
JAPANESE

✕ **Deko** デコ. Deko has no English menu, but the daily special, or *teishoku*, is a reliable choice. The central low tables of this boisterous bar are Japanese style; regular tables and chairs are in the back. The salmon-and-basil spring rolls are an excellent appetizer. It's between the Hakata train station and Yakuin subway station on Sumiyoshi-dori. ⊠ *B1 Rasa Bldg.,1–24–22 Takasago, Chuo-ku* ☎ *092/526–7070.*

¢
JAPANESE
★

✕ **Horin** 鳳凛. To prepare for a big night in Tenjin, this is a convenient, delicious, and inexpensive place to grab some tonkotsu ramen beforehand. For less than ¥800 you can dive into a big bowl of thin noodles in a steamy, pork-based soup garnished with sliced pork, chopped onions, slivers of ginger, and whatever other toppings you choose. The most recommended and popular topping is the sliced *kikurage* ("tree jellyfish" or black mushrooms)—high in protein, full of vitamin B. It's on a corner, just off the south side of Kokutai-dori, two blocks west of Haruyoshi Bridge, on the way to all-night fun in the Tenjin district. ⊠ *3–21–15 Haruyoshi, Chuo-ku* ☎ *092/716–6755* ⊕ *www.ramen-hourin.jp* ⊟ *No credit cards.*

$
JAPANESE
★

✕ **Ichi-ran** 一蘭. Folks in Fukuoka wait in long lines to get their fix of distinctive extra-thin noodles swimming in a rectangular black box of pork-bone broth topped with tasty slices of *char-shu*, or roasted pork, *negi* (green onions), and sprinkles of *togarashi* (red pepper). Additional toppings such as kikurage, extra pork, or boiled eggs can be added for ¥100 each. The clerk gives you an order form (with English), and you indicate exactly how you like it, from the amount of shredded garlic to the fat content (locals go for more fat to get that sweet flavor they adore). You then buy a ticket from the machine inside the door. The clerk will help you if you are new to this gig. Hang onto it until you are seated in back at a private cubicle with a curtain that conceals all but the smells of the intoxicating substance you are about to receive. You place your ticket and order form on the counter below the curtain, and moments later the goods appear. The noodles taste best when ordered slightly chewy, and the soup is flavorful even with a light fat content. There are several branches, including one in the basement of the Hakata Station complex (and even some in Tokyo), but the best one is in Canal City. ⊠ *B1F 1–2– 22 Sumiyoshi, Hakata-ku* ☎ *092/263–2201* ▭ *No credit cards.*

WHERE TO STAY

Hotel reviews have been condensed for this book. Please go to Fodors. com for full reviews of each property.

$$ 🏨 **Canal City Fukuoka Washington Hotel** キャナルシテイ福岡ワシントンホテル.
HOTEL This is no ordinary Washington Hotel; it's much classier than others members of the chain. **Pros:** great value; located almost as conveniently as the Hyatt but much cheaper; flat-screen TVs. **Cons:** limited English spoken; some really small rooms; carpets could use some sprucing up. ⊠ *1–2–20 Sumiyoshi, Hakata-ku* ☎ *092/282–8800* 🖷 *092/282–0757* ⊕ *www.fukuoka-wh.com* ⤵ *423 rooms* ⌂ *In-room: a/c, refrigerator. In-hotel: 2 restaurants, laundry facilities, Internet terminal* ⦿ *No meals.*

$$$$ 🏨 **Fukuoka Grand Hyatt Hotel** グランド・ハイアット・福岡. Far and away
HOTEL the best digs in town, the Grand Hyatt overlooks—or rather, looks
★ into—the Canal City entertainment complex. **Pros:** the coolest spot to base yourself, bar none; feels like you're in a space movie. **Cons:** there have been reports of indifferent service, tricky charges, and facility glitches; could use better soundproofing. ⊠ *1–2–82 Sumiyoshi, Canal City, Hakata-ku* ☎ *092/282–1234* 🖷 *092/282–2817* ⊕ *www.fukuoka. grand.hyatt.com* ⤵ *370 rooms, 14 suites* ⌂ *In-room: a/c, Internet. In-hotel: 4 restaurants, bars, pool, gym* ⦿ *No meals.*

$$$–$$$$ 🏨 **Hakata Excel Hotel Tokyu** 博多エクセルホテル東急. This is an upscale,
HOTEL Western-style hotel located near the Nakasu Kawabata Station (on the way into town from the airport or five minutes out from Hakata Station; use Exit 1). **Pros:** great location; free breakfast. **Cons:** perhaps a bit bland and businesslike for some. ⊠ *4–6–7 Nakasu, Hakata-ku* ☎ *092/262–0109* 🖷 *092/262–5578* ⊕ *www.hakata-e.tokyuhotels.co.jp/ ja/index.html* ⤵ *176 rooms, 2 suites* ⌂ *In-room: a/c, refrigerator, Internet. In-hotel: 2 restaurants, bar, Internet terminal* ⦿ *Breakfast.*

$ 🏨 **Toyoko Inn Hakata Nishinakasu** 東横イン博多西中洲. There are more
HOTEL than 250 Toyoko Inn hotels are all over Japan, and for budget travel-
Fodor's Choice ers they are clearly the best option, offering excellent accommodations
★ and facilities for the lowest prices in highly central locations. **Pros:** five minutes to Hakata Station and Naka River; nice, free toiletries set; free breakfast. **Cons:** rooms are adequate but not overly large; late check-in. ⊠ *1–16 Nishinakasu, Chuo-ku, Fukuoka-ken* ☎ *092/739–1045* 🖷 *092/739–1046* ⊕ *www.toyoko-inn.com/e_hotel/00044/index.html* ⤵ *260 rooms* ⌂ *In-room: a/c, refrigerator, Internet. In-hotel: restaurant, laundry facilities, Internet terminal, Wi-Fi hotspot* ⦿ *Breakfast.*

NIGHTLIFE

Fukuoka seems forever in the throes of an ongoing party—perhaps in a heroic endeavor to put off the inevitable hangover—but the surest places for memorable nightlife action are the Nakasu and Tenjin areas, which run along the Naka-gawa. Nakasu is on the east side of the river; Tenjin is on the west.

Propeller Drive プロペラドライブ. To be seen with the in crowd, be sure to drop by the bar and café known as Propeller Drive. It's open late every night, and you are practically guaranteed to see some of the prettiest and most stylishly dressed women in the world—Hakata Bi-jin—as well as a few confident guys who are invigorated rather than intimidated by this. It's fancy, but there's no cover charge. All three floors have white stucco walls, and the second floor has a wonderful overhang with tables where you can sit and enjoy the lovely view. Countless intricately framed mirrors reflect the light of crystal chandeliers. ⊠ *1–13–30 Imaizumi, Chuo-ku* ☎ *092/715–6322.*

SHOPPING

Fukuoka is known for two traditional folk crafts: Hakata *ningyo* (dolls) and Hakata *obi* (kimono sashes). Made of fired clay, hand-painted with bright colors and distinctive expressions, Hakata ningyo represent children, women, samurai, and geisha. The obi are made of a local silk that has a slightly coarse texture; bags and purses made of this silk make excellent souvenirs.

Kyushu has a rich ceramics tradition. The shops and kilns of Arita, Karatsu, and Imari and other towns of Saga Prefecture, in particular, continue to produce fine pottery, especially a delicate-looking but surprisingly tough type of porcelain. The earthenware of Karatsu, particularly the fine tea ceremony wares, are much admired by ceramics collectors both within and outside Japan.

Iwataya 岩田屋. The seventh floor of the department store carries the most complete selection of local merchandise, including Hakata dolls, silk, and ceramics. From the Tenjin subway station, take Exit W-5 and follow the street straight for two blocks. ⊠ *2–5–35 Tenjin, Chuo-ku* ☎ *092/721–1111* ⊕ *www.i.iwataya-mitsukoshi.co.jp.*

Kawabata Shotengai 川端商店街 *(Kawabata Shopping Arcade)*. Traditional Edo-style restaurants and shops selling quaint souvenirs line the stretching along the Naka-gawa from the Nakasu-Kawabata subway station to Canal City.

NAGASAKI 長崎

154 km (96 mi) southwest of Fukuoka (Hakata Station).

Blessed with a breathtaking location, Nagasaki is strung together on a long series of hillocks in a scenic valley that follows the arms of the Urakami River down into a gentle harbor. Unlike Hiroshima, the city was left with no suitably intact reminders of the atomic bombing, and perhaps for this reason, there were apparently no compunctions about rebuilding the town right up to the edge of a tiny ground-zero circle with a stark steel monument at its center. Still, relatively new as it all may be, everything here exudes flavors of Nagasaki's international history, from the city's lively and compact Chinatown to the European-style mansions and Catholic churches on the hillsides.

In the mid-16th century, Portuguese missionaries, including Saint Francis Xavier, came ashore to preach throughout Kyushu. This new and altruistic religion—coinciding with the arrival of firearms—threatened to spread like an epidemic through the impoverished and restive masses of the feudal system, and, in 1597, to give bite to a new decree by Chief Minister Toyotomi to stifle worship, 26 followers were publicly crucified in Nagasaki, an act that brought condemnation from the world. This cruel and shocking display was followed not long after by Tokugawa's nationwide edict making the practice of Christianity a capital offense.

All foreigners were expelled except the Dutch, who, considered to be lacking overt propensities to convert anything but profits on trades, were sequestered on an island, Dejima. Of the local population, only merchants and prostitutes were allowed direct interactions with them. The Dutch took over the considerable trade brokering between China and Japan formerly done by the Portuguese. Though the rest of Japan was strangled by isolation and starved for foreign goodies, Nagasaki continued to prosper by making use of this tiny but important offshore loophole in the Tokugawa anti-trade policy out in the harbor. This arrangement lasted until 1859, when insular Japan was forced to open up to the outside world.

Once other ports became popular, the city lost much of its special status. Centuries later, Mitsubishi decided to concentrate its arms manufacturing and shipbuilding capabilities here; the industrial presence and bad weather over the primary target of Kokura in northern Kyushu made Nagasaki the target for the second atomic bomb drop in 1945.

The city isn't small, but as it lies in a long winding valley you experience it in small, manageable increments. Similarities with San Francisco are frequently touted, and the comparison is not far off—although the posters advertising whale-bacon and manga remind you of where you are.

GETTING HERE AND AROUND

Nagasaki Airport is approximately one hour by bus or car from Nagasaki. A regular shuttle bus travels between Nagasaki Airport and Nagasaki Station and costs ¥1,200. All Nippon Airways and Japan Airlines fly daily from Haneda Airport in Tokyo to Nagasaki Airport (1¾ hours). From Osaka the flights are about 1¼ hours.

The **Kyushu Kyuko Bus Company** runs buses between Fukuoka's Tenjin Bus Center and **Nagasaki Bus Terminal;** the trip takes two hours. The **Nagasaki Ken-ei Bus Company** can get you to Unzen (¥1,900), a string of hot springs on the Shimabara Peninsula, in two hours, and direct to Kumamoto in three hours for ¥3,600.

The JR Kamome Express train costs ¥4,710 and takes one hour, 51 minutes from Fukuoka's Hakata Station to **Nagasaki Station.** To get to Kumamoto from Nagasaki, take the JR Kamome to Tosu (two hours) and switch to the Tsubame Relay (one hour). Note that unless you have

This godlike man with outstretched arms stands at the center of Nagasaki's Heiwa Koen.

a free ride with a RailPass, at ¥6,770, it's going to be nearly double the cost of the bus and will take almost the same amount of time.

Nagasaki is small enough to cover on foot; otherwise, the streetcar system is the most convenient mode of transportation. Stops are posted in English, and lines extend to every attraction in town. You can purchase a one-day streetcar pass (¥500) at tourist offices and major hotels. Otherwise, pay ¥100 as you get off the streetcar at any stop. If you wish to transfer from one streetcar to another, get a *norikae kippu* (transfer ticket) from the driver of the first one. Local buses are not as convenient, and the routes, timetables, and fares are complicated.

One-hour **cruises** of Nagasaki Harbor depart from Nagasaki-ko (Nagasaki Port) at 10:30, noon, 1:30, and 3; the cost is ¥1,300.

Airport Information Nagasaki Airport (✉ *Mishima-machi, Omura-city* ☎ *0120/029–222 or 03/5435–0750*).

Bus Contacts Kyushu Kyuko Bus Company (☎ *092/734–2500*). **Nagasaki Ken-ei Bus Company** (☎ *095/823–6155*).

Bus Depot Nagasaki Bus Terminal (✉ *3–1 Daikoku-machi* ☎ *095/826–6221*).

Train Station Nagasaki Station (✉ *1–89 Onoue-machi* ☎ *095/826–4336*).

Tour Information Cruises (☎ *095/824–0088* 💺 *¥1,300*).

VISITOR INFORMATION

The **City Tourist Information Center** provides English assistance, maps, and brochures. The **Nagasaki Prefectural Tourist Information Center** is across the street from Nagasaki Station. Use the pedestrian bridge on the second floor of the station to reach it. English travel information for the entire prefecture, including maps and bus schedules, are available.

Contacts City Tourist Information Center (✉ *Inside Nagasaki Station, 1–1 Onoue-machi* ☎ *095/823–3631* ⊕ *www1.city.nagasaki.nagasaki.jp* ⊘ *Daily 8–8*). **Nagasaki Prefectural Tourist Information Center** (✉ *2F Nagasaki Ken-ei Bus Terminal Bldg., 3–1 Daikoku-machi* ☎ *095/828–7875* ⊕ *www.nagasaki-tabinet. com* ⊘ *Daily 9–5:45*).

EXPLORING NAGASAKI

While most of the interesting sights, restaurants, and shopping areas are south of Nagasaki Station, the Peace Park and the Atomic Bomb Museum are to the north, about 10 to 15 minutes by streetcar or taxi.

Dejima 出島. When the government deported foreigners from Japan in the mid-17th century, Dutch traders were the only Westerners allowed to remain—but they were relegated to and confined on this artificial island in Nagasaki Harbor. Here you can see a 450-year-old mix of Dutch housing styles that is popular among Japanese tourists. Take Streetcar 1 to the Dejima stop. ✉ *6–3 Dejima-machi* ☎ *095/821–7200* ⊕ *www1.city.nagasaki.nagasaki.jp/dejima* ✐ *¥500* ⊘ *Daily 8–6*.

Genbaku Shiryokan 原爆資料館 *(Atomic Bomb Museum)*. The spiral staircase of this museum takes you down into a dark, depressing collection of video loops, dioramas, and exhibits that demonstrate the devastating effects of the bomb that was detonated here. English audio tours are available, though what you see is already too much to handle. The continuous, unblinking film footage is absolutely nauseating at several points, and a melted and blasted wall clock, as surreal as any Dalí painting, sears its way into your conscience. To get to the museum, take Streetcar 1 from Nagasaki Station to the Hamaguchi stop. ✉ *7–8 Hirano-machi* ☎ *095/844–1231* ⊕ *www1.city.nagasaki. nagasaki.jp/peace* ✐ *¥200, audio guide ¥150* ⊘ *Apr. and Sept.–Mar., daily 8:30–5:30; May–Aug., daily 8:30–6:30 (to 8 Aug. 7–9)*.

Fodor'sChoice **Glover Garden** グラバー邸. Glover contains an impressive assortment of
★ 19th-century Western houses. Wooden verandas, Greco-Roman porticos and arches, and other random elements of European architecture adorn these houses, which are often crowned with Japanese-style roofs. The main attraction is the former mansion (1863) of Thomas Glover, a prominent Scottish merchant who introduced steam locomotives and industrialized coal mining to Japan. Escalators whisk you up the steep hillside to the gardens, where you can admire the views of Nagasaki and the harbor. Take Streetcar 5 to Oura Tenshudo-shita and follow the signs. ✉ *8-1 Minami Yamate-machi* ☎ *095/822–8223* ⊕ *www.glover-garden.jp/miru.html* ✐ *¥600* ⊘ *Apr. 29–May 5, July 17–Oct. 9, daily 8–9:30; Dec. 23–25, daily 8–9; all other dates, daily 8–6*.

Heiwa Koen 平和公園 *(Peace Park)*. Nagasaki's Peace Park was built on the grounds of an old prison that was destroyed in the atomic blast. In the middle is a large statue of a godlike man sitting with one arm stretched to the sky and one to the land. A short distance down the hill, **Hypocenter Koen** 原爆落下中心地 marks the bomb's "hypocenter."

Glover Garden has a large koi pond.

A solitary pillar was erected to mark the exact epicenter, and there is curiously little distance separating this from anything else. In contrast to the looming Hiroshima dome, when you came upon the spot you might not immediately recognize its significance. But as you get closer the significance of the solemn pillar becomes starkly clear. From Nagasaki Station, take either Streetcar 1 or 3 for the 10-minute ride to the Matsuya-machi stop. 🚋 *Free* 🕐 *Park never closes.*

Koshi-byo 孔子廟 *(Confucian Shrine).* The bright red shrine was built in 1893 by the Chinese residents of Nagasaki. The small museum displays artifacts on loan from Beijing's Palace Museum of Historical Treasures and National Museum of Chinese History. The closest streetcar stop is Ishi-bashi; look for the signs leading to the shrine. ✉ *10-36 Oura-machi* ☎ *095/824–4022* ⊕ *www4.cncm.ne.jp/~rekidai-museum* 🚋 *¥600* 🕐 *Daily 8:30–5:30.*

Oranda-zaka オランダ坂 *(Holland Slope).* This is a good place to wander on the way to Chinatown and Glover Garden. It's a cobblestone incline with restored wooden houses originally built by Dutch residents in the late 19th century. Many become shops and tearooms in summer. To get here, follow the street on the southeast side of the Confucian Shrine.

Oura Tenshu-do 大浦天主堂 *(Oura Catholic Church).* The church survived the bomb that leveled much of the city farther up the valley. It was constructed in 1865 to commemorate the death of 26 Christians crucified in 1597, victims of Toyotomi's gruesome message of religious intolerance. It's the oldest Gothic-style building in Japan. Below the entrance to Glover Garden, the church is a five-minute walk from the

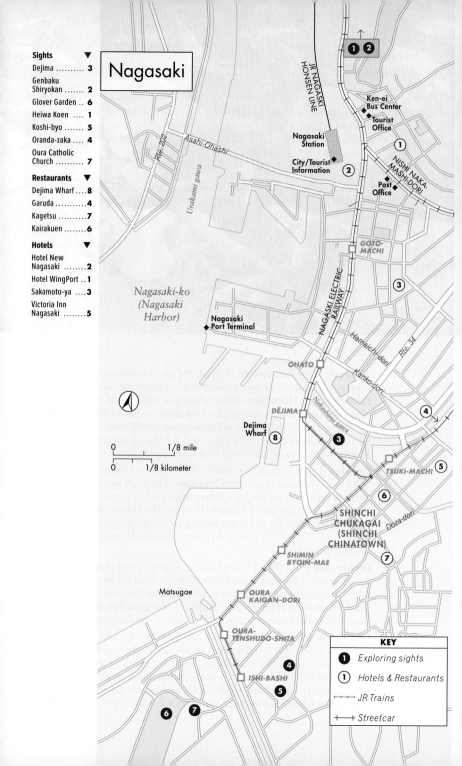

Nagasaki

Nagasaki-ko
(Nagasaki
Harbor)

Nagasaki
Port Terminal

JR NAGASAKI HONSEN LINE

Ken-ei
Bus Center

Tourist
Office

Nagasaki
Station

City/Tourist
Information

Post
Office

NISHI NAKA-MASHI-DORI

Rte. 202

Asahi-Ohashi

Urakami gawa

GOTO-MACHI

NAGASAKI ELECTRIC RAILWAY

Hamaichi-dori

Rte. 34

OHATO

Kanko-dori

DEJIMA

Dejima
Wharf

Nakashima gawa

TSUKI-MACHI

SHINCHI
CHUKAGAI
(SHINCHI
CHINATOWN)

Doza-dori

SHIMIN
BYOIN-MAE

Matsugae

OURA
KAIGAN-DORI

OURA-
TENSHUDO-SHITA

ISHI-BASHI

0   1/8 mile
0   1/8 kilometer

KEY

❶ *Exploring sights*

① *Hotels & Restaurants*

+++ *JR Trains*

+++ *Streetcar*

August 9, 1945

On August 9, 1945, two days after the blast at Hiroshima, Nagasaki fell victim to a second atomic bomb because of bad weather. The plane, named *Bock's Car*, was supposed to drop the Fat Man, a new and experimental plutonium bomb, on the war industry complexes in Kokura. A delay in hooking up with *Bock's Car*'s B-29 escorts meant that when they reached Kokura, bad weather had rolled in and blocked their view. So they headed over to the secondary target, Nagasaki and its vital shipyards, and dropped the bomb there.

More powerful than the uranium bomb dropped on Hiroshima, the Fat Man's core of plutonium, surrounded by TNT, imploded. The runaway fission chain reaction released the heat- and light-wave radiation of a small sun over the target, which in turn delivered a blast pressure of tons per square inch. Virtually nothing within miles of the blast was left standing, or even recognizable. Nagasaki's hilly topography and conformity to undulating river valley floors had made it a less desirable target, but it did help save a number of residential areas from total destruction. Meanwhile, 6.7 square km (2.59 square mi) were obliterated, 74,884 people were killed in the blast or died shortly thereafter, and another 74,909 were injured. The effects of radioactivity caused the deaths of an estimated 70,000 others within five years.

Oura Tenshu-do-shita streetcar stop. ⊠ *5–3 Minami Yamate-machi* ☎ *095/823–2628* ⊕ *www1.bbiq.jp/oourahp* ⊠ *¥300* ⊘ *Daily 8–6.*

WHERE TO EAT

$$
ECLECTIC
✕ **Dejima Wharf** 出島ワーフ. Warm nights draw crowds to the outdoor terraces of this trendy two-story wooden complex on the pier next to Nagasaki Port. You'll find a sprawl of tantalizing seafood restaurants downstairs; a quiet pub serving pasta dishes, pizza, and cocktails at the north end of the second floor; and a family restaurant with burgers and Japanese noodle and rice dishes on the south end of the second floor. ⊠ *Dejima Wharf* ☎ *095/828–3939.*

$
ITALIAN
✕ **Garuda** ガルダ. Authentic pizza and pasta are the mainstays at this Italian restaurant in the Shian-bashi entertainment quarter (east of Chinatown). From rustic wooden tables upstairs you watch the narrow streets below. Takeout is also available. From the Shian-bashi tram stop, head two blocks north into the arcade and another two blocks east. ⊠ *1–20 Kajiya-machi* ☎ *095/826–1302* ⊟ *No credit cards.*

$$$$
JAPANESE
✕ **Kagetsu** 花月. This quiet hilltop retreat is Nagasaki's most prestigious restaurant. Dishes are served as *kaiseki* (Kyoto-style multicourse meals) or *shippoku*, an elaborate course blending Asian and European elements. Lunch runs from ¥5,200 to ¥11,000; dinners start at ¥11,000. The interior wooden beams date to 1618, when Kagetsu was reputedly a high-class brothel. According to another local legend, Meiji Restoration leader Ryoma Sakamoto once took a chunk out of a wooden

pillar with his sword during a brawl, leaving a still visible gash. ✉ *2–1 Maruyama-cho* ☎ *095/822–0191.*

$ ✕ **Kairakuen** 会楽園. This ornate Chinese restaurant is a local favorite, and
CHINESE it's easy to see, smell, and taste why. It serves the best *chanpon*—Naga-
★ saki's signature dish of Chinese-style noodles, vegetable, and pork-based broth—in town. The reasonable price is an added bonus. Mama-san speaks English if given the chance, and Papa-san sits like Buddha watching over the customers. It's just inside the entrance to Chinatown, on the left. Take the streetcar to Tsuki-machi and walk a couple of blocks south. ✉ *10–16 Shinchi-machi* ☎ *095/822–4261* ⊕ *www.kairakuen.tv.*

WHERE TO STAY

Hotel reviews have been condensed for this book. Please go to Fodors. com for full reviews of each property.

$$$$ 🏨 **Hotel New Nagasaki** ホテルニュー長崎. Glossy marble and massive
HOTEL slabs of granite dominate this popular and upscale hotel. **Pros:** you
★ can't get closer to the station; great shopping and more next door.
Cons: a bit too lively and beehive-like for solitude seekers. ✉ *14–5 Daikoku-machi* ☎ *095/826–8000* 🖷 *095/823–2000* ⊕ *www.newnaga. com* 🛏 *130 rooms* ⚷ *In-room: a/c, Internet. In-hotel: 3 restaurants, pool, gym* ⚟ *No meals.*

$–$$ 🏨 **Hotel WingPort** ホテルウィングポート. Computer rentals and in-room
HOTEL Internet access make the WingPort popular with business travelers. **Pros:** spacious rooms; clean; location. **Cons:** light sleepers beware—noises travel well here. ✉ *9–2 Daikoku-machi* ☎ *095/833–2800* 🖷 *095/833– 2801* ⊕ *www.wingport.com/index.html* 🛏 *200 rooms* ⚷ *In-room: a/c, Internet. In-hotel: restaurant* ⚟ *No meals.*

$$$$ 🏨 **Sakamoto-ya** 坂本屋. Established in 1895, this wooden ryokan is the
RYOKAN oldest lodging in town, and it seems to have changed very little over time. **Pros:** private aromatic wooden bathtubs; private gardens. **Cons:** baths are not hot springs (though nice); no Internet access. ✉ *2–13 Kanaya-machi* ☎ *095/826–8211* 🖷 *095/825–5944* ⊕ *www.sakamotoya. co.jp* 🛏 *14 Japanese-style rooms* ⚷ *In-room: a/c. In-hotel: restaurant* ⚟ *Some meals.*

$$ 🏨 **Victoria Inn Nagasaki** ホリデイイン長崎. For value and location—with
HOTEL a dash of style and sophistication—this is the place. Leather chairs, vintage sofas, antique telephones, and dark oil paintings in the lobby are reminiscent of an old European drawing room. **Pros:** in the thick of things; comfortable and stylish; friendly, capable staff. **Cons:** some single rooms have no view; room service only available from 5 to 10 pm. ✉ *6–24 Doza-machi* ☎ *095/828–1234* 🖷 *095/828–0178* ⊕ *www. victoria-inn.jp/index.html* 🛏 *87 rooms, 6 suites* ⚷ *In-room: a/c, refrigerator. In-hotel: restaurant, room service, bar* ⚟ *No meals.*

SHOPPING

Castella sponge cake, the popular souvenir of Nagasaki, was introduced by the Portuguese in the mid-16th century. The original recipe called for just eggs, flour, and sugar, but it's been tinkered with over time. Every sweet shop and souvenir store in town has its own specially flavored recipe, but you're advised to stick with the good old plain version—a delightful treat with coffee or tea.

SHOPPING AREAS

Everyone converges at **Amu Plaza (Amu Puraza)** アムプラーザ as the sun sets. Towering over Nagasaki Station, this is where the newest shops and restaurants are, and a multi-theater movie complex is inside. It's thoroughly modern, and a striking contrast to the city's old-fashioned style.

Not far from Dejima, **Hamano-machi** 浜野町 is the major shopping district in downtown Nagasaki. This covered arcade stretches over four blocks and contains numerous department stores, cake shops, cafés, pharmacies, and fashion boutiques.

Fukusaya 福砂屋. This bakery has been in business since the Meiji period. When you say *castella* in Nagasaki, most people think of this shop and its distinctive yellow packaging. There's a branch on the first floor of the New Nagasaki Hotel, next to Nagasaki Station. ✉ *3–1 Funadaiku-machi* ☎ *095/821–2938* ⊕ *www.castella.co.jp.*

KUMAMOTO 熊本

118 km (73 mi) south of Fukuoka (Hakata).

Kumamoto is situated nearly midway along the curve of the west coast of Kyushu. From here you can go to Nagasaki to the west, Fukuoka to the north, Aso-san to the east, and Kagoshima to the south on the new high-speed train line.

The town has many sights of its own, including the nationally famous Suizen-ji Garden, but the most renowned is the castle once deemed impregnable. Kiyomasa Kato ushered in the 17th century with the construction of a mighty fortress that was even bigger than the current replica, and he and his son held sway here until the 1630s. The Hosokawa clan then took over, and for the next few centuries Kumamoto was a center of the Tokugawa governmental authority. In 1877, the real "Last Samurai," Saigo Takamori, brought his army of rebels here to battle untested Meiji government conscripts holed up inside. Things were looking grim. Then Takamori ordered his starving men to butcher their horses for raw and ready food. Strengthened, they did breach the castle 53 days into the siege, but reinforcements forced them to backpedal as much of the castle and compound were destroyed in a huge conflagration. It may have been the first time raw horseflesh (*ba-sashi*) was eaten in Japan, but locals continue to devour it to help their stamina.

A number of notable folks had homes which can still be seen in town, including the writers Lafcadio Hearn and Soseki Natsume, both of whom lived here for brief periods while teaching English.

GETTING HERE AND AROUND

The Kyushu-Sanko bus makes the 50-minute run from **Kumamoto Airport** to JR Kumamoto Station for ¥670. Flights on ANA, JAL, and Sky Net Asia (SNA) connect Tokyo's Haneda Airport with Kumamoto Airport (1¾ hours). ANA and JAL fly the hour-long route from Osaka's Itami Airport eight times a day.

The Nagasaki Ken-ei Bus (from Nagasaki Ken-ei Bus Terminal) costs ¥3,600 and takes three hours to Kumamoto City Kotsu Center. Kyushu-Sanko buses leaving from Kumamoto City Kotsu Center take three hours, 15 minutes to Kagoshima, via change at Hotoyoshi for ¥3,650. There's also a Kyushu Sanko bus route linking the *onsen* (thermal baths) paradise of Yufuin and Kumamoto in 4½ hours for ¥3,450, and from April to October a trip via Aso-san (90-minute-stop for Aso sightseeing) can be done for ¥5,800 in about five hours (reservations strongly recommended on this route).

A sightseeing bus, also operated by Kyushu-Sanko, makes a four-hour scenic trip (¥3,790) that starts at Fugen-dake and Shimabara, then ferries across Ariake Bay to Kumamoto-ko (Kumamoto Port) before ending the journey at Kumamoto City Kotsu Center.

The JR Tsubame or Ariake Express from Fukuoka's Hakata Station stops at **Kumamoto Station** and takes 1¼ hours, ¥3,740. From Nagasaki, take JR to Tosu and change to the train for Kumamoto (three hours; ¥ 6,170).

This is one spread-out city, and buses get stuck in all the traffic, so your best bet is to hop a streetcar. Tram lines (Nos. 2 and 3) connect the major areas of the city. The fare is a flat ¥150; pay as you get off. From the Kumamoto Eki-mae streetcar stop in front of the train station it's a 10-minute ride downtown. One-day travel passes, good for use on streetcars and city buses, are available for ¥500 from the City Tourist Information Office. There is also a Castle Loop Bus that connects a string of sights around the castle with a stop across from the main train station and runs every 30 minutes from 8:30 to 5 daily. Tickets (¥130 single stop, or ¥300 for the day) can be bought at the tourist office in the station or at the Kotsu Center Bus Terminal near the castle.

Airport Information Kumamoto Airport (✉ *1802–2 Oyatsu, Mashiki-machi* ☎ *096/232–2311*).

Bus Contacts Kyushu-Sanko Buses (☎ *096/355–2525*).

Bus Depot Kumamoto City Kotsu Center (✉ *3–10 Sakura-machi* ☎ *096/354–6411*).

Train Station Kumamoto Station (✉ *3–15–1 Kasuga* ☎ *096/211–2406*).

VISITOR INFORMATION

The **City Tourist Information Office** can provide maps and information in English. The city's Web site, Visit Kumamoto, also has good descriptions of major sights.

CONTACTS

City Tourist Information Office (✉ *JR Kumamoto Station, 3–15–1 Kasuga* ☎ *096/352–3743* ⊙ *Daily 8:30–7*). **Visit Kumamoto** (⊕ *www.visitkumamoto.com*).

Towering Kumamoto-jo was built in 1607 but largely destroyed in 1877; it has since been rebuilt.

EXPLORING KUMAMOTO

In most Japanese cities the hive of activity is around the station. However, very little of interest surrounds JR Kumamoto Station; the bulk of the town's attractions are to the northeast, squeezed in between the Tsuboi and Shira rivers. Most of what constitutes downtown huddles around the old castle, up there.

★ **Kumamoto-jo** 熊本城 *(Kumamoto Castle)*. The towering, ominous castle was completed in 1607, having been designed and built by Kiyomasa Kato (1562–1611), the area's feudal lord or *daimyo*. Gracefully curved, white-edged roofs rest atop the mysterious black keep. The wide stone base has *mushagaeshi*, concave walls with stout platform overhangs, situated under slanted windows perfect for unleashing rock falls, one of many clever features to prevent intrusion. The top floor of the reconstructed castle commands an excellent view of Kumamoto, and exhibits include samurai weapons and armor arrayed to evoke images of the fearless warriors charging into battle. To get here, board Streetcar 2, get off at the Kumamoto-jo-mae stop, and walk up the tree-lined slope. Volunteer guides conduct tours in English. ⊠ *1-1 Honmaru, Kumamoto-shi* ☎ *096/352–5900* ⊕ *www.manyou-kumamoto.jp/castle* ⊠ ¥500; ¥640 *for combined admission to castle and Hosokawa Mansion, purchase ticket at castle* ⊙ Apr.–Oct., *daily 8:30–6;* Nov.–Mar., *daily 8:30–5.*

Kyu-Hosokawa Gyobu-tei 旧細川刑部邸 *(Hosokawa Mansion)*. This private home was built in 1646 for the Hosokawa family, who took power at the behest of Tokugawa in 1611—and whose local lineage produced Japan's former Prime Minister Morihiro Hosokawa (served 1993–94). ⊠ *3–1 Furukyo-machi* ☎ *096/352–6522* ⊕ *www.manyou-kumamoto.*

jp/contents.cfm?id=436 🎫 *¥300; ¥640 for combined admission to mansion and Kumamoto Castle; purchase ticket at castle* ⊙ *Apr.–Oct., daily 8:30–5:30; Nov.–Mar., daily 8:30–4:30.*

Suizen-ji Joju-en 水前寺成趣園 *(Suijzen-ji Garden).* Created in the mid-17th century, the garden was originally part of the sprawling villa of the ruling Hosokawa family. An undulating hummock of lush green grass representing Japan—there's even a Fuji-san-like cone in about the right place—is beside a pond surrounded by a network of stone bridges. The garden is dotted with impeccably trimmed bushes and trees. A tiny old teahouse gives welcome respite from the sun's glare and tour-bus groups' clatter. Also on the grounds is Izumi Jinja (Izumi Shrine), which houses the tombs of several eminent Hosokawa clan members. To get to the garden, take Streetcar 2 or 3 east from the castle to the Suizen-ji Joju-en-mae stop. ⊠ *8–1 Suizenji-koen* ☎ *096/383–0074* ⊕ *www.suizenji.or.jp* 🎫 *¥400* ⊙ *Mar.–Oct., daily 7:30–6; Nov.–Feb., daily 8:30–5.*

OFF THE BEATEN PATH

Takachiho 高千穂. If you're looking for someplace that most tourists never venture to see, this village—the mythological heart of the country—is worth the trouble. This is the place where the goddess Amaterasu's grandson is said to have descended to Earth to establish the Japanese Imperial Family. It's a spot on the radar of many Japanese tourists, especially those who travel to spiritual places around the country, but it has not really been discovered by the vast majority of tourists. Reaching Takachiho is not easy, and that has kept the town from becoming an overdeveloped tourist trap, but it is well worth the journey. In the most northerly part of Miyazaki Prefecture, about 80 km (49 mi) southeast of the Kumamoto, the town is most easily reached by rental car since the train line is no longer operating. The drive is only a couple of hours, and as public transportation is minimal in the town, you can use your car to get around up on arrival. An overnight stay is recommended to see a good selection of the many sights available and enjoy the atmosphere (*see Where to Eat and Where to Stay, below*). There is a direct bus to Takachiho from Kumamoto that takes about three hours (¥2,300 one-way, ¥4,000 round-trip). You can pay on the bus or get a round-trip ticket from the vending machine in the Kumamoto bus terminal. Buses leave at 9:10 am and arrive at midday and then depart at 4:40 pm, arriving in Kumamoto around 7:30. But a day trip, while possible, doesn't really give you a good enough sense of the place; an overnight is recommended.

WHERE TO EAT

$$
JAPANESE

✕**Aoyagi** 青柳. The extensive menu includes regional favorites—*ba-sashi* (raw horse meat) and *karashi renkon* (lotus root stuffed with fiery chili and mustard powder, sliced and fried tempura style)—in addition to various types of sushi and tofu dishes. You can relax in a booth, or sit at the counter and admire the skilled chefs. It's tucked behind the Daiei department store, not far from the Shi-yakusho-mae streetcar stop. ⊠ *1–2–10 Shimotori* ☎ *096/353–0311* ⊕ *aoyagi.ne.jp* ⊙ *Daily 11:30–10.*

$$
JAPANESE

✕**Sobadokoro Ten'an** そば処天庵. If you find yourself in Takachiho, for a real treat in the middle of the day visit the wonderful soba shop run by Sayoko Kojima. The soba and soup are delicious and are served with different kinds of tempera and other dishes made with vegetables that Kojima grows organically. During the daytime this is a tourist spot popular with day-trippers, but if you can go back at night, you can mingle with the locals who also gather there to drink shochu and partake of the incredible soba. ✉ *1180 Mitai, Takachiho-cho, Nishiusuki-gun* ☎ *0982/72–3023* ⚲ *Reservations essential* ⊟ *No credit cards* ⊙ *Closed Sun.*

$$$$
FRENCH
★
✕ **Suganoya** 菅乃屋. When in Kumamoto, do as the locals do—eat some ba-sashi! If you order the Nishiki Set (¥6,300), you can get it served in all its forms: there's a starter of raw tidbits with garlic, ginger, and assorted dunking sauces; or a finale of *hari-hari nabe,* a soup of thinly sliced delicately flavored meat (still horse), and vegetables cooked in a folded-paper vessel that doesn't burn. Sit at the bar for a delightful atmosphere of friendly frenzy, or kick back at one of the secluded tables. ✉ *L2F Lion Parking Biru, 2–12 Joto-machi* ☎ *096/355–3558* ⊕ *www. suganoya.com/info-kamidori.html.*

WHERE TO STAY

Hotel reviews have been condensed for this book. Please go to Fodors. com for full reviews of each property.

$$$–$$$$
HOTEL
🏨 **Hotel New Otani Kumamoto** ホテルニューオータニ熊本. It's not as over-the-top as its big-city counterparts, but this hotel is endowed with the same crisp service and all the amenities. **Pros:** unlike everything else in town, it's close to the station; Internet access in lobby. **Cons:** it's close to the station, all right—but nothing else is. ✉ *1–13–1 Kasuga* ☎ *096/326–1111* 🖷 *096/326–0800* ⊕ *www.newotani.co.jp/en* ⌨ *130 rooms* ⚲ *In-room: a/c. In-hotel: 4 restaurants, room service, bar* ⦿ *No meals.*

$$–$$$
HOTEL
★
🏨 **Kumamoto Hotel Castle** 熊本ホテルキャッスル. Just across from the castle, rooms here are done in dark wood and traditional enough to please anyone, but the service is excellent and modern. **Pros:** great staff; great location. **Cons:** confusing lobby arrangement makes an intimidating first impression. ✉ *4–2 Joto-machi* ☎ *096/326–3311* 🖷 *096/326–3324* ⌨ *185 rooms* ⚲ *In-room: a/c. In-hotel: 5 restaurants, bars* ⦿ *No meals.*

$$$$
RYOKAN
🏨 **Shinsen** 神仙. If you decide to overnight in Takachiho, Shinsen claims to be the best ryokan in town. **Pros:** devoted and friendly service; convenient location. **Cons:** expensive; the hot springs are a bit too hot. ✉ *1127–5 Mitai, Takachiho-cho, Nishiusuki-gun* ☎ *0982/72–2257* ⊕ *www.takachiho-shinsen.co.jp* ⌨ *6 Japanese-style rooms, 4 combination rooms* ⚲ *In-room: a/c, safe, refrigerator, Internet. In-hotel: room service, parking (free)* ⦿ *Some meals.*

¢–$
HOTEL
★
🏨 **Toyoko Inn Kumamoto Karashima Koen** 東横イン辛島公園. There are more than 250 Toyoko Inn hotels all over Japan, and for budget travelers they are clearly the best option, offering excellent accommodation facilities for the lowest prices in highly central locations. **Pros:** free breakfast; Internet access in lobby; excellent location; laundry facilities. **Cons:** late check-in (4 pm). ✉ *1–24 Koyaima-machi, Kumamoto-ken* ☎ *096/322–1045* 🖷 *096/322–2045* ⊕ *www.toyoko-inn.com/e_hotel/00077/index.html* ⌨ *153 rooms* ⚲ *In-room: a/c. In-hotel: restaurant, laundry facilities, Wi-Fi hotspot* ⦿ *Breakfast.*

SHOPPING

Kumamoto's most famous product is *Higo zogan,* or Higo inlay. A unique form of metalwork originally employed in the decoration of swords, scabbards, and gunstocks of the Hosokawa clan, it consists of black steel delicately inlaid with silver and gold, and it is now used to make fashionable jewelry that does not come cheap; a simple pendant can run ¥8,000, and prices for large pieces reach ¥700,000 and more. Other local products include gold paper lanterns, dolls, tops, and fine cutlery.

Dento Kogei-kan (*Kumamoto Traditional Crafts Center*). *This is* the best place to buy zogan and regional handicrafts. It's in a redbrick building across from the Akazu-mon entrance to the castle. ⊠ *3–35 Chiba-jo-machi* ☎ *096/324–4930* ⊕ *cyber.pref.kumamoto.jp/kougei* ☉ *Oct.– June, Tues.–Sun. 9–5; July–Sept., Tues.–Sun. 9–6.*

ASO-SAN 阿蘇山 (MT. ASO)

Aso-san comprises the world's largest caldera—128 km (80 mi) in circumference, from 18 km to 24 km (11 to 15 mi) wide in places—formed after a massive lava-dome collapse some 100,000 years ago. Inside the crater are seven settlements, not to mention herds of cows and horses. The emerald-green grasses that nourish them thrive in the fertile volcanic soil. The crater area, officially named the Aso-Kuju (Mt. Aso National Park), contains five volcanic cones; one is the still-active Naka-dake, and it sticks up out of the side of the taller Taka-dake just east of the crater's center. There's no mistaking the sulfurous stench of the mighty belches that gust freely from its mouth.

GETTING HERE AND AROUND

Kyushu-Sanko buses make frequent runs between Kumamoto City Kotsu Center, the Aso Nishi cable-car station at Asosan-jo, and Kurokawa Onsen. The Kyushu bus continues from Kurokawa Onsen to Yufuin and Beppu.

The JR Hohi Line runs between Kumamoto Station and **JR Aso Station** (¥1,680, express; ¥1,080, local) and also connects Aso to Kagoshima (¥7,400). From JR Aso Station you must board a **Ky Sanko** bus (40 minutes; ¥540 one-way) to get to Aso-San Nishi Station. Buses run every one to two hours starting at 8:30; the last bus down is at 7:44. From there you can walk 30 minutes to the crater or take the **Aso Nishi Cable Car** (4 minutes) to the terminus at Kako Nishi (West Crater). Aso-san makes an excellent stopover on the way to Yufuin from Kumamoto. The JR Odan Line also connects JR Aso Station to Yufuin via change in Oita (¥4,850).

If you start early, you can make Aso-san a day trip. You have until 9 for the last Kumamoto-bound train, but the last bus back to distant Aso Station is at 5. If you want to spend more time in the park, spend the night in one of the many mountain pensions clustered in the southern half.

Bus Contacts Kyushu Bus Co. (☎ *096/325–0100*).

Train Station JR Aso Station (⊠ *1444-2 Kurokawa, Aso-cho* ☎ *0967/34–0101*).

VISITOR INFORMATION

Stop by the **Aso Station Information Center** to get your bearings and check conditions. The mountain's emissions occasionally take the lives of tourists, and park officials will shut things down when the alarm is raised.

Contact Aso Station Information Center (✉ *Inside JR Aso Station* ☎ *0967/34–0751* ⏱ *Thurs.–Tues. 9–5*).

EXPLORING ASO-SAN

Aso Kazan Hakubutsukan 阿蘇火山博物館 *(Aso Volcano Museum)*. The museum is across from the Kusasenri parking lot and rest area. Want to see what's happening inside the volcano? Two heat-impervious cameras were inserted into the most active part of the volcano, and museum visitors can watch what's being recorded in there. Another display explains that Japan sits on the busiest tectonic plate junction in the world and that these fault lines are visible from space. ✉ *1930 Akamizu, Aso* ☎ *0967/34–2111* ⊕ *www.asomuse.jp* 🎫 *¥840* ⏱ *Daily 9–5.*

Kusasenri 草千里. A 35-minute ride from the JR Aso Station on the Kyushu Sanko bus line, this bowl-shape meadow is where the region's cows and horses graze on the lush grass and wade in shallow marshes. If you have time, hike along an easy trail that goes 5½ km (3½ mi) around the base of Kijima-dake. It takes an hour or so, and provides excellent views of the otherworldly terrain. You could also march the 3 km (2 mi) straight across the rugged lava plain to the foot of Naka-dake. ■**TIP**→ For several trails of other lengths and difficulty in the area, pick up the "Aso Trekking Route Map" at the information center in JR Aso Station.

Fodor's Choice **Naka-dake** 中岳. This caldera is reason enough to visit Mt. Aso National
★ Park. Inside the crater, a churning ash-gray lake bubbles and spits scalding, reeking steam. Naka-dake's rim is a 30-minute walk from the bottom of the **Aso Nishi Cable Car** at Asosan-jo; the cable car takes you up in four minutes. You can skirt around some of the lip, but the northern reaches have been out of bounds since 1997, when toxic fumes seeped out and killed two tourists. If rumbling turns to shaking, and steam and smoke turn to sizable ash fall, know where the bunkerlike shelters are located. These were built after a dozen people perished in a sudden eruption some 50 years ago. ✉ *Aso-san Cable Car, 808–5 Kurokawa, Aso869-2225* ☎ *0967/34–0411* 🎫 *¥1,000 round-trip, ¥500 one-way.*

WHERE TO STAY

There are more than 50 lodging outfits in and around Aso National Park to choose from.

Hotel reviews have been condensed for this book. Please go to Fodors. com for full reviews of each property.

$$ 🏠 **Pension Angelica** ペンションアンジェリカ. The main appeal of this
INN manor in the woods is the hospitality of the Tatsuji family. **Pros:** heartwarming hosts; homemade bread; fresh air and quiet. **Cons:** have to hustle to get there early; long way to go if your stay is short. ✉ *1800 Shirakawa, Minami-aso-mura, Aso-gun* ☎🖷 *0967/62–2223* ⊕ *www.*

This churning, bubbling lake is found in the crater of Naka-dake in Mt. Aso National Park.

pensionangelica.com ⇱ *7 rooms, 2 with bath ⚘ In-room: a/c. In-hotel: restaurant, bar, spa, Internet terminal* ⏶⏷ *Some meals.*

$$$
RYOKAN

⊞ **Yamaguchi Ryokan** 山口旅館. From the outdoor baths of this rustic lodge you can watch mineral water meander down the rocky cliffs of the green mountainside. Don't be shy—mixed bathing is often practiced here. **Pros:** about as isolated as one can get in this country; awe-inspiring baths and falls; rated by some as Best Outdoor Baths in Japan; indoor baths are great, too. **Cons:** perhaps a little too isolated and certainly not suitable if you want to do any exploring outside the ryokan; food not as stunning as the baths. ✉ *2331 Kawayo, Aso-gun, Minami-Aso-mura* ☎ *0967/67–0006* ⎙ *0967/67–1694* ⊕ *www.tarutama.jp* ⇱ *35 Japanese-style rooms ⚘ In-room: a/c.* ⏶⏷ *Some meals.*

KAGOSHIMA 鹿児島

171 km (106 mi) south of Kumamoto, 289 km (180 mi) south of Hakata/Fukuoka.

Kagoshima is a laid-back, flowery, palm-lined southern getaway on the Satsuma Peninsula with mild weather, outgoing people, and a smoking volcano out in the bay. Ancient relics believed to date back to 9,000 BC indicate that humans have been in the area a very long time indeed. It became a center of trade with Korea and China and was an important fortress town from the mid-16th century until the Meiji Restoration. This is where Saigo Takamori and his rebel followers (reduced to a few hundred from 40,000) made their last stand against the new Emperor on September 24, 1877, chased here after having sacked Kumamoto Castle. Facing 300,000

11

well-supplied troops, they had no chance, and Takamori was injured in the fight. Rather than face capture, he ordered one of his own men to cut off his head. Reviled and vilified during the rush to modernization, he was posthumously pardoned and honored as a national hero.

Today, the area is famous for growing the world's smallest mandarin oranges (only an inch across) and the largest white daikon radishes— grown in the rich volcanic soil, these can span 3 feet and weigh in at more than 100 pounds. There's also *kurobuta,* a special breed of black pig that locals convert into breaded, fried cutlets called *tonkatsu* (*ton* is pork; *katsu* means cutlet).

GETTING HERE AND AROUND

The flight between Tokyo's Haneda Airport and **Kagoshima Airport** takes 1¾ hours. From Osaka the flight takes about one hour. The **Airport Limousine** picks up passengers every 10 minutes (until 9 pm) at Bus Stop No. 2 outside the Kagoshima Airport. From downtown, catch it in the terminal in the Nangoku Nissei Building, across the street from the East (Sakura-jima) Exit from JR Kagoshima **Chuo** Station. The 40-minute trip costs ¥1,200.

Frequent buses make the four-hour trip for ¥5,300 from Fukuoka (departing from Hakata Kotsu Bus Center and Tenjin Bus Center) to **Kagoshima Chuo Station.** Trains to the same station arrive on the JR Tsubame and Relay Tsubame Limited Express lines from Fukuokata's Hakata Station and Kumamoto via Shin-Yatsushiro.

For the past hundred years the easiest way to get around Kagoshima has been by streetcar. A ¥160 fare will take you anywhere on the trusty old network. One-day travel passes for unlimited rides on streetcars and buses cost ¥600. You can buy one at the Kagoshima-Chuo Station Tourist Information Center, or on a streetcar or bus. Buses get around, but are run by five competing outfits on a complicated system.

To visit Sakura-jima, you must take a ferry from Kagoshima Port; it runs 24 hours a day. To get to the pier from Kagoshima Chuo Station, take Bus East–4 or 5 for the short ¥180 ride.

Airport Information Kagoshima Airport (☏ *099/558–4686*).

Airport Transfer Airport Limousine (☏ *099/247–2341*).

Bus and Train Station Kagoshima Chuo Station (✉ *1–1 Chuo-cho* ☏ *099/256–1585*).

Ferry Ports Kagoshima Port (✉ *4–1 Shin-machi, Hon-ko* ☏ *099/223–7271*).

VISITOR INFORMATION

The **Kagoshima-Chuo Station Tourist Information Center** is on the second floor of the station's Sakura-jima Exit. An English-speaking person is on hand to arm you with maps and info or help you make hotel reservations.

Contact Kagoshima-Chuo Station Tourist Information Center (✉ *1–1 Chuo-cho* ☏ *099/253–2500* ✆ *Daily 8:30–7*).

EXPLORING KAGOSHIMA

★ **Sakura-jima** 桜島. Across Kinko Bay rises this volcano, and you can often see it spewing thick plumes of dust and smoke. Its last big eruption was in 1955, but the far side of the cone sometimes lets loose with explosive burps that light the night sky red and cover the town in a blanket of ash. There are scattered lodgings and hot springs, as well as winding paths up to old lava plateaus with great views over the crater or back toward town. The ferry port is at the foot of the volcano. There are four to six ferries per hour, with fewer connections after 9 pm. The one-way fare is ¥150, and the trip takes only 10–15 minutes. ⌧ *Sakura-jima Port, 61–4 Yokoyama-cho, Sakura-jima* ☎ *099/293-2525.*

OFF THE BEATEN PATH

Ibusuki Tennen Sunamushi Onsen (and Sand-Bath Center Saraku) 指宿天然砂むし温泉と砂楽. This laid-back seaside resort is at the southern tip of the Satsuma Peninsula and may provide your one chance to try a therapeutic hot-sand bath. At the bath, you buy your ticket and rent a *yukata*, or cotton robe—the small towel is yours to keep—on the second floor of the main "Saraku" Sand Bath Hall, and then go down into the locker rooms (separate sexes) to remove your clothes and change into the robe before heading to the beach. Stand in line and wait for an assistant to call you over. They'll scoop a place for you and show how to wrap your head and neck in the towel. They will then bury you in hot, mildly sulfur-smelling sand with their shovels. It'll get squirmy, but stay in the Zen zone for at least 10 minutes. Fifteen will give you a full charge—if you can take it! Aside from giving you a powerful dose of joint-penetrating heat, the stimulating, sweaty experience is also guaranteed to cleanse your pores and soften your skin. It's a highly scenic one-hour trip south of Kagoshima on the Ibusuki Nanohana local train line. Exit Ibusuki Station and follow the signs to the natural hot sand bathing spot, a 15- to 20-minute walk or five-minute cab ride to the beach. ⌧ *5–25–18 Yu-no-hama, Ibusuki* ☎ *0993/23–3900* ⌧ *¥1,000, including towel and robe rental* ⊙ *Daily 8:30–noon and 1–8:30.*

WHERE TO EAT AND STAY

Hotel reviews have been condensed for this book. Please go to Fodors. com for full reviews of each property.

$$$
JAPANESE
★
✕ **Kumaso-tei** 熊襲亭. Enjoy the best of Satsuma specialties in a maze of private and semiprivate Japanese-style rooms. There's an English photo menu, and deluxe set meals range from ¥3,360 to ¥10,500. Highlights include *kibinago* (raw herring), *satsuma-age* (fish cakes filled with potato or *gobo*, burdock root), and kurobuta tonkatsu (breaded, fried pork cutlets from locally bred black pigs). From the Tenmonkan-dori streetcar stop, walk four blocks north through the covered arcade and turn left; the restaurant will be on the right. ⌧ *6–10 Higashi Sengoku-cho* ☎ *099/222-6356* ⊕ *www.kumasotei.com.*

$$$–$$$$
RESORT
Fodor's Choice
★
▨ **Furusato Kanko Hotel** ふるさと観光ホテル. This hotel is on Sakura-jima, and the *rotemburo* (outdoor bath) offers amazing views. **Pros:** spectacular ocean-side baths; great for a romantic hideaway. **Cons:** you won't want to reenter the rat race after a dose of this place's magic. ⌧ *1076–1 Furusato-machi, Kagoshima-ken* ☎ *099/221-3111* 🖷 *099/221-2345*

You can be buried in hot, black volcanic sand at Sandbath Center Sraku

⊕ *www.furukan.co.jp* ↪ *38 Japanese-style rooms* △ *In-room: a/c. In-hotel: restaurant, bar, pool* ⋔ *Some meals.*

$$$–$$$$

HOTEL

⊡ **Shiroyama Kanko Hotel** 城山観光ホテル. Also called Castle Park Hotel in brochures, the hotel is on Shiro-yama, site of Takamori's last stand. **Pros:** panoramic views; great baths; free Wi-Fi. **Cons:** nothing but relaxation happening here; it'll be hard to give it up when the time comes. ⊠ *1–41 Shinshoin-cho* ☎ *099/224–2211* 🖷 *099/224–2222* ⊕ *www.shiroyama-g.co.jp* ↪ *365 rooms* △ *In-room: a/c. In-hotel: 6 restaurants, bar* ⋔ *No meals.*

$–$$

HOTEL

⊡ **Sun Days Inn Kagoshima** サンデイズイン鹿児島. This sleek business hotel offers excellent value, style, and convenience. **Pros:** spanking new and clean; top value for the yen. **Cons:** could use a nice bath to compete with its rivals; meals in the restaurant are a bit small for Westerners. ⊠ *9–8 Yamanokuchi-cho* ☎ *099/227–5151* 🖷 *099/227–4667* ⊕ *www.sundaysinn.com/index.html* ↪ *351 rooms* △ *In-room: a/c. In-hotel: restaurant, bar* ⋔ *No meals.*

KIRISHIMA-YAKU KOKURITSU KOEN 霧島屋久国立公園

43 km (106 mi) northeast of Kagoshima

This mountainous, volcanic region northeast of Kagoshima is one of two possible places (according to Japanese myth) where Amaterasu's grandson descended to earth (*see also* ⇨ *Takachiho in Kumamoto, above*). The national park, part of which is on Kyushu and part on an off-shore island, is dotted with good hiking trails and interesting shrines in addition to the sacred mountain, Mt. Takachiho-no-mine. Because of the paucity of public transportation and difficulty reaching here, it's probably worth spending the night. This way you can maximize your time. ✉ *1-6-22 Onoue, Kumamoto-shi, Kumamoto* ☎ *096/214–0311.*

GETTING HERE AND AROUND

From Kagoshima, take a local (one hour) or express (50 minutes) train to Kirishima Jingu Station. There are also direct buses from Kagoshima Airport to Kirishima Jingu Station. There are buses into the national park from there, though once you have arrived, it's much easier to get around if you have private transportation. You might consider renting a car in Kagoshima.

EXPLORING KIRISHIMA-YAKU KOKURITSU KOEN

Kirishima Jingu 霧島神宮. The original shrine was established in the 6th century, but the present structure was built under the patronage of the Shimazu clan in 1715. It is wonderfully appointed with views as far away as Sakura-jima. The shrine is dedicated to Ninigi-no-mikoto, the legendary god who landed on the peak of Takachiho-no-mine nearby. This imposing beautiful shrine inscribed in an incredible setting is well worth a visit. ✉ *2608–5 Kirishima-taguchi, Kirishima* ☎ *0995/57–0001* ⊕ *www.kirishimajingu.or.jp* ▱ *Free* ☉ *Daily 8–6.*

Takachiho-no-mine 高千穂峰. Both Mt. Takachiho-no-mine and Takachiho (*see ⇨ Kumamoto, above*) claim to be the places where Amaterasu's grandson Ninigi-no-mikoto descended to Earth to establish the Japanese Imperial Family. The dispute has never been settled, either legally or spiritually. Both places remain very spiritual and worthy of a visit. For Takchiho-no-mine you must climb to the peak (the round-trip takes about three hours). One a clear day, you can see the surrounding craters of other mountains in Kirishima National Park.

WHERE TO EAT AND STAY

Hotel reviews have been condensed for this book. Please go to Fodors. com for full reviews of each property.

$$$
JAPANESE

✕ **Ichi Nii San** いちにいさん. The novel idea behind this restaurant is to serve pork shabu-shabu in soba broth. The broth imparts a delicate flavor to the thinly sliced pork, which is served with seasonal vegetables. In the black-pork shabu-shabu course you can enjoy an excellent sampling of the best of the restaurant and get to choose ramen or soba to finish off your meal. The idea has been so successful that the restaurant is now a small chain with branches in Tokyo and Hokkaido and is planning to expand further. ✉ *540–3 Kokubunoguchin-ishi, Kirishima* ☎ *0995/48–8123* ⊕ *ichiniisan.jp/access/kagoshima/kokubu.html.*

$$$$
RYOKAN
Fodor'sChoice
★

▥ **Myoken Ishiharaso** 妙見石原荘. Ishiharaso is in a valley alongside a river of such ferocious rapids that you might feel you're being plunged right into the drama of nature upon arrival. **Pros:** Updated building; beautiful hot spring; excellent food. **Cons:** Requires transportation. ✉ *4376 Hayatocho Kareigawa, Kirishima* ☎ *0995/77–2111* ⊕ *www. m-ishiharaso.com* ▱ *15 Japanese-style rooms, 2 Western-style rooms,*

2 combination rooms ♿ In-room: a/c, safe (some), refrigerator, DVD (some), Internet (some). In-hotel: room service, spa, Internet terminal, parking (free) 🍽 Some meals.

YUFUIN 湯布院

★ *135 km (84 mi) southeast of Hakata/Fukuoka.*

Southwest of the majestic twin peaks of Yufu-dake, this tranquil village resembles a checkered quilt. Forests nestle up to clusters of galleries, eclectic cafés, local crafts shops, and rustic lodgings. Most of the year, Yufuin is a relatively peaceful area, but things heat up in July and August with the arrival of national music and film festivals.

Yufuin has suffered from fewer of the pitfalls of modern tourism than the nearby and overdeveloped Beppu. But it wasn't an accident. City planners and investors went to Europe and came back with ideas about how to set up a quaint and lovely spa town—and how *not to*. The town has blossomed into a quieter, more sedate getaway than its garish counterpart to the east. Relatively unadorned natural baths with great views can be found here, as can a thriving arts-and-crafts industry and fantastic food.

GETTING HERE AND AROUND

The closest airport is **Oita Airport**. The flight to Oita Airport from Tokyo's Haneda Airport takes 1½ hours; the flight from Osaka's Itami Airport takes 1 hour. From the airport to Yufuin, buses run six times daily (8–8, ¥1,500; 55 minutes).

The *Kujugo*, run by **Kyushu Odan Teiki Kanko Bus**, travels between Kumamoto and Beppu three times daily (8:40 am, 9:50 am, and 2:30 pm), stopping in Yufuin along the way. The one-way fare from Kumamoto to Yufuin (3¾ hours) is ¥5,800.

JR Yufuin-no-Mori Express trains run three times daily between Fukuoka's Hakata Station and **Yufuin Station**; they take two hours, 10 minutes and cost ¥4,440.

Airport Information Oita Airport (✉ *Shimobaru, Aki-machi, Kunisaki* ☎ *0978/67–1174*).

Airport Transfer Oita Kotsu Bus Company (☎ *097/534–7455*).

Bus Contacts Kyushu Odan Teiki Kanko Bus (☎ *096/355–2525*).

Train Station Yufuin Station (✉ *8–2 Kawakita* ☎ *0977/84–2021*).

VISITOR INFORMATION

To enjoy the best of Yufuin in a day, start by picking up an English map at **Yufuin Tourist Information Office.** For more-detailed information, visit the **Yufuin Tourist Center,** a five-minute walk from the station. Bicycles can be rented from either office.

Contact Yufuin Tourist Center (✉ *2863 Kawakami* ☎ *0977/85–4464* ⏲ *Daily 9–6*). **Yufuin Tourist Information Office** (✉ *In Yufuin Station, 8–2 Kawakita* ☎ *0977/84–2446* ⏲ *Daily 9–7*).

EXPLORING YUFUIN

Kinrin-ko 金麟湖 *(Lake Kinrin)*. In winter, steam rises from the surface of this thermal lake in the east end of town. Warm up with a dip in one of the many bathhouses along its shores.

Kuso-no-Mori 空想の森. From Yufuin Station, take the five-minute taxi ride north to this collection of art galleries along the foot of Yufu-dake.

OFF THE
BEATEN
PATH

Usa Jingu 宇佐神宮. Usa Jingu is the main shrine of all the Hachiman shrines in Japan and well worth a visit. It rests inside a huge precinct with many sights to see including lovely ponds with lotus and sub-shrines. You should leave an hour to see the shrine while enjoying a pleasant stroll. Historically there was a long tradition in Japan of building temples and shrines in the same precinct (abolished in the Meiji period), and this is said to be the first place to do so. It is a place of great historical importance and has long received imperial patronage. Usa is a two-train ride from Yufuin (change at Oita and get off at Usa). From Usa, it is a short taxi or bus ride to the shrine. If you take the bus, get on the bus bound for Yotsukaichi and get off at the stop Usa Hachiman. From Oita Airport, the shrine is a one-hour drive. There is also a bus service from the airport via Oita Kotsu Kaisoku Limousine Bus. ✉ *2859 Minamiusa* ☏ *0978/37–0001* ⊕ *www.usajinguu.com* ✉ *Free* ☉ *Daily 6 am–9 pm.*

Yu-no-tsubo 湯の坪. Close to the train station, this neighborhood is a long shopping street lined with traditional Japanese wooden buildings, where you can mill in and out of artsy craft shops and souvenir stalls, or relax in one of the many coffee shops or tearooms.

Yutaka Isozaki Gallery 由夛加磯崎ギャラリー. On most days an artist is painting at the large wooden table in the center of this gallery. Small cards with inspirational messages and illustrations such as persimmons and wildflowers make original souvenirs (¥300–¥2,000). For a unique memento of old Japan, you can sift through clothing made from antique kimonos at the rear of the gallery or piles of antique cotton and silk textiles in **Folk Art Gallery Itoguruma,** the little shop to the right of the entrance. ✉ *1266–21 Kawakami* ☏ *0977/85–4750* ☉ *Daily 9–6.*

WHERE TO EAT

$$$$
JAPANESE
★

✕ **Budoya** 葡萄屋. Part of the pricey Yufuin Tamanoyu hotel, which was until 1975 a lodging for Zen Buddhist monks, this restaurant retains an air of solemnity. The first level has stone floors, thick wooden tables, and windows overlooking a thicket of wildflowers and tall grass. Upstairs, rooms have tatami floors and bamboo-mat ceilings. For a splurge, try the *amiyaki* course (¥11,025), with tender charcoal-grilled beef, seasonal vegetables, and homemade *kabosu* (lime) sherbet. ✉ *Yunotsubo, Yufuin-cho, Yufu* ☏ *0977/84–2158* ⊕ *www.tamanoyu.co.jp/publicspace/index.html.*

$$$–$$$$
FRENCH
Fodor'sChoice
★

✕ **Inaka no Nichiyobi** 田舎の日曜日. For a once-in-a-lifetime eating experience, visit this restaurant run by the Nakayama couple. It's situated in an amazing lofty space within walking distance of Lake Kinrin. But what makes it special is the incredibly delicious menu that features an unusual combination of French and macrobiotic cooking. The steak and

There are several public bathhouses along the shores of Yufuin's Kinrin-ko thermal lake.

fish courses, both followed by exquisite appetizers, are especially recommended, but the macrobiotic is every bit as delicious. Everything is so beautifully presented and good that you feel refreshed and an incredible sense of well-being at the end of the meal, not to mention pleasantly full. You may also want to try the incredible curry that was so good the Emperor and Empress of Japan requested it be served to them a second time. ⊠ *2717–6 Kawakami, Yufuin-cho, Yufu* ☎ *0977/84–3831* ⊕ *www.inakanonichiyoubi.com* ☾ *Closed Tues.*

$$$$
FRENCH
✕ **Moustache** レストランムスタシュ. Started by a Japanese chef who wanted to create a European atmosphere in the shadow of Yufu-dake, Moustache is a café and restaurant with a flair for hearty, country French–style fare. Food can be ordered in set courses or à la carte. The *masu*, or sea trout, is highly recommended. ⊠ *1264–7 Kawakami, Yufuin-cho* ☎ *0977/84–5155* ⊕ *www.moustache-yufuin.com* ☾ *Closed Mon.*

WHERE TO STAY

Hotel reviews have been condensed for this book. Please go to Fodors. com for full reviews of each property.

$$$–$$$$
RYOKAN
🏠 **Onyado Yufu Ryochiku** 御宿由布両築. In winter, when not submerged in the mineral waters here, you can toast yourself by the burning coals in the *irori* (sunken hearth) in the lobby of this 1925 inn. **Pros:** charming, tranquil atmosphere; locks on mineral bath doors mean they can be made private. **Cons:** no Internet; not much except bathing going on. ⊠ *1097–1 Kawakami, Yufuin-cho, Yufu, Oita-ken* ☎ *0977/85–2526* 🖷 *0977/85–4466* ⊕ *www.tentacle.jp* ⤺ *8 Japanese-style rooms without bath, 2 houses* ☖ *In-room: a/c* ⍩ *Some meals.*

Sanso Murata is a ryokan that blends Western and Japanese influences.

$$$–$$$$
INN

🏠 **Pension Momotaro** ペンション桃太郎. The owners of this interesting and very rustic pension make every effort to make you feel at home; they'll even take you to the station when you depart. Both Western-style and Japanese-style rooms are available in the main building, and four charming A-frame cottages are on the premises—each with hot spring water piped into the bath and shower. **Pros:** funky little shacks; private baths inside; open-air bath with views of Yufu-dake. **Cons:** cottages like tents in a yard; might be too much like "camp" for some. ✉ *1839–1 Kawakami, Yufuin-cho, Yufu, Oita-ken* ☎ *0977/85–2187* 🖷 *0977/85–4002* 🛏 *6 Western-style rooms, 4 Japanese-style rooms, 4 chalets* ♨ *In-room: a/c. In-hotel: restaurant* ▤ *No credit cards* ❙○❙ *Some meals.*

$$$$
RYOKAN
Fodor's Choice
★

🏠 **Sanso Murata** 山荘無量塔. Murata is a truly unique and special place that mixes the best of Western and Japanese accommodation to perfection. **Pros:** incredible food; marvelous staff; real taste and atmosphere. **Cons:** noise from boiler, air-cleaner, and heaters can disturb the majestic silence; very expensive (albeit worth the cost). ✉ *1264–2 Yufuin-cho Kawakami, Yufu* ☎ *0977/84–5000* ⊕ *www.sansou-murata.com* 🛏 *12 combination rooms* ♨ *In-room: a/c, safe, refrigerator, DVD, Internet. In-hotel: room service, spa, parking (free)* ❙○❙ *Some meals.*

Okinawa

WORD OF MOUTH

"The Peace Park and Museum are awesome—I've never been to anyplace more moving or filled with hope. The Navy HQ—not so interesting (to me). Suicide Cliffs—not so depressing. . . . The Peace Museum is stunningly moving and educational. I didn't find it at all depressing and I learned a lot."

—kotoanne

WELCOME TO OKINAWA

TOP REASONS TO GO

★ **Local Flavors:** Okinawa's food, music, art, and local spirit combine powerful influences from all over Asia with funky, homegrown flavors.

★ **Tragic History:** Moving memorials tell the poignant story of the chaos that ravaged this idyllic landscape during World War II's fierce final battle.

★ **Getting Wild:** Snorkeling, diving, trekking, sailing, fishing, whale-watching, and kayaking are in your reach in Japan's most pristine and enticing natural vistas.

★ **Dazzling Reefs:** Okinawa's abundant reefs are home to varied marine life thriving in clear, warm seas. Dive with manta rays and hammerhead sharks or simply glide over gardens of hard and soft corals.

1 **Okinawa Honto.** Naha's Kokusai Street and Shuri Castle are a great introduction to the area. More captivating are the war memorials on the southern peninsula, and the diving and snorkeling spots, active artisan workshops, and wild scenery to the north.

2 **Kerama Islands.** Dazzling coral reefs and white beaches are only a stone's throw away from Naha's port. Though close to Okinawa's mainland, infrequent ferry times make planning ahead essential, but the vivid blue ocean makes these islands well worth the hassle.

3 **Miyako Islands.** A 45-minute flight from Naha, Miyako Island has arguably the best beaches in Japan. Along with snorkeling, diving and great beach-side accommodation, Miyako offers a whole lot of R&R.

4 **Yaeyama Islands.** An hour flight from Naha, Ishigaki is a great place to visit and a launch point for the surrounding sights including time-forgotten villages on Taketomi Island and the reefs and forests of untamed Iriomote. It's the perfect mixture of developed getaways and seriously off-the-map adventure.

GETTING ORIENTED

Island-hopping outside Okinawa Honto means traveling among several disparate clusters of islands; Okinawa Prefecture is a conflation of smaller archipelagoes gerrymandered together, not a steady string of pearls. Traverse the long distances by plane and use ferries to get from one nearby island to another; on the islands themselves you'll enjoy the most freedom with your own transportation, but whether a bicycle or an automobile is more appropriate depends on the size of the island.

OKINAWA'S WORLD WAR II SIGHTS

The Battle of Okinawa is one of the most tragic events in modern history. Caught between two warring nations, the people of Okinawa were killed by a "Typhoon of Steel" and the brutal inhumanity of war.

(This page above) Himeyuri Peace Museum; (opposite page upper right) Okinawa Peace Memorial Park; (opposite page bottom left) Sugar Loaf Hill in Naha

By late March 1945, American forces began the assault on Okinawa, a pivotal stepping-stone to attacking the Japanese mainland. Japan's strategy was to drag out the conflict and force a war of attrition. Every sector of Okinawa's civilian population was mobilized into the front lines of the fighting. The initial bombardment by the U.S. was described as a "Typhoon of Steel." Artillery rained down so heavily that the bombs changed the very topography of the island. Horrific losses were followed by an awful land war. Okinawans who survived the shelling and flame-throwers succumbed to starvation, disease, suicide, or the brutality of retreating Japanese troops. The final battle of the war claimed roughly 240,000 lives—more than half of them civilian—over a quarter of Okinawa's population. The memorials commemorating these events and the quest for world peace are Okinawa's most poignant landmarks.

THE FUTENMA ISSUE

The U.S. Marine Corps Air Station Futenma is Okinawa's most controversial U.S. military base. It is surrounded by a residential area, and locals wanted it closed. In 1996, the U.S. and Japanese governments agreed to move the base to Henoko in northern Okinawa. Many Okinawans have opposed the move, citing environmental concerns, and want no military bases in Okinawa.

SIGHTS IN OKINAWA HONTO

In Naha City, **Sugar Loaf Hill** was a heavily defended strategic point on General Mitsuru Ushijima's Shuri Line. American Marines made repeated frontal assaults, losing thousands of men before capturing the hill on May 18, 1945. The hill is now dwarfed by the DFS Building (Duty-Free Store) just west of Omoro-machi Monorail Station. A plaque marks the spot where so many men died.

Just south of Naha City is the **Underground Headquarters of the Japanese Imperial Navy** (⊠ *236 Tomishiro, Tomishiro-son*). Visitors can explore the tunnels in which Imperial Navy Vice Admiral Minoru Ota lived with 4,000 men. You can see the various rooms, including the commander's office, but perhaps the most unnerving sights are the gouges in the walls and roof from grenades when the officers took their own lives.

Farther south, **Himeyuri Peace Museum** tells the tragic story of Okinawan schoolgirls who were mobilized as field nurses during the conflict. Harrowing accounts of their experiences convey the horrors of war.

Peace Memorial Park is located at Mabuni Hill, and it's here where the final acts of the Battle of Okinawa took place. There are three main areas to the park. The **Peace Memorial Museum** tells the

history of the Battle of Okinawa and the resulting desire of Okinawans for world peace. Outside is the **Cornerstone of Peace**, line after line of low black, granite walls are inscribed with the names of more than 240,000 Okinawans, Japanese, Americans, Koreans, North Koreans, British, and Taiwanese who perished during the conflict. June 23 is Okinawa Memorial Day, when services, held at the Cornerstone of Peace, are usually attended by the Japanese Prime Minister. The **Peace Memorial Hall** houses a 10-meter statue of a person praying. The artist, Shinzan Yamada, began the project when he was 72, and the work took him 18 years. The statue sits on a six-petal flower representing the six continents to symbolize the global search for peace.

AN UNDERWATER MEMORIAL

One war memorial on Okinawa is far more difficult to visit. The USS *Emmons* was a U.S. destroyer that was hit by five kamikaze planes on April 6, 1945. The following day the ship was sunk before it drifted into enemy-controlled territory. In 2000, the Japanese Coast Guard discovered the wreck, and then in early 2001 it was found by local American divers. The *Emmons* lies at a depth of around 50 meters, just off Kouri Island. A few dive shops on Okinawa do offer recreational dives to view the wreck, but the depth and strong currents mean this is only an option for advanced divers.

Updated by
Chris Willson

You'll swear you've hit a different country: let the tropical climate get you ready for sun-kissed beaches and crystal blue waters, deserted islands ringed by rainbow-hue coral reefs, verdant jungle trails, and funky port towns full of laid-back, fun-loving islanders: it's all here welcoming you to Okinawa, Japan's most diverse and exciting destination.

Naha, Okinawa's capital, is geographically closer to Taiwan than to any of Japan's main islands, but deeper distinctions of culture and history are what really set the islands apart. Okinawa's indigenous population comprises an ethnic group independent from the mainland Japanese, and local pride lays much heavier with Okinawa's bygone Ryukyu Kingdom than it ever will with the Empire of the Rising Sun. Island culture today forms an identity around its Ryukyu roots but also reflects the centuries of cross-cultural influence brought to Okinawa on successive tides of imperialism. Ships from ancient Polynesia, Ming China, Edo Japan, and most recently wartime America brought the ravages of conquest and the joys of new tradition (snake-skin instruments, the stir-fry, salarymen, and Spam). Okinawa's melting pot is sharply different from mainland Japan's commercial culture of appropriation and pastiche, touching every element of island life and lending flavor to the music, language, cuisine, architecture, arts, and lifestyle that define the archipelago.

The Okinawan archipelago spans about 700 km (435 mi) of ocean, reaching from south of Kyushu's Kagoshima Prefecture to just east of Taiwan. Of the hundreds of islands only a handful are inhabited, and even the settled ones sport more jungle and beach than they do road and city. More than 90% of the population, numbering about 1.3 million, lives on Okinawa Honto, the largest and most developed island of the chain. Honto is notorious for also housing the bulk of the Japan's American military presence, though unless you're here visiting a friend in uniform, your focus will be the island's beaches, moving war memorials, natural escapes, and the World Heritage castles and monuments of the Ryukyu Kingdom.

With limited time to spend in Okinawa, we recommend you choose one of the three main island groups to explore instead of trying to cram it all in. Many travelers make the mistake of staying put on Honto, but while its sights are terrific, you'll find more great fun, diverse adventure, and welcoming islander hospitality as you get farther away from the mainland. Okinawa rewards a traveler's intrepid spirit, so cast away your map and head out into the wild blue yonder.

12

PLANNING

WHEN TO GO

The best time to visit Okinawa will depend on your goals. In general, avoid mid-May to mid-June, which is the rainy season. The subtropical climate means the temperatures in winter rarely drop below 15°C (59°F), and because of this Okinawa celebrates the arrival of cherry blossom in January. For marine sports including scuba diving, July to October is the best time since the water temperature is around 25°C–28°C (77°F–82°F) and the southerly breezes are not strong. However, July to September is also typhoon season, so the fantastic weather can be interrupted by several days of heavy rains and ferocious winds.

For those interested in Okinawan culture, try to schedule your trip to coincide with one of the many festivals, such as the Shuri Castle Festival (New Year), Naha dragon-boat races (March), Eisa festivals (August), or Naha Festival & Tug of War (October).

GETTING HERE AND AROUND

Naha is the most common entry point to Okinawa, with flights taking roughly two hours and departing regularly from most major airports in Japan (although no direct flights from Sapporo) and several nearby international hubs (Hong Kong, Taipei, Seoul, Shanghai). Most odysseys through Okinawa begin here before moving farther into the archipelago, but there's no reason not to start farther out and work your way back: flights connect directly to Miyako Airport from Osaka-Itami and Tokyo-Haneda, and to Ishigaki from Osaka-Kansai, Kobe, and Tokyo-Haneda. Flying from Naha to either one takes around an hour. Travel agents anywhere in the country can arrange tickets for you. Booking early can get you a significant discount. It is also worth checking on the prices of flight hotel packages that, if booked more than two weeks in advance, can be cheaper than the flight alone.

Public transportation in Okinawa leaves a lot to be desired. Naha is serviced by a handy monorail running from the airport through the city and terminating at Shuri Castle, taking less than an hour end-to-end with trains running about every 10 minutes. Outside the city things are less promising. The story is the same on each of the islands: yes, buses link to urban centers and popular tourist destinations, but schedules are inconvenient, hard to decipher, and confining. Budget for rental cars to make the most of your time on the larger islands.

CLOSE UP

On the Menu

Okinawa's famously long-lived and hearty population has made the "Okinawa Diet" a buzzword among Slow-Food enthusiasts and others interested in healthful eating. Islanders aren't sure where the secret of their longevity lies, but do your best to try it all: is it in the knobbly, green bitter *goya* (bitter melon); delicious tofu-like *fu*; salty *mozuku* seaweed; abundant tropical fruits like pineapple, mango, and papaya; conscientious consumption of every single part of the pig; *champlu* stir-fry dishes; alien-looking fish and crustaceans, sometimes still wriggling; delicious white *soki*-soba noodles, tastiest in a hot pork-stock soup with soft soki rib meat lining the bowl; Thai rice or the blindingly potent *awamori* liquor it's distilled into; aromatic, *koregusu* hot sauce, made from red chilies pickled in awamori; cloying *kokuto* black sugar; savory *umi-budo* sea grapes; purple *beni-imo* potatoes; or a mix of it all?

ABOUT THE RESTAURANTS

Okinawa's culinary history doesn't have the same pedigree as the haute cuisine of Kyoto or Tokyo. A similar aristocratic tradition hasn't prevailed here, and prized local ingredients like soba, pork, and *mozuku* seaweed aren't necessarily expensive or hard to produce. This isn't to say that Okinawan cuisine falls short on rare delicacies or delicious cooking but simply that great, true-blue Okinawan food can be had on the cheap, anywhere. Greasy-spoon joints will have fare as traditional and as tasty as the fancy gourmet establishments, so go enjoy!

■TIP→ One effect of the American military presence has been to increase English-language proficiency throughout Okinawa. Most restaurants and hotels will have some English-speaking staff, so feel confident about going into any establishment for a meal or to inquire about a stay.

ABOUT THE HOTELS

Lodgings range from no-frills beach shacks to lavish resorts. Most of the Japanese tourists visiting Okinawa have purchased packages that combine flights, a rental car, and hotel accommodation. Some chose to remain in Naha, but the majority stay at one of the large resort hotels on the west coast, many of which are on the Yomitan Peninsula or in Onna Village. The high-end resorts often have their own golf courses, fine restaurants, and even wedding chapels. However, you don't have to spend large amounts of money to find paradise. You'll get friendly service, meet interesting locals, and receive knowledgeable recommendations for tours by staying at smaller, local-run hotels and inns.

⇨ *For a short course on accommodations in Japan, see Accommodations in Travel Smart.*

WHAT IT COSTS IN YEN					
	¢	$	$$	$$$	$$$$
RESTAURANTS	under ¥800	¥800–¥1,000	¥1,000–¥2,000	¥2,000–¥3,000	over ¥3,000
HOTELS	under ¥8,000	¥8,000–¥12,000	¥12,000–¥18,000	¥18,000–¥22,000	over ¥22,000

Restaurant prices are per person for a main course, set meal, or equivalent combinations of smaller dishes. Hotel prices are for a double room, excluding 5% tax and tip.

12

VISITOR INFORMATION

Multilingual Contact Center (☎ *098/916–6180 English 24 hrs, 098/916–6181 Chinese 24 hrs, 098/916–6182 Korean 9 am–midnight*). **Okinawa Convention and Visitors Bureau** (⊕ *www.okinawastory.jp/en*).

OKINAWA HONTO 沖縄本島

1,558 km (968 mi) southwest of Tokyo, 1,145 km (711 mi) southwest of Osaka. By air: 2½ hrs from Tokyo, 2 hrs from Osaka. Weekly or daily connections with most major domestic airports.

Arriving from the Japanese mainland onto Okinawa Honto brings a fresh wave of culture shock. The exciting urban landscape of Naha, the bizarre American-esque strip malls, chain diners, mammoth resorts, and funky dive shops all grafted seamlessly onto the place's laid-back, tropical vibe.

Naha's sights make for a great day or two, and some great bars and restaurants offer a good scene after dark. But rather than indulging too much in Naha's nightlife, take advantage of the early daylight to drive out to Honto's other sights. To the south, moving war memorials tell the valuable story of Okinawa's tragic history in World War II. North of Naha, small towns sprawling up the coast are cut at intervals by resort hotels and some great treasures: active artisan enclaves, sweet diving spots, and the phenomenal Churaumi Aquarium. Beyond, the road opens out to the lush, empty northern peninsula. Scenic overviews, rocky karsts, mangrove forests, and waterfalls make for a great day trip. You can see most of the sights on Okinawa Honto in about three or four days: a two-night stay in Naha lets you spend one in the city and one circling the southern peninsula, a following night near a beach up north lets you hit the sights along the coast getting there, and a day in the northernmost natural parks gets you back to Naha for a night out before the flight or ferry to your next destination.

NAHA 那覇

Orchids growing in the airport lounges are the first sign you've come to a very different sort of place. Okinawa's capital city is the center of commerce, tourism, and youthful enterprise in the region. People here are more laid-back than elsewhere in Japan, with business suits replaced by brightly colored Kariyushi shirts, and you'll probably have

Who's Who

Encoded into islander speech are delineations for who comes from where. Ethnic Ryukyu are *shimanchu*—written with the Chinese-Japanese ideographs to literally mean island-people and pronounced in Okinawa's dialect. Ethnic Japanese by contrast are *yamatochu*, reflecting Japan's archaic name, Yamato. Everyone else in the world? *Naichu*, or mainlanders. These systems are all relative, however. More-obscure islands hold denizens of Okinawa's capital Naha to be *naichu*, while on the bigger landmasses they differentiate between *yamanchu* and *uminchu*, mountain folks and sea people. By the time you go home, Okinawa's beach life may make you a dedicated uminchu, but for the moment be happy with what you are: *tabinchu* means traveler.

an easy time feeling relaxed and energized by the city's verve as you tour the sights. Naha's appeal has a short half-life, however, and you may quickly tire of the students on school trips swarming the sidewalks, the chintzy souvenir shops and arcades, and the traffic congestion. Enjoy the wonderful sights before moving out to explore the rest of the island.

GETTING HERE AND AROUND

Japan Airlines (JAL) and All Nippon Airways (ANA) fly to Naha from most major Japanese destinations, with tickets usually running between ¥20,000 and ¥30,000, but discounts for booking in advance can bring the price as low as ¥9,000. Ferries between Naha and Kansai, Tokyo and southern Kyushu have fares expensive enough to make flying worthwhile, especially in light of the time you save: compare a two-hour flight from Tokyo versus a four-day boat ride with at best a ¥10,000 difference in price. Naha also has flights to Miyako, Ishigaki, and Yonaguni, all farther out in the archipelago. The flights within Okinawa are often run by (or code-shared with) the regional arms of JAL and ANA: JTA and ANK.

Getting to the city is easy thanks to the clean, convenient monorail. The line begins at the airport, Naha Kuko, and weaves through the city before terminating at the castle Shuri-jo. Shopping, accommodations, and activities are all centered around on bustling Kokusai Street in the middle of town. Depending on which end your hotel is closest to, you'll get off at the Kencho-mae, Miebashi, or Makishi Station. Everything you need is in within walking distance or a few monorail stops away. Trains run about every 10 minutes from 6 am until about 11:30 pm, and fares are ¥130–¥260 per trip.

When it's time to leave the city, ask your hotel for the closest rental-car place; Naha is denser with these than with noodle shops. It is also very easy to rent a car from the airport on arrival. Most companies offer a similar selection of sensible subcompact cars, but if you want to cruise in style check out the vehicles at Celeb Rent-a-Car. You will need to show an international driver's license or a Japanese driver's license to rent a vehicle.

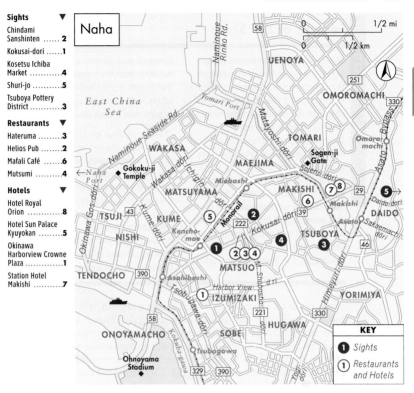

Airline Information ANA (☎ 0570/029–709 ⊕ *www.ana.co.jp*). **JAL** (☎ 0120/747–222 ⊕ *www.jal.co.jp/en*).

Car Rentals Celeb Rent-a-Car (☎ 0120/859–337 ⊕ *www.celeb-r.com/index. html*). **Japaren** (☎ 098/861–3900). **Nippon Rent-a-Car** (☎ 098/868–4554). **OTS Rent-a-Car** (☎ 0120/343–732).

VISITOR INFORMATION

Before you leave the airport, equip yourself with good local maps, time schedules, and service information at the **tourist Information Desk** in the main lobby of the airport. In the city, stop by Naha City Tourist Information Center a few yards down from the Kokusai Street Starbucks.

Contacts Naha Airport Information Desk (*Naha Airport Terminal Bldg. 1, Kakamimizu 150* ☎ 098/857–6884). **Naha City Tourist Information Center** (✉ *Okiei-dori, 2–1–4 Makishi [near Kokusai-dori Starbucks]* ☎ 098/868–4887).

WHAT TO SEE

Chindami Sanshinten ちんだみ 三線店. You shouldn't leave Okinawa without hearing the unique sound of sanshin music. And you shouldn't leave Naha without taking a peek into one of the most highly regarded sanshin-maker's shops in the country, close by Kokusai-dori. Higa-san will give you a free lesson to fill whatever time you have, and several ranks of beginner-oriented sets let you choose a good arrangement if

Legend of the Shisa

Shisa, the lion-like talismans protecting doorways and adorning rooftops throughout the islands, have quite a history. It's said that during the reign of one of the ancient Ryukyu kings a terrible dragon was terrorizing Naha, destroying settlements and devouring townsfolk. When the king encountered the dragon, a local shaman and his boy gave the king some advice they had received in dreams. The boy took hold of a pendant the king wore around his neck, a lion-like figurine that had been a gift from a Chinese emissary. Held aloft toward the dragon, the figure cracked forth a ferocious roar, so powerful it toppled boulders from the heavens to pin the dragon to the shallow seabed, where it died and became part of the islands, now a park near Naha.

These days shisa are Okinawa's most iconic image. Homes and businesses display them in pairs, one on either side of their entranceways, the open-mouthed one scaring off evil spirits, the closed-mouth partner keeping in good spirits. These good-luck totems are popular souvenirs and come in myriad shapes and descriptions; which style you display will depend on the character of your home.

you want to take one home. (If purchasing a sanshin, it is important to buy one made with fake snakeskin. It is illegal to import sanshin made with real snakeskin (usually that of the Burmese python) into many countries, and your new instrument could be confiscated and destroyed at customs. Chindami Sanshinten is on the side street off Kokusai-dori that abuts the south side of the JAL City Hotel. ⊠ *1–2–18 Makishi* ☎ *098/869–2055* ⊕ *www.chindami.com* ⊗ *Daily 10–8.*

Kokusai-dori 国際通り. You're sure to get caught up in the buzzing, infectious beat of Kokusai Street, Naha's central hub for commerce, nightlife, restaurants, souvenirs, and people-watching. A day's wander or a night's crawl along Kokusai Street will give an eye-popping introduction to Okinawa's varied demographics, from the crew-cut military personnel to teeney-boppers out clubbing, from street musicians to octogenarians on shopping trips. The schlock shops can be overwhelming, but those selling everything from high-proof snake liquor to pickled pig's ears carry an irresistible charm. Shisa figurines depicting the fantastic lion-dog creature of Okinawan legend seem to come in every shape and size, from giant ceramic sculptures to plastic trinkets.

NEED A BREAK?

Blue Seal. While strolling down Naha's Kokusai Street, stop by one of the Blue Seal ice-cream shops that pop up along the strip—a soft-serve swirl of vanilla and *beni imo* (purple yam) at an outdoor patio chair is the finest way to beat the heat. The shops are hard to miss, and there are no fewer than six of them between the Kencho Mae and Makishi monorail stations. ⊕ *en. blueseal.co.jp/shop_kokusaidori.html.*

★ **Kosetsu Ichiba Market** 那覇公設市場. Three covered shopping arcades snake out from Kokusai-dori, filled with shops specializing less in trinkets and more in snack-foods and produce. Sample deep-fried ball

Kosetsu Ichiba Market is filled with produce and food stands, including this fish monger.

doughnuts, leaf-wrapped mochi, and tropical fruit drinks on your way to the expansive market that awaits you at the first big intersection on Ichiba Chuo Street. Passing between outdoor fruit stalls into an unassuming doorway leads you to a carnival of delightful and grotesque butchers' counters, fishmongers, and pickle sellers. Pigs' faces stare ghoulishly down from racks displaying every other part of the animal (including some things you likely never thought anyone could eat), displays rivaled only by multicolor shellfish, neon eels, and giant crustaceans so shockingly exotic they seem like they were pinched from Churaumi Aquarium.

★ **Shuri-jo** 首里城. The sprawling, grandiose seat of the ancient Ryukyu Kingdom is far more reminiscent of Beijing's Forbidden City than Kyoto's Imperial Palace and deserves an afternoon of exploration. A marvel for the eyes from the bright red walls and roof tiles to the massive gray and white walls ringing the vast stone courtyard, the original 15th-century castle was once part of an even more extensive property, but was mostly leveled during World War II when the Japanese Imperial Army made the complex its local headquarters. After reconstruction in 1992, Shuri Castle was named a UNESCO World Heritage Site. It's a 10-minute walk from Shuri Station, the last stop on the monorail; follow the signs from the station. ⊠ *1–2 Kinjo-cho, Shuri* ☎ *098/886–2020* ⊕ *oki-park.jp/shurijo-park/english/index.html* ✆ *¥800* ⊙ *Daily 8:30–7.*

Tsuboya Pottery District 壷屋焼. More than 300 years of ceramic tradition are celebrated in this area behind Kokusai-dori's main drag. In more than 20 workshops around these hills Master Craftsman and Living Cultural Asset plaques hang on the walls between various examples of Okinawa's distinctive pottery, on sale ranging from cheap souvenirs to specials pieces for wealthy collectors. The famous Japanese potter Shoji Hamada came here in the 1920s and '30s and left with the inspiration for his notable works, but you may be more inspired by what you find in the nearby pottery museum than what you see on sale—some of the dishes and shisa statues can be kitschy, although the bits of broken pottery whimsically accenting walls and doorways in Gaudí-esque embellishment are a lot of fun. Some workshops are open to visitors, but you'll have a better view of it all one-hour's drive north of Naha at the pottery collective **Yachimun no Sato.**

> ## OKINAWA POTTERY
>
> Walking through stalls of nearly identical terra-cotta shisa statues in the Tsuboya district, you may think that Okinawa's pottery tradition is a newfangled tourist gimmick: don't be fooled. Stop into Kiyomasa Toki for a look at 320 years of unbroken tradition. Take home a keepsake and you'll be in good company: during the 2000 G8 summit in Okinawa, dignitaries dined at Shuri Castle off plates made by Takashi Kobashikawa. The dignataries also received a plate as a gift from the city.

Kiyomasa Toki was begun by a mandate from the old Shuri Emperor to a distant forbear of the kiln's current master, Takashi Kobashikawa, himself a government-designated Master of Traditional Crafts. "The pots shapes change generation to generation with the hands of the individual potters," says Takashi, but the freewheeling geometrics and whimsical fish pattern in a unique red-and-blue glaze were perfected generations ago and are lovingly celebrated in new pieces with every firing. Bearing left out of the Heiwa-dori arcade, go 200 meters until a small incline leads you up to the red-and-black sign. Mugs and tankards are around ¥4,000, cup and saucer sets from around ¥5,000; larger bowls and platters scale from affordable to astronomical. Wrapping and shipping services are available. ⊠ *Tsuboya 1-16-7* ☎ *098/862–3654* ⊙ *Daily 10–7.*

The small but heartfelt **Tsuboya Pottery Museum** has exhibits illustrating the history of the region's earthenware production, including representative pieces from all periods, and a reproduction of a traditional Okinawan house, showing Tsubo-yaki tableware and kitchen utensils. Next to the museum is an intact 19th-century climbing kiln, called a *noborigama*. Recent attention to providing more-detailed English explanations has made the experience more exciting and informative. To get to the pottery district, walk through Heiwa-dori, the left-hand arcade, until it empties out into Yachimun-dori. ⊠ *1–9–32 Tsuboya* ☎ *098/862–3761* ⊕ *www.edu.city.naha.okinawa.jp/tsuboya* ⊙ *Daily 10–6.*

WHERE TO EAT

$$$
IZAKAYA
✕ **Hateruma** 波照間. This lively izakaya-style restaurant with Okinawan food on a helpful picture menu also has fun, live music and dance shows most nights of the week at 6:30, 8, and 9. It's on Kokusai-dori a few blocks south of the Starbucks. It's open until midnight. ⊠ *1–2–30 Makishi* ☎ *098/863–8859* ⊟ *No credit cards.*

$$
ECLECTIC
✕ **Helios Pub** ヘリオスパブ. This microbrewery and pub serves up five tasty home brews along with hearty snacks like Okinawan seafood salad, a goya omelet, and herb-seasoned bratwurst sausages. Wood

floors and thick roof beams, brick pillars, and hanging sheaves of barley don't exactly scream, "Okinawa," but it's a great place for a hearty comfortable meal. Two blocks south of Starbucks on Kokusai-dori. ⊠ *1–2–25 Makishi* ☎ *098/863–7227.*

$–$$
CAFÉ

✕ **Mafali Cafe** マファリカフェ. Hidden on the second floor of a building north (behind) the Makishi Station monorail tracks on Kokusai-dori is a laid-back oasis of good food, great music, and chill staff and clientele. A decent drink selection is backed by a surprisingly varied food menu, with curry soups, alligator steaks, and taco rice. Coffee and cake sets are a great excuse to get out of the weather in the daytime, and on most weekend nights you'll find live shows or DJs. Depending on what you're looking for, it's probably even more fun as a nightspot than as a lunch café. ⊠ *2F Asato 1–1–3* ☎ *098/894–4031* ☉ *Closed Wed. No lunch Mon.–Tues. and Thurs.–Sat.* ⊟ *No credit cards.*

¢
JAPANESE

✕ **Mutsumi** むつみ. This greasy-spoon counter place has been serving some of the best Okinawan fare on the island since 1958, with endearing, hand-drawn renderings on the walls serving as a handy picture menu. Everything is twice as big and three times as filling as it looks, with soup and rice included. Walking north on Kokusai-dori one block past Starbucks, make a left onto the cobbled street just before the Mitsukoshi department store main entrance; it's the unassuming place on your left. And it's open continuously until 2 am. ⊠ *2–1–16 Makishi* ☎ *098/867–0862* ☉ *Closed Thurs.* ⊟ *No credit cards.*

WHERE TO STAY

Hotel reviews have been condensed for this book. Please go to Fodors. com for full reviews of each property.

$$$
HOTEL

🏨 **Hotel Royal Orion** ホテルロイヤルオリオン. You couldn't ask for a better place to find this reasonable, classy Western hotel. **Pros:** great location; good rates; helpful tour desk. **Cons:** traffic noise from Kokusai-dori. ⊠ *1–2–21 Asato* ☎ *098/866–5533* ⊕ *www.royal-orion.co.jp* ➽ *209 rooms* ⌂ *In-room: a/c, safe, refrigerator. In-hotel: 3 restaurants* ℺ *No meals.*

$–$$
HOTEL

🏨 **Hotel Sun Palace Kyuyokan** ホテルサンパレス. Earth-tone tiles and rounded balconies overflowing with tropical flowers welcome you to this appealing riverside hotel. **Pros:** good location; near but not overwhelmed by the city. **Cons:** no Wi-Fi service. ⊠ *2–5–1 Kumoji* ☎ *098/863–4181* 🖷 *098/861–1313* ⊕ *www.palace-okinawa.com* ➽ *62 Western-style rooms, 10 Japanese/Western style rooms* ⌂ *In-room: a/c, Internet. In-hotel: restaurant* ℺ *No meals.*

$$$$
HOTEL

🏨 **Okinawa Harborview Crowne Plaza** 沖縄ハーバービュクラウンプラザ. One of Naha's finest, this spiffy hotel caters to the higher-end market, from the pool's careful nighttime lighting scheme to the dark woods of the lobby. **Pros:** elegant facilities; spacious rooms, quiet area. **Cons:** 10-minute walk to Kokusai-dori. ⊠ *2–46 Izumizaki* ☎ *098/853–2111* 🖷 *098/833–6422* ⊕ *www.harborview.co.jp* ➽ *352 rooms* ⌂ *In-room: a/c. In-hotel: 4 restaurants, bar, pool, laundry service* ℺ *No meals.*

$$
HOTEL

🏨 **Station Hotel Makishi** ステーションホテル牧志. Right where Kokusai-dori quiets down, you'll find a stark white-tiled lobby leading up to improbably spacious, accommodating guest rooms at this high-rise, Western-style hotel. **Pros:** large rooms; hotel has Internet service. **Cons:**

no double beds. ✉ *1–2–25 Asato* ☎ *098/862–8001* 🌐 *www.hotel-makishi.com* *79 rooms* *In-room: a/c, safe, refrigerator, Internet. In-hotel: restaurant, laundry facilities* *No meals.*

NIGHTLIFE

You can't visit Okinawa without hearing the entrancing, energetic sound of the sanshin, Okinawa's banjo-like string instrument. A fretless lacquered neck with three strings on a body traditionally made from snakeskin wrapped around a tight drum produces a sound at once upbeat and melancholic—and wholly otherworldly if you've grown up anywhere but here. Music is one of the most celebrated parts of Okinawa's culture, and you might easily fall in love with the mesmerizing sanshin. If you don't have a solid idea of what Okinawan music can really sound like at its best, ask to hear some Kadekaru Rinsho, a master of traditionally inspired songs, or something by modern folk-pop group Begin (they're kind of Okinawa's Beatles), or just go out drinking later into the night than you're used to. The izekaya Hateruma on Kokusai-dori has live shows of Okinawan music most nights.

Black Harlem. Stop here for the smooth, relaxed atmosphere, and sample some of the 10,000 soul records the owner, Takeshi, has on display behind the bar. If you're tired of hearing the sanshin and would rather chill out to Marvin Gaye and the Isley Brothers, this is your place. There's usually a cover of ¥500. ✉ *6F Cosmo Bldg., 2–7–22 Makishi* ☎ *098/866–8912* 🌐 *www.geocities.jp/soulbar_black_harlem* ⏲ *9 pm–6 am.*

Bomba Latina. You can enjoy the spirit of Latin America while you're in Okinawa. Food choices include Peruvian ceviche and Mexican tacos, while the drinks menu includes South American classics such as Inca Kola and Pisco. ✉ *2F Miyazato Bldg., 2–7–26 Makishi* ☎ *098/863–5028* 🌐 *www.bombalatina.jp* ⏲ *Daily noon–4 am.*

Eager Beaver. Paul Patry's new Canadian Pub is a welcome addition to Okinawa. With a relaxed, friendly atmosphere, it's a place where you can settle down with a pint, play foosball and darts, or watch sports on TV. There's a good selection of international beers and food, including fish and chips, nachos, and French-Canadian *poutine* (fries topped with fresh cheese curds and brown gravy). ✉ *1F Friends Bldg., 3–19–21 Makishi* ☎ *098/938–3838* 🌐 *www.eagerbeaverokinawa.com* ⏲ *Tues.–Sun., 7 pm–3 am.*

Live House Kento's. In Naha's admittedly seedier area, Matsuyama, Live House Kento's has been going strong for decades with mostly 1950s and '60s cover bands in great getups rocking a stage so warmly neoned out it feels like the whole bar is inside a Wurlitzer jukebox: there's a whole lotta shakin' goin' on. Most nights have performances with entry fee ¥1,500. It's a famous spot, so anyone can point the way. Walking from Kokusai-dori, follow Ichigin-dori north until you get to the bustling Matsuyama intersection and hang a left at the Lawson convenience store. ✉ *BF Matsu-machi Peatsuti Bldg., 1–14–19 Matsuyama* ☎ *098/868–1268* 🌐 *kentos-okinawa.com* ⏲ *Daily* 6 pm–*3* am.

Rehab. This is the best of Naha's foreigner hang-out bars, and it's easily the most fun place in town to relax for a few drinks at the end of your night. Rehab and its owner Paul Patry are institutions in Naha's

The sanshin is covered by snakeskin (sometimes fake).

nightlife. Come in to hear stories from Norwegian ship captains on leave, multilingual local businessmen, the convivial barmaids or Paul himself, the most gregarious person within city limits. Paul is also a great resource for arranging sailing cruises, reef walking, diving, kayaking, and more. ⊠ *3A Kakazu Bldg., 2–4–14 Makishi* ☎ *098/864–0646* ⊕ *www.rehabokinawabar.com* ☺ *Daily 7–2.*

SOUTH OF NAHA

There are at least three good reasons to explore Okinawa's southern spur. The culture park **Okinawa World** is an interactive trip through the islands' Ryukyu past, with restored houses, a large limestone cave, and traditional performances. More than the ancient Ryukyu culture, however, it is Okinawa's history during World War II that will resonate most with visitors. Himeyuri Peace Museum and Okinawa Peace Memorial Museum trace Okinawa's tragic story. Caught between American and Japanese militaries during the last months of the war, Okinawa suffered an astronomical toll in lost lives and resources. Like Hiroshima's **Atomic Bomb Dome,** these sights are important not only to local history, but also for their message teaching the value of peace to all.

GETTING HERE AND AROUND

Bus routes will take you past all the sights, but infrequent schedules will rush you or leave you bored. It's an easy drive from the city, though—every sight is on Route 331—so renting a car is highly advisable. Bus schedules change year to year.

WHAT TO SEE

Fodor's Choice
★

Himeyuri Peace Museum ひめゆり平和祈念資料館. This moving museum tells the story of 240 students from a girls' high school near Naha. Mobilized as field nurses in the war's final months, the girls' hellish experience tending to wounded Japanese soldiers in hidden caves near the city are retold in an intensely poignant series of dioramas, textual explanations, and displays. Photographs and journals show the girls' innocence and hope before the war, providing a moving counterpoint to the artifacts and diaries that highlight the ghastly conditions they endured during the fighting. Photographs of each girl drive home the waste and finality of the war's tragic effects. The museum is very clear about its message: "we must continue to tell our stories of a war filled with insanity and brutality, now that the post-war generations, who have no idea what war is, have formed the majority of the population . . . threats to peace in both domestic and international politics cannot be ignored." It's 60 minutes from Naha via Bus 32 or 89 (¥550), with a change in Itoman to Bus 82 (¥270). Buses depart hourly and continue on to the Peace Memorial. ⊠ *671–1 Aza-Ihara, Itoman* ☎ *098/997–2100* ⊕ *www.himeyuri.or.jp* ▣ *¥300* ☽ *Daily 9–5.*

Okinawa Peace Memorial Museum 沖縄県立平和公園. Rows of black granite blocks inscribed with the names of the thousands who lost their lives in the fighting cover the rolling, green hills around this excellent museum complex. Inside, several exhibits designed specifically for children provide a rare opportunity to focus on global issues, while other areas explore and document the various facets of the momentous Battle of Okinawa. Interesting exhibits highlighting each side's tactical perspective and the progress of the fighting are offset by more-personal displays of what life was like on the ground during the chaos and testimonies of survivors (unfortunately, only a few of these are translated). A diorama showing life in American-occupied postwar Okinawa offers further insight into local history. It is 80 minutes from Naha via bus; change from Bus 89 to 82 at Itoman Terminal. The total cost is ¥900. ⊠ *614–1 Aza-Mibuni, Itoman* ☎ *098/997–3844* ⊕ *www.peace-museum.pref.okinawa.jp* ▣ *¥300* ☽ *Daily 9–5.*

Okinawa World おきなわワールド. It's worth spending a few hours at Okinawa World to get a quick overview of local culture. There are tropical fruit orchards and workshops for glassblowing, pottery, textile weaving, dying, and printing. Traditional Eisa dance performances take place several times a day. The main attraction is Gyokusendo Cave, the second-longest limestone cave in Japan. Visitors can walk through an 890-meter section of the cave and marvel at the giant stalactites and stalagmites. From Naha Bus terminal take Bus 54 or 83 and get off at Gyokusendo-mae. ⊠ *1336 Maekawa, Tamagusku, Nanjo City* ☎ *098/949–7421* ⊕ *www.gyokusendo.co.jp* ▣ *¥1,600* ☽ *Daily 9–6.*

Underground Imperial Navy Headquarters (*Kyu Kaigun Shireibu-go*). The cold, clammy tunnels are where a dramatic end came to Admiral Ota and 174 of his men on June 13, 1945. He and six of his top officers killed themselves to escape capture or death by American forces. The grenade blasts that killed the rest of Ota's men left visible shrapnel damage on the walls. An information desk has pamphlets in English, but the staff is unlikely to speak anything but Japanese. It's 25 minutes from the Naha Bus Terminal via buses No. 33, 46, or 101. Get off at the Tomigusuku-Jōshi Kōen-mae (Tomigusuku Castle Park) bus stop, and walk 10 minutes uphill to the ticket gate. ✉ *236 Aza Tomishiro, Tomishiro-shi* ☎ *098/850–4055* 💴 *¥420* ⊙ *Daily 8:30–5.*

12

NORTH OF NAHA

WHAT TO SEE

★ **Churaumi Aquarium** 美ら海水族館. The most impressive aquarium in Japan has the biggest saltwater tank in the world and is a wonderland for the eyes. A pioneering coral-breeding experiment has tons of information about the fragile tropical ecosystem, while tanks hold dangerous sharks, freaky deep-water species, and myriad other wondrous inhabitants of the sea. The star attraction is the 10-meter-deep tank, big enough to give free play space for three majestic whale sharks, a dozen giant, graceful mantas, and schools of fish big and small from the nutrient-rich pacific. This tank is deep enough to allow the whale sharks to feed in their natural, vertical position. Viewing them from below is a breathtaking experience. Take the highway Bus 111 from Naha Terminal to Nago (¥1,940; 90 minutes), and change to Bus 65, 66, or 70 (¥790; 60 minutes). Driving is faster: take the expressway one hour to Nago and continue on Route 58 to 449 and then 114 (about another hour) to Ocean Expo Park. ■TIP➔ In addition to the Aquarium, Ocean Expo Park also houses a great Oceanic Culture Museum and Traditional Okinawa Village Arboretum. ✉ *424 Ishikawa, Motobu-cho, Kunigami-gun* ☎ *0980/48–3748* ⊕ *oki-churaumi.jp* 💴 *¥1,800* ⊙ *Mar.–Sept., daily 8:30–7; Oct.–Feb., daily 8:30–5:30.*

Kongou Sekirinzan Boulder Park 金剛石林山. This great nature preserve lets you wander through the eerie land-before-time rock formations and gorgeous limestone spires of Japan's only tropical karst. Of the three trails, the longer "Strange and Big Rock Course" marked in yellow is nowhere near as challenging or time-consuming as the park rangers make it out to be, and with its varied terrain more reminiscent of Papua New Guinea or Indonesia, the hour you'll spend trail-walking will be highly rewarding. It's all the way up Route 58 just before the road ends, about an hour from Nago. After leaving the karst continue 10 minutes to Hedo Misaki, Okinawa's northernmost tip, for more otherworldly cliffs and rock formations and a great scenic lookout before coming back down the coast. ✉ *973 Hedo, Kunigami Village* ☎ *0980/41–8111* ⊕ *www.sekirinzan.com* 💴 *¥800* ⊙ *Apr.–Sept., daily 9–5; Oct.–Mar., daily 9–4.*

Ryukyu Mura 琉球村. This cultural park showcases Okinawa's roots, with reconstructed buildings, music lessons, foods, frequent variety performances, and a show featuring the poisonous Habu viper. Until Okinawa hosted the G8 Summit in 2000, Habu versus mongoose fights were a popular attraction; thankfully the fighting is now CGI (and 3D). Many of the park staff are elderly Okinawan ladies who epitomize the health and vitality of the Ryukyu Islands. ✉ *1130 Yamada, Onna Village* ☎ *098/965–1234* ⊕ *www.ryukyumura.co.jp* 💴 *¥840* ⊙ *Daily 9–5.*

Yachimun no Sato Pottery Village やちむんの里. This enclave of pottery studios, workshops, and giant wood-fired kilns (and the occasional glassblower's forge) meanders through a woodsy jumble of dirt lanes and Ryukyu-style houses. You can glimpse artisans at work crafting bowls, dishes, and sculptures in any number of distinctive styles as you wander around the tiny village. It's great for sightseeing or gift-shopping as the pieces created here are sold in the adjoining shops. Hidden away at the back is the studio of Omine-san, an excellent potter who, along with his three sons, produces pieces for everyday use, for the tea ceremony, and as works of art. The village is an hour north of Naha in Yomitan Village past Kadena base; turn left onto Route 12 from Route 58 and follow the signs. ⊠ *2653–1 Zakimi, Yomitan-son* ☎ *098/958–1020 for Yomitan Village Community Store.*

WHERE TO STAY

Hotel reviews have been condensed for this book. Please go to Fodors. com for full reviews of each property.

$$$$ ▥ The Busena Terrace. This luxurious resort is arguably the best in
Fodor's Choice Okinawa, if not Japan, but it's extraordinarily expensive. **Pros:** great
★ location; luxurious; excellent facilities. **Cons:** limited number of staff
RESORT speak English for such a major resort. ⊠ *1808 Kise, Nago* ☎ *0980/51–1333* ⊕ *www.terrace.co.jp* ⇝ *410 rooms* ⌂ *In-room: a/c, refrigerator, Internet. In-hotel: restaurants, room service, bars, beachfront, water sports, gym, laundry service* ▮⊙▮ *No meals.*

$–$$ ▥ **Lue on the Beach** オン・ザ・ビーチ・ルー. This bungalow hideaway just
HOTEL south of the Churaumi Aquarium is a quiet, laid-back alternative to the bigger resorts. **Pros:** great location; isolated beach; good restaurant. **Cons:** slim menu; no double beds; spartan rooms. ⊠ *2626–1 Motobu* ☎ *0980/47–3535* ⊕ *www.luenet.com* ⇝ *12 rooms, 12 condos* ⌂ *In-room: a/c, refrigerator. In-hotel: restaurant, beachfront* ▮⊙▮ *No meals.*

SPORTS AND THE OUTDOORS
DIVING AND SNORKELING

Island Club Okinawa. Island Club Okinawa is a marine sports company that helps time-pressed tourists fit as much adventure into their day as possible. Staff are friendly but have varying levels of English ability. Single- or multi-activity courses include snorkeling, kayaking, starlight healing, and even a "discover scuba" class. Island Club is located near Cape Maeda on the Yomitan Peninsula. ⊠ *590–1 Onna-son, Yamada* ☎ *098/963–0166* ⊕ *www.okinawa123.jp.*

Natural Blue Diving Company. There are many diving shops in Okinawa, but few instructors can speak English. This can make it difficult to go on fun dives—and almost impossible to do a certification course. Natural Blue Diving Company, however, is run by Yasu, a bilingual diving instructor who studied marine biology in Florida. He bases his diving and snorkeling trips around Cape Maeda on the Yomitan Peninsula (close to Ryukyu Mura). Cape Maeda is one of Okinawa's most popular dive spots, with an interesting cave. Yasu also does snorkeling and diving with whale sharks, but it should be noted that these sharks are kept in an ocean net and aren't free. Reservations are essential, and credit cards are not accepted. ⊠ *1279–25 Yomitan-son* ☎ *090/9497–7374* ⊕ *www.natural-blue.net.*

KERAMA ISLANDS 慶良間諸島

35 km (22 mi) west of Naha by ferry.

The Kerama Islands have many pristine beaches, and divers rate the coral and clear water off their coasts highly. There are two main islands, Tokashiki and Zamami, along with many more small, uninhabited islets. You can experience the best of the Keramas in a day trip or two from Naha. Eating and drinking establishments are scattered over the two islands, so you won't lack for sustenance.

GETTING HERE AND AROUND

From Naha's Tomari Port you can catch ferries to both Tokashiki and Zamami. The ferry *Kerama* reaches Tokashiki-jima in 70 minutes. The fare is ¥1,620 and leaves daily at 10 am. Marine Liner *Tokashiki* is the express ferry running twice daily, which costs ¥2,430. Always call Tokashiki-son Renrakusho to confirm schedules.

To get to Zamami-jima you have also two choices: the high-speed *Queen Zamami* ferry reaches the island in 50 minutes, sometimes stopping at Aka-jima along the way. The fare is ¥3,140 per person, and there are two or three departures daily. The slower *Zamami-maru* ferry reaches the island in two hours and makes only one daily run. The fare is ¥2,120. Call Zamami-son Renrakusho for schedules.

Once you're on one of the islands, you can rent bicycles or scooters from vendors at the piers. Bicycles rent for about ¥500 per hour, scooters ¥3,000 per day. Zamami-jima also has car-rental agencies.

Car Rental Asagi Rent-a-Car (✉ *Zamami-Town* ☎ *098/896–4135*).

Ferry Information Tokashiki-son Renrakusho (☎ *098/868–7541*). **Zamami-son Renrakusho** (☎ *098/868–4567*).

VISITOR INFORMATION

At Zamami's harbor you can duck into the **tourist information office** in the cluster of buildings to the left of the ferry exit for information in English on boat tours, bike rentals, and diving outfitters.

Contact Zamami Tourist Information Office (✉ *Zamami-Town Chisaki 1–1* ☎ *098/987–2277* ⊙ *Daily 9–5*).

TOKASHIKI-JIMA 渡嘉敷島

The largest of the Kerama Islands, Tokashiki gets the most tourist traffic from Naha. Two lovely beaches with clean, white sand are on the west side: Tokashiki Beach, in the center of the coast, and Aharen Beach, toward the south.

ZAMAMI-JIMA 座間味島

For great snorkeling, try **Furuzamami Beach** (a short walk south of the harbor and village. In summer, there are snorkel rentals and showers. There's also a restaurant, and shuttle buses run to and from the pier and other beaches.

WHALE-WATCHING

On Zamami, late January through March is prime whale-watching season, and during those months you can join two-hour boat tours for ¥5,000. From land, the north shore gives you the best chance of seeing whale tails and fin-slapping humpback antics—bring your best binoculars.

Zamami Whale Watching Association. Weather permitting, boats head out from Zamami port daily at 10:30 am and 12:30 pm. You can arrange these tours from Zamami Island or, more commonly and conveniently, from Tomari Port in Naha. ☎ *098/987–2277* ⊕ *www.vill.zamami. okinawa.jp/whale/english.htm.*

MIYAKO ISLANDS 宮古諸島

300 km (186 mi) southwest of Okinawa Honto.

Some intensive beach therapy can be engaged in here. In the southwest corner of the main island, Miyako-jima, is Maehama, perhaps Japan's finest beach, and across the bridge on the adjacent tiny island of Kurima-jima lies the gorgeous Nagama Beach. Throughout the Miyako islands you can find bright white sand and emerald, turquoise, and cobalt waters. If you're traveling to Miyako-jima in July or August, or during a Japanese holiday, book your lodging in advance.

GETTING HERE AND AROUND

Japan TransOcean Air (part of JAL) and **ANK** (part of ANA) fly from Naha (45 minutes, 11 flights daily) and Ishigaki Island to Miyako-shoto. From the airport to Hirara, a taxi costs about ¥1,300. There are also direct flights with JTA from Tokyo Haneda and Osaka Itami.

Passenger ferries from Naha to Miyako-jima and Ishigaki-jima are no longer in operation. From Hirara Port Miyako ferries make short trips to nearby Irabu-jima, Shimoji-jima, Tarama-jima, and Minna-jima. Tickets can be bought in the Hirara ferry terminal. Boats generally leave every half hour for the 10-minute trip to Irabu-jima (¥410). Boats to the other islands depart less often.

Buses on Miyako-jima depart from two terminals in Hirara and travel the coastal roads around the island. Buses to the north of the island and Ikema-jima (35 minutes from Hirara) depart from the Yachiyo bus station. Buses heading south to Maehama (25 minutes from Hirara) and Cape Higashi-henna (50 minutes from Hirara) depart from the Miyako Kyoei terminal. Buses run every couple of hours from morning to early evening.

Taxi use on Miyako-jima is convenient and reasonable (for Japan). A taxi for the 10-km (6-mi) trip to Maehama Beach should cost ¥5,000 or less. There are several taxi companies; most drivers speak

> **CAUTION**
>
> Although following the coastal roads is straightforward enough, driving in the interior of Miyako-jima requires time and patience, and should not be attempted after dark. Signage is confusing, and the endless sugarcane fields look identical.

12

limited English but will be able to get you to the major sights without any problems.

For car rentals, reserving in advance is essential. **Nippon Rent-a-Car** will pick you up at the airport or ferry terminal. Rates are expensive, beginning at ¥8,085 per day. Perhaps the best option for getting around the island is by scooter (¥3,000–¥4,000 per day) or motorbike (¥6,500 per day). Nippon Rent-a-Car also rents motorbikes, and you can arrange for one to be dropped at your hotel.

Airline Information ANA (☎ 0570/029–709 ⊕ www.ana.co.jp). **JAL** (☎ 0120/747–222 ⊕ www.jal.co.jp/en).

Car Rental Nippon Rent-a-Car (☎ 0980/72–0919, 0120/17–0919 toll-free).

VISITOR INFORMATION

Whether you arrive by plane or ferry, stop in at the **Tourist Information Desk** in Hirara City for help on travel, tour, and lodging arrangements.

Contact Tourist Information Desk (✉ 1697–128 Aza Shimosato, Hirara ☎ 0980/72–0899 airport, 098/073–1881 ferry ⊙ Daily 9–6).

HIRARA CITY 平良

On the main island of Miyako-jima, sprawling, unremarkable Hirara, population 48,000, doesn't have much to see but offers plenty of budget accommodations.

WHAT TO SEE

Boraga Beach 保良泉ビーチ. Here, on the southern shore of the island, a swimming pool filled with water from a cold natural spring is next to a picturesque stretch of sand. Snorkel gear and kayak rentals can be arranged through the pool complex, which includes a refreshment stand. Check out the cave with the pumpkin-shape rock formation.

OFF THE BEATEN PATH

Higashi-henna Zaki 東平安名岬 (Cape Higashi-henna). If you're in the southern corner of Miyako-jima and you have a couple of hours to spare, take a leisurely walk out to see Cape Higashi-henna's surreal landscape. A twisty, narrow road atop a spine of rock leads through a thatch of green grass out to a lonely, perfectly lovely lighthouse. The 2-km (1-mi) peninsula retains an impressive, end-of-the-earth feeling; and in spring the ground is covered with trumpet lilies. The multicolor coral can be viewed from above. Allow about one hour to walk from the Bora bus stop at Boraga Beach. If you rent a scooter in Hiraga, you can ride to the end of the road next to the lighthouse.

Ikema-jima 池間島. Connected to the northwestern corner of Miyako-jima by a bridge, this small island, ringed by a scenic coastal road, has fine views above and below the sea. A distinctive rock formation shaped like a whale tail poised to slap the water lies offshore (and is prominent in postcards). The island is 35 minutes by bus from Hirara.

Irabu-jima 伊良部島. This small, rural island, only a 15-minute boat ride (¥410) from Hirara Port, has two more gorgeous and secluded beaches: **Toguchi-no-hama** and **Sawada-no-hama**.

Maehama Beach on Miyako-jima may very well be Japan's best beach.

OFF THE
BEATEN
PATH

Tori-ike 通り池. If you travel across one of the several small bridges from Irabu-jima to Shimoji-jima, and proceed to its west side, beyond the oversize runway where ANA sometimes trains its jumbo-jet pilots to take off and land the unbelievably noisy things, you can check out Tori-ike, a deep, mysteriously dark cenote connected by underwater caverns to the sea. It's a justly celebrated spot for diving.

Fodor's Choice
★
Maehama Beach 前浜ビーチ. Maehama, or as you may see on local signs, "Yonaha Maehama," is regarded by many as Japan's best beach, and it lives up to its reputation. White sand stretches for miles on a smooth, shallow shelf extending far into the warm, clear water. Take on your friends or the locals at beach volleyball; there can be fewer better locations in the world to play a game. A tiny slice of Maehama can keep you entertained all day, but it actually stretches for 7 km (4 mi). At the Tokyu Resort are water-sports equipment rentals and a marina. The beach is 25 minutes from Hirara via bus.

Nagamahama Beach 長間浜ビーチ. A lovely and often deserted beach on the west side of tiny Kurima-jima, Nagamahama can be reached via the bridge just southeast of Maehama. This is a fantastic place to spend the day snorkeling and picnicking on the fine white sand.

Sunayama Beach 砂山ビーチ. This beach has an enormous sand dune (*suna-yama* means "sand mountain"), out of which juts a marvelously rugged natural stone arch. The snorkeling is as good as at Maehama, and the beach is only a few kilometers (15 minutes by bus) north of Hirara.

Yoshino Beach 吉野ビーチ. The water here is said to have the highest concentration of colorful fish in all of Miyako-shoto; needless to say, it's an awesome spot to snorkel. The beach is just north of

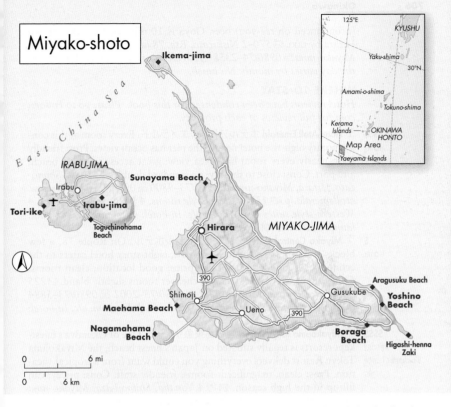

Miyako-shoto

East China Sea

IKEMA-JIMA

IRABU-JIMA

Irabu

Tori-ike

Irabu-jima

Toguchinohama
Beach

Sunayama Beach

Hirara

MIYAKO-JIMA

390

Shimoji

Maehama Beach

Ueno

390

Nagamahama
Beach

Gusukube

Aragusuku Beach

Yoshino
Beach

Boraga
Beach

Higashi-henna
Zaki

0   6 mi
0   6 km

125°E   KYUSHU

Yaku-shima   30°N

Amami-o-shima

Tokuno-shima

Kerama
Islands   OKINAWA
                 HONTO
   Map Area

Yaeyama Islands

Higashi-henna-misaki. If Yoshino Beach is packed with busloads of tourists, try Aragusuku Beach, a little farther north.

WHERE TO EAT

¢ ✕ **Chuzan** 中山. This simple tavern serves inexpensive Okinawa favor-
ASIAN ites such as *goya champuru* (a stir-fry using bitter melon); Korean-style *bibimbap,* a delicious, tangy, healthful dish of kimchi, bean sprouts, spinach, and other vegetables stirred into rice; and a plate of *katsuo* (bonito) sashimi big enough for two or three people. A couple of blocks east from the port, it's on the left side of McCrum-dori before it meets Route 83. There's no lunch served, but it does open by 4 pm if you're eating off-hours. ⊠ *McCrum-dori, Hirara, Miyako-jima* ☎ *0980/73–1959* ▤ *No credit cards* ☉ *No lunch.*

¢ ✕ **Goya** 郷家. The wooden walls of this rustic establishment are full of
JAPANESE alcoves holding treasures and knickknacks from dolls to farm imple-
★ ments to ancient jugs full of fresh *awamori* (rice liquor). Partially enclosed tatami-style rooms offer intimate dining and drinking experiences, while the beer hall–style area in front of the stage makes social-izing easy. There's live music nightly, and cheap, filling, delicious food. Tasty goya chips, *rafute* (bacon slow-cooked in a mix of awamori, soy sauce, brown sugar, and ginger root), and garlicky *gyoza* (fried meat dumplings) should be accompanied by large mugs of icy cold Orion

(pronounced oh-*ree*-yon) beer. Goya is 10 minutes from downtown Hirara by taxi. ✉ *570–2 Nishizato, Rte. 78 just past Rte. 390, Hirara, Miyako-jima* 🕿 *0980/74–2358* ▭ *No credit cards* ☾ *Closed 1 day a wk, the day varies by month. No lunch.*

WHERE TO STAY

Hotel reviews have been condensed for this book. Please go to Fodors. com for full reviews of each property.

$$$$
HOTEL
🏨 **Hotel Atoll Emerald** ホテルアトールエメラルド. Every room at this contemporary high-rise hotel next to the pier has ocean views. **Pros:** friendly staff; nearly every room has a sea view; great access to town, beach, and port. **Cons:** close to the city; no standard doubles. ✉ *108–7 Shimozato, Hirara, Miyako-jima* 🕿 *0980/73–9800* 🖷 *098/073–0303* ⊕ *www. atollemerald.jp* ☞ *133 Western-style rooms, 4 Japanese-style rooms, 4 Western-style suites* ☖ *In-room: a/c. In-hotel: 4 restaurants, bar, pool, laundry facilities* 🍽 *No meals.*

$
HOTEL
🏨 **Miyako Central Hotel** ミヤコセントラルホテル. On Route 78, a few blocks from the pier, this tidy, narrow, eight-story hotel caters to the economically minded. **Pros:** nice price; good location; clean rooms. **Cons:** rooms' views lack scenery; cheaper rooms slightly bland. ✉ *225 Nishizato, Hirara, Miyako-jima* 🕿 *0980/73–2002* 🖷 *0980/73–5884* ⊕ *www.cosmos.ne.jp/~mcentral* ☞ *62 rooms* ☖ *In-room: a/c. In-hotel: restaurant* 🍽 *No meals.*

$$$$
RESORT
Fodor's Choice
★
🏨 **Miyakojima Tokyu Resort** 宮古島東急リゾート. One of Okinawa's finest-kept resorts is regally situated on Japan's finest beach; the Miyakojima Tokyu Resort delivers everything you could want from a tropical vacation. **Pros:** clean, magnificent rooms; friendly staff. **Cons:** pricey; can fill up in the high season. ✉ *914 Yonaha, Shimoji-aza, Miyako-jima* 🕿 *0980/76–2109* 🖷 *0980/76–6781* ⊕ *www.tokyuhotels.co.jp* ☞ *205 Western-style rooms, 40 Japanese-style rooms, 3 Western-style suites* ☖ *In-room: a/c. In-hotel: 5 restaurants, bar, tennis courts, pools, beachfront, diving, water sports, bicycles, laundry service* 🍽 *Breakfast.*

DIVING AND SNORKELING

The Goodfellas Club on Route 390 just east of Route 192 in south Hirara offers diving trips in the waters around Miyako-jima. You can rent or buy snorkeling equipment at one of the many shops in Hirara or near the beaches. ✉ *869-1 Kugai, Hirara, Miyako-jima* 🕿 *0980/73–5483.*

NIGHTLIFE

Miyako-jima has a notoriously hard-drinking nightlife. A common boast is that Miyako-jima has more bars per person than in any other part of the country, which, given the Japanese fondness for drinking, likely means that Miyako-jima has one of the highest concentration of bars in the world. Countless nightspots adorn Hirara, especially in the blocks just east of the piers.

Bar Alchemist. This a good vibes bar with a piano, a telescope, and an endearing, eccentric owner. It's a couple of blocks south of the ferry terminal on the seafront road, upstairs above the A Dish restaurant. It's closed Monday, but other nights you might find live music. ✉ *215–3 Shimozato, Hirara* 🕿 *090/4582–4278.*

South Park. This spot bills itself as an "American shot bar." Cocktails are ¥700 (a bargain for Japan), and shots begin at ¥600. South Park is a bit of a hike east of the piers, near where Route 243 crosses Route 190. From the post office downtown, walk south five blocks then east for two blocks. Open daily 6 pm–1 am. ⊠ *638 Shimozato, Hirara* ☎ *0980/73–7980.*

12

YAEYAMA ISLANDS 八重山諸島

430 km (267 mi) southwest of Okinawa Honto.

This is Japan's final frontier. For a country so famous for its high-tech urban centers and overdeveloped, concreted natural vistas, Japan's farthest islands are a dramatic incongruity. The difference is like day and night, even between Ishigaki-jima, the most developed island, and Okinawa Honto. Ishigaki sports a tiny, funky port city, a few beaches, and very little else. The picturesque, sandy lanes of its neighbor Taketomi-jima have more lion-shape shisa statues than actual people. You're unlikely to make it to Yonaguni-jima, Japan's farthest shore, to dive the bizarre underwater "ruins," but the more easily accessible Iriomote-jima promises plenty of adventure: practically the entire island is protected national parkland, from the lush jungles and mangrove-lined rivers to the glittering, shimmering coral under the waves.

ISHIGAKI-JIMA 石垣島

1 hr by plane from Naha.

A day of beachside R&R and a night in Ishigaki City's fun bars and cheap restaurants may be all it takes to make you want to move here. You wouldn't be alone: most of Ishigaki's people are either escapees seeking asylum from Japan's business-driven culture or descendants of islanders repatriating themselves into their forebears' country.

GETTING HERE AND AROUND

Both **JTA (part of JAL)** and **ANK (part of ANA)** airlines make the 55-minute flight from Naha to Ishigaki-jima. JTA also has direct flights from Ishigaki to Nagoya, Osaka, and Tokyo. Late-night arrivals may miss the last bus to the city, but a taxi ride won't cost more than ¥1,000. From Ishigaki city, ferries connect to the surrounding islands. Only far-off Yonaguni-jima requires another flight.

Ishigaki City is small and walkable; pick up a map at your hotel or the bus center across from the port, where you'll also find pamphlets on attractions and vital ferry and bus schedules. Getting around the island by car and motor scooter is a snap—there's really no traffic and only a few roads—and rental places litter the town like sandal shops. Cars are expensive, but cheaper than on some islands; rentals typically range from ¥6,825 to ¥7,875 per day. Try **Ai-Ai**, kitty-corner to the post office, for bicycles, scooters, and motorcycles.

Airline Information ANA (☎ *0570/029–709* ⊕ *www.ana.co.jp.* **JAL** (☎ *0120/747–222* ⊕ *www.jal.co.jp/en.*

Bicycle Rentals Ai-Ai (☎ *0980/83–9530*) has one-day rentals from ¥1,000.

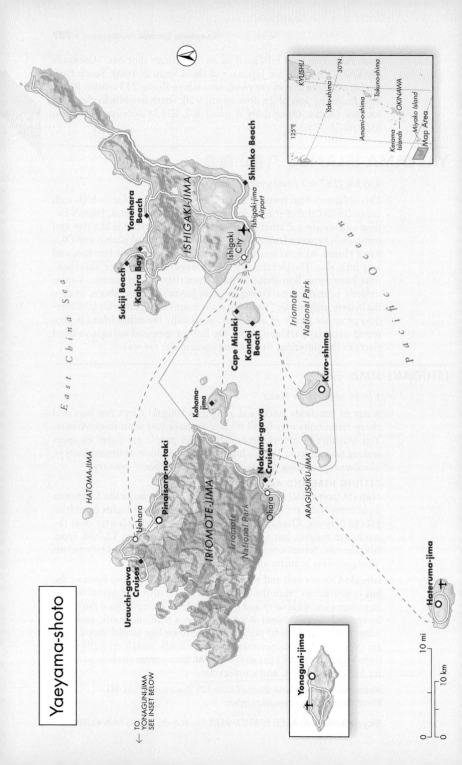

Yaeyama-shoto

East China Sea

ISHIGAKI-JIMA

Sukiji Beach
Kabira Bay
Yonehara Beach
Ishigaki City
Ishigaki-jima Airport
Shimko Beach

Iriomote National Park

HATOMA-JIMA

Uehara
Urauchi-gawa Cruises
Pinaisara-no-taki
IRIOMOTE-JIMA
Iriomote National Park
Ohara
Nakama-gawa Cruises

Cape Misaki
Kondoi Beach
Kohama-jima

Kuro-shima

ARAGUSUKU-JIMA

Pacific Ocean

Haterma-jima

Yonaguni-jima

← TO YONAGUNI-JIMA
SEE INSET BELOW

0   10 mi
0   10 km

KYUSHU
30°N
125°E
Yaku-shima
Amami-o-shima
Tokuno-shima
OKINAWA
Kerama Islands
Okinawa Island
Miyako Island
Map Area

Tamatorizaki Observation Point is on Ishigaki-jima's hilly northern peninsula.

Car Rentals Toyota Rent-a-Car (☎ *0980/82–0100*). **Nippon Rent-a-Car** (☎ *0980/82–3629*).

Visitor Information Ishigaki City Tourism Office (✉ *114 Hamasaki Town 1F, Ishigaki City* ☎ *0980/82–2809* ⏱ *Weekdays 8:30–5:30*).

WHAT TO SEE

Yonehara Beach 米原キャンプ場. The most idyllic beach on Ishigaki has great swimming and snorkeling off a hundred-meter-long stretch of clean, sparkling sand. Beach access involves walking through the Yonehara Campground, but as there are rarely any tents up even in the high season, the water will be more or less all yours. Behind a stand of trees in the campground the Orange House rents fins and snorkels; at low-tide the sea life will be beautiful if alarmingly close up, and in high tide the rainbow-color coral and alien-looking sea life are amazing. You can use the Orange House's shower when you return the equipment, and plates of tasty Okinawan yaki-soba will recharge you. If you can't bear to leave, rent a tent and a barbecue set there and catch the sunset. Yonehara is about one hour from Ishigaki by bus or a half hour by car on the island's northern shore.

Taketomi-jima 竹富島. It is just a 10-minute ferry trip from Ishigaki City to the quaint terra-cotta-roof Ryukyu cottages, sleepy lanes, and empty bright beaches of Taketomi Island. The cute little town is easily navigable by bicycle; ask one of the touts standing at the pier when you show up. Another fun option is the "old-fashioned" tour—meander between the narrow rock walls in the back of a water buffalo–drawn cart, and you'll be serenaded by the plonking sanshin and soaring voice

You can take a tour of Taketomi-jima on a water-buffalo cart.

of the cart's skilled grandfatherly driver. **Kondoi Beach** コンドイビーチ, about 15 minutes by bicycle from the center of town, has good swimming with showers and changing facilities. **Hoshizuna Beach** is famous for its star sand, which are, depending on who you ask, either the tiny exoskeletons of marine protozoa or the children of stars.

WHERE TO EAT AND STAY

Hotel reviews have been condensed for this book. Please go to Fodors. com for full reviews of each property.

$–$$
JAPANESE
★
☺

✕ **Buku Buku Cha-Ya Tea Shop** ぶくぶく茶屋. Two blocks up from Ishigakis City's main intersection and set back into an inviting wooden storefront, Buku Buku Tea Shop would be famous just for its kitchen, were it not for the rare traditional tea that really steals the show. Great lunch and dinner sets usually begin from a standard base like the *don-buri*—a rice bowl with stir-fried meat or vegetables served on top—but dishes are tweaked and specialized with locally grown vegetables and innovative styles of rice preparation and rare strains of rice to bowl over your palette. Tea is delightful by itself, too, when you try making it the Ryukyu way. A wooden bowl holds thick, black tea made from baked rice grains, but this isn't what you drink: with a big bamboo whisk, you'll whip it into a thick cloud of foam to spoon onto the drink of your choice; sharing one drink among friends so everyone looks equally foolish with a splash of foam on his nose is highly encouraged, and the drinks are delicious. ⊠ *238 Okawa, Ishigaki* ☎ *0980/87–8033* ▭ *No credit cards.*

$$$
IZAKAYA
Fodor's Choice
★

✕ **Usagi-Ya** うさぎや. Ishigaki's finest example of Okinawan izakaya cooking—where many small dishes add up to a sensational, weird meal—is offered here. Be sure to try something with delicious *fu,* a soft tofu-like bean paste if the crunchy pig's ears are too much for you, and curry favor with the staff by washing it down with golden Orion beer. Okinawa's proud local awamori is a fierce, island-made liquor distilled from rice. Food and drink here are terrific, but even better is the nightly floor show. From about 7 until the mood dies (or when the restaurant closes, around midnight), staff armed with guitars and snakeskin sanshin will go through every song in the archipelago's catalog, the moving traditional pieces balanced with rock-pop hits. Join in wherever the feeling hits you; Okinawan songs are built to involve boisterous shouting and clapping from the audience, so don't be shy! After the show, see how far you can get on one of the instruments. It's just off Ishigaki's main drag next to Shima-Soba. ⊠ *1F Nakamura Heights, 1–1 Ishigaki* ☎ *0980/88–5014* ⊟ *No credit cards.*

$$$$
RESORT

⊡ **Chisun Resort Ishigaki** チサンリゾート石垣. A member of the upscale Solaris Resort Group, the Chisun Ishigaki is pretty down to earth while being luxurious enough to let you really relax and enjoy your stay. **Pros:** gorgeous wood flooring; excellent decoration sense; big beds. **Cons:** no doubles; only one suite; not on the beach. ⊠ *1 Tonoshiro* ☎ *0980/82– 6161* ⊅ *83 rooms, 1 suite* ⌂ *In-room: a/c, safe, refrigerator, Internet. In-hotel: restaurant, laundry facilities* ⊚⊙ *No meals.*

$
HOTEL

⊡ **Hyper Hotel Ishigaki** ハイパーホテル石垣. Big beds, fluffy duvets, and a great location—it's a block east of the ferry dock—make Hyper Hotel a great choice despite the silly name and slightly grubby trimming. **Pros:** price; location; basic amenities covered. **Cons:** showing some age; gruff staff. ⊠ *1–2–3 Yashima-cho, Ishigaki* ☎ *0980/82–2000* ⊞ *0980/82–3933* ⊕ *www.hyper-ishigaki.co.jp* ⊅ *94 rooms* ⌂ *In-room: a/c. In-hotel: laundry facilities* ⊚⊙ *Breakfast.*

DIVING AND SNORKELING

Tom Sawyer. The scuba-diving and snorkeling around Ishigaki-jima is superb; you can find plenty of outfitters based in downtown Ishigaki, including this one. Trips include the coral reefs near Kabira-wan, Yonehara, and Cape Hirakubo. Lunch-inclusive outings cost around ¥13,000 plus ¥4,000 for scuba gear rental. The most famous diving spot on the island (and perhaps in Japan) is Manta Scramble near Kabira Bay. In autumn you can sit on the ocean floor and watch manta rays circle above you. ☎ *0980/83–4677.*

IRIOMOTE-JIMA 西表島

31 km (19 mi) west of Ishigaki-jima, 50 mins by ferry.

Surging brown rivers, dense green forests, and crystal blue seas are Iriomote's essential draws, and there's a surprising amount of helpful infrastructure in place to help you get the most fun out of it all. Skilled guides and tour companies make it easy and safe to explore the wilds of this pocket of primordial wilderness, and a few extremely nice lodging options let you enjoy some refined relaxation while you do. You'll want at least two nights—preferably three or four—to get the most out of Iriomote's varied environs, depending on what you want to try. It's all a blast. Returning even to two-horse Ishigaki after a few days jungle-trekking, sea-kayaking, sailing, snorkeling, scuba diving, or river cruising will feel like reemerging into civilization. ■TIP➜ **The post-office ATM may be working, but it's in your best interest to bring enough cash for your entire stay.**

GETTING HERE AND AROUND

Ferries from Ishigaki-jima connect to two ports on Iriomote-jima, southeastern Ohara and northern Uehara, in just under an hour. You want to head for Uehara, but in heavy weather, boats may not continue past Ohara. There are between 9 and 12 departures daily each way for ¥2,300.

The long road ringing Iriomote's northern half terminates in the west at Shirohara and the east in Funaura, and although infrequent buses connect them, all tour companies will take care of transporting you to and from your hotel or port of call at the time of your excursion. Rental scooters and cars are available, but there aren't really a lot of places to go; rely on your tour guides to get you around, and center your meals on your lodging.

WHERE TO STAY

Hotel reviews have been condensed for this book. Please go to Fodors. com for full reviews of each property.

$$$$
HOTEL
★

🏨 **Nilaina Resort** ニ ラ イ ナ リ ゾ ー ト. "Resort" is a misnomer as it a small lodge, but Nilaina has a perfect location, with rooms that look out onto the jungle. **Pros:** diverse customer base; friendly staff; price includes transfers and service. **Cons:** no doubles. ⊠ *10–425 Uehara* 🕾 *0980/85–6400* ⊕ *www.nilaina.com* ⤳ *3 rooms* ⏃ *In-room: no phone, a/c, no TV. In-hotel: restaurant, bar* ⦿ *Breakfast.*

$$–$$$
INN

🏨 **Pension Hoshinosuna** ペンション星の砂. The price could be double for what the hotel offers: bright rooms mostly facing the ocean, excellent breakfast and dinner in the dining room, and a facade backing onto a clean beach with good swimming and gorgeous sunset views. **Pros:** great access; diverse clientele, fantastic location. **Cons:** rooms aren't plush; no doubles. ⊠ *289–1 Uehara* 🕾 *0980/85–6448* ⊕ *www.hoshinosuna. ne.jp* ⤳ *11 rooms* ⏃ *In-room: a/c, safe, refrigerator. In-hotel: restaurant* ⦿ *Some meals.*

SPORTS AND THE OUTDOORS

BOAT TOURS

Urauchi-gawa Cruises. If you go with your guide at Simamariasibi, take one of the boat tours up Iriomote's Amazon. The Urauchi River is the sole reason many day-trippers come to the island, and boats navigate up the broad, coffee-color water through mangroves and ferns to an impressive waterfall, all for ¥1,500. Allow three hours for the round-trip. Kayak rentals can also be negotiated from the boat operators if you want to go it on your own. The first boats depart at 9 am, and the last depart at 4 pm. Since this is the most popular activity for visitors to Iriomote-jima, you'll find plenty of boats as well as frequent buses to Urauchibashi, the mouth of the river, if you arrive at Uehara port in the early part of the day.

DID YOU KNOW?

A 16-km (10-mi) walking trail cuts directly through the dense interior jungle of Iriomote-jima. Local trekking companies can lead you on a guided hike through the bush.

DIVING

Waterman Tours. If burly diving instructor Tokoku-san's beach-bum appearance doesn't immediately inspire confidence, his experienced, skilled instructional manner will win you over in no time. Some two decades of teaching diving courses in the United States, Mexico, New Caledonia, and here on Iriomote give him a sensitivity to people's different learning styles when approaching diving for the first time. His guidance will put you at ease, and his courses through reefs and rocks will thrill you. Tokoku offers fun dives but not certification courses to English speakers. ⊠ *538–1 Uehara* ☏ *0980/85–6005* ✉ *From ¥4,000 for snorkeling, from ¥12,500 for diving (full gear rental ¥5,000).*

HIKING

Fodor'sChoice
★

Simamariasibi. Trekking tours through Iriomote's *Predator*-like jungle is fun and exotic, especially with a tour guide so thoroughly knowledgeable about the island's trails and conscientious about his customer's safety and enjoyment. Nagasawa-san moved to Iriomote from Tokyo more than a decade ago with a background in ecology and environmental engineering. He learned the ins and outs of Iriomote's riddled interior by going boar-hunting with local men during the winter off-season, and focuses his tours away from the regular, frequented tour spots to really let you feel immersed in nature. Along the way he'll point out a surprising amount of information about the jungle and reveal some very special overlooks and locations. Nagasawa-san offers a variety of trekking packages to suit every level of conditioning and interest among customers, beginning at ¥9,000 and including lunch and transportation, all detailed on his Web site. ⊠ *972 Taketomi-cho* ☏ *0980/84–8408* ⊕ *www.simamariasibi.com.*

KAYAKING

Good Outdoor. This company offers sea kayaking courses. The owner doesn't speak much English but is welcoming to foreign visitors. ⊠ *607 Iriomote* ☏ *0980/84–8116* ⊕ *www16.ocn.ne.jp/~g-o-d* ✉ *From ¥10,000 for a 6- to 7-hr course.*

Mansaku Tour Service. Sea kayaking is a terrific way to experience some of the best of what Iriomote has to offer. Tours set off where the road ends at Shirahama; from there it's into the waves. After navigating some shore points and smaller straights and islets, you'll weave in and out of the mangrove-lined estuaries along the coast. You won't really hit the open ocean, but the scenery is wonderful, and it's enough of a workout if you are not accustomed to rowing. Your guide Mansaku-san is decently conversant in English and skilled at creating a fun atmosphere during the trip. If the weather is good you can snorkel off the kayaks into the crystal clear bay. Longer camping tours and lure-fishing are available as well. ⊠ *10–75 Uehara #201, Iriomote* ☏ *0980/85–6222* ⊕ *www.cosmos.ne.jp/mansaku/eindex.html* ✉ *Sea-kayak and snorkeling from ¥10,500 for a full-day tour.*

Tohoku

WORD OF MOUTH

"We loved Kakunodate and Lake Tazawa. They are both at altitude so would be a little cooler in July. Lots of people also do the Sendai to Matsushima area. Aomori and the Oirase stream is nice along with Lake Towadako. It is cooler in the mountains with a lot of ryokan in the area. Lots of area to explore in Northern Tohoku."
—hawaiiantraveler

WELCOME TO TOHOKU

TOP REASONS TO GO

★ **Summer Festivals:** Tohoku hosts a number of raucous, tumultuous, and exciting festivals every summer, the Tanabata Matsuri being the top draw.

★ **Coastal Beauty:** Matsushima Bay's 250 islands near Sendai are beautiful, but the coast is postcard-pretty virtually anywhere.

★ **Seafood and Vegetables:** The freshest seafood you'll ever eat is presented in many ways, all of them tasty. *Sansai* (wild mountain vegetables) are a specialty of the region.

★ **Country Life:** Tohoku claims some of the cleanest water in the country, which helps produce high-quality rice, noodles, apples, cherries, and beef and dairy cattle.

★ **Mountain Adventures:** The many fine mountain playgrounds are made all the more appealing by the relative absence of people using them.

1 Sendai. The city of fun-loving, livable, navigable, stylish people and a haven of great shopping, friendly people, and fine eateries hosts the immense and colorful Tanabata Matsuri, a four-night, three-day festival that swells the town to three times its normal size.

2 Northern Tohoku. By branching out from the Shinkansen hub of Morioka, you'll come across traditional iron-ware teakettles, grand old castles, lovingly preserved samurai houses, sparkling lakes, and huge national parks with mountains to climb, hiking trails for all abilities, large virgin forests, and hot springs galore.

3 West Coast Tohoku. Mountains give way to fertile plains that extend to the Sea of Japan. While you will find an occasional castle, everywhere you explore you'll encounter the best food, local women nationally celebrated for their legendary fairness, mountains often buried in powder snow, and countless onsen.

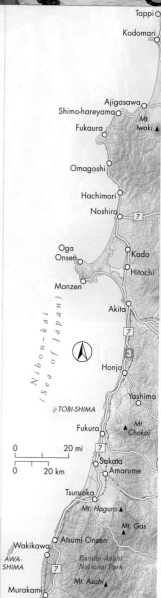

GETTING ORIENTED

Tohoku, like the rest of Honshu, is riven by a series of dramatic chains of densely forested mountains. Not only will their rugged beauty take your breath away, they can also make travel difficult. If you allow for this, you won't be overly frustrated. Tohoku is comprised of six prefectures, and stretches from Fukushima, just a short train ride from Tokyo, to the remote and rugged Aomori, the northernmost tip of Honshu, within easy striking distance of Hokkaido. This broad swath of territory encompasses mountain ranges, primitive forests, stunning seacoasts, well-preserved feudal villages, sacred glaciated peaks and secluded temples, relaxing hot springs, and bottomless lakes in the craters of volcanoes.

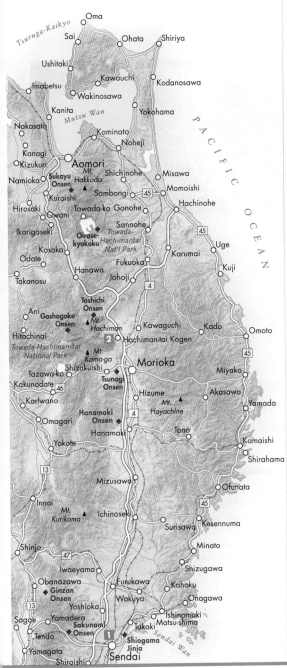

TOHOKU'S HINABITA ONSEN

The Tohoku region has some 650 *onsen* (thermal spas) that are mostly located or "hidden" in remote mountain villages. Traveling here (particularly in winter) is not always easy, but soaking in a relaxing onsen while you are surrounded by snow will remind you why it was worth the trouble to visit.

(This page above) Nyuto Onsen in Tazawa; (opposite page upper right) Ginzan onsen, Yamagata, at night; (opposite page bottom left) a large hot-spring resort in Sukayu Onsen, Aomori

When you hear Japanese talk about Tohoku's onsen, there is one word you cannot miss: *hinabita*. The word means rustic, and for many, it's this simple charm that makes the onsen here so enjoyable. Tohoku's hinabita onsen are a magnet for connoisseurs. To enjoy it fully, an overnight stay is recommended. Nearly all onsen have adjoining lodgings, and most will pick you up at a nearby train station or bus stop. Many ryokan in the region welcome not only visitors but also long-term guests, who stay for months for *touji* (therapeutic purposes) in spartan quarters where they do their own cooking and make their own beds. Touji has been practiced since the 17th century and is still popular, particularly among cancer patients as an alternative medicine.

HOW TO ONSEN

Sit on a small stool and scrub thoroughly with liquid soap from head to toe as if you haven't bathed for years. This is no joke. Just as taking your shoes off at the door prevents dirt from coming into a house, bathing first helps keep the onsen clean. This isn't as much about meticulous hygiene (though the Japanese are known to be obsessive in that regard), but about keeping dirt and bacteria out of the onsen.

13

AOMORI

Sukayu Onsen. Milky, highly acidic water floods into the large cedar bathhouse known as a *sennin-buro,* a 1,000-person bath. Designated as a national health resort, Sukayu draws many touji travelers to its curative waters. It has a reputation for the best mix-bathing in the nation. The trip from Aomori takes 70 minutes, or one hour from Oirase. ✣ *From JR Aomori Station, take the JR bus bound for Towada-ko; from Oirase Gorge, take the bus bound for JR Aomori Station, but get off at the Sukayu Onsen stop* ⊕ *www.sukayu.jp.*

IWATE

Hanamaki Onsenkyo. Among 14 onsen that collectively make up this district, Osawa and Namari stand out for their quality and well-kept ryokans offering comfort and long-cherished histories. Osawa is 40 minutes by bus from Iwate's Hanamaki Airport, Namari 50 minutes. From Morioka, Osawa is 70 minutes, Namari 80 minutes. Arrange for a shuttle from the bus station to your ryokan. ✣ *From Iwate Hanamaki Airport, take the "Airport liner" bus bound for Hanamaki Minami Onsenkyo Houmen. From JR Morioka Station, take the Iwatekoutsu bus bound for Shin-Namari Onsen to save time and money. If you arrive either at JR Hanamaki Station or Shin-Hanamaki Station, take a bus or free shuttle* ⊕ *www.kankohanamaki.ne.jp/en/spa/index.html.*

TAZAWA

Nyuto. A mecca for onsen buffs, Nyuto actually consists of seven different onsen and represents the most charming hinabita onsen in Tohoku. Each onsen has well-managed ryokan, and guests can purchase a pass (¥1,500) that allows them to ride free shuttles operating among the seven and to use almost all facilities. Nyuto is 47 minutes from Tazawa-ko, 35 minutes from Tsurunoyu. ✣ *From JR Tazawa-ko Station or Tazawa Lake, take the Ugokoutsu bus bound for Nyuto Onsen. From Tsurunoyu, get off at Alpa Komakusa Station, where you can get a free pickup or walk 5 km (3 mi)* ⊕ *www.nyuto-onsenkyo. com/english/eng_qkamura.html.*

YAMAGATA

Ginzan. Ginzan is known its unique landscape and distinguished Taisho-era (1912–26) architectural design. A magnificent wooden four-story ryokan is depicted in Miyazaki's animated film *Spirited Away.* Hanagasa dance shows take place Saturday evenings from May to October. Ginzan is 45 minutes from Oishida, a bit over two hours from Sendai. ✣ *From JR Oishida Station, take the Hanagagsa-go bus bound for Ginzan Onsen. From Sendai, hop on the Yamako bus leaving Platform 22 for Shinjyo and get off at Obanazawa Machiaijyo Station, where you switch to the Hanagasa-go bus to Ginzan Onsen stop* ⊕ *www.ginzanonsen.jp.*

Updated by
Noriko Kitano

Tohoku translates as "east–north," and a visit can do more than shift your physical coordinates. Though the Shinkansen has made getting up here easier, it is still a world away from the crowded south. In Tohoku, the mountain villages are more remote, the forests more untamed, and the people more reserved—but still quite friendly.

Wild as the northeastern territory can be, Sendai sets things in balance, right on the doorstep of the great wilderness. This attractive modern city of a million, with wide, shady boulevards, covered walkways, and shopping complexes, puts on perhaps the country's biggest festival, Tanabata, every summer in early August, in honor of an ancient legend of star-crossed lovers. It attracts more than 3 million people, and it caters to them surprisingly well.

Beyond Sendai you won't find another city as large or lively until you hit Sapporo in Hokkaido, and the countryside looms all around. In comfort and convenience, you can ride the Akita Shinkansen to places like Lake Tazawa, Japan's deepest lake—a powder-blue reflection of sky that sits nestled in a caldera surrounded by virgin stands of beech trees draped in sweet-smelling vines, and steep hills studded with blue-green pines preside over all. Samurai history lives on virtually everywhere in the region, but especially in the well-preserved dwellings and warehouses that now play host to curious tourists in Kakunodate, a town also famous for its hundreds of lovely, ancient *shidare-zakura,* or dangling-branch cherry trees.

Tohoku cherishes its forever-frontier status, and has plenty of low-key cities and timeless small towns full of folks who work hard in the cool summers and somehow bide their time through the fierce winters. Many ski areas collect neck-high powder snow, making for great skiing and snowboarding. There are also broad, bountiful plains that stretch between mountains and ocean, and they yield a bounty of treats, from the sweetest apples and tastiest tomatoes to the perfect rice and purest water that go into some of the best *karakuchi* (crisp, dry) sake in

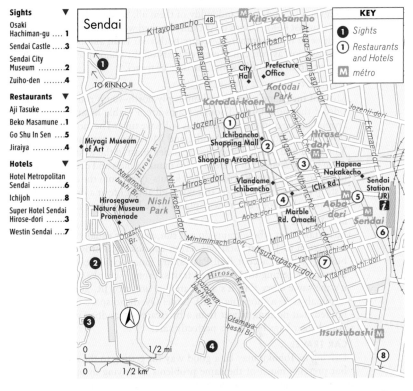

Sights ▼
Osaki
Hachiman-gu **1**
Sendai Castle ...**3**
Sendai City
Museum **2**
Zuiho-den **4**

Restaurants ▼
Aji Tasuke **2**
Beko Masamune ..**1**
Go Shu In Sen **5**
Jiraiya **4**

Hotels ▼
Hotel Metropolitan
Sendai **6**
Ichijoh **8**
Super Hotel Sendai
Hirose-dori **3**
Westin Sendai ...**7**

the land. As a bonus, you're sure never to be far from an onsen—there seems to be one in each and every municipality!

Although the east coast of Tohoko was hit hard by the March 11, 2011 earthquake and tsunami, the area rebounded quickly, with most hotels and tourist attractions open for business just two months after the quake.

PLANNING

WHEN TO GO

The north and west have Japan's fiercest winters; transportation slows down significantly, even grinding to a halt during prolonged sieges of snowfall. Along the Pacific and around Sendai, however, things are decidedly milder. Fall colors in the region are fantastic, and spring brings spectacular blossoms of cherry trees. Summer is cooler with less humidity than in most of Japan.

It would be a hectic rush, but festival freaks could conceivably see all of Tohoku's big summer festivals in a single whirlwind visit, starting with Hirosaki's Neputa Matsuri (August 1–7), Aomori's Nebuta Matsuri (August 2–7), Goshogawara's Tachi Neputa (August 4–8), Akita's Kanto Matsuri (August 3–7), Yamagata's Hana-gasa Festival

(August 5–7, and the granddaddy of them all, Sendai's Tanabata Mat-suri (August 6–8). Things do get fully booked well ahead (often as early as three to four months), so secure both your train and hotel reservations as soon as you can. Reserved seats on the Shinkansenare usually sell out up to a month before the date of travel.

GETTING HERE AND AROUND

Most of the island's trains and buses ply north–south routes on either side of the mountains. Though trains are a viable means of getting around up here, in some cases a bus will save time. The most important travel routes fan out from Sendai and Morioka in the east, and from Yamagata and Tsuruoka on the Japan Sea coast in the west. Routes are often highly scenic, but there are also many tunnels and occasional boring stretches where the road or track cuts away from the coast or into a steep ravine. A journey in Tohoku is all about life at a different pace, so expect those out-of-the-way places to be hard to reach.

BUS TRAVEL

Buses take over where trains do not run, and they usually depart from and return to JR train stations. From Morioka to Hirosaki, highway buses (JR buses accept Rail Passes) are more convenient (and twice as fast) for getting to Akita than trains. From Tsuruoka to Yamagata, it's the same story (but it's a private bus line, not JR, and one of the terminals is in a shopping mall). Note: Overhead space is so severely limited that nothing bigger than a briefcase or handbag will fit. Store your bigger bags below, it's perfectly safe.

CAR TRAVEL

Driving in Tohoku may be a good way for getting to the remote spots but presents much of the same problems as driving in other parts of Japan, and then some: absence of proper signage (especially in English); inclement weather; following tour buses on narrow, winding roads, one-lane roads; and getting nearly run off the highways by big trucks driven by daredevils. Although gas, tolls, and car rentals make driving expensive, some areas, such as Hachiman-tai, can be explored enjoyable by car.

Most rental cars are equipped with a car navigation system (which is in Japanese but with English handbooks) so navigation may not be not as difficult as you would think. However, the speeds are limited to 80 kph to 100 kph on expressways, 30 kph to 40 kph on secondary roads and in urban areas, making travel considerably slower than the Shinkansen. The approximate driving times from Tokyo (assuming you can clear the metropolitan area in 2 hours) are 6 hours to Sendai, 8–10 hours to Morioka, and 10–11 hours to Aomori.

All major towns have car-rental agencies. Nippon Rent-A-Car is the one most frequently represented. Other car-rental companies include JR Eki, Toyota, and Nissan Rent-A-Car. These outfits usually have offices near major train stations, and even smaller ones. All you need is a valid International Driver's License (available from AAA in the United States) and your home state or country's license. ■ TIP→ Note that maps are not provided by car-rental agencies; be sure to obtain bilingual maps in Tokyo or Sendai.

Contacts JR Eki (☏ *0800/888–4892 toll-free*).

Nippon Rent-A-Car (☏ *03/3485–7196 English service desk, 0120/00–4123 toll-free* ⊕ *www.nipponrentacar.co.jp/english/index.html*).

Toyota (☏ *0800/700–0815 toll-free* ⊕ *rent.toyota.co.jp/en/index.html*).

TRAIN TRAVEL

The best way to get to Tohoku from Tokyo is on the Tohoku Shinkansen trains, all of which are included in the JR Pass. The fastest Hayate run to Aomori, and the slower Yamabiko Shinkansen run to Sendai and Morioka; the Tsubasa run to Yamagata; and the Komachi go to Akita. Shinkansen lines don't go farther north than the west-coast city of Akita. Elsewhere in Tohoku, JR local trains are slower and less frequent (every two hours rather than every hour during the day) when they cross the region's mountainous spine. Most trains and many buses are owned by Japan Railways, so a JR Rail Pass will be a worthwhile purchase. Be aware that most trains stop running before midnight. Overhead racks are adequate for small packs, but you should stow larger items in spaces at the ends of cars. In Japan no one is ever likely to touch your bags, even if left unattended.

DISCOUNTS AND DEALS

Northern Tohoku (Aomori, Iwate, and Akita prefectures) has an excellent way for foreigners staying in Japan one year or less to see the sights of the prefecture: the Northern Tohoku Welcome Card gets you discounts on public buses (50%), at hotels (10%), and at museums (discount varies). The free card is available upon presentation of your passport after filling out a short application form. For complete information in English, visit the Northern Tohoku Welcome Card Web site.

Contact Northern Tohoku Welcome Card (⊕ *www.northern-tohoku.gr.jp/welcome*).

ABOUT THE RESTAURANTS

Tohoku's a great place for fresh food, whether from the fields, mountains, forests, or seas. Restaurants range from local sake shacks to upscale sushi bars and steak houses, and dress may be street-casual to office attire, but rarely will it be formal. Menus may not always be in English, but you can find window displays full of plastic representations of the menu. Credit cards are widely accepted in cities, but they are rarely accepted in the countryside. In many restaurants you'll take your shoes off at the entry and place them in a cubicle.

ABOUT THE HOTELS

Hotels in Tohoku run the gamut from minuscule to behemoth, and often reflect local character. No matter the destination, make advance lodging reservations for the busy summer season. Hotels in the larger cities have the standard amenities, and, as is common in Japan, provide free toothbrushes, hair articles, robes, slippers, plentiful towels, hair dryers, and more. Most large hotels offer a choice of Japanese or Western breakfast; though it is not often included in the rates, it's seldom more than ¥1,500–¥2,000 per person. Casual clothes are usually fine, but as in most Asian countries, shorts on men are not nearly as widely seen as in the West.

CLOSE UP

On the Menu

Visitors seeking culinary excellence and diversity will not be disappointed in Tohoku. Restaurants in the region serve the freshest assortment of seafood, in sushi, sashimi, grilled, broiled, and boiled versions, as well as a bounty of seaweed and generous offerings of wild mountain vegetables (*sansai*) and mushrooms (*kinoko*) in season. *Hinaijidori,* or special local chicken, is a year-round treat and so is the marbled, exquisitely tender beef known as *Yonezawa-gyu*—very expensive, but well worth it!

In Sendai, don't be afraid to try the local delicacy—grilled or braised beef tongue, *gyu-tan,* which tastes like a juicy and less chewy version of well-seasoned beef jerky. In Morioka, try the *reimen,* or cold, chewy ramen-type egg noodles served in a big bowl with a slice of beef, a helping of kimchi, half a boiled egg, slices of cucumber, and a large wedge of watermelon. In Akita, locals are fond of *inaniwa* udon noodles that are flatter, whiter, and more tender than the usual udon. In Kakunodate, *sakura,* or cherry blossoms, are mixed into the flour, and the result is a mildly sweet noodle, as edible as it is pink! Don't miss the truly unique *kiritampo* (hot pot) made with chicken, local vegetables, and distinctive tubular rice cakes that have been formed and cooked onto sticks of bamboo or cedar. Yamagata has its distinctive rounded, chewy soba and incomparable beef. The local sake is uniformly excellent throughout the region, thanks to the quality rice and water.

WHAT IT COSTS IN YEN					
	¢	$	$$	$$$	$$$$
RESTAURANTS	under ¥800	¥800–¥1,000	¥1,000–¥2,000	¥2,000–¥3,000	over ¥3,000
HOTELS	under ¥8,000	¥8,000–¥12,000	¥12,000–¥18,000	¥18,000–¥22,000	over ¥22,000

Restaurant prices are per person for a main course, set meal, or equivalent combinations of smaller dishes. Hotel prices are for a double room with private bath, excluding service and 5% tax.

VISITOR INFORMATION

Individual towns have offices that provide local information. The largest and most helpful tourist centers, which provide information on all of Tohoku, are at the Sendai Station. In Tokyo each prefecture has an information center with English brochures and maps. In summer the local Japan Travel Bureau at the train station in each major tourist area, or at major hotels, can make arrangements for scenic bus tours. The offices in Tokyo, Kyoto, and Sendai arrange tours, some in English.

Contacts Japan Travel Bureau (☎ 022/221–4422). **JNTO Tourist Information Center in Tokyo** (*TIC* ✉ *Tokyo Kotsu Kaikan, 2–10–1 Yurakucho, Chiyoda-ku* ☎ *03/3201–3331* Ⓜ *Yuraku-cho Line and JR Yamanote Line, Yuraku-cho Station*). **Prefecture Information Offices in Tokyo** (☎ *03/5212–9115 for Akita* ☎ *03/5276–1788 for Aomori* ☎ *03/3524–8289 for Iwate, 03/3504–8711 for Yamagata*).

SENDAI 仙台

352 km (219 mi) north of Tokyo.

Sendai is Tohoku's largest city, and its 1.3 million residents enjoy the big-city feel. Meanwhile, they can relax in knowing that Sendai is as safe and easygoing as a small town. Devastated by World War II, Sendai has since become a thoroughly modern and well-planned city, with wide boulevards and a surprising amount and variety of greenery. It's the economic and educational capital of the region, hosting a broad range of industries and universities such as prestigious Tohoku University. In recent decades the city has become a magnet for international students, teachers, and workers, and this has helped foster Sendai's energetic and affable atmosphere.

The city's origins can largely be traced to the story of the "one-eyed dragon," local warlord Masamune Date (1567–1636). Affectionately nicknamed for both his one working eye (he was blinded in the other during a childhood bout with smallpox) and his valor in battle, Masamune established a dynasty in Sendai that maintained its position as one of the three most powerful *daimyo* (feudal lord) families during the shogun period. In later life, his talents expanded: he engineered a canal linking two rivers, improving the transport of rice; and in an effort to further trade with Europe, he dispatched an emissary to Rome and the Vatican.

EXPLORING SENDAI

A convenient entry point for striking out into the region, Sendai has its noteworthy sights and is a fun place to spend a day or two poking around, shopping, and enjoying good restaurants. Walkers and people-watchers will love Sendai; it seems as if the whole city is within a quick stroll. Thousands of shops, bars, restaurants, and cafés line glittering arcades that stretch in all directions. Spiffy hotels and glitzy department stores are well located. Not far from the station, and slicing cleanly through the downtown entertainment area, are three broad avenues: Aoba-dori, Hirose-dori, and Jozen-ji-dori. There's also Chuo-dori shopping street, and all of these conveniently intersect and are linked by the wide shopping arcade of Ichiban-cho.

GETTING HERE AND AROUND

Sendai Airport is well connected, with numerous daily flights to and from every major airport in Japan, and destinations in Asia and the Pacific as well.

But the easiest way to get to Sendai from Tokyo is the Shinkansen. From Tokyo, the Hayate Shinkansen rockets to Sendai in only one hour, 40 minutes, for ¥10,590.

If you have time, the JR Express bus from Tokyo to Sendai is inexpensive (¥4,500–¥5,500) and takes approximately six hours; departures leaving Tokyo from JR Shinjyuku Station at midnight arrive in Sendai at 5:40 am. There are also two cheaper daytime departures from JR Shinjyuku Station at 8 am and 2:10 pm (¥3,000).

Tanabata Matsuri (Tanabata Festival)

Tohoku's Tanabata festival, one of the largest in Japan, is held every year from August 6 to 8 (heralded by massive fireworks over the river the night of the fifth), when Sendai's population triples. The festival is believed to have evolved from a Chinese legend of a weaver girl (the star Vega in her afterlife) and her cowherd boyfriend (the star Altair, in his). As lovers tend to do, they slowly went mad, and began to spend their time idly, living as if in a dream. The jealous ruler became irate and banished them to the far sides of his kingdom (the Milky Way). But he relented, perhaps remembering some foolish love affair of his own, and allowed them to meet on one day a year: the seventh day of the seventh month.

Why the people here celebrate this quintessentially cosmic love story on the sixth day of the eighth month is probably more closely linked with a need to give restive subjects time off to party in a time of great heat. Whatever the background, the festival creates a great reservoir of energy. Colorful streamers flutter from every perch in town. To walk along the arcades with the endless streamers brushing down against your face, neck, and shoulders—as you bump against and smile back at other enraptured souls also seduced by the whole grand pageant—is to feel glad to be alive and in Sendai at such a wonderful time.

From 5 pm on the evening of the 6th, parades, dances, events, and demonstrations of festival spirit are held nightly through the eighth, along a short stretch of Jozen-ji-dori between Kotodai Park and Bansui-dori. The tourist information office in Sendai Station can help with more details, also contained in countless pamphlets.

The Willer Express bus also runs from Tokyo to Sendai and takes approximately five hours in the daytime, six hours in the evening (¥4,500–¥5,500). Five departures leave Tokyo at either JR Tokyo, Shinjyuku, or Ikebukuro Station between 7:40 am and 11:35 pm. The big advantage of the Willer Express buses is their larger choice of comfortable seats. On most routes you can choose from Business class to Economy class.

Returning to Tokyo from Sendai, all night buses depart from JR Sendai Station between 11 pm and midnight and arrive in Tokyo between 5 am and 8 am. Reservations are required.

Once you get to the city, take Sendai Loople, a limited-access bus that stops at Zuiho-den (15 minutes from the station) and Osaki Hachiman-gu (43 minutes) and other major sights. A full-day pass costs ¥600 which gives you discounts at some sights including Zuiho-den; single rides cost ¥250. Buses depart from the West Exit of JR Sendai Station (Platform 15-3) every 15–20 minutes from 9 to 4. The Sendai subway runs roughly north–south only, and its stations are far from the most interesting sights. It's really only of use to resident commuters.

Contacts JR Express bus (☎ 022/256-6646). **Willer Express** (☎ 050/5536-4767 ⊕ travel.willer.co.jp).

Sendai's colorful Tanabata Matsuri is one of the biggest festivals in Japan.

ESSENTIALS

The Sendai City Tourist Information Center on the second floor of Sendai JR Station has English-speakers who will gladly recommend hotels and restaurants. They also provide essential maps with walking and bus routes; there is also an Internet café with coin-operated, multilingual terminals (12 languages; 15 minutes for ¥100).

Contact Sendai City Tourist Information Center (☎ 022/222–4069 ⊙ *Daily 8:30–8*).

WHAT TO SEE

Osaki Hachiman-gu 大崎八幡宮. This was one of the few structures left standing in Sendai after World War II. Built in Yonezawa in 1527, the shrine pleased Masamune Date so much that he had it brought to Sendai in 1607. Nestled among trees, it is an elegant structure, with bright-metal ornamentation over subdued black lacquer. The main building has been designated a National Treasure. It's in the northwest section of the city, about 43 minutes from the station by the Loople and 30 minutes from the Zuiho-den area. ⊠ *4–6–1 Hachiman, Aoba-ku* ☎ *022/234–3606* ☎ *Free* ⊙ *Daily dawn–dusk*.

Rinno-ji 輪王寺 *(Rinno Temple)*. Interested in Zen meditation? This temple, with a quintessentially Japanese garden, holds *zazen-kai* (Zen meditation class) on Saturday evenings. In June, the garden is a blaze of color; azaleas, irises, water lilies, gnarled pines, and bamboos harmonize with each other. It's best to visit in the evening when tranquillity returns after flocks of visitors left. The garden is a 30-minute walk from **Osaki Hachiman Jinja**, northwest of the city center, and if you come directly from Sendai Station, take the JR train to Kita-Sendai Station and walk 10 minutes. ✉ *1–14–1 Kitayama, Aoba-ku* ☎ *022/234–5327* ⊕ *www.rinno-ji.or.jp* 🖭 *¥300* ⊙ *Daily 8–5.*

Sendai Castle 仙台城 *(Sendai-jo).* Views of the city and ruined stone walls await those who hike or take a bus up Aoba-yama to the castle known as Aoba-jo. A restored guardhouse and ruins are all that remain today. The Date dynasty kept its residence here for nearly three centuries after beginning construction of the once-grand castle around 1600. Sadly, it was all pulled down during the Meiji Restoration. **Gokoku Jinja** (Gokoku Shrine) is now the main feature of the area. Near the observation terrace is a statue of the city's founder and favorite ruler, Masamune Date, mounted on a horse. In clear weather the Pacific Ocean can be seen far off to the right. Take the Sendai Loople and get off at the "Sendai-jo ato" stop. ✉ *1 Kawauchi, Aoba-ku* ☎ *022/214–8259* ⊕ *www.sendaijyo.com* 🖭 *Free* ⊙ *Daily dawn–dusk.*

Sendai City Museum 仙台市博物館 *(Sendai-shi Hakubutsukan).* The museum at the foot of the hill beneath Aoba Castle displays cultural artifacts, including pottery, paintings, and armor relating to the history of the Date family and the city, and hosts special exhibitions. It's three minutes' walk from Hakubutsukan Kokusai Center-mae stop. ✉ *26 Kawauchi, Aoba-ku* ☎ *022/225–3074* 🖭 *¥400* ⊙ *Tues.–Sun. 9–4:45, last entry at 4:15; closed Mon. and the day following a national holiday.*

SS (Sendai Sumitomo) 30 Building 住友生命仙台中央ビル. Visitors who want to see the sights from on high can do so from the observatory deck on the top floor of this 30-story skyscraper. ✉ *4–6–1 Chuo, Aoba-ku* ☎ *022/267–4465* 🖭 *Free* ⊙ *Daily 7 am–11 pm.*

Zuiho-den 瑞鳳殿. Not your ordinary cold gray slab of stone memorial, the grand mausoleum of Masamune Date, the most revered ruler of ancient Sendai, was made in the showy style of the Momoyama period (16th century), where figures of people, birds, and flowers are carved and inlaid in natural colors. Looking like the world's fanciest one-story pagoda, there is so much gold leaf that in the right light it practically glows. Having burned during the firebombing in 1945, Zuiho-den was reconstructed in a five-year period beginning in 1974. During the excavation, Masamune Date's well-preserved remains were found and have been reinterred in what appears to be a perfect replica of the original hall. It's a 10-minute walk from the Zuiho-den stop. The mausoleum is a short walk up the hill. From Sendai Castle it's a 10-minute bus ride or a 30-minute walk down Aoba-yama and across the Hirose-gawa (Hirose River). ✉ *23–2 Otamayashita, Aoba-ku* ☎ *022/262–6250* ⊕ *www.zuihoden.com* 🖭 *¥550* ⊙ *Feb.–Nov., daily 9–4:30; Dec. and Jan., daily 9–4.*

WHERE TO EAT

Sendai has hundreds of great restaurants, but the highest concentrations are found along the parallel streets Ichiban-cho, Inari-koji, and Kokubun-cho. Most places display their menus in their windows, along with the prices. Also, within the JR Station is the underground mall called S-pall, which includes small branches of established restaurants.

13

$$ ✗ **Aji Tasuke** 味太助. This birthplace of grilled beef tongue proudly serves
JAPANESE excellent and inexpensive Japanese meals. A ¥1,400 *teishoku* (combo)
gets you the full set of three slices of grilled beef tongue and pickled
cabbage, oxtail soup, and a bowl of barley mixed with rice. From the
Ichiban-cho Exit of the Mitsukoshi department store, turn left, walk
to the first narrow street, turn right, then go left at the next corner; Aji
Tasuke is 50 yards ahead on the left, next to a small shrine. ⊠ *4–4–13
Ichiban-cho, Aoba-ku* ☎ *022/225–4641* ⊕ *www.aji-tasuke.co.jp* ▭ *No
credit cards* ⊙ *Closed Tues.*

$$–$$$ ✗ **Beko Masamune** べこ政宗. The fearless, meat-loving gourmet should
SEAFOOD stop here. Fatty raw beef tongue sushi and sashimi—served with a
hint of wasabi—that melt smoothly in the mouth are served here. For
¥1,510 you get the full cow's-tongue set: grilled and seasoned with miso,
soy sauce, or salt; a tasty bowl of oxtail soup; and a healthful mix of
steamed rice and barley. Substitute skewers of chicken or sirloin for the
tongue if you're less adventurous. Earthen walls, dark passages, and
intimate lighting conjure up a romantic setting. It's a few minutes' walk
from the station, at the entrance of the Clis Road/ Hapina Nakaka-cho
(Chuo-dori) arcade, on the second floor—look for the red sign with the
black cow's head. ⊠ *1–8–32 Chuo, Aoba-ku* ☎ *022/217–1151* ⊕ *www.
rinno-ji.or.jp* ⊙ *No lunch Sun.*

$–$$ ✗ **Go Shu In Sen** 御酒印船. A good place for cheap seafood and sake, you
SEAFOOD can't beat their lunch sets. For ¥770 you get the grilled fish of the day
(on the 5th, 15th, and 25th of the month, you get the day's special for
¥500 at lunch, ¥730 otherwise). All lunch sets come with a bottomless
coffee and rice. At dinner, all-you-can-drink is ¥980 an hour, and your
best bet is sashimi by the bucket. Go Shu In Sen is in the basement of
the Shonai Bank Building, a couple of minutes from the JR Station, on
Aoba-dori, near where it meets Atago Kamisugi-dori. ⊠ *3–1–24 Chuo,
Aoba-ku* ☎ *022/225–6868* ⊙ *No lunch Sun.*

$$$$ ✗ **Jiraiya** 地雷也. A curtain next to a big red paper lantern leads to this
JAPANESE inviting Sendai gem where *kinki* (deepwater white fish) are carefully
grilled on a charcoal fire. Writers, intellectuals, and celebrities often
drop by to enjoy the expensive fish. A whole fish (¥6,000) can be shared
by two people, as can the kinki set (¥7,000): kinki, tempura, sashimi,
oyster, soup, and homemade ice cream. If you don't eat your full portion of kinki initially, the fish bones and leftovers will be incorporated
into your soup course. Nothing is wasted. It's just off Ichiban-cho,
near Hirose-dori. ⊠ *2–1–15 Kokubun-cho, Aoba-ku* ☎ *022/261–2164*
⊕ *www.jiraiya.com* ⊙ *Closed Sun.*

WHERE TO STAY

$$$$ ▦ **Hotel Metropolitan Sendai** ホテルメトロポリタン仙台. This upscale hotel
HOTEL adjacent to the railway station offers great value for its price range, and
most rooms will make you feel at home. **Pros:** unbeatably convenient;
20% off with JR Rail Pass; 10% off with JR East Pass. **Cons:** traffic
noise might disturb light sleepers. ⊠ *1–1–1 Chuo, Aoba-ku* ☎ *022/268–
2525* 🖷 *022/268–2521* ⊕ *www.s-metro.stbl.co.jp/english/index.html*
🛏 *292 Western-style rooms, 3 Japanese-style rooms* ♿ *In-room: a/c.
In-hotel: 3 restaurants, bar* ◎ *No meals.*

$$$$
RYOKAN

🏠 **Ichijoh** 一條. The old and new are elegantly juxtaposed in this upscale ryokan. **Pros:** sophisticated ryokan experience; excellent meals; all rooms have a private bath. **Cons:** not much shopping or museum visiting around; requires a Rail Pass to stay here. ⌧ *1–48 Kamasaki, Shiroishi* ☎ *0224/26–2151* ⊕ *www.ichijoh.co.jp* ↵ *14 Western-style rooms, 10 Japanese-style rooms* ⌂ *In-room: a/c, safe, refrigerator, Internet. In-hotel: restaurant, bar, Wi-Fi hotspot, parking (free)* ⦿*some meals.*

¢–$
HOTEL

🏠 **Super Hotel Sendai Hirose-dori** スーパーホテル仙台・広瀬通り. This budget hotel is best for active people who won't plan to spend much time in the room. **Pros:** unbeatable price; complimentary breakfast. **Cons:** teensy bathrooms may remind you of an airplane's lavatory. ⌧ *2–9–23 Chuo, Aoba-ku* ☎ *022/224–9000* ⊕ *www.superhoteljapan.com/en* ↵ *180 rooms* ⌂ *In-room: a/c, safe, refrigerator, Internet. In-hotel: laundry facilities, Internet terminal, parking (paid)* ⦿*Breakfast.*

$$$$
HOTEL

🏠 **Westin Sendai** ウェスティン仙台. An aroma of white tea hovers in the air on the 26th floor of this hotel, where the black-and-gold reception lobby is located. Opened in 2010, this is one of most luxurious hotels in Sendai. **Pros:** impeccably clean, modern rooms. **Cons:** no single rooms; Internet is expensive at ¥1,000/night/room; hotel feels isolated from the liveliness of downtown. ⌧ *1–9–1, Ichiban-cho, Aoba-ku* ☎ *022/722–1234* ⊕ *www.westin-sendai.com* ↵ *292 rooms* ⌂ *In-room: a/c, safe, refrigerator. In-hotel: 2 restaurants, room service, bar, gym, spa, laundry service, Internet terminal, Wi-Fi hotspot, parking (paid)* ⦿*EP.*

SHOPPING

Sendai is the unofficial capital of the Tohoku region, and you can find many well-known regional crafts of Miyagi Prefecture here: *kokeshi* dolls, Shiroishi's *washi* handmade paper, and Sendai's Tansu chests. Heading west out of the station, follow the elevated walkways across the busy street below to where the main shopping begins in earnest.

The best variety of shops may be found along the popular Clis Road arcade. Or if you are pressed for time, drop down into S-pall Mall at Sendai Station.

The Asaichi, or Farmer's Market, is an east–west alley positioned midway in the big block that sits near the Hotel Green Well, a five-minute walk from JR Sendai Station's West Exit. It's busy from early morning to night, and you'll be able to see, hear, smell, and taste it all.

Furusato. This store carries all kinds of Tohoku souvenirs. ⌧ *B1F Sendai Station, 1–1–1 Chuo, Aoba-ku* ☎ *022/267–4023.*

Shimanuki. This store is tops for folk crafts and snacks from around Tohoku. It's open Monday through Saturday from 10 to 8:30. The main branch is in the mall at Sendai Station, but there's another branch in Ichiban-cho. ⌧ *B1F Sendai Station, 1–1–1 Chuo, Aoba-ku* ☎ *022/267–4021.*

SIDE TRIPS FROM SENDAI

MATSU-SHIMA 松島

30 km (19 mi) northeast of Sendai.

Matsu-shima and its bay are the most popular coastal resort destinations in Tohoku. Matsu-shima owes this distinction to the Japanese infatuation with oddly shaped rocks, which the bay has in abundance. Hordes come to see the 250 small, pine-clad islands scattered about the bay. Long ago it was such a sublime and tranquil scene that it was fondly written of by the 17th-century haiku poet Basho. Although Matsu-shima's outermost islands sheltered it from the worst of the March 11, 2011 tsunami, many hotels and shops on the waterfront were badly damaged and may be under construction through the end of 2011. However, transportation and most major tourist sights are open as usual.

GETTING HERE AND AROUND

If you can avoid weekends or holidays and obtain a good vantage point—consider renting a bicycle from one of the shops and pedaling up into the hills—you can indeed feel your cares float away, and the islands themselves may seem to bob and sway on the gentle breeze-driven swells. The key sights are within easy walking distance of each other. To get here, take the JR from Sendai (25 minutes northeast; ¥400). For maps and info, visit the tourist office at the end of the Matsu-shima Kaigan Pier.

ESSENTIALS

Visitor Information Matsu-shima Town Office (☎ *022/354–2263*).

WHAT TO SEE

Godai-do 五大堂. Just to the right of the ferry pier in Matsu-shima is this small temple constructed in 1609 at the behest of Masamune Date. The temple is on a tiny islet connected to the shore by two small arched bridges. Animals are carved in the timbers beneath the temple roof and among the complex supporting beams.

Fukurajima 福浦島. From Godai-do it's a short walk across the 250-yard pedestrian bridge near the Matsu-shima Century Hotel to the islet of Fukurajima. For the ¥200 toll you can walk away from the crowds to enjoy a picnic in the park with views across the bay.

Zuigan-ji 瑞巌寺. Matsu-shima's main temple dates from 828, but the present structure was rebuilt to meet Masamune Date's tastes in 1609. Zuigan-ji is perhaps the most representative Zen temple in the Tohoku region. The main hall is a large wooden structure with elaborately carved wood panels and paintings (now faded) of some of Date's favorite totems: flowers, birds, and trees. Except during holidays, when the crowds are heavy, the relaxing temple grounds are full of trees, including two plum trees brought back from Korea in 1592 by Masamune Date after a failed military venture. The natural caves surrounding the temple are filled with Buddhist statues that novices carved from the rock face as part of their training. Zuigan-ji is down the street

Matsu-shima's Godai-do temple is on a tiny islet connected to the mainland via two small bridges.

from Godai-do, across Route 45 and the central park. ☎ 022/354–2023 ⊕ *www.zuiganji.or.jp* ✉ *¥700* ☉ *Apr.–Sept., daily 8–4; Oct. and Mar., daily 8–4:30; Dec. and Jan., daily 8–3:30; Nov. and Feb., daily 8–4.*

WHERE TO STAY

Although most travelers come to Matsu-shima on a day trip, spending the night is well worth the expense if you can afford the locally expensive hotel rates. There are also many good restaurants in the town, though they, too, are overpriced and often full of pushy tour-bus groups. For this reason, many people just wait to have a good meal when they return to Sendai; however, if you do stay, the hotels all have good restaurants.

$$$$ 🏯 **Hotel Ichinobo** ホテル一の坊. This posh, expensive resort hotel has a
HOTEL gorgeous garden that stays illuminated at night. **Pros:** luxurious touches from top to bottom; friendly, helpful staff. **Cons:** tourist attractions are not within walking distance; price can be prohibitive. ✉ *1–4 Takagi Aza Hama* ☎ *022/353–3333* 🖶 *022/353–3339* ⊕ *www.ichinobo.com/ matsushima* 🛏 *20 Western-style rooms, 104 Japanese-style rooms* ⚙ *In-room: a/c. In-hotel: restaurant, pool* ❙❙❙ *Some meals.*

$ 🏯 **Resort Inn Matsushima** リゾートイン松島. Casual and family-friendly,
HOTEL this affordable hotel is a great option for budget travelers. **Pros:** laid-back atmosphere; free parking. **Cons:** room sofas are tacky; not flashy compared to other hotels. ✉ *17 Sanjukari, Matsu-shima Aza* ☎ *022/355–0888* 🖶 *022/353–0889* ⊕ *www.resort-inn.jp* 🛏 *29 rooms* ⚙ *In-room: a/c, Wi-Fi, Internet. In-hotel: Internet terminal, Wi-Fi hotspot* ❙❙❙ *Breakfast.*

$$$$
RYOKAN 🖼 **Shoan** 松庵. A plush sedate ryokan sits quietly on the edge of the peninsula, called Oku-Matsushima. Many regulars stay several nights because of its sublime dinner, great privacy, and breathtaking views. **Pros:** peaceful hideaway; impeccable personal attention; great natural surroundings **Cons:** very expensive; baths are relaxing but not exactly onsen. ⊠ *1 Umeki, Tetaru,* ☎ *022/354–3111* ⊕ *www.shoan-umine. com* ⊅ *11 rooms* 🔥 *In-room: a/c, safe, refrigerator. In-hotel: restaurant, room service, bar, laundry service, Wi-Fi hotspot, parking (free)* ❑ *Some meals.*

13

YAMADERA 山寺

49 km (30 mi) west of Sendai.

If you'd like to see one of Japan's most revered—and scenic—temple complexes, come up here on an easy day trip from Sendai.

GETTING HERE AND AROUND

Reach Yamadera from Sendai on the JR Senzan Line (¥820), or from Yamagata City on the same line (¥230). Once you leave the station, you'll find a tourist information office near the bridge, but no English is spoken there.

WHAT TO SEE

Hoju-san 宝珠山 *(Mt. Hoju).* If you are expecting just another mundane temple, you will certainly be surprised. Yamadera is like something conjured out of the ethereal mists of an ancient Japanese charcoal painting. Built in the year 860, Yamadera's ambitious complex of temples is perched high on the upper slopes of Mt. Hoju, from where you can enjoy divine vistas. Belonging to the Tendai Buddhists, who believe in the existence of "Buddha-nature" within all living things, Yamadera attracts a steady stream of pilgrims. Just inside the temple-complex entrance is **Kompon Chu-do,** the temple where the sacred Flame of Belief has burned constantly for 1,100 years. Near Kompon Chu-do is a statue of the Japanese poet **Matsuo Basho** (1644–94), whose pithy and colorful haiku related his extensive wanderings throughout Japan. During a visit to the temple, he wrote, "Stillness . . . the sound of cicadas sinks into the rocks" and buried the poem on the spot.

The path continues up many steps—nearly 1,100 of them, well tended though they be. At the summit is **Oku-no-in,** the hall dedicated to the temple founder, Jikaku Daishi. But if you've come this far, keep going. Of all the temples hanging out over the valley, the view from **Godai-do** is the best. The path becomes crowded in summer and slippery in winter.

To get to the temple complex, walk through the village from the station, cross the bridge, and turn right. Allow 1 to 1½ hours for a leisurely climb up and a careful tramp down. On the way back to the station, pick up refreshments at the shop to the right of the bridge, where you can sit and see the river. ☎ *023/695–2816 for Yamadera Tourist Association* ❑ *¥300 to climb mountain.*

Sakunami Onsen 作並温泉. If you are looking for a stopover between Yamadera and Sendai, this relaxing hot spring is just off the train line.

EN
ROUTE

Sakunami is only 32 minutes (¥480) by local express from Sendai Station, close enough to be an alternative spot to spend the night.

Ginzan Onsen 銀山温泉 Ginzan is another relaxing hot spring between Yamagata and Sendai, but this one is more isolated than Sakunami. It's about two to three hours from Sendai by bus.

WHERE TO STAY

$$$$
RYOKAN

🏠 **Iwamatsu Ryokan** 岩松旅館. Situated along Hirose River, this old, large ryokan has rooms that peer out over the stream and mountains. **Pros:** traditional comfort in remote setting; free parking. **Cons:** non-aficionados may not appreciate its simple charms; although rooms have private baths, there are no Western-style rooms; little English is spoken. ✉ *Sakunamionsen, Motoyu* ☎ *022/395–2211* 🖷 *022/395–2020* ⊕ *www. iwamatu-ryokan.com* ⤷ *91 Japanese-style rooms* ♨ *In-room: no a/c. In-hotel: restaurant* ❎ *Some meals.*

HIRAIZUMI 平泉

120 km (75 mi) north of Sendai.

A culture of gold flourished in Hiraizumi in the late 11th and 12th centuries, when the Oshu Fujiwara family, a then-powerful clan, chose to move here. Massive temple- building projects were carried out so as to create a peaceful society based on the principles of Buddhism. Hiraizumi evokes Kyoto in many ways, especially in its similar topography. In its heyday, the city served as a convenient base to transport gold, fine horses, and other materials by land and sea, and trading it made the Oshu Fujiwara family prosper. Hiraizumi, then-called Mutsu, supplied much of the gold to decorate images of the Buddha and tactfully traded with the capital Kyoto and even China.

For its magnificent Golden Hall and its lovely Buddhist Jodo Garden, Hiraizumi is a worthwhile day trip from Sendai.

GETTING HERE AND AROUND

The nearest station is JR Hiraizumi Station. From Sendai, the *Yamabiko* Shikkansen rockets to Ichinoseki Station (31 minutes; ¥3,920) then you hop on the local train one stop for Hiraizumi. It's also accessible by local trains (two hours; ¥1,890) and by express buses (90 minutes; ¥1,700).

Tourist Information Hiraizumi Tourist Information Office (☎ *0191/46–2110* ⊗ *Daily 9–5:30*).

WHAT TO SEE

Chuson-ji 中尊寺. Founded in 850, the highlight of this temple is its Konjiki-do (Golden Hall), which was completed in 1124. The first Ohu Fujiwara lord Kiyohara commissioned many temples and pagodas during his reign, perhaps as many as 40, not to mention residences for 300 priests. Nearly all were destroyed by fire except for Konjiki-do, and it is the only structure in Chuson-ji that remains unchanged. More than 3,000 objects have survived and are now housed in the treasure house. It's a 20-minute walk from JR Hiraizumi Station or a 10-minute bus ride. ✉ *202 Koromonoseki* ☎ *0191/46–2211* ⊕ *www.chusonji.or.jp* 🎟 *¥800* ⊗ *Apr.–mid-Nov., daily 8–5; mid-Nov.–Mar., daily 8:30–4:30.*

Motsu-ji毛越寺. Although founded in 850, Motsu-ji's main buildings were commissioned by the second Fujiwara lord in the 12th century and completed by his son. There were originally 40 halls and pagodas as well as residences for 500 priests, but as at Chuson-ji, most of the buildings were destroyed by fire in 1226. However, its remaining Heian-period **Jodo Garden** still provides a beautiful scenery as it was landscaped to depict the Amida Buddha's Pure Land. ⊠ *58 Osawa* ☎ *0191/46–2331* ⊕ *www.motsuji.or.jp* ⤳ *¥500* ⊙ *Daily 8:30–5 (early Nov.–early Apr. 8:30–4:30).*

13

YAMAGATA 山形

63 km (39 mi) west of Sendai, 120 km (75 mi) southeast of Tsuruoka.

Yamagata, or Mountain Terrain, is the capital of the prefecture of the same name (and the Sister City of Boulder, Colorado). It's a community of a quarter-million souls who enjoy one of the most visually stunning locations in Japan. Everywhere you look there are arrayed lovely mountains, a play of light and shadow shifting across their sculpted flanks and lofty summits. Connoisseurs of soba and mountain vegetables will be delighted, as will fans of sweet, perfectly marbled beef. Yamagata Prefecture is the only prefecture to be 100% thermal—having at least one onsen, or hot spring, in each of its 44 municipalities. Mt. Zao was once a popular ski resort, but it has become less fashionable as skiers have shifted to more-favored slopes in Hokkaido.

During the **Hana-gasa Festival** (August 5–7), some 10,000 dancers from the region dance through the streets in traditional costume and *hanagasa,* hats so named for the safflowers (locally called *benibana*) decorating them. It's based on an old ritual to promote fertility and ensure a rich harvest. Floats are interspersed among the dancers, and stalls provide food and refreshments.

GETTING HERE AND AROUND

The train is your best bet for getting to Yamagata. The JR Senzan Line from Sendai takes about one hour (¥1,110 or buy a W-ticket for ¥1,500, which allows one person to make a round-trip or two people a one-way trip from Sendai); via the Tsubasa Shinkansen it's 2½ hours from Tokyo (¥11,030). If you're coming from Tsuruoka, you can take the non–JR bus from S-mall (two hours; ¥2,400). Yamagata is easy to navigate, so walking is the way to go unless you need to head farther afield. You can pick up free maps and brochures from the Yamagata Tourist Information Office opposite the ticket turnstiles inside Yamagata JR Station.

ESSENTIALS

Tourist Information Yamagata Tourist Information Office (☎ *023/631–7865* ⊙ *Daily 9–5:30*).

WHERE TO EAT

$–$$
JAPANESE

✕**Mitsuya** 三津屋. A short walk from the station will put you in front of some fine and slightly chewy Yamagata soba noodles. Everything is good here, but in summer try the *hiyashi-dori* soba (with cold chicken). Head south (right) from the East Station Exit, and keep to the street that follows along the tracks until you can cross over them and turn to

In summer, hiking is a popular pastime in the mountains around Yamagata, which host skiers in the winter.

the right. Then it's just a hop to the traditional black-wood-and-white-stucco building on the left. It is also located on the first floor of S-pal Mall at JR Yamagata Station. ✉ *1–1–75 Uwa-machi* ☎ *023/644–4973* ⊕ *www.soba328.com* ▭ *No credit cards* ⊘ *Closed Tues.*

$$$–$$$$

JAPANESE

★

✕ **Sagoro** 佐五郎. If you have never indulged in some strictly top-end sukiyaki, shabu-shabu, or steak—or if you have and want to feel that way again—Sagoro will serve you a full dose of some excellent Yonezawa and Yamagata beef. The staff is polite and service is efficient. This will not only fill you up, but you may gush for days about the beef's impossible tenderness and its impeccable marbling of such ineffably sweet fat. Although most dishes are pricey in this sophisticated, upscale setting, there are some relative bargains. A simple plate of *shoga-yaki* (beef sautéed in ginger sauce; ¥1,785), with *oshinko moriawase* (pickled vegetables; ¥735), rice, and soup can make for a fairly reasonable meal. Go three blocks east from the station. Turn left. Look for the meat shop, and you'll see the black bull on the sign above the street next to it. Take the stairs up one flight to heaven. ✉ *1–6–10 Kasumi-cho* ☎ *023/631–3560* ⊕ *www.sagoro.jp* ⊘ *Closed Sun.*

$–$$

SOBA

✕ **Shojiya** 庄司屋. Yamagata is famous for soba, and **Shojiya** is the oldest soba restaurant in Yamagata. This newly opened branch is a good place to enjoy the famous noodles. For lunch or a light dinner, try tempura soba (¥1,440) or *nameko* soba (with mushrooms; ¥990). The immediate area is as interesting as the restaurant; you can see restored irrigation channels where five dams were built in 1623 to control flooding, and nearby are traditional kimono and green-tea shops. It's a 10-minute walk from the JR Station. ✉ *2–7–6 Nanoka-machi* ☎ *023/673–9636* ⊕ *www.shojiya.jp* ▭ *No credit cards* ⊘ *Closed Mon.*

WHERE TO STAY

$$$$
RYOKAN

🔲 **Fujiya** 藤屋. A renovation completed in 2006 transformed Fujiya from a traditional to a modern ryokan. **Pros:** excellent service; fabulous food. **Cons:** too expensive and too contemporary for some; a little far from Yamagata unless you have a JR pass. ✉ *433 Shinpata, Ginzan, Obanazawa* ☎ *0237/28–2141* 📠 *0237/28–2140* ⊕ *www.fujiya-ginzan. com/english* 🛏 *8 rooms* ⚟ *In-room: a/c, safe, refrigerator, Wi-Fi (some). In-hotel: restaurant, room service, laundry service, Wi-Fi hotspot, parking (free)* ⦿ *Some meals.*

$$$
HOTEL

🔲 **Hotel Metropolitan Yamagata** ホテルメトロポリタン山形. Yamagata's best-located upscale hotel is on your right as you exit the east side of the station. **Pros:** central location to beat all; nice views out front. **Cons:** some daytime distractions with the busy station next door; breakfast is served in a room with no windows and is rather small and pricey. ✉ *1–1–1 Kasumi-cho* ☎ *023/628–1111* 📠 *012/628–1166* ⊕ *www. metro-yamagata.jp* 🛏 *116 rooms* ⚟ *In-room: a/c. In-hotel: restaurant, bar* ⦿ *No meals.*

13

NORTHERN TOHOKU 北東北

MORIOKA 盛岡

184 km (114 mi) north of Sendai.

Morioka is a busy commercial and industrial city ringed by mountains, but it's more of a travel hub than a destination to visit; for that reason, a one-day (or even half-day) stopover is usually sufficient to give travelers a glimpse of the city's greenery and attractions. A nice, expansive park surrounds a ruined castle, and an ancient cherry tree has proven it belongs here by rooting itself into the crack of a huge granite slab in front of the district courthouse. But the city's major draw is the locally produced *Nambu-tetsu,* a special type of cast iron forged into functional and highly ornamental wares. The most popular are heavy iron kettles. They are expensive, because they're specially tempered not to rust. As tea connoisseurs know, once conditioned, these pots soften the water by leeching out unwanted minerals and chemicals while adding the taste and health benefits of elemental iron. They will go on doing it forever, too, if properly cared for. Many locals are still using kettles from centuries past. Dozens of shops throughout the city sell Nambu-tetsu, but the main shopping streets are Saien-dori and O-dori, which pass right by Iwate Koen (Iwate Park).

GETTING HERE AND AROUND

From Sendai, the quickest way to reach Morioka is the Hayate Shinkansen (45 minutes; ¥6,290); the cheapest way to get there is the express bus (two hours, 40 minutes; ¥2,850) Both run many times a day from Sendai. If you want to fly from Osaka or Sapporo, Morioka (whose Hanamaki Airport is 53 minutes by bus, ¥1,000, from downtown) has two or three flights daily from Osaka's Itami Airport (one hour, 25 minutes; ¥35,200–¥37,400) by JAL. There are also flights from Sapporo's Chitose Airport.

To get to downtown Morioka from the JR Morioka Station, you can walk or take the convenient loop bus, called Denden-mushi, which goes to the shopping area on the far side of the river past the park; the bus departs every 10 to 15 minutes between the hours of 9 and 7 from Bus Stop 15 or 16 in front of JR Morioka Station (¥100 for one ride, ¥300 for the day pass).

VISITOR INFORMATION AND TOURS

The Northern Tohoku Tourist Information Center is on the second floor of JR Morioka Station, and the English-speaking staff can give you maps and other information on the three prefectures of Iwate, Akita, and Aomori. The office can also help arrange accommodations with the members of a ryokan union.

Contacts Iwate Kanko Bus Company (☎ 019/651–3355).

Northern Tohoku Tourist Information Center (☎ 019/625–2090 ⊘ Daily 9–5:30).

> ## HORSING AROUND
>
> If you happen to be in town on the second Saturday in June, a small festival called **Chagu-chagu Umako**—named for the noise the big horses' bells make—features 100 locally bred and gaily decorated Nambu-koma horses brought from nearby Takizawa Village to parade around in front of the station. The horses clomp through the streets between 9:30 and 2 on that day only.

WHAT TO SEE

Gozaku ござ九. This wealthy merchant's house was built sometime between the Edo and Meiji periods (1600–1868) and has a distinguished historical presence. It is now a miscellaneous store carrying lots of bamboo baskets and straw sandals. Behind the store is a willow tree and the river, quite a scenic view. It's located in front of Kamasada Iron Casting Studio. ⊠ 1–31 Konya-cho ☎ 019/622–7129 ⊘ Mon.–Sat. 8:30–5:30.

Hoonji Temple 報恩寺 五百羅漢 (500 Disciples of Buddha). On the outskirts of Mt. Atagoyama is a temple district where a dozen temples are clustered. This one houses 499 statues, including Marco Polo and Kublai Khan, that were carved between 1731 and 1735. Behind Hoonji are a small cemetery and a tranquil Japanese garden. Monks ring a bell periodically; the sounds echo through the premises and the city. ⊠ 31–5 Nakasugawa-machi ☎ 019/641–4415 ☞ ¥300 ⊘ Daily 9–4.

Iwate Koen 岩手公園. This park is large enough to get lost in, with varied landscapes, an astonishing variety of artfully placed flowers and trees, shady groves, streams, and colors in every season. It's a good place for a romantic walk. In 1597, the 26th Lord of Nambu had a fine castle built here, but all that remains are ruined walls. To reach the park from JR Morioka Station, cross Kai-un-bashi and walk straight down the middle of the three roads that meet there.

Kamasada Iron Casting Studio 釜足南部鉄器. At the studio, five casters create the fine iron work, and their products are as authentic and beautiful as Nanbu-tekki can be. Designed by resident master caster Nobuho Miya, a saucepan with a wooden handle is elegantly traditional yet modern. Equally attractive teakettles come in all sizes and prices; a small one is about ¥3,500. All neatly displayed wares are for sale, but if you want to place a special order for something such as a door plate, your piece will be produced in two months' time and can be shipped anywhere. To get there, go half a block down the tiny street that extends in front of the venerable and well-known Azuma-ya soba restaurant (⇨ *Where to Eat*). ⊠ *2–5 Konya-cho* ☎ *019/622–3911* 🖷 *019/622–3912* 🕑 *Mon.–Sat. 9–5:30.*

Kogensha 光原社. Have a look around this store, which specializes in quality folk crafts like lacquerware, kites, dyed fabrics, and pottery. The main shop is composed of several small buildings around a courtyard. You can walk through the courtyard to a small *kohee-kan* (coffee shop) and farther on to the river. Along the wall to the left are poems by famous local poet Kenji Miyazawa. To get to Kogensha from Morioka Station, walk left to the stoplight in front of the Hotel Metropolitan Morioka, turn right, and cross the river on Asahi-bashi. Take the first left into a funky little street that leads to the main shop, 50 yards down on the left. There's also a branch shop across the street that sells basketry and wooden bowls. ⊠ *2–18 Zaimoku-cho* ☎ *019/622–2894* 🕑 *Daily 10–6; closed 15th of month and the following day if the 15th is either Sat. or Sun.*

WHERE TO EAT

$$–$$$
SOBA
★
✕**Azuma-ya** 東屋. Hearty soba is made from plentiful northern Japanese buckwheat, and Azuma-ya is easily Morioka's most famous place to eat these healthful noodles. The second level is devoted to the courageous and hearty of appetite, where *wanko* soba courses—you can attack and devour all the soba you desire—start at ¥2,600. Down on the first floor, popular dishes such as hand-kneaded cold tempura soba (¥1,260) and pork cutlet in a rice bowl (\900) are speedily served. The *maneki-neko* (decorative beckoning cats) are mascots to keep customers coming back, and they (more than 50 of them), seem to be doing their job. Azuma-ya is near the bus center, along the small street across the busy road from the Naka-san department store, on the other side of the river from Iwata Park; it's 15 minutes from the train station on foot. ⊠ *1–8–3 Naka-no-hashi-dori* ☎ *019/622–2252* ⊕ *www.wankosoba-azumaya. co.jp* ▭ *No credit cards.*

$$$–$$$$
SEAFOOD
✕**Banya Nagasawa** 番屋ながさわ. When you slide open the door, your eye may notice the two-story fish tank with piles of shells and the fish freezer packed with greenlings, flounders, sea breams, and a frightening-looking red, pop-eyed fish that might make you recoil. But you'll instantly know what you'll be served here: all manner of grilled shellfish and fish, crisp and brown on the outside but white and tender inside. You'll be eating *warabi* (fiddle ferns) in spring, and drinking excellent local sake with friendly regulars. To reach Banya Nagasawa from the train station, follow O-dori to the Iwate Bank and turn right at the statue of Takuboku Ishikawa. The restaurant is 2½ blocks ahead on the right, across from the Hotel New Carina. From the station you can also follow Saien-dori to the Saien police box and turn left; the restaurant will be on your left. ⊠ *2–6–1 Saien* ☎ *019/622–2646* 🕑 *Closed Sun. and mid-Aug. No lunch.*

$$–$$$
JAPANESE

✕ **Daido-En** 大同苑. Reimen are clear, slippery noodles made from flour, starch, and water. They came from Korea and are frequently combined with spicy kimchi. Here, the reimen is spicy, all right, and it comes with half a boiled egg, green onions, cucumber pickles, a slice or two of meat, and a fat wedge of watermelon. Quality local beef, Maezawa-gyu, is available for at-table *yaki-niku* grilling, too. It's in the entertainment district, halfway between the station (three blocks) and Iwate Park. ✉ *2–6–19 Saien* ☎ *019/654–5588* ⊕ *www.daido-en.jp* ▭ *No credit cards* ☽ *No dinner.*

WHERE TO STAY

$$$$
RYOKAN

🛏 **Fujisan Ryokan** 藤三旅館. The main reason to stay here is have the opportunity to steep in Namari Onsen, **Pros:** storied 600-year history; good meals; ability to experience Namari Onsen. **Cons:** loud announcements break the peaceful moments; although a stop on the Shinkansen line from Tokyo, Hanamaki is about 40 km (25 mi) south of Morioka. ✉ *75–1 Namari, Nakadaira, Hanamaki* ☎ *0198/25–2311* 🖷 *0198/25–2312* ⊕ *www.namari-onsen.co.jp* ⟿ *36 Japanese-style rooms, 6 with bath* ♿ *In-room: a/c, safe, refrigerator. In-hotel: parking (free)* ¶◎¶ *Some meals.*

$$$–$$$$
HOTEL

🛏 **Morioka Grand Hotel** 盛岡グランドホテル. This pleasingly secluded hotel is near the top of a wooded hill with a breezy view over the rolling green hills that surround the otherwise ordinary-looking city. **Pros:** tranquillity reigns; great views. **Cons:** most rooms are dated; a bit far from the action; the attached wedding chapel may strike some as strange and tacky. ✉ *1–10 Atagoshita* ☎ *019/625–2111* 🖷 *019/625–1003* ⟿ *5 Japanese-style rooms, 21 Western-style rooms, 1 suite* ♿ *In-room: a/c. In-hotel: 2 restaurants, bar* ¶◎¶ *No meals.*

$
RYOKAN

🛏 **Ryokan Kumagai** 旅館熊ヶ井. This friendly and cozy Japanese inn attracts many backpackers and budget-minded travelers. **Pros:** reasonable rates; festive though basic atmosphere. **Cons:** a bit rustic; no private baths. ✉ *3–2–5 Osawakawara* ☎ *019/651–3020* 🖷 *019/626–0096* ⊕ *www.kumagairyokan.com* ⟿ *8 Japanese-style rooms without bath* ♿ *In-room: a/c. In-hotel: restaurant* ¶◎¶ *No meals.*

$$$$
RYOKAN

🛏 **Shikitei** 四季亭. A half-hour bus ride from JR Morioka Station takes you to this quiet onsen town called Tsunagi and this upscale ryokan, which offers the relaxation of a hot spring as well as a wonderful culinary experience. **Pros:** excellent meals including Matsuzaka beef. **Cons:** nothing to do but relax; not all rooms have a private bath. ✉ *137 Tsunagi, Yunodate* ☎ *019/689–2021* 🖷 *019/689–2159* ⊕ *www.shikitei.jp* ⟿ *22 Japanese-style rooms, 16 with bath* ♿ *In-room: a/c, safe, refrigerator. In-hotel: room service, laundry service, parking (free)* ¶◎¶ *Some meals.*

TAZAWA-KO AND KAKUNODATE 田沢湖と角館

Japan's deepest lake, Tazawa-ko (Lake Tazawa), and the traditional town of Kakunodate are good side-trips into Tohoku's wilder interior, approachable from either Morioka or the west-coast city of Akita. For a little thermal relaxation in a very rustic setting, forge on to the old spa town of Nyuto Onsen, just north of Lake Tazawa.

TAZAWA-KO 田沢湖

40 km (25 mi) west of Morioka, 87 km (54 mi) east of Akita.

GETTING HERE AND AROUND

A 12-minute bus ride (¥350) from the JR Tazawa-ko Station gets you to the Tazawa-ko-han center on the eastern lakeshore. A very small and shallow swimming area is a short distance to the northwest along the road. A 30-minute bus ride from JR Tazawa-ko Station via Tazawa-ko-han takes you to Tazawa-ko Kogen (Tazawa-ko Plateau) for ¥600. The journey offers spectacular views of the lake. Once there, you can rent your own paddleboat or rowboat. You'll want sunscreen and a hat or sunshade in summer. There's also regular bus service around the lake and bicycles available for rent (¥500 to ¥800 per hour, with two hours usually sufficient for the loop) at the Tazawa-ko-han bus terminal and at many lodgings in the area.

13

VISITOR INFORMATION

The Tazawa-ko Tourist Information Office to the left of the JR Tazawa-ko Station has maps and bus schedules; it's open daily from 8:30 to 6:30.

Contact Tazawa-ko Tourist Information Office (☎ *0187/43–2111*).

WHAT TO SEE

Nyuto Onsen 乳頭温泉. Accessible by bus from Tazawa-ko are several small, unspoiled, mountain hot-spring spas. Most of these have only one inn, and you'll have to take your meals there. It's advisable to arrange accommodations before you arrive if you plan to stay the night, and the Tazawa-ko Tourist Information Office can help arrange this.

★ **Tazawa-ko** 田沢湖町. The clear waters and forested slopes of Tazawa-ko (Lake Tazawa), Japan's deepest lake, create a mystical quality that greatly appeals to the Japanese. According to legend, the great beauty from Akita, Takko Hime, sleeps in the water's deep, disguised as a dragon. The lake never freezes over in winter because Takko Hime and her dragon husband churn the water with their passionate lovemaking. The scientific reason is this: Tazawa-ko has been measured to a depth of 426 meters (1,397 feet), and its depth is what prevents it from turning over or freezing. Though clear enough to allow you to see a startling 90 meters (300 feet) or more down into it, the mineral-blue water is too acidic to support anything but a few hardy fish. A scenic 20-km-long (12-mi-long) two-lane road rings the crater lake, and a great afternoon activity is to cycle completely around it in a refreshing, leisurely loop. Bicycles can be rented at the bus station.

Near the bus stop and roadhouse there may be some traffic in summer, but it is generally sporadic; once you get away from there the road and the exhilarating mountain air are all yours. Clearly, all around you here is perched precariously on the lip of a flooded, cliff-walled abyss. In winter, the Tazawa area is a popular downhill skiing destination, and the gleaming deep blue of the mesmerizing lake steals the show in every view from the lifts or trails.

Tazawa-ko is the deepest lake in Japan.

WHERE TO STAY

$–$$ ⓘ **Kuroyu Onsen** 黒湯温泉. Among seven nearby rustic ryokan in Nyuto,
RYOKAN   this one is the least touristy and most cozy. **Pros:** great retreat; great
service. **Cons:** light sleepers may be surprised at how loud nature is
at night (bring earplugs); no private baths. ✉ *2–1 Tazawa-ko, Obo-
nai, Semboku* ☎ *0187/46–2214* 🖷 *0187/46–2280* ⊕ *www.kuroyu.com*
💤 *42 Japanese-style rooms without bath* ⚲ *In-room: a/c (some), kitchen
(some), refrigerator (some). In-hotel: restaurant, laundry facilities, parking (free)* ⊙ *Closed mid-Nov.–mid-Apr.* ⦿ *Some meals.*

KAKUNODATE 角館

★   *19 km (12 mi) southwest of Tazawa-ko; 59 km (37 mi) southwest of
Morioka; 69 km (43 mi) east of Akita City.*

The little samurai town of Kakunodate, sometimes called "Little
Kyoto," was founded in 1620 by Yoshikatsu Ashina, the local lord,
who chose it for its defensible position and reliable water sources. It
has remained an outpost of traditional Japan, and it is consistently
regarded as one of the very best places for seeing cherry blossoms in
spring. The whole town is full of *shidare-zakura* (weeping cherry trees),
descended from the same trees that adorn Kyoto, and their pink flowers
grace the dark-wood gates, walls, and roofs of ancient samurai houses.
The trees were brought by the daughter of the noble Sanjonishi family,
who fell in love with Yoshiaki Jr. and brought some saplings with her
from Kyoto. Along the banks of Hinokinai-gawa (Hinokinai River),
these living jewel factories dangle a 2-km-long (1-mi-long) pink curtain.
From September 7 to 9, a loud Kakunodate festival takes place here.

GETTING HERE AND AROUND

Kakunodate can be reached from Tazawa-ko on JR Komachi Shinkansen (¥1,000) or JR Tazawa-ko Line (¥320). From Morioka take the JR Komachi Shinkansen (¥2,260) or the JR Tazawa-ko Line (¥1,110). Akita City is 43 minutes away on the Komachi Shinkansen (¥2,940) or accessible ¥1,280 by JR Ou and Tazawa-ko lines (¥1,280). On local trains, the trip to Akita City takes 90 minutes to two hours because the trains halt at Oomagari station for a half hour or so.

BARK SHOPPING

Shops in Kakunodate are the best places in Tohoku to pick up the locally made *kabazaiku*, or cherry-bark veneer items—everything from warmly translucent maroon lamp shades to tiny, intricate business-card holders. If you're looking to score great and unique souvenirs and crafts, this is an important tip to remember, since anything you're likely to find in the hokey souvenir shops in the big cities will be overpriced and fake.

VISITOR INFORMATION

The Kakunodate Tourist Information Center is in an old *kura*-style (warehouse-like) building, adjacent to the tea shop by the station, and the English-speaking staff have maps and information about the samurai houses and walks in town, and can recommend nearby lunch or dinner options. It also has an Internet terminal with printers that travelers are free to use. Coin lockers are also located inside.

Contact Kakunodate Tourist Information Center (☎ 0187/54–2700 ⊙ Daily 9–5:30).

WHAT TO SEE

Aoyagi-ke 青柳家. Several well-preserved samurai houses date from the founding of the town. The most renowned and largest is *Aoyagi Manor*, which functions as a museum and even a bit of a shopping center (there are a lot of restaurants and gift shops located here). The house displays an extensive collection of swords, armor, guns, and silk kimono wedding gowns as well as all kinds of historical artifacts to pore over, such as farm implements and household items. It also exhibits a large number of war documents, photos, and uniforms from the Sino-Japanese War (1894–95) to the Pacific War (1941–45). It's a 15-minute walk northwest from the station. ⊠ *3 Shimo-cho, Omote-machi 014-0325* ☎ *0187/54–3257* ⊕ *www.samuraiworld.com* ✉ *¥500* ⊙ *Apr.–Nov., daily 9–5; Dec.–Mar., daily 9–4.*

Ishiguro-ke 石黒家. Direct descendents of the Ishiguro family open part of their residence to let people to observe their oldest samurai house in Kakunodate. They lead tours around the house explaining the ornamented doors and the vestibule; the family's 12th-generation successor, Naonobu, explains them with English handouts. These are the only tatami-mat rooms visitors can enter. In the rear, the armory and historical documents, such as a German text on anatomy, are exhibited. The beautiful cherry tree in the garden is nearly three centuries old. ⊠ *1 Shimo-cho, Omote-machi, Senboku* ☎ *0187/55–1496* ✉ *¥300* ⊙ *Daily 9–5.*

WHERE TO STAY

$$$$
HOTEL
🛏 **Forukuroro (Folklore) Kakunodate** フォルクローロ角館. Located next to the station, this low-rise hotel looks to be part of the station itself. **Pros:** convenient if you need to catch an early-morning train. **Cons:** very far away from samurai houses; nothing going on in the area after dusk; rooms are uninspiring. ⊠ *14 Nakasugaawa, Senboku* ☎ *0187/53–2070* 🖷 *0187/53–2118* ⊕ *hotel.eki-net.com/e/index.html* 🛏 *26 rooms* ⚙ *In-room: a/c* ❙❉❙ *Breakfast.*

$$
HOTEL
🛏 **Kakunodate Plaza Hotel** 角館プラザホテル. There are two main reasons to stay in this hotel: the location and the reasonably priced, spacious rooms. **Pros:** great location; great value **Cons:** the property is out-dated; no elegant touches. ⊠ *46 Yoko-machi Senboku* ☎ *0187/54–2727* 🖷 *0187/54–2732* 🛏 *34 Western-style rooms, 2 Japanese-style rooms* ⚙ *In-room: a/c, refrigerator, Internet. In-hotel: bar, Internet terminal, parking (free)* ❙❉❙ *No meals.*

$$$$
RYOKAN
🛏 **Tamachi Bukeyashiki Hotel** 田町武家屋敷ホテル. The name may tell you this is a hotel, but it's actually the fanciest ryokan in town. **Pros:** genu-ine charm and luxury. **Cons:** a bit pricey for some. ⊠ *23 Omote-machi, Shimo-cho, Senboku* ☎ *0187/52–1700* 🖷 *0187/52/1701* ⊕ *www. bukeyashiki.jp* 🛏 *9 Western-style rooms, 3 Japanese-style rooms* ⚙ *In-room: a/c, safe, refrigerator. In-hotel: restaurant, laundry service, park-ing (free)* ❙❉❙ *Some meals.*

TOWADA–HACHIMAN-TAI NATIONAL PARK AND VICINITY

158 km (98 mi) northwest of Morioka.

GETTING HERE AND AROUND

The fastest way to Towada-ko is by one daily bus directly from Morioka Station (departs from the West Exit at 9:45 am; two hours, 15 min-utes; ¥2,200). The last stop on the bus is Towada-ko. Or you can take a JR bus from Aomori Station or Hachinohe Station. Mizuumi-go's route travels between Aomori and Towada-ko in two hours, 45 minutes (¥3,000). JR Oirase-go operates on the same route but also stops at Hachinohe Station (two hours, 15 minutes; ¥2,600). If you do not have a Japan Rail Pass, there is a two-day pass that covers the route from Aomori to Towada (¥4,600; can be used any time except October); it also lets you stop at other interesting sights such as Oirase Gorge. Local buses run along a network that links all the main spots, but service is frequently suspended during winter storms. See the Northern Tohoku Tourist Information Center for more info on routes, schedules, activi-ties, and places to stay in Towado-Hachiman-tai National Park. If you rent a car, driving in Hachiman-tai, on the Hachiman-tai Aspite Line, can be enjoyable except on winter days. The scenery is especially beau-tiful in early summer and fall.

WHAT TO SEE

Hachiman-tai Kogen 八幡平 *(Hachiman Plateau)*. Situated roughly between Lakes Tozawa and Towada, the Hachiman Plateau is a hum-mock of scantily covered geological activity suspended between vol-cano tops, and the geysers and mudboils remind you of all that goes on beneath us. But remember, there are always wonderful onsen for relaxing and recharging near such geothermally active places!

Oirase-kyokoku 奥入瀬峡谷 *(Oirase* [oh-*ee*-ra-seh] *Gorge)*. An excellent choice for a walk—if a bit crowded—is this gorge northeast of the lake at Nenokuchi. The carefully tended trail to the gorge follows the stream for a total of 9 km (5½ mi; about two hours, 40 minutes). A two-lane road parallels the river, and you can catch buses at intervals of about 2 km (1 mi). Buses go north to Aomori and south to Nenokuchi and Yasumi-ya. Though very popular with tour groups, especially in fall, this does take you through one of the most pristine areas of Tohoku. Be prepared for cold mist or rain, take a map of the river and bus stops, and find out the bus schedule before you start out.

Towada-Hachiman-tai National Park 十和田八幡平国立公園. For walking among the splendid and vast virgin beech, pine, and cedar forests covering the verdant valleys and mountainsides deep in the heart of Tohoku, you could not pick a better destination than Towada-Hachiman-tai National Park. The mountains afford sweeping panoramas over the park's gorges and valleys, crystal clear lakes like Towada-ko, gnarled and windswept trees, and volcanic mountain cones. The park straddles Aomori, Iwate, and Akita prefectures, and sprawls over 330 square mi. Hot springs and tiny villages lost in time are secreted away here, and the fresh tree-scented air promotes a feeling of true wilderness. Fall foliage can be spectacular, but this draws boisterous crowds.

Towada-ko 十和田湖 *(Lake Towada)*. Thanks to famous colors and a rumbling fleet of packed tour buses, the Lake Towada area is almost too popular in autumn. The lake fills a volcanic crater to a depth of 334 meters (1,096 feet), making it the third deepest in Japan. The crater is held aloft like a giant goblet 400 meters above the surrounding topography, giving it a dramatic illusory aspect. There are boat tours, and nearby Yasumi-ya Village facilities include a campsite. The lake borders remote reaches of Aomori and Akita prefectures, and it's not nearly as convenient or unhurried as Tazawa-ko.

WHERE TO STAY

$$$$
HOTEL
Oirase Keiryu Hotel. 奥入瀬渓流ホテル. Since it was once a ryokan, this resort hotel feels like a hybrid: two meals are served; yukata robes are provided (and you are encouraged to walk around in them); there are both Japanese- and Western-style rooms, but it's a large hotel. **Pros:** lots of activities, including photography classes and candlelit dining under stars. **Cons:** there are fees for all the extra programs; breakfast on the terrace costs an extra ¥1,500. ⊠ *231 Tochikubo, Okuse, Towada* ☎ *0176/74–2121* 🖷 *0176/74–2128* ⊕ *www.oirase-keiryuu.jp* 🗪 *36 Western-style rooms, 153 Japanese-style rooms* ⚃ *In-room: a/c, safe, refrigerator. In-hotel: restaurants, room service, laundry service, Wi-Fi hotspot, parking (free), some pets allowed* ⊗ *Closed end Nov.–end-Mar.* 🍴 *MAP.*

HIROSAKI 弘前

★ *47 km (30 mi) south of Aomori; 230 km (143 mi) northwest of Morioka.*

Hirosaki is one of northern Tohoku's most attractive cities. It's most famous for its sweet apples, and its only real cultural attraction is a small but photogenic, reconstructed castle. The town has a very appealing, easygoing nature, and this is suitably reflected in a local slang word, *azumashii* ("a feeling of coziness"). Perhaps owing to latitude and topography, there also a blue-tinged component to the light that is reminiscent of Santa Fe or Taos, New Mexico.

GETTING HERE AND AROUND

The easiest way to approach Hirosaki is to take a local train from Aomori (45 minutes; ¥650). If you are in a hurry, take Tsugaru-go (32 minutes; ¥1660). From Morioka, the fastest and cheapest way is to take the JR express highway bus (two hours, 15 minutes; ¥5,200 round-trip).

VISITOR INFORMATION

Hirosaki is compact and walkable, but finding your bearings in this ancient castle town can prove difficult, for the streets were designed to disorient invaders before they could get to the battlements. So, by all means, pick up a map at the Hirosaki City Tourist Information Center before setting out. It's on the right side of the train station as you exit.

Contact

Hirosaki City Tourist Information Center (✉ *1–1 Omote-cho* ☎ *0172/32–0524* ◷ *Jan. 4–Mar., daily 8–5; Apr.–Dec. 28, daily 8:45–6).*

WHAT TO SEE

Chosho-ji Temple and Zenrin-gai 長勝寺と禅林街. Thirty-three of the Souto Sect's Zen temples line up solemnly along a long avenue, at the end of which Chosho-ji temple stands dignified. The Tsugaru clan's family temple was originally built in Aji-gasawa in 1528, but it was moved here in 1610 to protect Hirosaki Castle. You'll see a large bell dating back from Kamakura period, a *Sanmon* gate meant to shake off greediness and complaining, and 500 statues depicting Buddha's disciples. ✉ *1–23–8 Nish-ishigemori* ☎ *0172/32–0813* 🎟 *\300* ◷ *Daily 9–4.*

Hirosaki Castle 弘前城 *(Hirosaki-jo).* The castle is situated atop a high stone base, guarded by deep moats, over which a red wooden bridge crosses in a picturesque curve. The original castle, completed in 1611, was set ablaze 16 years later by a lightning bolt. The present castle, of a smaller scale, dates back to 1810. When the more than 5,000

SHAMISEN

Shamisen literally means "three-tastes-strings," and this musical instrument is played and sounds somewhat like the American banjo. The sound-amplification board is traditionally made of tightly stretched dog or cat skin, and it is usually played with a large comblike plectrum made of tortoiseshell or ivory. The shamisen has recently been exposed to young Japanese audiences—and to Westerners—by popular bands like the Yoshida Brothers, who forgo tradition and play the instrument with the ferocity of a rock guitar.

Hirosaki-jo is surrounded by cherry blossoms each spring.

somei-yoshino cherry trees blossom, or when the maples turn, the setting is even more gorgeous. A snow-lantern festival with illuminated ice sculptures is held in early February. The castle is a 30-minute walk from the station on the northwest side of town, across the river. Take the ¥100 bus from the No. 2 stop and get off at the Shiyaku-sho-mae, or City Hall stop. ⊠ *2–1 Shimo-Shirogane-cho* ☎ *0172/33–8733* 🖼 *Grounds free, castle ¥300* 🕙 *Grounds daily 7 am–9 pm; castle Apr.– Nov., daily 9–5 (Apr. 23–May 5, daily 7–9).*

Hirosaki Sightseeing Information Center. South of the castle grounds, this center displays local industry, crafts, and regional art (free) and provides tourist information. ⊠ *1–1 Shimo-Shirogane-cho, Hirosaki Koen Mae* ☎ *0172/26–3600* 🖨 *0172/26–3601* 🕙 *Daily 8:45–6.*

Tsugaru-han Neputa Mura *(Tsugaru Peninsula Neputa Village).* On the northeast corner of the castle grounds, this museum exhibits the giant drums and floats used in the Neputa Festival. If you miss the real thing, come here to see the 40-foot fan-shape floats as they sleep off their hangovers from the mad midsummer revelry. In the workshop you can paint your own traditional kite, *Kingyo-neputa* (paper-and-frame goldfish) and *kokeshi* (traditional wooden dolls) to take home as souvenirs. It has a Japanese garden with the borrowed scenery method—combining it with outer scenic objects to complete a harmony—and a food court on the premise provides inexpensive hearty Japanese meals. From mid-May to October, you can borrow a free bicycle. ☎ *0172/39–1511* 🖼 *¥500* 🕙 *Apr.–Nov., daily 9–5; Dec.–Mar., daily 9–4.*

WHERE TO EAT

$$$
JAPANESE

✕**Anzu** 杏. Avant-garde performances of live Tsugaru-jamisen—the Japanese banjo—by young and promising performers and national champs are the main attraction here, more so even than the food. Jams take place evenings at 7:30 and 9:30. Arrive early to sit on cushions on the floor, in local style, and enjoy seasonal vegetables, sashimi, and such dishes as grilled eggplant (¥600) and grilled scallops (¥800). Although a good selection of Tsugaru sake helps provide a merry time, performers humbly ask you to be all-ears, if not totally quiet, when they play. ✉44–1 Oyakata ☎0172/32–6684 ▬No credit cards ☾Closed Sun. No lunch.

$$–$$$
JAPANESE

✕**Kikufuji** 菊富士. Tasty, healthful, and authentic dishes from the region are Kikufuji's specialty, from delicious vegetable stews like kenoshiru (vegetable soup) to the freshest seafood. The scallops brought in from the Mutsu Bay coast are superb, so try the hotateno-kaiyakimiso (scallops grilled in the shell). Because excellent dry, cold, local varieties of sake are available, dinner may be preferable here over lunch. It's a short taxi ride from JR Hirosaki Station, or a long walk out along the main northwest–southwest diagonal, near the stream crossing, and not far from the tall, freaky sci-fi building that contains Naka-san department store. ✉1 Sakamoto-cho ☎0172/36–3300 🖷0172/36–3319 ⊕www. kikufuji.co.jp ▬No credit cards.

$$$$
FRENCH

✕**Restaurant Yamazaki** レストラン山崎. Would you believe that people come here from all over Honshu solely for a cup of soup? Whether you scoff or not, the totally organic "miracle" apples that farmer Kimura Akinori raises and the dishes chef Yamazaki prepares using those apples keep attracting customers. So try the famous cold apple soup topped with crusted baked apple skins; it's got a very smooth and natural taste. In addition to apple dishes, the restaurant offers prix-fixe menus that include an hors d'oeuvre, soup, fish or meat, dessert, and coffee. Menus vary, but you can always count on carefully chosen fresh ingredients cooked and presented in elegant styles. ✉41 Oayakata-machi ☎0172/38–5515 🖷017/35–1236 ⊕r-yamazaki.com ✍Reservations essential ☾Closed Mon. and 3rd Sun. of month.

$$$–$$$$
JAPANESE

✕**Yamauta** 山唄. Traditional shamisen live performances with the addition of wailing Tsugaru vocals are expected here. The restaurant serves a teishoku set menu and three prix-fixe menus of regional foods that usually include grilled fish, yakitori, mozuku seaweed, and herring cooked with soy sauce (¥3,000–¥5,000). Live shamisen music shows start around 7 and 9. The restaurant is a five-minute walk past the Best Western Hotel New City Hirosaki from the train station. ✉1–2–4 O-machi ☎0172/36–1835 ▬No credit cards ☾Closed 1st and 3rd Mon. of month. No lunch.

WHERE TO STAY

$$–$$$
HOTEL

🛏**Best Western Hotel New City Hirosaki**ベストウエスタンホテルニューシティ弘前. One of the most pleasant lodgings in Hirosaki is located next to the JR Hirosaki Station and provides clean and comfortable rooms. **Pros:** well situated; great prices. **Cons:** a bit impersonal. ✉1–1–2 O-machi ☎0172/37–0700 🖷0172/37–1229 ⊕www.bestwestern.co.jp/hirosaki ⇄141 rooms ♿In-room: a/c. In-hotel: restaurants, bar ¶◎EP.

$$$$
HOTEL 🏨 **Hotel New Castle** ホテルニューキャッスル. The biggest advantage to this hotel is its location: a block and a half from Hirosaki Castle, and the saddest news is that many rooms are outdated. **Pros:** close to the quaint, photogenic castle (and the park's spectacular cherry blossoms in season). **Cons:** rooms and facilities are dated; sparse decor. ⊠ *24–1 Kamisayashi-machi* ☎ *0172/36–1211* 🖷 *0172/36–1210* ⇨ *58 Western-style rooms, 3 Japanese-style rooms* ⚲ *In-room: a/c. In-hotel: 2 restaurants* ⦿*No meals.*

13

AOMORI 青森

37 km (23 mi) northeast of Hirosaki.

Despite the horrible weather, Aomori may return to its busier heyday since the Hayate Shikansen now stops at JR Shin-Aomori Station, making a day trip from Tokyo and elsewhere on Honshu an easy task. In the land where over 35 feet of snowfall is typical, things tend to be low-key and many shops close early. But year-round, you can enjoy delicious seafood from Aomori Bay, including *Oma no Maguro* (tuna of Oma), as well as delicious fruits and vegetables (particularly garlic). And come every summer, the town cuts loose to throw the decidedly wild Nebuta Matsuri festival, a frenzied, utterly unaccountable period when normal gets thrown to the wind.

GETTING HERE AND AROUND

Aomori Airport has six daily flights from Tokyo's Haneda Airport by JAS, a JAL affiliate (one hour, 20 minutes; ¥32,000-one-way, ¥54,000 round-trip). Aomori also has two JAL flights from Osaka's Itami Airport, and three from Sapporo's Chitose Airport.

The Hayate runs 15 trains daily from Tokyo (three hours, five minutes; ¥16,370) and one daily from Morioka (one hour; ¥5,970). By JR local train it's 45 minutes (¥650) from Hirosaki. If red-eye transportation is your choice, take the Willer Express bus departing from Tokyo at 9:30 pm from JR Tokyo Station or at 10:20 pm from JR Shinjyku Station, arriving at JR Aomori Station at 8:50 am (¥5,300–¥6,500/way). The JR highway express bus departing from Tokyo at 10:30 pm arrives at Aomori at 6:30 am (¥8,500–¥9,000 one-way, ¥15,000 round-trip).

Contact Aomori Airport (⊠ *1–5 Kotani, Otaniaza, Oaza* ☎ *017/739–2121*).

VISITOR INFORMATION

The Aomori City Tourist Information Center is on the south end of Aomori Station. English maps and brochures for the city and prefecture are available, and you can apply for the discount Tohoku Welcome Card if you haven't done so online.

Contact Aomori City Tourist Information Center (⊠ *JR Aomori Station, 1–1–1 Yanagawa* ☎ *017/723–4670* 🕙 *Daily 8–5:30*).

WHAT TO SEE

Aomori's main event is its **Nebuta Matsuri Festival** ねぶた祭り, August 2–7, not to be confused with Hirosaki's Neputa Festival (residents of each locale tend to get annoyed when they are). Both are held in early August, and both have large, illuminated floats of gigantic samurai

figures paraded through the streets at night. Aomori's festival is one of Japan's largest, and is said to celebrate the euphoria of post-battle victory, and is thus encouraged to be noisier and livelier than you may have been exposed to in other Japanese festivals. Dancers, called *heneto,* run alongside the floats, dancing crazily, and you're encouraged to join in. Brace yourself, and enjoy!

Aomori Museum of Art 青森県立美術館. This new contemporary arts museum houses a collection of Aomori-related artists such as Munakata Shiko (1903–75), Nara Yoshitomo (1959–) and Terayama Shuji (1935–1983). Another highlight is Marc Chagall's three backdrops of the ballet *Aleko* (of his four backdrops, three are here while Act 3 belongs to the Philadelphia Museum of Art). Unlike many museums in which restaurants and gift shops are near the entrance and packed with people, the gift shop here sits quietly in a corner upstairs, seemingly asking visitors to enjoy art first before shopping. Outside, a statue of Aomori-ken (*ken* means both prefecture and dog) waits in front of his food dish. ⊠ *185 Chikano, Yasuda* ☎ *017/783–3000* 🖷 *017/783–5244* ⊕ *www.aomori-museum.jp* 🎫 *¥500* 🕑 *June–Sept., daily 9–6; Oct.–May daily 9:30–5.*

Auga アウガ. Many tourists arriving in Aomori head to the pyramid-shape ASPAM building, which offers gorgeous waterfront views, but at a price of ¥800, the entry fee for the observation lounge and Panorama Theater is pretty steep. Better is the Auga market complex, where fish, shellfish, preserved seaweed, smoked fish, and fish eggs—in short, all manner of marine organisms—are hawked by hundreds of shopkeepers in 80 stores. It's one block east of JR Aomori Station, on Shinmachi-dori, in the basement level of a modern building with distinctive crimson pillars. ⊠ *Shinmachi* 🕑 *Daily 5–3 (some shops open until 6).*

Nebuta-no-Sato, or Nebuta Village Museum ねぶたの里. If you can't visit during the Nebuta Festival, head to this museum in the southeast part of town, where glowing papier-mâché sculptures painted with the fierce countenances of warriors used in Aomori's festival are displayed. To get here, take the JR bus bound for Moyahills (25 minutes; ¥450) and get off at Nebuta-no-Sato Iriguchi stop, then walk 15 minutes. ☎ *017/738–1230* ⊕ *www.nebutanosato.co.jp* 🎫 *¥630* 🕑 *Apr.–Nov., daily 9–5:30 (closed during Nebuta Festival in early Aug.); Dec.–Mar., daily 10–5:30. Last entry 30 mins before closing.*

Sannai Maruyama Iseki 三内丸山遺跡. Interested in archeology? Want to know what it was like to live in Japan 5,500 years ago? This, one of the largest archaeological sites in Japan, features a reconstructed Jomon settlement that lasted for roughly 1,500 years, from 3500 BC to 2000 BC. After an extensive excavation, it was opened to the public and has attracted crowds of schoolchildren and others. Its interactive approach encourages visitors to try crafts making, Jomon fashion, and cuisine. ⊠ *350 Sannai Maruyama* ☎ *017/782–9462* ⊕ *sannaimaruyama.pref. aomori.jp* 🎫 *Free* 🕑 *Daily 9–5.*

WHERE TO EAT

$$$–$$$$ ✕ **Hide-zushi** 秀寿司. You're in a major seafood city, and if you want
SEAFOOD some of the best of what is available in that cold, clean water, then this is the place to get it. Excellent service and bright surroundings, not to

mention sea urchin, salmon roe, scallops, squid, tuna, and ark shell (a variety of clam) await your whetted appetite. ✉ *1–5 Tsutsumi-machi* ☎ *017/722–8888* ⊘ *Closed Sun.*

$$$–$$$$
SEAFOOD

✕ **Ippa-zushi** 一八寿司. What was once an early-20th-century warehouse is now a modern sushi restaurant. The sushi here is good, and the price is right, with a price list clearly hung in the wall. (Sushi beginners should be aware that some snobby, older establishments do not have prices on the menu and will expect you to eat what is brought to you and pay accordingly.) The casual atmosphere also makes it popular among business travelers. The fish served varies according to the season and availability, but tuna almost always appears. ✉ *1–10–11 Shinmachi* ☎ *017/722–2639* ⊘ *Closed 2nd and 4th Sun. of month.*

$$$–$$$$
JAPANESE

✕ **Mitsuishi** 三ッ石. If decent Japanese food is your desire without having to endure a tourist eatery, then this is the place. Crowded with locals, it has a convivial atmosphere. Sashimi *moriawase* (assorted sashimi; ¥1,200–¥2,500) is excellent for two or three. Grilled scallops and grilled chicken with herbs are also tasty and popular. The Mitsuishi-gozen (¥2,000) and Hime-kaiseki (¥3,000) set menus include sashimi, tempura, grilled fish, vegetables, rice, soup, and fruits. A sake list shows numerous kinds of sake. If you are in the mood to just drink and perhaps a small bite, take a seat at the bar, where the chef sometimes hands out complimentary snacks over the counter. As late night approaches things get busier and louder, but the staff comes to your table at top speed if you scream "Sumimasen!" It's three minutes from Hotel JAL. ✉ *2–7–36 Yasukata* ☎ *017/735–3314* ⊘ *Closed 3rd Sun. of month.*

$$–$$$
JAPANESE

✕ **Nishimura** 西むら. It would be hard to walk out of this Japanese restaurant hungry: the *danna* course (¥3,000), for example, includes abalone and sea-urchin soup, seaweed and fish, a mixed hot pot, and fried eggplant. *Shottusu nabe* and other local specialties are also recommended. On sunny days you should come for lunch. Both the great-value teishoku set menu and splendid bay views from the 10th floor of ASPAM are all yours. ✉ *1–5–19 Yasukata* ☎ *017/773–2880* ⊕ *www. michinokunishimura.com* ⊘ *Closed Sun.*

WHERE TO STAY

$$–$$$
HOTEL

🏨 **Hotel JAL City Aomori** ホテルジャルシテイ青森. This nine-story upscale art deco–style hotel curves around the corner as if it belonged in 1960s Miami Beach. **Pros:** good location; comfortable rooms. **Cons:** coin-op Internet terminal in the lobby looks cheap in this upscale hotel. ✉ *4–12 Yasukata, 2-chome* ☎ *017/732–2580* 🖷 *017/735–2584* ⊕ *aomori. jalcity.co.jp/index.php* ⇱ *167 rooms* ⚏ *In-room: a/c, Internet. In-hotel: 2 restaurants, bar, Internet terminal* ⫟◉⫟ *No meals.*

$$$
HOTEL

🏨 **Richmond Hotel Aomori** リッチモンドホテル青森. A good location and new, comfortable rooms make this a fine, moderately priced hotel option in Aomori. **Pros:** great rates; comfortable, modern rooms. **Cons:** no restaurant or café. ✉ *1–6–6 Nagashima* ☎ *017/732–7655* 🖷 *017/732–7656* ⊕ *www.richmondhotel.jp/aomori* ⇱ *177 rooms* ⚏ *In-room: a/c, safe, refrigerator, Internet. In-hotel: Internet terminal, parking (paid)* ⫟◉⫟ *No meals.*

TOHOKU WEST COAST

AKITA 秋田

186 km (116 mi) southwest of Aomori City; 148 km (92 mi) southwest of Hirosaki.

In the scenic, faraway realm of Akita, the peaks of the Dewa Sanchi (Dewa Range), marked by Mt. Taihei, march off to the east, and the Sea of Japan lies at the edge of the fertile plains that extend to the west. The region's history began in 733, during the turbulent Nara period, with the establishment of Dewa-no-saku, a fortress built on a hill in Takashimizu by the powerful Yamato clan. The area, set up to guard trade routes, soon gained strategic importance, and during the Heian era, soldiers and their families began spreading outward. The Ando and Satake families each built major bastions in the Yuwa and Kawabe districts after the Battle of Sekigahara in 1600. These municipalities, now merged, are considered to be the foundations of modern Akita City. Today the prefectural capital (population 324,000) is a lively, likable city full of delicious food from the mountains, plain, rivers, and sea.

The countryside is devoted to producing what locals feel is the best rice in Japan, and they certainly do make good sake with it. Additionally, the fruits and vegetables grown here are unbelievably cheap and flavorful. The combination of climate, pure water, and healthful food are said to make the women of Akita the fairest in the land—a matter of prefectural, even national, pride. In the Japanese media, "scientific" studies have been trotted out since the 19th century as proof of the Akita *bii-jin* (Akita beauty) phenomenon.

GETTING HERE AND AROUND

ANA and JAL fly to Akita Airport three to four times daily from Tokyo's Haneda Airport (65 minutes; ¥24,700). JAL also flies twice daily from Osaka's Itami Airport and three times from Sapporo's Shin-Chitose Airport. ANA flies twice daily from the Nagoya's Chubu International Airport.

If you're traveling regionally by rail, the Komachi Shinkansen from Tazawa-ko (one hour; ¥3,280); JR Kamoshika Express from Aomori City (two hours, 30 minutes; ¥5,450); or the JR Kamoshika Limited Express from Hirosaki (two hours; ¥4,940) are the most convenient trains. Traveling between Morioka and Akita is rather difficult; local trains take three to four hours (¥2,210) and involve additional waiting time. From Tokyo the JR Komachi Shinkansen will spirit you off to Akita in four hours (¥16,810). By bus, the JR Express bus Dream-Akita departs daily from JR Tokyo Station at 9:50 pm, arriving in JR Akita Station at 6:35 am (¥9,500), while the Willer Express leaves JR Tokyo Station at 9:40 pm, arriving at JR Akita Station at 7:45 am (¥5,500–¥6,300).

Airport Contact Akita Airport (✉ *Terminal Bldg., 49 Yamagomori Yuwatsu-bakigaw* ☎ *018/886–3366).*

VISITOR INFORMATION

The Akita City Tourist Information Center is on the second floor at the station, just across from the exit from the Shinkansen tracks, and supplies many colorful English-language pamphlets and lots of friendly advice.

Contact Akita City Tourist Information Center (✉ *JR Akita Station, 7–1–2 Naka-dori* ☎ *018/832–7941* ⊙ *Daily 9:30–7*).

WHAT TO SEE

Hirano Masakichi Bijutsukan 平野政吉美術館 *(Hirano Masakichi Museum of Fine Art)*. An aspiring artist and aviator fanatic, Masakichi Hirano was born in a wealthy land-owning family in Akita. His passion for art inspired him to acquire hundreds of paintings including many *ukiyoe* (Japanese wood-block prints) and nothing—including wars—stopped him from collecting. Under the distinctive copper-covered Japanese palace–style roof of the museum, a varied collection of 599 works donated by Hirano include 14 oil paintings by Tsuguji Fujita (1886–1968) and an excellent selection of Western art (94 masterpieces are here), with works by Toulouse-Lautrec and Picasso as well as a fantastic array of Goya etchings. However, the highlight is Fujita's enormous *Annual Events in Akita*. Fujita took just 15 days to complete the painting of three local festivals merged into a single scene, rendered on one of the world's largest canvases at the time, measuring 11 feet by 66 feet. The interior galleries provide an airy and minimalist aesthetic that allows the art to speak for itself. ✉ *1-chome* ☎ *018/833–5809* ⊕ *hirabi.m78.com* ✉ *¥610* ⊙ *Apr.–Sept., Tues.–Sun. 10–5:30; Oct.–Mar., Tues.–Sun. 10–5.*

OFF THE BEATEN PATH

Shirakami Sanmyaku 白神山脈. South of Mt. Iwaki, straddling Aomori Prefecture's border with Akita, are the Shirakami Mountains, site of the world's largest (42,000-acre) virgin beech forest, which is a UNESCO World Heritage Site. In keeping with the goal of preservation, access is provided by just a few tiny roads. The area is truly pristine and great for hiking, particularly in spring. There are several ways to get here, but the easiest way is to take the Konan bus from JR Hirosaki Station bound for Tsugaru Touge, getting off at Aqua Green Village, Anmon. (90 minutes; ¥1,600/one-way, ¥2,400/round-trip). If you only want to see the Mother tree (the forest's largest, and presumably oldest tree), get off at the last stop, Tsugaru Touge; the tree is a five-minute walk from there (two hours, 10 minutes; ¥1,800/one-way, ¥2,700/round-trip). Verify the bus schedule because so you won't miss your return as only a few buses run daily. ☎ *0176/36–5061 for Konan Bus* ⊕ *konanbus.com.*

BIG BAMBOO

Akita's **Kanto Festival** (August 3–6) celebrates ancient fertility rites with young men balancing 36-foot-long bamboo poles (*kanto*) hung with as many as 46 lighted paper lanterns on its eight crossbars—and weighing up to 110 pounds—against a special pouched strap on their waist, hip, back, or shoulder. The lanterns represent sacks full of rice, and a bountiful harvest is fervently prayed for and celebrated in anticipation of its arrival.

13

WHERE TO EAT

$$$–$$$$

JAPANESE

✕ **Inaniwa Kaiseki O-machi Sato Yousuke** 稲庭懐石大町佐藤養助. Noodles can only be called Inaniwa Udon if they are produced exclusively in Inaniwa. Established in 1860, this Inaniwa noodle empire has many restaurants and shops across the Tohoku region, but this one is for mature adults who want to sample regional foods and locally brewed sake. A casual, nine-course kaiseki (¥3,150–¥5,000) comes with its signature hand-kneaded shiny Inaniwa noodle, which has a firm al dente texture, and fresh fruits for dessert. Make big slurps and enjoy. ✉ *5–2–13 O-machi* ☎ *018/862–3777* ⊕ *www.sato-yoske.co.jp* ☉ *Closed Sun.*

$$–$$$

JAPANESE

★

✕ **Shukitei-Hinaiya** 酒季亭比内や. This restaurant is named after the local breed of chicken that goes into *Hinai-jidori kiritampo-nabe,* a hot pot made with *kiritampo,* or rice that's cooked, put onto skewers (usually cedar or bamboo), then grilled over a charcoal fire. The rice is then simmered in a pot with chicken and broth, seasonal vegetables, burdock root, green onions, and mushrooms (¥1,890). Tsukune-bou (skewered chicken meatballs, ¥390) is equally tasty. To get to Hinaiya, in the heart of the Kawabata entertainment district, walk one block from the river on Suzuran-dori; it's on the second floor. Noisy, fun-loving Hinaiya is conducive to partying, and even the fish swimming in the tank seem oblivious to their fate. ✉ *4–2–2 O-machi* ☎ *018/823–1718* ⊕ *www. inaniwa-g.co.jp*

WHERE TO STAY

$$$–$$$$

HOTEL

🏨 **Akita Castle Hotel** 秋田キャッスルホテル. At this writing, a massive renovation was underway at Akita Castle Hotel, scheduled to be completed by 2012, to make rooms more comfortable and spacious, level the uneven ceilings, and ensure that the bright rooms overlooking the moats of Senshu Park remain ever attractive. **Pros:** good location for sightseeing; nice ambience. **Cons:** a bit far from the station. ✉ *1–3–5 Naka-dori* ☎ *018/834–1141* 🖷 *018/834–5588* ⊕ *www.castle-hotel. co.jp* ⤢ *149 rooms* △ *In-room: a/c. In-hotel: 4 restaurants, bar* �‖ *No meals.*

$$–$$$

HOTEL

🏨 **Akita View Hotel** 秋田ビューホテル. The largest hotel in town, the Akita View is beside the Seibu department store. **Pros:** exciting location. **Cons:** rooms are on the small side. ✉ *2–6–1 Naka-dori* ☎ *018/832– 1111* 🖷 *018/832–0037* ⊕ *www.akitaviewhotel.jp* ⤢ *192 rooms* △ *In-room: a/c, Internet. In-hotel: 3 restaurants, bar, gym* �‖ *No meals.*

$$$

HOTEL

🏨 **Hotel Metropolitan Akita** メトロポリタンホテル秋田. Adjacent to the west side of JR Akita Station and ALS shopping mall, this hotel's location makes it a perfect choice for shopping and exploring sights. **Pros:** sleek and modern setting; 20% off for JR Rail Pass holders; business center. **Cons:** impersonal; chain-hotel feel at times. ✉ *7–2–1 Naka-dori* ☎ *018/831–2222* 🖷 *018/831–2290* ⊕ *www.metro-akita.jp* ⤢ *115 rooms* △ *In-room: a/c. In-hotel: 3 restaurants, bar* �‖ *No meals.*

TSURUOKA AND DEWA-SANZAN 鶴岡と出羽三山

132 km (82 mi) south of Akita

South of Akita along the Nihon-kai coast are small fishing villages where nets hang to dry only inches from train windows, vast plains of rice fields lead to faraway hills, rushing rivers and clear streams are full of fish, and, closer to Atsumi Onsen, you will be confronted with lofty forested mountains coming down to the endless crashing waves. Along the way is the town of Tsuruoka 鶴岡, once a castle stronghold of the Sakai family, which serves as a (bus) gateway to Yamagata City and the three mountains of Dewa-Sanzan that are held sacred by the *yama-bushi*, the popular name given to members of the ascetic and nature-loving Shugendo sect of "mountain warrior" Buddhists.

GETTING HERE AND AROUND

If you are considering visiting Tsuruoka from Tokyo, the most inexpensive way is by overnight highway bus. Willer Express leaves JR Tokyo Station at 10:30 pm or Shinjyuku at 11:15 pm and arrives at Tsuruoka at 7:15 am (¥5,000). Tsuruoka is 1½ hours south of Akita by JR Uetsu Line (¥2,210). It's easiest to get to the base of Haguro by bus (55 minutes), either from Bus Stop 2, in front of JR Tsuruoka Station, or from Stop 5, at Sho-Ko (Sho-nai Ko-tsu) Mall (it's not a JR bus); there are four departures in winter and at least hourly departures in summer. A fare of ¥800 will take you from the station to the Haguro Center village at the entrance to the peak itself. Most buses from Tsuruoka to Haguro Center continue to the summit, Haguro-san-cho, which is not much farther, but the fare jumps to ¥1,150.

VISITOR INFORMATION

The **Tsuruoka Tourist Information Office** is just to the right from the station exit. They speak some English, though most pamphlets about Dewa-Sanzan are in Japanese, but they can help with bus schedules and lodging arrangements.

Contact Tsuruoka Tourist Information Office (☎ 0235/25–7678 ☉ Daily 10–5).

WHAT TO SEE

Of the three holy mountains of Dewa-Sanzan, only Haguro-san has year-round access, but you can reach the others during the summer months. In summer only, Shonai Kotsu buses also depart from Yamagata Bus Terminal (confer with the Tourist Information Office, and *see Yamagata, above*), with stops at all three sacred mountains. Note that many of the bus companies conducting the trips to the mountains and towns in this area are not affiliated with JR, but they are generally not expensive.

Ga-san 月山. Buses leave JR Tsuruoka Station at 6 and 7 am in summer for the 90-minute trip (¥1,650) to the Ga-san Hachigome (Eighth Station) stop, from where you can hike three hours past the glaciers and wildflowers to the 1,984-meter (6,500-foot) summit of Ga-san, or Moon-mountain. From the top you can see the whole gorgeous gallery of mountains that is Yamagata, including one called Dewa-Fuji (after Mt. Fuji) for its shape, and to the Sea of Japan to the west.

Haguro-san 羽黒山. The climb up Mt. Haguro begins in Haguro Center, at the red **Zaishin Gate** (Zaishin-mon), then goes up 2,446 or so stone steps to the summit. The strenuous ascent cuts through ancient cedar trees that rise to dominate the sky. You'll pass a 14th-century five-story pagoda sitting alone in the forest. A tea shop, open from April through November, is situated at a perfect stop to take in the view.

This five-story wooden pagoda that can be found on Mt. Haguro was built without a single nail.

The trail is just over 1.7 km (about 1 mi) in all, and it may take you an hour to reach the 414-meter (1,400-foot) summit with its thatch-roof shrine, **Dewa-Sanzan Jinja.** You may happen upon one of the mysterious ceremonies held there—the initiation ritual of a yama-bushi (a "mountain warrior" who seeks power from ascetic practices and close bonds to nature) lasts nine grueling days, and it is said that if an apprentice wants to complete his training he must first prove that he can engage and destroy an imaginary demon. Up to nine buses a day make the 35-minute trip to Haguro Center from JR Tsuroka Station, many going to the summit for an extra cost (in July and August there are early-morning buses on weekdays). It is possible to stay overnight on the mountain at the temple-lodge of Sai-kan, which is attached by a long stairway to the Dewa-Sanzan Jinja.

Yudono-san 湯殿山. The last of the trio of peaks, Yudono-san, is 1,504 meters (5,000 feet) high, and is generally the last on pilgrims' rounds. You can descend on foot in a few hours from Ga-san, but it involves some exertion, kanji-sign navigational ability, and slippery metal ladders, and you'll want to talk with the tourist info folks about current conditions. Buses make the 80-minute (¥1,490) run between Tsuruoka and Sen-in-zawa, a trailhead for a short climb to the summit, where you must make a small monetary donation and be purified in a secret ritual that you are forbidden to photograph or tell anyone about. Once cleansed, don't miss the last bus back down to Tsuruoka, which leaves promptly at 4:30 pm.

WHERE TO EAT AND STAY

If you are staying overnight in Tsuruoka, you can stay in town or up on Haguro-san itself.

$$$$
ITALIAN

✕ **Al-chécciano** アルケチャーノ. Acclaimed executive chef and owner Masayuki Okuda prepares Italian dishes that are totally unique and a full of originality. His style of Italian comes with a commitment to the freshest Shonai-grown ingredients such as vegetables, fruits, fish, and meat. The menu varies, but pasta and everything else is reliably great. The aim here is to bring out all natural flavors and aromas of the Shonai foods by using few condiments, to create a perfectly combined dish where delicate flavors are more important than heavy sauces or big portions. In winter, try risotto with turnips, truffles, and cod *milt* (cod sperm). (Don't be afraid; it's the nation's winter delicacy). Prix-fixe meals starts at ¥3,500. A well-chosen wine list includes Italian and Japanese varietals. It's 20 minutes by taxi or by bus from JR Tsuruoka Staton. ✉ *83 Ichirizuka, Shimoyamazoe, Turuoka* ☎ *0235/78–7230* ⊕ *www.alchecciano.com* ⌘ *Reservations essential* ⊗ *Closed Mon.*

$–$$
HOTEL

▦ **Route Inn Tsuruoka Ekimae** ルートイン鶴岡. This hotel's location makes it a good base for visiting Dewa-Sanzan or exploring other cities in Yamagata Prefecture. **Pros:** a 30-second walk from the station; complimentary breakfast. **Cons:** surroundings are a bit austere. ✉ *1–17 Suehiro-machi, Tsuruoka* ☎ *0235/28–2055* ᕬ *0235/23–1180* ⊕ *www.route-inn.co.jp* ⇆ *152 rooms* ⌂ *In-room: a/c, safe, refrigerator, Internet. In-hotel: restaurant, laundry facilities, Internet terminal, parking (free)* ⑩ *Breakfast.*

$$
TEMPLE

▦ **Sai-kan** 斉館. This temple lodge connected to Dewa-Sanzan Jinja by a long stairway allows you to enjoy the shrine and scenery at the summit after most tourists have gone home. The cedar-lined approach is more than majestic, but inside, this *shukubo*, or monks' lodging, is spartan. **Pros:** great healthful food; tranquil Zen garden. **Cons:** 10-minute, uphill walk from bus stop. ✉ *Toge, Haguro-machi, Higashi Tagawa-gun* ☎ *0235/62–2357* ᕬ *0235/62–2352* ⊕ *www.dewasanzan.jp* ⇆ *200 futons* ⌂ *In-room: no no phone, a/c, no TV* ▭ *No credit cards* ⑩ *Some meals.*

Hokkaido

WORD OF MOUTH

"[Why not spend] a nice relaxing day and/or night at the hot springs in Sapporo? We got a package (spas, room, dinner) for $180 U.S. (for two people) . . . at the Daiichi Takimotokan. It truly was hot-spring heaven."

—usernameistaken

WELCOME TO HOKKAIDO

TOP REASONS TO GO

★ **The Beer:** Hokkaido has the Sapporo Beer brewery and local microbreweries in Otaru and Hakodate.

★ **The Slopes:** Deep powder and uncrowded lift lines are hallmarks of Hokkaido's ski resorts at Niseko, Rusutsu, and Furano.

★ **The Valley of Hell:** Sulfur-spewing springs at Noboribetsu, Toya, Akan, and Shiretoko volcanoes burst forth into vents and craters. Check out the ash flow from the eruption of Toya's Mt. Usu.

★ **The Last Frontier:** Salmon-fishing bears and red-crested cranes, alpine flowers, and vast forests hold modern Japan at bay. Although the most convenient way to see outback Hokkaido is by car, the vistas of mountains and plains are best viewed on foot or bike.

★ **Winter Wonderland:** Frigid winter nights are brightened by festivals. Out east, icebreakers cut through Arctic ice floes, and passengers spy seals and eagles.

1 Hakodate. Gateway to Hokkaido for train travelers, this bustling port and tourist city has 19th-century clapboard buildings, rattling streetcars, and the region's best public fish market.

2 Sapporo. Hokkaido's capital is modern, green, clean, and easy to navigate. At its heart is Odori Park, which hosts several popular festivals. The Susukino nightlife area is a blaze of neon and noise.

3 **Otaru and Niseko.** A historic harbor town, Otaru is now popular for its gentrified canal, cafés, shops, and restaurants. Niseko has the best powder snow for skiers and snowboarders from December to April.

4 **Shikotsu-Toya National Park.** Soaring mountains and deep lakes offer an escape into nature two hours from Sapporo. The region includes Shikotsu, one of Japan's deepest, prettiest lakes.

GETTING ORIENTED

14

Hokkaido is 90 minutes north by air from Tokyo, with high (up to 6,500 feet) volcanic mountains and expansive populated and cultivated plains in between. Summers are cooler and less humid, winters colder and snowier than elsewhere in Japan.

5 **Eastern Hokkaido.** The completely unpopulated tip of the Shiretoko Peninsula is a World Heritage Site. In the south are the Kushiro wetlands, while farther north, Ainu people at Lake Akan share their culture through song and dance.

6 **Central and Northern Hokkaido.** At the Daisetsu Mountains, in Hokkaido's center, cable cars lift visitors to flower-filled plateaus, and hiking trails promise panoramic views. To the far north are Rebun and Rishiri islands, friendly places with short summers, rare flowers, and creamy *uni* sea urchin.

WINTER SPORTS IN HOKKAIDO

Hokkaido is a fantastic winter wonderland. Ridiculous amounts of powder snow and great resorts delight skiers and boarders from both Japan and overseas.

(This page above) Scenic skiing at Niseko; (opposite page upper right) Huge snowfalls make for great downhill skiing in Hokkaido; (opposite page bottom left) Gondola lifts are numerous at Rusutsu.

Hokkaido is the northernmost of Japan's four main islands. In winter, cold Siberian winds bring huge amounts of snow throughout the winter months. For some locals it is a curse, (winter driving, once you've dug out your car, is slow and treacherous) but for skiers and boarders it is paradise. Those used to marginal pistes in other parts of the world let out whoops of joy as they float over the deep powder. Hokkaido has a quarter of Japan's landmass, but only one-twentieth of its population. The resorts are nowhere near as crowded as on mainland Japan, and although the Hokkaido secret is out, there's more than enough powder for everybody. And one of the great joys of winter sports in Japan is that after a long day on the slopes you can soak your aching muscles in a local *onsen* (thermal spa).

DOGSLEDDING

Although not a traditional method of transportation, several dogsled races take place in Hokkaido during the winter months. Major events include the Japan Cup Dogsled Competition held in Wakkanai (February) and the JFSS Cup International Dogsled Race held in Sapporo (March). If you'd like to get up close and personal with man's best friend, then you can give dog sledding a try at the Rusutsu resort area.

HOKKAIDO'S SKI RESORTS

More than 100 ski hills are dotted across Hokkaido. Some are small, used almost exclusively by locals, and have limited facilities. Others are vast resorts that attract and cater to visitors from around the world. Hokkaido's big three are Niseko, Rusutsu, and Furano but you can find great snow and a friendly welcome across the whole island.

FURANO

Furano, located in the center of island, is famous for its fields of lavender in summer, and skiing in winter. Heavy snowfalls provide plenty of light powder snow while the local town has found a good balance between welcoming visitors and maintaining its traditional charm. Furano is about an hour from Asahikawa Airport, or three hours from Chitose Airport.

RUSUTSU

Rusutsu is a large resort stretching out over East Mountain, West Mountain, and Mount Isola. Thirty-seven courses provide everything from smooth groomed runs to steep and deep off-piste powder. Numerous gondolas, quads, and pair lifts mean you shouldn't have to wait in line. The resort also provides a whole range of other winter activities from snowshoeing to horseback riding. Rusutsu is about 90 minutes from Chitose Airport.

14

NISEKO

The Niseko ski area is made up of several resorts, which when combined make it arguably the best place for skiing and snowboarding in Japan. Niseko Hirafu, Niseko Higashiyama (aka Niesko Village), and Niseko Annupuri are collectively known as Niseko United and can be skied on a single pass. This gives you access to 61 official ski runs, but locals and powder hounds know of many more unofficial runs that make the most of the huge snowfalls. The chairlifts at nearby Niseko Weiss closed many years ago and have been replaced by a surprisingly inexpensive snowcat service. The tracked vehicles shuttle you up the mountain, and let you enjoy the powder on the way down.

Over the last decade Niseko has gone through an amazing boom, with a large increase in the number of foreign visitors. The positive side of this is that you can get by with limited or no Japanese language ability; rental equipment includes large sizes; and there's a lively international scene with varied bars, accommodations, restaurants, and clientele. For those looking for a more traditional Japanese experience it is worth spending at least some time exploring the more remote corners of Hokkaido.

Updated by
Arudou Debito

Hokkaido is Japan with breathing space. People here don't put on the air-conditioning in summer—they open the windows. Outside, fragrant air, wild mountains, virgin forests, pristine lakes, and surf-beaten shores are all within easy reach of cities and towns.

Hokkaido's Japanese history is, compared to the mainland, relatively short. Born during the Meiji Restoration (1868–1912), Hokkaido was developed by Japan only to keep Russia from getting to it. Until then, this large northern island, comprising 20% of Japan's current landmass, had largely been left to the indigenous Ainu people, hunter-gatherers who had traded with the Japanese and Russians for centuries.

In the 1870s, after researching American and European agriculture, city design, and mining, Japan sent 63 foreign experts to harness Hokkaido's resources, introducing a soldier-farmer system to spur mainlanders north to clear and settle the land. Hokkaido was replete with coal and gold, herring shoals, and fertile soil conducive to dairy farming, potato growing, horse breeding, and even cold-climate rice planting. The legacy lives on—small holdings with silos and barns still anchor the rolling farmland, while flat landscapes with mountains on the horizon give stretches of Hokkaido a frontier flavor.

On the losing end of this colonization were the Ainu, who died by the thousands from disease, forced labor, and conflict with the Japanese. Forced assimilation and intermarriage has largely eliminated their way of life (although recent decades of activism have given the Ainu a modicum of public acceptance as a distinct ethnic minority).

Hokkaido's people—who call themselves *Dosanko*—can be quite open-minded. Many readily come to the rescue of foreign travelers with a warmth and directness that make up for language problems. Japanese tourists visit here for a less-traditional view of Japan, while others still settle here, seeking an alternative way of life as farmers, artists, outdoor adventure guides, and guesthouse owners.

However, because Hokkaido consists more of countryside than of culture-rich cities, the number of non-Japanese visitors has traditionally been small, and many locally promoted attractions—such as flower fields and dairy farms—may be of less interest to people from Western countries than the mountain scenery, wildlife, and volcanically active areas. Recently, visitors from China, Hong Kong, Taiwan, South Korea, and Australia have started to drop by in the hundreds of thousands to enjoy the snow and escape the summer heat.

Hokkaido remains a frontier in terms of geopolitics. In prominent places are signboards demanding the return of the southern four Kuril Islands, Japan-administered territory that Russia invaded in the final days of World War II. Japanese Self-Defense Force bases still dot the map as a Cold War–era deterrent, and travel to neighboring Russian air- and seaports is quite restricted. Nevertheless, a Russian business presence is noticeable in Hokkaido's northern and eastern fishing ports, where road signs in Wakkanai and Nemuro are in Japanese and Cyrillic; locals in Monbetsu, Abashiri, and Kushiro might first address Caucasians in Russian.

14

It's easy to romanticize Japan's Great White North as largely wild and untamed, but Hokkaido also has large cities (Sapporo's population is nearly 2 million, and nine other places have populations greater than 100,000), along with decent public transportation and first-world urban lifestyles. Beyond the cities, though, small-town life in Hokkaido is quiet, a tad cumbersome to explore without a car, and a bit stagnant— but for the adventurous visitor, wild beauty and open spaces abound.

The island is a geological wonderland: lava-seared mountains hide deeply carved ravines; hot springs, gushers, and steaming mud pools boil out of the ground; and crystal clear lakes fill the seemingly bottomless cones of volcanoes. Wild, rugged coastlines hold back the sea, and all around the prefecture, islands surface offshore. Half of Hokkaido is covered in forest, home to bears, owls, hawks, cranes, foxes, and other wildlife you would have trouble finding elsewhere in Japan.

Come to Hokkaido, and open your windows.

⇨ *See the glossary at the end of this book for definitions of the common Japanese words and suffixes used in this chapter.*

PLANNING

Hokkaido's expansiveness is daunting. The main sights—calderas, remote onsen, craggy coasts, dramatic mountains—are everywhere. Rather than rushing to see everything, consider balancing the natural with the urban, the inland with the coastal, and figure in the seasonal appropriateness of sights, activities, and available access.

WHEN TO GO

Hokkaido has Japan's most dramatic seasons. Recommended times to visit are May to September (if you are a summer person), January to March (if winter). January to March is snow, snow, snow. From late April to mid-May, Hokkaido offers Japan's last *sakura* (cherry blossoms), as well as a fireworks display of spring flowers all at once. May to September offers perfectly temperate summer weather (except for a sometimes wet July), a respite for people gasping under Asia's humidity.

However, hotel rooms can be more difficult to book in summer, and many scenic areas get crowded with tour groups and Japanese families. ■TIP➡ Avoid the middle of August, when Hokkaido celebrates Obon homecoming and travel prices spike. Late September ushers in brief but spectacular golden foliage, peaking in early October. The periods from November to December and late March to April offer predominately chilly drizzle, so avoid these times. Winter makes travel more difficult (some minor roads and attractions are closed), but Hokkaido is no less beautiful, with snow covering everything in ever-freshened mounds of white. Early February offers the unmissable Sapporo Snow Festival.

HOW MUCH TIME?

You'll need at least a week to experience Hokkaido, with a day or two in Sapporo and then a stay in one or two of the places recommended below. Distances are large, and a train or road trip across the island takes most of a day. Flying to a regional airport cuts down on unnecessary travel time. Make cars and hotel reservations in advance; outside Sapporo and Hakodate, finding people who speak enough English to do bookings can be difficult. Check on access for each destination when planning a winter trip.

GETTING HERE AND AROUND

The best way to explore Hokkaido is by train or car. Most car-rental companies allow different pickup and drop-off locations and will meet customers at trains, ferries, and local flights.

AIR TRAVEL

Domestic carriers Japan Airlines, All Nippon Airways (ANA), and the budget carriers Air Do and SkyMark connect major Japanese airports with Sapporo (New Chitose), Asahikawa, Hakodate, Abashiri (Memambetsu), Obihiro, and Kushiro. Flying across Hokkaido is a good way to cross the distances, particularly the far-flung eastern and northern regions. In winter, sudden changes in weather can divert or cancel flights, so plan adequate time for connections.

Japan Airlines (JAL), and All Nippon Airways link Hokkaido to Honshu by direct flights from Tokyo's Haneda Airport to Hakodate, Sapporo (New Chitose Airport), Asahikawa Airport, Abashiri (Memambetsu Airport), Nemuro (Nakashibetsu Airport), and Kushiro Airport. Two flights a day depart from Tokyo's Narita International Airport. Other major cities on Honshu have flights to Sapporo, as do several places in the Asia and Pacific region. The cost by air from Tokyo to Sapporo can be as low as ¥12,000 compared with ¥22,430 by train. Fly-stay packages from Tokyo (subsidized by the Hokkaido government) offering excellent deals for short trips are recommended. Some air travelers arriving in Japan on European flights can, with a change of planes at Tokyo, fly at no extra charge to Sapporo. If you're flying from overseas to Sapporo via Tokyo, book the domestic portion when you buy your international ticket; otherwise, you will fork out for what is, per mile, one of the most expensive domestic tickets in the world.

Airline Information Air Do (☎ 011/200–7333 ⊕ www.airdo.jp). **Air Hokkaido and Air Nippon** (☎ 0120/029–222 ⊕ www.ana.co.jp). **Hokkaido Air System** (☎ 0120/511–283). **Japan Airlines** (☎ 0570/025–071 international,

0120/747–002, 011/232–3690 domestic ⊕ www.jal.co.jp). **SkyMark**
(☎ 050/3116–7370 [Japanese language only] ⊕ www.skymark.co.jp).

BOAT AND FERRY TRAVEL

Ferries from Honshu connecting to Tomakomai, Hakodate, and Otaru
offer a leisurely way to arrive, while in Hokkaido boats connect the
islands of Rebun and Rishiri to the northern tip of Japan. In the far
east, ferries offer the best bear-viewing off the Shiretoko Peninsula.

The ferries are the cheapest way to travel to Hokkaido on paper, but
for only a few thousand yen more you can fly there within two hours
from the mainland. If slow travel is your style, there are ferries from
Niigata into Otaru, and services on the Pacific side (Nagoya, Oarai, Sendai, and Aomori) connect to Hakodate and Tomakomai. Other routes
include Shin Nihon-kai Ferry's Niigata to Otaru (¥6,200); Taiheiyo
Ferry's Sendai to Tomakomai (14-hour service for ¥8,000), and the
mammoth 39-hour Nagoya-Sendai-Tomakomai (¥10,500); Kawasaki
Kinkai Kisen's Hachinohe to Tomakomai (nine hours; ¥5,000); and
Seikan Ferry's service that crosses between Aomori and Hakodate (four
hours; ¥1,800).

First-class is usually double the second-class price, but the extra buys
you privacy and comfort, as most regular passengers stretch out on
communal carpeted areas with no beds. Outside the summer holiday
season, the ferries are mostly used by long-distance truck drivers and
the occasional budget backpacker and motorcyclist.

The most budget-conscious, if you don't mind a 24-hour journey, can
book Shosen Mitsui's Pacific Story package. This is a bus/ferry/bus service which connects Tokyo to Sapporo for only ¥9,900 (excluding July
18 to August 31), departing Tokyo mid-afternoon and reaching Sapporo
the following afternoon. Check the English Web site, and reserve tickets at the Tokyo or Shinjuku Highway bus terminals. Tickets can also
be bought for the Oarai-to-Tomakomai section only (¥8,500–¥14,000
depending on the season).

Boat and Ferry Contacts Kawasaki Kinkai Kisen *(☎ 03/3502–4838 ⊕ www.
kawakin.co.jp [Japanese language only]).* **Seikan Ferry** *(☎ 017/782–3671
⊕ www.seikan-ferry.co.jp [Japanese language only]).* **Shin Nihon-kai Ferry**
(☎ 03/3543–5500 ⊕ www.snf.jp/pdf/english.pdf). **Shosen Mitsui** *(☎ 03/3844–
1950 in Tokyo [Japanese language only]; 029/267–4133 in Orai [Japanese language only] ⊕ www.sunflower.co.jp).* **Taiheiyo Ferry** *(☎ 052/582–8611 ⊕ www.
taiheiyo-ferry.co.jp [Japanese language only]).*

BUS TRAVEL

Buses cover most of the major routes through the scenic areas. There
is, however, no English-language telephone service for buses in Hokkaido, so we suggest you find an interlocutor. The Sapporo International
Communication Plaza in Sapporo will supply bus-route and schedule
information and make telephone bookings if required.

CAR TRAVEL

Driving in Hokkaido is made easy, despite mountain bends and snow,
by wide roads and English-language signage that helps guide you to
wilder places. Toll highways at this writing link Sapporo only with

Asahikawa, but nearly complete (and recently cheapened) stretches can take you down to Hakodate and over to Obihiro. Otherwise, two-lane roads are the norm, and untimed stoplights can slow travel.

Most major auto-rental companies have offices at Sapporo's New Chitose Airport, in major cities, and in smaller tourist areas. JR Hokkaido arranges very good value travel packages, although service is available in English only at major stations such as Sapporo and Hakodate. Car rentals, depending on the season, can cost as little as ¥6,000 per day; reservations are best made through the ToCoo Web site for Mazda, Nissan, Toyota, MMC, and J-Net. August is peak holiday driving season, so book early. Don't forget to request an English-language navigation system (called *car-navi*).

Japanese are cautious drivers, and Hokkaido is the best place in Japan for driving, even though wide, straight roads, treacherous winter weather conditions, and most visitors' unfamiliarity with all of the above gives Hokkaido the worst traffic fatality figures in Japan. Beware of speed traps, especially in holiday periods: in apparently rural areas a hidden village can dictate urban speed limits of 50 to 60 kph.

Rental Agencies JR Hokkaido–Rent-a-Car (☎ 011/742–8211 ⊕ www.jrh-rentacar.jp [Japanese language only]). **Nippon Rent-a-Car** (☎ 03/3485–7196 ⊕ www.nipponrentacar.net/english). **ToCoo Car Rental** (☎ 03/5333–0246 ⊕ www2.tocoo.jp). **Toyota Rent-a-Car** (☎ 0123/40–0100 English ⊕ www. toyotarentacar.net/english).

Road Conditions Hokkaido Traffic Information (☎ 011/281–6511).

TRAIN TRAVEL

Japan Railways Hokkaido helps visitors enjoy the big country in comfort, with a three- or five-day Hokkaido Rail Pass and good English-language information at major stations. Although there are no Shinkasen bullet trains yet, superexpress trains connect Sapporo south to Hakodate (and on to Honshu), and north and east to Asahikawa, Kushiro, Abashiri, and Wakkanai. A three-day pass costs ¥14,000, five-day ¥18,000; Green superior cars cost ¥6,000 extra. Train and car packages are available.

The train journey from Tokyo to Sapporo can take as little as 10 hours including connections. This trip involves a combination of the Shinkansen train to Hachinohe (3 hours, 10 minutes), the northernmost point on the Tohoku Shinkansen Line, and a change to an express train for the remaining journey to Hakodate (2 hours, 20 minutes) and then on to Sapporo (3¼ hours). The JR Pass covers this route (the cost is ¥22,430 without the pass). The Hokutosei sleeper train provides greater comfort and eliminates the need to change trains, but the voyage takes 17 hours. The fare is ¥23,520 (¥9,450 for JR Pass holders).

Train Information Japan Railway Information Line (☎ 03/3423–0111 ⊕ www.jreast.co.jp/e). **JR Hokkaido Twinkle Plazas at main stations** (☎ 011/209–5030 ⊕ www.jrhokkaido.co.jp/global).

ABOUT THE RESTAURANTS

Hokkaido's regional food includes excellent seafood, beef, lamb, corn on the cob, and potatoes. Dining out is generally much cheaper than in Tokyo and Osaka. Look for lunch and dinner *tabehodai* (all-you-can-eat) smorgasbords (called *baikingu*, from the Viking; long story) ranging from ¥1,000 to ¥3,000. Many restaurants have picture menus or a visual display made of plastic in the window. Lead the waiter outside to the window display and point if necessary.

Outside the cities there may not be many dining choices in the evening, and many resort towns (where meals are included in hotel stays) may offer nothing but noodles and booze. Further, dinner reservations at guesthouses are required, and if you arrive without a reservation and are able to secure a room, you will generally have to eat elsewhere. Not to worry—you won't starve: There are 24-hour convenience stores (*konbini*) in any Hokkaido settlement, where you can pick up a bento box lunch, sandwiches, or just about any amenity necessary. While large hot-spring hotels often have huge buffet dinners, the smaller guesthouses excel in food that is locally caught, raised, and picked. Given the overall high quality of dining throughout Japan, you probably won't even need to leave your hotel to get a decent meal.

ABOUT THE HOTELS

Accommodations that are easily booked in English tend to be modern, characterless hotels built for Japanese tour groups. Gorgeous lobbies and sterile, cookie-cutter rooms are the norm, although more attractive hotels are appearing as Japanese seek out lodging with more personality. Guesthouses or pensions are a cheaper and friendlier option, with welcoming owners who strive to impress guests with the catch of the day or wild vegetables on the dinner menu. Many (but not all) guesthouses have Western-style beds. Although booking in Japanese is the norm, simple English faxes or emails via a Web site can work, too. Although you might not normally consider one, a youth hostel is also a decent alternative in Hokkaido, both for price and for the sense of spirit and camaraderie that you will not find in the more sterile hotels. However, some do not allow male-female couples to sleep in the same room. Hostels in towns and cities are usually clean and modern, and in the national parks, although in older buildings, they can be excellent touring bases.

Outside Sapporo and Hokkaido, most hot-spring hotels (onsen) charge on a per-person basis and include two meals, excluding service and tax, in their rates. If you don't want meals and wish to eat convenience-store food, you can often renegotiate the price (the word in Japanese is *sudomari*). Just remember that those hot-spring hotels and guesthouses are your best bet for dinner in remote areas. Also note that with Japan's prolonged recession, some hotels may actually be cheaper than listed in this guide.

Hostel Contact Hokkaido Youth Hostel Association (☎ *011/825–3389* ⊕ *www.youthhostel.or.jp/english*).

CLOSE UP

On the Menu

Hokkaido is known for its seafood—the prefecture's name means "the Road to the Northern Sea." *Shakeĕ* or *sakeĕ* (salmon), *ika* (squid), *uni* (sea urchin), *nishin* (herring), and *kai* (shellfish) are abundant, but the real treat is the fat, sweet scallop, *kai-bashira*, collected from northernmost Wakkanai. The other great favorite is crab, which comes in three varieties: *ke-gani* (hairy crab), *taraba-gani* (king crab), and Nemuro's celebrated *hanasaki-gani* (spiny king crab)—often to be had for a very reasonable price.

As for meat dishes, Hokkaido's most famous concoction, jingisukan, is thinly sliced mutton cooked on a dome-shape griddle. The name comes from the griddle's resemblance to helmets worn by Mongolian cavalry under Genghis Khan. Vegetables—usually onions, green peppers, and cabbage—are added to the sizzling mutton, and the whole mix is dipped in a tangy brown sauce.

As for Japanese "soul food," ramen is extremely popular and inexpensive; get some *gyoza* (pot stickers) or *chahan* (fried rice) with it. Local residents favor miso ramen, which uses a less-delicate variety of fermented soybean paste than miso soup. Ramen with *shio* (salt) or *shoyu* (soy sauce) soup base is also widely available.

WHAT IT COSTS IN YEN					
	¢	$	$$	$$$	$$$$
RESTAURANTS	under ¥800	¥800–¥1,000	¥1,000–¥2,000	¥2,000–¥3,000	over ¥3,000
HOTELS	under ¥8,000	¥8,000–¥12,000	¥12,000–¥18,000	¥18,000–¥22,000	over ¥22,000

Restaurant prices are per person for a main course, set meal, or equivalent combinations of smaller dishes. Hotel prices are for a double room, excluding service and 5% tax.

BANKS AND EXCHANGE SERVICES

Outside major cities there are no foreign exchange services. Local banks in Hokkaido towns are not user-friendly for foreign visitors. Sapporo, Hakodate, Asahikawa, and Kushiro have banks with exchange counters and automatic teller machines. Banks in Sapporo are concentrated on Eki-mae Dori, the wide main street linking Sapporo Station and the Odori shopping area. Banking hours are weekdays 10 am–3 pm.

Many establishments will not take credit cards, apart from large hotels, some restaurants, and gas stations. ■TIP➔ We recommend you get yen cash (as Japan is largely a cash-based society) from post office (yubinkyoku 郵便局) ATMs, found in every settlement. Post offices are open until 6 pm every day.

VISITOR INFORMATION

The Japan National Tourist Organization's Tourist Information Center (TIC) in Tokyo has free Hokkaido maps and brochures. It's the best place for travel information in English. If in Hokkaido already, get multilingual brochures and services at the Tourist Information Center found at the North Exit (*kita guchi* 北口) of JR Sapporo Station opposite Mister Donuts.

To really get out into Hokkaido and see its wild side, join a hiking tour with **Japan Adventures.** The Hokkaido Bush Pig, New Zealander Leon Roode, runs two- to seven-day camping and hiking trips for the novice and the hard-core hiker.

Tour Information Japan Adventures (✉ *Shinkawa 4-jo 10-chome 3–13, Kita-ku, Sapporo* ☎ *011/641–1115, 090/8275–5012 Leon direct* ⊕ *www.japan-adventures.com*).

Visitor Information Hokkaido-Sapporo Tourist Information Center (✉ *1F JR Sapporo Bldg., Kita, 6 Nishit 5, Chuo-ku, Sapporo* ☎ *011/222–4894* ⊕ *www.welcome.city.sapporo.jp* ☾ *Daily 8–9*).

Tourist Information Center (TIC) (✉ *B-1 Tokyo International Forum Bldg., 3-5-1 Marunochi, Chiyoda-ku, Tokyo* ☎ *03/3201–3331* ⊕ *www.jnto.go.jp*).

14

HAKODATE 函館

318 km (198 mi) south of Sapporo.

Facing out on two bays, Hakodate is a 19th-century port town, with clapboard buildings on sloping streets, a dockside tourist zone, streetcars, and fresh fish on every menu. In the downtown historic quarter, a mountain rises 1,100 feet above the city on the southern point of the narrow peninsula. Russians, Americans, Chinese, and Europeans have all left their mark; this was one of the first three Japanese ports the Meiji government opened up to international trade in 1859.

EXPLORING HAKODATE

The main sights around the foot of Mt. Hakodate can be done in a day, but the city is best appreciated with an overnight stay for the illumination in the historic area, the night views from either the mountain or the fort tower, and the fish market at dawn. City transport is easy to navigate and English information is readily available. Evening departure trains from Tokyo arrive here at dawn—perfect for fish-market breakfasts.

GETTING HERE AND AROUND

Hakodate is 3 hours south of Sapporo by express train and 2½ hrs north of Aomori by JR Rapid via the Seikan Tunnel.

Streetcars cost ¥200–¥250, and municipal buses cost ¥200–¥260. The sightseeing area is hilly, so save foot power by using a one- or two-day bus and streetcar pass (¥1,000/1,700), and borrow an audio walking guide (deposit ¥500) from the tourist center.

For sightseeing, hotel, and travel information in English stop at the Hakodate City Tourist Information Center inside the station building.

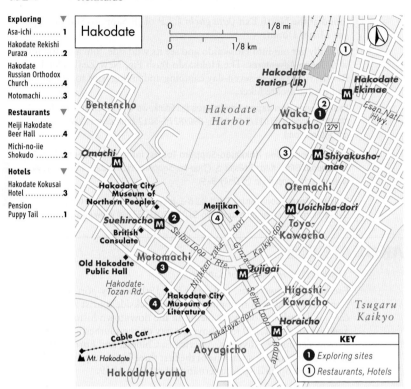

ESSENTIALS

Car Rental Mazda Car Rental (Hakodate Airport) (☎ 0138/59–0002,
03/5286–0712 English inquiries ⊕ www.mazda-rentacar.co.jp [Japanese
language only]).

Visitor Information Hakodate City Tourist Information Center (✉ 12–13
Wakamatsu-cho ☎ 0138/23–5440 ⏱ Apr.–Oct., daily 9–7; Nov.–Mar., daily 9–5).

WHAT TO SEE

Asa-ichi 朝市 *(Morning Market)*. Bright red crabs wave giant claws from
old fishing boats filled with water, squid dart furiously around restaurant tanks, and samples of dried octopus parts are piled high—it's all at
Hokkaido's largest public fish market one block from Hakodate Station.
It opens at dawn; if you can stomach it, try a fish-on-rice breakfast.
Asa-ichi, which also has a fruit-and-vegetable section, stays active until
mid-afternoon. ✉ *Asa-ichi, Wakamatsu-cho.*

Hakodate Rekishi Puraza 函館歴史プラザ *(Hakodate History Plaza)*. On
the cobbled waterfront of Moto-machi, redbrick warehouses now bustle
with 21st-century tourism: shops, restaurants, bars, harbor boat trips,
street entertainers, and glassblowing studios. In December it offers a
giant Canadian Christmas tree and nightly fireworks. This is a good
place to wind down, although most bars close at 10:30 pm. The plaza

Hakodate's Russian Orthodox Church dates from 1916.

is a 1½-km (1-mi) walk from Hakodate Station. ✉ *14–16 Suehiro-cho, about 750 ft northwest of Juji-gai streetcar stop* ☎ *0138/23–0350* ⏱ *Daily 9:30–7.*

Harisutosu Sei Kyokai 函館ハリストス正教会 *(Hakodate Russian Orthodox Church).* A green Byzantine dome and tower rise above this beautiful white church. The present building dates from 1916, and donations help with the upkeep of Hakodate's most exotic attraction. The Episcopal and Catholic churches are on either side. ✉ *3–13 Moto-machi* ☎ *0138/23–7387.*

Moto-machi Historic Area. Overlooking the western bay at the foot of Mt. Hakodate is a 2-square-km area of wide, sloping streets lined with the 19th-century churches, consulates, shops, and homes of the Japanese and foreigners who first opened up this part of Japan to commerce. Only the main historic buildings have English information, but many others have been converted into shops and cafés. Return here at night when the illuminated buildings, particularly in winter, show why Hakodate is a favorite Japanese romantic movie and TV drama location.

The most interesting historic buildings and museums are the arch-Victorian **Old Public Hall** (旧函館区公会堂; Kyu Hakodate-ku Kokaido), with the Emperor's Toilet; the **British Consulate** (旧イギリス領事館; Kyu Igirisu Ryojikan), a nice place for tea and scones; and the **Hakodate City Museum of Northern Peoples** (函館市北方民族資料館 Hakodate Hoppo Minzoku Shiryokan). They can be visited with combined tickets. Get off the streetcar at the Suehiro-cho stop and start at the museum, then walk 10 minutes up the Motoizaka Slope to the other two. There's lots more to see in the area even if you don't enter any buildings. ⊕ *www.*

hakodatekankou.com ✉ ¥300 for 1 site, ¥500 for 2, ¥720 for all 3 ⊙ Apr.–Oct., daily 9–7; Nov.–Mar., daily 9–5.

NEED A BREAK?

Kitchen and Cafe Hana キッチン＆カフェ華. More than 100 kimono-clad dolls watch guests with their coffees, teas, and traditional desserts in the tiny, two-room café in a house near the gates of the Old Public Hall. Shoes off at the door, please. ✉ 2–21 Funami-cho ☎ 0138/24–4700.

WHERE TO EAT

$$
SEAFOOD

✕ **Meiji Hakodate Beer Hall** 明治はこだてビアホール. This seaside hall in Hakodate History Plaza serves seafood specialties such as squid, octopus, and tofu shabu-shabu (cooked table-side by dipping the food into boiling water and then into a sauce) for ¥1,300, as well as three local brews (wheat beer, ale, and the slightly more bitter "alt" beer). Its spaciousness and conviviality are typical of Hokkaido, and although it's in a tourist complex, even locals like the wide range of Hokkaido's seasonal specialties. ✉ 5–22 Ote-machi ☎ 0138/23–8000.

$$
JAPANESE

✕ **Michi-no-iie Shokudo** 道乃家食堂. What do squid eyes taste like? Imagine the dog's chew toy, all slimy and gristly, add in an exploding juice ball, and you have the "eye-light" of the *ika-sashi ika-sumi don* set at ¥1,800. Did we mention that it's actually pretty good? And fresh—your squid is pulled flapping from the tank and returns minutes later sliced, with squid-ink black rice, delicious slivers of still-twitching flesh, soup, pickles, and two big black eyes. Wash it down with gray-squid ice cream for dessert. Too much information? Luckily, the restaurant has plenty of other seafood, and a picture menu for easy selection. It's on the Morning Market's closest corner to the station, first spot on the right in the restaurant-filled alleyway. ✉ Donburi Yokocho Ichiba, Asa-ichi ☎ 0138/22–6086 ▭ No credit cards ⊙ No meals.

WHERE TO STAY

Hotel reviews have been condensed for this book. Please go to Fodors. com for full reviews of each property.

$$$–$$$$
HOTEL

⊡ **Hakodate Kokusai Hotel** 函館国際ホテル. This bustling, modern hotel occupies three buildings a short walk from the station, the Morning Market area, and the History Plaza warehouses. **Pros:** walking distance from station fish market and waterfront Hakodate History Plaza. **Cons:** modern box hotel; tour group central. ✉ 5–10 Ote-machi ☎ 0138/23–5151 ⊟ 0138/23–0239 ⊕ www.hakodate.ne.jp/kokusaihotel (Japanese language only) ⇱ 304 Western-style rooms, 6 Japanese-style rooms ⊙ In-room: no a/c. In-hotel: 4 restaurants, room service, bars, laundry service, parking (free) ⊙ No meals.

¢
INN
★

⊡ **Pension Puppy Tail** ペンションパピィーテール. Decoupage decorations and garlands of silk flowers overwhelm and so does the family's welcoming manner. **Pros:** genuine family welcome; walking distance to station. **Cons:** from the station it's in the opposite direction to the sights;

some rooms very small. ✉ *30–16 Wakamatsu-cho* ☎ *0138/23–5858* 🖷 *0138/26–8239* ⊕ *www.p-puppytail.com* ⇆ *6 Western-style rooms, 13 Japanese-style rooms* ♿ *In-room: no a/c. In-hotel: restaurant* ⊟ *No credit cards* ⦿ *No meals.*

SAPPORO 札幌

318 km (197 mi) north of Hakodate.

Modern, openhearted Sapporo is a good planning base for any trip to Hokkaido's wilder regions, with plenty of English-language information and transport connections. Hokkaido's capital is also worth a few days' stay for its major snow (February), dance (June), and beer (July and August) festivals.

With 1.8 million inhabitants, it's four times larger than Asahikawa, the prefecture's next-largest city, but the downtown area can be crossed on foot in 25 minutes. Centered on the 11-block-long Odori Koen (park), an ideal people-watching place, it has wide streets and sidewalks and bustling shopping complexes. There is limited sightseeing, but there's enough to fill a day or two at a holiday's start or finish. Products from all over Hokkaido can be found, and the dining-out standards are high and relatively cheap.

GETTING HERE AND AROUND

AIR TRAVEL

Although there are no direct flights from the United States to Hokkaido, cheap international connections with All Nippon Airways (ANA) and Japan Airlines (JAL) can add domestic discounted connections to New Chitose Airport (Shin-Chitose Kuko, the most convenient to Sapporo) via Tokyo Narita or Haneda, Osaka Kansai, or Nagoya Centrair airports. More than 30 domestic routes link New Chitose, 40 km (25 mi) south of the city, to the rest of Japan, and flights from New Chitose to other parts of Asia are increasing through New Chitose's brand-new International Terminal.

For those without international connections, budget domestic commuter airlines Air Do (Haneda) and SkyMark (Kobe Airport) often have the least-expensive flights to Sapporo.

Japan Railways (JR) runs every 20 minutes or so between New Chitose Airport and downtown Sapporo. The trip into Sapporo is usually made by rapid-transit train (¥1,040; 40 minutes). Hokuto Bus and Chuo Bus run shuttle buses (¥820) that connect the airport with downtown hotels and Sapporo Station, twice every hour. The trip takes about 70 minutes but can be slower in winter. Train service is recommended. ■TIP➔ **Don't make the mistake of getting off at the suburban Shin-Sapporo Station, 10 minutes before Sapporo Station itself.**

CAR TRAVEL

Public transportation makes renting a car for Sapporo sightseeing unnecessary, but it's a good place to rent for setting out into the southern and western national parks. Trips farther north and east are best made by train; rent a car at the destination. In Sapporo, major car companies are clustered around Sapporo Station.

Car Rentals Honda Rent-a-Car (⊠ *1–2, Nishi 2, Kita 10, Sapporo Station* ☎ *011/737–5353* ⊕ *www.hondarent.com/english* ⊘ *Daily 8–7*). **Toyota Rent-a-Car** (⊠ *Sapporo Station East, 2–1 Higashi, Kita 5, Kita-ku* ☎ *0123/40–0110 [in English]* ⊕ *www.toyotarentacar.net* ⊘ *Daily 8–8*).

PUBLIC TRANSIT

Two circular bus routes connect many of the main sites. The Factory Line—bus stops are confusingly marked "Sapporo Walk"—connects downtown shops, the train station, the fish market, the Sapporo Factory, and the Sapporo Beer Garden. The *Sansaku* or Stroller Bus (May to October only) connects downtown with Maruyama Park and Okurayama Jump Hill. Rides on both cost ¥200 each time or ¥750 for a day pass. Tickets are available on the buses or from Chuo Bus counter at the JR Station or bus terminal.

Most of Sapporo's subway signs include English. There are three lines: the Namboku Line, the Tozai Line, and the Toho Line. They all intersect at Odori Station.

The basic fare, covering a distance of about three stations, is ¥200. A one-day open ticket (*ichi-nichi-ken*) for ¥1,000 provides unlimited subway (the subway alone would cost ¥800), bus, and streetcar access. Tickets are available at subway stations and the machines have English instructions. There are also prepaid "With You" cards (¥1,000, ¥3,000, ¥5,000, and ¥10,000 at vending machines) for multiday travel.

TAXI TRAVEL

Taxi meters start at ¥550 or ¥600, depending on the company. An average fare, such as from the JR Station to Susukino, runs about ¥800 ($7), but be aware the meter ticks up fast, especially after 9 pm. In winter most taxies are fitted with ski and board roof racks, and drivers are adept at stowing even the bulkiest winter gear.

VISITOR INFORMATION

Contact Hokkaido-Sapporo Food and Tourism Information Center (⊠ *Sapporo Station, Western Concourse, North Exit* ☎ *011/213–5088* ⊘ *Daily 8:30–8*).

EXPLORING SAPPORO

The name *Sapporo* is derived from a combination of Ainu words meaning "a river running along a reed-filled plain." In 1870 the governor of Hokkaido visited President Grant in the United States and requested that American advisers visit Hokkaido to help design the capital on the site of an Ainu village. As a result, Sapporo was built on a grid system with wide avenues and parks. Today, the downtown area has uncluttered streets and English signs. It's distinctly lacking in pre-Meiji historic sights.

WHAT TO SEE

Sapporo is easy to navigate. Eki-mae Dori (Station Road) runs south of the station, crossed east–west by Odori Koen (park), then continues south through the shopping district to the nightlife area Susukino and beyond to Nakajima Park. Addresses use the cardinal points: north, south, east, and west (*kita, minami, higashi,* and *nishi,* respectively).

Downtown sights are easily covered on foot in a few hours, using Odori subway station as the center point. Underground shopping malls linking the subway station with both Susukino and the TV Tower are bustling thoroughfares, especially in winter.

DOWNTOWN SAPPORO

Hokudai Shokubutsu-en 北大植物園 *(Botanical Gardens).* With more than 5,000 plant varieties, the gardens are a cool summer retreat, both for the shade and welcome green space. For nonbotanists, highlights include a small **Ainu Museum** with a grisly but fascinating 13-minute film of an Ainu bear-killing ceremony in Asahikawa in 1935, and a large stuffed husky dog sharing a room with bears and an Ezo wolf. This glassy-eyed hound is Taro, one of the canine survivors of Japan abandoned in a 1958 Antarctic expedition (a story brought to non-Japanese audiences in the Disney movie *Eight Below*). After his ordeal, Taro retired to Hokkaido University and died in 1970. ⊠ *Kita 3-jo, Nishi 8, Chuo-ku*

CLOSE UP

On the Calendar

One of Japan's best-known annual events, held for a week beginning February 5 or 6, is the **Sapporo Snow Festival** (*Sapporo Yuki Matsuri*). More than 300 lifelike ice sculptures as large as 130 feet high by 50 feet deep by 80 feet wide are created each year by the Japanese Self Defense Forces. Memorable statues include baseball star Matsui, cavorting whales, dinosaurs, and the Taj Mahal.

The festival began in 1950 with six statues commissioned by the local government to entertain Sapporo citizens depressed by the war and the long winter nights. Now the event is so large that the sculptures are spread around three different sections of the city: Odori Koen, Susukino, and the suburban Tsudome site. You'll also find ice slides for children. One highlight is the international teams of amateur and professional ice sculptors (some from countries without snow, such as Singapore), hired by major local businesses, who spend four days sculpting their creations. Although statues are roped off, taking photographs is no

problem. The festival attracts more than 2 million visitors each year, so book your stay well in advance.

During the **Yosakoi Festival** every second week of June, Sapporo's streets stage Japan's version of Carnival. Based on the Kochi Festival in Shikoku, more than 40,000 performers go wild in brightly colored costumes and face paint as they run, jump, and chant *soran* (a Hokkaido fishermen's folk song) through the city streets. A boisterous Japanese take on hip-hop crossed with aerobics, Yosakoi is far more exciting than the traditional *bon odori* community dancing. Dance teams wave enormous flags and snap *naruko* (wooden clappers) in the wake of giant trucks, mounted with powerful sound systems and *taiko* drummers in loincloths. Ticketed seats are available in the stands along the route in Odori Koen and at an outdoor stage, but they aren't necessary—most people just perch wherever they can get a vantage point. Dance teams also perform in Susukino at night.

✉ *May–Oct., gardens and greenhouse ¥400; Nov.–Apr., gardens free, greenhouse ¥110* ☉ *Apr.–Sept., daily 9–4; Oct. and Nov., daily 9–3:30; Dec.–Mar., weekdays 9–5.*

Nakajima Koen 中島公園 *(Nakajima Park)*. This green oasis is a 10-minute walk beyond Susukino's lights and contains **Hoheikan,** a white-and-blue Russian-influenced 19th-century imperial guesthouse; **Hasso-an Teahouse,** a simple, empty 17th-century teahouse in the Japanese garden on the right as you enter the park's northern side; a boating lake; and the concert hall Kitara, home of the Pacific Music Festival, started in 1990 by Leonard Bernstein.

Odori Koen 大通公園 *(Odori Park)*. This 345-foot-wide green belt bisects the city center. In summer people buy roasted or butter-covered corn on the cob and potatoes from food vendors and then sit down to watch the street performers, skateboarders, and each other. The Sapporo Beer Festival lasts three weeks in July and August, when every block becomes an outdoor beer garden, and thousands of drinkers enjoy a veritable bacchanal until 9 pm. The park also hosts the annual Sapporo Snow and Yosakoi festivals (*see On the Calendar box, above*). ✉ *Nishi 11-chome bus or subway stop, Odori.*

Sapporo International Communication Plaza 札幌国際交流プラザ *(Sapporo Kokusai Koryu Puraza)*. This is the best place for travel, nightlife, restaurant, and travel suggestions in Hokkaido and for meeting people who speak English. You can have something translated from Japanese into English. The salon with books, newspapers, and brochures in English is meant for informal socializing. Pick up a free copy of *What's On in Sapporo* at the salon information counter. The building faces the white Clock Tower; go through the glass doors under the second-floor balcony restaurant and take the elevator up. ✉ *3F Kita 1-jo, Nishi 3, Chuo-ku, Odori* ☎ *011/221–2105* ⊕ *www.plaza-sapporo. or.jp* ⊙ *Mon.–Sat. 9–5:30.*

14

Tanuki Koji 狸小路 *(Tanuki Mall)*. A *tanuki* is kind of like a raccoon crossed with a Tasmanian devil and is known in Japanese mythology for its libidinous nature. Tanuki Koji got its name because the area used to be frequented by prostitutes. Now a different breed of merchant in this kitschy covered arcade is eager to lighten the wallets of passersby, with small shops selling clothing, footwear, electronics, records, and touristy, Ainu-inspired souvenirs of Hokkaido. Tanuki Koji has considerably lower prices than the area's department stores. It's also the place to find Hokkaido specialties, from melon confections to dried salmon and seaweed, as well as the occasional belting street performer. ✉ *Minami 3-jo, extending from Nishi 1 to 7, Chuo-ku.*

Tokeidai 時計台 *(Clock Tower)*. For millions of Japanese, this little white-clapboard Russian-style meetinghouse defines Sapporo; it is used as the city's symbol on souvenir packaging, and its red Polaris symbol graces Sapporo Beer labels. Now almost lost like San Antonio's Alamo among modern office blocks, it was the 1878 drill hall for the pioneer students of Sapporo Agricultural College (now Hokkaido University). Inside are photographs and documents of city history and a clock from Boston. A little underwhelming, Tokeidai also serves as the landmark for the Sapporo International Communication Plaza information center across the street ✉ *Kita 1-jo, Nishi 2, Chuo-ku* 🎫 *¥200* ⊙ *Tues.–Sat. 9–5.*

ELSEWHERE IN SAPPORO

Hokkaido Jingu 北海道神宮 *(Hokkaido Shrine)*. Wash your hands and rinse your mouth at the stone basin first, then step up the gray stone steps. This 1871 Shinto shrine houses three gods deemed helpful in Hokkaido's development: the gods of land and nature, of land development, and of healing. Sapporo families bring babies, children, anxious students, young engaged couples, and even cars to Shinto ceremonies. In May this is Sapporo's main *hanami* (cherry-blossom) venue. It's a 15-minute walk from Maruyama subway station and shares the park with the zoo. ✉ *474 Miyagaoka, Maruyama Koen, Chuo-ku* ⊕ *www. hokkaidojingu.or.jp/eng/index.html*

★ **Hokkaido Kaitaku-no-mura** 北海道開拓の村 *(Historical Village of Hok-*
🕘 *kaido)*. Step back into 19th-century Hokkaido and see the herring-fleet dormitory where 60 fishermen appear to have just folded up their

CLOSE UP

The Beer

Sapporo means beer to drinkers around the world, and what would a visit to the city of the same name be without a little beer research?

Head to Sapporo Beer Museum, 2 km (1 mi) northeast of Sapporo Station for a cursory history lesson in the red-brick former factory, and then to the neighboring biergarten, where waiters in a cavernous noisy hall will rush to get a glass of the golden brew into your hands. Raise your glass—*Kampai* (Bottoms up)!

If you are in town in July and early August, join Sapporo Beer and other companies at the Sapporo Beer Garden festival in Odori Park in the city center: every night for three weeks thousands of revelers sit out under the trees with beer steins and snacks getting very lubricated. The faithful can do the factory tour and tasting at Hokkaido Brewery at Eniwa, near New Chitose Airport, where guides

(Japanese-language only) show the brewing process.

Brewmaster Seibei Nakagawa spent two years at the Berliner Brauerai studying German know-how and returned ready to put it all into practice. The first brewery was at the current Sapporo Factory shopping mall, and Sapporo Reisi (cold) Beer, with a red-and-black label bearing the red star symbol, first went on sale in 1877 (Sapporo's cold climate was a competitive advantage in the era before refrigeration).

Toriaezu biiru! (For the time being, beer!) is still the first order of business at parties, beer-hall barbecues, and campsite cookouts. Sapporo Beer dominates the market up here, but microbreweries offer interesting alternatives. Look for local brews, *ji-biiru*, particularly Otaru (factory tour available), Hakodate, and Taisetsu.

futons and left for a day's work; or the village clinic where a Dr. Kondo seems to have vanished, leaving his scary-looking birthing table and books behind. It's easy to spend a few hours walking in and out of 60 homes, shops, farms, and offices brought from all over Hokkaido in a park museum that preserves how ordinary people lived and worked. A ride down the main street in a horse-drawn trolley (summer) or sleigh (winter) costs ¥200. ■TIP→ Ask for the excellent, free, blue-color English guide at the ticket counter. The village is about 10 km (6 mi) outside Sapporo; easiest access is via an hour bus ride (¥260) from Sapporo Station on a Japan Rail Bus or a 10-minute taxi ride from Shin-Sapporo Station. ⊠ *1–50–1 Konopporo, Atsubetsu-cho, Atsubetsu-ku* ☎ *011/898–2692* 🖭 *¥830* ⊙ *Tues.–Sun. 9:30–4:30.*

Kaitaku Ki'nenkan 開拓記念館 *(Historical Museum of Hokkaido).* From mammoth molars on through Ainu and samurai-farmers, to bulky 1950s home electronics, the history of Hokkaido is meticulously exhibited in glass-case and map displays, which are a tad dry compared to the people's history in the Historical Village of Hokkaido 10 minutes away. But this is a thorough overview of how Meiji Japan realized that it had a northern island rich in coal, fish, and agricultural opportunities ripe for the picking. The village and museum are linked by a free shuttle bus

Sapporo is famous for its beer.

on Sunday, and the public bus from Sapporo stops at the museum first. ✉ *53–2 Konopporo, Atsubetsu-cho, Atsubetsu-ku* ☎ *011/898–0456* 💴 *¥450* ⏰ *Tues.–Sat. 9:30–4:30.*

Sapporo Beer Hokkaido Brewery サッポロビール北海道工場. Eniwa's branch of the Sapporo Brewery is a 20-minute local train ride from Chitose Airport, offers free tours all year. Tours (which are only in Japanese, but there is English signage) last 60 minutes and start at 9, 10, and 11 am and 1, 2, and 3 pm. Visitors receive a free beer at the tour's end. No reservations are necessary except for large groups. Hokkaido Brewery is served by Chuo Bus and trains stopping at Sapporo Beer Teien Station on the Chitose–Sapporo Line. Closures due to maintenance are frequent, so call to confirm open dates. ✉ *Sapporo Beer Hokkaido Brewery, 542–1 Toiso, Eniwa City* ☎ *0123/32–5811* 💴 *Free* ⏰ *Daily 9–11:45 and 1–3:50, no tours on weekends Nov.–Apr. and public holidays.*

Sapporoo Biiru-en to Hakubutsukan 札幌ビール園と博物館 *(Sapporo Beer Garden and Museum)*. Redbrick buildings overshadowed by a giant shopping mall make up the public face of Sapporo's most famous export. The original brewery buildings are at another nearby mall, Sapporo Factory, and now brewing takes place in Eniwa City near Chitose Airport. At the downtown Sapporo site a small museum with mostly Japanese-language-only information shows the development of bottle and label designs, and beer-poster pin-up ladies over the ages. For ¥100 for one kind or ¥400 for three, visitors can taste the brews: Black Label is most popular, Classic is only available in Hokkaido, and the original brew of Kaitakushi uses local hops.

In the evening the cavernous downtown Sapporo Biergarten is filled with serious drinkers tackling the *tabe-nomi-hodai* (all-you-can-eat-and-drink) feast of lamb barbecue and beer (¥3,570 per head). Recent menu additions include fish and vegetable dishes.

To get to the Sapporo Beer Garden and Museum, take a 15-minute Sapporo Walk circular bus from the station or Odori area (the same bus also stops at Sapporo Factory mall) or a ¥1,000 taxi ride. ⊠ *Sapporo Beer Garden and Museum, Kita 7-jo, Higashi 9, Higashi-ku* ☎ *011/731–4368 museum, 011/742–1531 restaurant* ⊕ *www.sapporobeer.jp (Japanese language only)* 🎟 *Free* ⊙ *Museum daily 9–5:30. Beer Garden daily 11:30–9:30.*

Sapporo Winter Sports Museum 札幌ウィンタースポーツミュージアム. Leap off a ski jump into the freezing air and land like a pro—or not. A realistic simulator has visitors comparing jump distances and style in the museum with a body-on approach at the base of the Olympic Okura Jump. The 1972 Winter Olympics and other Japanese sporting successes in skating, curling, and many forms of skiing are celebrated with displays interesting even to nonsporting types. Outside the museum, take the chairlift to the top of the real jump 300 meters above the city with a chilling view of what jumpers face before takeoff. It's a 15-minute bus ride from Maruyama Bus Terminal, City Bus Nishi 14 (¥200). ⊠ *1274 Miyanomori, Chuo-ku* ☎ *011/641–1972* 🎟 *¥600* ⊙ *May–Oct., daily 9–6; Nov.–Apr., daily 9:30–5.*

WHERE TO EAT

The greatest concentration of restaurants for nighttime dining is in the entertainment district of Susukino; good daytime choices are in the downtown department stores and the shopping complex around the JR Station. Hokkaido is known for its ramen, and Sapporo for its miso ramen. The city has more than 1,000 ramen shops, so it's not hard to find a noodle lunch. To track down the current ramen star shack look for the lines of enthusiastic youths outside otherwise unassuming restaurants; young Japanese use their mobile phones and the Internet to research the newest hot spot.

Soup curry—curry with more sauce than content—is currently touted domestically as a Sapporo creation, but the curry restaurants run by Indian and Nepali expats in the city are a better bet.

$$$–$$$$ ✕ **Daruma** だるま. Below the sign with a roly-poly red doll, this 40-year-
JAPANESE old establishment serves the freshest lamb barbecue *jingisukan* (¥700 a plate). At the end of the meal you're given hot tea to mix with the dipping sauce remaining from your meat. You drink the tea and sauce together: it's delicious! Be sure to wear your least-favorite clothes and don a paper bib (provided). ⊠ *Crystal Bldg., Minami 5, Nishi 4, Chuo-ku* ☎ *011/552–6013* ⚏ *Reservations not accepted* ⊟ *No credit cards* ⊙ *Closed Mon.* ⊠ *Noguchi Bldg., Minami 6, Nishi 4, Susukino* ☎ *011/533–8929* ⚏ *Reservations not accepted* ⊟ *No credit cards* ⊙ *Closed Tues.*

$$ ✕ **Ebi-Ten** 蛯天. In a narrow street between Pivot and 4-Chome Plaza
TEMPURA buildings (near Mitsukoshi department store downtown), Ebi-Ten (look

for the white signs) is on the first floor of a building next to the corner car park lot. The sliding doors behind a blue banner reveal a quiet, homey restaurant, managed for two generations by the very friendly Yamada-san, with years of tempura aroma seeped into the woodwork and Hokkaido taxidermy (look for the bear climbing a tree). Seating is available at the counter, tables, and tatami rooms with cushions. On offer: Japanese soul-food-style tempura, salad, and alcoholic beverages. This writer recommends the same meal he has eaten every time over 25 years: Tendon Setto—a rice bowl with seafood and veggies in season, a delicious homemade miso soup with mushrooms, and tsukemono pickles, with a big mug of green tea to wash it down (¥650). Beer with edamame (boiled salted soybeans) are also recommended as appetizers. This is an ideal downtown oasis for a relaxing, cheap dinner or lunch, where you can unwind and decompress from cultural overload. A basic English menu is available. ⊠ *Minami 2, Nishi 4, Chuo-ku* ☎ *011/271–2867* ⊟ *No credit cards.*

14

$$$$ ✕ **Kani Honke** かに本家. This crab-eating haven serves raw, steamed,
JAPANESE   boiled, and baked crustaceans from the Hokkaido (or Russian) seas.
★   The waitress will tell you whether the *ke-gani* (hairy crab), *taraba-gani* (king crab), or *zuwai-kani* (snow crab) is in season. The menu is in English and has photographs, so it's easy to choose from the set dinners, which start at ¥2,000. Wooden beams, tatami mats, and traditional decorations provide an authentic setting for the feast. There are two restaurants, one near the station and the other in Susukino. ⊠ *Station branch, Kita 3, Nishi 2* ☎ *011/222–0018* ⊠ *Susukino, Minami 6, Nishi 4* ☎ *011/551–0018* ☉ *No lunch weekdays.*

$$ ✕ **Keyaki** けやき. It's a mystery why some ramen restaurants are famous
JAPANESE   and millions are not. This ordinary-looking 10-stools-at-the-plastic-counter joint in Susukino has had lines of faithful outside since 2000 (a lifetime in ramen shop terms) and is still chopping, boiling, and serving its six-item menu: miso, *cha-shu* (pork slice), *negi* (leeks), butter corn, *karai* (spicy), and *nin-niku* (garlic). There's even a branch in the Ramen Museum in Yokohama. At the original shop you order while standing in line outside, pay when you claim a counter spot, and then wait for the cook to hand down the steaming bowl (topped generously with vegetables) from the raised and hidden kitchen. Ahhh. Maybe you'll deduce the secret of good ramen. It's open until 4 am. ⊠ *Minami 6, Nishi 3, Susukino* ☎ *011/552–4601* ⊟ *No credit cards.*

$$$–$$$$ ✕ **Sushi-zen** すし善. Hokkaido sushi is famed throughout Japan, and this
SUSHI   is the best in Hokkaido. It's the place locals take guests when they want
★   to impress them with a pure sushi experience. Sushi-zen operates three restaurants and a delivery service. To taste the best at bargain prices, visit the Maruyama branch the third Wednesday of every month when the trainee chefs' sushi is available for ¥200 apiece. ⊠ *Kita 1, Nishi 27, Maruyama, Chuo-ku* ☎ *011/644–0071* ⊠ *109 Bldg., Minami 4, Nishi 5, Chuo-ku* ☎ *011/521–0070* ⊠ *Minami 7, Nishi 4, Chuo-ku* ☎ *011/531–0069* ☉ *Closed Wed. (except for 3d Wed. at the Maryuma branch).*

$ ✕ **Zazi** ザジ. A casual downtown coffee shop with an English menu,
CAFÉ   this hangout is popular with students and expat customers. Favorites

include the Power Lunch (¥1,000 for two fried eggs, sausages, potatoes, salad, and bread), generous spaghetti plates, one-pot stews for ¥630, and homemade cakes. Only one busy cook works in the kitchen, so don't expect a speedy lunch. The restaurant opens at 10 am. ⊠ *Minami 2-jo, Nishi 5, Chuo-ku* 🕿 *011/221–0074* ▭ *No credit cards.*

WHERE TO STAY

Hotel reviews have been condensed for this book. Please go to Fodors. com for full reviews of each property.

$
INN
🏨 **Hotel Maki** ホテル牧. Need a "Welcome back!" after sightseeing? Help with booking hotels ahead? The Inada family does their best with simple English. **Pros:** genuine family welcome; home cooking. **Cons:** 15 minutes from downtown, in a residential area; 10 minutes from Horohira subway stop. ⊠ *1–20, Minami 13, Nishi 7, Chuo-ku* 🕿 *011/521–1930* 🖷 *011/531–6747* 🛏 *15 Japanese-style rooms (6 with bath)* ⚒ *In-room: no a/c. In-hotel: restaurant* ▭ *No credit cards* 🍽 *Multiple meal plans.*

$$$$
HOTEL
★
🏨 **Hotel Okura** ホテルオークラ. In the shopping heart of the city, one block from the Odori subway station, the Okura gets the balance between style and the personal connection just right. **Pros:** close to shopping; near public transportation; personal attention for a city hotel. **Cons:** limited public seating areas. ⊠ *Nishi 5, Minami 1, Chuo-ku* 🕿 *011/221–2333* 🖷 *011/221–0819* ⊕ *www.okura.com/hotels/sapporo/index.html* 🛏 *147 Western-style rooms* ⚒ *In-room: no a/c, Internet. In-hotel: 3 restaurants, bar* 🍽 *No meals.*

$$$–$$$$
HOTEL
★
🏨 **JR Tower Hotel Nikko Sapporo** JRタワーホテル日航札幌. Sapporo's skyscraper over the station puts the city at your feet from small, modern rooms with cream and brown furnishings and throw pillows. **Pros:** inside the station complex; city views. **Cons:** small, standard rooms; restaurants are crowded with nonguests. ⊠ *Sapporo Station JR Tower, Kita 5, Nishi 2, Chuo-ku* 🕿 *0120/58–2586 or 011/251–2222* 🖷 *011/251–6370* ⊕ *www.jrhotels.co.jp/tower* 🛏 *350 Western-style rooms* ⚒ *In-room: a/c, Internet. In-hotel: 3 restaurants, bar* 🍽 *No meals.*

$–$$
RYOKAN
🏨 **Nakamuraya Ryokan** 中村屋旅館. The small, family-run hotel is on a tree-lined street between government buildings near the botanical gardens. **Pros:** welcoming environment; foreign-guest friendly; quiet location. **Cons:** limited storage space; 10 minutes' walk to station and shopping area. ⊠ *Kita 3-jo, Nishi 7, Chuo-ku* 🕿 *011/241–2111* 🖷 *011/241–2118* ⊕ *www.nakamura-ya.com* 🛏 *29 Japanese-style rooms* ⚒ *In-room: no a/c, refrigerator. In-hotel: restaurant, Wi-Fi hotspot* 🍽 *Some meals.*

$$$–$$$$
HOTEL
★
🏨 **Sapporo Grand Hotel** 札幌グランドホテル. Classic European style with white-gloved bellhops, first-rate service, and modern conveniences like room refrigerators tastefully hidden away in wooden cabinets, Sapporo's grand old hotel has welcomed guests since 1934. **Pros:** useful halfway point between station and park; traditional, high-end service. **Cons:** small windows in main building; long walk from some rooms to public areas; you need to know what amenities you want when booking. ⊠ *Kita 1, Nishi 4, Chuo-ku* 🕿 *011/261–3311* 🖷 *011/231–0388* ⊕ *www.grand1934.com* 🛏 *560 Western-style rooms* ⚒ *In-room: a/c,*

Susukino is Sapporo's busy entertainment district.

safe, refrigerator, Internet (some). In-hotel: 8 restaurants, room service, bars ⏺ No meals.

NIGHTLIFE

★ **Susukino** すすきの. Sapporo's entertainment district is seven by seven mind-boggling blocks of neon and noise with more than 4,000 bars, nightclubs, and restaurants (in a constant state of flux; many will disappear and be replaced after this guide goes to print). Bars stay open late, some until 5 am, though restaurants often close before midnight. The seedier alleys are mostly west of Eki-mae Dori, but all of Susukino is safe. They can be cheap, too, if you ask for a *tabe-nomi hodai,* which might get you up to two hours of all-you-can-eat and drink for around ¥3,500. Bearing in mind that places go out of business all the time in Susukino (so there is no guarantee any bar will still be in existence as you read this), following are some places that will probably get you fed and sloshed with a minimum of fuss.

Blues Alley. Willie sings the blues at a casual basement bar (Thursday to Saturday). Hang out with a drink and keep the hand steady for a game of darts or pool in a bar where nobody is going to be put off by foreign customers. You'll have to look for it; it's hidden behind the KFC at the Susukino intersection. ⊠ *B1 Miyako Bldg., Minami 3-jo, Nishi 3, Susukino* ☎ *011/231–6166* ⏱ *Daily 6 pm–3 am.*

Brian Brew. With Guinness and Kilkenny available, this spot has food for expats such as fish-and-chips and meat pies. Sporting events

BARS 101

Nightlife comes in several kinds: clubs stocked with hostesses who make small talk (¥3,000 and up per hour, proving that talk is *not* cheap); *sunakku* bars (the word sounds like "snack," which translates into fewer hostesses and expensive *odoburu*, or hors d'oeuvres); izakaya, for both Japanese and Western food and drink; bars with entertainment, either karaoke or live music (not to mention "soapland," and *herusu* (health) massage parlors, which of course are not bars, and not recommended.

Signs that say "no charge" only mean that there's no charge to be seated; beware of hidden extras. Many bars add on charges for peanuts, female companionship, song, cold water, hand towels, etc. The term "free drink" refers to "drinking freely", i.e. all-you-can-drink specials that cost money. So unless you want a "laddish" male-oriented environment (sunakku are not for couples) dominated by baby talk with a hostess for a high price, stick to the izakaya and live bars.

are shown on big-screen TVs. ✉ *FA-S3 Bldg., Minami 3-jo, Nishi 3* ☎ *011/219–3556* ☾ *Daily 4 pm–2 am.*

Brits Beat Club. British rock and roll is played in five nightly sets (first at 9.30 pm) by bar owner Kazuaki and his band. The small bar serves cheap Brit fare, such as fish-and-chips and cottage pie, while the band plays everything from Beatles to Blur. There's a steep ¥2,100 cover charge, and the bar is open nightly 8–4. ✉ *2F Green Bldg. No. 4, Minami 5-jo, Nishi 3, Susukino* ☎ *011/531–8808.*

Rad Brothers. On Susukino's main street across from the Toyokawainari shrine one of Sapporo's veteran pickup joints can get packed. ✉ *Minami 7-jo, Nishi 3, Susukino* ☎ *011/561–3601.*

Saloon Maco. Stetson-wearing Japanese staff (and drinkers) sing country and pop karaoke, fortified by a no-time-limit *nomi-hodai* (all-you-can-drink plan) for ¥2,000. Pasta and salad dishes go for under ¥1,000. Look behind the JRA Building to find this bar. ✉ *2F Asano Bldg., Minami 3-jo, Nishi 4, Odori* ☎ *011/222–4828.*

St. John's Wood. Start the evening perched on a bar stool looking out upon Susukino's main intersection. Can a business call itself an Irish pub if there is no Guinness or Kilkenny? Never mind. This friendly, pay-at-the-counter pub serves beer, mint juleps, whiskeys, malts, plus haggis, fish-and-chips, and onion rings. ✉ *1F Keiai Bldg., Minami 4, Nishi 4, Susukino* ☎ *011/271–0085* ⊕ *www.sjw.k-ai.jp* ☾ *Daily 5 pm–2 am, until 5 am weekends.*

SHOPPING

Sapporo is known to some as Japan's largest small town, and shopping to some degree reflects that. Sapporoites, like Dosanko as a whole, seek to be comfortable, average, and middle-class. Prices are relatively cheap, and displays of wealth and prestige are rare. Although you'll find a number of stores that appeal to tourist money as well as gourmet markets (Hokkaido is more famous for its food and raw materials than its finished products), there are no high-end boutique quadrants as in, say, Ginza or Harajuku in Tokyo. The best shopping is along Eki-Mae Dori, between JR Sapporo Station and Susukino. Start at Stella Place, Daimaru, and Tokyu department stores around the station, then move south along the financial district to the underground shopping malls of Pole Town and Aurora Town (these will be connected underground with JR Sapporo come March 2011). Surface at Odori to find decent department stores like Mitsukoshi, Parco, and Marui Imai. Walk a little further south to find the cheap and kitchy Tanuki Koji arcade, which stretches for six blocks.

Kinokuniya 紀伊国屋. Outside Sapporo, finding English-language books is difficult, so you may want to browse in this expansive bookstore near the West Exit of Sapporo Station (across the street west from Daimaru department store) first; foreign magazines are on the first floor near the escalators, and fiction, nonfiction, and English-language teaching books are on the second floor. The children's section also has many Japanese titles in translation. ⊠ *Kita 5-jo, Nishi 6, Sapporo Station* ☎ *011/231–2131* ⊘ *Daily 10–9.*

OTARU AND NISEKO 小樽とニセコ

West of Sapporo, Meiji-era stone warehouses line a canal lighted at night by glowing lamps and filled by day with sightseers. Otaru is a medium-size touristy port city facing the Japan Sea. Its herring-fishing heyday between the 1870s and 1930s created the riches that built the banks, warehouses, and grand houses that give the city its historical visage.

The Niseko area lies over the mountains and extends into the hinterland, where the perfect cone of Mt. Yotei acts like the Eiffel Tower to a pastoral Paris, blessed with fertile land offering up fruit, potatoes, pumpkins, corn, and hot springs. In winter this is one of Japan's leading ski areas, and from May to October outdoor enthusiasts enjoy river rafting and hiking. Niseko is best experienced by car over two or three days. Adventure tours should be booked in advance.

OTARU 小樽

40 km (25 mi) west of Sapporo.

★ Otaru nets its wealth in tourists these days, but the canal where barges used to land the catch of the day is still the center of action for thousands of domestic and Asian visitors reeled in by images of a romantic weekend retreat. Non-Japanese from countries with 19th-century stone buildings of their own may be less impressed by the tourist strip along the canal, but rent a bike or walk away from the main drag and you can explore quaint neighborhoods and interesting buildings. The Otaru Snow Gleaming Festival (February 9–18), when thousands of snow lanterns light up the canal area and old buildings, is a quieter concurrent alternative to the blockbuster Sapporo Snow Festival.

GETTING HERE AND AROUND

Otaru is an easy day trip from Sapporo. Trains run every 20 minutes and take about 40 minutes (sit on the right facing forward for the best coast views); the ¥1,500 Sapporo–Otaru Welcome Pass from JR Hokkaido permits one-day travel on Sapporo subways and the JR train to and from Otaru.

Otaru also makes a good base for touring around Hokkaido by car. **Toyota Car Rental** is near Otaru Station. **Nippon Rent-a-Car** is downtown. Neither agency has English-speaking staff, so ask the tourist office or your hotel to help with reservations.

While you're in town explore by bike; **JR Rent Cycle,** just to the right of the station exit, offers pedal- (¥1,000 for two hours) or electric- (¥1,200 for two hours) powered rentals.

ESSENTIALS

Bike Rental JR Rent Cycle (☎ 0134/24–6300).

Car Rental Nippon Rent-a-Car (☎ 0134/32–0919 ⊙ Daily 8:30–7). **Toyota Car Rental** (☎ 0134/27–0100 ⊙ Daily 8–8).

VISITOR INFORMATION

The **Otaru Tourist Office** 小樽駅観光案内所 is to the left of the ticket gates inside the station. It has room availability lists for hotels. English is basic, but they try hard. The **Unga Plaza Tourist Office** 運河プラザ, by the canal, has city information and leaflets for further travel. From the station, walk down the main street for eight blocks; the office is in the stone buildings on the left before the canal.

Contacts Otaru Tourist Office (☎ 0134/29–1333 ⊙ Daily 9–6).

Unga Plaza Tourist Office (✉ 2–1–20 Ironai ☎ 0134/33–1661).

WHAT TO SEE

Canal and Sakae-machi Street Historic District 小樽運河と栄町歴史街 (*Otaru Unga to Sakae-machi Rekishi-gai*). The canal is sandwiched between a contemporary shopping area and the port, eight blocks downhill from the station. Former banks and trading homes have been converted into generally charming glass and clothing stores. Don't miss the music-box collection and the musical steam clock at Marchen Square on the eastern end of the Sakae-machi district. Hordes of bus tours descend on the strip, but for some quiet time, dive into one of the cool, dark stone buildings and escape 21st-century Japan. A one-day pass (¥750) on the replica trolley is a useful energy-saver; and sunburned rickshaw runners offer tours (starting at ¥3,000 for two people).

In the port you may see Russian, Chinese, and Korean (North as well as South) ships loaded up with used cars, bicycles, and refrigerators. The Russian presence is quite noticeable, and there has been a history of tension between locals and sailors at Otaru bathhouses. Summer sightseeing boats leave the dock just beyond the Chuo Bridge for a 25-minute, ¥550 trip to the Herring Mansion area. Boats also go for an hour beyond this area along the mineral-stained cliff coastline. For those ready to leave Hokkaido, there is also a ferry to Niigata.

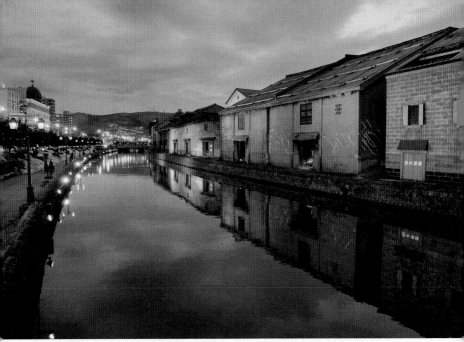

Otaru's canal is lined with 19th-century stone buildings.

Kyu Aoyama Bettei 旧青山別邸 *(Aoyama Villa)*. Gorgeous, gold-painted sliding doors and dark lacquered floors testify to the huge wealth of fishing millionaires, the Aoyamas. Teenage daughter Masae came home from a trip with another rich family in Honshu with big ideas about how her family could spend its fortune, and in 1917 her father commissioned the chief imperial carpenter and a team of top craftsmen to create a home and garden of sumptuousness rare in Hokkaido. The modern annex also has a good restaurant serving herring-on-rice lunches. Take bus No. 3 from the station to the Shukutsu 3-chome bus stop, then walk up the hill for about 1 km (½ mi). ✉ *3–63 Shukutsu* ☎ *0134/24–0024* 💴 *¥1,000* ⊘ *Apr.–Oct., daily 9–6; Nov.–Mar., daily 9–5.*

★ **Nishin Goten** 鰊御殿 *(Herring Mansion)*. Herring fishermen ate, slept, and dreamt of riches in this 1897 working base. On display are kitchen appliances, nets, and mislaid personal items of the men who toiled. Photographs of the Otaru coastline lined with ships, and beaches piled high with fish, reveal how the herring heydays brought riches to some— and put a serious dent in the Pacific fish stocks. ✉ *3–228 Shukutsu* ☎ *0134/22–1038* 💴 *¥200* ⊘ *Apr.–Nov., daily 9–5.*

☃ **Otaru Unga Kogeikan** 小樽運河工藝館 *(Otaru Canal Glass Factory)*. In the 19th century, Otaru craftsmen made glass buoys and gas lamps for the fishing fleets, some of which have floated across the Pacific and become collectors' items. Blow your own beer mug in the heat of the sandblasting room, laced with the color of your choice, in 10 minutes (beer glasses ¥2,310, tumblers ¥1,890). Reservations in advance are necessary; creations are ready the next day after cooling or can be shipped both domestically and internationally for ¥2,000 extra.

Children over 10 are welcome to try their hand in the furnace room. ✉ *2–1–19 Ironai* ☎ *0134/29–1112* ⊕ *www.otaru-glass.com* 🆓 *Free to factory shop* ⏱ *Oct.–Mar., daily 9:30–6; Apr.–Sept., daily 9–7.*

WHERE TO EAT

¢　✕ **Kita-no Ice Cream** 北のアイスクリーム. Beer ice cream anyone? Maybe
CAFÉ　you'd prefer sake ice cream? Or squid, cherry-blossom, or pumpkin? This Otaru institution serves up 20 unconventional varieties from an 1892 warehouse in an alleyway one block from the canal. ✉ *Ironai 1-chome* ☎ *0134/23–8983* ⊕ *www.kitanoice.com (Japanese language only)* ▭ *No credit cards.*

$$　✕ **Kita Togarashi** 北とうがらし. There's lamb barbecue heaven among
JAPANESE　all the sushi joints in Otaru at the easiest-to-find branch of a famous jingisukan restaurant. Plates of fresh, succulent lamb cost ¥700, and you cook them yourself on a dome-shape griddle with side orders of bean sprouts (*moyashi*) and leeks (*negi*). Along the canal, look for the tiny dive on the corner of the food-court complex opposite the group-photo spot. ✉ *1–1 Denuki, Ironai* ☎ *0134/33–0015* 🔖 *Reservations not accepted* ▭ *No credit cards.*

$$$$　✕ **Masazushi** 政寿司. This is sushi central in Otaru with this morning's
SUSHI　catch of herring, tuna, abalone, or salmon perched on quality vinegared rice. A good, quick lunch is the basic nine-piece-and-soup *Hamanasu* set (¥1,500) with seasonal changes, and staff will check your wasabi (horseradish) tolerance levels when taking the order. The restaurant is quiet and removed from the day-trip crowds during the day, and in the evening this is where local business leaders hold court in private rooms. There's also a canal-area branch called Zen-an, which often has a 30-minute wait. There are English menus and some English-speaking staff. ✉ *1–1–1 Hanazono, Sushi-ya* ☎ *0134/23–0011* ▭ *MC, V* ⏱ *Closed Wed.* ✉ *Zen-an, 1–2–1 Ironai, Canal Area* ☎ *0134/22– 0011* ⏱ *Closed Thurs.*

$$　✕ **Takeda** たけだ. Crab legs dripping juice and darkly gleaming red
JAPANESE　salmon eggs piled high on a bowl of rice are just two of Otaru's famous raw-fish options at this small family restaurant in the middle of the noisy fish market, just up the steps to the left of the station. The *Omakase-don* at ¥2,500 somehow gets eight kinds of fish into one bowl, although anyone hoping to still manage some sightseeing after lunch may prefer crab soup (¥200) and one portion of fish (¥400). There is no English spoken, but menus have plenty of pictures to choose from and point to. ✉ *3–10–16 Inaho, Sankaku Market, Otaru Station* ☎ *0134/22–9652* ▭ *No credit cards* ⏱ *No dinner.*

WHERE TO STAY

Hotel reviews have been condensed for this book. Please go to Fodors. com for full reviews of each property.

$$$–$$$$　🛏 **Authent Hotel** オーセントホテル. A former department store was
HOTEL　reborn as an elegant city-center hotel in the heart of the downtown
★　shopping area. **Pros:** located in town center; sunset views from piano bar. **Cons:** less-expensive rooms are boxlike; crowded with tour groups. ✉ *15–1, Inaho 2* ☎ *0134/24–8100* 🖨 *0134/27–8118* ⊕ *www.authent.*

co.jp ✑ *190 Western-style rooms, 5 Japanese-style rooms* ♿ *In-room: no a/c, Internet (some). In-hotel: 3 restaurants, bars* ⦿ *No meals.*

$$$–$$$$
HOTEL
★

🏨 **Grand Park Otaru** グランドパーク小樽. Overlooking Otaru Marina, 18 floors of a former Hilton chain hotel sit atop the huge WingBay shopping complex, giving easy access to outlet clothes bargains, movie theaters, a hot spring, and even a Ferris wheel. **Pros:** reliable service; handy shopping without leaving the building. **Cons:** out-of-the-way location; shopping mall atmosphere beyond the doors. ✉ *11–3 Otaru Chikko* ☎ *0134/21–3111, 0120/48–9852 toll-free* 🖨 *0134/21–3322* ⊕ *www. parkhotelgroup.com/gpot* ✑ *289 Western-style rooms* ♿ *In-room: a/c, safe, Internet. In-hotel: 3 restaurants, bars* ⦿ *No meals.*

$$$–$$$$
INN

🏨 **Otaru Furukawa** 小樽ふる川. Dark wooden beams, shadowy corridors, and antiques transform a modern canal-side building into a comfortable, old-fashioned Japanese inn—a rarity in Otaru. **Pros:** Old-Japan atmosphere; by the canal; Internet is free. **Cons:** tobacco smells in some rooms; overlooks main road. ✉ *1–2–15 Ironai* ☎ *0134/29–2345* ⊕ *www.otaru-furukawa.com* ✑ *43 Western-style rooms, 1 Japanese-style room, 2 suites* ♿ *In-room: no a/c. In-hotel: restaurant, Internet terminal* ⦿ *No meals.*

14

NISEKO ニセコ

73 km (45 mi) southwest of Otaru.

★ For the best skiing in Hokkaido, head for Niseko. This has been boomsville for Australian leisure developers, with foreign-owned holiday homes and apartments shooting up everywhere, particularly in Hirafu village. Direct flights between Chitose and Cairns, Australia, from November to April have revitalized Niseko, which had its heyday with Japanese skiers in the 1970s. Chinese tourism and speculative buying has also recently been making an impact.

Between the skiing and boarding on Mt. Annupuri and the conical Mt. Yotei is a gentle landscape of hot springs, dairy and vegetable farms, artists' workshops, and hiking trails. The Japanese love the outdoor farm and nature attractions, but for most Western visitors the adventure-sport opportunities are the real reason to come. Outdoor-adventure companies run by Australian and Canadian expats offer year-round thrills, including rafting (best from April to May), backcountry skiing, mountain biking, and bungee jumping.

Niseko is developing into a major self-catering vacation destination, meaning visitors provide their own food in exchange for access to a full kitchen. With most companies staffed by English-speaking expats, this offers an unusual-in-Japan stay opportunity. The Niseko area is hands-down the best place to discover the Hokkaido countryside, and it's easy to find an English-speaking guide.

GETTING HERE AND AROUND

Niseko is really a collection of villages near the town of Kutchan, a 2½-hour drive from New Chitose Airport. From November to May public buses go from the airport to the Niseko ski resorts almost hourly. In July and August, Chuo Bus Company has two buses a day. A one-way trip costs ¥2,300.

From Sapporo you can drive to the Niseko area in two hours, up and over Nakayama Pass. Trains from Sapporo to Kutchan depart hourly; the trip takes two hours and costs ¥1,790. You will probably have to switch trains in Otaru. From Kutchan seven trains a day go to the Hirafu and Niseko villages at the heart of the scenic area. Hotels and pensions pick up guests at these two stations. Travelers with no pickup arranged should go to Niseko Station because Hirafu is tiny and deserted once the train has gone (although there is a one-person hot-spring bath carved out of a tree trunk in a little building on the platform). In ski season there are shuttle buses connecting Kutchan, the villages, and the lift stations. Out of season public transport is limited and car hires make sense. Nippon Rental Car and Mazda Rent-A-Car 9–5 are both a five-minute walk from Niseko Station.

ESSENTIALS

Car Rental Mazda Rent-A-Car 9–5 (⊠ *74–4 Aza-Honcho* ☎ *0136/44–1188* ⊘ *Daily 9–5*) **Nippon Rental Car** (⊠ *247–7 Aza-Soga, Niseko-cho* ☎ *0136/43–2929* ⊘ *Apr.–Oct., daily 9–6; Nov.–Mar., daily 9–5*).

VISITOR INFORMATION

Down the street in front of Kutchan Station (three blocks and on the left) is the excellent **Machi-no-eki – PLAT,** run by the Kutchan Tourist Association, which has information, Internet access, hotel booking help, and event listings. In Niseko go to the **Niseko Hirafu Welcome Center** for accommodation help, tourist information, and essential heaters while waiting for the bus. It's next to the bus arrival/departure area at the top of Hirafu village, near the Hotel Niseko Alpen. The main self-catering companies are the **Niseko Company, Hokkaido Tracks,** and **Niseko Management Service.**

Self-Catering Companies Hokkaido Tracks (☎ *0136/23–3503* ⊕ *www.hokkaidotracks.com*). **The Niseko Company** (☎ *0136/21–7272* ⊕ *www.thenisekocompany.com*). **Niseko Management Service** (☎ *0136/21–7788* ⊕ *www.nisekomanagement.com*).

Skiing Information Niseko Grand Hirafu (⊕ *www.grand-hirafu.jp*). **Niseko United** (⊕ *www.niseko.ne.jp*). **Snow Japan** (⊕ *www.snowjapan.com*).

Contacts Machi-no-eki – PLAT (⊠ *Minami 1-jo, Nishi 4-chome, Kutchan* ☎ *0136/22–1121* ⊕ *www.niseko.co.jp*). **Niseko Hirafu Welcome Center** (⊠ *189–3 Aza-Yamada, Abuta-gun, Kutchan* ⊘ *Daily 10–6*).

WHERE TO EAT

$$
ECLECTIC
✗**Izakaya Bang Bang** 居酒屋ばんばん. Yakitori (sizzling meats on wood skewers) and other Hokkaido favorites, such as salmon and herring, accompany imports like spareribs and tacos. Your dining neighbors could become tomorrow's skiing or adventure-tour buddies, and your pension's staff may enjoy their evenings off here. In Hirafu village, Izakaya Bang Bang is definitely the place to be. English translations are on the menu. ⊠ *188–24 Aza-Yamada, Abuta-gun, Kutchan* ☎ *0136/22–4292* ⊕ *www.niseko.or.jp/bangbang.*

$$
AMERICAN
✗**Jo-Jo's.** Platters overflow with power food for adventurers—juicy hamburgers and generous salads, followed by home-baked cakes smothered in cream. A spacious laid-back restaurant on the second floor

of the Niseko Adventure Center, it's all soaring beams and big windows overlooking Yotei-san, and is busy all day with adventure guides and their nervous or elated customers. It's on the right, off the main road arriving in Hirafu village from Kutchan. ✉ *179–53 Aza-Yamada, Abuta-gunKutchan* ☎ *0136/23–2220* ▭ *No credit cards.*

WHERE TO STAY

Hotel reviews have been condensed for this book. Please go to Fodors. com for full reviews of each property.

¢–$

INN

▦ **Grand Papa** ぐらんぱぱ. In keeping with Niseko's wishful claim to be the St. Moritz of Asia, this Alpine-style pension at the bottom of Hirafu village has lots of dark wood and red carpeting. **Pros:** friendly family owners; casual atmosphere; home cooking. **Cons:** stairs, stairs, stairs—there's no elevator; limited rooms with baths; far from the lifts. ✉ *163 Aza-Yamada, Abuta-gun, Kutchan* ☎ *0136/23–2244* 🖶 *0136/23–2255* ⊕ *www.niseko-grandpapa.com* ⤶ *17 Western-style rooms, 3 with bath; 2 Japanese-style rooms without bath* ⚒ *In-room: a/c, Internet. In-hotel: restaurant, bar, bicycles* ❘◎❘ *Breakfast.*

$$$$

RESORT

▦ **Hilton Niseko Village** ヒルトンニセコビレッジ. Reopened as a Hilton in 2008, this resort hotel has wonderful views either of Mt. Yotei or the Higashiyama ski area. **Pros:** awesome views; 10-person teppan-yaki counter; ski valet and horseback riding available; great service. **Cons:** a 20-minute shuttle bus ride to après-ski life in Hirafu village; standard rooms small for the price. ✉ *Higashiyama Onsen, Niseko-cho, Abuta-gun* ☎ *0136/44–1111* ⊕ *www.hilton.co.uk/niseko* ⤶ *506 rooms* ⚒ *In-room: a/c, safe, refrigerator, Internet, Wi-Fi (some). In-hotel: 5 restaurants, room service, bars, golf course, tennis courts, gym, spa, children's programs (seasonal), laundry service, Internet terminal* ❘◎❘ *No meals.*

$$–$$$

HOTEL

▦ **Hotel Niseko Alpen** ホテル ニセコ アルペン. Smack-dab at the base of Grand Hirafu ski slopes is a modern hotel with English-speakers to help plan a Niseko stay. **Pros:** ski-in ski-out; close to village life; 20 steps from the bus terminal; onsen views. **Cons:** bland rooms; public areas crowded with skiers during the day in-season. ✉ *Aza Yamada 204, Abuta-gun, Kutchan* ☎ *0136/22–1105* 🖶 *0136/23–2202* ⊕ *www. grand-hirafu.jp* ⤶ *78 Western-style rooms, 15 Japanese-style rooms, 36 combination rooms* ⚒ *In-room: a/c, refrigerator, Internet. In-hotel: 2 restaurants, pool, spa, parking (free)* ❘◎❘ *No meals, Some meals.*

SPORTS AND THE OUTDOORS

HIKING

Mt. Yotei 羊蹄山 *(Yotei-san).* Climbing this Fuji look-alike takes four to six hours. Two trails lead up the mountain: the more-challenging **Hirafu Course** and the easier but still arduous **Makkari Course.** It's basically a stairway without switchbacks all the way up. Regardless of your approach, you'll find wildflowers in summer, and elderly Japanese chomping on bamboo shoots that grow wild on the hills. A hut at the top provides crude lodging. To get to the trails, take the bus from JR Kutchan Station 20 minutes to Yotei Tozan-guchi (hiking trail entrance) for the Hirafu Course or 40 minutes to the Yotei Shinzan Koen stop for the Makkari Course.

SKIING

From November to May, skiers and snowboarders enjoy 61 courses covering 47 km (30 mi) of powder in the Niseko area. There are five ski resorts, but the big three are Grand Hirafu, Higashiyama, and Annupuri. You can ski them all with a Niseko All-Mountain Pass costing ¥4,800 for one day or ¥8,800 for two days. Only the very top is above the tree line, and reaching Hirafu's big, off-trail bowl entails a 30-minute trek above the top chairlift. Nondrivers coming from Sapporo can buy package ski tours, including lunch and transportation by bus, for about ¥4,500. You can book tours at almost any city hotel. If you're driving to Niseko, check Sapporo convenience stores for discount lift tickets.

Annupuri Resort. This resort has wide, gently sloping runs that are kind to beginners and shaky intermediates. ☎ *0136/58–2080.*

Grand Hirafu. This is the largest of the Niseko ski resorts, with 34 courses, 27% of which are classed "expert." The longest run is more than 5 km (3 mi) long. A day pass to all three during peak season costs ¥5,500. There's more on seasonal rates at the Niseko Village Web site (⊕ *www.nisekovillage.com*). ☎ *0136/22–0109.*

Higashiyama Resort. Based at the Hilton Niseko Village, this resort has a superfast cable car that takes you to beautifully designed forested courses. You descend through the trees to the mountain base. ☎ *0136/44–1111.*

SPORTS OUTFITTERS

Niseko Adventure Centre (☎ *0136/23–2093* ⊕ *www.nac-web.com*) arranges river trips, mountain biking, and winter sport outings, and has an indoor rock-climbing wall at its village-center base. **SAS Hanazono Activity Center** (☎ *0136/21–3333* ⊕ *www.sas-net.com*) has rafting trips popular with school groups. The company also arranges hot-air ballooning, fishing, snowshoeing, and dogsled riding with a team of huskies.

SHIKOTSU-TOYA NATIONAL PARK 支笏洞爺国立公園

Mountains, forests, caldera lakes, hot-spring resorts, and volcanoes are virtually in Sapporo's backyard. Less than an hour from Sapporo, Route 230 passes the large hot-spring village Jozankei, then the mountains close in, and the road climbs to Nakayama Pass at 2,742 feet. On a clear day the view from the top is classic Hokkaido—farmland with the majestic Mt. Yotei in its midst, and on the southern horizon lie Lake Toya's volcanic crater and Noboribetsu hot springs, where the earth steams, rumbles, and erupts.

TOYAKO 洞爺湖

179 km (111 mi) southwest of Sapporo.

★ World leaders met here for the G8 Summit in 2008, but Lake Toya's most notable activity is still its recent volcanic events. At lunchtime

Scenic Lake Toya is in the vicinity of an active volcano that last erupted in 2000.

on March 28, 2000, Usu-san volcano exploded for the first time in 23 years, shooting a 10,500-foot-high cloud of ash and smoke over the quiet resort town of Lake Toya. About 16,000 farmers, hoteliers, and townspeople were evacuated. Amazingly, by July everyone came back, cleaned up their town, and reopened for business with still-smoking craters in their midst.

GETTING HERE AND AROUND
Usu-san is one of several peaks on Lake Toya's crater, a huge volcanic rim that dominates the landscape. Route 230 from Sapporo drops over the northern edge, and Route 453 from Lake Shikotsu and Noboribetsu and roads from the coast come in from the south. Volcanic activity is centered around the small town of Toyako Onsen, and a few kilometers around the lake at Showa Shin-san. A road rings the water, dotted with campsites and hot springs, and pleasure boats go out to three small islands where deer beg for snacks.

Direct buses from Sapporo to Toyako Onsen via Nakayama Toge Pass take 2½ hours (¥2,700). **Jotetsu Bus** runs between Sapporo and Toyako Onsen; reservations are necessary. **Donan Bus** makes the Sapporo to Toyako Onsen trip daily. Toyako Onsen is on the JR Sapporo–Hakodate Line. Disembark from the train at JR Toya Station for a 15-minute bus ride to the lake. There is a ¥100 shuttle bus four times a day round the lake, nonstop takes more than an hour. Sightseeing boats leave the pier for the 20-minute crossing to the islands. Bike rentals near the bus station cost ¥900 for two hours and ¥1,200 for three, the latter just enough time to cycle the circumference of the lake.

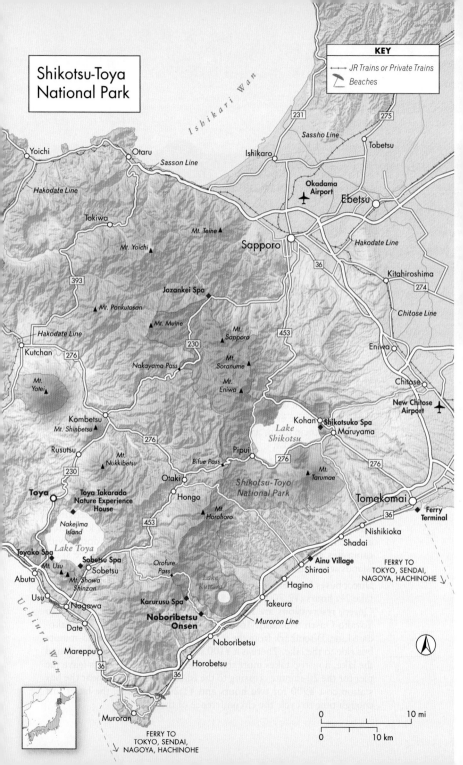

Shikotsu-Toya National Park

KEY
JR Trains or Private Trains
Beaches

Ishikari Wan

231
275
Sassho Line
Tobetsu
Ishikaro
Yoichi
Otaru
Sasson Line
Okadama Airport
Ebetsu
Hakodate Line
Tokiwa
Mt. Teine ▲
Sapporo
Hakodate Line
Kitahiroshima
Mt. Yoichi ▲
36
274
393
Jozankei Spa ◆
Chitose Line
Mt. Ponkutosan ▲
Mt. Muine ▲
Mt. Sapporo ▲
453
Hakodate Line
Kutchan
276
230
Mt. Soranume ▲
Eniwa
Nakayama Pass
Mt. Eniwa ▲
Chitose
Mt. Yotei ▲
New Chitose Airport ✈
Kombetsu
Kohan
Shikotsuko Spa ◆
Mt. Shinbetsu ▲
Lake Shikotsu
Maruyama
Rusutsu
276
Pipui
Mt. Nukkibetsu ▲
Bifue Pass
276
230
Otaki
Shikotsu-Toya National Park
276
Toya
Hongo
Mt. Tarumae ▲
Tomakomai
Toya Takarada Nature Experience House ◆
453
Mt. Horohoro ▲
36
Ferry Terminal ◆
Nakejima Island
Nishikioka
Lake Toya
Sobetsu Spa ◆
Shadai
Toyako Spa ◆
Sobetsu
Orofure Pass
Ainu Village ◆
FERRY TO TOKYO, SENDAI, NAGOYA, HACHINOHE ⟩
Mt. Usu ▲
Shiraoi
Abuta
Mt. Showa Shinzan ▲
Lake Kuttara
Hagino
Usu
Nagawa
Karurusu Spa ◆
Takeura
Date
Noboribetsu Onsen ◆
Muroron Line
Mareppu
Noboribetsu
36
Uchiura Wan
Horobetsu
36
Muroran

FERRY TO
TOKYO, SENDAI,
NAGOYA, HACHINOHE ⟩

0   10 mi
0   10 km

ESSENTIALS
Bus Information Donan Bus (☎ 011/261–3601). **Jotetsu Bus**
(☎ 011/572–3131).

VISITOR INFORMATION
Tourist Information, between the bus terminal and the lake, has English-speaking staff, and although officially unable to make hotel reservations, the Web site has access to online booking for some hotels. **Toya Guide Center** provides English-speaking guides for year-round excursions such as Canadian canoeing on the lake, walking the volcano, deer spotting, and waterfall walking.

Tour Information Toya Guide Center (✉ 402 Toya-cho, Abuta-gun, Toyako
☎ 0142/82–5002 ⊕ www.toya-guide.com).

Visitor Information Toyako Onsen Tourist Information (✉ 144 Toyako OnsenToyako-cho, Abuta-gun ☎ 0142/74–2446 ⊕ www.laketoya.com).

14

WHAT TO SEE

☉ **Kazan Kagaku-kan** 洞爺湖ビジターセンター 火山科学館 *(Volcanic Science Museum and Visitor Center)*. Rumbling sound tracks and shaking floors re-create the 1977 and 2000 eruptions in a small, official information center. Though there's a good explanation of the science and the geography, the museum is less useful in describing the impact on residents' lives. It's left of the bus terminal. ✉ 142–5 Toyako-Onsen, Toyako-cho
☎ 0142/75–2555 ⊕ www.toyako-vc.jp 🎟 ¥600 ☉ Daily 9–5.

★ **Nishiyama Kakogun Sansakuro** 西山火口群散策路 *(Nishiyama Crater
☉ Trail)*. A brand-new fire station, a school, and houses stand at crazy angles amid the solidified ash flows where the 2000 eruption reached the edges of Toyako Onsen. Walkways wind up into the still steaming hills. Although not as exciting as Hawaiian lava-flow hikes, it's an impressive scene of what can happen when you live next to a volcano. Buses from Toya Station to the onsen stop at the trailhead. The trail is accessible from the coast or from the lakeside above the village.
✉ 3–4–5 Takashaga-dori, between Abuta and Toyako 🎟 Free ☉ Apr.–Nov., daily.

Toyako Onsen 洞爺湖温泉. Fireworks enjoyed over sake from a rooftop hot spring after a pleasant dinner of local produce—this is why thousands of Japanese come to the one-street town year-round. From April 28 to October 31 the 30-minute, nightly fireworks are the highlight of any stay. A waterside walk in front of the wall of hotels is quiet before the bus groups arrive late afternoon. Be advised, however, that hotel staff may be resistant to changing the food-and-drink options they offer to their tour-bus-regimented guests. Moreover, if you overstay your welcome in certain banquet areas, cleaning ladies will come in and start vacuuming.

OFF THE BEATEN PATH

Showa Shin-san 昭和新山. Beginning with an earthquake in 1943, Showa Shin-san rose suddenly from a farmer's wheat field. Kept secret by authorities during the war as a potentially unlucky symbol, it continued growing to its present height of 1,319 feet by 1945. It is privately owned by the family of the village postmaster. A cable-car ride (¥1,450) up the eastern flank of Mt. Usu (2,400 feet) provides great views of the mountain, Lake Toya, and the sea in Funka (Eruption) Bay. Avoid, however, the Bear Ranch at the base, a depressing tourist attraction and a disgrace in a region that won World Heritage status for its efforts to preserve the bears' habitat.

WHERE TO EAT AND STAY

Hotel reviews have been condensed for this book. Please go to Fodors. com for full reviews of each property.

$$–$$$ ✗**Biyotei** びようてい. A European-style restaurant amid a garden in the
CONTINENTAL heart of the village, Biyotei has a stone floor, low beams, log table legs, and sepia family photos of the 60-plus years in business. The menu is in English, and the sizzling hamburger platters are the best choices. ✉ *36–12 Toyako Onsen, Abuta-gun* ☎ *0142/75–2311.*

¢–$ 🖼 **Lakeside Spa Toya Kawanami** 湖畔の宿洞爺かわなみ. Lake and fire-
HOTEL work show views are available from almost all rooms at this family-run hotel. **Pros:** peaceful getaway from the resort village; English-speaking owners; friendly service. **Cons:** old buildings being upgraded; no lake views from small hot spring; no private baths. ✉ *53 Toyako Onsen, Sobetsu-cho, Usu-gun* ☎ *0142/75–2715* ⊕ *www.kawanami.jp* ⇨ *50 Japanese-style rooms* ⚭ *In-room: no a/c (some), refrigerator. In-hotel: restaurant, bar, spa, laundry facilities, Internet terminal* ¶⊙| *Some meals.*

$$$$ 🖼 **The Windsor Hotel** ウインザーホテル. Visible for miles around—the
HOTEL hotel looks like a giant luxury cruise ship perched on the rim of the
Fodor's Choice Toya volcano—the Windsor is the best hotel in Hokkaido for location
★ and service. **Pros:** top service; top views; chance to spot Asian celebs on private holidays. **Cons:** top prices; some restaurants closed unexpectedly during quiet season. ✉ *Shimizu, Toyako Onsen, Abuta-cho* ☎ *0120/29–0500 or 0142/73–1111* 🖷 *0142/73–1210* ⊕ *www.windsor-hotels.co.jp* ⇨ *395 Western-style rooms, 3 Japanese-style rooms* ⚭ *In-room: a/c, Wi-Fi. In-hotel: 14 restaurants, bars, golf courses, tennis courts, pool, gym, spa, bicycles, Internet terminal* ¶⊙| *No meals.*

NOBORIBETSU ONSEN 登別温泉

53 km (32 mi) east of Toya-ko, 100 km (62 mi) south of Sapporo.

If you want to see how many Japanese people prefer to relax, this is the place to go. Noboribetsu Onsen is Hokkaido's most famous spa. The town claims that some 34,300 gallons of geothermally heated water are pumped out every hour, making it the most prodigious hot spring in Asia. Not a quaint little hot-spring town, Noboribetsu caters to Japanese-style onsen tourism (i.e., soak, eat, soak, get drunk, soak, carouse, canoodle, soak), meaning services are limited once you step outside your hotel. The hotels are good, but the town is basically tourist shops; come here expecting good hot water and conveyer-belt-style Japanese service.

GETTING HERE AND AROUND

Noboribetsu City is one hour south of Sapporo by JR Limited Express. From the JR Station in there, a shuttle bus serves Noboribetsu Onsen. Don't confuse Noboribetsu Onsen with Noboribetsu, an industrial city that is 13 minutes by bus from its namesake spa town. If you are coming from Sapporo, arrange a tour through your hotel, Japan Railways, or the Sapporo International Communication Plaza.

Donan Bus travels from Sapporo to Noboribetsu Onsen; the trip takes 1 hour, 20 minutes (¥1,900; reservations advised). From June to late October, three buses per day make the 1¼-hour run between Toyako Onsen and Noboribetsu Onsen; only one bus runs per day the rest of the year (¥1,530; reservations necessary). Heavy snows keep the road closed until spring.

ESSENTIALS

Bus Contact Donan Bus (☎ 011/261–3601).

WHAT TO SEE

★ **Jigokudani** 地獄谷 *(Valley of Hell)*. A volcanic crater in a bow-shape valley, Jigokudani has hundreds of multicolor geysers, pulsing like the heartbeat of Earth itself, or, rather, its handy-dandy sulfur vent. Not to worry, though; the walkways to photo ops have handrails and are very safe. It's a short walk from all Noboribetsu hotels and worth a look. There's no admission fee or formal open hours.

WHERE TO STAY

Hotel reviews have been condensed for this book. Please go to Fodors. com for full reviews of each property.

$–$$
HOTEL
☐ **Dai-ichi Takimoto-kan** 第一滝本館. Contemplate Hell while soaking the soul in one of the 12 different pools overlooking Jigokudani, as more than 1,000 guests a night tuck in at this prime example of Japanese mass tourism. **Pros:** hot water to ease every known condition; crab-crazy buffets; free Wi-Fi. **Cons:** mass tourism; noisy with groups. ⊠ 55 *Noboribetsu Onsen, Noboribetsu* ☎ 0120/940–489 📠 0143/84–2202 ⊕ *www.takimotokan.co.jp* ⟿ 16 *Western-style rooms, 383 Japanese-style rooms* ⌂ *In-room: a/c. In-hotel: 3 restaurants, room service, bars, pool, laundry service, Internet terminal, Wi-Fi hotspot* ⦿ *Some meals.*

$$$–$$$$
HOTEL
☐ **Ryotei Hanayura** 旅亭花ゆら. This is an idyllic peaceful hot-spring hotel: floor-to-ceiling lobby windows look out on a small canyon and river, and the hotel hot springs on the top floor bubble gently among rocks and trees. **Pros:** peaceful, dignified environment. **Cons:** rooms a little poky; 10 minutes' walk from Valley of Hell. ⊠ 100 *Noboribetsu Onsen, Noboribetsu* ☎ 0143/84–2322 📠 0143/84–2035 ⊕ *www. hanayura.com* ⟿ 58 *rooms* ⌂ *In-room: no a/c, safe, refrigerator. In-hotel: restaurant, spa* ⦿ *Some meals.*

NIBUTANI 二風谷

★ *40 km (24 mi) east of Tomakomai, 115 km (71 mi) southeast of Sapporo.*

Nibutani is one of the last places in Hokkaido with a sizable Ainu population—or at least part Ainu, as few pure-blooded Ainu are left. The tiny village, which is nothing more than some scattered homes along a main road, has two museums and a handful of souvenir shops. It's a very long day trip from Sapporo, and if you have toured native people's centers in North America it may feel like more of the same, but it is where you can find the best, nontouristy collection of Ainu art and artifacts in Hokkaido.

GETTING HERE AND AROUND

Nibutani is hard to reach by public transport. It involves an early train from Sapporo, a change, and then a local bus—all costing about ¥6,000 round-trip. The Tourist Office in Sapporo has information on the current public transport connections if this is your only option. Otherwise, you're better off renting a car for the day. See Exploring Sapporo for car rental information.

WHAT TO SEE

Kayano Shigeru Nibutani Shiryo-kan 萱野茂 二風谷アイヌ資料館 *(Kayano Shigeru Nibutani Ainu Archive).* This museum puts a spotlight on artifacts, particularly Ainu clothing and items used in sacred rites collected by the late prominent Ainu activist and Nibutani resident Shigeru Kayano. Until his death in 2006, Kayano traveled extensively, and the archive contains presents to the Ainu from other indigenous peoples. The museum is across the main road from the Culture Museum. ⊠ *54 Nibutani, Biratori-cho* ☎ *0145/72–3215* ⊡*¥400, ¥700 joint ticket with Nibutani Ainu Culture Museum* ⊘ *Mid-Jan.–mid-Dec., Tues.– Sun. 9:30–4:30.*

Fodor'sChoice **Nibutani Ainu Bunka Hakubutsukan** 二風谷アイヌ文化博物館 *(Nibutani*
★ *Ainu Culture Museum).* This museum is an excellent resource for information about the Ainu, and it's sadly unknown to many Japanese. Ainu artifacts, such as shoes of salmon skin, water containers made from animal bladders, and heavy blue-and-black embroidered coats are displayed, as well as implements used in *iyomante,* an Ainu ritual that sent the spirit of the bear back to the nonhuman world. There is an hour-long movie in English and translated books on sale. A selection of videos lets you listen to eerie traditional Ainu chants and songs. ⊠ *Off Rte. 237, 55 Nibutani, Biratori-cho* ☎ *0145/72–2892* ⊡*¥400, ¥700 joint ticket with Kayano Shigeru Nibutani Ainu Archive* ⊘ *Mid- Jan.–mid-Dec., Tues.–Sun. 9:30–4:30.*

CENTRAL HOKKAIDO

Breathtaking and often snowy Daisetsu-san is Japan's largest national park and home to Mt. Asahi-dake, Hokkaido's highest peak, at 7,311 feet. Roads in the region skirt through farmland and flower fields to circle the mountains north and south, and cable cars lift visitors onto mountain plateaus with steaming volcanic vents, alpine flower meadows, and awe-inspiring views. Allow at least two days for reaching the area and enjoying its grandeur. Asahikawa is the largest city and the transport gateway to the park. Staying-over places are Biei and Furano for gentle countryside and Soun-kyo Gorge and Asahidake for mountain grandeur.

CLOSE UP

Hokkaido's First Inhabitants

Once upon a time in *Ainumosir* (human being peaceful land), *aynu* (human beings) lived in *kotan* (villages), raising their families on a diet of *ohaw* (salmon, meat, or plants) and *sayo* (millet and other grains). They honored the god Okikurmikamu, and told *yukar* (epic poems) to remember the interwoven lives of human and the spirit world, particularly of bears and owls. Sometimes they traded kelp, salmon, and herring with the *sisam,* the neighbors north or south.

Around the 15th century life changed. The southern sisam—the Japanese— began arriving in greater numbers and building trading posts along the far south coast. As the Japanese moved north and solidified their presence on the island, the aynu—regarded as "hairy people"—became forced laborers.

In 1869 the new Meiji Government lumped Ainu together with Japanese as "commoners," and the Ainu language and lifestyle were outlawed. Along with intermarriages, this nearly obliterated the culture. The Hokkaido Former Aborigine Protection Law sliced up land ownership, dispossessing many Ainu of ancestral homesteads.

But the Ainu have fought back. By the 1980s Ainu were calling for basic human rights, drawing support from indigenous groups in other countries. The United Nations made 1993 the Year of Indigenous Peoples, which bolstered their efforts, and a victory was achieved in 1994 when leading activist Shigeru Kayano of Nibutani was elected the first Ainu to Japan's House of Councilors. In May 1997, the national government passed belated legislation acknowledging the existence of Ainu as a minority group (a landmark event in Japan's purportedly "homogeneous" society), requiring local and national governments to respect their dignity by promoting Ainu culture and traditions. The act stopped short of certifying Ainu as an indigenous ethnic group, due to concerns about aboriginal rights to land and natural resources.

Visitors to Hokkaido may find it hard to recognize full-blooded Ainu outside the tourist centers of Shiraoi, Nibutani, and Akan. Some 24,000 people declare themselves Ainu. Most Japanese have little interest in Ainu affairs, beyond buying cute wooden carvings as souvenirs. Otherwise well-informed, worldly Japanese hosts may be surprised, and a little embarrassed, by foreigners' interest in Ainu. Today, Ainu tourist parks are being revamped as cultural centers. Ainu language is taught at 14 locations, and Shiro Kayano is continuing his father's monthly Ainu radio broadcasts (FM-Pipaushi).

The best places to learn more about Ainu culture and politics are the Nibutani Ainu Culture Museum and the Kayano Shigeru Nibutani Ainu Archive; the Poroto Kotan and Ainu Museum, Shiraoi; and the Akan Ainu Kotan cultural performances.

Foundation for Research and Promotion of Ainu Culture
アイヌ文化振興・研究 (*FRPAC* ⊠ *7F Presto 1.7, Kita 1-jo, Nishi 7-chome, Sapporo* ☎ *011/271–4171* ⊕ *www.frpac.or.jp*) has English-language information.

14

DAISETSU-SAN NATIONAL PARK 大雪山国立公園

★

50 km (31 mi) east of Asahikawa

Daisetsu-san National Park is the geographical center of Hokkaido and the largest of Japan's national parks. It contains the very essence of rugged Hokkaido: vast plains, soaring mountain peaks, hidden gorges, cascading waterfalls, wildflowers, forests, hiking trails, wilderness, and onsen. Daisetsu-san, which means great snow mountains, refers to the park's five major peaks, whose altitudes approach 6,560 feet.

GETTING HERE AND AROUND

Soun-kyo village and canyon are 90 minutes northeast of Asahikawa by car on Route 39. The highway skirts the northern side of the park, and Soun-kyo is the gateway. You can catch a bus directly to Soun-kyo Onsen (¥1,900) from in front of Asahikawa's JR Station. If you are using a JR Pass, you can save money and time by taking the train to Kamikawa Station and transferring to the Dohoku Bus for the 30-minute run to Soun-kyo. Bicycles can be rented for ¥1,000 a day in the village, and a short cycling trail along the old road by the river is a peaceful way to enjoy the gorge. From July to September a ¥390 bus ride connects the village with the Daisetsu dam and lake.

VISITOR INFORMATION

The **Soun-kyo Tourist Office**, in the bus terminal, provides hiking maps and information on sightseeing and lodging. English is spoken.

Contact Soun-kyo Tourist Office (☎ 0165/85–3350 ⊕ www.sounkyo.net).

WHAT TO SEE

★ **Soun-kyo** 層雲峡 *(Soun-kyo Gorge)*. As you follow the main route through the park, the first place to go is this 24-km (15-mi) ravine extending into the park from its northeast entrance. For an 8-km (5-mi) stretch, sheer cliff walls rise on both sides of the canyon as the road winds into the mountains. In winter and early spring, forbidding stone spires loom as if in judgment; in other seasons they thrust through glorious foliage. Soun-kyo Onsen is at the halfway point of the ravine.

On the park's west side, two **spa towns** serve as summer hiking centers and winter ski resorts. **Shirogane Onsen,** at 2,461 feet, has had especially good skiing since its mountain, Tokachi-dake, erupted in 1962 and 1988, creating a superb ski bowl. At **Asahi-dake Onsen** you can take a cable car (¥2,800 round-trip) up Asahi-dake to an altitude of 5,250 feet, and hike for two hours to the 7,513-foot summit. In late spring and early summer the slopes are carpeted with alpine flowers. Serious skiers come for Japan's longest ski season.

Soun-kyo Onsen village tries hard to be attractive. In summer, the pedestrian-friendly main street is full of flower boxes, and the guesthouses and souvenir shops do their best to add charm to what is basically a copycat concrete Alpine village. Activities take place in resort hotels, not in the village, and during the day most people are hiking through the park. From Late January to March, the frozen river is illuminated for the Ice Waterfall Festival. ■TIP➔ Watch your petrol tank, as there is no gas station in town.

Daisetsu-zan National Park has some of Hokkaido's most rugged scenery.

WHERE TO STAY

There's no lodging within the township of Soun-kyo Onsen 層雲峡温泉 if you want to stay in the northern part of the park. Because Soun-kyo's hotels are almost exclusively ryokan, where meals are included in your lodging cost, other dining opportunities in town are severely limited. A list of hotels and onsen is on the English page of the Soun-kyo Tourist Office. Rates tend to be 20% lower in winter.

Hotel reviews have been condensed for this book. Please go to Fodors. com for full reviews of each property.

$$–$$$
HOTEL ⊞ **Choyo Tei** 層雲峡朝陽亭. Perched on a bluff halfway up the side of the gorge, this hotel has the best views of any in the park. **Pros:** service and food quality on par with other large hotels; big baths. **Cons:** public areas make you feel like you're in a Japanese resort town. ⊠ *Soun-kyo Onsen, Kamikawa* ☎ *01658/5–3241* ⊕ *www.choyotei.com* ⌗ *5 Western-style rooms, 257 Japanese-style rooms* ⌂ *In-room: no a/c. In-hotel: 3 restaurants, bar* ⦿*l Some meals.*

$–$$
INN ⊞ **Resort Pension Yamanoue** 山の上. This modern guesthouse is in the center of the village's flower-filled pedestrian area. **Pros:** in village center; expansive dinners. **Cons:** guests have to use hot springs next door, not in-house. ⊠ *Soun-kyo Onsen, Kamikawa* ☎ *0165/85–3206* ⊟ *01658/ 5–3207* ⊕ *www.tabi-hokkaido.co.jp/p.yamanoue* ⌗ *14 Japanese-style rooms without bath* ⌂ *In-room: a/c. In-hotel: restaurant* ⦿*l Some meals.*

¢
HOTEL ⊞ **Soun-kyo Youth Hostel** 層雲峡ユースホステル. Between the big hotels—but at a fraction of the price and with a more-personal welcome—this 40-year-old hostel is a good base for mountain hiking. **Pros:** foreigner friendly; hiking conditions news provided; discounted use of the big

hotel onsens. **Cons:** early-morning bustle among hikers prevents sleeping in. ✉ *Soun-kyo Onsen, Kamikawa* ☎ *01658/5–3418* 📠 *01658/5–3186* ⊕ *www.youthhostel.or.jp/sounkyo* 🛏 *12 rooms with shared bath* 🛆 *In-room: no phone, no a/c, no TV. In-hotel: restaurant, Internet terminal, Wi-Fi hotspot* ═ *No credit cards* 🍽 *Multiple meal plans.*

HIKING

★ **Kuro-dake** 黒岳. Technology helps even the most reluctant up the mountains: a cable car and chair lift (¥2,200 round-trip) rise up the side of the gorge above the village to 4,264 feet. Hikers can march one more hour to the top of Kuro-dake, 2,244 feet higher. From here, numerous well-marked trails lead either across volcanic gravel or low shrub plateaus. Crimson foliage sets the slopes ablaze in September. Between June and mid-October, the cable car starts at 6 am, and experienced hikers can cross the range to Asahi-dake, then take its cable car down to Asahi-dake Onsen in one long day. But Daisetsu's beauty is best enjoyed slowly, and you may encounter deer, foxes, and bears. While most trails are busy during the summer months, care should be taken on quieter midweek or early-season visits when bear cubs—and bear mamas—are around.

ASAHIKAWA 旭川

136 km (84 mi) northwest of Sapporo.

Asahikawa, Hokkaido's second-largest city, is the principal entrance to Daisetsu-san National Park. It is not terribly cosmopolitan; daytime life centers around a pedestrian shopping area and at night the entertainment district is raucously full of men from the farming hinterland. Travelers pass through its station, bus terminal, or airport on their way to more beautiful places, but a small Ainu museum and a winter festival in February are worthwhile if the schedule dictates a one-night stay.

GETTING HERE AND AROUND

Trains leave Sapporo for Asahikawa twice an hour and the journey takes about one hour, 30 minutes. The Hokkaido Expressway also connects the two cities and takes just under two hours to drive. Domestic airlines from Haneda (Tokyo), Osaka, and Nagoya fly into Asahikawa Airport, 10 km (6 mi) from the city center, making it a good entry point for a holiday in central and eastern Hokkaido. There are car rentals at the airport and station.

ESSENTIALS

Car Rentals Toyota Car Rental (✉ *9–396–2 Miyashita-dori, Station area* ☎ *0166/23–0100* ⊕ *rent.toyota.co.jp/top.asp*).

Visitor Information Asahikawa Tourism (✉ *5F Okuno Bldg., 3-jo-dori 7-chome* ⊕ *www.asahikawa-tourism.com*).

WHERE TO EAT AND STAY

Far from the sea, Asahikawa is not known for name-brand cuisine, with two notable exceptions: ramen and *tonkatsu* (breaded, deep-fried pork cutlet). Asahikawa ramen features a distinctively salty pork broth and thin noodles prized by ramen connoisseurs. Several noodle shops pepper the area around the station.

Hotel reviews have been condensed for this book. Please go to Fodors. com for full reviews of each property.

$–$$
JAPANESE

✕ **Takada-ya** 高田屋. Tonkatsu with soba noodles, tempura with noodles, and curry with noodles are served at this traditionally decorated restaurant favored by shoppers and business people alike. At lunchtime there's a no-smoking rule to allow full appreciation of the soba. Diners are seated in booths and entertained with quiet jazz, and free *bancha* (roasted green tea) is served with all meals. It's on the main street three blocks from the station, opposite the Okuno department store. No English is spoken, but the menu has pictures. ⊠ *3-jo-dori 8-chome* ☎ *0166/29–0811* ▭ *No credit cards.*

¢–$
HOTEL

🏠 **Washington Hotel** ワシントンホテル. Anyone forced to stay the night in Asahikawa can make do with this bright, busy hotel with small motel-type rooms located across the street from the station. **Pros:** at the station; near restaurants. **Cons:** small, characterless rooms. ⊠ *7 Miyashita-dori* ☎ *0166/23–7111* 🖷 *0166/26–6767* ⊕ *www.wh-rsv.com* ➴ *260 Western-style rooms* ⌂ *In-room: no a/c. In-hotel: 2 restaurants* ☻ *Breakfast.*

14

BIEI AND FURANO 美瑛と富良野

Biei: 23 km (15 mi) east of Asahikawa. Furano: 31 km (19 mi) farther south.

Flower fields and small farms at the base of the Daisetsu-san mountain range attract thousands of domestic and East Asian visitors hoping to get a taste of the simple country life. Although Western visitors may not be so wowed by lavender and potato fields, or by the art galleries and cutesy coffee shops that dot the region, it makes an attractive stopover area while driving to central or east Hokkaido between late May and September. Biei is a small modern village with neighboring rolling hills and a patchwork of crop fields (potato, corn, soba, sunflowers) to cycle around; Furano is a small town famous throughout Japan for its lavender farms (when in bloom) and its ski resort.

GETTING HERE AND AROUND

Trains from Asahikawa depart every hour and reach Biei in 30 minutes and Furano in 70 minutes. In July and August there are special trains, sightseeing buses, and bus or train packages from Sapporo, which combine Biei and Furano flowers with a popular zoo at Asahikawa. Check with JR Hokkaido and Chuo Bus for details.

VISITOR INFORMATION

Outside Furano Station, flower farm information, shuttle buses, and help with hotel searches are available at the Furano Tourist Association.

Contact Furano Tourist Association (⊠ *1–26 Hinode-machi, Furano* ☎ *0167/23–3388* ⊕ *www.furano.ne.jp/kankou* ⊗ *Daily 9–5*).

WHAT TO SEE

Farm Tomita ファーム富田. In Japanese eyes, lavender is possibly the leading souvenir and image of Hokkaido, and this is the farm where it all started—back in 1903. Now thousands of visitors come to see fields of lavender, poppies, cosmos, herbs, and marigolds. *Irodori* is the field with flowers planted in seven strips, each a different color. Lavender peak season is early July to early August, and during this time the Lavender Bataké Station—seven minutes closer than Nakafurano Station—is open. JR Hokkaido and Chuo Bus offer packages for one-day visits in summer. ⊠ *Hokusei, Nakafurano-cho, Sorachi-gun* ☏ *0167/39–3939* ⊕ *www.farm-tomita.co.jp* ⊷ *Free* ⊙ *Daily 8:30–5.*

EASTERN HOKKAIDO 道東

Bears and eagles rule the mountains of Shiretoko National Park. Farther inland are the mysterious lakes of Akan National Park, where Ainu people hold on to their pre-Japanese culture with spirit worship, music, and dance. South, around Kushiro, are the vast wetland breeding grounds of the striking *tancho-zuru* (red-crested crane). On the eastern coast flowers carpet the land in the short summer, while in winter creaking ice floes nudge against the shore, providing a temporary home to seals and seabirds. Unfortunately, the ice is getting thinner and the viewing season shorter—this is the front line of global warming.

Japan's last frontier is also a hotbed of international politics. Japan and Russia are engaged in bitter disputes over islands and fishing and mineral rights. Russian sailors hang around fishing ports, and signboards across the region proclaim, "Return the Northern Territories!" This is Japan's campaign to reclaim the Kurile islands, some just kilometers off its eastern shore, that were occupied by the Soviets in the closing days of World War II.

There are regional airports in Kushiro and Memanbetsu, and express trains reach Abashiri and Kushiro. The largest city is Kushiro, famous for its morning fish market, but more beautiful touring bases include Akan Onsen and Abashiri, and the small fishing town of Utoro, halfway up the Shieroko Peninsula.

ABASHIRI 網走

517 km (321 mi) east of Sapporo.

A good touring base for eastern Hokkaido, Abashiri is a small town in the shadow of Tento-san. On the town outskirts are shallow coastal lakes with flowers and seabirds. Bicycles can be rented for slow sightseeing. The whaling fleet sets out from here on "research" trips ("research" is the official word, common parlance would call it "hunting") under Japan's interpretation of IWC rules, which keeps Japan at loggerheads with conservationists. Winters are harsh: visitors bundle up for boat tours through the ryuhyo (ice floes) that jam up on its shores and stretch out to sea as far as the eye can see.

GETTING HERE AND AROUND

The significant distance from Sapporo to Abashiri makes it advisable to take one of the four daily so-called express trains out. This is a five-hour-plus trip, sometimes chugging along at almost walking speeds through the northern Daisetsu mountain area, then a dead-end turn at Engaru, where passengers must stand and turn the seats to face forward again.

Abashiri has enough sights for a day or more as you set out to cycle the 27-km (17-mi) lakeside cycling road (or the equally easy 40-km [25-mi] one-way cycle along Lake Notoro to Tokoro town). There are seven buses a day from the station, circling the sights on Tento-san; a day pass costs ¥900. Be careful if you arrive on the morning train from Sapporo that gets in at 12:46 pm because you'll only have eight minutes to run for bus stop Number 2, or face a two-hour wait for the next bus. Tourist office staff will keep bags for ¥300 per item. After taking in Abashiri's sights, rent a car or go by bus to the Shiretoko, Akan, or Kushiro Marsh areas.

14

VISITOR INFORMATION

Some staff members at the **Abashiri Tourist Association**, adjoining the JR Station, speak English. This is where to find information about transportation and lodging in the area. At the station, inside the JR Hokkaido car rental office you'll find **Bicycle–Ekimae Rental**, where you can rent a bike for ¥500 an hour, from June to September.

Contacts Abashiri Tourist Association (☎ *0152/44–5849* ⊕ *www.abakanko. jp).* JR Travel Center Abashiri Branch (☎ *0152/43–4261).*

Bicycle Rental Bicycle–Ekimae Rental (☎ *0152/43–6197).*

WHAT TO SEE

★ **Abashiri Kangoku Hakubutsukan** 網走監獄博物館 *(Prison Museum).* Spartan cells line the central corridors in five wooden prison blocks, showing how the convicts who built much of early Hokkaido lived out their years. Used between 1912 and 1984, the prison is now a park museum with the blocks, watchtowers, and preserved farm buildings. Only the most heinous criminals were banished to this forbidding northern outpost, the Alcatraz of Japan. English information is entertainingly lost in translation, but anguished-looking mannequins illustrate the grimness of life behind bars, and how grimmer it was for some who did escape. ✉ *1–1 Yobito* ☎ *0152/45–2411* ⊕ *www.kangoku.jp* 🎫 *¥1,050* ⊗ *Apr.– Oct., daily 8–6; Nov.–Mar., daily 9–5.*

Hoppo Minzoku Hakubutsukan 北方民族博物館 *(Hokkaido Museum of Northern Peoples).* Hokkaido is the most southerly point of the northern community of the Ainu. This museum's delightful exhibits link indigenous people, such as the Ainu, Inuits, and Sami (or Lapps) in a way that shows surprising community and similarity over wide spaces. Displays compare and contrast the kitchen implements, clothes, and hunting tools of various cultures from northern Japan, the neighboring Russian island of Sakhalin, and the northern parts of America and Eurasia. English-language pamphlets are available. Of particular interest are the on-site videos depicting life in the frozen north (such as dressing children for the outdoors, or building an igloo)—and look for the alien-like fish-skin suit! The museum is 5 km (3 mi)—a 10-minute drive—from JR Abashiri Station on Tento-san. By bus, take the "Shinai kanko Shisetsu Meguri" 市内観光施設めぐり to the Hoppo Minzoku Hakubutsukan Mae stop 北方民族博物館前. ⊠ *309–1 Shiomi* ☎ *0152/45–3888* ⊕ *www.hoppohm.org* 🖅 *¥800* 🕙 *Tues.–Sun. 9:30–4:30.*

WHERE TO EAT AND STAY

Hotel reviews have been condensed for this book. Please go to Fodors. com for full reviews of each property.

¢
CAFÉ
✕ **Bangaichi Cafe** 番外地カフェ. This small windowless café above a main-street shop looks unpromising from its stair entrance, but inside is a cocoon of peace with sofas, warm lighting, and jazz. The menu includes hemp and raisin scones, fresh-brewed coffee, cheese on toast, and parfaits. ⊠ *2F Honma Bldg., Nishi 2, Minami 4* ☎ *0152/43–7110* 🖃 *No credit cards.*

$$$–$$$$
JAPANESE
✕ **Nakazushi** 中鮨. Rotarian Kanio Nakano presides over the Ohotsuku-kai's freshest catch in a small restaurant near the Abashiri Central Hotel run for more than 40 years by the same family. Depending on the season, Nakano-san has salmon roe on rice, sea urchin, and the plump, juicy Abashiri scallop. *Tsuchi-kujira* (Baird's beaked whale) is sometimes on the menu. Although Nakano-san doesn't speak English, he's aware of the whale-meat debate and can make substitutions if you let him know your no-whale preference through gestures. ⊠ *Minami 2, Nishi 2* ☎ *0152/43–3447* 🖃 *No credit cards.*

$–$$
HOTEL
🛏 **Abashiri Central Hotel** 網走セントラルホテル. Luxury awaits you at this downtown hotel, which seems a world away from small-town Abashiri. **Pros:** town center; foreigner friendly service. **Cons:** could be anywhere in the world; boring views. ⊠ *7, Minami 2-jo, Nishi 3* ☎ *0152/44–5151* 🖷 *0152/43–5177* ⊕ *www.abashirich.com* 📞 *94 Western-style rooms, 2 Japanese-style rooms* ⚭ *In-room: no a/c, Internet, Wi-Fi. In-hotel: restaurant, bar* 🍴 *No meals.*

$$$–$$$$
★
HOTEL
🛏 **Hotel Abashiri-ko-so** ホテル網走湖荘. Waterbirds and mist drift by the windows of the big but friendly hotel on the shore of Lake Abashiri, a few kilometers from town. It has the usual noise of Japanese resort hotels—game corners, tour groups, and karaoke rooms. **Pros:** lakeside; ideal for bird-watching. **Cons:** out of town; used by tour groups. ⊠ *Abashiri Kohan Onsen* ☎ *0152/48–2245* 🖷 *0152/48–2828* ⊕ *www. abashirikoso.com* 📞 *37 Western-style rooms, 20 Japanese-style rooms, 100 combination rooms* ⚭ *In-room: no a/c. In-hotel: 3 restaurants, bars* 🍴 *Some meals.*

SIGHTSEEING CRUISES

Ice Breaker Sailing from Aurora Terminal 流氷観光砕氷船「おーるら号」運航. If you really want to break the ice in future conversations, try some bird- and seal-watching (weather permitting) from late January to April, or a trip to Shiretoko National Park in the summer months. The icebreakers *Aurora 1* and *2* sail from Aurora Terminal at the east end of the port, letting you inspect winter ryuhyo at close range for ¥3,000. In summer, the same company takes you around Shiretoko from Utoro Port 80 km (50 mi) away. Travel agencies in Tokyo and Sapporo and JR Hokkaido offer ice-floe/hot-spring package tours that always include this boat trip. ⊠ *Minami 3, Nishi 4, Aurora Port* ☎ *0152/45–3888* ⊕ *www.ms-aurora. com* 🖅 *¥3,000–¥6,500* 🕙 *Jan. 20–early Apr. for ice 9–6, Apr. 28–Oct. 25 treks around Shiretoko 9–6.*

SHIRETOKO NATIONAL PARK 知床国立公園

Fodor'sChoice *50 km (31 mi) east of Abashiri.*

★

Shiretoko National Park is a World Heritage Site and a highlight of any trip to Hokkaido. If you have the time to get out there, do so. The village of Utoro is the center of visitor activity. It was a simple working fishing village, but now with the World Heritage Site status it has become a boomtown with a large hotel zone built on a bluff above the center.

The spectacular national park on the Shiretoko Peninsula is worlds away from modern Japan: brown bears hook salmon out of tumbling rivers; Blackiston's fish owls and Steller's sea eagles glide the skies; and a steaming hot river tumbles to the sea. However, with World Heritage Site designation came mass tourism. The bid to control and preserve has resulted in strict rules, and limited shuttle-bus access to the last few kilometers of peninsula road—which may give some visitors an unwelcome Jurassic Park feel to the visit.

Most tour buses whisk visitors in and out in 24 hours—with an overnight stay in a big hotel in Utoro's hotel zone and quick photo stops at Shiretoko Five Lakes, the Nature Center, and maybe a boat tour. Time your sightseeing at these places during the noon–1 pm tour lunch break or late in the day, and head for the places off the tour route. The magic of Shiretoko is found just beyond the bus park hordes. Shiretoko is lovely but local weather, even in summer, is fickle. A Shiretoko stay (and hiking plans) can be marred by mists and rain.

If you visit outside the summer crush—June and September are good times—Shiretoko is a remarkable, untouched pocket of wilderness in a heavily industrialized and technologically advanced nation. Note: Some sites close from November to April.

GETTING HERE AND AROUND

From Sapporo to Abashiri it's a five-hour express train, then a local train to Shari, and finally a 55-minute bus ride to Utoro. With connections the trip takes seven hours. Depending on the season, about seven daily bus connections go from Shari to Utoro. Buses from Abashiri and the airports in Kushiro and Memanbetsu also connect to Utoro. Kushiro and Abashiri have several car-rental companies, and Shari has only one (Nippon Rent-a-Car). Coming from Kushiro it's a two-hour drive to the ugly fishing village of Rausu on the south side of the peninsula, and then a 30-minute drive over the Shiretoko Pass (closed November–April) to Utoro.

From Sapporo the twice-daily Eagle Liner bus takes seven hours (¥15,000 round-trip), departing Sapporo Chuo Bus Terminal at 9 am and 11:15 pm. Reservations with Chuo Bus are necessary and can be made at the terminal behind the TV Tower in Sapporo, where the bus departs. Utoro and Rausu are also connected by four buses daily, although, aside from its fantastic views of Russian-occupied Kunashiri Island, a visit to the disappointing town of Rausu is not highly recommended.

14

From the end of April to the end of October, one-hour shuttle-bus trips link Utoro with the Nature Center and Shiretoko Five Lakes, running three times a day (¥900). If you are coming by car, park at the Nature Center and board the shuttle. The 12-km (7-mi) dirt road to Kamui-wakka Onsen waterfall is open to shuttle buses only between July 13 and September 20 (closed in winter). Be careful of wildlife when driving; Shiretoko is full of grazing deer that favor cleared roadside verges and are largely unperturbed by vehicles.

Apart from hiking, a boat is the best way to see the wildest parts. From late April to October, several boat companies in Utoro harbor offer one- to three-hour trips (¥3,000–¥8,000) out along the peninsula, beneath soaring 600-foot cliffs to the tip of the cape. Early-morning and late-afternoon trips on a small boat offer the best chances to see bears come down to the beaches to forage. On the Rausu side, boats head out into the Nemuro Straits along Russia's Kunashiri Island, and summer is the best time for whale-watching. A stay of at least one night is recommended for hiking, hot springs, wildlife spotting, and silence. We recommend CafeFox Cruises out of Utoro and Ever Green Nature Cruises out of Rausu.

ESSENTIALS
Boat Tours CafeFox Cruises (🖷 0152/24–2680 ⊕ www.hitcolour.com/cafefox/ cruise). **Ever Green Nature Cruises** (🖷 0153/87–4002 ⊕ www.e-shiretoko.com).

Bus Contact Chuo Bus (Eagle Liner) (☎ 011/231–0500 [Japanese language only]).

Tour Information Shiretoko Nature Office (🖷 0152/22–5041 ⊕ www.sno.co.jp [Japanese language only]).

Shiretoko Naturalist's Association (Shinra) (☎ 0152/22–5522 ⊕ www.shinra. or.jp [Japanese language only]).

VISITOR INFORMATION
In Utoro, pick up information about the park, its sights, and access at **Utoro-Shiretoko Michi-no-eki**, a two-minute walk from the bus terminal on the waterfront. On the Rausu side, information can be found at the **Rausu Visitor Center.** Don't forget to check out the hourly 8-meter-high geyser in the woods out back.

Contacts Rausu Visitor Center (✉ Yunosawa, Rausu ☎ 0153/87–2828).

Utoro-Shiretoko Michi-no-eki (✉ 186 Banchi 8, Utoro Nishi ☎ 0152/22–5000 ☉ Daily 8–6).

WHAT TO SEE
☼ **Kamuiwakka Onsen** カムイワッカ温泉. *Kamui* means "spirit" or "god" in the Ainu language, and there's something wondrous, almost otherworldly, about this tumbling hot waterfall on the north shore under Io-zan (Mt. Io, as in Sulphur Mountain). Hot water rushes down the mountain through a series of multicolor falls and pools. Wear shoes that can get wet as you will scramble up over slippery rocks to a couple of pools higher upstream; park staff are there to help you up down and caution you not to go much farther than the roped-off third pool. Access in summer is by bus only: get tickets at the Nature Center (*see below*), not at Shiretoko Goko.

Fodor's Choice
★

Kamuiwakka Onsen is filled by a series of waterfalls.

Mt. Rausu 羅臼岳. Snow-covered from October to June and towering 5,448 feet along the spine of the peninsula, Mt. Rausu provides the real getaway from the crowds. The most accessible trailhead is 5 km (3 mi) east of Utoro behind the Hotel Chi-no-hate; if you are a fast hiker, you can walk for one hour, 20 minutes to a 1,920-foot rocky outcrop, then another two hours to the top. From there trails head west (two hours) along the peninsula to meet the Utoro-Rausu highway at Shiretoko Pass, or go over the ridge and down to Rausu (three hours). Check weather conditions before hiking, sign the trailhead books, and fix a bear bell to your backpack.

Aching muscles can be soaked in open-air hot springs waiting at the end of the hike: **Iwaobetsu Onsen** 岩尾別温泉, just below the Hotel Chi-no-hate car park, has four steaming rocky pools in a forest with no changing hut and a strong likelihood of sitting naked with strangers. Near the trailhead and campsite on the Rausu side, look for **Kuma-no-yu** 熊ノ湯, two boiling pools areas for men and women separated by some unfortunate concrete and rusty pipes, but fenced in for privacy.

Shiretoko Goko 知床五湖 (*Five Lakes*). Twenty minutes uphill from Utoro by car—and on every tour bus route in the region—a collection of small lakes hides in the forest on a precipice above the ocean. It takes just over an hour to walk round all five lakes on boardwalk paths. Most tour groups only reach the first two, and the others are sometimes closed due to the presence of bears. The lakes are pretty reflecting pools for the mountains, but crowds do disturb the idyll a bit, so plan on doing all five if you have the time.

Shiretoko National Park Nature Center. Park your car here and get bus tickets for Shiretoko Goko and Kamuiwakka. Crowds swarm the center for a big-screen film show, souvenir shopping, and a restaurant, but you might be more interested in the latest information about animal and plant sightings. The 2-km (1-mi) trail behind the center offers a peaceful trek to the Furepe Waterfall where the day visitors hardly venture. Bears have been spotted on this trail in the early morning. The Nature Center is 3 km (2 mi) from Utoro, at the junction of the roads leading to Iwaobetsu and the Shiretoko Pass/Rausu. ⊠ *531 Iwaobetsu, Shari-cho, Utoro* ☎ *0152/24–2114* ⊕ *www.shiretoko.or.jp* ☯ *Apr. 30–Oct. 20, daily 8–5:40; Oct. 21–Apr. 19, daily 9–4.*

WHERE TO EAT

$$ ✕ **Matsuda Suisan: Tabi no Eki** 松田水産・旅の駅. This bustling village eat-
JAPANESE ery serves steaming crab curry, golden sea urchin on rice, and anything else they can make out of this morning's catch. They often give free crab legs to suck on while you wait. It's by the entrance to the harbor next to the Shiretoko Grand Hotel; picture menus are available for easy ordering. ⊠ *151 Utoro Higashi, Shari-choo* ☎ *0152/24–2910* ▭ *No credit cards.*

WHERE TO STAY

Hotel reviews have been condensed for this book. Please go to Fodors. com for full reviews of each property.

¢–$ 🛏 **Iruka (Dolphin) Hotel** いるかホテル. Owned by a diver/wildlife pho-
HOTEL tographer, this hotel guesthouse sits waterside in Utoro. **Pros:** personal welcome; great food; nature-spotting advice. **Cons:** slow to respond to email reservation enquiries; small rooms. ⊠ *5 Utoro-Nishi, Shari-cho* ☎ *0152/24–2888* 🖷 *0152/24–2788* ⊕ *www.iruka-hotel.com* ⤶ *13 rooms* ⌂ *In-room: a/c. In-hotel: diving* ▭ *No credit cards* ❍▮ *Some meals.*

$$–$$$ 🛏 **Shiretoko Daiichi Hotel** 知床第一ホテル. Beneath vast sunset ceiling
HOTEL murals, replica antique furniture stands toe-deep in plush carpets decorated with regional flowers—as far as Japanese hotel stays go, it doesn't get much better than this. **Pros:** luxury; best place for sunset view; pig-out dining. **Cons:** Hokkaido's nature can oddly feel a bit distant; tour group frenzy in the lobby. ⊠ *306 Utoro Onsen, Shari-cho* ☎ *0152/24– 2334* 🖷 *0152/24–2261* ⊕ *www.shiretoko-1.com (Japanese language only)* ⤶ *238 rooms, 178 Japanese-style rooms, 41 Western-style rooms, 19 combination rooms* ⌂ *In-room: no a/c. In-hotel: 3 restaurants, bars, Internet terminal* ❍▮ *Some meals.*

AKAN NATIONAL PARK 阿寒国立公園

58 km (36 mi) southeast of Abashiri.

Volcanoes rise from primeval forests, and lakeside beaches bubble with hot springs in a national park that is unfairly outshone by its neighbors Daisetsu and Shiretoko. In Akan's northern forests, strange, cylindrical algae bob on the surface of Lake Akan. Ainu men pluck and blow eerie music from traditional instruments, while women dancers duck and weave in honor of the red-crested white cranes that fly in every winter, breeding on the wetland on the park's southern border. In summer, it's a hiker's heaven of trails and hot springs; in winter, the lakes freeze over and ice festivals spill out onto the frozen expanses.

GETTING HERE AND AROUND

There are about six buses (¥2,650; 90 minutes) a day to Akanko Lake from Kushiro Airport and station. You can also catch a bus from Akanko to Abashiri if you change buses in Bihoro. One bus a day also connects Akan to Soun-kyo.

Akan Bus Co. has escorted bus tours (Japanese-language only) from May to the end of October, departing from Kushiro Station for Akanko, the crane-watching areas, Lake Mashuko, and Kawayu Onsen. Since there are so few options to see this part of Japan, such tours may be unavoidable for those who don't want to drive themselves. On the Web site, look at the route map under "Sightseeing Bus." Reservations are required.

ESSENTIALS

Bus Contact Akan Bus Co. (☎ 0154/37–2221 ⊕ www.akanbus.co.jp [Japanese language only]).

WHAT TO SEE

Akan Kohan 阿寒湖畔. The small town on the lakeshore is a major stop on regional bus tours, with giant hotels blocking off the lake from the main road running through the town. Kitschy souvenir shops sell endless rows of carved Ainu-style bears, and bottles containing *marimo* (algae) that may never grow. At the northern end of the town is the Ainu village, one cobbled street lined by shops and restaurants, with the Culture Performance Center and a small museum at the top. From May to October there are excellent 30-minute, traditional dance performances five times a day, and the 9 pm show features *yukara* (chanted epic poems). Performances cost ¥1,100.

★ **Akanko** 阿寒湖 *(Lake Akan)*. Chugging tour boats with noisy Japanese commentaries and even speedboats disturb the waters below smoking volcanoes Me-Akan and O-Akan (Mr. and Mrs. Akan). But out on Churui Island, silence is green among Akanko's strangest inhabitants, *marimo,* as they nestle peacefully in display tanks. Marimo are spherical colonies of green algae that may be as small as a Ping-Pong ball or as large as a soccer ball (the latter taking up to 500 years to form). Rare life forms, marimo can only be found in Lake Yamanaka, near Fuji-san, and in a few lakes in North America, Siberia, and Switzerland. These strange algae act much like submarines, bobbing to the lake surface when bright sunshine increases their photosynthesis, then diving below during inclement weather when light levels drop.

SMELT FISHING

Lake Akan in winter is dotted with ice holes. Fishermen crouch in subzero temperatures to hook *wakasagi* (pond smelt) from the depths. Visitors can slide across the lake and try their luck, fortified with *amasaké,* a delicious—and alcoholic—drink made from sweetened brown rice. The successful can head back to the shore where stall holders are on hand to mince the catch for a raw meal or fry or grill it. Grilled *wakasagi* often appears on the winter menus of Hokkaido izakaya. Wakasagi fishing costs ¥800 for adults and ¥400 for kids. The gear includes a chair and your own personal ice hole.

14

Smelt-fishing through holes chopped in the ice is a popular wintertime activity at Lake Akan.

Between May and October you can enjoy the lake from a canoe with the help of the **Akan Nature Center,** which offers two- or eight-person Canadian canoes for a 45-minute beginner course (¥2,100), a 90-minute adventure course (¥5,300), or for the strong-of-arm the 2½-hour Yaitai Island course (¥8,400). Reserve one day in advance by calling, or emailing in simple English. The center is in Akan Kohan, near the Ainu village and next to Spa Inn Yamaguchi on the north end of the town street. ☎ *0154/67–2081 for canoe tour reservations* ⊕ *www.akan.co.jp.*

★ **Kushiro Shitsugen** 釧路湿原 *(Kushiro Marsh).* Graceful red-crested cranes preen and breed in protected Kushiro Marsh, which constitutes 60% of Japan's remaining marshlands. These rare cranes, whose feathers were thought to bring good luck, were ruthlessly hunted at the beginning of the 20th century and were even believed extinct until a handful of survivors were discovered in 1924. They have slowly regenerated and now number about 650. The crane—long-legged, long-billed, with a white body trimmed in black and a scarlet cap on its head—is a symbol of long life and happiness. Legends hold that the birds live 1,000 years, and indeed, in captivity some have made it to a rather impressive 80 years of age. They pair for life, making them the symbol of an ideal couple and are frequently alluded to in Japanese wedding speeches.

November to March is the best season for wild-crane watching, because this is when the birds fly in from Russia, China, and Korea and gather at feeding stations such as Tsurumidai, off Route 53. In summer, nesting birds retreat deep into the swamps to raise their chicks, and can only be spotted with binoculars.

Canoe paddlers on the Kushiro River have a chance to see cranes and other birds: canoe rental companies are at Lake Toro, off Route 391, and by the Norroko-go, a slow sightseeing train from Kushiro (July and August only). The marshland comprises 71 square mi and viewing areas with wooden walkways and observation towers are located off Routes 53 and 359.

The **Akan Rando Tanchono Sato** あかんランド丹頂の里 (*Tancho no Sato Crane Home*) is about one hour south of Lake Akan, near the Tancho-zuru bus stop on the Akan-kohan–Kushiro bus route. Here you can watch a feeding and visit the center's units for egg hatching, chick rearing, and bird medical care. ✉ *23–40 Akan-cho* ☎ *0154/66–4011.*

WHERE TO STAY

Hotel reviews have been condensed for this book. Please go to Fodors. com for full reviews of each property.

¢–$ 🏯 **Spa Inn Yamaguchi** 民宿山口. The mynah bird, Taro, may screech a
MINSHUKU   welcome as you enter this small home. **Pros:** cheap; friendly. **Cons:** well-worn rooms; thin walls; old, shared baths; no lake views. ✉ *5–3–2 Akan-ko Onsen, Akan-cho* ☎ *0154/67–2555* ⊕ *www.tabi-hokkaido. co.jp/~yamaguchi* ◻ *10 Japanese-style rooms without bath* ⚲ *In-room: no phone, a/c. In-hotel: restaurant* ▭ *No credit cards* ⦿ *Some meals.*

NORTHERN HOKKAIDO 道北

Travelers with more time might trek north to Soya-misaki, Japan's northernmost cape, for the stark beauty of the Rebun and Rishiri islands. Wakkanai, the regional center, is a rather unpleasant fishing town 396 km (246 mi) north of Sapporo. Use it as the jumping-off point to the islands and to the coastal grasslands to the south. The best season is late May to early September.

THE NORTHERN CAPE AND ISLANDS

Wakkamai is 396 km (246 mi) north of Sapporo.

Japan's northernmost point is windy and empty. In the short summer season, tiny alpine flowers bloom in coastal grasslands and on rocky outcrops overlooking the sea. In winter, little happens as people batten down the hatches. Come here only when you've already seen Daisetsu and Shiretoko. Visitors journey here for the hiking, flowers, bragging rights of having seen Japan's northernmost extremity, and the solitude found in such edge-of-the-world places.

GETTING HERE AND AROUND

From June through August, Air Nippon flies from Shin-Chitose Airport directly to Rishiri Airport (45 minutes) on Rishiri. There are also buses year-round from Sapporo to Wakkanai (six hours), and then ferry connections to both Rishiri and Rebun islands.

Heart Land Ferry has boats that make the daily two-hour crossing to Rebuno and the 100-minute crossing to Rishirio. In summer there are four or five daily ferries, two daily in winter. Fares to Rebun are ¥4,080 for first class and ¥2,400 second class. Fares to Rishiri are ¥3,660 and ¥2,180 respectively. A ferry between the two islands costs ¥880.

ESSENTIALS

Ferry Information Heart Land Ferry (☎ 0162/23–3780).

WHAT TO SEE

Rebun-to 礼文島 *(Rebun Island)*. This is the older of two Sea of Japan islands created by an upward thrust of Earth's crust. Along the east coast there are numerous villages anchoring fleets of uni boats just off-shore; prickly sea urchins are spotted through bottomless boxes held over the side of the boat and then raked in.

The coast has an eight-hour hiking trail, and cliffs stave off the surging waters of the Nihon-kai. Inland, more than 300 species of wild alpine flowers blanket the mountain meadows—by mid-June in such profusion that each step seems to crush a dozen of the delicate blossoms; look for the white-pointed *usuyo-kiso* (roughly meaning "dusting of snow"), found only on Rebun.

★ **Rishiri-to** 利尻島 *(Rishiri Island)*. The island is the result of a submarine volcano whose cone now rises 5,640 feet out of the water. The scenery is wilder than on Rebuno, and though it's a larger island, Rishirio has fewer inhabitants. The rugged terrain makes it hard to support life and figures for hardier climbing. The intermediate **Kutsugata Course** (four hours to the top for fit hikers; plan on six) on the west side of the island takes you past patches of wildflowers—including the buttercup-like *botan kimbai* and the vibrant purple *hakusan chidori*—and numerous bird species. Cycling around the island is also an option (four hours if not too windy).

Soya-misaki 宗谷岬 *(Cape Soya)*. This is the end of Japan. Behind lies a world of sushi, cherry blossoms, and bowing—ahead across frigid waters is Russia's Sakhalin Island (sometimes visible) and who knows what. This lonely but significant spot is the site of several monuments marking the end of Japan's territory, as well as a memorial to a Korean airliner downed by the Soviet military north of here in 1982. A public bus makes the hour-long run between Wakkanai and Cape Soya six times a day. It's worth going to if you've come up this far.

WHERE TO STAY

Hotel reviews have been condensed for this book. Please go to Fodors. com for full reviews of each property.

$–$$ **Hera-san-no Ie** へらさんの家. This is a good base for Rishiri hikes.
INN **Pros:** friendly welcome; up-to-date hiking advice. **Cons:** not much to do but eat dinner and sleep. ✉ *Oshitomari, Rishiri-Fuji-cho* ☎ *0163/82–2361* ⊕ *www.rishiri-yume.com* ⌨ *8 Japanese-style rooms without bath, 3 Western-style rooms* ⌂ *In-room: no a/c. In-hotel: restaurant* ⊟ *No credit cards* ❦ *Some meals.*

¢ **Pension Unii** ペンションうーにー. This sky-blue building is at the top
INN of the cliffs above Rebun's ferry terminal. **Pros:** good views; sea urchin (provided you like it) at every meal. **Cons:** no English spoken; steep climb up from the harbor. ✉ *Kafuka-Irifune, Rebun-cho* ☎ *0163/86–1541* ⊕ *www.p-uni.burari.biz (Japanese language only)* ⌨ *9 Western-style rooms, 1 Japanese-style room* ⌂ *In-room: no a/c. In-hotel: restaurant* ⊟ *No credit cards* ❦ *Some meals.*

UNDERSTANDING JAPAN

Books and Movies

Vocabulary and Menu Guide

BOOKS AND MOVIES

BOOKS

Fiction and Poetry. The great classic of Japanese fiction is the *Tale of Genji*, written by Lady Murasaki Shikibu of the Heian court around the year 1000 and regarded by many as the world's first novel. From the same period is *The Pillow Book of Sei Shonagon*, the stylish and stylized diary of life at court. Required background reading for both is historian Ivan Morris's outstanding *The World of the Shining Prince*.

For the Edo period, Howard Hibbett's *Floating World in Japanese Fiction* gives an excellent selection with commentaries. The racy prose of late-17th-century Ihara Saikaku is well translated in *Five Women Who Loved Love*.

The key figures in early modern Japanese fiction are Tanizaki Junchiro (*The Makioka Sisters* and *Some Prefer Nettles),* Nobel Prize winner Kawabata Yasunari (*Snow Country, The Sound of the Mountain, A Thousand Cranes*), and Soseki Natsume (*Botchan, I Am a Cat*). For the postwar period, read Mishima Yukio (*The Sea of Fertility, The Temple of the Golden Pavilion*), Abe Kobo (*Woman in the Dunes*), and Endo Shusaku (*The Samurai*).

Among the novelists at work in Japan today is Murakami Hiroki, whose *Wild Sheep Chase* and numerous short stories are often bizarre and humorous blends of magical realism and science fiction. Yoshimoto Banana's *Kitchen* and other novels are escapist fun. Nobel Prize winner Oe Kenzaburo's *A Personal Matter* is a compelling novelistic coming-to-terms with his relationship with his handicapped son.

Haiku, the 5-7-5 syllable form that the monk Matsuo Basho honed in the 17th century, especially in his *Narrow Road to the Deep North*, is perhaps the best known genre of Japanese poetry; two fine small collections of poems by Basho and other haiku masters are the beautifully illustrated *Monkey's Raincoat* and *A Net of Fireflies*. Three volumes of translations by Kenneth Rexroth, including *One Hundred Poems from the Japanese* and *Women Poets of Japan,* cover other genres of poetry and numerous authors from the last 1,000 years.

Travel Narratives. Two travel narratives stand out as superb introductions to Japanese history, culture, and people: Donald Richie's *The Inland Sea* and Leila Philip's eloquent *Road Through Miyama*.

History and Society. Two excellent surveys are Richard Storry's *A History of Modern Japan* and George Sansom's *Japan: A Short Cultural History*. Oliver Statler's *Japanese Inn* takes one family enterprise to trace 400 years of social change.

Yamamoto Tsunetomo's *Hagakure* is an 18th-century guide to the Way of the Samurai. Few books get closer to the realities of everyday life in early-modern rural Japan than Dr. Saga Junichi's 1970s collection of interviews, *Memories of Silk and Straw*.

Fine studies of the Japanese mind are to be found in Doi Takeo's *The Anatomy of Dependence*, and Nakane Chie's *Japanese Society*. Karel van Wolferen's *The Enigma of Japanese Power* is an enlightening book on the Japanese sociopolitical system. Alex Kerr's *Lost Japan,* the first work by a foreigner to win the Shincho Gakugei literature prize, examines the directions of Japanese society past and present.

Religion. The classic gateways to this subject are Suzuki Daisetsu's seminal *Introduction to Zen Buddhism* and *Zen and Japanese Culture*. Stuart D. Picken has written books on both major Japanese religions: *Shinto: Japan's Spiritual Roots* and *Buddhism: Japan's Cultural Identity*.

Art, Architecture, and Crafts. The *Japan Arts Library* series has separate volumes on castles, teahouses, screen painting, and wood-block prints. Nishi Kazuo and Hozumi Kazuo's *What Is Japanese*

Architecture? treats the subject historically and has examples of buildings you will actually see on your travels.

Crafts and individual artisans are well-illustrated in the *Japan Crafts Sourcebook;* in *Inside Japanese Ceramics;* in *Shoji Hamada,* on one of Japan's most revered potters; and in *The Living Traditions of Old Kyoto.*

MOVIES

Western viewers have typically encountered Japanese cinema in the work of directors Mizoguchi Kenji, Ozu Yasujiro, and Kurosawa Akira. Three of Mizoguchi's finest films explore the role of women in feudal Japan: *The Life of Oharu* (1952), *Ugetsu* (1953), and *Sansho the Bailiff* (1954). Ozu's films—among them *Late Spring* (1949), *Early Summer* (1951), and *Tokyo Story* (1953)—explore traditional Japanese values in the everyday lives and relationships of middle-class families. Kurosawa's *Rashomon* (1950), a 12th-century murder story told by four different narrators, inspired a worldwide interest in Japanese cinema. Among his other classic period films are *Seven Samurai* (1954), *Yojimbo* (1961), *Red Beard* (1965), and *Kagemusha* (1980).

The next wave of postwar filmmakers include Ichikawa Kon, who directed two powerful antiwar movies, *The Burmese Harp* (1956) and *Fires on the Plain* (1959); Teshigahara Hiroshi, best known for his allegorical *Woman in the Dunes* (1964), based on a novel by Abe Kobo; and Imamura Shohei, who made *The Ballad of Narayama* (1983), about life and death in an Edo-period mountain village, and *Black Rain* (1989), which deals with the atomic bombing of Hiroshima.

More recent Japanese filmmakers winning acclaim abroad are Itami Juzo and Suo Masayuki. Itami's work includes *Tampopo* (1986), a highly original comedy about food; and *Minbo no onna* (1992), which dissects the world of Japanese gangsters. Suo's *Shall We Dance?* (1997) is a bittersweet comedy about a married businessman who escapes his daily routine by taking ballroom dance lessons.

Akin to the samurai films are Japanese gangster flicks. Though they date back to such Kurosawa classics as *Drunken Angel* (1948) and *Stray Dog* (1949), an edgy gangster genre emerged in the 1990s led by Beat Takeshi Kitano. His films *Fireworks* (1997) and *Zatoichi* (2003) have won awards at the Venice Film Festival. There are many Japanese gangster films, including a whole exploitative subset that mixes extreme violence with basically soft-core porn.

Those interested in Japanese anime should start with the Academy Award–winning picture *Spirited Away* (2002) by Hayao Miyazaki. Other modern anime pioneers include Tezuka Osamu, Mamoru Oshii, and Katsuhiro Otomo.

Recently, Japanese horror has also enjoyed international popularity. Focusing more on anticipation and psychological horror than blood-spurting special effects—though some can be quite gruesome, such as the hair-raising *Audition* (1999), directed by cult favorite Takashi Miike—Japanese horror tends to hinge on an eerie feeling of unseen threat and inescapable doom; they typically involve ghosts (by convention, women in white dresses and long hair) or poltergeists, seeking revenge for some wrong revealed as the movie progresses. The horror hits, *Ringu* (Nakata Hideo, 1998) and *Ju-on: The Grudge* (Shimizu Takashi, 2003) are representative of this genre; both have been remade by American directors for wider audiences. —Updated by Jared Lubarsky.

ABOUT JAPANESE

To read and write Japanese you need a command of some 2,000 *kanji* (ideogram characters derived from Chinese) and two syllablic alphabets, called *hiragana* and *katakana*. The pronunciation of all the *kanji* and their various inflections can be rendered in either alphabet, although *katakana* is normally used for the spelling of foreign loan-words.

The alphabets are comprised of four types of syllables: the single vowels *a, i, u, e,* and *o* (pronounced ah, ee, ooh, eh, and oh); vowel-consonant pairs like *ka, ni, hu,* or *ro*; the single consonant *n* (which punctuates, for example, the upbeats of the word for bullet train, *Shinkansen: shee-n-ka-n-se-n*); and compounds like *kya, chu,* and *ryo*—also each one syllable. Thus Tōkyō, the capital city, has only two syllables—*tō* and *kyō*—not three. Likewise pronounce Kyōto *kyō-to*, not *kee-oh-to*. The Japanese *r* is rolled so that it sounds like a bounced *d*. There is no *l*-sound in the language, and the Japanese have great difficulty in distinguishing *l* from *r*, whether spoken or written.

No diphthongs. Paired vowels in Japanese words are not slurred together, as in the English *coin, brain,* or *stein.* The Japanese separate them, as in *mae* (*ma*-eh), which means in front of; *kōen* (ko-en); and *tokei* (to-*keh*-ee), which means clock or watch.

Macrons. Many Japanese words, when rendered in *romaji* (Roman letters) require a macron, or bar, over certain vowels to indicate whether it is pronounced long or short. The macrons in Tōkyō, for example, direct you to double the length of the *o*, as if you're saying it twice: to-o-*kyo*-o. Likewise, when you see double consonants, as in the city name Nikkō, double up on the *k*s—as you would with "bookkeeper"—and elongate the *o*.

Emphasis. Some books state that the Japanese emphasize all syllables in their words equally. This is not true. Take the words *sayōnara* and *Hiroshima.* Americans are likely to stress the downbeats: sa-yo-*na*-ra

and *hi*-ro-*shi*-ma. The Japanese actually emphasize the second beat in each case: sa-*yō*-na-ra (note the macron) and hi-ro-shi-ma. Metaphorically speaking, the Japanese don't so much stress syllables as pause over them or race past them: Emphasis is more a question of speed than weight. In the vocabulary below, we indicate emphasis by italicizing the syllable that you should stress.

Note also the unstressed pronunciations. The word *desu* roughly means "is." It looks like it has two syllables, but the Japanese race past the final *u* and just say "dess." Likewise, some verbs end in -*masu*, which is pronounced "mahss." Similarly, the character *shi* is often quickly pronounced "sh," as in the phrase meaning "pleased to meet you:" ha-ji-me-*mash(i)*-te.

Hyphens. Throughout this book we have hyphenated certain words to help you recognize meaningful patterns and vocabulary elements. This isn't conventional; it is practical. Seeing *Eki-mae-dōri* (literally "Station Front Avenue") this way instead of run together in a single word, for example, makes it easier to register the terms for "station" and "avenue" for use elsewhere. You'll also run across a number of sight names that end in -*jingu* or -*jinja* or –*taisha*, all of which mean "Shinto shrine."

Structure. Japanese sentences are structured back-to-front, ie. subject-object-verb instead of subject-verb-object as in English. "I am going to Tokyo" would translate literally in Japanese as "Tokyo to I'm going."

Note: placing an "o" before words like *tera* (*otera*) and *shiro* (*oshiro*) makes the word honorific. The meaning is clear enough without it, but omitting the polite form would be exceedingly un-Japanese.
—Updated by Jared Lubarsky.

ESSENTIAL PHRASES

BASICS

Yes/No	*ha*-i/*ii*-e	はい / いいえ
Please	o-ne-*gai* shi-masu	お願いします
Thank you (very much)	(*dō*-mo) a-*ri*-ga-tō go-*zai*-ma su	（どうも）ありがとうございます
You're welcome	*dō* i-ta-shi-ma-shi-te	どういたしまして
Excuse me	su-mi-ma-*sen*	すみません
Sorry	*go*-men na-*sai*	ごめんなさい
Good morning	o-*ha*-yō *go*-zai-ma-su	おはようございます
Good day/afternoon	kon-*ni*-chi-wa	こんにちは
Good evening	kom-*ban*-wa	こんばんは
Good night	o-*ya*-su-mi na-*sai*	おやすみなさい
Good-bye	sa-*yō*-na-ra	さようなら
Mr./Mrs./Miss	-san	〜さん
Pleased to meet you	*ha*-ji-me-*mashi*-te	はじめまして
How do you do?	*dō*-zo yo-*ro*-shi-ku	どうぞよろしく

NUMBERS

The first reading is used for reading numbers, as in telephone numbers, and the second is often used for counting things.

1	*i*-chi / hi-*to*-tsu	一 / 一つ	10	jū / tō	十
2	ni / fu-*ta*-tsu	二 / 二つ	11	*jū*-i-chi	十一
3	san / *mit*-tsu	三 / 三つ	12	*jū*-ni	十二
4	yon (shi) / *yot*-tsu	四 / 四つ	13	*jū*-san	十三
5	go / i-*tsu*-tsu	五 / 五つ	14	*jū*-yon	十四
6	*ro*-ku / *mut*-tsu	六 / 六つ	15	*jū*-go	十五
7	*na*-na / *na*-na-tsu	七 / 七つ	16	*jū*-ro-ku	十六
8	*ha*-chi / *yat*-tsu	八 / 八つ	17	*jū*-shi-chi	十七
9	kyū / *ko*-ko-no-*tsu*	九 / 九つ	18	*jū*-ha-chi	十八

19	jū-kyū	十九	70	na-na-jū	七十
20	ni-jū	二十	80	ha-chi-jū	八十
21	ni-jū-i-chi	二十一	90	kyū-jū	九十
30	san-jū	三十	100	hya-ku	百
40	yon-jū	四十	1000	sen	千
50	go-jū	五十	10,000	i-chi-man	一万
60	ro-ku-jū	六十	100,000	jū- man	十万

DAYS OF THE WEEK

Sunday	ni-chi yō-bi	日曜日
Monday	ge-tsu yō-bi	月曜日
Tuesday	ka yō-bi	火曜日
Wednesday	su-i yō-bi	水曜日
Thursday	mo-ku yō-bi	木曜日
Friday	kin yō-bi	金曜日
Saturday	dō yō-bi	土曜日
Weekday	hei-ji-tsu	平日
Weekend	shū-ma-tsu	週末

MONTHS

January	i-chi ga-tsu	一月
February	ni ga-tsu	二月
March	san ga-tsu	三月
April	shi ga-tsu	四月
May	go ga-tsu	五月
June	ro-ku ga-tsu	六月
July	shi-chi ga-tsu	七月
August	ha-chi ga-tsu	八月
September	ku ga-su	九月
October	jū ga-tsu	十月
November	jū-i-chi ga-tsu	十一月
December	jū-ni ga-tsu	十二月

USEFUL EXPRESSIONS, QUESTIONS, AND ANSWERS

Do you speak English?	*ei*-go ga wa-*ka*-ri-ma-su *ka*	英語がわかりますか。
I don't speak Japanese.	*ni*-hon-go ga wa-*ka*-ri-ma-*sen*	日本語がわかりません。
I don't understand.	wa-*ka*-ri-ma-*sen*	わかりません。
I understand.	wa-*ka*-ri-ma-shi-*ta*	わかりました。
I don't know.	*shi*-ri-ma-*sen*	知りません。
I'm American (British).	wa-*ta*-shi wa a-*me*-ri-ka (i-*gi*-ri-su) jin *desu*	私はアメリカ (イギリス) 人です。
What's your name?	o-*na*-ma-e wa *nan* desu *ka*	お名前はなんですか。
My name is . . .	. . . to *mo*-shi-*ma*-su	～と申します。
What time is it?	i-ma *nan*-ji desu *ka*	今何時ですか。
How?	*dō* yat-te	どうやって。
When?	*i*-tsu	いつ。
Yesterday/today/tomorrow	ki-*nō*/kyō/*ashi*-ta	昨日 / 今日 / 明日
This morning	*ke*-sa	けさ
This afternoon	*kyō* no *go*-go	今日の午後
Tonight	*kom*-ban	今晩
Excuse me, what?	su-*mi*-ma-*sen*, *nan* desu *ka*	すみません、何ですか。
What is this/that?	*ko*-re/*so*-re wa *nan* desu *ka*	これ / それは何ですか。
Why?	*na*-ze desu *ka*	なぜですか。
Who?	*da*-re desu *ka*	だれですか。
I am lost.	*mi*-chi ni ma-yo-i-*mashi*-ta	道に迷いました。
Where is [place]	[place] wa *do*-ko desu *ka*	はどこですか
. . . train station?	e-ki	駅
. . . subway station?	chi-*ka*-te-tsu-no eki	地下鉄の駅
. . . bus stop?	*ba*-su *no*-ri-*ba*	バス乗り場
. . . taxi stand?	*ta*-ku-shi-i *no*-ri-*ba*	タクシー乗り場
. . . airport?	kū-kō	空港
. . . post office?	*yū*-bin-*kyo*-ku	郵便局

. . . bank?	*gin*-kō	銀行
. . . the [name] hotel?	[name] ho-*te*-ru	ホテル
. . . elevator?	e-re-bē-tā	エレベーター
Where are the restrooms?	*to*-i-re wa *do*-ko desu *ka*	トイレはどこですか。
Here/there/over there	*ko*-ko/*so*-ko/*a*-so-ko	ここ / そこ / あそこ
Left/right	hi-*da*-ri/*mi*-gi	左 / 右
Straight ahead	mas-*su*-gu	まっすぐ
Is it near (far)?	chi-*ka*-i (*tō*-i) desu *ka*	近い（遠い）ですか。
Are there any rooms?	*he*-ya *ga* a-ri-masu *ka*	部屋がありますか。
I'd like [item]	[item] ga ho-*shi*-i no desu ga	がほしいのですが。
. . . newspaper	*shim*-bun	新聞
. . . stamp	*kit*-te	切手
. . . key	*ka*-gi	鍵
I'd like to buy [item]	[item] o kai-*ta*-i no desu ga	を買いたいのですが。
. . . a ticket to [destination]	[destination] *ma*-de no *kip*-pu	までの切符
Map	*chi*-zu	地図
How much is it?	i-*ku*-ra desu *ka*	いくらですか。
It's expensive (cheap).	ta-*ka*-i (ya-*su*-i) de su *ne*	高い（安い）ですね。
A little (a lot)	su-*ko*-shi (*ta*-ku-san)	少し（たくさん）
More/less	*mot*-to o-ku/ su-ku-na-ku	もっと多く / 少なく
Enough/too much	*jū*-bun/ō-su-*gi*-ru	十分 / 多すぎる
I'd like to exchange	*ryō*-ga e shi-*te* i-*ta*-da-ke-masu *ka*	両替していただけ ますか。
. . . dollars to yen	*do*-ru o *en* ni	ドルを円に
. . . pounds to yen	*pon*-do o *en* ni	ポンドを円に
How do you say. in Japanese?	ni-*hon*-go de wa [word] wa *dō* i-i-masu *ka*	日本語で.はどう言い ますか。
I am ill/sick.	wa-*ta*-shi wa *byō*-ki desu	私は病気です。

Please call a doctor/an ambulance.	*i*-sha/kyū-kyū-sha o *yon*-de ku-da-*sa*-i	医者を呼んでください。
Please call the police.	*ke*-i-sa-tsu o *yon*-de ku-da-*sa*-i	警察を呼んでください。
Help!	*ta*-su-*ke*-te	助けて！

USEFUL WORDS

airport	kūkō	空港
bay	wan	湾
beach	-hama	浜
behind	ushiro	後ろ
bridge	hashi or -bashi	橋
Bullet train, literally "new trunk line"	Shinkansen	新幹線
castle	shiro or -jō	城
cherry blossoms	sakura	桜
city or municipality	-shi	市
department store	depāto (deh-pah-to)	デパート
district	-gun	郡
east	higashi	東
exit	deguchi or -guchi	出口
festival	matsuri	祭
foreigner	gaijin (more politely: gai-koku-jin)	外人
garden	niwa	庭
gate	mon or torii	門 / 鳥居
hill	oka	丘
hot-spring spa	onsen	温泉
in front of	mae	前
island	shima or -jima/-tō	島
Japanese words rendered in roman letters	rōmaji	ローマ字

lake	mizumi or -ko	湖
main road	kaidō or kōdō	街道 / 公道
morning market	asa-ichi	朝市
mountain	yama or –san	山
museum	bijutsukan for art; hakubut-sukan for natural history, etc.	博物館
north	kita	北
park	kōen	公園
peninsula	-hantō	半島
plateau	kōgen	高原
pond	ike or -ike	池
prefecture	-ken/-fu	県 / 府
pub	izakaya	居酒屋
river	kawa or -gawa	川 / 河
sea	umi or -nada	海
section or ward	-ku	区
shop	mise or -ya	店 / 屋
shrine	jinja or -gu	神社 / 宮
south	minami	南
street	michi or -dō	道
subway	chikatetsu	地下鉄
temple	tera or -ji/-in	寺 / 院
town	machi	町
train	densha	電車
train station	eki	駅
valley	tani	谷
west	nishi	西

MENU GUIDE

RESTAURANTS

BASICS AND USEFUL EXPRESSIONS

a bottle of	*ip*-pon	一本
a glass/cup of	*ip*-pai	一杯
ashtray	*ha*-i-*za*-ra	灰皿
bill/check	kan-*jō*	勘定
bread	pan	パン
breakfast	*chō*-sho-ku	朝食
butter	ba-*tā*	バター
cheers!	kam-*pai*	乾杯!
chopsticks	*ha*-shi	箸
cocktail	*ka*-ku-*te*-ru	カクテル
Does that include dinner?	*Yū*-sho-ku *ga* tsu-ki- ma-su-ka	夕食が付きますか。
fork	*fō*-ku	フォーク
I am diabetic.	wa-ta-*shi* wa tō-*nyō*-byō de su	私は糖尿病です。
I am dieting.	*da*-i-et-to *chū* desu	ダイエット中です。
I am a vegetarian.	*saisho*-ku shu-*gi*-sha/ beji-*tari*-an de-su	菜食主義者 / ベジタリアンです。
I cannot eat [item]	[item] wa *ta*-be-ra- re-ma-*sen*	は食べられません。
I'd like to order.	*chū*-mon o shi-*tai* desu	注文をしたいです。
I'd like [item]	[item] o o-ne-*gai*-shi-ma su	をお願いします。
I'm hungry.	o-na-ka ga *su*-i-te i-*ma su*	お腹が空いています。
I'm thirsty.	*no*-do ga ka-*wa*-i-te i-*ma su*	喉が渇いています。
It's tasty (not good)	o-i-shi-i (ma-*zu*-i) desu	おいしい(まずい)です。
knife	*na*-i-fu	ナイフ
lunch	*chū*-sho-ku	昼食
menu	me-nyū	メニュー

napkin	*na*-pu-*kin*	ナプキン
pepper	ko-*shō*	こしょう
plate	*sa*-ra	皿
Please give me [item]	[item] o ku-da-*sa*-i	をください。
salt	*shi*-o	塩
set menu	*te*-i-sho-ku	定食
spoon	su-*pūn*	スプーン
sugar	sa-tō	砂糖
wine list	*wa*-i-n *ri*-su-to	ワインリスト
What do you recommend?	o-su-su-me *ryō*-ri wa *nan* desu *ka*	おすすめ料理は何ですか。

MEAT DISHES

gyōza	minced pork spiced with ginger and garlic in a Chinese wrapper and fried or steamed	ギョウザ
hayashi raisu	beef flavored with tomato and brown sauce with onions and peas over rice	ハヤシライス
kara-age	deep-fried chicken	から揚げ
karē-raisu	curried rice: thick curry gravy typically containing beef over white rice	カレーライス
katsu-karē	curried rice with tonkatsu	カツカレー
niku-jaga	beef and potatoes stewed together with soy sauce	肉じゃが
okonomi-yaki	a Japanese pancake made from a batter of flour, egg, cabbage, and meat or sea-food, griddle-cooked and sprinkled with green onions and a Worcestershire-soy-based sauce	お好み焼き

oyako-domburi (oyako-don)	literally, "mother and child bowl": cooked chicken and egg in broth over rice	親子どんぶり（親子丼）
rōru kyabetsu	rolled cabbage; beef or pork rolled in cabbage and cooked	ロールキャベツ
shabu-shabu	thin slices of beef swirled for an instant in boiling water flavored with soup stock and then dipped into a thin sauce	しゃぶしゃぶ
shōga-yaki	pork cooked with ginger	しょうが焼き
shūmai	shrimp or pork wrapped in a light dough and steamed (originally Chinese)	シュウマイ
subuta	sweet-and-sour pork, originally a Chinese dish	酢豚
sukiyaki	one-pot meal of thinly sliced beef, green onions, mushrooms, thin noodles, and tofu simmered in a mixture of soy sauce, mirin, and a little sugar	すき焼き
sutēki	steak	ステーキ
tanin-domburi (tannin-don)	literally, "strangers in a bowl": similar to oyako-domburi, but with beef instead of chicken	他人どんぶり（他人丼）
tonkatsu	breaded deep-fried pork cutlets	トンカツ
yaki-niku	thin slices of beef marinated then barbecued over an open fire at the table.	焼き肉

| yaki-tori | bits of chicken on skewers with green onions, marinated in sweet soy sauce and grilled | 焼き鳥 |

SEAFOOD DISHES

age-zakana	deep-fried fish	揚げ魚
aji	horse mackerel	あじ
asari no sakamushi	clams steamed with rice wine	あさりの酒蒸し
buri	yellowtail	ぶり
dojo no yanagawa-nabe	loach cooked with burdock root and egg in an earthen dish	どじょうの柳川鍋
ebi furai	deep-fried breaded prawns	海老フライ
ika	squid	イカ
iwashi	sardines	いわし
karei furai	deep-fried breaded flounder	かれいフライ
katsuo no tataki	bonito lightly braised, eaten with chopped ginger and scallions and thin soy sauce	かつおのたたき
maguro	tuna	まぐろ
nizakana	soy-simmered fish	煮魚
saba no miso-ni	mackerel stewed with soybean paste	さばの味噌煮
samma	saury pike	さんま
sashimi	fresh raw fish served sliced thin on a bed of white radish with a saucer of soy sauce and horseradish	刺身
sawara	Spanish mackerel	さわら
shake / sāmon	salmon	しゃけ / サーモン
shimesaba	mackerel marinated in vinegar	しめさば

shio-yaki	fish sprinkled with salt and broiled until crisp	塩焼き
tako	octopus	たこ
ten-jū	deep-fried prawns served over rice with sauce	天重
teri-yaki	fish basted in soy sauce and broiled	照り焼き
una-jū	eel marinated in a slightly sweet soy sauce, charcoal-broiled and served over rice	うな重
yaki-zakana	broiled fish	焼き魚

SUSHI

aji	horse mackerel	あじ
ama-ebi	sweet shrimp	甘えび
anago	conger eel	あなご
aoyagi	round clam	あおやぎ
chirashi zushi	a variety of seafood arranged on the top of a bowl of rice	ちらし寿司
ebi	shrimp	えび
futo-maki	big roll with egg and pickled vegetables	太巻き
hamachi	yellowtail	はまち
hirame	flounder	ひらめ
hotate-gai	scallop	ほたて貝
ika	squid	いか
ikura	salmon roe	いくら
kani	crab	かに
kappa-maki	cucumber roll	かっぱ巻き
kariforunia-maki	California roll, with crabmeat and avocado (originally American)	カリフォルニア巻き
kazunoko	herring roe	数の子

kohada	shad	こはだ
maguro	tuna	まぐろ
maki zushi	raw fish, vegetables, or other ingredients rolled in sushi rice and wrapped in dried seaweed	巻き寿司
miru-gai	giant clam	みる貝
nigiri zushi	rice shaped by hand into bite-sized cakes and topped with raw or cooked fish or other ingredients	にぎり寿司
saba	mackerel	さば
shake / sāmon	salmon	しゃけ / サーモン
shinko-maki	a type of pickle rolled in rice and wrapped in seaweed	新香巻き
tai	red snapper	たい
tako	octopus	たこ
tamago	egg	玉子
tekka-maki	small bits of tuna rolled in rice and wrapped in seaweed	鉄火巻き
toro	fatty tuna	とろ
uni	sea urchin	うに

VEGETABLE DISHES

aemono	vegetables dressed with sauces	和えもの
daigaku imo	fried yams in a sweet syrup	大学いも
gobō	burdock root	ごぼう
hōrenso	spinach	ほうれん草
kabocha	pumpkin	かぼちゃ
kimpira gobō	carrots and burdock root, fried with soy sauce	きんぴらごぼう

kyūri	cucumber	きゅうり
negi	green onions	ねぎ
nimono	vegetables simmered in a soy- and sake-based sauce	煮物
oden	street food of various types of fish cakes, vegetables, and boiled eggs simmered in a soy fish stock	おでん
o-hitashi	boiled vegetables with soy sauce and dried shaved bonito or sesame seeds	おひたし
renkon	lotus root	れんこん
satoimo	taro root	さといも
su-no-mono	vegetables seasoned with vinegar	酢の物
takenoko	bamboo shoots	タケノコ
tempura	vegetables, shrimp, or fish deep-fried in a light batter and dipped into a thin sauce with grated white radish	天ぷら
tsukemono	Japanese pickles made from white radish, eggplant, or other vegetables	漬け物
yasai itame	stir-fried vegetables	野菜炒め

EGG DISHES

chawan mushi	vegetables, shrimp, etc., steamed in egg custard	茶碗蒸し
medama-yaki	fried eggs, sunny-side up	目玉焼き
omuraisu	omelet with rice inside	オムライス
yude tamago	boiled eggs	ゆで卵

TOFU DISHES

agedashi dōfu	deep-fried plain tofu garnished with spring onions, dipped in hot broth	揚げだし豆腐
hiya-yakko	cold tofu with soy sauce and grated ginger	冷やっこ
mābō dōfu	tofu and ground pork in a spicy sauce (originally Chinese)	マーボー豆腐
tofu no dengaku	tofu broiled on skewers and flavored with miso	豆腐の田楽
yu-dōfu	boiled tofu with green onions	湯豆腐

RICE DISHES

chāhan	fried rice with vegetables and pork	チャーハン (炒飯)
chimaki	sticky rice wrapped in bamboo skin	ちまき
gohan	steamed white rice	ご飯
okayu	rice porridge	お粥
onigiri	triangular balls of rice with fish or vegetables inside and wrapped in sheets of dry seaweed	おにぎり

SOUPS

miso shiru	thin broth containing tofu, mushrooms, or other ingredients in a soup flavored with miso or soybean paste	みそ汁
suimono	clear broth, often including fish and tofu	吸い物
tonjiru	pork soup with vegetables	豚汁

NOODLES

hiyamugi	similar to sōmen, but thicker	ひやむぎ

rāmen	Chinese noodles in soy sauce, miso, or salt-flavored broth, often with chāshū (roast pork)	ラーメン
soba	buckwheat noodles served in a broth or, during the summer, cold on a bamboo mesh (called zaru soba)	そば
sōmen	summer dish of very thin wheat noodles, usually served cold with a tsuyu or thin sauce	そうめん
udon	broad flour noodles that can be lunch in a light broth, or a meal (nabe-yaki udon) when meat, chicken, egg, and vegetables are added	うどん
yaki-soba	noodles fried with beef and cabbage, garnished with pickled ginger and vegetables	焼きそば

FRUIT

anzu	apricot	あんず
budō	grapes	ぶどう
ichigo	strawberries	いちご
ichijiku	figs	いちじく
kaki	persimmon	柿
kuri	chestnuts	栗
kurumi	walnuts	くるみ
mikan	tangerine (mandarin orange)	みかん
momo	peach	桃
nashi	Japanese pear	梨
ringo	apple	リンゴ

sakurambo	cherry	さくらんぼ
suika	watermelon	西瓜

DESSERT

kōhii zerii	coffee-flavored gelatin	コーヒーゼリー
purin	caramel pudding	プリン
wagashi	sweet bean-paste confection	和菓子
yōkan	sweet bean-paste jelly	ようかん

DRINKS

ALCOHOLIC

biiru	beer	ビール
chūhai	shōchū mixed with soda water, lemon juice, or other flavoring	チューハイ
nama biiru	draft beer	生ビール
sake	rice wine, also called Nihonshu, which can be semi-sec (amaku-chi) or dry (karaku-chi), usually served warm (atsukan), although purists prefer it cold	酒, 日本酒
shōchū	spirit distilled from potatoes	焼酎

NONALCOHOLIC

jasumin cha	jasmine tea	ジャスミン茶
jūsu	juice, but can also mean any soft drink	ジュース
kō-cha	black tea	紅茶
kōhii	coffee	コーヒー
nihon cha	Japanese green tea	日本茶
ūron cha	Oolong tea	ウーロン茶

Travel Smart
Japan

WORD OF MOUTH

"The JR pass is a deal only IF you travel extensively (we abused ours both times, practically robbing JR!). As someone else says, it is a waste to use it in Tokyo, unless it just happens to work for you."

—usernameistaken

GETTING HERE AND AROUND

▌ AIR TRAVEL

Flying time to Japan is 13¾ hours from New York, 12¾ hours from Chicago, and 9½ hours from Los Angeles. Japan Airlines' GPS systems allow a more direct routing, which reduces its flight times by about 30 minutes. Your trip east, because of tailwinds, can be about 45 minutes shorter.

You can fly nonstop to Tokyo from Chicago, Detroit, New York, Los Angeles, San Francisco, Portland (OR), Seattle, Minneapolis, and Washington, DC.

You can also fly nonstop to Osaka from Chicago, Detroit, Pittsburgh, and San Francisco. Because of the distance, fares to Japan tend to be expensive, usually around $1,200 for a seat in coach.

Both of Japan's major carriers offer reduced prices for flights within the country, which are real cost- and time-savers if your trip includes destinations such as Kyushu or Hokkaido, though tickets must be booked outside Japan and there are restrictions on use in peak times. JAL offers the Yokoso Japan Airpass; ANA has the Visit Japan Fare. Cathay Pacific offers a pass that includes 18 cities throughout Asia.

All domestic flights in Japan are no-smoking.

Air Pass Information Visit Japan Fare (☎ 800/235–9262 All Nippon Airways in U.S. ⊕ www.anaskyweb.com). **Yokoso Japan Airpass** (☎ 800/525–3663 Japan Airlines ⊕ www.jal.co.jp/yokoso).

TRAVEL TIMES FROM TOKYO			
To	By Air	By Car or Bus	By Train
Osaka	1¼ hours	7–8 hours	2½ hours
Hiroshima	1½ hours	10 hours	5 hours
Kyoto	1¼ hour	7 hours	2½ hours

TRAVEL TIMES FROM TOKYO			
Fukuoka	2 hours	14 hours	6 hours
Sapporo	1½ hours	15 hours	10 hours
Naha (Okinawa)	3 hours	NA	NA

▌TIP➔ Ask the local tourist board about hotel and local transportation packages that include tickets to major museum exhibits or other special events.

AIRPORTS

The major gateway to Japan is Tokyo's Narita Airport (NRT), 80 km (50 mi) northeast of the city. The new Haneda Airport International Terminal, which opened in 2010, offers flights to major international cities and is only 20 km (12 miles) south of central Tokyo. International flights also use Kansai International Airport (KIX) outside Osaka to serve the Kansai region, which includes Kobe, Kyoto, Nara, and Osaka. In 2005 Centrair Airport (NGO) near Nagoya opened to take even more of the strain off Narita. Fares are generally cheapest into Narita, however. A few international flights use Fukuoka Airport, on the island of Kyushu; these include Continental flights from Guam, JAL from Honolulu, and flights from other Asian destinations. New Chitose Airport, outside Sapporo on the northern island of Hokkaido, handles some international flights, mostly to Asian destinations such as Seoul and Shanghai. Most domestic flights to and from Tokyo are out of Haneda Airport.

Tokyo Narita's Terminal 2 has two adjoining wings, north and south. When you arrive, your first task should be to convert your money into yen; you need it for transportation into Tokyo. In both wings ATMs and money-exchange counters are in the wall between the customs inspection area and the arrival lobby. Both terminals have a Japan National Tourist Organization tourist information center, where you can get free maps, brochures, and other visitor information. Directly across from the customs-area exits at both terminals are the ticket counters for airport limousine buses to Tokyo.

If you have a flight delay at Narita, take a local Keisei Line train into Narita town 15 minutes away, where a traditional shopping street and the beautiful Narita-san Shinsho-ji Temple are a peaceful escape from airport noise.

Flying into Haneda provides visitors with quicker access to downtown Tokyo, which is a short monorail ride away. Stop by the currency exchange and Tourist Information Desk in the second floor arrival lobby before taking a train into the city. There are also numerous jade-uniformed concierge staff on hand to help passengers with any questions.

If you plan to skip Tokyo and center your trip on Kyoto or central or western Honshu, Kansai International Airport (KIX) is the airport to use. Built on reclaimed land in Osaka Bay, it's laid out vertically. The first floor is for international arrivals; the second floor is for domestic departures and arrivals; the third floor has shops and restaurants; and the fourth floor is for international departures. A small tourist information center on the first floor of the passenger terminal building is open daily 9–5. Major carriers are Air Canada, Japan Airlines, and Northwest Airlines. The trip from KIX to Kyoto takes 75 minutes by JR train; to Osaka it takes 45–70 minutes.

Airport Information Centrair (Chubu) Airport (NGO) (☎ 0569/38–1195 ⊕ www.centrair.jp). **Fukuoka Airport (FUK)** (☎ 092/621–0303 ⊕ www.fuk-ab.co.jp). **Haneda Airport (HND)** (☎ 03/6428-0888 [International], 03/5757–8111[Domestic] ⊕ www.haneda-airport.jp/en). **Kansai International Airport (KIX)** (☎ 0724/55–2500 ⊕ www.kansai-airport.or.jp). **Narita Airport (NRT)** (☎ 0476/34–8000 ⊕ www.narita-airport.jp). **New Chitose Airport (CTS)** (☎ 0123/23–0111 ⊕ www.new-chitose-airport.jp).

GROUND TRANSPORTATION

Known as "The Gateway to Japan," Narita is the easiest airport to use if you are traveling to Tokyo. It takes about 90 minutes—a time very dependent on city traffic—by taxi or bus. The *Keisei Skyliner* and *Japan Railways NEX* are the easiest ways to get into the city. If you are arriving with a Japan Rail Pass and staying in Tokyo for a few days, it is best to pay for the transfer into the city and activate the Rail Pass for travel beyond Tokyo.

Directly across from the customs-area exits at both terminals are the ticket counters for buses to Tokyo. Buses leave from platforms just outside terminal exits, exactly on schedule; the departure time is on the ticket. The Friendly Airport Limousine offers the only shuttle-bus service from Narita to Tokyo.

Japan Railways trains stop at both Narita Airport terminals. The fastest and most comfortable is the Narita Limited Express (NEX), which makes 23 runs a day in each direction. Trains from the airport go directly to the central Tokyo Station in just under an hour, then continue to Yokohama and Ofuna. Daily departures begin at 7:43 am; the last train is at 9:43 pm. In addition to regular seats, there is a first-class Green Car and private, four-person compartments. All seats are reserved, and you'll need to reserve one for yourself in advance, as this train fills quickly.

The Keisei Skyliner train runs every 20–30 minutes between the airport terminals and Keisei-Ueno Station. The trip takes around 40 minutes. The first Skyliner leaves Narita for Ueno at 8:17 am, the last at 10:18 pm. From Ueno to Narita the first Skyliner is at 6:30 am, the last at 5:45 pm. There's also an early train from the airport, called the Morning Liner, which leaves at 7:49 am and costs ¥1,400.

Contacts Airport Transport Service Co. (☎ 03/3665–7232 in Tokyo, 0476/32–8080 for Terminal 1, 0476/34–6311 for Terminal 2). **IAE Co** (☎ 0476/32–7954 for Terminal 1, 0476/34–6886 for Terminal 2). **Japan**

TRAVEL TIMES FROM TOKYO				
From Narita	**To**	**Fares**	**Times**	**Notes**
Friendly Airport Limousine (buses)	Various $$$$ hotels in Tokyo & JR Tokyo and Shinjuku train stations	¥2,400–¥3,800	Every hr until 11:30 pm	70–90 mins, can be longer in traffic
Friendly Airport Limousine (buses)	Tokyo City Air Terminal (TCAT)	¥2,900	Every 10–20 mins from 6:55 am to 11 pm	
Narita Limited Express (NEX)	Central Tokyo Station, then continue to Yoko-hama and Ofuna	One-way fare ¥2,940; Green Car ¥4,980; private compartment (four people) ¥5,380 per person	Daily departures begin at 7:43 am; the last train is at 9:43 pm	All seats are reserved
Kaisoku (rapid train on JR's Narita Line)	Tokyo Station, by way of Chiba	¥1,280; ¥2,210 Green Car	16 departures daily, starting at 7 am	Trip takes 1 hr, 27 mins
Keisei Skyliner train	Keisei-Ueno Station	¥2,400	Every 20–30 mins, 7:49 am–10:18 pm	All seats are reserved
Taxi	Central Tokyo	¥20,000 or more		
From Haneda	**To**	**Fares**	**Times**	**Notes**
Tokyo Monorail	Central Tokyo	¥470	Every 20 min, 5:13 am–midnight	Trip takes 25–30 minutes. Connect to other major stations via the Yamanote Line at Hamamatsucho Station
Taxi	Central Tokyo	¥5000–¥6000		

Railways (☎ 03/3423–0111 for JR East InfoLine ⊗ Weekdays 10–6). **Keisei Railway** (☎ 03/3831–0131 for Ueno information counter, 0476/32-8505 at Narita Airport).

TRANSFERS BETWEEN AIRPORTS
Transfer between Narita and Haneda, the international and domestic airports, is easiest by the Friendly Limousine Bus, which should take 75 minutes and costs ¥3,000. Train transfers involve two changes.

Contacts Friendly Airport Limousine
(☎ 03/3665–7220 ⊕ www.limousinebus.co.jp).

FLIGHTS
Japan Airlines (JAL) and United Airlines are the major carriers between North America and Narita Airport in Tokyo; American Airlines, Delta Airlines, and All Nippon Airways (ANA) also link North American cities with Tokyo's Haneda and Narita Airports. Most of these airlines also fly into and out of Japan's two other international airports, Kansai International Airport, located south of Osaka and Centrair, near Nagoya.

Airline Contacts All Nippon Airways
(☎ 800/235–9262, 0120/02-9222 in Japan for domestic flights, 0120/02-9333 in Japan for

international flights ⊕ www.anaskyweb.com).
American (☎ 800/433-7300, 03/3298-7677
in Japan ⊕ www.aa.com). **Delta Airlines**
(☎ 800/221-1212 for U.S. reservations,
800/241-4141 for international reservations ⊕ www.delta.com). **Japan Airlines**
(☎ 800/525-3663, 0120/25-5931 international
in Japan, 0120/25-5971 domestic in Japan
⊕ www.jal.co.jp). **United** (☎ 800/864-8331,
0120/11-4466 in Japan ⊕ www.united.com).

■ BOAT TRAVEL

Ferries connect most of the islands of
Japan. Some of the more-popular routes
are from Tokyo to Tomakomai or Kushiro in Hokkaido; from Tokyo to Shikoku;
and from Tokyo or Osaka to Kyushu. You
can purchase ferry tickets in advance from
travel agencies or before boarding. The
ferries are inexpensive and are a pleasant,
if slow, way of traveling. Private cabins
are available, but it's more fun to travel in
the economy class, where everyone sleeps
on the carpeted floor in one large room.
Passengers eat, drink, and enjoy themselves in a convivial atmosphere. There
is little English information for local ferries, apart from three companies serving
the Inland Sea between Osaka/Kobe and
Kyushu. *For information on local ferries,
see the Essentials sections for individual
towns within each chapter.*

Information Hankyu Ferry (⊕ www.han9f.
co.jp). **Kansai Ferry** (⊕ www.kanki.co.jp). **Mei-
mon Taiyo Ferry** (⊕ www.cityline.co.jp).

■ BUS TRAVEL

Japan Railways (JR) offers a number of
long-distance buses that are comfortable and inexpensive. You can use Japan
Rail Passes (⇨ *Train Travel, below)* on
some, but not all, of these buses. Routes
and schedules are constantly changing,
but tourist information offices will have
up-to-date details. It's now possible to
travel from Osaka to Tokyo for as little
as ¥5,000 one-way. Buses are generally
modern and very comfortable, though

overnight journeys are best avoided.
Nearly all are now no-smoking. Foreign
travelers are not often seen on these buses,
and they remain one of the country's best-
kept travel secrets. Japan Rail Passes are
not accepted by private bus companies.
City buses outside Tokyo are quite convenient, but be sure of your route and destination, because the bus driver probably
won't speak English.

Local buses have a set cost, anywhere
from ¥100 to ¥200, depending on the
route and municipality, in which case
you board at the front of the bus and
pay as you get on. On other buses cost
is determined by the distance you travel.
You take a ticket when you board at the
rear door of the bus; it bears the number
of the stop at which you boarded. Your
fare depends on your destination and is
indicated by a board at the front of the
bus. Japan Railways also runs buses in
some areas that have limited rail service.
Remember, these buses are covered by the
JR Pass, even if some JR reservation clerks
tell you otherwise. Bus schedules can be
hard to fathom if you don't read Japanese,
however, so it's best to ask for help at a
tourist information office. The Nihon Bus
Association has information about routes
and which companies have English Web
information.

Reservations are not always essential,
except at peak holiday times and on the
most popular routes, like Tokyo–Osaka.

Bus Information JR Kanto Bus (☎ 03/3516-
1950 ⊕ www.jrbuskanto.co.jp). **Nihon Bus
Association** (⊕ www.bus.or.jp/e/index.html).
Nishinihon JR Bus (☎ 06/6466-9990 ⊕ www.
nishinihonjrbus.co.jp). **Willer Express** (⊕ www.
willerexpress.com).

■ CAR TRAVEL

You need an international driving permit
(IDP) to drive in Japan. IDPs are available from the American Automobile
Association. These international permits, valid only in conjunction with your
regular driver's license, are universally

recognized; having one may save you a problem with local authorities. By law, car seats must be installed if the driver is traveling with a child under six.

Major roads in Japan are sufficiently marked in roman type, and on country roads there's usually someone to ask for help. However, it's a good idea to have a detailed map with town names written in *kanji* (Japanese characters) and *romaji* (romanized Japanese).

Car travel along the Tokyo–Kyoto–Hiroshima corridor and in other built-up areas of Japan is not as convenient as the trains. Roads are congested, gas is expensive (about ¥250 per liter), and highway tolls are exorbitant (tolls between Tokyo and Kyoto amount to ¥10,550). In major cities, with the exception of main arteries, English signs are few and far between, one-way streets often lead you off the track, and parking is often hard to find.

That said, a car can be the best means for exploring cities outside the metropolitan areas and the rural parts of Japan, especially Kyushu and Hokkaido. Consider taking a train to those areas where exploring the countryside will be most interesting and renting a car locally for a day or even half a day. Book ahead in holiday seasons. Car rental rates in Tokyo begin at ¥6,300 a day and ¥37,800 a week, including tax, for an economy car with unlimited mileage.

Local Agencies Japan Railways Group (⊕ *www.japanrail.com*). **ToCoo!** (☎ *03/5333–0246* ⊕ *www2.tocoo.jp*).

Major Agencies Avis (☎ *800/331–1084* ⊕ *www.avis.com*). **Budget** (☎ *800/472–3325* ⊕ *www.budget.com*). **Hertz** (☎ *800/654–3001* ⊕ *www.hertz.com*). **National Car Rental** (☎ *800/227–7368* ⊕ *www.nationalcar.com*).

GASOLINE

Gas stations are plentiful along Japan's toll roads, and prices are fairly uniform across the country. Credit cards are accepted everywhere and are even encouraged—there are discounts for them at some places. Self-service stations have recently become legal, so if you pump your own gas you may get a small discount. Often you pay after putting in the gas, but there are also machines where you put money in first and then use the receipt to get change back. Staff will offer to take away trash and clean car windows. Tipping is not customary.

PARKING

There is little on-street parking in Japan. Parking is usually in staffed parking lots or in parking towers within buildings. Expect to pay upward of $3 per hour. Parking regulations are strictly enforced, and illegally parked vehicles are towed away. Recovery fees start at $300 and increase hourly.

ROAD CONDITIONS

Roads in Japan are often narrower than those in the United States, but they're well maintained in general. Driving in cities can be troublesome, as there are many narrow, one-way streets and little in the way of English road signs except on major arteries. Japanese drivers stick to the speed limit, but widely ignore bans on mobile phone use and dashboard televisions, and ignore rules on baby seats. Wild boars are not uncommon in rural districts, and have been known to block roads and ram into cars in the mountainous city of Kobe and in Kyushu, especially at night. From December to April northern areas are snow covered.

ROADSIDE EMERGENCIES

Emergency telephones along highways can be used to contact the authorities. A nonprofit service, JHelp.com, offers a free, 24-hour emergency assistance hotline. Car-rental agencies generally offer roadside assistance services. Mobile phones are now so widespread that local drivers can call for help from the middle of nowhere.

Emergency Services Police (☎ *110*). **Fire** (☎ *119*). **JHelp.com** (☎ *0570/00–0911*).

RULES OF THE ROAD

In Japan people drive on the left. Speed limits vary, but generally the limit is 80 kph (50 mph) on highways, 40 kph (25 mph) in cities. Penalties for speeding are severe. By law, car seats must be installed if the driver is traveling with a child under six, while the driver and all passengers in cars must wear seat belts at all times. Driving while using handheld phones is illegal.

Many smaller streets lack sidewalks, so cars, bicycles, and pedestrians share the same space. Motorbikes with engines under 50 cc are allowed to travel against automobile traffic on one-way roads. Fortunately, considering the narrowness of the streets and the volume of traffic, most Japanese drivers are technically skilled. However, they may not allow quite as much distance between cars as you're used to. Be prepared for sudden lane changes by other drivers. When waiting at intersections after dark, many drivers, as a courtesy to other drivers, turn off their main headlights to prevent glare.

Starting in 2006 there has been a nationwide crackdown on drunk driving, following a spate of horrific, headlining-grabbing accidents, so it's wisest to avoid alcohol entirely if you plan to drive.

▍ TAXI TRAVEL

Taxis are an expensive way of getting around cities in Japan, though nascent deregulation moves are easing the market a little. In Tokyo, for instance, first 2 km (1 mi) cost ¥710 and it's ¥80 for every additional 280 meters (400 yards). If possible, avoid using taxis during rush hours (7:30 am–9:30 am and 5 pm–7 pm).

In general, it's easy to hail a cab: do not shout or wave wildly—simply raise your hand if you need a taxi. Japanese taxis have automatic door-opening systems, so do not try to open the taxi door. Stand back when the cab comes to a stop—if you are too close, the door may slam into you. When you leave the cab, do not try to close the door; the driver will do it automatically. Only the curbside rear door opens. A red light on the dashboard (visible through the front window) indicates an available taxi, and a green light indicates an occupied taxi.

Drivers are for the most part courteous, though not necessarily chatty. Unless you're going to a well-known destination such as a major hotel, it's advisable to have a Japanese person write out your destination in Japanese. Your hotel concierge will do this for you. Remember, there is no need to tip.

▍ TRAIN TRAVEL

Riding Japanese trains is one of the pleasures of travel in the country. Efficient and convenient, trains run frequently and on schedule. The Shinkansen (bullet train), one of the fastest trains in the world, connects major cities north and south of Tokyo. It is only slightly less expensive than flying, but is in many ways more convenient because train stations are more centrally located than airports (and, if you have a Japan Rail Pass, it's extremely affordable).

Other trains, though not as fast as the Shinkansen, are just as convenient and substantially cheaper. There are three types of train services: *futsu* (local service), *tokkyu* (limited express service), and *kyuko* (express service). Both the tokkyu and the kyuko offer a first-class compartment known as the Green Car. Smoking is allowed only in designated carriages on long-distance and Shinkansen trains. Local and commuter trains are entirely no-smoking.

Because there are no porters or carts at train stations, it's a good idea to travel light when getting around by train. Savvy travelers often have their main luggage sent ahead to a hotel that they plan to reach later in their wanderings. It's also good to know that every train station, however small, has luggage lockers, which cost about ¥300 for 24 hours.

If you plan to travel by rail, it may be advantageous to buy a Japan Rail Pass, which offers unlimited travel on Japan Railways (JR) trains. You can purchase one-, two-, or three-week passes. A one-week pass is less expensive than a regular round-trip ticket from Tokyo to Kyoto on the Shinkansen. You must obtain a rail pass voucher prior to departure for Japan (you cannot buy them in Japan), and the pass must be used within three months of purchase. The pass is available only to people with tourist visas, as opposed to business, student, and diplomatic visas.

When you arrive in Japan, you must exchange your voucher for the Japan Rail Pass. You can do this at the Japan Railways desk in the arrivals hall at Narita Airport or at JR stations in major cities. When you make this exchange, you determine the day that you want the rail pass to begin, and, accordingly, when it ends. You do not have to begin travel on the day you make the exchange; instead, pick the starting date to maximize use. The Japan Rail Pass allows you to travel on all JR-operated trains (which cover most destinations in Japan) but not lines owned by other companies.

The JR Pass is also valid on buses operated by Japan Railways (⇨ *Bus Travel, above*). You can make seat reservations without paying a fee on all trains that have reserved-seat coaches, usually long-distance trains. The Japan Rail Pass does not cover the cost of sleeping compartments on overnight trains (called blue trains), nor does it cover the newest and fastest of the Shinkansen trains, the *Nozomi,* which make only one or two stops on longer runs. The pass covers only the *Hikari* Shinkansen, which make a few more stops than the *Nozomi,* and the *Kodama* Shinkansen, which stop at every station along the Shinkansen routes.

Japan Rail Passes are available in coach class and first class (Green Car), and as the difference in price between the two is relatively small, it's worth the splurge for first class, for real luxury, especially on the Shinkansen. A one-week pass costs ¥28,300 coach class, ¥37,800 first class; a two-week pass costs ¥45,100 coach class, ¥61,200 first class; and a three-week pass costs ¥57,700 coach class, ¥79,600 first class. Travelers under 18 pay lower rates. The pass pays for itself after one Tokyo–Kyoto round-trip Shinkansen ride. Contact a travel agent or Japan Airlines to purchase the pass.

Many travelers assume that rail passes guarantee them seats on the trains they wish to ride. Not so. If you're using a rail pass, there's no need to buy individual tickets, but you should book seats ahead. You can reserve up to two weeks in advance or just minutes before the train departs. If you fail to make a train, there's no penalty, and you can reserve again.

Seat reservations for any JR route may be made at any JR station except those in the tiniest villages. The reservation windows or offices, *midori-no-madoguchi,* have green signs in English and green-stripe windows. If you're traveling without a Japan Rail Pass, there's a surcharge of approximately ¥500 (depending upon distance traveled) for seat reservations, and if you miss the train you'll have to pay for another reservation. When making your seat reservation you may request a no-smoking or smoking car. Your reservation ticket shows the date and departure time of your train as well as your car and seat number. Notice the markings painted on the platform or on little signs above the platform; ask someone which markings correspond to car numbers. If you don't have a reservation, ask which cars are unreserved. Unreserved tickets can be purchased at regular ticket windows. There are no reservations made on local service trains. For traveling short distances, tickets are usually sold at vending machines. A platform ticket is required if you go through the wicket gate onto the platform to meet someone coming off a train. The charge is ¥140 (the tickets are ¥130 in Tokyo and Osaka).

Most clerks at train stations know a few basic words of English and can read roman script. Moreover, they are invariably helpful in plotting your route. The complete railway timetable is a mammoth book written only in Japanese; however, you can get an English-language train schedule from the Japan National Tourist Organization *(JNTO ⇨ Visitor Information, below)* that covers the Shinkansen and a few of the major JR Limited Express trains. JNTO's booklet *The Tourist's Handbook* provides helpful information about purchasing tickets in Japan. The Jorudan Route Finder is a good online source for searching train times and prices.

Information Japan Railways Group (✉ *1 Rockefeller Plaza, Suite 1410, New York, NY* ☎ *212/332–8686* ⊕ *www.japanrail.com*).

Jorudan Route Finder (⊕ *www.jorudan.co.jp/ english*).

Buying a Pass Japan Rail Pass (⊕ *www. japanrailpass.net*).

Train Information JR Hotline (☎ *03/3423– 0111*) is an English-language information service, open weekdays 10–6.

ESSENTIALS

▌ ACCOMMODATIONS

Overnight accommodations in Japan run from luxury hotels to *ryokan* (traditional inns) to youth hostels and even capsules. Western-style rooms with Western-style bathrooms are widely available in large cities, but in smaller, out-of-the-way towns it may be necessary to stay in a Japanese-style room—an experience that can only enhance your stay.

Large chain and business hotels usually quote prices based on rooms and occupancy. Traditional *minshuku* (Japanese bed-and-breakfasts) and ryokan prices are generally per-person and include dinner and breakfast. If you do not want dinner at your hotel, it is usually possible to renegotiate the price. Stipulate, too, whether you wish to have Japanese or Western breakfasts, if any. Japanese-style rooms generally have tatami flooring and a futon instead of a bed. Rarely do they have a private bath or shower; guests bath in communal baths, following a particular etiquette, and baths are frequently only open a few hours a day. When you make reservations at a non-city hotel, you are usually expected to take breakfast and dinner at the hotel—this is the rate quoted to you unless you specify otherwise. In this guide, properties are assigned price categories based on the range between their least and most expensive standard double rooms at high season (excluding holidays).

A travel agent based in Japan can help you make reservations and other travel arrangements, and this is a particularly useful service since some hotels and ryokan do not have Web sites in English.

Japan Hotel.net, J-Reserve, Rakuten Travel, and Tabiplaza, an offshoot of Nippon Travel Agency, offer a wide range of accommodations from big city luxury to out-of-the-way family guesthouses. Budget Japan Hotels offers big discounts on cheaper rooms at major hotels.

Online Accommodations Budget Japan Hotels (⊕ www.budgetjapanhotels.com). Japan Hotel.net (⊕ www.japanhotel.net). J-Reserve (⊕ www.japan-hotel-reserve. com). Rakuten Travel (⊕ www.travel.rakuten. co.jp/en). Tabiplaza (⊕ www.tabiplaza.net/ japanhotels).

Japan Travel Agents IACE Travel (✉ 3F Kounan Okamoto Bldg., Kounan, Minato-ku, Tokyo ☎ 03/5282–1522 ⊕ www.iace-usa.com ✉ 18 E. 41st St., New York, NY ☎ 800/872–4223). JTB Sunrise Tours (✉ 2–3–11 Higashi-Shinagawa, Shinagawa-ku, Tokyo ☎ 03/5796–5454 ⊕ www.jtbusa.com). Nippon Travel Agency (✉ Shimbashi Ekimae Bldg., Number 1, Shimbashi, Minato-ku, Tokyo ⊕ www. ntainbound.com ✉ 1025 W. 190th St., Suite 300, Gardena, CA ☎ 310/768–0017).

APARTMENT AND HOUSE RENTALS

In addition to the agents listed here, English-language newspapers and magazines such as the *Hiragana Times, Metropolis, Kansai Scene, or Tokyo Weekender* may be helpful in locating a rental property. Note that renting apartments or houses in Japan is not a common way to spend a vacation, and weekly studio-apartment rentals may be fully booked by local business travelers.

The range of online booking services for Japan is expanding, although most of the accommodation booked this way is large and impersonal and staff in the hotel may not speak any English. Also check the location carefully to avoid incurring unforeseen extra costs and hassles in trying to reach the sights from a suburban hotel.

Contacts The Mansions (☎ 03/5414–7070, 03/5575–3232). Sakura House—Apartments (☎ 03/5330–5250 ⊕ www.sakura-house.com). Weekly Mansion Tokyo (⊕ www.wmt-tokyo. com).

Rental Listings **Kansai Scene** (⊕ *www. kansaiscene.com*). **Metropolis** (☎ *03/3423– 6932* ⊕ *www.metropolis.co.jp*).

Exchange Clubs **Home For Exchange** (⊕ *www.homeforexchange.com*); $59 for a 1-year online listing.

HOME VISITS

Through the home visit system travelers can get a sense of domestic life in Japan by visiting a local family in their home. The program is voluntary on the home-owner's part, and there's no charge for a visit. The system is active in many cities throughout the country, including Tokyo, Yokohama, Nagoya, Kyoto, Osaka, Hiroshima, Nagasaki, and Sapporo. To make a reservation, apply in writing for a home visit at least a day in advance to the local tourist information office of the place you are visiting. Contact the Japan National Tourist Organization (⇨ *Visitor Information, below)* before leaving for Japan for more information on the program.

INEXPENSIVE ACCOMMODATIONS

JNTO publishes a listing of some 700 accommodations that are reasonably priced. To be listed, properties must meet Japanese fire codes and charge less than ¥8,000 per person without meals. For the most part, the properties charge ¥5,000–¥6,000. These properties welcome foreigners (many Japanese hotels and ryokan do not like to have foreign guests because they might not be familiar with traditional-inn etiquette). Properties include business hotels, ryokan of a very rudimentary nature, minshuku (Japanese bed-and-breakfasts), and pensions. It's the luck of the draw whether you choose a good or less-than-good property. In most cases rooms are clean but very small. Except in business hotels, shared baths are the norm, and you are expected to have your room lights out by 10 pm.

Many establishments on the list of reasonably priced accommodations—and many that are not on the list—can be reserved through the nonprofit organization Wel-

come Inn Reservation Center. Reservation forms are available from your nearest JNTO office (⇨ *Visitor Information, below)*. The Japanese Inn Group, which provides reasonable accommodations for foreign visitors, can be reserved through this same service. The center must receive reservation requests at least one week before your departure to allow processing time. If you are already in Japan, the Tourist Information Centers (TICs) at Narita Airport and Kansai International Airport and in downtown Tokyo and Kyoto can make immediate reservations for you at these Welcome Inns. Telephone reservations are not accepted.

Contacts **Japanese Inn Group** (☎ *03/3252– 1717* ⊕ *www.japaneseinngroup.com*). **Welcome Inn Reservation Center** (✉ *10F, Tokyo Kotsu Kaikakan Bldg., 2–10–1 Yuraku-cho, Chiyoda-ku, Tokyo* ⊕ *www.itcj.jp* ☼ *Closed 2nd and 4th Tues. of month)*.

TEMPLES

You can also arrange accommodations in Buddhist temples, known as *shukubo*. JNTO has lists of temples that accept guests and you can arrange for your stay here as well. A stay at a temple generally costs ¥3,000–¥9,000 ($37–$110) per night, including two meals. Some temples offer instruction in meditation or allow you to observe their religious practices, while others simply offer a room. The Japanese-style rooms are very simple, and range from beautiful, quiet havens to not-so-comfortable, basic cubicles. For specific information on temple lodging in the Kii Mountain range in southern Japan, try contacting the Shukubo Temple Lodging Cooperative.

Contacts Shukubo Temple Lodging Cooperative (☎ *03/3231–5310* ⊕ *www.shukubo.net*).

■ ADDRESSES

The simplest way to decipher a Japanese address is to break it into parts. For example: 6-chome 8–19, Chu o-ku, Fukuoka-shi, Fukuoka-ken. In this address the "chome" indicates a precise area (a block, for example), and the numbers following "chome" indicate the building within the area. Note that buildings aren't always numbered sequentially; numbers are often assigned as buildings are erected. Only local police officers and mail carriers in Japan seem to be familiar with the area defined by the chome. Sometimes, instead of "chome," "machi" (town) is used. Written addresses in Japan also have the opposite order of those in the West, with the city coming before the street. "Ku" refers to a ward (a district) of a city, "shi" refers to a city name, and "ken" indicates a prefecture, which is roughly equivalent to a state in the United States. It's not unusual for the prefecture and the city to have the same name, as in the above address. There are a few geographic areas in Japan that are not called ken. One is greater Tokyo, which is called Tokyo-to. Other exceptions Kyoto and Osaka, which are followed by the suffix "-fu"—Kyoto-fu, Osaka-fu. Hokkaido, Japan's northernmost island, is also not considered a ken. Not all addresses conform exactly to the above format. Rural addresses, for example, might use "gun" (county) where city addresses have "ku" (ward). Even Japanese people cannot find a building based on the address alone. If you get in a taxi with a written address, do not assume the driver will be able to find your destination. Usually, people provide very detailed instructions or maps to explain their exact locations. It's always

good to know the location of your destination in relation to a major building or department store.

■ COMMUNICATIONS

INTERNET

Phone jacks are the same in Japan as in the United States. Many hotels have ADSL or Ethernet connections for high-speed Internet access. Ethernet cables are usually available at hotels if you don't bring your own. Wireless Internet access (Wi-Fi) is increasingly available for free at certain coffee shops and in many hotel lobbies across the country. There are Internet cafés in many cities, often doubling as manga (comic book) libraries where you can rent a relaxation room with massage chair, computer, and desk.

Contacts Cybercafes (⊕ *www.cybercafes. com*) lists more than 4,000 Internet cafés worldwide.

PHONES

The country code for Japan is 81. When dialing a Japanese number from outside Japan, drop the initial "0" from the local area code.

CALLING WITHIN JAPAN

Public telephones are a dying species in cell-phone-happy Japan. But there are usually public telephones near convenience stores, stations, and of course in hotel lobbies. Phones accept ¥100 coins as well as prepaid telephone cards. Domestic long-distance rates are reduced as much as 50% after 9 pm (40% after 7 pm). Telephone cards, sold in vending machines, hotels, and a variety of stores, are tremendously convenient.

Operator assistance at 104 is in Japanese only. Weekdays 9–5 (except national holidays) English-speaking operators can help you at the toll-free NTT Information Customer Service Centre.

Contacts Directory Assistance (☎ *104*). **NTT Information Customer Service Centre** (☎ *0120/36–4463*).

CALLING OUTSIDE JAPAN

Many gray, multicolor, and green phones have gold plates indicating, in English, that they can be used for international calls. Three Japanese companies provide international service: KDDI (001), Japan Telecom (0041), and IDC (0061). Dial the company code + country code + city/area code and number of your party. Telephone credit cards are especially convenient for international calls. For operator assistance in English on long-distance calls, dial 0051.

The country code for the United States is 1.

Japan has several telephone companies for international calls, so make a note of all the possible access code numbers to use to connect to your U.S. server before departure.

Access Codes AT&T Direct (☎ 800/222–0300). **MCI WorldPhone** (☎ 800/444–4444). **Sprint International Access** (☎ 800/877–4646).

CALLING CARDS

Telephone cards for ¥1,000 ($12) can be bought at station kiosks or convenience stores and can be used in virtually all public telephones. For international calls, look for phones that accept KDDI prepaid cards valued between ¥1,000 and ¥7,000. Cards are available from convenience stores.

MOBILE PHONES

Japan is the world leader in mobile-phone technology, but overseas visitors cannot easily use their handsets in Japan because it is a non-GSM country. Best to rent a phone from one of the many outlets at Narita, Kansai, and Nagoya airports. Softbank sells 3G SIM cards so you can use your own number in Japan. Most company rental rates start at ¥525 a day, excluding insurance. Check the airport Web sites for the current companies. Phones can be ordered online or by fax, or rented for same-day use.

Contacts G-call (⊕ www.g-call.com). **JALABC Rental Phone** (⊕ www.jalabc.com/rental/ domestic_eng/index.html). **Softbank** (⊕ www.softbank-rental.jp).

▮ CUSTOMS AND DUTIES

Japan has strict regulations about bringing firearms, pornography, and narcotics into the country. Anyone caught with drugs is liable to be detained, refused reentry into Japan, and deported. Certain fresh fruits, vegetables, plants, and animals are also illegal. Nonresidents are allowed to bring in duty-free: (1) 400 cigarettes or 100 cigars or 500 grams of tobacco; (2) three 760-milliliter bottles of alcohol; (3) 2 ounces of perfume; (4) other goods up to ¥200,000 value.

Getting through customs at a Japanese airport goes more smoothly if you are well dressed, clean-shaven, and as conventional-looking as possible. Visitors arriving off flights from other Asian countries are particularly scrutinized for narcotics.

Japan Information Ministry of Finance, Customs and Tariff Bureau (☎ 03/3581–4111 ⊕ www.customs.go.jp).

U.S. Information U.S. Customs and Border Protection (⊕ www.cbp.gov).

▮ DAY TOURS AND GUIDES

The Japan National Tourist Organization (JNTO) sponsors a Goodwill Guide program in which local citizens volunteer to show visitors around; this is a great way to meet Japanese people. These are not professional guides; they usually volunteer both because they enjoy welcoming foreigners to their town and because they want to practice their English. You will have to negotiate the itinerary with the guide. The services of Goodwill Guides are free, but you should pay for their travel costs, their admission fees, and any meals you eat with them while you are together. To participate in this program, make arrangements for a Goodwill Guide in advance through JNTO in the United States or through the tourist office in the area where you want the guide to meet you. The program operates in 75 towns and cities, including Tokyo, Kyoto, Nara, Nagoya, Osaka, and Hiroshima. Bookings can be done through their Web site.

The Japan National Tourist Organization can also put you in touch with various local volunteer groups that conduct tours in English; you need only to pay for the guide's travel expenses, admission fees to cultural sites, and meals if you eat together. Assume that the fee will be ¥25,000–¥30,000 for a full eight-hour day.

Contacts Goodwill Guides (⊕ *www. jnto.go.jp/eng/arrange/essential/list_ volunteerGuides_a-n.html*). **Japan Guide Association** (☎ *03/3213–2706* ⊕ *www.jga21c. or.jp*). **Japan National Tourist Organization** (☎ *03/3201–3331* ⊕ *www.japantravelinfo.com*).

▮ ELECTRICITY

The electrical current in Japan is 100 volts, 50 cycles alternating current (AC) in eastern Japan, and 100 volts, 60 cycles in western Japan; the United States runs on 110-volt, 60-cycle AC current. Wall outlets in Japan accept plugs with two flat prongs, as in the United States, but do not accept U.S. three-prong plugs.

Consider making a small investment in a universal adapter, which has several types of plugs in one lightweight, compact unit. Most laptops and mobile phone chargers are dual voltage (i.e., they operate equally well on 110 and 220 volts), so require only an adapter. These days the same is true of small appliances such as hair dryers. Always check labels and manufacturers' instructions to be sure. Don't use 110-volt outlets marked for shavers only for high-wattage appliances such as hair dryers.

Contacts Steve Kropla's Help for World Travelers (⊕ *www.kropla.com*) has information on electrical and telephone plugs around the world. **Walkabout Travel Gear** (⊕ *www.*

walkabouttravelgear.com) has a good coverage of electricity under "adapters."

▮ EMERGENCIES

Assistance in English is available 24 hours a day on the toll-free Japan Helpline.

The following embassy and consulate is open weekdays, with one- to two-hour closings for lunch. Call for exact hours.

Contacts U.S. Embassy and Consulate (✉ *1–10–5 Akasaka, Minato-ku, Toranomon* ☎ *03/3224–5000* ⊕ *tokyo.usembassy.gov* Ⓜ *Namboku Line, Tameike-Sanno Station [Exit 13]*).

General Emergency Contacts Ambulance and Fire (☎ *119*). **Japan Helpline** (☎ *0120/46–1997 or 0570/00–0911*). **Police** (☎ *110*)

▮ HEALTH

Japan is a safe, clean country for travelers with good drinking water and no major water- or insect-borne diseases. Drugs and medications are widely available at drugstores, although the brand names and use instructions will be in Japanese, so if on regular medication, take along enough supplies to cover the trip. As with any international travel, be sure to bring your prescription or a doctor's note just in case. Condoms are sold widely, but they may not have the brands you're used to. Speak with your physician and/or check the CDC or World Health Organization

Web sites for health alerts, particularly if you're pregnant or traveling with children or have a chronic illness.

SPECIFIC ISSUES IN JAPAN

Tap water is safe everywhere in Japan. Medical treatment varies from highly skilled and professional at major hospitals to somewhat less advanced in small neighborhood clinics. At larger hospitals you have a good chance of encountering English-speaking doctors who have been partly educated in the West.

Mosquitoes can be a minor irritation during the rainy season, though you are never at risk of contracting anything serious like malaria. If you're staying in a ryokan or any place without air-conditioning, anti-mosquito coils or an electric-powered spray will be provided. Dehydration and heatstroke could be concerns if you spend a long time outside during the summer months, but isotonic sports drinks are readily available from the nation's ubiquitous vending machines.

General Information and Warnings U.S. Department of State (⊕ *www.travel.state. gov*).

OVER-THE-COUNTER REMEDIES

It may be difficult to buy the standard over-the-counter remedies you're used to, so it's best to bring with you any medications (in their proper packaging) you may need. Medication can only be bought at pharmacies in Japan, but every neighborhood seems to have at least one. Ask for the *yakyoku*. Pharmacists in Japan are usually able to manage at least a few words of English, and certainly are able to read some, so have a pen and some paper ready, just in case. In Japanese, aspirin is *asupirin* and Tylenol is *Tairenoru*. Following national regulations, Japanese drugs contain less potent ingredients than foreign brands, so the effects can be disappointing; check advised dosages carefully.

▌ HOURS OF OPERATION

General business hours in Japan are weekdays 9–5. Many offices also open at least half the day on Saturday, but are generally closed Sunday.

Banks are open weekdays from 9 to at least 3, some now staying open until 4 or 5. As with shops, there's a trend toward longer and later opening hours.

Gas stations follow usual shop hours, though 24-hour stations can be found near major highways.

Museums generally close Monday and the day following national holidays. They are also closed the day following special exhibits and during the weeklong New Year's celebrations.

Department stores are usually open 10–7, but close one day a week, varying from store to store. Other stores are open from 10 or 11 to 8 or 9. There's a trend toward longer and later opening hours in major cities, and 24-hour convenience stores, many of which now have ATM facilities, can be found across the entire country.

HOLIDAYS

As elsewhere, peak times for travel in Japan tend to fall around holiday periods. You want to avoid traveling during the few days before and after New Year's; during Golden Week, which follows Greenery Day (April 29); and in mid-July and mid-August, at the time of Obon festivals, when many Japanese return to their hometowns (Obon festivals are celebrated July or August 13–16, depending on the location). Note that when a holiday falls on a Sunday, the following Monday is a holiday.

Japan's national holidays are January 1 (*Ganjitsu*, New Year's Day); the second Monday in January (*Senjin-no-hi*, Coming of Age Day); February 11 (*Kenkoku Kinen-bi*, National Foundation Day); March 20 or 21 (*Shumbun-no-hi*, Vernal Equinox); April 29 (*Midori-no-hi*, Green Day); May 3 (*Kempo Kinen-bi*, Constitution Day); May 5 (*Kodomo-no-hi*,

Children's Day); the third Monday in July (*Umi-no-hi,* Marine Day); the third Monday in September (*Keiro-no-hi,* Respect for the Aged Day); September 23 or 24 (*Shubun-no-hi,* Autumnal Equinox); the second Monday in October (*Taiiku-no-hi,* Sports Day); November 3 (*Bunka-no-hi,* Culture Day); November 23 (*Kinro Kansha-no-hi,* Labor Thanksgiving Day); December 23 (*Tenno Tanjobi,* Emperor's Birthday).

▌ MAIL

The Japanese postal service is very efficient. Airmail between Japan and the United States takes between five and eight days. Surface mail can take anywhere from four to eight weeks. Express service is also available through post offices.

Although there are numerous post offices in every city, it's probably best to use the central post office near the main train station, because the workers speak English and can handle foreign mail. Some of the smaller post offices are not equipped to send packages. Post offices are open weekdays 9–5 and Saturday 9–noon. Some central post offices have longer hours, such as the one in Tokyo, near Tokyo Eki (train station), which is open 24 hours year-round. Most hotels and many convenience stores also sell stamps.

The Japanese postal service has implemented the use of three-numeral-plus-four postal codes, but its policy is similar to that in the United States regarding zip-plus-fours; that is, addresses with the three-numeral code will still arrive at their destination, albeit perhaps one or two days later. Mail to rural towns may take longer.

It costs ¥110 to send a letter by air to North America. An airmail postcard costs ¥70. Aerograms cost ¥90.

To get mail, have parcels and letters sent "poste restante" to the central post office in major cities; unclaimed mail is returned after 30 days.

SHIPPING PACKAGES

FedEx has drop-off locations at branches of Kinko's in all major cities. A 1-kilogram (2.20-pound) package from central Tokyo to Washington, DC, would cost about ¥7,200, and take two days to be delivered.

The Japanese postal service is very efficient, and domestic mail rarely goes astray. To ship a 5-kilogram (11.02-pound) parcel to the United States costs ¥10,150 if sent by airmail, ¥7,300 by SAL (economy airmail), and ¥4,000 by sea. Allow a week for airmail, two to three weeks for SAL, and up to six weeks for packages sent by sea. Large shops usually ship domestically, but not overseas.

Express Services FedEx (☎ *0120/003–200 toll-free, 043/298–1919* ⊕ *www.fedex.com/ jp_english*).

▌ MONEY

Japan is expensive, but there are ways to cut costs. This requires, to some extent, an adventurous spirit and the courage to stray from the standard tourist paths. One good way to hold down expenses is to avoid taxis (they tend to get stuck in traffic anyway) and try the inexpensive, efficient subway and bus systems; instead of going to a restaurant with menus in English and Western-style food, go to places where you can rely on your good old index finger to point to the dish you want, and try food that the Japanese eat.

ITEM	AVERAGE COST
Cup of Coffee	¥250–¥600
Glass of Wine	¥500
Glass of Beer	¥300–¥600
Sandwich	¥300
One-Mile Taxi Ride in Capital City	¥660
Museum Admission	¥1,000

ATMS AND BANKS

ATMs at many Japanese banks do not accept foreign-issue debit or credit cards. Citibank has centrally located branches in most major Japanese cities and ATMs that are open 24 hours. UFJ and Shinsei banks are members of the Plus network, as are some convenience store cash machines. Post offices have ATMs that accept Visa, MasterCard, American Express, Diners Club, and Cirrus cards. Elsewhere, especially in more-rural areas, it's difficult to find suitable ATMs. PIN numbers in Japan are comprised of four digits. In Japanese an ATM is commonly referred to by its English acronym, while a PIN is *ansho bango*. Because of a spate of ATM crimes allegedly involving "foreigners" asking for help, Japanese bank customers may react badly to requests for assistance. Instead, contact bank staff by using the phone next to the ATM. Many machines also have English on-screen instructions.

CREDIT CARDS

MasterCard and Visa are the most widely accepted credit cards in Japan. When you use a credit card you'll be asked if you intend to pay in one installment as most locals do, say *hai-ikkai* (Yes, one time) just to fit in, even if you plan differently once you get home. Many vendors don't accept American Express. Cash is still king in Japan, especially at smaller businesses—even in large cities like Osaka and Tokyo.

Reporting Lost Cards American Express (☎ 0120/02–0120 for Japan office ⊕ www. americanexpress.com). **Diners Club** (☎ 0120/07–4024 for Japan office ⊕ www. dinersclub.com). **MasterCard** (☎ 00531/11–3886 Japan office ⊕ www.mastercard.com). **Visa** (☎ 00531/11–1555 for Japan office ⊕ www.visa.com).

CURRENCY AND EXCHANGE

The unit of currency in Japan is the yen (¥). There are bills of ¥10,000, ¥5,000, ¥2,000, and ¥1,000. Coins are ¥500, ¥100, ¥50, ¥10, ¥5, and ¥1. Japanese currency floats on the international monetary exchange, so changes can be dramatic.

∎ TIP→ Even if a currency-exchange booth has a sign promising no commission, rest assured that there's some kind of huge, hidden fee. And as for rates, you're almost always better off getting foreign currency at an ATM or exchanging money at a bank.

∎ RESTROOMS

The most hygienic restrooms are found in hotels and department stores, and are usually clearly marked with international symbols. You may encounter Japanese-style toilets, with bowls recessed into the floor, over which you squat facing the top. This may take some getting used to, but it's completely sanitary as you don't come into direct contact with the facility. If you can't face a squat, check out the last cubical in the row because it may be a Western-style toilet.

In many homes and Japanese-style public places, there will be a pair of slippers at the entrance to the restroom. Change into these before entering the room, and change back when you exit.

Many public toilets don't have toilet paper, though there are dispensers where packets can be purchased for ¥50 or so. Many locals accept the free tissue packets that are handed out as advertisements in the center of town for this reason. Similarly, paper towel dispensers and hand dryers are not always installed, so bring a small handkerchief or washcloth with you, as well as some hand sanitizer.

Find a Loo The Bathroom Diaries (⊕ www. thebathroomdiaries.com) is flush with unsanitized info on restrooms the world over—each one located, reviewed, and rated.

∎ PACKING

Pack light, because porters can be hard to find and storage space in hotel rooms may be tiny. What you pack depends more on the time of year than on any dress code. For travel in the cities, pack as you would for any American or European city. At more expensive restaurants and nightclubs men usually need to wear a jacket and tie. Wear conservative-color clothing at business meetings. Casual clothes are fine for sightseeing. Jeans are as popular in Japan as they are in the United States, and are perfectly acceptable for informal dining and sightseeing.

Although there are no strict dress codes for visiting temples and shrines, you will be out of place in shorts or immodest outfits. For sightseeing leave sandals and open-toe shoes behind; you'll need sturdy walking shoes for the gravel pathways that surround temples and fill parks. Make sure to bring comfortable clothing that isn't too tight to wear in traditional Japanese restaurants, where you may need to sit on tatami-matted floors. For beach and mountain resorts pack informal clothes for both day and evening wear. Central and southern Japan are hot and humid June to September, so pack cotton clothing. Winter daytime temperatures in northern Japan hover around freezing, so gloves and hats are necessary, and clip-on shoe spikes can be bought locally.

Japanese do not wear shoes in private homes or in any temples or traditional inns. Having shoes you can quickly slip in and out of is a decided advantage. Take wool socks (checking first for holes!) to help you through those shoeless occasions in winter.

All lodgings provide a thermos of hot water and bags of green tea in every room. For coffee you can call room service, buy very sweet coffee in a can from a vending machine, or purchase packets of instant coffee at local convenience stores. If you're staying in a Japanese inn, they probably won't have coffee.

Take along small gift items, such as scarves or perfume sachets, to thank hosts (on both business and pleasure trips), whether you've been invited to their home or out to a restaurant.

▌PASSPORTS

Hotels in Japan require foreign guests to show passports at check-in, but police are unlikely to ask foreign visitors for on-the-spot identification, although crime crackdowns on nightlife areas of big cities and political tensions with North Korea or Russia can alter local circumstances in some areas.

U.S. Passport Information U.S. Department of State (☎ 877/487–2778 ⊕ travel.state.gov/ passport).

▌SAFETY

Even in its major cities Japan is a very safe country, with one of the lowest crime rates in the world. You should, however, keep an eye out for pickpockets and avoid unlighted roads at night like anywhere else. The greatest danger is the possibility of being caught up in an earthquake and its resulting tsunami. Earthquake information is broadcast (in Japanese) as news flashes on television within minutes, and during major disasters national broadcaster N.H.K. broadcasts information in English on radio and television. Minor tremors occur every month, and sometimes train services are temporarily halted. Check emergency routes at hotels and higher ground if staying near coastal areas.

▌TIP➜ **Distribute your cash, credit cards, IDs, and other valuables between a deep front pocket, an inside jacket or vest pocket, and a hidden money pouch. Don't reach for the money pouch once you're in public.**

▌TAXES

A 5% national consumption tax is added to all hotel bills. Another 3% local tax is added to the bill if it exceeds ¥15,000 (about $184). You may save money by paying for your hotel meals separately rather than charging them to your bill.

At first-class, full-service, and luxury hotels, a 10% service charge is added to the bill in place of individual tipping. At more expensive ryokan, where individualized maid service is offered, the service charge is usually 15%. At business hotels, minshuku, youth hostels, and economy inns, no service charge is added to the bill.

There's an across-the-board, nonrefundable 5% consumption tax levied on all sales, which is included in the ticket price. Authorized tax-free shops will knock the tax off purchases over ¥10,000 if you show your passport and a valid tourist visa. A large sign is displayed at such shops. A 5% tax is also added to all restaurant bills. Another 3% local tax is added to the bill if it exceeds ¥7,500 (about $92). At more expensive restaurants a 10%–15% service charge is added to the bill. Tipping is not customary.

▌ TIME

All of Japan is in the same time zone, which is 14 hours ahead of New York, and 17 hours ahead of San Francisco. Daylight saving time is not observed, although government officials are now pushing to introduce the concept over the next several years.

▌ TOURS

Tokyo and Kyoto feature on almost every tour of Japan, while Hiroshima, Nara, and Nikko are normally the secondary destinations. Read brochures carefully and try to see through the inevitable pictures of cherry trees and geisha—to check whether what is planned fits your idea of a holiday. Is it temple after temple? Does the tour include experiences such as sushi and sumo—or are they only pricey options? Is the domestic travel by bullet train, plane, or bus? Japan can be quite a culture shock, so resist the temptation to pack in too much, and go for tours that include half days of freedom, because just stepping outside the hotel into the local streets is likely to provide some unimagined sights and experiences.

Along with the usual destinations, General also goes to the Inland Sea, some ancient onsen towns and World Heritage sites; Kintetsu promises to get you closer to the world of geisha in Kyoto. IACE and Nippon Express Travel USA have tours that look to modern Japan by taking in the Tokyo Anime Festival and the Comic Market (side trip to techie-paradise Akihabara) and architecture old and new. Even the big companies try to get visitors off the beaten track: Explorient goes to the Kiso Valley near Nagoya.

Japan is daunting for first-time visitors and anyone without Japanese-language skills, so a package tour is a great way to get into the country and find your feet. However, beware of expensive optional tours such as tea ceremonies, Kabuki tours, and night views. Local tourist offices can probably tell you how to have the same experience more economically.

Recommended Companies Explorient Travel Services (☎ 800/785–1233 ⊕ www.explorient.com). **General** (☎ 800/221–2216 ⊕ www.generaltours.com). **IACE** (☎ 866/735–4223 ⊕ www.iace-asia.com). **Kintetsu** (☎ 800/422–381 ⊕ www.kintetsu.com). **Nippon Express Travel USA** (☎ 212/319–9021 New York; 415/412–1822 San Francisco ⊕ www.nipponexpresstravel.us./jp/index.htm).

SPECIAL-INTEREST TOURS

ART

Japan is overflowing with art—from pottery and painting to the precise skills of flower arranging and calligraphy. Many tours include museums and art galleries, but only some get you right into the artists' studios with English-language help to understand their skills and the chance to try your hand.

Contacts Absolute Travel (☎ 800/736–8187 ⊕ www.absolutetravel.com). **Smithsonian Journeys** (☎ 800/528–8147 ⊕ www.smithsonianjourneys.org).

CYCLING

Most airlines accommodate bikes as luggage, provided they're dismantled and boxed.

Cycling is popular in Japan, but local bike-rental shops may not have frames large enough for non-Japanese cyclists. For more information on cycling in Japan see the Japan Cycling Navigator.

Contacts Aloha Bike (☎ *0558/22–1516* ⊕ *www.alohabike.com*). **Japan Cycling Navigator** (⊕ *www.japancycling.org*). **One Life Japan** (☎ *03/3231–5310 or 03/3361–1338* ⊕ *www.onelifejapan.com*).

DIVING

Okinawa, Kyushu, and the islands and peninsular south of Tokyo are all popular diving areas. If you are a novice diver, make sure that a dive leader's "English spoken" means real communication skills. Dive Japan has lists of dive services and locations.

Contact Dive Japan (⊕ *www.divejapan.com*).

ECOTOURS

Whales, monkeys, bears, and cranes— Japan does have fauna and flora to appreciate slowly, but English-language tours are limited. Naturalist Mark Brazil, who writes extensively about wild Japan, leads ecotours through Zegrahm Eco Expeditions.

Contacts Zegrahm Eco Expeditions (☎ *800/628–8747* ⊕ *www.zeco.com*).

GOLF

Japan's love affair with golf does not make it any easier for non-Japanese-speaking visitors to reserve a game unless introduced by a club member. Japan Golf Tours takes guided groups from the United States, and Golf in Japan, put together by golfing expats, helpfully lists more than 2,000 courses that welcome foreign golfers.

Contacts Golf in Japan (⊕ *www.golf-in-japan. com*). **Japan Golf Tours** (☎ *03/3295–8141* ⊕ *www.japan-golf-tours.com*).

HIKING

Japan has well-marked trails, bus-train connections to trailheads, and hidden sights to be discovered. Millions of Japanese are avid and well-equipped hikers.

English information is growing, so check local tourist offices for details. Visit Outdoor Japan's Web site for all outdoor activities. Quest Japan, run by an experienced British hiker, has a range of tours in all seasons.

Contacts Outdoor Japan (⊕ *www. outdoorjapan.com*). **Quest Japan** (⊕ *www. questjapan.co.jp*).

MOTORCYCLE TOURS

For bikers, a motorcycle tour is by far the best way to see Japan's unique countryside. The roads are excellent and Japan has a thriving motorcycle tour culture. Though road signs are often marked in English, this isn't often the case inxral areas. The Japan Biker F.A.Q. has information on riding in Japan, and Sasa Trails offers customized motorcycle tours throughout the country.

Contacts Japan Biker F.A.Q. (⊕ *www. thejapanfaq.com/bikerfaq-toc.html*). **Sasa Trails** (☎ *050/5532–9570* ⊕ *sasatrails.com*).

LANGUAGE PROGRAMS

There is no better way to learn the language than to immerse yourself by studying Japanese in Japan, with classes, a homestay, and cultural tours on which to put the newfound skills into action. The Japanese Information and Culture Center (JICC) Web site has good links to schools and procedures for study-abroad programs.

Contacts Japan Information and Culture Center (JICC) (☎ *877/338–8687* ⊕ *www. us.emb-japan.go.jp*).

❚ TIPPING

Tipping is not common in Japan. It's not necessary to tip taxi drivers, or at hair salons, barbershops, bars, or nightclubs. A chauffeur for a hired car usually receives a tip of ¥500 for a half-day excursion and ¥1,000 for a full-day trip. Porters charge fees of ¥250–¥300 per bag at railroad stations and ¥200 per piece at airports. It's not customary to tip employees of hotels, even porters, unless a special service has been rendered. In such cases, a gratuity of ¥2,000–¥3,000 should be placed in an envelope and handed to the staff member discreetly.

■ VISITOR INFORMATION

The Japan National Tourism Organization (JNTO) has an office in Tokyo. The JNTO-affiliated International Tourism Center of Japan also has more than 140 counters/offices nationwide. Look for the sign showing a red question mark and the word "information" at train stations and city centers. Needing help on the move? For recorded information 24 hours a day, call the Teletourist service.

Japan National Tourism Organization (JNTO) Contacts Japan (✉ 2–10–1 Yurakucho, 1-chome, Chiyoda-ku, Tokyo ☎ 03/3502–1461). **United States** (✉ 11 W. 42nd St., 19th floor, New York, NY ☎ 212/757–5640 ✉ 340 E. 2nd St., Little Tokyo Plaza, Suite 302, Los Angeles, CA ☎ 213/623–1952 ⊕ www.japantravelinfo.com).

Teletourist Service Tokyo (☎ 03/3201–2911).

Tourist Information Centers (TIC) Tokyo International Forum B1 (✉ 3–5–1 Marunouchi, Chiyoda-ku, Tokyo ☎ 03/3201–3331 ✉ Main Terminal Bldg., Narita Airport, Chiba Prefecture ☎ 0476/34–6251 ✉ 2F JR Kyoto Station Bldg., Hachijo-guchi, Minami-ku, Kyoto ☎ 075/343–6655 ✉ Kansai International Airport, Osaka ☎ 0724/56–6025).

ONLINE TRAVEL TOOLS

Online cultural resources and travel-planning tools abound for travelers to Japan. Aside from the expected information about regions, hotels, and festivals, Web Japan has offbeat info such as the location of bargain-filled ¥100 shops in Tokyo and buildings designed by famous architects. Another good source for all-Japan information and regional sights and events is Japan-guide.com.

Urban Rail maintains a useful subway navigator, which includes the subway systems in Tokyo and the surrounding areas. The Metropolitan Government Web site is an excellent source of information on sightseeing and current events in Tokyo.

Check out the Web sites of Japan's three major English-language daily newspapers: the *Asahi Shimbun*, *Daily Yomiuri*, and the *Japan Times*. Expats share insider knowledge on the magazine site *Metropolis*; it has up-to-date arts, events, and dining listings. In the Kansai region, *Kansai Scene* is definitely worth a look.

Avoid being lost in translation with the help of Japanese-Online, a series of online language lessons that will help you pick up a bit of Japanese before your trip. (The site also, inexplicably, includes a sampling of typical Japanese junior-high-school math problems.) Order Japan's tastiest with confidence by checking translations on the Tokyo Food Page.

All About Japan Web Japan (⊕ web-jpn.org).

Currency Conversion Google (⊕ www.google.com). **Oanda.com** (⊕ www.oanda.com). **XE.com** (⊕ www.xe.com).

English-Language Media Sources *Asahi Shimbun* (⊕ www.asahi.com/english). ***Daily Yomiuri*** (⊕ www.yomiuri.co.jp/dy). ***Japan Times*** (⊕ www.japantimes.co.jp). ***Kansai Scene*** (⊕ www.kansaiscene.com). ***Metropolis*** (⊕ www.metropolis.co.jp)..

Transportation Hitachi's "Hyperdia-timetable" (⊕ www.hyperdia.com). **Jorudan's "Japanese Transport Guide"** (⊕ www.jorudan.co.jp/english). **Metropolitan Government** (⊕ www.metro.tokyo.jp). **Urban Rail** (⊕ www.urbanrail.net).

INDEX

A

A-Bomb Dome (Gembaku Domu), *562, 572–573*
Abashiri, *806–808*
Abashiri Kangoku Hakubutsu-kan (prison museum), *807*
Adashino Nembutsu-ji, *440*
Accommodations, *846–848*
Addresses, *848*
Advertising Museum Tokyo, *123–124*
Aichiya ✕ , *312*
Air travel and airports, *838–841*
Hokkaido, 766–767, 775, 815
Japan Alps and the North Chubu Coast, 355, 363, 379, 381, 388, 392
Kansai region, 489–490
Kobe, 547
Kyoto, 403
Kyushu, 651, 653, 656, 666, 673, 677
Nagoya, Ise-Shima, and the Kii Peninsula, 321, 324
Nara, 519
Okinawa, 687, 690, 702, 707
Osaka, 492
Shikoku, 603
Tohoku, 725, 737, 749, 755
Tokyo, 99–100
Western Honshu, 565
Yokohama, 302
Akahadayaki (shop), *528*
Akan Kohan, *813*
Akan National Park, *812–815*
Akanko (lake), *813*
Akasaka district, Tokyo, *90, 150, 152–153, 174–175*
Akechi-daira (Akechi Plain), *282*
Akita, *753–755*
Ama-no-Iwato Shrine, *649*
Ama-no-Yasugawara (cave), *649*
America-mura (America Village), *500*
Ame-ya Yoko-cho Market, *111, 211*
Amitie ✕ , *638*
Amusement centers, *121–122, 143, 149, 267, 278*
ANA Crowne Plaza Hotel Hiroshima 📷 , *583*
Anraku-ji Temple, *420–421*

Antiques, *207, 208, 232, 400, 475, 476, 560*
Aomori, *719, 749, 751–752*
Aomori Museum of Art, *751*
Aoyagi-ke (samurai house), *743*
Aoyama, Harajuku and Shibuya districts, Tokyo, *90, 133–135, 138–139, 153, 156–157, 195–196, 208–211*
Aoyama Villa (Kyu Aoyama Bettei, *Hokkaido), 789*
APA Hotel Eki-mae 📷 , *385*
Apartment and house rentals, *846–847*
Apple Store, *216*
Aquariums. ⇨ *See* Zoos and aquariums
Aragawa ✕ , *455*
Asahikawa, *804–805*
Arashiyama, *401, 438, 440, 442–444, 461*
Archaeology Museum (Hida Minzoku Kokokan), *375*
Arimatsu Tie-Dyeing Village, *327*
Art House Project, *617*
Arts, *58–61*
Kyoto, 470–472
Osaka, 514
Tokyo, 192–194
Asa-ichi (market), *389, 772*
Asahi-dake Onsen, *802*
Asakusa district, Tokyo, *116, 118–122, 157–158, 178–179, 198, 211–213*
Asakusa Jinja, *118*
Asama-san (volcano), *359*
Ashi-no-ko (Lake Ashi), *263–264, 265*
Aso Nishi cable car, *671*
Aso Volcano Museum (Aso Kazan Hakubutsukan), *671*
Aso-san (Mt. Aso), *646, 670–672*
Atami Plum Garden (Atami Bai-en), *252*
Atami Taikanso 📷 , *253–254*
ATMs, *853*
Atomic Bomb Museum (Gembaku Shiryokan), *660*
Atsuta Jingu (shrine), *327*
Auga (building complex), *751*
Authent Hotel 📷 , *790–791*
Awa Odori Kaikan (dance festival), *621*

Awa Washi Dento (paper museum), *621*
Azuma-ya ✕ , *739*

B

Bamboo forest, *444*
Bamboo ware, *475–476*
Bampaku Koen (Senri Expo Park), *498*
Banks. *853*
Bars
Kanazawa, 386
Kobe, 558–559
Kyoto, 472–474
Kyushu, 657
Matsuyama, 640
Okinawa, 696–697, 706–707
Osaka, 514
Sapporo, 785–786
Shikoku, 624
Takayama, 377
Tokyo, 195, 196, 198, 200, 202–203
Baseball, *16, 72–73, 135, 332–333, 515, 638*
Basha-michi, *306*
Beaches, *15, 252–253, 257, 299, 630–631*
Bears (music club), *18*
Beer halls and pubs, *196, 204*
Belfry (Asakusa), *118*
Benessee House Museum, *618*
Benzaiten, *111–112*
Bicycling, *19, 600, 616, 643–644, 701, 707, 731, 855–856*
Biei, *805–806*
Blue Seal ✕ , *692*
Boat and ferry travel, *841*
Hokkaido, 767, 810, 815
Japan Alps and the North Chubu Coast, 395
Kyushu, 659, 673
Okinawa, 690, 701, 702, 703, 709, 712
Shikoku, 603, 616, 634
Western Honshu, 565
Yokohama, 303
Bookstores, *108–109, 207, 229, 231, 233*
Bookstores of Jimbo-cho, *108–109*
Boraga Beach, *703*
Botanical Gardens (Shokubutsu-en), *777*
Botchan Stadium, *638*

PHOTO CREDITS

1, Gavin Hellier/age fotostock. 2-3, JTB Photo/age fotostock. 5, Steve Vidler / age fotostock. Chapter 1: Experience Japan. 8-9, JTB Photo / age fotostock. 10, Nikada/iStockphoto. 11 (left), Gunma prefecture/ JNTO. 11 (right), Kobe Convention & Visitors Association. 12, Budoya. 13 (left), Aomori Prefecture/ JNTO. 13 (right), Dmitry Petelin/Wikimedia Commons. 14 (left), Wikimedia Commons. 14 (top right), JNTO. 14 (bottom right), Tibor Bognar/age fotostock. 15 (top left), Chi King/Flickr. 15 (bottom left), Thomas La Mela/Shutterstock. 15 (right), Imre Cikajlo/iStockphoto. 16, The Other View/Flickr. 17 (left), Yasufumi Nishi/ JNTO. 17 (right), Japan Ryokan Association/ JNTO. 18, Daderot/Wikimedia Commons. 19 (left), Hokkaido Tourism Organization/ JNTO. 19 (right), Oilstreet/Wikimedia Commons. 23 (top), Yasufumi Nishi/ JNTO. 23 (bottom), Gavin Hellier/age fotostock. 24, rudiuk/Shutterstock. 25, Grand Hyatt Fukuoka 27 (left), Nuno Silva/iStockphoto. 27 (right), Lorenzo Colloreta/ iStockphoto. 34, iStockphoto. 35, Yasufumi Nishi/ JNTO. 37, Robert Churchill/iStockphoto. 38, Jay-Turbo/Shutterstock. 39, Bernard Gagnon/Wikimedia Commons. 40, Javier Larrea / age fotostock. 41, Steve Vidler / age fotostock. 42 (top left), 663highland/Wikimedia Commons. 42 (bottom left), Public domain. 42 (right), Javier Larrea / age fotostock. 43 (top left), Fedor Selivanov/Shutterstock. 43 (bottom left), Razvan Radu-Razvan Photography/iStockphoto. 43 (center), Rachelle Burnside/Shutterstock. 43 (right), CAN BALCIOGLU/Shutterstock. 44 (left), Neale Cousland/Shutterstock. 44 (top right), Ilya D. Gridnev/Shutterstock. 44 (bottom right), Wikimedia Commons. 45 (left), Yasufumi Nishi/JNTO. 45 (top right), Dr_Flash/Shutterstock. 45 (bottom right), Tataroko/Wikimedia Commons. 46 (top left), tci / age fotostock. 46 (bottom left), Tibor Bognar / age fotostock. 46 (right), Jochen Tack / age fotostock. Chapter 2: A Japanese Culture Primer. 47, JNTO. 48, thinboyfatter/Flickr. 49, Kagawa Prefecture/ JNTO. 49 (inset), sevenke/Shutterstock. 50, JNTO. 51, Payless Images/Shutterstock. 52 (top), JNTO. 52 (bottom), Saga Prefecture/JNTO. 53 (all), Hokkaido Tourism Organization/JNTO. 54 (top and bottom), Nagano Prefecture/JNTO. 55 (top), JNTO. 55 (bottom), Jill Battaglia/iStockphoto. 56 (top), Tondo Soesanto Soegondo/Shutterstock. 56 (bottom), svry/Shutterstock. 57, Kanazawa City/JNTO. 58 and 59 (top), JNTO. 59 (bottom), Photo Japan / age fotostock. 60, Okinawa Convention & Visitors Bureau/JNTO. 61, Ishikawa Prefecture/ JNTO. 62, Ishikawa Prefecture Tourist Association and Kanazawa Convention Bureau/ JNTO. 63 (left), su.bo/Flickr. 63 (right), Nagano Prefecture/ JNTO. 64, Jim Epler/iStockphoto. 65, Iwate Prefecture/JNTO. 66, Iain Masterton / age fotostock. 67 (bottom left), JNTO. 67 (top right), Nagano Prefecture/ JNTO. 68, Christophe Boisvieux / age fotostock. 69, chrisho/ iStockphoto. 70, John Warburton-Lee Photography / Alamy. 71 (bottom left), Juri Pozzi/iStockphoto. 71 (top right), Japan Ryokan Association/ JNTO. 72, Steve Silver / age fotostock. 73 (bottom left), FOTOSEARCH RM / age fotostock. 73 (top right), _Yuki_K_ /Flickr. 74, Steve Silver / age fotostock. 75 (bottom left), Kodokan/ JNTO. 75 (top right), Steve Silver / age fotostock. 76, Kevin O'Hara / age fotostock. 77 (bottom left), strikeael/Flickr. 77 (top right), Oote Boe / age fotostock. 78, Kanazawa City/ JNTO. 79 (bottom left), simonhn/Flickr. 79 (top right), jonrawlinson/Flickr. 80, Mitchell Coster / age fotostock. 81 (bottom left), Okayama Prefecture/JNTO. 81 (top right), Noriko Kitano. 82 and 83 (bottom), Yasufumi Nishi/ JNTO. 83 (top), thinboyfatter/Flickr. 84, Y.Shimizu/ JNTO. 85 (bottom left), Yasufumi Nishi/ JNTO. 85 (top right), JNTO. 86, PSno7/Shutterstock. 87, Yasufumi Nishi/ JNTO. 88, Christopher Heschong/Flickr. Chapter 3: Tokyo. 89, JNTO. 90, Cheng Chang/iStockphoto. 91 (top left), Lluís Casas/Flickr. 91 (bottom right), Akira Okada/ JNTO. 92, ton koene/age fotostock. 93 (bottom left), Lukas Kurtz/Flickr. 93 (top right), luisvilla/Flickr. 94, Christian Kober/age fotostock. 95 (bottom left), Karl Baron/Flickr. 95 (top right), jetalone/Flickr. 96, JNTO. 97 (bottom left), alvarez/ iStockphoto. 97 (top right), Eneri LLC/iStockphoto. 98, Y. Shimizu. 105, Tibor Bognar/age fotostock. 111, Chie Ushio. 120, MeeRok/Shutterstock. 126, Tifonimages/Shutterstock. 132, MIKI Yoshihito/ Flickr. 142, Sylvain Grandadam/age fotostock. 146, Iain Masterton/age fotostock. 159, Tableaux. 166, Inakaya/INAKAYA GINZA SHOP. 181 (top left), GINZA YOSHIMIZU. 181 (middle left), Prince Hotels. 181 (bottom left), Park Hyatt Tokyo. 181 (top right), Hotel Claska. 181 (middle right), Gran-bell Hotel Shibuya. 181 (bottom right), Park Hotel Tokyo. 189, José Fuste Raga/age fotostock. 197, conbon33/Flickr. 205, José Fuste Raga/age fotostock. 210, Edmund Sumner/VIEW/age fotostock. 215, Kimtaro/Flickr. 219, VH / age fotostock. 220 (top left), ton koene / age fotostock. 220 (bottom left), idealisms/Flickr. 220 (top right), Andrew Currie/Flickr. 220 (bottom right), JTB Photo / age fotostock. 221 (center left) robcocquyt/Shutterstock. 221 (top), Sylvain Grandadam / age fotostock. 221 (bottom left), José Fuste Raga / age fotostock. 221 (right) bptakoma/Flickr. 222, Kimtaro/Flickr. 223 (top) JNTO. 223 (bottom) dichohecho/Flickr. 224 (top left), Ron Koeberer / age fotostock. 224 (bottom) Gianni Muratore / Alamy. 224 (top right), ton koene / age fotostock. 225, Boaz Rottem / age fotostock. 226 (top), LIMI feu SS 2010 collection. 226 (center), N.HOOLYWOOD. 226 (bottom), Somarta. 228, ehnmark/Flickr. Chapter 4: Side Trips from Tokyo. 235, JNTO. 236 (bottom), Odakyu Electric Railway/JNTO. 236 (top) and 237 (top left), Aschaf/Flickr. 237 (top right), Yasufumi Nishi/ JNTO. 237

(bottom), H.L.I.T./Flickr. 238, ototadana/Flickr. 242-43, JTB Photo / age fotostock. 242 (bottom), Banzai Hiroaki/Flickr. 243 (top and bottom), flickr.com/diloz. 244 (top and bottom), Wikimedia Commons. 245 (top), Vidler Steve / age fotostock. 245 (bottom), Odakyu Electric Railway/JNTO. 246 (top left, right 3, and right 4), jetalone/Hajime NAKANO/Flickr . 246 (bottom left), flickr.com/diloz. 246 (right 2), imgdive/Banzai Hiroaki/Flickr. 246 (top right), skyseeker/Flickr. 247, Azlan DuPree/Flickr. 248 (top), flickr.com/diloz. 248 (center), jetalone/Hajime NAKANO/Flickr. 248 (bottom), By imgdive/ Banzai Hiroaki/Flickr . 249, JTB Photo / age fotostock. 250, Attila JANDI/Shutterstock. 259, Terraxplorer/iStockphoto. 262, Christian Goupi/age fotostock. 264 and 274, JTB Photo/age fotostock. 276, Vladimir Khirman/iStockphoto. 279, Imre Cikajlo/iStockphoto. 281, Tony Waltham/age fotostock. 290, 297 and 298, Aschaf/Flickr. 307, Yasufumi Nishi/ JNTO. 310, matteusus/iStockphoto. Chapter 5: Nagoya, Ise-Shima, and the Kii Peninsula. 315, Christian Goupi / age fotostock. 316, Aschaf/Flickr. 317 (top left), 663highland/Wikimedia Commons. 317 (bottom right), ThorstenS/Wikimedia Commons. 318-19, TOYOTA MOTOR CORPORATION. 320, brytta/iStockphoto. 326, 335 and 340, JTB Photo / age fotostock. 347, Christophe Boisvieux / age fotostock. Chapter 6: The Japan Alps and the North Chubu Coast. 349, JNTO. 350, Nagano Prefecture/ JNTO. 351 (top left), Gunma prefecture/ JNTO. 351 (bottom right), Justin Lancaster/Shutterstock. 352 and 353 (bottom left), JNTO. 353 (top right), microstock8/Shutterstock. 354, rumpleteaser/Flickr. 361, Nagano Prefecture/ JNTO. 364, David Poole / age fotostock. 368, Nagano Prefecture/ JNTO. 371, Tibor Bognar / age fotostock. 373 and 382, 663highland/Wikimedia Commons. 387 and 392, JTB Photo / age fotostock. 396, Paolo Negri / age fotostock. Chapter 7: Kyoto. 399, Kyoto Convention Bureau /JNTO. 400, Salawin Chanthapan/Shutterstock. 401 (top), Fg2/Wikimedia Commons. 401 (bottom), gwydionwilliams/Flickr. 402, Aschaf/ Flickr. 405, Sylvain Grandadam / age fotostock. 411, Matt Comeaux/iStockphoto. 413, JNTO. 414, MShades/Chris Gladis/Flickr. 415, Christian Goupi / age fotostock. 416 (top), rudiuk/Shutterstock. 416 (bottom), PlusMinus/Wikimedia Commons. 417 (top left), RachelH_/Flickr. 417 (bottom left), Wikimedia Commons. 417 (top right), whitefield_d/whity/Flickr. 417 (bottom right), rudiuk/Shutterstock. 418 (top left), Lonnie Duka / age fotostock. 418 (bottom left), JTB Photo / age fotostock. 418 (top right), John Weiss/Flickr. 418 (bottom right), shisho_1975/Shinji WATANABE/Flickr. 419, Christophe Boisvieux / age fotostock. 421, JNTO. 428, Richard T Nowitz / age fotostock. 435, Fg2/Wikimedia Commons. 439, Iain Masterton / age fotostock. 440, Tibor Bognar / age fotostock. 448, José Fuste Raga / age fotostock. 451, Kikunoi. 460, Somushi Tea House. 464 (top), Hyatt Hotels. 464 (bottom left), Kyoto Brighton. 464 (bottom right), Hotel Granvia Kyoto. 468, Klaus-Werner Friedric / age fotostock. 471, Klaus-Werner Friedric / age fotostock. 473, Jeremy Hoare / Alamy. 479, Atlantide SNC / age fotostock. Chapter 8: The Kansai Region. 481, JTB Photo / age fotostock. 482 (bottom left), photofriday/ Shutterstock. 482 (top right), Bernard Gagnon/Wikimedia Commons. 483 (top left), Martin Mette/ Shutterstock. 483 (bottom right), Neale Cousland/Shutterstock. 484, Fred Hsu/Flickr. 485 (bottom left), DoNotLick/Flickr. 485 (top right), blogefl/Flickr. 486, Iain Masterton / age fotostock. 487 (bottom left), Hokkaido Tourism Organization/ JNTO. 487 (top right), beggs/Flickr. 488, Aschaf/Flickr. 495, RinzeWind/Flickr. 497, McPHOTO / age fotostock. 501, José Fuste Raga / age fotostock. 508 and 512, The Ritz-Carlton, Osaka. 524, Laitr Keiows/Shutterstock. 529, Nara Visitors Bureau. 537, Nara Hotel. 539 (left), Kyoto Convention Bureau /JNTO. 539 (top right), tehcheesiong/Shutterstock. 539 (bottom right), glimmerous/Eve/Flickr. 539 (bottom center), Claudia van Dijk/Shutterstock. 540 (top), JTB Photo / age fotostock. 540 (bottom), Naoto Takai/Flickr. 541 (top left), Wikimedia Commons. 541 (middle left), Ehime Prefecture/JNTO. 541 (bottom left), Ishikawa Prefecture Tourist Association and Kanazawa Convention Bureau/JNTO. 541 (bottom center), Saga Prefecture/JNTO. 541 (middle center), Ishikawa Prefecture Tourist Association and Kanazawa Convention Bureau/JNTO. 541 (bottom center), Nagano Prefecture/JNTO. 541 (top right), Naoto Takai/Flickr. 541 (middle right), Okayama-ken Kanko Renmei/JNTO. 541 (bottom right), Japan Convention Services, Inc./JNTO. 542 (top left), Naomi Hasegawa/Shutterstock. 542 (bottom left), Craig Hanson/Shutterstock. 542 (top right), Friedensreich Hundertwasser/Wikimedia Commons. 542 (bottom right), ma_shimaro/Flickr. 543 (top left), NH/Shutterstock. 543 (bottom left), takayuki/Shutterstock. 543 (top right and bottom right), JTB Photo / age fotostock. 544 (top left), Tomomarusan/WIkimedia Commons. 544 (bottom left), DKPugh/ Shutterstock. 544 (top right), willem!/Wikimedia Commons. 544 (bottom right), maxstockphoto/Shutterstock. 549, Kobe Convention & Visitors Association. 553, Tibor Bognar / age fotostock. 559, Crowne Plaza Kobe. Chapter 9: Western Honshu. 561, JNTO. 562 (left), Okayama Prefecture.The Best 100 Images of Okayama/JNTO. 562 (right), shrk/Flickr. 563 (top), NASAblueshift/Flickr. 563 (bottom), jfeuchter/Flickr. 564, JNTO. 568, Okayama-ken Kanko Renmei/JNTO. 574-75, JNTO. 576, Brent Winebrenner / age fotostock. 577 (all), JNTO. 578 (top), JNTO. 578 (bottom), Ewing Galloway / age fotostock. 579 (top), FOTOSEARCH RM / age fotostock. 579 (bottom left and bottom right), Wikimedia Commons. 580, JNTO. 585, Dave Collins / age fotostock. 591, JTB Photo / age fotostock.

595, JNTO. Chapter 10: Shikoku. 599, JTB Photo / age fotostock. 600 (top)ighland/Wikimedia Commons. 600 (bottom)Flickr. 601 (top and bottom), JNTO. 602, Randym/Shutterstock. 609 (left), JTB Photo / age fotostock. 609 (top right), Reggaeman/Wikimedia Commons. 609 (bottom right), Wikimedia Commons. 610 (left and right), 663highland/Wikimedia Commons. 611 (top left and top right), Reggaeman/Wikimedia Commons. 611 (bottom), PHGCOM/Wikimedia Commons. 612 (left, top right, and bottom right), Reggaeman/Wikimedia Commons. 612 (top center), Wikimedia Commons. 613, Ehime Prefecture/JNTO. 617, Edmund SumnerVIEW / age fotostock. 625, Mike Crane/stockstudioX/iStockphoto. 628, Mark Treston/HappyRaft. 635, Tibor Bognar / age fotostock. 643, JNTO. Chapter 11: Kyushu. 645, Kagoshima Prefectural Tourist Federation/ JNTO. 646, Paolo Gianti/Shutterstock. 647 (left), TANAKA Juuyoh/Flickr. 647 (right), Hourin. 648, JTB Photo / age fotostock. 649 (bottom), Filip Fuxa/Shutterstock. 649 (top), JTB Photo / age fotostock. 650, Jordan Austin/Flickr. 659, Burak Demir/iStockphoto. 661, Lukas Kurtz/Flickr. 667, koi88/Shutterstock. 672, Igorberger/Wikimedia Commons. 675, JNTO. 679, JTB Photo / age fotostock. 680, Sanso Murata. Chapter 12: Okinawa. 681, Nancy Kennedy/Shutterstock. 682, Ippei Naoi/iStockphoto. 683 (top), Sam DCruz/Shutterstock. 683 (bottom left), Simamariasibi. 683 (bottom right), Sharon Kennedy/Shutterstock. 684, Okinawa Convention & Visitors Bureau. 685 (bottom), Okinawa Convention & Visitors Bureau. 685 (top), mdid/Flickr. 686, Simamariasibi. 693-704, Okinawa Convention & Visitors Bureau. 709 and 710, JTB Photo / age fotostock. 713, Simamariasibi. Chapter 13: Tohoku. 715, Yasufumi Nishi/ JNTO. 716 (bottom), JNTO. 716 (top), Yasufumi Nishi/ JNTO. 717, kakutani/Flickr. 718-19, JTB Photo / age fotostock. 720 and 727, Yasufumi Nishi/ JNTO. 732, JTB Photo / age fotostock. 736, Yamagata Prefecture/JNTO. 742, JTB Photo / age fotostock. 747, JayTurbo/Shutterstock. 750, Yasufumi Nishi/ JNTO. 757, Crown of Lenten rose/Wikimedia Commons. Chapter 14: Hokkaido. 759, JTB Photo / age fotostock. 760 (top), Yasufumi Nishi/ JNTO. 760 (bottom), Mukasora/Wikimedia Commons. 761, Yasufumi Nishi/ JNTO. 762 and 763 (bottom), JNTO. 763 (top), Furano Tourism Association/ JNTO. 764, Y.Shimizu/ JNTO. 773, Tibor Bognar / age fotostock. 781, Hokkaido Tourism Organization/ JNTO. 785, Y. Shimizu. 789, Chi King/Flickr. 795, JTB Photo / age fotostock. 803, Yasufumi Nishi/ JNTO. 811 and 814, JTB Photo / age fotostock.

ABOUT OUR WRITERS

Paul Bosley is originally from Shaker Heights, Ohio, and has spent some time living in Chicago and Oregon. He lives just south of Kyoto in Uji city, where he enjoys hiking with his wife. He updated Kyoto's dining, lodging, nightlife, and shopping for this edition.

Charles Canning taught English for 10 years at three different universities in Japan. He is currently enrolled in the PhD program in creative writing at the University of Adelaide. *The 89th Temple* is his first novel. He contributed essays on baseball and religion for this edition.

Arudou Debito is a 23-year resident of Hokkaido, a *Japan Times* columnist, and a naturalized Japanese citizen. He keeps a daily blog on life and human rights in Japan at *www.debito.org*. He revised the Hokkaido chapter.

Paige Ferrari has worked for Radar, MSN's Wonderwall entertainment portal, and many Web sites. She recently finished a two-year stay in Japan and updated the Western Honshu chapter.

Nagoya updater **Rob Goss** has lived in Tokyo since 1999. Writing on Japan-related topics that range from travel and culture to business and finance, Rob is a regular contributor to *Time, Eurobiz Japan,* and numerous other publications around the globe.

Noriko Kitano is a freelance journalist and researcher at *The Times UK,* a daily newspaper in Tokyo. She has published two books: a collection of essays on monasteries in Romania, and a book on cultural designs in Romania, Bulgaria, and Greece. She is currently writing about East Timor and updated our coverage of Tohoku.

A 30-year veteran of Japan, **Jared Lubarsky** teaches comparative cultures and literature at Josai International University in Chiba Prefecture, and writes for a variety of travel publications and magazines. He wrote much of our new Japanese culture chapter as well as coverage of traditional crafts.

Peter McMillan, originally from Ireland, has lived in Japan for 20 years. He is a Professor of Kyorin University in Tokyo where he teaches art, writing, poetry and translation in Faculty of Foreign studies and Graduate School. He is a poet and print-maker as well as a translator. He updated Kyushu for this edition.

Robert Morel lived in Western and Central Japan for four years, and has crossed the country both by train and bicycle. He now lives in a charmingly neglected neighborhood in Tokyo, where he teaches and writes. He updated our Kansai region coverage.

Aidan O'Connor was the food columnist for *Time Out Kansai* for more than 12 years and has contributed to other editions of *Fodor's Japan.* For this edition, he wrote our feature on Japanese cuisine.

Annamarie Sasagawa grew up in the wilds of northern British Columbia and is now a proud resident of Tokyo's Shinjuku ward. She is a travel writer and tour leader. She updated our Japan Alps and Shikoku coverage for this edition.

Christal Whelan, PhD, is a Kyoto-based author and anthropologist, as well as a columnist on Japanese culture for *The Daily Yomiuri* newspaper. Having published widely on Japanese religion, her current interests include the interpretation of fashion and the social impacts of new technologies. She updated our Kyoto exploring coverage.

Chris Willson is a travel writer and photographer who lives in Okinawa. His Web site is *www.travel67.com*. He updated the Okinawa chapter for this edition.

Our coverage of Tokyo was updated by several writers, including **Brett Bull, Nicholas Coldicott, Misha Janette,** and **Kevin Mcgue** (who also updated the Sidetrips from Tokyo chapter).